Lecture Notes in Computer Science 13503

More information about this series at https://link.springer.com/bookseries/558

Lejla Batina · Joan Daemen (Eds.)

Progress in Cryptology - AFRICACRYPT 2022

13th International Conference
on Cryptology in Africa, AFRICACRYPT 2022
Fes, Morocco, July 18–20, 2022
Proceedings

Springer

Editors
Lejla Batina 🆔
Radboud University
Nijmegen, The Netherlands

Joan Daemen 🆔
Radboud University
Nijmegen, Gelderland, The Netherlands

ISSN 0302-9743   ISSN 1611-3349 (electronic)
Lecture Notes in Computer Science
ISBN 978-3-031-17432-2   ISBN 978-3-031-17433-9 (eBook)
https://doi.org/10.1007/978-3-031-17433-9

This Springer imprint is published by the registered company Springer Nature Switzerland AG
The registered company address is: Gewerbestrasse 11, 6330 Cham, Switzerland

Preface

This volume contains the papers accepted for presentation at Africacrypt 2022, the 13th International Conference on the Theory and Application of Cryptographic Techniques in Africa. The aim of this series of conferences is to provide an international forum for practitioners and researchers from industry, academia, and government agencies for a discussion of all forms of cryptography and its applications. The initiative of organizing Africacrypt started in 2008 and it was first held in Morocco. Subsequent yearly events were held in Tunisia, South Africa, Senegal, Morocco, and Egypt. This year, on the initiative of Abderrahmane Nitaj and with the great support of Sidi Mohamed Ben Abdellah University, Fes, Morocco, Africacrypt 2022, which is organized in cooperation with the International Association for Cryptologic Research (IACR), was held in Fes, during July 18–20.

We received 68 submissions authored by researchers from countries from all over the world, including Australia and the Americas. After a double-blind reviewing process that included online discussion and involved 46 Program Committee members and 37 external reviewers, we decided to accept 25 papers resulting in an acceptance rate of around 37%. All submitted papers received at least three reviews. We thank the Program Committee and the external reviewers for their diligent work and fruitful discussions and we thank the authors of all submitted papers for supporting the conference.

The conference program featured two keynote speakers, Lilya Budaghyan from the University of Bergen, Norway, and Matthieu Rivain from Cryptoexperts, France. We were happy that they both agreed to attend and deliver their keynotes physically. The technical program was also enriched by a poster session organized by Stjepan Picek. We thank Stjepan for taking this part of the program fully out of our hands and taking care of submissions, final versions, and chairing the poster session.

The General Chairs, Lhoussain El Fadil of Sidi Mohamed Ben Abdellah University, Fes, Morocco, and Abderrahmane Nitaj, and the local organizing committee were a pleasure to work with. Special thanks goes to Konstantina Miteloudi who created and set up the conference website and executed all the updates, almost instantly. Solane El hirsch is thanked for collecting all the accepted papers' final versions to be processed by Springer. We thank the staff at Springer for their help with the proceedings' production. Without our sponsors, in particular the Technology Innovation Institute from Abu Dhabi as a platinum sponsor, not all of the support for speakers and local organization facilities would have been possible and we thank them for that.

Acting as program chairs for Africacrypt 2022 was a privilege and a great experience, thanks go to all those people that helped us make this conference a big success.

July 2022

Lejla Batina
Joan Daemen

Organization

Africacrypt 2022 was organized by Sidi Mohamed Ben Abdellah University, Fes, Morocco, in cooperation with the International Association for Cryptologic Research (IACR).

General Chairs

Lhoussain El Fadil   Sidi Mohamed Ben Abdellah University, Morocco
Abderrahmane Nitaj   Université de Caen Normandie, France

Program Chairs

Lejla Batina   Radboud University, The Netherlands
Joan Daemen   Radboud University, The Netherlands

Invited Speakers

Lilya Budaghyan   University of Bergen, Norway
Matthieu Rivain   Cryptoexperts, France

Honorary Committee

Redouane Mrabet   Sidi Mohamed Ben Abdellah University, Morocco
Mohammed Benlemlih   Sidi Mohamed Ben Abdellah University, Morocco

Organizing Committee

Lhoussain El Fadil   Sidi Mohamed Ben Abdellah University, Morocco
Siham Ezzouak   Sidi Mohamed Ben Abdellah University, Morocco
Hicham Amakdouf   Sidi Mohamed Ben Abdellah University, Morocco
Abdelhakim Chillali   Sidi Mohamed Ben Abdellah University, Morocco
Omar Kchit   Sidi Mohamed Ben Abdellah University, Morocco
Asmae El Baz   Sidi Mohamed Ben Abdellah University, Morocco
Moha Ben Taleb Elhamam   Sidi Mohamed Ben Abdellah University, Morocco
Amine Marzouki   Sidi Mohamed Ben Abdellah University, Morocco
Laghrissi Zakaria   Sidi Mohamed Ben Abdellah University, Morocco

Program Committee

Najwa Aaraj	TII, Abu Dhabi, UAE
Greg Alpár	Open University, The Netherlands
Estuardo Alpirez-Bock	Radboud University, The Netherlands
Riham AlTawy	University of Victoria, Canada
Giorgia Azzurra Marson	NEC Labs Europe, Germany
Hatem M. Bahig	Ain Shams University, Egypt
Hussain Ben-Azza	Moulay Ismail University, Morocco
Shivam Bhasin	Nanyang Technical University, Singapore
Nina Bindel	University of Waterloo, Canada
Sebastien Canard	Orange Labs, France
Celine Chevalier	CRED, University of Paris, France
Tingting Cui	Hangzhou Dianzi University, China
Luca De Feo	IBM Zürich, Switzerland
Christoph Dobraunig	Intel, Austria
Nadia El Mrabet	École des Mines de Saint-Étienne, France
Georgios Fotiadis	University of Luxembourg, Luxembourg
Emmanuel Fouotsa	University of Bamenda, Cameroon
Gina Gallegos-Garcia	IPN, Mexico
Guang Gong	University of Waterloo, Canada
Lorenzo Grassi	Radboud University, The Netherlands
Javier Herranz	BarcelonaTech, Spain
Akinori Hosoyamada	NTT, Japan
Tetsu Iwata	Nagoya University, Japan
Juliane Kramer	Technical University Darmstadt, Germany
Patrick Longa	Microsoft, Redmond, USA
Marc Manzano	SandboxAQ, Spain
Sarah McCarthy	University of Waterloo, Canada
Marine Minier	University of Lorraine, France
Mainack Mondal	IIT Kharagpur, India
Abderrahmane Nitaj	Université de Caen Normandie, France
Anca Nitulescu	École normale supérieure - PSL, France
Yanbin Pan	Chinese Academy of Sciences, China
Christophe Petit	Université Libre de Bruxelles, Belgium
Elizabeth A. Quaglia	Royal Holloway, University of London, UK
Joost Renes	NXP Semiconductors, The Netherlands
Yann Rotella	Université Paris-Saclay, France
Simona Samardjiska	Radboud University, The Netherlands
Ali Aydin Selçuk	TOBB University of Economics and Technology, Turkey
Dave Singelee	KU Leuven, Belgium
Ling Song	Jinan University, Guangzhou, China

Djiby Sow   University of Dakar, Senegal
Pontelimon Stanica   Naval Postgraduate School, USA
Fernando Virdia   ETH Zürich, Switzerland
Vanessa Vitse   Université Grenoble Alpes, France

Additional Reviewers

Khalid Abdelmoumen   Oscar Lapointe
Ismail Afia   Kalikinkar Mandal
Adrien Benamira   Soundes Marzougui
Murat Burham Ilter   Simon-Philippe Merz
Craig Costello   Michael Naehrig
Debaiyoti Das   Kamil Otal
Fatih Demirbaş   Stjepan Picek
Sayon Duttagupta   Kirthivaasan Puniamurthy
Sébastien Duval   Shahram Rasoolzadeh
Samed Düzlü   Sayandeep Saha
Mehmet Emin Gönen   Ugur Sen
Seyed Fargad Aghili   Ragvendra Singh Rohit
Shihui Fu   Patrick Struck
Pierre Galissant   Marloes Venema
Fei Guo   Charlotte Weitkämper
James Howe   Jun Xu
Samuel Jaques   Sophia Yakoubov
Péter Kutas   Mengce Zheng
Virginie Lallemand

Contents

Post-quantum (Crypt)analysis

Side-Channel Attacks

Protocols and Foundations

Public Key (Crypt)analysis

Symmetric Cryptography

Construction of Recursive MDS Matrices Using DLS Matrices

Kishan Chand Gupta[1], Sumit Kumar Pandey[2], and Susanta Samanta[1]([⊠]) [ID]

[1] Applied Statistics Unit, Indian Statistical Institute,
203, B.T. Road, Kolkata 700108, India
{kishan,susantas_r}@isical.ac.in

[2] Computer Science and Engineering, Indian Institute of Technology Jammu,
Jagti, PO Nagrota, Jammu 181221, India

Abstract. Many block ciphers and hash functions use MDS matrices because of their optimal branch number. On the other hand, MDS matrices generally have a high implementation cost, which makes them unsuitable for lightweight cryptographic primitives. In this direction, several sparse matrix structures like companion, GFS, and DSI matrices are proposed to construct recursive MDS matrices. The key benefit of these matrices is their low fixed XOR, and the diffusion layer can be made by recursively executing the implementation of the matrices, which takes a few clock cycles. In this paper, we propose a new class of sparse matrices called Diagonal-like sparse (DLS) matrices and the DSI matrix is a particular type of DLS matrix. We prove that for an n-MDS DLS matrix of order n, the fixed XOR (say $\mathcal{K}$) should be at least equal to the $\left\lceil \frac{n}{2} \right\rceil$. We also show that an n-MDS DLS matrix over $\mathbb{F}_{2^r}$ with $\mathcal{K} = \left\lceil \frac{n}{2} \right\rceil$ is a permutation similar to some n-MDS sparse DSI matrix. We propose another type of sparse matrices called generalized DLS (GDLS) matrices. Next, we introduce some lightweight recursive MDS matrices of orders $4, 5, 6$, and 7, using GDLS matrices, that can be implemented with $22, 30, 31$, and 45 XORs over $\mathbb{F}_{2^8}$, respectively. The results match the best known lightweight recursive MDS matrices of orders 4 and 6 and beat the best known matrices of orders 5 and 7. Also, the proposed 4-MDS GDLS matrix over $\mathbb{F}_{2^4}$ has a XOR count of 10, which meets the best known result.

Keywords: Diffusion layer · MDS matrix · Permutation matrix · XOR count

1 Introduction

Claude Shannon in his paper "Communication Theory of Secrecy Systems" [25] introduced the concepts of confusion and diffusion. These concepts are essential to the design of block ciphers and hash functions. Confusion is achieved by using nonlinear functions such as Sboxes and Boolean functions to make the statistical relationship between the ciphertext and the message too complex for

L. Batina and J. Daemen (Eds.): AFRICACRYPT 2022, LNCS 13503, pp. 3–27, 2022.
https://doi.org/10.1007/978-3-031-17433-9_1

the attacker to exploit. Diffusion ensures that each bit of the message and each bit of the secret key has an effect on many bits of the ciphertext and that after a few rounds, all the output bits are dependent on all the input bits. In many block ciphers and hash functions, the diffusion property is achieved by a linear layer which can be represented as a matrix with the property that a small change in the input causes the maximum change in the output. This can be accomplished through the use of MDS matrices. For example, the block cipher AES [6] uses an MDS matrix in its MixColumn operation.

However, ensuring strong diffusion power generally results in a high hardware implementation cost, and in addition to security, an essential secondary criterion for a lightweight cryptographic primitive is efficient implementation in hardware and software. Thus to reduce the implementation cost, recursive MDS matrices are proposed which can be implemented in a serialized manner. A matrix B is said to be recursive MDS if the matrix B^q is MDS for some positive integer q. The matrix B^q can be implemented by recursively executing the implementation of B, requiring q many clock cycles. Such matrices based on the companion matrices were first used in the PHOTON [8] family of hash functions. The key advantage of the companion matrix is that just the last row of it accounts for its hardware implementation cost, making it more suitable for lightweight primitives. Following that, the Generalized-Feistel-Structure (GFS) [27], Diagonal-Serial-Invertible (DSI) [26], and sparse DSI matrices [26] were proposed.

Many works have been done over the years to construct recursive MDS matrices. One way to classify the techniques used to construct recursive MDS matrices is based on whether the matrix is constructed directly or a search method is employed by enumerating some search space. Direct constrictions use some coding theoretic techniques. Augot et al. [1] employed shortened BCH codes, and Berger [4] used Gabidulin codes in their method. Then, in a series of works [12–14], the authors proposed many approaches for the construction of recursive MDS matrices from the companion matrices over finite fields. Recently, in [16], authors have proposed several methods for the direct construction of recursive MDS matrices defined over finite commutative rings. While in search methods for finding efficiently implementable recursive MDS matrices, elements of the matrix are judiciously selected such that the entries can be implemented with fewer XOR gates. In some early studies [27,28], the entries of the matrix B are chosen from $\mathbb{F}_2[L]$. Then, by symbolically computing the determinants of all square submatrices of B^q and replacing L with a suitable field element $\alpha \in \mathbb{F}_{2^r}$ or a linear transformation, such that the resultant matrix becomes MDS. In [26], search ideas are used to find lightweight recursive MDS matrices from companion and DSI matrices. In [21,24], the authors obtained some lightweight recursive MDS matrices by increasing the number of iterations. However, these matrices are not useful for low latency purposes because if B^q is MDS for an order n matrix B, where $q > n$, the matrix B must be applied q times in the serialized implementation of the diffusion layer. So the best case is to see whether B^n is MDS or not.

It is worth mentioning that recently a lot of attention has been paid to the search for efficiently implementable MDS matrices by global optimization techniques. For instance see [2, 7, 19, 20, 29]. So we can categorize the search methods into two ways: local optimization and global optimization.

In local optimizations, designers mainly focus on the selection of matrix entries with low d-XOR/s-XOR counts. Whereas in global optimizations, given a matrix A, we can obtain an estimation of its hardware cost by finding a good linear straight-line program corresponding to A with state-of-the-art automatic tools based on a certain SLP heuristic [5]. A globally optimized implementation can be significantly cheaper than the local optimization because common intermediate values can be computed once and reused. However, in this paper, we consider the local optimization technique as the cost of a lightweight MDS matrix (locally optimized) may be cheaper in the globally optimized technique.

Contributions. In this paper, we introduce a new type of sparse matrix called the Diagonal-like sparse (DLS) matrix and the DSI matrix is a specific type of DLS matrix. We prove that the value of fixed XOR ($\mathcal{K}$) should be at least $\left\lceil \frac{n}{2} \right\rceil$ for an n-MDS DLS matrix of order n. The exhaustive search using a naive way of finding a higher-order recursive MDS matrix using DLS matrices is impractical. In this regard, we present some theoretical results that are used to narrow the search space to a small domain. Then, after an exhaustive search in the restricted domain, we notice that for $n = 5, 6, 7, 8$ and $\mathcal{K} = \left\lceil \frac{n}{2} \right\rceil, \left\lceil \frac{n}{2} \right\rceil + 1, \ldots, n - 1$, there is no n-MDS DLS matrix of order n over field $\mathbb{F}_{2^4}$. We also show that an n-MDS DLS matrix with $\mathcal{K} = \left\lceil \frac{n}{2} \right\rceil$ is a permutation similar to some n-MDS sparse DSI matrix over $\mathbb{F}_{2^r}$. Thus the existence of n-MDS DLS matrices with the lowest fixed XOR implies the existence of n-MDS sparse DSI matrices over $\mathbb{F}_{2^r}$ and vice versa.

We propose another type of sparse matrices called generalized DLS (GDLS) matrices and using these matrices, we introduce some lightweight recursive MDS matrices of orders 4, 5, 6, and 7 that can be implemented with 22, 30, 31, and 45 XORs over $\mathbb{F}_{2^8}$, respectively. The results are the same as with the best known lightweight recursive MDS matrices of orders 4 and 6, but the results are better than the best known matrices of orders 5 and 7. In addition, the proposed 4-MDS GDLS matrix over $\mathbb{F}_{2^4}$ has a XOR count of 10, which is consistent with the best known result. Besides searching over $\mathbb{F}_{2^4}$ and $\mathbb{F}_{2^8}$, we also provide some efficient n-MDS GDLS matrices over $GL(8, \mathbb{F}_2)$ for orders $n = 4, 5$, and 6. The implementation costs of those matrices are 18, 28, and 30, respectively. Table 1 compares our results to the known results.

Outline. The rest of the paper is organized as follows. Section 2 contains definitions and preliminaries. Section 3 discusses DLS matrices. In this section, we give some theoretical results to restrict the search space to a smaller domain for finding n-MDS DLS matrices of order n. In Sect. 4, we extend the definition of DLS matrices to propose a class of sparse matrices called GDLS matrices. Some lightweight recursive MDS matrices of orders 4, 5, 6, and 7, using GDLS matrices, are proposed in this section.

Table 1. Comparison of n-MDS matrices of order n

Order n	Input	Matrix Type	Field/Ring	XOR	References
4	4-bit	Sparse DSI	$\mathbb{F}_{2^4}/\text{0x13}$	10	[26]
4	4-bit	GFS	$GL(4, \mathbb{F}_2)$	10	[27]
4	4-bit	Companion	$\mathbb{F}_{2^4}/\text{0x13}$	15	[18]
4	4-bit	Companion	$GL(4, \mathbb{F}_2)$	15	[27]
4	4-bit	GDLS	$\mathbb{F}_{2^4}/\text{0x13}$	10	Section 4.1
4	8-bit	Sparse DSI	$[\mathbb{F}_{2^4}/\text{0x13}]^2$	2×10	[26]
4	8-bit	GFS	$GL(8, \mathbb{F}_2)$	18	[27]
4	8-bit	Companion	$\mathbb{F}_{2^4}/\text{0x11d}$	33	[18]
4	8-bit	Companion	$GL(8, \mathbb{F}_2)$	27	[27]
4	8-bit	Sparse DSI	$GL(8, \mathbb{F}_2)$	18	[21]
4	8-bit	GDLS	$\mathbb{F}_{2^8}/\text{0x1c3}$	22	Remark 6
4	8-bit	GDLS	$GL(8, \mathbb{F}_2)$	18	Remark 7
5	4-bit	Companion	$GL(4, \mathbb{F}_2)$	19	[27]
5	4-bit	Companion	$\mathbb{F}_{2^4}/\text{0x13}$	18	[8]
5	4-bit	Companion	$\mathbb{F}_{2^4}/\text{0x13}$	18	[26]
5	4-bit	GDLS	$\mathbb{F}_{2^4}/\text{0x13}$	26	Section 4.2
5	8-bit	Companion	$GL(8, \mathbb{F}_2)$	35	[27]
5	8-bit	Sparse DSI	$\mathbb{F}_{2^8}/\text{0x1c3}$	31	[26]
5	8-bit	Sparse DSI	$GL(8, \mathbb{F}_2)$	30	[21]
5	8-bit	GDLS	$\mathbb{F}_{2^8}/\text{0x1c3}$	30	Section 4.2
5	8-bit	GDLS	$GL(8, \mathbb{F}_2)$	**28**	Remark 8
6	4-bit	Companion	$GL(4, \mathbb{F}_2)$	25	[27]
6	4-bit	Companion	$\mathbb{F}_{2^4}/\text{0x13}$	28	[8]
6	4-bit	Companion	$\mathbb{F}_{2^4}/\text{0x13}$	25	[26]
6	8-bit	Companion	$GL(8, \mathbb{F}_2)$	45	[27]
6	8-bit	Companion	$\mathbb{F}_{2^8}/\text{0x11b}$	57	[8]
6	8-bit	Sparse DSI	$\mathbb{F}_{2^8}/\text{0x1c3}$	31	[26]
6	8-bit	GDLS	$\mathbb{F}_{2^8}/\text{0x1c3}$	31	Section 4.3
6	8-bit	GDLS	$GL(8, \mathbb{F}_2)$	**30**	Remark 9
7	4-bit	Companion	$GL(4, \mathbb{F}_2)$	30	[27]
7	4-bit	Companion	$\mathbb{F}_{2^4}/\text{0x13}$	31	[8]
7	4-bit	Companion	$\mathbb{F}_{2^4}/\text{0x13}$	30	[26]
7	8-bit	Companion	$GL(8, \mathbb{F}_2)$	54	[27]
7	8-bit	Sparse DSI	$\mathbb{F}_{2^8}/\text{0x1c3}$	54	[26]
7	8-bit	Sparse DSI	$\mathbb{F}_{2^8}/\text{0x1c3}$	47	[17]
7	8-bit	GDLS	$\mathbb{F}_{2^8}/\text{0x1c3}$	**45**	Section 4.4
8	4-bit	Companion	$GL(4, \mathbb{F}_2)$	37	[27]
8	4-bit	Companion	$\mathbb{F}_{2^4}/\text{0x13}$	47	[8]
8	4-bit	Companion	$\mathbb{F}_{2^4}/\text{0x13}$	36	[26]
8	4-bit	Companion	$\mathbb{F}_{2^4}/\text{0x13}$	41	[18]
8	8-bit	Companion	$GL(8, \mathbb{F}_2)$	65	[27]
8	8-bit	Companion	$[\mathbb{F}_{2^4}/\text{0x13}]^2$	2×36	[26]

2 Definition and Preliminaries

In this section, we have provided an overview of the concepts and definitions that will be used throughout the paper.

2.1 Finite Fields and MDS Matrices

Let $\mathbb{F}_2 = \{0, 1\}$ be the finite field of two elements, $\mathbb{F}_{2^r}$ be the finite field of 2^r elements and $\mathbb{F}_{2^r}^n$ be the set of vectors of length n with entries from the finite field $\mathbb{F}_{2^r}$. Elements of $\mathbb{F}_{2^r}$ can be represented as polynomials of degree less than r over $\mathbb{F}_2$. For example, let $\beta \in \mathbb{F}_{2^r}$, then β can be represented as $\sum_{i=0}^{r-1} b_i \alpha^i$, where $b_i \in \mathbb{F}_2$ and α is the root of the constructing polynomial of $\mathbb{F}_{2^r}$. Again if α be a primitive element of $\mathbb{F}_{2^r}$, all the nonzero elements of $\mathbb{F}_{2^r}$ can be expressed as the power of α. Therefore $\mathbb{F}_{2^r} = \{0, 1, \alpha, \alpha^2, \alpha^3, \ldots, \alpha^{2^r-1}\}$. We also use a hexadecimal representation of a finite field $\mathbb{F}_{2^r}$ throughout the paper. For instance, $\mathbb{F}_{2^4}/0x13$ denotes the finite field $\mathbb{F}_{2^4}$ constructed by the polynomial $x^4 + x + 1$. Note that $\mathbb{F}_{2^r}$ and $\mathbb{F}_2^r$ are isomorphic when both of them are regarded as vector spaces over $\mathbb{F}_2$. The isomorphism is given by $x = (x_1\alpha_1 + x_2\alpha_2 + \cdots + x_r\alpha_r) \rightarrow (x_1, x_2, \cdots, x_r)$, where $\{\alpha_1, \alpha_2, \ldots, \alpha_r\}$ is a basis of $\mathbb{F}_{2^r}$. A square matrix is a matrix with the same number of rows and columns. An $n \times n$ matrix is known as a matrix of order n.

An MDS matrix provides optimal diffusion that has useful applications in cryptography. The idea comes from coding theory, in particular from maximum distance separable (MDS) code.

Definition 1. *Let $\mathbb{F}$ be a finite field and p and q be two integers. Let $x \rightarrow B \times x$ be a mapping from $\mathbb{F}^p$ to $\mathbb{F}^q$ defined by the $q \times p$ matrix B. We say that B is an MDS matrix if the set of all pairs $(x, B \times x)$ is an MDS code i.e. a linear code of dimension p, length $p + q$, and minimal distance $q + 1$.*

In this context, we state two important theorems from coding theory.

Theorem 1 *(The Singleton bound)* [22, page 33]. *Let C be an $[n, k, d]$ code. Then $d \leq n - k + 1$.*

Definition 2. *A code with $d = n - k + 1$ is called maximum distance separable code or MDS code in short.*

Theorem 2 *[22, page 321]. An $[n, k, d]$ code C with generator matrix $G = [I \mid B]$, where B is a $k \times (n - k)$ matrix, is MDS if and only if every square submatrix (formed from any i rows and any i columns, for any $i = 1, 2, \ldots, min\{k, n - k\}$) of B is nonsingular.*

The following fact is another way to characterize an MDS matrix.

Fact 1. *A square matrix B is an MDS matrix if and only if every square submatrices of B are nonsingular.*

Definition 3 [16]. *Let q be a positive integer. A matrix B is said to be recursive MDS or q-MDS if the matrix $M = B^q$ is MDS. If B is q-MDS then we say B yields an MDS matrix.*

Example 1. For example, the matrix

$$B = \begin{bmatrix} 0 & 1 & 0 & 0 \\ 0 & 0 & 1 & 0 \\ 0 & 0 & 0 & 1 \\ 1 & \alpha & 0 & 0 \end{bmatrix}$$

is 22-MDS, where α is a primitive element of the field $\mathbb{F}_{2^4}/0x13$ and α is a root of $x^4 + x + 1$.

Lemma 1. *If B is q-MDS, then B^T and B^{-1} are also q-MDS.*

Definition 4. *A matrix $D = (D)_{i,j}$ is said to be diagonal if $(D)_{i,j} = 0$ for $i \neq j$. By setting $d_i = (D)_{i,i}$, we denote the diagonal matrix D as $diag(d_1, d_2, \ldots, d_n)$. It is obvious to see that the determinant of D is $det(D) = \prod_{i=1}^{n} d_i$. Hence the diagonal matrix D is nonsingular if and only if $d_i \neq 0$ for $1 \leq i \leq n$.*

Lemma 2 [10, Corollary 1]. *Let A be an MDS matrix, then for any nonsingular diagonal matrices D_1 and D_2, $D_1 A D_2$ will also be an MDS matrix.*

Corollary 1. *Let B be a recursive MDS matrix, then for any nonsingular diagonal matrix D, DBD^{-1} will also be a recursive MDS matrix.*

Definition 5. *Let ρ be an element of the symmetric group S_n (set of all permutations over the set $\{1, 2, \ldots, n\}$). Then by $\rho = [i_1, i_2, i_3, \ldots, i_n]$, where $1 \leq i_j \leq n$ for $j = 1, 2, 3, \ldots, n$, we mean $\rho = \begin{pmatrix} 1 & 2 & 3 & \ldots & n \\ i_1 & i_2 & i_3 & \ldots & i_n \end{pmatrix}$ i.e. $1 \rightarrow i_1$, $2 \rightarrow i_2, \ldots, n \rightarrow i_n$.*

Then the product of two permutations $\rho_1 = [i_1, i_2, i_3, \ldots, i_n]$ and $\rho_2 = [j_1, j_2, j_3, \ldots, j_n]$ is given by $\rho_1 \cdot \rho_2 = [i_{j_1}, i_{j_2}, i_{j_3}, \ldots, i_{j_n}]$ and the inverse of a permutation $\rho = [i_1, i_2, i_3, \ldots, i_n]$ is the permutation $\delta = [j_1, j_2, j_3, \ldots, j_n]$ such that $\rho \cdot \delta = \delta \cdot \rho = [1, 2, 3, \ldots, n]$.

Example 2. For the two permutations $\rho_1 = [2, 3, 4, 5, 1, 6]$ and $\rho_2 = [1, 4, 3, 2, 6, 5]$ over S_6, their product is given by

$$\rho_1 \cdot \rho_2 = [2, 5, 4, 3, 6, 1] \text{ and } \rho_2 \cdot \rho_1 = [4, 3, 2, 6, 1, 5].$$

The inverse of the permutation $\rho_1 = [2, 3, 4, 5, 1, 6]$ is given by $\delta = [5, 1, 2, 3, 4, 6]$.

Definition 6. *A permutation matrix P of order n related to a permutation $\rho = [i_1, i_2, i_3, \ldots, i_n]$ is the binary matrix which is obtained from the identity matrix of order n by permuting the rows (or columns) according to the permutation ρ.*

Throughout the paper, for permutation matrices, we will consider the row permuted identity matrix. For example, the permutation matrix P related to the permutation $[4, 2, 3, 1]$ is given by

$$P = \begin{bmatrix} 0 & 0 & 0 & 1 \\ 0 & 1 & 0 & 0 \\ 0 & 0 & 1 & 0 \\ 1 & 0 & 0 & 0 \end{bmatrix}.$$

Note that a permutation matrix is invertible and the inverse of P is the transpose of P, i.e. $P^{-1} = P^T$. The product of two permutation matrices is a permutation matrix.

Lemma 3 [10, Corollary 4]. *If M is an MDS matrix, then for any permutation matrices P and Q, PMQ is an MDS matrix.*

Corollary 2. *Let B be a recursive MDS matrix, then for any permutation matrix P, PBP^{-1} will also be a recursive MDS matrix.*

We will call a matrix M_1 to be diagonal (permutation) similar to a matrix M_2 if $M_1 = DM_2D^{-1}$ ($M_1 = PM_2P^{-1}$) for some nonsingular diagonal matrix D (permutation matrix P). Thus diagonal/permutation similar of a q-MDS matrix is again a q-MDS matrix.

Definition 7. *Let ρ be an element of the symmetric group S_n. Then ρ is called a k length cycle or k-cycle, written $(j_1\ j_2\ j_3\ \cdots\ j_k)$, if $\rho = \begin{pmatrix} j_1 & j_2 & j_3 & \cdots & j_k \\ j_2 & j_3 & j_4 & \cdots & j_1 \end{pmatrix}$ i.e. $j_1 \to j_2,\ j_2 \to j_3,\ \cdots\ ,j_k \to j_1$.*

2.2 XOR Count

In the past, it was widely believed that the hardware implementation costs of finite field elements with low Hamming weights were lower. As of 2014, the authors of [18] proposed an approach to estimate implementation costs by counting the number of XOR gates (d-XOR gates) required to implement the field element based on the multiplicative matrices of the elements. According to them, higher Hamming weight elements can be implemented at a lower cost than previously thought. To better estimate the cost of hardware implementation, the authors of [15] suggested a metric called s-XOR. In this study, we use this metric to calculate the implementation cost of the diffusion matrices given in that paper and to compare the implementation costs of the matrices, we use the table in [26, App. B].

Definition 8 [15]. *The s-XOR count of an element $\alpha \in \mathbb{F}_{2^r}$, denoted by s-XOR($\alpha$), is the minimum number of XOR operations for implementing the field element multiplication, where the minimum is taken over all implementation sequences.*

Example 3. Any element b in $\mathbb{F}_{2^4}/\text{0x13}$, can be written as $b = b_0 + b_1 \cdot \alpha + b_2 \cdot \alpha^2 + b_3 \cdot \alpha^3$, where α is a primitive element of the field $\mathbb{F}_{2^4}$ and is a root of $x^4 + x + 1$ i.e. $\alpha^4 + \alpha + 1 = 0$. Then by the multiplication of b by $\beta = \alpha^3 + \alpha^2 + \alpha + 1$ we have

$$(b_0 + b_1 \cdot \alpha + b_2 \cdot \alpha^2 + b_3 \cdot \alpha^3) \cdot (\alpha^3 + \alpha^2 + \alpha + 1)$$
$$= (b_0 + b_1 + b_2 + b_3) + b_0 \cdot \alpha + (b_0 + b_1) \cdot \alpha^2 + (b_0 + b_1 + b_2) \cdot \alpha^3.$$

Thus in vector form the above product looks like

$$((b_0 \oplus b_1 \oplus b_2) \oplus b_3, \; b_0, \; (b_0 \oplus b_1), \; (b_0 \oplus b_1) \oplus b_2),$$

in which there is 6 XOR. Therefore the d-XOR count of $\beta = \alpha^3 + \alpha^2 + \alpha + 1$ is 6 but it is easy to see that multiplication with β can be implemented with only 3 XOR operations since the results of previous steps can be reused. Therefore, we have s-XOR$(\beta) = 3$.

To measure the implementation cost of a diffusion matrix, one has to add the XOR count of all the entries in that matrix. For an MDS matrix, the implementation cost is high for its fixed XOR. For matrices like Hadamard or cyclic matrices, the absence of any zero entries is a prerequisite for being MDS. If a row contains k_i nonzero field elements, these k_i many elements must be summed together, which costs a fixed number of XOR counts of $(k_i - 1)r$ over the field $\mathbb{F}_{2^r}$. Thus, if there are $k_1, k_2, \ldots, k_n$ nonzero elements in the n rows of an n order matrix, the matrix's fixed XOR count is $\sum_{i=1}^{n}(k_i - 1)r$ over $\mathbb{F}_{2^r}$. The number $\mathcal{K} = \sum_{i=1}^{n}(k_i - 1)$ will be referred to as a fixed XOR of a matrix throughout the paper. Thus for an MDS matrix of order n fixed XOR $\mathcal{K} = n(n-1)$.

Other Notations: Here are the other notations used in the paper.

1. The (i,j)-th entry of a matrix A is denoted by $(A)_{i,j}$.
2. We denote by $|A|$ for the number of nonzero entries in the matrix A and $|A| \leq |B|$ means the number of nonzero elements in A is less than or equal to the number of nonzero elements in B.
3. For two $m \times n$ matrices A and B, we symbolize $A \cong B$ if $(A)_{i,j} \neq 0$ implies $(B)_{i,j} \neq 0$.
4. $\mathbb{F}_2[L]$ denotes the set of polynomials of L over $\mathbb{F}_2$.
5. For simplicity, we use nonzero positions in each row of a binary matrix as a representation of the matrix. For example, $[[1, 2, 3], [1, 3], [2]]$ represents the binary matrix $\begin{bmatrix} 1 & 1 & 1 \\ 1 & 0 & 1 \\ 0 & 1 & 0 \end{bmatrix}$.

An MDS matrix must have all its entries nonzero. Therefore, any $n \times n$ matrix cannot be MDS if the number of nonzero entries is less than n^2. In the following section, we are using this fact to obtain some interesting results.

3   Construction of MDS Matrices from DLS Matrices

First, let us recall some sparse matrix structures that are used to construct recursive MDS matrices. The advantage of such matrices is that they are particularly well suited for lightweight implementations: the diffusion layer can be implemented by recursively executing the implementation of the sparse matrices, requiring some clock cycles. Such matrices based on the companion matrices were used in the PHOTON [8] family of hash functions and LED block cipher [9] because they can be implemented by a simple LFSR. Later, Generalized-Feistel-Structure (GFS) [27] and Diagonal-Serial-Invertible (DSI) [26] matrices were proposed.

Definition 9. *Let* $g(x) = a_1 + a_2x + \ldots + a_nx^{n-1} + x^n \in \mathbb{F}_{2^r}[x]$ *be a monic polynomial of degree* n. *The companion matrix* C_g *associated to the polynomial* g *is given by*

$$C_g = \begin{bmatrix} 0 & 1 & 0 & \ldots & 0 \\ \vdots & & \ddots & & \vdots \\ 0 & 0 & \ldots\ldots & & 1 \\ a_1 & a_2 & \ldots\ldots & & a_n \end{bmatrix}.$$

We sometimes use the notation $Comp(a_1, a_2, \ldots, a_n)$ to represent the companion matrix C_g.

Definition 10 [26, Definition 5]. *Let* $\mathbf{a} = [a_1 \ a_2 \ \cdots \ a_n]$ *and* $\mathbf{b} = [b_1 \ b_2 \ \cdots \ b_{n-1}]$ *where* $a_i, b_j \in \mathbb{F}_{2^r}$ *for* $1 \le i \le n$ *and* $1 \le j \le n - 1$. *A Diagonal-Serial-Invertible (DSI) matrix* D *is determined by two vectors* $\mathbf{a}$ *and* $\mathbf{b}$ *defined as follows:*

$$(D)_{i,j} = \begin{cases} a_1, & i = 1, j = n \\ a_i, & i = j + 1 \\ b_i, & i = j \le n - 1 \\ 0, & otherwise. \end{cases}$$

Definition 11 [26, Definition 6]. *A DSI matrix* $D = DSI(a_1, a_2, \ldots, a_n; b_1, b_2, \ldots, b_{n-1})$ *of order* n *is sparse if it satisfies:*

$$\begin{cases} b_2 = b_4 = \ldots = b_{n-2} = 0, & \text{if } n \text{ is even} \\ b_2 = b_4 = \ldots = b_{n-3} = 0, & \text{if } n \text{ is odd.} \end{cases}$$

Example 4. An example of a sparse DSI matrix of order 4 and 5 are given below:

$$\begin{bmatrix} b_1 & 0 & 0 & a_1 \\ a_2 & 0 & 0 & 0 \\ 0 & a_3 & b_3 & 0 \\ 0 & 0 & a_4 & 0 \end{bmatrix}, \qquad \begin{bmatrix} b_1 & 0 & 0 & 0 & a_1 \\ a_2 & 0 & 0 & 0 & 0 \\ 0 & a_3 & b_3 & 0 & 0 \\ 0 & 0 & a_4 & b_4 & 0 \\ 0 & 0 & 0 & a_5 & 0 \end{bmatrix}.$$

3.1   Diagonal-Like Sparse (DLS) Matrices

Definition 12. *Let $\rho = [i_1, i_2, i_3, \ldots, i_n]$ be a permutation such that $i_k \neq k$ for $k = 1, 2, \ldots, n$, D_1 be a nonsingular diagonal matrix and D_2 be a diagonal matrix (may be singular). Then we will call the matrix $B = PD_1 + D_2$ as the diagonal-like sparse (DLS) matrix, where P is the permutation matrix of order n related to the permutation ρ. We will denote these matrices as $DLS(\rho; D_1, D_2)$.*

Example 5. An example of a DLS matrix of order 4 is given by

$$DLS(\rho; D_1, D_2) = PD_1 + D_2 = \begin{bmatrix} 0 & 0 & 0 & 1 \\ 0 & 0 & 1 & 0 \\ 1 & 0 & 0 & 0 \\ 0 & 1 & 0 & 0 \end{bmatrix} \cdot \begin{bmatrix} a & 0 & 0 & 0 \\ 0 & b & 0 & 0 \\ 0 & 0 & c & 0 \\ 0 & 0 & 0 & d \end{bmatrix} + \begin{bmatrix} e & 0 & 0 & 0 \\ 0 & 0 & 0 & 0 \\ 0 & 0 & f & 0 \\ 0 & 0 & 0 & 0 \end{bmatrix} = \begin{bmatrix} e & 0 & 0 & d \\ 0 & 0 & c & 0 \\ a & 0 & f & 0 \\ 0 & b & 0 & 0 \end{bmatrix},$$

where P is the permutation matrix related to $\rho = [3, 4, 2, 1]$ and $D_1 = diag(a, b, c, d)$ and $D_2 = diag(e, 0, f, 0)$.

Remark 1. Note that the DSI matrix is a particular type of DLS matrix. More specifically, for $\rho = [2, 3, 4, \ldots, n-1, n, 1]$ and a nonsingular diagonal matrix D_1, if $D_2 = diag(b_1, b_2, \ldots, b_{n-1}, 0)$ then we call $DLS(\rho; D_1, D_2)$ a DSI matrix and if $D_2 = diag(b_1, 0, b_3, \ldots, 0, b_{n-1}, 0)$ (when n is even) or $D_2 = diag(b_1, 0, b_3, \ldots, b_{n-2}, b_{n-1}, 0)$ (when n is odd), then $DLS(\rho; D_1, D_2)$ is called a sparse DSI matrix of order n.

Now we will discuss some results on the DLS matrices for the construction of recursive MDS matrices from this.

For a DSI matrix M of order n, M^k contains at least one zero for $0 \leq k < n$ and $n \geq 2$. In [11, Theorem 4], authors proved this by a combinatorial argument. In Theorem 3, we have used the same combinatorial argument to show that for a DLS matrix $M = DLS(\rho; D_1, D_2)$ of order n, M cannot be k-MDS for $0 \leq k < n - 1$. For this, we need the following lemmas.

Lemma 4. *For any permutation matrix P related to some permutation ρ and any diagonal matrix D, we have $DP = PD_1$ for some diagonal matrix D_1. Also, the number of nonzero entries in D and D_1 are same.*

Proof. Let P be a permutation matrix related to the permutation $\rho = [i_1, i_2, i_3, \ldots, i_n]$ and $D = diag(d_1, d_2, \ldots, d_n)$. By the pre-multiplication of P with D i.e. by PD, the rows of D are permuted according to the permutation ρ. Also by post-multiplication of P, the columns of D are permuted. Since P is obtained from the identity matrix of order n by permuting the rows according to ρ, the j-th column of P is the i_j-th column of the identity matrix for $j = 1, 2, \ldots, n$. Thus we have $(DP)_{i_j, j} = d_{i_j}$ for $j = 1, 2, \ldots, n$ and $(DP)_{i,j} = 0$ for others i, j. Also, for $j = 1, 2, \ldots, n$, we have $(PD)_{i_j, j} = d_j$ and $(PD)_{i,j} = 0$ for others i, j. Therefore we have $DP = PD_1$ where $D_1 = diag(d_{i_1}, d_{i_2}, \ldots, d_{i_n})$.

Also since each $d_{i_j} = d_v$ for some $v \in \{1, 2, \ldots, n\}$, the number of nonzero entries in D and D_1 are same.   □

Lemma 5. *Let $M = P + D_2$ be an $n \times n$ matrix, where D_2 is a diagonal matrix (may be singular) and P is a permutation matrix. Then*

$$M^r \leqq P^r + P^{r-1}D + P^{r-2}D + \ldots + PD + D_*$$

for $r \geq 2$, where D denotes some nonsingular diagonal matrix and $D_* = D_2^2$.

Proof. We will prove this result using mathematical induction. We have

$$M^2 = (P + D_2)(P + D_2) = P^2 + PD_2 + D_2P + D_2^2.$$

By Lemma 4, we have $D_2P = PD_3$ for some diagonal matrix D_3 and so if D_2 is a singular diagonal matrix, then $D_2 + D_3$ may be nonsingular. Therefore

$$M^2 \leqq P^2 + PD_2 + PD_3 + D_* \leqq P^2 + PD + D_*.$$

Thus the result is true for $r = 2$. Assume that the result is true for $r = k$. Now, $M^{k+1} = M^k(P + D_1)$. Therefore we have

$$\begin{aligned}
M^{k+1} &\leqq (P^k + P^{k-1}D + P^{k-2}D + \ldots + PD + D_*)(P + D_2) \\
&\leqq P^{k+1} + P^kD_2 + P^{k-1}DP + P^{k-1}DD_2 + P^{k-2}DP \\
&\quad + P^{k-2}DD_2 + \ldots + PDP + PDD_2 + D_*P + D_*D_2 \\
&\leqq P^{k+1} + P^kD_2 + P^{k-1}PD + P^{k-1}D_* + P^{k-2}PD + \ldots \\
&\quad + PPD + PD_* + PD_{2*} + D_*, \text{ where } D_*P = PD_{2*} \\
&= P^{k+1} + P^k(D_2 + D) + P^{k-1}(D_* + D) + \ldots + P(D_* + D_{2*}) \\
&\quad + D_* \\
&\leqq P^{k+1} + P^kD + P^{k-1}D + \ldots + PD + D_*.
\end{aligned}$$

This completes the proof. □

Theorem 3. *Given a DLS matrix $M = DLS(\rho; D_1, D_2)$ of order $n \geq 2$, for $k < n - 1$, the number of nonzero elements in M^k is less than n^2 and hence M^k is not MDS.*

Proof. We have $M = DLS(\rho; D_1, D_2) \leqq P + D_2$, where P is the permutation matrix corresponding to ρ. From Lemma 5, we have

$$\begin{aligned}
|M^k| &\leq |P^k + P^{k-1}D + \ldots + PD + D_*| \\
&\leq |P^kD| + |P^{k-1}D| + \ldots + |PD| + |D_*|.
\end{aligned} \tag{1}$$

Since power of a permutation matrix is again a permutation matrix, we have

$$|M^k| \leq \underbrace{|D| + |D| + \ldots + |D|}_{k \text{ times}} + |D_*| \leq kn + n. \tag{2}$$

Now for $k < n - 1$, we have

$$|M^k| < (n - 1)n + n = n^2 \implies |M^k| < n^2.$$

Hence M^k is not MDS for $k < n - 1$. □

Corollary 3. *For a DLS matrix $M = DLS(\rho; D_1, D_2)$ of order $n \geq 2$, if ρ is not an n-cycle, then M^k is not MDS for $k \leq n$.*

Proof. If ρ is not an n-cycle, then it is a product of disjoint cycles in S_n. Suppose that $\rho = \rho_1 \rho_2 \ldots \rho_v$, where ρ_i is a r_i-cycle in S_n for $i = 1, 2, \ldots, v$ and $v \in \{2, 3, \ldots, \lfloor \frac{n}{2} \rfloor\}$. Now from Eq. 2, for $k \leq n$, we have $|M^k| \leq n^2 + n$.

But by the definition of the DLS matrix, ρ has no fixed points, we have $2 \leq r_i \leq n - 2$ and $r_1 + r_2 + \ldots + r_v = n$. Now for the permutation matrix P related to ρ, $P^{r_i} D$ has r_i nonzero elements in the diagonal. Also D_* has n many nonzero elements in the diagonal and so we can eliminate the counting of the nonzero elements in the diagonal of $P^{r_i} D$ as $P^{r_i} D$ has r_i many nonzeros in the diagonal. Also as $v \leq \lfloor \frac{n}{2} \rfloor$, at least two multiples of some r_i occurs in the set $\{2, 3, \ldots, n\}$. Thus $P^{r_i} D$ and $P^{2r_i} D$ have at least r_i nonzero elements in the same diagonal position. Therefore we have

$$|M^n| \leq n^2 + n - (r_1 + r_2 + \ldots + r_v) - r_i \leq n^2 - 2.$$

Hence if ρ is not an n-cycle, then M^k is not MDS for $k \leq n$.   □

Remark 2. If D_2 is singular, having at least one zero in the diagonal then from Eq. 1 we have,

$$|M^k| \leq |P^k D| + |P^{k-1} D| + \ldots + |PD| + |D_{i=0}|$$
$$\leq \underbrace{n + n + \ldots + n}_{k \text{ times}} + (n - 1) = kn + n - 1.$$

where $D_{i=0}$ be some diagonal matrix with zero only at the i-th diagonal position for some $i \in \{1, 2, \ldots, n\}$. Thus for $k \leq n - 1$, we have $|M^k| \leq n^2 - 1$. Therefore if D_2 is singular (even if ρ is n-cycle), a DLS matrix of order $n \geq 2$, cannot be k-MDS for $k \leq n - 1$.

If D_2 is nonsingular, then the fixed XOR count for a DLS matrix is n. Whereas for the companion matrix, DSI matrix and sparse DSI matrix, the fixed XOR is $n-1$, $n-1$, and $\lceil \frac{n}{2} \rceil$ respectively. However, we can reduce the number of nonzero elements for D_2 in the DLS matrices to get a recursive MDS matrix from this. In this context, we have proved in Theorem 4 that in an n-MDS DLS matrix $DLS(\rho; D_1, D_2)$ of order n, D_2 must have at least $\lceil \frac{n}{2} \rceil$ nonzero elements. Thus for an n-MDS DLS matrix of order n, the fixed XOR can be reduced to $\lceil \frac{n}{2} \rceil$.

Lemma 6. *Let $M = P + D_2$ be an $n \times n$ matrix, where D_2 is a diagonal matrix having at most $t = \lceil \frac{n}{2} \rceil - 1$ nonzero elements and P is permutation matrix. Then*

$$M^r \leq P^r + P^{r-1} D + P^{r-2} D + \ldots + PD_{i=0} + D_{\{t\}=0}$$

for $r \geq 2$, where D denotes some nonsingular diagonal matrix, $D_{i=0}$ be some diagonal matrix with zero only at the i-th diagonal position for some $i \in \{1, 2, \ldots, n\}$ and $D_{\{t\}=0}$ be some diagonal matrix with t many zeros in the diagonal.

Proof. We will prove this result using mathematical induction. We have

$$M^2 = (P + D_2)(P + D_2) = P^2 + PD_2 + D_2P + D_2^2.$$

By Lemma 4, we have $D_{\{t\}=0}P = PD'_{\{t\}=0}$ for some diagonal matrix $D'_{\{t\}=0}$ with t many zeros in the diagonal and so $D_{\{t\}=0} + D'_{\{t\}=0}$ has at least one zero in the diagonal. Therefore

$$M^2 \leq P^2 + PD_{\{t\}=0} + PD'_{\{t\}=0} + D_{\{t\}=0} \leq P^2 + PD_{i=0} + D_{\{t\}=0}.$$

Therefore the result is true for $r = 2$. Assume that the result is true for $r = k$. Now, $M^{k+1} = M^k(P + D_2)$. Therefore we have

$$\begin{aligned}
M^{k+1} &\leq (P^k + P^{k-1}D + P^{k-2}D + \ldots + PD_{i=0} + D_{\{t\}=0})(P + D_{\{t\}=0}) \\
&\leq P^{k+1} + P^k D_{\{t\}=0} + P^{k-1}DP + P^{k-1}DD_{\{t\}=0} + \ldots + \\
&\quad + PD_{i=0}P + PD_{i=0}D_{\{t\}=0} + D_{\{t\}=0}P + D_{\{t\}=0} \\
&\leq P^{k+1} + P^k D_{\{t\}=0} + P^k D + P^{k-1}D_{\{t\}=0} + \ldots + P^2 D'_{j=0} \\
&\quad + PD_{\{t\}=0} + PD'_{\{t\}=0} + D_{\{t\}=0},
\end{aligned}$$

where $D_{i=0}P = PD'_{j=0}$ for some $D'_{j=0}$ and $D_{\{t\}=0}P = PD'_{\{t\}=0}$ for some diagonal matrix $D'_{\{t\}=0}$ with t many zeros in the diagonal. Thus we have

$$\begin{aligned}
M^{k+1} &\leq P^{k+1} + P^k(D_{\{t\}=0} + D) + \ldots + P(D_{\{t\}=0} + D'_{\{t\}=0}) + D_{\{t\}=0} \\
&\leq P^{k+1} + P^k D + \ldots + PD_{i=0} + D_{\{t\}=0}.
\end{aligned}$$

This completes the proof of the lemma.   □

Remark 3. If D_2 has $t = \lceil \frac{n}{2} \rceil$ nonzero elements then $D_{\{t\}=0} + D'_{\{t\}=0}$ may be nonsingular. For example, let $\rho = [2, 4, 1, 3]$ and $D = diag(a_1, 0, 0, a_4)$, where $a_1, a_4 \in \mathbb{F}_{2^r}^*$. Then we have $DP = PD'$, where $D' = diag(0, a_4, a_1, 0)$. Thus $D + D' = diag(a_1, a_4, a_1, a_4)$, which is nonsingular. Hence if D_2 has $t = \lceil \frac{n}{2} \rceil$ nonzero elements, then Lemma 6 will be modified as follows.

$$M^r \leq P^r + P^{r-1}D + P^{r-2}D + \ldots + PD + D_{\{t\}=0}$$

for $r \geq 2$, where D denotes some nonsingular diagonal matrix.

Theorem 4. *For an n-MDS DLS matrix $DLS(\rho; D_1, D_2)$ of order n, D_2 must have at least $\lceil \frac{n}{2} \rceil$ nonzero elements and ρ will be an n-cycle.*

Proof. Let $M = DLS(\rho; D_1, D_2)$ and D_2 has at most $t = \lceil \frac{n}{2} \rceil - 1$ nonzero elements. We have $M \leq P + D_2$, where P is the permutation matrix corresponding to ρ. From Lemma 6, we have

$$M^n \leq (P + D_2)^n \leq P^n + P^{n-1}D + P^{n-2}D + \ldots + PD_{i=0} + D_{\{t\}=0}.$$

Therefore, we have

$$|M^n| \le |P^n + P^{n-1}D + P^{n-2}D + \ldots + PD_{i=0} + D_{\{t\}=0}|$$
$$\le |P^n| + |P^{n-1}D| + |P^{n-2}D| + \ldots + |PD_{i=0}| + |D_{\{t\}=0}|.$$

Case 1: ρ is an n-cycle of S_n.

Then we have $P^n = I$, where I is the identity matrix of order n. Thus we have

$$|M^n| \le |I + P^{n-1}D + P^{n-2}D + \ldots + PD_{i=0} + D_{\{t\}=0}|$$
$$\le |I + D_{\{t\}=0}| + |P^{n-1}D| + |P^{n-2}D| + \ldots + |PD_{i=0}|.$$

Note that $|I + D_{\{t\}=0}| = n$ and $|PD_{i=0}| = n - 1$. Hence

$$|M^n| \le \underbrace{n + n + \ldots + n}_{n-1 \text{ times}} + (n-1) = (n-1)n + (n-1) = n^2 - 1 < n^2.$$

In that case, if D_2 has $\lceil \frac{n}{2} \rceil$ nonzero elements, then by Remark 3, we have

$$|M^n| \le |I + P^{n-1}D + P^{n-2}D + \ldots + PD + D_{\{t\}=0}|$$
$$\le |I + D_{\{t\}=0}| + |P^{n-1}D| + |P^{n-2}D| + \ldots + |PD|$$
$$= n \cdot n = n^2.$$

Thus if D_2 has $\lceil \frac{n}{2} \rceil$ nonzero elements, then $DLS(\rho; D_1, D_2)$ of order n can potentially be n-MDS.

Case 2: ρ is not an n-cycle.

Then $\rho = \rho_1 \rho_2 \ldots \rho_v$, where ρ_i is a r_i length cycle in S_n for $i = 1, 2, \ldots, v$ and $v \in \{2, 3, \ldots, \lfloor \frac{n}{2} \rfloor\}$. Also, since by the definition of the DLS matrix, ρ has no fixed point, we have $2 \le r_i \le n - 2$ and $r_1 + r_2 + \ldots + r_v = n$. Now for the permutation matrix P related to ρ, $P^{r_i}D$ has r_i nonzero elements in the diagonal. Also, as $v \le \lfloor \frac{n}{2} \rfloor$, at least two multiples of some r_i occurs in the set $\{2, 3, \ldots, n\}$. Thus $P^{r_i}D$ and $P^{2r_i}D$ have at least r_i nonzero elements in the same diagonal position. Thus we have

$$|M^n| \le |P^n| + |P^{n-1}D| + |P^{n-2}D| + \ldots + |PD_{i=0}| + |D_{\{t\}=0}|$$
$$\le |P^n| + |P^{n-1}D| + |P^{n-2}D| + \ldots + |PD_{i=0}|$$
$$\le (n-1)n + (n-1) - r_i$$
$$\le (n-1)n + (n-1) - 2 = n^2 - 3 < n^2.$$

In that case, if D_2 has $\lceil \frac{n}{2} \rceil$ nonzero elements, then we have

$$|M^n| \le n \cdot n - r_i \le n^2 - 2 < n^2.$$

Therefore $DLS(\rho; D_1, D_2)$ of order n can be n-MDS only when D_2 has at least $\lceil \frac{n}{2} \rceil$ nonzero elements and ρ is an n-cycle. $\qquad \square$

3.2 Equivalence Classes of DLS Matrices to Construct Recursive MDS Matrices

If the DLS matrix $DLS(\rho; D_1, D_2)$ of order n has a fixed XOR of k, the diagonal of D_2 has k nonzero elements. Since there are ${}^nC_k$ arrangements for the k nonzero elements in the diagonal of D_2, the search space for finding a recursive MDS matrix from the DLS matrices over the field $\mathbb{F}_{2^r}$ is $D(n) \cdot {}^nC_k \cdot (2^r)^{(n+k)}$, where $D(n)$[1] is the number of derangements for n different objects. However, we have reduced the search space drastically by defining some equivalence classes of DLS matrices to construct recursive MDS matrices. Finally, we show that the existence of n-MDS DLS matrices over $\mathbb{F}_{2^r}$ with $\mathcal{K} = \lceil \frac{n}{2} \rceil$ implies the existence of n-MDS sparse DSI matrices over $\mathbb{F}_{2^r}$.

Theorem 5. *Let $a_1, a_2, \ldots, a_n, a'_1, a'_2, \ldots, a'_n \in \mathbb{F}_{2^r}^*$ such that $a = \prod\limits_{i=1}^{n} a_i = \prod\limits_{i=1}^{n} a'_i$ for some $a \in \mathbb{F}_{2^r}^*$. Then for any diagonal matrix D_2 over $\mathbb{F}_{2^r}$, the DLS matrix $M = DLS(\rho; D_1, D_2)$ of order n is n-MDS if and only if $M' = DLS(\rho; D'_1, D_2)$ is n-MDS, where $D_1 = diag(a_1, a_2, \ldots, a_n)$ and $D'_1 = diag(a'_1, a'_2, \ldots, a'_n)$.*

Proof. Suppose $\rho = [i_1, \; i_2, \; i_3, \; \ldots, \; i_n]$ and P is the permutation matrix corresponding to ρ.

Now for any nonsingular diagonal matrix $D = diag(d_1, d_2, \ldots, d_n)$, we have

$$DMD^{-1} = D(PD_1 + D_2)D^{-1} = DPD_1D^{-1} + D_2.$$

Now by Lemma 4, we have $DP = PD'$ where $D' = diag(d_{i_1}, d_{i_2}, \ldots, d_{i_n})$. Thus we have

$$DMD^{-1} = P(D'D_1D^{-1}) + D_2.$$

If $D'D_1D^{-1} = D'_1$, then we have

$$DMD^{-1} = PD'_1 + D_2 = M'. \tag{3}$$

Now if $D'D_1D^{-1} = D'_1$, we have $D'D_1 = D'_1D$. Therefore we have

$$\left.\begin{aligned} a_1 d_{i_1} &= a'_1 d_1 \\ a_2 d_{i_2} &= a'_2 d_2 \\ &\;\;\vdots \\ a_n d_{i_n} &= a'_n d_n \end{aligned}\right\} \implies \left\{\begin{aligned} d_1 &= a_1 d_{i_1}(a'_1)^{-1} \\ d_2 &= a_2 d_{i_2}(a'_2)^{-1} \\ &\;\;\vdots \\ d_n &= a_n d_{i_n}(a'_n)^{-1}. \end{aligned}\right. \tag{4}$$

From Corollary 3, we know that a DLS matrix of order n can be n-MDS only when ρ is n-cycle. Thus from above, we have

$$a_1 a_2 \ldots a_n = a'_1 a'_2 \ldots a'_n = a.$$

Now choosing $d_1 = 1$, from Eq. 4, we get the values of other d_j's in terms of a_i's and a'_i's for $j = 2, 3, \ldots, n$. Also from Eq. 3, we can say that M is n-MDS if and only if M' is n-MDS. $\qquad\square$

---

[1] The value of $D(n)$ is $1, 2, 9, 44$ and 265 for $n = 2, 3, 4, 5$ and 6 respectively.

Corollary 4. *Let $a_1, a_2, \ldots, a_n \in \mathbb{F}_{2^r}^*$ such that $a = \prod_{i=1}^{n} a_i$ for some $a \in \mathbb{F}_{2^r}^*$. Then for any diagonal matrix D_2 over $\mathbb{F}_{2^r}$, the DLS matrix $M = DLS(\rho; D_1, D_2)$ of order n is n-MDS if and only if $M' = DLS(\rho; D_1', D_2)$ is n-MDS, where $D_1 = diag(a_1, a_2, \ldots, a_n)$ and $D_1' = diag(a, 1, 1, \ldots, 1)$.*

In [17, Theorem 8], authors proved the same result as Theorem 5 and Corollary 4 for a fixed permutation $\rho = [2, 3, 4, \ldots, n-1, n, 1]$. However, we have seen that the result holds for any n-cycle permutation.

Lemma 7. *Let $M_1 = DLS(\rho_1; D_1, D_2)$ be a DLS matrix of order n and $\rho_2 \in S_n$ is conjugate with ρ_1, then M_1 is n-MDS if and only if $M_2 = DLS(\rho_2; D_1', D_2')$ is n-MDS, where D_1' and D_2' are some diagonal matrices.*

Proof. Since ρ_1 and ρ_2 are conjugate, we have $\sigma \rho_1 \sigma^{-1} = \rho_2$, for some $\sigma \in S_n$. Let P_1, P_2 and P be the permutation matrices related to ρ_1, ρ_2 and σ respectively. Then we have

$$PM_1P^{-1} = P(P_1D_1 + D_2)P^{-1} = PP_1D_1P^{-1} + PD_2P^{-1}$$
$$= PP_1P^{-1}D_1' + PP^{-1}D_2',$$

where $D_1P^{-1} = P^{-1}D_1'$ and $D_2P^{-1} = P^{-1}D_2'$ for some diagonal matrices D_1' and D_2'. Thus we have $PM_1P^{-1} = P_2D_1' + D_2' = M_2$. Since $PM_1P^{-1} = M_2$, from Corollary 2 we can say that M_1 is n-MDS if and only if M_2 is n-MDS. □

Remark 4. We know that a DLS matrix $DLS(\rho_1; D_1, D_2)$ can be n-MDS only when ρ is an n-cycle. Also, the n-cycles in S_n are conjugate to each other. Thus for finding the n-MDS DLS matrices, we need to check only for the DLS matrices related to a particular n-cycle ρ.

Now consider $\mathbb{D}(n, \mathbb{F}_{2^r})$ to be the set of all DLS matrices $DLS(\rho; D_1, D_2)$ of order n, with fixed XOR of k, over the field $\mathbb{F}_{2^r}$ and define

$$\mathbb{D}'(n, \mathbb{F}_{2^r}) = \{B \in \mathbb{D}(n, \mathbb{F}_{2^r}) : B = P'D_1' + D_2'\},$$

where P' is the permutation matrix related to the n length cycle $[2, 3, 4, \ldots, n-1, n, 1]^2$, $D_1' = diag(a, 1, 1, \ldots, 1)$ and D_2' is a diagonal matrix containing k nonzero elements.

3.3 Equivalence of DLS Matrices with Sparse DSI Matrices

In this section, we show that the existence of n-MDS DLS matrices with $\mathcal{K} = \lceil \frac{n}{2} \rceil$ over $\mathbb{F}_{2^r}$ implies the existence of n-MDS sparse DSI matrices over $\mathbb{F}_{2^r}$.

By Corollary 4 and Remark 4, we can say that in order to search for n-MDS matrices from the set $\mathbb{D}(n, \mathbb{F}_{2^r})$, it is enough to search for n-MDS matrices from the set $\mathbb{D}'(n, \mathbb{F}_{2^r})$. For the fixed XOR k, D_2 has ${}^nC_k$ many choices of

---

[2] By Remark 4, any n length cycle can be chosen for the set $\mathbb{D}'(n, \mathbb{F}_{2^r})$.

arrangements of the k nonzero elements. However, in [11, Theorem 5], authors proved that if $\rho = [2, 3, 4, \ldots, n-1, n, 1]$ and D_2 has any two consecutive zero entries[3], $B = PD_1 + D_2$ must contain a zero element when raised to power n i.e. B cannot be n-MDS, where P is the permutation matrix of order n related to the permutation ρ and D_1 is a nonsingular matrix. For the n-MDS DLS matrix $DLS(\rho; D_1, D_2)$ with $\rho = [2, 3, 4, \ldots, n-1, n, 1]$ and $\mathcal{K} = \lceil \frac{n}{2} \rceil$, there are n and 2 eligible arrangements of the nonzero elements in D_2 when n is odd and even respectively. However, we show that for all such eligible arrangements, $DLS(\rho; D_1, D_2)$ is permutation similar to some sparse DSI matrix.

Consider $\mathbb{D}''$ be the set of all DLS matrices $DLS(\rho; D_1, D_2)$ with $\rho = [2, 3, 4, \ldots, n-1, n, 1]$, $\mathcal{K} = \lceil \frac{n}{2} \rceil$, and the eligible arrangements of nonzero elements in D_2. It can be observed that any DLS matrix $B \in \mathbb{D}''$ are permutation similar to some sparse DSI matrix of order n. More specifically, we have

$$Q \cdot DLS(\rho; D_1, D_2) \cdot Q^{-1} = D_s,$$

where Q is the permutation matrix of order n related to the permutation $\sigma = \rho^k$ for some $k = 1, 2, \ldots, n$ and D_s denotes some sparse DSI matrix of order n.

Therefore any DLS matrices $B \in \mathbb{D}''$ is n-MDS over $\mathbb{F}_{2^r}$ implies that there is an n-MDS sparse DSI matrix over $\mathbb{F}_{2^r}$. Hence, by Remark 4 and Table 4 of [17], we have the results for the existence of n-MDS DLS matrices over $\mathbb{F}_{2^r}$ for $n = 4, 5, 6, 7, 8$ listed in Table 2.

Table 2. n-MDS DLS matrix of order n over the field $\mathbb{F}_{2^r}$ with $\mathcal{K} = \lceil \frac{n}{2} \rceil$ ("DNE" stands for does not exist).

Order n	Over field $\mathbb{F}_{2^4}$	Over field $\mathbb{F}_{2^5}$	Over field $\mathbb{F}_{2^6}$	Over field $\mathbb{F}_{2^7}$	Over field $\mathbb{F}_{2^8}$
4	Exists	Exists	Exists	Exists	Exists
5	DNE	Exists	Exists	Exists	Exists
6	DNE	DNE	DNE	Exists	Exists
7	DNE	DNE	DNE	DNE	Exists
8	DNE	DNE	DNE	DNE	DNE

Companion matrices of order n have $\mathcal{K} = n-1$, whereas DLS matrices can be n-MDS if $\mathcal{K} = \lceil \frac{n}{2} \rceil$. In [26], the authors have provided some examples of efficient companion matrices that are n-MDS over the field $\mathbb{F}_{2^4}$ for $n = 5, 6, 7$, and 8. But from Table 2, we can see that there are no n-MDS DLS matrices with $\mathcal{K} = \lceil \frac{n}{2} \rceil$ over the field $\mathbb{F}_{2^4}$ for $n = 5, 6, 7$, and 8. Next, we increase the value of $\mathcal{K}$ from $\lceil \frac{n}{2} \rceil$ to $n-1$, to check whether there are n-MDS DLS matrices over the field $\mathbb{F}_{2^4}$. For this, we reduce the search space using Corollary 4 and Remark 4 and then perform an exhaustive search in the restricted domain. We observe that

---

[3] Note that here the first and n-th diagonal elements are also considered as consecutive entries.

there are no n-MDS DLS matrices over the field $\mathbb{F}_{2^4}$ for $n = 5, 6, 7$, and 8 and $\mathcal{K} = \lceil \frac{n}{2} \rceil, \lceil \frac{n}{2} \rceil + 1, \ldots, n - 1$.

4   Construction of MDS Matrices from Generalized DLS Matrices

In this section, we extend Definition 12 to propose a class of sparse matrices called as GDLS matrices. Then we propose some lightweight recursive MDS matrices of orders $4, 5, 6$, and 7, using GDLS matrices.

Definition 13. *Let $\rho_1 = [i_1, i_2, i_3, \ldots, i_n]$ and $\rho_2 = [j_1, j_2, j_3, \ldots, j_n]$ be two permutations such that $i_k \neq j_k$ for $k = 1, 2, \ldots, n$, D_1 be a nonsingular diagonal matrix and D_2 be a diagonal matrix (may be singular). Then we will call the matrix $B = P_1 D_1 + P_2 D_2$ as the generalized DLS (GDLS) matrix, where P_1 and P_2 are the permutation matrices of order n related to the permutation ρ_1 and ρ_2 respectively. We will denote these matrices as $GDLS(\rho_1, \rho_2; D_1, D_2)$.*

Remark 5. Note that GDLS matrix is row permuted matrix of DLS matrix. More specifically, we have

$$GDLS(\rho_1, \rho_2; D_1, D_2) = P_2(P_2^{-1} P_1 D_1 + D_2) = P_2 \cdot DLS(\rho; D_1, D_2)$$

where $P = P_2^{-1} P_1$ is the permutation matrix of order n related to the permutation $\rho = \rho_2^{-1} \rho_1$. Thus $GDLS(\rho_1, \rho_2; D_1, D_2)$ is row permuted $DLS(\rho_2^{-1} \rho_1; D_1, D_2)$.

Example 6. However, a $GDLS(\rho_1, \rho_2; D_1, D_2)$ matrix of order n is n-MDS does not imply that $DLS(\rho_2^{-1} \rho_1; D_1, D_2)$ is n-MDS. For $\rho_1 = [2, 3, 4, 1], \rho_2 = [3, 2, 1, 4]$ and $D_1 = diag(1, 1, 1, \alpha^2), D_2 = diag(\alpha^{-1}, 0, \alpha^{-1}, 0)$, we have the 4-MDS GDLS matrix

$$M = GDLS(\rho_1, \rho_2; D_1, D_2) = P_1 D_1 + P_2 D_2$$

$$= \begin{bmatrix} 0 & 0 & \alpha^{-1} & \alpha^2 \\ 1 & 0 & 0 & 0 \\ \alpha^{-1} & 1 & 0 & 0 \\ 0 & 0 & 1 & 0 \end{bmatrix} = \begin{bmatrix} 0 & 0 & 1 & 0 \\ 0 & 1 & 0 & 0 \\ 1 & 0 & 0 & 0 \\ 0 & 0 & 0 & 1 \end{bmatrix} \begin{bmatrix} \alpha^{-1} & 1 & 0 & 0 \\ 1 & 0 & 0 & 0 \\ 0 & 0 & \alpha^{-1} & \alpha^2 \\ 0 & 0 & 1 & 0 \end{bmatrix}$$

$$= P_2 DLS(\rho_2^{-1} \rho_1; D_1, D_2),$$

where $\rho_2^{-1} \rho_1 = [2, 1, 4, 3]$, α is a primitive element of $\mathbb{F}_{2^4}/0x13$ and α is a root of $x^4 + x + 1$. But the DLS matrix $DLS(\rho_2^{-1} \rho_1; D_1, D_2)$ is not 4-MDS.

Also, note that diagonal/permutation similar matrix of a DLS matrix is again a DLS matrix. So the structure of the GDLS matrix is important for constructing recursive MDS matrices.

To find lightweight recursive MDS matrices, we looked through the GDLS matrices of order n whose entries are from the set $\{1, \alpha, \alpha^{-1}, \alpha^2, \alpha^{-2}, \alpha^3, \alpha^{-3}\}$, where α is a primitive element of the field $\mathbb{F}_{2^r}$. First, we start with $\mathcal{K} = \lceil \frac{n}{2} \rceil$ and if we do not find any n-MDS GDLS matrix, then we increase the value of $\mathcal{K}$. Even with the set $\{1, \alpha, \alpha^{-1}, \alpha^2, \alpha^{-2}, \alpha^3, \alpha^{-3}\}$, the search space for finding n-MDS matrices of order $n \geq 5$ is large. Hence, we perform a random search to obtain n-MDS matrices of order $n = 5, 6, 7, 8$. But, the proposed 4-MDS matrix of order 4 is found by exhaustive search. Although we could not obtain n-MDS matrices from $\mathbb{F}_{2^4}$ for $n = 6, 7, 8$, and 8-MDS matrix over $\mathbb{F}_{2^8}$, there is still hope of getting such n-MDS matrices. To calculate the implementation costs of the matrices given in that paper, we use the table from [26, App. B].

4.1   Construction of 4×4 Recursive MDS Matrices

In this section, we propose a GDLS matrix of order 4 that yields a recursive MDS matrix. The proposed GDLS matrix is constructed by the permutations $\rho_1 = [4, 3, 1, 2]$, $\rho_2 = [2, 1, 4, 3]$ and with the value of $\mathcal{K} = 2$.

For $\rho_1 = [4, 3, 1, 2], \rho_2 = [2, 1, 4, 3]$ and diagonal matrices $D_1 = diag(\alpha, 1, 1, 1)$, $D_2 = diag(1, \alpha, 0, 0)$, we have the GDLS matrix of order 4 over $\mathbb{F}_{2^4}$ as follows

$$B = GDLS(\rho_1, \rho_2; D_1, D_2) = \begin{bmatrix} 0 & \alpha & 1 & 0 \\ 1 & 0 & 0 & 1 \\ 0 & 1 & 0 & 0 \\ \alpha & 0 & 0 & 0 \end{bmatrix},$$

where α is a primitive element of $\mathbb{F}_{2^4}/0x13$ and α is a root of $x^4 + x + 1 = 0$. The matrix B is a 4-MDS matrix with a XOR count of $(1 + 1) + 2 \cdot 4 = 10$.

Remark 6. If we consider α to be a root of $x^8 + x^7 + x^6 + x + 1$ which is the constructing polynomial of $\mathbb{F}_{2^8}$, then B is 4-MDS over the field $\mathbb{F}_{2^8}$ and its XOR count will be $(3 + 3) + 2 \cdot 8 = 22$.

Remark 7. Since there is no trinomial irreducible polynomial of degree 8 over $\mathbb{F}_2$, elements with XOR count 1 in $\mathbb{F}_{2^8}$ are not possible (see [3, Theorem 2]). But over rings, we can have elements with a XOR count of 1.

Consider the GDLS matrix $B_{4,8} = GDLS(\rho_1, \rho_2; D_1, D_2)$ over $\mathbb{F}_2[L]$, where $\rho_1 = [4, 3, 1, 2], \rho_2 = [2, 1, 4, 3]$, $D_1 = diag(L, 1, 1, 1)$, $D_2 = diag(1, L, 0, 0)$.

Then it is easy to verify that $B_{4,8}^4$ is MDS over $\mathbb{F}_2[L]$. The set of minors of $B_{4,8}^4$ are

$$\{1, L, L^2, L^2 + 1, L^2 + L, L^3, L^3 + 1, L^3 + L, L^3 + L^2, L^3 + L^2 + L, L^4, L^4 + L^2,$$
$$L^4 + L^3 + 1, L^4 + L^3 + L, L^4 + L^3 + L^2, L^4 + L^3 + L^2 + 1, L^5, L^5 + L^2, L^5 + L^3,$$
$$L^5 + L^3 + L, L^5 + L^4, L^5 + L^4 + L, L^5 + L^4 + L^2, L^5 + L^4 + L^3 + L, L^6, L^6 + L^4 + L^2,$$
$$L^6 + L^5, L^7, L^8 + L^3\}$$

whose factors are

$$\{1, L, L^2, L+1, L^2+L+1, L^3+L+1, L^3+L^2+1, L^4+L^3+1, L^4+L^3+L^2+L+1\}. \tag{5}$$

Now, consider the binary matrix $C_{4,8} = [[2], [3], [4], [5], [6], [7], [8], [1, 3]]$ which is the companion matrix of $x^8 + x^2 + 1$ over $\mathbb{F}_2$. Then using $L = C_{4,8}$, the given elements in 5 are nonsingular matrices over $\mathbb{F}_2$. In addition, the implementation cost of $C_{4,8}$ is 1 XOR. Hence, $B_{4,8}$ is 4-MDS over $GL(8, \mathbb{F}_2)$ and the implementation cost of $B_{4,8}$ is $(1 + 1) + 2 \cdot 8 = 18$ XORs.

4.2   Construction of 5×5 Recursive MDS Matrices

In this section, we propose a GDLS matrix of order 5 that yields a recursive MDS matrix over $\mathbb{F}_{2^8}$. This GDLS matrix has the lowest XOR count among the existing recursive MDS matrices of order 5 over $\mathbb{F}_{2^8}$. Also, we provide an example of a 5-MDS GDLS matrix over $\mathbb{F}_{2^4}$.

For $\rho_1 = [3, 4, 5, 1, 2], \rho_2 = [5, 3, 1, 2, 4]$ and diagonal matrices $D_1 = diag(1, 1, \alpha^{-1}, 1, 1)$, $D_2 = diag(\alpha, 0, 1, 0, 1)$, we have the GDLS matrix of order 5 over $\mathbb{F}_{2^8}$ as follows

$$B = GDLS(\rho_1, \rho_2; D_1, D_2) = \begin{bmatrix} 0 & 0 & 1 & 1 & 0 \\ 0 & 0 & 0 & 0 & 1 \\ 1 & 0 & 0 & 0 & 0 \\ 0 & 1 & 0 & 0 & 1 \\ \alpha & 0 & \alpha^{-1} & 0 & 0 \end{bmatrix},$$

where α is a primitive element of $\mathbb{F}_{2^8}/0x1c3$ and α is a root of $x^8 + x^7 + x^6 + x + 1$. The matrix B is a 5-MDS matrix with a XOR count of $(3 + 3) + 3 \cdot 8 = 30$, outperforming the best known results for a 5-MDS matrix over $\mathbb{F}_{2^8}$.

We have observed that there is no 5-MDS DLS matrix of order 5 over the field $\mathbb{F}_{2^4}$ with $\mathcal{K} = 3$ and $\mathcal{K} = 4$. However, we have 5-MDS GDLS matrix of order 5 over the field $\mathbb{F}_{2^4}$ with $\mathcal{K} = 4$. For example for $\rho_1 = [4, 2, 3, 5, 1], \rho_2 = [2, 4, 1, 3, 5]$ and diagonal matrices $D_1 = diag(\alpha, \alpha^3, 1, \alpha^2, \alpha^3)$, $D_2 = diag(1, 1, \alpha^{-1}, 1, 0)$, we have the GDLS matrix of order 5 over $\mathbb{F}_{2^4}$ as follows

$$B = \begin{bmatrix} 0 & 0 & \alpha^{-1} & 0 & \alpha^3 \\ 1 & \alpha^3 & 0 & 0 & 0 \\ 0 & 0 & 1 & 1 & 0 \\ \alpha & 1 & 0 & 0 & 0 \\ 0 & 0 & 0 & \alpha^2 & 0 \end{bmatrix},$$

where α is a primitive element of $\mathbb{F}_{2^4}/0x13$ and α is a root of $x^4 + x + 1$. It can be verified that B is 5-MDS over $\mathbb{F}_{2^4}$ with XOR count of $(1+1+2+3+3)+4 \cdot 4 = 26$.

Remark 8. Consider the GDLS matrix $B_{5,8} = GDLS(\rho_1, \rho_2; D_1, D_2)$ over $\mathbb{F}_2[L]$, where $\rho_1 = [3, 4, 5, 1, 2], \rho_2 = [5, 3, 1, 2, 4]$, $D_1 = diag(1, 1, L-1, 1, 1)$ and $D_2 = diag(L, 0, 1, 0, 1)$. Then it can be verified that $B_{5,8}$ is 5-MDS over $\mathbb{F}_2[L]$. Let $\mathbb{S}_5$ be the set of factors of the minors of $B_{5,8}^5$. It is easy to check that the polynomial $L^8 + L^7 + L^2 + L + 1 \notin \mathbb{S}_5$.

Now, consider the binary matrix $C_{5,8} = [[8], [1, 2], [2, 8], [3], [4], [5], [6], [7]]$ whose minimal polynomial is $x^8 + x^7 + x^2 + x + 1$. Then using $L = C_{5,8}$, the elements in $\mathbb{S}_5$ are nonsingular matrices over $\mathbb{F}_2$. In addition, the implementation cost of $C_{5,8}$ is 2 XORs. Also, $C_{5,8}^{-1}$ can be implemented with 2 XORs. Hence $B_{5,8}$ is 5-MDS over $GL(8, \mathbb{F}_2)$ and the implementation cost of $B_{5,8}$ is $(2+2)+3 \cdot 8 = 28$ XORs.

4.3   Construction of 6×6 Recursive MDS Matrices

In this section, we propose a GDLS matrix of order 6 that yields a recursive MDS matrix over $\mathbb{F}_{2^8}$.

For $\rho_1 = [6, 1, 2, 3, 4, 5], \rho_2 = [5, 6, 1, 2, 3, 4]$ and diagonal matrices $D_1 = diag(1,\ 1,\ \alpha,\ 1,\ 1,\ 1), D_2 = diag(1,\ 0,\ 1,\ 0,\ \alpha^2,\ 0)$, we have the GDLS matrix of order 6 over $\mathbb{F}_{2^8}$ as follows

$$B = GDLS(\rho_1, \rho_2; D_1, D_2) = \begin{bmatrix} 0 & 1 & 1 & 0 & 0 & 0 \\ 0 & 0 & \alpha & 0 & 0 & 0 \\ 0 & 0 & 0 & 1 & \alpha^2 & 0 \\ 0 & 0 & 0 & 0 & 1 & 0 \\ 1 & 0 & 0 & 0 & 0 & 1 \\ 1 & 0 & 0 & 0 & 0 & 0 \end{bmatrix},$$

where α is a primitive element of $\mathbb{F}_{2^8}/0x1c3$ and α is a root of $x^8 + x^7 + x^6 + x + 1$. The matrix B is a 6-MDS matrix with a XOR count of $(3+4)+3 \cdot 8 = 31$, which corresponds to the best result for a 6-MDS matrix over $\mathbb{F}_{2^8}$.

Remark 9. Consider the GDLS matrix $B_{6,8} = GDLS(\rho_1, \rho_2; D_1, D_2)$ over $\mathbb{F}_2[L]$, where $\rho_1 = [6, 1, 2, 3, 4, 5], \rho_2 = [5, 6, 1, 2, 3, 4]$ and $D_1 = diag(1, 1, L, 1, 1, 1)$, $D_2 = diag(1, 0, 1, 0, L^2, 0)$. Then it can be verified that $B_{6,8}$ is 6-MDS over $\mathbb{F}_2[L]$. Let $\mathbb{S}_6$ be the set of factors of the minors of $B_{6,8}^6$. It is easy to check that the polynomial $L^8 + L^7 + L^2 + L + 1 \notin \mathbb{S}_6$. Then using $L = C_{5,8}$ from Remark 8 the elements in $\mathbb{S}_6$ are nonsingular matrices over $\mathbb{F}_2$. The binary matrix $C_{5,8}^2$ can be implemented with 4 XORs. Hence $B_{6,8}$ is 6-MDS over $GL(8, \mathbb{F}_2)$ and the implementation cost of $B_{6,8}$ is $(2 + 4) + 3 \cdot 8 = 30$ XORs.

Following that, we looked for a 6-MDS GDLS matrix over $\mathbb{F}_{2^4}$, but we could not find a 6-MDS matrix of order 6 in $\mathbb{F}_{2^4}$.

4.4   Construction of 7×7 Recursive MDS Matrices

In this section, we propose a GDLS matrix of order 7 that yields a recursive MDS matrix over $\mathbb{F}_{2^8}$.

For $\rho_1 = [7, 1, 2, 3, 4, 5, 6], \rho_2 = [3, 2, 5, 4, 7, 6, 1]$ and diagonal matrices $D_1 = diag(1,\ \alpha^{-2},\ \alpha^{-2},\ 1,\ \alpha^3,\ 1,\ 1), D_2 = diag(1, 0, 1, 0, 1, 0, 1)$, we have the GDLS matrix of order 7 over $\mathbb{F}_{2^8}$ as follows

$$B = GDLS(\rho_1, \rho_2; D_1, D_2) = \begin{bmatrix} 0 & \alpha^{-2} & 0 & 0 & 0 & 0 & 1 \\ 0 & 0 & \alpha^{-2} & 0 & 0 & 0 & 0 \\ 1 & 0 & 0 & 1 & 0 & 0 & 0 \\ 0 & 0 & 0 & 0 & \alpha^3 & 0 & 0 \\ 0 & 0 & 1 & 0 & 0 & 1 & 0 \\ 0 & 0 & 0 & 0 & 0 & 0 & 1 \\ 1 & 0 & 0 & 0 & 1 & 0 & 0 \end{bmatrix},$$

where α is a primitive element of $\mathbb{F}_{2^8}/0x1c3$ and α is a root of $x^8 + x^7 + x^6 + x + 1$. The matrix B is a 7-MDS matrix with a XOR count of $(5 + 4 + 4) + 4 \cdot 8 = 45$, outperforming the best known results for a 7-MDS matrix over $\mathbb{F}_{2^8}$.

After that, we searched for a 7-MDS GDLS matrix over $\mathbb{F}_{2^4}$ but could not get a 7-MDS matrix of order 7 in $\mathbb{F}_{2^4}$.

As 4 and 8 are the most commonly used diffusion layer matrix sizes, we look for an 8-MDS GDLS matrix of order 8 over $\mathbb{F}_{2^4}$ and $\mathbb{F}_{2^8}$. However, we were unable to find a GDLS matrix of order 8, which corresponds to 8-MDS.

4.5 Importance of GDLS Matrices

In this section, we look at the importance of GDLS matrices for the construction of recursive MDS matrices.

1. The popular DSI matrix is a particular type of GDLS matrix. Also, note that the GFS matrix structure used in [27] is a particular type of GDLS matrix. More specifically, for $\rho_1 = [n, 1, 2, 3, \ldots, n-1]$, $\rho_2 = [1, n, 3, 2, 5, 4, 7, \ldots, n-1, n-2]$, a nonsingular diagonal matrix $D_1 = diag(L_1, 1, L_3, 1, \ldots, L_{n-1}, 1)$ and $D_2 = diag(0, L_2, 0, L_4, 0, \ldots, 0, L_n)$ we have $GDLS(\rho_1, \rho_2; D_1, D_2)$ as the GFS matrix in [27]. In addition, each GFS matrix structure used in [23] to construct MDS matrices can be viewed as a GDLS matrix.
2. Also, the GFS matrix structure utilized in [23,27] only exists for even orders, whereas our GDLS matrix structure exists for all orders, allowing us to obtain improvements on several parameters that were not possible with the GFS matrix structure.
3. From Table 2 and later discussions, we know that there are no n-MDS DLS matrices over $\mathbb{F}_{2^4}$ for $n = 5, 6, 7, 8$ with $\mathcal{K} = \lceil \frac{n}{2} \rceil, \lceil \frac{n}{2} \rceil + 1, \ldots, n-1$. However, we know that there are 5-MDS GDLS matrices over $\mathbb{F}_{2^4}$ with a fixed XOR of 4. Also, the diagonal (or permutation) similar matrix of a DLS matrix is again a DLS matrix. So the structure of the GDLS matrix is important for constructing recursive MDS matrices.
4. In [11, Theorem 2], authors prove that there does not exist any n-MDS matrix of order n with a fixed XOR of 1 for $n \geq 3$. Thus, the example of the 4-MDS GDLS matrix in Sect. 4.1 has the lowest possible fixed XOR count. Since the diffusion matrix of order 4 is perhaps the most frequently utilized matrix size for the diffusion layer, the 4-MDS GDLS matrix is an excellent contender for designing lightweight ciphers.

5. Using GDLS matrices, we provide some lightweight recursive MDS matrices of orders $5, 6$, and 7 over $\mathbb{F}_{2^8}$. The results match those of the best known lightweight recursive MDS matrices of order 6 and outperform those of orders 5 and 7.

5   Conclusion and Future Work

In this paper, we introduce a new type of sparse matrix called the Diagonal-like sparse (DLS) matrix and we see that the DSI matrix is a specific type of DLS matrix. We also show that the fixed XOR $(\mathcal{K})$ for an n-MDS DLS matrix of order n should be at least $\left\lceil \frac{n}{2} \right\rceil$. We present some theoretical results on DLS matrices and some of those results are used to narrow the search space for finding n-MDS DLS matrices over the field $\mathbb{F}_{2^r}$. Finally, we show that the existence of n-MDS DLS matrices over $\mathbb{F}_{2^r}$ with $\mathcal{K} = \left\lceil \frac{n}{2} \right\rceil$ implies the existence of n-MDS sparse DSI matrices over $\mathbb{F}_{2^r}$. We extend the definition of the DLS matrix to define some class of sparse matrices called GDLS matrices. Using GDLS matrices, we introduce some efficient recursive MDS matrices of orders $4, 5, 6$, and 7 that can be implemented with $22, 30, 31$, and 45 XORs over $\mathbb{F}_{2^8}$. The results are the same as with the best known lightweight recursive MDS matrices of orders 4 and 6, but the results are better than the best known matrices of orders 5 and 7.

Our investigations in this paper open up many possibilities for future work.

1. We see that 8-MDS DLS matrices do not exist over $\mathbb{F}_{2^8}$ with the lowest fixed XOR of 4. So it could be a future work to find an 8-MDS DLS matrix of order 8 over $\mathbb{F}_{2^8}$ with a higher fixed XOR.
2. We have provided some theoretical results on DLS matrices in order to narrow the search space for finding n-MDS DLS matrices over the field $\mathbb{F}_{2^r}$. So it could be a future work to provide theoretical results on GDLS matrices for reducing the search space. As 4 and 8 are the most commonly used diffusion layer matrix sizes, we look for an 8-MDS GDLS matrix of order 8 over $\mathbb{F}_{2^4}$ and $\mathbb{F}_{2^8}$. However, we were unable to find a GDLS matrix of order 8, which corresponds to 8-MDS. So it could be a future work to find 8-MDS GDLS matrices of order 8 over $\mathbb{F}_{2^4}$ and $\mathbb{F}_{2^8}$.
3. By the composition of different GFS matrices, the authors in [23] have constructed some lightweight MDS matrices of even orders (for orders 4, 6, and 8). We know the GDLS matrix structure exists for all orders. So it could be a future work to use GDLS matrices for such constructions for finding lightweight MDS matrices of any order.
4. There are many direct constructions of recursive MDS matrix from companion matrices. So it can be a problem for further research to find a direct construction method for recursive MDS matrices from a DLS or GDLS matrix.

Acknowledgments. We are thankful to the anonymous reviewers for their valuable comments. We also wish to thank Sandip Kumar Mondal and Samir Kundu for providing several useful and valuable suggestions. Susanta Samanta is supported by the project "Study and Analysis of IoT Security" by NTRO under the Government of India at R.C. Bose Centre for Cryptology and Security, Indian Statistical Institute, Kolkata.

References

1. Augot, D., Finiasz, M.: Direct construction of recursive MDS diffusion layers using shortened BCH codes. In: Cid, C., Rechberger, C. (eds.) FSE 2014. LNCS, vol. 8540, pp. 3–17. Springer, Heidelberg (2015). https://doi.org/10.1007/978-3-662-46706-0_1
2. Banik, S., Funabiki, Y., Isobe, T.: More results on shortest linear programs. In: Attrapadung, N., Yagi, T. (eds.) IWSEC 2019. LNCS, vol. 11689, pp. 109–128. Springer, Cham (2019). https://doi.org/10.1007/978-3-030-26834-3_7
3. Beierle, C., Kranz, T., Leander, G.: Lightweight multiplication in $GF(2^n)$ with applications to MDS matrices. In: Robshaw, M., Katz, J. (eds.) CRYPTO 2016. LNCS, vol. 9814, pp. 625–653. Springer, Heidelberg (2016). https://doi.org/10.1007/978-3-662-53018-4_23
4. Berger, T.P.: Construction of recursive MDS diffusion layers from Gabidulin codes. In: Paul, G., Vaudenay, S. (eds.) INDOCRYPT 2013. LNCS, vol. 8250, pp. 274–285. Springer, Cham (2013). https://doi.org/10.1007/978-3-319-03515-4_18
5. Boyar, J., Matthews, P., Peralta, R.: Logic minimization techniques with applications to cryptology. J. Cryptol. **26**(2), 280–312 (2012). https://doi.org/10.1007/s00145-012-9124-7
6. Daemen, J., Rijmen, V.: The Design of Rijndael: AES - The Advanced Encryption Standard. Information Security and Cryptography, Springer, Heidelberg (2002). https://doi.org/10.1007/978-3-662-04722-4
7. Duval, S., Leurent, G.: MDS matrices with lightweight circuits. IACR Trans. Symm. Cryptol. **2018**(2), 48–78 (2018)
8. Guo, J., Peyrin, T., Poschmann, A.: The PHOTON family of lightweight hash functions. In: Rogaway, P. (ed.) CRYPTO 2011. LNCS, vol. 6841, pp. 222–239. Springer, Heidelberg (2011). https://doi.org/10.1007/978-3-642-22792-9_13
9. Guo, J., Peyrin, T., Poschmann, A., Robshaw, M.: The LED block cipher. In: Preneel, B., Takagi, T. (eds.) CHES 2011. LNCS, vol. 6917, pp. 326–341. Springer, Heidelberg (2011). https://doi.org/10.1007/978-3-642-23951-9_22
10. Gupta, K.C., Pandey, S.K., Ray, I.G., Samanta, S.: Cryptographically significant MDS matrices over finite fields: a brief survey and some generalized results. Adv. Math. Commun. **13**(4), 779–843 (2019)
11. Gupta, K.C., Pandey, S.K., Samanta, S.: A few negative results on constructions of MDS matrices using low XOR matrices. In: Bhasin, S., Mendelson, A., Nandi, M. (eds.) SPACE 2019. LNCS, vol. 11947, pp. 195–213. Springer, Cham (2019). https://doi.org/10.1007/978-3-030-35869-3_14
12. Gupta, K.C., Pandey, S.K., Venkateswarlu, A.: On the direct construction of recursive MDS matrices. Designs Codes Cryptogr. **82**, 77–94 (2017)
13. Gupta, K.C., Pandey, S.K., Venkateswarlu, A.: Towards a general construction of recursive MDS diffusion layers. Designs Codes Cryptogr. **82**, 179–195 (2017)
14. Gupta, K.C., Pandey, S.K., Venkateswarlu, A.: Almost involutory recursive MDS diffusion layers. Designs Codes Cryptogr. **87**, 609–626 (2019)
15. Jean, J., Peyrin, T., Sim, S.M., Tourteaux, J.: Optimizing implementations of lightweight building blocks. IACR Trans. Symm. Cryptol. **2017**(4), 130–168 (2017)
16. Kesarwani, A., Pandey, S.K., Sarkar, S., Venkateswarlu, A.: Recursive MDS matrices over finite commutative rings. Discret. Appl. Math. **304**, 384–396 (2021)
17. Kesarwani, A., Sarkar, S., Venkateswarlu, A.: Exhaustive search for various types of MDS matrices. IACR Trans. Symm. Cryptol. **2019**(3), 231–256 (2019)

18. Khoo, K., Peyrin, T., Poschmann, A.Y., Yap, H.: FOAM: searching for hardware-optimal SPN structures and components with a fair comparison. In: Batina, L., Robshaw, M. (eds.) CHES 2014. LNCS, vol. 8731, pp. 433–450. Springer, Heidelberg (2014). https://doi.org/10.1007/978-3-662-44709-3_24
19. Kranz, T., Leander, G., Stoffelen, K., Wiemer, F.: Shorter linear straight-line programs for MDS matrices. IACR Trans. Symm. Cryptol. **2017**(4), 188–211 (2017)
20. Li, S., Sun, S., Li, C., Wei, Z., Lei, H.: Constructing low-latency involutory MDS matrices with lightweight circuits. IACR Trans. Symm. Cryptol. **2019**(1), 84–117 (2019)
21. Li, S., Sun, S., Shi, D., Li, C., Lei, H.: Lightweight iterative MDS matrices: how small can we go? IACR Trans. Symm. Cryptol. **2019**(4), 147–170 (2019)
22. MacWilliams, F.J., Sloane, N.J.A.: The Theory of Error Correcting Codes. North-Holland Publishing Co., Amsterdam (1977)
23. Sajadieh, M., Mousavi, M.: Construction of MDS matrices from generalized Feistel structures. Des. Codes Crypt. **89**, 1433–1452 (2021)
24. Sarkar, S., Syed, H., Sadhukhan, R., Mukhopadhyay, D.: Lightweight design choices for LED-like block ciphers. In: Patra, A., Smart, N.P. (eds.) INDOCRYPT 2017. LNCS, vol. 10698, pp. 267–281. Springer, Cham (2017). https://doi.org/10.1007/978-3-319-71667-1_14
25. Shannon, C.E.: Communication theory of secrecy systems. Bell Syst. Tech. J. **28**(4), 656–715 (1949)
26. Toh, D., Teo, J., Khoo, K., Sim, S.M.: Lightweight MDS serial-type matrices with minimal fixed XOR count. In: Joux, A., Nitaj, A., Rachidi, T. (eds.) AFRICACRYPT 2018. LNCS, vol. 10831, pp. 51–71. Springer, Cham (2018). https://doi.org/10.1007/978-3-319-89339-6_4
27. Wu, S., Wang, M., Wu, W.: Recursive diffusion layers for (lightweight) block ciphers and hash functions. In: Knudsen, L.R., Wu, H. (eds.) SAC 2012. LNCS, vol. 7707, pp. 355–371. Springer, Heidelberg (2013). https://doi.org/10.1007/978-3-642-35999-6_23
28. Xu, H., Tan, L., Lai, X.: On the recursive construction of MDS matrices for lightweight cryptography. In: Huang, X., Zhou, J. (eds.) ISPEC 2014. LNCS, vol. 8434, pp. 552–563. Springer, Cham (2014). https://doi.org/10.1007/978-3-319-06320-1_40
29. Yang, Y., Zeng, X., Wang, S.: Construction of lightweight involutory MDS matrices. Des. Codes Crypt. **89**(7), 1453–1483 (2021). https://doi.org/10.1007/s10623-021-00879-3

FUTURE: A Lightweight Block Cipher Using an Optimal Diffusion Matrix

Kishan Chand Gupta[1], Sumit Kumar Pandey[2], and Susanta Samanta[1(✉)]

[1] Applied Statistics Unit, Indian Statistical Institute,
203, B.T. Road, Kolkata 700108, India
{kishan,susantas_r}@isical.ac.in
[2] Computer Science and Engineering, Indian Institute of Technology Jammu,
Jagti, PO Nagrota, Jammu 181221, India

Abstract. In this work, we present FUTURE, a new 64-bit lightweight SPN-based block cipher. FUTURE encrypts data in a single clock cycle with a very low implementation cost compared to other block ciphers in unrolled fashion. The advantage of an unrolled implementation is that there are no sequential elements, such as registers, in the implementation and hence no clock. While designing FUTURE in a completely unrolled fashion, the goal was to keep the implementation costs low along with minimal latency. Security is the most essential aspect of a cryptographic primitive. However, in addition to security, an essential secondary criterion for a lightweight cryptographic primitive is efficient implementation in hardware and software. Most lightweight block ciphers refrain from the use of MDS matrices in the round function, and as a result, they need more rounds for full encryption. Using MDS matrices in a lightweight block cipher is a challenging task due to its high implementation cost. The lightweight block cipher FUTURE overcomes this challenge by judiciously choosing a very lightweight MDS matrix, which is a composition of 4 sparse matrices. We also use a lightweight cryptographically significant Sbox which is a composition of 4 Sboxes.

Keywords: Lightweight cryptography · Block cipher · Substitution-permutation network · MDS matrix

1 Introduction

AES [21], SHA-256 [31] and RSA [33] are some of the most widely used cryptography methods, and they work well on systems with reasonable processing power and memory capabilities. But these primitives are not suitable in constrained environments such as RFID tags, sensor networks, contactless smart cards, medical services gadgets, etc. For this purpose in the recent decade, a large number of lightweight cryptographic primitives have been suggested and deployed on resource-constrained devices. While there is no precise meaning of the term lightweight cryptography, it is normally perceived as cryptography with

L. Batina and J. Daemen (Eds.): AFRICACRYPT 2022, LNCS 13503, pp. 28–52, 2022.
https://doi.org/10.1007/978-3-031-17433-9_2

a solid spotlight on efficiency. Here efficiency can be assessed by different models like hardware cost, power utilization, latency, etc., and their blends.

A block cipher converts plaintext blocks of a fixed length n (for the most part $n = 64$ or 128) to ciphertext blocks with the length n under the influence of a secret key k. More precisely, a block cipher is a set of Boolean permutations working on n-bit vectors. This set contains a Boolean permutation for each value of the secret key k. Also, block ciphers are fundamentally arranged into two sorts: Feistel structure and substitution-permutation network (SPN) structure. Feistel structures (e.g. TWINE [42], Piccolo [39]) generally apply a round function to just one half of the block due to which they may be implemented in hardware with minimal cost. However as Feistel structures inject non-linearity in just one half of the block in every round, such designs require more executions of round functions than SPN structures in order to preserve the security margins.

Due to the large deployment of low-resource devices and expanding need to provide security among such devices, lightweight cryptography has become a popular topic. Thus, research on designing and analyzing lightweight block ciphers has got a great deal of attention. Initial lightweight block ciphers such as PRESENT [10] and KATAN [22] focused mainly on the chip area and employed simple round functions as their primary building blocks. With the advent of lightweight block ciphers, this field expanded dramatically in terms of possibilities. At this point, we have specialized ciphers that are optimized for code size, latency, energy and power. For example we have SIMON and SPECK [6] for code-size, PRINCE [11] and MANTIS [7] for latency and MIDORI [3] and GIFT [4] for energy. Furthermore, the cost of implementing decryption with encryption has been optimized for some block ciphers. Such as in MIDORI all the components are involutory and PRINCE has α-reflection property.

Also, many lightweight block cipher such as LED [24], MIDORI and SKINNY [7] adopt the general structure of AES round function and tweak its components to improve their performances.

There have also been attempts to create lightweight tweakable block ciphers, a block cipher with an extra input called tweak. This primitive supports better encryption modes and efficient constructions of authenticated encryption. SKINNY, MANTIS, CRAFT [8], QARMA [2] are some examples of such primitives. Also for CRAFT, design considerations were made to ensure that its implementations were resistant to Differential Fault Analysis (DFA) attacks.

Also, it is worth mentioning that MDS matrices provide maximum diffusion in block ciphers. Whereas most of the lightweight block ciphers do not employ MDS matrices in a round function due to their high cost. As a consequence, they need more rounds to achieve security against some well-known attacks like differential, impossible differential, and linear. So it is challenging to use MDS matrices in a lightweight block cipher. Our proposed lightweight block cipher FUTURE overcomes this challenge by choosing a suitable MDS matrix.

2   Definition and Preliminaries

Let $\mathbb{F}_2 = \{0, 1\}$ be the finite field of two elements, $\mathbb{F}_{2^r}$ be the finite field of 2^r elements and $\mathbb{F}_{2^r}^n$ be the set of vectors of length n with entries from the finite field $\mathbb{F}_{2^r}$. A square matrix is a matrix with the same number of rows and columns. An $n \times n$ matrix is known as a matrix of order n.

In the following section, we will discuss some fundamental definitions and properties of MDS matrices. For a comprehensive overview of various theories on the construction of MDS matrices, readers may look at [25].

2.1   MDS Matrix

The diffusion properties of an MDS matrix make it useful in cryptography. The concept originates from coding theory, specifically from maximum distance separable (MDS) codes.

Theorem 1. *[29, page 321] An $[n, k, d]$ code C with generator matrix $G = [I \mid A]$, where A is a $k \times (n - k)$ matrix, is MDS if and only if every square submatrix (formed from any i rows and any i columns, for any $i = 1, 2, \ldots, min\{k, n - k\}$) of A is nonsingular.*

The following fact is another way to characterize an MDS matrix.

Fact 1. *A square matrix A is an MDS matrix if and only if every square submatrices of A are nonsingular.*

The diffusion power of a linear transformation (specified by a matrix) is measured by its branch numbers [21, pages 130–132].

Definition 1. *[21, page 132] The Differential branch number $\beta_d(M)$ of a matrix M of order n over finite field $\mathbb{F}_{2^r}$ is defined as the minimum number of nonzero components in the input vector x and the output vector Mx as we range over all nonzero $x \in (\mathbb{F}_{2^r})^n$ i.e. $\beta_d(M) = \min\limits_{x \neq 0}(w(x) + w(Mx))$, where $w(x)$ denotes the weight of the vector x i.e. number of nonzero components of the vector x.*

Definition 2. *[21, page 132] The Linear branch number $\beta_l(M)$ of a matrix M of order n over finite field $\mathbb{F}_{2^r}$ is defined as the minimum number of nonzero components in the input vector x and the output vector $M^T x$ as we range over all nonzero $x \in (\mathbb{F}_{2^r})^n$ i.e. $\beta_l(M) = \min\limits_{x \neq 0}(w(x) + w(M^T x))$, where $w(x)$ denotes the weight of the vector x i.e. number of nonzero components of the vector x.*

Remark 1. [21, page 132] Note that the maximal value of $\beta_d(M)$ and $\beta_l(M)$ are $n + 1$. In general $\beta_d(M) \neq \beta_l(M)$ but if a matrix has the maximum possible differential or linear branch number, then both branch numbers are equal.

Therefore the following fact is another characterization of MDS matrix.

Fact 2. *[21] A square matrix A of order n is MDS if and only if $\beta_d(A) = \beta_l(A) = n + 1$.*

For simplicity, in this paper, we will consider the differential branch number only and we will call this simply the branch number.

Some definitions and properties of Boolean functions and Sboxes are revisited in the following section. For a comprehensive overview of Boolean functions, we recommend [12,20].

2.2 Boolean Function and Sbox

An n-variable Boolean function is a map $g : \mathbb{F}_2^n \to \mathbb{F}_2$. The support of a Boolean function g is denoted by $Sup(g)$ and is defined to be $Sup(g) = \{x : g(x) = 1\}$. The weight of g is denoted by $w(g)$ and is defined to be $w(g) = |Sup(g)|$. A function g is said to be balanced if $w(g) = 2^{n-1}$.

A Boolean function can be represented by its binary output vector containing 2^n elements, referred to as the truth table. Another way of representing g is by its algebraic normal form:

$$g(x) = \bigoplus_{(\alpha_{n-1}, \alpha_{n-2}, \dots, \alpha_1, \alpha_0) \in \mathbb{F}_2^n} A_g(\alpha_{n-1}, \alpha_{n-2}, \dots, \alpha_1, \alpha_0) x_{n-1}^{\alpha_{n-1}} x_{n-2}^{\alpha_{n-2}} \dots x_1^{\alpha_1} x_0^{\alpha_0}$$

where $x = (x_{n-1}, x_{n-2}, \dots, x_1, x_0) \in \mathbb{F}_2^n$ and $A_g(x_{n-1}, x_{n-2}, \dots, x_1, x_0)$ is a Boolean function.

The nonlinearity of a Boolean function is a key parameter in cryptography. This quantity measures the Hamming distance[1] of a Boolean function from the set of all affine functions. If A_n be the set of all n-variable affine functions, the nonlinearity of an n-variable Boolean function is given by $nl(g) = \min\limits_{l \in A_n} d(g, l)$.

The maximum nonlinearity achievable by an n-variable Boolean function is $2^{n-1} - 2^{(n-2)/2}$. Functions achieving this value of nonlinearity are called bent and can exist only when n is even [34].

Definition 3. *An $n \times m$ Sbox is a mapping $S : \mathbb{F}_2^n \to \mathbb{F}_2^m$.*

Then, to each $x = (x_{n-1}, x_{n-2}, \dots, x_1, x_0) \in \mathbb{F}_2^n$ some $y = (y_{m-1}, y_{m-2}, \dots, y_1, y_0) \in \mathbb{F}_2^m$ is assigned by $S(x) = y$. The $n \times m$ Sbox S can be considered as a vectorial Boolean function comprising m individual Boolean functions $f_{m-1}, f_{m-2}, \dots, f_1, f_0 : \mathbb{F}_2^n \to \mathbb{F}_2$, where $f_i(x) = y_i$ for $i = 0, 1, 2, \dots, m-1$. These functions are referred to as the coordinate Boolean functions of the Sbox. Thus we can write $S(x) = (f_{m-1}(x), f_{m-2}(x), \dots, f_1(x), f_0(x))$.

It is well known that most of desirable cryptographic properties of the Sbox can be defined also in terms of all non-trivial linear combinations of the coordinate functions, referred to as the Sbox component Boolean functions $g_c : \mathbb{F}_2^n \to \mathbb{F}_2$, where $g_c = c_{m-1} f_{m-1} \oplus \dots \oplus c_1 f_1 \oplus c_0 f_0$ and $c = (c_{m-1}, \dots, c_1, c_0) \in \mathbb{F}_2^m \setminus \{0\}$.

To avoid trivial statistical attacks, an Sbox should be regular (balanced). An $n \times m$ Sbox S with $n \geq m$ is said to be regular if, for each its output $y \in \mathbb{F}_2^m$, there are exactly 2^{n-m} inputs that are mapped to y. Clearly, each bijective $n \times n$ Sbox S is always regular since it represents a permutation. It is well known that

---

[1] The Hamming distance $d(f, g)$ between two functions f and g, defined on a same set A, is defined to be the size of $\{x \in A : f(x) \neq g(x)\}$.

an $n \times m$ Sbox with $n \geq m$ is regular if and only if all its component Boolean functions are balanced [38].

The nonlinearity of an Sbox is a fundamental parameter in cryptography. The nonlinearity of S, denoted by $nl(S)$, is given by the minimal nonlinearity among the nonlinearities of the component Boolean functions i.e. $nl(S) = \min_{c \in \mathbb{F}_2^m \setminus \{0\}} nl(g_c)$.

The best known nonlinearity of a 4-variable balanced Boolean function is 4 [12, Table 3.2]. Thus the maximum nonlinearity of an 4×4 bijective Sbox is 4.

In this paper, we are discussing about $n \times n$ bijective Sboxes and we will call these as n-bit Sboxes.

Definition 4. *For an n-bit Sbox, the difference distribution table (DDT) of S is the table of size $2^n \times 2^n$ of integers $\delta_S(a, b)$ defined by*

$$\delta_S(a, b) = \# \{x \in \mathbb{F}_2^n : S(x \oplus a) \oplus S(x) = b\}$$

The differential uniformity of S, denoted by δ_S, is the highest value in the DDT, i.e. $\delta_S = \max_{a, b \in \mathbb{F}_2^n, a \neq 0} \delta_S(a, b)$ and $\frac{\delta_S}{2^n}$ is called the maximal probability of a differential of the Sbox S.

An Sbox should have low differential uniformity to increase block cipher immunity to differential cryptanalysis [9].

Definition 5. *For an n-bit Sbox, the linear approximation table (LAT) of S is the table of size $2^n \times 2^n$ of integers $L_S(a, b)$ defined by*

$$L_S(a, b) = \# \{x \in \mathbb{F}_2^n : x \cdot a \oplus S(x) \cdot b = 0\} - 2^{n-1},$$

where '$\cdot$' denotes the bitwise logical AND.

The maximal absolute bias of a linear approximation of an Sbox is given by $\frac{L_S}{2^n}$, where $L_S = \max_{a, b \in \mathbb{F}_2^n, a \neq 0} |L_S(a, b)|$.

As with the differential uniformity, the lower value of L_S is required to increase the block cipher's resistance to linear cryptanalysis [30].

Now we will discuss the design specification of the block cipher FUTURE.

3   Structure of FUTURE

FUTURE is a new SPN-based block cipher and consists of 10 rounds in a fully unrolled fashion. It accepts 128-bit keys and has a block size of 64-bit.

3.1   Round Function

Each encryption round of FUTURE is composed of four different transformations in the following order: SubCell, MixColumn, ShiftRow and AddRoundKey (see illustration in Fig. 1). The final round of the block cipher is slightly different,

MixColumn operation is removed here. The cipher receives a 64-bit plaintext $P = b_0b_1b_2 \ldots b_{62}b_{63}$ as the cipher state I, where b_0 is the most significant bit. The cipher state can also be expressed as 16 4-bit cells as follows:

$$I = \begin{bmatrix} s_0 & s_4 & s_8 & s_{12} \\ s_1 & s_5 & s_9 & s_{13} \\ s_2 & s_6 & s_{10} & s_{14} \\ s_3 & s_7 & s_{11} & s_{15} \end{bmatrix},$$

i.e. $s_i \in \{0,1\}^4$. The i-th round input state is defined as I_i, namely $I_0 = P$.

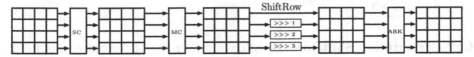

Fig. 1. The round function applies four different transformations: SubCells (SC), Mix-Columns (MC), ShiftRows (SR) and AddRoundKey (ARK).

Nonlinear Transformation SubCell. SubCell is a nonlinear transformation in which 4-bit Sbox S is applied to every cell of the cipher internal state.

$$s_i \leftarrow S(s_i) \quad \text{for } i = 0, 1, \ldots, 15.$$

where S is a 4-bit Sbox applied to every cell of the cipher internal state. The Sbox S is a composition of four low hardware cost Sboxes S_1, S_2, S_3 and S_4 i.e. $S(s_j) = S_1 \circ S_2 \circ S_3 \circ S_4(s_j)$ for $j = 0, 1, \ldots, 15$.

The Sboxes in hexadecimal notation are given by the following Table 1.

Table 1. Specifications of FUTURE Sbox

x	0	1	2	3	4	5	6	7	8	9	a	b	c	d	e	f
$S_4(x)$	0	1	2	3	4	5	6	7	8	9	e	f	c	d	a	b
$S_3(x)$	0	1	2	3	4	d	6	f	8	9	a	b	c	5	e	7
$S_2(x)$	1	3	0	2	5	7	4	6	9	a	8	b	d	e	c	f
$S_1(x)$	0	1	2	3	4	7	6	5	8	9	a	b	c	f	e	d
$S(x)$	1	3	0	2	7	e	4	d	9	a	c	6	f	5	8	b

Linear Transformation MixColumn. The MixColumn is a linear operation that operates separately on each of the four columns of the state. FUTURE uses an MDS matrix M for the MixColumns operation. We have

$$(s_i, s_{i+1}, s_{i+2}, s_{i+3}) \leftarrow M \cdot (s_i, s_{i+1}, s_{i+2}, s_{i+3})^t$$

for $i = 0, 4, 8, 12$. The MDS matrix M is given by

$$M = \begin{bmatrix} \alpha^3 & \alpha^3+1 & 1 & \alpha^3 \\ \alpha+1 & \alpha & \alpha^3+1 & \alpha^3+1 \\ \alpha & \alpha+1 & \alpha^3 & \alpha^3+1 \\ \alpha^3+1 & \alpha^3+1 & \alpha^3 & 1 \end{bmatrix}$$

which is constructed by composition of 4 sparse matrices M_1, M_2, M_3 and M_4 of order 4 i.e. $M = M_1 M_2 M_3 M_4$, where

$$M_1 = \begin{bmatrix} 0 & 0 & 1 & 1 \\ 1 & 0 & 0 & 0 \\ 1 & 1 & 0 & 0 \\ 0 & 0 & 1 & 0 \end{bmatrix}, M_2 = \begin{bmatrix} 0 & 0 & 1 & \alpha \\ 1 & 0 & 0 & 0 \\ \alpha^3+1 & 1 & 0 & 0 \\ 0 & 0 & 1 & 0 \end{bmatrix}, M_3 = \begin{bmatrix} 0 & 0 & 1 & 1 \\ 1 & 0 & 0 & 0 \\ \alpha^3+1 & 1 & 0 & 0 \\ 0 & 0 & 1 & 0 \end{bmatrix} \text{ and } M_4 = M_1.$$

(1)

The multiplications between matrices and vectors are performed over $\mathbb{F}_{2^4}$ defined by the primitive polynomial $x^4 + x + 1$ and α is a primitive element which is a root of $x^4 + x + 1$.

Cell Permutation ShiftRow. ShiftRow rotates row i of the array state i cell positions to the right for $i = 0, 1, 2, 3$. We have,

$$\begin{bmatrix} s_0 & s_4 & s_8 & s_{12} \\ s_1 & s_5 & s_9 & s_{13} \\ s_2 & s_6 & s_{10} & s_{14} \\ s_3 & s_7 & s_{11} & s_{15} \end{bmatrix} \leftarrow \begin{bmatrix} s_0 & s_4 & s_8 & s_{12} \\ s_{13} & s_1 & s_5 & s_9 \\ s_{10} & s_{14} & s_2 & s_6 \\ s_7 & s_{11} & s_{15} & s_3 \end{bmatrix}.$$

i.e. $s_i \leftarrow 13 \cdot s_i \pmod{16}$ for $i = 0, 1, \ldots, 15$.

Note that in the ShiftRow operation of AES [21] and LED [24], the row i of the array state is rotated i cell positions to the left, for $i = 0, 1, 2, 3$.

AddRoundKey. Given round key RK_i for $1 \leq i \leq 10$, the i-th 64-bit round key RK_i is XORed to the state S.

Data Processing. The data processing part of FUTURE for encryption consisting of 10 rounds. The encryption function F takes a 64-bit data $X \in \{0, 1\}^{64}$, whitening keys $WK \in \{0, 1\}^{64}$ and 10 round keys $RK_i \in \{0, 1\}^{64}$ ($1 \leq i \leq 10$) as the inputs and outputs a 64-bit data $Y \in \{0, 1\}^{64}$. F is defined as follows:

$$F = \begin{cases} \{0,1\}^{64} \times \{0,1\}^{64} \times \left\{\{0,1\}^{64}\right\}^{10} \to \{0,1\}^{64} \\ (X, WK, RK_1, RK_2, \ldots, RK_{10}) \to Y. \end{cases}$$

The Round Key Evolution and Round Constants. FUTURE uses a 128-bit secret key $K = k_0 k_1 \ldots k_{127}$. It splits K in two equal parts K_0 and K_1 for the round key and whitening key generation i.e. $K = K_0 \| K_1$, where $K_0 = k_0 k_1 \ldots k_{63}$ and $K_1 = k_{64} k_{65} \ldots k_{127}$ are two 64-bit keys. It uses K_0 as whitening key and the round key RK_i ($1 \leq i \leq 10$) generation is as follows (see Fig. 2):

$$RK_i = \begin{cases} K_0 \leftarrow K_0 \lll (5 \cdot \frac{i}{2}) & \text{if } 2 \mid i \\ \\ K_1 \leftarrow K_1 \lll (5 \cdot \lfloor \frac{i}{2} \rfloor) & \text{if } 2 \nmid i \end{cases}$$

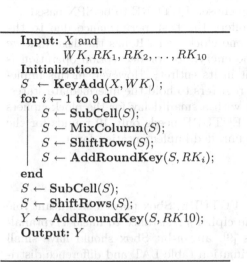

Algorithm 1: Encryption Function of FUTURE

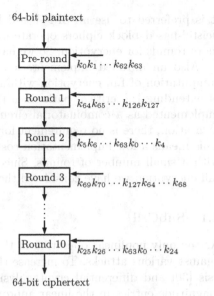

Fig. 2. Round key generation

where $K_i \lll j$ means the 64-bit word obtained by a j-bit left rotation (left cyclic shift) of K_i.

For FUTURE a single bit "1" is XORed into each 4-bit cell (in different positions) of every round except the 5th and 10th round. We define the round constants in Table 2.

Table 2. The round constants for the N-th round of FUTURE

Rounds (N)	Round constant
1, 6	0x1248248148128124
2, 7	0x2481481281241248
3, 8	0x4812812412482481
4, 9	0x8124124824814812
5, 10	0x0000000000000000

In the following section we justify the decisions we took during the design of FUTURE.

4   Design Decision

The design choice of round function for FUTURE has been inspired by the existing block ciphers, however all the components of FUTURE are new. Sometimes it is preferred to use an SPN-based block cipher over a Feistel-based one, as Feistel-based block ciphers operate on just half of the state, which results in more rounds for encryption. So we have chosen FUTURE to be SPN-based.

Also an unrolled implementation offers the best performance due to the computation of full encryption within one clock cycle. It has the disadvantage of extending the critical path since the encryption or decryption operation is implemented as a combinatorial circuit in its entirety. However, in this implementation, there is no requirement for registers to hold the intermediate states. This means a low implementation cost with a small delay for the block ciphers with a small number of rounds. Since FUTURE needs only 10 rounds for the full encryption we have considered the unrolled implementation for it.

4.1   SubCell

As the only nonlinear operation in the FUTURE, Sbox plays a significant role against various attacks. To increase the cipher's resistance to linear cryptanalysis [30] and differential cryptanalysis [9], any n-bit Sbox should have small magnitude entries in the linear approximation table LAT and difference distribution table DDT respectively, not counting the first entry in the first row. In other words, the maximal absolute bias of a linear approximation and the maximal probability of a differential of an Sbox should be low. One other criteria is the absence of fixed points for increasing resistance against statistical attacks. Also, the cost of the Sbox, i.e., its area and critical path, is a significant portion of the entire cost. As a result, selecting an Sbox that optimizes such expenses is important for the design of a lightweight block cipher.

For the SubCell operation, we use a 4-bit Sbox that is extremely efficient in terms of hardware and also meets the following criteria:

1. Nonlinearity of the Sbox is 4 (which is optimal).
2. The maximal probability of a differential is 2^{-2} and there are exactly 24 differentials with probability 2^{-2}.
3. The maximal absolute bias of a linear approximation is 2^{-2} and there are exactly 36 linear approximations with absolute bias 2^{-2}.
4. There is no fixed point.

FUTURE Sbox S is a composition of four Sboxes S_1, S_2, S_3 and S_4 (See Table 1). The algebraic normal form of the coordinate Boolean functions of S is given by

$$l_3(x) = x_0x_1x_3 \oplus x_0x_2 \oplus x_3$$
$$l_2(x) = x_1x_3 \oplus x_2$$
$$l_1(x) = x_0x_2x_3 \oplus x_0x_2 \oplus x_0 \oplus x_1x_2 \oplus x_2$$
$$l_0(x) = x_0x_1x_3 \oplus x_0x_2 \oplus x_0x_3 \oplus x_1 \oplus 1.$$

Thus we can see that the maximal and minimal algebraic degree of S are 3 and 2 respectively.

To find lightweight 4-bit Sboxes, we chose to explore circuits systematically from the bottom-up approach, starting with the identity function's circuit (or by bit wiring of the circuit) and adding gates sequentially. We have decided to choose only NAND, XOR, and XNOR gates as some popular block ciphers like SKINNY [7] and Piccolo [39] use lightweight 4-bit Sboxes that can be implemented by a minimum number of these logic gates. First, we have searched for the circuits representing a 4-bit Sbox that can be implemented by (i) one XOR/XNOR gate or by (ii) one NAND gate followed by one XOR/XNOR gate. As a result, we have the two sets of 4-bit Sboxes, T_1 and $T_2{}^2$, where T_1 contains the Sboxes implemented by one XOR/XNOR gate and T_2 contains the Sboxes implemented by one NAND and one XOR/XNOR gate. Next, we search for the Sboxes with low hardware cost and good cryptographic properties by composition of 2, 3 or 4 different Sboxes from the set $T_1 \cup T_2$. We obtain the FUTURE Sbox which is a composition of 4 Sboxes with 4 NAND, 3 XNOR and 1 XOR gates with is the lowest hardware cost for our search of 4-bit Sboxes with the optimal nonlinearity of 4.

During the search of an Sbox for FUTURE with this composition method, we only concentrate on the nonlinearity of the resulting Sbox. The nonlinearity of the Sboxes S_1, S_2, S_3 and S_4 are zero, whereas the resulting Sbox S has 4, which is the maximum value for a balanced 4-bit Sbox. The main concern for choosing such a composition method was to reduce implementation cost for the Sbox S. The hardware cost for S_1, S_2, S_3 and S_4 are very low. More specifically, they can be implemented with 4 NAND, 3 XNOR, and 1 XOR gates only (see Figure: 4, 5, 6 and 7), resulting in a low hardware cost (12 GE in UMC 180nm 1.8 V [1]) for the Sbox S.

With this method, the implementation cost of an Sbox with the standard Sbox criteria (like balancedness, maximum nonlinearity, small value of δ_S and L_S etc.) may be reduced significantly. We believe that this is the first time to use this composition type Sbox with maximum nonlinearity and some useful cryptographic properties.

Also, it is worth mentioning that the 4-bit Sboxes used in SKINNY and Piccolo have the same nonlinearity and hardware cost as the FUTURE Sbox. But FUTURE Sbox is the new one and it is constructed by the composition of four lightweight Sboxes with zero nonlinearity. Also, it is not always trivial to get an Sbox with good cryptographic properties by the composition of four such lightweight Sboxes. We decided to use the newly constructed Sbox.

4.2 MixColumn

Almost MDS matrix (or binary matrix with slightly lower branch number) has efficient implementation features. But its diffusion speed is slower and the minimum number of active Sboxes in each round is lower than the ciphers that

---

^{2} Some Sboxes of the sets T_1 and T_2 are given in the full version of the paper. Also, note that we are not doing an exhaustive search to find all such Sboxes. More specifically, we have taken only 24 such elements from both T_1 and T_2, and the Sboxes S_1, S_2, S_3, and S_4, used to construct the FUTURE Sbox, are taken from the 48 Sboxes.

employ the MDS matrix as part of MixColumn. The diffusion speed is measured by the number of rounds taken to achieve full diffusion, i.e. all output cells are affected by all input cells. FUTURE requires only 2 rounds for the full diffusion (See Fig. 3).

For hardware efficiency, most of the lightweight block ciphers in the literature use almost MDS matrix or binary matrix with a much lower branch number, which results in more rounds for achieving security against various attacks, including differential, impossible differential, and linear. Whereas FUTURE needs only 10 rounds for resisting such attacks by using an MDS matrix.

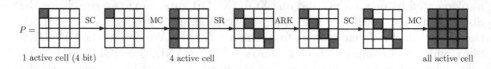

1 active cell (4 bit)   4 active cell   all active cell

Fig. 3. Full diffusion of FUTURE.

MDS matrices are not sparse. But they can be constructed from sparse matrices by recursive method i.e. using a sparse matrix several times resulting in a very low hardware cost.

The MDS matrix in FUTURE is a composition of 4 different lightweight sparse matrices M_1, M_2, M_3 and M_4 (see Eq. 1 of Sect. 3.1). These matrices are of the form

$$\begin{bmatrix} 0 & 0 & m_1 & m_2 \\ m_3 & 0 & 0 & 0 \\ m_4 & m_5 & 0 & 0 \\ 0 & 0 & m_6 & 0 \end{bmatrix},$$

where $m_i \in \mathbb{F}_{2^4}$ for $i = 1, 2, \ldots, 6$.

The idea of constructing MDS matrices in such a fashion was first introduced in [35] and we are the first to take advantage of this method in the design of FUTURE. More specifically, we have fixed $m_1 = m_3 = m_6 = 1$ and perform an exhaustive search ($5^{12} \approx 2^{28}$ choices) over the set $\{1, \alpha, \alpha^2, \alpha^{-1}, \alpha^{-2}\}$ to obtain $M = M_1 M_2 M_3 M_4$ as an MDS matrix.

The implementation cost for the MDS matrix M is minimized due to the low implementation cost of M_1, M_2, M_3 and M_4. Note that to construct an MDS matrix in this method, the implementation cost is calculated by the sum of the implementation costs of M_1, M_2, M_3, and M_4.

We will now demonstrate how selecting specific elements from a finite field constructed by a specific irreducible polynomial improves multiplication efficiency.

The Primitive Polynomial $x^4 + x + 1$. The multiplications between the matrices M_1, M_2, M_3 and M_4 and vectors are performed over the field $\mathbb{F}_{2^4}$ constructed by the primitive polynomial $x^4 + x + 1$. The entries of these matrices are from the set $\{0, 1, \alpha, \alpha^3 + 1 = \alpha^{-1}\}$, where α is a primitive element of $\mathbb{F}_{2^4}$ and is a root of $x^4 + x + 1$ i.e. $\alpha^4 + \alpha + 1 = 0$.

Any element b in $\mathbb{F}_{2^4}$ can be written as $b = b_0 + b_1 \cdot \alpha + b_2 \cdot \alpha^2 + b_3 \cdot \alpha^3$. Then by the multiplication of b by $\alpha^3 + 1$ we have

$$(b_0 + b_1 \cdot \alpha + b_2 \cdot \alpha^2 + b_3 \cdot \alpha^3) \cdot (\alpha^3 + 1) = (b_0 + b_1) + b_2 \cdot \alpha + b_3 \cdot \alpha^2 + b_0 \cdot \alpha^3.$$

Thus in vector form the above product looks like $(b_0 \oplus b_1, b_2, b_3, b_0)$, in which there is 1 XOR. Therefore the XOR count of $\alpha^3 + 1$ i.e. the XORs required to implement the multiplication of $\alpha^3 + 1$ with an arbitrary element $b \in \mathbb{F}_{2^4}$ is 1. Similarly we have $b \cdot \alpha = (b_3, b_0 \oplus b_3, b_1, b_2)$. Hence the XOR count of α is 1. Also, the XOR count of 1 is 0 and there is no other nonzero element in the field with an XOR count of ≤ 1.

Thus for the suitable choice of the constructing polynomial and entries of the matrices, the implementation cost of the MDS matrix M is reduced significantly. More specifically, FUTURE requires 35 XORs for the implementation of the MDS matrix (See Sect. 6.2).

The Table 3 provides a comparison of the cost of the FUTURE MDS matrix with the matrices[3] used in the linear layer of some popular block ciphers. From Table 3, we can see that PRINCE and MIDORI use an Almost MDS matrix with a low implementational cost of 24 XORs. But for achieving security against various attacks they need more rounds than FUTURE. The linear layers in PRESENT and GIFT are a bit permutation of the state. As a result, the linear layer is created with simple wire shuffling and requires no hardware. But for resisting some fundamental attacks like linear cryptanalysis, differential cryptanalysis etc., they need a large number of rounds than MIDORI and PRINCE. For the case of SKINNY and CRAFT, the binary matrix is of branch number 2

Table 3. Comparison of cost of the linear layers.

Block cipher	Linear layer	Cost
AES	MDS matrix	108 XORs
LED	Recursive MDS matrix	14 XORs
FUTURE	MDS matrix	35 XORs
Piccolo	MDS matrix	52 XORs
PRINCE	$(M^{(0)}, M^{(1)})$Almost MDS matrix	24 XORs
MIDORI	Almost MDS matrix	24 XORs
SKINNY	Binary matrix with branch number 2	12 XORs
CRAFT	Binary matrix with branch number 2	12 XORs
PRESENT	Bit permutation	0
GIFT	Bit permutation	0

---

[3] Each matrix in the Table 3 has an input size of 16 bits, except for the AES, which has an input size of 32 bits.

and needs only 12 XORs for implementation. For this, they attain full diffusion after 6th and 7th rounds respectively, which is 2 for FUTURE. Also, the cost of implementing the MDS matrix of LED is low. However, the companion matrix in LED needs to be applied 4 times in the serialized implementation of the diffusion layer to get the MDS matrix, i.e., if we implement the MDS matrix in a single clock cycle, its cost will be $4 \times 14 = 56$ XORs. The FUTURE MDS matrix M is implemented in a single clock cycle with 35 XOR gates. Since FUTURE is implemented in a fully unrolled fashion, M is preferred over the others in terms of XOR gates and security parameters.

4.3   Round Key

For the key scheduling, we are mainly concerned about reducing hardware costs. Note that the key scheduling function in FUTURE is implemented as a bit permutation of the master key. It is, therefore, possible to create this module through simple wire shuffling and it takes up no hardware cost.

5   Security Analysis

The security of FUTURE against various cryptanalysis techniques is discussed in this section.

5.1   Differential and Linear Cryptanalysis

The most frequent and fundamental security analysis of a block cipher is to determine a cipher's resistance to differential and linear cryptanalysis. We computed the lower limits on the minimum number of active Sboxes involved in a differential or linear characteristic to measure the resistance against differential and linear attacks.

Mixed Integer Linear Programming (MILP) is used in this study to derive lower limits for the minimum number of active Sboxes in both Differential and Linear Cryptanalysis for various numbers of rounds. The outcomes[4] are outlined in Table 4. Also, the MILP solution gives us the actual differential or linear characteristics, which permits us to find out the actual differential probability and correlation potential from the DDT and LAT[5] of FUTURE Sbox respectively.

Differential Cryptanalysis. If $2^{-\delta}$ be the maximum probability of the differential propagation in a single Sbox and N_s be the number of active Sboxes in a differential characteristic, then attack with the differential characteristic of a block cipher becomes infeasible if N_s satisfies the following condition [36, Section 4.2.12]:

$$2^{\delta \cdot N_s} > 2^b \implies \delta \cdot N_s > b,$$

---

[4] Here we have done the bit-based MILP and we could not find any solution for the higher number of rounds ($n \geq 6$) by the MILP model due to its long-running time.

[5] The DDT and LAT are provided in the full version.

Table 4. The minimum number of active Sbox for N rounds of FUTURE

Rounds (N)	1	2	3	4	5
Differential cryptanalysis	1	5	9	25	26
Linear cryptanalysis	1	5	9	25	26

where b is the bit-length of the block size of the block cipher. For FUTURE, $b = 64$ and $\delta = 2$ and hence we must have $N_s > 32$. This is obtained by at most 7 rounds[6] for FUTURE.

However for the 4-round FUTURE, we have searched 50 different single characteristics with the minimum number of active Sboxes (which is 25) with no Sbox activity pattern. Here we have observed that among these 50 characteristics the highest probability is 2^{-62}. Next we have fixed the input and output differences of the characteristic with highest probability and search for different single characteristics with the same Sbox activity pattern. Here we have found that only 2 characteristics are possible and the highest probability is also 2^{-62}. Also, from DDT, we can observe that there are only 24 differentials with probability 2^{-2} and whereas there are 72 differentials with probability 2^{-3}. Hence we expect that the probability of any possible differential characteristic will be lower than 2^{-63} when we have 5 rounds. Therefore, we believe that full rounds of FUTURE are strong enough to resist differential cryptanalysis.

Linear Cryptanalysis. Given a linear characteristic with a bias ϵ, $4\epsilon^2$ is defined as the correlation potential. For an adversary to perform linear cryptanalysis on an n-bit block cipher, the correlation potential must be more than 2^{-n}.

Similar to the differential, for the 4th round of FUTURE, we have searched 50 different single linear characteristics with the minimum number of active Sboxes with no Sbox activity pattern. Among which, the highest correlation potential is 2^{-74}. Next, with the same input and output masking of the highest correlation potential, we search for 10 more different single characteristics which follow the same Sbox activity pattern. We observe that it has a linear hull effect (average correlation potential) of $2^{-73.66}$. Also, from LAT, we can observe that there are exactly 36 linear approximations with absolute bias 2^{-2} and whereas there are 96 linear approximations with absolute bias 2^{-3}. So we expect that for 5-round FUTURE, the correlation potential will be lower than 2^{-64}. Hence, we believe that 10-round FUTURE is sufficient to resist linear cryptanalysis.

5.2 Impossible Differential Attacks

A differential $(\Delta x, \Delta y)$ is supposed to be an impossible differential on an encryption function F if, for all plaintexts x, $F(x) + F(x + \Delta x) \neq \Delta y$. Such a difference over a reduced round version of the cipher can be used for a key-recovery attack

---

[6] Since the minimum number of active Sboxes in round 3 and round 4 are 9 and 25 respectively, for 7th round FUTURE there will be at least 34 active Sboxes.

on the cipher in some more rounds and this is done by eliminating all the keys that produce intermediate state values with differences Δx and Δy, i.e. intermediate state values that match the impossible differential. Note that for the resistance of FUTURE against impossible differential attack, we have used the similar approach as in GIFT [4]. We looked for impossible differentials in the reduced-round versions of FUTURE using the Mixed-Integer Linear Programming method [19,37]. We thoroughly test input and output differences that meet the following conditions.

1. The input difference activates just one of the first 4 Sboxes.
2. The output difference activates only one of the 16 Sboxes.

There are $4 \times 15 = 60$ such input differences in the first case and for the second case, there are $16 \times 15 = 240$ such output differences. We thus examined the $14,400$ set of pairs of input and output differences.

Our search results show that for 4-round FUTURE, there are only 267 impossible differentials out of the $14,400$ choices. We then extend this search procedure to 5 rounds and found that there does not exist any impossible differential from the $14,400$ pairs. So full rounds of FUTURE are strong enough to resist the impossible differential attack.

5.3 Boomerang Attack

The boomerang attack [44] is a type of differential attack in which the attacker does not attempt to cover the entire block cipher with a single differential characteristic with high probability. Instead, the attacker first divides the cipher into two sub-ciphers, then finds a boomerang quartet with high probability. The probability of constructing a boomerang quartet is denoted as $\hat{p}^2\hat{q}^2$, where

$$\hat{p} = \sqrt{\sum_{\beta} \Pr^2[\alpha \to \beta]},$$

and α and β are input and output differences for the first sub-cipher and $\hat{q}$ for the second sub-cipher. This attack is effective when an n-bit cipher satisfies $\hat{p}^2\hat{q}^2 \le 2^{-n}$.

The value of $\hat{p}^2$ is bounded by the maximum differential characteristic probability, i.e., $\hat{p}^2 \le \max_{\beta} \Pr[\alpha \to \beta]$ and $\hat{q}^2$ as well. Let p, q be the maximum differential trail probability for the first and the second sub-ciphers. Then, p, q are bounded by $2^{-2 \cdot N_s}$, where N_s is the minimum number of active Sboxes in each sub-cipher. From Table 4, we can see that any combination of two sub-ciphers for FUTURE consisting of 8 rounds has at least 32 active Sboxes in total. Hence, we conclude that the full round of FUTURE is secure against boomerang attacks.

5.4 Integral Attack

We first search for integral distinguishers for the round reduced versions of FUTURE by using the (bit-based) division property [43] and using the Mixed-Integer Linear Programming approach described in [41,45]. We first evaluate the propagation of the division property for the Sbox. The algebraic normal form of FUTURE Sbox is given by

$$y_3 = x_0 x_1 x_3 \oplus x_0 x_2 \oplus x_3$$
$$y_2 = x_1 x_3 \oplus x_2$$
$$y_1 = x_0 x_2 x_3 \oplus x_0 x_2 \oplus x_0 \oplus x_1 x_2 \oplus x_2$$
$$y_0 = x_0 x_1 x_3 \oplus x_0 x_2 \oplus x_0 x_3 \oplus x_1 \oplus 1.$$

and the propagation of the division property is summarized as Table 5.

Table 5. The possible propagation of the division property for FUTURE Sbox

u \ v	0	1	2	3	4	5	6	7	8	9	a	b	c	d	e	f
0	×	×	×	×	×	×	×	×	×	×	×	×	×	×	×	×
1		×	×	×		×	×	×	×	×	×	×	×	×	×	×
2		×	×	×	×	×	×	×	×	×	×	×	×	×	×	×
3		×		×		×	×	×	×	×	×	×	×	×	×	×
4		×	×	×	×	×	×	×	×	×	×	×	×	×	×	×
5		×	×		×	×	×	×	×	×	×	×	×	×	×	×
6		×	×		×	×	×		×	×	×		×	×	×	×
7							×		×	×		×	×	×	×	×
8		×	×	×	×	×	×	×	×	×	×	×	×	×	×	×
9		×	×		×	×	×	×	×	×	×	×	×	×	×	×
a		×		×	×	×	×	×	×	×	×	×	×	×	×	×
b		×		×	×	×	×	×	×	×	×	×	×	×	×	×
c			×	×		×	×	×		×	×	×	×	×	×	×
d			×	×		×	×	×			×	×		×	×	×
e										×	×		×	×	×	×
f																×

Here, let u and v be the input and output division property, respectively. The propagation from u to v labeled × is possible. Otherwise, the propagation is impossible.

Taking into account the effect of MixColumn, we evaluated the propagation of the division property on the reduced-round FUTURE. To search for the longest integral distinguisher, we choose only one bit in plaintext as constant and the others are active. For example, in the 6th round we have a distinguisher $ACA^{62} \rightarrow B^{64}$. But we could not find any distinguisher for the 7th round by MILP model due to its long running time. So we can not conclude whether there is an integral distinguisher in the 7th round or not. We also checked that there is no distinguisher from the 8th round[7]. So we are expecting that full rounds of FUTURE is secure against integral attack.

5.5 Invariant Subspace Attacks

The invariant subspace attack [26,27] exploits a subspace A and constants u, v such that $F(u \oplus A) = v \oplus A$, where F is a round transformation of a block cipher. For the round key $r_k \in A \oplus u \oplus v$, $F \oplus r_k$ maps the subspace $u \oplus A$ onto itself, because $F(u \oplus A) \oplus r_k = v \oplus A \oplus r_k = u \oplus A$. However, we can avoid this invariant subspace by using appropriate round constants.

By Sect. 3.3 of [28], if RC be the constants on a single cell over all rounds, then the designer can choose RC such that there is no 2-dimensional subspace V of $\mathbb{F}_{2^4}$ satisfying $RC \subseteq V$ for the resistance of invariant subspace attack on AES-like ciphers with MDS MixColumn layer.

Recall that FUTURE is an AES-like ciphers with MDS MixColumn layer which uses round constants 0, 1, 2, 4, 8 in each output of a cell. Also, there is no 2-dimensional subspace V such $\{0, 1, 2, 4, 8\} \subseteq V$. Hence in FUTURE, the invariant subspace attack cannot be found for an arbitrary number of rounds.

5.6 Meet-in-the-Middle Attacks

This section shows the security of FUTURE against the meet-in-the-middle attacks. We have used an approach which is similar to the methods used in the block ciphers MIDORI [3] and SKINNY [7]. The maximum number of rounds that can be attacked can be evaluated by considering the maximum length of three features: partial-matching, initial structure, and splice-and-cut.

a. **Partial-Matching:** Partial-matching can not work if the number of rounds reaches full diffusion in each of the forward and backward directions. In FUTURE, full diffusion is achieved after 2 rounds forwards and backwards. Thus, the number of rounds used for partial-matching is upper bounded by $(2 - 1) + (2 - 1) + 1 = 3$.

b. **Initial Structure:** The condition for the initial structure is that key differential trails in the forward direction and those in the backward direction do not share active Sboxes. For FUTURE, since any key differential affects all 16 Sboxes after at least 4 rounds in the forward and the backward directions, there is no such differential which shares active Sbox in more than 4 rounds. Thus, the number of rounds used for the initial structure is upper bounded by $(4 - 1) = 3$.

c. **Splice-and-Cut:** Splice-and-cut may extend the number of attack rounds up to the smaller number of full diffusion rounds minus one, which is $(2 - 1) = 1$.

Therefore we can conclude that the meet-in-the-middle attack may work up to $3 + 3 + 1 = 7$ rounds. Hence full round FUTURE is sufficient to resist meet-in-the-middle attacks.

---

[7] For finding an r round division trail $(a_0^0, a_1^0, \ldots, a_{63}^0) \to \cdots \to (a_0^r, a_1^r, \ldots, a_{63}^r)$ by the MILP technique, we fixed the output $(a_0^r, a_1^r, \ldots, a_{63}^r)$ of the rth round by the unit vectors (64 cases) and check whether the MILP model is feasible or not.

5.7 Algebraic Attacks

FUTURE Sbox has algebraic degree 3 and from Table 4 we see that for 4-round differential characteristic, there are at least 25 active Sboxes. So we have $3 \times 25 \times \lfloor \frac{10}{4} \rfloor = 150 > 64$, where 64 is the block size and 10 is the number of rounds in FUTURE. Also, the FUTURE Sbox is described by 21 quadratic equations in the 8 input/output-bit variables over $\mathbb{F}_2$. The key schedule of FUTURE does not need any Sbox. Thus the 10-round cipher is described by $10 \times 16 \times 21 = 3360$ quadratic equations in $10 \times 16 \times 8 = 1280$ variables.

The general problem of solving a system of multivariate quadratic equations is NP-hard. However the systems derived for block ciphers are very sparse since they are composed of a small number of nonlinear systems connected by linear layers. Nevertheless, it is unclear whether this fact can be exploited in a so-called algebraic attack. Some specialized techniques such as XL [16] and XSL [17] have been proposed, though flaws in both techniques have been discovered [13, 23]. Instead the practical results on the algebraic cryptanalysis of block ciphers have been obtained by applying the Buchberger and F4 algorithms within Magma. Also, recently there are some practical results [46] on algebraic cryptanalysis by using ElimLin [15, 18] and SAT solver techniques [5, 40].

Now note that the entire system for a fixed-key AES permutation consists of 6400 equations in 2560 variables and whereas in FUTURE these numbers are roughly half of that in AES. Simulations on small-scale variants of the AES showed that except for very small versions, one quickly encounters difficulties with time and memory complexity [14]. So we believe that algebraic attacks do not threaten FUTURE.

6 Hardware Implementations, Performance and Comparison

In this section, we will discuss the hardware implementation cost of FUTURE in both FPGA and ASIC design.

6.1 FPGA Implementation

Nowadays, FPGAs are used more and more for high-performance applications, even in the field of security and cryptographic applications. Since there are a wealth of different FPGA vendors available, we decided to implement our designs on various FPGA boards provided by Xilinx. The hardware implementation of FUTURE is written in VHDL and is implemented on both Virtex-6 and Virtex-7. More specifically, the FPGA results are obtained after place-and-route (PAR) on the Xilinx Virtex-6 (xc6vlx240t-2ff1156) and Virtex-7 (xc7vx415t-2ffg1157) in Xilinx ISE. In Table 6 the implementation results are given. Note that for the comparison of FUTURE with other block ciphers (in fully unrolled implementations), we used the VHDL codes available at https://github.com/KULeuven-COSIC/UnrolledBlockCiphers.

Table 6. Comparison of size, critical path and throughput on FPGA.

Cipher	Virtex-6			Virtex-7		
	Size (Slices)	Critical Path (ns)	Throughput (Gbit/s)	Size (Slices)	Critical Path (ns)	Throughput (Gbit/s)
KATAN 64/80	2550	47.33	1.35	2550	42.11	1.52
PRESENT 64/80	2089	29.21	2.19	2089	26.27	2.44
PRESENT 64/128	2203	32.55	1.97	2203	29.03	2.20
SIMON 64/128	2688	27.31	2.34	2688	25.30	2.53
SPECK 64/128	3594	50.29	1.27	3594	48.31	1.32
PRINCE	1244	16.38	3.91	1244	14.79	4.33
FUTURE	**1240**	**15.94**	**4.01**	**1241**	**14.53**	**4.40**

6.2   ASIC Implementation

In order to estimate the hardware cost for an ASIC platform, we will consider the use of the Synopsys Design Compiler using the UMCL18G212T3 [1] ASIC standard cell library, i.e. UMC 0.18µm. In Table 7 we describe the area requirements and corresponding gate count in this library (for details, check [32]). Also, note that Gate equivalent (GE) is a measure of the area requirements of integrated circuits (IC). It is derived by dividing the area of the IC by the area of a two-input NAND gate with the lowest driving strength.

Table 7. Area requirements and corresponding gate count

Standard cell	Area in μm^2	GE
NAND	9.677	1
NOR	9.677	1
AND/OR	12.902	1.33
XOR/XNOR	25.805	2.67
NOT	6.451	0.67

But as discussed in [39], some libraries provide special gates that further save the area. Namely, in this library, the 4-input AND-NOR and 4-input OR-NAND gates with two inputs inverted can be used to directly compute an XOR or an XNOR. Since both cells cost 2 GE instead of 2.67 GE required for XOR or XNOR, we can save 0.67 GE per XOR or XNOR gate. Now we will discuss the cost for each module of a single round FUTURE using the above mentioned implementation techniques.

Cost of FUTURE Sbox. Recall that FUTURE Sbox S is a composition of four Sboxes S_1, S_2, S_3 and S_4 i.e. $S(x) = S_1 \circ S_2 \circ S_3 \circ S_4(x)$. We can see that $S_4(x) = (x_3, x_1 x_3 \oplus x_2, x_1, x_0)$, $S_3(x) = (x_0 x_2 \oplus x_3, x_2, x_1, x_0)$, $S_2(x) =$

$(x_3, x_2, x_0, x_0x_3 \oplus x_1 \oplus 1)$ and $S_1(\mathrm{x}) = (x_3, x_2, x_0x_2 \oplus x_1, x_0)$. Thus they can be implemented as follows:

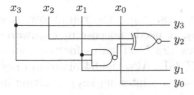

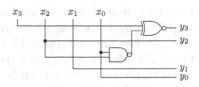

Fig. 4. Sbox S_4 **Fig. 5.** Sbox S_3

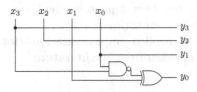

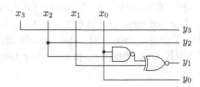

Fig. 6. Sbox S_2 **Fig. 7.** Sbox S_1

Here $y_3y_2y_1y_0$ and $x_3x_2x_1x_0$ denotes the 4-bit output and input respectively of the Sboxes. Thus to implement the Sbox of FUTURE, we need 4 NAND, 3 XNOR and 1 XOR gates only. Therefore FUTURE Sbox can be implemented with $(4 \times 1 + 3 \times 2 + 1 \times 2) = 12$ GE.

Therefore SubCell operation for a single round FUTURE takes $16 \times 12 = 192$ GE for implementation.

Cost of FUTURE MDS Matrix The MDS matrix in FUTURE is a composition of 4 different lightweight sparse matrices M_1, M_2, M_3 and M_4 (see Eq. 1 of Sect. 3.1). Thus the cost for implementation of the matrices are given below:

(a) cost for implementing M_4 and $M_1 = 8$ XORs (1 has no multiplication cost and $2 \times 4 = 8$ for two fixed XORs).
(b) cost for implementing $M_3 = 8 + 1 = 9$ XORs (the multiplication cost of $\alpha^3 + 1$ is 1 XOR).
(c) cost for implementing $M_2 = 8 + 1 + 1 = 10$ XORs (the multiplication cost of α and $\alpha^3 + 1$ is 1 XOR).

Therefore MDS matrix for FUTURE needs 35 XOR gates. As a result, it can be implemented with $35 \times 2 = 70$ GE and MixColumn operation for a single round FUTURE takes $4 \times 70 = 280$ GE for implementation.

Cost of ShiftRow. Since ShiftRow is nothing but a permutation of the whole state, this module is constructed by a simple wire shuffle and takes no area at all.

Cost of Key Schedule and Round Constants. Since the round keys are obtained by only bit wiring of the master key, it needs no cost in hardware. Whereas, for the full encryption FUTURE uses 128 NOT gates for the round constants. Therefore it takes $128 \times 0.67 = 85.76$ GE. Also the 64-bit round key is xored with the entire state in each round (also for whitening key) resulting in a $64 \times 2 = 128$ GE cost for this operation in each single round.

Cost for the Full Encryption of FUTURE. Since FUTURE is implemented in a fully unrolled fashion, it does not need any extra logic and state register. Thus FUTURE can be implemented with $9 \times (192 + 280 + 128) + (192 + 128) + 128 + 85.76 = 5933.76$ GE only. Of course, these numbers depend on the library used, but we expect that it will take less area than our estimations.

In Table 8, we list the hardware cost of unrolled implementations for FUTURE and compare it to other block ciphers taken from the literature.

Table 8. Comparison of the hardware cost of unrolled implementations for FUTURE and other 64-bit block ciphers with 128 bit key on ASIC platform

Ciphers	Area (GE)
LED-64–128	111496
PRESENT-64–128	56722
PICCOLO-64–128	25668
SKINNY-64–128	17454
MANTIS$_5$	8544
PRINCE	8512
FUTURE	**5934**

The Table 8 contains the cost estimations of FUTURE along with the cost of other ciphers obtained from Table 12 and Table 24 of [7]. It should be pointed out that SKINNY and MANTIS are tweakable block ciphers, whereas the others are not.

It will be inappropriate to compare the hardware cost of the unrolled version of a rolled block cipher with a large number of rounds because the hardware cost of making the rolled version into the unrolled version will be very high. That's why we are not comparing the hardware cost of FUTURE with the recent block ciphers like GIFT [4] and CRAFT [8].

In Table 6, we compare FUTURE with some block ciphers in the FPGA platform and Table 8 compares its hardware cost with some block ciphers in the ASIC platform. A better approach would be to compare our block cipher with other block ciphers in both FPGA and ASIC implementations. But we are comparing some block ciphers in FPGA and other block ciphers in ASIC because of the unavailability of their hardware codes in the literature.

7 Conclusions

One of the fundamental primitives for cryptographic applications is block ciphers. In this work, we have proposed a new SPN-based lightweight block cipher, FUTURE, that is designed for minimal latency with low hardware implementation cost. For the perfect diffusion, it employs an MDS matrix in the round function. Whereas, due to the high cost of MDS matrices, most lightweight block ciphers do not use such matrices in their round function. But FUTURE optimizes the cost of the MDS matrix by taking advantage of a particular type of MDS matrix construction. By judiciously choosing the FUTURE Sbox as a composition of four lightweight Sboxes, we have reduced the implementation cost significantly. Also, FUTURE shows its resistance to fundamental attacks. We believe that FUTURE will be a secure lightweight block cipher.

Acknowledgments. We are thankful to the anonymous reviewers for their valuable comments. We would also like to thank Gaurav Bansal, Manas Ghai and Rajat Khanna for their help. Susanta Samanta is supported by the project "Study and Analysis of IoT Security" by NTRO under the Government of India at R.C.Bose Centre for Cryptology and Security, Indian Statistical Institute, Kolkata.

A Test Vectors

Plaintext	Key ($K = K_0||K_1$)	Ciphertext
0x0000000000000000	0x00000000000000000000000000000000	0x298650c13199cdec
0x0000000000000000	0x0000000000000000111111111111111111	0x4aa41b330751b83d
0xffffffffffffffff	0x00102030405060708090a0b0c0d0e0f	0x68e030733fe73b8a
0xffffffffffffffff	0xffffffffffffffffffffffffffffffff	0x333ba4b7646e09f2
0x6162636465666768	0x00000000000000000000000000000000	0xcc5ba5e52038b6df
0x5353414d414e5441	0x0519283201091364502938776394887 1	0x5ce1b8d8d01a9310

References

1. Virtual Silicon Inc. 0.18 μm VIP Standard Cell Library Tape Out Ready, Part Number: UMCL18G212T3, Process: UMC Logic 0.18 μm Generic II Technology: 0.18 μm (2004)

2. Avanzi, R.: The QARMA block cipher family. almost MDS matrices over rings with zero divisors, nearly symmetric even-mansour constructions with non-involutory central rounds, and search heuristics for low-latency s-boxes. IACR Trans. Symmetric Cryptology, **2017**(1), 4–44 (2017)

3. Banik, S., et al.: Midori: a block cipher for low energy. In: Iwata, T., Cheon, J.H. (eds.) ASIACRYPT 2015. LNCS, vol. 9453, pp. 411–436. Springer, Heidelberg (2015). https://doi.org/10.1007/978-3-662-48800-3_17

4. Banik, S., Pandey, S.K., Peyrin, T., Sasaki, Yu., Sim, S.M., Todo, Y.: GIFT: a small present. In: Fischer, W., Homma, N. (eds.) CHES 2017. LNCS, vol. 10529, pp. 321–345. Springer, Cham (2017). https://doi.org/10.1007/978-3-319-66787-4_16

5. Bard, G.V., Courtois, N.T., Jefferson, C.: Efficient methods for conversion and solution of sparse systems of low-degree multivariate polynomials over GF(2) via SAT-Solvers. Cryptology ePrint Archive, Report 2007/024 (2007). https://ia.cr/2007/024

6. Beaulieu, R., Shors, D., Smith, J., Treatman-Clark, S., Weeks, B., Wingers, L.: The SIMON and SPECK lightweight block ciphers. In: Proceedings of the 52nd Annual Design Automation Conference, DAC 2015, pp. 1–6 (2015)

7. Beierle, C., et al.: The SKINNY family of block ciphers and its low-latency variant MANTIS. In: Robshaw, M., Katz, J. (eds.) CRYPTO 2016. LNCS, vol. 9815, pp. 123–153. Springer, Heidelberg (2016). https://doi.org/10.1007/978-3-662-53008-5_5

8. Beierle, C., Leander, G., Moradi, A., Rasoolzadeh, S.: CRAFT: lightweight tweakable block cipher with efficient protection against DFA attacks. IACR Trans. Symmetric Cryptology **2019**(1), 5–45 (2019)

9. Biham, E., Shamir, A.: Differential cryptanalysis of DES-like cryptosystems. J. Cryptol. 4(1), 3–72 (1991). https://doi.org/10.1007/BF00630563

10. Bogdanov, A., et al.: PRESENT: an ultra-lightweight block cipher. In: Paillier, P., Verbauwhede, I. (eds.) CHES 2007. LNCS, vol. 4727, pp. 450–466. Springer, Heidelberg (2007). https://doi.org/10.1007/978-3-540-74735-2_31

11. Borghoff, J., et al.: PRINCE – a low-latency block cipher for pervasive computing applications. In: Wang, X., Sako, K. (eds.) ASIACRYPT 2012. LNCS, vol. 7658, pp. 208–225. Springer, Heidelberg (2012). https://doi.org/10.1007/978-3-642-34961-4_14

12. Carlet, C.: Boolean Functions for Cryptography and Coding Theory. Cambridge University Press, Cambridge (2021)

13. Cid, C., Leurent, G.: An analysis of the XSL algorithm. In: Roy, B. (ed.) ASIACRYPT 2005. LNCS, vol. 3788, pp. 333–352. Springer, Heidelberg (2005). https://doi.org/10.1007/11593447_18

14. Cid, C., Murphy, S., Robshaw, M.J.B.: Small scale variants of the AES. In: Gilbert, H., Handschuh, H. (eds.) FSE 2005. LNCS, vol. 3557, pp. 145–162. Springer, Heidelberg (2005). https://doi.org/10.1007/11502760_10

15. Courtois, N.T., Bard, G.V.: Algebraic cryptanalysis of the data encryption standard. In: Galbraith, S.D. (ed.) Cryptography and Coding 2007. LNCS, vol. 4887, pp. 152–169. Springer, Heidelberg (2007). https://doi.org/10.1007/978-3-540-77272-9_10

16. Courtois, N., Klimov, A., Patarin, J., Shamir, A.: Efficient algorithms for solving overdefined systems of multivariate polynomial equations. In: Preneel, B. (ed.) EUROCRYPT 2000. LNCS, vol. 1807, pp. 392–407. Springer, Heidelberg (2000). https://doi.org/10.1007/3-540-45539-6_27

17. Courtois, N.T., Pieprzyk, J.: Cryptanalysis of block ciphers with overdefined systems of equations. In: Zheng, Y. (ed.) ASIACRYPT 2002. LNCS, vol. 2501, pp. 267–287. Springer, Heidelberg (2002). https://doi.org/10.1007/3-540-36178-2_17

18. Courtois, N.T., Sepehrdad, P., Sušil, P., Vaudenay, S.: ElimLin algorithm revisited. In: Canteaut, A. (ed.) FSE 2012. LNCS, vol. 7549, pp. 306–325. Springer, Heidelberg (2012). https://doi.org/10.1007/978-3-642-34047-5_18

19. Cui, T., Chen, S., Jia, K., Fu, K., Wang, M.: New automatic search tool for impossible differentials and zero-correlation linear approximations. Cryptology ePrint Archive, Report 2016/689 (2016). https://ia.cr/2016/689

20. Cusick, T.W., Stanica, P.: Cryptographic Boolean Functions and Applications, 2nd edn. Academic Press, Cambridge (2017)

21. Daemen, J., Rijmen, V.: The Design of Rijndael: AES - The Advanced Encryption Standard. Information Security and Cryptography, Springer, Heidelberg (2002)

22. De Cannière, C., Dunkelman, O., Knežević, M.: KATAN and KTANTAN — a family of small and efficient hardware-oriented block ciphers. In: Clavier, C., Gaj, K. (eds.) CHES 2009. LNCS, vol. 5747, pp. 272–288. Springer, Heidelberg (2009). https://doi.org/10.1007/978-3-642-04138-9_20

23. Diem, C.: The XL-algorithm and a conjecture from commutative algebra. In: Lee, P.J. (ed.) ASIACRYPT 2004. LNCS, vol. 3329, pp. 323–337. Springer, Heidelberg (2004). https://doi.org/10.1007/978-3-540-30539-2_23

24. Guo, J., Peyrin, T., Poschmann, A., Robshaw, M.: The LED block cipher. In: Preneel, B., Takagi, T. (eds.) CHES 2011. LNCS, vol. 6917, pp. 326–341. Springer, Heidelberg (2011). https://doi.org/10.1007/978-3-642-23951-9_22

25. Gupta, K.C., Pandey, S.K., Ray, I.G., Samanta, S.: Cryptographically significant MDS matrices over finite fields: a brief survey and some generalized results. Adv. Math. Commun. **13**(4), 779–843 (2019)

26. Leander, G., Abdelraheem, M.A., AlKhzaimi, H., Zenner, E.: A cryptanalysis of PRINTCIPHER: the invariant subspace attack. In: Rogaway, P. (ed.) CRYPTO 2011. LNCS, vol. 6841, pp. 206–221. Springer, Heidelberg (2011). https://doi.org/10.1007/978-3-642-22792-9_12

27. Leander, G., Minaud, B., Rønjom, S.: A generic approach to invariant subspace attacks: cryptanalysis of robin, iSCREAM and Zorro. In: Oswald, E., Fischlin, M. (eds.) EUROCRYPT 2015. LNCS, vol. 9056, pp. 254–283. Springer, Heidelberg (2015). https://doi.org/10.1007/978-3-662-46800-5_11

28. Liu, Y., Rijmen, V.: New observations on invariant subspace attack. Inf. Process. Lett. **138**, 27–30 (2018)

29. MacWilliams, F.J., Sloane, N.J.A.: The Theory of Error Correcting Codes. North-Holland Publishing Co., Amsterdam-New York-Oxford (1977)

30. Matsui, M.: Linear cryptanalysis method for DES cipher. In: Helleseth, T. (ed.) EUROCRYPT 1993. LNCS, vol. 765, pp. 386–397. Springer, Heidelberg (1994). https://doi.org/10.1007/3-540-48285-7_33

31. U.S. Department of Commerce, National Institute of Standards, and Technology. Secure Hash Standard - SHS: Federal Information Processing Standards Publication 180-4. CreateSpace Independent Publishing Platform, North Charleston, SC, USA (2012). https://csrc.nist.gov/publications/fips/fips180-4/fips-180-4.pdf

32. Axel Poschmann. Lightweight cryptography - cryptographic engineering for a pervasive world. Cryptology ePrint Archive, Report 2009/516 (2009). https://ia.cr/2009/516

33. Rivest, R.L., Shamir, A., Adleman, L.: A method for obtaining digital signatures and public-key cryptosystems. Commun. ACM **21**(2), 120–126 (1978)

34. Rothaus, O.S.: On "bent" functions. J. Comb. Theor. Ser. A **20**(3), 300–305 (1976)
35. Sajadieh, M., Mousavi, M.: Construction of MDS matrices from generalized Feistel structures. Des. Codes Crypt. **89**, 1433–1452 (2021)
36. Sakiyama, K., Sasaki, Y., Li, Y.: Security of Block Ciphers: From Algorithm Design to Hardware Implementation. Wiley Publishing, 1st edition (2015)
37. Sasaki, Yu., Todo, Y.: New impossible differential search tool from design and cryptanalysis aspects. In: Coron, J.-S., Nielsen, J.B. (eds.) EUROCRYPT 2017. LNCS, vol. 10212, pp. 185–215. Springer, Cham (2017). https://doi.org/10.1007/978-3-319-56617-7_7
38. Seberry, J., Zhang, X.-M., Zheng, Y.: Relationships among nonlinearity criteria. In: De Santis, A. (ed.) EUROCRYPT 1994. LNCS, vol. 950, pp. 376–388. Springer, Heidelberg (1995). https://doi.org/10.1007/BFb0053452
39. Shibutani, K., Isobe, T., Hiwatari, H., Mitsuda, A., Akishita, T., Shirai, T.: *Piccolo*: an ultra-lightweight blockcipher. In: Preneel, B., Takagi, T. (eds.) CHES 2011. LNCS, vol. 6917, pp. 342–357. Springer, Heidelberg (2011). https://doi.org/10.1007/978-3-642-23951-9_23
40. Soos, M., Nohl, K., Castelluccia, C.: Extending SAT solvers to cryptographic problems. In: Kullmann, O. (ed.) SAT 2009. LNCS, vol. 5584, pp. 244–257. Springer, Heidelberg (2009). https://doi.org/10.1007/978-3-642-02777-2_24
41. Sun, L., Wang, W., Wang, M.Q.: MILP-aided bit-based division property for primitives with non-bit-permutation linear layers. IET Inf. Secur. **14**(1), 12–20 (2020)
42. Suzaki, T., Minematsu, K., Morioka, S., Kobayashi, E.: *TWINE*: a lightweight block cipher for multiple platforms. In: Knudsen, L.R., Wu, H. (eds.) SAC 2012. LNCS, vol. 7707, pp. 339–354. Springer, Heidelberg (2013). https://doi.org/10.1007/978-3-642-35999-6_22
43. Todo, Y., Morii, M.: Bit-based division property and application to SIMON family. In: Peyrin, T. (ed.) FSE 2016. LNCS, vol. 9783, pp. 357–377. Springer, Heidelberg (2016). https://doi.org/10.1007/978-3-662-52993-5_18
44. Wagner, D.: The boomerang attack. In: Knudsen, L. (ed.) FSE 1999. LNCS, vol. 1636, pp. 156–170. Springer, Heidelberg (1999). https://doi.org/10.1007/3-540-48519-8_12
45. Xiang, Z., Zhang, W., Bao, Z., Lin, D.: Applying MILP method to searching integral distinguishers based on division property for 6 lightweight block ciphers. In: Cheon, J.H., Takagi, T. (eds.) ASIACRYPT 2016. LNCS, vol. 10031, pp. 648–678. Springer, Heidelberg (2016). https://doi.org/10.1007/978-3-662-53887-6_24
46. Yeo, S.L., Le, D.-P., Khoo, K.: Improved algebraic attacks on lightweight block ciphers. J. Cryptogr. Eng. **11**(1), 1–19 (2020). https://doi.org/10.1007/s13389-020-00237-4

A Small GIFT-COFB: Lightweight Bit-Serial Architectures

Andrea Caforio[1(✉)], Daniel Collins[1], Subhadeep Banik[2],
and Francesco Regazzoni[2,3]

[1] LASEC, Ecole Polytechnique Fédérale de Lausanne, Lausanne, Switzerland
{andrea.caforio,daniel.collins}@epfl.ch
[2] Universita della Svizzera Italiana, Lugano, Switzerland
subhadeep.banik@usi.ch
[3] University of Amsterdam, Amsterdam, The Netherlands
f.regazzoni@uva.nl

Abstract. GIFT-COFB is a lightweight AEAD scheme and a submission to the ongoing NIST lightweight cryptography standardization process where it currently competes as a finalist. The construction processes 128-bit blocks with a key and nonce of the same size and has a small register footprint, only requiring a single additional 64-bit register. Besides the block cipher, the mode of operation uses a bit permutation and finite field multiplication with different constants. It is a well-known fact that implementing a hardware block cipher in a bit-serial manner, which advances only one bit in the computation pipeline in each clock cycle, results in the smallest circuits. Nevertheless, an efficient bit-serial circuit for a mode of operation that utilizes finite field arithmetic with multiple constants has yet to be demonstrated in the literature.

In this paper, we fill this gap regarding efficient field arithmetic in bit-serial circuits, and propose a lightweight circuit for GIFT-COFB that occupies less than 1500 GE, making it the to-date most area-efficient implementation of this construction. In a second step, we demonstrate how the additional operations in the mode can be executed concurrently with GIFT itself so that the total latency is significantly reduced whilst incurring only a modest area increase. Finally, we propose a first-order threshold implementation of GIFT-COFB, which we experimentally verify resists first-order side-channel analysis. (For the sake of reproducibility, the source code for all proposed designs is publicly available [14]).

Keywords: GIFT-COFB · Serial · ASIC · Threshold implementation

1 Introduction

Resource-constrained devices have become pervasive and ubiquitous commodities in recent years to the extent that the task of securing such gadgets has spawned a dedicated branch of cryptographic research. Lightweight cryptography is a discipline that comprises the creation, analysis and implementation of

© The Author(s), under exclusive license to Springer Nature Switzerland AG 2022
L. Batina and J. Daemen (Eds.): AFRICACRYPT 2022, LNCS 13503, pp. 53–77, 2022.
https://doi.org/10.1007/978-3-031-17433-9_3

resource-optimized cryptographic primitives in terms of criteria such as circuit area, power consumption and latency.

This proliferation of low-resource devices and their security requirements spurred the NIST Lightweight Cryptography competition [1]. Commencing in 2018 and recently entering its ultimate round with ten competing candidate designs, the competition can nowadays be considered the essential driving force in this research field. GIFT-COFB [9,10] is one the finalists and thus an efficient implementation of this construction on hardware and software platforms is both timely and useful. The designers of this scheme have provided results for round-based circuits, i.e., which perform one round of the underlying block cipher encryption algorithm per clock cycle. However, such circuits, although they consume less energy [6], induce a higher hardware footprint in gate count. Consequently, the minimum circuit area of GIFT-COFB remains unexplored.

A popular technique to reduce the hardware footprint of circuits is serialization. Serialized circuits operate with a datapath of width much less than the specified block size of the cipher, and therefore allow for specific resources of the circuit to be reused several times in each round. The byte-serial circuit (i.e., which advances one byte in the computation pipeline in each clock cycle) for AES-128 [16] by Moradi et al. [21], with area equivalent to around 2400 GE, remained for many years the most compact implementation of this block cipher. The implementation was subsequently extended to support both encryption and decryption capabilities as well as different key sizes [2,7,8].

A first generic technique to obtain bit-serial block cipher implementations, termed *bit-sliding*, was proposed in a work by Jean et al. [20] yielding, at the time, the smallest circuits for the ciphers AES-128, SKINNY [11] and PRESENT [13]. However, all these circuits required more clock cycles than the block size of the underlying block ciphers to execute one encryption round. The circuit for PRESENT was further compacted in [4] with a technique that made it possible to execute one round in exactly 64 clock cycles which is equal to the block size. This endeavour of computing a round function in the same number cycles as there are bits in the internal state was successfully extended to other ciphers including AES-128, SKINNY and GIFT-128 [3]. This was achieved by not treating the round as a monolithic entity by deferring some operations to the time allotted to operations of the next round. Additionally, the authors proposed bit-serial circuits for some modes of operation such as SAEAES [22], SUNDAE-GIFT [5], Romulus [18], SKINNY-AEAD [12]. It is important to note that the canon of bit-serial works has pushed implementations to a point where the corresponding circuits are predominantly comprised of storage elements with almost negligible amounts of combinatorial parts that implement the actual logic of the algorithm.

1.1 Contributions

Unlike the bit-serial AEAD implementations proposed in [3], GIFT-COFB involves finite field arithmetic for which there is no straightforward mapping into a bit-serial setting that is both circuit area and latency efficient. In this paper, we fill this gap by proposing *three* bit-serial circuits that stand as the to-date most area-efficient GIFT-COFB implementations known in the literature. More specifically, our contributions are summarized as follows:

1. GIFT-COFB-SER-S: This circuit represents an effective transformation of the *swap-and-rotate* GIFT-128 scheme into the GIFT-COFB mode of operation minimizing its area footprint.
2. GIFT-COFB-SER-F: Subsequently, we observed that the interspersing of block cipher invocations with calls to the finite field module as found in the baseline GIFT-COFB design can be reordered by leveraging its inherent mathematical structure in order to further optimize the overall latency of GIFT-COFB-SER-S while only incurring a modest area increase.
3. GIFT-COFB-SER-TI: In a natural progression, we design a bit-serial first-order threshold implementation based on GIFT-COFB-SER-F whose security is experimentally verified through statistical tests on signal traces obtained by measuring the implemented circuit on a SAKURA-G side-channel evaluation FPGA board.
4. We synthesise all of the proposed schemes on ASIC platforms using multiple standard cell libraries and compare our results to existing bit-serial implementations of NIST LWC candidate submissions, indicating our designs are among the smallest currently in the competition. A brief overview of the synthesis results is tabulated in Table 1.

Table 1. Synthesis results overview for lightweight block cipher based NIST LWC competitors using the STM 90 nm cell library at a clock frequency of 10 MHz. Latency and energy correspond to the encryption of 128 bits of AD and 1024 message bits. Highlighted schemes are NIST LWC finalists. A more detailed breakdown, including figures for the TSMC 28 nm and NanGate 45 nm processes, is given in Table 2.

	Datapath	Area	Latency	Power	Energy	Reference
	Bits	GE	Cycles	µW	nJ	
SUNDAE-GIFT	1	1201	92544	55.48	513.4	[3]
SAEAES	1	1350	24448	84.47	206.5	[3]
Romulus	1	1778	55431	82.28	456.1	[3]
SKINNY-AEAD	1	3589	72960	143.7	1048	[3]
GIFT-COFB	128	3927	400	156.3	6.254	[9]
GIFT-COFB-SER-S	1	1443	54784	50.11	275.8	Section 3
GIFT-COFB-SER-F	1	1485	51328	62.15	319.8	Section 4
GIFT-COFB-SER-TI	1	3384	51328	158.1	813.5	Section 5

1.2 Roadmap

Section 2 introduces preliminaries and the description of the GIFT-COFB AEAD scheme. Section 3 delves into the complexities of implementing finite field multiplication and presents the first bit-serial circuit for GIFT-COFB. In Sect. 4, we present a modified circuit in which the finite field operations are absorbed in the last encryption round of the GIFT-128 block cipher. Section 5 presents the circuit for the first order threshold implementation of GIFT-COFB and experimental results for leakage detection in which we do not observe any first-order leakage. Section 6 shows our implementation results. Section 7 concludes the paper.

2 Preliminaries

For the remainder of this paper, we denote by upper-case letters bitvectors, e.g., $X = x_{n-1}x_{n-2}\cdots x_1x_0$ represents a vector of length n composed of individual bits x_i and ϵ the empty string. We use $\|$ to indicate a concatenation of two bitvectors. $\lll i$ signifies the leftward rotation of a bitvector by i positions, whereas $\ll i$ is the leftward logical shift. For any binary string X and bit b, $b * X = X$ if $b = 1$ and $0^{|X|}$ if $b = 0$.

2.1   GIFT-COFB

GIFT-COFB is a block-cipher-based authenticated encryption mode that integrates GIFT-128 as the underlying block cipher with an 128-bit key and state. The construction adheres to the *COmbined FeedBack* mode of operation [15] which provides a processing rate of 1, i.e., a single block cipher invocation per input data block. The mode only adds an additional 64-bit state L to the existing block cipher registers and thus ranks among the most lightweight AEAD algorithms in the literature.

In the following, let $n = 128$ and denote by E_K a single GIFT-128 encryption using key $K \in \{0,1\}^n$. Furthermore, $N \in \{0,1\}^n$ signifies a nonce and A represents a list of n-bit associated data blocks of size $a \geq 0$. Analogously, let M be a list of n-bit plaintext blocks of size $m \geq 0$. GIFT-COFB intersperses E_K calls with that of several component functions. In particular, it uses a truncation procedure $\mathrm{Trunc}_k(x)$ that retrieves the k most significant bits of an n-bit input and a padding function $\mathrm{Pad}(x)$ that extends inputs whose lengths are not a multiple of n as follows:

$$\mathrm{Pad}(x) = \begin{cases} x & \text{if } x \neq \epsilon \text{ and } |x| \bmod n = 0 \\ x\|10^{(n-(|x| \bmod n)-1)} & \text{otherwise.} \end{cases}$$

Additionally, the internal state enters a feedback function between encryptions composed of two rotations of an input $X = (X_0, X_1)$ where $X_i \in \{0,1\}^{n/2}$ such that

$$\mathrm{Feed}(X) = (X_1, X_0 \lll 1).$$

Alongside the execution of Feed, the auxiliary state L is updated through a multiplication over the finite field $\mathrm{GF}(2^{64})$ generated by the root of the polynomial $p_{64}(x) = x^{64} + x^4 + x^3 + x + 1$. Consequently, the doubling of an element

$z = z_{63}z_{62}\cdots z_0 \in \mathrm{GF}(2^{64})$, i.e., the multiplication by the primitive element $\alpha = x = 0^{62}10$, is conveniently calculated as

$$\alpha \cdot z = \begin{cases} z \ll 1 & \text{if } z_{63} = 0 \\ (z \ll 1) \oplus 0^{59}11011 & \text{otherwise.} \end{cases} \tag{1}$$

By leveraging this multiplication, we can similarly triple an element z by calculating $(1 + \alpha) \cdot z$. The encryption of the last block of both A and M is preceded by the multiplication of L by 3^x and 3^y respectively, where

$$x = \begin{cases} 1 & \text{if } |A| \bmod n = 0 \text{ and } A \neq \epsilon, \\ 2 & \text{otherwise;} \end{cases} \qquad y = \begin{cases} 1 & \text{if } |M| \bmod n = 0 \text{ and } M \neq \epsilon, \\ 2 & \text{otherwise.} \end{cases}$$

All other encryptions lead to a multiplication of L by 2, excluding the initial encryption of the nonce. Ultimately, the mode of operation produces a ciphertext C of size $|C| = |M|$ and a tag $T \in \{0,1\}^n$. A graphical diagram of GIFT-COFB is given in Fig. 1.

2.2   Swap-and-Rotate Methodology

Swap-and-rotate is a natural progression of the bit-sliding technique with a particular focus on reducing the latency of an encryption round such that the number of required cycles is equal to the bit-length of the internal state. This technique was first successfully demonstrated on PRESENT and GIFT-64 by Banik et al. [4] and refined for other block ciphers in a follow-up work [3]. The core idea behind the technique lies in the reliance on a small number of flip-flop pairs that swap two bits in-place at specific points in time during the round function computation while the state bits are rotating through the register pipeline one position per clock cycle.

For simplicity, we represent an n-bit pipeline, i.e., shift register, as a sequence of individual flip-flops such that $\mathrm{FF}_{n-1} \leftarrow \mathrm{FF}_{n-2} \leftarrow \cdots \leftarrow \mathrm{FF}_1 \leftarrow \mathrm{FF}_0$. A swap is a hard-wired connection between two flip-flops $\mathrm{FF}_i, \mathrm{FF}_j$ that, when activated, exchanges the stored bits in registers FF_i and FF_j and takes effect in the following clock cycle (shown in Fig. 2). Feature-rich cell libraries normally offer a specific register type, a so-called scan-flip-flop, that enriches a normal d-flip-flop with an additional input value in order to implement this functionality more efficiently than simply multiplexing the input bits. However, if one flip-flop is part of multiple swaps, there is usually no other solution than placing an additional multiplexer in front of a regular d-flip-flop.

Depending on the block cipher, *swap-and-rotate* may be sufficient to fully implement the linear layer without any additional logic, especially in the case of simple bit permutations like those found in PRESENT or the bit-sliced variant

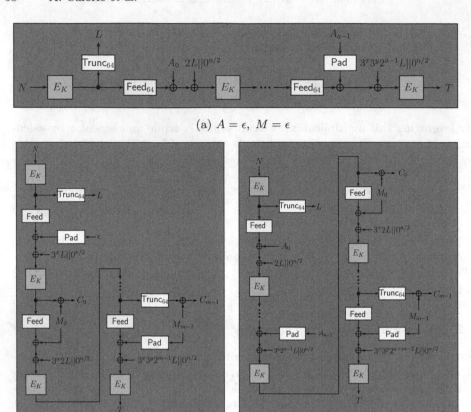

(a) $A = \epsilon$, $M = \epsilon$

(b) $A = \epsilon$, $M \neq \epsilon$ (c) $A \neq \epsilon$, $M \neq \epsilon$

Fig. 1. Schematic depiction of GIFT-COFB mode of operation for all associated data and plaintext sizes. We remark that an empty associated data input will always be padded to a full block, hence the minimum number of encryption calls is two.

of GIFT which is used in GIFT-COFB.[1] Considering the latter, a reinterpretation of GIFT-128, the state bits $x_{127} \cdots x_1 x_0$ are partitioned into four lanes such that

$$S_3 = x_{127}x_{126} \cdots x_{97}x_{96}, \qquad S_2 = x_{95}x_{94} \cdots x_{65}x_{64},$$
$$S_1 = x_{63}x_{62} \cdots x_{33}x_{32}, \qquad S_0 = x_{31}x_{30} \cdots x_1 x_0.$$

The bit permutation Π now reduces to four independent sub-permutations $\Pi_3, \Pi_2, \Pi_1, \Pi_0$ that act on each lane

$$\Pi(x_{127} \cdots x_0) = \Pi_3(x_{127} \cdots x_{96})\Pi_2(x_{95} \cdots x_{64})\Pi_1(x_{63} \cdots x_{32})\Pi_0(x_{31} \cdots x_0).$$

This fact was then exploited in [3] to compute each sub-permutation while the corresponding bits are advancing through $\mathbf{FF}_i$ for $96 \leq i \leq 127$. More specifi-

---

[1] A detailed description of the bit-sliced GIFT representation can be found in the GIFT-COFB white paper [9].

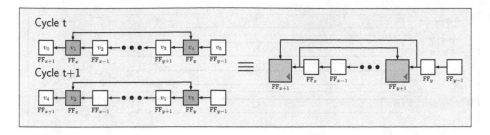

Fig. 2. The fundamental concept of *swap-and-rotate*. When a swap is active as shown by a colored box on FF_x and FF_y, then the operation performed in the pipeline swaps the contents of FF_x and FF_y and then rotates. The construct can be achieved by using scan flip-flops wired as shown above. The large green boxes on the right denote scan flip-flops. (Color figure online)

cally, the plaintext is loaded into FF_0 throughout cycles 0–127. In cycles 96–127, the S-box layer of the first round and the swaps that calculate Π_3 are active. Subsequently, the swaps corresponding to Π_2, Π_1, Π_0 are active during the cycles 128–159, 160–191 and 192–224 respectively, concluding the calculation of the first round function. This pattern repeats for the remaining rounds until the 40-th and ultimate round which starts executing in cycle 5088. The first ciphertext bits are made available at FF_{127} from cycle 5120 until the last bit has exited the pipeline in cycle 5248. Hence, a full encryption takes exactly $(40+1) \cdot 128 = 5248$ cycles. A schematic timeline diagram is given Fig. 3.

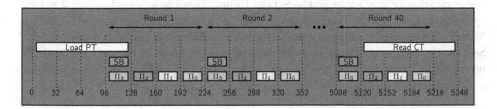

Fig. 3. Timeline diagram of the *swap-and-rotate* GIFT-128 implementation; the numbers in the x-axis denote clock cycles.

Another peculiarity of the bit-sliced GIFT-128 variant is that the 4-bit S-box is not applied to adjacent bits of the state but to the first bits of each lane, i.e., $x_{96}, x_{64}, x_{32}, x_0$. Summa summarum, the circuit for the state pipeline is compact and simple as shown in Fig. 4.[2]

---

[2] Note that there is an equally efficient circuit for the key schedule pipeline. An exact breakdown of all the swaps in the state pipeline is given in Appendix A.

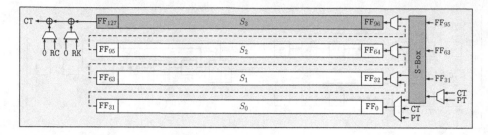

Fig. 4. The *swap-and-rotate* GIFT-128 state pipeline circuit. There are in total 9 swaps over 12 flip-flops. Their exact placement and activity cycles are given in Appendix A.

3 GIFT-COFB-SER-S

In this section, we lay the groundwork for our bit-serial GIFT-COFB circuits and describe how to efficiently implement the field multiplication as well as the feedback function. In the process, we integrate the obtained component circuits with the *swap-and-rotate* module described in Sect. 2.2 which yields the first lightweight bit-serial GIFT-COFB circuit. This is straightforward in the sense that there is a clear separation between the execution of the GIFT-128 encryption, the calculation of Feed and the addition of L to the internal state, alongside the loading of the plaintext as part of the next encryption. Meaning that, after the ciphertext has completely exited the pipeline, these three operations are each performed in 128 separate cycles during which the GIFT-128 pipeline executes the identity function, i.e., the state bits rotate through the shift register without the activation of any swap or the S-box. Hence, there is an overhead of 3×128 cycles between encryption invocations. We denote this circuit by GIFT-COFB-SER-S which will be the basis for the latency-optimized variant, presented in Sect. 4, that circumvents those periodic 384 *penalty* cycles with only a marginal increase in circuit area.[3] The exact sequence of operations between encryptions is described in Fig. 5.

3.1 Implementing the Feedback Function

Recall the feedback function as detailed in Sect. 2.2, i.e.,

$$\text{Feed}(X_0, X_1) = (X_1, X_0 \lll 1).$$

It is a bit-permutation belonging to the symmetric group over a set of 128 elements and executes two operations sequentially:

1. Swapping of the upper and lower halves of the word $(X_0, X_1) \rightarrow (X_1, X_0)$.
2. Leftward rotation of the lower half X_0 by one position.

---

[3] The letters S and F in GIFT-COFB-SER-S and GIFT-COFB-SER-F stand for slow and fast respectively.

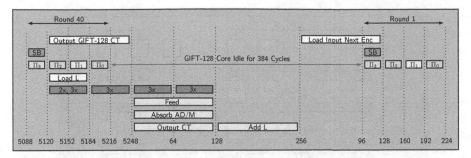

Fig. 5. Timeline diagram and cycle-by-cycle description of GIFT-COFB-SER-S for two successive encryptions. Note the interval of 3×128 idle cycles between encryptions.

Cycles	Operations
0-5087	The nonce is fed into the state pipeline bit by bit in cycles 0 to 127. Thereafter, the first 39 rounds of GIFT-128 are executed.
5088-5247	Round 40 executes during cycles 5088-5216. The resulting ciphertext bits exit the pipeline during cycles 5120-5247. We read the first 64-bits of the ciphertext into the L register during cycles 5120-5183 while executing the first multiplication during the same period.
For each additional data block, the following cycles are executed sequentially:	
0-127	After the ciphertext has fully exited the state pipeline, we start executing the feedback function for 128 cycles. In parallel, we can absorb the input data block and, if needed, produce the ciphertext bits. Subsequent multiplications of L are performed if required.
128-255	The state after the above is now XORed with the content of the L register and the result is written back, bit by bit, into the state register.
0-5247	A new encryption starts after L has been added to the cipher state.

Proposition 1. *Using two swaps over four flip-flops, it is possible to fully implement both subroutines of the subroutine Feed in exactly 128 clock cycles.*

Proof. A schematic cycle-by-cycle diagram of the feedback function is depicted in Fig. 6. The first swap $FF_0 \leftrightarrow FF_1$ is active from cycles 2 to 64. As a result, the state at clock cycle 64 is given as $x_{63}x_{62}\cdots x_1x_0x_{126}x_{125}\cdots x_{64}x_{127}$. Note that this is already the output of Feed if the two least significant bits were swapped, which is then done in cycle 64. The second swap $FF_{127} \leftrightarrow FF_{63}$ is active from cycle 64 to 127 which effectively computes the identity function over 64 cycles. One can thus see that after 128 cycles that the register contains the intended output of the Feed function. $\square$

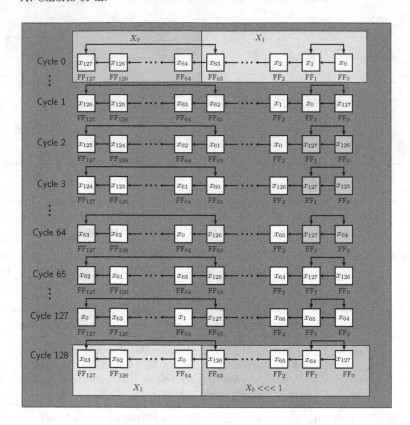

Fig. 6. Cycle-by-cycle execution diagram of the feedback function. Green marked registers denote active swaps that execute $X_0 \lll 1$ while yellow registers mark active swaps that perform $(X_0, X_1) \rightarrow (X_1, X_0)$. Note that when a swap is active as shown by a colored box on $\mathtt{FF}_x$ and $\mathtt{FF}_y$, then the operation performed in the pipeline is a) swap contents of $\mathtt{FF}_x$ and $\mathtt{FF}_y$ and then b) rotate. The construct can be achieved by using scan flip-flops wired as shown in Fig. 2. (Color figure online)

Absorbing Data Blocks and Outputting the Ciphertext. In order to avoid having to pass the message block bits twice to the circuit, once to produce the AEAD ciphertext and once for absorption into the state, i.e., $\mathrm{Feed}(X) \oplus M$, this absorption is performed in parallel to the execution of the feedback function. Note that if $X = x_{127}x_{126} \cdots x_0$ and $M = m_{127}m_{126} \cdots m_0$, then the i-th bit u_i of $\mathrm{Feed}(X) \oplus M$ is given as:

$$u_i = \begin{cases} m_i \oplus x_{i-64} & \text{if } 64 \leq i < 128, \\ m_i \oplus x_{i+63} & \text{if } 0 < i \leq 63, \\ m_i \oplus x_{127} & \text{if } i = 0 \end{cases}$$

By inspection of Fig. 6, one can see that in order to execute the above seamlessly, the data bits must be added to $\mathtt{FF}_{63}$. This is because, for any i, the state bit x_{i-64} (for $64 \leq i < 128$), x_{i+63} (for $0 < i \leq 63$) and x_{127} (for $i = 0$) is always present at FF_{63} at clock cycle i. Thus, to implement the above, we need one additional XOR gate before the 63rd flip-flop in the state register. Additionally, FF_{127} always contains the most significant bit of $X \lll i$ at any cycle $i \in [0, 127]$, thus the ciphertext, which is computed as $M \oplus X$, is extracted by adding the input data bit with FF_{127}. In Fig. 7, we present the state pipeline circuit of GIFT-COFB-SER-S that integrates the swaps of the feedback function, and the additional XOR gates for the data absorption and ciphertext creation.

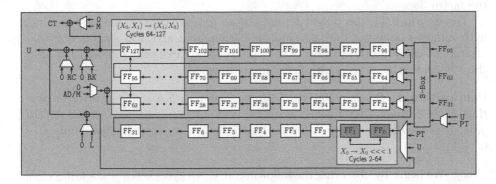

Fig. 7. GIFT-COFB-SER-S state pipeline.

3.2 Multiplication by 2 and 3

GIFT-COFB multiplies the auxiliary state L between encryptions by either the factor 2 or 3^x for $1 \leq x \leq 4$ depending on the associated data and message block sizes and padding. If it were not for the period right after the initial encryption of the nonce N in which L has to be loaded and updated in a short time interval, this would not be too much of an issue as there is ample time to calculate the multiplication while the encryption core is busy. In the following, we demonstrate how to efficiently multiply L by 2 or 3 in 64 cycles, yielding a maximum latency of 256 clock cycles for any factor 3^4.

Let $L = l_{63}l_{62} \cdots l_1 l_0$ be the individual bits of the register. On a 64-bit shift register, multiplication by 2 has the following form:

$$2 \times l_{63}l_{62} \cdots l_0 = (L \ll 1) \oplus (l_{63} * 0^{59}11011)$$

which, in plain terms, is simply a leftward shift by one position and the addition of the most significant bit l_{63} to four lower bits. On the other hand, the multiplication by three is more involved as $3 \times L = (2 \times L) \oplus L$ and is thus given as

$$3 \times l_{63}l_{62} \cdots l_0 = (L \ll 1) \oplus (l_{63} * 0^{59}11011) \oplus L.$$

A single-cycle implementation of this function necessitates 64 additional 2-input XOR gates that would incur roughly 128 GE in most standard libraries, which is a considerable overhead for a bit-serial circuit. Note that technically $3\times$ can be implemented with zero additional gates, if one is prepared to pay with latency. This is because $p_{64}(x)$ is a primitive polynomial, and since the element 2 is the root of $p_{64}(x)$ it must generate the cyclic multiplicative group of the finite field. With some arithmetic, it can be deduced that $3 = 2^d$ where $d = 9686038906114705801$ in this particular representation of the finite field. The discrete logarithm d of 3 is an integer of the order of 2^{63}, hence executing the multiplication by 2 over d would, in theory, compute the multiplication by the factor 3.

Disregarding this theoretical detour, our actual goal consists in implementing, with minimal circuitry, both the multiplication by 2 and 3 in such a way that after 64 clock cycles the first bit of the updated state exits the pipeline and after the 128 cycles the entire multiplication has finished.

Proposition 2. *By equipping the L shift register with a single auxiliary d-flip-flop, three 2-input NAND gates, one 2-input XOR gate and one 2-input XNOR gate, it is possible to multiply L by either 2 or 3, i.e., by the polynomials x or $(x + 1)$.*

Proof. We begin by observing the following: if $V = v_{63}v_{62}\cdots v_0 = 2 \times l_{63}l_{62}\cdots l_0$ and $W = w_{63}w_{62}\cdots w_0 = 3 \times l_{63}l_{62}\cdots l_0$, where v_i, w_i are given as

$$
v_i = \begin{cases} l_{i-1} \oplus l_{63} & \text{if } i \in \{1,3,4\}, \\ l_{63} & \text{if } i = 0, \\ l_{i-1} & \text{otherwise} \end{cases}
\qquad
w_i = \begin{cases} l_{i-1} \oplus l_{63} \oplus l_i & \text{if } i \in \{1,3,4\}, \\ l_{63} \oplus l_i & \text{if } i = 0, \\ l_{i-1} \oplus l_i & \text{otherwise.} \end{cases}
$$

It is immediately evident that for all three cases v_i and w_i differ only by the XOR of the term l_i. In cycle 0, bit l_{63} is first stored in an auxiliary register, which we hereafter refer to as Aux. Using this fact, we show how to update the register. Then we calculate each update bit as follows, where α, β and γ are signals defined below:

$$u = (\alpha \cdot \text{Aux}) \oplus (\beta \cdot \text{FF}_{63}) \oplus (\gamma \cdot \text{FF}_{62}). \tag{2}$$

Identity function. It is simply a rotation of the L register; $\alpha = \beta = \gamma = 0$.

Multiplication by 2. Signal α is used to add l_{63}, which is stored in Aux in cycle 0, to the output bit. β is always 0 for multiplication by 2. γ is 1 for all but cycle 63 in order to implement a left shift (and not left rotate). Consequently, we have

$$
\alpha = \begin{cases} 1 & \text{cycles } 59, 60, 62, 63, \\ 0 & \text{otherwise;} \end{cases}
\qquad \beta = 0; \qquad
\gamma = \begin{cases} 1 & \text{cycle} \neq 63, \\ 0 & \text{otherwise.} \end{cases} \tag{3}
$$

Recall the doubling function (1). If the update function u were to simply be $\gamma \cdot \text{FF}_{62}$, then after 64 cycles, the register would store $l_{63}\cdots l_0 \ll 1$. Now if we added l_{63} to the LFSR update in cycles 59, 60, 62, 63, then after 64 cycles, the

LFSR state would be $(l_{63} \cdots l_0 \ll 1) \oplus (l_{63} * 0^{59}11011)$ which is the output of the doubling function.

Multiplication by 3. α, and γ as above and always $\beta = 1$. Adding $\beta \cdot \mathsf{FF}_{63}$ to the update function enables the output to be $(l_{63} \cdots l_0 \ll 1) \oplus (l_{63} * 0^{59}11011) \oplus (l_{63} \cdots l_0)$, which is the output of the tripling function.

Using (2), we can implement both multiplications by factors 2 and 3 in 64 cycles using one auxiliary d-flip-flop, three 2-input NAND gates and one 2-input XOR gates and one 2-input XNOR gate. A diagram of the resulting circuit is shown in Fig. 8. □

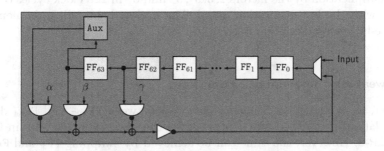

Fig. 8. Implementation of the bit-serial multiplication by 2 and 3.

3.3 GIFT-COFB-SER-S Total Latency

It can be seen that the encryption of the nonce takes 5248 cycles. Thereafter, every additional block takes $256 + 5248 = 5504$ cycles to process. Thus if the padded associated data and message consist of B blocks in total, then the time taken to produce the ciphertext and tag is $T_S = 5248 + 5504 \cdot B$ clock cycles.

4 GIFT-COFB-SER-F

The proposed bit-serial circuit from the previous section already represents the to-date most area-efficient GIFT-COFB implementation. However, as our bit-serial interpretation respects the natural order of operations as given in the specification of the mode of operation, it has a significantly elevated latency. This is mainly due to the encryption core being idle during 3×128 clock cycles between successive invocations which means that if we want to do away with those penalty cycles, the calculation of Feed, the update and addition of L, the addition of incoming associated data and message bits and the loading of the next encryption state all have to occur in parallel. This means that during 128 cycles while the GIFT ciphertext bits $c_i^{(j)}$ for datablock j leave the pipeline, the newly entering bits $v_i^{(j+1)}$ for data block $j+1$ at FF_0 are necessarily of the form

$$v_i^{(j+1)} = c_i^{(j)} \oplus \mathsf{RK}_i \oplus \mathsf{RC}_i \oplus L_i^{(j+1)} \oplus D_i^{(j+1)}, \tag{4}$$

where $\mathsf{RK}_i \oplus \mathsf{RC}_i$ denote the i-th bit of the last round key, $L_i^{(j+1)}$ denotes the i-th bit of the L register to be added before the $(j+1)$-th data block and $D_i^{(j+1)}$ is the i-th bit of the $(j+1)$-th data block. In this section, we describe three requisite tweaks to GIFT-COFB-SER-S that let us achieve this goal.

1. Change the swaps of Feed described in Sect. 3.1 as to enable its execution in parallel to the ciphertext bits leaving the state pipeline.
2. Reorder the incoming data bits as well as L such that they can be seamlessly added to the exiting ciphertext bits.
3. Enrich the L circuit from Sect. 3.2 with additional logic in order to compute the multiplication by the factors $2, 3, 3^2, 3^3$ and 3^4 in 128 clock cycles concurrently with the last encryption round. The updated time diagram alongside a cycle-by-cycle description is given in Fig. 9.

4.1 Tweaking the Feedback Function

Note that, as explained in Sect. 3.1, the swap between FF_{127} and FF_{64} during the calculation of the Feed function preserves the state over 64 cycles in GIFT-COFB-SER-S. However, the same can be achieved by swapping FF_x and FF_{x-63} for any x. Since we execute Feed concurrently with the last GIFT encryption round, we want the bit exiting the pipeline at FF_{127} to be the output of the GIFT encryption routine in the same order as in GIFT-COFB-SER-S. Swapping out FF_{127} and FF_{64}, however, disrupts that order. Thus, we replace the swap $\mathsf{FF}_{127} \leftrightarrow \mathsf{FF}_{64}$ with the swap $\mathsf{FF}_{63} \leftrightarrow v_i^{(j)}$, where $v_i^{(j)}$ is the i-th bit of the j-th incoming block as defined above.

A side effect of this choice affects the S-box inputs of just the first round of every new encryption with an incoming data block. In GIFT-COFB-SER-F, in the first S-box invocation of a new encryption, inputs are now of the form FF_{95}, $v_i^{(j)}$, $\mathsf{FF}_{31}, \mathsf{FF}_{63}$ instead of $\mathsf{FF}_{95}, \mathsf{FF}_{63}, \mathsf{FF}_{31}, v_i^{(j)}$ due to the $\mathsf{FF}_{63} \leftrightarrow v_i^{(j)}$ swap. As a result, we need two more multiplexers that swap FF_{63} and $v_i^{(j)}$ before entering into the S-box during cycles 96 to 127. The resulting circuit for GIFT-COFB-SER-F is depicted in Fig. 10.

4.2 Reordering Data Bits

The absorption of associated data/message bits and L normally occurs after the computation of the feedback function. However, we have to do it with the last encryption round, which involves some re-ordering of data bits and L. Consider the inverse transformation of Feed:

$$\text{Feed}^{-1}(X_0, X_1) = ((X_1 \ggg 1), X_0).$$

Note that Feed is a linear function, we have since $\text{Feed}^{-1}(L, 0^{64}) = 0^{64} \| L$:

$$\text{Feed}(X \oplus \text{Feed}^{-1}(D) \oplus \text{Feed}^{-1}(L, 0^{64})) = \text{Feed}(X) \oplus D \oplus L \| 0^{64}.$$

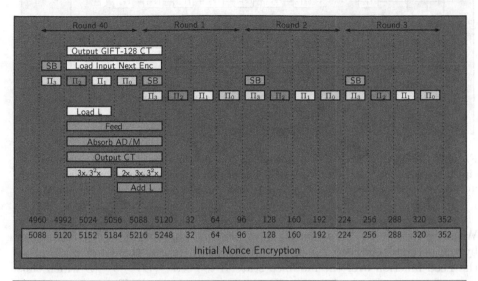

Cycles	Operations
0-5087	The nonce is fed into the state pipeline bit by bit in cycles 0 to 127. Thereafter, the first 39 rounds of **GIFT**-128 are executed.
5088-5247	Round 40 executes during cycles 5088-5216. The resulting ciphertext bits exit the pipeline during cycles 5120-5247. We read the first 64-bits of the ciphertext into the L register during cycles 5120-5183 while executing the first multiplication during the same period such that in the second 64 cycles it is added back to the cipher state. In the same 128 cycles, we also execute Feed and add the data bits.
For each additional data block, the following cycles are executed sequentially:	
0-4959	We perform the first 39 rounds of the new encryption call.
4960-4991	The first 32 cycles of the last round of the encryption call.
4992-5119	We execute the following in parallel: we finish executing the encryption call, we load the new cipher state, perform multiplication of L, execute Feed, absorb data bits and the (updated) L, output the ciphertext and start executing round 1 of the next encryption call.

Fig. 9. Timeline diagram of **GIFT-COFB-SER-F**. Note that the initial 128 cycles to load the nonce cannot be parallelized with other functions, hence the initial encryption of the nonce takes 5248 cycles.

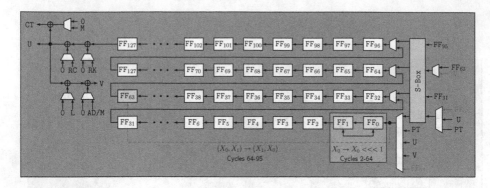

Fig. 10. GIFT-COFB-SER-F state pipeline. U denotes the input bit during intermediate cipher rounds and V the input during the first round of a new encryption. Wires marked in red enable the concurrent execution of Feed and the S-box. (Color figure online)

We need to re-order the incoming data bits and the output of the L function by the permutation Feed^{-1} before adding it to the state, thereafter performing the Feed function over the modified state $X \oplus \text{Feed}^{-1}(D) \oplus 0^{64} \| L$ which thus correctly computes the input to the next encryption call. This comes with a convenient side effect:

Proposition 3. *Placing the addition of L before Feed yields 64 spare cycles that can be used to perform the finite field multiplications.*

Proof. When we add the string Feed$^{-1}(L, 0^{64}) = 0^{64} \| L$, the first 64 cycles are spent adding the zero string. These 64 cycles can be used to load L into its register and simultaneously multiply it by either $2, 3, 3^2, 3^3$ or 3^4 such that in cycle 64 the first correctly updated bits exit L and the entire register is updated in a total of 128 cycles. □

4.3 Enhancing the Multiplier

We proceed to demonstrate that the assertion from the previous proposition, namely that after 64 cycles the first correctly multiplied bit exits the L pipeline, can be integrated into the existing multiplier from Sect. 3.2 with modest overhead.

Proposition 4. *By equipping the L shift register with four auxiliary d-flip-flops, nine 2-input NAND gates, eight 2-input XOR gates and one 2-input XNOR gate, it is possible to multiply L by either $2, 3, 3^2, 3^3$ or 3^4 in 128 cycles.*

Proof. Again let $L = l_{63}l_{62} \cdots l_0$ be the individual state, then the multiplication by 3^2 is written as

$$3^2 \times l_{63}l_{62} \cdots l_0 = (L \ll 2) \oplus (l_{63} * 0^{58}110110) \oplus L \oplus (l_{62} * 0^{59}11011)$$

Recall the multiplication circuit for the factors 2 and 3 from Sect. 3.2. We re-introduce signals α, β, γ as α_0, β_0 and γ_0, and to capture multiplication by 3^2 we further add δ_0 and α_1. Let Aux0 be the register that stores l_{63} in cycle 0, and analogously denote by Aux1 the auxiliary register that stores l_{62} in the same cycle. Then, the circuit for the multiplication by the factors 2, 3, 3^2 can be written as

$$u = (\alpha_0 \cdot \text{Aux0}) \oplus (\alpha_1 \cdot \text{Aux1}) \oplus (\beta_0 \cdot \text{FF}_{63}) \oplus (\gamma_0 \cdot \text{FF}_{62}) \oplus (\delta_0 \cdot \text{FF}_{61}).$$

In order to compute the multiplication by the higher factors 3^3 and 3^4, we equip the L pipeline with a second 3^2 circuit at the beginning that continuously overwrites register FF_2, which is therefore a scan flip-flop, as the bits enter the pipeline. In cycle 2, the values FF_2 and FF_1 are l_{63} and l_{62} respectively, which are stored in this cycle in auxiliary flip-flops Aux2 and Aux3. The updated bit for these cases can be written as:

$$u' = (\alpha_2 \cdot \text{Aux2}) \oplus (\alpha_3 \cdot \text{Aux3}) \oplus (\beta_1 \cdot \text{FF}_2) \oplus (\delta_1 \cdot \text{FF}_0).$$

The resulting circuit full multiplier is shown in Fig. 11.

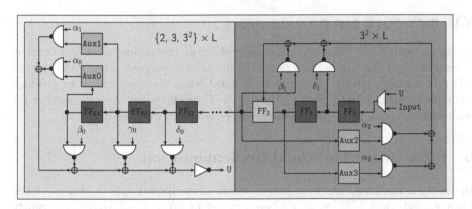

Fig. 11. L state pipeline that performs the multiplication by the factors 2, 3, 3^2, 3^3 and 3^4.

As before in Sect. 3.2, we give an exact list of activation cycles for each control signal below.

Identity function: All signals are set to 0.

Multiplication by 2. We have $\alpha_0 = \alpha$, $\beta_0 = \beta$ and $\gamma_0 = \gamma$ where α, β, γ are as in (3), additionally $\delta_0 = \alpha_1 = 0$. Since only the left half of the diagram is relevant, all other signals are 0.

Multiplication by 3. As in multiplication by 2 except for $\beta_0 = 1$.

Multiplication by 3^2. As above, only the left portion of the diagram is used. δ_0 steers the addition of l_{61}, and is active except for the last two cycles. α_0 enables the addition of l_{63}, similarly α_1 enables the addition of l_{62}. Furthermore, γ_0 is always 0 as it is only used in the multiplication by 3 and β_0 is always 1. In summary, we have

$$\alpha_0 = \begin{cases} 1 & \text{cycles } 58, 59, 61, 62, \\ 0 & \text{otherwise;} \end{cases} \qquad \alpha_1 = \begin{cases} 1 & \text{cycles } 59, 60, 62, 63, \\ 0 & \text{otherwise;} \end{cases}$$

$$\delta_0 = \begin{cases} 1 & \text{cycle} < 62, \\ 0 & \text{otherwise;} \end{cases} \qquad \beta_0 = 1; \quad \gamma_0 = 0.$$

Multiplication by 3^3. We first use the 3^2 multiplier on the right in the diagram that executes on newly entered bits then finish with a multiplication by 3 by the left multiplier. As we always update FF_2 for the factor 3^2, the activation cycles of the signals α_2, α_3, β_1 and δ_1 are analogous to the signals α_0, α_1, β_0 and δ_0 in the left 3^2 multiplication module except they occur 62 cycles before.

Multiplication by 3^4. The first phase is exactly as in the case of multiplication by 3^3, and the second phase is exactly as in multiplication by 3^2.   □

4.4 GIFT-COFB-SER-F Total Latency

It can be seen from Fig. 9 that the encryption of the nonce takes 5248 cycles. Thereafter every additional block takes 5120 cycles to process. Thus if the padded AD and message consist of B blocks in total, then the time taken to produce the ciphertext and Tag is $T_F = 5248 + 5120 \cdot B$ clock cycles. We can see that for each block of data processed we save $\frac{T_S - T_F}{B} = 384$ clock cycles.

5 First-Order Threshold Implementation

In Boolean masking, sensitive values x are decomposed into s shares of the form x_i such that $\sum_0^{s-1} x_i = x$ where any set of up to $s - 1$ shares are jointly independent of x. This technique can be used to provide security guarantees when an adversary can query up to $d = s - 1$ wires in a circuit at any one point in time, i.e., to provide d-th order security. In the following, we restrict our attention to the case where $d = 1$.

Threshold implementations [23] are a family of masking schemes which provide provable first-order security guarantees even in the presence of hardware glitches [17]. In a threshold implementation (TI) of a given design, n-ary Boolean functions (i.e., sub-functions of the design) $f(x_{n-1}, ..., x_0) = z$ are divided into s components f_i such that $\sum_0^{s-1} f_i = f$. We consider sharings of values f that are *non-complete*, i.e., each f_i is independent of at least one value x_j, and *uniform*, i.e., for all x_i the number of sets $\{x_{n-1}, ..., x_0\}$ which satisfies for a given $(y_{k-1}, ..., y_0)$ both $\sum_i x_i = x$ and $f(x) = (y_{k-1}, ..., y_0)$ is constant. We also assume that maskings are uniform, i.e., for each x, each valid masking $\{x_{n-1}, ..., x_0\}$ such that $\sum_i x_i = x$ occurs with the same probability.

5.1 GIFT-COFB-SER-TI First-Order Threshold Implementation

We first note that the GIFT S-box S is cubic and can be decomposed into two quadratic S-boxes S_F and S_G from $\{0,1\}^4 \rightarrow \{0,1\}^4$ such that $S = S_F \circ S_G$. Since S_F and S_G are quadratic, they can be masked using a direct sharing approach using three shares for a first-order threshold implementation such that

$$S_G = S_{G_1} \oplus S_{G_2} \oplus S_{G_3}; \quad S_F = S_{F_1} \oplus S_{F_2} \oplus S_{F_3},$$

where $S_{G_1}, S_{G_2}, S_{G_3}$ and $S_{F_1}, S_{F_2}, S_{F_3}$ are the component function of S_F and S_G respectively. This approach was used in [19] from which we take the proposed non-complete and uniform first-order TI. We provide the algebraic expression of the component functions in Appendix B.

Consequently, our implementation uses three shares for the state and L registers while the key and round constant pipeline remain unshared. The only challenge in constructing the circuit is to place the S_{F_i} and S_{G_i} substitution boxes such that they correctly compute the masked GIFT S-box in consonance with the other operations done in parallel. This can readily be achieved by noting that we can replace the unmasked S and replace it with S_{G_i}, and place S_{F_i} after the first flip-flop of each lane, i.e., $FF_0, FF_{32}, FF_{64}, FF_{96}$, which executes for 32 cycles starting in cycle 97 of each round. A schematic of one of the three shares of the state pipeline is shown in Fig. 13 (Fig. 12).

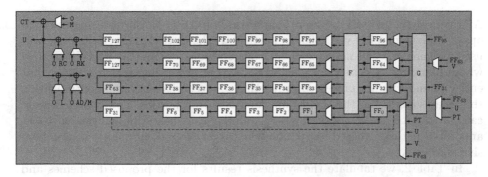

Fig. 12. One of the three state pipeline shares of the GIFT-COFB-SER-TI circuit.

5.2 Evaluation

We applied the TVLA methodology [24] and performed non-specific t-tests (using Welsh's t-test) to validate the first-order security of our threshold implementation GIFT-COFB-SER-TI. We took a threshold of $|t| > 4.5$ for any value of t computed to reject the null hypothesis that GIFT-COFB-SER-TI encryption operations admit indistinguishable mean power consumption in the case that the input is either uniform or fixed.

We used the SAKURA-G side-channel evaluation board[4] with two Spartan 6 FPGA cores, one which performed GIFT-COFB-SER-TI operations clocked at a slow 1.5MHz and the other that interfaces between the cryptographic core and a computer (which generates pre-masked shares for the DUT). To prevent unintended optimisations that could lead to leakage during synthesis, we added DONT_TOUCH, KEEP and KEEP_HIERARCHY constraints to our code. Measurements were taken with a Tektronix MSO44 at 625MS/s taking 3000 data points per trace, which corresponds to 7 cycles of S-box evaluation (the only non-linear component of GIFT-COFB) in the second round of the first GIFT encryption call, i.e., while GIFT is encrypting the nonce. During testing, we reset the cryptographic core between each GIFT-COFB encryption and interleaved encryptions with random and fixed inputs. A sample trace is shown in Fig. 13a.

As a measure to ensure our setup was calibrated properly, we first performed a t-test in the leaky *masks off* setting, which is as follows. Recall that GIFT-COFB-SER-TI is a three-share TI. Then, in the masks off setting, one input value is set to the original input (fixed or random) and the other two to constant values (the zero vector here). We present the results in Fig. 13b revealing that significant, potentially exploitable leakage was detected with just 20 thousand traces. Then, with masks on (i.e., with uniform masking used), we found no evidence of leakage with 10,000,000 traces, evident in Fig. 13c.

6   Implementation

All the investigated schemes were synthesized on ASIC platforms using the Synopsys Design compiler v2019.03. In particular, the compile_ultra directive was used to generate the netlists for all constructions except GIFT-COFB-SER-TI whose hierarchy is conserved via the no_autoungroup flag which ensures that entity boundaries are preserved preventing any security-degrading optimization that may violate the threshold implementation properties. Power figures were calculated with the Synopsys Power Compiler that bases its analysis on back-annotated netlists created by running the target circuits through a comprehensive testbench.

In Table 2, we tabulate the synthesis results for the proposed schemes and other bit-serial AEAD schemes for three different cell libraries. Namely, the relatively recent TSMC 28 nm process, the high-leakage NanGate 45 nm library and the comparably large STM 90 nm library.

Naturally, due to the increased complexity of both Feed and the multiplier, GIFT-COFB-SER-F incurs a slightly larger circuit area than GIFT-COFB-SER-S which is offset by the latency savings as part of the parallelization of all component functions. We note that both GIFT-COFB-SER-S and GIFT-COFB-SER-F significantly undercut Romulus, the only other lightweight block cipher scheme among the NIST LWC finalists, in both area and power/energy.

---

[4] https://satoh.cs.uec.ac.jp/SAKURA/hardware/SAKURA-G.html.

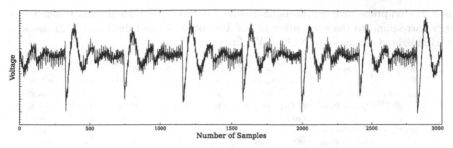

(a) A sample trace taken over 7 cycles.

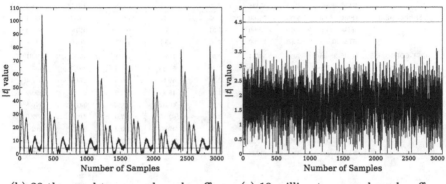

(b) 20 thousand traces and masks off.   (c) 10 million traces and masks off.

Fig. 13. Sample trace (top) and t-test results for the GIFT-COFB-SER-TI circuit (bottom). The red lines correspond to a threshold of $|t| = 4.5$. (Color figure online)

7   Conclusion

In this paper, we investigated bit-serial architectures for the AEAD mode GIFT-COFB, a finalist in the NIST lightweight cryptography competition. In the process, we propose two architectures: the first follows a natural order of operations in which the finite field operations and other state updates are performed in the time period between 2 successive calls to the encryption module. The second absorbs all these operations in the last 128 cycles of the encryption operation, and saves 384 clock cycles in the processing of every block of associated data or message. We then extended the second architecture to construct a first order threshold implementation of GIFT-COFB. We verify the first-order security claims by performing statistical tests on power traces resulting from an implementation of the circuit on the SAKURA-G FPGA platform.

Acknowledgements. This project is partially supported by the European Union Horizon 2020 research and innovation program under the CPSoSAware project (grant 871738).

Table 2. Comprehensive synthesis figures for bit-serial AEAD schemes. Latency and energy correspond to the encryption of 128 bits of associated data and 1024 message bits. Highlighted schemes are NIST LWC finalists.

Scheme	Library	Area (GE)	Latency (Cycles)	Critical Path (ns)	Power (μW)		Energy (nJ)	
					10 MHz	100 MHz	10 MHz	100 MHz
SUNDAE-GIFT	TSMC 28 nm	1732	92544	0.54	15.06	139.8	138.8	128.6
	NanGate 45 nm	1913	92544	1.28	52.42	271.71	485.1	251.4
	STM 90 nm	1201	92544	1.91	55.48	504.0	513.4	466.4
SAEAES	TSMC 28 nm	1927	24448	1.63	18.66	187.9	45.62	45.7
	NanGate 45 nm	2073	24448	3.05	61.16	329.7	149.5	80.6
	STM 90 nm	1350	24448	5.20	84.47	779.26	206.5	190.5
Romulus	TSMC 28 nm	2601	55431	0.54	24.16	225.2	133.9	124.8
	NanGate 45 nm	2878	55431	1.25	42.99	387.8	238.3	214.5
	STM 90 nm	1778	55431	2.29	82.28	796.8	456.1	441.2
SKINNY-AEAD	TSMC 28 nm	5335	72960	0.85	42.12	421.3	307.3	307.4
	NanGate 45 nm	5976	72960	1.31	167.4	861.2	1218	628.3
	STM 90 nm	3589	72960	2.02	143.7	1437	1048	1048
GIFT-COFB-SER-S	TSMC 28 nm	2095	54784	0.97	15.61	144.1	85.52	79.31
	NanGate 45 nm	2308	54784	1.40	55.25	245.5	302.7	135.1
	STM 90 nm	1443	54784	2.97	50.11	495.3	274.5	272.4
GIFT-COFB-SER-F	TSMC 28 nm	2148	51328	1.12	18.83	174.9	96.89	89.99
	NanGate 45 nm	2365	51328	2.22	66.62	343.55	342.8	176.8
	STM 90 nm	1485	51328	3.66	62.15	627.0	319.8	322.6
GIFT-COFB-SER-TI	TSMC 28 nm	4821	51328	1.15	42.30	393.2	217.7	202.3
	NanGate 45 nm	5317	51328	2.31	149.01	777.4	766.7	400.0
	STM 90 nm	3384	51328	3.74	158.1	1437	813.5	739.4

A   Swap-and-Rotate GIFT-128 State Pipeline

In Table 3, we give the exact placement and activation periods of the nine swaps that implement the *swap-and-rotate* GIFT-128 permutation Π as specified in the work by Banik et al. [3].

Table 3. *Swap-and-rotate* listing of all swaps and their activation cycles.

Swap	Cycles
$FF_{96} \leftrightarrow FF_{97}$	Cycle mod 8 = 5
$FF_{96} \leftrightarrow FF_{98}$	Cycle mod 8 = 5
$FF_{96} \leftrightarrow FF_{99}$	Cycle mod 8 = 5 or Cycle mod 8 = 7
$FF_{99} \leftrightarrow FF_{101}$	6, 7, 10, 11, 14, 15, 18, 19, 22, 23, 26, 27, 30, 31, 34 35, 72, 73, 80, 81, 88, 89, 96, 97
$FF_{99} \leftrightarrow FF_{103}$	0, 1, 42, 43, 50, 51, 58, 59, 66, 67, 104, 105, 112, 113, 120, 121
$FF_{99} \leftrightarrow FF_{105}$	74, 75, 82, 83, 90, 91, 98, 99
$FF_{105} \leftrightarrow FF_{111}$	6, 7, 18, 19, 28, 29, 38, 39, 50, 51, 60, 61, 70, 71, 82, 83, 92, 93, 102, 103, 114, 115, 124, 125
$FF_{105} \leftrightarrow FF_{117}$	4, 5, 26, 27, 36, 37, 58, 59, 68, 69, 90, 91, 100, 101, 122, 123
$FF_{105} \leftrightarrow FF_{123}$	2, 3, 34, 35, 66, 67, 98, 99

B   ANF Equations of the 3-Share GIFT-128 S-Box

Below we list the exact ANF equations for all component functions of the 3-share first-order threshold implementation of the GIFT S-box as proposed in [19].

$$S_{G_1}(a_2, b_2, c_2, d_2, a_3, b_3, c_3, d_3) = a_3 + b_3 + b_2c_2 + b_2c_3 + b_3c_2,$$
$$c_3 + 1,$$
$$b_3 + a_2c_2 + a_2c_3 + a_3c_2,$$
$$a_3 + b_3 + c_3 + d_3 + a_2b_2 + a_2b_3 + a_3b_2;$$
$$S_{G_2}(a_1, b_1, c_1, d_1, a_3, b_3, c_3, d_3) = a_1 + b_1 + b_1c_3 + b_3c_1 + b_3c_3,$$
$$c_1,$$
$$b_1 + a_1c_3 + a_3c_1 + a_3c_3,$$
$$a_1 + b_1 + c_1 + d_1 + a_1b_3 + a_3b_1 + a_3b_3;$$
$$S_{G_3}(a_1, b_1, c_1, d_1, a_2, b_2, c_2, d_2) = a_2 + b_2 + b_1c_1 + b_1c_2 + b_2c_1$$
$$c_2,$$
$$b_2 + a_1c_1 + a_1c_2 + a_2c_1,$$
$$a_2 + b_2 + c_2 + d_2 + a_1b_1 + a_1b_2 + a_2b_1;$$
$$S_{F_1}(a_2, b_2, c_2, d_2, a_3, b_3, c_3, d_3) = d_3 + a_2b_2 + a_2b_3 + a_3b_2,$$
$$b_3 + c_3 + d_3 + a_2d_2 + a_2d_3 + a_3d_2 + 1,$$
$$a_3 + b_3,$$
$$a_3 + 1;$$
$$S_{F_2}(a_1, b_1, c_1, d_1, a_3, b_3, c_3, d_3) = d_1 + a_1b_3 + a_3b_1 + a_3b_3,$$
$$b_1 + c_1 + d_1 + a_1d_3 + a_3d_1 + a_3d_3,$$
$$a_1 + b_1,$$
$$a_1;$$
$$S_{F_3}(a_1, b_1, c_1, d_1, a_2, b_2, c_2, d_2) = d_2 + a_1b_1 + a_1b_2 + a_2b_1,$$
$$b_2 + c_2 + d_2 + a_1d_1 + a_1d_2 + a_2d_1,$$
$$a_2 + b_2,$$
$$a_2.$$

References

1. Nist lightweight cryptography project. https://csrc.nist.gov/projects/lightweight-cryptography
2. Balli, F., Banik, S.: Six shades of AES. In: Buchmann, J., Nitaj, A., Rachidi, T. (eds.) AFRICACRYPT 2019. LNCS, vol. 11627, pp. 311–329. Springer, Cham (2019). https://doi.org/10.1007/978-3-030-23696-0_16
3. Balli, F., Caforio, A., Banik, S.: The area-latency symbiosis: towards improved serial encryption circuits. IACR Trans. Cryptogr. Hardw. Embed. Syst. **2021**(1), 239–278 (2021). https://doi.org/10.46586/tches.v2021.i1.239-278

4. Banik, S., Balli, F., Regazzoni, F., Vaudenay, S.: Swap and rotate: lightweight linear layers for spn-based blockciphers. IACR Trans. Symmetric Cryptol. **2020**(1), 185–232 (2020). https://doi.org/10.13154/tosc.v2020.i1.185-232

5. Banik, S., et al.: Sundae-gift v1.0. NIST Lightweight Cryptography Project **1**, 157–161 (2019). https://csrc.nist.gov/Projects/lightweight-cryptography/round-2-candidates

6. Banik, S., Bogdanov, A., Regazzoni, F.: Exploring energy efficiency of lightweight block ciphers. In: Dunkelman, O., Keliher, L. (eds.) SAC 2015. LNCS, vol. 9566, pp. 178–194. Springer, Cham (2016). https://doi.org/10.1007/978-3-319-31301-6_10

7. Banik, S., Bogdanov, A., Regazzoni, F.: Atomic-AES: a compact implementation of the AES Encryption/Decryption core. In: Dunkelman, O., Sanadhya, S.K. (eds.) INDOCRYPT 2016. LNCS, vol. 10095, pp. 173–190. Springer, Cham (2016). https://doi.org/10.1007/978-3-319-49890-4_10

8. Banik, S., Bogdanov, A., Regazzoni, F.: Compact circuits for combined AES Encryption/Decryption. J. Cryptogr. Eng. **9**(1), 69–83 (2017). https://doi.org/10.1007/s13389-017-0176-3

9. Banik, S., et al.: GIFT-COFB v1.0. NIST lightweight cryptography project (2019). https://csrc.nist.gov/Projects/lightweight-cryptography/round-2-candidates

10. Banik, S., Pandey, S.K., Peyrin, T., Sasaki, Y., Sim, S.M., Todo, Y.: GIFT: a small present - towards reaching the limit of lightweight encryption. In: Proceedings of Cryptographic Hardware and Embedded Systems - CHES 2017–19th International Conference, Taipei, Taiwan, 25–28 September 2017, pp. 321–345 (2017). https://doi.org/10.1007/978-3-319-66787-4_16

11. Beierle, C., et al.: The SKINNY family of block ciphers and its low-latency variant MANTIS. In: Robshaw, M., Katz, J. (eds.) CRYPTO 2016, Part II. LNCS, vol. 9815, pp. 123–153. Springer, Heidelberg (2016). https://doi.org/10.1007/978-3-662-53008-5_5

12. Beierle, C., et al.: Skinny-aead and skinny-hash. NIST Lightweight Cryptography Project (2019). https://csrc.nist.gov/Projects/lightweight-cryptography/round-2-candidates

13. Bogdanov, A., et al.: PRESENT: an ultra-lightweight block cipher. In: Paillier, P., Verbauwhede, I. (eds.) CHES 2007. LNCS, vol. 4727, pp. 450–466. Springer, Heidelberg (2007). https://doi.org/10.1007/978-3-540-74735-2_31

14. Caforio, A., Collins, D., Banik, S., Regazzoni, F.: A small GIFT-COFB: lightweight Bit-Serial Architectures (Repository) (5). https://github.com/qantik/cofbserial

15. Chakraborti, A., Iwata, T., Minematsu, K., Nandi, M.: Blockcipher-based authenticated encryption: how small can we go? J. Cryptol. **33**(3), 703–741 (2019). https://doi.org/10.1007/s00145-019-09325-z

16. Daemen, J., Rijmen, V.: The Design of Rijndael: AES - The Advanced Encryption Standard. Information Security and Cryptography, Springer, Heidelberg (2002). https://doi.org/10.1007/978-3-662-04722-4

17. Dhooghe, S., Nikova, S., Rijmen, V.: Threshold implementations in the robust probing model. In: Proceedings of ACM Workshop on Theory of Implementation Security Workshop, pp. 30–37 (2019)

18. Iwata, T., Khairallah, M., Minematsu, K., Peyrin, T.: Romulus v1.2. NIST lightweight cryptography project (2019). https://csrc.nist.gov/Projects/lightweight-cryptography/round-2-candidates

19. Jati, A., Gupta, N., Chattopadhyay, A., Sanadhya, S.K., Chang, D.: Threshold implementations of GIFT: a trade-off analysis. IEEE Trans. Inf. Forensics Secur. **15**, 2110–2120 (2020). https://doi.org/10.1109/TIFS.2019.2957974

20. Jean, J., Moradi, A., Peyrin, T., Sasdrich, P.: Bit-sliding: a generic technique for bit-serial implementations of spn-based primitives. In: Fischer, W., Homma, N. (eds.) CHES 2017. LNCS, vol. 10529, pp. 687–707. Springer, Cham (2017). https://doi.org/10.1007/978-3-319-66787-4_33
21. Moradi, A., Poschmann, A., Ling, S., Paar, C., Wang, H.: Pushing the limits: a very compact and a threshold implementation of AES. In: Paterson, K.G. (ed.) EUROCRYPT 2011. LNCS, vol. 6632, pp. 69–88. Springer, Heidelberg (2011). https://doi.org/10.1007/978-3-642-20465-4_6
22. Naito, Y., Matsui M., Sakai, Y., Suzuki, D., Sakiyama, K., Sugawara, T.: SAEAES. NIST Lightweight Cryptography Project (2019). https://csrc.nist.gov/Projects/lightweight-cryptography/round-2-candidates
23. Nikova, S., Rijmen, V., Schläffer, M.: Secure hardware implementation of nonlinear functions in the presence of glitches. J. Cryptol. **24**(2), 292–321 (2010). https://doi.org/10.1007/s00145-010-9085-7
24. Schneider, T., Moradi, A.: Leakage assessment methodology. In: Güneysu, T., Handschuh, H. (eds.) CHES 2015. LNCS, vol. 9293, pp. 495–513. Springer, Heidelberg (2015). https://doi.org/10.1007/978-3-662-48324-4_25

Attribute and Identity Based Encryption

Identity-Based Encryption in DDH Hard Groups

Olivier Blazy[1] and Saqib A. Kakvi[2(✉)]

[1] LIX, CNRS, Inria, École Polytechnique, Institut Polytechnique de Paris,
91120 Palaiseau, France
olivier.blazy@polytechnique.edu
[2] Royal Holloway, University of London, London, UK
kakvi@rhul.ac.uk

Abstract. The concept of Identity-Based Encryption was first introduced by Shamir (CRYPTO 1984) but were not realised until much
later by Sakai, Ohgishi and Kasahara (SCIS 2000), Boneh and Franklin
(CRYPTO 2001) and Cocks (IMACC 2001). Since then, Identity-Based
Encryption has been a highly active area of research. While there have
been several instantiations of Identity-Based Encryption and its variants,
there is one glaring omission: there have been no instantiations in plain
Decisional Diffie-Hellman groups. This seemed at odds with the fact that
we can instantiate almost every single cryptographic primitive in plain
Decisional Diffie-Hellman groups. An answer to this question came in a
result by Papakonstantinou, Rackoff and Vahlis (EPRINT 2012), who
showed that it is *impossible* to instantiate an Identity-Based Encryption in
plain DDH groups. The impossibility result was questioned when Döttling
and Garg (CRYPTO 2017) presented an Identity-Based Encryption based
on the Decisional Diffie-Hellman problem. However, this result did not dis-
prove the impossibility result, as it requires the use of garbled circuits,
which are inherently interactive. This type of scheme is not covered by
the impossibility result, but it does raise some questions. In this paper, we
answer some of those questions by constructing an Identity-Based Encryption scheme based on the Decisional Diffie-Hellman problem. We achieve
this by instantiating the generic construction based on Witness Encryption by Garg, Gentry, Sahai and Waters (STOC 2013), with some minor
changes. To this end, we construct the first unique signature scheme in
Decisional Diffie-Hellman groups, to the best of our knowledge. The unique
signature scheme, and as a result, our Identity-Based Encryption scheme,
is inefficient, but this is unavoidable. Our construction does not completely
contradict the impossibility result but instead shows that the statement
was too strong, and the result only rules out efficient constructions.

Keywords: Identity-based encryption · Unique signatures · Generic
constructions · DDH · Impossibility results

1 Introduction

Identity-Based Encryption (IBE) was first proposed by Shamir [43] and is a generalisation of standard Public Key Encryption (PKE), wherein instead of each

© The Author(s), under exclusive license to Springer Nature Switzerland AG 2022
L. Batina and J. Daemen (Eds.): AFRICACRYPT 2022, LNCS 13503, pp. 81–102, 2022.
https://doi.org/10.1007/978-3-031-17433-9_4

user generating a public key themselves, their unique identifier, such as their e-mail address, would serve as their public key. The corresponding secret key for decryption is derived from the public identity and a master secret key, which is held by a trusted third party. Despite being posited in the 80s, the first constructions came at the turn of the millennium with a factoring-based scheme due to Cocks [16] and the pairing-based schemes due to Boneh and Franklin [10] and Sakai, Ohgishi and Kasahara [40]. A few years later, an IBE scheme based on lattice problems was introduced by Gentry, Peikert and Vaikuntanathan [26]. Since then, IBE schemes have been an active area of research, with several interesting results.

Despite all the results and advances in the field of IBEs, there is one glaring omission; there is no IBE scheme that is secure in plain Decisional Diffie-Hellman (DDH) groups. Given this, one might think that parings are somehow crucial for the constructions of IBEs and that it may not be possible to construct IBEs in plain DDH groups. Further evidence to this end was provided by the impossibility result of Papakonstantinou, Rackoff, and Vahlis [37], who showed that it is impossible to construct a weakly secure IBE scheme in the Generic Group Model (GGM). We will refer to this as the PRV impossibility result henceforth. Given that this weakly secure scheme cannot exist in this idealised model, it follows that no fully secure scheme can exist in this idealised model. This cast further doubts upon the possibility of such a scheme being realised in the standard model. However, recent developments present a glimmer of hope and may show a methodology to construct an IBE in DDH groups.

The seminal work of Garg, Gentry, Sahai and Waters [23] not only introduced the very powerful primitive of Witness Encryption (WE), but they also showed how to use it to construct several other primitives generically. In particular, Garg et al. showed how to *generically* construct a weakly secure IBE scheme from a WE scheme and a unique signature scheme. If we assume that both the generic construction and the impossibility result are correct, this would mean that at least one of the constituent components cannot be instantiated. However, if we can show an instantiation of these components, then either the impossibility result is correct and the DDH problem is not hard, or the impossibility result is somehow flawed. Given this, that means that at least one of the following statements is true:

1. There is no unique signature scheme in DDH groups.
2. There is no secure WE in DDH groups.
3. The DDH problem is not hard.
4. The PRV impossibility result is incorrect.

We now take this list and examine each statement and begin to eliminate the incorrect from the list. Once we have removed all the incorrect statements, we will know where we stand. We can show that the first two statements are not true by instantiating a WE scheme and a unique signature scheme in DDH groups. Once we have these, we can then apply the transformation to them to construct an IBE scheme. Given this, we can then look at the third and fourth items on our list.

We begin by showing a unique signature scheme in DDH groups. To the best of our knowledge, there are no deterministic signatures in plain DDH groups. The most commonly used Diffie-Hellman-based signatures are variants of the Digital Signature Algorithm (DSA) [42], which requires randomness. DSA builds upon the early work of ElGamal [22] and Schnorr [41], both of which are randomised. Even the tightly secure standard model signatures of Blazy et al. [8] rely on the randomness of Chameleon Hash Functions to be secure. This is not surprising since it was shown that any deterministic signature in the standard model cannot have a tight security reduction [17,31]. Indeed, not only can signatures in DDH groups not be tight, but they can also not be short as shown by Döttling et al. [21]. This means that we can do no better than a non-tight, non-short signatures. Keeping this in mind, we construct a unique signature scheme by combining the discrete logarithm-based collision resistant hash function of Chaum, van Heijst and Pfitzmann [13] with the tree-based signature construction of Merkle [35] in Sect. 3.1.

The next item on the list is the WE, which at first glance seems like a daunting task as all known constructions of WE (and variants thereof) [2,12,15,23] rely on either indistinguishability Obfuscation (iO) [5] or extractable Obfuscation (eO) [12], neither of which have an instantiation in DDH groups. While it might seem that we have hit a wall, we are saved by another primitive, namely Smooth Projective Hash Functions (SPHFs), which were first introduced by Cramer and Shoup [19]. There are several known constructions of SPHFs in DDH groups [19,24], for a variety of languages. Furthermore, it has been shown that an SPHF for some language $\mathcal{L}$ can be used to construct a WE scheme for $\mathcal{L}$ [1,7]. We note that this generic transformation does not give rise to a generic WE scheme, but rather a WE for the given language $\mathcal{L}$. We describe the language and the related SPHF in more detail in Sect. 3.2. We then show how to build a WE scheme from our SPHF. Therefore we know that the second item on our list is also not true.

Given that we have a unique signature and a WE in DDH groups, we also have an IBE in DDH groups. At this point, we must note that our scheme is a proof of concept and is inefficient. Although the scheme could be optimized to some degree, this inefficiency is unavoidable. This is due to the fact that our unique signature scheme cannot be efficient, as was demonstrated by Döttling et al. [21]. However, this will be a key point in showing the limits of the PVR result.

We now look at the third and fourth items on our list simultaneously. Our IBE construction and the PRV impossibility result directly contradict one another. This means that either the PRV impossibility result is correct and our IBE construction gives an adversary against the DDH problem, which would mean that the DDH problem is not hard. The other possibility is that the DDH problem is still hard, which would mean that the PRV impossibility result is incorrect. Here we note that the PVR result and the result of Döttling et al. [21] have a similar high-level idea; they show that with sufficiently many queries, one can recover the secret key. Therefore, we see that the PVR impossibility result is incorrect and the statement they show is somewhat weaker. Specifically, the PVR result only rules out *efficient* IBEs. We discuss this in Sect. 4.

1.1 Our Contributions

The core result of the paper is an IBE in DDH groups. To build this, we proceed in the following steps:

- Firstly, we need to build a unique signature scheme secure under the DDH assumption. The first step is to build a one-time signature. We achieve this by treating the hash function of Chaum, van Heijst and Pfitzmann [13] as Chameleon Hash Function [33] and applying the techniques of Mohassel [36].
- The next step in constructing our signatures is amplifying our one-time signature to a k-time signature for sufficiently large k. We achieve this using a variant of Merkle's tree-based signatures [35]. To be in a purely DDH setting, we rely again on the hash function by Chaum, van Heijst and Pfitzmann [13].
- Secondly, we construct a witness encryption using SPHFs. The original generic construction of Garg et al. [23] uses the Goldreich-Levin hardcore predicate [27], but we cannot use this in the GGM, as we are required to do XORs and the SPHFs for this type of circuit require interactivity. To work around this, we replace the Goldreich-Levin hardcore predicate with a Katz-Wang style DDH proof of membership [32], for which we can build efficient SPHFs. It is clear to see that our replacement satisfies the original generic construction at the cost of being specific to DDH hard groups.
  We then use the well-known WE construction from an SPHF.
- Finally, we combine these two using our modified version of the generic construction of Garg et al. [23] to build a selectively secure IBE in the GGM.

Once we have our IBE scheme, this gives us a first indication that the PVR impossibility result is incorrect. It is not a direct contradiction as our construction is not tight and has large keys and ciphertexts. However, as we discuss in Sect. 4, this shows that the result only extends to *efficient* instantiations.

1.2 Related Work

Identity-Based Encryption schemes have been widely studied since their introduction by Shamir in [43]; while the design of IBEs has been studied extensively [10,45], there is a lack of generic design which could be leveraged to achieve a construction natively under a given hypothesis. Chen and Wee [14] and Blazy, Kiltz and Pan [9] proposed a generic design of IBEs by using affine MACs as a building block. However, their constructions, while leading to (almost) tight IBEs, require the use of pairings, which puts them outside pure DDH groups. More recently, Döttling and Garg [20] proposed a construction of IBE under DDH using Garbled Circuits and Pedersen-like multi-commitments. Their construction was the first to try and bridge the gap. However, Garbled Circuits, while being a useful building block, are inherently interactive, which does not match with the classical definitions of IBE. In the standard definition, neither the encryptors nor the recipients are expected to actively interact with the authority to produce/decrypt a new ciphertext. Thus, this IBE is not ruled out by the PVR impossibility result. Our construction is similar to that of Döttling and Garg [20], but we use WE instead of garbled circuits and thus do not require interactivity.

2 Preliminaries

2.1 Notations and Conventions

We denote our security parameter as λ. For all $n \in \mathbb{N}$, we denote by 1^n the n-bit string of all ones. For any bit string a, we define $a[i]$ as the ith most significant bit of a. For any element x in a set S, we use $x \in_R S$ to indicate that we choose x uniformly random in S. We denote the set of all integers with $\mathbb{Z}$ and the set of all primes as $\mathbb{P}$. We denote the set of k-bit integers as $\mathbb{Z}[k]$ and the set of all k-bit primes as $\mathbb{P}[k]$. All algorithms may be randomised. For any algorithm A, we define $x \xleftarrow{\$} A(a_1, \dots, a_n)$ as the execution of A with inputs $a_1, \dots, a_n$ and fresh randomness and then assigning the output to x. For conciseness, we will write PPT for Probabilistic Polynomial Time.

2.2 Identity-Based Key Encryption

We recall syntax of an Identity-Based Encryption scheme.

Definition 1 (Identity-Based Key Encryption). *An Identity-Based Encryption $\mathcal{IBE}$ consists of four PPT algorithms $\mathcal{IBE} = (\mathcal{IBE}.\mathsf{Setup}, \mathcal{IBE}.\mathsf{KeyGen}, \mathcal{IBE}.\mathsf{Encrypt}, \mathcal{IBE}.\mathsf{Decrypt})$ with the following properties.*

- *The probabilistic key generation algorithm $\mathcal{IBE}.\mathsf{Setup}(1^\lambda)$ returns the (master) public/secret keys $(\mathsf{pk}, \mathsf{msk})$.*
- *The probabilistic user secret key generation algorithm $\mathcal{IBE}.\mathsf{KeyGen}(\mathsf{msk}, \mathsf{ID})$ returns a secret key $\mathsf{sk}_{\mathsf{ID}}$ for identity $\mathsf{ID} \in \mathfrak{I}$.*
- *The probabilistic encapsulation algorithm $\mathcal{IBE}.\mathsf{Encrypt}(\mathsf{pk}, \mathsf{ID}, m)$ returns a ciphertext c with respect to the $\mathsf{ID} \in \mathfrak{I}$.*
- *The deterministic decryption algorithm $\mathcal{IBE}.\mathsf{Decrypt}(\mathsf{sk}_{\mathsf{ID}}, \mathsf{ID}, c)$ returns a plaintext m or the reject symbol $\perp$.*

For correctness we require that for all $\lambda \in \mathbb{N}$, all pairs $(\mathsf{pk}, \mathsf{msk})$ generated by $\mathcal{IBE}.\mathsf{Setup}(1^\lambda)$, all $\mathsf{ID} \in \mathfrak{I}$, all $\mathsf{sk}_{\mathsf{ID}}$ generated by $\mathcal{IBE}.\mathsf{KeyGen}(\mathsf{msk}, \mathsf{ID})$ and all (c) generated by $\mathcal{IBE}.\mathsf{Encrypt}(\mathsf{pk}, \mathsf{ID}, m)$ for all m:

$$\Pr[\mathcal{IBE}.\mathsf{Decrypt}(\mathsf{sk}_{\mathsf{ID}}, \mathsf{ID}, c) = m] = 1.$$

2.3 Signature Schemes

We first recall the definition of a unique signature scheme.

Definition 2. *A digital signature scheme $\mathcal{SIG}$ with message space $\mathfrak{M}$ and signature space $\mathfrak{S}$ is defined as a triple of PPT algorithms $\mathcal{SIG} = (\mathsf{KeyGen}, \mathsf{Sign}, \mathsf{Verify})$:*

- *KeyGen takes as an input the unary representation of our security parameter 1^λ and outputs a signing key sk and verification key pk.*
- *Sign takes as input a signing key sk, message $m \in \mathfrak{M}$ and outputs a signature $\sigma \in \mathfrak{S}$.*
- *Verify is a deterministic algorithm, which on input of a public key and a message-signature pair $(m, \sigma) \in \mathfrak{M} \times \mathfrak{S}$ outputs 1 (accept) or 0 (reject).*

We say $\mathcal{SIG}$ is correct if for any $\lambda \in \mathbb{N}$, all $(\mathsf{pk}, \mathsf{sk}) \leftarrow_s \mathsf{KeyGen}(1^\lambda)$, all $m \in \mathfrak{M}$, and all $\sigma \leftarrow_s \mathsf{Sign}(\mathsf{sk}, m)$ we have that

$$\Pr[\mathsf{Verify}(\mathsf{pk}, m, \sigma) = 1] = 1.$$

We say $\mathcal{SIG}$ is a unique signature scheme if $\forall m \in \mathfrak{M}, \exists! \ \sigma \in \mathfrak{S}$ such that $\mathsf{Verify}(\mathsf{pk}, m, \sigma) = 1$.

2.4 Witness Encryption

Witness Encryption (WE) is a generalisation of public key encryption where anybody in possession of a valid witness w that some statement x is in a specified language can decrypt all ciphertexts encrypted under x. The first witness encryption scheme was presented by Garg et al. [23]. We now recall the definition of WE.

Definition 3. *A Witness Encryption scheme $\mathcal{WE}$ for some language $\mathcal{L}$ is defined by the two PPT algorithms $\mathcal{WE} = (\mathsf{Encrypt}, \mathsf{Decrypt})$:*

- *$\mathsf{Encrypt}$ takes as an input the unary representation of our security parameter 1^λ, an instance x and a message m and outputs a ciphertext c.*
- *$\mathsf{Decrypt}$ takes as input a ciphertext c and a witness w and outputs m if $(x, w) \in \mathcal{L}$ and $\perp$ otherwise.*

We say $\mathcal{WE}$ is correct if for all messages m and for all pairs $(x, w) \in \mathcal{L}$, we have:

$$\Pr[\mathsf{Decrypt}(\mathsf{Encrypt}(1^\lambda, x, m), w) = m] = 1$$

2.5 Smooth Projective Hash Functions

When building our Witness Encryption, we require Smooth Projective Hash Functions (SPHF). They were proposed by Cramer and Shoup in [19]. SPHFs can be evaluated them in two ways: using the (secret) hashing key on a public element or using the (public) projected key on a word on a special subset of its domain with a secret witness.

A Smooth Projective Hash Function system over a language $\mathcal{L} \subset X$ onto a set $\mathcal{S}$ is defined by the five following algorithms:

- Setup(1^λ) generates the global parameters of the protocol and the description of an $\mathcal{NP}$ language $\mathcal{L}$.
- HashKG($\mathcal{L}$) generates a hashing key hk.
- ProjKG(hk, $\mathcal{L}, C$) derives the projection key hp, possibly depending on the word C.
- Hash(hk, $\mathcal{L}, C$) outputs the hash value of C from hk.
- ProjHash(hp, $\mathcal{L}, C, w$) outputs the hash value of the word C from the projection key hp and the witness w that $C \in \mathcal{L}$.

A Smooth Projective Hash Function SPHF should satisfy the following properties:

- *Correctness*: Let $W \in \mathcal{L}$ and w a witness of this membership. Then, for all hashing keys hk and associated projection keys hp we have Hash(hk$\mathcal{L}, W$) = ProjHash(hp, $\mathcal{L}, W, w$).
- *Smoothness*: For all $W \in X \backslash \mathcal{L}$ the following distributions are statistically indistinguishable:

$$\Delta_0 = \left\{ (\mathcal{L}, \text{prm}, W, \text{hp}, v) \ \middle| \ \begin{array}{l} \text{prm} = \text{Setup}(1^\lambda), \text{hk} = \text{HashKG}(\mathcal{L}), \\ \text{hp} = \text{ProjKG}(\text{hk}, \mathcal{L}, W), v = \text{Hash}(\text{hk}, \mathcal{L}, W) \end{array} \right\}$$

$$\Delta_1 = \left\{ (\mathcal{L}, \text{prm}, W, \text{hp}, v) \ \middle| \ \begin{array}{l} \text{prm} = \text{Setup}(1^\lambda), \text{hk} = \text{HashKG}\mathcal{L}, \\ \text{hp} = \text{ProjKG}(\text{hk}, \mathcal{L}, W), v \xleftarrow{\$} \mathcal{S} \end{array} \right\}.$$

This is formalized by

$$\text{Adv}_{\text{SPHF}}^{\text{StdM}}(1^\lambda) = \sum_{V \in \mathbb{G}} \left| \Pr_{\Delta_1}[v = V] - \Pr_{\Delta_0}[v = V] \right| \text{ is negligible.}$$

- *Pseudo-Randomness*: If $W \in \mathcal{L}$, then without a witness of membership the two previous distributions should remain computationally indistinguishable: for any adversary $\mathcal{A}$ within reasonable time and a negligible function ϵ, we have

$$Adv_{\text{SPHF},\mathcal{A}}^{\text{pr}}(1^\lambda) = |\Pr_{\Delta_1}[\mathcal{A}(\mathcal{L}, \text{prm}, W, \text{hp}, v) = 1] - \Pr_{\Delta_0}[\mathcal{A}(\mathcal{L}, \text{prm}, W, \text{hp}, v) = 1]|$$
$$\leqslant \epsilon$$

2.6 The Generic Group Model

The Generic Group Model was first proposed by Shoup [44], as a way to show lower bounds for *generic* algorithms solving the discrete logarithm problem, such as Pollard's Rho method [39]. Shoup presented a model wherein an adversary only interacts with group elements via oracles for all the operations. To facilitate this, the adversary was given a random encoding as a unique tag for each element. The adversary can then use these encodings to make oracles queries on the relevant elements. This model was then extended by Maurer [34], by replacing the random encodings with indices of their locations in the oracle's internal table.

One may wonder as to which model is better suited for use in cryptographic proofs. The answer to this was provided by Jager and Shwenk [28], who show the two models to be equivalent. They achieve this by reducing algorithms in model to the other. As the PVR impossibility result was stated in Shoup's model, we will also use Shoup's model for consistency.

Definition 4 (Generic Group Algorithm in Shoup's Model [44]). *A generic group algorithm $\mathcal{A}$ is a (possibly probabilistic) algorithm which takes as input a r-tuple of encoded group elements $([x_1], \dots, [x_r])$, $x_i \in \mathbb{G}, 1 \le i \le r$. The algorithm may query a generic group oracle $\mathcal{O}$ to perform computation operations in some set Π and relations in some set Σ on encoded group elements.*

Normally one considers the sets $\Pi = \{\odot\}, \Sigma = \{\equiv\}$, that is the group operation and equality testing. This leads to the most basic instantiation of the GGM we can think of or at least, the most intuitive. Algorithmically, we have:

- $\mathcal{O}_{\mathbb{G}}$: The oracle for encoding group elements.
- $\mathcal{O}_{\odot}$: The oracle for performing the group operation.
- $\mathcal{O}_{\equiv}$: The oracle for testing equality of group elements.

It must be noted that these oracles are stateful with regards to elements. That is to say, if we compute the same element twice, then the results of both those computations is the same.

3   Construction

3.1   Unique Signatures Based on DDH

We now present the signature we will employ in the generic construction of our IBE scheme. Recall that the generic construction of Garg et al. [23] requires a *unique* signature scheme. When constructing such a scheme, there are two significant hurdles. Firstly, it is known that no unique signature scheme in the standard model can be tightly secure, as shown by Coron [17,18] and Kakvi and Kiltz [30,31]. Secondly, the recent result of Döttling et al. [21] showed that no unique signature in a DDH group can be short.

Given these restrictions, it is not surprising that there is no known direct construction of DDH-based unique signatures, but only generic ones. We will use one such generic construction, specifically the tree-based signature scheme of Merkle [35]. However, we will deviate slightly from the original construction due to the fact that we cannot use standard collision-resistant hash functions, so we need to adapt our scheme to fit this. The basic building tool for this is the Discrete Logarithm-based (chameleon) hash function due to Chaum, van Heijst and Pfitzmann [13].

Hash Function Based on Discrete Logarithm. We now recall the collision resistant hash function due to Chaum, van Heijst and Pfitzmann [13] based on the discrete logarithm problem, which will we denote as $\mathcal{CVHPH}$. The hash function requires a seed $s = (g, h)$, which will be passed to the hash evaluation algorithm each time. Unlike normal hash functions that can take arbitrarily large values, $\mathcal{CVHPH}$ maps two $\mathbb{Z}_p^*$ elements to one $\mathbb{Z}_p^*$ element i.e. $\mathcal{CVHPH} : \mathbb{Z}_p^* \times \mathbb{Z}_p^* \to \mathbb{Z}_p^*$. We note that this hash function is closely related to the commitment scheme of Pedersen [38], as was used by Döttling and Garg [20], and it can be extended to larger input sizes in a similar manner. We now present the hash function in Fig. 1.

Scheme $\mathcal{CVHPH}$

KeyGen(1^λ)
$p \in_R \mathbb{P}[\lambda]$
$g, h \in_R \mathbb{Z}_p^*$
return $s = (p, g, h)$
Hash$(s, (x_1, x_2))$
return $y = g^{x_1} h^{x_2} \mod p$

Fig. 1. The $\mathcal{CVHPH}$ hash function

We can see that we get collision-resistance from the discrete logarithm problem (DLog). If we can find $(x_1, x_2) \neq (y_1, y_2)$, we can find the discrete logarithm of h in base g as $\log_g h = \frac{y_1 - x_1}{x_2 - y_2}$. Recall that if DDH is hard, then DLog is also hard.

One-Time Signatures. After their introduction of chameleon hash functions by Krawczyk and Rabin [33], it became clear that $\mathcal{CVHPH}$ can also be viewed as a Chameleon Hash Function. We will use this fact to build a one-time signature, using the well-known method of Mohassel [36]. We will give the explicit instantiation of the one-time signature scheme, which we call the $\mathcal{CVHPOTS}$ scheme. For clarity, we write the scheme mod a prime q instead of mod p so as to distinguish the two usages. We now present the one-time signature scheme in Fig. 2.

Now that we have our one-time signature scheme, we can start to build it into a full-fledged signature scheme. There are two tree-based transformations of one-time signatures to full signatures that one would consider in this situation, namely that of Merkle [35] using hash functions and that of Blazy et al. [8] using chameleon hash functions. However, neither of these approaches is directly applicable to our scenario for separate reasons. The Merkle [35] transformation relies on cryptographic collision-resistant hash functions, which is an assumption we cannot make, as it would take us out of the pure Generic Group Model. On the other hand, the transformation of Blazy et al. [8] does not require this

Scheme $\mathcal{CVHPOTS}$

KeyGen(1^λ)
$q \in_R \mathbb{P}[\lambda]$
$g, \alpha, \hat{m}, \hat{r} \in_R \mathbb{Z}_q^*$
$h = g^\alpha \mod q$
$z = g^{\hat{m}} h^{\hat{r}} \mod q$
return $\mathsf{vk} = (q, g, h, z), \mathsf{sk} = (\alpha, \hat{m}, \hat{r})$
Sign(sk, m)
return $\sigma = (\hat{m} - m)\alpha^{-1} + \hat{r} \mod q$
Verify(pk, m, σ)
if $(g^m h^\sigma == z \mod q)$
$\quad$ return 1
else
$\quad$ return 0

Fig. 2. The $\mathcal{CVHPOTS}$ one-time signature scheme.

assumption, but creates signatures that are not unique. Therefore, we take ideas from both schemes and create a tree-based transformation that is tailored to our purposes.

We first begin by outlining the general structure of both tree-based signatures. Both schemes build a binary tree of depth d and then associate each leaf with a one-time signature verification key. The leaf is then an authentication of the OTS verification key. Each parent node is the authentication of its children, leading all the way up to the root node. The root node is published as the verification key, potentially with some additional public parameters. In the scheme of Merkle [35], the authentication is the hash value, whereas in Blazy et al. [8] the authentication is a two-tier signature [6]. We will primarily follow the transformation of Merkle, with a modification at the leaves.

The primary hurdle in our setting is that the Merkle transformation relies on hash functions $\mathcal{CRHF} : \{0,1\}^* \to \{0,1\}^\ell$, which allows them to deal with values of arbitrary size. However, we have $\mathcal{CVHPH} : \mathbb{Z}_p^* \times \mathbb{Z}_p^* \to \mathbb{Z}_p^*$, which means that we can only hash pairs of group elements. While this does fit in with the intermediate nodes, we run into the issue that our OTS verification keys consist of 3 group elements and the modulus. To get around this, we employ a hash function with a sufficiently large modulus p such that q can also be hashed, by having the bit size of p be a constant factor larger than the bit size of q (For simplicity, we will use 2). We will then hash p, g and h, z to get intermediate hash values $\eta_1 = \mathcal{CVHPH}.\mathsf{Hash}(s, (q, g)), \eta_2 = \mathcal{CVHPH}.\mathsf{Hash}(s, (h, z))$. We then take the hash of these intermediate values to get the label of the corresponding leaf as $\mathcal{CVHPH}.\mathsf{Hash}(s, (\eta_1, \eta_2))$. This is conceptually similar to just adding an additional level to our tree.

We now establish some notation for our trees. We label all nodes of our tree as $\mathtt{Node}_{i,j}$ with i being the depth and j being the position, with the left-most nodes being labelled 0 and the right most being labelled $2^i - 1$. The root node it therefore labelled as $\mathtt{Node}_{0,0}$. We also label the leaves of our tree $\mathtt{Node}_{d,0}, \ldots, \mathtt{Node}_{d,2^d-1}$ as $\mathtt{Leaf}_0, \ldots, \mathtt{Leaf}_{2^d-1}$ from left to right. We assume there is an efficient algorithm that returns the path and co-path to any leaf $\mathtt{Leaf}_i$, which we call $\mathtt{TreePath}(i)$. We now present the final signature scheme in Fig. 3.

3.2   Witness Encryption Based on DDH

The next ingredient needed for our generic IBE construction is a witness encryption (WE) scheme. Since its introduction by Garg et al. [23], there have been some follow-up constructions [2,12,15,46], but crucially all of these have relied on either indistinguishability obfuscation [5], or extractability obfuscation [12]. These are undesirable as the initial constructions were based on multi-linear maps, which were first introduced by Boneh and Silverberg [11], which are out of the scope of the GGM. While there have been recent works on building obfuscation from other assumptions [3,4,25,29], none of these falls within the GGM. Therefore, we must look for another way to construct a witness encryption scheme.

We will use the generic construction of a Witness Encryption scheme from a Smooth Projective Hash Function (SPHF). The generic construction was proposed by Abdalla, Benhamouda and Pointcheval [1], which we now briefly recall. To encrypt a message m under an instance x generates and new set of SPHF keys and computes the hash of the instance. The hash is used as a one-time pad and is XOR'd with the message to provide a ciphertext. The ciphertext and the projective key are then sent to the receiver. Given the projective key, the receiver can recompute the hash value with the correct witness, which they can then use to decrypt the ciphertext.

Now that we have the basic idea for our Witness Encryption, we now need to define our language. For this, we will work in a way similar to Katz-Wang signatures [32]. Natively our signatures are verified by checking that: $h^\sigma = g^{-m} \prod B_i^{m_i}$, instead, we are going to double those parameters, with $\hat{h}, \hat{g}, A_i$ by picking $\alpha \overset{\$}{\leftarrow} \mathbb{Z}_p$ and setting $\log_{A_i}(B_i) = \log_{\hat{h}}(h) = \log_{\hat{g}}(g) = \alpha$, intuitively now in addition to verifying the equation, $h, \hat{h}, h^\sigma, \hat{h}^\sigma$ form a DDH tuple, and the signature simply becomes a witness of this fact.

SPHF for the Verification of Signatures. The language $\mathcal{L}_{\mathsf{vk}}$, we need to handle with an SPHF is the verification equation. That we know the (unique) σ such that $g^{-m} \cdot B_i(m[i]) = h^\sigma$ and $\log_{\hat{h}}(h) = \log_{\hat{g}}(g)$. The B_i is uniquely determined by the depth at which the SPHF is computed relatively to a node or a leaf.

In other words, writing $G = g^{-m} \cdot B_i^{m[i]}, \hat{G} = \hat{g}^{-m} \cdot \prod A_i^{m[i]}$, we need the witness σ such that $G, \hat{G}, h, \hat{h}$ is a DDH tuple.

- HashKG(M, vk): Outputs hk $= \lambda, \mu \xleftarrow{\$} \mathbb{Z}_p$, hp $= h^\lambda \hat{h}^\mu$
- Hash(hk, M, vk): Outputs $G^\lambda \hat{G}^\mu$
- ProjHash(hp, M, vk, σ): Outputs hp$^\sigma$.

This SPHF is Smooth, and it should be noted, that the person in charge of the SPHF can compute Hash without receiving data from the prover.

The Witness Encryption Scheme. To achieve a Witness Encryption from an SPHF, one classically outputs a word presumably in the language, compute on Hash on it, and XOR this hash with the message to encrypt. Anyone possessing a witness the word is in the language, can then decrypt by computing the Projected Hash.

A final step is thus to combine the previous construction for every level of the tree, so $d + 1$ times. For the witness encryption, we are going to need to handle the language where words are a tuple of (Identity, $\hat{h}$), and the witness is the deterministic signature on the given identity. We use the SHPFs described above and combine them into one SPHF for our final language, which we call $\mathcal{SPHF}$.

Given an instance $x = (\text{ID}, \hat{h})$, we run our combined SPHF $\mathcal{SPHF}$ to get a hashing key and a projection key. We then use the hashing key to compute the hash of the instance x, which is a single element in $\mathbb{Z}_p^*$. We use this hash as a mask and multiply it with the message, to get our masked message. Our ciphertext consists of the masked message and the projection key. Our projection key consists of $d + 1$ group elements. With the masked message, and the helper generator $\hat{h}$, this gives a total ciphertext size of $d + 3$ group elements to transmit.

On receipt of a ciphertext, the user can use their secret key sk$_{\text{ID}}$ as the witness and recompute the mask using the projection key. With this they can then unmask message, which is returned. We now give the complete witness encryption scheme $\mathcal{WE}$ below in Fig. 4.

The resulted (projected) hashes are each a group element that will serve as a mask.

3.3   Modified Generic Construction

We now recall the generic construction of IBE due to Garg et al. [23]. Before we begin we must establish some notation. We define our ID space such that all identities can be expressed as bitstrings of length at most d, for some public parameter d, that is to say $\mathcal{IBE}.\mathfrak{I} \subseteq \{0,1\}^d$. Additionally, we note that we do not restrict ourselves to single bit messages, as is the case of the Witness Encryption of Garg et al. [23] or the IBE of Papakonstantinou, Rackoff, and Vahlis [37], but instead consider the more general case where messages can be longer. For simplicity, we consider messages that are single group elements. We now give a high-level explanation of the scheme.

We first discuss the Setup and KeyGen algorithms together as they both rely on the same primitive. Let $\mathcal{USIG} = \{\mathcal{USIG}.\text{Gen}, \mathcal{USIG}.\text{Sign}, \mathcal{USIG}.\text{Verify}\}$

be the secure signature scheme with unique signatures from Sect. 3.1 such we can sign all our identities, i.e. the depth of our tree is the same as the public parameter d. This is required as the user secret keys $\mathsf{sk_{ID}}$ are simply a signature on the corresponding identity ID. It is easy to see that the IBE public parameters pp are the signature verification key vk and the IBE master secret key msk is the signature signing key sk. Here we note that the master secret key is 2^d one-time signing keys, each of which is $3 \ \mathbb{Z}_q^*$ elements. This means we have a total size of $2^d \cdot 3\lambda/ = 2^{d-1} \cdot 3\lambda$ bits. Additionally, user secret keys consist of $d+1$ elements from $\mathbb{Z}_p*$, one $\lambda/2$-bit prime q and four elements from $\mathbb{Z}_q*$. Since we know $q < p$, we pad q and all elements in $\mathbb{Z}_q*$ with leading 0's to be λ bits long for simplicity. Thus we know that our user secret keys are $\ell = (d+6)\lambda$ bits long.

Now we discuss the Encrypt algorithm. We pick a random value α and compute $\hat{h} = h^\alpha$, where h is from our hash function seed. We then combine this with the ID to create an instance for the witness encryption scheme $\mathcal{WE}$ from Sect. 3.2. Recall our language for the witness encryption is verifying our Katz-Wang like signatures [32] with proof of membership. To encrypt, the user simply runs the WE encryption procedure and receives the ciphertext $\hat{C}$. Recall that this contains projection key, the masked message and the randomness. We combine this with our identity to form our IBE ciphertext.

Finally, we discuss the Decrypt algorithm. Once the receiver has the IBE ciphertext, they can use their secret key to WE decryption algorithm to decrypt the ciphertext $\hat{C}$ and recover the message. Having given a high-level description of the IBE, we now present the full scheme.

Proof Idea. Our construction allows us to achieve a secure IBE under the DDH assumption. As we are building on the construction of Garg et al. proof [23], the arguments of security follow in a straightforward manner. We will first provide a high level idea; then we provide a more detailed sketch proof.

Any adversary that is able to break the IBE scheme must fall into one of two categories:

1. *The adversary is able to generate secret keys themselves.* Since the adversary never sees the secret key for the target identity ID^*, this is equivalent to forging a signature, which in turn would break the DLog assumption.
2. *The adversary is able to distinguish the encryption of their message from a random encryption.* This is directly equivalent to breaking the underlying WE built from the SPHF, which in turn would break the DDH assumption.

We now give a brief sketch as to how we achieve this. In the first game hop, we would move from generating user secret keys to querying the signature security game for all the ID requests. This way, we are able to provide a user secret key oracle without the master secret key. Here the challenge ciphertext would be generated normally. From the view of the adversary this is identical to the normal game.

The next game hop would be to switch the generator $\hat{h}$ to a random value so that $(G, \hat{G}, h, \hat{h})$ is no longer a valid DDH tuple. The difference to the previous game is negligible, under the DDH assumption, as a significant advantage loss compared to the previous game would imply a distinguisher for DDH challenges.

Additionally, in this game, there is no valid signature that would be a valid witness for any statements, hence the adversary can do no better than random guessing. Thus the advantage of the adversary in the game is effectively 0.

Detailed Proof

Theorem 5. *Our construction allows to achieve a secure IBE under the DDH assumption.*

Proof. In this proof, we are going to build a simulator $\mathcal{B}$ using an adversary $\mathcal{A}$ against our IBE to either break the unforgeability or our signature scheme, or the pseudo-randomness of the underlying SPHF. In both cases, this would lead to breaking a DDH challenge.

We start from a game $\mathcal{G}_0$. This is the real game, everything is generated honestly. The adversary is allowed to query user secret keys, and wins if he can decrypt a challenge ciphertext on a chosen identity if and only if he never queries a user secret key for this id. $\mathsf{Adv}^{\mathcal{G}_0} = \mathsf{Adv}^{\mathsf{real}}$

In game $\mathcal{G}_1$, we now use the signature Osign oracle to answer the $\mathsf{UserKey}$ Queries. As, the challenge identity is not allowed to be queries, this game is indistinguishable of the previous one (under appropriate simulation in the signature security proof). $|\mathsf{Adv}^{\mathcal{G}_1} - \mathsf{Adv}^{\mathcal{G}_0}| \leq \mathsf{Adv}_{\mathsf{uf}}$

In game $\mathcal{G}_2$, we forget the signature secret key we were no longer using. As this is just some internal memory state of the simulator this is strictly equivalent to the previous game. $\mathsf{Adv}^{\mathcal{G}_2} = \mathsf{Adv}^{\mathcal{G}_1}$

In game $\mathcal{G}_3$, we now alter the challenge ciphertext. Instead of using a word in the language, we switch it to outside the language (as in the Katz-Wang signatures), hence the adversary has to lose the game (except with negligible probability). We use the secret Hash key hk from the SPHF to produce the valid output. Under DDH, this game is indistinguishable from the previous one. $|\mathsf{Adv}^{\mathcal{G}_3} - \mathsf{Adv}^{\mathcal{G}_2}| \leq \mathsf{Adv}^{\mathsf{DDH}}$

At this stage, there is no valid user secret key possible for the description, hence, the security relies purely on the smoothness of the SPHF. And so $\mathsf{Adv}^{\mathcal{G}_3} \leq \varepsilon$. □

Which leads to the conclusion $\mathsf{Adv}^{\mathsf{real}} \leq \mathsf{Adv}^{\mathsf{uf}} + \mathsf{Adv}^{\mathsf{DDH}} + \varepsilon = \mathcal{O}(\mathsf{Adv}^{\mathsf{DDH}})$ (Fig. 5).

KeyGen$(1^\lambda, d)$

$s \leftarrow_\$ \mathcal{CVHPH}.\mathsf{KeyGen}(1^\lambda)$

for $i \in [\![0, 2^d - 1]\!]$
    $\mathsf{vk}_i, \mathsf{sk}_i \leftarrow_\$ \mathcal{CVHPOTS}.\mathsf{KeyGen}(1^{\lambda/2})$
    parse $\mathsf{vk}_i = (q_i, g_i, h_i, z_i)$
    $\eta_{i,1} = \mathcal{CVHPH}.\mathsf{Hash}(s, (q_i, g_i))$
    $\eta_{i,2} = \mathcal{CVHPH}.\mathsf{Hash}(s, (h_i, z_i))$
    $\mathsf{Leaf}_i = \mathcal{CVHPH}.\mathsf{Hash}(s, (\eta_{i,1}, \eta_{i,2}))$
next i

for $i \in [\![d - 1, 0]\!]$
    for $j \in [\![0, 2^i - 1]\!]$
        $\mathsf{Node}_{i,j} = \mathcal{CVHPH}.\mathsf{Hash}(s, (\mathsf{Node}_{i+1,2j-1}, \mathsf{Node}_{i+1,2j}))$
    next j
next i

$\mathsf{vk} = (s = (p, g, h), \mathsf{Node}_{0,0}), \mathsf{sk} = (\mathsf{sk}_0, \mathsf{sk}_1, \cdots, \mathsf{sk}_{2^d - 1})$
return $(\mathsf{vk}, \mathsf{sk})$

Sign(sk, m)

parse m as an integer $\in [\![0, 2^d - 1]\!]$
$(\mathsf{Node}_{0,0}, \cdots \mathsf{Leaf}_m) \leftarrow \mathsf{TreePath}(m)$
$\hat{\sigma} = \mathcal{CVHPOTS}.\mathsf{Sign}(\mathsf{sk}_m, m)$
return $\sigma = (\hat{\sigma}, \mathsf{vk}_m, \mathsf{Node}_{0,0}, \cdots \mathsf{Leaf}_m)$

Verify(vk, m, σ)

parse $\mathsf{vk} = (s, \mathsf{Node}_{0,0})$
parse $\sigma = (\hat{\sigma}, \mathsf{vk}_m = (q_m, g_m, h_m, z_m), \mathsf{Node}'_{0,0}, \cdots \mathsf{Leaf}'_m)$

if $(\mathcal{CVHPOTS}.\mathsf{Verify}(\mathsf{vk}_m, m, \hat{\sigma}) = 0)$
    return 0
end if

$\eta_1 = \mathcal{CVHPH}.\mathsf{Hash}(s, (q_m, g_m))$
$\eta_2 = \mathcal{CVHPH}.\mathsf{Hash}(s, (h_m, z_m))$
if $(\mathsf{Leaf}'_m \neq \mathcal{CVHPH}.\mathsf{Hash}(s, (\eta_1, \eta_2)))$
    return 0

for $\mathsf{Node}_{i,j} \in (\mathsf{Node}_{0,0}, \cdots \mathsf{Leaf}_m)$
    if $\mathsf{Node}_{i,j} \neq \mathcal{CVHPH}.\mathsf{Hash}(s, (\mathsf{Node}_{i+1,2j-1}, \mathsf{Node}_{i+1,2j})$
        return 0
next $\mathsf{Node}_{i,j}$

if $(\mathsf{Node}'_{0,0} = \mathsf{Node}_{0,0})$ then
    return 1
else
    return 0

Fig. 3. The unique signature scheme based on DDH

Scheme $\mathcal{WE}$

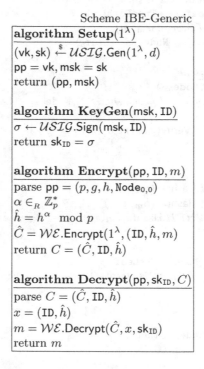

$\textbf{Encrypt}(1^\lambda, x = (\text{ID}, \hat{h}), m)$

prm $\leftarrow_\$ \mathcal{SPHF}.\text{Setup}(1^\lambda)$
For all i:
 $G_i = g^{-\text{ID}} \cdot B_i(\text{ID}_i),$
 $\hat{G}_i = \hat{g}^{-\text{ID}} \cdot A_i(\text{ID}(i))$
 $\text{hk}_i \leftarrow_\$ \mathcal{SPHF}.\text{HashKG}(\mathcal{L}_{\text{vk}})$
 $\text{hp}_i = \mathcal{SPHF}.\text{ProjKG}(\text{hk}_i)$
 $H_i = \mathcal{SPHF}.\text{Hash}(\text{hk}_i, G_i, \hat{G}_i)$
$\hat{C} = m \cdot \prod H_i$
return $C = ((\text{hp}_i)_{i\in[n+1]}, \hat{C}, \hat{h})$

$\textbf{Decrypt}(C, \text{ID}, \sigma)$

parse $C = (\text{hp}, \hat{C}, \hat{h})$
$\hat{H} = \prod \mathcal{SPHF}.\text{ProjHash}(\text{hp}_i, \mathcal{L}_{\text{vk}}, \sigma)$
return $M = \hat{C} \cdot \hat{H}^{-1} \mod p$

Fig. 4. The witness encryption scheme for $\mathcal{L}_{\text{vk}}$

Scheme IBE-Generic

$\textbf{algorithm Setup}(1^\lambda)$

$(\text{vk}, \text{sk}) \xleftarrow{\$} \mathcal{USIG}.\text{Gen}(1^\lambda, d)$
$\text{pp} = \text{vk}, \text{msk} = \text{sk}$
return (pp, msk)

$\textbf{algorithm KeyGen}(\text{msk}, \text{ID})$

$\sigma \leftarrow \mathcal{USIG}.\text{Sign}(\text{msk}, \text{ID})$
return $\text{sk}_{\text{ID}} = \sigma$

$\textbf{algorithm Encrypt}(\text{pp}, \text{ID}, m)$

parse $\text{pp} = (p, g, h, \text{Node}_{0,0})$
$\alpha \in_R \mathbb{Z}_p^*$
$\hat{h} = h^\alpha \mod p$
$\hat{C} = \mathcal{WE}.\text{Encrypt}(1^\lambda, (\text{ID}, \hat{h}, m)$
return $C = (\hat{C}, \text{ID}, \hat{h})$

$\textbf{algorithm Decrypt}(\text{pp}, \text{sk}_{\text{ID}}, C)$

parse $C = (\hat{C}, \text{ID}, \hat{h})$
$x = (\text{ID}, \hat{h})$
$m = \mathcal{WE}.\text{Decrypt}(\hat{C}, x, \text{sk}_{\text{ID}})$
return m

Fig. 5. The generic construction of an IBE scheme [23]

4   Discussion

Now that we have shown that we can construct an IBE in the GGM, albeit a somewhat inefficient one, we now consider how this affects the PVR impossibility result. It would seem at first glance that the PVR result is incorrect as we have proven a result directly contrary to theirs. While at a high level, this does seem to be true, as there are several subtle details of the PVR impossibility which we need to examine more closely to get a more complete answer. We will give a high level overview of the PVR impossibility result and then we will show where problems may arise and how we provide an alternative formulation of the result. We believe that the result is not a general impossibility result, but more likely rules out *tightly secure and efficient* constructions. This is in line with the recent results of Döttling et al. [21], who show that no unique signature can be "short" using similar techniques. We now recap the PVR impossibility result.

4.1   The PVR Impossibility Result [37]

We will now give a high-level overview of the PVR impossibility result and discuss how it relates to our construction. For a more detailed description, we refer the reader to the original paper [37]. We begin by introducing the notation needed for the PVR impossibility result. In the impossibility result, IBE schemes are parametrised by the prime modulus p and 3 additional values $m, n \in \mathbb{Z}, \varepsilon \in (0.5, 1]$. The value n is the bit-size of the master secret key msk and the bit size of the randomness used in encryption. The value m is the maximum number of GGM oracle queries by any of the IBE algorithms and is also the upper bound on the number of group elements output by any IBE algorithm. Finally, ε is the correctness error; that is to say, a valid ciphertext is correctly decrypted with probability $\geq \varepsilon$.

The first step in the impossibility result is to transform an IBE scheme to a so-called Restricted IBE (RIBE), which has no group elements in the secret key. To this end, Papakonstantinou, Rackoff, and Vahlis introduce a transformation that turns any (p, m, n, ε)-IBE scheme into a $(p, \mathrm{poly}(m), \mathrm{poly}(n), \varepsilon - \frac{1}{\mathrm{poly}(n)})$-RIBE [37]. The RIBE key generation algorithm first runs the IBE key generation algorithm to get $\mathsf{sk_{ID}}$. The algorithm then generates a large number of ciphertexts and uses $\mathsf{sk_{ID}}$ to decrypt them. By observing the queries and responses made during these decryption procedures, the algorithm can rewrite all the secret key elements as sums of the public key elements and the ciphertext elements. Using this, the secret key elements can all be rewritten as these sums of public elements. The decryption procedure is modified to accept these new keys. It must be noted that any RIBE that results from this transformation, as some of the secret information may be lost in the transformation. However, the resulting RIBE is a secure IBE scheme.

The next step is to show an attacker against a (p, m, n, ε)-RIBE. For this attack, we have an additional parameter $c > 0$. The RIBE attacker receives $k_1 \in_R [\![n^{2c}, 2n^{2c}]\!]$ user secret keys $\mathsf{sk_{ID_1}}, \ldots, \mathsf{sk_{ID_{k_1}}}$ for identities $\mathsf{ID_1}, \ldots, \mathsf{ID_{k_1}}$ of its choice and a challenge ciphertext C^* under the identity ID^* of its choice.

It uses these secret keys to construct a partial master secret key msk'. The adversary now generates a large number of ciphertexts for some other identities $\mathsf{ID}_{k_1+1}, \ldots, \mathsf{ID}_{k_1+k_2}$, with $k_2 \in_R \in_R [\![n^{2c}, 2n^{2c}]\!]$, which it uses to learn "frequently accessed elements". With all this information the adversary builds a simulated secret key $\mathsf{sk}_{\mathsf{ID}^*}$ using the information it has collected. Once it has a simulated secret key $\mathsf{sk}_{\mathsf{ID}^*}$, it attempts to decrypt the challenge ciphertext. The adversary succeeds with a probability equal to the correctness error of the RIBE. We now recall the theorem statement of the attacker.

Theorem 6 (Thm. 1 in [37]). *Let $\mathcal{RIBE} = (\mathsf{Setup}, \mathsf{KeyGen}, \mathsf{Encrypt}, \mathsf{Decrypt})$ be a restricted (p, m, n, ε)-IBE, then for every $c > 0$ and sufficiently large n, there exists and adversary which breaks the security of $\mathcal{RIBE}$ with $\mathsf{poly}(m, n)$ queries and advantage $\varepsilon - \frac{1}{2} - \frac{1}{n^c}$.*

4.2   Shortcomings of the PVR Impossibility Result

We now look at how the PVR impossibility result works with our scheme and where it fails. First, we establish what our parameters are. We see that $n = |\mathsf{msk}| = 2^d \cdot 3 \cdot \lambda/2 = 2^{d-1} \cdot 3\lambda$, as we have 2^d one time signing keys, each with 3 elements of size $\lambda/2$. Next, we have that $m = |C| = d+3$. Finally, it is clear to see we have $\varepsilon = 1$. Even before we apply the RIBE transformation, a problem starts to become evident. The attacker requires k_1 secret keys, where $k_1 \in [\![n^{2c}, 2n^{2c}]\!]$, which if we plug in our value of n and use the minimal value $c = 1$, this gives us $k_1 \in [\![(2^{d-1} \cdot 3\lambda)^2, 2(2^{d-1} \cdot 3\lambda)^2]\!] = [\![2^{2d-2} \cdot 9\lambda^2, 2^{2d-1} \cdot 18\lambda^2]\!]$, which is larger than the total number of valid user secret keys 2^d. While at first glance it seems possible that we could reduce this by using smaller moduli for our signatures, but we would have to make them so small as to be impractical. Furthermore, we note that these figures are for our base IBE and not for the reduced IBE that results from the transformation, where the parameters are polynomial in the original parameters.

Therefore, it is clear that the PVR does not apply to our case. However, based on this, it is not possible to completely discount the result, as our scheme does not expose any flaws in the core methodology of the attack. It seems most likely that the result only applies to "compact" IBEs, for some appropriate definition of compact. This seems the most likely result, as it fits in perfectly with the recent impossibility by Döttling et al. [21], which states that there are no "short" unique signatures in the GGM. The impossibility of "compact" IBEs combined with the generic construction of Garg et al. [23], immediately implies the impossibility of "short" unique signatures, as shown by Döttling et al. [21].

This idea is further reinforced by the number of oracle queries that are required be the adversary. The attacker against a (p, n, m, ε)-RIBE requires $\mathsf{poly}(n, m)$ queries to the oracles. As n and m, this number also grows, especially considering both n and m are polynomially larger than the parameters from the original IBE. As the number of queries approaches $\sqrt{p}$, the RIBE attack starts to be less efficient than the generic attacks on DDH/DLog, such as that of Pollard [39]. Therefore, for the attack to be a valid attack on the IBE system, the parameters n, m must be as small as possible, that is to say the IBE must be "compact". Therefore, it seems that the PVR impossibility result only holds for "compact" IBEs.

Another aspect that is overlooked by the PVR impossibility result is the tightness of the security reduction. If the IBE is tightly secure, then any attack on the IBE would result in an attack on the underlying assumption, in our case DDH and/or DLog. However, our scheme is not tight and our loss is in the number in secret key queries, which are signing queries to our unique signature. Therefore even if the attack were successful against our IBE scheme, it would not necessarily lead to an attack on DDH/DLog. This is further compounded by the fact that the attack is not always successful. While it might be tempting to assume that this rules out any tight IBE in the GGM, it is not clear that this is the case. The loss in our scheme is unavoidable, as any unique signature cannot be tight, but that does not mean that there does not exist an IBE scheme where there is no loss.

5 Conclusions

We have constructed the first IBE scheme in a DDH only group by using the generic construction of Garg et al. [23]. To do this, we showed the first unique signature scheme in DDH only groups and combined that with known results on SPHFs to obtain our IBE. The resulting IBE is not very efficient but serves as a counter-example to the impossibility result of Papakonstantinou, Rackoff, and Vahlis [37]. We showed that while our construction contradicts the impossibility result, it does not fully negate it and it seems that the result only rules out all IBEs with small parameters. This is reinforced by the impossibility result of short signatures by Döttling et al. [21]. Thus, while the PVR impossibility result does not rule out *all possible* IBEs in DDH only groups, it does rule out all *practical* IBEs. Therefore, while the result is mildly overstated, it is still correct for all practical purposes.

References

1. Abdalla, M., Benhamouda, F., Pointcheval, D.: Disjunctions for hash proof systems: new constructions and applications. In: Oswald, E., Fischlin, M. (eds.) EUROCRYPT 2015, Part II. LNCS, vol. 9057, pp. 69–100. Springer, Heidelberg (2015). https://doi.org/10.1007/978-3-662-46803-6_3
2. Abusalah, H., Fuchsbauer, G., Pietrzak, K.: Offline witness encryption. In: Manulis, M., Sadeghi, A.-R., Schneider, S. (eds.) ACNS 2016. LNCS, vol. 9696, pp. 285–303. Springer, Cham (2016). https://doi.org/10.1007/978-3-319-39555-5_16
3. Agrawal, S.: Indistinguishability obfuscation without multilinear maps: new methods for bootstrapping and instantiation. In: Ishai, Y., Rijmen, V. (eds.) EUROCRYPT 2019, Part I. LNCS, vol. 11476, pp. 191–225. Springer, Cham (2019). https://doi.org/10.1007/978-3-030-17653-2_7

4. Ananth, P., Jain, A., Lin, H., Matt, C., Sahai, A.: Indistinguishability obfuscation without multilinear maps: new paradigms via low degree weak pseudorandomness and security amplification. In: Boldyreva, A., Micciancio, D. (eds.) CRYPTO 2019, Part III. LNCS, vol. 11694, pp. 284–332. Springer, Cham (2019). https://doi.org/10.1007/978-3-030-26954-8_10

5. Barak, B., et al.: On the (im)possibility of obfuscating programs. In: Kilian, J. (ed.) CRYPTO 2001. LNCS, vol. 2139, pp. 1–18. Springer, Heidelberg (2001). https://doi.org/10.1007/3-540-44647-8_1

6. Bellare, M., Shoup, S.: Two-tier signatures, strongly unforgeable signatures, and Fiat-Shamir without random oracles. In: Okamoto, T., Wang, X. (eds.) PKC 2007. LNCS, vol. 4450, pp. 201–216. Springer, Heidelberg (2007). https://doi.org/10.1007/978-3-540-71677-8_14

7. Benhamouda, F., Blazy, O., Ducas, L., Quach, W.: Hash proof systems over lattices revisited. In: Abdalla, M., Dahab, R. (eds.) PKC 2018, Part II. LNCS, vol. 10770, pp. 644–674. Springer, Cham (2018). https://doi.org/10.1007/978-3-319-76581-5_22

8. Blazy, O., Kakvi, S.A., Kiltz, E., Pan, J.: Tightly-secure signatures from chameleon hash functions. In: Katz, J. (ed.) PKC 2015. LNCS, vol. 9020, pp. 256–279. Springer, Heidelberg (2015). https://doi.org/10.1007/978-3-662-46447-2_12

9. Blazy, O., Kiltz, E., Pan, J.: (Hierarchical) identity-based encryption from affine message authentication. In: Garay, J.A., Gennaro, R. (eds.) CRYPTO 2014, Part I. LNCS, vol. 8616, pp. 408–425. Springer, Heidelberg (2014). https://doi.org/10.1007/978-3-662-44371-2_23

10. Boneh, D., Franklin, M.: Identity-based encryption from the Weil pairing. In: Kilian, J. (ed.) CRYPTO 2001. LNCS, vol. 2139, pp. 213–229. Springer, Heidelberg (2001). https://doi.org/10.1007/3-540-44647-8_13

11. Boneh, D., Silverberg, A.: Applications of multilinear forms to cryptography. Cryptology ePrint Archive, Report 2002/080 (2002). https://eprint.iacr.org/2002/080

12. Boyle, E., Chung, K.-M., Pass, R.: On extractability obfuscation. In: Lindell, Y. (ed.) TCC 2014. LNCS, vol. 8349, pp. 52–73. Springer, Heidelberg (2014). https://doi.org/10.1007/978-3-642-54242-8_3

13. Chaum, D., van Heijst, E., Pfitzmann, B.: Cryptographically strong undeniable signatures, unconditionally secure for the signer. In: Feigenbaum, J. (ed.) CRYPTO 1991. LNCS, vol. 576, pp. 470–484. Springer, Heidelberg (1992). https://doi.org/10.1007/3-540-46766-1_38

14. Chen, J., Wee, H.: Fully, (almost) tightly secure IBE and dual system groups. In: Canetti, R., Garay, J.A. (eds.) CRYPTO 2013, Part II. LNCS, vol. 8043, pp. 435–460. Springer, Heidelberg (2013). https://doi.org/10.1007/978-3-642-40084-1_25

15. Chvojka, P., Jager, T., Kakvi, S.A.: Offline witness encryption with semi-adaptive security. In: Conti, M., Zhou, J., Casalicchio, E., Spognardi, A. (eds.) ACNS 2020, Part I. LNCS, vol. 12146, pp. 231–250. Springer, Cham (2020). https://doi.org/10.1007/978-3-030-57808-4_12

16. Cocks, C.: An identity based encryption scheme based on quadratic residues. In: Honary, B. (ed.) Cryptography and Coding 2001. LNCS, vol. 2260, pp. 360–363. Springer, Heidelberg (2001). https://doi.org/10.1007/3-540-45325-3_32

17. Coron, J.S.: Optimal security proofs for PSS and other signature schemes. Cryptology ePrint Archive, Report 2001/062 (2001), https://eprint.iacr.org/2001/062

18. Coron, J.-S.: Optimal security proofs for PSS and other signature schemes. In: Knudsen, L.R. (ed.) EUROCRYPT 2002. LNCS, vol. 2332, pp. 272–287. Springer, Heidelberg (2002). https://doi.org/10.1007/3-540-46035-7_18

19. Cramer, R., Shoup, V.: Universal hash proofs and a paradigm for adaptive chosen ciphertext secure public-key encryption. In: Knudsen, L.R. (ed.) EUROCRYPT 2002. LNCS, vol. 2332, pp. 45–64. Springer, Heidelberg (2002). https://doi.org/10.1007/3-540-46035-7_4

20. Döttling, N., Garg, S.: Identity-based encryption from the Diffie-Hellman assumption. In: Katz, J., Shacham, H. (eds.) CRYPTO 2017, Part I. LNCS, vol. 10401, pp. 537–569. Springer, Cham (2017). https://doi.org/10.1007/978-3-319-63688-7_18

21. Döttling, N., Hartmann, D., Hofheinz, D., Kiltz, E., Schäge, S., Ursu, B.: On the impossibility of short algebraic signatures. Cryptology ePrint Archive, Report 2021/738 (2021). https://ia.cr/2021/738

22. ElGamal, T.: A public key cryptosystem and a signature scheme based on discrete logarithms. IEEE Trans. Inf. Theory **31**, 469–472 (1985)

23. Garg, S., Gentry, C., Sahai, A., Waters, B.: Witness encryption and its applications. In: Boneh, D., Roughgarden, T., Feigenbaum, J. (eds.) 45th ACM STOC, pp. 467–476. ACM Press (2013). https://doi.org/10.1145/2488608.2488667

24. Gennaro, R., Lindell, Y.: A framework for password-based authenticated key exchange. In: Biham, E. (ed.) EUROCRYPT 2003. LNCS, vol. 2656, pp. 524–543. Springer, Heidelberg (2003). https://doi.org/10.1007/3-540-39200-9_33, https://eprint.iacr.org/2003/032.ps.gz

25. Gentry, C., Jutla, C.S., Kane, D.: Obfuscation using tensor products. Cryptology ePrint Archive, Report 2018/756 (2018). https://eprint.iacr.org/2018/756

26. Gentry, C., Peikert, C., Vaikuntanathan, V.: Trapdoors for hard lattices and new cryptographic constructions. In: Ladner, R.E., Dwork, C. (eds.) 40th ACM STOC, pp. 197–206. ACM Press (2008). https://doi.org/10.1145/1374376.1374407

27. Goldreich, O., Levin, L.A.: A hard-core predicate for all one-way functions. In: 21st ACM STOC, pp. 25–32. ACM Press (1989). https://doi.org/10.1145/73007.73010

28. Jager, T., Schwenk, J.: On the analysis of cryptographic assumptions in the generic ring model. In: Matsui, M. (ed.) ASIACRYPT 2009. LNCS, vol. 5912, pp. 399–416. Springer, Heidelberg (2009). https://doi.org/10.1007/978-3-642-10366-7_24

29. Jain, A., Lin, H., Matt, C., Sahai, A.: How to leverage hardness of constant-degree expanding polynomials over $\mathbb{R}$ to build $i\mathcal{O}$. In: Ishai, Y., Rijmen, V. (eds.) EUROCRYPT 2019, Part I. LNCS, vol. 11476, pp. 251–281. Springer, Cham (2019). https://doi.org/10.1007/978-3-030-17653-2_9

30. Kakvi, S.A., Kiltz, E.: Optimal security proofs for full domain hash, revisited. In: Pointcheval, D., Johansson, T. (eds.) EUROCRYPT 2012. LNCS, vol. 7237, pp. 537–553. Springer, Heidelberg (2012). https://doi.org/10.1007/978-3-642-29011-4_32

31. Kakvi, S.A., Kiltz, E.: Optimal security proofs for full domain hash, revisited. J. Cryptol. **31**(1), 276–306 (2017). https://doi.org/10.1007/s00145-017-9257-9

32. Katz, J., Wang, N.: Efficiency improvements for signature schemes with tight security reductions. In: Jajodia, S., Atluri, V., Jaeger, T. (eds.) ACM CCS 2003, pp. 155–164. ACM Press (2003). https://doi.org/10.1145/948109.948132

33. Krawczyk, H., Rabin, T.: Chameleon signatures. In: NDSS 2000. The Internet Society (2000)

34. Maurer, U.: Abstract models of computation in cryptography. In: Smart, N.P. (ed.) Cryptography and Coding 2005. LNCS, vol. 3796, pp. 1–12. Springer, Heidelberg (2005). https://doi.org/10.1007/11586821_1

35. Merkle, R.C.: A certified digital signature. In: Brassard, G. (ed.) CRYPTO 1989. LNCS, vol. 435, pp. 218–238. Springer, New York (1990). https://doi.org/10.1007/0-387-34805-0_21

36. Mohassel, P.: One-time signatures and chameleon hash functions. In: Biryukov, A., Gong, G., Stinson, D.R. (eds.) SAC 2010. LNCS, vol. 6544, pp. 302–319. Springer, Heidelberg (2011). https://doi.org/10.1007/978-3-642-19574-7_21
37. Papakonstantinou, P.A., Rackoff, C.W., Vahlis, Y.: How powerful are the DDH hard groups? Cryptology ePrint Archive, Report 2012/653 (2012). https://eprint.iacr.org/2012/653
38. Pedersen, T.P.: Non-interactive and information-theoretic secure verifiable secret sharing. In: Feigenbaum, J. (ed.) CRYPTO 1991. LNCS, vol. 576, pp. 129–140. Springer, Heidelberg (1992). https://doi.org/10.1007/3-540-46766-1_9
39. Pollard, J.M.: A Monte Carlo method for factorization. BIT Numer. Math. **15**(3), 331–334 (1975)
40. Sakai, R., Ohgishi, K., Kasahara, M.: Cryptosystems based on pairing. In: SCIS 2000, Okinawa, Japan (2000)
41. Schnorr, C.P.: Efficient identification and signatures for smart cards. In: Brassard, G. (ed.) CRYPTO 1989. LNCS, vol. 435, pp. 239–252. Springer, New York (1990). https://doi.org/10.1007/0-387-34805-0_22
42. Kerry , C.F. (Secretary), Romine, C. (Director): FIPS PUB 186–4 federal information processing standards publication digital signature standard (DSS) (2013)
43. Shamir, A.: Identity-based cryptosystems and signature schemes. In: Blakley, G.R., Chaum, D. (eds.) CRYPTO 1984. LNCS, vol. 196, pp. 47–53. Springer, Heidelberg (1985). https://doi.org/10.1007/3-540-39568-7_5
44. Shoup, V.: Lower bounds for discrete logarithms and related problems. In: Fumy, W. (ed.) EUROCRYPT 1997. LNCS, vol. 1233, pp. 256–266. Springer, Heidelberg (1997). https://doi.org/10.1007/3-540-69053-0_18
45. Waters, B.: Efficient identity-based encryption without random oracles. In: Cramer, R. (ed.) EUROCRYPT 2005. LNCS, vol. 3494, pp. 114–127. Springer, Heidelberg (2005). https://doi.org/10.1007/11426639_7
46. Zhandry, M.: How to avoid obfuscation using witness PRFs. In: Kushilevitz, E., Malkin, T. (eds.) TCC 2016, Part II. LNCS, vol. 9563, pp. 421–448. Springer, Heidelberg (2016). https://doi.org/10.1007/978-3-662-49099-0_16

TinyABE: Unrestricted Ciphertext-Policy Attribute-Based Encryption for Embedded Devices and Low-Quality Networks

Marloes Venema[1](✉) and Greg Alpár[1,2]

[1] Radboud University, Nijmegen, The Netherlands
{m.venema,g.alpar}@cs.ru.nl
[2] Open University of the Netherlands, Heerlen, The Netherlands

Abstract. Ciphertext-policy attribute-based encryption (CP-ABE) has attracted much interest from the practical community to enforce access control in distributed settings such as the Internet of Things (IoT). In such settings, encryption devices are often constrained, having small memories and little computational power, and the associated networks are lossy. To optimize both the ciphertext sizes and the encryption speed is therefore paramount. In addition, the master public key needs to be small enough to fit in the encryption device's memory. At the same time, the scheme needs to be expressive enough to support common access control models. Currently, however, the state of the art incurs undesirable efficiency trade-offs. Existing schemes often have linear ciphertexts, and consequently, the ciphertexts may be too large and encryption may be too slow. In contrast, schemes with small ciphertexts have extremely large master public keys, and are generally computationally inefficient.

In this work, we propose TinyABE: a novel CP-ABE scheme that is expressive and can be configured to be efficient enough for settings with embedded devices and low-quality networks. In particular, we demonstrate that our scheme can be configured such that the ciphertexts are small, encryption is fast and the master public key is small enough to fit in memory. From a theoretical standpoint, the new scheme and its security proof are non-trivial generalizations of the expressive scheme with constant-size ciphertexts by Agrawal and Chase (TCC'16, Eurocrypt'17) and its proof to the unbounded setting. By using techniques of Rouselakis and Waters (CCS'13), we remove the restrictions that the Agrawal-Chase scheme imposes on the keys and ciphertexts, making it thus more flexible. In this way, TinyABE is especially suitable for IoT devices and networks.

Keywords: Attribute-based encryption · Ciphertext-policy attribute-based encryption · Short ciphertexts · Efficient encryption

1 Introduction

Attribute-based encryption (ABE) is an advanced type of public-key encryption in which the key pairs are associated with attributes rather than individu-

© The Author(s), under exclusive license to Springer Nature Switzerland AG 2022
L. Batina and J. Daemen (Eds.): AFRICACRYPT 2022, LNCS 13503, pp. 103–129, 2022.
https://doi.org/10.1007/978-3-031-17433-9_5

als [42]. In *ciphertext-policy ABE* (CP-ABE), messages are encrypted under an access policy [15]. Subsequently, the ciphertexts can be decrypted by a single secret key that is associated with a set of attributes that satisfies the policy. In contrast, in *key-policy ABE* (KP-ABE), ciphertexts are associated with sets of attributes and secret keys with access policies [29]. CP-ABE has proven to be a valuable primitive in the enforcement of fine-grained access control on a cryptographic level [15,33,43]. It allows the encrypting device to determine who gets access to the plaintext, without requiring an online trusted third party to act as an intermediary [48]. Instead, it requires a trusted entity to issue secret keys to eligible users, which can be used to access the data for which those are authorized. In this way, the device can directly and securely share its data via any (potentially untrusted) network. Recently, the European Telecommunications Standards Institute (ETSI) has published two specifications regarding the high-level requirements for ABE [25], and how ABE can increase data security and privacy [26]. In these specifications, ETSI focuses on several use cases, one of which considers data access control in the Internet of Things (IoT), in particular. An important requirement that ETSI imposes on ABE is that an IoT device should be able to encrypt, but not necessarily decrypt. To this end, the public keys and ciphertexts should be small, and encryption should be efficient. ETSI also requires the scheme to support expressive policies [25]. Such policies include Boolean formulas, consisting of AND and OR gates, over attributes; and the attributes may be strings or numerical values. The policies may also be large, because they could specify that a decryption key should be generated within a certain time interval, whose description may require several attributes.

According to RFC8576[1], IoT devices and networks are characterized by small memory, low computational power, and high packet loss rates. Unfortunately, many ABE schemes—including those considered by ETSI [25]—have ciphertexts sizes and encryption costs that grow linearly in the number of attributes [2, 5]. As a result, these schemes are not suitable for IoT applications [27]. First, encryption may simply consume too much time, requiring almost one second per attribute [44]. Second, even for small policies, the ciphertexts may be so large that they have to be fragmented across more than one data packet during transmission. This results in an increased probability that at least one of the packets is dropped, and subsequently increases the expected time that it takes for the message to successfully arrive at the receiver [39]. Third, the ciphertext may not fit in memory. The computation of one ciphertext would therefore need to be split into parts, and the partial ciphertexts need to be streamed out of the device, like in [32]. This may further complicate issues with packet loss.

To mitigate issues with the size, ABE schemes with sufficiently short ciphertexts can be deployed. Several schemes with constant-size ciphertexts have been proposed [1,10,11,21,24,31]. However, many of these schemes have restricted policies [21,24,31], supporting only AND-gates or threshold functions, and therefore have a limited expressivity. Others are bounded [1,10,11], supporting only limited sizes for the sets or policies associated with the ciphertexts. More impor-

---

[1] https://tools.ietf.org/html/rfc8576.

tantly, the efficiency of these bounded schemes depends heavily on the bounds. Hence, choosing these bounds to be sufficiently high for some given practical setting is not a suitable option either.

In this work, we mitigate these limitations by proposing a scheme with a trade-off feature. Upon setup, the system parameters can be chosen such that the desired efficiency trade-off between the sizes of the keys and the ciphertexts, as well as the computational costs of the algorithms can be attained. In particular, one can optimize encryption so that it can be performed on IoT devices. Furthermore, one can configure the ciphertexts to be small enough for a specific setting, i.e., to fit in memory of IoT devices or in one Ethernet packet for some given number of attributes. One can also configure the master public key to be small enough to fit in memory. This makes TinyABE especially suitable for IoT.

1.1   Our Contributions

Our main contribution is TinyABE, a new CP-ABE scheme that simultaneously can satisfy several desirable properties:

- **Expressivity:** The scheme supports monotone span programs (MSPs), which includes Boolean formulas consisting of both AND and OR gates;
- **Large-universeness:** Any string can be used as attribute;
- **Unboundedness:** No bounds are posed on the parameters, including the attribute sets associated with the keys and the policy lengths;
- **Configurable:** The system parameters can be chosen such that the scheme attains the required efficiency, for example
  - **Short ciphertexts:** The scheme can be configured such that the ciphertexts are sufficiently small for scenarios involving low-quality networks;
  - **Efficient encryption:** The scheme can be configured such that encryption is fast, even on resource-constrained devices.

We achieve this by making the expressive CP-ABE scheme with constant-size ciphertexts by Agrawal and Chase (AC16) [1] unbounded. As a result, our scheme is parametrized, and can be configured to provide the desired efficiency trade-off. Special cases of our scheme include AC16, and the CP-ABE scheme with constant-size ciphertexts by Attrapadung (Att19) [8]. TinyABE can thus be viewed as a generalization of AC16 to the unbounded setting. We also provide two secondary contributions:

- *Security proof:* We generalize Agrawal and Chase's [3] proof for AC16 [1] to the unbounded setting using Rouselakis and Waters' [41] techniques;
- *Performance analysis:* We analyze the efficiency of our scheme with a focus on practice. In particular, we obtain the most efficient encryption algorithm compared to other expressive and unbounded schemes.

2   High-level Overview and Details About TinyABE

Our Construction. TinyABE is a generalization of the Agrawal-Chase scheme (AC16) [1,3] to the unbounded setting, using the partitioning techniques by Attrapadung et al. (AHM+16) [9], and by using the proof techniques by Rouselakis and Waters (RW13) [41]. By generalizing AC16, we can make it more efficient. Although AC16 supports expressive policies and attains constant-size ciphertexts, it is bounded in parameters N_1 and N_2, where N_1 and N_2 denote the upper bounds on the number of rows and columns of the access structure, respectively. Importantly, the scheme's efficiency depends on these parameters. Whereas the ciphertext sizes are constant, the master public key grows by a factor $N_1 N_2$, and the secret keys grow by a factor $N_1^2 N_2$. As a result, the master public key is already so large for $N_1 = N_2 = 32$, i.e., 103 kilobytes (KB), that it does not fit in memory of many embedded devices. By making AC16 unbounded, the efficiency depends differently on these factors. We make the AC16 scheme unbounded by using a similar approach as AHM+16. Roughly, we partition the sets of rows and columns in smaller subsets of maximum sizes $\hat{n}_1$ and $\hat{n}_2$, respectively, and apply the AC16 scheme to the partitions. The master public key and secret keys then also grow in factors $\hat{n}_1 \hat{n}_2$ and $\hat{n}_1^2 \hat{n}_2$, respectively, but $\hat{n}_1$ and $\hat{n}_2$ can be much smaller to attain small ciphertexts. Although our ciphertexts are not constant-size, they shrink by a factor $\mathcal{O}(\min(\hat{n}_1, \hat{n}_2))$ compared to schemes with linear-size ciphertexts, such as RW13. Thus, even for small choices of $\hat{n}_1$ and $\hat{n}_2$, our ciphertexts are much smaller than RW13 ciphertexts. Whereas RW13 ciphertexts might only fit in memory or in one Ethernet packet for a maximum policy length of 33 or 3, respectively, TinyABE can support larger policy lengths. For example, in the same settings, it supports maximum policy lengths of 298 (for $\hat{n}_1 = \hat{n}_2 = 3$), and 100 (for $\hat{n}_1 = \hat{n}_2 = 13$), respectively, while the associated master public keys are only 2.3, and 19 KB, respectively.

Security Proof: The AC17 Framework. We formulate our scheme and proofs in the AC17 [3] framework, which considers a commonly-used abstraction of pairing-based encryption schemes: pair encoding schemes (PES) [7]. Essentially, a PES condenses a scheme to "what happens in the exponent". The AC17 framework simplifies security analysis, whilst achieving strong security guarantees, by reducing the effort of proving security to performing simple linear algebra [47]. In part, we use this framework, because we generalize AC16, and its only proofs in the full-security setting are given in this framework [3,8]. In contrast, other expressive CP-ABE schemes with constant-size ciphertexts [10,12] have larger keys than AC16 and are therefore less efficient.

Improving the Partitioning Approach. We improve on the partitioning approach used for the KP-ABE scheme of Attrapadung et al. (AHM+16) [9], which is unbounded, supports expressive policies, and can be configured to have small ciphertexts. Specifically, AHM+16 generalizes the first expressive KP-ABE scheme with constant-size ciphertexts of Attrapadung, Libert and de Panafieu

(ALP11) [11] to the unbounded setting. Concretely, their approach consists of the partitioning of the attribute set (to be used during encryption) into subsets of maximum size n_k, where n_k is the bound on the attribute set inherited from ALP11. Before our work, a CP-ABE scheme attaining similar characteristics remained an open problem. In fact, the first expressive CP-ABE schemes with constant-size ciphertexts [1,10] were proposed four years after the introduction of ALP11. Presumably, the reason for this delay is the difficulty in simultaneously achieving these properties in the ciphertext-policy setting. On the one hand, the entire access policy—which is two-dimensional—needs to be embedded in one ciphertext component. On the other hand, the decrypting user—who has an attribute set satisfying the policy—may not have keys for all attributes used in the access policy. These difficulties also translate to the unbounded setting: to make AC16 unbounded, we need to partition in two dimensions instead of one. In addition, we want to embed the entire policy in one ciphertext component, like AC16. This is unlike AHM+16, which embeds each partitioned subset in a separate ciphertext component, and thus still requires a linear number of operations during encryption. In contrast, the costs of computing our ciphertext component embedding the policy are essentially upper-bounded by a constant.

Performance Analysis. We show that TinyABE offers advantages over other schemes by analyzing the storage and computational costs. In this analysis, we take into account the limitations of constrained devices and low-quality networks. To this end, we select two configurations of TinyABE, which we compare with RW13 and AC16. Our first configuration provides sufficiently small public keys and ciphertexts for IoT devices, whilst attaining an efficient encryption algorithm. For example, in Sect. 6.3, we estimate the encryption costs on some IoT devices. For policies of length 100, encryption with RW13 takes over a minute, while encryption with our scheme takes only 7.6 s. Moreover, while the master public key of AC16 is almost a megabyte in size, our master public key is only 2.25 kilobytes, and thus fits easily in memory of constrained devices. Our second configuration ensures that, for policy lengths of up to 100 attributes, the ciphertexts fit in one Ethernet packet, which has a maximum transmission unit of 1500 bytes. In contrast, RW13 ciphertexts are too large.

Expressive, Large-Universe, Unbounded and Efficient. TinyABE is simultaneously expressive and unrestricted while it is configurable. Therefore, it can be configured to be efficient enough for practical applications involving IoT devices and networks. Our scheme supports large universes, so it can efficiently support any strings as attributes, and does not require that, in the setup, public keys are generated for each attribute. The scheme is also unbounded[2], which implicitly ensures that it attains a better efficiency, even for large policies, compared to bounded schemes. In contrast, the efficiency of bounded schemes with

---

[2] Note that our scheme is also unbounded in that it satisfies the "multi-use" property, meaning that attributes may occur any number of times in the access policies.

constant-size ciphertexts [1,8] depends heavily on the choice of these bounds. Finally, because our scheme supports monotone span programs, it can enforce any fine-grained policies on encrypted data. Practitioners therefore do not need to restrict themselves to less expressive solutions in IoT settings anymore [27,34].

Expressive and Efficient CP-ABE Scheme for IoT. Several schemes have been introduced over the years. Some can attain sufficiently short ciphertexts for some specific practical context. In particular, we consider schemes that can be configured to be small enough to fit e.g., in memory of constrained devices or in Ethernet packets, even for large policies. As Table 1a shows, all of the CP-ABE schemes of this kind incur a trade-off: either they are not expressive, or they impose bounds (and by extension, they are inefficient). In contrast, TinyABE is the first CP-ABE scheme to overcome these limitations. Furthermore, compared to expressive schemes with ciphertext sizes that grow at least in the size of the policy or set (see Table 1b), TinyABE can be configured to have a more efficient encryption. As such, it is feasible to implement ABE on IoT devices (see Sect. 6.3), which are mainly assumed to be required to encrypt and not decrypt.

3 Preliminaries

3.1 Notation

If an element is chosen uniformly at random from a finite set S, then we denote this as $x \in_R S$. For integers $a < b$, we denote $[a, b] = \{a, a + 1, ..., b - 1, b\}$, $[b] = [1, b]$ and $\overline{[b]} = [0, b]$. We use boldfaced variables $\mathbf{A}$ and $\mathbf{v}$ for matrices and vectors, respectively. We denote $a : \mathbf{A}$ to substitute variable a by a matrix or vector $\mathbf{A}$. We define $\mathbf{1}_{i,j}^{d_1 \times d_2} \in \mathbb{Z}_p^{d_1 \times d_2}$ as the matrix with 1 in the i-th row and j-th column, and 0 everywhere else, and similarly $\mathbf{1}_i^{d_1}$ and $\overline{\mathbf{1}}_i^{d_2}$ as the row and column vectors with 1 in the i-th entry and 0 everywhere else.

3.2 Access Structures

We represent access policies $\mathbb{A}$ by linear secret sharing scheme (LSSS) matrices, which support monotone span programs [14,30]. In particular, Boolean formulas can be efficiently converted into LSSS matrices [35].

Definition 1 (Access structures represented by LSSS matrices [30]). *An access structure can be represented as a pair $\mathbb{A} = (\mathbf{A}, \rho)$ such that $\mathbf{A} \in \mathbb{Z}_p^{n_1 \times n_2}$ is an LSSS matrix, where $n_1, n_2 \in \mathbb{N}$, and ρ is a function that maps the rows of $\mathbf{A}$ to attributes in the universe. For some vector $\mathbf{v} = (s, v_2, ..., v_{n_2}) \in_R \mathbb{Z}_p^{n_2}$, the i-th secret generated by matrix $\mathbf{A}$ is $\lambda_i = \mathbf{A}_i \mathbf{v}^\mathsf{T}$, where $\mathbf{A}_i$ denotes the i-th row of $\mathbf{A}$. In particular, if S satisfies $\mathbb{A}$, then there exist a set of rows $\Upsilon = \{i \in [n_1] \mid \rho(i) \in S\}$ and coefficients $\varepsilon_i \in \mathbb{Z}_p$ for all $i \in \Upsilon$ such that $\sum_{i \in \Upsilon} \varepsilon_i \mathbf{A}_i = (1, 0, ..., 0)$, and thus, $\sum_{i \in \Upsilon} \varepsilon_i \lambda_i = s$ holds. If S does not satisfy $\mathbb{A}$, there exists $\mathbf{w} = (1, w_2, ..., w_{n_2}) \in \mathbb{Z}_p^{n_2}$ such that $\mathbf{A}_i \mathbf{w}^\mathsf{T} = 0$ for all $i \in \Upsilon$ [14].*

Table 1. Comparison of ABE schemes with short and linear ciphertexts, respectively. For each scheme, we list whether they are CP, the expressivity (expr.), whether they are large-universe (LU), and whether they support unbounded (unb) policies or sets. For the schemes with short ciphertexts, we also give the asymptotic complexity of the storage costs of their master public keys (MPK), secret keys (SK) and ciphertexts (CT). We consider a scheme to have short ciphertexts if their asymptotic sizes are smaller than linear in the number of attributes, i.e., $\mathcal{O}(|\mathcal{S}|)$ or $\mathcal{O}(|\mathbb{A}|)$. Note that we have only listed schemes that are structurally different, i.e., that have a different PES. For instance, the KP-ABE scheme in [41] has the same PES as the KP-ABE scheme in [36].

Scheme	CP	Expr.	LU	Unb. $|\mathbb{A}|$	Unb. $|\mathcal{S}|$	Sizes MPK	Sizes SK	Sizes CT
EMN+09 [24]	✓	AND	✗	✓	✓	$\mathcal{O}(|\mathcal{U}|)$	$\mathcal{O}(1)$	$\mathcal{O}(1)$
HLR10 [31]	✓	Threshold	✗	✓	✓	$\mathcal{O}(|\mathcal{U}|)$	$\mathcal{O}(|\mathcal{U}|)$	$\mathcal{O}(1)$
CZF11 [21]	✓	AND	✗	✓	✓	$\mathcal{O}(|\mathcal{U}|)$	$\mathcal{O}(|\mathcal{U}|)$	$\mathcal{O}(1)$
ALP11 [11]	✗	(N)MSP	✓	✓	✗	$\mathcal{O}(N_k)$	$\mathcal{O}(N_k|\mathbb{A}|)$	$\mathcal{O}(1)$
CCL+13 [20]	✗	Threshold	✗	✓	✓	$\mathcal{O}(|\mathcal{U}|)$	$\mathcal{O}(|\mathcal{U}||\mathbb{A}|)$	$\mathcal{O}(1)$
Tak14 [45]	✗	NMSP	✓	✗	✗	$\mathcal{O}(N_k)$	$\mathcal{O}(N_k|\mathbb{A}|)$	$\mathcal{O}(1)$
AHY15 [10]	✓	(N)MSP	✓	✗	✗	$\mathcal{O}((N_kN_1)^2\lambda)$	$\mathcal{O}((N_kN_1)^4\lambda^2)$	$\mathcal{O}(1)$
AHM+16 [9]	✗	MSP	✓	✓	✓	$\mathcal{O}(n_k)$	$\mathcal{O}(n_k|\mathbb{A}|)$	$\mathcal{O}(\frac{|\mathcal{S}|}{n_k})$
AC16 [1,3]	✓	MSP	✓	✗	✗	$\mathcal{O}(N_1(N_2+N_k))$	$\mathcal{O}(|\mathcal{S}|N_1^2(N_2+N_k))$	$\mathcal{O}(1)$
Att19 [8]	✓	NMSP	✓	✗	✓	$\mathcal{O}(N_1N_2)$	$\mathcal{O}(|\mathcal{S}|N_1^2N_2)$	$\mathcal{O}(1)$
AT20 [12]	✓	(N)MSP	✓	✗	✓	$\mathcal{O}((N_2+N_k\lambda)^2)$	$\mathcal{O}((N_2+N_k\lambda)^4)$	$\mathcal{O}(1)$
LL20b [37]	✗	MSP	✓	✓	✗	$\mathcal{O}(N_k)$	$\mathcal{O}(N_k|\mathbb{A}|)$	$\mathcal{O}(1)$
TinyABE	✓	MSP	✓	✓	✓	$\mathcal{O}(\hat{n}_1(\hat{n}_2+n_k))$	$\mathcal{O}(\hat{n}_1^2(\hat{n}_2+\hat{n}_k)\frac{|\mathcal{S}|}{n_k})$	$\mathcal{O}(\min(\frac{n_1}{\hat{n}_1},\frac{n_2}{\hat{n}_2}))$

(a)ABE with short ciphertexts.

Scheme	CP	LU	Unb. $|\mathbb{A}|$	Unb. $|\mathcal{S}|$
GPSW06 [29]	✗	✗	✓	✓
BSW07 [15]	✓	✓	✓	✓
Wat11-I [50]	✓	✗	✓	✓
Wat11-IV [50]	✓	✓	✓	✓
LW11 [36]	✗	✓	✓	✓
RW13 [41]	✓	✓	✓	✓
FAME [2]	✓	✓	✓	✓
ABGW17 [5]	✓	✓	✓	✓
TKN20 [46]	✓	✓	✓	✓
TinyABE	✓	✓	✓	✓

(b) ABE with linear-sized keys and ciphertexts that support MSPs.

Notes: $\mathcal{U}$ = universe; $\mathbb{A}$ = access policy; $\mathcal{S}$ = set of attributes;
(N)MSP = (non-)monotone span program, n_1, n_2 = number of rows, columns of $\mathbb{A}$;
N_1, N_2, N_k = maximum bounds on $n_1, n_2, |\mathcal{S}|$;
$\hat{n}_1, \hat{n}_2, n_k$ = maximum partition sizes of $n_1, n_2, |\mathcal{S}|$

3.3   Ciphertext-policy ABE

Definition 2 (Ciphertext-policy ABE [15]). *A ciphertext-policy ABE (CP-ABE) scheme consists of four algorithms:*

- Setup(λ) → (MPK, MSK): *The setup takes as input a security parameter λ. It outputs the master public-secret key pair (MPK, MSK).*
- KeyGen(MSK, $\mathcal{S}$) → SK$_{\mathcal{S}}$: *The key generation takes as input a set of attributes $\mathcal{S}$ and the master secret key MSK. It outputs a secret key SK$_{\mathcal{S}}$.*
- Encrypt(MPK, $\mathbb{A}$, M) → CT$_{\mathbb{A}}$: *The encryption takes as input a message M, a policy $\mathbb{A}$ and the master public key MPK. It outputs a ciphertext CT$_{\mathbb{A}}$.*
- Decrypt(SK$_{\mathcal{S}}$, CT$_{\mathbb{A}}$) → M': *The decryption takes as input the ciphertext CT$_{\mathbb{A}}$ with access policy $\mathbb{A}$, and a secret key SK$_{\mathcal{S}}$ with attribute set $\mathcal{S}$. It succeeds and outputs a message M' if $\mathcal{S}$ satisfies $\mathbb{A}$. Otherwise, it fails.*

The scheme is correct if successful decryption of a ciphertext always yields the original message.

Large-universe and Unbounded ABE. A scheme supports large universes if it does not impose bounds on the universe, which consists of all attributes that can be used in the scheme. We call the scheme unbounded, if it supports large universes and additionally does not impose bounds on the sets $\mathcal{S}$ and policies $\mathbb{A}$, or on the number of times $|\rho^{-1}(\text{att})|$ that one attribute att occurs in a policy.

3.4   Security Model

Definition 3 (Full IND-CPA-security for CP-ABE [15]). *We define the game between challenger and attacker as follows:*

- **Setup phase:** *The challenger runs the Setup algorithm and sends the master public key MPK to the attacker.*
- **First query phase:** *The attacker queries secret keys for the sets of attributes $\mathcal{S}_1, ..., \mathcal{S}_{n_1}$.*
- **Challenge phase:** *The attacker specifies two equal-length messages M_0 and M_1, and an access structure $\mathbb{A}^*$ such that none of the sets $\mathcal{S}_i$ satisfies it, and sends these to the challenger. The challenger flips a coin, i.e., $\beta \in_R \{0, 1\}$, encrypts M_β under $\mathbb{A}^*$, and sends the resulting ciphertext to the attacker.*
- **Second query phase:** *The attacker queries secret keys for the sets of attributes $\mathcal{S}_{n_1+1}, ..., \mathcal{S}_{n_2}$ with the restriction that none of the sets $\mathcal{S}_i$ satisfy access structure $\mathbb{A}^*$.*
- **Decision phase:** *The attacker outputs a guess β' for β.*

The advantage of the attacker is defined as $|\Pr[\beta' = \beta] - \frac{1}{2}|$. A CP-ABE scheme is fully secure if all polynomial-time attackers have at most a negligible advantage in this security game.

3.5   Pairings (or Bilinear Maps)

We define a pairing to be an efficiently computable map e on three groups $\mathbb{G}, \mathbb{H}$ and $\mathbb{G}_T$ of prime order p, so that $e \colon \mathbb{G} \times \mathbb{H} \to \mathbb{G}_T$, with generators $g \in \mathbb{G}, h \in \mathbb{H}$ is such that for all $a, b \in \mathbb{Z}_p$, it holds that $e(g^a, h^b) = e(g, h)^{ab}$ (bilinearity), and for $g^a \neq 1_{\mathbb{G}}, h^b \neq 1_{\mathbb{H}}$, it holds that $e(g^a, h^b) \neq 1_{\mathbb{G}_T}$, where $1_{\mathbb{G}'}$ denotes the unique identity element of the associated group $\mathbb{G}'$ (non-degeneracy).

3.6 Pair Encoding Schemes

Definition 4 (Pair encoding schemes (PES) [3]). *A pair encoding scheme for a predicate family* $P_\kappa \colon \mathcal{X}_\kappa \times \mathcal{Y}_\kappa \to \{0,1\}$, *indexed by* $\kappa = (p, \mathrm{par})$, *where* par *specifies some parameters, is given by four deterministic polynomial-time algorithms as described below.*

- Param(par) $\to n$: *On input* par, *the algorithm outputs* $n \in \mathbb{N}$ *that specifies the number of common variables, which are denoted as* $\mathbf{b} = (b_1, ..., b_n)$.
- EncKey$(y, p) \to (m_1, m_2, \mathbf{k}(\mathbf{r}, \hat{\mathbf{r}}, \mathbf{b}))$: *On input* $p \in \mathbb{N}$ *and* $y \in \mathcal{Y}_\kappa$, *this algorithm outputs a vector of polynomials* $\mathbf{k} = (k_1, ..., k_{m_3})$ *defined over non-lone variables* $\mathbf{r} = (r_1, ..., r_{m_1})$ *and lone variables* $\hat{\mathbf{r}} = (\hat{r}_1, ..., \hat{r}_{m_2})$. *Specifically, the polynomial* k_i *is expressed as*

$$k_i = \delta_i \alpha + \sum_{j \in [m_2]} \delta_{i,j} \hat{r}_j + \sum_{j \in [m_1], k \in [n]} \delta_{i,j,k} r_j b_k,$$

  for all $i \in [m_3]$, *where* $\delta_i, \delta_{i,j}, \delta_{i,j,k} \in \mathbb{Z}_p$.
- EncCt$(x, p) \to (w_1, w_2, \mathbf{c}(\mathbf{s}, \hat{\mathbf{s}}, \mathbf{b}))$: *On input* $p \in \mathbb{N}$ *and* $x \in \mathcal{X}_\kappa$, *this algorithm outputs a vector of polynomials* $\mathbf{c} = (c_1, ..., c_{w_3})$ *defined over non-lone variables* $\mathbf{s} = (s, s_2, ..., s_{w_1})$ *and lone variables* $\hat{\mathbf{s}} = (\hat{s}_1, ..., \hat{s}_{w_2})$. *Specifically, the polynomial* c_i *is expressed as*

$$c_i = \sum_{j \in [w_2]} \eta_{i,j} \hat{s}_j + \sum_{j \in \overline{[w_1]}, k \in [n]} \eta_{i,j,k} s_j b_k,$$

  for all $i \in [w_3]$, *where* $\eta_{i,j}, \eta_{i,j,k} \in \mathbb{Z}_p$.
- Pair$(x, y, p) \to (\mathbf{E}, \overline{\mathbf{E}})$: *On input* p, x, *and* y, *this algorithm outputs two matrices* $\mathbf{E}$ *and* $\overline{\mathbf{E}}$ *of sizes* $(w_1 + 1) \times m_3$ *and* $w_3 \times m_1$, *respectively.*

A PES is correct for every $\kappa = (p, \mathrm{par})$, $x \in \mathcal{X}_\kappa$ *and* $y \in \mathcal{Y}_\kappa$ *such that* $P_\kappa(x, y) = 1$, *it holds that* $\mathbf{s}\mathbf{E}\mathbf{k}^\mathsf{T} + \mathbf{c}\overline{\mathbf{E}}\mathbf{r}^\mathsf{T} = \alpha s$.

Definition 5 (Symbolic property [3]). *A pair encoding scheme* $\Gamma = (\mathrm{Param}, \mathrm{EncKey}, \mathrm{EncCt}, \mathrm{Pair})$ *for a predicate family* $P_\kappa \colon \mathcal{X}_\kappa \times \mathcal{Y}_\kappa \to \{0,1\}$ *satisfies the* (d_1, d_2)-*selective symbolic property for positive integers* d_1 *and* d_2 *if there exist deterministic polynomial-time algorithms* EncB, EncS, *and* EncR *such that for all* $\kappa = (p, \mathrm{par})$, $x \in \mathcal{X}_\kappa$ *and* $y \in \mathcal{Y}_\kappa$ *with* $P_\kappa(x, y) = 0$, *we have that*

- EncB$(x) \to \mathbf{B}_1, ..., \mathbf{B}_n \in \mathbb{Z}_p^{d_1 \times d_2}$;
- EncR$(x, y) \to \mathbf{r}_1, ..., \mathbf{r}_{m_1} \in \mathbb{Z}_p^{d_1}, \mathbf{a}, \hat{\mathbf{r}}_1, ..., \hat{\mathbf{r}}_{m_2} \in \mathbb{Z}_p^{d_2}$;
- EncS$(x) \to \mathbf{s}_0, ..., \mathbf{s}_{w_1} \in \mathbb{Z}_p^{d_2}, \hat{\mathbf{s}}_1, ..., \hat{\mathbf{s}}_{w_2} \in \mathbb{Z}_p^{d_1}$;

such that $\langle \mathbf{s}_0, \mathbf{a} \rangle \neq 0$, *and if we substitute*

$$\hat{s}_{i'} : \hat{\mathbf{s}}_{i'}^\mathsf{T} \quad s_i b_j : \mathbf{B}_j \mathbf{s}_i^\mathsf{T} \quad \alpha : \mathbf{a} \quad \hat{r}_{k'} : \hat{\mathbf{r}}_{k'} \quad r_k b_j : \mathbf{r}_k \mathbf{B}_j,$$

for $i \in [w_1], i' \in [w_2], j \in [n], k \in [m_1], k' \in [m_2]$ *in all the polynomials of* $\mathbf{k}$ *and* $\mathbf{c}$ *(output by* EncKey *and* EncCt, *respectively), they evaluate to* $\mathbf{0}$.

Similarly, a pair encoding scheme satisfies the (d_1, d_2)-co-selective symbolic security property if there exist EncB, EncR, EncS *that satisfy the above properties but where* EncB *and* EncR *only take y as input, and* EncS *takes x and y as input.*

A scheme satisfies the (d_1, d_2)-symbolic property if it satisfies the (d'_1, d'_2)-selective and (d''_1, d''_2)-co-selective properties for $d'_1, d''_1 \leq d_1$ and $d'_2, d''_2 \leq d_2$.

Agrawal and Chase [3] prove that any PES satisfying the (d_1, d_2)-symbolic property can be transformed in a fully secure ABE scheme.

4 Our Construction: TinyABE

We present our construction. To this end, in Sect. 4.1, we give a step-by-step description on how these layering techniques can be applied, by first carefully reviewing the scheme. Roughly, we use the techniques of Attrapadung et al. [8,9] to remove the bounds on the attribute sets used in the key generation. Then, we apply the layering techniques to the ciphertext policy, by using the partitioning approach of Attrapadung et al. (AHM+16) [9]. However, unlike in AHM+16 [9], we need to partition in two "directions" due to the two-dimensional nature of access policies. In particular, for each policy, we split the set of rows in subsets of maximum size $\hat{n}_1$, and the set of columns in subsets of maximum size $\hat{n}_2$. Then, for each subset, we use a fresh "randomizer". These randomizers are appropriately applied to the ciphertext component of AC16 that embeds the policy. To this end, we identify which parts of this ciphertext component correspond to the rows and which to the columns:

$$C'' = \underbrace{\prod_{j \in [n_1], k \in [n_2]} g^{sA_{j,k}b_{j,k}}}_{\text{columns}} \underbrace{\prod_{i \in \overline{[n_k]}, j \in [n_1]} g^{s\rho(j)^i b'_{i,j}}}_{\text{rows}},$$

where $g^{b_{j,k}}$ and $g^{b'_{i,j}}$ denote public keys, and s is a random integer during encryption under access structure $\mathbb{A} = (\mathbf{A}, \rho)$ with $\mathbf{A} \in \mathbb{Z}_p^{n_1 \times n_2}$. For example, for each partitioned subset $\mathcal{S}'_l$ of $[n_1]$, we use a fresh randomizer s_l to compute partial ciphertext $\prod_{i \in \overline{[n_k]}, j \in \mathcal{S}'_l} g^{s_l \rho(j)^i b'_{i,j}}$. In the scheme, we use mappings τ_1 and τ_2 to partition the rows and columns, respectively, in sets of maximum size $\hat{n}_1$ and $\hat{n}_2$. Furthermore, we define the mappings $\hat{\tau}_1$ and $\hat{\tau}_2$ to map each row and column, respectively, that are in the same partition to a unique set of public keys.

4.1 Removing the Bounds from AC16

We show how to make AC16 [1] unbounded, by analyzing the scheme and showing, in steps, how the bounds can be removed by introducing more randomness.

The AC16 Scheme. We briefly review the AC16 scheme [1]. Specifically, the secret keys SK and ciphertexts CT are of the form

$$\text{SK} = (\{K_{1,j} = g^{r_j}, K_{2,j,k} = g^{r_j b_{j,k} - v_k}, K_{3,j,j',k} = g^{r_j b_{j',k}},$$

$$K_{4,j,\text{att}} = g^{r_j \sum_{i \in \overline{[n_k]}} x_{\text{att}}^i b'_{i,j}}, K_{5,i,j,j'} = g^{r_j b'_{i,j'}}\}_{i \in \overline{[n_k]}, j,j' \in [\hat{n}_1], j \neq j', \atop k \in [\hat{n}_2], \text{att} \in \mathcal{S}}),$$

$$\text{CT} = \left(C = M \cdot e(g,g)^{\alpha s}, C' = g^s, \right.$$

$$\left. C'' = \prod_{j \in [n_1], k \in [n_2]} g^{s A_{j,k} b_{j,k}} \prod_{i \in \overline{[n_k]}, j \in [n_1]} g^{s \rho(j)^i b'_{i,j}} \right)$$

where $g^{b_{j,k}}$ and $g^{b'_{i,j}}$ denote public keys, $v_1 = \alpha$ is the master-key, $r_j, v_k \in_R \mathbb{Z}_p$ are randomly chosen integers during the key generation for set $\mathcal{S}$ with $|\mathcal{S}| \leq n_k$, and s is a randomly chosen integer during encryption for access structure $\mathbb{A} = (\mathbf{A}, \rho)$ with $\mathbf{A} \in \mathbb{Z}_p^{n_1 \times n_2}$ such that $n_1 \leq N_1$ and $n_2 \leq N_2$ and $\rho \colon [n_1] \to \mathbb{Z}_p$, where $N_1, N_2 \in \mathbb{N}$ denote bounds on the policy size. Furthermore, x_{att} denotes the unique representation of an attribute att (represented as a string) in $\mathbb{Z}_p$, which can be generated with a collision-resistant hash function $\mathcal{H} \colon \{0,1\}^* \to \mathbb{Z}_p$.

Intuitively, decryption using a key SK for set $\mathcal{S}$ of a ciphertext CT with access policy $\mathbb{A}$ works by "singling out" each row $j \in \Upsilon = \{j' \in [n_1] \mid \rho(j') \in \mathcal{S}\}$, i.e., $e(g,g)^{r_j s(\sum_{k \in [\hat{n}_2]} A_{j,k} b_{j,k} + \sum_{i \in \overline{[n_k]}} \rho(j)^i b'_{i,j})}$ from C'' (and $K_{1,j}$). From this, $e(g,g)^{\sum_{k \in [\hat{n}_2]} A_{j,k} v_k}$ can be retrieved by using C', $K_{2,j,k}$ and $K_{4,j,\rho(j)}$. More concretely, this can be done because the secret keys are constructed in a specific way. That is, for each $j, j' \in [\hat{n}_1]$, it embeds the product $r_j b_{j',k}$, but only in the case that $j = j'$, it also embeds the secret v_k (where $v_1 = \alpha$). Similarly, for $j = j'$, only the secrets $r_j \sum_i x_{\text{att}}^i b'_{i,j}$ are given for those attributes att that are in the set $\mathcal{S}$. For $j \neq j'$, we can reconstruct $r_j \sum_i x_{\text{att}}^i b'_{i,j'}$ for any attribute $\overline{\text{att}}$. To decrypt, we have to retrieve $e(g,g)^{\alpha s}$, for which we would need to pair $K_{2,j,k}$ with C' to obtain $e(g,g)^{r_j b_{j,k} s - v_k s}$. Then, the question is how we can cancel out $e(g,g)^{r_j b_{j,k} s}$. Roughly, we want to "single out" the j-th row of the access policy in the ciphertext component C''. Then, we pair $K_{1,j} = g^{r_j}$ with C'', and cancel out all resulting components $e(g,g)^{r_j s(A_{j',k} b_{j',k} + \rho(j')^i b'_{i,j'})}$ for $j \neq j'$ by using $K_{3,j,j',k}$ and $K_{5,i,j,j'}$ and pairing them with C'. Note that we just argued that we can reconstruct these components (regardless of the fact that, possibly, $\rho(j') \notin \mathcal{S}$). This leaves us with components $e(g,g)^{r_j s(\sum_{k \in [\hat{n}_2]} A_{j,k} b_{j,k} + \sum_{i \in \overline{[n_k]}} \rho(j)^i b'_{i,j})}$. Then, we can only cancel $\prod_{i \in [n_k]} e(g,g)^{r_j s \rho(j)^i b'_{i,j}}$ if $\rho(j) \in \mathcal{S}$ (by pairing $K_{4,j,\text{att}}$ with C'), which subsequently yields $\prod_{k \in [\hat{n}_2]} e(g,g)^{r_j s A_{j,k} b_{j,k}}$. By combining this with $e(g,g)^{r_j b_{j,k} s - v_k s}$, we can obtain $e(g,g)^{\alpha s}$. For these last steps, we use the following LSSS property (Definition 1). If $\mathcal{S}$ satisfies $\mathbb{A}$, then there exist $\varepsilon_j \in \mathbb{Z}_p$ for all $j \in \Upsilon = \{j \in [n_1] \mid \rho(j) \in \mathcal{S}\}$ such that $\sum_{j \in \Upsilon} \varepsilon_j \mathbf{A}_j = (1, 0, ..., 0)$ for rows $\mathbf{A}_j$ of matrix $\mathbf{A}$. Thus, computing $\prod_{k \in [\hat{n}_2]} (e(g,g)^{r_j b_{j,k} s - v_k s})^{\varepsilon_j A_{j,k}}$ yields

$\prod_{j\in\Upsilon,k\in[\hat{n}_2]} e(g,g)^{r_j\varepsilon_j A_{j,k}b_{j,k}s}e(g,g)^{-\alpha s}$. We finally obtain $e(g,g)^{\alpha s}$ by raising $\prod_{k\in[\hat{n}_2]} e(g,g)^{r_j s A_{j,k}b_{j,k}}$ to the power ε_j for each $j\in\Upsilon$.

Removing the Bound on Set $\mathcal{S}$. First, we remove the bound n_k on set $\mathcal{S}$, which is simpler than removing the bounds on the access policy. In fact, this has already been done by Attrapadung [8], so we only briefly review his version of the scheme. Note that this method also resembles the method used in the AHM+16 scheme [9]. The general idea is that the set $\mathcal{S}$ is partitioned in arbitrary sets of maximum size n_k. For each partition, we use the randomness provided by r_j and the public keys to embed the partition like in the original scheme. However, because we have $m = \left\lceil \frac{|\mathcal{S}|}{n_k} \right\rceil$ partitions, we need m fresh sets of randomness $\{r_j\}_{j\in[\hat{n}_1]}$ for each partition. Hence, the keys look like this:

$$\mathrm{SK} = \{K_{1,j,l} = g^{r_{j,l}}, K_{2,j,k,l} = g^{r_{j,l}b_{j,k}-v_k}, K_{3,j,j',k,l} = g^{r_{j,l}b_{j',k}},$$

$$K_{4,j,\mathrm{att}} = g^{r_{j,\iota(\mathrm{att})} \sum_{i\in\overline{[n_k]}} x_{\mathrm{att}}^i b'_{i,j}}, K_{5,i,j,j',l} = g^{r_{j,l}b_{i,j'}}\}_{j,j'\in[\hat{n}_1],j\neq j',k\in[\hat{n}_2],}$$
$$\scriptstyle i\in\overline{[n_k]},l\in[m],\mathrm{att}\in\mathcal{S}$$

where $\iota\colon \mathcal{S} \to [m]$ maps the attributes of $\mathcal{S}$ into partitions. To ensure that the partitions are small enough, we place a restriction on ι, i.e., $|\iota^{-1}(l)| \leq n_k$ for all $l \in [m]$. Note here that the key component $K_{4,j,\mathrm{att}}$ only uses the randomizer $r_{j,l}$ corresponding to the partition in which x_{att} is mapped with ι. Furthermore, decryption is similar as in the AC16 scheme, though a little more care should be taken into picking the correct randomizer $r_{j,l}$.

Removing the Bound from Policy $\mathbb{A}$. It is considerably more difficult to remove the bounds on the access policy $\mathbb{A}$. Again, we need to introduce fresh randomness for each partition. However, we need to partition in two directions: the rows and the columns. Hence, we partition the access policy $\mathbb{A} = (\mathbf{A}, \rho)$ by splitting the rows in $m'_1 = \left\lceil \frac{n_1}{\hat{n}_1} \right\rceil$ partitions of maximum size $\hat{n}_1$, and the columns in $m'_2 = \left\lceil \frac{n_2}{\hat{n}_2} \right\rceil$ partitions of maximum size $\hat{n}_2$. In addition, we define the associated mappings $\tau_\beta\colon [n_\beta] \to [m'_\beta]$ for $\beta \in \{1,2\}$ that output the indices of the partitions in which the rows (for $\beta = 1$) and columns (for $\beta = 2$) are mapped. For each partition $l_\beta \in [m'_\beta]$, we introduce a randomizer s_{β,l_β}. In addition, we need to ensure that each row $j \in [n_1]$ in one partition uses a unique set of public parameters $\{g^{b_{j',k}}, g^{b'_{i,j'}}\}_{i\in\overline{[n_k]},k\in[\hat{n}_2]}$ (with $j' \in [\hat{n}_1]$). Similarly, we need to ensure that each column $k \in [n_2]$ in one partition uses a unique set $\{b_{j,k'}\}_{j\in[n_1]}$ (with $k' \in [\hat{n}_2]$). We thus define the corresponding mappings $\hat{\tau}_\beta\colon [n_\beta] \to [\hat{n}_\beta]$ such that $\hat{\tau}_\beta$ is injective on the subdomain $\tau_\beta^{-1}(l_\beta)$ for each $l_\beta \in [m'_\beta]$.

Then, we consider how we can apply any randomness in the ciphertext without causing incorrectness or insecurity. To this end, we analyze the AC16 ciphertext component C'', which is

$$\underbrace{\prod_{j\in[n_1],k\in[n_2]} g^{sA_{j,k}b_{j,k}}}_{C''_{\mathbf{A}}} \cdot \underbrace{\prod_{i\in\overline{[n_k]},j\in[n_1]} g^{s\rho(j)^i b'_{i,j}}}_{C''_{\rho}}.$$

For both parts $C''_{\mathbf{A}}$ and C''_{ρ}, we analyze with which randomness the randomness s needs to be replaced. As shown, the part associated with the access policy, i.e., $C''_{\mathbf{A}}$, is necessary to retrieve the secret $e(g,g)^{sA_{j,k}v_k}$, such that eventually $e(g,g)^{\alpha s}$ can be retrieved by computing $\prod_{j\in\Upsilon,k\in[n_2]} e(g,g)^{\varepsilon_j sA_{j,k}v_k}$. Note that, here, it is important that s is associated with $k = 1$ to ensure correctness of the scheme. However, for $k > 1$, we can use a different randomness. In short, for the $C''_{\mathbf{A}}$ part, we use the randomness associated with the m'_2 column partitions, which yields the transformation:

$$C''_{\mathbf{A}} \mapsto \prod_{j\in[n_1],k\in[n_2]} g^{s_{2,\tau_2(k)}A_{j,k}b_{\hat{\tau}_1(j),\hat{\tau}_2(k)}},$$

where we require that $s_{2,\tau_2(1)} = s$ to ensure correctness.

As shown, the part of C'' associated with the attribute mapping ρ, i.e., C''_{ρ}, ensures that the message is, albeit indirectly, sufficiently blinded. That is, in the "singling out" of row j, we could only obtain $\prod_k e(g,g)^{r_j sA_{j,k}b_{j,k}}$ (now: $\prod_k e(g,g)^{r_{j,\iota(\rho(j))}s_{2,\tau_2(k)}A_{j,k}b_{\hat{\tau}_1(j),\hat{\tau}_2(k)}}$) if we could cancel out $e(g,g)^{r_j s\rho(j)^i b'_{i,j}}$. This only worked if $\rho(j) \in \mathcal{S}$. In this case, using a fresh set $\{b'_{i,j}\}_{i\in\overline{[n_k]}}$ for each row j ensures that there is sufficient randomness for the entire partition. As such, it is straightforward that the C''_{ρ} part needs to be randomized for each partition of $\hat{n}_1$ rows, like in the removal of the bound on $\mathcal{S}$. For the row partitions, we had introduced the random integers s_{1,l_1} for each partition $l_1 \in [m'_1]$, and substituting s for these yields:

$$C''_{\rho} \mapsto \prod_{i\in\overline{[n_k]},j\in[n_1]} g^{s_{1,\tau_1(j)}\rho(j)^i b'_{i,\hat{\tau}_1(j)}}.$$

Finally, we point out that the randomizers s_{1,l_1} and s_{2,l_2} are only used in combination with the public keys $b'_{i,j}$ and $b_{j,k}$, respectively. In our proofs, it becomes clear that we can therefore set $s_{2,l_2} = s_{1,l_2}$ for all $l_2 \in [m'_2]$.

4.2 The Scheme

We give our scheme in the selective-security setting. A fully secure variant can be obtained by applying the AC17 [3] transformation to our PES (Sect. 4.3).

Definition 6 (TinyABE). *TinyABE is defined as follows.*

- Setup(λ): *On input the security parameter λ, the algorithm generates three groups $\mathbb{G}, \mathbb{H}, \mathbb{G}_T$ of prime order p with generators $g \in \mathbb{G}$ and $h \in \mathbb{H}$,* *and chooses a pairing* $e: \mathbb{G} \times \mathbb{H} \to \mathbb{G}_T$. *It sets the universe of attributes* $\mathcal{U} = \mathbb{Z}_p$, *and chooses* $\hat{n}_1 \in \mathbb{N}$ *and* $\hat{n}_2 \in \mathbb{N}$ *as the maximum number of rows and columns that fit into one partition, respectively. It also chooses* $n_k \in \mathbb{N}$, *which is the maximum partition size of the keys. It then generates random* $\alpha, b_{j,k}, b'_{i,j} \in_R \mathbb{Z}_p$ *for all* $i \in \overline{[n_k]}, j \in [\hat{n}_1], k \in [\hat{n}_2]$. *It outputs* $\mathrm{MSK} = (\alpha, \{b_{j,k}, b'_{i,j}\}_{i \in \overline{[n_k]}, j \in [\hat{n}_1], k \in [\hat{n}_2]})$ *as the master secret key and publishes the domain parameters* $(p, \mathbb{G}, \mathbb{H}, \mathbb{G}_T, \hat{n}_1, \hat{n}_2, n_k)$ *and the master public key as*

$$\mathrm{MPK} = (g, h, A = e(g,h)^{\alpha}, \{B_{j,k} = g^{b_{j,k}}, B'_{i,j} = g^{b'_{i,j}}\}_{i \in \overline{[n_k]}, j \in [\hat{n}_1], k \in [\hat{n}_2]}).$$

– KeyGen(MSK, $\mathcal{S}$): *On input a set of attributes* $\mathcal{S}$, *the algorithm computes* $m = \left\lceil \frac{|\mathcal{S}|}{n_k} \right\rceil$, *defines a partition mapping* $\iota: \mathcal{S} \to [m]$ *such that* $|\iota^{-1}(l)| \le n_k$ *for each* $l \in [m]$, *and generates random integers* $r_{j,l}, v_k \in_R \mathbb{Z}_p$ *for each* $j \in [\hat{n}_1], k \in [2, \hat{n}_2], l \in [m]$, *setting* $v_1 = \alpha$ *and computes the secret key as*

$$\mathrm{SK}_{\mathcal{S}} = (\{K_{1,j,l} = h^{r_{j,l}}, K_{2,j,k,l} = h^{r_{j,l} b_{j,k} - v_k}, K_{3,j,j',k,l} = h^{r_{j,l} b_{j',k}},$$

$$K_{4,j,\mathrm{att}} = h^{r_{j,\iota(\mathrm{att})} \sum_{i \in \overline{[n_k]}} x_{\mathrm{att}}^i b'_{i,j}}, K_{5,i,j,j',l} = h^{r_{j,l} b'_{i,j'}}\}_{\substack{j,j' \in [\hat{n}_1], j \ne j', k \in [\hat{n}_2], \\ i \in \overline{[n_k]}, l \in [m], \mathrm{att} \in \mathcal{S}}}).$$

– Encrypt(MPK, $\mathbb{A}$, M): *Message* $M \in \mathbb{G}_T$ *is encrypted under* $\mathbb{A} = (\mathbf{A}, \rho)$ *with* $\mathbf{A} \in \mathbb{Z}_p^{n_1 \times n_2}$ *and* $\rho: [n_1] \to \mathcal{U}$ *by computing* $m'_1 = \left\lceil \frac{n_1}{\hat{n}_1} \right\rceil$ *and* $m'_2 = \left\lceil \frac{n_2}{\hat{n}_2} \right\rceil$, *and defining partition mappings for each* $\beta \in [2]$: $\tau_\beta: [n_\beta] \to [m'_\beta]$ *such that* $|\tau_\beta^{-1}(l_\beta)| \le \hat{n}_\beta$ *for each* $l_\beta \in [m'_\beta]$. *For* τ_2, *we require that* $\tau_2(1) = 1$. *Define* $\hat{\tau}_\beta: [n_\beta] \to [\hat{n}_\beta]$ *such that* $\hat{\tau}_\beta$ *is injective on the subset* $\tau_\beta^{-1}(l_\beta)$ *for each* $l_\beta \in [m'_\beta]$. *Then, generate random integers* $s, s_{l'} \in_R \mathbb{Z}_p$ *for each* $l' \in [2, \max(m'_1, m'_2)]$, *and specifically set* $s_1 = s$, *and compute the ciphertext as*

$$\mathrm{CT}_{\mathbb{A}} = \big(C = M \cdot A^s, \{C_{l_1} = g^{s_{l_1}}\}_{l_1 \in [m'_1]}$$

$$C' = \prod_{j \in [n_1], k \in [n_2]} B_{\hat{\tau}_1(j), \hat{\tau}_2(k)}^{s_{\tau_2(k)} A_{j,k}} \prod_{i \in \overline{[n_k]}, j \in [n_1]} (B'_{i, \hat{\tau}_1(j)})^{s_{\tau_1(j)} \rho(j)^i} \big).$$

– Decrypt(SK$_{\mathcal{S}}$, CT$_{\mathbb{A}}$): *Suppose that* $\mathcal{S}$ *satisfies* $\mathbb{A}$, *let* $\Upsilon = \{j \in [n_1] \mid \rho(j) \in \mathcal{S}\}$. *Then,* $\{\varepsilon_j \in \mathbb{Z}_p\}_{j \in \Upsilon}$ *exist with* $\sum_{i \in \Upsilon} \varepsilon_j \mathbf{A}_j = (1, 0, ..., 0)$ *(Definition 1). Then, the plaintext* M *is retrieved by computing* $C \cdot C_2 \cdot C_3 \cdot C_4 \cdot C_5 / C_1$, *where*

$$C_1 = \prod_{j \in \Upsilon} e(C', K_{1, \hat{\tau}_1(j), \iota(\rho(j))}^{\varepsilon_j}), C_2 = \prod_{j \in \Upsilon, k \in [n_2]} e(C_{\tau_2(k)}, K_{2, \hat{\tau}_1(j), \hat{\tau}_2(k), \iota(\rho(j))}^{\varepsilon_j A_{j,k}}),$$

$$C_3 = \prod_{j \in \Upsilon, j' \in [n_1] \setminus \{j\}, k \in [n_2]} e(C_{\tau_2(k)}, K_{3, \hat{\tau}_1(j), \hat{\tau}_1(j'), \hat{\tau}_2(k), \iota(\rho(j))}^{\varepsilon_j A_{j',k}}),$$

$$C_4 = \prod_{j \in \Upsilon} e(C_{\tau_1(j)}, K_{4, \hat{\tau}_1(j), \rho(j)}^{\varepsilon_j}),$$

$$C_5 = \prod_{i \in \overline{[n_k]}, j \in \Upsilon, j' \in [n_1] \setminus \{j\}} e(C_{\tau_1(j')}, K_{5, i, \hat{\tau}_1(j), \hat{\tau}_1(j'), \iota(\rho(j))}^{\varepsilon_j \rho(j')^i}).$$

The scheme is correct (see the full version [49]).

4.3   The Associated Pair Encoding Scheme

To prove security, we define the pair encoding of TinyABE, for which we use the variables $\hat{n}_1, \hat{n}_2, n_k, \mathcal{S}, \iota, \rho, \tau_1, \tau_2, \hat{\tau}_1, \hat{\tau}_2, n_1, n_2, \lambda_i, m, m_1', m_2'$ from Definition 6.

Definition 7 (PES for TinyABE).

- Param(par) $\rightarrow \hat{n}_1(\hat{n}_2 + n_k)$. Let $\mathbf{b} = (\{b_{j,k}, b_{i,j}'\}_{i \in \overline{[n_k]}, j \in [\hat{n}_1], k \in [\hat{n}_2]})$.
- EncK$(\mathcal{S}) \rightarrow \mathbf{k}(\mathbf{r}, \hat{\mathbf{r}}, \mathbf{b})$, where

$$\mathbf{k}(\mathbf{r}, \hat{\mathbf{r}}, \mathbf{b}) = (\{k_{2,j,k,l} = r_{j,l}b_{j,k} - v_k, k_{3,j,j',k,l} = r_{j,l}b_{j',k},$$

$$k_{4,j,\text{att}} = r_{j,\iota(\text{att})} \sum_{i \in [n_k]} x_{\text{att}}^i b_{i,j}', k_{5,i,j,j',l} = r_{j,l}b_{i,j'}\}_{\substack{i \in \overline{[n_k]}, j,j' \in [\hat{n}_1], j \neq j', \\ k \in [\hat{n}_2], l \in [m], \text{att} \in \mathcal{S}}}),$$

and $\mathbf{r} = (\{r_{j,l}\}_{j \in [n_1], l \in [m]})$ are non-lone variables and $\hat{\mathbf{r}} = (\{v_k\}_{k \in [2, n_2]})$ are lone variables.

- EncC$((\mathbf{A}, \rho)) \rightarrow \mathbf{c}(\mathbf{s}, \hat{\mathbf{s}}, \mathbf{b}) = (c')$, where

$$c' = \sum_{j \in [n_1], k \in [n_2]} s_{\tau_2(k)} A_{j,k} b_{\hat{\tau}_1(j), \hat{\tau}_2(k)} + \sum_{i \in \overline{[n_k]}, j \in [n_1]} s_{\tau_1(j)} \rho(j)^i b_{i, \hat{\tau}_1(j)}'$$

and we have non-lone variables $\mathbf{s} = (\{s_{l'}\}_{l' \in [\max(m_1', m_2')]})$.

Theorem 1. *The PES for TinyABE in Definition 7 satisfies the symbolic property (Definition 5).*

5   Security Proof

We prove security of TinyABE (Definition 7) by proving symbolic security of our PES. This yields a fully secure scheme with the generic transformation in the AC17 [3] framework. In particular, we prove the selective and co-selective security properties (Definition 5) in Sects. 5.2 and 5.3, respectively. Before that, we show in Sect. 5.1 how we combine the AC17 [4] symbolic proofs of AC16 [1], and the selective security proofs of RW13 [41].

5.1   "Unbounding" the AC17 Proof of AC16

We elevate the AC17 [4] proof of the AC16 [1] (see the full version [49] for a summary) to the unbounded setting by applying the techniques of Rouselakis and Waters [41]. (Note that, although we explain our methodology for the selective property, it is similar for the co-selective property.) Roughly speaking, with their layering techniques, we embed all row attributes that are mapped to the same public-key components $b_{i,j}'$ and $b_{j,k}$ for $j \in [\hat{n}_1]$ in these public-key components. Then, we use the individual randomness techniques of Rouselakis and Waters shared by all row attributes in the same row partition to ensure that only the attribute layer associated with the partition is singled out in the challenge phase. We do something similar for the column partitions.

More specifically, for the challenge ciphertext polynomials to evaluate to $\mathbf{0}$ (as needed for the symbolic property (Definition 5)), we require the following substitutions. The public key $b'_{i,j}$ "embeds" all rows $j' \in [n_1]$ that are mapped to row $j \in [\hat{n}_1]$ with $\hat{\tau}_1$. For each of these rows (and their corresponding attribute), the individual randomness associated with its partition—to which it is mapped with τ_1—is used. Similarly, the substituted public key $b_{j,k}$ "embeds" all columns that are mapped to column $k \in [\hat{n}_2]$, which are randomized with the individual randomness for each corresponding partition. In this way, during the "challenge phase", the layers associated with the ciphertext partitions $l_1 \in [m'_1]$ and $l_2 \in [m'_2]$ (for the rows and columns, respectively) can be singled out for each public-key variable $b_{j,k}$ and $b'_{i,j}$. This works, because each public-key component only uses each partition randomness at most once (due to the restriction that $\hat{\tau}_\beta$ is injective on each subdomain $\tau_\beta^{-1}(l_\beta)$ with $l_\beta \in [m'_\beta]$).

For the "key query phase", the AC17 proof is adapted as follows. We embed another individual randomness, for each row $j' \in [n_1]$ that is mapped to row $j \in [\hat{n}_1]$, in the public-key variables $b'_{i,j}$, and we embed another individual randomness associated with the i-th coefficient. In particular, we embed the same polynomial as in the AC17 proof, but instead we embed one for each row j' that is mapped to j with $\hat{\tau}_1$. That is, we define an n_k-degree polynomial that yields 0 if $\rho(j')$ is plugged in. We embed the polynomials for which the roots are the attributes in the partition—like in the AC17 proof—for each row attribute. This ensures that the substituted encoding associated with $K_{4,j,\mathrm{att}}$ evaluates to $\mathbf{0}$.

5.2   The Selective Property

Our PES satisfies the selective security property. Let $\chi_{1,j} = \{j' \in [n_1] \mid \hat{\tau}_1(j') = \hat{\tau}_1(j)\}$ and $\chi_{2,k} = \{k' \in [n_2] \mid \hat{\tau}_2(k') = \hat{\tau}_2(k)\}$ for all $j \in [\hat{n}_1], k \in [\hat{n}_2]$. Let Υ as before and set $\overline{\Upsilon} = [n_1] \setminus \Upsilon$. Because $\mathcal{S}$ does not satisfy $\mathbb{A}$, there exists $\mathbf{w} = (1, w_2, ..., w_{n_2}) \in \mathbb{Z}_p^{n_2}$ such that $\mathbf{A}_j \mathbf{w}^\mathsf{T} = 0$ for all $j \in \Upsilon$ (Definition 1). Let $\hat{G}_{j,k}(x_{\mathrm{att}}) = \sum_{i \in [n_k]}(x_{\mathrm{att}}^i - \rho(j)^i)\mathbf{1}_{(i,j,k),\tau_1(j)}^{d_1 \times d_2}$ for all $j \in [n_1], k \in [n_2]$. Let $\Psi_l = \{\mathrm{att} \in \mathcal{S} \mid \iota(\mathrm{att}) = l\}$ be the l-th partition of $\mathcal{S}$ for all $l \in [m]$. Then, for each $l \in [m]$, we define $G_l(x_{\mathrm{att}}) = \prod_{\mathrm{att}' \in \Psi_l}(x_{\mathrm{att}} - x_{\mathrm{att}'}) = \sum_{i=0}^{n_k} u_{i,l} x_{\mathrm{att}}^i$. We make the following substitutions:

$$b'_{0,j} \ : \ \sum_{j' \in \chi_{1,j}, k' \in [n_2]} A_{j',k'}\left(\mathbf{1}_{(j',k'),\tau_1(j')}^{d_1 \times d_2} - \sum_{i' \in [n_k]} \rho(j')^{i'} \mathbf{1}_{(i',j',k'),\tau_1(j')}^{d_1 \times d_2}\right)$$

$$b'_{i,j} \ : \ \sum_{j' \in \chi_{1,j}, k' \in [n_2]} A_{j',k'}\mathbf{1}_{(i,j',k'),\tau_1(j')}^{d_1 \times d_2}$$

$$b_{j,k} \ : \ -\sum_{k' \in \chi_{2,k}} \mathbf{1}_{(j,k),\tau_2(k')}^{d_1 \times d_2}, \quad s_{l'} \ : \ \overline{\mathbf{1}}_{l'}^{d_2}, \quad v_k \ : \ -w_k\left(\sum_{k' \in \chi_{2,k}} \overline{\mathbf{1}}_{\tau_2(k')}^{d_2}\right)$$

$$r_{j,l} \ : \ \sum_{k' \in [n_2]} w_{k'}\left(\mathbf{1}_{(j,k')}^{d_1} - \sum_{i' \in [n_k], j' \in \chi_{1,j} \cap \overline{\Upsilon}} \frac{u_{i',l}}{G_l(\rho(j'))}\mathbf{1}_{(i',j',k')}^{d_1}\right)$$

for all $i \in [n_k], j \in [\hat{n}_1], k \in [\hat{n}_2], l \in [m], l' \in [\max(m'_1, m'_2)]$, where the row indices (j, k) and (i, j, k) are mapped injectively in the interval $[(n_k + 2)n_1 n_2]$. We have $d_1 = (n_k + 2)n_1 n_2$ and $d_2 = \max(m'_1, m'_2)$. It follows quickly that the polynomials evaluate to $\mathbf{0}$ (see the full version [49]).

5.3 The Co-selective Property

For the co-selective property, we generalize the co-selective proof by Agrawal and Chase [4]. In this proof, the coefficients of the polynomials $G_l(x_{att})$ are embedded in the variables $b'_{i,j}$. We make the following substitutions:

$$
b'_{i,j} : \sum_{l \in [m]} u_{i,l} \mathbf{1}^{d_1 \times d_2}_{(j,l),(1,j,l)}, \quad b_{j,k} : \sum_{l \in [m]} \mathbf{1}^{d_1 \times d_2}_{(j,l),(2,k)}, \quad v_k : \overline{\mathbf{1}}^{d_2}_{(2,k)},
$$

$$
r_{j,l} : \mathbf{1}^{d_1}_{j,l}, \quad s_{l'} : \sum_{k \in \tau_2^{-1}(l')} w_k \overline{\mathbf{1}}^{d_2}_{2,\hat{\tau}_2(k)} - \sum_{j \in \tau_1^{-1}(l') \cap \overline{\Upsilon}, l \in [m]} \frac{\mathbf{A}_j \mathbf{w}^\mathsf{T}}{G_l(\rho(j))} \overline{\mathbf{1}}^{d_2}_{(1, \hat{\tau}_1(j), l)}
$$

for all $i \in [n_k], j \in [\hat{n}_1], k \in [\hat{n}_2], l \in [m], l' \in [\max(m'_1, m'_2)]$, where the row indices (j, l) are mapped injectively in the interval $[d_1]$, and the column indices $(1, j, l)$ and $(2, k)$ in the interval $[d_2]$, where $d_1 = \hat{n}_1 m$ and $d_2 = \hat{n}_1 m + \hat{n}_2$. It follows quickly that the polynomials go to $\mathbf{0}$ (see the full version [49]).

6 Performance Analysis

We analyze the performance of TinyABE for two configurations relevant to IoT settings. To illustrate the efficiency trade-offs and the advantages of TinyABE more clearly, we compare the efficiency of the two configurations with two large-universe CP-ABE schemes: one with linear-size ciphertexts and one with constant-size ciphertexts. In particular, we compare RW13 [41], which is an unbounded CP-ABE scheme with linear-size ciphertexts, and the version of AC16 [1] with unbounded attribute sets and constant-size ciphertexts: Att19 [8]. To effectively compare the efficiency of all relevant schemes, we run benchmarks for various group operations in RELIC [6], and extrapolate the computational costs of the schemes by counting the number of operations required by the algorithms. In particular, we use the pairing-friendly elliptic-curve group BLS12-381 [13,17] for our analysis. For this curve, Scott has recently performed measurements on several IoT devices [44], which we will use in our analysis in Sect. 6.3. RELIC [6] supports efficient constant-time implementations for "regular" exponentiations and two special types of exponentiation: fixed-base and multi-base exponentiation. In a fixed-base exponentiation, the base g to be exponentiated in g^x is fixed after setup, and as such, a precomputation table can be made to speed up the computation [19]. In a multi-base exponentiation, the product of multiple exponentiations, e.g., $g_1^{x_1} \ldots g_n^{x_n}$, is computed [38]. We have run these benchmarks on a 1.6 GHz Intel i5-8250U processor[3] (see the full version [49]).

---

[3] Our code is available as a Jupyter notebook at https://github.com/mtcvenema/tinyabe.

We compare the schemes as follows. For a fair comparison, we place all of them in the selective-security and prime-order setting. We then convert the schemes to the asymmetric setting using the same optimization approaches [40]. For each scheme, we optimize the encryption efficiency[4], e.g., by placing each ciphertext component in $\mathbb{G}$. (In the full version [49], we give a full description of RW13. Att19 is a special case of TinyABE, where $\hat{n}_1$ and $\hat{n}_2$ are the upper bounds on the access policies used during encryption.) Afterwards, we convert the results to match the most efficient variant in the full-security setting by applying the generic transformation in the AC17 [3] framework, which incurs roughly twice the costs. To obtain the most efficient implementation of encryption and decryption, we assume that the access policies used during encryption are Boolean formulas. Any Boolean formula can be converted to an LSSS matrix with matrix entries $A_{j,k}$ in $\{-1, 0, 1\}$, and coefficients ε_j in $\{0, 1\}$ [35].

6.1   Computational Costs of TinyABE

We list the computational costs of the key generation, encryption and decryption algorithms by listing the number of group operations required by these (see the full version [49] for further details on our analysis):

- **Key generation:** $\hat{n}_1(m + \hat{n}_1\hat{n}_2 m + |\mathcal{S}| + n_k(\hat{n}_1 - 1)m)$ fixed-base exponentiations in $\mathbb{H}$;
- **Encryption:** one exponentiation in $\mathbb{G}_T$, m fixed-base exponentiations in $\mathbb{G}$, one $(n_k \min(\hat{n}_1, |\Upsilon|))$-multi-base exponentiation in $\mathbb{G}$, the minimum of the following two costs:
  - one $(\hat{n}_1\hat{n}_2)$-multi-base exponentiation in $\mathbb{G}$;
  - one m_2'-multi-base exponentiation in $\mathbb{G}$ and $n_1 n_2$ multiplications in $\mathbb{G}$;
  and the minimum of the following two costs:
  - one $\hat{n}_1$-multi-base-exponentiation in $\mathbb{G}$;
  - one m_1'-multi-base exponentiation and n_1 multiplications in $\mathbb{G}$.

(Note that the ciphertext component C' can be computed in multiple ways, which we show in more detail in the full version [49]. Specifically, the costs are upper bounded by a constant.)

- **Decryption:** one $(m_1' + 1)$-multi-pairing operation, and $|\Upsilon|\hat{n}_1 n_2 + n_k n_1$ exponentiations and $(|\Upsilon| - 2)n_k n_1 + 2|\Upsilon|$ multiplications in $\mathbb{H}$.

To convert these costs to the full-security setting (using the most efficient transformation in [3]), we multiply the costs in $\mathbb{G}$ and $\mathbb{H}$ by a factor 2.

---

[4] In the full version [49], we explain how a more balanced encryption-decryption efficiency can be attained.

Two Configurations of TinyABE. To investigate the feasibility of TinyABE in IoT settings, we analyze the efficiency of TinyABE for two configurations, i.e.,

1. where encryption is optimal: $(n_k, \hat{n}_1, \hat{n}_2) = (1, 3, 3)$;
2. where ciphertexts are small: $(n_k, \hat{n}_1, \hat{n}_2) = (1, 13, 13)$.

In particular, for the latter configuration, the ciphertexts are small enough such that they fit in one Ethernet packet for policy sizes $|\mathbb{A}| \leq 100$. In the full version [49], we give further details on how the parameters can be chosen.

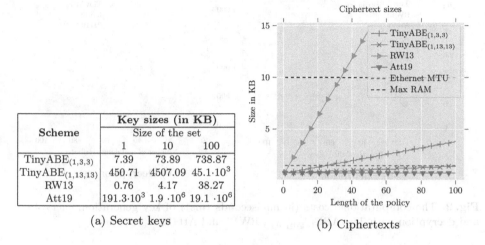

Scheme	Key sizes (in KB)		
	Size of the set		
	1	10	100
TinyABE$_{(1,3,3)}$	7.39	73.89	738.87
TinyABE$_{(1,13,13)}$	450.71	4507.09	$45.1 \cdot 10^3$
RW13	0.76	4.17	38.27
Att19	$191.3 \cdot 10^3$	$1.9 \cdot 10^6$	$19.1 \cdot 10^6$

(a) Secret keys

(b) Ciphertexts

Fig. 1. The key and ciphertext sizes of TinyABE$_{(n_k, \hat{n}_1, \hat{n}_2)}$, RW13 and Att19.

6.2   Comparison with RW13 and AC16/Att19

We compare the efficiency of TinyABE with RW13, a scheme with linear-size ciphertexts and Att19, the variant of AC16 with constant-size ciphertexts that is unbounded in sets $\mathcal{S}$. In particular, we focus on the ciphertext size and encryption efficiency, as ultimately, we want to optimize the scheme for low-quality networks and resource-constrained encryption devices. For all schemes, we require that they can support any $|\mathbb{A}|, |\mathcal{S}| \leq 100$, thus we set the upper bounds N_1, N_2 of Att19 on the number of rows and columns to $N_1 = N_2 = 100$. Because the key sizes and the key generation costs are linear and the differences between the schemes are large, we put those results in tables, and the rest in graphs.

Storage Costs. As Fig. 1 shows, our secret keys are generally much larger than RW13. Nevertheless, our ciphertexts are much smaller. Our scheme's configurations never exceed the maximum RAM size, and TinyABE$_{(1,13,13)}$ never exceeds the maximum transmission unit (MTU), which we show to be beneficial

Scheme	Key generation costs (in ms)		
	Size of the set		
	1	10	100
TinyABE$_{(1,3,3)}$	20.3	202.8	$2 \cdot 10^3$
TinyABE$_{(1,13,13)}$	$1.2 \cdot 10^3$	$12.4 \cdot 10^3$	$123.7 \cdot 10^3$ (≈ 2 minutes)
RW13	2.1	11.4	105.1
Att19	$525.3 \cdot 10^3$ (> 8 minutes)	$5.3 \cdot 10^6$ (> 1 hour)	$52.5 \cdot 10^6$ (> 14 hours)

(a) Key generation

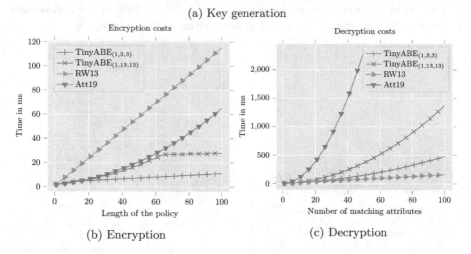

(b) Encryption   (c) Decryption

Fig. 2. The computational costs (in milliseconds (ms)) of key generation, encryption and decryption with TinyABE$_{(n_k, \hat{n}_1, \hat{n}_2)}$, RW13 and Att19.

in Sect. 6.3. Compared to Att19, our keys are much smaller, while our ciphertexts are marginally larger. Importantly, our master public key is, at most, 19.13 KB, in contrast to the 957 KB of Att19. In Sect. 6.3, we show that our scheme can thus be used in resource-constrained devices while Att19 cannot.

Computational Costs. Similarly, Fig. 2 shows that our key generation and decryption costs are higher than RW13, but our encryption is much more efficient. We show in Sect. 6.3 that this gain in encryption efficiency can make a difference between deployment or not, as it reduces the encryption timings on resource-constrained devices from minutes to mere seconds. (Also note that our key generation can be extended to an online/offline variant (see the full version [49]). This allows the authority that generates keys to prepare many keys in advance (e.g., 0.7-44 MB per 100 attributes for $(n_k, \hat{n}_1, \hat{n}_2) \in \{(1, 3, 3), (1, 13, 13)\}$), which mitigates any potential issues caused by the large costs.) Moreover, all of our configurations outperform Att19, notably reducing the key generation costs to more feasible timings. While Att19 takes at least eight minutes to compute a key, our scheme never requires more than two minutes, even for large sets.

Comparison with Other Linear-Sized Schemes. The main reason why we compare our scheme with RW13 is because it is closely related to our scheme, and because it has linear-size ciphertexts and it is unbounded. In addition, to illustrate the advantages of TinyABE in IoT settings, we want to compare mainly its encryption (and the public key and ciphertext sizes) with a linear-sized scheme such as RW13. Because encryption with other popular large-universe schemes [2,5,15] is roughly as efficient as RW13 (see the full version [49]), we expect that TinyABE compares similarly as favorably to those schemes as to RW13.

6.3   Advantages in Low-Quality Networks and Constrained Devices

We showcase some practical advantages of TinyABE in IoT settings.

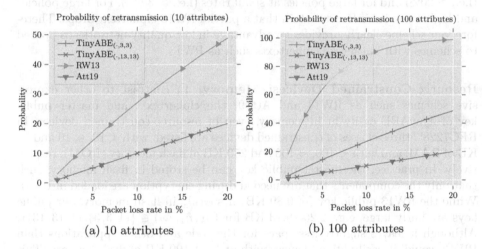

(a) 10 attributes   (b) 100 attributes

Fig. 3. The probability that a partial ciphertext needs to be retransmitted for various packet loss rates.

Packet Loss in Low-Quality Networks. One of the main features of TinyABE is that the ciphertexts can be configured to be small, which is beneficial in low-quality networks. In general, large ciphertexts may increase the risk that at least one of the packets is dropped during transmission, in which case the dropped packets need to be retransmitted [39], delaying the message's time of arrival. This may be problematic for resource-constrained devices, such as IoT devices, because their communication channels are often characterized by high packet loss rates (see RFC8576[5]). Furthermore, they may not be able to fit the ciphertext in memory, and risk having to recompute the ciphertexts (which may be slow).

---

[5] https://tools.ietf.org/html/rfc8576.

Through an example, we briefly illustrate that the increase in size of the ciphertext may increase the probability that one of the packets drops. For this example, we use a similar approach as in [39]. We consider the maximum transmission unit (MTU) of an Ethernet connection, i.e., 1500 bytes, and consider varying packet loss rates between 1% and 20%, with steps of 1%. In general, if we consider the shortest round-trip time, then the expected additional time incurred by re-transmitting a packet is 6.193 ms. In comparison, we can encrypt a message under a policy of length 20 with our least efficient configuration of our scheme in that time (Fig. 2), so this additional overhead is relevant in practice. To illustrate the effect of packet loss on the efficiency of the scheme, we analyze the probability that at least a part of the ciphertext is dropped in Fig. 3. As the figures show, TinyABE never exceeds 50%, even for large policies and high packet loss rates. In contrast, for small policies, RW13 exceeds 50% at high rates (i.e., $> 20\%$) and for large policies at small rates (i.e., $> 3.5\%$). For large policies and high rates, it is almost certain that a partial RW13 ciphertext drops. Therefore, our scheme clearly provides an advantage in low-quality networks compared to schemes with linear-size ciphertexts such as RW13.

Resource-Constrained Devices: Memory. In contrast to other expressive schemes such as RW13 and Att19, the ciphertexts and master public key of TinyABE easily fit in memory, even of resource-constrained devices. In RFC7228[6], three classes of constrained devices are listed: with < 10, ≈ 10 and 50 KB of RAM, and with < 100, ≈ 100 and 250 KB of flash memory (ROM), respectively. In practice, the master public key can be stored in flash memory, such that only the components that are needed during encryption are loaded in RAM. While the RW13 public key (of 0.89 KB) fits easily in flash memory, our public keys are fairly large, e.g., 2.25-19.13 KB for $(n_k, \hat{n}_1, \hat{n}_2) \in \{(1, 3, 3), (1, 13, 13)\}$. Although it leaves slightly less space for the code and other applications than RW13 would, it easily fits in devices with at least 100 KB of flash memory. This is not the case for the Att19 scheme, as the master public key of 957 KB is much larger than 100 KB for maximum policy length 30 or higher.

Additionally, while the ciphertexts of our scheme as well as the RW13 scheme would easily fit in 50 KB of RAM (even for large policies), it would be more problematic for devices with only 10 KB of RAM to fit RW13 ciphertexts. In fact, a ciphertext with policy length 33 already pushes the limit of 10 KB, and leaves no space for anything else, such as payload, additional overhead incurred by the computation, or optimization through precomputation. As such, trade-offs need to be made, e.g., by limiting the size of the access policy or by streaming out partially computed ciphertexts. In contrast, TinyABE's ciphertexts easily fit in 10 KB of memory, even for large policies. For $\hat{n}_1 = 3$ and policy length $n_1 = 100$, the size of the ciphertext is 3.84 KB. For $\hat{n}_1 = 13$, the size of the ciphertext is 1.41 KB, which leaves an ample 8.59 KB of memory for e.g., the payload and optimization through precomputation. In this way, we may be able to gain some significant speedup [28]. Furthermore, because the ciphertext fits

---

[6] https://tools.ietf.org/html/rfc7228.

entirely in memory, the device can retain it, until it has been notified by the intended receiver that the ciphertext has arrived successfully.

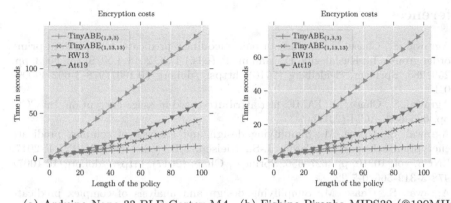

(a) Arduino Nano 33 BLE Cortex-M4   (b) Fishino Piranha MIPS32 (@120MHz)

Fig. 4. Conservative estimates of the encryption costs on two IoT devices.

Resource-constrained Devices: Speed. As shown, for some parameter choices, our scheme provides fast encryption, even for large inputs. For instance, for $(n_k, \hat{n}_1) = (1, 3)$, our encryption algorithm is several factors faster than RW13, which may be desirable for resource-constrained devices. Recently, Scott [44] tested the performance of some operations on the BLS12-381 curve on IoT devices. These results show that the devices with the slowest and fastest timings would approximately require 1.175 and 0.075 s, respectively, per exponentiation in $\mathbb{G}$. In Fig. 4, we estimate the encryption costs for the two fastest devices measured in [44]. For the fastest device, our most efficient configuration requires only 7.6 s to encrypt with a policy of length 100, while RW13 requires one minute and 15 s.

7 Future Work

Our work paves the way for further improvements of ABE in IoT settings. While we have theoretically analyzed the feasibility of implementing our schemes in practical settings such as low-quality networks and embedded devices, it would be useful to empirically test them. Notably, our conservative estimates for the IoT devices in Sect. 6.3 are based on the benchmarks in [44]. By implementing the scheme—possibly using optimizations (e.g., through precomputation [28]) that have not been used in [44] or using curves with more efficient arithmetic in $\mathbb{G}$ [23]—it may perform even better than our estimates suggest. Finally, because our scheme is proven secure in the AC17 [3] framework, its security relies on a q-type assumption [16,18]. Even though existing attacks [22] have not been shown to break that specific q-type assumption, from a theoretical point of view, it might be preferable to rely on non-parametrized assumptions [12,37].

References

1. Agrawal, S., Chase, M.: A study of pair encodings: predicate encryption in prime order groups. In: Kushilevitz, E., Malkin, T. (eds.) TCC 2016. LNCS, vol. 9563, pp. 259–288. Springer, Heidelberg (2016). https://doi.org/10.1007/978-3-662-49099-0_10
2. Agrawal, S., Chase, M.: FAME: fast attribute-based message encryption. In: CCS, pp. 665–682. ACM (2017)
3. Agrawal, S., Chase, M.: Simplifying design and analysis of complex predicate encryption schemes. In: Coron, J.-S., Nielsen, J.B. (eds.) EUROCRYPT 2017. LNCS, vol. 10210, pp. 627–656. Springer, Cham (2017). https://doi.org/10.1007/978-3-319-56620-7_22
4. Agrawal, S., Chase, M.: Simplifying design and analysis of complex predicate encryption schemes. Cryptology ePrint Archive, Report 2017/233 (2017)
5. Ambrona, M., Barthe, G., Gay, R., Wee, H.: Attribute-based encryption in the generic group model: automated proofs and new constructions. In: CCS, pp. 647–664. ACM (2017)
6. Aranha, D.F., Gouvêa, C.P.L., Markmann, T., Wahby, R.S., Liao, K.: RELIC is an Efficient LIbrary for Cryptography. https://github.com/relic-toolkit/relic
7. Attrapadung, N.: Dual system encryption via doubly selective security: framework, fully secure functional encryption for regular languages, and more. In: Nguyen, P.Q., Oswald, E. (eds.) EUROCRYPT 2014. LNCS, vol. 8441, pp. 557–577. Springer, Heidelberg (2014). https://doi.org/10.1007/978-3-642-55220-5_31
8. Attrapadung, N.: Unbounded dynamic predicate compositions in attribute-based encryption. In: Ishai, Y., Rijmen, V. (eds.) EUROCRYPT 2019. LNCS, vol. 11476, pp. 34–67. Springer, Cham (2019). https://doi.org/10.1007/978-3-030-17653-2_2
9. Attrapadung, N., Hanaoka, G., Matsumoto, T., Teruya, T., Yamada, S.: Attribute based encryption with direct efficiency tradeoff. In: Manulis, M., Sadeghi, A.-R., Schneider, S. (eds.) ACNS 2016. LNCS, vol. 9696, pp. 249–266. Springer, Cham (2016). https://doi.org/10.1007/978-3-319-39555-5_14
10. Attrapadung, N., Hanaoka, G., Yamada, S.: Conversions among several classes of predicate encryption and applications to ABE with various compactness tradeoffs. In: Iwata, T., Cheon, J.H. (eds.) ASIACRYPT 2015. LNCS, vol. 9452, pp. 575–601. Springer, Heidelberg (2015). https://doi.org/10.1007/978-3-662-48797-6_24
11. Attrapadung, N., Libert, B., de Panafieu, E.: Expressive key-policy attribute-based encryption with constant-size ciphertexts. In: Catalano, D., Fazio, N., Gennaro, R., Nicolosi, A. (eds.) PKC 2011. LNCS, vol. 6571, pp. 90–108. Springer, Heidelberg (2011). https://doi.org/10.1007/978-3-642-19379-8_6
12. Attrapadung, N., Tomida, J.: Unbounded dynamic predicate compositions in ABE from standard assumptions. In: Moriai, S., Wang, H. (eds.) ASIACRYPT 2020. LNCS, vol. 12493, pp. 405–436. Springer, Cham (2020). https://doi.org/10.1007/978-3-030-64840-4_14
13. Barreto, P.S.L.M., Lynn, B., Scott, M.: Constructing elliptic curves with prescribed embedding degrees. In: Cimato, S., Persiano, G., Galdi, C. (eds.) SCN 2002. LNCS, vol. 2576, pp. 257–267. Springer, Heidelberg (2003). https://doi.org/10.1007/3-540-36413-7_19

14. Beimel, A.: Secure schemes for secret sharing and key distribution. Ph.D thesis, Ben Gurion University (1996)
15. Bethencourt, J., Sahai, A., Waters, B.: Ciphertext-policy attribute-based encryption. In: S&P, pp. 321–334. IEEE (2007)
16. Boneh, D., Boyen, X., Goh, E.-J.: Hierarchical identity based encryption with constant size ciphertext. In: Cramer, R. (ed.) EUROCRYPT 2005. LNCS, vol. 3494, pp. 440–456. Springer, Heidelberg (2005). https://doi.org/10.1007/11426639_26
17. Bowe, S.: Bls12-381: New zk-snark elliptic curve construction. https://blog.z.cash/new-snark-curve/
18. Boyen, X.: The uber-assumption family. In: Galbraith, S.D., Paterson, K.G. (eds.) Pairing 2008. LNCS, vol. 5209, pp. 39–56. Springer, Heidelberg (2008). https://doi.org/10.1007/978-3-540-85538-5_3
19. Brickell, E.F., Gordon, D.M., McCurley, K.S., Wilson, D.B.: Fast exponentiation with precomputation. In: Rueppel, R.A. (ed.) EUROCRYPT 1992. LNCS, vol. 658, pp. 200–207. Springer, Heidelberg (1993). https://doi.org/10.1007/3-540-47555-9_18
20. Chen, C., et al.: Fully secure attribute-based systems with short ciphertexts/signatures and threshold access structures. In: Dawson, E. (ed.) CT-RSA 2013. LNCS, vol. 7779, pp. 50–67. Springer, Heidelberg (2013). https://doi.org/10.1007/978-3-642-36095-4_4
21. Chen, C., Zhang, Z., Feng, D.: Efficient ciphertext policy attribute-based encryption with constant-size ciphertext and constant computation-cost. In: Boyen, X., Chen, X. (eds.) ProvSec 2011. LNCS, vol. 6980, pp. 84–101. Springer, Heidelberg (2011). https://doi.org/10.1007/978-3-642-24316-5_8
22. Cheon, J.H.: Security analysis of the strong Diffie-Hellman problem. In: Vaudenay, S. (ed.) EUROCRYPT 2006. LNCS, vol. 4004, pp. 1–11. Springer, Heidelberg (2006). https://doi.org/10.1007/11761679_1
23. Clarisse, R., Duquesne, S., Sanders, O.: Curves with fast computations in the first pairing group. In: Krenn, S., Shulman, H., Vaudenay, S. (eds.) CANS 2020. LNCS, vol. 12579, pp. 280–298. Springer, Cham (2020). https://doi.org/10.1007/978-3-030-65411-5_14
24. Emura, K., Miyaji, A., Nomura, A., Omote, K., Soshi, M.: A ciphertext-policy attribute-based encryption scheme with constant ciphertext length. In: Bao, F., Li, H., Wang, G. (eds.) ISPEC 2009. LNCS, vol. 5451, pp. 13–23. Springer, Heidelberg (2009). https://doi.org/10.1007/978-3-642-00843-6_2
25. ETSI: ETSI TS 103 458 (V1.1.1). Technical specification, European Telecommunications Standards Institute (ETSI) (2018)
26. ETSI: ETSI TS 103 532 (V1.1.1). Technical specification, European Telecommunications Standards Institute (ETSI) (2018)
27. ETSI: Even more advanced cryptography - industry applications and use cases for advanced cryptography. Technical report, European Telecommunications Standards Institute (ETSI) (2020)
28. Fujii, H., Aranha, D.F.: Curve25519 for the Cortex-M4 and beyond. In: Lange, T., Dunkelman, O. (eds.) LATINCRYPT 2017. LNCS, vol. 11368, pp. 109–127. Springer, Cham (2019). https://doi.org/10.1007/978-3-030-25283-0_6
29. Goyal, V., Pandey, O., Sahai, A., Waters, B.: Attribute-based encryption for fine-grained access control of encrypted data. In: CCS. ACM (2006)
30. Goyal, V., Pandey, O., Sahai, A., Waters, B.: Attribute-based encryption for fine-grained access control of encrypted data. Cryptology ePrint Archive, Report 2006/309 (2006)

31. Herranz, J., Laguillaumie, F., Ràfols, C.: Constant size ciphertexts in threshold attribute-based encryption. In: Nguyen, P.Q., Pointcheval, D. (eds.) PKC 2010. LNCS, vol. 6056, pp. 19–34. Springer, Heidelberg (2010). https://doi.org/10.1007/978-3-642-13013-7_2

32. Hülsing, A., Rijneveld, J., Schwabe, P.: ARMed SPHINCS. In: Cheng, C.-M., Chung, K.-M., Persiano, G., Yang, B.-Y. (eds.) PKC 2016. LNCS, vol. 9614, pp. 446–470. Springer, Heidelberg (2016). https://doi.org/10.1007/978-3-662-49384-7_17

33. Kamara, S., Lauter, K.: Cryptographic cloud storage. In: Sion, R., et al. (eds.) FC 2010. LNCS, vol. 6054, pp. 136–149. Springer, Heidelberg (2010). https://doi.org/10.1007/978-3-642-14992-4_13

34. Kumar, S., Hu, Y., Andersen, M.P., Popa, R.A., Culler, D.E.: JEDI: many-to-many end-to-end encryption and key delegation for IoT. In: 28th USENIX Security Symposium, pp. 1519–1536. USENIX Association (2019)

35. Lewko, A., Waters, B.: Decentralizing attribute-based encryption. Cryptology ePrint Archive, Report 2010/351 (2010)

36. Lewko, A., Waters, B.: Unbounded HIBE and attribute-based encryption. In: Paterson, K.G. (ed.) EUROCRYPT 2011. LNCS, vol. 6632, pp. 547–567. Springer, Heidelberg (2011). https://doi.org/10.1007/978-3-642-20465-4_30

37. Lin, H., Luo, J.: Succinct and adaptively secure ABE for ABP from k-Lin. In: Moriai, S., Wang, H. (eds.) ASIACRYPT 2020. LNCS, vol. 12493, pp. 437–466. Springer, Cham (2020). https://doi.org/10.1007/978-3-030-64840-4_15

38. Möller, B.: Algorithms for multi-exponentiation. In: Vaudenay, S., Youssef, A.M. (eds.) SAC 2001. LNCS, vol. 2259, pp. 165–180. Springer, Heidelberg (2001). https://doi.org/10.1007/3-540-45537-X_13

39. Paquin, C., Stebila, D., Tamvada, G.: Benchmarking post-quantum cryptography in TLS. In: Ding, J., Tillich, J.-P. (eds.) PQCrypto 2020. LNCS, vol. 12100, pp. 72–91. Springer, Cham (2020). https://doi.org/10.1007/978-3-030-44223-1_5

40. de la Piedra, A., Venema, M., Alpár, G.: ABE squared: accurately benchmarking efficiency of attribute-based encryption. TCHES **2022**(2), 192–239 (2022)

41. Rouselakis, Y., Waters, B.: Practical constructions and new proof methods for large universe attribute-based encryption. In: CCS, pp. 463–474. ACM (2013)

42. Sahai, A., Waters, B.: Fuzzy identity-based encryption. In: Cramer, R. (ed.) EUROCRYPT 2005. LNCS, vol. 3494, pp. 457–473. Springer, Heidelberg (2005). https://doi.org/10.1007/11426639_27

43. Santos, N., Rodrigues, R., Gummadi, K.P., Saroiu, S.: Policy-sealed data: a new abstraction for building trusted cloud services. In: USENIX Security Symposium, pp. 175–188. USENIX Association (2012)

44. Scott, M.: On the deployment of curve based cryptography for the internet of things. Cryptology ePrint Archive, Report 2020/514 (2020)

45. Takashima, K.: Expressive attribute-based encryption with constant-size ciphertexts from the decisional linear assumption. In: Abdalla, M., De Prisco, R. (eds.) SCN 2014. LNCS, vol. 8642, pp. 298–317. Springer, Cham (2014). https://doi.org/10.1007/978-3-319-10879-7_17

46. Tomida, J., Kawahara, Y., Nishimaki, R.: Fast, compact, and expressive attribute-based encryption. Des. Codes Cryptogr. **89**(11), 2577–2626 (2021). https://doi.org/10.1007/s10623-021-00939-8

47. Venema, M., Alpár, G.: A bunch of broken schemes: a simple yet powerful linear approach to analyzing security of attribute-based encryption. In: Paterson, K.G. (ed.) CT-RSA 2021. LNCS, vol. 12704, pp. 100–125. Springer, Cham (2021). https://doi.org/10.1007/978-3-030-75539-3_5

48. Venema, M., Alpár, G., Hoepman, J.H.: Systematizing core properties of pairing-based attribute-based encryption to uncover remaining challenges in enforcing access control in practice. Des. Codes Cryptogr. (2022). https://doi.org/10.1007/s10623-022-01093-5

49. Venema, M., Alpár, G.: TinyABE: Unrestricted ciphertext-policy attribute-based encryption for embedded devices and low-quality networks. Cryptology ePrint Archive, Report 2022/569 (2022)

50. Waters, B.: Ciphertext-policy attribute-based encryption: an expressive, efficient, and provably secure realization. In: Catalano, D., Fazio, N., Gennaro, R., Nicolosi, A. (eds.) PKC 2011. LNCS, vol. 6571, pp. 53–70. Springer, Heidelberg (2011). https://doi.org/10.1007/978-3-642-19379-8_4

Symmetric Cryptanalysis

Cryptanalysis of Reduced Round SPEEDY

Raghvendra Rohit[1(✉)] and Santanu Sarkar[2]

[1] Cryptography Research Centre, Technology Innovation Institute, Abu Dhabi, UAE
raghvendra.rohit@tii.ae
[2] Indian Institute of Technology Madras, Chennai, India
santanu@iitm.ac.in

Abstract. SPEEDY is a family of ultra low latency block ciphers proposed by Leander, Moos, Moradi and Rasoolzadeh at TCHES 2021. Although the designers gave some differential/linear distinguishers for reduced rounds, a concrete cryptanalysis considering key recovery attacks on SPEEDY was completely missing. The latter is crucial to understand the security margin of designs like SPEEDY which typically use low number of rounds to have low latency. In this work, we present the first third-party cryptanalysis of SPEEDY-r-192, where $r \in \{5, 6, 7\}$ is the number of rounds and 192 is block and key size in bits. We identify cube distinguishers for 2 rounds with data complexities 2^{14} and 2^{13}, while the differential/linear distinguishers provided by designers has a complexity of 2^{39}. Notably, we show that there are several such cube distinguishers, and thus, we then provide a generic description of them. We also investigate the structural properties of 13-dimensional cubes and give experimental evidence that the partial algebraic normal form of certain state bits after two rounds is always the same. Next, we utilize the 2 rounds distinguishers to mount a key recovery attack on 3 rounds SPEEDY. Our attack require $2^{17.6}$ data, $2^{25.5}$ bits of memory and $2^{52.5}$ time. Our results show that the practical variant of SPEEDY, i.e., SPEEDY-5-192 has a security margin of only 2 rounds. We believe our work will bring new insights in understanding the security of SPEEDY.

Keywords: SPEEDY · Cube attacks · Block cipher

1 Introduction

Lightweight ciphers are designed with the aim of achieving implementation-specific properties such as low gate count, low latency, and low power and energy consumption. It is often difficult to obtain all these properties in a single design, and thus, the spectrum of lightweight ciphers (considering gate count, latency, power and energy) is too wide and continuously evolving. Some of the ciphers targeting low gate count are block ciphers, for example, PRESENT [10], KATAN [13], LED [17], Piccolo [26], SIMON [7] and GIFT [6], and stream ciphers such as Grain [21], Mickey [3] and Trivium [14].

© The Author(s), under exclusive license to Springer Nature Switzerland AG 2022
L. Batina and J. Daemen (Eds.): AFRICACRYPT 2022, LNCS 13503, pp. 133–149, 2022.
https://doi.org/10.1007/978-3-031-17433-9_6

The second key property is the latency which is defined as the time taken between the moment an input data is given to cipher and the corresponding output is obtained. Low latency is highly desirable in applications like encryption of memory bus and storage systems where entire encryption and decryption should take place within the shortest possible delay. Since for many stream ciphers, the high number of clock cycles are required for the initialization phase, these are not suitable for low latency.

The first lightweight block cipher in literature which was aimed for low latency is PRINCE [11]. The design principles of PRINCE with slight variations were later adopted in QARMA [2] and PRINCEv2 [12]. Mantis is another family of low latency tweakable block ciphers [8]. Another block cipher, Midori [4], whose primary aim was low energy, also has relatively small latency.

Very recently, Leander *et al.* proposed SPEEDY [25]. It is a family of ultra low latency block ciphers that targets high-end CPUs and efficient hardware implementations (in terms of latency). In particular, one instance SPEEDY-6-192 consists of 6 rounds with 192-bit block and 192-bit key. The authors showed that its execution time is faster in hardware than any other known encryption primitives like Even-Mansour block cipher with Gimli as its core primitive [9,16] and Orthros pseudorandom function [5]. From security perspective, the authors claimed 128-bit security for SPEEDY-6-192. They also claimed that 7 rounds SPEEDY with 192-bit block and 192-bit key achieves full 192-bit security. Moreover, they proposed a 5-round variant SPEEDY-5-192 and mentioned that "SPEEDY-5-192 provides a decent security level that is sufficient for many practical applications ($\geq 2^{128}$ time complexity when data complexity is limited to $\leq 2^{64}$)".

In this paper, we investigate the security of SPEEDY for reduced rounds using cube attack. We unveil new distinguishers, their structural properties, and key recovery attacks on SPEEDY which were not reported before. Table 1 gives a summary of attacks on SPEEDY till date. In what follows, we summarize our contributions.

Our Contributions. We report the first third-party security evaluation of the SPEEDY family of block ciphers. In particular, we present practical distinguishers for 2 rounds, and key recovery attacks that can reach up to 3 rounds for all three instances of SPEEDY. We now list our contributions.

1. **Practial distinguishers for 2 rounds:** We identify generic 14-dimensional cubes whose cube-sum[1] in rows 1, 2 and 3 of state (arranged in 6 rows and 32 columns) after two full rounds is always zero. We also find 13-dimensional cubes for which cube-sum value of state bits after 2 rounds at indices $i, 31 + i$ and $62 + i$ is always equal, for all $32 \leq i \leq 63$. Moreover, we provide experimental evidence for the same and conjecture that the partial algebraic normal form of these bits $(i, 31 + i$ and $62 + i)$ is always the same. In total, we find 32 such cubes for both cases.

The source codes of the distinguishers are available on request for verification.

---

[1] XOR-ing the evaluation of a state bit at all possible 2^{14} values of cube variables.

Table 1. Summary of attacks on SPEEDY

Distinguishers					
Method	#Rounds	Data	Time	Memory (bits)	Source
Differential and linear[†]	2	2^{39}	2^{39}	-	[25]
	3	2^{69}	2^{69}	-	[25]
Cube	2	2^{14}	2^{14}	-	Sect. 3.2
Cube	2	2^{13}	2^{13}	-	Sect. 3.3
Key recovery					
Method	#Rounds	Data	Time	Memory (bits)	Source
Integral	3	$2^{17.6}$	$2^{52.5}$	$2^{25.2}$	Sect. 4.1

†: No exact trails are provided in the paper. The data in column 3, for instance, 2^{39} corresponds to the upper bound on the probability (2^{-39}) of a differential (linear) trail.

2. **Key recovery attack on 3 rounds:** We present a key recovery attack on 3-round SPEEDY with $2^{17.6}$ data, $2^{25.5}$ bits of memory and $2^{52.5}$ time. To achieve this, we use the 2-round distinguisher (with cube size 14) and append one round (from decryption side) for key recovery. It is worth noting that a 2-round differential distinguisher (from designers) can be used to mount a key-recovery attack on 3 rounds. However, the attack complexities will be larger than our proposed 3-round cube attack.

Our key recovery attack is applicable to all three instances of SPEEDY, i.e., SPEEDY-5-192, SPEEDY-6-192 and SPEEDY-7-192, reduced to 3 rounds. Interestingly, after our attack, the security margin of SPEEDY-5-192 is reduced to only 2 rounds.

Outline of the Paper. The rest of the paper is organized as follows. Section 2 gives the specification of SPEEDY and the basics of Boolean functions and cube attacks. In Sect. 3, we present our low data complexity distinguishers for 2 rounds of SPEEDY along with their structural properties. Section 4 gives a detailed analysis of key recovery attacks on 3 rounds SPEEDY. Finally, we conclude the paper with relevant research directions in Sect. 5.

2   Preliminaries

In this section, we first describe the specification of SPEEDY along with its instances and their security claims. We then briefly recall basic theory of Boolean functions and cube attacks which are required for our attacks on SPEEDY.

2.1 Specification of **SPEEDY**

SPEEDY is a family of ultra low latency block ciphers proposed by Leander *et al.* at TCHES 2021 [25]. SPEEDY-r-6ℓ denotes one instance of this family with block and key size 6ℓ and r rounds. It takes as inputs a 6ℓ-bit plaintext P and a 6ℓ-bit secret key K and outputs the 6ℓ-bit ciphertext C after applying the round function $\mathcal{R}_j$ sequentially r times for $j = 0, \cdots, r-1$.

We consider the 6ℓ-bit state as a $6 \times \ell$ binary matrix. In the original design specification, the authors considered the state as a $\ell \times 6$ matrix. However, for the simplicity of analysis and efficient software implementation[2], we choose to view the state as a $6 \times \ell$ matrix. The round function $\mathcal{R}_j$ and key schedule are then modified accordingly, and the test vectors are matched with the author's implementation to verify the correctness of our representation.[3] A high level overview of SPEEDY is shown in Fig. 1 where the round function is given by

$$\mathcal{R}_j = \begin{cases} \mathsf{RK}^{r-1} \circ \mathsf{SB} \circ \mathsf{SR} \circ \mathsf{SB} \circ \mathsf{RK}^r & \text{for the last round,} \\ \mathsf{RK}^j \circ \mathsf{SB} \circ \mathsf{SR} \circ \mathsf{SB} \circ \mathsf{SR} \circ \mathsf{MR} \circ \mathsf{AC} & \text{otherwise.} \end{cases} \quad (1)$$

Note that to keep consistency between Fig. 1 and Eq. 1, we perform the operations from left to right for an input of 6ℓ-bit state.

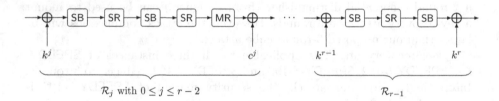

$$\mathcal{R}_j \text{ with } 0 \leq j \leq r-2 \qquad\qquad \mathcal{R}_{r-1}$$

Fig. 1. r rounds of **SPEEDY** block cipher

We now describe the core components of the round function following our representation of SPEEDY. We use $X = x_0, \cdots, x_{6\ell-1}$ and $Y = y_0, \cdots, y_{6\ell-1}$ to represent intermediate states. We sometimes write $X = X_0\|X_1\|X_2\|X_3\|X_4\|X_5$ and $Y = Y_0\|Y_1\|Y_2\|Y_3\|Y_4\|Y_5$ where $X_i = (x_{\ell \cdot i}, \cdots, x_{\ell \cdot i+31})$ and $Y_i = (y_{\ell \cdot i}, \cdots, y_{\ell \cdot i+31})$ denote the i-th row of X and Y, respectively. The operations SB, SR, MR, AC and RK are explained in detail as follows.

SubBox (SB). A 6-bit Sbox is applied on each of the columns (see Fig. 2). Let $(x_0, x_1, x_2, x_3, x_4, x_5)$ and $(y_0, y_1, y_2, y_3, y_4, y_5)$ denote the input and output of the Sbox, respectively. Then the Sbox is given in Table 2. Note that here x_i and y_i are the bits of row X_i and Y_i, respectively.

---

[2] From point of cryptanalysis.

[3] Test vectors are provided along with the codes.

Y_0
Y_1
Y_2
Y_3
Y_4
Y_5

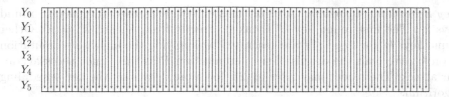

Fig. 2. SubBox SB

Table 2. SPEEDY SBox

x_0x_1	$x_2x_3x_4x_5$															
	0	1	2	3	4	5	6	7	8	9	a	b	c	d	e	f
0	08	00	09	03	38	10	29	13	0c	0d	04	07	30	01	20	23
1	1a	12	18	32	3e	16	2c	36	1c	1d	14	37	34	05	24	27
2	02	06	0b	0f	33	17	21	15	0a	1b	0e	1f	31	11	25	35
3	22	26	2a	2e	3a	1e	28	3c	2b	3b	2f	3f	39	19	2d	3d

ShiftRows (SR). As shown in Fig. 3, the i-th row of state Y is rotated left by i bits. We have, $Y_i \leftarrow Y_i \lll i$ for $0 \leq i \leq 5$ where $\lll$ is a left cyclic shift operation.

Y_0
$Y_1 \lll 1$
$Y_2 \lll 2$
$Y_3 \lll 3$
$Y_4 \lll 4$
$Y_5 \lll 5$

Fig. 3. ShiftRows SR

MixRows (MR). A cyclic binary matrix is multiplied to each row of the state. When $\ell = 32$, we have the 192 version. For this version, given an input $(x_0, \cdots, x_{31}) \in \mathbb{F}_2^{32}$, MR computes the output $(y_0, \cdots, y_{31}) \in \mathbb{F}_2^{32}$ as follows.

$$y_i = x_i \oplus x_{i+1} \oplus x_{i+5} \oplus x_{i+9} \oplus x_{i+15} \oplus x_{i+21} \oplus x_{i+26}, \text{ for } 0 \leq i \leq 31, \quad (2)$$

where the subscripts are computed modulo 32.

Add Constant (AC). A 6ℓ-bit round constant c^j is XORed to the state, i.e., $Y = X \oplus c^j$. The round constants following our representation of state are given in Appendix A.

Add Round Key (RK). A 6ℓ-bit round key k^j is XORed to the state, i.e., $Y = X \oplus k^j$.

Key Scheduling Algorithm. A 6ℓ-bit master key K is used to generate round keys k^j. The first round key k^0 is taken directly from K, i.e., $k^0 = K$. Other round keys k^j for $1 \leq j \leq r$ are generated by applying the bit-wise permutation P on k^j. We omit the details of the permutation P as this is not necessary for our attack. The reader may refer to [25] for more details on the key scheduling algorithm.

In the following, we denote $(x_0^j, \cdots, x_{191}^j)$ and $(k_0^j, \cdots, k_{191}^j)$ as the input state to j-th round and j-th round key, respectively.

2.2   SPEEDY Instances and Security Claims

The authors chose $\ell = 32$ and provided three instances of SPEEDY, namely SPEEDY-5-192, SPEEDY-6-192 and SPEEDY-7-192. They expect that SPEEDY-6-192 and SPEEDY-7-192 provide 128-bit security and 192-bit security, respectively. For SPEEDY-5-128, the claimed time complexity is at least 2^{128} when data is limited to 2^{64}.

2.3   Cube Attacks

It is well known that $\mathbb{F}_2^n$ is a vector space of dimension n over the field $\mathbb{F}_2 = \{0, 1\}$. A Boolean function f in n variables is a map from $\mathbb{F}_2^n$ to $\mathbb{F}_2$. Let $\mathbb{B}_n$ be the set of all n-variable Boolean functions, then we have $|\mathbb{B}_n| = 2^{2^n}$. A Boolean function $f \in \mathbb{B}_n$ can be expressed as a polynomial in n variables over $\mathbb{F}_2$ as

$$f(x_0, \cdots, x_{n-1}) = \sum_{a \in \mathbb{V}_n} C_a x_0^{a_0} \cdots x_{n-1}^{a_{n-1}}, \tag{3}$$

is called as algebraic normal form (ANF for short) of f, where $C_a \in \mathbb{F}_2$, $a = (a_0, \cdots, a_{n-1})$ and $\mathbb{V}_n$ is the set consisting of all possible values of a. The number of variables in the highest order monomial with non-zero coefficient is called the algebraic degree, or simply the degree of f. In the ANF form of any random element of $\mathbb{B}_n$, each monomial (and in particular, the highest degree monomial $x_0 \cdot x_1 \cdots x_{n-1}$) appears with probability $\frac{1}{2}$.

Let $v = (v_0, \cdots, v_{m-1})$ be m public variables and $k = (k_0, \cdots, k_{n-1})$ be n secret variables. Then, in the context of symmetric ciphers, each output bit can be regarded as a Boolean function $f : \mathbb{F}_2^m \times \mathbb{F}_2^n \to \mathbb{F}_2$ given by

$$f(v, k) = \sum_{u \in \mathbb{V}_m} \sum_{w \in \mathbb{V}_n} C_{u,w} v_0^{u_0} \cdots v_{m-1}^{u_{m-1}} k_0^{w_0} \cdots k_{n-1}^{w_{n-1}}, \tag{4}$$

where $u_i, w_j, \in \mathbb{F}_2$ for $0 \leq i \leq m - 1$ and $0 \leq j \leq n - 1$ and $C_{u,w} \in \mathbb{F}_2$.

The cube attack proposed in [15,30] analyzes a keyed Boolean function as a black-box polynomial which is tweakable in public variables. Given a set of indices $\mathcal{I} = \{i_0, \cdots, i_{d-1}\} \subseteq \{0, \cdots, m - 1\}$ and $\bar{\mathcal{I}} = \{0, \cdots, m - 1\} \setminus \mathcal{I}$, Eq. 4 can be viewed as

$$f(v, k) = v_{i_0} \cdots v_{i_{d-1}} \cdot t(\underset{i \in \bar{\mathcal{I}}}{v_i}; k_0, \cdots, k_{n-1}) + q(v_0, \cdots, v_{m-1}, k_0, \cdots, k_{n-1}), \tag{5}$$

where each monomial in the Boolean function q misses at least one variable from $v[\mathcal{I}] = \{v_i \mid i \in \mathcal{I}\}$. Following the terminology of cube attacks, we denote $\mathcal{I}$, $v[\mathcal{I}]$ and a Boolean function $t(\cdot)$ as the *cube indices* set, *cube variables* set, and the *superpoly* of cube monomial $\prod_{i \in \mathcal{I}} v_i$, respectively.

One can see that XOR-ing the evaluation of f at all possible 2^d values of $v_{i_0}, \cdots, v_{i_{d-1}}$ (called as *cube sum* and given by $\mathcal{C}_{v[\mathcal{I}]}$), we have

$$\bigoplus_{\mathcal{C}_{v[\mathcal{I}]}} f(v,k) := \sum_{(v_{i_0}, \ldots, v_{i_{d-1}}) \in \mathbb{F}_2^d} f(v,k) = t(\underset{i \in \mathcal{I}}{v_i}; k_0, \cdots, k_{n-1}). \tag{6}$$

Cube tester [1] is an algorithm which can distinguish a cipher from random source. The presence of monomials, balancedness, constantness, presence of linear variables, presence of neutral variables are some testing properties which can detect non-randomness in superpoly of a Boolean function. Recently, cube attacks have gained attention due to the introduction of the division property [27,29] based automated techniques which can provide information of a superpoly [18–20,22,23,28].

3   Practical Distinguishers for Two Rounds SPEEDY

In this section, we present (experimental) practical distinguishers for two full rounds of SPEEDY. We first explain our core observation behind the distinguishers. Next, we present two generic distinguishers with data complexities 2^{14} and 2^{13}. We also unveil some unexpected properties of the second distinguisher and show that for certain state bits, a part of the algebraic normal form of these state bits is always the same. In the end, we discuss the possibility (with current challenges) of their proof.

3.1   Core Idea of Distinguishers

Our main idea is to reduce the algebraic degree of the output bits after 1 full round, i.e., SB∘SR∘SB∘SR∘MR. Note that the degree of the output bits in rows 0, 1, 2, 3, 4 and 5 after 1 round are 19, 15, 13, 13, 13 and 20, respectively. To reduce these degrees, we look at the ShiftRows property of the round function, i.e., row i is cyclically left shifted by i bits (for $0 \le i \le 5$).

For instance, consider 6 cube variables in the 0-th Sbox as shown in Fig. 4. After the SB operation, the output bits 0, 32, 64, 96, 128 and 160 have algebraic degrees of 5, 3, 3, 3, 4 and 5, respectively. Now, after the SR operation, these monomials will shift to Sboxes 0, 31, 30, 29, 28 and 27. Applying SB on these Sboxes will not change the algebraic degree as the monomials are in distinct Sboxes. Now, since SR ∘ MR ∘ AC is a linear operation, the algebraic degree of the state bits after 1 round is at most 5. The diffusion of these cube variables is shown in Fig. 4.

To have further degrees of freedom, we select another 6 cube variables in the 6-th Sbox as the last shift offset is 5. Thus, after round 1, the algebraic degree of state bits in 12 cube variables is at most 5 (compared to 12).

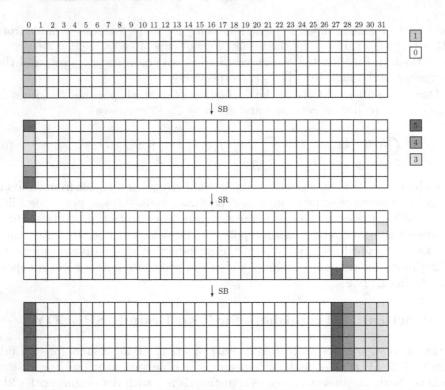

Fig. 4. Diffusion of cube variables for SB ∘ SR ∘ SB. SR ∘ MR ∘ AC is omitted as it is linear and will not affect the degree. The colors represent the degree value as shown on the right side of the figure.

3.2   Distinguishers with 2^{14} Data

Recall that x_i^2 denotes the i-th bit of state after 2 rounds. We find multiple cube indices sets $\mathcal{I}$ with $|\mathcal{I}| = 14$ such that

$$\bigoplus_{\mathcal{C}_{v[\mathcal{I}]}} x_i^2 = 0, \quad \text{for all } i \in \{32, \cdots, 127\}. \tag{7}$$

We start with an example of one such $\mathcal{I}$ in Example 1.

Example 1. Consider $\mathcal{I} = \{0, 32, 64, 96, 128, \ 160, 6, 38, 70, 102, 134, 166, 12, 18\}$ as shown in Fig. 5. Experimentally we checked the validity of $\mathcal{I}$ with 2^{16} random keys and for each key we set random non-cube variables. In all 2^{16} experiments, the superpolies at positions $\{32, \cdots, 127\}$ (green squares in Fig. 5) after 2 rounds are always zero.

We now give a generic description of such $\mathcal{I}$'s in Observation 1.

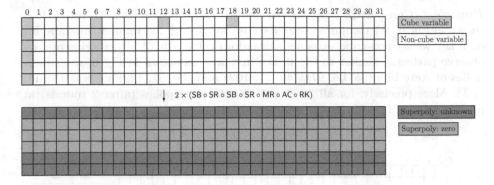

Fig. 5. A 2-round cube distinguisher with 2^{14} data (Color figure online)

Observation 1 (Generic 14-dimensional cube). *Let $0 \le n \le 31$. Define*

$$\mathcal{S}_n := \{n, 32 + n, 64 + n, 96 + n, 128 + n, 160 + n\}$$
$$\mathcal{S}_{6+n \bmod 32} := \{i, 32 + i, 64 + i, 96 + i, 128 + i, 160 + i \mid i \equiv 6 + n \bmod 32\}$$
$$\mathcal{S}_{12+n \bmod 32} := \{12 + n \bmod 32\}$$
$$\mathcal{S}_{18+n \bmod 32} := \{18 + n \bmod 32\}$$
$$\mathcal{I}_n := \mathcal{S}_n \bigcup \mathcal{S}_{6+n \bmod 32} \bigcup \mathcal{S}_{12+n \bmod 32} \bigcup \mathcal{S}_{18+n \bmod 32}.$$

(8)

Then

$$\bigoplus_{\mathcal{C}_{v[\mathcal{I}_n]}} x_i^2 = 0, \text{ for all } i \in \{32, \cdots, 127\}.$$

(9)

Experimental Verification of Observation 1. For $0 \le n \le 31$, and for each $\mathcal{I}_n$, we take 2^{16} random keys and set non-cube variables as some random values. We then check the value of superpolies at positions $\{32, \cdots, 127\}$ after 2 rounds. In total, we have $2^{16} \cdot 2^5 \cdot (32 \times 3)$ superpolies. We observed that all superpolies are equal to zero.

Remark 1. The distinguisher presented in Observation 1 is very unique. For instance, one may think of first choosing 4 Sboxes which are at a distance of 6, and then select 14 (out of 4×6) variables in these Sboxes as cube variables. But this approach does not give a similar distinguisher. A counter example is $\mathcal{I} = \{0, 32, 64, 96, 128, 160, 6, 38, 70, 102, 134, 166, 12, 30\}$.

3.3 Distinguishers with 2^{13} Data

The 14 size cube in the previous section gives a distinguisher with probability 1. Thus, it is normal to see if we decrease the cube dimension what is the impact on probability. Accordingly, we remove 1 variable from the 14 size cube and observe the behavior of superpolies. We start with an example of 13-dimensional cube and then provide the general description of such cubes.

Example 2. Consider $\mathcal{J} = \{0, 32, 64, 96, 128,\ 160, 6, 38, 70, 102, 134, 166, 12\}$ as shown in Fig. 6. We computed the cube sum for $\mathcal{J}$ with 2^{16} random keys and for each key we set non-cube variables as random values. In all 2^{16} experiments, we observe patterns[4] similar to Fig. 6. For instance, as shown in Fig. 6, the super-polies of state bits (35, 66, 97), (40, 71, 102) and (60, 91, 122) are equal to (1, 1, 1). More precisely, for all $32 \le i \le 63$, the superpolies (after 2 rounds) at positions $i, (i-1) + 32, (i-2) + 64$ are always equal.

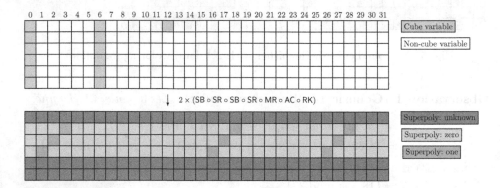

Fig. 6. A 2-round cube distinguisher with 2^{13} data

Now, analogous to Observation 1, we give a generic description of 13-dimensional cubes in Observation 2.

Observation 2 (Generic 13-dimensional cube). *Let $0 \le n \le 31$. Define*

$$\mathcal{S}_n := \{n, 32 + n, 64 + n, 96 + n, 128 + n, 160 + n\}$$
$$\mathcal{S}_{6+n \bmod 32} := \{i, 32 + i, 64 + i, 96 + i, 128 + i, 160 + i \mid i \equiv 6 + n \bmod 32\}$$
$$\mathcal{S}_{12+n \bmod 32} := \{12 + n \bmod 32\}$$
$$\mathcal{J}_n := \mathcal{S}_n \bigcup \mathcal{S}_{6+n \bmod 32} \bigcup \mathcal{S}_{12+n \bmod 32}.$$

$$(10)$$

Then

$$\bigoplus_{\mathcal{C}_{v[\mathcal{J}_n]}} x_i^2 = \bigoplus_{\mathcal{C}_{v[\mathcal{J}_n]}} x_{i+31}^2 = \bigoplus_{\mathcal{C}_{v[\mathcal{J}_n]}} x_{i+62}^2, \ \textit{for all } i \in \{32, \cdots, 63\}. \qquad (11)$$

Experimental Verification of Observation 2. For $0 \le n \le 31$, and for each $\mathcal{J}_n$, we take 2^{16} random keys and set non-cube variables as some random values. We then check the value of superpolies (after 2 rounds) corresponding to the triplet $(i, i + 31, i + 62)$ for $32 \le i \le 63$. In total, we have $2^{16} \cdot 2^5$ triplets. We observed that in each triplet, superpolies values are always equal.

---

[4] This is one of the example of a pattern.

Observations on the Distinguisher. It is somewhat unexpected that superpolies in the triplet $(i, i+31, i+62)$ are always equal. Our experimental results suggest that this behavior happens for almost all keys (we further checked Observation 2 for another 2^{20} keys). Since $(i, i+31, i+62)$ can be $(0, 0, 0)$ or $(1, 1, 1)$, it can be argued that the superpolies are not constant. We believe this happens only if the partial algebraic normal (containing the cube monomial and superpoly) of these state bits after 2 rounds is always same. Since we can not prove this fact theoretically (albeit this holds experimentally), we present it as conjecture below.

Conjecture 1. Let $0 \le n \le 31$ and $\mathcal{J}_n$ as defined in Observation 2. Then for all $i = 32, \cdots, 63$, the ANF of state bits $i, i + 31$ and $i + 62$ is given by

$$x_i^2 = f_i + (\prod_{j \in \mathcal{J}_n} v_j) \cdot t_i$$

$$x_{i+31}^2 = f_{i+31} + (\prod_{j \in \mathcal{J}_n} v_j) \cdot t_i \qquad (12)$$

$$x_{i+62}^2 = f_{i+62} + (\prod_{j \in \mathcal{J}_n} v_j) \cdot t_i$$

where t_i is the superpoly corresponding to cube indices $\mathcal{J}_n$ and f_i, f_{i+31}, f_{i+62} are Boolean functions similar to the Boolean function q in Eq. 5.

3.4   Discussion on the Proofs of Distinguishers

In all our experimental results related to Observation 1 and 2, we did not find a counter example, i.e., a key for which these two observations do not hold. Thus, we expected that they could be proved mathematically. As such, we tried the following two approaches for the proofs.

SAGE Based Proof. We set the cube variables and 192 key bits as symbolic variables. Then, we checked the maximum degree in cube variables after round 2. Because of the high algebraic degree (including key variables), our SAGE code always ran out of memory. Thus, we chose to find the degree by selecting a random key and setting non-cube variables as zero. We find that for 14-dimensional cube, the degree is at most 13 in rows 1, 2 and 3 of the state. For 13-dimensional cube, we find that the algebraic degree is at most 12 in majority of the state bits. This provides another evidence for our experimental distinguishers.

Division Property Based Proof. We modeled the three subset bit based division property [19,31] propagation of one round SPEEDY using MILP. We find that even for a single round, the superpolies of a 5-dimensional cube are too dense. Since the algebraic degree of 1 round is at most 20, we expect that this tool may become slow for two consecutive rounds.

The source codes of the SAGE implementation and the division property models are also available to readers on request.

4   Key Recovery Attacks

In this section, we present a 3-round key recovery attack that is applicable to SPEEDY-5-192, SPEEDY-6-192 and SPEEDY-7-192. Our attack is based on the principles of integral cryptanalysis [24] and utilize the 2-round distinguishers as described before. Before proceeding to the attack, we first recall some notations that will be used throughout this section.

The vectors $(x_0^j, \ldots, x_{191}^j)$ and $(k_0^j, \ldots, k_{191}^j)$ denote the input state at j-th round and j-th round key, respectively. Also, $(x_0^0, \ldots, x_{191}^0)$ and $(x_0^r, \ldots, x_{191}^r)$ represent the plaintext and the ciphertext, respectively. Further, note that recovering a round key is equivalent to recovering the master key. In our attacks, we aim to recover the last round key k^r which is also the post-whitening key.

4.1   3-Round Key Recovery Attack

Figure 7 shows the high level overview of the 3-round key recovery attack on SPEEDY. We use a 2-round cube distinguisher (cube size 14, Example 1) and append 1-round for the key recovery. In our attack, we use the fact that each state bit after $\mathsf{SB}^{-1} \circ \mathsf{SR}^{-1} \circ \mathsf{SB}^{-1}$ depends only on 36 bits of key and 36 bits of the ciphertext. For instance, the bits in column 0 depends on the ciphertext and last round key bits from columns 0, 31, 30, 29, 28 and 27. More precisely, a column i after $\mathsf{SB}^{-1} \circ \mathsf{SR}^{-1} \circ \mathsf{SB}^{-1}$ depends on columns $i, i-1, \cdots, i-5$ of ciphertext and key k^3.[5] Thus, in order to do partial decryption with mutually disjoint subkey bits (see Eq. 13), we choose columns 0, 6, 12, 18 and 24. We match the decrypted value of a state bit with the cube sum value in bits 1, 2 and 3 for each of these columns (see green squares in Fig. 7).

We now explain the detailed attack steps along with their respective complexities. For $i = 0, 6, 12, 18$ and 24, we first define

$$
\begin{aligned}
\mathsf{SK}[i] := \{ \; & k_i^3, k_{32+i}^3, k_{64+i}^3, k_{96+i}^3, k_{128+i}^3, k_{160+i}^3, \\
& k_{i-1}^3, k_{31+i}^3, k_{63+i}^3, k_{95+i}^3, k_{127+i}^3, k_{159+i}^3, \\
& k_{i-2}^3, k_{30+i}^3, k_{62+i}^3, k_{94+i}^3, k_{126+i}^2, k_{158+i}^3, \\
& k_{i-3}^3, k_{29+i}^3, k_{61+i}^3, k_{93+i}^3, k_{125+i}^3, k_{157+i}^3, \\
& k_{i-4}^3, k_{28+i}^3, k_{60+i}^3, k_{92+i}^3, k_{124+i}^3, k_{156+i}^3, \\
& k_{i-5}^3, k_{27+i}^3, k_{59+i}^3, k_{91+i}^3, k_{123+i}^3, k_{155+i}^3 \; \}
\end{aligned}
\tag{13}
$$

as partial bits of k^3. While computing $\mathsf{SK}[i]$, the subscripts of key bits are taken modulo 192. Note that $\mathsf{SK}[i]$'s are mutually disjoint. Similarly, we define mutually disjoint sets for the ciphertext bits as follows.

---

[5] Column numbers taken modulo 32.

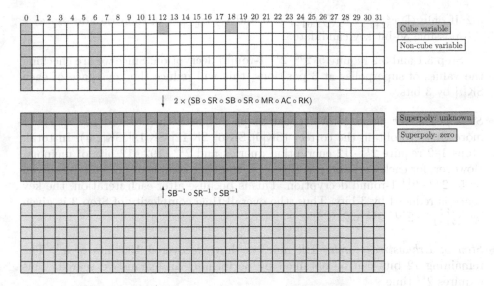

Fig. 7. An overview of the 3-round key recovery attack. After partial decryption, a matching is done at positions as shown by green squares (after 2 rounds from the encryption side). (Color figure online)

$$CT[i] := \{ x_i^3, x_{32+i}^3, x_{64+i}^3, x_{96+i}^3, x_{128+i}^3, x_{160+i}^3,$$
$$x_{i-1}^3, x_{31+i}^3, x_{63+i}^3, x_{95+i}^3, x_{127+i}^3, x_{159+i}^3,$$
$$x_{i-2}^3, x_{30+i}^3, x_{62+i}^3, x_{94+i}^3, x_{126+i}^3, x_{158+i}^3,$$
$$x_{i-3}^3, x_{29+i}^3, x_{61+i}^3, x_{93+i}^3, x_{125+i}^3, x_{157+i}^3, \qquad (14)$$
$$x_{i-4}^3, x_{28+i}^3, x_{60+i}^3, x_{92+i}^3, x_{124+i}^3, x_{156+i}^3,$$
$$x_{i-5}^3, x_{27+i}^3, x_{59+i}^3, x_{91+i}^3, x_{123+i}^3, x_{155+i}^3 \}$$

The attack steps proceed as follows.

Step 1: Setting cube and non-cube variables. For $\mathcal{I} = \{0, 32, 64, 96, 128, 160, 6, 38, 70, 102, 134, 166, 12, 18\}$, set $x_i^0 = v_i$ for $i \in \mathcal{I}$, and set x_i^0 as a random bit, for $i \in \{0, \cdots, 191\} \setminus \mathcal{I}$.

Step 2. Querying **SPEEDY** *oracle and storing ciphertexts.* Let $v = (v_0, v_{32}, \cdots, v_{12}, v_{18})$. For $v = 0$ to $2^{14} - 1$, query 3-round **SPEEDY** oracle and store the ciphertexts in the set $\mathcal{C}$. This step requires 2^{14} encryption queries (1 query = 3-round **SPEEDY**) and $2^{14} \cdot 192$ bits of memory.

Step 3. Key recovery phase. For $i = 0, 6, 12, 18, 24$, we recover key bits as follows.

3.1 For each guess sk_i of $SK[i]$, we compute the values $\bigoplus x_{32+i}^2, \bigoplus x_{64+i}^2$ and $\bigoplus x_{96+i}^2$ by partially decrypting all 2^{14} ciphertexts in $\mathcal{C}$. Note that while doing the partial decryption, we only need the information of 36 bits of each ciphertext. The latter is captured by the set $CT[i]$ (see Eq. 14).

3.2 If only $\bigoplus x^2_{32+i} = 0, \bigoplus x^2_{64+i} = 0$ and $\bigoplus x^2_{96+i} = 0$, then we add sk_i as a possible 36-bit key candidate.

Step 3.1 and 3.2 require $5 \cdot 2^{36} \cdot 2^{14}$ 1-round decryption. Since we are checking the values of superpolies at 3 positions, this will reduce the key space of each $\mathsf{SK}[i]$ by 3 bits.

Step 4: Further filtering. We repeat Steps 1–3 with the reduced key space 11 more times to obtain the correct $(\mathsf{SK}[0], \mathsf{SK}[6], \mathsf{SK}[12], \mathsf{SK}[18], \mathsf{SK}[24])$. In total, Steps 1–2 require $2^{14} \cdot 12$ encryption queries and $2^{14} \cdot 192 \cdot 12$ bits of memory. However, for each iteration $j = 12, \cdots, 1$, the time complexity of Step 3 is given by $5 \cdot 2^{3 \cdot j} \cdot 2^{14}$ 1-round decryption. This is because after each iteration, the key space is reduced by 3 bits. Thus, the overall time complexity of Step 3 is given by $\sum_{j=1}^{12} 5 \cdot 2^{3 \cdot j} \cdot 2^{14} \approx 2^{52.52}$.

Step 5: Exhaustive search. Till now, we have recovered 180 bits of k^3. The remaining 12 bits can be obtained by performing an exhaustive search. This requires 2^{12} time.

Combining Steps 1–5, the entire 3-round attack has the following complexities.

$$\text{Data} = 2^{14} \cdot 12 \approx 2^{17.58}$$
$$\text{Memory} = 2^{14} \cdot 192 \cdot 12 \approx 2^{25.16} \text{ bits} \qquad (15)$$
$$\text{Time} = 2^{52.52} + 2^{12} \approx 2^{52.52}.$$

4.2 On Improving Number of Rounds for Key Recovery

It is natural to ask whether we can attack 4-round SPEEDY. Based on our current analysis, we do not see a direct way to attack 4 rounds.

The reasons are as follows: (1) We are unaware of the existence of a 2.5 and 3 round distinguisher with a complexity at most 2^{64}, and (2) the exact ANF of 1 and 1.5 rounds in forward and backward directions is extremely complicated and of high degree.

5 Conclusion

In this work, we have presented the first third-party cryptanalysis of SPEEDY family of block ciphers. We identified multiple distinguishers (in total 32+32) for 2 rounds with data complexities 2^{14} and 2^{13}. Our second distinguisher (13-dimensional cubes) revealed an unexpected property that the partial algebraic normal form of certain state bits after 2 rounds is always equal, for which we also provided the experimental evidence. We then gave a key recovery attack on 3-round SPEEDY which requires $2^{17.6}$ data, $2^{25.5}$ bits of memory and $2^{52.5}$ time.

Although our findings may not appear to be novel, they did cover 60% and 50% rounds of SPEEDY-5-192 and SPEEDY-6-192 for the first time in the literature. We expect many more unidentified distinguishers for 2 rounds. To find them, it is important to investigate and understand the theoretical properties of the current 2-round distinguishers. Furthermore, it would be interesting to see if there are any 2.5 or 3-round cube distinguishers. Our initial analysis shows that this may require a non-trivial effort because of the high growth in algebraic degree. Overall, we believe there are lot of unanswered questions and this work (being the first one apart from designers) will provide new insights to the community in further understanding the security of SPEEDY.

Acknowledgements. The authors would like to thank the reviewers of Africacrypt 2022 for providing us with insightful comments to improve the quality of the paper.

A SPEEDY Round Constants

In Table 3, we list the first 6 round constants of SPEEDY.

Table 3. Round constants of SPEEDY

Round j	c^j
0	0x3903501c, 0x22145a05, 0xb46705b0, 0x2269408a, 0x5b9954ce, 0xe150791e
1	0x3a21067b, 0x32801fbe, 0x35c8cee9, 0x0d33c971, 0xfd8f9408, 0x22b25e82
2	0xbf3984a2, 0xa5b365cd, 0x5d54b65f, 0x0ff7e9ee, 0x4012012d, 0x1a5d9cd5
3	0x8eb8aff6, 0xc16d9463, 0x1ddb3cda, 0xa19c9865, 0x535f36d7, 0x5f9f7fac
4	0xe17adece, 0x3cc44c83, 0x85ccd8e4, 0xc7b3b8d5, 0xe481006d, 0x4cc7691c
5	0x7873963c, 0xc98a9bb3, 0x8006f8e7, 0x6f7cbba0, 0x4def0a1c, 0x0785d9ae

References

1. Aumasson, J.-P., Dinur, I., Meier, W., Shamir, A.: Cube testers and key recovery attacks on reduced-round MD6 and Trivium. In: Dunkelman, O. (ed.) FSE 2009. LNCS, vol. 5665, pp. 1–22. Springer, Heidelberg (2009). https://doi.org/10.1007/978-3-642-03317-9_1
2. Avanzi, R.: The QARMA block cipher family. Almost MDS matrices over rings with zero divisors, nearly symmetric even-mansour constructions with non-involutory central rounds, and search heuristics for low-latency s-boxes. IACR Trans. Symmetric Cryptol. **2017**(1), 4–44 (2017). https://doi.org/10.13154/tosc.v2017.i1.4-44
3. Babbage, S., Dodd, M.: The MICKEY stream ciphers. In: Robshaw, M., Billet, O. (eds.) New Stream Cipher Designs. LNCS, vol. 4986, pp. 191–209. Springer, Heidelberg (2008). https://doi.org/10.1007/978-3-540-68351-3_15
4. Banik, S., et al.: Midori: a block cipher for low energy. In: Iwata, T., Cheon, J.H. (eds.) ASIACRYPT 2015, Part II. LNCS, vol. 9453, pp. 411–436. Springer, Heidelberg (2015). https://doi.org/10.1007/978-3-662-48800-3_17

5. Banik, S., Isobe, T., Liu, F., Minematsu, K., Sakamoto, K.: Orthros: a low-latency PRF. IACR Trans. Symmetric Cryptol. **2021**(1), 37–77 (2021). https://doi.org/ 10.46586/tosc.v2021.i1.37-77

6. Banik, S., Pandey, S.K., Peyrin, T., Sasaki, Y., Sim, S.M., Todo, Y.: GIFT: a small present. In: Fischer, W., Homma, N. (eds.) CHES 2017. LNCS, vol. 10529, pp. 321–345. Springer, Cham (2017). https://doi.org/10.1007/978-3-319-66787-4_16

7. Beaulieu, R., Shors, D., Smith, J., Treatman-Clark, S., Weeks, B., Wingers, L.: The SIMON and SPECK families of lightweight block ciphers. IACR Cryptology ePrint Archive, p. 404 (2013). http://eprint.iacr.org/2013/404

8. Beierle, C., et al.: The SKINNY family of block ciphers and its low-latency variant MANTIS. In: Robshaw, M., Katz, J. (eds.) CRYPTO 2016, Part II. LNCS, vol. 9815, pp. 123–153. Springer, Heidelberg (2016). https://doi.org/10.1007/978-3-662-53008-5_5

9. Bernstein, D.J., et al.: GIMLI: a cross-platform permutation. In: Fischer, W., Homma, N. (eds.) CHES 2017. LNCS, vol. 10529, pp. 299–320. Springer, Cham (2017). https://doi.org/10.1007/978-3-319-66787-4_15

10. Bogdanov, A., et al.: PRESENT: an ultra-lightweight block cipher. In: Paillier, P., Verbauwhede, I. (eds.) CHES 2007. LNCS, vol. 4727, pp. 450–466. Springer, Heidelberg (2007). https://doi.org/10.1007/978-3-540-74735-2_31

11. Borghoff, J., et al.: PRINCE – a low-latency block cipher for pervasive computing applications. In: Wang, X., Sako, K. (eds.) ASIACRYPT 2012. LNCS, vol. 7658, pp. 208–225. Springer, Heidelberg (2012). https://doi.org/10.1007/978-3-642-34961-4_14

12. Božilov, D., et al.: PRINCEv2 - more security for (almost) no overhead. In: Dunkelman, O., Jacobson, M.J., Jr., O'Flynn, C. (eds.) SAC 2020. LNCS, vol. 12804, pp. 483–511. Springer, Cham (2021). https://doi.org/10.1007/978-3-030-81652-0_19

13. De Cannière, C., Dunkelman, O., Knežević, M.: KATAN and KTANTAN—a family of small and efficient hardware-oriented block ciphers. In: Clavier, C., Gaj, K. (eds.) CHES 2009. LNCS, vol. 5747, pp. 272–288. Springer, Heidelberg (2009). https:// doi.org/10.1007/978-3-642-04138-9_20

14. De Cannière, C., Preneel, B.: Trivium. In: Robshaw, M., Billet, O. (eds.) New Stream Cipher Designs. LNCS, vol. 4986, pp. 244–266. Springer, Heidelberg (2008). https://doi.org/10.1007/978-3-540-68351-3_18

15. Dinur, I., Shamir, A.: Cube attacks on tweakable black box polynomials. In: Joux, A. (ed.) EUROCRYPT 2009. LNCS, vol. 5479, pp. 278–299. Springer, Heidelberg (2009). https://doi.org/10.1007/978-3-642-01001-9_16

16. Even, S., Mansour, Y.: A construction of a cipher from a single pseudorandom permutation. J. Cryptol. **10**(3), 151–161 (1997). https://doi.org/10.1007/ s001459900025

17. Guo, J., Peyrin, T., Poschmann, A., Robshaw, M.: The LED block cipher. In: Preneel, B., Takagi, T. (eds.) CHES 2011. LNCS, vol. 6917, pp. 326–341. Springer, Heidelberg (2011). https://doi.org/10.1007/978-3-642-23951-9_22

18. Hao, Y., Leander, G., Meier, W., Todo, Y., Wang, Q.: Modeling for three-subset division property without unknown subset - improved cube attacks against Trivium and Grain-128AEAD. In: Canteaut, A., Ishai, Y. (eds.) EUROCRYPT 2020, Part I. LNCS, vol. 12105, pp. 466–495. Springer, Cham (2020). https://doi.org/10.1007/ 978-3-030-45721-1_17

19. Hebborn, P., Lambin, B., Leander, G., Todo, Y.: Lower bounds on the degree of block ciphers. In: Moriai, S., Wang, H. (eds.) ASIACRYPT 2020, Part I. LNCS, vol. 12491, pp. 537–566. Springer, Cham (2020). https://doi.org/10.1007/978-3-030-64837-4_18

20. Hebborn, P., Lambin, B., Leander, G., Todo, Y.: Strong and tight security guarantees against integral distinguishers. Cryptology ePrint Archive, Report 2021/1502 (2021). https://ia.cr/2021/1502

21. Hell, M., Johansson, T., Maximov, A., Meier, W.: The grain family of stream ciphers. In: Robshaw, M., Billet, O. (eds.) New Stream Cipher Designs. LNCS, vol. 4986, pp. 179–190. Springer, Heidelberg (2008). https://doi.org/10.1007/978-3-540-68351-3_14

22. Hu, K., Sun, S., Todo, Y., Wang, M., Wang, Q.: Massive superpoly recovery with nested monomial predictions. IACR Cryptology ePrint Archive, p. 1225 (2021). https://eprint.iacr.org/2021/1225

23. Hu, K., Sun, S., Wang, M., Wang, Q.: An algebraic formulation of the division property: revisiting degree evaluations, cube attacks, and key-independent sums. In: Moriai, S., Wang, H. (eds.) ASIACRYPT 2020, Part I. LNCS, vol. 12491, pp. 446–476. Springer, Cham (2020). https://doi.org/10.1007/978-3-030-64837-4_15

24. Knudsen, L., Wagner, D.: Integral cryptanalysis. In: Daemen, J., Rijmen, V. (eds.) FSE 2002. LNCS, vol. 2365, pp. 112–127. Springer, Heidelberg (2002). https://doi.org/10.1007/3-540-45661-9_9

25. Leander, G., Moos, T., Moradi, A., Rasoolzadeh, S.: The SPEEDY family of block ciphers engineering an ultra low-latency cipher from gate level for secure processor architectures. IACR Trans. Cryptogr. Hardw. Embed. Syst. 2021(4), 510–545 (2021). https://doi.org/10.46586/tches.v2021.i4.510-545

26. Shibutani, K., Isobe, T., Hiwatari, H., Mitsuda, A., Akishita, T., Shirai, T.: *Piccolo*: an ultra-lightweight blockcipher. In: Preneel, B., Takagi, T. (eds.) CHES 2011. LNCS, vol. 6917, pp. 342–357. Springer, Heidelberg (2011). https://doi.org/10.1007/978-3-642-23951-9_23

27. Todo, Y.: Structural evaluation by generalized integral property. In: Oswald, E., Fischlin, M. (eds.) EUROCRYPT 2015, Part I. LNCS, vol. 9056, pp. 287–314. Springer, Heidelberg (2015). https://doi.org/10.1007/978-3-662-46800-5_12

28. Todo, Y., Isobe, T., Hao, Y., Meier, W.: Cube attacks on non-blackbox polynomials based on division property. In: Katz, J., Shacham, H. (eds.) CRYPTO 2017, Part III. LNCS, vol. 10403, pp. 250–279. Springer, Cham (2017). https://doi.org/10.1007/978-3-319-63697-9_9

29. Todo, Y., Morii, M.: Bit-based division property and application to SIMON family. In: Peyrin, T. (ed.) FSE 2016. LNCS, vol. 9783, pp. 357–377. Springer, Heidelberg (2016). https://doi.org/10.1007/978-3-662-52993-5_18

30. Vielhaber, M.: Breaking One.Fivium by AIDA an algebraic iv differential attack. Cryptology ePrint Archive, Report 2007/413 (2007). https://ia.cr/2007/413

31. Xiang, Z., Zhang, W., Bao, Z., Lin, D.: Applying MILP method to searching integral distinguishers based on division property for 6 lightweight block ciphers. In: Cheon, J.H., Takagi, T. (eds.) ASIACRYPT 2016, Part I. LNCS, vol. 10031, pp. 648–678. Springer, Heidelberg (2016). https://doi.org/10.1007/978-3-662-53887-6_24

And Rijndael?
Automatic Related-Key Differential Analysis of Rijndael

Loïc Rouquette[1,5(✉)], David Gérault[2,3], Marine Minier[4], and Christine Solnon[1]

[1] CITI, INRIA, INSA Lyon, 69621 Villeurbanne, France
{loic.rouquette,christine.solnon}@insa-lyon.fr
[2] University of Surrey, Guildford, UK
[3] TII, Abu Dhabi, UAE
[4] LORIA, Université de Lorraine, 54000 Nancy, France
marine.minier@loria.fr
[5] LIRIS, UMR5201 CNRS, 69621 Villeurbanne, France

Abstract. Finding optimal related-key differential characteristics for a given cipher is a problem that hardly scales. For the first time, we study this problem against the 25 instances of the block cipher Rijndael, which are the little brothers of the AES. To achieve this, we adapt and improve an existing approach for the AES which is based on Constraint Programming.

The attacks presented here overpass all the previous cryptanalytic results of Rijndael. Among all our results, we obtain a 12-round (out of 13 rounds) related-key differential attack for Rijndael with a block size equal to 128 bits and a key size equal to 224 bits. We also obtain an 11-round related-key differential characteristic distinguisher for Rijndael with a block size equal to 160 bits and a key size equal to 256 bits leading to an attack on 12 rounds (out of 14 rounds).

Keywords: Related-key differential characteristics · Constraint Programming (CP) · Automatic tools · Rijndael

1 Introduction

Cryptanalysis aims at finding non-random properties and distinguishers against classical cryptographic primitives. In particular, *differential cryptanalysis* [5] is a powerful tool against block and stream ciphers. It studies the propagation of the difference $\delta X = X \oplus X'$ between two plaintexts X and X' through the cipher E or a part of the cipher, where $\oplus$ is the exclusive OR (XOR). If the distribution of the output difference $\delta C = E_K(X) \oplus E_K(X')$ is non uniform over all the keys K, then an adversary has a distinguisher and can exploit this non-uniformity to guess part of the key K faster than exhaustive search. Most of the times, the distinguisher is constructed on a reduced number of rounds. Today, differential cryptanalysis is a public knowledge, and block ciphers have proven security bounds against differential attacks. Hence, [4] proposed to consider differences not only between the plaintexts X and X' but also between the keys K and K' to mount *related-key*

© The Author(s), under exclusive license to Springer Nature Switzerland AG 2022
L. Batina and J. Daemen (Eds.): AFRICACRYPT 2022, LNCS 13503, pp. 150–175, 2022.
https://doi.org/10.1007/978-3-031-17433-9_7

attacks. In this case, the cryptanalyst is interested in finding *optimal related-key differentials*, *i.e.*, input and output differences that maximize the probability of obtaining the output difference given the input difference. In other words, we search for δX, δK, and δC that maximize the probability that δC is equal to $E_K(X) \oplus E_{K \oplus \delta K}(X \oplus \delta X)$ for a plaintext X and a key K.

Finding an optimal related-key differential characteristic is a highly combinatorial problem that hardly scales. To simplify this problem, Knudsen [16] introduced *truncated differential characteristics* where byte or nibble differences are abstracted by single bits that indicate if there is a difference at a given position or not. Thus, the search for related-key differential characteristics is divided into two steps as done in [6,10]. In Step 1, each byte or nibble difference is abstracted by a Boolean value and the aim of this step is to find the trail which minimizes the number of active S-boxes. The goal here is to find the positions of the differences. Then, for each solution found at Step 1, Step 2 aims at instantiating each Boolean value into a valid byte or nibble difference while maximizing the overall probability of the differential characteristic crossing the S-boxes. However, some truncated differential characteristics found at Step 1 may not be valid (*i.e.*, there do not exist byte or nibble values corresponding to these difference positions). Scaling from the AES to Rijndael can only be made with a tight model for Step 1. Models described in [6,10] do not scale when increasing the block size and the key size. Only the model described in [13] has a sufficiently small number of solutions found at Step 1 to hope that the computational time will be reasonable.

In this paper, we show how to adapt the two-step solving process of [13] dedicated to the AES to compute optimal related-key differential characteristics for Rijndael [8]. Both steps are solved with Constraint Programming (CP) solvers[1]: Picat-SAT for Step 1 and Choco for Step 2. We improve the approach of [13] by better interleaving Steps 1 and 2 and exploiting bounds to stop the search sooner. We also improve the Step 2 process of [13] by decomposing the constraints associated with MixColumns. These improvements allow us to compute the optimal differential characteristics for all Rijndael instances but one within a reasonable amount of time.

Rijndael is a family of block ciphers (more precisely it is composed of 25 instances of the same cipher where the block size and the key size vary) originally proposed at the AES competition. But the NIST only retained as a standard its 128-bit-block version under the key sizes 128, 192 and 256 bits. Studying the security of Rijndael is interesting to enlighten the AES standardization process. Among the most interesting results, we obtain a 12-round (over 13 rounds) related-key differential distinguisher and a 12-round (over 13 rounds) attack for Rijndael with a block size equal to 128 bits and a key size equal to 224 bits. We also obtain an 11-round related-key differential distinguisher for Rijndael with a block size equal to 160 bits and a key size equal to 256 bits leading to an attack on 12 rounds out of 14.

---

[1] The code is available here: https://gitlab.inria.fr/lrouquet/cp-differential-cryptanalysis/-/tree/AfricaCrypt22.

When looking at the state of the art concerning the cryptanalysis of Rijndael, some of the results are in the single key scenario [11,15,18,19,25,27] or in the related-key scenario [26] and none of those attacks exceeds 10 rounds.

The rest of this paper is organized as follows: in Sect. 2, we recall the full description of Rijndael; in Sect. 3, we detail the methods and our CP models. in Sect. 4, we sum up all the related-key differential characteristics distinguishers we obtained, give all resolution times and compare them with those of [13]; in Sect. 5, we present two attacks based on the most efficient distinguishers and finally, in Sect. 6, we conclude this paper.

2   Rijndael

Rijndael-C_{len}-K_{len}(where C_{len} is the block size and K_{len} is the key size) is a set of 25 different SPN block ciphers designed by Joan Daemen and Vincent Rijmen [9]. Each instance varies according to the block size (128, 160, 192, 224 or 256 bits) and to the key size (128, 160, 192, 224 or 256 bits) but the ciphering process is the same for all variants, except for the ShiftRows operation (given in Table 1) and the number of rounds (given in Table 2). It has been chosen as the new advanced encryption standard by the NIST [1] with a 128-bit block size and a key length that can be set to 128, 192 or 256 bits. The number of rounds N_r depends on the text size C_{len} and on the key size K_{len} and varies between 10 and 14. For all the versions, the current block at the input of the round i is represented by a $4 \times N_b$ matrix of bytes X_i where $N_b = (C_{len}/32)$ is the number of columns and where each byte at row j and column k is denoted by $X_i[j,k]$. The round function, repeated $N_r - 1$ times, involves four elementary mappings, all linear except the first one. Round i consists of the following transformations:

SubBytes. A bytewise transformation is applied on each byte of the current
  block using an 8-bit to 8-bit non linear S-box, denoted by SBOX: $SX_i[j,k] =$
  SBOX$(X_i[j,k])$, $\forall j \in [0,3], \forall k \in [0, N_b - 1]$.
ShiftRows. A linear mapping rotates to the left all the rows of the current matrix
  SX_i. The values of the shifts denoted P_{N_b} (given in Table 1) depend on N_b:
  $Y_i[j,k] = SX_i[j, (P_{N_b}[j] + k) \mod N_b]$, $\forall j \in [0,3], \forall k \in [0, N_b - 1]$.
MixColumns is a linear multiplication of each column of the current state by a
  constant matrix M in the Galois field GF(2^8), that provides the corresponding
  column of the new state. For a given column $k \in [0, N_b - 1]$, if we denote by
  $\otimes$ the multiplication in GF(2^8), we have:

$$Z_i[l,k] = \sum_{j \in [0,3]} M[l,j] \otimes Y_i[j,k]$$

with M the 4×4 circulant matrix defined by its first row $= [2,3,1,1]$
AddRoundKey performs a bitwise XOR between the subkey RK_i of round i and the
  current state Z_i: $X_{i+1}[j,k] = Z_i[j,k] \oplus RK_i[j,k]$, $\forall j \in [0,3], \forall k \in [0, N_b - 1]$.

The subkeys RK_i are generated from the master key K using a KeySchedule algorithm composed of byte shifting, SBOX substitutions and XORs which is fully

---

Algorithm 1: Rijndael KeySchedule function

---

input : A key matrix K of $[4; N_k]$ bytes
output: The expanded key WK of $[4; N_b \times (N_r + 1) - 1]$ bytes
for $k \in [0, N_b]$ **and** $j \in [0, 3]$ **do**
$\quad\lfloor\ $ WK$[j, k] \leftarrow$ K$[j, k]$;

for $k \in [N_b, N_b \times (N_r + 1) - 1]$ **do**
$\quad$ **if** $k \mod N_k = 0$ **then**
$\qquad$ WK$[0, k] =$ WK$[0, k - N_k] \oplus$ SBOX(WK$[1, k$ - $1]$) **for** $j \in [1, 3]$ **do**
$\qquad\lfloor\ $ WK$[j, k] =$ WK$[j, k$ - $N_k] \oplus$ SBOX(WK$[(j + 1) \mod 4, k$ - $1]$) ;

$\quad$ **else if** $k > 6 \wedge k \mod N_k = 4$ **then**
$\qquad$ **for** $j \in [0, 3]$ **do**
$\qquad\lfloor\ $ WK$[j, k] =$ WK$[j, k$ - $N_k] \oplus$ SBOX(WK$[j, k$ - $1]$);

$\quad$ **else**
$\qquad$ **for** $j \in [0, 3]$ **do**
$\qquad\lfloor\ $ WK$[j, k] =$ WK$[j, k$ - $N_k] \oplus$ WK$[(j + 1) \mod 4, k$ - $1]$;

return WK

Table 1. ShiftRows table $P_{C_{len}}$. This table specifies the required number of byte shifts to the left according to the row number, e.g., $P_{224}[3] = 4$.

	Row			
	0	1	2	3
P_{128}	0	1	2	3
P_{160}	0	1	2	3
P_{192}	0	1	2	3
P_{224}	0	1	2	4
P_{256}	0	1	3	4

Table 2. The number of rounds N_r of Rijndael-C_{len}-K_{len}.

C_{len}	128	160	192	224	256
$K_{len} = 128$	10	11	12	13	14
$K_{len} = 160$	11	11	12	13	14
$K_{len} = 192$	12	12	12	13	14
$K_{len} = 224$	13	13	13	13	14
$K_{len} = 256$	14	14	14	14	14

described in Algorithm 1. We denote by $N_k = K_{len}/32$ the number of columns of the master key K. Note that each subkey RK_i is extracted from a main register WK in the following way: $RK_i[j, k] = WK[j, (i + 1) \times N_b + k]$, $\forall j \in [0, 3], \forall k \in [0, N_b - 1]$.

Those $Nr - 1$ rounds are surrounded at the top by an initial key addition with the subkey RK_0 and at the bottom by a final transformation composed by a call to the round function where the MixColumns operation is omitted.

Our notations are summarized below.

- X_i: the state at the beginning of round i. Note that X_i is also the state after applying the AddRoundKey function on the previous round X_{i-1};
- SX_i: the state of round i, after applying SubBytes;
- Y_i: the state of round i, after applying ShiftRows;

- Z_i: the state of round i, after applying MixColumns.
- RK_i: the subkey of round i.

3   The Solving Process

In this section, we describe how to compute the optimal related-key differential characteristics for Rijndael by adapting and improving the approach introduced in [13] for the AES. We first recall some basic principles of CP; then we describe the two-step solving process; finally, we describe the CP models associated with each of these two steps.

3.1   Constraint Programming

CP is a generic framework for solving Constraint Satisfaction Problems (CSPs), *i.e.*, finding an assignment of values to variables such that (i) each variable is assigned to a value that belongs to its domain, and (ii) a given set of constraints is satisfied. Each constraint is a relation between some variables which restricts the set of values that may be assigned simultaneously to these variables. This relation may be defined in intention, by using mathematical operators, or in extension, by listing all allowed tuples. For example, let us consider the constraint that ensures that the sum of three variables x_1, x_2, and x_3 is different from 1. This constraint may be defined in intention by using operators $+$ and $\neq$: $x_1 + x_2 + x_3 \neq 1$ or it may be defined in extension by using a table constraint: $\langle x_1, x_2, x_3 \rangle \in \mathsf{T}_{\mathsf{sum} \neq 1}$ where $\mathsf{T}_{\mathsf{sum} \neq 1}$ is a table which enumerates every triple of values the sum of which is different from 1. For example, if the domain of x_1, x_2, and x_3 is $\{0, 1\}$, then $\mathsf{T}_{\mathsf{sum} \neq 1}$ contains the following triples: $\langle 0, 0, 0 \rangle, \langle 0, 1, 1 \rangle, \langle 1, 0, 1 \rangle, \langle 0, 1, 1 \rangle$, and $\langle 1, 1, 1 \rangle$.

CP may also be used to solve Constrained Optimisation Problems (COPs), *i.e.*, CSPs with an additional objective function that must be optimised. CSPs and COPs are defined by using a modelling language such as MiniZinc [20]. Then, they can be solved by CP solvers such as, Choco [21], Gecode [12], Chuffed [7], or Picat-SAT [28]. We refer the reader to [22] for more details on CP.

SAT is a special case of CSP, where all variables have boolean domains and all constraints are logical formulae (clauses). Also, MILPs (Mixed Integer Linear Programs) are special cases of COPs where all variables have numerical domains, constraints are linear inequalities, and the objective function is linear. To compute differential characteristics with SAT or MILP solvers, it is necessary to model the problem by means of logical formulae (for SAT) or linear inequalities (for MILP). In particular, the non linear DDT associated with an S-box must be represented by a large number of clauses (for SAT) or inequalities (for MILP), and the resulting models hardly scale [2,17,24].

When using CP, constraints do not need to be linear and DDTs are modelled in a straightforward way by using table constraints. In particular, [13] recently showed that CP solvers can compute optimal differential characteristics very efficiently and outperform the dedicated approaches of [6] and [10] for the AES.

Algorithm 2: Computation of optimal related-key differential characteristics for Rijndael.

Input: The size K_{len} of the key, the size C_{len} of the block and the number r of
rounds
Output: An optimal related-key differential characteristic S^*
begin

$\quad NB_{\text{SBOX}} \leftarrow Step1\text{-}opt(N_k, N_b, r)$ where $N_k = K_{len}/32$ and $N_b = C_{len}/32$
$\quad UB \leftarrow 2^{-6 \cdot NB_{\text{SBOX}}}$
$\quad LB \leftarrow 0$
$\quad$**while** $LB < UB$ **do**
$\quad\quad S_1 \leftarrow Step1\text{-}next(N_k, N_b, r, NB_{\text{SBOX}})$
$\quad\quad$**if** $S_1 \neq null$ **then**
$\quad\quad\quad S_2 \leftarrow Step2(N_k, N_b, r, LB, S_1)$
$\quad\quad\quad$**if** $S_2 \neq null$ **then**
$\quad\quad\quad\quad S^* \leftarrow S_2$
$\quad\quad\quad\quad LB \leftarrow probability$ of S_2
$\quad\quad$**else**
$\quad\quad\quad NB_{\text{SBOX}} \leftarrow NB_{\text{SBOX}} + 1$
$\quad\quad\quad UB \leftarrow 2^{-6 \cdot NB_{\text{SBOX}}}$
$\quad$**return** S^*

3.2 Two-Step Solving Process

Finding the best related-key differential characteristic is a highly combinatorial
problem. To improve the scalability of the attack, Knudsen has introduced truncated differentials [16]. The core idea is to solve the problem in two steps: In Step
1, we compute a truncated differential characteristic S_1 where each differential
byte δA of the ciphering process is replaced with a boolean variable ΔA that
indicates whether δA contains a difference or not (*i.e.*, $\Delta A = 0 \iff \delta A = 0$
and $\Delta A = 1 \iff \delta A \in [\![1, 2^8 - 1]\!]$); In Step 2, we instantiate S_1 into a differential characteristic S_2: for each boolean variable ΔA, if ΔA is equal to 0 in
S_1, then δA is equal to 0 in S_2; otherwise δA must belong to $[\![1, 2^8 - 1]\!]$. Note
that some truncated characteristics cannot be instantiated to a characteristic
because some abstractions are done at Step 1.

As SBOX is the only non-linear operation, the probability of a differential characteristic only depends on the values of the differential bytes that pass through
S-boxes, under the Markov assumption that rounds are independent. We denote
δ_{SB} this set of bytes (including those in the key schedule), and Δ_{SB} the corresponding set of boolean variables.

A theoretical upper bound on the probability of the best differential characteristic may be computed by searching for the truncated differential characteristic which minimises the number of active S-boxes $NB_{\text{SBOX}} = \#\{\Delta A \mid \Delta A \in
\Delta_{SB} \wedge \Delta A = 1\}$. As 2^{-6} is the maximal differential probability of the Rijndael
SBOX, the best probability is upper bounded by $UB = 2^{-6 \cdot NB_{\text{SBOX}}}$.

UB may be larger than the actual best probability because it may be possible
that the best truncated differential characteristic cannot be instantiated into a

differential characteristic, or because some non null differential bytes that go through S-boxes have a probability equal to 2^{-7} instead of 2^{-6}. Hence, the best differential characteristic is searched by alternating Step 1 and Step 2 in an iterative process which is described in Algorithm 2. First, we call *Step1-opt* to compute NB_{SBOX}, a lower bound of the number of active S-boxes in a truncated differential, and this number is used to compute a first upper bound UB on the probability. The lower bound LB on the probability is initialised to 0. Then, at each iteration of the while loop, we call *Step1-next* to compute the next truncated differential characteristic with NB_{SBOX} active S-boxes: each time this function is called, it returns a new Step 1 solution with NB_{SBOX} active S-boxes until they all have been computed (in this latter case, *Step1-next* returns *null*). If a new Step 1 solution S_1 has been computed, then *Step2* is called to search for the differential characteristic S_2 corresponding to S_1 whose probability is larger than LB and maximal: if such a characteristic exists, then the best characteristic S^* is updated to S_2 and LB is updated to the probability of S_2. When *Step1-next* returns *null*, all truncated characteristics with NB_{SBOX} active S-boxes have been enumerated. In this case, we increment NB_{SBOX} and update consequently the upper bound UB. We stop iterating when UB becomes smaller than or equal to LB: in this case S^* is equal to the optimal differential characteristic.

Algorithm 2 is different from the one used in [13]: it avoids computing useless Step 1 solutions by updating LB and UB and stopping the process when $LB \geq UB$. *Step1-opt*, *Step1-next* and *Step2* are implemented with CP solvers and the corresponding CP models are described in the next two sections.

3.3   Step 1

Both *Step1-opt* and *Step1-next* compute truncated differential characteristics: *Step1-opt* searches for the truncated characteristic that minimises NB_{SBOX}, whereas *Step1-next* searches for the next truncated characteristic given NB_{SBOX}. Both problems share the same constraints which are described in this section. *Step1-opt* is a COP which is obtained by adding the objective function: *minimise* NB_{SBOX}. *Step1-next* is a CSP which is obtained by assigning the variable NB_{SBOX} to the optimal solution of *Step1-opt*.

A key point for Algorithm 2 to be efficient is to avoid as much as possible computing truncated characteristics which cannot be instantiated at Step 2. To this aim, we consider the model introduced in [13] which is tighter than the model of [14], *i.e.*, it computes fewer truncated characteristics that cannot be instantiated at Step 2. This model has been defined for the AES, and we show in this section how to extend it to Rijndael.

Constraints Associated with Rijndael Transformations. A basic Step 1 model for Rijndael is displayed in Model 1. Constraint (A1) relates NB_{SBOX} with the number of active S-boxes. The other constraints are derived from Rijndael round function transformations.

$$NB_{\text{SBOX}} = \sum_{\Delta A \in \Delta_{SB}} \Delta A \tag{A1}$$

$$\forall i \in [0, N_r - 1], \forall j \in [0, 3], \forall k \in [0, N_b - 1], \tag{A2}$$

$$\Delta SX_i[j, k] = \Delta X_i[j, k]$$
$$\forall i \in [0, N_r - 2], \forall j \in [0, 3], \forall k \in [0, N_b - 1], \tag{A3}$$

$$\Delta Y_i[j, k] = \Delta SX_i[j, P_{N_b}[j] + k \mod N_b]$$
$$\forall i \in [0, N_r - 2], \forall k \in [0, N_b - 1], \tag{A4}$$

$$\sum_{j \in [0,3]} \Delta Z_i[j, k] + \sum_{j \in [0,3]} \Delta Y_i[j, k] \in \{0, 5, 6, 7, 8\}$$
$$\forall i \in [0, N_r - 2], \forall j \in [0, 3], \forall k \in [0, N_b - 1], \tag{A5}$$

$$\Delta RK_i[j, k] = \Delta WK[j, (i + 1) \times N_b + k]$$
$$\Delta X_{i+1}[j, k] + \Delta Z_i[j, k] + \Delta RK_i[j, k] \neq 1$$

$$\forall \omega \in [N_b, N_b \times (N_r + 1) - 1] \text{ such that } \text{isSbCol}(\omega), \forall j \in [0, 3], \tag{A6}$$

$$\Delta SWK[j, \omega] = \Delta WK[j, \omega]$$

where predicate $\text{isSbCol}(\omega)$ is $\omega \geq Nk - 1 \wedge \omega < N_b \times (N_r + 1) - 1 \wedge$
$$(\omega \mod N_k = N_k - 1 \vee (N_k > 6 \wedge \omega \mod N_k = 3))$$

$$\forall j \in [0, 3], \forall \omega \in [N_b, N_b \times (N_r + 1) - 1], \tag{A7}$$

$$\text{if } \omega \mod N_k = 0 : \Delta WK[j, \omega] + \Delta WK[j, \omega - N_k] + \Delta SWK[(j + 1) \mod 4, \omega - 1] \neq 1$$
$$\text{else if } N_k > 6 \wedge k \mod N_k = 4 : \Delta WK[j, \omega] + \Delta WK[j, \omega - N_k] + \Delta SWK[j, \omega - 1] \neq 1$$
$$\text{else} : \Delta WK[j, \omega] + \Delta WK[j, \omega - N_k] + \Delta WK[j, \omega - 1] \neq 1$$

Model 1: Basic step 1 model for Rijndael.

SubBytes: As SBOX is bijective, there is an output difference if and only if there is an input difference. The SubBytes transformation at Boolean level is thus abstracted by an identity mapping ΔX_i and ΔSX_i (Constraint (A2)).

ShiftRows: As ShiftRows is just a shift at byte level, its abstraction in Step 1 is directly expressed as the equivalent shift as defined in Constraint (A3).

MixColumns: Multiplications of MixColumns cannot be mapped into the Boolean domain as the coefficients of M belong to $GF(2^8)$. Thus, instead of encoding multiplications, we exploit the *MDS* (*Maximum Distance Separable*) property of the MixColumns transformation as defined in Constraint (A4).

AddRoundKey: It is a simple XOR between bytes of the current state Z_i and bytes of the subkey RK_i. It is modelled by constraint (A5) which prevents every triple of boolean variables involved in a same XOR from having exactly one difference. This constraint also relates variables associated with the subkey RK_i with variables associated with the expanded key WK.

KeySchedule: the whole KeySchedule process of Rijndael is described in Algorithm 1. The variables that pass through SBOXes are unchanged, as stated in Constraint (A6). XORs are modelled by Constraint (A7) which prevents every triple of boolean variables involved in a same XOR from having exactly one difference.

However, this simple model generates many truncated characteristics which cannot be instantiated at Step 2. This mainly comes from the fact that XORs performed by `AddRoundKey` and `KeySchedule` are modelled by constraints which simply prevent the sum of differences to be equal to 1. Thus, we show how to refine this in the next two paragraphs.

Inference of New XOR Equations from the `KeySchedule`. In Model 1, every XOR equation $\delta A \oplus \delta B \oplus \delta C = 0$ is represented by a sum constraint $\Delta A + \Delta B + \Delta C \neq 1$. This simple model is not sharp enough and generates a lot of truncated solutions that cannot be instantiated at Step 2. For example, the two XOR equations $\delta A \oplus \delta B \oplus \delta C = 0$ and $\delta B \oplus \delta C \oplus \delta D = 0$ are represented by the two sum constraints $\Delta A + \Delta B + \Delta C \neq 1$ and $\Delta B + \Delta C + \Delta D \neq 1$. When reasoning at the byte level, we easily infer that we cannot have $\delta A = 0$ and $\delta D \neq 0$, whatever the values of δB and δC are. However, when reasoning at the boolean level, the two sum constraints may be satisfied when $\Delta A = 0$ and $\Delta D = 1$ (*e.g.*, when $\Delta B = \Delta C = 1$).

To sharpen the Step 1 model and reduce the number of Step 1 solutions that cannot be instantiated at Step 2, we generate new XOR equations from the initial set of equations, by XORing them. These new equations do not change the set of solutions at the byte level. However, at the boolean level, they remove some of the truncated solutions that cannot be instantiated at Step 2. For example, when XORing the two XOR equations of our previous example, we obtain the equation $\delta A \oplus \delta D = 0$. When adding the constraint $\Delta A + \Delta D \neq 1$ to the two sum constraints, we prevent the search from generating solutions with $\Delta A = 0$ and $\Delta D = 1$.

This trick has been introduced in [13] for the AES, and we extend it to Rijndael in a straightforward way. More precisely, we consider the set of all XOR equations coming from the `KeySchedule` (this set corresponds to Constraint (A7) of Model 1). From this set, we generate all possible equations that involve no more than 4 variables by recursively XORing these equations[2]. This set of new equations is denoted EXTXOR.

Introduction of *diff* Variables. As done in [13], we also introduce *diff* variables to reason on differences at the byte level: every variable $diff_{A,B}$ is a boolean variable which is true if $\delta A \neq \delta B$, and false otherwise. *diff* variables are associated with variables involved in the `KeySchedule`, in `AddRoundKey` and in `MixColumns`. This new Model is presented in Model 2.

---

[2] We do not generate equations with more than 4 variables as the number of new equations grows exponentially with respect to their size.

Each variable $diff_{A,B}$ is related with ΔA and ΔB by ensuring: $diff_{A,B} + \Delta A + \Delta B \neq 1$. In other words, $diff_{A,B} = 0$ whenever $\Delta_A = \Delta_B = 0$ and $diff_{A,B} = 1$ whenever $\Delta_A \neq \Delta_B$. This corresponds to Constraints (E1) (for KeySchedule) and (E2) (for the MixColumns). These constraints also ensure symmetry, $i.e.$, $diff_{A,B} = diff_{B,A}$. Constraints (E3) and (E4) ensure transitivity ($i.e.$, if $\delta A = \delta B$ and $\delta B = \delta C$, then $\delta A = \delta C$) by constraining the sum of the corresponding $diff$ variables to be different from 1.

Constraint (E5) relates $diff$ variables associated with the subkey RK_i with $diff$ variables associated with the expanded key WK.

Constraints (E6) and (E7) are associated with the new XOR equations in ExtXOR. Two cases are considered: equations with three variables in Constraint (E6), and equations with four variables in Constraint (E7). In both cases, if at least one variable involved in the equation belongs to Δ_{SB}, then the constraint simply prevents the sum of the variables to be equal to 1. Otherwise, we exploit $diff$ variables to tighten the constraint.

Finally, Constraints (E8) and (E9) ensure the MDS property of MixColumns on differences between pairs of columns (this constraint is partly equivalent with the linear incompatibility of [10]). Indeed, the MDS property holds between each input and output column before and after applying MixColumns but it also holds when XORing different columns. More precisely, if $i_1, i_2 \in [0, r - 2]$ are two round numbers, and $k_1, k_2 \in [0, 3]$ are two column numbers, for every row $j \in [0, 3]$, we have

$$\delta Z_{i_1}[j][k_1] \oplus \delta Z_{i_2}[j][k_2] = \left(\bigoplus_{l=0}^{3} M[j][l] \cdot \delta Y_{i_1}[l][k_1] \right) \oplus \left(\bigoplus_{l=0}^{3} M[j][l] \cdot \delta Y_{i_2}[l][k_2] \right)$$
$$= \bigoplus_{l=0}^{3} M[j][l] \cdot (\delta Y_{i_1}[l][k_1] \oplus \delta Y_{i_2}[l][k_2])$$

Therefore, the MDS property also holds for the result of the XOR of two different columns. This is modelled by Constraint (E8). This constraint removes many Step 1 solutions that cannot be instantiated at Step 2. In a rather similar way, Constraint (E9) is derived by XORing equations coming from AddRoundKey.

$\forall \omega_1, \omega_2 \in [0, N_b \times (N_r + 1) - 1], \forall j \in [0, 3]$ where $\omega_2 > \omega_1$ (E1)

$$\mathit{diff}_{WK[j,\omega_1], WK[j,\omega_2]} + \Delta WK[j, \omega_1] + \Delta WK[j, \omega_2] \neq 1$$

$$\mathit{diff}_{WK[j,\omega_1], WK[j,\omega_2]} = \mathit{diff}_{WK[j,\omega_2], WK[j,\omega_1]}$$

$\forall i_1, i_2 \in [0, N_r - 2], \forall j \in [0, 3], \forall k_1, k_2 \in [0, N_b - 1]$ where $(i_2, k_2) > (i_1, k_1)$ (E2)

$$\mathit{diff}_{Y_{i_1}[j,k_1], Y_{i_2}[j,k_2]} + \Delta Y_{i_1}[j, k_1] + \Delta Y_{i_2}[j, k_2] \neq 1$$

$$\mathit{diff}_{Y_{i_1}[j,k_1], Y_{i_2}[j,k_2]} = \mathit{diff}_{Y_{i_2}[j,k_2], Y_{i_1}[j,k_1]}$$

$$\mathit{diff}_{Z_{i_1}[j,k_1], Z_{i_2}[j,k_2]} + \Delta Z_{i_1}[j, k_1] + \Delta Z_{i_2}[j, k_2] \neq 1$$

$$\mathit{diff}_{Z_{i_1}[j,k_1], Z_{i_2}[j,k_2]} = \mathit{diff}_{Z_{i_2}[j,k_2], Z_{i_1}[j,k_1]}$$

$\forall \omega_1, \omega_2, \omega_3 \in [0, N_b \times (N_r + 1) - 1], \forall j \in [0, 3]$ where $\omega_3 > \omega_2 > \omega_1$ (E3)

$$\mathit{diff}_{WK[j,\omega_1], WK[j,\omega_2]} + \mathit{diff}_{WK[j,\omega_1], WK[j,\omega_3]} + \mathit{diff}_{WK[j,\omega_2], WK[j,\omega_3]} \neq 1$$

$\forall i_1, i_2, i_3 \in [0, N_r - 2], \forall j \in [0, 3], \forall k_1, k_2, k_3 \in [0, N_b - 1]$ where $(i_3, k_3) > (i_2, k_2) > (i_1, k_1)$ (E4)

$$\mathit{diff}_{Y_{i_1}[j,k_1], Y_{i_2}[j,k_2]} + \mathit{diff}_{Y_{i_2}[j,k_2], Y_{i_3}[j,k_3]} + \mathit{diff}_{Y_{i_3}[j,k_3], Y_{i_1}[j,k_1]} \neq 1$$

$$\mathit{diff}_{Z_{i_1}[j,k_1], Z_{i_2}[j,k_2]} + \mathit{diff}_{Z_{i_2}[j,k_2], Z_{i_3}[j,k_3]} + \mathit{diff}_{Z_{i_3}[j,k_3], Z_{i_1}[j,k_1]} \neq 1$$

$\forall i_1, i_2 \in [0, N_r - 1], \forall j \in [0, 3], \forall k_1, k_2 \in [0, N_b - 1]$ (E5)

$$\mathit{diff}_{RK_{i_1}[j,k_1], RK_{i_2}[j,k_2]} = \mathit{diff}_{WK[j,(i_1+1) \times N_b + k], WK[j,(i_2+1) \times N_b + k]}$$

For each equation $\delta_{B1} \oplus \delta_{B2} \oplus \delta_{B3} = 0$ in ExtXOR,   (E6)

$$\text{if } \{\Delta_{B1}, \Delta_{B2}, \Delta_{B3}\} \cap \Delta_{SB} \neq \emptyset \text{ then } \Delta_{B1} + \Delta_{B2} + \Delta_{B3} \neq 1$$

$$\text{if } \{\Delta_{B1}, \Delta_{B2}\} \cap \Delta_{SB} = \emptyset \text{ then } \mathit{diff}_{B1, B2} = \Delta_{B3}$$

$$\text{if } \{\Delta_{B2}, \Delta_{B3}\} \cap \Delta_{SB} = \emptyset \text{ then } \mathit{diff}_{B2, B3} = \Delta_{B1}$$

$$\text{if } \{\Delta_{B1}, \Delta_{B3}\} \cap \Delta_{SB} = \emptyset \text{ then } \mathit{diff}_{B1, B3} = \Delta_{B2}$$

For each equation $\delta_{B1} \oplus \delta_{B2} \oplus \delta_{B3} \oplus \delta_{B4} = 0$ in ExtXOR,   (E7)

$$\text{if } \{\Delta_{B1}, \Delta_{B2}, \Delta_{B3}, \Delta_{B4}\} \cap \Delta_{SB} \neq \emptyset \text{ then } \Delta_{B1} + \Delta_{B2} + \Delta_{B3} + \Delta_{B4} \neq 1$$

$$\text{else } \mathit{diff}_{B1, B2} = \mathit{diff}_{B3, B4}$$

$$\mathit{diff}_{B1, B3} = \mathit{diff}_{B2, B4}$$

$$\mathit{diff}_{B1, B4} = \mathit{diff}_{B2, B3}$$

$\forall i_1, i_2 \in [0, N_r - 2], \forall k_1, k_2 \in [0, N_b - 1]$ where $(i_2, k_2) > (i_1, k_1)$ (E8)

$$\sum_{j \in [0,3]} \mathit{diff}_{Y_{i_1}[j,k_1], Y_{i_2}[j,k_2]} + \sum_{j \in [0,3]} \mathit{diff}_{Z_{i_1}[j,k_1], Z_{i_2}[j,k_2]} \in \{0, 5, 6, 7, 8\}$$

$\forall i_1, i_2 \in [0, N_r - 2], \forall j \in [0, 3], \forall k_1, k_2 \in [0, N_b - 1]$ where $(i_2, k_2) > (i_1, k_1)$ (E9)

$$\mathit{diff}_{RK_{i_1}[j,k_1], RK_{i_2}[j,k_2]} + \mathit{diff}_{Z_{i_1}[j,k_1], Z_{i_2}[j,k_2]} + \Delta X_{i_1+1}[j, k_1] + \Delta X_{i_2+1}[j, k_2] \neq 1$$

Model 2: Additional constraints for the refined Step 1 model for Rijndael.

Incomplete Step 1 Solutions. As pointed out in [13], some AES instances have a huge number of Step 1 solutions. Many of these solutions have exactly the same values for the boolean variables in Δ_{SB} (corresponding to S-boxes), and they only differ on values of other boolean variables (that do not correspond to S-boxes). For example, when the key has 192 bits and the number of rounds is equal to 10, there are 27,548 different Step 1 solutions. However, there are only 7 different assignments of values to the variables in Δ_{SB}.

As Rijndael is a generalisation of the AES, this is also true for Rijndael. Hence, as proposed in [13], we enumerate incomplete solutions such that only the variables in Δ_{SB} are assigned.

3.4   Step 2

Given a Step 1 solution (corresponding to a truncated characteristic), Step 2 aims at searching for the corresponding characteristic which has the largest probability, and such that this largest probability is larger than the best probability found so far (LB).

The CP model used to solve Step 2 is described in Model 3. For each boolean variable ΔA of Step 1, this model uses an integer variable δA to represent the corresponding differential byte. If this byte passes through an S-box $(i.e., \delta A \in \delta_{SB})$, then the initial domain of δA depends on the value of ΔA in the Step 1 solution: If $\Delta A = 0$, then δA is assigned to 0; Otherwise the domain of δA is $[\![1, 255]\!]$. For each variable $\delta A \notin \delta_{SB}$, the domain of δA is $[\![0, 255]\!]$ as the associated boolean variable ΔA is not assigned in the Step 1 solution.

SBOX. We introduce new variables in order to represent probabilities associated with S-boxes. More precisely, for each byte $\delta A \in \delta_{SB}$ that passes through an S-box, we introduce an integer variable p_A. This variable represents the binary logarithm of the probability to observe the output difference δSA given the input difference δA. We consider the binary logarithm of the probability (instead of the probability), in order to avoid rounding errors. As the probability for Rijndael S-boxes is 0, 2^{-7}, 2^{-6}, or 1, and as we only consider values with non null probabilities, the values that may be assigned to p_A are -7, -6, and 0.

Constraint (C2) of Model 3 relates input differences, output differences and probabilities for the S-boxes applied on the plaintext, whereas Constraint (C9) relates them for the S-boxes in the KeySchedule. In both cases, we use a table constraint which ensures that the triple of variables belongs to a table denoted T_{SBOX}: This table contains a triple $\langle \delta_{in}, \delta_{out}, p \rangle$ for each couple of differential bytes $(\delta_{in}, \delta_{out})$ such that the DDT content for $(\delta_{in}, \delta_{out})$ is different from 0, and such that p is equal to: $\log_2(\frac{\#\{(X,X') \in [\![0,255]\!]^2 | (X \oplus X' = \delta_{in}) \wedge (\text{SBOX}(X) \oplus \text{SBOX}(X') = \delta_{out})\}}{256})$.

Objective Function. We introduce an integer variable *obj* to represent the binary logarithm of the probability of the differential characteristic. The objective function is: *maximise obj*. The actual probability is computed as 2^{obj}.

$$obj = \sum_{\delta A \in \delta_{SB}} p_A \tag{C1}$$

$$obj > LB$$

$$\forall i \in [0, N_r - 1], \forall j \in [0, 3], \forall k \in [0, N_b - 1], \tag{C2}$$

$$\langle \delta X_i[j,k], \delta SX_i[j,k], p_{X_i}[j,k] \rangle \in \mathsf{T_{SBOX}}$$

$$\forall i \in [0, N_r - 1], \forall j \in [0, 3], \forall k \in [0, N_b - 1], \tag{C3}$$

$$\delta Y_i[j,k] = \delta SX_i[j, P_{N_b}[j] + k \mod N_b]$$

$$\forall i \in [0, N_r - 1], \forall k \in [0, N_b - 1], \forall j \in [0, 3], \forall v \in \{2, 3\} \tag{C4}$$

$$\langle \delta Y_i[j,k], v\delta Y_i[j,k] \rangle \in \mathsf{T_{MULv}}$$

$$\forall i \in [0, N_r - 1], \forall k \in [0, N_b - 1], \tag{C5}$$

$\langle 2\delta Y_i[0,k], 3\delta Y_i[1,k], a_i[k] \rangle \in \mathsf{T_\oplus}$	$\langle \delta Y_i[2,k], \delta Y_i[3,k], b_i[k] \rangle \in \mathsf{T_\oplus}$	$\langle a_i[k], b_i[k], \delta Z_i[0,k] \rangle \in \mathsf{T_\oplus}$
$\langle \delta Y_i[0,k], 2\delta Y_i[1,k], c_i[k] \rangle \in \mathsf{T_\oplus}$	$\langle 3\delta Y_i[2,k], \delta Y_i[3,k], d_i[k] \rangle \in \mathsf{T_\oplus}$	$\langle c_i[k], d_i[k], \delta Z_i[1,k] \rangle \in \mathsf{T_\oplus}$
$\langle \delta Y_i[0,k], \delta Y_i[1,k], e_i[k] \rangle \in \mathsf{T_\oplus}$	$\langle 2\delta Y_i[2,k], 3\delta Y_i[3,k], f_i[k] \rangle \in \mathsf{T_\oplus}$	$\langle e_i[k], f_i[k], \delta Z_i[2,k] \rangle \in \mathsf{T_\oplus}$
$\langle 3\delta Y_i[0,k], \delta Y_i[1,k], g_i[k] \rangle \in \mathsf{T_\oplus}$	$\langle \delta Y_i[2,k], 2\delta Y_i[3,k], h_i[k] \rangle \in \mathsf{T_\oplus}$	$\langle g_i[k], h_i[k], \delta Z_i[3,k] \rangle \in \mathsf{T_\oplus}$

$$\forall i \in [0, N_r - 1], \forall k \in [0, N_b - 1], \forall j \in [0, 3], \forall v \in \{9, 11, 13, 14\} \tag{C6}$$

$$\langle \delta Z_i[j,k], v\delta Z_i[j,k] \rangle \in \mathsf{T_{MULv}}$$

$$\forall i \in [0, N_r - 1], \forall k \in [0, N_b - 1], \tag{C7}$$

$\langle 14\delta Z_i[0,k], 11\delta Z_i[1,k], m_i[k] \rangle \in \mathsf{T_\oplus}$	$\langle 13\delta Z_i[2,k], 9\delta Z_i[3,k], n_i[k] \rangle \in \mathsf{T_\oplus}$	$\langle m_i[k], n_i[k], \delta Y_i[0,k] \rangle \in \mathsf{T_\oplus}$
$\langle 9\delta Z_i[0,k], 14\delta Z_i[1,k], o_i[k] \rangle \in \mathsf{T_\oplus}$	$\langle 11\delta Z_i[2,k], 13\delta Z_i[3,k], p_i[k] \rangle \in \mathsf{T_\oplus}$	$\langle o_i[k], p_i[k], \delta Y_i[1,k] \rangle \in \mathsf{T_\oplus}$
$\langle 13\delta Z_i[0,k], 9\delta Z_i[1,k], q_i[k] \rangle \in \mathsf{T_\oplus}$	$\langle 14\delta Z_i[2,k], 11\delta Z_i[3,k], r_i[k] \rangle \in \mathsf{T_\oplus}$	$\langle q_i[k], r_i[k], \delta Y_i[2,k] \rangle \in \mathsf{T_\oplus}$
$\langle 11\delta Z_i[0,k], 13\delta Z_i[1,k], s_i[k] \rangle \in \mathsf{T_\oplus}$	$\langle 9\delta Z_i[2,k], 14\delta Z_i[3,k], t_i[k] \rangle \in \mathsf{T_\oplus}$	$\langle s_i[k], t_i[k], \delta Y_i[3,k] \rangle \in \mathsf{T_\oplus}$

$$\forall i \in [0, N_r - 1], \forall j \in [0, 3], \forall k \in [0, N_b - 1], \tag{C8}$$

$$\langle \delta X_{i+1}[j,k], \delta Z_i[j,k], \delta WK[j, (i+1) \times N_b + k] \rangle \in \mathsf{T_\oplus}$$

$$\forall \omega \in [N_b, N_b \times (N_r + 1) - 1] \text{ such that } \mathtt{isSbCol}(\omega), \forall j \in [0,3], \tag{C9}$$

$$\langle \delta WK[j, \omega], \delta SWK[j, \omega], p_{WK}[j, \omega] \rangle \in \mathsf{T_{SBOX}}$$

where predicate $\mathtt{isSbCol}(\omega)$ is $\omega \geq Nk - 1 \wedge \omega < N_r \times (N_k + 1) - 1 \wedge$
$(\omega \mod N_k = N_k - 1 \vee (N_k > 6 \wedge \omega \mod N_k = 3))$

$$\forall j \in [0, 3], \forall \omega \in [N_b, N_b \times (N_r + 1) - 1], \tag{C10}$$

if $\omega \mod N_k = 0$ then $\langle \delta WK[j, \omega], \delta WK[j, \omega - N_k], \delta SWK[(j+1) \mod 4, \omega - 1] \rangle \in \mathsf{T_\oplus}$
elsif $N_k > 6 \wedge k \mod N_k = 4$ then $\langle \delta WK[j, \omega], \delta WK[j, \omega - N_k], \delta SWK[j, \omega - 1] \rangle \in \mathsf{T_\oplus}$
else $\langle \delta WK[j, \omega], \delta WK[j, \omega - N_k], \delta WK[j, \omega - 1] \rangle \in \mathsf{T_\oplus}$

Model 3: Step 2 model for Rijndael.

Constraint (C1) of Model 3 ensures that obj is equal to the sum of every p_A such that δA is a byte that passes through an S-box. It also ensures that obj is strictly greater than the current lower bound LB.

ShiftRows. Constraint (C3) of Model 3 is the straightforward translation of ShiftRows.

MixColumns. Constraints (C4) to (C7) represent the `MixColumns` operation. We introduce new integer variables to represent the result of applying the Galois Field multiplication to a byte: for each value $v \in \{2, 3\}$, and each byte $\delta Y_i[j, k]$, the variable $v\delta Y_i[j, k]$ is constrained to be equal to $v \otimes \delta Y_i[j, k]$ by the table constraint (C4), where $\mathsf{T}_{\texttt{MULv}}$ contains every couple $(\delta A, \delta B) \in [\![0, 255]\!]^2$ such that $\delta B = v \otimes \delta A$. Then, Constraint (C5) ensures that $\delta Z_i[j, k]$ is equal to the result of XORing four bytes (corresponding to the bytes at column k of δY_i multiplied by the coefficients at row j of M). Again, this is done by using table constraints. The main novelty with respect to the model introduced in [13] for the AES is that we do not use a single table containing every tuple of five bytes such that the XOR of these bytes is equal to 0, as this table is very large (2^{40} tuples of five bytes). Instead, we introduce new variables (denoted $a_i[k]$, $b_i[k]$, etc.), and we decompose the relation into three constraints such that each constraint ensures that the XOR of three variables is equal to zero. For example, the relation

$$\delta Z_i[0, k] \oplus 2\delta Y_i[0, k] \oplus 3\delta Y_i[1, k] \oplus \delta Y_i[2, k] \oplus \delta Y_i[3, k] = 0$$

is decomposed into the three following constraints:

$$\langle 2\delta Y_i[0, k], 3\delta Y_i[1, k], a_i[k] \rangle \in \mathsf{T}_\oplus$$
$$\langle \delta Y_i[2, k], \delta Y_i[3, k], b_i[k] \rangle \in \mathsf{T}_\oplus$$
$$\langle a_i[k], b_i[k], \delta Z_i[0, k] \rangle \in \mathsf{T}_\oplus$$

where $\mathsf{T}_\oplus$ is the table which contains every triple $(\delta A, \delta B, \delta C) \in [\![0, 255]\!]^3$ such that $\delta A \oplus \delta B \oplus \delta C = 0$. This decomposition allows us to remove some variables and simplify constraints when we know that some variables are equal to 0. For example, if $\Delta Y_i[0, k] = 0$ in the truncated characteristic, then we infer that $2\delta Y_i[0, k] = 0$ (because $2 \otimes 0 = 0$) and $a_i[k] = 3\delta Y_i[1, k]$ (because $0 \oplus \delta Y_i[1, k] \oplus a_i[k] = 0$). Hence, in this case the three previous constraints are replaced with: $\langle \delta Y_i[2, k], \delta Y_i[3, k], b_i[k] \rangle \in \mathsf{T}_\oplus$ and $\langle 3\delta Y_i[1, k], b_i[k], \delta Z_i[0, k] \rangle \in \mathsf{T}_\oplus$.

Constraints (C6) and (C7) are redundant constraints that model the `MixColumns`$^{-1}$ operation: They do not change the solutions, but they speed up the solution process by allowing the solver to propagate in both forward (from the plaintext to the ciphertext) and backward (from the ciphertext to the plaintext) directions.

AddRoundKey. Constraint (C8) is a straightforward implementation of `AddRoundKey`, using table $\mathsf{T}_\oplus$.

KeySchedule. Constraints (C9) and (C10) model the `KeySchedule`. Constraint (C9) models the S-boxes of the `KeySchedule` (as described in Sect. 3.4). Constraint (C10) models the XORs of the `KeySchedule`, using table $\mathsf{T}_\oplus$. Note that we do not represent XORs with constants as they are cancelled by differential cryptanalysis.

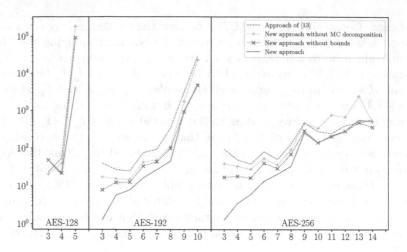

Fig. 1. Comparison of the approach of [13] (in green) with our new approach (in red), our new approach without `MixColumns` decomposition (in orange), and our new approach without exploiting bounds (in purple). Each point (x, y) corresponds to an AES instance (with $K_{len} = 128$ on the left, $K_{len} = 192$ in the middle, and $K_{len} = 256$ on the right): y gives the CPU time in seconds needed to solve it (logscale) when there are $N_r = x$ rounds. (Color figure online)

4   Results

The Step 1 model is implemented with the MiniZinc 2.4.3 modelling language[3]. This language is accepted by many CP solvers and preliminary experiments have shown us that the best performing solver is Picat-SAT[4] 2.8.6: This solver first translates the MiniZinc model into a SAT instance and then uses the Lingeling SAT solver to solve the SAT instance. The Step 2 model is implemented and solved with the CP library Choco[5] v4.10.2.

In Fig. 1, we compare solving times of the approach of [13] with those of our new approach on the AES instances in order to evaluate the interest of our two modifications, i.e., (i) the interleaving of Steps 1 and 2 and the active use of LB and UB to stop the search whenever LB $\geq$ UB (see Sect. 3.2), and (ii) the decomposition of the `MixColumns` constraint into 3 smaller table constraints (see Sect. 3.4). For this experiment, all runs have been performed on a single core of an Intel Xeon CPU E3 at 3.50 GHz with 4 cores under a Linux Ubuntu 20.04.1 (Focal Fossa) using at most 16 GB of RAM. There are two instances for which our new approach needs slightly more time than the approach of [13]: AES-128 when $N_r = 3$ (48 s instead of 23 s) and AES-256 when $N_r = 13$ (567 s instead of 479 s). For the 21 remaining instances our new approach is faster and, in some cases the difference is very large, e.g., 4,217 s instead of 95,389 s for AES-128

---

[3] https://github.com/MiniZinc/MiniZincIDE/releases/tag/2.4.3.

[4] http://picat-lang.org/download/picat28_6_linux64.tar.gz.

[5] https://github.com/chocoteam/choco-solver/releases/tag/4.10.2.

when $N_r = 5$, or 5,163 s instead of 30,059 s for AES-192 when $N_r = 10$. To evaluate the interest of each of our two modifications separately, we also display our new approach without (ii), and our new approach without (i). In many cases, each modification improves the solution process, and the combination of these two modifications is even better. However, modification (i) deteriorates the solution process when $N_r \geq 10$ for AES-256. This comes from the fact that, for these instances, the optimal solution is strictly smaller than $2^{-6 \cdot NB_{sbox}}$ so that the lower bound LB cannot be used to stop the search.

We give in Tables 3 and 4 the results of Algorithm 2 for every key length $K_{len} \in \{128, 160, 192, 224, 256\}$, every block size $C_{len} \in \{128, 160, 192, 224, 256\}$, and every number of rounds $N_r \in [\![3, x]\!]$ where x is the maximum number of rounds authorized (i.e., the maximal number of rounds for which NB_{SBOX} is smaller than the key length divided by 6 and the number of active S-boxes in the plaintext part is smaller than the block length divided by 6). For this experiment, all runs have been performed on a single core of an Intel Xeon E5-2630 v4 at 3.10 Ghz with 10 cores under a Linux Debian 10 (Buster) using at most 16 GB of RAM (default JVM configuration). This architecture was provided by the Grid5000 cluster [3].

Please note that there is a slight difference between the model used for Fig. 1 and the model used for Tables 3 and 4. Indeed, the model in [13] ignores the SBOXes of the last round subkey. When the key has 128 or 256 bits, this does not change anything. However, when the key has 192 bits this may change results. To allow a fair comparison with [13], we also ignore the SBOXes of the last round key in all models compared in Fig. 1. However, in Tables 3 and 4, we do consider the SBOXes of the last round subkey. Therefore, when the key has 192 bits and the text 128 bits, some probabilities may be greater than those reported in [13], e.g., for the instance Rijndael-128-192 with 7 rounds the maximal probability is 2^{-84} instead of 2^{-78}.

One instance (when $C_{len} = 128$, $K_{len} = 160$, and $N_r = 8$) is still not completely solved at the time we submit the paper, after 38 days of computation. For this instance, the output value of *Step1-opt* is 23. *Step1-enum* has enumerated 7 truncated characteristics with 23 active S-boxes and none of them can be instantiated into a Step 2 characteristic. So far, we have enumerated 213 truncated characteristic with 24 active S-boxes and none of them can be instantiated into a Step 2 characteristic. Hence, for this instance the current upper bound is $UB = 2^{-150}$. We have computed 189 instances with 25 active S-boxes and 1048 instances with 26 active S-boxes and the smaller probability is $LB = 2^{-160}$.

All other instances have been solved within a reasonable amount of time: 82 are solved within 1,000 s; 24 need more than 1,000 s and less than 10,000 s (i.e., less than three hours); 10 need more than 10,000 s and less than 100,000 s (i.e., less than 28 h); and finally 2 need more than 28 h and less than 3 days.

In Tables 3 and 4, o_1 is the output value of *Step1-opt* (called at line 1 of Algorithm 2), i.e., the initial value of NB_{SBOX}; p is the output value of Algorithm 2, i.e., the probability of the optimal related-key differential characteristic; and time is the total CPU time spent by Algorithm 2 in seconds (this time both includes the running times of Picat-SAT and of Choco). We also report the number o_2 of active S-boxes in the optimal differential characteristic. In most cases (91 out of 122 cases), $o_1 = o_2$ and $p > 2^{-6 \cdot (o_1+1)}$. In these cases, Algorithm 1 has enumerated Step 1 solutions for only one value of NB_{SBOX}, and LB became larger than or equal to UB the first time NB_{SBOX} has been incremented.

In 17 cases (marked with ^{c} just after o_2), $o_1 = o_2$ but it has been necessary to increment NB_{SBOX} at least once in order to check that no better characteristic can be found with more active S-boxes. For example, when $C_{len} = 128$, $K_{len} = 224$, and $r = 9$, the best differential characteristic has 22 active S-boxes and its probability is 2^{-139}. As $2^{-139} < 2^{-6 \cdot 23}$, Algorithm 1 has incremented NB_{SBOX} in order to check that it is not possible to have a larger probability (equal to 2^{-139}) with 23 active S-boxes.

In 2 cases (marked with ! just after o_2), $o_2 \geq o_1 + 1$ because none of the step 1 truncated characteristic with o_1 active S-boxes can be instantiated into a Step 2 characteristic. In these two cases, Algorithm 1 has incremented NB_{SBOX} in order to enumerate Step 1 solutions with $o_1 + 1$ active S-boxes and find the best differential characteristic.

Finally, in 13 cases (marked with ↑ just after o_2), $o_2 \geq o_1 + 1$ because a better characteristic has been found with $o_1 + n$ active S-boxes (though at least one Step 1 solution can be instantiated into a Step 2 solution).

5   Attacks

We describe in this section the best attacks we could mount based on the distinguishers found in the previous section. More precisely, two particular distinguishers have a real interest in terms of attacks. The first one is an 11-round related-key differential characteristic distinguisher on Rijndael-128-224 (presented in Table 5 that allows us to mount an attack on 12 rounds (out of 13) of this cipher. There also exists a 12-round distinguisher for Rijndael-128-224 but due to its very low probability (equal to 2^{-127}) for the data path, we do not manage to transform this distinguisher into an attack. And second, we also mount an attack on 12 rounds of Rijndael-160-256 (it has 14 rounds) based on the 11-round related-key differential characteristic distinguisher (presented in Table 6).

5.1   Attack on 12 Rounds of Rijndael-128-224

First, remember that the 12th round of Rijndael-128-224 is the last round for our attack so it does not contain a MixColumns operation. We base our attack on the distinguisher presented in Table 5. This distinguisher has a probability equal to 2^{-169}: 2^{-103} coming from the state and 2^{-66} coming from the key.

Thus, the attack process is the following one. We submit $M = 2^{103+\epsilon}$ pairs of plaintexts X and X' with the difference specified in the first line of Table 5 under the keys K and $K' = K \oplus \delta K$ with the difference specified in the first line (second column) of Table 5. Then a possible propagation of the difference is the one shown in Table 5, and we obtain the corresponding ciphertexts C and C'.

Table 3. Summary of the best related-key differential characteristics for Rijndael when $C_{len} \in \{128, 160\}$. The time is given in seconds.

Results when $C_{len} = 128$ and $K_{len} \in \{128, 160, 192\}$

	$K_{len} = 128$				$K_{len} = 160$				$K_{len} = 192$			
	o_1	o_2	p	time	o_1	o_2	p	time	o_1	o_2	p	time
$Nr = 3$	5	5	2^{-31}	13	4	4	2^{-24}	5	1	1	2^{-6}	1
$Nr = 4$	12	12	2^{-75}	31	5	5	2^{-30}	21	4	4	2^{-24}	6
$Nr = 5$	17	17	2^{-105}	8,304	10	10	2^{-60}	12	5	5	2^{-30}	8
$Nr = 6$					17	17	2^{-108}	641	10	10	2^{-60}	17
$Nr = 7$					19	19	2^{-120}	1,089	14	14	2^{-84}	46
$Nr = 8$					23	$\geq 24!$	$2^{-160} \leq p \leq 2^{-150}$	$> 10^6$	18	18	2^{-108}	83
$Nr = 9$									24	24	2^{-146}	1,800

Results when $C_{len} = 128$ and $K_{len} \in \{224, 256\}$

	$K_{len} = 224$				$K_{len} = 256$			
	o_1	o_2	p	time	o_1	o_2	p	time
$Nr = 3$	1	1	2^{-6}	1	1	1	2^{-6}	1
$Nr = 4$	3	3	2^{-18}	3	3	3	2^{-18}	3
$Nr = 5$	6	6	2^{-36}	8	3	3	2^{-18}	5
$Nr = 6$	8	8	2^{-48}	14	5	5	2^{-30}	13
$Nr = 7$	13	13	2^{-78}	35	5	5	2^{-30}	18
$Nr = 8$	18	18	2^{-112}	1,593	10	10	2^{-60}	32
$Nr = 9$	22	22^c	2^{-139}	2,425	15	15	2^{-92}	346
$Nr = 10$	24	24^c	2^{-151}	1,834	16	16	2^{-98}	159
$Nr = 11$	27	27^c	2^{-169}	1,823	20	20	2^{-122}	330
$Nr = 12$	34	34^c	2^{-212}	9,561	20	20	2^{-122}	277
$Nr = 13$					24	24	2^{-146}	420
$Nr = 14$					24	24	2^{-146}	557

Results when $C_{len} = 160$ and $K_{len} \in \{128, 160, 192\}$

	$K_{len} = 128$				$K_{len} = 160$				$K_{len} = 192$			
	o_1	o_2	p	time	o_1	o_2	p	time	o_1	o_2	p	time
$Nr = 3$	9	9	2^{-54}	6	5	5	2^{-30}	880	4	4	2^{-24}	4
$Nr = 4$	18	18	2^{-112}	49,501	10	10	2^{-60}	11	6	6	2^{-36}	7
$Nr = 5$					17	17	2^{-107}	621	9	9	2^{-54}	15
$Nr = 6$					21	22!	2^{-138}	36,788	15	15	2^{-90}	62
$Nr = 7$									19	19	2^{-117}	600
$Nr = 8$									23	23	2^{-141}	2,059

Results when $C_{len} = 160$ and $K_{len} \in \{224, 256\}$

	$K_{len} = 224$				$K_{len} = 256$			
	o_1	o_2	p	time	o_1	o_2	p	time
$Nr = 3$	2	2	2^{-12}	2	1	1	2^{-6}	2
$Nr = 4$	5	5	2^{-31}	16	4	4	2^{-24}	4
$Nr = 5$	10	10	2^{-60}	18	6	6	2^{-36}	14
$Nr = 6$	15	15	2^{-90}	40	12	12	2^{-72}	42
$Nr = 7$	20	20	2^{-124}	402	15	15	2^{-93}	226
$Nr = 8$	24	24	2^{-148}	783	20	20	2^{-124}	755
$Nr = 9$	30	30^c	2^{-190}	13,081	23	23^c	2^{-146}	2,284
$Nr = 10$					27	27^c	2^{-169}	4,927
$Nr = 11$					32	32^c	2^{-204}	15,497

Table 4. Summary of the best related-key differential characteristics for Rijndael when $C_{len} \in \{192, 224, 256\}$. The time is given in seconds.

Results when $C_{len} = 192$ and $K_{len} \in \{128, 160, 192\}$

	$K_{len} = 128$				$K_{len} = 160$				$K_{len} = 192$			
	o_1	o_2	p	time	o_1	o_2	p	time	o_1	o_2	p	time
$Nr = 3$	9	9	2^{-54}	7	6	6	2^{-37}	20	5	5	2^{-30}	199
$Nr = 4$					15	15	2^{-94}	92	9	9	2^{-54}	15
$Nr = 5$					19	19	2^{-118}	183	14	15↑	2^{-90}	146
$Nr = 6$									19	19	2^{-117}	864
$Nr = 7$									25	25	2^{-153}	2,101

Results when $C_{len} = 192$ and $K_{len} \in \{224, 256\}$

	$K_{len} = 224$				$K_{len} = 256$			
	o_1	o_2	p	time	o_1	o_2	p	time
$Nr = 3$	4	4	2^{-24}	7	1	1	2^{-6}	2
$Nr = 4$	8	8	2^{-48}	13	5	5	2^{-30}	10
$Nr = 5$	15	15	2^{-95}	387	12	12	2^{-72}	84
$Nr = 6$	16	17↑	2^{-103}	1,349	17	17	2^{-106}	452
$Nr = 7$	24	24^c	2^{-157}	11,908	18	18	2^{-112}	551
$Nr = 8$	32	33↑^{c}	2^{-205}	91,983	24	24	2^{-149}	951
$Nr = 9$					29	29	2^{-179}	3,397
$Nr = 10$					38	38^c	2^{-236}	88,076

Results when $C_{len} = 224$ and $K_{len} \in \{128, 160, 192\}$

	$K_{len} = 128$				$K_{len} = 160$				$K_{len} = 192$			
	o_1	o_2	p	time	o_1	o_2	p	time	o_1	o_2	p	time
$Nr = 3$	9	9	2^{-54}	13	9	9	2^{-54}	9	6	6	2^{-37}	39
$Nr = 4$					19	19^c	2^{-122}	2,742	13	13	2^{-78}	35
$Nr = 5$									20	20	2^{-124}	1,040
$Nr = 6$									28	29↑	2^{-179}	18,632

Results when $C_{len} = 224$ and $K_{len} \in \{224, 256\}$

	$K_{len} = 224$				$K_{len} = 256$			
	o_1	o_2	p	time	o_1	o_2	p	time
$Nr = 3$	6	6	2^{-36}	8	4	4	2^{-24}	10
$Nr = 4$	13	13	2^{-79}	121	8	8	2^{-48}	22
$Nr = 5$	16	17↑	2^{-103}	1,562	15	16↑	2^{-97}	3,267
$Nr = 6$	23	23^c	2^{-150}	1,511	18	19↑	2^{-115}	5,049
$Nr = 7$	31	31^c	2^{-196}	49,429	20	21↑	2^{-128}	1,378
$Nr = 8$					28	30↑	2^{-182}	18,377
$Nr = 9$					37	37^c	2^{-241}	210,290

Results when $C_{len} = 256$ and $K_{len} \in \{128, 160, 192\}$

	$K_{len} = 128$				$K_{len} = 160$				$K_{len} = 192$			
	o_1	o_2	p	time	o_1	o_2	p	time	o_1	o_2	p	time
$Nr = 3$	9	9	2^{-54}	15	9	9	2^{-54}	13	9	9	2^{-54}	12
$Nr = 4$					20	21↑	2^{-130}	4,157	18	18	2^{-110}	824
$Nr = 5$									24	24	2^{-148}	4,624

Results when $C_{len} = 256$ and $K_{len} \in \{224, 256\}$

	$K_{len} = 224$				$K_{len} = 256$			
	o_1	o_2	p	time	o_1	o_2	p	time
$Nr = 3$	6	6	2^{-37}	33	5	5	2^{-30}	34
$Nr = 4$	18	18^c	2^{-115}	65,672	13	13	2^{-79}	276
$Nr = 5$	28	29!	2^{-179}	455,210	16	17↑	2^{-103}	3,084
$Nr = 6$					20	21↑	2^{-128}	2,170
$Nr = 7$					27	29↑	2^{-176}	9,237
$Nr = 8$					37	37^c	2^{-240}	191,581

Table 5. The Best related key differential characteristic we found on 11 rounds of Rijndael-128-224 with probability equal to 2^{-169}. The four words represent the four rows of the state and are given in hexadecimal notation. Note that the last round does not contain the `MixColumns` operation.

Round	$\delta X_i = X_i \oplus X_i'$ (before SBOX) δSBX_i (after SBOX)	δRK_i	Pr(States)	Pr(Key)
$i=0$	005D005D 00A300A3 00A300A3 00FE00FE	015C005D 00A300A3 00A300A3 00FE00FE	–	–
$i=1$	01010000 00000000 00000000 00000000 1F1F0000 00000000 00000000 00000000	21210001 1F1F0000 1F1F0000 21210000	$2^{-2\times6}$	–
2	1F1F0001 00000000 00000000 00000000 A3A3001F 00000000 00000000 00000000	5D5D0021 A3A3001F A3A3001F FEFE0021	$2^{-3\times6}$	–
3	0000001F 00000000 00000000 00000000 000000A3 00000000 00000000 00000000	0000015C 000000A3 000000A3 000000FE	2^{-6}	–
4	00001F1F 00000000 00000000 00000000 00001F1F 00000000 00000000 00000000	01013E3E 00001F1F 00001F1F 00002121	$2^{2\times(-6)}$	2^{-6}
5	01010000 00000000 00000000 00000000 1FA30000000000000000000000000000	3E5C0001 1FA300001FA3000021FE0000	2^{-6-7}	$2^{-6-3\times7}$
6	00010001 0000000000000000000000000000 001F001F 00000000 0000000000000000	003E003E 001F001F001F001F00210021	$2^{2\times(-6)}$	$2^{-6-3\times7}$
7	0000000000000000 00000000 00000000 0000000000000000 00000000 00000000	01010000 00000000 00000000 00000000	–	–
8	01010000 00000000 00000000 00000000 1F1F0000 00000000 00000000 00000000	3E3E0001 1F1F0000 1F1F0000 21210000	$2^{2\times(-6)}$	–
9	00000001 00000000 00000000 00000000 0000001F 00000000 00000000 00000000	0000003E 0000001F 0000001F 00000021	2^{-6}	–
10	00000000 00000000 00000000 00000000 00000000 00000000 0000000000000000	00000101 00000000 00000000 00000000	–	–
11	0000010100000000 00000000 00000000 00001F1F 00000000 0000000000000000	01012121 00001F1F00001F1F 00002121	$2^{2\times(-6)}$	2^{-6}
Output	01013E3E 00001F1F 00001F1F00002121			

We know from Table 5 that the output of the 11th round (and the beginning of the 12th round) is of the form $\delta X_{12} = \begin{pmatrix} 01 & 01 & 1F & 1F \\ 0 & 0 & 0 & 0 \\ 0 & 0 & 0 & 0 \\ 0 & 0 & 0 & 0 \end{pmatrix}$. After passing through

SubBytes and ShiftRows, it becomes: $\delta SX_{12} = \begin{pmatrix} ? & ? & ? & ? \\ 0 & 0 & 0 & 0 \\ 0 & 0 & 0 & 0 \\ 0 & 0 & 0 & 0 \end{pmatrix}$. From the keysched-

ule, the subkey difference δK_{12} will be of the form $\begin{pmatrix} 21 & A \oplus 01 & A & A \oplus 01 \\ 1F & B & B & B \\ 1F & C & C & C \\ 21 & D & D & D \end{pmatrix}$

where A, B, C and D are unknown difference. Thus the difference between C

and C' will be of the form $\delta C = \begin{pmatrix} ? & ? & ? & ? \\ 1F & B & B & B \\ 1F & C & C & C \\ 21 & D & D & D \end{pmatrix}$.

So the attack works as follows:

1. We filter on the values $1F$, $1F$, and 21 at positions $(1,0)$, $(2,0)$, and $(3,0)$ in δC before the last ShiftRows. It remains $2^{103+\epsilon-24} = 2^{79+\epsilon}$ pairs of plaintexts/ciphertexts. Moreover, we know that the three bytes at positions $(1,1), (1,2)$ and $(1,3)$ must be equal (this remark also holds for the second and the third rows). This leads to another filter of 48 bits.
2. We guess the byte value of K_{12} at position $(0,0)$ with a cost of 2^8. Then, we decipher this byte from C and C' to check if it is equal to 01 at the input of the 12th round. Then, it filters 2^{-8} values. Moreover, the known byte at position $(0,0)$ in K_{12} gives us the difference D (due to the keyschedule construction).
3. We can guess the byte at position $(1,0)$ in K_{12} and check the value at the input of the 12th round at position $(1,0)$, by deciphering from C and C'. Then, it filters 2^{-8} values. Moreover, we can compute the difference A.
4. We can guess the three bytes at positions $(0,1)$, $(0,2)$, and $(0,3)$ in K_{12} and check the value at the input of the 12th round at the same position knowing the difference A, by deciphering from C and C'. Then, it filters 2^{-24} values.
5. We can guess the byte at position $(3,0)$ in K_{12} and check the value at the input of the 12th round at position $(3,0)$, by deciphering from C and C'. Then, it filters 2^{-8} values.
6. We can guess the byte at position $(2,0)$ in K_{12} and check the value at the input of the 12th round at position $(2,0)$, by deciphering from C and C'. Then, it filters 2^{-8} values.

Then, we have guessed 7 bytes of the subkey K_{12}, 56 bits of key, and we have filtered an equivalent of 72 bits, leading to keep $2^{103+\epsilon-72} = 2^{31+\epsilon}$ pairs of plaintexts/ciphertexts. After guessing the 7-byte difference in the subkey K_{12}, $\delta_{K_{12}}$ is fully determined. Thus, guessing the bytes of one key state could determine the bytes of the related-key state.

The related-key differential characteristic given in Table 5 has a probability to happen for the state part equals to 2^{-103}. Thus, if we use 2^{104} plaintexts/ciphertexts in the related-key differential attack on 12 rounds of Rijndael-128-224, then the right difference of the 56 bits of the last subkey will be counted at least twice on average whereas the probability that a bad key appears twice is really low (around $2^{32-72} = 2^{-40}$). The success probability computed using the results of [23] is around 97%. The time complexity of the attack is about 2^{105} encryptions and the attack succeeds if the key follows the characteristic described in Table 5. In other words, we have a set of weak keys of size $2^{224-66} = 2^{158}$.

The 168 remaining bits of the master key can be guessed through guessing more bytes in K_{11} and in K_{12} and filtering according to the remaining values in δX_{11} and the SBoxes of the key schedule.

5.2   Attack on 12 Rounds of Rijndael-160-256

In the same way, from the related-key differential characteristic distinguisher on 11-round of Rijndael-160-256 presented in Table 6, we can easily mount a 12-round attack against Rijndael-160-256 that has 14 rounds. Note that the 12th round does not contain the MixColumns operation as it is the last round

Table 6. The Best related key differential characteristic we found on 11 rounds of Rijndael-160-256 with probability equal to 2^{-204}. The four words represent the four rows of the state and are given in hexadecimal notation. Note that the last round does not contain the MixColumns operation.

Round	$\delta X_i = X_i \oplus X_i'$ (before SBOX) δSBX_i (after SBOX)	δRK_i	Pr(States)	Pr(Key)
$i=0$	E094E0E082 7000700041 1400700041 701F9000C3	E000E0E000 7000700041 7000700041 70909000C3	–	–
$i=1$	0094000082 0000000000 6400000000 008F000000	008282E0E0 0041007070 0041007070 00C3000090	$2^{4\times(-6)}$	2^{-6}
	0041000070 0000000000 2000000000 0010000000			
2	000082D000 0000000000 0000000000 0000000000	00E0828200 0000414100 0000414100 0000C3C300	$2^{2\times(-7)}$	2^{-6}
	0000414100 0000000000 0000000000 0000000000			
3	00E0000000 0000000000 0000000000 0000000000	82E00000E0 0070000000 0070000000 0090000000	2^{-7}	2^{-6-7}
	0070000000000000000 0000000000 0000000000			
4	82000000E0 0000000000 0000000000 0000000000	00828200E0 4100000070 4100000070 C300000090	$2^{2\times(-7)}$	–
	4100000070 0000000000 0000000000 0000000000			
5	8282820000 0000000000 0000000000 0000000000	E0E0000082 7070700000 7070700000 9090900000	$2^{3\times(-6)}$	$2^{3\times(-7)}$
	7070700000 0000000000 0000000000 0000000000			
6	0000E00082 0000000000 0000000000 0000000000	0000E000E0 0000700070 0000700070 0000900090	2^{-6-7}	–
	0000700070 0000000000 0000000000 0000000000			
7	0000000000 0000000000 0000000000 0000000000	E082000000 0000000000 0000000000 0000000000	–	2^{-6}
	0000000000 0000000000 0000000000 0000000000			
8	E082000000 0000000000 0000000000 0000000000	E0E000E000 7070000000 7070000000 9090000000	2^{-6-7}	2^{-6}
	7070000000 0000000000 0000000000 0000000000			
9	000000E000 0000000000 0000000000 0000000000	000000E000 0000007000 0000007000 0000009000	2^{-7}	–
	0000007000 0000000000 0000000000 0000000000			
10	0000000000 0000000000 0000000000 0000000000	00E0828282 0000000000 0000000000 0000000000	–	2^{-6}
	0000000000 0000000000 0000000000 0000000000			
11	00E0828282 0000000000 0000000000 0000000000	82E0E0E000 0070707070 0070707070 00E0E0E0E0	$2^{4\times(-6)}$	2^{-6}
	0082707070 0000000000 0000000000 0000000000			
Output	?????????? 00F20000?? 00F20000?? 000D0000??			

of our attack. The 11-round related-key differential characteristic distinguisher presented in Table 6 has a probability equal to 2^{-204}: 2^{-128} coming from the difference in the state and 2^{-76} coming from the key.

Thus, the attack process is the following one. We submit $M = 2^{128+\epsilon}$ pairs of plaintexts X and X' with the difference specified in the first line of Table 6 under the keys K and $K' = K \oplus \delta K$ with the difference specified in the first line (second column) of Table 6. Then a possible propagation of the difference is the one shown in Table 6. Then, we obtain the corresponding ciphertexts C and C'.

Then, we know from Table 6 that the output of the 11th round (and the beginning of the 12th round) is of the form

$$\delta X_{12} = \begin{pmatrix} 82 & FF & 0 & 0 & E0 \\ 0 & F2 & 0 & 0 & 0 \\ 0 & F2 & 0 & 0 & 0 \\ 0 & ED & 70 & 70 & 70 \end{pmatrix}.$$ After passing through SubBytes and ShiftRows,

it becomes: $\delta SX_{12} = \begin{pmatrix} ? & ? & 0 & 0 & ? \\ ? & 0 & 0 & 0 & 0 \\ 0 & 0 & 0 & 0 & ? \\ ? & ? & 0 & ? & ? \end{pmatrix}$. From the keyschedule, the subkey differences δK_{12} will be of the form $\begin{pmatrix} 82 & 0 & 82 & 0 & F \\ A & A & A & A & D \\ B & B & B & B & E \\ C & C & C & C & E0 \end{pmatrix}$ where A, B, C, D, E and F are

unknown difference. Thus the difference between C and C' will be of the form

$$\delta C = \begin{pmatrix} ? & ? & 82 & 0 & ? \\ ? & A & A & A & D \\ B & B & B & B & ? \\ ? & ? & C & ? & ? \end{pmatrix}.$$

So the attack works as follows:

1. For all the $2^{128+\epsilon}$ encrypted pairs of plaintexts/ciphertexts, we filter on the values 82 and 0 at positions $(0,2)$ and $(0,3)$ in δC. This filters 2^{-16} values. Then, it remains $2^{112+\epsilon}$ encrypted pairs of plaintexts/ciphertexts.
2. We guess the three bytes at positions $(1,4)$, $(2,4)$, and $(3,4)$ in K_{11} for a cost of 2^{24}. This gives us the values of differences A, B and C. With those known values, we filter on δSX_{12} on the 8 positions that are equal to 0 after removing A, B, and C (positions $(1,1),(1,2),(1,3),(2,0),(2,1),(2,2),(2,3)$ and $(3,2)$). This filters 2^{-64} values.
3. We guess 6 bytes of K_{12} (those at positions $(0,0),(0,1),(1,0),(3,0),(3,1)$ and $(3,3)$). We filter the corresponding 2^{-48} values on δX_{12} (before the SBOXes) at the same positions.
4. We guess the byte at position $(2,3)$ in K_{12} to get one new byte in δK_{12} at position $(1,4)$ equal to D and check if the difference is equal to 0 at position $(1,4)$ in δX_{12}. It filters 2^{-8} values.
5. We guess the byte at position $(3,4)$ in K_{12} to filter one byte of value in δX_{12} at position $(3,4)$. We guess another byte at position $(2,4)$ in K_{12} to filter the byte value at position $(2,4)$ in δX_{12}. And finally, we guess the two bytes at positions $(1,3)$ and $(0,4)$ in K_{12} to filter the byte value at position $(0,4)$ in δX_{12}.

We have guessed a total of 112 key bits and we have filtered, in the initial step 16 bits and the equivalent of 32 bits in the second step and the last step leading to stay with $2^{80+\epsilon}$ pairs of plaintexts/ciphertexts.

The related-key differential characteristic given in Table 6 has a probability to happen for the state part equals to 2^{-128}. Thus, if we use 2^{129} plaintexts/ciphertexts in the related-key differential attack on 12 rounds of Rijndael-160-256, then the right difference of the 112 bits of the last subkey will be counted at least twice on average whereas the probability that a bad key appears twice is really low (around $2^{81-112} = 2^{-31}$). The success probability computed using the results of [23] is around 97% also. The time complexity of the attack is about 2^{130} encryptions and the attack succeeds if the key follows the characteristic described in Table 6. In other words, we have a set of weak keys of size $2^{256-76} = 2^{180}$.

The 144 remaining bits of the master key can be guessed through guessing more bytes in K_{11} and in K_{12} and filtering according the remaining values in δX_{11} and the SBoxes of the key schedule.

6 Conclusion

In this paper, we have extended and improved the models initially proposed in [13] for the AES to the 25 instances of Rijndael. This allowed us to compute optimal related-key differential characteristics for all Rijndael instances but one (and provide upper and lower bounds for the remaining one). We sum up in Table 7 the best attacks described in this paper.

Table 7. Summary of the best related-key differential attacks we found on different Rijndael instances. The last column displays the number of keys for which the attack works.

Instance	Nb rounds	Nr	Time	Number of keys
Rijndael-128-224	12	13	2^{105}	2^{158}
Rijndael-160-256	12	14	2^{130}	2^{180}

Those results are obtained using a two-step strategy that is feasible in terms of memory usage and time consumption. This strategy is modelled in MiniZinc, and it is solved by combining two solvers: Picat-SAT for Step 1 and Choco for Step 2. It essentially means that we could today automate a big part of cryptanalysis through the use of generic solvers: we have gone from the artisan age of cryptanalysis to its industrial age.

Acknowledgements. This work has been partly funded by the ANR under grant Decrypt ANR-18-CE39-0007.

References

1. FIPS 197, Advanced Encryption Standard (AES), p. 51 (2001)
2. Ahmed Abdelkhalek, Yu., Sasaki, Y.T., Tolba, M., Youssef, A.M.: MILP modeling for (large) s-boxes to optimize probability of differential characteristics. IACR Trans. Symmetric Cryptol. **2017**(4), 99–129 (2017)
3. Balouek, D., et al.: Adding virtualization capabilities to the Grid'5000 testbed. In: Ivanov, I.I., van Sinderen, M., Leymann, F., Shan, T. (eds.) CLOSER 2012. CCIS, vol. 367, pp. 3–20. Springer, Cham (2013). https://doi.org/10.1007/978-3-319-04519-1_1
4. Biham, E.: New types of cryptanalytic attacks using related keys. In: Helleseth, T. (ed.) EUROCRYPT 1993. LNCS, vol. 765, pp. 398–409. Springer, Heidelberg (1994). https://doi.org/10.1007/3-540-48285-7_34
5. Biham, E., Shamir, A.: Differential cryptanalysis of feal and N-hash. In: Davies, D.W. (ed.) EUROCRYPT 1991. LNCS, vol. 547, pp. 1–16. Springer, Heidelberg (1991). https://doi.org/10.1007/3-540-46416-6_1
6. Biryukov, A., Nikolić, I.: Automatic search for related-key differential characteristics in byte-oriented block ciphers: application to AES, Camellia, Khazad and Others. In: Gilbert, H. (ed.) EUROCRYPT 2010. LNCS, vol. 6110, pp. 322–344. Springer, Heidelberg (2010). https://doi.org/10.1007/978-3-642-13190-5_17

7. Chu, G., Stuckey, P.J.: Chuffed solver description (2014). http://www.minizinc. org/challenge2014/description_chuffed.txt
8. Daemen, J., Rijmen, V.: AES Proposal: Rijndael (1999)
9. Daemen, J., Rijmen, V.: The Design of Rijndael: AES - The Advanced Encryption Standard. Springer, Berlin (2002). https://doi.org/10.1007/978-3-662-04722-4. OCLC: 751525895
10. Fouque, P.-A., Jean, J., Peyrin, T.: Structural evaluation of AES and chosen-key distinguisher of 9-round AES-128. In: Canetti, R., Garay, J.A. (eds.) CRYPTO 2013. LNCS, vol. 8042, pp. 183–203. Springer, Heidelberg (2013). https://doi.org/10.1007/978-3-642-40041-4_11
11. Galice, S., Minier, M.: Improving integral attacks against Rijndael-256 up to 9 rounds. In: Vaudenay, S. (ed.) AFRICACRYPT 2008. LNCS, vol. 5023, pp. 1–15. Springer, Heidelberg (2008). https://doi.org/10.1007/978-3-540-68164-9_1
12. Gecode Team. Gecode: Generic constraint development environment (2006). http://www.gecode.org
13. Gerault, D., Lafourcade, P., Minier, M., Solnon, C.: Computing AES related-key differential characteristics with constraint programming. Artif. Intell. **278**, 103183 (2020)
14. Gerault, D., Minier, M., Solnon, C.: Constraint programming models for chosen key differential cryptanalysis. In: Rueher, M. (ed.) CP 2016. LNCS, vol. 9892, pp. 584–601. Springer, Cham (2016). https://doi.org/10.1007/978-3-319-44953-1_37
15. Nakahara, J., Jr., Pavão, I.C.: Impossible-differential attacks on large-block Rijndael. In: Garay, J.A., Lenstra, A.K., Mambo, M., Peralta, R. (eds.) ISC 2007. LNCS, vol. 4779, pp. 104–117. Springer, Heidelberg (2007). https://doi.org/10.1007/978-3-540-75496-1_7
16. Knudsen, L.R.: Truncated and higher order differentials. In: Preneel, B. (ed.) FSE 1994. LNCS, vol. 1008, pp. 196–211. Springer, Heidelberg (1995). https://doi.org/10.1007/3-540-60590-8_16
17. Liu, G., Ghosh, M., Song, L.: Security analysis of SKINNY under related-tweakey settings (long paper). IACR Trans. Symmetric Cryptol. **2017**(3), 37–72 (2017)
18. Liu, Y., et al.: Improved impossible differential cryptanalysis of large-block Rijndael. Sci. China Inf. Sci. **62**(3), 32101:1–32101:14 (2019)
19. Minier, M.: Improving impossible-differential attacks against Rijndael-160 and Rijndael-224. Des. Codes Cryptogr. **82**(1–2), 117–129 (2017)
20. Nethercote, N., Stuckey, P.J., Becket, R., Brand, S., Duck, G.J., Tack, G.: MiniZinc: towards a standard CP modelling language. In: Bessière, C. (ed.) CP 2007. LNCS, vol. 4741, pp. 529–543. Springer, Heidelberg (2007). https://doi.org/10.1007/978-3-540-74970-7_38
21. Prud'homme, C., Fages, J.-G., Lorca, X.: Choco Documentation. TASC, INRIA Rennes, LINA CNRS UMR 6241, COSLING S.A.S. (2016)
22. Rossi, F., van Beek, P., Walsh, T.: Handbook of Constraint Programming (Foundations of Artificial Intelligence). Elsevier Science Inc., New York (2006)
23. Selçuk, A.A.: On probability of success in linear and differential cryptanalysis. J. Cryptol. **21**(1), 131–147 (2008)
24. Sun, L., Wang, W., Wang, M.: More accurate differential properties of LED64 and Midori64. IACR Trans. Symmetric Cryptol. **2018**(3), 93–123 (2018)
25. Wang, Q., Gu, D., Rijmen, V., Liu, Y., Chen, J., Bogdanov, A.: Improved impossible differential attacks on large-block Rijndael. In: Kwon, T., Lee, M.-K., Kwon, D. (eds.) ICISC 2012. LNCS, vol. 7839, pp. 126–140. Springer, Heidelberg (2013). https://doi.org/10.1007/978-3-642-37682-5_10

26. Wang, Q., Liu, Z., Toz, D., Varici, K., Dawu, G.: Related-key rectangle cryptanalysis of Rijndael-160 and Rijndael-192. IET Inf. Secur. **9**(5), 266–276 (2015)
27. Zhang, L., Wu, W., Park, J.H., Koo, B.W., Yeom, Y.: Improved impossible differential attacks on large-block Rijndael. In: Wu, T.-C., Lei, C.-L., Rijmen, V., Lee, D.-T. (eds.) ISC 2008. LNCS, vol. 5222, pp. 298–315. Springer, Heidelberg (2008). https://doi.org/10.1007/978-3-540-85886-7_21
28. Zhou, N.-F., Kjellerstrand, H.: The Picat-SAT compiler. In: Gavanelli, M., Reppy, J. (eds.) PADL 2016. LNCS, vol. 9585, pp. 48–62. Springer, Cham (2016). https://doi.org/10.1007/978-3-319-28228-2_4

Breaking PANTHER

Christina Boura[✉], Rachelle Heim Boissier[✉], and Yann Rotella[✉]

Laboratoire de mathématiques de Versailles, Université Paris-Saclay, UVSQ, CNRS, 78000 Versailles, France
{christina.boura,rachelle.heim,yann.rotella}@uvsq.fr

Abstract. PANTHER is a sponge-based lightweight authenticated encryption scheme published at Indocrypt 2021. Its round function is based on four Nonlinear Feedback Shift Registers (NFSRs). We show here that it is possible to fully recover the secret key of the construction by using a single known plaintext-ciphertext pair and with minimal computational resources. Furthermore, we show that in a known ciphertext setting an attacker is able with the knowledge of a single ciphertext to decrypt all plaintext blocks expect for the very first ones and can forge the tag with only one call and probability one. As we demonstrate, the problem of the design comes mainly from the low number of iterations of the round function during the absorption phase. All of our attacks have been implemented and validated.

Keywords: Cryptanalysis · Panther · Duplex construction · NFSR · Key recovery · Forge

1 Introduction

PANTHER is a sponge-based lightweight AEAD scheme designed by Bhargavi, Srinivasan and Lakshmy [3] and published at Indocrypt 2021. This construction works on a 328-bit state, divided as an outer part of rate $r = 64$ bits and an inner part of capacity $c = 264$ bits. The state is updated by iterating a function F that is composed of four interconnected NFSRs of sizes 19, 20, 21 and 22 nibbles respectively. This function is iterated 92 times for the initialization and the finalization part and only 4 times after the absorption of associated data (AD) or plaintext blocks or after the extraction of a block of the tag. The authors present their construction as lightweight, even if no concrete performance comparison is given with similar AEAD schemes.

A preliminary security analysis of PANTHER against various attacks is given in the document and the authors conclude that their construction is immune against all of the explored cryptanalysis techniques. They claim thus a security of $2^{c/2} = 2^{132}$. However, we show in this article that PANTHER has an important flaw that permits devastating attacks against it. More precisely, we demonstrate that due to the low number of iterations of the function F in all the middle computations, some public information goes directly into the inner state. This

© The Author(s), under exclusive license to Springer Nature Switzerland AG 2022
L. Batina and J. Daemen (Eds.): AFRICACRYPT 2022, LNCS 13503, pp. 176–188, 2022.
https://doi.org/10.1007/978-3-031-17433-9_8

fact has several consequences. In the known plaintext model, the attacker is for example able to inverse the state and to recover the secret key. In the known ciphertext (only) mode, it is possible to recover all plaintext blocks but the first six ones and also to forge the tag. A particularity of all our attacks is that they only need a single plaintext/ciphertext or a single ciphertext and the computation time is equivalent (or sometimes even smaller) to one encryption with PANTHER. As we will show, the main conclusion of this paper is that when using shift registers to build permutation-based constructions, one should at least take as many rounds as the size of the registers.

The rest of the paper is organized as follows. In Sect. 2 we provide the specifications of PANTHER and introduce some notations. Next, in Sect. 3 we describe our central observation on the diffusion of the cipher. Section 4 is dedicated to our attacks and finally we briefly describe in Sect. 5 their implementation.

2   Specification of PANTHER

The design of PANTHER is based on the sponge construction [1,2]. Its central component is a function called F that applies to a 328-bit state. The state S is divided into a r-bit outer part $\overline{S}$ and a c-bit inner part $\widehat{S}$, where $r = 64$ is called the rate and $c = 264$ the capacity. The encryption works as follows.

Initialization Phase. First, in the initialization phase, the 128-bit key and the 128-bit initial value (IV) are loaded to the state. More precisely, if we denote by k_i, $0 \leq i < 128$, the 128 bits of the secret key K, by iv_i, $0 \leq i < 128$, the 128 bits of the IV and by $\overline{x}$ the Boolean complement of the binary value x, the initial state is loaded with the following vector:

$$(k_0, \ldots, k_{127}, iv_0, \ldots, iv_{127}, \overline{k_0}, \ldots, \overline{k_{63}}, 1, 1, 1, 1, 1, 1, 1, 0).$$

The state is then updated 92 times by the function F.

Absorption Phase. Both associated data and plaintexts are then processed in the absorption phase. First, associated data (AD) are incorporated to the state. This part processes data that only needs to be authenticated and not necessarily encrypted. This is done by dividing the data into k blocks AD_i of 64 bits each, XORing each block to the outer part of the state and by applying next the permutation F four times. This is repeated until all the AD blocks have been absorbed. This part can of course be omitted if there is no associated data to authenticate. Next, plaintext blocks are processed and ciphertext blocks are generated. For this, the plaintext is divided into n blocks of 64 bits and each block is absorbed by the outer part of the state. Once a plaintext block P_i is absorbed, a 64-bit ciphertext block C_i is immediately generated by outputting the outer part of the state. Four iterations of the permutation F are next applied for all blocks except for the last one.

Finalization Phase. Once all plaintext blocks have been processed, the finalization mode is activated, during which the tag is generated. For this, 92 rounds of the permutation F are first applied to the state. Then, the outer part of the state is outputted as a first block of the tag and four rounds of the permutation F are next applied. The other blocks of the tag are generated in the same manner until a tag of the desired length is obtained. This procedure can be visualized in Fig. 1.

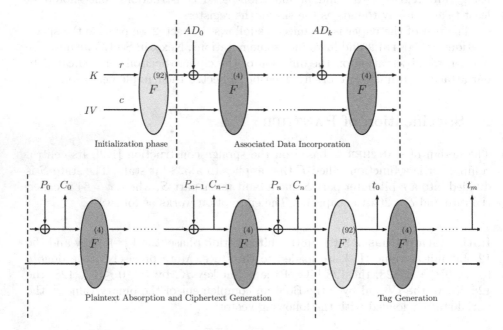

Fig. 1. PANTHER's global structure

2.1   State Update Function F

The cipher's function F applies to the 328-bit state. This state can be seen as 82 nibbles split into four unequally-sized registers P, Q, R and S. The register P contains the 19 nibbles $P_{18}, \ldots, P_0$, the register Q the 20 nibbles $Q_{19}, \ldots, Q_0$, the register R the 21 nibbles $R_{20}, \ldots, R_0$ and finally the register S the 22 nibbles $S_{21}, \ldots, S_0$. The outer part $\overline{S}$ is composed by the last four nibbles of each register:

$$\overline{S} = (P_{15}, P_{16}, P_{17}, P_{18}, Q_{16}, Q_{17}, Q_{18}, Q_{19}, R_{17}, R_{18}, R_{19}, R_{20}, S_{18}, S_{19}, S_{20}, S_{21}).$$

We use the following notation to denote an arbitrary state of PANTHER, where everything left to the symbol $\parallel$ is the outer state.

$$P_{18}||P_{17}||P_{16}||P_{15}\;\big\|\;P_{14}||...||P_0$$

$$Q_{19}||Q_{18}||Q_{17}||Q_{16}\;\big\|\;Q_{15}||Q_{14}||...||Q_0$$

$$R_{20}||R_{19}||R_{18}||R_{17}\;\big\|\;R_{16}||R_{15}||R_{14}...||R_0$$

$$S_{21}||S_{20}||S_{19}||S_{18}\;\big\|\;S_{17}||S_{16}||S_{15}||S_{14}||...||S_0$$

This state is then loaded into four interconnected NFSRs, each NFSR containing the values of the registers P, Q, R and S respectively, as can be seen in Fig. 2. We provide here the full specification of the round function, even if most of these details are not needed to understand our attack nor have any effect on it.

The function F can be described as follows. First the 4-bit values f_p, f_q, f_r and f_s, each one corresponding to the feedback polynomial of the corresponding NFSR are computed:

$$f_p = P_0 \oplus P_7 \oplus P_{10} \oplus P_6 \otimes P_{18}$$
$$f_q = Q_0 \oplus Q_4 \oplus Q_6 \oplus Q_7 \oplus Q_{15} \oplus Q_3 \otimes Q_7$$
$$f_r = R_0 \oplus R_1 \oplus R_{15} \oplus R_{17} \oplus R_{19} \oplus R_{13} \otimes R_{15}$$
$$f_s = S_0 \oplus S_1 \oplus S_4 \otimes S_{10} \oplus S_{11} \otimes S_{18}$$

Here, the symbol $\otimes$ corresponds to the multiplication in the field $GF(2^4)$, where the field is constructed by using the polynomial $x^4 + x^3 + 1$. Next, four interconnection polynomials, g_p, g_q, g_r and g_s, mixing nibbles from different registers are computed:

$$g_p = Q_9 \oplus R_{10} \oplus S_{12}$$
$$g_q = P_4 \oplus R_2 \oplus S_5$$
$$g_r = P_{12} \oplus Q_{11} \oplus S_{16}$$
$$g_s = P_{16} \oplus Q_{17} \oplus R_2$$

Next one computes the 4-bit values ℓ_1, ℓ_2, ℓ_3 and ℓ_4, each one corresponding to the XOR of the values f_* and g_* together with a constant rc_i:

$$\ell_1 = f_p \oplus g_p \oplus rc_1$$
$$\ell_2 = f_q \oplus g_q \oplus rc_2$$
$$\ell_3 = f_r \oplus g_r \oplus rc_3$$
$$\ell_4 = f_s \oplus g_s \oplus rc_4,$$

where the constant values are $rc_1 = 7, rc_2 = 9, rc_3 = \mathtt{b}, rc_4 = \mathtt{d}$ given in hexadecimal notation. After this, the vector $[\ell_1, \ell_2, \ell_3, \ell_4]^T$ is multiplied by a Toeplitz MDS matrix T_p to create the 16-bit vector $[d_1, d_2, d_3, d_4]^T = T_p \times [\ell_1, \ell_2, \ell_3, \ell_4]^T$.

A 4-bit S-box Sb is then applied to each one of the nibbles d_1, d_2, d_3 and d_4 and the resulting 16-bit vector is then multiplied again by the matrix T_p:

$$[t_1, t_2, t_3, t_4]^T = T_p \times [Sb[d_1], Sb(d_2), Sb(d_3), Sb(d_4)]^T.$$

As the specification of the matrix T_p is not relevant to our attack, we omit its description here. Finally, the registers P, Q, R and S are shifted by one nibble to the right and the most-significant nibbles of each NFSR are updated by the values t_1, t_2, t_3 and t_4:

$$P \gg 1, Q \gg 1, R \gg 1, S \gg 1$$
$$P_{18}, Q_{19}, R_{20}, S_{21} = t_1, t_2, t_3, t_4$$

F is applied successively a certain number of times n_r, where the value of n_r depends on the phase considered. In the initialization phase and before the first block of tag is outputted, n_r equals 92, while for all other applications of F, n_r equals 4.

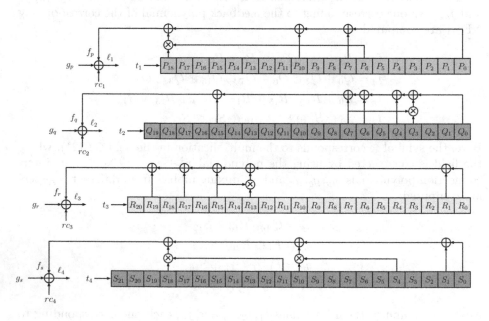

Fig. 2. Function F

3 Main Observation on PANTHER

In this section, we make an observation on PANTHER that is at the core of all the attacks provided next. The property that we exhibit is, as we will show, caused by the low number of applications of the state update function F in the plaintext absorption and ciphertext generation phase and has as a consequence to greatly alter the security of the cipher.

3.1   An Observation on F^4

As stated above, our main observation stems from the very low number $n_r = 4$ of times F is applied between each ciphertext output. We thus exhibit a very simple observation on F^4.

We begin by studying one application of F. Let us denote the input nibbles to F by:

$$P_{18}||P_{17}||P_{16}||P_{15} \,\big\|\, P_{14}||\cdots||P_0 \tag{1}$$

$$Q_{19}||Q_{18}||Q_{17}||Q_{16} \,\big\|\, Q_{15}||Q_{14}||\cdots||Q_0$$

$$R_{20}||R_{19}||R_{18}||R_{17} \,\big\|\, R_{16}||R_{15}||R_{14}\cdots||R_0$$

$$S_{21}||S_{20}||S_{19}||S_{18} \,\big\|\, S_{17}||S_{16}||S_{15}||S_{14}||\cdots||S_0$$

As can be observed in Fig. 2, because of the action of the four NFSRs to the state, the output of F is of the form:

$$X_0||P_{18}||P_{17}||P_{16} \,\big\|\, P_{15}||\cdots||P_1 \tag{2}$$

$$Y_0||Q_{19}||Q_{18}||Q_{17} \,\big\|\, Q_{16}||Q_{15}||\cdots||Q_1$$

$$Z_0||R_{20}||R_{19}||R_{18} \,\big\|\, R_{17}||R_{16}||R_{15}||\cdots||R_1$$

$$T_0||S_{21}||S_{20}||S_{19} \,\big\|\, S_{18}||S_{17}||S_{16}||S_{15}||\cdots||S_1$$

where X_0, Y_0, Z_0, T_0 are 4-bit values depending on the input nibbles. As the exact expression of these values has no impact on our attacks we do not provide their details here, but those can be found in Sect. 2.1.

Thus, note that each time the state is updated, only one nibble per register is modified. The values of the other nibbles remain unchanged, they are simply shifted. As a consequence, after four state updates, only four nibbles per register have been properly modified whilst all the others remain unchanged and are simply shifted to the right. By repeating the same analysis for the following rounds, we can see that the output of F^4 is of the form:

$$X_3||X_2||X_1||X_0 \,\big\|\, P_{18}||\cdots||P_4 \tag{3}$$

$$Y_3||Y_2||Y_1||Y_0 \,\big\|\, Q_{19}||Q_{18}||\cdots||Q_4$$

$$Z_3||Z_2||Z_1||Z_0 \,\big\|\, R_{20}||R_{19}||R_{18}||\cdots||R_4$$

$$T_3||T_2||T_1||T_0 \,\big\|\, S_{21}||S_{20}||S_{19}||S_{18}||\cdots||S_4$$

where the X_i, Y_i, Z_i, T_i for $0 \le i \le 3$ depend on the nibbles of the input state (again, their actual expression is not of interest, for more details see the specification of F in Sect. 2.1).

In particular, note that the outer part nibbles of the initial state are among those nibbles that have not been modified, but simply shifted into the inner part. For a more visual representation, we colour in red the nibbles of the outer part of the input that have been moved to the inner part of the output of F^4:

$$X_3||X_2||X_1||X_0 \, \Big\| \, P_{18}||P_{17}||P_{16}||P_{15}|| \cdots ||P_4 \tag{4}$$

$$Y_3||Y_2||Y_1||Y_0 \, \Big\| \, Q_{19}||Q_{18}||Q_{17}||Q_{16}||Q_{15}|| \cdots ||Q_4$$

$$Z_3||Z_2||Z_1||Z_0 \, \Big\| \, R_{20}||R_{19}||R_{18}||R_{17}||R_{16}||R_{15}|| \cdots ||R_4$$

$$T_3||T_2||T_1||T_0 \, \Big\| \, S_{21}||S_{18}||S_{17}||S_{16}||S_{17}||S_{16}||S_{15}|| \cdots ||S_4$$

3.2   Consequences in a Known Ciphertext only Setting

At the end of the initialisation phase, the state is *a priori* unknown since the key has been mixed in with the IV by the application of F^{92}. The absorption of the associated data which follows does not reveal anything about the state at the beginning of the plaintext absorption/ciphertext generation phase either. However, as soon as ciphertext blocks start to be outputted, an attacker has knowledge of the outer part of the input state to each application of F^4.

If we recall the observations on F^4 made above, the outer part of the input state to F^4 is not modified but simply shifted into the inner state. Let $C = C_0|| \cdots ||C_{n-1}$ be the known ciphertext of an unknown padded plaintext $M = M_0|| \cdots ||M_{n-1}$ where $|C_i| = |M_i| = 64$ for $0 \le i < n$. An output of one ciphertext block C_{i-1} thus not only leaks information on the outer part of the state at the entry of F^4, but also on the inner part of the output of F^4. As the next message block M_i is then XORed only to the outer part of the output state, when the next ciphertext block C_i is outputted, the attacker knows not only the outer part of the state but also 64 bits of the inner state. As more ciphertext blocks are outputted, more information on the inner state is given to the attacker. Once 6 consecutive ciphertext blocks $C_{i-1}, \ldots, C_{i+4}$ have been outputted, the attacker knows the whole inner state and the whole outer state. The property is illustrated in Fig. 3 with $C_0, \ldots, C_5$.

We show this property in a more formal way for the first ciphertext outputs $C_0, \ldots, C_5$. We consider the state at the beginning of the plaintext absorption and ciphertext generation. In the following, we use the color blue to put forward what the attacker knows (which corresponds to the ciphertext blocks). Once the first ciphertext is outputted, the entry to F^4 is as follows:

$$C_3^0||C_2^0||C_1^0||C_0^0 \, \Big\| \, P_{14}|| \cdots ||P_0$$

$$C_7^0||C_6^0||C_5^0||C_4^0 \, \Big\| \, Q_{15}||Q_{14}|| \cdots ||Q_0$$

$$C_{11}^0||C_{10}^0||C_9^0||C_8^0 \, \Big\| \, R_{16}||R_{15}||R_{14}|| \cdots ||R_0$$

$$C_{15}^0||C_{14}^0||C_{13}^0||C_{12}^0 \, \Big\| \, S_{17}||S_{16}||S_{15}||S_{14}|| \cdots ||S_0$$

After the application of F^4, the state is of the following form:

$$X_3||X_2||X_1||X_0 \, \Big\| \, C_3^0||C_2^0||C_1^0||C_0^0||P_{14}||\cdots||P_4$$

$$Y_3||Y_2||Y_1||Y_0 \, \Big\| \, C_7^0||C_6^0||C_5^0||C_4^0||Q_{15}||Q_{14}||\cdots||Q_4$$

$$Z_3||Z_2||Z_1||Z_0 \, \Big\| \, C_{11}^0||C_{10}^0||C_9^0||C_8^0||R_{16}||R_{15}||R_{14}||\cdots||R_4$$

$$T_3||T_2||T_1||T_0 \, \Big\| \, C_{15}^0||C_{14}^0||C_{13}^0||C_{12}^0||S_{17}||S_{16}||S_{15}||S_{14}||\cdots||S_4$$

The message is then XORed to the nibbles in blue, and the outer part thus takes the value of the outputted C^1. Therefore, the state has the following form just before the next application of F^4:

$$C_3^1||C_2^1||C_1^1||C_0^1 \, \Big\| \, C_3^0||C_2^0||C_1^0||C_0^0||P_{14}||\cdots||P_4$$

$$C_7^1||C_6^1||C_5^1||C_4^1 \, \Big\| \, C_7^0||C_6^0||C_5^0||C_4^0||Q_{15}||Q_{14}||\cdots||Q_4$$

$$C_{11}^1||C_{10}^1||C_9^1||C_8^1 \, \Big\| \, C_{11}^0||C_{10}^0||C_9^0||C_8^0||R_{16}||R_{15}||R_{14}||\cdots||R_4$$

$$C_{15}^1||C_{14}^1||C_{13}^1||C_{12}^1 \, \Big\| \, C_{15}^0||C_{14}^0||C_{13}^0||C_{12}^0||S_{17}||S_{16}||S_{15}||S_{14}||\cdots||S_4$$

As C_2 is outputted, the attacker knows 128 bits of the inner state as well as the whole outer state. This phenomenon goes on iteratively: as more consecutive ciphertexts get known, more information is given to the attacker. Once the attacker knows the 6 first ciphertext blocks $C_0, \ldots, C_5$, the attacker knows the whole inner state and the whole outer state. For a visual representation of the property, see Fig. 3. In general, leaks on the value of the inner state of a sponge-based cipher have a devastating effect on the security. In the case of PANTHER, the attacker recovers the value of the whole inner state and, depending on the attack settings, controls or knows the outer state. Unsurprisingly, this weakness will allow an attacker to mount extremely powerful key-recovery, plaintext-recovery and forging attacks as described in the next section.

4   Cryptanalysis of PANTHER

In this section, we show how the observation of Sect. 3 allows us to mount three attacks including a known plaintext key recovery attack, a known ciphertext-only attack and a chosen ciphertext-only forge. Note that each of these three attacks is extremely powerful, as they simply require the knowledge of either one plaintext/ciphertext pair or of a single ciphertext.

4.1   Key-Recovery Attack with One Plaintext/Ciphertext Pair

We start by describing the most powerful of our attacks, namely a known plaintext attack which recovers the full key with a single plaintext/ciphertext pair. This attack, as also all the following ones, is memoryless and its time complexity

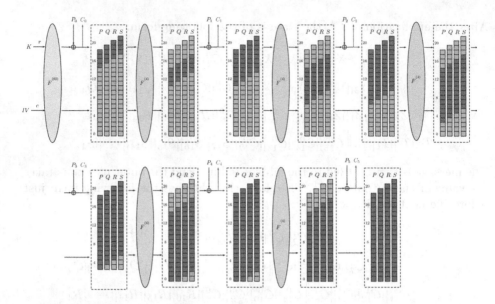

Fig. 3. Attack on PANTHER. The blue nibbles correspond to the nibbles known to the attacker, while the grey nibbles are values that are a priori unknown. (Color figure online)

is equivalent to a single encryption or decryption with PANTHER. This attack is a direct consequence of our observation from Sect. 3.

The only constraint on the pair is that the padded message M must contain at least six 64-bit blocks. As shown in Sect. 3, the attacker recovers the full state as soon as she knows six consecutive ciphertext blocks. Once the full state is known, one can recover the full key as F is a permutation and its inverse can be very easily computed. As the attacker can invert F and knows all the message blocks M_i (and the optional associated data blocks), she can recover the initial state and thus the key. The fact that F is a permutation is not explicitly mentioned by the authors. Thus, we provide a short proof at the end of this section. From this proof one can easily deduce how to invert F.

We've shown that with only one plaintext/ciphertext pair, an attacker can recover the key with a very easy and straightforward procedure. The attack is memoryless and, as for time, it is equivalent to a single encryption or decryption with PANTHER.

Proof that F is a Permutation. Let

$$I = P_{18}||\cdots||P_0||Q_{19}||\cdots||Q_0||S_{20}||\cdots||S_0||R_{21}||\cdots||R_0 \in \mathbb{F}_2^{328}$$

be an input to F, and let

$$O = P'_{18}||\cdots||P'_0||Q'_{19}||\cdots||Q'_0||S'_{20}||\cdots||S'_0||R'_{21}||\cdots||R'_0$$

be its image by F. We show that I is uniquely determined by O.

First, note that all $P_i, 0 < i \leq 18$, $Q_j, 0 < j \leq 19$, $R_k, 0 < k \leq 20$ and $S_\ell, 0 < \ell \leq 21$ are uniquely determined by O since

$$P_i = P'_{i-1} \quad \text{for} \quad 0 < i \leq 18$$
$$Q_j = Q'_{j-1} \quad \text{for} \quad 0 < j \leq 19$$
$$R_k = R'_{k-1} \quad \text{for} \quad 0 < k \leq 20$$
$$S_\ell = S'_{\ell-1} \quad \text{for} \quad 0 < \ell \leq 21$$

Thus, we now only need to show that P_0, Q_0, R_0 and S_0 are uniquely determined by O. First, note that $(P'_{18}, Q'_{19}, R'_{20}, S'_{21})$ uniquely determines the value of

$$\ell_1 = P_0 \oplus P_7 \oplus P_{10} \oplus P_6 \otimes P_{18} \oplus Q_9 \oplus R_{10} \oplus S_{12} \oplus rc_1$$
$$\ell_2 = Q_0 \oplus Q_4 \oplus Q_6 \oplus Q_7 \oplus Q_{15} \oplus Q_3 \otimes Q_7 \oplus P_4 \oplus R_2 \oplus S_5 \oplus rc_2$$
$$\ell_3 = R_0 \oplus R_1 \oplus R_{15} \oplus R_{17} \oplus R_{19} \oplus R_{13} \otimes R_{15} \oplus P_{12} \oplus Q_{11} \oplus S_{16} \oplus rc_3$$
$$\ell_4 = S_0 \oplus S_1 \oplus S_4 \otimes S_{10} \oplus S_{11} \otimes S_{18} \oplus P_{16} \oplus Q_{17} \oplus R_2 \oplus rc_4$$

as both the matrix T_p and the S-box Sb are invertible (T_p being MDS). Since the $P_i, 0 < i \leq 18$, $Q_j, 0 < j \leq 19$ $R_k, 0 < k \leq 20$ and $S_\ell, 0 < \ell \leq 21$ are also uniquely determined by O as shown just above, it comes that

$$P_0 = \ell_1 \oplus P_7 \oplus P_{10} \oplus P_6 \otimes P_{18} \oplus Q_9 \oplus R_{10} \oplus S_{12} \oplus rc_1$$
$$Q_0 = \ell_2 \oplus Q_4 \oplus Q_6 \oplus Q_7 \oplus Q_{15} \oplus Q_3 \otimes Q_7 \oplus P_4 \oplus R_2 \oplus S_5 \oplus rc_2$$
$$R_0 = \ell_3 \oplus R_1 \oplus R_{15} \oplus R_{17} \oplus R_{19} \oplus R_{13} \otimes R_{15} \oplus P_{12} \oplus Q_{11} \oplus S_{16} \oplus rc_3$$
$$S_0 = \ell_4 \oplus S_1 \oplus S_4 \otimes S_{10} \oplus S_{11} \otimes S_{18} \oplus P_{16} \oplus Q_{17} \oplus R_2 \oplus rc_4$$

are also uniquely determined by O. We've shown that F is injective which is sufficient to prove that it is a permutation. Further, it is easy to see from this proof how to invert F.

4.2   Plaintext-Recovery Attack with One Known Ciphertext

In this section, we show how our observation on F^4 also allows one to mount attacks in a known ciphertext only setting. Even if this attack does not recover the secret key, it is nevertheless devastating as it allows the attacker to recover full plaintext blocks. More precisely, for any padded message $M = M_0 || \cdots || M_{n-1}$ where $|M_i| = 64$ for all i and such that $n \geq 6$, one can fully recover all plaintext blocks from the seventh on.

As shown in the previous sections, knowing the six first ciphertext blocks allows one to recover the full state. Thus, the attacker also knows the full state after another application of F^4, that is when the rest of the plaintext blocks $M_i, i \geq 6$ are absorbed. To recover these blocks, the attacker only needs to XOR the known ciphertext block $C_i, i \geq 6$ to the outer part of the state after each application of F^4. With only known ciphertext of sufficient length, an attacker can recover the whole plaintext except for the first 384 bits. This attack is also memoryless and requires only one ciphertext. Concerning the time complexity, it is striking that this attack is more efficient than a decryption since one does not need to go through the initialisation phase and the absorption of the associated data.

4.3 Forging Attacks

Last but not least, our observation on F^4 can also allow one to launch forging attacks both in a known plaintext and in a known ciphertext only setting.

To begin, an attacker with access to plaintext/ciphertext pairs can recover the key with the method described in Sect. 4.1. Thus, she can generate a valid tag for any chosen plaintext and any chosen ciphertext.

In the known ciphertext only setting, let us consider a ciphertext C composed of n blocks of 64 bits with $n \geq 6$ and let T be the valid tag for C. As explained in Sect. 3.2, when six consecutive ciphertext blocks are outputted, the full state is known by the attacker. In particular, the value of the last six ciphertext blocks fully determines the state at the end of the absorption phase. Thus, for any ciphertext C' composed of m blocks such that $m \geq 6$, if the six last blocks of C' are equal to those of C, the two states will fully collide at the end of the ciphertext generation phase, and thus at the beginning of the tag generation phase. It stems that T is also a valid tag for C'.

As the other attacks presented above, this forging attack is very powerful as it is memoryless and requires only one valid ciphertext/tag pair. The time complexity is also negligible, as the attacker does not even need to apply F once. The forged ciphertexts can have any length as long as they have at least 6 blocks, and only the last 6 blocks are constrained. As a consequence, one can build as many valid ciphertext/tag pairs as they wish. Forging is thus not only possible but also very easy and with a large degree of freedom for the attacker.

5   Implementation

All of the described attacks need negligible memory and computational ressources and can thus easily be implemented. Therefore, we implemented all of them in C in order to confirm their validity. Our code is accessible online[1].

Our program works in the following way. First, a random 128-bit key, a random 128-bit initial value (IV) and a random 512-bit plaintext are generated. Since PANTHER has a rate of 64 bits, the plaintext is processed in 8 blocks. The code does not generate associated data as our attacks work regardless. The plaintext is then encrypted with the key and IV and the corresponding ciphertext and tag are returned. The three attacks are then launched.

---

[1] https://github.com/panthercryptanalyst/Panther-cryptanalysis.

Key Recovery. First, we implemented a function that takes as input the plaintext/ciphertext pair and returns the secret key. The program verifies that the key returned matches with the random secret key that was generated.

Plaintext Recovery. Second, we implemented a function that takes as input the ciphertext and returns all plaintext blocks but the first six. Once the plaintext blocks are recovered, the program verifies that they match the actual plaintext encrypted.

Forge. Lastly, we implemented a function that takes as input the ciphertext and returns a forged ciphertext which has the same tag. We then implemented a function that checks whether the forged ciphertext is valid. This function takes as input the key and the IV. It works as a decryption function on the forged ciphertext and returns the valid 128-bit tag for the forged ciphertext. The program then verifies that the forged ciphertext tag matches the initial ciphertext tag.

5.1   Repairing PANTHER

The main problem in the cipher's design comes from the fact that the number of rounds that the function F needs to be iterated in the middle computation was wrongly estimated. While determining the least number of rounds for the cipher to resist all known attacks is not an easy task, a minimum requirement is that the function F^r provides full diffusion, in the sense that at the end of the computation every output bit depends on all input bits. Computing the minimal round r ensuring a full diffusion for F^r is an easy procedure that we implemented. The code can be found together with the attacks code. This simple computation permitted us to affirm that the minimal number of rounds for reaching full diffusion is 46.

We can therefore conclude that at least 46 rounds are needed in the middle part of the cipher in order to resist the presented attacks. Of course, this minimal number of rounds does not necessarily guarantee the resistance of the cipher against other attacks, for example those exploiting a low algebraic degree. To determine this, a more in-depth analysis of the structure of F is required but such an analysis is out-of-scope of the current article.

6   Conclusion

In this paper we showed several devastating attacks in different scenarios against the AEAD scheme PANTHER. All of our attacks are extremely powerful as they are memoryless, require a single plaintext/ciphertext or a single ciphertext and have negligible execution time. This work shows that this design cannot be used in its current form to securely transmit data. We also demonstrate that special care is required when combining the sponge construction with an NFSR-based update function. More precisely, the inner part should always remain secret in sponge-like constructions, hence, when using shift registers, the number of rounds should at least be the size of the register, so that all bits in the inner part cannot be deduced from the ciphertext.

We believe that modifying PANTHER in order for it to resist our attacks requires to greatly increase the number of rounds of the update function (from 4 to at least 46) in order to get full diffusion. However, in this scenario, the lightweight character of the cipher will very probably not be ensured any more, limiting thus the interest of someone to use it.

Acknowledgements. The authors are partially supported by the French Agence Nationale de la Recherche through the SWAP project under Contract ANR-21-CE39-0012.

References

1. Bertoni, G., Daemen, J., Peeters, M., Assche, G.V.: Sponge functions. In: ECRYPT Hash Workshop 2007, May 2007. https://keccak.team/files/SpongeFunctions.pdf
2. Bertoni, G., Daemen, J., Peeters, M., Assche, G.V.: Cryptographic sponge functions (2011). https://keccak.team/files/CSF-0.1.pdf
3. Bhargavi, K.V.L., Srinivasan, C., Lakshmy, K.V.: Panther: a sponge based lightweight authenticated encryption scheme. In: Adhikari, A., Küsters, R., Preneel, B. (eds.) INDOCRYPT 2021. LNCS, vol. 13143, pp. 49–70. Springer, Cham (2021). https://doi.org/10.1007/978-3-030-92518-5_3

Automated Key Recovery Attacks on Round-Reduced Orthros

Muzhou Li[1,2], Ling Sun[1,2], and Meiqin Wang[1,2,3(✉)]

[1] Key Laboratory of Cryptologic Technology and Information Security, Ministry of Education, Shandong University, Jinan, China
muzhouli@mail.sdu.edu.cn, {lingsun,mqwang}@sdu.edu.cn
[2] School of Cyber Science and Technology, Shandong University, Qingdao, China
[3] Quan Cheng Shandong Laboratory, Jinan, China

Abstract. Orthros is a low-latency keyed pseudo-random function designed by Banik *et al.* in FSE 2022. It adopts the parallel structure composed of two keyed permutations. Both branches take the same 128-bit input and their outputs are XORed to generate the final 128-bit output. Benefiting from this special structure, it's security is hard to evaluate, especially for key recovery attacks. In its specification, the most effective distinguisher proposed is a 7-round integral one. However, it can only lead to key recovery attacks worse than exhaustive attack. Besides, there is no key recovery attack presented in the design document. Therefore, we are motivated to see whether a valid key recovery attack exists and how powerful it can be. In this paper, we aim to proceed differential and differential-linear key recovery attacks on Orthros. To deal with the special structure, we introduce two automated key recovery attack frameworks that work for such two-branch ciphers. With the help of them, we finally got a 7-round differential-linear key recovery attack and a 6-round differential one. Both attacks are the first key recovery attacks on this cipher. However, they are so far from threatening its full-round security.

Keywords: Differential-linear · Differential · Automated key recovery attack

1 Introduction

As a subfield of symmetric-key cryptography, lightweight primitives used under strong resource-restricted circumstances have drawn a lot of attentions in recent years. Latency is a typical metric which affects the response time of cryptographic primitives. In FSE 2022, Banik *et al.* proposed a 128-bit low-latency keyed pseudo-random function called Orthros [2]. Its overall structure is a sum of two keyed permutations, which has been adopted in the design of two hash functions: RIPEMD-160 [12] and Grøstl [14]. Relying on this special structure, the permutation in each branch is designed to be rather weak as a stand-alone block cipher. Designers claim that this weakness can be overcame since outputs of these two branches are not given to the adversary clearly.

An extensive security analysis under different cryptographic methods is introduced in [2]. Among all these results, the longest effective distinguisher is a 7-round integral one with 127 active bits in the input. However, we cannot proceed valid key recovery

L. Batina and J. Daemen (Eds.): AFRICACRYPT 2022, LNCS 13503, pp. 189–213, 2022.
https://doi.org/10.1007/978-3-031-17433-9_9

attacks based on it, as explained[1] by the designers [2]. Meanwhile, there is no key recovery attack given in its specification.

The difficulty of mounting key recovery attacks comes from the unique feature of taking the sum of two branch outputs. As pointed out by the designers [2], the common way of appending several rounds after the distinguisher is quite hard for Orthros since the adversary has to guess the output of each branch. In this case, it costs more than the exhaustive attack. The other way is prepending some rounds before the distinguisher. Thus, one has to construct the set of plaintext (pairs) suitable for both branches, especially in differential-like attacks. Meanwhile, due to the different key schedule adopted in each branch, a lot of to-be-guessed key bits are involved. This motivates us to check whether a valid key recovery attack can be implemented and how powerful it can be.

In this paper, we focus on mounting attacks with differential and differential-linear distinguishers. Differential cryptanalysis was proposed by Eli Biham and Adi Shamir in 1991 [6,7], and has been one of the most effective methods on symmetric primitives. It investigates how many plaintext pairs (M, M') fulfilling the same input difference $\Delta_{in} = M \oplus M'$ can make their corresponding ciphertexts C and C' satisfy the fixed output difference Δ_{out} in the same time. With this distinguisher, one can mount key recovery attacks by adding some rounds before or after it. For Orthros, one can only prepend several rounds before. To proceed attacks in this case, one has to construct a set of plaintext pairs (M, M') where $M \oplus M'$ follows a specific active pattern determined by the input difference Δ_{in}. This pattern indicates which bit of $M \oplus M'$ can have non-deterministic difference. Such bit is referred as the active bit. A common way to build such set is choosing plaintexts that taking all possible values in those active bits while fixed in others. With these plaintexts, one can obtain the plaintext pair by taking any two of them. One can see that these generated pairs fulfill the active pattern. Meanwhile, this pattern influences the data complexity of corresponding key recovery attack. Since the input difference Δ_{in} influences this active pattern, the data complexity of the attack is determined by the choice of Δ_{in}. With this set, we can figure out the right key since the number of plaintext pairs fulfilling the distinguisher for the right key guess is much higher than that under wrong key guesses.

Since Orthros adopts the structure of summing two branch outputs, the distinguisher is composed of two input differences $(\Delta_{in}^1, \Delta_{in}^2)$ and an output difference Δ_{out}. As shown above, two active patterns $ActP^1$ and $ActP^2$, respectively decided by Δ_{in}^1 and Δ_{in}^2, will be obtained. If these two patterns are not equal, one needs to traverse more plaintext bits in order to construct the set suitable for both branches than dealing with the case when only one branch is considered. Thus, to avoid unnecessary cost of data complexity, we aim to choose Δ_{in}^1 and Δ_{in}^2 so that $ActP^1 = ActP^2$. Relation between input differences and active patterns can be achieved by considering active pattern propagation properties of each basic operations, which has been exploited for other ciphers in [13,18,22]. When deducing this relation, we can also realize which key bits are involved. Inspired by [13,18], we unify the procedure of deducing the relation, the restriction $ActP^1 = ActP^2$, general searching progress of distinguishers into one framework, and also evaluate the attack complexity following a predefined attack procedure in this framework.

---

[1] We gave a more detailed explanation on such integral attacks in Appendix A.

Differential-Linear cryptanalysis on Orthros is another aspect focused in this paper. This method is a combination of differential and linear attacks, which was proposed by Langford and Hellman [15]. Similar with differential cryptanalysis, it also utilizes plaintext pairs satisfying a fixed input difference Δ_{in}, but checks how many ciphertext pairs (C, C') fulfilling the linear approximation $\Gamma_{out} \cdot C \oplus \Gamma_{out} \cdot C' = 0$. When mounting this kind of key recovery attacks on Orthros, one has to construct the set of plaintext pairs in the same way with that in proceeding differential attacks. Hence, the automated key recovery framework for differential cryptanalysis is similar with mounting differential-linear attacks except for some necessary modifications.

Implementing above two frameworks with an automatic searching tool, we obtain a 7-round differential-linear attack and a 6-round differential one. Attack complexities of these two attacks are illustrated in Table 1. Detailed attack procedures as well as those two frameworks can be found in Sect. 3 and 4. Note that these two frameworks can also be utilized in attacking other two-branch ciphers by considering their active pattern propagation properties in the key recovery phase.

Table 1. The first key recovery attacks on Orthros

Attack type	Round	Distinguisher		Time	Data	Memory	Reference
Differential-Linear Attack	7	6-round	$\text{Cor} = 2^{-46}$	2^{106}	2^{95} CP	2^{29} bits	Sect. 3
Differential Attack	6	5-round	$\text{Pr} = 2^{-112}$	2^{120}	2^{115} CP	2^{29} bits	Sect. 4

Time complexity is evaluated by encryption units; CP is short for Chosen Plaintexts.

2 Preliminaries

2.1 Specification of Orthros

Orthros [2] is a 128-bit low-latency keyed pseudo-random function designed by Banik *et al.* in FSE 2022. Its structure is a sum of two 128-bit keyed permutations called Branch1 and Branch2, as shown in Fig. 1. In both branches, the same 128-bit key K is adopted. A 128-bit plaintext M is firstly copied into two 128-bit states and then encrypted under Branch1 and Branch2 with K, respectively. At last, a 128-bit ciphertext C is obtained by XORing these two 128-bit outputs of each branch.

Both Branch1 and Branch2 are 12-round SPN-based ciphers whose round function consists of an Sbox layer, a bit or nibble permutation, matrix multiplication, the round-key addition and the constant addition. Before the first round of each branch, there is also a key addition operation where whitening keys are XORed with the state.

These two branches adopt the same Sbox layer consisting of 32 parallel 4-bit Sboxes shown in Table 2. While for the bit or nibble permutation, they are different. Branch1 (resp. Branch2) adopts the bit permutation P_{br1} (resp. P_{br2}) and nibble permutation P_{nr1} (resp. P_{nr2}). Taking these two permutations used in Branch1 as an example. Denote the most significant bit of the state as 0-th bit. The i-th bit of the state before P_{br1} will be the $P_{br1}(i)$-th bit of the state after P_{br1}, while the j-th nibble of the state before P_{nr1} is placed in the $P_{nr1}(j)$-th nibble after P_{nr1}. Detailed descriptions of these permutations

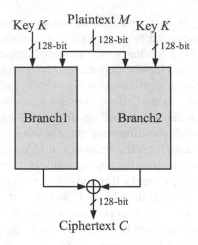

Fig. 1. Structure of Orthros [2]

are shown in Appendix C (Table 5 and 6). Note that the bit permutation is used in the first four rounds, and the nibble permutation is adopted in the next seven rounds, while there is no permutation utilized in the final round. The matrix multiplication is also the same for both branches, where eight 4×4 matrix M_b are applied on these 32 nibbles. Each matrix updates four consistent nibbles $(a_{4i}, a_{4i+1}, a_{4i+2}, a_{4i+3})$, $0 \le i \le 7$, with

$$a'_{4i} \leftarrow a_{4i+1} \oplus a_{4i+2} \oplus a_{4i+3},$$
$$a'_{4i+1} \leftarrow a_{4i} \oplus a_{4i+2} \oplus a_{4i+3},$$
$$a'_{4i+2} \leftarrow a_{4i} \oplus a_{4i+1} \oplus a_{4i+3},$$
$$a'_{4i+3} \leftarrow a_{4i} \oplus a_{4i+1} \oplus a_{4i+2}.$$

In other words, M_b is an almost MDS matrix defined as

$$M_b = \begin{pmatrix} 0 & 1 & 1 & 1 \\ 1 & 0 & 1 & 1 \\ 1 & 1 & 0 & 1 \\ 1 & 1 & 1 & 0 \end{pmatrix}.$$

Note that in the final round, there is no matrix multiplication, too. The addition of round-key or constant is the XOR operation between the internal state and the 128-bit round key or the 128-bit predefined constant.

Orthros utilizes two linear key schedules $KSF1$ and $KSF2$, which only consist of bit permutations P_{bk1} and P_{bk2}. In $KSF1$, P_{bk1} is adopted to generate whitening and round keys utilized in Branch1, while for $KSF2$, P_{bk2} is used for Branch2. Given the 128-bit key K, $KSF1$ (resp. $KSF2$) firstly updates its value using P_{bk1} (resp. P_{bk2}), and then generates the whitening key WK^1 (resp. WK^2). After that, $KSF1$ (resp. $KSF2$) will output each round key RK_r^1 (resp. RK_r^2) after updating its state using the permutation. Descriptions of P_{bk1} and P_{bk2} are given in Appendix C (Table 7).

Table 2. 4-bit Sbox utilized in Orthros [2]

x	0	1	2	3	4	5	6	7	8	9	a	b	c	d	e	f
$S(x)$	1	0	2	4	3	8	6	d	9	a	b	e	f	c	7	5

In [2], designers have evaluated its security using several common cryptanalytic methods. Among all of these results, a 7-round distinguisher based on integral cryptanalysis [20, 21] is the longest effective one. However, key recovery attacks based on it cost more than the exhaustive attack, as remarked by designers [2]. To make it clear, we proposed a further investigation of integral attacks on Orthros in Appendix A. Meanwhile, designers clarified that the difficulty of recovering keys comes from the special structure of taking the sum of two branch outputs [2]. Due to this structure, common strategy of appending several rounds after the distinguisher is not suitable here, since one of the branch outputs has to be guessed in order to reverse the ciphertext. And this costs more than the exhaustive search. Hence, one can only add several rounds before the distinguisher. In this case, one has to construct the set of plaintext (pairs) suitable for both branches. Besides, a lot of to-be-guessed key bits are involved due to different key schedules utilized in each branch.

2.2 Differential Cryptanalysis

In 1991, Eli Biham and Adi Shamir proposed differential cryptanalysis [6, 7] to mount attacks on the Data Encryption Standard (DES) [1]. It's a chosen-plaintext attack where one queries many plaintext pairs satisfying a fixed input difference Δ_{in} and aims to obtain a specific output difference Δ_{out} of corresponding ciphertext pairs.

To determine which difference pairs $(\Delta_{in}, \Delta_{out})$ should be utilized and estimate the cost of proceeding attacks, one need to evaluate the probability

$$\Pr\{\Delta_{in} \rightarrow \Delta_{out}\} = \frac{\#\{M \mid E(M) \oplus E(M \oplus \Delta_{in}) = \Delta_{out}\}}{2^n},$$

where $E : \mathbb{F}_2^n \rightarrow \mathbb{F}_2^n$ is (several rounds of) the encryption function. Generally, in differential analysis, the attacker will try to find difference pairs with the highest probability. Those difference pairs are referred as the differentials. Besides, a differential is regarded as an effective one if it has the probability more than 2^{-n}. Differentials with $\Delta_{in} = 0$ (resp. $\Delta_{out} = 0$) are trivial solutions since this leads to $\Delta_{out} = 0$ (resp. $\Delta_{in} = 0$) with probability one. These differentials cannot be used to mount attacks.

Given a non-trivial effective differential, one can proceed key recovery attacks by adding several rounds before or after it. In order to check how many pairs satisfying the differential, key bits involved in those added rounds should be guessed. Number of pairs fulfilling the differential for the right key guess is expected to be much higher than that for a wrong key guess. Hence, one can figure out the right key or some bits of it.

As we can see, the cornerstone of differential cryptanalysis is the differential with high probability. However, it's extremely hard or impractical to evaluate the probability $\Pr\{\Delta_{in} \rightarrow \Delta_{out}\}$ following its definition when n is large enough. To deal with this, Biham and Shamir introduced the notation of differential trail [6, 7].

A differential trail contains a series of differences of input states and output states of each round. Assume that there are R rounds. Denote the input difference of the i-th round as α_i where $0 \leq i \leq R-1$, then α_{i+1} is also the output difference of the i-th round. Thus, all trails satisfying that $\alpha_0 = \Delta_{in}$ and $\alpha_R = \Delta_{out}$ comprise the differential $(\Delta_{in}, \Delta_{out})$. Hence, the probability of the differential can be evaluated by

$$\Pr\{\Delta_{in} \to \Delta_{out}\} = \sum_{(\alpha_0, \alpha_1, \cdots, \alpha_R) \text{ with } \alpha_0 = \Delta_{in},\ \alpha_R = \Delta_{out}} \prod_{i=0}^{R-1} \Pr\{\alpha_i \to \alpha_{i+1}\},$$

where the probability $\Pr\{\alpha_i \to \alpha_{i+1}\}$ for each round can be obtained by investigating difference propagation properties of each basic operations in the round function.

For most ciphers such as DES, there is always a dominant trail in the differential. In other words, $\Pr\{\Delta_{in} \to \Delta_{out}\}$ is very close to the probability of this dominant trail. Therefore, the approach of finding the best differential is to find the trail with the highest probability. Complexities of attacks using this differential can be evaluated by the probability of this dominant trail. For other ciphers that may not have the dominant trail, we can also adopt the same approach. Although attack complexities may be overestimated in this case, validities of these attacks are not influenced.

2.3   Differential-Linear Cryptanalysis

Differential-Linear cryptanalysis is another chosen-plaintext attack which was proposed by Langford and Hellman [15]. It's a combined method of differential and linear attacks.

Linear cryptanalysis is a known-plaintext attack proposed by Matsui [16] in 1993. Denote $a \cdot b$ as the inner product of two n-bit values a and b, i.e. $a \cdot b = \oplus_{i=0}^{n-1} a_i b_i$. To mount linear attacks, one has to find a linear approximation between some bits of plaintext M, ciphertext $C = E(M)$ and key K, which is $\Gamma_{in} \cdot M \oplus \Gamma_{out} \cdot E(M) \oplus \Lambda \cdot K = 0$. In the context of linear cryptanalysis, Γ_{in}, Γ_{out} and Λ are referred as masks. Efficiency of such approximation is evaluated by the correlation

$$\text{Cor}\{\Gamma_{in} \to \Gamma_{out}\} = 2\frac{\#\{M \mid \Gamma_{in} \cdot M \oplus \Gamma_{out} \cdot E(M) \oplus \Lambda \cdot K = 0\}}{2^n} - 1.$$

Similar with differential attack, to find such approximation efficiently, one always tries to find a linear trail which contains not only Γ_{in} and Γ_{out} but also masks before and after each round. Note that $\Lambda \cdot K$ only changes the symbol of $\text{Cor}\{\Gamma_{in} \to \Gamma_{out}\}$. Hence, one always ignores this term and focuses on the approximation $\Gamma_{in} \cdot M \oplus \Gamma_{out} \cdot E(M) = 0$.

In a differential-linear attack, the adversary also considers plaintext pairs (M, M') satisfying a fixed input difference $\Delta_{in} = M \oplus M'$, which is same with that utilized in the differential cryptanalysis. However, in this case, the attacker checks whether corresponding ciphertexts (C, C') fulfill the approximation $\Gamma_{out} \cdot (C \oplus C') = 0$. Effectiveness of this differential-linear distinguisher $(\Delta_{in}, \Gamma_{out})$ is defined as the correlation

$$\text{Cor}\{\Delta_{in} \to \Gamma_{out}\} = 2\frac{\#\{M \mid \Gamma_{out} \cdot E(M) \oplus \Gamma_{out} \cdot E(M \oplus \Delta_{in})\}}{2^n} - 1.$$

To find such distinguisher efficiently, the cipher E is split into two parts E_0 and E_1 with $E(M) = E_1(E_0(M))$, as shown in Fig. 2(a). For the first part E_0, one will try to find an

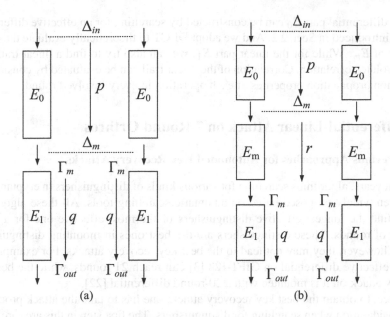

Fig. 2. Structure of differential-linear distinguisher

effective differential (Δ_{in}, Δ_m). Assume that its probability is p, we have

$$\Pr\{E_0(M) \oplus E_0(M \oplus \Delta_{in}) = \Delta_m\} = p.$$

While for the second part E_1, a linear approximation (Γ_m, Γ_{out}) is exploited. Denote its correlation as q. For each plaintext pair $(M, M \oplus \Delta_{in})$,

$$\text{Cor}\{\Gamma_m \cdot E_0(M) \oplus \Gamma_{out} \cdot E(M) = 0\} = q,$$
$$\text{Cor}\{\Gamma_m \cdot E_0(M \oplus \Delta_{in}) \oplus \Gamma_{out} \cdot E(M \oplus \Delta_{in}) = 0\} = q.$$

Assuming the independence of E_0 and E_1 as well as

$$\Pr\{\Gamma_m \cdot E_0(M) \oplus \Gamma_m \cdot E_0(M \oplus \Delta_{in}) = 0 \mid E_0(M) \oplus E_0(M \oplus \Delta_{in}) \neq \Delta_m\} = \frac{1}{2},$$

one can obtain $\text{Cor}\{\Gamma_m \cdot E_0(M) \oplus \Gamma_m \cdot E_0(M \oplus \Delta_{in}) = 0\} = (-1)^{\Gamma_m \cdot \Delta_m} p$. With the help of piling-up lemma [16], correlation of the differential-linear distinguisher can be obtained using above three approximations, which is $(-1)^{\Gamma_m \cdot \Delta_m} pq^2$.

However, above two assumptions may not hold in practice. To tackle this problem, a middle part E_m is often added. Thus, the whole cipher is now split into three parts E_0, E_m and E_1, as illustrated in Fig. 2(b). One can experimentally evaluate the correlation of the middle part $r = \text{Cor}\{\Gamma_m \cdot E_m(x) \oplus \Gamma_m \cdot E_m(x \oplus \Delta_m) = 0\}$ or use the Differential-Linear Connectivity Table (DLCT) [4] in a theoretical way. Thus, correlation of the differential-linear distinguisher can be computed as prq^2. The distinguisher is regarded to be effective for the n-bit cipher if this value is larger than $2^{-\frac{n}{2}}$.

The differential part E_0 can be constructed by searching for an effective differential trail, as introduced in Sect. 2.2. And we adopt DLCT to theoretically evaluate the effectiveness of E_m. While for the linear part E_1, we can also try to find a linear trail with high absolute correlation. Correlation of the linear trail can be evaluated by considering correlation propagation properties of each operation in every involved round.

3   Differential-Linear Attack on 7-Round Orthros

3.1   Previous Approaches for Automated Key Recovery Attacks

In recent years, algorithms searching for various kinds of distinguishers in cryptanalysis have been widely proposed based on automatic searching tools. All these algorithms aim to find the longest effective distinguishers or the most effective one for a given number of rounds. These distinguishers are the best ones in mounting distinguishing attacks, however, they may not lead to the best key recovery attacks. For example, the longest effective differential on GIFT-128 [3] can reach 21 rounds, while the best key recovery attack on it is mounted with a 20-round differential [22].

Hence, to obtain the best key recovery attack, one has to take the attack procedure into consideration when searching for distinguishers. The first step in this area are taken by Derbez et al. [11], Shi et al. [19] and Chen et al. [8] for Demirci-Selçuk Meet-in-the-Middle attack, where the distinguisher and key recovery phase are constructed in a uniform searching algorithm.

Recently, Zong et al. introduced a two-step strategy to search for key-recovery-attack friendly differential and linear distinguishers [22]. To gain such distinguishers, not all bits of the plaintext or ciphertext should be activated by the input or output differences (resp. linear masks). Meanwhile, involved key bits in these added rounds should be as less as possible. Under above two considerations, they can firstly filter out some input and output differences (resp. masks) and then only focus on searching trails fulfilling these differences (resp. masks). After obtaining satisfied distinguishers, they will try to manually mount attacks with them and evaluate complexities of these attacks.

Later in [18], Qin et al. proposed a new approach for differential-like attacks where the key recovery phase and distinguisher searching process are constructed in a unified algorithm. Their approach is achieved with a predefined attack framework. Similar with [22], they also consider how active bits of input or output differences propagate to the plaintext or ciphertext, and construct this propagation procedure in the algorithm. Meanwhile, involved key bits can be recognized and then attack complexity can be evaluated roughly with a deterministic formula. However, as pointed out by Dong et al. [13], time complexity in this approach was not evaluated thoroughly, especially for rectangle attacks. Hence, Dong et al. restudied this approach by considering all time consuming parts together with a refined attack framework for rectangle attacks [13].

Inspired by [13,18], we adopt a similar approach to mount key recovery attacks on Orthros with the differential-linear cryptanalysis automatically. Different with [13,18], our attack framework can be used on ciphers adopting the parallel structure, such as Orthros, while they only focus on ciphers with only one branch. In following sections, we firstly construct the framework of mounting differential-linear attacks on Orthros, and then show how to implement this framework with automatic searching tools. At last, we can achieve the first key recovery attack on it.

3.2   Framework of Mounting Key Recovery Attacks on Orthros

In the differential-linear cryptanalysis, our aim is to check how many plaintext pairs fulfill the distinguisher $(\Delta_{in}, \Gamma_{out})$ after guessing several key bits involved in the added rounds. Generally, these plaintext pairs are constructed under several *structures*. In each structure, one chooses plaintext M taking all possible values on all active bits while fixed in others. These active bits can be identified since they are uniquely determined by the input difference Δ_{in}. Such a combination of active and non-active bits are referred as *active pattern* in this paper. Denote N_{ActP} as the number of active bits in the active pattern of the plaintexts. We can construct

$$\frac{N_{ActP}(N_{ActP} - 1)}{2} \approx \frac{1}{2}(N_{ActP})^2$$

pairs in each structure, which has zero differences in non-active bits but unknown differences in active bits. For each pair, one can guess corresponding key bits and then check whether it satisfies the trail. If so, the counter of these key bits will be increased by one. After checking all constructed pairs, the key corresponding to the counter which has the most biased value compared to half the number of constructed plaintext pairs is regarded as the right one. With one or two extra pairs, the full key can be recovered.

As mentioned in Sect. 2.1, due to the special structure adopted by Orthros, key recovery attack on it can be mounted only by adding several rounds before the differential-linear distinguisher. Besides, this distinguisher is also different with the one used to attack other primitives. It contains two input differences: Δ_{in}^1 for Branch1 and Δ_{in}^2 for Branch2, and an output mask Γ_{out}. Therefore, when using it to mount attacks, one has to construct the set of plaintext pairs suitable for both branches, simultaneously. In other words, constructed pairs should fulfill the active pattern derived from Δ_{in}^1 and that derived from Δ_{in}^2 in the same time. To minimize the data complexity, the best way to generate these pairs is restricting that these two active patterns are the same.

In order to ensure the same active pattern for these two branches, one has to deduce the relation between the input differences and them. Given input differences Δ_{in}^1 and Δ_{in}^2, one can obtain output differences Δ^1 and Δ^2 of the Sbox layer in the last key recovery round for each branch with certainty, as illustrated in Fig. 3. Hence, the active pattern is actually determined by Δ^1 and Δ^2.

Since we aim to get the active pattern of plaintexts, we have to compute the input active pattern of each operation given its output pattern. For the Sbox layer, if at least one output bit of an Sbox is active, all input bits of the same Sbox are considered to be active ones. Otherwise, they are all non-active. For the bit or nibble permutation, active pattern will propagates following its inverse. As for the matrix multiplication, propagation rules can be deduced after splitting it into several COPY and XOR operations. For each COPY operation, the input x_{in} is copied into two branches x_{out_1} and x_{out_2} with $x_{in} = x_{out_1} = x_{out_2}$. If at least one of these two branches is active, its input is also active. While for the XOR operation, the output $x_{out} = x_{in_1} \oplus x_{in_2}$, where x_{in_1} and x_{in_2} are two

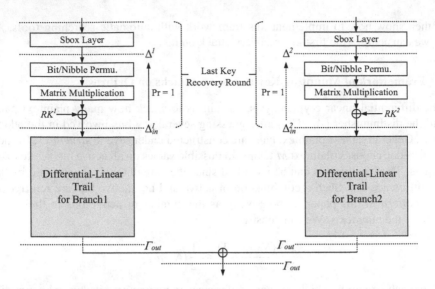

Fig. 3. Extended differential-linear distinguisher for Orthros

inputs. In this case, these two input bits are active if the output bit is active, while they are non-active if the output one is non-active. The round-key addition operation should also be considered since it indicates which key bits need to be guessed. In other words, if the key bit is active, we have to guess its value in the key recovery phase. As for the constant addition operation, one can ignore it since the extra input is a predefined constant.

With above propagation properties of active pattern, we can construct the relation between Δ^1 (resp. Δ^2) and its corresponding active pattern of plaintext Act_P^1 (resp. Act_P^2). Recall that for Orthros, we require that $Act_P^1 = Act_P^2$. To find distinguishers fulfilling this condition, we have to combine these propagation properties of active patterns with common searching process together. Meanwhile, we can realize which key bits are involved since this is indicated by the round-key addition operation. Thus, complexity of corresponding key recovery attack can be evaluated in the same time, given a predefined attack procedure. Since bit permutations utilized in Orthros can ensure the 2.5-round full diffusion [2], at most two rounds can be prepended to mount valid attacks. We show in Appendix B that it's highly unlikely that there exist valid attacks when two rounds are added. Hereafter, we only consider adding one round.

Assuming that an extended differential-linear distinguisher $(\Delta^1, \Delta^2, \Gamma_{out})$ with correlation c is obtained. The best way we can do to mount key recovery attacks based on it is to follow the procedure illustrated in Fig. 4 and described in Algorithm 1.

As shown in Line 10–15 of this algorithm, plaintext pairs (M, M') are constructed such that they fulfill the difference Δ^1 in Branch1. On average, they will satisfy the difference Δ^2 in Branch2 with probability $2^{-N_{ActP}}$. Besides, to ensure that V can recommend the right value of these N_{tot} bits, number of ciphertext pairs left in Line 20 should be at least c^{-2}. For each structure, one can obtain about $2^{2N_{ActP}-1}$

Algorithm 1: Key Recovery Attack Procedure on Orthros by Adding One Round

---

    // N_{tot}: number of involved master key bits;
    // N_{com}: number of common master key bits deduced from WK^1 and WK^2;
    // N_{ActP}: number of active bits in the active pattern of plaintexts;
    // $X[i]$: the i-th nibble of X, where X can be differences or values.

1 Allocate a counter array V_k with size $2^{N_{tot}}$, and initialize it to zeros;

2 **for** m structures **do**

      // In each structure, chosen plaintexts M take all possible
      values for active bits while fixed in others. Different
      structures take different values in those fixed bits.

3   Allocate an array V_m with size $2^{N_{ActP}}$, and initialize it to zeros;

4   **for** $2^{N_{ActP}}$ plaintexts M **do**

5   Query ciphertexts C for M and store (M,C) in V_m indexed by M;

6   **for** $2^{N_{ActP}}$ plaintexts M **do**

7   **for** $2^{N_{ActP}}$ possible values of WK^1 **do**

8   Deduce N_{ActP} bits of master key K from WK^1, and denote them as K^1;

9   Compute known bits of X^1 with WK^1 and M;

            // Construct M' such that (M,M') fulfills difference Δ^1.

10   **for** $i \leftarrow 0$ **to** 31 **do**

11   **if** $\Delta^1[i] \neq 0$ **then**

12   Compute $(X^1[i])' = X^1[i] \oplus \Delta^1[i]$;

                  // $S^{-1}[]$ is the inverse function of the Sbox.

13   Set the i-th nibble of M' as $S^{-1}[(X^1[i])'] \oplus WK^1[i]$;

14   **else**

15   Let the i-th nibble of M' equal to the i-th nibble of M;

16   Squeeze N_{ActP}-bit of WK^2 out with (M,M') and Δ^2;

17   Get N_{ActP} bits of master key K from WK^2, and denote them as K^2;

18   **if** K^1 and K^2 share same values on these N_{com} bits **then**

19   Compute these N_{tot} key bits from K^1 and K^2, and denote its value as k;

20   Find ciphertexts C and C' from V_m with index M and M', respectively;

21   **if** $\Gamma_{out} \cdot C \oplus \Gamma_{out} \cdot C' = 0$ **then**

22                   $V[k] \leftarrow V[k] + 1$;

23 **for** $2^{N_{tot}}$ k in V **do**

24      $V[k] \leftarrow |V[k] - c^{-2}2^{-1}|$;

25 Find the most largest one in V and output corresponding N_{tot} bits as the right key guess;

26 Query for a new (M,C);

27 **for** all possible values of remaining $(128\text{-}N_{tot})$ key bits **do**

28   Check whether it's the right key according to (M,C), and output it if so;

(M, M')

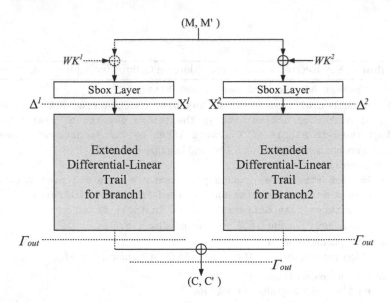

Fig. 4. Key recovery attack procedure on Orthros by adding one round

pairs. Note that in Line 18, a $2^{-N_{com}}$ condition is used to filter out pairs. Thus, we need $m = 2c^{-2}2^{N_{com}}2^{-N_{ActP}}$ structures due to $m2^{2N_{ActP}-1} = c^{-2}2^{N_{ActP}}2^{N_{com}}$. Data complexity is $D = m2^{N_{ActP}}$ chosen plaintexts. Time complexity is mainly determined by Line 5, 13 and 28. For Line 5 and 28, we need $m2^{N_{ActP}} + 2^{128-N_{tot}}$ encryption units, while for Line 13, it costs $m2^{N_{ActP}}2^{N_{ActP}} \times \frac{N_{ActP}}{4\times32}$ times of proceeding the Sbox layer. Assuming that we're attacking an R-round cipher and the proceeding cost of Sbox layer equals to half of one-round encryption. Thus in total, time complexity is about $T = m2^{N_{ActP}} + 2^{128-N_{tot}} + m2^{N_{ActP}}2^{N_{ActP}} \times \frac{N_{ActP}}{4\times32} \times \frac{1}{2R}$ full-round encryptions. We also need $128 \times 2^{N_{tot}}$ bits to store the counter V and another $256 \times 2^{N_{ActP}}$ bits for V_m.

3.3   Implement Our Framework with STP

Nowadays, many cryptanalytic results have been proposed with automatic searching tools. Among all of them, the Boolean Satisfiability Problem (SAT) [9]/Satisfiability Modulo Theories (SMT) problem [5] solver STP[2] has been playing an important role. The application of STP was firstly suggested by Mouha and Preneel [17]. It is a decision procedure to confirm whether there is a solution to a set of equations. These equations must follow the rule of input language parsed by STP[3].

To implement our differential-linear attack framework, equations describing the distinguisher searching process should be combined with those depicting the key recovery

---

[2] https://stp.github.io/.

[3] STP supports two kinds of input languages, here we use the CVC language to describe our model. For more information, please refer to https://stp.readthedocs.io/en/latest/cvc-input-language.html.

process in a unified searching algorithm. Besides, the evaluation of attack complexities is also constructed by several equations in this algorithm under a predefined attack procedure.

Modeling the Distinguisher Searching Process. Since we aim to mount attacks using differential-linear distinguishers, both difference and mask propagation properties of each component in the round function should be depicted in this part. As for the Sbox in middle part E_m, DLCT is utilized to evaluate its effectiveness. Meanwhile, propagation probability or correlation of each Sbox is also recorded.

For the Sbox layer, the differential distribution table (DDT), linear approximation table (LAT) and DLCT are adopted to describe its propagation properties. These tables are illustrated in Appendix D (Table 8, 9 and 10).

Property 1 *(Sbox Layer). Let Δ_{in}, Δ_{out}, Γ_{in} and Γ_{out} respectively represent the 4-bit input/output difference and input/output mask. Denote the propagation probability and correlation as p and c, separately. Then for each Sbox,*

(1) difference propagation: $p = DDT(\Delta_{in}, \Delta_{out})/16$ and $p \neq 0$;
(2) mask propagation: $c = LAT^*(\Gamma_{in}, \Gamma_{out})/8$ and $c \neq 0$;
(3) differential-linear: $c = DLCT^*(\Delta_{in}, \Gamma_{out})/8$ and $c \neq 0$.

Elements in LAT^* (resp. $DLCT^*$) are absolute values of those in LAT (resp. DLCT).

Property 2 *(Bit Permutation). Let Δ_{in}^i and Δ_{out}^i respectively be the i-th bit of 128-bit input and output differences. Then we have $\Delta_{out}^j = \Delta_{in}^i$, where $j = P_{br1}(i)$ for Branch1 and $j = P_{br2}(i)$ for Branch2. The relation also holds for masks Γ_{in} and Γ_{out}.*

Property 3 *(Nibble Permutation). Denote $\Delta_{in}[i]$ and $\Delta_{out}[i]$ as the i-th nibble of 128-bit input and output differences, separately. Then the relation is $\Delta_{out}[j] = \Delta_{in}[i]$ with $j = P_{nr1}(i)$ for Branch1 and $j = P_{nr2}(i)$ for Branch2, which also holds for masks.*

The matrix multiplication operation can be described through several 1-bit COPY and XOR operations. Thus, we directly present equations for them.

Property 4 *(1-bit COPY)*

(1) Let Δ_{in} be the input difference, while Δ_{out_1} and Δ_{out_2} are output differences. Then the relation between them is $\Delta_{out_1} = \Delta_{out_2} = \Delta_{in}$.
(2) Denote Γ_{in}, Γ_{out_1} and Γ_{out_2} as the 1-bit input mask and two output masks, respectively. Then the relation is $\Gamma_{in} = \Gamma_{out_1} \oplus \Gamma_{out_2}$.

Property 5 *(1-bit XOR)*

(1) Let Δ_{in_1} and Δ_{in_2} respectively represent input differences, and the output difference is Δ_{out}. Then we have $\Delta_{out} = \Delta_{in_1} \oplus \Delta_{in_2}$.
(2) Denote Γ_{in_1}, Γ_{in_2} and Γ_{out} as corresponding masks. Then $\Gamma_{in_1} = \Gamma_{in_2} = \Gamma_{out}$.

Modeling the Key Recovery Process. Equations depicting active pattern propagation properties for each operation are constructed here. These properties have already been explained in Sect. 3.2. When describing them, the bit taking the value 1 means that it's active, while it's a non-active bit if its value is 0.

Property 6 *(Active Pattern Propagation: Sbox Layer). Let Act_{in} and Act_{out} denote the 4-bit input and output active pattern of each Sbox, respectively. Then $Act_{in} = 0x0$ if $Act_{out} = 0x0$. Otherwise, $Act_{in} = 0xF$.*

Property 7 *(Active Pattern Propagation: Bit Permutation). Denote Act_{in}^i and Act_{out}^i as the i-th bit of the 128-bit input and output active pattern as Act_{in} and Act_{out}, respectively. Then $Act_{in}^i = Act_{out}^j$, where $j = P_{br1}(i)$ for Branch1 and $j = P_{br2}(i)$ for Branch2.*

Property 8 *(Active Pattern Propagation: Nibble Permutation). Let $Act_{in}[i]$ and $Act_{out}[i]$ respectively denote the i-th nibble of the 128-bit input and output active pattern. Then we have $Act_{in}[i] = Act_{out}[j]$, where $j = P_{nr1}(i)$ for Branch1 and $j = P_{nr2}(i)$ for Branch2.*

Property 9 *(Active Pattern Propagation: COPY). Let Act_{in} be the 1-bit input active pattern, while Act_{out_1} and Act_{out_2} are output active patterns. Then $Act_{in} = Act_{out_1} | Act_{out_2}$, where "$|$" represents the OR operation.*

Property 10 *(Active Pattern Propagation: XOR). Denote Act_{in_1} and Act_{in_2} as input active patterns, while the output active pattern is Act_{out}. Then $Act_{in_1} = Act_{in_2} = Act_{out}$.*

With Property 9 and 10, one can deduce the active pattern propagation property of the matrix multiplication operation. At the same time, according to Property 10, if the i-th bit of the state after the round-key addition operation is active, we have to guess the i-th round key bit. Since the key schedule is linear, one can realize which master key bit is involved.

Evaluating the Attack Complexity. As discussed in Sect. 3.2, data complexity of this attack is $D = m2^{N_{ActP}}$ chosen plaintexts where $m = 2c^{-2}2^{N_{com}-N_{ActP}}$. Besides, it costs $T = m2^{N_{ActP}}(1 + \frac{N_{ActP}}{R}2^{N_{ActP}-8}) + 2^{128-N_{tot}}$ encryption units. Memory complexity is $2^{N_{tot}+7} + 2^{N_{ActP}+8}$ bits. Note that total correlation c of the differential-linear distinguisher can be evaluated with Property 1. N_{tot}, N_{com} and N_{ActP} can be obtained following their definitions, which are explained in Algorithm 1. To gain valid attack results, we set $c > 2^{-n/2}$, $D < 2^n$ and $T < T_{th}$ for some expected threshold T_{th}.

After setting the number of rounds covered by E_0, E_1 and key recovery phase, one can generate corresponding equations with Property 1 to 10 and these three restrictions on attack complexities. Putting all these equations into STP, one can get a valid attack with time complexity less than T_{th} or realize that no satisfied attack exists.

3.4   Key Recovery Attack on 7-Round Orthros

Following the automatic searching procedure introduced in Sect. 3.3, we obtain a 7-round valid attack with time complexity 2^{106} encryption units, where 2^{95} chosen plaintexts are utilized. This attack is mounted based on a 6-round distinguisher with correlation $c = 2^{-46}$. As far as we know, this is the best key recovery attack on Orthros.

To make it clear, we illustrate the 6-round extended differential-linear distinguisher in Table 3. Its differential part E_0 contains the second and third round, while the linear part E_1 covering the fifth to seventh round is connected with E_0 by a one-round E_m. The first row in each branch shows the output difference of the Sbox layer in the key recovery round. From Table 3, one can see that only the 14-, 26- and 30-th nibble are active and thus $N_{ActP} = 12$. Meanwhile, we know that $WK^1[14]$, $WK^1[26]$, $WK^1[30]$, $WK^2[14]$, $WK^2[26]$ and $WK^2[30]$ need to be guessed. With known bits of WK^1, the 23-, 32-, 37-, 43-, 46-, 52-, 61-, 69-, 82-, 85-, 96- and 98-th master key bit are obtained. While from known bits of WK^2, we can get the 22-, 30-, 46-, 59-, 65-, 73-, 85-, 100-, 102-, 107-, 110- and 113-th master key bit. Hence, there are $N_{tot} = 22$ master key bits obtained. Among these bits, the 46- and 85-th key bit are common bits, thus $N_{com} = 2$. Therefore, data complexity of this key recovery attack is $D = 2^{95}$ chosen plaintexts. Time complexity is $T \approx 2^{106}$ encryptions of 7-round Orthros. Memory complexity is about 2^{29} bits. Detailed key recovery procedure has been shown in Algorithm 1 and Fig. 4. Note that this reduced version of Orthros we attack here is composed of four rounds using the bit permutation, followed by two rounds utilizing the nibble permutation and the last round is the final round.

4   Differential Attack on Orthros

As we have mentioned several times, key recovery attacks on Orthros can be mounted only by adding some rounds before the distinguisher. Due to the similarity between differential and differential-linear attacks, we can slightly modify the automatic searching procedure introduced in Sect. 3.3 to search for valid differential attacks.

Assuming that we have obtained an extended differential distinguisher $(\Delta^1, \Delta^2, \Delta_{out})$ with probability p, where Δ^1 and Δ^2 are output differences of the Sbox layer in the last key recovery round, as shown in Fig. 3. With this distinguisher, one can mount the key recovery attack by prepending some rounds before it. Similar with the differential-linear attack, we need an array V to count the number of plaintext pairs (M, M') who fulfills that $C \oplus C' = \Delta_{out}$. Different with the differential-linear attack, the right key is recommended by the largest value in V. By adding one round before, we can mount a differential attack following the similar procedure with Algorithm 1, where the condition in Line 21 is replaced by $C \oplus C' = \Delta_{out}$ and Line 23, 24 are removed. Therefore, attack complexities can be evaluated similarly with those of the differential-linear attack introduced in Sect. 3.2, however, $m = 2p^{-1}2^{N_{com}-N_{ActP}}$ in this case.

With the help of STP, we implemented above automated searching procedure. As a result, a 6-round key recovery attack with $T = 2^{120}$ and $D = 2^{115}$ is found. It relies on a 5-round differential distinguisher with probability $p = 2^{-112}$, which is depicted in Table 4. From this table, one can deduce that $N_{ActP} = 12$, $N_{tot} = 22$ and $N_{com} = 2$. Thus, attack complexities can be evaluated. The 6-round Orthros we attacked comprises four rounds utilizing the bit permutation, followed by one round using the nibble permutation and the final round.

Table 3. 6-round extended differential-linear distinguisher

ROUND	Diff./Mask	Branch1																																Pr/Cor
1	$\Delta S_{out}(\Delta^1)$	-	-	-	-	-	-	-	-	-	-	-	-	-	2	-	-	-	-	-	-	-	-	-	-	2	-	-	-	8	-			Pr = 1
2	ΔS_{in}	-	-	-	-	-	-	-	-	-	-	-	-	-	-	-	-	-	-	-	-	-	1	-	-	-	-	-	-	-	-			2^{-3}
	ΔS_{out}	-	-	-	-	-	-	-	-	-	-	-	-	-	-	-	-	-	-	2	-	-	-	-	-	-	-	-						
3	ΔS_{in}	-	-	-	-	4	4	4	-	-	-	-	-	-	-	-	-	-	-	-	-	-	-	-	-	-								2^{-6}
	ΔS_{out}	-	-	-	-	6	6	6	-	-	-	-	-	-	-	-	-	-	-	-	-	-	-											
4	ΔS_{in}	3	3	-	3	4	-	4	4	4	4	-	4	-	-	-	-	2	2	-	2	-	-	-	-	-	-	-	8	8	-	8		Cor = 1
	ΓS_{out}	-	-	-	-	-	-	-	-	-	-	-	8	-	5	-	-	-	-	-	4	3	2	-	8	-	2	-	-	-	-	-		
5	ΓS_{in}	4	-	-	-	-	-	-	-	-	-	-	-	-	-	-	-	-	-	-	4	-	-	-	-	2	-	-	-	-	-			2^{-3}
	ΓS_{out}	4	-	-	-	-	-	-	-	-	-	-	-	-	-	-	-	-	-	-	4	-	-	-	-	4	-	-	-	-	-			
6	ΓS_{in}	-	-	-	-	-	-	-	-	-	-	-	4	-	-	-	-	-	-	-	-	-	-	-	-	-	-							2^{-1}
	ΓS_{out}	-	-	-	-	-	-	-	-	-	-	-	A	-	-	-	-	-	-	-	-	-	-											
7	ΓS_{in}	-	-	-	-	-	-	-	-	-	-	A	A	-	A	-	-	-	-	-	-	-	-											2^{-3}
	$\Gamma S_{out}(\Gamma_{out})$	-	-	-	-	-	-	-	-	-	-	7	7	-	7	-	-	-	-	-	-	-												

ROUND	Diff./Mask	Branch2																																Pr/Cor
1	$\Delta S_{out}(\Delta^2)$	-	-	-	-	-	-	-	-	-	-	-	8	-	-	-	-	-	-	-	-	-	-	-	1	-	-	-	2	-				Pr = 1
2	ΔS_{in}	-	-	-	-	-	-	1	-	-	-	-	-	-	-	-	-	-	-	-	-	-	-	-	-	-	-	-	-	-				2^{-3}
	ΔS_{out}	-	-	-	-	-	-	2	-	-	-	-	-	-	-	-	-	-	-	-	-	-	-	-	-	-	-							
3	ΔS_{in}	-	-	-	-	-	-	-	-	-	-	-	-	8	-	8	8	-	-	-	-	-	-	-	-	-	-							2^{-6}
	ΔS_{out}	-	-	-	-	-	-	-	-	-	-	-	-	8	-	8	8	-	-	-	-	-	-	-	-	-								
4	ΔS_{in}	-	-	-	-	-	-	-	-	-	-	-	4	6	2	6	-	-	-	-	-	-	1	1	1	-	-	-	-	-				Cor = 1
	ΓS_{out}	2	5	2	-	-	-	4	-	1	1	2	-	-	4	-	1	5	4	1	-	-	-	-	-	-	2	-						
5	ΓS_{in}	-	-	-	-	-	-	2	-	-	-	D	-	-	-	-	-	2	-	-	-	-	-	-	-	-	-							2^{-3}
	ΓS_{out}	-	-	-	-	-	-	F	-	-	-	F	-	-	-	-	-	-	F	-	-	-	-	-	-	-	-							
6	ΓS_{in}	-	-	-	-	-	-	-	-	-	-	-	-	-	-	-	F	-	-	-	-	-	-	-	-	-	-							2^{-1}
	ΓS_{out}	-	-	-	-	-	-	-	-	-	-	-	-	-	-	-	C	-	-	-	-	-	-	-	-									
7	ΓS_{in}	-	-	-	-	-	-	-	-	-	-	-	C	C	-	C	-	-	-	-	-	-	-	-	-	-								2^{-3}
	$\Gamma S_{out}(\Gamma_{out})$	-	-	-	-	-	-	-	-	-	-	-	7	7	-	7	-	-	-	-	-	-	-	-	-									
Output	Γ_{out}	-	-	-	-	-	-	-	-	-	-	-	7	7	-	7	-	-	-	-	-	-	-	-	-	-								$c = 2^{-46}$

Note: Symbol "-" denotes the corresponding difference or mask is zero.

Table 4. 5-round extended differential trail

ROUND	Difference	Branch1	Pr
1	$\Delta S_{out}(\Delta^1)$	- - - - - - - - - - - - - - 2 - - - - - - - - - - - - 2 - - - - 8 -	1
2	ΔS_{in}	- 1 - - - - - - - -	2^{-3}
	ΔS_{out}	- 2 - - - - - - - -	
3	ΔS_{in}	- - - - 4 4 4 -	2^{-9}
	ΔS_{out}	- - - - 8 2 4 -	
4	ΔS_{in}	- - - - - - 4 4 - 8 8 - 8	2^{-14}
	ΔS_{out}	- - - - - - 9 8 - 8 1 - 4	
5	ΔS_{in}	- - - - - - - - 2 - 2 - - - - - - - - - B A 1 B 1 - 1 1 - - - -	2^{-24}
	ΔS_{out}	- - - - - - - - 3 - 2 - - - - - - - - - 2 B 3 B 2 - B B - - - -	
6	ΔS_{in}	- - B B - 2 - - B B - - - - - - - - - - - 3 3 - - - - - - - - -	2^{-14}
	ΔS_{out}	- - F F - 5 - - F F - - - - - - - - - - - E E - - - - - - - - -	

ROUND	Difference	Branch2	Pr
1	$\Delta S_{out}(\Delta^2)$	- - - - - - - - - - - - - - 8 - - - - - - - - - - - 1 - - - 2 -	1
2	ΔS_{in}	- - - - - - - 1 -	2^{-3}
	ΔS_{out}	- - - - - - - 2 -	
3	ΔS_{in}	- - - - - - - - - - - - - - 8 - 8 8 - - - - - - - - - - - - -	2^{-8}
	ΔS_{out}	- - - - - - - - - - - - - - 4 - 4 8 - - - - - - - - - - - - -	
4	ΔS_{in}	- - - - - 2 2 2 - - - - 4 - 4 - - - - - - - - - - - - - - - -	2^{-13}
	ΔS_{out}	- - - - - 4 8 4 - - - - 8 - 4 - - - - - - - - - - - - - - - -	
5	ΔS_{in}	- 2 2 2 - - - - - - - - - - - - - - - - 2 2 - 5 5 - 5 - - - -	2^{-16}
	ΔS_{out}	- 5 5 5 - - - - - - - - - - - - - - - - 5 5 - 5 5 - 5 - - - -	
6	ΔS_{in}	- - - - - 5 - - - - 5 - - 5 - 5 - - - - - - - - - - - - - - -	2^{-8}
	ΔS_{out}	- - - - - 5 - - - - 5 - - 9 - 5 - - - - - - - - - - - - - - -	
Output	Δ_{out}	- - F F - - - - F F 5 - - 9 - 5 - - - - - E E - - - - - - - -	2^{-112}

Note: Symbol "-" denotes the corresponding difference is zero.

5 Conclusion and Future Work

Due to the special overall structure that composed of two parallel permutations, key recovery attacks on Orthros are hard to be proceeded. In this paper, we proposed two automated key recovery attack frameworks on it utilizing differential and differential-linear cryptanalyses. We firstly exploit the relation between the input difference and the active pattern of plaintexts, and then combine it with common distinguisher searching progress as an unified algorithm. Meanwhile, the relation also indicates which key bits need to be guessed in the attack. Thus, attack complexities can be evaluated under a predefined attack procedure and also depicted in the searching algorithm. Implementing this unified algorithm with the automatic searching tool STP, we achieve a 7-round key recovery attack based on the differential-linear distinguisher with time complexity 2^{106} encryption units, where 2^{95} chosen plaintexts are used. Besides, a 6-round differential attack is also obtained which needs 2^{115} chosen plaintexts and 2^{120} encryption units. A potential way to improve these two attacks may be using the probability of differentials rather than that of dominant differential trail to evaluate attack complexities, as we have mentioned in Sect. 2.2. The actual probability of a differential is often evaluated by summing the probabilities of all significant trails comprising it. However, the automatic searching tools can return only one trail in this differential at a time. Besides, they can come up with another trail after we add some extra equations in the searching algorithm to exclude previous outputted trails. In other words, the common distinguisher searching process implemented with automatic tools cannot be constructed as a unified algorithm. Thus, there seems to be no way of combining it with key recovery attack procedures as a single searching algorithm. Whether there is another way to unify them as one algorithm is uncertain, and we leave this as the future work.

Acknowledgments. The authors would like to thank the anonymous reviewers for their valuable comments and suggestions to improve the quality of the paper. The research leading to these results has received funding from the National Natural Science Foundation of China (Grant No. 62032014, Grant No. 62002201, Grant No. 62002204), the National Key Research and Development Program of China (Grant No. 2018YFA0704702, Grant No. 2021YFA1000600), the Major Basic Research Project of Natural Science Foundation of Shandong Province, China (Grant No. ZR202010220025), and the Program of Qilu Young Scholars (Grant No. 61580082063088) of Shandong University.

A   Integral Key Recovery Attacks on Orthros

In this section, we show that there is no integral key recovery attacks can be mounted for more than 6 rounds with complexities better than the exhaustive attack. Hence, our proposed 7-round differential-linear attack is the best key recovery one.

The 7-round integral distinguishers given in the design document [2] have 127 active bits in the input. One of them can make all output bits after 7 rounds balanced when the 0-th bit is constant and the remaining 127 bits take all possible 2^{127} values. As pointed out by designers, these 7-round distinguishers cannot be used to mount key recovery attacks on 8-round Orthros. When adding one round after the distinguisher, one has to guess one of the branch outputs in order to reverse the ciphertext. In this case, it costs more than the exhaustive attack. If we try to prepend one round before it, we have to traverse all 2^{128} inputs which is also not better than the exhaustive attack.

Another way is proceeding a 7-round attack based on a 6.5-round distinguisher. The first round of this distinguisher contains all operations except for the Sbox layer[4], while the others are composed of all operations. By adding the Sbox layer and the whitening key addition operation before such distinguisher, we try to mount a 7-round attack. To find the distinguisher in each branch, we constructed an automatic searching algorithm following the way introduced in [10]. As a result, we found several 6.5-round distinguishers which hold for both branches. Among these distinguishers, the best ones have 5 bits fixed and take all possible values on the other 123 bits. These five bits cover a full output of a Sbox S_1 (4-bit) and one bit of the output of another Sbox S_2.

Without loss of generality, assuming that S_1 is the i-th Sbox while S_2 is the j-th Sbox. In this case, we have to traverse all inputs of the added Sbox layer except for the i-th Sbox to check whether the distinguisher holds. Meanwhile, to get these 124-bit input to the Sbox layer in Branch1, the 4-bit whitening key $WK^1[j]$ should be guessed, where $WK^1[j]$ denotes the j-th nibble of WK^1. As for Branch2, another 4-bit whitening key $WK^2[j]$ also needs to be guessed. According to bit permutations utilized in the key schedule of Orthros, there is at most one common bit in $WK^1[j]$ and $WK^2[j]$. Hence, we have to guess 7 master key bits for each input. Recall that we need to traverse 2^{124}

---

[4] That is what we mean by 0.5 round.

inputs. Therefore, such an attack costs $2^{124} \cdot 2^7 = 2^{131}$ full-round encryptions of Orthros, which is worse than the exhaustive attack which needs 2^{128} full-round encryptions.

B   Differential-Like Attacks Considering Two Rounds Prepended

Since the active pattern of plaintexts affects the data complexity of key recovery attack, we wonder how many bits will be activated from randomly chosen input differences. The relation between the active pattern and input differences can be deduced with active pattern propagation properties of each operation. To find the minimal number of activated bits, we construct this deducing procedure into several equations following Property 6–10 and solve them with the automatic searching tool STP. Note that we don't make any restriction on these two input differences. As a result, we obtain that at least 22 nibbles (i.e. 88 bits) will be activated when two rounds are prepended.

Key recovery attack framework in this case is illustrated in Fig. 5. In this attack, the best way we can do to construct plaintext pairs is following the strategy utilized in Algorithm 1. For each structure, we choose 2^{88} plaintexts M which takes all possible values in these 88 activated bits while fixed in others. For each plaintext M, we encrypt it under 2^{88} guessed values of WK^1. After applying the first Sbox layer, one can obtain 88-bit Y^1. Then one can achieve $(Y^1)' = Y^1 \oplus \alpha^1$, where α^1 is deduced from Δ^1 and

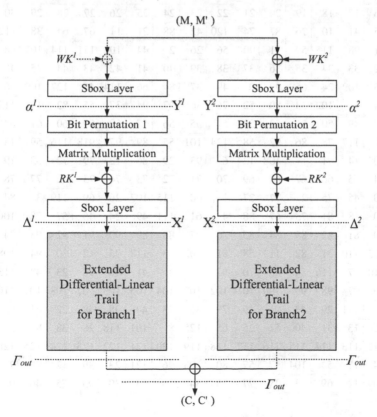

Fig. 5. Key recovery attack on Orthros considering two rounds

takes more than one possible value. With the 88-bit $(Y^1)'$, one can obtain M' by applying the inverse of Sbox layer.

Note that the above procedure has already cost at least $T = 2^{88} \cdot 2^{88} \cdot \frac{22}{32} \approx 2^{175.46}$ times of proceeding the Sbox layer. Assuming that the proceeding cost of Sbox layer equals to $\frac{1}{2}$ one-round encryption and we're mounting attacks on an R-round Orthros, this procedure costs $T \cdot \frac{1}{2} \cdot \frac{1}{R} \geq T \cdot \frac{1}{2} \cdot \frac{1}{12} \approx 2^{170.87}$ full-round encryptions. This costs much worse than the exhaustive attack where time complexity is 2^{128} full-round encryptions.

C Permutations Adopted in Orthros

Bit and nibble permutations used in the round function of Orthros are shown in Table 5 and 6, while Table 7 describes bit permutations utilized in key schedules.

Table 5. Bit permutations P_{br1} and P_{br2} adopted in Orthros [2]

i	0	1	2	3	4	5	6	7	8	9	10	11	12	13	14	15
P_{br1}	6	46	62	126	70	52	28	14	36	125	72	83	106	95	4	35
P_{br2}	20	122	74	62	119	35	15	66	9	85	32	117	21	83	127	106
i	16	17	18	19	20	21	22	23	24	25	26	27	28	29	30	31
P_{br1}	25	41	10	76	87	74	120	42	88	21	11	67	64	38	112	50
P_{br2}	11	98	115	59	71	90	56	26	2	44	103	121	114	107	68	16
i	32	33	34	35	36	37	38	39	40	41	42	43	44	45	46	47
P_{br1}	85	109	24	65	99	0	49	37	8	66	114	47	127	100	56	40
P_{br2}	84	1	102	33	80	52	76	36	27	94	37	55	82	12	112	64
i	48	49	50	51	52	53	54	55	56	57	58	59	60	61	62	63
P_{br1}	13	117	78	86	92	58	124	101	55	89	97	918	116	59	15	13
P_{br2}	105	14	91	17	108	124	6	93	29	86	123	79	72	53	19	99
i	64	65	66	67	68	69	70	71	72	73	74	75	76	77	78	79
P_{br1}	20	45	75	2	77	27	1	60	115	107	26	69	119	3	84	51
P_{br2}	50	18	81	73	67	88	4	61	111	49	24	45	57	78	100	22
i	80	81	82	83	84	85	86	87	88	89	90	91	92	93	94	95
P_{br1}	123	110	31	82	113	53	81	102	63	118	93	12	30	94	108	32
P_{br2}	110	47	116	54	60	70	97	39	3	41	48	96	23	42	113	87
i	96	97	98	99	100	101	102	103	104	105	106	107	108	109	110	111
P_{br1}	5	111	29	43	91	19	79	33	73	44	98	48	22	61	68	105
P_{br2}	126	13	31	40	51	25	65	125	8	101	118	28	38	89	5	104
i	112	113	114	115	116	117	118	119	120	121	122	123	124	125	126	127
P_{br1}	34	71	54	104	17	57	80	103	96	121	23	39	122	90	7	16
P_{br2}	109	120	69	43	7	77	58	34	10	63	30	95	75	46	0	92

Table 6. Nibble permutations P_{nr1} and P_{nr2} adopted in Orthros [2]

j	0	1	2	3	4	5	6	7	8	9	10	11	12	13	14	15
$P_{nr1}(j)$	10	27	5	1	30	23	16	13	21	31	6	14	0	25	11	18
$P_{nr2}(j)$	26	13	7	11	29	0	17	21	23	5	18	25	12	10	28	2
j	16	17	18	19	20	21	22	23	24	25	26	27	28	29	30	31
$P_{nr1}(j)$	15	28	19	24	7	8	22	3	4	29	9	2	26	20	12	17
$P_{nr2}(j)$	14	19	24	22	1	8	4	31	15	6	27	9	16	30	20	3

Table 7. Bit permutations P_{bk1} and P_{bk2} adopted in Orthros [2]

i	0	1	2	3	4	5	6	7	8	9	10	11	12	13	14	15
P_{bk1}	0	53	87	73	22	95	99	48	61	36	108	1	124	67	119	93
P_{bk2}	76	30	53	35	31	46	2	79	11	125	110	87	39	91	14	101
i	16	17	18	19	20	21	22	23	24	25	26	27	28	29	30	31
P_{bk1}	54	103	69	112	16	111	94	122	31	66	33	83	47	3	65	62
P_{bk2}	97	118	36	48	29	80	57	115	49	18	74	85	61	82	105	126
i	32	33	34	35	36	37	38	39	40	41	42	43	44	45	46	47
P_{bk1}	123	9	101	19	5	58	89	37	38	51	28	106	82	76	121	4
P_{bk2}	70	12	47	111	51	17	66	1	60	96	116	71	81	114	104	15
i	48	49	50	51	52	53	54	55	56	57	58	59	60	61	62	63
P_{bk1}	70	7	42	92	104	80	45	75	114	17	2	97	46	107	63	18
P_{bk2}	42	124	100	4	113	44	75	89	23	0	84	107	32	26	88	8
i	64	65	66	67	68	69	70	71	72	73	74	75	76	77	78	79
P_{bk1}	109	15	127	43	13	59	29	125	77	11	50	30	12	90	118	64
P_{bk2}	69	121	38	94	37	86	54	21	62	123	41	10	16	95	117	65
i	80	81	82	83	84	85	86	87	88	89	90	91	92	93	94	95
P_{bk1}	20	35	57	10	124	56	68	91	116	21	84	98	52	81	126	34
P_{bk2}	45	50	72	20	109	58	7	67	108	28	3	55	92	103	24	5
i	96	97	98	99	100	101	102	103	104	105	106	107	108	109	110	111
P_{bk1}	105	27	120	74	6	85	40	72	113	41	23	49	79	55	102	8
P_{bk2}	77	9	27	102	122	6	106	22	99	34	90	56	43	83	120	64
i	112	113	114	115	116	117	118	119	120	121	122	123	124	125	126	127
P_{bk1}	117	39	88	26	25	110	14	32	115	100	86	71	78	44	96	60
P_{bk2}	78	59	119	93	40	98	52	68	112	33	63	25	19	73	127	13

D   DDT, LAT and DLCT for the Sbox of Orthros

We illustrate DDT, LAT and DLCT for its Sbox in Table 8, 9 and 10, respectively.

Table 8. Differential distribution table $DDT(\Delta_{in}, \Delta_{out})$

Δ_{in}	Δ_{out}															
	0	1	2	3	4	5	6	7	8	9	a	b	c	d	e	f
0	16															
1		2	2	4		2	2					4				
2			2	2	4	4			2	2						
3		2	2		2		2			2	2			4		
4			2		2		4		2	2		2	2			
5			2	2		4				4					2	2
6		2	2		2			2					2	2	2	2
7		2					2	4		2		4	2			
8		2			2				4	2	4		2			
9				2			2		2	2	2	2				4
a		2			2				2	2	2			2	4	
b			2			2		2		2	2		2			4
c		2	2	2		2				2			2	2	2	
d		2		2			2	2	2	2				2		2
e						2	4	2	4					2		2
f				2	4			2					2	2	2	2

Note: Blank grid denotes the corresponding element is zero.

Table 9. Linear approximation table $LAT(\Gamma_{in}, \Gamma_{out})$

Γ_{in} \ Γ_{out}	0	1	2	3	4	5	6	7	8	9	a	b	c	d	e	f
0	8															
1		-4	-4		2	-2	2	-2	2	2	-2	-2				
2			2	2	4		2	-2	-2	-2			2	-2		4
3		-4	2	-2	-2	-2					2	2	2	-2	-4	
4		2		-2	4	-2		-2		2	4	2		2		-2
5		-2	4	-2	2		-2		-2		-2	-4		2		-2
6		-2	2	-4		2	2		2		2	-2		4	2	
7		2	2		-2	-4	4	-2		-2	-2		-2			-2
8		2	2		2		2	4	2	-2		2	-4			-2
9		2	-2	-4		-2	-2		2	-4		-2	2			2
a		-2		2	2		2	4	2	-4	2		2			-2
b		-2		2		-2	-4	-2		-2		2		-2	4	-2
c			2	2	-2	2		-4	4		2	-2	2	2		
d			-2	-2		4	2	-2	-2	-2		2	-2			-4
e				-2	-2	2	2	-2	2		2	-2	4		4	
f											4	-4	-4	-4		

Table 10. Differential-linear connectivity table $DLCT(\Delta_{in}, \Gamma_{out})$

Δ_{in} \ Γ_{out}	0	1	2	3	4	5	6	7	8	9	a	b	c	d	e	f
0	8	8	8	8	8	8	8	8	8	8	8	8	8	8	8	8
1	8	-4	-4		4	-4	-4	4	4			-4				
2	8		4			-4		4						-4	-8	
3	8		-4	-4			-4	4					4			-4
4	8	4			-4			4	-4	-4	-4					
5	8	-4		-4										4	-8	4
6	8			-4		-4						4				-4
7	8			-4		-4		-4	-4						8	
8	8	4	4		4			-4	-4	-4			-4	-4		
9	8	-4	-4	4			-4	-4								4
a	8			-4		-4		-4			4	4				-4
b	8		-4		4			-4	4			-4		-4		
c	8			-4			-4				-4		4			
d	8	-4				4						-4		-4		
e	8			-4	4	4	4					-4	-4	-4	-4	
f	8			4	-4	-4	-4					4				-4

References

1. FIPS 46-3: Data encryption standard. National Institute of Standards and Technology (1977). https://csrc.nist.gov/csrc/media/publications/fips/46/3/archive/1999-10-25/documents/fips46-3.pdf
2. Banik, S., Isobe, T., Liu, F., Minematsu, K., Sakamoto, K.: Orthros: a low-latency PRF. IACR Trans. Symmetric Cryptol. **2021**(1), 37–77 (2021). https://doi.org/10.46586/tosc.v2021.i1.37-77
3. Banik, S., Pandey, S.K., Peyrin, T., Sasaki, Y., Sim, S.M., Todo, Y.: GIFT: a small present. In: Fischer, W., Homma, N. (eds.) CHES 2017. LNCS, vol. 10529, pp. 321–345. Springer, Cham (2017). https://doi.org/10.1007/978-3-319-66787-4_16
4. Bar-On, A., Dunkelman, O., Keller, N., Weizman, A.: DLCT: a new tool for differential-linear cryptanalysis. In: Ishai, Y., Rijmen, V. (eds.) EUROCRYPT 2019. LNCS, vol. 11476, pp. 313–342. Springer, Cham (2019). https://doi.org/10.1007/978-3-030-17653-2_11
5. Barrett, C.W., Sebastiani, R., Seshia, S.A., Tinelli, C.: Satisfiability modulo theories. In: Biere, A., Heule, M., van Maaren, H., Walsh, T. (eds.) Handbook of Satisfiability, Frontiers in Artificial Intelligence and Applications, vol. 185, pp. 825–885. IOS Press (2009). https://doi.org/10.3233/978-1-58603-929-5-825
6. Biham, E., Shamir, A.: Differential cryptanalysis of DES-like cryptosystems. In: Menezes, A.J., Vanstone, S.A. (eds.) CRYPTO 1990. LNCS, vol. 537, pp. 2–21. Springer, Heidelberg (1991). https://doi.org/10.1007/3-540-38424-3_1
7. Biham, E., Shamir, A.: Differential cryptanalysis of DES-like cryptosystems. J. Cryptol. **4**(1), 3–72 (1991). https://doi.org/10.1007/BF00630563
8. Chen, Q., Shi, D., Sun, S., Hu, L.: Automatic Demirci-Selçuk meet-in-the-middle attack on SKINNY with key-bridging. In: Zhou, J., Luo, X., Shen, Q., Xu, Z. (eds.) ICICS 2019. LNCS, vol. 11999, pp. 233–247. Springer, Cham (2020). https://doi.org/10.1007/978-3-030-41579-2_14
9. Cook, S.A.: The complexity of theorem-proving procedures. In: Harrison, M.A., Banerji, R.B., Ullman, J.D. (eds.) Proceedings of the 3rd Annual ACM Symposium on Theory of Computing, Shaker Heights, Ohio, USA, 3–5 May 1971, pp. 151–158. ACM (1971). http://doi.acm.org/10.1145/800157.805047
10. Cui, J., Hu, K., Wang, Q., Wang, M.: Integral attacks on Pyjamask-96 and round-reduced Pyjamask-128. In: Galbraith, S.D. (ed.) CT-RSA 2022. LNCS, vol. 13161, pp. 223–246. Springer, Cham (2022). https://doi.org/10.1007/978-3-030-95312-6_10
11. Derbez, P., Fouque, P.-A.: Automatic search of meet-in-the-middle and impossible differential attacks. In: Robshaw, M., Katz, J. (eds.) CRYPTO 2016. LNCS, vol. 9815, pp. 157–184. Springer, Heidelberg (2016). https://doi.org/10.1007/978-3-662-53008-5_6
12. Dobbertin, H., Bosselaers, A., Preneel, B.: RIPEMD-160: a strengthened version of RIPEMD. In: Gollmann, D. (ed.) FSE 1996. LNCS, vol. 1039, pp. 71–82. Springer, Heidelberg (1996). https://doi.org/10.1007/3-540-60865-6_44
13. Dong, X., Qin, L., Sun, S., Wang, X.: Key guessing strategies for linear key-schedule algorithms in rectangle attacks. IACR Cryptology ePrint Archive, p. 856 (2021). https://eprint.iacr.org/2021/856
14. Gauravaram, P., et al.: Grøstl - a SHA-3 candidate. In: Handschuh, H., Lucks, S., Preneel, B., Rogaway, P. (eds.) Symmetric Cryptography, 11.01. - 16 January 2009. Dagstuhl Seminar Proceedings, vol. 09031. Schloss Dagstuhl - Leibniz-Zentrum für Informatik, Germany (2009). http://drops.dagstuhl.de/opus/volltexte/2009/1955/
15. Langford, S.K., Hellman, M.E.: Differential-linear cryptanalysis. In: Desmedt, Y.G. (ed.) CRYPTO 1994. LNCS, vol. 839, pp. 17–25. Springer, Heidelberg (1994). https://doi.org/10.1007/3-540-48658-5_3

16. Matsui, M.: Linear cryptanalysis method for DES cipher. In: Helleseth, T. (ed.) EURO-CRYPT 1993. LNCS, vol. 765, pp. 386–397. Springer, Heidelberg (1994). https://doi.org/10.1007/3-540-48285-7_33
17. Mouha, N., Preneel, B.: Towards finding optimal differential characteristics for ARX: application to Salsa20. Cryptology ePrint Archive, Report 2013/328 (2013). https://eprint.iacr.org/2013/328
18. Qin, L., Dong, X., Wang, X., Jia, K., Liu, Y.: Automated search oriented to key recovery on ciphers with linear key schedule applications to boomerangs in SKINNY and ForkSkinny. IACR Trans. Symmetric Cryptol. **2021**(2), 249–291 (2021). https://doi.org/10.46586/tosc.v2021.i2.249-291
19. Shi, D., Sun, S., Derbez, P., Todo, Y., Sun, B., Hu, L.: Programming the Demirci-Selçuk meet-in-the-middle attack with constraints. In: Peyrin, T., Galbraith, S. (eds.) ASIACRYPT 2018. LNCS, vol. 11273, pp. 3–34. Springer, Cham (2018). https://doi.org/10.1007/978-3-030-03329-3_1
20. Todo, Y.: Structural evaluation by generalized integral property. In: Oswald, E., Fischlin, M. (eds.) EUROCRYPT 2015. LNCS, vol. 9056, pp. 287–314. Springer, Heidelberg (2015). https://doi.org/10.1007/978-3-662-46800-5_12
21. Todo, Y., Morii, M.: Bit-based division property and application to SIMON family. In: Peyrin, T. (ed.) FSE 2016. LNCS, vol. 9783, pp. 357–377. Springer, Heidelberg (2016). https://doi.org/10.1007/978-3-662-52993-5_18
22. Zong, R., Dong, X., Chen, H., Luo, Y., Wang, S., Li, Z.: Towards key-recovery-attack friendly distinguishers: application to GIFT-128. IACR Trans. Symmetric Cryptol. **2021**(1), 156–184 (2021). https://doi.org/10.46586/tosc.v2021.i1.156-184

Post-quantum Cryptography

Dilithium for Memory Constrained Devices

Joppe W. Bos [ID], Joost Renes [ID], and Amber Sprenkels[✉] [ID]

NXP Semiconductors, Leuven, Belgium
{joppe.bos,joost.renes}@nxp.com, amber@electricdusk.com

Abstract. We investigate the use of the Dilithium post-quantum digital signature scheme on memory-constrained systems. Reference and optimized implementations of Dilithium in the benchmarking framework pqm4 (Cortex-M4) require 50–100 KiB of memory, demonstrating the significant challenge to use Dilithium on small Internet-of-Things platforms. We show that compressing polynomials, using an alternative number theoretic transform, and falling back to the schoolbook method for certain multiplications reduces the memory footprint significantly. This results in the first implementation of Dilithium for which the recommended parameter set requires less than 7 KiB of memory for key and signature generation and less than 3 KiB of memory for signature verification. We also provide benchmark details of a portable implementation in order to estimate the performance impact when using these memory reduction methods.

Keywords: Post-quantum cryptography · Dilithium · Memory optimization

1 Introduction

Digital signatures are one of the essential building blocks in our cybersecurity infrastructure. These cryptographic algorithms need to be computed on different platforms in the ecosystem: ranging from high-end cloud servers to resource constrained embedded devices. Especially the number of Internet-of-Things (IoT) devices, which has steadily outgrown the number of humans living on this planet and is expected to keep increasing [21], highlights the importance of being able to compute security primitives on such constrained devices.

Currently, the most commonly used digital signature schemes are RSA [27] and variants of (EC)DSA [14,22]. However, with the possibility of a quantum computer being realized, the security of RSA and (EC)DSA is threatened. Cryptography designed to run on our current platforms and which is secure against such a quantum threat is called *post-quantum* or *quantum safe* cryptography (PQC). In an effort to standardize such algorithms, the US National Institute of Standards and Technology (NIST) put out a call for proposals [23] to submit candidate algorithms in 2016. As of July 2020, seven out of fifteen remaining

L. Batina and J. Daemen (Eds.): AFRICACRYPT 2022, LNCS 13503, pp. 217–235, 2022.
https://doi.org/10.1007/978-3-031-17433-9_10

candidates have been marked as finalists, of which a subset is expected to be selected for standardization around May 2022. One of the three finalists for digital signatures is CRYSTALS–Dilithium [6,19], which will be the focus of this paper.

Dilithium signing has two main practical drawbacks for embedded devices. The first one is the variable signing time, which follows a geometric distribution. When using the parameter set targeting NIST security level 3, the probability that the signing time is more than twice the expected average is approximately 14 percent. This is significant and will have a real impact on many performance requirements for various use-cases. The second drawback relates to the memory requirements which are significantly higher for virtually all PQC schemes compared to the classical digital signature counterparts. This can not only attributed to relatively large key and signature sizes, but also heavy use of stack space for the storage of intermediate data. For example, the embedded benchmarking platform *pqm4* [10,11] (which executes on the ARM Cortex-M4) initially reported memory requirements for Dilithium in the range of 50–100 KiB for the original reference as well as the optimized implementations.

Dilithium has received a significant amount of attention from the cryptographic community. One direction of study comes from an applied cryptographic engineering perspective: how can one realize efficient implementations in practice for a selected target platform. Often the single most important optimization criterion is latency: the algorithm needs to execute as fast as possible, at the possible expense of other important metrics. Examples include the AVX2-based implementations from [6] and [7]; or the implementation from [25], which requires up to 175 KiB of memory.

Instead, we target platforms that have significantly less memory and computational power. Typical examples are platforms which are based on ARM Cortex-M0(+) cores. Such platforms are typical for a large family of IoT applications. Products in this range include the LPC800 series by NXP (4–16 KiB of SRAM), STM32F0 by ST (4–32 KiB of SRAM), and the XMC1000 by Infineon (16 KiB of SRAM). It is clear that PQC implementations with memory requirements of well over 50 KiB do not fit on these platforms and will not be able to sign nor verify digital post-quantum signatures.

In this paper we investigate whether it is possible to execute Dilithium on such memory-constrained devices that often have up to 8 KiB of SRAM and, if so, which performance penalty is incurred. Recently, there have been promising results in this direction [1,8]. Most notably the third strategy from [8] manages to run the recommended parameter set of Dilithium in just below 10 KiB: this is a remarkable achievement but still too large for many devices with only 8 KiB of SRAM, especially when you take into account that other applications will require memory as well.

Our Contribution. We present a new pure-C implementation for Dilithium that is optimized for low-memory usage. In Sects. 3 and 4, we investigate different methods for reducing the memory usage of the Dilithium algorithm. In particular, we come up with methods to reduce the amount of memory needed to store the **w** vector and the amount of memory needed to compute $c \cdot s_1$, $c \cdot s_2$, and $c \cdot t_0$. For all operations (KeyGen, Sign, and Verify), we propose an efficient allocation of the variables used during the algorithm. Then in Sect. 5, we measure the achieved memory usage and the impact on the performance of the algorithm on the Cortex-M4 platform using the pqm4 [10] framework.

2 Preliminaries

In this paper, we follow the same notation as the Dilithium specification [19]. We let R and R_q respectively denote the rings $\mathbb{Z}[X]/(X^n + 1)$ and $\mathbb{Z}_q[X]/(X^n + 1)$, for q an integer. Throughout this document, the value of n will always be 256 and q will be the prime $8380417 = 2^{23} - 2^{13} + 1$. Scalars and polynomials are written in a regular font (a), vectors are written in lowercase bold (**a**), and matrices are written in uppercase bold (**A**). All values in the NTT domain are written with a hat ($\hat{a}$), $\circ$ denotes coefficient-wise multiplication between two polynomials, and $\|a\|_\infty$ denotes the infinity norm of a.

In the remaining part of this work we describe optimization strategies for the Dilithium signature algorithm. One of the techniques used is to reuse memory space that is used by another value at some point during the computation to reduce the overall memory requirement. In the context of programming languages, a variable's *lifetime* is the time from which it is *initialized* until the last time it is *used*. After a variable has been used for the last time, it is *dead*. This is not the same as *allocation*, which means that a certain part of memory has been reserved for the storage of a variable. When the lifetimes of two variables overlap this means that, at some point in the algorithm, both variables are alive at the same time. As a consequence, such overlapping lifetimes mean that both variables cannot share the same memory location.

2.1 Dilithium

One approach to construct digital signatures comes from the realm of lattice-based cryptography. A particular problem used as a security foundation is known as the Learning With Errors (LWE) problem [26] introduced by Regev, which relates to solving a "noisy" linear system modulo a known integer. This problem can be used as the basis for a signature scheme, as shown by Lyubashevsky [18], by improving on their idea to apply Fiat-Shamir with aborts [13,17] to lattices.

The Ring Learning With Errors (R-LWE) [20,24] is a variant of this approach which works in the ring of integers of a cyclotomic number field and offers significant storage and efficiency improvements compared to LWE. Yet another approach to address certain shortcomings in both LWE and R-LWE and allows one to interpolate between the two. This Module Learning with Errors problem (M-LWE) [5,16] takes the R-LWE problem and, informally, replaces the single ring element with module elements over the same ring. Using this intuition, R-LWE can be seen as M-LWE with module rank 1. A practical instantiation

Table 1. Overview of the relevant Dilithium parameters (taken from [19]).

NIST security level	2	3	5
q [modulus]	8380417	8380417	8380417
(k, ℓ) [dimensions of $\mathbf{A}$]	$(4,4)$	$(6,5)$	$(8,7)$
η [secret key range]	2	4	2
τ [Hamming weight of c]	39	49	60
d [dropped bits from $\mathbf{t}$]	13	13	13
γ_1 [$\mathbf{y}$ coefficient range]	2^{17}	2^{19}	2^{19}
γ_2 [low-order rounding range]	$(q-1)/88$	$(q-1)/32$	$(q-1)/32$
β [range of $c\mathbf{s_1}$ and $c\mathbf{s_2}$]	78	196	120
Public key size (bytes)	1312	1952	2592
Secret key size (bytes)	2528	4000	4864
Signature size (bytes)	2420	3293	4595

of M-LWE with various (practical) improvements resulted in the CRYSTALS–Dilithium [6,19] digital signature algorithm.

The key generation is listed in Algorithm 1, the signature generation in Algorithm 2, and the signature verification in Algorithm 3.

The main mathematical building blocks in Dilithium are polynomials in $R_q = \mathbb{Z}_q[X]/(X^n + 1)$. These polynomials consist of $n = 256$ elements modulo $q < 2^{23}$. So far, all previous Dilithium implementations have stored polynomials in a buffer of 256 (u)int32_ts. This counts up to 1024 bytes $\hat{=}$ 1 KiB per polynomial. This explains why Dilithium implementations generally require a significant amount of memory: all of KeyGen, Sign, and Verify use $k \cdot \ell$ polynomials to store $\mathbf{A}$; add to that four vectors of length k, and you have already reached a total memory use of $\{32, 54, 88\}$ KiB.

It should be noted that not all polynomials require this much memory. The situation is different for $(\mathbf{s_1}, \mathbf{s_2}) \in S_\eta^\ell \times S_\eta^k$ which are uniformly random numbers in the range $\{-\eta, \ldots, +\eta\}$. Since $\eta = \{2, 4, 2\}$ for Dilithium-$\{2,3,5\}$ this means each coefficient can be stored using $\{3, 4, 3\}$ bits respectively. Hence, the polynomial $\mathbf{s}_{x,i}$ requires only $\{96, 128, 96\}$ bytes of memory. However, when this polynomial is stored naively in the NTT domain then one cannot use this property and the full 1024 bytes are needed, requiring $\{10.7, 8.0, 10.7\}$ times more memory.

3   Dilithium Signature Generation

The digital signature generation in Dilithium requires a significant amount of memory. To illustrate, the fastest implementation reported on the benchmark results from pqm4[1] requires ≈ 49, ≈ 80 and ≈ 116 KiB for Dilithium-$\{2,3,5\}$ respectively. In this section we outline the proposed techniques to reduce the memory requirements.

---

[1] Accessed February 14, 2022 using revision 3bfbbfd3.

Algorithm 1. Dilithium key generation (taken from [19])

Output: A public/secret key pair (pk, sk).
1: $\zeta \leftarrow \{0,1\}^{256}$
2: $(\rho, \rho', K) \in \{0,1\}^{256} \times \{0,1\}^{512} \times \{0,1\}^{256} := H(\zeta)$
3: $\mathbf{A} \in R_q^{k \times \ell} := \mathsf{ExpandA}(\rho)$ $\triangleright$ $\mathbf{A}$ is generated in NTT domain as $\hat{\mathbf{A}}$
4: $(\mathbf{s_1}, \mathbf{s_2}) \in S_\eta^\ell \times S_\eta^k := \mathsf{ExpandS}(\rho')$
5: $\mathbf{t} := \mathbf{A}\mathbf{s_1} + \mathbf{s_2}$ $\triangleright$ Compute $\mathbf{A}\mathbf{s_1}$ as $\mathsf{NTT}^{-1}(\hat{\mathbf{A}} \cdot \mathsf{NTT}(\mathbf{s_1}))$
6: $(\mathbf{t_1}, \mathbf{t_0}) := \mathsf{Power2Round}_q(\mathbf{t}, d)$
7: $tr \in \{0,1\}^{256} := H(\rho \parallel \mathbf{t_1})$
8: **return** $(pk = (\rho, \mathbf{t_1}), sk = (\rho, K, tr, \mathbf{s_1}, \mathbf{s_2}, \mathbf{t_0}))$

Algorithm 2. Dilithium signature generation (taken from [19])

Input: Secret key sk and a message M.
Output: Signature $\sigma = \mathsf{Sign}(sk, M)$.
1: $\mathbf{A} \in R_q^{k \times \ell} := \mathsf{ExpandA}(\rho)$ $\triangleright$ $\mathbf{A}$ is generated in NTT domain as $\hat{\mathbf{A}}$
2: $\mu \in \{0,1\}^{512} := H(tr \parallel M)$
3: $\kappa := 0, (\mathbf{z}, \mathbf{h}) := \bot$
4: $\rho' \in \{0,1\}^{512} := H(K \parallel \mu)$ (or $\rho' \leftarrow \{0,1\}^{512}$ for randomized signing)
5: **while** $(\mathbf{z}, \mathbf{h}) = \bot$ **do** $\triangleright$ Pre-compute $\hat{\mathbf{s}}_1 := \mathsf{NTT}(\mathbf{s_1})$, $\hat{\mathbf{s}}_2 := \mathsf{NTT}(\mathbf{s_2})$, and
       $\hat{\mathbf{t}}_0 := \mathsf{NTT}(\mathbf{t_0})$
6:     $\mathbf{y} \in S_{\gamma_1}^\ell := \mathsf{ExpandMask}(\rho', \kappa)$
7:     $\mathbf{w} := \mathbf{A}\mathbf{y}$ $\triangleright$ $\mathbf{w} := \mathsf{NTT}^{-1}(\hat{\mathbf{A}} \cdot \mathsf{NTT}(\mathbf{y}))$
8:     $\mathbf{w_1} := \mathsf{HighBits}_q(\mathbf{w}, 2\gamma_2)$
9:     $\tilde{c} \in \{0,1\}^{256} := H(\mu \parallel \mathbf{w_1})$
10:    $c \in B_\tau := \mathsf{SampleInBall}(\tilde{c})$ $\triangleright$ Store c in NTT representation as $\hat{c} = \mathsf{NTT}(c)$
11:    $\mathbf{z} := \mathbf{y} + c\mathbf{s_1}$ $\triangleright$ Compute $c\mathbf{s_1}$ as $\mathsf{NTT}^{-1}(\hat{c} \cdot \hat{\mathbf{s}}_1)$
12:    $\mathbf{r_0} := \mathsf{LowBits}_q(\mathbf{w} - c\mathbf{s_2}, 2\gamma_2)$ $\triangleright$ Compute $c\mathbf{s_2}$ as $\mathsf{NTT}^{-1}(\hat{c} \cdot \hat{\mathbf{s}}_2)$
13:    **if** $\|\mathbf{z}\|_\infty \geq \gamma_1 - \beta$ or $\|\mathbf{r_0}\|_\infty \geq \gamma_2 - \beta$ **then**
14:        $(\mathbf{z}, \mathbf{h}) := \bot$
15:    **else**
16:        $\mathbf{h} := \mathsf{MakeHint}_q(-c\mathbf{t_0}, \mathbf{w} - c\mathbf{s_2} + c\mathbf{t_0}, 2\gamma_2)$ $\triangleright$ Compute $c\mathbf{t_0}$ as $\mathsf{NTT}^{-1}(\hat{c} \cdot \hat{\mathbf{t}}_0)$
17:        **if** $\|c\mathbf{t_0}\|_\infty \geq \gamma_2$ or the # of 1's in $\mathbf{h}$ is greater than ω **then**
18:            $(\mathbf{z}, \mathbf{h}) := \bot$
19:    $\kappa := \kappa + \ell$
20: **return** $\sigma = (\tilde{c}, \mathbf{z}, \mathbf{h})$

Algorithm 3. Dilithium signature verification (taken from [19])

Input: Public key pk, message M and signature σ.
Output: Signature verification $\mathsf{Verify}(pk, M, \sigma)$: true if σ is a valid signature of M
    using pk and false otherwise.
1: $\mathbf{A} \in R_q^{k \times \ell} := \mathsf{ExpandA}(\rho)$ $\triangleright$ $\mathbf{A}$ is generated in NTT Representation as $\hat{\mathbf{A}}$
2: $\mu \in \{0,1\}^{512} := H(H(\rho \parallel \mathbf{t_1}) \parallel M)$
3: $c \in B_\tau := \mathsf{SampleInBall}(\tilde{c})$
4: $\mathbf{w_1'} := \mathsf{UseHint}_q(\mathbf{h}, \mathbf{A}\mathbf{z} - c\mathbf{t_1} \cdot 2^d, 2\gamma_2)$
5: **return** $[\![\|\mathbf{z}\|_\infty < \gamma_1 - \beta]\!]$ and $[\![c = H(\mu \parallel \mathbf{w_1'})]\!]$ and $[\![\# \text{ of 1's in } \mathbf{h} \text{ is } \leq \omega]\!]$

3.1   Streaming A and y

In Dilithium's signature generation algorithm the matrix $\mathbf{A}$ requires $k \cdot \ell$ KiB: by far the largest contributor to memory. A straightforward optimization is to not generate the entire matrix $\mathbf{A}$ but only generate the elements of $\mathbf{A}$ and $\mathbf{y}$ on-the-fly when they are needed. This approach was proposed and discussed already in [8, Strategy 3].

The expected memory reduction of this optimization is $k \cdot \ell$ KiB for $\mathbf{A}$, and ℓ KiB for $\mathbf{y}$; in practice this means a saving of $\{20, 35, 63\}$ KiB, for Dilithium-$\{2,3,5\}$ respectively. This optimization comes at a performance price: the matrix $\mathbf{A}$ needs to be regenerated again from ρ on every iteration of the rejection-sampling loop. Moreover, $\mathbf{y}$ needs to be generated twice during each iteration of the rejection-sampling loop; once for computing $\mathbf{w} = \mathbf{A}\mathbf{y}$, and once for computing $\mathbf{z} = \mathbf{y} + c\mathbf{s_1}$ later on. In [8], the authors report a slowdown factor of around $3.3 - 3.9$ compared to precomputing $\mathbf{A}$ and $\mathbf{y}$ completely.[2]

3.2   Compressing w

Another significant contributor to the overall memory requirements is the vector $\mathbf{w}$. This could be resolved if one could compute and use a single element at a time during the signature generation. Unfortunately, this is not possible due to the overlapping lifetimes of $\mathbf{w}$ and c, as identified in [8]. In line 9 of Algorithm 2, c is computed from $\mathbf{w_1} = \mathsf{HighBits}(\mathbf{w})$. On lines 12 and 16, the values $\mathbf{r_0}$ and $\mathbf{h}$ depend on c and the complete vector $\mathbf{w}$. This means that either *all* elements of $\mathbf{w}$ must be retained between computing c and computing $\mathbf{r_0}$ and $\mathbf{h}$, or $\mathbf{w} = \mathbf{A}\mathbf{y}$ must be computed twice during each iteration of the rejection-sampling loop. Recomputing the matrix-vector multiplication in every loop iteration will roughly double the execution time of the signing algorithm; although a viable direction to reduce memory we deemed this performance impact too large. Instead, we explore the other option where all elements of $\mathbf{w}$ have to be alive at the same time at the cost of storing k polynomials.

One polynomial has $n = 256$ coefficients, which are all bounded by $q = 2^{23} - 2^{13} + 1$. In previous works, implementations have always used 32-bit data-types for storing these coefficients. Instead, we use a *compressed* representation for storing $\mathbf{w}$. Instead of using 32-bit registers for storing $\mathbf{w}$ coefficients, the approach is to explicitly reduce them modulo q, reducing each coefficient to 24 bits and next pack the 256 24-bit coefficients into a 768-byte array. The (24-bit) compressed coefficients reduce the amount of storage that is used for storing $\mathbf{w}$ from $k \cdot 1024$ bytes to $k \cdot 768$ bytes, which results in a reduction of $\{1.0,1.5,2.0\}$ KiB for Dilithium-$\{2,3,5\}$, respectively. Packing and unpacking coefficients of $\mathbf{w}$ adds a little overhead during the matrix-vector multiplication.

It should be noted that one could compress each coefficient into 23 bits instead of 24 bits. This would save an additional 32 bytes per polynomial. However, working with the 23-bit format (packing and unpacking) is significantly

---

[2] These numbers are for NIST round-2 Dilithium and do not directly apply to the round-3 version.

more cumbersome and therefore slower compared to the 24-bit format for align-
ment reasons and the need for more expensive reductions during the computation of $\mathbf{w}$. This explains why we compress to 24 bits for the results presented in
Sect. 5.

3.3 Compressing $c \cdot \mathbf{s}_1$, $c \cdot \mathbf{s}_2$, and $c \cdot \mathbf{t}_0$

The multiplications of the challenge $c \in B_\tau$ with the polynomials $\mathbf{s}_1 \in S_\eta^\ell$,
$\mathbf{s}_2 \in S_\eta^k$, and $\mathbf{t}_0 \in S_{2^d}^k$, are typically computed using NTTs (see line 11, line 12
and line 16 of Algorithm 2). As the values of $\mathbf{s}_1$, $\mathbf{s}_2$ and $\mathbf{t}_0$ are static throughout
a whole signing computation, it is computationally most efficient to pre-compute
the NTTs on all these elements, and store $\hat{\mathbf{s}}_1$, $\hat{\mathbf{s}}_2$ and $\hat{\mathbf{t}}_0$ in memory before entering
the rejection-sampling loop. Avoiding the storage of these elements reduces the
total memory used by $2k + \ell$ KiB; i.e., {12,17,23} KiB for Dilithium-{2,3,5},
respectively. Indeed, this would naively imply a performance loss as the NTTs
need to be computed several times (at least once for each aborted signature).
However, the routine using (inverse) NTTs on-the-fly needs at least 1.75 KiB of
space: 1 KiB is needed to compute the (inverse) NTT for one operand, while
0.75 KiB is needed to store the other operand in (24-bit) compressed form. We
find that, for the computation of $\mathbf{s}_1$, $\mathbf{s}_2$ and $\mathbf{t}_0$, we do not necessarily need to
use the regular NTT. For most values involved, there is a lot of structure that
can be exploited. In the remainder of this section we discuss three different ideas
to compute $c \cdot \mathbf{s}_1, c \cdot \mathbf{s}_2$ and $c \cdot \mathbf{t}_0$ with lower memory requirements than using
regular NTTs.

Sparse Polynomial Multiplication. The most obvious choice for polynomial multiplication is the schoolbook approach. At first glance, using schoolbook multiplication actually requires *more* memory compared to NTT-based multiplication
because one cannot do the multiplication in-place. However, when using schoolbook multiplication, one does not need to store the right-hand-side operand
polynomials ($\mathbf{s}_1$, $\mathbf{s}_2$, and $\mathbf{t}_0$) completely. We can multiply their coefficients in a
streaming fashion, unpacking them "lazily" from the secret key. Apart from using
a small buffer we have now removed the need to store any full element from $\mathbf{s}_1$,
$\mathbf{s}_2$ and $\mathbf{t}_0$. Although one still needs 1.0 KiB for the accumulator polynomial,
only 68 bytes are required for storing the challenge c; as well as a small buffer of
32 bytes, which is used to unpack polynomial coefficients more efficiently from
the secret key. This adds up to 1124 bytes total: a reduction of a factor 1.37
compared to using an NTT.

Furthermore, one can reduce the computational as well as the memory complexity by exploiting the regular structure of the challenge c [2,28]. Recall that
the challenge polynomial has exactly τ non-zero coefficients that are either ± 1,
where $\tau \in \{39, 49, 60\}$ depending on the Dilithium parameter set. Therefore,
when multiplying c with some other polynomial, one really only needs to multiply each coefficient from the right-hand side operand with τ coefficients in c.
Skipping the multiplications with the zero-elements is not a security concern
(e.g., from a timing leakage perspective) since the challenge value c is public.

Using this property, one can use a data structure for c that allows for fast iteration over all the non-zero coefficients. We use a single 64-bit datatype which indicates for each of the τ non-zero positions whether it is a $+1$ or a -1; and an array of τ bytes which stores positions of the non-zero coefficients. The benefit of storing the indices of all non-zero coefficients, as opposed to storing a bit-string with bits set for each non-zero coefficient, is the fast iteration over the non-zero indices. If we store a bit for every coefficient in c, we have to do a conditional addition/subtraction of the coefficient in the other operand for *every* coefficient of c, i.e., n times. By only storing the non-zero indices, we only have to do the addition/subtraction τ times and avoid computing any multiplications. Hence, this polynomial multiplication with c can be done using $\tau \cdot n$ additions or subtractions only.

Alternative Number Theoretic Transforms. When computing $c \cdot \mathbf{s_1}$ and $c \cdot \mathbf{s_2}$ one can use a different-sized NTT over a smaller prime as described in [1]. The idea is that all coefficients of both $c\mathbf{s_1}$ and $c\mathbf{s_2}$ are bounded by $\pm \tau \cdot \eta = \pm \beta$. This allows computing the polynomial product with modulus $q' = 257$ for Dilithium-$\{2,5\}$, and $q' = 769$ for Dilithium-3. Since the coefficients in the product are bounded by $\pm \beta$, they will not overflow when computing them modulo $q' \geq 2\beta$. In [1], this improves the performance of the NTT-based multiplications because—with $q' = 257$—some of the multiplications with twiddle factors become cheaper. Moreover, [1] still uses 32-bit registers for all values, which provides so much headroom that it eliminates the need for any intermediate Barrett reductions in both NTT algorithms. However, the small-modulus NTTs also allows one to store all coefficients in 16-bit variables; computing an NTT in half the amount of memory at the cost of reintroducing the intermediate Barrett reductions. When using this technique, the memory requirement of $c \cdot \mathbf{s_1}$ and $c \cdot \mathbf{s_2}$ is reduced to 1.0 KiB: 0.5 KiB for the first operand and product, and another 0.5 KiB for the second operand.

Kronecker Substitution. By applying (generalizations of) Kronecker substitution [9,15] to $c \cdot \mathbf{s_1}$ and $c \cdot \mathbf{s_2}$ one can reduce the polynomial multiplication to the integer multiplications $c(2^\lambda) \cdot \mathbf{s_1}(2^\lambda)$ and $c(2^\lambda) \cdot \mathbf{s_2}(2^\lambda)$ modulo $2^{256\lambda} + 1$. The application of Kronecker substitution to lattice-based cryptography has been studied [3,4], but its use for $c \cdot \mathbf{s_1}$ and $c \cdot \mathbf{s_2}$ has not been considered yet. In order to retrieve the coefficients of the resulting polynomial, we require that $2^\lambda \geq 2\beta$. This means we can select $\lambda = 8$ for Dilithium-$\{2,5\}$ and $\lambda = 9$ for Dilithium-3, transforming the full polynomial multiplication into a single 2048-bit multiplication and a 2304-bit multiplication respectively. This requires 256 or 288 bytes for each of the two inputs and result polynomials: assuming the result can overwrite one of the inputs this means 512 or 576 bytes in total. Additionally one can use the more general Kronecker+ method [4] to improve the performance further (the optimal setting depending on the platform).

Although Kronecker substitution works perfectly well on the regular central processing unit it is particularly suitable for small systems that typically have dedicated hardware to perform (public-key) cryptographic operations in a timely manner. For RSA or elliptic-curve cryptography (ECC), such co-processors come in the form of large-integer multipliers that are heavily optimized for performing integer (modular) multiplications.

3.4 Variable Allocation

After applying the memory optimizations described above we analyzed efficient memory allocation schemes during the Dilithium signature generation algorithm. This showed that one can reuse the 1 KiB memory location that is used for doing computations on non-compressed polynomials. On top of that, we need 128 bytes for storing μ and ρ'; and 68 bytes for storing c, as described earlier ($\tilde{c}$ is stored solely in the output buffer). The complete memory allocation of the signature generation algorithm is listed in Fig. 1.

When looking at Fig. 1 one can observe that the memory bottle-neck is shared between multiple subroutines. We see no trivial way to further optimize the allocation of variables in memory. The only time-memory tradeoff that could still be performed is to keep a single element of $\mathbf{w}$ at a time. Following the recommendations from [8] we dismiss this approach because it requires us to compute all elements of $\mathbf{w}$ *twice* during each iteration of the rejection sampling loop. This would not only require expanding all elements of $\mathbf{A}$ *and* $\mathbf{y}$ twice, one would also need to recompute $\hat{\mathbf{y}} = \mathsf{NTT}(\mathbf{y})$ and $\mathbf{w} = \mathsf{NTT}^{-1}(\hat{\mathbf{w}})$. Because the matrix multiplication is already a dominating factor in the signing algorithm, this optimization would likely result in another slowdown by a factor two. Its gains in terms of memory consumption would be $(k-1) \cdot 768$ bytes, i.e., $\{2.25, 3.75, 5.25\}$ KiB for Dilithium-$\{2,3,5\}$, so it might be worthwhile if one can compensate for or cope with this performance penalty.

3.5 Summary of Optimizations

In this section we have described a large number of (possible) optimizations that can be applied to optimize the signature generation algorithm. For clarity, let us summarize which optimizations were selected for use in our implementation:

- we generate the elements of $\mathbf{A}$ and $\mathbf{y}$ on-the-fly, as described in Sect. 3.1;
- for storing $\mathbf{w}$, we use the compressed format described in Sect. 3.2;
- for computing $c \cdot \mathbf{t_0}$, we use *Sparse polynomial multiplication* (Sect. 3.3);
- for computing $c \cdot \mathbf{s_1}$ and $c \cdot \mathbf{s_2}$ we use the *small-modulus* NTTs from [1] (Sect. 3.3); and
- we use the variable allocation described by Fig. 1 and Sect. 3.4.

4 Dilithium Key Generation and Signature Verification

Both the Dilithium key generation and verification algorithms are fundamentally different from the signature algorithm with the most important difference that there is no rejection-sampling loop. Therefore, there is no performance benefit to precomputing the matrix $\mathbf{A}$ in these algorithms, which already reduces

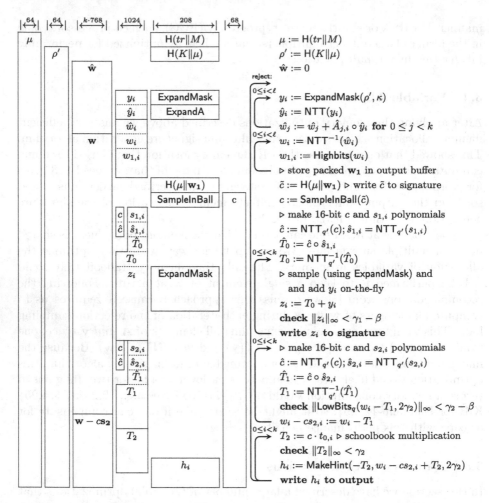

Fig. 1. Memory allocation of the Dilithium signature generation algorithm. Horizontal direction shows the memory slots that are used. Vertical direction shows the progression in time. The boxes indicate the lifetimes of the variables used in the algorithm. Dotted barriers denote that a variable is *renamed*, i.e., it is modified in-place. Arrows in the algorithm indicate loops that iterate over some range, except for the loop annotated by reject:, which indicates which code is repeated when a signature in the Sign algorithm is aborted. All temporary values are denoted by a T_i.

the memory requirement naturally. Moreover, in both KeyGen and Verify there are no polynomials for which it makes sense to precompute the NTT representation to speed-up the algorithms. This makes both algorithms significantly more lightweight in terms of memory compared to the signature generation, even without any further optimizations.

It is common that the key generation algorithm is executed on the same device where one performs the signature generation algorithm. Therefore, we do not attempt to reduce the memory footprint of KeyGen to the maximum extent, but instead try and minimize the memory footprint of max(KeyGen, Sign). In other words, we optimize the memory use of KeyGen, until it is at least as low as the memory use of Sign which we try to optimize as much as possible.

4.1   Key Generation

When following the same strategy for computing the multiplication $\mathbf{A} \cdot \mathbf{s_1}$ in the key generation algorithm as in the signing algorithm one can already remove the need for ℓ different memory slots for polynomials. Using this optimization in combination with careful scheduling the other memory (see Fig. 2) already means that all variables used in KeyGen use less memory than the signature generation algorithm. Hence, there is no reason to sacrifice any performance to optimize the KeyGen algorithm further.

Let us outline some memory improvements for the interested reader who has requirements to reduce the memory even further. One idea comes up from the observation that one can transpose the order in which the multiplication in $\mathbf{t} = \mathbf{As_1} + \mathbf{s_2}$ is performed. Recall that in the Sign algorithm, the lifetime of c overlaps with the lifetimes of all elements in $\mathbf{w}$ (where $\mathbf{w}$ is the output of the matrix-vector multiplication) which limits the potential to reduce memory. However, in the KeyGen algorithm there is no (equivalent to) c, i.e., there is no variable that causes the lifetimes of the elements in $\mathbf{t}$ to overlap. Hence, the elements in $\mathbf{t}$ do not have to be alive at the same time and can be computed in a streaming fashion. With this optimization one can reduce the memory by $(k - 1)$ KiB, saving $\{3.0, 4.5, 6.0\}$ for Dilithium-{2,3,5}, respectively.

4.2   Signature Verification

In the setting of the Dilithium signature verification algorithm we are interested in minimizing the memory usage as much as possible. There are many embedded applications that only use signature verification: e.g., secure boot implementations or in the case of public-key infrastructures.

The optimizations one can apply to the signature verification algorithm follow the same pattern as those of Sign and KeyGen. In particular, it is possible to verify any signature using only two slots for storing polynomials, of which one is 1.0 KiB and one is 768 bytes, using the optimizations from Sect. 4.1. Apart from the 1.75 KiB for storing two polynomials, one still needs twice the space for storing the SHA-3 state (208 bytes) plus one compressed challenge polynomial c (68 bytes). This sums up to a minimum of 2276 bytes of required memory for such an approach in the Dilithium verification algorithm. In contrast to the KeyGen and Sign algorithms, the memory usage of the Verify algorithm is independent from any of the Dilithium parameters.

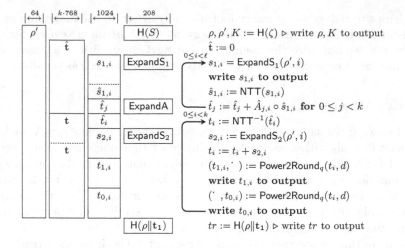

Fig. 2. Memory allocation of the Dilithium key generation algorithm. Horizontal direction shows the memory slots that are used. Vertical direction shows the progression in time. The boxes indicate the lifetimes of the variables used in the algorithm. Dotted barriers denote that a variable is *renamed*, i.e., it is modified in-place. Arrows in the algorithm indicate loops that iterate over some range.

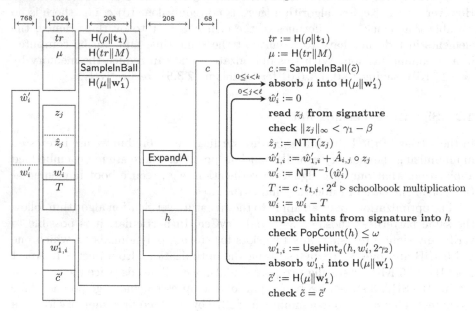

Fig. 3. Memory allocation of the Dilithium signature verification algorithm. Horizontal direction shows the memory slots that are used. Vertical direction shows the progression in time. The boxes indicate the lifetimes of the variables used in the algorithm. Dotted barriers denote that a variable is *renamed*, i.e., it is modified in-place. Arrows in the algorithm indicate loops that iterate over some range. All temporary values are denoted by a T_i.

5   Results and Discussion

Our Implementation. Using the Dilithium reference implementation[3] as a starting point, we wrote a new implementation for Dilithium, in which we applied the techniques described in Sects. 3 and 4. Because we are only interested in validating the memory reduction techniques and *not* focused on performance we have opted to write a cross-platform implementation in pure C. Correspondingly, our implementation does not include any architecture-specific optimizations. Moreover, our implementation as well as the implementations we compare against are not hardened in any fashion except for the prevention of (cache-)timing attacks.

Our implementation introduces many new internal data types that are optimized for a lower memory footprint; like compressed polynomials (with 24-bit coefficients and 16-bit coefficients) and the compressed challenge. We implemented the $q' \in \{257, 769\}$ NTTs for $c \cdot s_1$ and $c \cdot s_2$ multiplications, and we implemented the schoolbook multiplication for the $c \cdot t_0$ and $c \cdot t_1$ multiplications. We improved the implementation such that parts can be called in a streaming fashion. For example, the matrix-vector multiplication and ExpandA routines have been merged into a single non-buffering function; and almost all packing/unpacking functions have been refactored to allow for (un)packing polynomials in small chunks. Because of the tight memory budget we have removed some local stack allocations from all internal Dilithium routines. Instead, one memory block is allocated on the stack in the root functions (i.e., `dilithium_keygen`, `dilithium_signature`, and `dilithium_verify`) and passed to the internal functions.

As opposed to the previous works that only support a single Dilithium variant at a time, selected using C preprocessor macros at compile time, our implementation integrates all variants at the same time, and the variant is selected by the user at runtime as in typical in cryptographic software libraries.

Results. We integrated our implementation into a local fork of the benchmarking framework pqm4 [10].[4] We compared the memory footprint and the execution times of our implementation to those of the Dilithium implementation in PQClean [12], the Dilithium-round-3 updated port of [8] in pqm4, and the recent implementation results from [1].[5]

It should be noted that all of these implementations have different goals and implementation methods, so evaluating the benchmarking results is not as straightforward as just comparing performance numbers. Firstly, the PQClean implementation has been published as a "clean" implementation of Dilithium. Its main goal is to provide an implementation of Dilithium, written purely in C, that works cross-platform and follows best coding practices. It has been written with performance in mind and ensures a running time independent of secret-key related material. However, it does not include any platform-optimized assembly

---

[3] https://github.com/pq-crystals/dilithium.
[4] Commit hash e47864b3, forked on 8 Oct 2021.
[5] As of early 2022, this implementation has replaced the port of [8] in pqm4.

code which has the potential to greatly improve the performance. On the other side, there are the pqm4 [8] and [1] implementations. These implementations are specifically hand-crafted for the ARM Cortex-M4 platform and are highly optimized for performance (i.e., reducing the number of required cycles) and large parts of these implementations are written in Armv7 assembly. Some attention is paid to reducing memory in "Strategy 3" from [8]; unfortunately it is hard to compare directly since the paper presents numbers for the round-2 parameters of Dilithium which are significantly different compared to the latest (Round 3) ones. As an indication, the round-2 Dilithium-3 memory usage of signature verification and generation using this strategy are in both settings 10 KiB: significantly less compared to previous work but still too large for the embedded devices we target in this paper.

Our implementation is designed with a different goal in mind: it is a cross-platform C implementation that optimizes in the first place for memory usage to ensure it can execute on memory constrained (≤ 8 KiB) platforms. It makes a significant amount of sacrifices in terms of performance and does not contain any routines that are specially optimized for the Cortex-M4 (the techniques presented in this paper are platform independent). Therefore we expect the pqm4 implementation from [8] and the implementation from [1] to outperform our implementation on the Cortex-M4: we use a slower approach and a generic implementation. In order to assess the impact of the proposed techniques we remove the optimized assembly implementation from the equation and compare to the generic PQClean implementation. We include the performance figures of the other implementations for the sake of completeness.

An overview of the results is provided in Table 2. The testing platform that we used is the STM32F4 Discovery board, which is based on the STM32F407 microcontroller. Our implementation was benchmarked using the pqm4 framework. To obtain the cycle counts we measured 10 000 executions and computed the average. The results for the pqm4 [8] and [1] implementations are based on the results listed in [1].

The pqm4 method for measuring a scheme's memory usage is to first fill the stack with dummy values, then run the algorithm, and count how many dummy values were overwritten. The speed of the scheme is measured by measuring how much the SysTick timer has advanced while running the algorithm. The SysTick timer is clocked with the same frequency as the CPU, so this gives us the algorithm's latency in number of cycles (cc). In order to eliminate the influence of the chip's flash latency on the benchmarking results, the STM32F4 chip is clocked at 24 MHz, and the flash wait-states are set to zero. The code was compiled using GCC version 9.2.1,[6] with optimization level -Os.

In Table 3 we have listed the code sizes for all the implementations that we compare in Table 2. We have measured these code sizes using the same settings as for the memory/performance measurements. Because the [8] pqm4 and the [1] implementations are optimized for speed, we have listed their code sizes for the

---

[6] arm-none-eabi-gcc (15:9-2019-q4-0ubuntu1) 9.2.1 20191025 (release) [ARM /arm-9-branch revision 277599].

Table 2. Memory usage and cycle counts for Dilithium in kibibytes (KiB) and kilocycles (kcc). The [8] (pqm4) and [1] are implementations that include optimized assembly for Cortex-M4; PQClean [12] and **This work** are pure-C implementations. K, S, and V correspond to the signing primitives KeyGen, Sign, and Verify respectively. All cycle counts were averaged over 10 000 iterations.

	Variant		Dilithium-2		Dilithium-3		Dilithium-5	
			KiB	kcc	KiB	kcc	KiB	kcc
			Total ≤ 8		Total ≤ 8		Total ≤ 8	
With asm	[8] (pqm4)	K	37.1	1 602	59.6	2 835	95.7	4 835
		S	47.9	4 219	72.3	6 742	112.3	8 960
		V	35.2	1 579	56.6	2 700	90.8	4 718
	[1]	K	37.1	1 598	59.6	2 830	95.7	4 828
		S	47.9	4 083	67.4	6 624	113.3	8 726
		V	35.2	1 572	56.6	2 692	90.8	4 707
C only	PQClean [12]	K	37.4	2 025	59.4	3 504	–[a]	–[a]
		S	50.7	8 034	77.7	12 987	–[a]	–[a]
		V	35.4	2 223	56.4	3 666	–[a]	–[a]
	This work	K	4.9 ✓	2 927	6.4 ✓	5 112	7.9 ✓	8 609
		S	5.0 ✓	18 470	6.5 ✓	36 303	8.1	44 332
		V	2.7 ✓	4 036	2.7 ✓	7 249	2.7 ✓	12 616

[a] Implementation disabled because the device does not have enough RAM to support it.

optimization levels -O3 and -Os. In these metrics, the contribution of symmetric primitives—e.g., the size of the SHAKE code—has been excluded.

Discussion. The memory footprints reported in Table 2 for the presented techniques are close to the lower bounds provided earlier. The discrepancy in memory use is around 0.4 KiB of memory for all algorithms. The largest contributor to this additional memory use is the execution of SHAKE. The SHAKE code, which has been unadapted from the Dilithium reference implementation uses around 300 bytes of stack. The last 100 bytes are found in call-tree information and temporary buffers used during the packing and unpacking of polynomials into bit-arrays.

Table 2 clearly shows that the proposed techniques pay off. The states of both Dilithium-2 and Dilithium-3 for signature generation, verification and key generation easily fit into 8 KiB. It should be noted that none of the other high-speed implementations can execute on devices even with 32 KiB of memory. The amount of headroom arguably allows for plenty of other tasks to run on the device; 3.0 KiB in the case of Dilithium-2 and 1.4 KiB for Dilithium-3. The memory footprint of Dilithium-5 signing *just* exceeds 8 KiB. For Verify, the memory footprint is reduced to 2.7 KiB.

This is of course only half of the story. The memory reduction techniques have a clear impact on the performance of the scheme. When comparing cycle

Table 3. Code sizes of the implementations from Table 2 expressed in bytes. Opt-level denotes the optimization level that was used. Contribution of Keccak and AES code is excluded from all implementations.

Implementation	Opt-level	Dilithium-2	Dilithium-3	Dilithium-5
[8] (pqm4)	-O3	10 564	10 092	–[a]
[1]	-O3	18 448	19 916	18 262
[8] (pqm4)	-Os	9 700	9 276	–[a]
[1]	-Os	17 408	19 012	17 234
PQClean	-Os	6 986	6 534	–[b]
This work	-Os	**10 091**[c]	**10 091**[c]	**10 091**[c]

[a] Not reported by pqm4.
[b] Implementation disabled because the device does not have enough RAM to support it.
[c] Implementation includes support for all Dilithium variants.

counts to those of the PQClean implementation (which is the implementation most similar to ours), one observes a factor 2.3–2.8 slowdown for Sign and a factor 1.8–2.0 slowdown for Verify. For both algorithms, the difference in performance is due to the overhead from the (24-bit) bit-packing operations in the matrix-vector multiplication, and the slower schoolbook method for multiplying ct_0. For Dilithium-3 signing there is some additional overhead, because the $q' = 769$ NTTs are somewhat slower than the $q' = 257$ NTTs in the other variants.

Optimization efforts from [8] and [1] have lead to a 43%–44% reduction of cycles in Sign compared to the PQClean implementation. Similarly, one can expect that future performance enhancements will be able to improve the performance of our implementation of the memory reduction techniques as well. Depending on the platform, integrating more optimized assembly implementations for SHAKE, (inverse) NTT, and challenge multiplication could result in significant performance gains. In particular, many of the values in the challenge multiplication are 8 bits, This is suitable for parallel computation using SIMD instructions, which are not used in our C-implementation.

More importantly, many of the memory constrained devices come equipped with dedicated cryptographic coprocessors for symmetric primitives (such as SHAKE) as well as for big-number arithmetic. When one is able to make use of these coprocessors, the execution times could be reduced drastically: especially because SHAKE remains a dominating component of the Dilithium execution time as well as the polynomial multiplication [4].

Although the reduction of the run-time state has a big impact on the execution speed of the algorithm, we see from the results in Table 3 that this is not the case for the code size. The code for our new implementation is slightly bigger than the PQClean code, but about the same size as the optimized implementations.[7] Moreover, we must take into account that our implementation supports *all* variants of Dilithium at the same time, so a slight increase is actually expected.

6   Conclusions and Future Work

Although there is considerable performance impact when implementing Dilithium in a low-memory environment, we have shown that such low-memory Dilithium implementations are feasible in practice. In particular, we broke the 8 KiB memory barrier for Dilithium-2 and Dilithium-3. Dilithium-5 uses a *little* bit more memory than 8 KiB but we have shown that there are still time-memory tradeoffs that can be applied, even though these tradeoffs are relatively expensive in terms of performance.

When earlier work (like [25]) was published, it was not clear whether Dilithium was a scheme that could even be considered for memory constrained devices. Then [8] showed that the Dilithium algorithms could reasonably fit into 16 KiB of memory. In this paper, we show that most variants of Dilithium can even fit into 8 KiB without a very drastic impact on performance. More so, we reduced the memory footprint for Dilithium verification below 3 KiB. For memory-constrained devices, storing Dilithium's public keys and signatures has arguably become a bigger challenge than storing its run-time state.

References

1. Abdulrahman, A., Hwang, V., Kannwischer, M.J., Sprenkels, A.: Faster Kyber and Dilithium on the Cortex-M4. In: Applied Cryptography and Network Security: 20th International Conference, ACNS 2022, pp. 853–871. Rome, Italy, 20–23 June 2022. Proceedings Jun 2022. https://doi.org/10.1007/978-3-031-09234-3_42
2. Akleylek, S., Bindel, N., Buchmann, J., Krämer, J., Marson, G.A.: An efficient lattice-based signature scheme with provably secure instantiation. In: Pointcheval, D., Nitaj, A., Rachidi, T. (eds.) AFRICACRYPT 2016. LNCS, vol. 9646, pp. 44–60. Springer, Cham (2016). https://doi.org/10.1007/978-3-319-31517-1_3
3. Albrecht, M.R., Hanser, C., Hoeller, A., Pöppelmann, T., Virdia, F., Wallner, A.: Implementing RLWE-based schemes using an RSA co-processor. IACR TCHES **2019**, 169–208 (2018). https://doi.org/10.13154/tches.v2019.i1.169-208. https://tches.iacr.org/index.php/TCHES/article/view/7338
4. Bos, J.W., Renes, J., van Vredendaal, C.: Polynomial multiplication with contemporary co-processors: beyond Kronecker, Schönhage-Strassen & Nussbaumer (to appear). In: USENIX Security Symposium. USENIX Association (2022). https://eprint.iacr.org/2020/1303
5. Brakerski, Z., Gentry, C., Vaikuntanathan, V.: (Leveled) fully homomorphic encryption without bootstrapping. In: Goldwasser, S. (ed.) ITCS 2012, pp. 309–325. ACM (2012). https://doi.org/10.1145/2090236.2090262

---

[7] It is clear that the hand-written assembly in the [8] and [1] implementations—which is very aggressively loop-unrolled—comes at a significant cost in code size.

6. The CRYSTALS-Dilithium team: A lattice-based digital signature scheme. IACR TCHES **2018**(1), 238–268 (2018). https://doi.org/10.13154/tches.v2018.i1.238-268. https://tches.iacr.org/index.php/TCHES/article/view/839
7. Faz-Hernández, A., Kwiatkowski, K.: Introducing CIRCL: an advanced cryptographic library. Cloudflare (2019). https://github.com/cloudflare/circl. v1.1.0 Accessed Feb 2022
8. Greconici, D.O.C., Kannwischer, M.J., Sprenkels, A.: Compact Dilithium implementations on Cortex-M3 and Cortex-M4. IACR TCHES **2021**(1), 1–24 (2021). https://doi.org/10.46586/tches.v2021.i1.1-24. https://tches.iacr.org/index.php/TCHES/article/view/8725
9. Harvey, D.: Faster polynomial multiplication via multipoint Kronecker substitution. J. Symb. Comput. **44**(10), 1502–1510 (2009). https://doi.org/10.1016/j.jsc.2009.05.004
10. Kannwischer, M.J., Rijneveld, J., Schwabe, P., Stoffelen, K.: PQM4: Post-quantum crypto library for the ARM Cortex-M4. https://github.com/mupq/pqm4
11. Kannwischer, M.J., Rijneveld, J., Schwabe, P., Stoffelen, K.: PQM4: testing and benchmarking NIST PQC on ARM Cortex-M4. Workshop Record of the Second PQC Standardization Conference (2019)
12. Kannwischer, M.J., Schwabe, P., Stebila, D., Wiggers, T.: Improving software quality in cryptography standardization projects. Cryptology ePrint Archive, Report 2022/337 (2022). https://eprint.iacr.org/2022/337
13. Kiltz, E., Lyubashevsky, V., Schaffner, C.: A concrete treatment of Fiat-shamir signatures in the quantum random-oracle model. In: Nielsen, J.B., Rijmen, V. (eds.) EUROCRYPT 2018. LNCS, vol. 10822, pp. 552–586. Springer, Cham (2018). https://doi.org/10.1007/978-3-319-78372-7_18
14. Koblitz, N.: Elliptic curve cryptosystems. Math. Comput. **48**, 203–209 (1987). https://doi.org/10.1090/S0025-5718-1987-0866109-5
15. Kronecker, L.: Grundzüge einer arithmetischen Theorie der algebraischen Grössen. J. für die reine und angewandte Mathematik **92**, 1–122 (1882). https://doi.org/10.1515/9783112342404-001
16. Langlois, A., Stehlé, D.: Worst-case to average-case reductions for module lattices. Des. Codes Crypt. **75**(3), 565–599 (2014). https://doi.org/10.1007/s10623-014-9938-4
17. Lyubashevsky, V.: Fiat-Shamir with aborts: applications to lattice and factoring-based signatures. In: Matsui, M. (ed.) ASIACRYPT 2009. LNCS, vol. 5912, pp. 598–616. Springer, Heidelberg (2009). https://doi.org/10.1007/978-3-642-10366-7_35
18. Lyubashevsky, V.: Lattice signatures without trapdoors. In: Pointcheval, D., Johansson, T. (eds.) EUROCRYPT 2012. LNCS, vol. 7237, pp. 738–755. Springer, Heidelberg (2012). https://doi.org/10.1007/978-3-642-29011-4_43
19. Lyubashevsky, V., et al.: CRYSTALS-DILITHIUM. Technical Report, National Institute of Standards and Technology (2020). https://csrc.nist.gov/projects/post-quantum-cryptography/round-3-submissions
20. Lyubashevsky, V., Peikert, C., Regev, O.: On ideal lattices and learning with errors over rings. In: Gilbert, H. (ed.) EUROCRYPT 2010. LNCS, vol. 6110, pp. 1–23. Springer, Heidelberg (2010). https://doi.org/10.1007/978-3-642-13190-5_1
21. Maayan, G.D.: The IoT rundown for 2020: stats, risks, and solutions. https://securitytoday.com/Articles/2020/01/13/The-IoT-Rundown-for-2020.aspx
22. Miller, V.S.: Use of elliptic curves in cryptography. In: Williams, H.C. (ed.) CRYPTO 1985. LNCS, vol. 218, pp. 417–426. Springer, Heidelberg (1986). https://doi.org/10.1007/3-540-39799-X_31

23. National Institute of Standards and Technology: Post-quantum cryptography standardization. https://csrc.nist.gov/Projects/Post-Quantum-Cryptography/Post-Quantum-Cryptography-Standardization

24. Peikert, C., Regev, O., Stephens-Davidowitz, N.: Pseudorandomness of ring-LWE for any ring and modulus. In: Hatami, H., McKenzie, P., King, V. (eds.) 49th ACM STOC, pp. 461–473. ACM Press (2017). https://doi.org/10.1145/3055399.3055489

25. Ravi, P., Gupta, S.S., Chattopadhyay, A., Bhasin, S.: Improving speed of Dilithium's signing procedure. In: Belaïd, S., Güneysu, T. (eds.) CARDIS 2019. LNCS, vol. 11833, pp. 57–73. Springer, Cham (2020). https://doi.org/10.1007/978-3-030-42068-0_4

26. Regev, O.: On lattices, learning with errors, random linear codes, and cryptography. In: Gabow, H.N., Fagin, R. (eds.) 37th ACM STOC, pp. 84–93. ACM Press (2005). https://doi.org/10.1145/1060590.1060603

27. Rivest, R.L., Shamir, A., Adleman, L.M.: A method for obtaining digital signatures and public-key cryptosystems. Commun. Assoc. Comput. Mach. **21**(2), 120–126 (1978). https://dl.acm.org/doi/10.1145/359340.359342

28. Wang, W., Tian, S., Jungk, B., Bindel, N., Longa, P., Szefer, J.: Parameterized hardware accelerators for lattice-based cryptography. IACR TCHES **2020**(3), 269–306 (2020). https://doi.org/10.13154/tches.v2020.i3.269-306. https://tches.iacr.org/index.php/TCHES/article/view/8591

Lattice-Based Inner Product Argument

Veronika Kuchta[1]([✉]), Rajeev Anand Sahu[2], and Gaurav Sharma[3]

[1] The University of Queensland, Brisbane, Australia
v.kuchta@uq.edu.au
[2] University of Luxembourg, Esch-sur-Alzette, Luxembourg
[3] Université libre de Bruxelles, Bruxelles, Belgium

Abstract. In this paper we put forth the first lattice-based construction of an inner product argument. The inner product argument can serve as a key building block for reducing computation and communication in the arithmetic circuit satisfiability. The only existing inner product arguments are based on the discrete-log problem which leaves them vulnerable to quantum cryptanalysis. An equivalent idea in the lattice-based setting is interesting to explore, especially in the view of the upcoming quantum computing scenario. The underlying lattice commitment on a vector of ℓ ring elements, is computationally binding and hiding assuming hardness of M-LWE and M-SIS problems. The crux idea is to split the vector into s chunks each having ℓ/s ring elements. In contrast to the existing inner product arguments, our commitment includes randomness which guarantees the hiding property of the commitment. The proposed lattice-based inner product argument requires logarithmic communication in the length of the witness for both the prover and the verifier except to a relaxation factor ℓ^3 of the extracted witness. Moreover, we present an optimized inner product argument in which the size of the initial commitment can be further reduced using the properties of ring isomorphism and splitting rings. The idea is to split each witness into chunks, laying them into separate rings that are isomorphic to the ring $\mathcal{R}_q$, commit to these ring elements and prove the security of the scheme by its reduction to the security of the underlying commitment scheme.

1 Introduction

The ongoing process of post-quantum cryptography standardization by NIST and the recent quantum supremacy achieved by Google [2] witnesses the urgent need of quantum-resistant primitives. In line of research to handle the advent of quantum computers, the family of lattice-based constructions [30] is believed to be a promising candidate. The lattice-based protocols enjoy provable security under hardness of certain lattice problems with achieving relatively efficient implementations. In comparison to the key-exchange, encryption and signature schemes [12,14,15] the privacy-preserving protocols using lattices are less explored due to challenges in devising reasonable zero-knowledge proof (ZKP).

Zero-Knowledge Proof. The ZKP techniques, introduced by Goldwasser, Micali and Rackoff [18] have been recognized as useful tools for achieving authenti-

© The Author(s), under exclusive license to Springer Nature Switzerland AG 2022
L. Batina and J. Daemen (Eds.): AFRICACRYPT 2022, LNCS 13503, pp. 236–268, 2022.
https://doi.org/10.1007/978-3-031-17433-9_11

cation and privacy. Particularly in the blockchain technology, these ZKP techniques have been instrumental in achieving security. The goal of a ZKP between a prover $\mathcal{P}$ and verifier $\mathcal{V}$ is that it is impossible for the verifier to gain any additional information besides the fact the prover wants to convey. A ZKP requires *completeness*– the prover can prove a correct statement, *soundness*– the prover cannot convince the verifier for a false statement and *zero-knowledge*– the verifier learns nothing beyond the fact that the prover's statement is true or false. Usually a zero-knowledge proof can only achieve statistical soundness while the one achieving computational soundness is referred to as zero-knowledge argument (ZKA). Kilian [23] demonstrated that a ZKA can have lower communication complexity than a ZKP. Among the exhaustive works on ZKA, the work of Groth [19] based on the discrete logarithm assumption is comparatively relevant to set a pointer on the state-of-the art ZKP. His protocol has a communication complexity proportional to the square root of the circuit size. This motivates to achieve better results [20, 21]. Recently Groth's inner product arguments [21] has attracted attention for achieving privacy in blockchain. However, the efficiency of inner product argument has been a prime concern for practical applications.

Inner Product Arguments. Recently, Bootle et al. [10] proposed a similar result with 5 moves over 7 moves of [19]. Their construction is solely based on the discrete logarithm assumption and unlike the traditional setup, requires only a small common reference string independent of the circuit. Basically in [10] they have proposed an inner product argument and employed it to construct zero-knowledge proof for arithmetic circuit satisfiability. The basic idea of the original inner product argument introduced in [10] provides an argument of knowledge of two vectors $\mathbf{a}, \mathbf{b} \in \mathbb{Z}_q^n$, where for the generators $\mathbf{g}, \mathbf{h} \in \mathbb{G}^n$ holds $A = \mathbf{g}^\mathbf{a}, B = \mathbf{g}^\mathbf{b}$, and $\mathbf{a} \cdot \mathbf{b} = z$ for a given $z \in \mathbb{Z}_q$ and $A, B \in \mathbb{G}$. In the mentioned paper the authors showed how to reduce the communication cost from being linear in n to logarithmic in n. In another work by Bünz et al. [13], the inner product argument is improved and presented as Bulletproofs. In comparison to $6 \log_2 n$ of [10], they have demonstrated the argument with communication complexity of $2 \log_2 n$ for n being the vector dimension.

Lattice-Based Zero-Knowledge Arguments. The first lattice-based version of a zero-knowledge proof was presented by Goldreich and Goldwasser [17], where they proved complements of the approximate shortest vector problem and approximate closest vector problem. In a later work, Micciancio and Vadhan [29] provided an optimization of these problems by constructing new statistical zero-knowledge proofs. The first zero-knowledge identification protocol based on the hardness of syndrome decoding for a linear code was introduced by Stern [32] which was later used for further constructions of lattice-based proofs [24, 25]. The protocol in [32] and its adaptations achieve constant soundness error, however, these proofs are required to be run in several parallel repetitions. An alternative approach "Fiat-Shamir with Aborts (FSwA)" was introduced by Lyubashevsky [26] to build zero-knowledge proofs. This method has been further used in many constructions which benefit from high efficiency as they produce a soundness error of $1 - 2^{-\lambda}$ with only one repetition, for the security parameter

λ. This approach is used to prove a relaxed relation about the knowledge of a secret element s and a short ring vector c while working over a polynomial ring $\mathcal{R}_q = \mathbb{Z}_q[X]/(X^n + 1)$, such that $\mathbf{As} = \mathbf{ct}$, where $\mathbf{t} \in \mathcal{R}_q$. However, this kind of relaxation makes zero-knowledge proofs less practical. To avoid this issue, a new approach was introduced in [4], where the challenge space is given by a set of two elements $\{0, 1\}$. The schemes using this binary challenge space are considered to be less efficient when proving fewer relations. Benhamouda et al. [9] introduced a new challenge space consisting of monomial challenges, such as $X^i \in \mathcal{R}$ in the Ring-LWE setting. Esgin et al. [16] provided a short one-out-of-many proofs from lattices that proves knowledge of a secret which associates with one of the public values. They used the new challenge space from [9] which allowed them to reduce the number of repetitions to achieve a negligible soundness error. Unfortunately, the one-shot technique is not suitable for our protocol, therefore we stick to the monomial challenge space and repeat our protocol $\lambda/|\log(\mathcal{CH})|$ times. In [6] a new zero-knowledge argument of knowledge for general arithmetic circuits was proposed. It is based on the complex "MPC-in-the-head" paradigm [22].

Zero-Knowledge Proofs Evolving Blockchain. Recently, the properties of zero-knowledge proof have found significant impact on blockchain application. For a secure financial transaction the blockchain requires anonymity and confidentiality. The anonymity hides the identity of participants while confidentiality conceals the transaction amount. The blockchain's mechanism provides partial anonymity, hence there have been efforts to achieve confidentiality or privacy. Now, each transaction should carry along a validity proof. In this view the zero-knowledge proofs are viable options to achieve privacy within the blockchain frame. Among the existing zero-knowledge proofs zk-SNARKs, zk-STARKs and Bulletproofs are the candidate choices with their pros and cons. For example Zcash, Ethereum etc. use zk-SNARK for privacy. Further, there are also associated challenges in the view whether these proofs are realized with or without trusted setup. The generation of common reference string (CRS) in trusted setup relies on randomness and leakage of this randomness enables false proofs therefore counterfeit coins can be created by a malicious party. Also, the protocols with no trusted setup have their own challenges. For instance, the proof size of STARK in [8] is practically unacceptable. Thus for blockchain applications the zero-knowledge arguments of knowledge without trusted setup are primarily significant and short proof size are especially preferable. Bulletproofs [13]– short non-interactive zero-knowledge argument of knowledge without trusted setup– derives efficient zero-knowledge proofs suitable for range proof. The Bulletproof reduces the proof size to verify a witness. Monero– a cryptocurrency with dedicated privacy– uses Bulletproofs to aggregate all the range proofs of a confidential transaction and collectively prove their validity. Additionally, utilizing constraint systems on the top of Bulletproofs can support confidential multi-asset transactions. The deployment of Bulletproof in bitcoin can reduce the size of unspent transaction outputs (UTXOs) by a factor of 10. Yet, construction of zero-knowledge arguments in the lattice-based setting is rather challenging on many fronts. For example achieving a succinct proof is one of the main bottlenecks. However, very recently some of the leading work [3,11] have been benefited by the advantage of *folding techniques* to reduce the witness size sufficiently small by repeating the reduction. Both of the constructions [3,11] realise lattice-based arguments. Unlikely [11], in [3] Attema et al. have reduced the knowledge error achieving compact soundness error leveraging parallel repetition of multi-round public-coin protocols.

Our Contribution. Recently, efficient ZKP for circuit satisfiability have been achieved leveraging the advantage of inner product arguments. The existing inner product arguments are based on computation of discrete logarithm (DL). However, all the primitives based on factoring or DL problems would be insecure in the presence of large scale quantum computers. Considering this fact and motivated from the introductory inner product argument [10], in this paper we present an efficient lattice-based inner product argument which is quantum-secure with assuming the computational binding and hiding properties of the underlying commitment scheme. Our lattice-based scheme requires only logarithmic communication and computation costs except a polynomial relaxation factor of the extracted witness. In order to optimise the computational cost, we investigate some of the advanced algebraic properties of polynomial ring $\mathcal{R}_q$. Furthermore, we propose an optimization of our inner product argument where we decompose each witness from $\mathcal{R}_q$ into chunks defined in the different rings $\mathcal{R}_{q,j}$ where $j \in [0, \kappa - 1]$ and κ being the number of rings after the first round of decomposition. In other words, two integers x and y which are both encoded into a polynomial over $\mathcal{R}_q$ will be decomposed into smaller pieces x_i, y_i, respectively such that the multiplication of these two integers can be computed over smaller subrings $\mathcal{R}_{q,j}$. A possible application of such optimized inner product argument is integer multiplication where the prover convinces the verifier of knowledge of two secret integers x and y and their product $xy = z$. With our optimized protocol we are able to multiply two integer x and y faster and more efficient. We prove the security of our proposed optimized inner product argument under the binding and hiding property of the underlying commitment scheme.

As ZKP brings relevant security in blockchain transactions, the efficiency is an important concern. Inner product argument is an effective building block to reduce communication complexity in cryptographic constructions which has been recently instrumental for blockchain application [10]. As we propose a lattice-based inner product argument with logarithmic communications to realize efficient ZKP, this construction is quite suitable for blockchain. Particularly, similar to Bulletproof, our scheme can leverage an efficient range proof relying on lattice commitment and optimized inner product argument which can be further utilized to verify whether the wallet balance of both the transacting participants is positive and also the transaction amount is greater than zero. Moreover, the presented construction is secure against quantum attacks.

Our Techniques. In our contribution we develop new techniques to construct an inner product argument from lattices. A detailed list of notations we use throughout the paper is given in Table 1.

Table 1. Important notations

Notation	Description
$\mathcal{R}_q = \mathbb{Z}_q[X]/(X^n + 1)$	Polynomial ring
q	Prime modulus defining $\mathcal{R}_q$
n	Degree of polynomials in $\mathcal{R}_q$
m	The number of columns in a linear system
λ	Security parameter
δ	Root Hermite factor
$\mathcal{CH}$	Set of challenges
$\beta_{(\cdot)}$	Euclidean norm of a randomness $\mathbf{r}$ in a zero-knowledge argument
$\mathcal{B}$	Infinity norm of a randomness $\mathbf{r}$ in a zero-knowledge argument
$x \leftarrow_\$ X$	Element x is sampled at uniform random from a finite set X
$\mathsf{Com}_{ck}(x, r)$	Commitment on a message x with randomness r and a commitment key ck
d	Number of rows in a commitment
$\mathfrak{D}_\sigma^n$	n-dimensional discrete Normal distribution with standard deviation σ
ℓ	The length of the input strings to the protocol in Sect. 3
s_ν	The number of chunks at level ν in Sect. 3.1
ℓ_ν	The length of the witness at level ν in Sect. 3.1
$(\hat{\cdot})$	Initial input to the protocol in Sect. 3, e.g. $\hat{\mathbf{a}}, \hat{\mathbf{r}}_a, \hat{\mathbf{A}}, \hat{\mathbf{B}}$, etc.
$(\cdot)'_\nu$	Compressed input at level ν, e.g. $\mathbf{a}'_\nu, \mathbf{b}'_\nu$, etc.
$\mathfrak{C}_{a,s}, \mathfrak{C}_{a,s_\nu}$	Commitment matrix to the initial input $\hat{\mathbf{a}}$ or $\mathbf{a}'$ at level ν
$\mathbb{A}_\nu$	Commitment to $\mathbf{a}'_\nu$ with randomness $\mathbf{r}'_\nu$ at the recursion level ν
$\mathbb{A}_{k_\nu}$	Diagonal commitment to the k_ν-th diagonal in the matrix $\mathfrak{C}_{a,s_\nu}$
κ	Number of rings in the first decomposition round (Chap. 5)
$\Phi(m)$	m^{th} cyclotomic polynomial
$\mathfrak{m}$	Minimal polynomial
$\mathcal{R}_{q,j}$	j-th component of $\mathcal{R}_q$ after the first ring decomposition for all $j \in [0, \kappa - 1]$
$f_j(X) = (X^{\phi(m)/\kappa} - r_j)$	Irreducible polynomial with a zero r_j
$(\tilde{\cdot})$	Input to the protocol in Sect. 4, e.g. $\tilde{\mathbf{a}}, \tilde{\mathbf{r}}_a, \tilde{\mathbf{A}}, \tilde{\mathbf{B}}$, etc.
κ_1	Number of rings $(\mathcal{R}_{q,j})_{j_1}$ after the second ring decomp., $\forall j_1 \in [0, \kappa_1 - 1]$
$\psi_{i \mapsto j}$	Ring isomorphism (Sect. 4.2) between the rings $\mathcal{R}_{q,i}$ and $\mathcal{R}_{\mathrm{II},\mid}$
$\tilde{\mathfrak{C}}_{a,\kappa}, \tilde{\mathfrak{C}}_{b,\kappa}$	Commitment matrix to the initial input $\tilde{\mathbf{a}}$ or $\tilde{\mathbf{a}}$ at the first level
$((\tilde{\cdot})_j)_{j_1}$	Input to the protocol after the second ring decomposition, e.g. $(\tilde{\mathbf{a}}_j)_{j_1}$, etc.

Lattice-Based Inner Product Argument. Our first contribution is the inner product argument. This is the first construction based on a lattice assumption. We define a lattice commitment on a vector of ℓ ring elements, i.e. $\hat{\mathbf{a}} \in \mathcal{R}_q^\ell$ by following the idea from [10]. We first split the vector into s chunks $\mathbf{a}'_i \in (\mathcal{R}_q)^{\ell/s}$ where each chunk consists of ℓ/s ring elements. The public parameters are given by a concatenation of ℓ elements $\mathbf{A}'_\iota$ and ℓ elements $\mathbf{B}'_\iota$ for $\iota \in [1, \ell]$. Similar procedure is adopted for the randomness $\hat{\mathbf{r}}_a \in (\mathcal{R}_q^{m \times 1})^\ell$. The lattice-based commitment is defined as $\mathbb{A} = \mathsf{Com}_{\hat{\mathbf{A}}, \hat{\mathbf{B}}}(\hat{\mathbf{a}}, \hat{\mathbf{r}}_a) = \sum_{i=1}^s (\mathbf{A}'_i \mathbf{r}'_{a,i} + \mathbf{B}'_i \mathbf{a}'_i)$. The main trick of this recursive proof is to build a matrix $\mathfrak{C}_{a,s}$ with coefficients being $c_{i,j} = \mathbf{A}'_i \mathbf{r}'_{a,j} + \mathbf{B}'_i \mathbf{a}'_j$, where i, j runs from 1 to s. The prover's part of this protocol contains the computation of the diagonal commitments $\mathbb{A}_k = \mathbf{A}'_i \mathbf{r}'_{a,i+k} + \mathbf{B}'_i \mathbf{a}'_{i+k}$

of the matrix $\mathfrak{C}_{a,s}$, where $k = 1 - s, \ldots, s - 1$. The prover communicates $2s - 1$ diagonal commitments of size $n \log q$ to the verifier. Upon receiving a challenge from the verifier, the prover employs it in computing the new commitment $\mathbb{A}' = \sum_{k=1-s}^{s-1} \mathbb{A}_k x^k$ with the new secret $\mathbf{a}' = \sum_{k=1}^{s} \mathbf{a}'_i x^i$ which only consists of ℓ/s ring elements and is shorter than the initial witness $\hat{\mathbf{a}} \in \mathcal{R}_q^\ell$. The security of this protocol relies on the binding and hiding properties of the underlying commitment scheme, where the binding and hiding properties are secured by the hardness of the underlying module-based learning with error problem (M-LWE) and the module-based short integer solution problem (M-SIS). We use the challenge space consisting of monomials X^ι for all $\iota \in [0, 2n]$, we need to repeat our proof $\lambda/|\log(\mathcal{CH})|$-times to achieve a negligible soundness error. Furthermore, we note that we prove a relaxed relation of the inner product since the extracted witness consists of the initial witness multiplied by a relaxation factor which is equal to ℓ^3. The Euclidean norm of the extracted witness is $\ell^3 \sqrt{mn} B$. This result is the first construction of a lattice-based inner product argument. In our second contribution we try to explore possible ways to optimize the first result.

Lattice-Based Inner Product Over the Splitting Rings. We present our second contribution which provides an optimization in our inner product argument. The main challenge of this contribution is to show that the size of the initial commitment can be reduced using the properties of ring isomorphisms and splitting rings. Our protocol takes as input two witnesses $\tilde{\mathbf{a}}, \tilde{\mathbf{b}} \in \mathcal{R}_q$, and we are interested in their inner product. By representing these polynomials over the ring $\mathcal{R}_q$ via their coefficients and writing them into coefficient vectors, we obtain two vectors for which we can compute the inner product.

Our first idea is to split each witness into chunks defined over different rings that are isomorphic to the ring $\mathcal{R}_q$. We follow an approach used in [28] which splits a given polynomial $\Phi_m(X)$ into irreducible factors $f_j(X) = (X^{\phi(m)/\kappa} - r_j)$ defined over the rings $\mathcal{R}_{q,j}$ of $\mathcal{R}_q$, where $\tilde{r}_j \in \mathbb{Z}_{q_j}$ is a zero of $f_j(X)$. In Sect. 4.1, we show how to split the witnesses $\tilde{\mathbf{a}}, \tilde{\mathbf{b}}, \tilde{\mathbf{r}}_{\tilde{a}}, \tilde{\mathbf{r}}_{\tilde{b}}$ and the corresponding public parameters $\tilde{\mathbf{A}}, \tilde{\mathbf{B}}, \tilde{\mathbf{C}}, \tilde{\mathbf{D}}$ into the chunks over $\mathcal{R}_{q,j}$. While computing the diagonal commitments which are given as $\tilde{\mathbb{A}}_k = \sum_{i=\max(1,1-k)}^{\min(\kappa,\kappa-k)} (\tilde{\mathbf{A}}_i \tilde{\mathbf{r}}_{a,i+k} + \tilde{\mathbf{B}}_i \tilde{\mathbf{a}}_{i+k})$, where the products $\tilde{\mathbf{A}}_i \tilde{\mathbf{r}}_{a,i+k}$ are consisting of factors from two different rings $\mathcal{R}_{q,i}$ and $\mathcal{R}_{q,i+k}$. In order to be able to multiply two different ring elements from different rings we introduce a ring isomorphism in Sect. 4.2. The initial idea comes from [31] and it defines the following isomorphism $\psi_{i \mapsto j}(\tilde{\mathbf{a}})$ which is a fixed zero of $f_i = (X^{\phi(m)/\kappa} - r_i)$ in $\mathbb{Z}_q[X]/(X^{\phi(m)/\kappa} - r_i)$, where $\phi(m) = n$. This isomorphism enables multiplication and addition between different rings. The splitting procedure can proceed in multiple rounds until the polynomial is fully split, i.e. splits into a product of degree-one polynomials. During our construction we observed that a single split up round does not provide a significant efficiency improvement to the original inner product argument protocol. Thus we applied the splitting up procedure for one more round, i.e. we split each $\mathcal{R}_{q,j}$ into κ_1 rings $(\mathcal{R}_{q,j})_{j_1}$, where $j_1 \in [1, \kappa_1 - 1]$. It is an interesting research question to be addressed in our future research whether more split-up rounds would lead to further efficiency improvements and what would be the maximal number of rounds.

We exploit algebraic properties of a ring structure and show that a commitment to the initial witness $\tilde{\mathbf{a}}$ is isomorphic to $\sum_{j=0}^{\kappa-1} \sum_{j_1=0}^{\kappa_1-1} (\tilde{\mathbf{g}}_j)_{j_1}$, where $(\tilde{\mathbf{g}}_j)_{j_1} = (\tilde{\mathbf{A}}_j)_{j_1} \cdot (\tilde{\mathbf{r}}_{\tilde{a},j})_{j_1} + (\tilde{\mathbf{B}}_j)_{j_1}(\tilde{\mathbf{a}}_j)_{j_1}$. This means that our commitment to $\tilde{\mathbf{a}}$ is isomorphic to a shorter commitment of length $n/(\kappa\kappa_1)$. Using this property we can build more efficient inner product protocol with improved computational cost. We achieve an improvement in computational and communication cost. After applying the isomorphism from Sect. 4.2 we prove that the initial commitment of length $n \log q$ is isomorphic to a commitment of length $n/(\kappa\kappa_1) \log q$. The prover communicates $(\kappa\kappa_1)$ diagonal commitments to the verifier in the first round after the split up. We emphasize that the optimized inner product argument helps to shorten the proof length significantly by a multiple factor between 6 and 10 in dependence of the different parameter sets which we show in corresponding sections on the inner product argument and the optimized inner product argument.

2   Preliminaries

Definition 1 ($\mathsf{M} - \mathsf{SIS}_{q,n,m,\beta}$ [27]). *Let $\mathcal{R}_q$ be some ring and $\mathcal{K}$ a uniform distribution over $\mathcal{R}_q^{n \times m}$. Given a random matrix $\mathbf{A} \in \mathcal{R}_q^{n \times m}$ sampled from $\mathcal{K}$, find a non-zero vector $\mathbf{v} \in \mathcal{R}_q^m$ such that $\mathbf{A}\mathbf{v} = \mathbf{0}$ and $\|\mathbf{v}\|_2 \leq \beta$.*

Definition 2 ($\mathsf{M} - \mathsf{LWE}_{q,n,m,\chi}$ [27]). *Let χ be a distribution over $\mathcal{R}_q$ and $\mathbf{s} \leftarrow_\$ \chi^n$ be a secret key. The $\mathsf{M} - \mathsf{LWE}_{q,\mathbf{s}}$ distribution is obtained by sampling $\mathbf{a} \leftarrow_\$ \mathcal{R}_q^n$, an error $e \leftarrow_\$ \chi$ and outputting $(\mathbf{a}, \langle \mathbf{a}, \mathbf{s} \rangle + e)$. The goal is to distinguish between m given samples which are either from $\mathsf{M} - \mathsf{LWE}_{q,\mathbf{s}}$ or from the uniform distribution $\mathcal{U}(\mathcal{R}_q^n, \mathcal{R}_q)$.*

Rejection Sampling technique was first introduced by Lyubashevsky [27] and is significant for the zero-knowledge property of a ZKP as it provides independence of prover's responses from the secret values. In other words, the distribution of those responses has to be independent of the secret key. Below we recall Lyubashevsky's theorem on rejection sampling which requires only a constant number of iterations before outputting a value.

Theorem 1 ([27]). *Let V be a subset of $\mathbb{Z}^l$ in which all elements have norms less than T, and let h be a probability distribution over V. Then, for any constant M, there exists a value $\sigma = 12T$, such that the output distribution of the following algorithms A and F are statistically close:*

Algorithm A: *(1) $\mathbf{v} \leftarrow_\$ h$, (2) $\mathbf{z} \leftarrow_\$ \$\mathcal{D}_{\mathbf{v},\sigma}^l$, (3) Output $(\mathbf{z}, \mathbf{v})$ with probability* $\min\left(\exp\left(\frac{-2\langle \mathbf{z}, \mathbf{v} \rangle + \|\mathbf{v}\|^2}{2\sigma^2}\right), 1 \right).$

Algorithm F: *(1) $\mathbf{v} \leftarrow_\$ h$, (2) $\mathbf{z} \leftarrow_\$ \mathcal{D}_\sigma^l$, (3) Output $(\mathbf{z}, \mathbf{v})$ with probability $1/M$.*

Moreover, the probability that A outputs something is exponentially close to that of F, i.e. $1/M$.

Lemma 1 ([9]). *Let* $\mathcal{R} = \mathbb{Z}[X]/(X^n + 1)$ *where* $n > 1$ *is a power of* 2 *and* $0 < i, j < 2n - 1$. *Then all the coefficients of* $2(X^i - X^j)^{-1} \in \mathcal{R}$ *are in* $\{-1, 0, 1\}$. *This implies that* $\|2(X^i - X^j)^{-1}\| \leq \sqrt{n}$.

In [16] Esgin et al. have presented the generalization of Lemma 1 which states that for all monomial challenges $x_i = X^{\iota_i}$ for $0 \leq \iota_i \leq 2n - 1$ the following relation holds for the zero-coefficient of a Vandermonde matrix:

$$\|2^k a_0\| = \left\| \prod_{i=1}^{k} \frac{2}{x_i - x_0} \right\| = \left\| \prod_{i=1}^{k} 2\left(X^{\iota_i} - X^{\iota_0}\right)^{-1} \right\| \leq n^{k-1/2} \qquad (1)$$

Challenge Space. We define the challenge space $\mathcal{CH}$ being a set of monomials $X^\iota \in \mathcal{R}_q$ for $\iota \in [0, 2n]$, i.e. $\mathcal{CH} = \{x \in \mathcal{R}_q : x = X^\iota, 0 \leq \iota \leq 2n - 1\}$.

Lemma 2. *(Lemma 4.4 in [27])*

- *For any* $\alpha > 0, Pr[|z| > \alpha\sigma; z \leftarrow D_\sigma] \leq 2 \exp\left(-\alpha^2/2\right)$.
- *For any* $\alpha > 1, Pr[\|\mathbf{z}\| > \alpha\sigma\sqrt{m}, \mathbf{z} \leftarrow D_\sigma^m] \leq \alpha^m \exp\left(\frac{m(1-\alpha^2)}{2}\right)$.

In particular: $Pr[|z| > 12\sigma : z \leftarrow D_\sigma] < 2^{-100}$ *and* $Pr[\|\mathbf{z}\| > 5\sigma : z \leftarrow D_\sigma^n] < 2^{-100}$, *if* $n \geq 7$.

Zero-Knowledge Arguments of Knowledge [7]. Let $\mathcal{P}$ be the prover and $\mathcal{V}$ be the verifier which are both PPT algorithms. The PPT algorithm KeyGen generates the public parameters pp. Note, that in this paper the public parameter is represented by the commitment key of our lattice-based commitment. Furthermore, let R be a relation and w be a witness for the statement x. Then, the language is defined as $L_{pp} = \{x|\exists w : (pp, x, w) \in \mathsf{R}\}$, which is the set of statements x that have a witness w in the relation R. When prover $\mathcal{P}$ interacts with $\mathcal{V}$, the output of the interaction is denoted by a transcript tr which consists of the initial message from the prover, the challenge from the verifier and the answer from the prover and the decision from the verifier.

Definition 3 (Argument of knowledge). *The system* (KeyGen, $\mathcal{P}, \mathcal{V}$) *is called an argument of knowledge for the relation* R *if it satisfies the three properties: completeness,* $k + 1$-*special soundness and special honest verifier zero-knowledge which are defined below.*

Definition 4 (Completeness). *The system* (KeyGen, $\mathcal{P}, \mathcal{V}$) *is complete if for all non-uniform PPT adversaries* $\mathcal{A}$ *holds that:*

$$\Pr\left[\begin{array}{l} pp \leftarrow \mathsf{KeyGen}(1^\lambda); (x, w) \leftarrow \mathcal{A}(pp) : \\ (pp, x, w) \notin R \vee \langle \mathcal{P}(pp, x, w), \mathcal{V}(pp, x)\rangle = 1 \end{array}\right] = 1 - \alpha.$$

where α *is completeness error.*

The second property called $k + 1$-special soundness is relaxed meaning that the verifier is only convinced of the argument of knowledge of a witness w for a relaxed relation R'.

Definition 5 ($k + 1$-Special Soundness). *A system* $(\mathsf{KeyGen}, \mathcal{P}, \mathcal{V})$ *is* $k + 1$ *special sound if for all probabilistic polynomial time* $\mathcal{P}^*$ *there exists an extractor* $\mathcal{E}$, *such that for all non-uniform polynomial time interactive adversaries* $\mathcal{A}$ *holds:*

$$\Pr\left[\begin{array}{l} pp \leftarrow \mathsf{KeyGen}(1^\lambda); (x, s) \leftarrow \mathcal{A}(pp); \\ trs \leftarrow \langle \mathcal{P}^*(pp, x, s), \mathcal{V}(pp, x) \rangle : \mathcal{A}(trs) = 1 \end{array} \right]$$

$$\approx \Pr\left[\begin{array}{l} pp \leftarrow \mathsf{KeyGen}(1^\lambda); (x, s) \leftarrow \mathcal{A}(pp); \\ (trs_i, w) \leftarrow \mathcal{E}^{\langle \mathcal{P}^*(pp, x, s), \mathcal{V}(pp, x) \rangle}(pp, x) : \mathcal{A}(trs) = 1 \\ and \ if \ \forall i \in [0, k] \ trs_i \ is \ accepting, \ then \ (pp, x, w) \in \mathsf{R} \end{array} \right].$$

Definition 6 (Special Honest Verifier Zero-Knowledge). *An argument is called a perfect special honest verifier zero-knowledge (SHVZK) argument for a relation* R *if there exists a probabilistic polynomial time simulator* $\mathcal{S}$ *such that for all interactive non-uniform polynomial time adversaries* $\mathcal{A}$ *we have*

$$\Pr\left[\begin{array}{l} pp \leftarrow \mathsf{KeyGen}(1^\lambda); (x, w, \rho) \leftarrow \mathcal{A}(pp); trs \leftarrow \\ \langle \mathcal{P}(pp, x : \rho), \mathcal{V}(pp, x; \rho) \rangle : (pp, x, w) \in \mathsf{R} \wedge \mathcal{A}(trs) = 1 \end{array} \right]$$

$$\approx \Pr\left[\begin{array}{l} pp \leftarrow KG(1^\lambda); (x, w, \rho) \leftarrow \mathcal{A}(pp); \\ trs \leftarrow \mathcal{S}(pp, x, \rho) : (pp, x, w) \in \mathsf{R} \wedge \mathcal{A}(trs) = 1 \end{array} \right],$$

where s *denotes the state of* $\mathcal{P}^*$ *including the randomness. This means that whenever* $\mathcal{P}^*$ *manages to provide a convincing argument while being in stage* s, *the emulator is able to extract a witness* w.

Definition 7 (Public coin). *An argument* $(\mathsf{KeyGen}, \mathcal{P}, \mathcal{V})$ *is called a public coin if the verifier picks the challenges uniformly at random and independent of the prover's messages. It means that the challenges correspond to the verifier's randomness* ρ.

Commitment Scheme. For our construction we use the lattice-based commitment scheme introduced in [5]. The commitment achieves computational binding and computational hiding security. The hiding property relies on the hardness of $\mathsf{M-LWE}_{q,n,m,\chi}$ and the binding property relies on the hardness of $\mathsf{M-SIS}_{q,n,m,\beta}$. The opening algorithm in our commitment scheme is relaxed, meaning that there exists a relaxation factor $\mathsf{d} \in \mathcal{R}_q$ such that ROpen checks if $\mathsf{d} \cdot \mathsf{C} = \mathsf{Com}_{ck}(\mathbf{x}, \mathbf{r})$. The instantiation of an unbounded-message commitment is given in the following definition.

Definition 8. *Let* $n, m, q, \mathcal{B}$ *be positive integers. Let* $\mathcal{U}(x)$ *denote the uniform distribution of any input* x. *The relaxed commitment of a message* $\mathbf{x} \in \mathcal{R}_q^{n'}$ *is defined as:*

KeyGen: *Create* $(\mathbf{A}_1, \mathbf{A}_2) \in \mathcal{R}_q^{\nu \times m} \times \mathcal{R}_q^{n' \times m}$. *Public parameters are:* $\mathbf{A}_1 = [\mathbf{I}_\nu \| \mathbf{A}_1']$, *where* $\mathbf{A}_1' \leftarrow_{\$} \mathcal{R}_q^{\nu \times (m-\nu)}$ *and* $\mathbf{A}_2 = [\mathbf{0}^{n' \times \nu} \| \mathbf{I}_{n'} \| \mathbf{A}_2']$, *where* $\mathbf{A}_2' \leftarrow_{\$} \mathcal{R}_q^{n' \times (m-\nu-n')}$. *Set the commitment key* $ck = \mathbf{A} = \begin{bmatrix} \mathbf{A}_1 \\ \mathbf{A}_2 \end{bmatrix}$, *which is used to commit to* $\mathbf{x} \in \mathcal{R}_q^{n'}$.

Com: *To commit to a message* $\mathbf{x} \in \mathcal{R}_q^{n'}$, *choose a random polynomial vector* $\mathbf{r} \leftarrow_s \mathcal{U}(\{-\mathcal{B}, \ldots, \mathcal{B}\}^{mn})$ *and output the commitment*

$$C := \mathrm{Com}_{ck}(\mathbf{x}, \mathbf{r}) = \mathbf{A} \cdot \mathbf{r} + \mathrm{enc}(\mathbf{x}), \text{ where } \mathrm{enc}(\mathbf{x}) = \begin{bmatrix} \mathbf{0}^{\nu} \\ \mathbf{x} \end{bmatrix} \in \mathcal{R}_q^{\nu+n'}.$$

ROpen: *A valid opening of a commitment* C *is a tuple consisting of* $\mathbf{x} \in \mathcal{R}_q^{n'}$, $\mathbf{r} \in \mathcal{R}_q^m$ *and* $\mathbf{d} \in \Delta\mathcal{CH}$. *The verifier checks that* $\mathbf{d} \cdot C = \mathbf{A} \cdot \mathbf{r} + \mathbf{d} \cdot \mathrm{enc}(\mathbf{x})$, *and that* $\|\mathbf{r}\| \leq \beta$. *Otherwise return* 0.

Throughout the rest of the paper we assume $n' = \nu = 1$. Security of this commitment scheme has been proved in [5] and is stated in the following lemma.

Lemma 3. *If* $\mathsf{M} - \mathsf{LWE}_{q, m-\nu-n', \nu+n', \mathcal{U}(\{-\mathcal{B}, \ldots, \mathcal{B}\}^{mn})}$ *problem is hard then the above commitment scheme is computationally hiding. If* $\mathsf{M} - \mathsf{SIS}_{q,n,m,\beta}$ *problem is hard, then our commitment scheme is computationally* γ_{bind}−*binding with respect to the relaxation factor* d.

3   Lattice-Based Inner Product

In this section we provide the inner product protocol which is inherited from its discrete-log construction and applied to the lattice setting. Let $\hat{\mathbf{a}} \in \mathcal{R}_q^{\ell}$, i.e. $\hat{\mathbf{a}} = (\mathbf{a}_1, \ldots, \mathbf{a}_\ell)^{tr}$ where each $\mathbf{a}_\eta \in \mathcal{R}_q = \mathbb{Z}_q[X]/(X^n + 1)$, $\eta \in [1, \ell]$ for $\mathbf{a}_\eta = \sum_{j=0}^{n-1} a_{\eta,j} X^j$. We want to prove knowledge of $\hat{\mathbf{a}} = (\mathbf{a}_1, \ldots, \mathbf{a}_\ell)^{tr} \in \mathcal{R}_q^{\ell}$. For this, we split $\hat{\mathbf{a}}$ into s chunks of length ℓ/s, i.e. $\hat{\mathbf{a}} = (\mathbf{a}_1', \ldots, \mathbf{a}_s')^{tr}$ with $\mathbf{a}_i' \in \mathcal{R}_q^{\ell/s}$ for $i \in [1, s]$. We let $\hat{\mathbf{A}}$ and $\hat{\mathbf{B}}$ be a concatenation of ℓ public parameters $\mathbf{A}_\eta \in \mathcal{R}_q^{d \times m}$ and $\mathbf{B}_\eta \in \mathcal{R}_q^{d}$ for $\eta \in [1, \ell]$, respectively and the randomness be a concatenation of the ℓ chunks $\mathbf{r}_{a,i}'$ of size ℓ/s. We further set $\hat{\mathbf{A}} = [\mathbf{A}_1 \| \ldots \| \mathbf{A}_\ell]$ and $\hat{\mathbf{B}} = [\mathbf{B}_1 \| \ldots \| \mathbf{B}_\ell]$, $(\hat{\mathbf{r}}_a) = (\mathbf{r}_{a,1}, \ldots, \mathbf{r}_{a,\ell})^{tr}$. It holds $\hat{\mathbf{A}} \in \mathcal{R}_q^{d \times m} \times \cdots \times \mathcal{R}_q^{d \times m} = (\mathcal{R}_q^{d \times m})^{\ell}$, $\hat{\mathbf{B}} \in \mathcal{R}_q^{d} \times \cdots \times \mathcal{R}_q^{d} = \mathcal{R}_q^{d\ell}$ and $\hat{\mathbf{r}}_a \in \mathcal{R}_q^{m \times 1} \times \cdots \times \mathcal{R}_q^{m \times 1} = (\mathcal{R}_q^{m \times 1})^{\ell}$. In order to commit to $\hat{\mathbf{a}} \in \mathcal{R}_q^{\ell}$ we split $\hat{\mathbf{r}}_a$ into s chunks $\mathbf{r}_{a,i}' \in (\mathcal{R}_q^{m \times 1})^{\ell/s}$ for $i \in [1, s]$ and the s public parameters $\mathbf{A}_i' \in (\mathcal{R}_q^{d \times m})^{\ell/s}$, $\mathbf{B}_i' \in \mathcal{R}_q^{d \times \ell/s}$. The commitment to $\hat{\mathbf{a}}$ is given using a randomness $\hat{\mathbf{r}}_a$ as follows:

$$\mathbb{A} = \mathrm{Com}_{\hat{\mathbf{A}}, \hat{\mathbf{B}}}(\hat{\mathbf{a}}, \hat{\mathbf{r}}_a) = \hat{\mathbf{A}} \cdot \hat{\mathbf{r}}_a + \hat{\mathbf{B}} \cdot \hat{\mathbf{a}} = \sum_{i=1}^{s} (\mathbf{A}_i' \cdot \mathbf{r}_{a,i}' + \mathbf{B}_i' \cdot \mathbf{a}_i') \tag{2}$$

Similar to [10], the prover's target is to replace $\mathbb{A} := \mathrm{Com}_{\hat{\mathbf{A}}, \hat{\mathbf{B}}}(\hat{\mathbf{a}}, \hat{\mathbf{r}}_a)$ by $\mathbb{A}'$, which is a commitment to a shorter vector $\mathbf{a}' = \sum_{i=1}^{s} \mathbf{a}_i' x^i$ for a given challenge $x \in \mathcal{CH}$. The challenge space consists of monomials $x = X^\iota$ for $\iota \in [0, 2n-1]$. The prover defines a matrix as follows:

$$\mathfrak{C}_{a,s} = \begin{bmatrix} \mathbf{A}_1' \cdot \mathbf{r}_{a,1}' + \mathbf{B}_1' \cdot \mathbf{a}_1' & \cdots & \mathbf{A}_1' \cdot \mathbf{r}_{a,s}' + \mathbf{B}_1' \cdot \mathbf{a}_s' \\ \vdots & \ddots & \vdots \\ \mathbf{A}_s' \cdot \mathbf{r}_{a,1}' + \mathbf{B}_s' \cdot \mathbf{a}_1' & \cdots & \mathbf{A}_s' \cdot \mathbf{r}_{a,s}' + \mathbf{B}_s' \cdot \mathbf{a}_s' \end{bmatrix}$$

In the next equation we define diagonal commitments $\mathbb{A}_k$ which are computed as a sum of the elements in the corresponding diagonal k of the above matrix:

$$\mathbb{A}_k = \sum_{i=\max(1,1-k)}^{\min(s,s-k)} \mathbf{A}'_i \mathbf{r}'_{a,i+k} + \mathbf{B}'_i \mathbf{a}'_{i+k}, \quad \text{for} \quad k = 1 - s, \ldots, s - 1$$

It holds that $\mathbb{A}_0 = \mathbb{A}$ is a commitment defined via a central diagonal trace. After receiving a challenge $x \leftarrow_s \mathcal{CH}$ from the verifier, the prover computes:

$$\mathbf{A}' = \sum_{i=1}^{s} \mathbf{A}'_i x^{-i}, \quad \text{and} \quad \mathbf{B}' = \sum_{i=1}^{s} \mathbf{B}'_i x^{-i} \tag{3}$$

which are the new public parameters of the new commitment on a shorter secret $\mathbf{a}'$ with the corresponding randomness $\mathbf{r}'_a = \sum_{i=1}^{s} \mathbf{r}'_{a,i} x^i$. The new commitment is computed using the received challenge x and the diagonal commitments $\mathbb{A}_k$ for all k running over the matrix diagonals $k = 1 - s, \ldots, s - 1$:

$$\mathbb{A}' = \sum_{k=1-s}^{s-1} \mathbb{A}_k x^k = \mathrm{Com}_{\mathbf{A}',\mathbf{B}'}(\mathbf{a}', \mathbf{r}'_a) = \mathbf{A}' \mathbf{r}'_a + \mathbf{B}' \mathbf{a}'. \tag{4}$$

Similarly, for $\hat{\mathbf{b}} = (\mathbf{b}'_1, \ldots, \mathbf{b}'_s)^{tr}$ compute $\mathbb{B} = \mathrm{Com}_{\hat{\mathbf{C}}, \hat{\mathbf{D}}}(\hat{\mathbf{b}}, \hat{\mathbf{r}}_b)$, with public parameters $\hat{\mathbf{C}} = [\mathbf{C}'_1 || \ldots || \mathbf{C}'_\ell] \in \left(\mathcal{R}_q^{d \times m}\right)^\ell$ and $\hat{\mathbf{D}} = [\mathbf{D}'_1 || \ldots || \mathbf{D}'_\ell] \in \mathcal{R}_q^{d\ell}$. Using the received challenge x, the new public parameters are computed similarly to (3): $\mathbf{C}' = \sum_{i=1}^{s} \mathbf{C}'_i x^i$ and $\mathbf{D}' = \sum_{i=1}^{s} \mathbf{D}'_i x^i$. Similar to the matrix $\mathfrak{C}_{a,s}$ the prover generates a matrix $\mathfrak{C}_{b,s}$ and computes the diagonal commitments $\mathbb{B}_k$ as a sum of elements in the k-th diagonal of $\mathfrak{C}_{b,s}$: $\mathbb{B}_k = \sum_{i=\max(1,1-k)}^{\min(s,s-k)} \left(\mathbf{C}'_i \mathbf{r}'_{b,i+k} + \mathbf{D}'_i \mathbf{b}'_{i+k}\right)$, for $k = 1 - s, \ldots, s - 1$. The new commitment $\mathbb{B}'$ is computed using all diagonal commitments $\mathbb{B}_k$ and the received challenge x as: $\mathbb{B}' = \sum_{k=1-s}^{s-1} \mathbb{B}_k x^k = \mathrm{Com}_{\mathbf{C}',\mathbf{D}'}(\mathbf{b}', \mathbf{r}'_b) = \mathbf{C}' \mathbf{r}'_b + \mathbf{D}' \mathbf{b}'$, where $\mathbf{b}' = \sum_{i=1}^{s} \mathbf{b}'_i x^{-i}$ and $\mathbf{r}'_b = \sum_{i=1}^{s} \mathbf{r}'_{b,i} x^{-i}$ are the new secrets which have a shorter length than the initial ones.

3.1   The Protocol

In this section we present the main protocol for the zero-knowledge inner product argument. The relation we want to prove with its corresponding relaxed version are given as follows:

$$\mathsf{R}_{\beta_{ip}} = \left\{ (\hat{\mathbf{a}}, \hat{\mathbf{b}}, \hat{\mathbf{r}}_a, \hat{\mathbf{r}}_b), (\mathbb{A}_\nu, \mathbb{B}_\nu, z_\nu) : \hat{\mathbf{a}} \cdot \hat{\mathbf{b}} = \sum_{i=1}^{s_\nu} \mathbf{a}'_i \mathbf{b}'_i = z_\nu, \|\hat{\mathbf{r}}_a\| \leq \beta_{ip}, \|\hat{\mathbf{r}}_b\| \leq \beta_{ip} \right\}$$

$$\mathsf{R}'_{\beta'_{ip}} = \left\{ (\hat{\mathbf{a}}', \hat{\mathbf{b}}', \hat{\mathbf{r}}'_a, \hat{\mathbf{r}}'_b, \mathsf{d}), (\mathbb{A}_\nu, \mathbb{B}_\nu, z_\nu) : \hat{\mathbf{a}}' \cdot \hat{\mathbf{b}}' = \mathsf{d}^{\ell_\nu / s_\nu} \sum_{i=1}^{s_\nu} \mathbf{a}'_i \mathbf{b}'_i = z_\nu, \|\hat{\mathbf{r}}_a\| \leq \beta'_{ip}, \right.$$

$$\left. \|\hat{\mathbf{r}}'_b\| \leq \beta'_{ip} \right\}.$$

Note, that the above description considers only the first level of recursion. Here, we use the notation s_ν to indicate the number of chunks at level $\nu \in [1, \mu]$.

Common Input: Public parameters $\mathbf{A}'_i, \mathbf{C}'_i \in (\mathcal{R}_q^{d \times m})^{\ell_\nu / s_\nu}$, $\mathbf{B}'_i, \mathbf{D}'_i \in \mathcal{R}_q^{d \times (\ell_\nu / s_\nu)}$ for $i \in [1, s_\nu]$, commitments to $\hat{a}$ and $\hat{b}$ given as $\mathbb{A}, \mathbb{B}$, respectively. Let $\ell = s_\mu \cdot s_{\mu-1} \cdot \ldots \cdot s_1$ with $\ell := \ell_\mu$, $s_\mu := s$, $\ell_\mu / s_\mu = \ell_{\mu-1}$, and $\ell_\nu / s_\nu = \ell_{\nu-1}$ for any $\nu \in [2, \mu]$.

Prover's Witness: The witness is given by two strings each consisting of ℓ ring elements in $\mathcal{R}_q$: $\hat{a} = (a_1, \ldots, a_\ell)^{tr}$, $\hat{b} = (b_1, \ldots, b_\ell)^{tr}$, where each $a_\eta, b_\eta \in \mathcal{R}_q, \eta \in [1, \ell]$ and the corresponding randomnesses $\hat{r}_a = (r_{a,1}, \ldots, r_{a,\ell})^{tr}$, $\hat{r}_b = (r_{b,1}, \ldots, r_{b,\ell})^{tr}$. In the first recursion step the prover splits $\hat{a}$ and $\hat{b}$ into s_ν chunks, where each chunk is $\mathbf{a}'_i, \mathbf{b}'_i \in \mathcal{R}_q^{\ell_\nu / s_\nu}$, for all $i \in [1, s_\nu]$. The same splitting procedure is applied to the randomnesses $\mathbf{r}'_{a,i}, \mathbf{r}'_{b,i} \in (\mathcal{R}_q^{m \times 1})^{\ell_\nu / s_\nu}$. The prover commits to $\hat{a}, \hat{b}$ and their inner product as follows:

$$\mathbb{A}_\nu = \mathrm{Com}_{\hat{\mathbf{A}}, \hat{\mathbf{B}}}(\hat{a}, \hat{r}_a) = \sum_{i=1}^{s_\nu} (\mathbf{A}'_i \cdot \mathbf{r}'_{a,i} + \mathbf{B}'_i \cdot \mathbf{a}'_i),$$

$$\mathbb{B}_\nu = \mathrm{Com}_{\hat{\mathbf{C}}, \hat{\mathbf{D}}}(\hat{b}, \hat{r}_b) = \sum_{i=1}^{s_\nu} (\mathbf{C}'_i \cdot \mathbf{r}'_{b,i} + \mathbf{D}'_i \cdot \mathbf{b}'_i),$$

and it holds $\hat{a} \cdot \hat{b} = \sum_{i=1}^{s_\nu} \mathbf{a}'_i \mathbf{b}'_i = z_\nu$.

Argument: if $\mu = 1$: The prover sends $(\mathbf{a}_1, \ldots \mathbf{a}_{s_\nu}, \mathbf{b}_1, \ldots, \mathbf{b}_{s_\nu})$ to the verifier.

Recursive Step ν: if $\mu \neq 1$: The prover sends diagonal commitments and the corresponding inner products $\mathbb{A}_{1-s_\nu}, \mathbb{B}_{1-s_\nu}, z_{1-s_\nu}, \ldots, \mathbb{A}_{s_\nu-1}, \mathbb{B}_{s_\nu-1}, z_{s_\nu-1}$ to the verifier, where for $k_\nu = 1 - s_\nu, \ldots, s_\nu - 1$:

$$\mathbb{A}_{k_\nu} = \sum_{i=\max(1, 1-k_\nu)}^{\min(s_\nu, s_\nu - k_\nu)} \mathbf{A}'_i \mathbf{r}'_{a, i+k_\nu} + \mathbf{B}'_i \mathbf{a}'_{i+k_\nu},$$

$$\mathbb{B}_{k_\nu} = \sum_{i=\max(1, 1-k_\nu)}^{\min(s_\nu, s_\nu - k_\nu)} \mathbf{C}'_i \mathbf{r}'_{b, i+k_\nu} + \mathbf{D}'_i \mathbf{b}'_{i+k_\nu},$$

$$z_{k_\nu} = \sum_{i=\max(1, 1-k_\nu)}^{\min(s_\nu, s_\nu - k_\nu)} \mathbf{a}'_i \cdot \mathbf{b}'_{i+k_\nu}$$

Challenge: The verifier sends a monomial challenge $x \leftarrow \mathcal{CH}$ to the prover.

Response: If $\mu = 1$: The prover sends $\mathbf{a}_1, \ldots, \mathbf{a}_\ell, \mathbf{b}_1, \ldots, \mathbf{b}_\ell$ to the verifier.

Rejection Sampling: The prover aborts with probability $1 - \mathbf{p}_{ip}$, where

$$\mathbf{p}_{ip} := \frac{\mathfrak{D}_{\sigma_{ip}}^{mn}(\mathbf{r}'_a)}{\mathfrak{D}_{\{x^j \cdot (\tilde{\mathbf{r}}_{a,j})_\ell\}_{j \in [1, s_\nu]}, \sigma_{ip}}^{mn}(\mathbf{r}'_a)}.$$

Verification: If $\mu = 1$: Verifier checks whether the following equations are satisfied: $\mathbb{A}_\nu = \sum_{i=1}^{s_\nu}(\mathbf{A}'_i\mathbf{r}_{a,i} + \mathbf{B}'_i\mathbf{a}_i)$, $\mathbb{B}_\nu = \sum_{i=1}^{s_\nu}(\mathbf{C}'_i\mathbf{r}_{b,i} + \mathbf{D}'_i\mathbf{b}_i)$, $\sum_{i=1}^{s_\nu}\mathbf{a}_i\mathbf{b}_i = z_\nu$. If $\mu \neq 1$: Prover and verifier compute a reduced commitment given by $\mathbf{A}', \mathbf{B}', \mathbf{C}', \mathbf{D}', \mathbb{A}'_\nu, \mathbb{B}'_\nu, z'_\nu, s_{\mu-1}, \ldots, s_1$ such that the following equations are satisfied for all $\nu \in [2, \mu]$:

$$\mathbf{A}'_\nu = \sum_{i=1}^{s_\nu}\mathbf{A}'_i x^{-i}, \quad \mathbf{B}'_\nu = \sum_{i=1}^{s_\nu}\mathbf{B}'_i x^{-i}, \quad \mathbf{C}'_\nu = \sum_{i=1}^{s_\nu}\mathbf{C}_i x^i, \quad \mathbf{D}'_\nu = \sum_{i=1}^{s_\nu}\mathbf{D}'_i x^i \quad (5)$$

$$\mathbb{A}'_\nu = \sum_{k_\nu=1-s_\nu}^{s_\nu-1}\mathbb{A}_{k_\nu} x^{k_\nu}, \quad \mathbb{B}'_\nu = \sum_{k_\nu=1-s_\nu}^{s_\nu-1}\mathbb{B}_{k_\nu} x^{-k_\nu}, \quad z'_\nu = \sum_{k_\nu=1-s_\nu}^{s_\nu-1}z_{k_\nu} x^{-k_\nu} \quad (6)$$

The prover computes a new witness $\mathbf{a}'_\nu = \sum_{i=1}^{s_\nu}\mathbf{a}'_i x^i$ and $\mathbf{b}'_\nu = \sum_{i=1}^{s_\nu}\mathbf{b}'_i x^{-i}$ and their corresponding randomnesses $\mathbf{r}'_{a,\nu} = \sum_{i=1}^{s_\nu}\mathbf{r}_{a,i}x^i$ and $\mathbf{r}'_{b,\nu} = \sum_{i=1}^{s_\nu}\mathbf{r}_{b,i}x^{-i}$. The prover proceeds the recursion on these small witnesses.

3.2 Security Analysis

Theorem 2. *Assuming that our commitment scheme is computationally hiding and β_{ip}-binding with $\beta_{ip} < \min\{q, 2^{2\sqrt{n \log q \log \delta}}\}$, where δ denotes a root Hermite factor, then our inner product protocol with the rejection sampling probability p_{ip} is a complete, $k + 1$ special-sound and special honest verifier zero-knowledge argument of knowledge.*

Proof. We prove the three security properties discussed in Definition 3.

Completeness: In order to prove this property we need to show that the verification Eq. 5 are satisfied. We show this only for the first verification equation of $\mathbb{A}'$. We take $\mathbb{A}_{k_\nu}$ defined in the recursive step of the protocol and insert it into the equation:

$$\mathbb{A}'_\nu = \sum_{k_\nu=1-s_\nu}^{s_\nu-1}\mathbb{A}_{k_\nu} x^{k_\nu} = \sum_{k_\nu=1-s_\nu}^{s_\nu-1}\left(\sum_{i=\max(1,1-k_\nu)}^{\min(s_\nu,s_\nu-k_\nu)}\mathbf{A}'_i\mathbf{r}'_{a,i+k_\nu} + \mathbf{B}'_i\mathbf{a}'_{i+k_\nu}\right)x^{k_\nu}$$

We compare it with the following equation of $\mathbb{A}'$ which is a commitment on $\mathbf{a}'$ with randomness $\mathbf{r}'_a$ using public parameters $\mathbf{A}', \mathbf{B}'$:

$$\mathbb{A}'_\nu = \mathrm{Com}_{\mathbf{A}',\mathbf{B}'}(\mathbf{a}',\mathbf{r}'_a) = \mathbf{A}'\mathbf{r}'_a + \mathbf{B}'\mathbf{a}' = \sum_{i=1}^{s_\nu}\mathbf{A}'_i x^{-i}\cdot\sum_{i=1}^{s_\nu}\mathbf{r}'_{a,i}x^i + \sum_{i=1}^{s_\nu}\mathbf{B}'_i x^{-i}\cdot\sum_{i=1}^{s_\nu}\mathbf{a}'_i x^i$$

Expanding the above products carefully we can see that the verification equation $\mathbb{A}'_\nu = \sum_{i=1}^{s_\nu}\mathbb{A}'_i x^{-i}$ is correct. We also have to show the shortness of the new randomness $\mathbf{r}'_a$ and $\mathbf{r}'_b$. The Euclidean norm is $\|\mathbf{r}'_{a,\nu}\| = \|\sum_{i=1}^{s_\nu}\mathbf{r}'_{a,i}x^i\| \leq \sqrt{n}s_\nu\beta_{ip}$.

$(2s_\nu - 1)$ **-Special Soundness:** We prove soundness using the induction. When $\mu = 1$ the prover reveals a witness which passes the verification phase. Induction guarantees that in the recursive step, if a M-SIS relation holds for $\mathbf{A}'_i, \mathbf{B}'_i$ for $i \in$

$[1, s_\nu]$, then there is also a non-trivial solution to the M-SIS relation for $\mathbf{A}', \mathbf{B}'$. The same argument is used for the public parameters $\mathbf{C}'_i, \mathbf{D}'_i$ for $i \in [1, s_\nu]$. From the inductive step follows that we can obtain the witness $\mathbf{a}', \mathbf{b}'$ which satisfy

$$\mathbb{A}'_\nu = \sum_{k_\nu=1-s_\nu}^{s_\nu-1} \mathbb{A}_{k_\nu} x^{k_\nu} = \left(\sum_{i=1}^{s_\nu} \mathbf{A}'_i x^{-i}\right) \cdot \mathbf{r}'_{a,\nu} + \left(\sum_{i=1}^{s_\nu} \mathbf{B}'_i x^{-i}\right) \cdot \mathbf{a}',$$

$$\mathbb{B}'_\nu = \sum_{k_\nu=1-s_\nu}^{s_\nu-1} \mathbb{B}_{k_\nu} x^{k_\nu} = \left(\sum_{i=1}^{s_\nu} \mathbf{C}'_i x^{i}\right) \cdot \mathbf{r}'_{b,\nu} + \left(\sum_{i=1}^{s_\nu} \mathbf{D}'_i x^{i}\right) \cdot \mathbf{b}',$$

$$z_\nu = \mathbf{a}' \cdot \mathbf{b}' = \sum_{k_\nu=1-s_\nu}^{s_\nu-1} z_{k_\nu} x^{-k_\nu}$$

Taking $2s_\nu - 1$ challenges $x_1, \ldots, x_{2s_\nu-1}$, for all $\gamma \in [1, 2s_\nu - 1]$ we compute

$$\sum_{k_\nu=1-s_\nu}^{s_\nu-1} \mathbb{A}_{k_\nu} x_\gamma^{k_\nu} = \left(\sum_{i=1}^{s_\nu} \mathbf{A}'_i x_\gamma^{-i}\right) \cdot \sum_{i=1}^{s_\nu} \mathbf{r}'_{a,i} x_\gamma^{i} + \left(\sum_{i=1}^{s_\nu} \mathbf{B}'_i x^{-i}\right) \cdot \sum_{i=1}^{s_\nu} \mathbf{a}'_i x_\gamma^{i}.$$

Remember that each $\mathbf{a}'_i \in \mathcal{R}_q^{\ell_\nu/s_\nu}$, i.e. $\mathbf{a}'_i = (\mathbf{a}'_{i,1}, \ldots, \mathbf{a}'_{i,\ell_\nu/s_\nu})$ and each $\mathbf{r}'_{a,i} \in (\mathcal{R}_q^{m\times 1})^{\ell_\nu/s_\nu}$, i.e. $\mathbf{r}'_{a,i} = (\mathbf{r}'_{a,i,1}, \ldots, \mathbf{r}'_{a,i,\ell_\nu/s_\nu})$. It implies the following equation system for all $\gamma \in [1, 2s_\nu - 1]$:

$$\sum_{k_\nu=1-s_\nu}^{s_\nu-1} \begin{bmatrix} \mathbb{A}_{k_\nu,1} \\ \vdots \\ \mathbb{A}_{k_\nu,\ell_\nu/s_\nu} \end{bmatrix} x_\gamma^{k_\nu} = \sum_{i=1}^{s_j} \mathbf{A}' \begin{bmatrix} \mathbf{r}'_{a,i,1} \\ \vdots \\ \mathbf{r}'_{a,i,\ell_\nu/s_\nu} \end{bmatrix} x_\gamma^{i} + \sum_{i=1}^{s_\nu} \mathbf{B}' \begin{bmatrix} \mathbf{a}'_{i,1} \\ \vdots \\ \mathbf{a}'_{i,\ell_\nu/s_\nu} \end{bmatrix} x_\gamma^{i}.$$

The above equation system can be expanded to ℓ_ν/s_ν systems for each vector component $\tau \in [1, \ell_\nu/s_\nu]$, where for all $\gamma \in [1, 2s_\nu - 1]$ each of these systems has the following representation:

$$\sum_{k_\nu=1-s_\nu}^{s_\nu-1} \mathbb{A}_{k_\nu,\tau} x_\gamma^{k_\nu} = \sum_{i=1}^{s_\nu} \mathbf{A}'_{x,\tau} \mathbf{r}'_{a,i,\tau} x_\gamma^{i} + \sum_{i=1}^{s_\nu} \mathbf{B}'_{x,\tau} \mathbf{a}'_{i,\tau} x_\gamma^{i}.$$

Knowing $\mathbf{a}'$, we can compute $\sum_{k_\nu=1-s_\nu}^{s_\nu-1} \mathbb{A}_{k_\nu,\tau} x_\gamma^{k_\nu} - \mathbf{B}'_{x_\gamma,\tau} \cdot \mathbf{a}'_{x_\gamma,\tau}$, where $\mathbf{A}'_{x_\gamma,\nu,\tau} = \sum_{i=1}^{s_\nu} \mathbf{A}'_{i,\tau} x_\gamma^{-i}$ and $\mathbf{B}'_{x_\gamma,\nu,\tau} = \sum_{i=1}^{s_\nu} \mathbf{B}'_{i,\tau} x_\gamma^{-i}$ being the τ-th component of $\mathbf{A}'_{x_\gamma,\nu} = \sum_{i=1}^{s_\nu} \mathbf{A}'_i x_\gamma^{-i}$ and $\mathbf{B}'_{x_\gamma,\nu} = \sum_{i=1}^{s_\nu} \mathbf{B}'_i x_\gamma^{-i}$ respectively and $\mathbf{a}'_{x_\gamma,\nu,\tau} = \sum_{i=1}^{s_\nu} \mathbf{a}_{i,\tau} x_\gamma^{i}$ being the τ-th component of $\mathbf{a}_{x_\gamma,\nu}$. For a fixed vector component τ we get $2s_\nu - 1$ equations using the challenges $x_1, \ldots, x_{2s_\nu-1}$ holds:

$$\sum_{k_\nu=1-s_\nu}^{s_\nu-1} \mathbb{A}_{k_\nu,\tau} x_\gamma^{k_\nu} - \mathbf{B}'_{x_\gamma,\tau} \cdot \mathbf{a}'_{x_\gamma,\tau} = \left(\sum_{i=1}^{s_\nu} \mathbf{A}'_{i,\tau} x_\gamma^{-i}\right) \cdot \sum_{i=1}^{s_\nu} \mathbf{r}_{a,i,\tau} x_\gamma^{i}$$

We define the left side of each i-th of the $2s_\nu - 1$ equations above as $\mathcal{A}_{i,\tau} := \sum_{k_\nu=1-s_\nu}^{s_\nu-1} \mathbb{A}_{k_\nu,\tau} x_i^{k_\nu} - \mathbf{B}'_{x_i,\tau} \cdot \mathbf{a}'_{x_i,\tau}$ and rewrite the right side of the equations above as $\sum_{k_\nu=1-s_\nu}^{s_\nu-1} \mathbf{R}_{k_\nu,\tau} x^{k_\nu}$, where $\mathbf{R}_{k_\nu,\tau} = \sum_{\iota-i=k_\nu} \mathbf{A}'_{i,\tau} \mathbf{r}_{\iota,a,\tau}$. We obtain the following system of equations for $\gamma \in [1, 2s_\nu - 1]$:

$$\mathcal{A}_{1,\tau} = \sum_{k_\nu=1-s_\nu}^{s_\nu-1} \mathbf{R}_{k_\nu,\tau} x_1^{k_\nu} = \mathbf{R}_{1-s_\nu,\tau} x_\gamma^{1-s_\nu} + \ldots + \mathbf{R}_{s_\nu-1,\tau} x_\gamma^{s_\nu-1} \qquad (7)$$

Next, we define a generalised Vandermonde matrix as follows:

$$V_{2s_\nu-1} = \begin{bmatrix} x_1^{1-s_\nu} & x_1^{2-s_\nu} & \cdots & x_1^{s_\nu-2} & x_1^{s_\nu-1} \\ \vdots & \vdots & \ddots & \vdots & \vdots \\ x_{2s_\nu-1}^{1-s_\nu} & x_{2s_\nu-1}^{2-s_\nu} & \cdots & x_{2s_\nu-1}^{s_\nu-2} & x_{2s_\nu-1}^{s_\nu-1} \end{bmatrix} \qquad (8)$$

We can represent the equation system in (7) using the above Vandermonde matrix $V_{2s_\nu-1}$ and setting $\widehat{\mathbf{R}}_\tau = (\mathbf{R}_{1-s_\nu,\tau}, \ldots, \mathbf{R}_{0,\tau}, \ldots, \mathbf{R}_{s_\nu-1,\tau})$ and $\widehat{\mathcal{A}}_\tau = (\mathcal{A}_{1,\tau}, \ldots, \mathcal{A}_{2s_\nu-1,\tau})$ for all $\tau \in [1, \ell_\nu/s_\nu]$ as follows:

$$\begin{bmatrix} \widehat{\mathcal{A}}_1 \\ \vdots \\ \widehat{\mathcal{A}}_{\ell_i/s_i} \end{bmatrix} := \sum_{k_\nu=1-s_\nu}^{s_\nu-1} \mathbb{A}_{k_\nu} x_1^{k_\nu} - \mathbf{B}'_{x_i} \cdot \mathbf{a}'_{x_i} = \begin{bmatrix} V_{2s_\nu-1} \cdot \widehat{\mathbf{R}}_1 \\ \vdots \\ V_{2s_\nu-1} \cdot \widehat{\mathbf{R}}_{\ell_\nu/s_\nu} \end{bmatrix} = V_{2s_\nu-1} \begin{bmatrix} \widehat{\mathbf{R}}_1 \\ \vdots \\ \widehat{\mathbf{R}}_{\ell_\nu/s_\nu} \end{bmatrix} \qquad (9)$$

The inverse of the Vandermonde matrix $V_{2s_\nu-1}$ is small, therefore we can multiply the last equation by it i.e. $V_{2s_\nu-1}^{-1} \cdot \widehat{\mathcal{A}}_\tau$ and obtain $\widehat{\mathbf{R}} = [\widehat{\mathbf{R}}_1| \ldots |\widehat{\mathbf{R}}_{\ell_\nu/s_\nu}]$.

Now we want to compute the growth of the relaxation factor from the bottom of the tree till its root. Since we use monomial challenges, the determinant of Vandermonde matrix is given by $\det(V_{2s_\nu-1}) = \mathsf{d}^{2s_\nu-1}$. Since we use a monomial challenge set as defined in the preliminaries, the determinant of the Vandermonde matrix at the first recursive step is $\mathsf{d} = 2$. We assumed that at each level ν we split the given string of length ℓ_ν into s_ν chunks. Let $\ell_0 = \ell$ and $\ell_\nu/s_\nu = \ell_{\nu-1}$. The splitting continues until we obtain one ring element in each string. Let's consider the worst case, where the previous string always splits into 2, i.e. $s_\nu = s = 2$. There are in total $\log(\ell)/\log(s)$ levels in the tree. Then there are $\log(\ell)/\log(s) \overset{s=2}{=} \log(\ell)$ levels of splitting if we set $s_\nu = s = 2$. The length of the input string at level ν is $\ell_\nu = \ell_{\nu-1}/s$. Since at each level i the relaxation factor is dependent on the Vandermonde matrices with $\det = \mathsf{d}^{2s-1}$, this relaxation factor is $\mathsf{d}_\nu = \mathsf{d}_{\nu+1}^{2s-1}$. At level $\nu - 1$ this relaxation factor is $\mathsf{d}^{2s-1} \cdot \mathsf{d}^{2s-1} = \mathsf{d}^{2(2s-1)}$. Let $\mathsf{d}_{\log(\ell)/\log(s)}$ be the relaxation factor at the bottom of the tree. It holds $\mathsf{d}_{\log(\ell)/\ell s} = \mathsf{d}^{2s-1}$. Continuing until the top of the tree we get the following relaxation factor:

$$\mathsf{d}_0 = \mathsf{d}^{2s-1} \cdot \ldots \cdot \mathsf{d}^{2s-1} = \mathsf{d}^{(2s-1) \cdot \log(\ell)/\log(s)} \qquad (10)$$

For the worst case, where $s = 2$ it holds

$$\mathsf{d}^{(2s-1) \cdot \log(\ell)/\log(s)} \overset{s=2}{=} \mathsf{d}^{3\log(\ell)} \overset{\mathsf{d}=2}{=} \ell^3 \qquad (11)$$

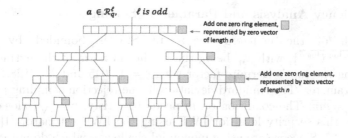

Fig. 1. Splitting tree

Note: if ℓ is odd, then we extend it by a zero element such that $\ell + 1$ is divisible by 2. Whenever ℓ_ν is odd in the following levels, 1 will be added as an extension of the string. It means that in total there are $\log(\ell)/\log(s)$ levels in a splitting tree (Fig. 1).

Extracted Witness Length. The length of the extracted witness at level $\nu - 1$ is given as a product of the extracted witness in level ν multiplied by the corresponding relaxation factor at level ν:

$$\|\mathsf{Ext.Wit.}\|_{\nu-1} = \|\mathsf{Ext.Wit.}\|_\nu \cdot \mathsf{d}^{(2s_\nu - 1)} = \|\mathsf{Ext.Wit.}\|_{\nu+1} \cdot \mathsf{d}^{(2s_{\nu+1} - 1)} \cdot \mathsf{d}^{(2s_\nu - 1)} =$$
$$\dots = \|\mathsf{Ext.Wit.}\|_{bot} \cdot \mathsf{d}^{(2s_\nu - 1)} \cdots \mathsf{d}^{(2s_{bot} - 1)} \tag{12}$$

This implies that the length of the witness at the top of the tree assuming that $s_\nu = s = 2$ is given as follows:

$$\|\mathsf{Ext.Wit.}\|_{top} = \|\mathsf{Ext.Wit.}\|_{bot} \cdot \mathsf{d}^{(2s-1) \cdot \left(\frac{\log(\ell)}{\log(s)}\right)} \overset{s=2}{=} \|\mathsf{Ext.Wit.}\|_{bot} \cdot \mathsf{d}^{3\log\ell} \tag{13}$$

Since $\mathsf{d} = 2$ (in case of monomials), it holds $\|\mathsf{Ext.Wit.}\|_{bot} \cdot \ell^3$. At the bottom of the tree we extract one ring element in $\mathcal{R}_q$ which has an upper bound $\|\mathsf{Ext.Wit.}\|_\infty \leq \mathcal{B}$. Using this in Eq. 14 implies:

$$\|\mathsf{Ext.Wit.}\|_{top} = \|\mathsf{Ext.Wit.}\|_{bot} \cdot \mathsf{d}^{\mathcal{O}(\log(\ell))} \overset{d=2}{\leq} \ell^3 \sqrt{mn}\mathcal{B} \tag{14}$$
$$\leftrightarrow \log(\|\mathsf{Ext.Wit.}\|_{top}) \leq 3\log(\ell) + \log(\sqrt{mn}\mathcal{B}) = \mathcal{O}(\log(\ell)) \tag{15}$$

Special Honest Verifier Zero-Knowledge (SHVZK). To prove the zero-knowledge property of our protocol, we need to show how to simulate the protocol transcript. The public transcript in the real protocol is given by $\mathbf{A}', \mathbf{B}', \mathbf{C}', \mathbf{D}', \mathbb{A}_\nu, \mathbb{B}_\nu, \mathbb{A}_{k_\nu}, \mathbb{B}_{k_\nu}, z_{k_\nu}, s_{\mu-1}, \dots, s_1, x$. In the simulated protocol the simulator chooses uniformly at random $\mathbf{A}', \mathbf{B}', \mathbf{C}', \mathbf{D}' \in (\mathcal{R}_q^{d \times m})^{\ell_\nu}, \mathbb{A}_\nu, \mathbb{B}_\nu, \mathbb{A}_{k_\nu}, \mathbb{B}_{k_\nu} \in \mathcal{R}_q^d, z_{k_\nu}, s_{\mu-1}, \dots, s_1, x$. Using the challenge x the simulator computes $\mathbf{A}'_\nu = \sum_{i=1}^{s_\nu} \mathbf{A}'_i x^{-i}, \mathbf{B}'_\nu = \sum_{i=1}^{s_\nu} \mathbf{B}'_i x^{-i}, \mathbf{C}'_\nu = \sum_{i=1}^{s_\nu} \mathbf{C}'_i x^i, \mathbf{D}'_\nu = \sum_{i=1}^{s_\nu} \mathbf{D}'_i x^i$. Taking $\mathbb{A}_{k_\nu}, \mathbb{B}_{k_\nu}$ the simulator computes the values $\mathbb{A}'_\nu = \sum_{k_\nu = 1 - s_\nu}^{s_\nu - 1} \mathbb{A}_{k_\nu} x^{k_\nu}, \mathbb{B}'_\nu = \sum_{k_\nu = 1 - s_\nu}^{s_\nu - 1} \mathbb{B}_{k_\nu} x^{-k_\nu}$, and $z_\nu = \sum_{k_\nu = 1 - s_\nu}^{s_\nu - 1} z_{k_\nu} x^{-k_\nu}$ which are computationally indistinguishable from the real protocol output. $\square$

3.3   Efficiency Analysis and Parameters Setting

The length of the non-zero vector in SIS is bounded by $\beta_{ip} \leq \min\{q, 2^{2\sqrt{n\log q \log \delta}}\}$, with β_{ip} being the Euclidean norm of the extracted witness, δ being the root's Hermite factor with $\delta = 1.0045$ and $\lambda = 128$ being the security parameter. The standard deviation in the rejection sampling procedure is $\sigma_{ip} = \mathcal{B}_{ip}\sqrt{mn}$. The condition on m needs to satisfy $m = \sqrt{(n\log q)(\log \delta)}$. We balance this security level for LWE using the LWE estimator [1]. We set $q = 2^{36}$, $n = 2^8$. Since we are using monomial challenges which do not guarantee a negligible soundness error, we need to repeat our protocol $\lambda/|\log(\mathcal{CH})|$ times which is equal to $128/8 = 16$. The communication cost is computed as follows: The prover computes $2\sum_{\nu=2}^{\mu}(2s_\nu - 1) + 2s_1$ diagonal commitments $\mathbb{A}_{k_\nu}, \mathbb{B}_{k_\nu}$ for $\nu = 1, \ldots, \mu$ of length $(2\sum_{\nu=2}^{\mu}(2s_\nu - 1) + 2s_1)\log q$ for each commitment. Even though the statements are getting shorter with each round of iteration, the total size of the communicated commitments remains the same. The total computational cost is $(2\sum_{\nu=2}^{\mu}(2s_\nu - 1) + 2s_1)\log(q) + \mathcal{B}_{ip}s_\nu\sqrt{mn}$. Thus it is required to look for optimizations which we present in the following section. We compute the communication cost for the worst case of s_ν, i.e. $s_\nu = 2$. Since this is the first lattice-based inner product argument, we provide a table of different parameter sets to demonstrate the change of the proof size with growing modulus q (refer Table 2).

4   Optimized Inner Product Argument

In the introduction section we have briefly discussed the importance of inner product arguments towards the efficiency. We further aim to improve the communication efficiency while dealing with polynomial ring elements by continuing the chunking technique up into each ring element. This is done by splitting the initial ring $\mathcal{R}_q$ into components and committing to the elements in the ring components. In Theorem 3 we show that a commitment over $\mathcal{R}_q$ is isomorphic to the sum of commitments over $\mathcal{R}_{q,j}$ for all $j \in [0, \kappa-1]$. In this section we provide an optimized version of the lattice-based inner product argument whose discrete log version was introduced in the mentioned work [10]. In contrast to that argument we consider ring elements $\mathbf{a}, \mathbf{b} \in \mathcal{R}_q = \mathbb{Z}_q[X]/(X^n+1)$ and perform the splitting of these elements in the ring $\mathcal{R}_q$. To do so, we apply the technique from [28] to partially split the ring.

4.1   Splitting Rings

In this section we provide a detailed description on how to split a ring $\mathcal{R}_q$ into the components $\mathcal{R}_{q,j}$ for $j \in [0, \kappa - 1]$. Our idea is based on the results in [28] where the authors showed that for the particular case $\Phi_m(X) = X^n + 1$, where Φ_m is the mth cyclotomic polynomial, the function $X^n + 1$ can split into several irreducible factors without affecting the optimal challenge set.

Detailed Description. We assume that q is chosen so that the polynomial $\Phi_m(X) = \prod_{j=1}^{d} f_j(X) \mod q = X^n + 1$ factors into κ irreducible polynomials of the form $f_j(X) = (X^{\phi(m)/\kappa} - r_j)$ for distinct $r_j \in \mathbb{Z}_{q_j}^*$, where r_j is a zero of $f_j(X)$. It holds $m = \prod p_j^{e_j}$, where $e_j \geq 1$ and $\kappa = \prod p_j^{g_j}$ for $1 \leq g_j \leq e_j$. Then according to the Chinese remainder theorem the following isomorphism holds:

$$\mathbb{Z}_q[X]/(X^n + 1) \cong \mathbb{Z}_q[X]/f_1(X) \times \cdots \times \mathbb{Z}_q[X]/f_\kappa(X) \tag{16}$$

Since $\mathbf{a} \in \mathcal{R}_q$, its polynomial representation is given as follows: $\mathbf{a} = \sum_{i=0}^{\phi(m)-1} a_i X^i$. Next, we define polynomials $\overline{\mathbf{a}}_i$ for $0 \leq i < \phi(m)/\kappa - 1$ as: $\overline{\mathbf{a}}_i = \sum_{j=0}^{\kappa-1} a_{j\phi(m)/\kappa+i} X^j$ with $\mathrm{Coef}(\overline{\mathbf{a}}_i) = (a_i, a_{\phi(m)/\kappa+i}, \ldots, a_{(\kappa-1)\phi(m)/\kappa+i})$. Polynomial $\mathbf{a}$ can be expressed in terms of $\overline{\mathbf{a}}_i$ as $\mathbf{a} = \sum_{i=0}^{\phi(m)/\kappa-1} \overline{\mathbf{a}}_i (X^{\phi(m)/\kappa}) \cdot X^i$. Reducing $\mathbf{a} \mod f_j$ yields: $\mathbf{a} \mod (X^{\phi(m)/\kappa} - r_j) = \sum_{i=0}^{\phi(m)/\kappa-1} \overline{\mathbf{a}}_i(r_j) \cdot X^i = \tilde{\mathbf{a}}_j$ for all $j \in [0, \kappa - 1]$. The vector $\tilde{\mathbf{a}}_j$ can be evaluated in r_j, which returns an element in $\mathcal{R}_{q,j}$:

$$\tilde{\mathbf{a}}_j = (\overline{\mathbf{a}}_0(r_j), \ldots, \overline{\mathbf{a}}_{\phi(m)/\kappa-1}(r_j)) = \left(a_{j\frac{\phi(m)}{\kappa}}, a_{j\frac{\phi(m)}{\kappa}+1}, \ldots, a_{(j+1)\frac{\phi(m)}{\kappa}-1} \right),$$

then collecting all $\tilde{\mathbf{a}}_j$ into a vector for all $j \in [0, \kappa - 1]$ returns: $\tilde{\mathbf{a}} = (\tilde{\mathbf{a}}_0, \ldots, \tilde{\mathbf{a}}_{\kappa-1}) \in (\mathcal{R}_{q,0} \times \cdots \times \mathcal{R}_{q,\kappa-1})$ where each ring is defined as $\mathcal{R}_{q,j} = \mathbb{Z}_q[X]/(X^{\phi(m)/\kappa} - r_j)$. The public parameters $\mathbf{A}, \mathbf{B}$ which are the inputs to the protocol, will be split into κ sub-parameters over the components $\mathcal{R}_{q,0}, \ldots, \mathcal{R}_{q,\kappa-1}$ as follows: We have $\mathbf{A} \in \mathcal{R}_q^{1 \times m}$ and $\mathbf{B} \in \mathcal{R}_q$, i.e. $\mathbf{A} = (\mathbf{A}^{(1)}, \ldots, \mathbf{A}^{(m)}) \in \mathcal{R}_q \times \cdots \times \mathcal{R}_q$. Each ring element $\mathbf{A}^{(i)}, i \in [1, m]$ is split into κ components $\mathbf{A}_j^{(i)} \in \mathcal{R}_{q,j}$, for $j \in [0, \kappa - 1]$, i.e. $\mathbf{A}^{(i)} \cong (\mathbf{A}_0^{(i)}, \ldots, \mathbf{A}_{\kappa-1}^{(i)}) \in \mathcal{R}_{q,0} \times \cdots \times \mathcal{R}_{q,\kappa-1}$. We concatenate the m component elements over the same component rings, i.e. set $\tilde{\mathbf{A}}_j = (\mathbf{A}_j^{(1)}, \ldots, \mathbf{A}_j^{(m)}) \in \mathcal{R}_{q,j}^{1 \times m}$. Similarly we deal with $\mathbf{B}$ and $\mathbf{r}_a$ to obtain $\tilde{\mathbf{B}}_j \in \mathcal{R}_{q,j}, \tilde{\mathbf{r}}_{a,j} \in \mathcal{R}_{q,j}^m$. Then a commitment to $\tilde{\mathbf{a}}$ is computed by choosing a randomness $\tilde{\mathbf{r}}_{\tilde{a},j} \in (\mathcal{R}_{q,j})^m$, where $\mathcal{R}_{q,j} = \mathbb{Z}_q[X]/(X^{\phi(m)/\kappa} - r_j)$ and public parameters $\tilde{\mathbf{A}}_j \in (\mathcal{R}_{q,j})^{1 \times m}, \tilde{\mathbf{B}}_j \in \mathcal{R}_{q,j}$, where $\tilde{\mathbf{A}} = (\tilde{\mathbf{A}}_0, \ldots, \tilde{\mathbf{A}}_{\kappa-1})$ and $\tilde{\mathbf{B}} = (\tilde{\mathbf{B}}_0, \ldots, \tilde{\mathbf{B}}_{\kappa-1}), \tilde{\mathbf{r}}_{\tilde{a}} = (\tilde{\mathbf{r}}_{\tilde{a},0}, \ldots, \tilde{\mathbf{r}}_{\tilde{a},\kappa-1})^{tr}$. Before we define the commitment on $\tilde{\mathbf{a}}$ we set up a function which takes as input different ring elements from the ring components $\mathcal{R}_{q,j}, j \in [0, \kappa - 1]$ performs a computation over these ring components (i.e. addition, multiplication) and outputs an element from one of those ring components. Without loss of generality we assume that the output of CRT is an element of the last ring component $\mathcal{R}_{q,\kappa-1}$. We recall important properties of CRT computations to see how an element over one ring component $\mathcal{R}_{q,j}$ can be transferred into an element over another ring component $\mathcal{R}_{q,j'}$, where $j \neq j'$. Here, r_j denotes the zeros of $f_j(X) = (X^{\phi(m)/\kappa} - r_j)$ for all $j \in [0, \kappa - 1]$. There is an isomorphism

$$\psi_{i \mapsto j} : \mathbb{Z}_q[X]/(X^{\phi(m)/\kappa} - r_i) \rightarrow \mathbb{Z}_q[X]/(X^{\phi(m)/\kappa} - r_j),$$

where $\psi_{i \mapsto j}(r_i)$ is a fixed zero of $f_i(X) = (X^{\phi(m)/\kappa} - r_i)$ in polynomial ring $\mathbb{Z}_q[X]/(X^{\phi(m)/\kappa} - r_j)$, i.e. $f_i(\psi_{i \mapsto j}(X)) \cong 0 \mod f_j(X)$ (Fig. 2).

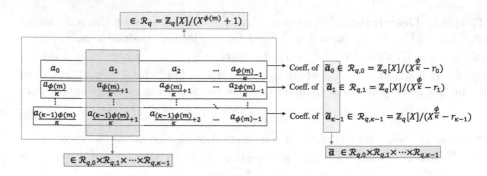

Fig. 2. Representation of $\mathbf{a} \in \mathcal{R}_q$

Definition 9 (CRT-Function). *Let $\mathcal{R}_{q,j} = \mathbb{Z}_q[X]/(X^{\phi(m)/\kappa} - r_j)$ be a component of the ring $\mathcal{R}_q = \mathbb{Z}_q[X]/(X^n + 1)$. The CRT function is defined over the ring elements $\mathbf{p}_j \in \mathcal{R}_{q,j}$ as follows:*

$$\mathrm{CRT}_{r_0}^{r_{\kappa}-1} : \mathcal{R}_{q,0} \times \cdots \times \mathcal{R}_{q,\kappa-1} \rightarrow \mathcal{R}_{q,\kappa-1},$$

$$\mathrm{CRT}_{r_0}^{r_{\kappa}-1}(\{\mathbf{p}_j\}) = \sum_{j=0}^{\kappa-2} \psi_{j \mapsto j+1}(\mathbf{p}_j) + \mathbf{p}_{\kappa-1}$$

Using this CRT function we define the commitment on $\tilde{\mathbf{a}}$ as follows:

$$\tilde{\mathbb{A}} = \mathrm{Com}_{\tilde{\mathbf{A}}, \tilde{\mathbf{B}}}(\tilde{\mathbf{a}}, \tilde{\mathbf{r}}_{\tilde{a}}) = \mathrm{CRT}_{r_0}^{r_{\kappa}-1}\left(\{\tilde{\mathbf{A}}_j \cdot \tilde{\mathbf{r}}_{\tilde{a},j} + \tilde{\mathbf{B}}_j \cdot \tilde{\mathbf{a}}_j\}_{j \in [0,\kappa-1]}\right).$$

Let $\mathbf{b} \in \mathcal{R}_q$ be a polynomial with the following representation $\mathbf{b} = \sum_{i=0}^{\phi(m)-1} b_i X^{-i}$ shorter polynomials $\overline{\mathbf{b}}_i$ for $0 \leq i < \phi(m)/\kappa - 1$ as: $\overline{\mathbf{b}}_i = \sum_{j=0}^{\kappa-1} b_{j\phi(m)/\kappa+i} X^{-j}$ with $\mathrm{Coef}(\overline{\mathbf{b}}_i) = \left(b_i, b_{\phi(m)/\kappa+i}, \ldots, b_{(\kappa-1)\phi(m)/\kappa+i}\right)$. Similar to $\mathbf{a}$, also $\mathbf{b}$ can be expressed in terms of the $\overline{\mathbf{b}}_i$ as follows: $\mathbf{b} = \sum_{i=0}^{\phi(m)/\kappa-1} \tilde{\mathbf{b}}_i(X^{\phi(m)/\kappa}) \cdot X^{-i}$. Using the same approach as for $\tilde{\mathbf{a}}_j$, we evaluate the coefficient $\tilde{\mathbf{b}}_i(X^{\phi(m)/\kappa})$ in r_j and obtain the following vector in $\mathcal{R}_{q,j}$:

$$\tilde{\mathbf{b}}_j = \left(\overline{\mathbf{b}}_0(r_j), \ldots, \overline{\mathbf{b}}_{\phi(m)/\kappa-1}(r_j)\right) = \left(b_{j\frac{\phi(m)}{\kappa}}, b_{j\frac{\phi(m)}{\kappa}+1}, \ldots, b_{(j+1)\frac{\phi(m)}{\kappa}-1}\right).$$

In the same manner we define a commitment to $\tilde{\mathbf{b}} = (\tilde{\mathbf{b}}_0, \ldots, \tilde{\mathbf{b}}_{\kappa-1})^{tr}$. A commitment to $\tilde{\mathbf{b}}$ is computed picking a randomness $\tilde{\mathbf{r}}_{\tilde{b},j} \in (\mathcal{R}_{q,j})^m$, where $\mathcal{R}_{q,j} = \mathbb{Z}_q[X]/(X^{\phi(m)/\kappa} - r_j)$ and public parameters $\tilde{\mathbf{C}}_j \in (\mathcal{R}_{q,j})^{1 \times m}, \tilde{\mathbf{D}}_j \in \mathcal{R}_{q,j}$, where $\tilde{\mathbf{C}} = (\tilde{\mathbf{C}}_0, \ldots, \tilde{\mathbf{C}}_{\kappa-1})$ and $\tilde{\mathbf{D}} = (\tilde{\mathbf{D}}_0, \ldots, \tilde{\mathbf{D}}_{\kappa-1}), \tilde{\mathbf{r}}_{\tilde{b}} = (\tilde{\mathbf{r}}_{\tilde{b},0}, \ldots, \tilde{\mathbf{r}}_{\tilde{b},\kappa-1})^{tr}$. The commitment is defined similar as above: $\tilde{\mathbb{B}} = \mathrm{Com}_{\tilde{\mathbf{C}}, \tilde{\mathbf{D}}}(\tilde{\mathbf{b}}, \mathbf{r}_{\tilde{b}}) = \mathrm{CRT}_{r_0}^{r_{\kappa}-1}(\{\tilde{\mathbf{C}}_j \cdot \tilde{\mathbf{r}}_{\tilde{b},j} + \tilde{\mathbf{D}}_j \cdot \tilde{\mathbf{b}}_j\}_{j \in [0,\kappa-1]})$. We can add up the different ring elements to reconstruct the commitment $\mathrm{Com}_{\tilde{\mathbf{A}}, \tilde{\mathbf{B}}}(\tilde{\mathbf{a}}, \tilde{\mathbf{r}}_a) = \tilde{\mathbf{A}} \cdot \tilde{\mathbf{r}}_a + \tilde{\mathbf{B}} \cdot \tilde{\mathbf{a}}$ as follows:

$$\tilde{\mathbf{A}} \cdot \tilde{\mathbf{r}}_{\tilde{a}} + \tilde{\mathbf{B}} \cdot \tilde{\mathbf{a}} = \sum_{i=0}^{\kappa-1} \tilde{\mathbf{g}}_i(r_i) \frac{(X^{\phi(m)} + 1)}{(X^{\phi(m)/\kappa} - r_i)} \left(\frac{(X^{\phi(m)/\kappa} - r_i)}{(X^{\phi(m)} + 1)} \mod \prod_{j \neq i}(X^{\phi(m)/\kappa} - r_j)\right)$$

where $\tilde{\mathbf{g}}_i = \tilde{\mathbf{A}}_i \cdot \tilde{\mathbf{r}}_{\tilde{a},i} + \tilde{\mathbf{B}}_i \cdot \tilde{\mathbf{a}}_i$. Similarly, for $\tilde{\mathbf{h}}_i = \tilde{\mathbf{C}}_i \cdot \tilde{\mathbf{r}}_{\tilde{b},i} + \tilde{\mathbf{D}}_i \cdot \tilde{\mathbf{b}}_i$:

$$\tilde{\mathbf{C}} \cdot \tilde{\mathbf{r}}_{\tilde{b}} + \tilde{\mathbf{D}} \cdot \tilde{\mathbf{b}} = \sum_{i=0}^{\kappa-1} \tilde{\mathbf{h}}_i(r_i) \frac{(X^{\phi(m)} + 1)}{(X^{\phi(m)/\kappa} - r_i)} \left(\frac{(X^{\phi(m)/\kappa} - r_i)}{(X^{\phi(m)} + 1)} \right) \quad \mathrm{mod} \prod_{j \neq i} (X^{\phi(m)/\kappa} - r_j) \Big)$$

Similar to the protocol in previous section we define the matrices $\tilde{\mathfrak{C}}_{a,\kappa}, \tilde{\mathfrak{C}}_{b,\kappa}$ which constitute the diagonal commitments to $\tilde{\mathbf{a}}_j, \tilde{\mathbf{b}}_j$, respectively:

$$\tilde{\mathfrak{C}}_{a,\kappa} = \begin{bmatrix} \tilde{\mathbf{A}}_0 \cdot \tilde{\mathbf{r}}_{a,0} + \tilde{\mathbf{B}}_0 \cdot \tilde{\mathbf{a}}_0 & \cdots & \tilde{\mathbf{A}}_0 \cdot \tilde{\mathbf{r}}_{a,\kappa-1} + \tilde{\mathbf{B}}_0 \cdot \tilde{\mathbf{a}}_{\kappa-1} \\ \vdots & \ddots & \vdots \\ \tilde{\mathbf{A}}_{\kappa-1} \cdot \tilde{\mathbf{r}}_{a,0} + \tilde{\mathbf{B}}_{\kappa-1} \cdot \tilde{\mathbf{a}}_0 & \cdots & \tilde{\mathbf{A}}_{\kappa-1} \cdot \tilde{\mathbf{r}}_{a,\kappa-1} + \tilde{\mathbf{B}}_{\kappa-1} \cdot \tilde{\mathbf{a}}_{\kappa-1} \end{bmatrix}$$

$$\tilde{\mathfrak{C}}_{b,\kappa} = \begin{bmatrix} \tilde{\mathbf{C}}_0 \cdot \tilde{\mathbf{r}}_{b,0} + \tilde{\mathbf{D}}_0 \cdot \tilde{\mathbf{b}}_0 & \cdots & \tilde{\mathbf{C}}_0 \cdot \tilde{\mathbf{r}}_{b,\kappa-1} + \tilde{\mathbf{D}}_0 \cdot \tilde{\mathbf{b}}_{\kappa-1} \\ \vdots & \ddots & \vdots \\ \tilde{\mathbf{C}}_{\kappa-1} \cdot \tilde{\mathbf{r}}_{b,0} + \tilde{\mathbf{D}}_{\kappa-1} \cdot \tilde{\mathbf{b}}_0 & \cdots & \tilde{\mathbf{C}}_{\kappa-1} \cdot \tilde{\mathbf{r}}_{b,\kappa-1} + \tilde{\mathbf{D}}_{\kappa-1} \cdot \tilde{\mathbf{b}}_{\kappa-1} \end{bmatrix} \quad (17)$$

The corresponding diagonal commitments are defined as follows for all:

$$\tilde{\mathbb{A}}_k = \sum_{i=\max(1,1-k)}^{\min(\kappa,\kappa-k)} (\tilde{\mathbf{A}}_i \tilde{\mathbf{r}}_{a,i+k} + \tilde{\mathbf{B}}_i \tilde{\mathbf{a}}_{i+k}), \quad \tilde{\mathbb{B}}_k = \sum_{i=\max(1,1-k)}^{\min(\kappa,\kappa-k)} (\tilde{\mathbf{C}}_i \tilde{\mathbf{r}}_{b,i+k} + \tilde{\mathbf{D}}_i \tilde{\mathbf{b}}_{i+k}),$$

$$z_k = \sum_{i=\max(1,1-k)}^{\min(\kappa,\kappa-k)} \tilde{\mathbf{a}}_i \cdot \tilde{\mathbf{b}}_{i+k}, \quad \forall k = 1 - \kappa, \ldots, \kappa - 1$$

4.2 Ring Isomorphism

The entries of the matrices $\tilde{\mathfrak{C}}_{a,\kappa}, \tilde{\mathfrak{C}}_{b,\kappa}$ are combinations of the elements from the different rings. Multiplication and addition of such elements are not a straightforward task. In order to perform these computations we first need to show that the different components are isomorphic to each other. More concrete, we want to show how to compute the product of two ring elements $\tilde{\mathbf{A}}_i$ and $\tilde{\mathbf{a}}_j$ which are defined in two different components $\mathcal{R}_{q,i}$ and $\mathcal{R}_{q,j}$, respectively. We use the idea of splitting fields and the corresponding isomorphisms which were defined in [31]. Let $\psi_{i \mapsto j}(\tilde{\mathbf{a}}_j)$ be a fixed zero of $(X^{\phi(m)/\kappa} - r_i)$ in $\mathbb{Z}_q[X]/(X^{\phi(m)/\kappa} - r_j)$, i.e. it holds $(\psi_{i \mapsto j}(\tilde{\mathbf{a}}_j)^{\phi(m)/\kappa} - r_i) \cong 0 \mod (X^{\phi(m)/\kappa} - r_j)$. Applying this isomorphism we can multiply two elements from different components as follows:

$$\tilde{\mathbf{A}}_i \cdot \tilde{\mathbf{r}}_{a,j} = \psi_{i \mapsto j}(\tilde{\mathbf{A}}_i) \cdot \tilde{\mathbf{r}}_{a,j} \quad \mathrm{mod} (X^{\phi(m)/\kappa} - r_j)$$

In order to speed up the computation we further decompose each ring $\mathcal{R}_{q,j} = \mathbb{Z}_q[X]/(X^{\phi(m)/\kappa} - r_j)$ into the rings $(\mathcal{R}_{q,j})_{j_1} = \mathcal{R}_{q,j}/(X^{\phi(m)/(\kappa \cdot \kappa_1)} - r_{j_1})$ where $j_1 \in [0, \kappa_1 - 1]$. Let $f_{j_1}(X) = (X^{\phi(m)/(\kappa \kappa_1)} - r_{j_1})$, then there is an isomorphism

$$\psi_{j \mapsto j_1} : \mathcal{R}_{q,j} \to (\mathcal{R}_{q,j})_{j_1}, \quad f_j(r_j) \mapsto f_j(\psi_{j \mapsto j_1}(r_{j_1})) \quad (18)$$

where $\psi_{j \mapsto j_1}(r_{j_1})$ is a fixed root of f_j in $(\mathcal{R}_{q,j})_{j_1}$. The decomposition of $\mathcal{R}_{q,j}$ is as follows: For $\tilde{a}_j \in \mathcal{R}_{q,j}$ we already know $\tilde{a}_j = \sum_{i=0}^{\phi(m)/\kappa-1} \overline{a}_i(r_j)X^i = \sum_{i=0}^{\phi(m)/\kappa-1} a_{j\frac{\phi(m)}{\kappa}+i}X^i$. After reducing it modulo $(X^{\phi(m)/(\kappa\kappa_1)} - r_{j_1})$ we get

$$\tilde{a}_j \mod (X^{\phi(m)/(\kappa\kappa_1)} - r_{j_1}) = \sum_{i=0}^{\phi(m)/(\kappa\kappa_1)-1} \tilde{a}_{j,i}(r_{j_1}) \cdot X^i = (\tilde{a}_j)_{j_1}.$$

Similar to the first split up of the ring we define public parameters $(\tilde{A}_j)_{j_1}, (\tilde{C}_j)_{j_1} \in (\mathcal{R}_{q,j})_{j_1}^{1 \times m}, (\tilde{B}_j)_{j_1}, (\tilde{D}_j)_{j_1} \in (\mathcal{R}_{q,j})_{j_1}$ and $(\tilde{r}_{j,a})_{j_1}, (\tilde{r}_{j,b})_{j_1} \in (\mathcal{R}_{q,j})_{j_1}^{m \times 1}$. Components of each element $(\tilde{a}_j)_{j_1}$ are $(\tilde{a}_{j,0}(r_{j_1}), \ldots, \tilde{a}_{j,\phi(m)/(\kappa\kappa_1)-1}(r_{j_1}))$. Let $(\tilde{g}_j)_{j_1} := (\tilde{A}_j)_{j_1} \cdot (\tilde{r}_{\tilde{a},j})_{j_1} + (\tilde{B}_j)_{j_1} \cdot (\tilde{a}_j)_{j_1}$ and $(\tilde{h}_j)_{j_1} := (\tilde{C}_j)_{j_1}(\tilde{r}_{\tilde{b},j})_{j_1} + (\tilde{D}_j)_{j_1}(\tilde{b}_j)_{j_1}$. We commit to $\tilde{a}$ using the following compression which returns a commitment in $(\mathcal{R}_{q,j})_{j_1}$ for all $j_1 \in [0, \kappa_1 - 1]$:

$$\tilde{A} = \mathrm{Com}_{\tilde{A},\tilde{B}}(\tilde{a}, \tilde{r}_{\tilde{a}}) \cong \mathrm{CRT}_{r_0}^{r_{\kappa-1}}\left(\mathrm{CRT}_{r_0'}^{r_{\kappa_1-1}'}\left((\tilde{g}_j)_0, \ldots, (\tilde{g}_j)_{\kappa_1-1}\right)\right) \tag{19}$$

We define the argument inside of the last equality in (19) as follows:

$$\mathrm{CRT}_{r_0'}^{r_{\kappa_1-1}'}\left((\tilde{g}_j)_0, \ldots, (\tilde{g}_j)_{\kappa_1-1}\right) = \sum_{j_1=0}^{\kappa_1-1} \psi_{j_1 \mapsto j_1+1}\left((\tilde{g}_j)_{j_1}\right). \tag{20}$$

Applying the isomorphism defined above we obtain

$$\tilde{A} = \mathrm{Com}_{\tilde{A},\tilde{B}}(\tilde{a}, \tilde{r}_{\tilde{a}}) = \sum_{j=0}^{\kappa-1} \psi_{i \mapsto i+k}\left(\sum_{j_1=0}^{\kappa_1-1} \psi_{j_1 \mapsto j_1+1}\left((\tilde{g}_j)_{j_1}\right)\right).$$

Components of each element $(\tilde{b}_j)_{j_1}$ are $(\tilde{b}_{j,0}(r_{j_1}), \ldots, \tilde{b}_{j,\phi(m)/(\kappa\kappa_1)-1}(r_{j_1}))$. The commitment to $\tilde{b}$ is similarly defined and is denoted as $\tilde{B} = \mathrm{Com}_{\tilde{C},\tilde{D}}(\tilde{b}, \tilde{r}_{\tilde{b}})$. Building a protocol from these data would not provide any improvement to the protocol in Sect. 3. The reason is that at each reduction level j the prover has to commit to s_j secrets where each commitment size is ℓ_j/s_j. This means that the total commitment size is again ℓ_j without leading to any improvement in computational cost. In order to overcome this issue our idea is to exploit the algebraic structure of our commitment scheme. What we would like to achieve is to reduce the computational cost, which is possible if we can reduce the length of our commitments. We develop this idea in the coming section.

4.3 Algebraic Structure of Our Commitment $\tilde{A}$

In this section we explore the algebraic structure of our commitment scheme given in Definition 8. Let $\mathcal{R}_q = \mathbb{Z}_q[X]/(X^{\phi(m)} + 1)$. We assume that $\mathcal{R}_q$ splits partially into the following κ ring components $\mathcal{R}_{q,j}$ for $j \in [0, \kappa]$ where $\mathcal{R}_{q,j} = \mathbb{Z}_q[X]/(X^{\phi(m)/\kappa} - r_j)$. Then we split each component $\mathcal{R}_{q,j}$ one more time into κ_1 ring components $(\mathcal{R}_{q,j})_{j_1}$ for $j_1 \in [0, \kappa_1 - 1]$ where each component $(\mathcal{R}_{q,j})_{j_1} = \mathbb{Z}_q[X]/(X^{\phi(m)/(\kappa\kappa_1)} - r_{j_1}^{(1)})$, where $r_{j_1}^{(1)}$ is a zero of polynomial $f_{j_1} = (X^{\phi(m)/(\kappa\kappa_1)} - r_{j_1}^{(1)})$ after the first split-up round. The splitting continues until a ring is fully split. In order to clarify the notations we define the rings $\mathcal{R}_{q,j}$ after the first split as $\mathcal{R}_{q,j_1}^{(1)}$ where the upper index denotes the round of splits. After the θ's split-up round we have $\kappa_{\theta-1}$ rings $\mathcal{R}_{q,j_\theta}^{(\theta)} = (\dots(\mathcal{R}_{q,j})_{j_1}\dots)_{j_{\theta-1}} = \mathbb{Z}_q[X]/(X^{\phi(m)/(\kappa\kappa_1\cdots\kappa_{\theta-1})} - r_{j_\theta}^{(\theta)})$. We have to show that for $j_\iota \in [0, \theta]$ there is an isomorphism between the initial commitment on $\mathbf{a}^{(0)} := \mathbf{a}$ with randomness $\mathbf{r}^{(0)} := \mathbf{r}$ and public parameters $\mathbf{A}^{(0)} := \mathbf{A}, \mathbf{B}^{(0)} := \mathbf{B}$.

$$\mathrm{Com}_{\mathbf{A}^{(0)},\mathbf{B}^{(0)}}(\mathbf{a}^{(0)}, \mathbf{r}^{(0)}) \cong \sum_{j_1=0}^{\kappa-1} \cdots \sum_{j_\iota=0}^{\kappa_\iota-1} \mathrm{Com}_{\tilde{\mathbf{A}}_{j_\iota}^{(\iota)},\tilde{\mathbf{B}}_{j_\iota}^{(\iota)}}(\tilde{\mathbf{a}}_{j_\iota}^{(\iota)}, \tilde{\mathbf{r}}_{j_\iota}^{(\iota)}) \tag{21}$$

According to the field extension theory the following relation holds:

$$\mathcal{R}_q \subseteq \mathcal{R}_q[r_{j_1}^{(1)}] \subseteq \mathcal{R}_q[r_{j_1}^{(1)}, r_{j_2}^{(2)}] \subseteq \dots \subseteq \mathcal{R}_q[r_{j_1}^{(1)}, r_{j_2}^{(2)}, \dots, r_{j_\theta}^{(\theta)}] =: L \tag{22}$$

where $r_{j_\iota}^{(\iota)}$ is a fixed root of $f_{j_\iota} := (X^{\phi(m)/(\kappa\kappa_1\cdots\kappa_\iota)} - r_{j_\iota}^{(\iota)})$ in $\mathcal{R}_{q,j_\iota}^{(\iota)}$. $[L : \mathcal{R}_q]$ is a field extension of $\mathcal{R}_q$. A value $r_{j_\iota}^\iota \in L$ is called algebraic over $\mathcal{R}_q$, if there is a polynomial $g \in \mathcal{R}_q$ such that $g(r_{j_\iota}^{(\iota)}) = 0$.

Let $[L : \mathcal{R}_q]$ be a field extension and $r_{j_\iota}^\iota \in L$ algebraic over $\mathcal{R}_q$. Then there exists a well-defined polynomial $\mathfrak{m}_r \in \mathcal{R}_q$ of lowest degree such that $\mathfrak{m}_r(r_{j_\iota}^\iota) = 0$ which is called a minimal polynomial of $r_{j_\iota}^\iota$ over $\mathcal{R}_q$.

Given a field extension $[L : \mathcal{R}_q]$ and an algebraic $r_{j_\iota}^\iota \in L$ over $\mathcal{R}_q$ with a minimal polynomial $\mathfrak{m}_r \in \mathcal{R}_q$ there exists a map $\Phi_r : \mathcal{R}_q \to L$ which is given by the following function: $\Phi_r(f) = g(r_{j_\iota}^{(\iota)})$ and $\mathcal{R}_q/\ker(\Phi_r) \cong \mathcal{R}_q[r_{j_\iota}^{(\iota)}]$ or equivalently for a minimal polynomial $\mathfrak{m}_r$ holds the following evaluation isomorphism:

$$\mathcal{R}_q/(\mathfrak{m}_{r_\iota}) \cong \mathcal{R}_q[r_{j_\iota}^{(\iota)}]. \tag{23}$$

In order to show that (21) holds, we prove the following theorem.

Theorem 3. *For a given field extension $[L : \mathcal{R}_q]$ for which (22) holds, a commitment $\mathrm{Com}_{\mathbf{A}^{(0)}}(\mathbf{a}^{(0)}, \tilde{\mathbf{r}}^{(0)}) \in \mathcal{R}_q$ is isomorphic to $\sum_{j_1=0}^{\kappa-1} \cdots \sum_{j_\theta=0}^{\kappa_\theta-1} \mathrm{Com}_{\tilde{\mathbf{A}}_{j_\theta}^\theta}$ $(\tilde{\mathbf{a}}_{j_\theta}^{(\theta)}, \tilde{\mathbf{r}}_{j_\theta}^{(\theta)})$ if and only if the following isomorphism is correct:*

$$\mathcal{R}_q \cong \mathcal{R}_{q,j_\iota}^{(\iota)}\left[\bigoplus_{\iota=1}^\theta\right] := \mathcal{R}_q\left[\sum_{\iota=1}^\theta \chi_\iota r_{j_\iota}^{(\iota)}\right], \quad \chi_\iota \in \mathcal{R}_q. \tag{24}$$

Proof. Let $\mathfrak{m}_{r_\iota}^{(\iota-1)}$ be a minimal polynomial of $r_{j_\iota}^{(\iota)}$ over $\mathcal{R}_{q,j_{\iota-1}}^{(\iota-1)}$. Then from (25) we get the following isomorphism:

$$\mathcal{R}_{q,j_{\iota-1}}^{(\iota-1)}/(\mathfrak{m}_{r_\iota}^{(\iota-1)}) \cong \mathcal{R}_{q,j_{\iota-1}}^{(\iota-1)}[r_{j_\iota}^{(\iota)}]. \tag{25}$$

Let us define $\mathcal{R}_{q,\chi}^{(\iota-1,\iota)} := \mathcal{R}_{q,\chi}[r_{j_{\iota-1}}^{(\iota-1)} + \chi_\iota r_{j_\iota}^{(\iota)}]$ and apparently $\mathcal{R}_{q,\chi}[r_{j_{\iota-1}}^{(\iota-1)} + \chi_\iota r_{j_\iota}^{(\iota)}] = \mathcal{R}_q[r_{j_{\iota-1}}^{(\iota-1)}, r_{j_\iota}^{(\iota)}]$. Furthermore holds

$$\mathcal{R}_q[r_{j_1}^{(1)}, r_{j_2}^{(2)}, \ldots, r_{j_\theta}^{(\theta)}] = \mathcal{R}_{q,\chi}[r_{j_1}^{(1)} + \chi_2 r_{j_2}^{(2)} + \cdots + \chi_\theta r_{j_\theta}^\theta]$$

The main statement of this theorem can be derived from the following graph:

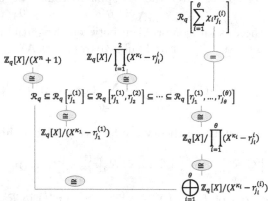

4.4   Correctness of the Inner Product

The main challenge of our protocol which we present in Sect. 3.1 is to show that the product of two ring elements $\mathbf{a} \cdot \mathbf{b}$ is isomorphic to $\tilde{\mathbf{a}} \cdot \tilde{\mathbf{b}}$ which is equal to the sum of the products $\tilde{\mathbf{a}}_j(r_j) \cdot \tilde{\mathbf{b}}_j(r_j)$ in the rings $\mathcal{R}_{q,j}$, then holds $\tilde{\mathbf{a}} \cdot \tilde{\mathbf{b}} = \sum_{j=1}^{\kappa-1} \tilde{\mathbf{a}}_j \cdot \tilde{\mathbf{b}}_j$, where κ is the number of rings after the first ring decomposition.

Let $f = \sum_{i=0}^{n-1} \lambda_i X^i$ be a polynomial of degree $n-1$ and $ZC(f) = \lambda_0$ denote the zero coefficient of this polynomial. In the next theorem we prove equality of the zero-coefficient in a polynomial represented by $\mathbf{a} \cdot \mathbf{b}$ and the inner product of coefficients of this polynomial.

Theorem 4. *Let* $\mathbf{a}, \mathbf{b} \in \mathcal{R}_q$ *with* $\mathtt{Coef}(\mathbf{a}) = (a_0, \ldots, a_{n-1})$, $\mathtt{Coef}(\mathbf{b}) = (b_0, \ldots, b_{n-1})$, *then these ring elements can also be represented as*

$$\mathbf{a} = \sum_{i=1}^{\phi(m)/\kappa-1} \overline{\mathbf{a}}_i(X^{\phi(m)/\kappa})X^i, \quad \mathbf{b} = \sum_{i=1}^{\phi(m)/\kappa-1} \overline{\mathbf{b}}_i(X^{\phi(m)/\kappa})X^{-i}, \qquad (26)$$

where the coefficients are defined as follows: $\overline{\mathbf{a}}_i = \sum_{j=0}^{\kappa-1} a_{j\phi(m)/\kappa+i}X^j$ *and* $\overline{\mathbf{b}}_i = \sum_{j=0}^{\kappa-1} b_{j\phi(m)/\kappa+i}X^{-j}$. *After evaluating* $\overline{\mathbf{a}}_i, \overline{\mathbf{b}}_i$, *in* r_j *we define:*

$$\tilde{\mathbf{a}}_j = \sum_{i=1}^{\phi(m)/\kappa-1} \overline{\mathbf{a}}_i(r_j)X^i \text{ and } \tilde{\mathbf{b}}_j = \sum_{i=1}^{\phi(m)/\kappa-1} \overline{\mathbf{b}}_i(r_j)X^{-i}. \qquad (27)$$

The zero coefficient of the inner product of $\mathbf{a}$ *and* $\mathbf{b}$ *is defined using the polynomials in* (27): $ZC(\mathbf{a} \cdot \mathbf{b}) = \langle \mathtt{Coef}(\mathbf{a}), \mathtt{Coef}(\mathbf{b}) \rangle$.

Proof. First we expand the sums from (27): $\tilde{\mathbf{a}}_j = \overline{\mathbf{a}}_1(r_j) + \overline{\mathbf{a}}_2(r_j)X + \ldots + \overline{\mathbf{a}}_{\phi(m)/\kappa-1}(r_j)X^{\kappa-1}$ and $\tilde{\mathbf{b}}_j = \overline{\mathbf{b}}_1(r_j) + \overline{\mathbf{b}}_2(r_j)X^{-1} + \ldots + \overline{\mathbf{b}}_{\phi(m)/\kappa-1}(r_j)X^{-(\kappa-1)}$. For all $i \in [1, \phi(m)/\kappa - 1]$ we set $\overline{\mathbf{a}}_i(r_j) = \sum_{j=0}^{\kappa-1} a_{j\frac{\phi(m)}{\kappa}+i} r_j^j$, i.e.: polynomials $\tilde{\mathbf{a}}_j, \tilde{\mathbf{b}}_j$ are encoded into the following vectors: $\text{enc}(\tilde{\mathbf{a}}_j) = \left(\sum_{j=0}^{\kappa-1} a_{j\frac{\phi(m)}{\kappa}+1} r_j^j, \sum_{j=0}^{\kappa-1} a_{j\frac{\phi(m)}{\kappa}+2} r_j^j, \ldots, \sum_{j=0}^{\kappa-1} a_{(j+1)\frac{\phi(m)}{\kappa}} r_j^j \right)$. Similar for $\overline{\mathbf{b}}_i$ we get the following evaluation in r_j: $\overline{\mathbf{b}}_i(r_j) = \sum_{j=0}^{\kappa-1} b_{j\frac{\phi(m)}{\kappa}+i} r_j^{-j}$, with coefficient vector: $\text{enc}(\tilde{\mathbf{b}}_j) = \left(\sum_{j=0}^{\kappa-1} b_{j\frac{\phi(m)}{\kappa}+1} r_j^{-j}, \ldots, \sum_{j=0}^{\kappa-1} b_{(j+1)\frac{\phi(m)}{\kappa}} r_j^{-j} \right)$.

Then for all $j \in [0, \kappa - 1]$ the product $\tilde{\mathbf{a}}_j \cdot \tilde{\mathbf{b}}_j$ is equal to the inner product of its encoding vectors:

$$\sum_{j=0}^{\kappa-1} a_{j\frac{\phi(m)}{\kappa}+1} r_j^j \sum_{j=0}^{\kappa-1} b_{j\frac{\phi(m)}{\kappa}+1} r_j^{-j} + \ldots + \sum_{j=0}^{\kappa-1} a_{j\frac{\phi(m)}{\kappa}+1} r_j^j \sum_{j=0}^{\kappa-1} b_{(j+1)\frac{\phi(m)}{\kappa}} r_j^{-j}$$

$$+ \ldots + \sum_{j=0}^{\kappa-1} a_{(j+1)\frac{\phi(m)}{\kappa}} r_j^j \sum_{j=0}^{\kappa-1} b_{j\frac{\phi(m)}{\kappa}+1} r_j^{-j} + \ldots + \sum_{j=0}^{\kappa-1} a_{(j+1)\frac{\phi(m)}{\kappa}} r_j^j \sum_{j=0}^{\kappa-1} b_{(j+1)\frac{\phi(m)}{\kappa}} r_j^{-j}$$

The zero coefficient of this product is computed by the following formula

$$ZC(\tilde{\mathbf{a}}_j \cdot \tilde{\mathbf{b}}_j) = \sum_{j=0}^{\kappa-1} a_{j\frac{\phi(m)}{\kappa}+1} r_j^j \sum_{j=0}^{\kappa-1} b_{j\frac{\phi(m)}{\kappa}+1} r_j^{-j} + \ldots + \sum_{j=0}^{\kappa-1} a_{(j+1)\frac{\phi(m)}{\kappa}} r_j^j \sum_{j=0}^{\kappa-1} b_{(j+1)\frac{\phi(m)}{\kappa}} r_j^{-j}$$

After extending the multiplication of the above equation, we obtain

$$\sum_{j=0}^{\kappa-1} a_{j\frac{\phi(m)}{\kappa}+1} b_{j\frac{\phi(m)}{\kappa}+1} + \sum_{j=0}^{\kappa-1} a_{j\frac{\phi(m)}{\kappa}+1} r_j^j \sum_{\chi \neq j}^{\kappa-1} b_{\chi\frac{\phi(m)}{\kappa}+1} r_\chi^{-\chi} + \sum_{j=0}^{\kappa-1} a_{j\frac{\phi(m)}{\kappa}+2} b_{j\frac{\phi(m)}{\kappa}+2}$$

$$+ \sum_{j=0}^{\kappa-1} a_{j\frac{\phi(m)}{\kappa}+2} r_j^j \sum_{\chi \neq j}^{\kappa-1} b_{\chi\frac{\phi(m)}{\kappa}+2} r_\chi^{-\chi} + \ldots + \sum_{j=0}^{\kappa-1} a_{(j+1)\frac{\phi(m)}{\kappa}} r_j^j \sum_{\chi \neq j}^{\kappa-1} b_{(\chi+1)\frac{\phi(m)}{\kappa}} r_\chi^{-\chi}$$

For $i \in [1, \phi(m)/\kappa - 1]$ we get the equality $ZC(\mathbf{a} \cdot \mathbf{b}) = \sum_{i=1}^{\phi(m)/\kappa-1} ZC(\tilde{\mathbf{a}}_i \cdot \tilde{\mathbf{b}}_i) = \langle \text{Coef}(\mathbf{a}), \text{Coef}(\mathbf{b}) \rangle$.

4.5   Zero-Knowledge Inner Product Argument over Splitting Rings

After introducing the building blocks and techniques for our main protocol, we move to our second main contribution of our paper by presenting a zero-knowledge inner product argument which is defined over splitting rings. The relation we want to prove with its corresponding relaxed version are given as follows:

$$R_{\beta_{oip}} = \left\{ (\tilde{\mathbf{a}}, \tilde{\mathbf{b}}, \tilde{\mathbf{r}}_a, \tilde{\mathbf{r}}_b), (\mathbb{A}, \mathbb{B}, z) : \tilde{\mathbf{a}} \cdot \tilde{\mathbf{b}} = \sum_{i=1}^{\kappa} \tilde{\mathbf{a}}_i \tilde{\mathbf{b}}_i' = z, \|\tilde{\mathbf{r}}_a\| \le \beta_{oip}, \|\tilde{\mathbf{r}}_b\| \le \beta_{oip} \right\}$$

$$R'_{\beta'_{oip}} = \left\{ (\tilde{\mathbf{a}}', \tilde{\mathbf{b}}', \tilde{\mathbf{r}}_a', \hat{\mathbf{r}}_b', d), (\mathbb{A}_\nu, \mathbb{B}, z_\nu) : \hat{\mathbf{a}}' \cdot \tilde{\mathbf{b}}' = d^{\frac{n}{\kappa \kappa_1}} \sum_{i=1}^{\kappa} \mathbf{a}_i' \mathbf{b}_i' = z', \|\tilde{\mathbf{r}}_a\| \le \beta'_{oip}, \right.$$
$$\left. \|\tilde{\mathbf{r}}_b'\| \le \beta'_{oip} \right\}.$$

The protocol consists of the following steps:

Common Input: The public parameters are given as follows: $(\tilde{\mathbf{A}}_j)_{j_1}, (\tilde{\mathbf{C}}_j)_{j_1} \in (\mathcal{R}_{q,j})_{j_1}^{1 \times m}, (\tilde{\mathbf{B}}_j)_{j_1}, (\tilde{\mathbf{D}}_j)_{j_1} \in (\mathcal{R}_{q,j})_{j_1}$. We set $\tilde{\mathbf{A}} = (\tilde{\mathbf{A}}_0, \ldots, \tilde{\mathbf{A}}_{\kappa-1})$, $\tilde{\mathbf{B}} = (\tilde{\mathbf{B}}_0, \ldots, \tilde{\mathbf{B}}_{\kappa-1})$, $\tilde{\mathbf{C}} = (\tilde{\mathbf{C}}_0, \ldots, \tilde{\mathbf{C}}_{\kappa-1})$, $\tilde{\mathbf{D}} = (\tilde{\mathbf{D}}_0, \ldots, \tilde{\mathbf{D}}_{\kappa-1})$, where for all $j \in [0, \kappa - 1]$ holds:

$$\tilde{\mathbf{A}}_j \cong ((\tilde{\mathbf{A}}_j)_0, \ldots, (\tilde{\mathbf{A}}_j)_{\kappa_1-1}), \quad \tilde{\mathbf{B}}_j \cong ((\tilde{\mathbf{B}}_j)_0, \ldots, (\tilde{\mathbf{B}}_j)_{\kappa_1-1})$$
$$\tilde{\mathbf{C}}_j \cong ((\tilde{\mathbf{C}}_j)_0, \ldots, (\tilde{\mathbf{C}}_j)_{\kappa_1-1}), \quad \tilde{\mathbf{D}}_j \cong ((\tilde{\mathbf{D}}_j)_0, \ldots, (\tilde{\mathbf{D}}_j)_{\kappa_1-1}).$$

Commitments to $\tilde{\mathbf{a}}$ and $\tilde{\mathbf{b}}$ given as $\tilde{\mathbf{A}}, \tilde{\mathbf{B}}$, respectively. Let $n = \kappa_\mu \cdot \kappa_{\mu-1} \cdot \ldots \cdot \kappa_1$ with the factors of n being defined as $\kappa_\mu = \kappa, \kappa_{\mu-1} = \kappa_1, \ldots, \kappa_\mu$ and $z = z_0 = \sum_{i=0}^{\kappa-1} \tilde{\mathbf{a}}_i \tilde{\mathbf{b}}_i$, where the upper index indicates the rounds of splitting the polynomial ring.

Prover's Witness: $\tilde{\mathbf{a}}, \tilde{\mathbf{b}} \in \mathcal{R}_q$, with the respective polynomial representation $\sum_{i=0}^{n-1} a_i X^i, \sum_{i=0}^{n-1} b_i X^{-i}$. Next, we define $\tilde{\mathbf{a}}_j, \tilde{\mathbf{b}}_j$ for $0 \le j < \kappa - 1$ as:

$$\tilde{\mathbf{a}}_j = \sum_{i=0}^{\kappa-1} a_{j\phi(m)/\kappa+i} X^i, \quad \tilde{\mathbf{b}}_j = \sum_{i=0}^{\kappa-1} b_{j\phi(m)/\kappa+i} X^{-i}$$

with coefficients:

$$\mathtt{Coef}(\tilde{\mathbf{a}}_j) = \left(a_{j\phi(m)/\kappa}, \ldots, a_{(j+1)\phi(m)/\kappa-1} \right),$$
$$\mathtt{Coef}(\tilde{\mathbf{b}}_j) = \left(b_{j\phi(m)/\kappa}, b_{j\phi(m)/\kappa+1}, \ldots, b_{(j+1)\phi(m)/\kappa-1} \right)$$

are coefficients of $\tilde{\mathbf{a}}_j, \tilde{\mathbf{b}}_j$, respectively.

For the secrets $\tilde{\mathbf{a}}$ and $\tilde{\mathbf{b}}$ we apply the splitting technique over the same rings $\mathcal{R}_{q,j} = \mathbb{Z}_q[X]/(X^{\phi(m)/\kappa} - r_j)$ for all $j \in [0, \kappa - 1]$ as introduced above. First we set: $\tilde{\mathbf{a}} \cong (\tilde{\mathbf{a}}_0, \ldots, \tilde{\mathbf{a}}_{\kappa-1}), \tilde{\mathbf{b}} \cong (\tilde{\mathbf{b}}_0, \ldots, \tilde{\mathbf{b}}_{\kappa-1}) \in (\mathcal{R}_{q,0} \times \cdots \times \mathcal{R}_{q,\kappa-1})$, with the corresponding randomnesses $\tilde{\mathbf{r}}_a, \tilde{\mathbf{r}}_b \in \mathcal{R}_q^{m \times 1}$ which are split up over the ring $\mathcal{R}_q$ such that holds: $\tilde{\mathbf{r}}_{\tilde{a}} \cong (\tilde{\mathbf{r}}_{\tilde{a},1}, \ldots, \tilde{\mathbf{r}}_{\tilde{a},\kappa-1})$ and $\tilde{\mathbf{r}}_{\tilde{b}} \cong (\tilde{\mathbf{r}}_{\tilde{b},1}, \ldots, \tilde{\mathbf{r}}_{\tilde{b},\kappa-1}) \in (\mathcal{R}_{q,0}^m, \ldots, \mathcal{R}_{q,\kappa-1}^m)$. For each component of $\tilde{\mathbf{a}}_j, \tilde{\mathbf{r}}_{\tilde{a},j}, \tilde{\mathbf{b}}_j, \tilde{\mathbf{r}}_{\tilde{b},j}$ the following isomorphism holds:

$$\tilde{\mathbf{a}}_j \cong ((\tilde{\mathbf{a}}_j)_0, \ldots, (\tilde{\mathbf{a}}_j)_{\kappa_1-1}), \quad \tilde{\mathbf{b}}_j \cong ((\tilde{\mathbf{b}}_j)_0, \ldots, (\tilde{\mathbf{b}}_j)_{\kappa_1-1}).$$
$$\tilde{\mathbf{r}}_{\tilde{a},j} \cong ((\tilde{\mathbf{r}}_{\tilde{a},1})_0, \ldots, (\tilde{\mathbf{r}}_{\tilde{a},1})_{\kappa_1-1}), \quad \tilde{\mathbf{r}}_{\tilde{b},j} \cong ((\tilde{\mathbf{r}}_{\tilde{b},1})_0, \ldots, (\tilde{\mathbf{r}}_{\tilde{b},1})_{\kappa_1-1}).$$

Let

$$(\tilde{\mathbf{g}}_j)_{j_1} = (\tilde{\mathbf{A}}_j)_{j_1}(\tilde{\mathbf{r}}_{\tilde{a},j})_{j_1} + (\tilde{\mathbf{B}}_j)_{j_1}(\tilde{\mathbf{a}}_j)_{j_1}$$
$$(\tilde{\mathbf{h}}_j)_{j_1} = (\tilde{\mathbf{C}}_j)_{j_1}(\tilde{\mathbf{r}}_{\tilde{b},j})_{j_1} + (\tilde{\mathbf{D}}_j)_{j_1}(\tilde{\mathbf{b}}_j)_{j_1}.$$

The description of commitment $\tilde{\mathbb{B}}$ is skipped as it is similar to that of $\tilde{\mathbb{A}}$.

$$\tilde{\mathbb{A}} = \mathrm{Com}_{\tilde{\mathbf{A}},\tilde{\mathbf{B}}}(\tilde{\mathbf{a}}, \mathbf{r}_{\tilde{a}}) = \sum_{j=0}^{\kappa-1}\sum_{j_1=0}^{\kappa_1-1}\left((\tilde{\mathbf{A}}_j)_{j_1}\cdot(\tilde{\mathbf{r}}_{\tilde{a},j})_{j_1} + (\tilde{\mathbf{B}}_j)_{j_1}(\tilde{\mathbf{a}}_j)_{j_1}\right)$$

$$\cong \mathrm{CRT}_{r_0}^{r_{\kappa}-1}\left(\mathrm{CRT}_{r_0'}^{r_{\kappa_1}'-1}\left((\tilde{\mathbf{g}}_j)_0,\ldots,(\tilde{\mathbf{g}}_j)_{\kappa_1-1}\right)\right) = \sum_{j=0}^{\kappa-1}\psi_{j\mapsto j+1}\left(\sum_{j_1=0}^{\kappa_1-1}\psi_{j_1\mapsto j_1+1}\left((\tilde{\mathbf{g}}_j)_{j_1}\right)\right),$$

$$ZC(\mathbf{a}\cdot\mathbf{b}) = \sum_{j=0}^{\kappa-1}\sum_{j_1=0}^{\kappa_1-1}ZC\left((\tilde{\mathbf{a}}_j)_{j_1}\cdot(\tilde{\mathbf{b}}_j)_{j_1}\right) = \langle\mathrm{Coef}(\mathbf{a}),\mathrm{Coef}(\mathbf{b})\rangle$$

Argument: if $\mu = 1$

- Prover sends $(a_1,\ldots a_{\phi(m)/\kappa-1}, b_1,\ldots, b_{\phi(m)/\kappa-1})$ to the verifier.
- Verifier checks: $\tilde{\mathbb{A}} = \sum_{i=1}^{j_1}(A_i r_{a,i} + B_i a_i)$, $\tilde{\mathbb{B}} = \sum_{i=1}^{j_1}(C_i r_{b,i} + D_i b_i)$ and $\sum_{i=1}^{j_1}a_i b_i = z$.

Recursive Step: if $\mu \neq 1$: the prover sends $\tilde{\mathbb{A}}_{1-s},\tilde{\mathbb{B}}_{1-s},z_{1-s},\ldots,\tilde{\mathbb{A}}_{s-1},\tilde{\mathbb{B}}_{s-1},$ z_{s-1} to the verifier, where it holds $[(\cdot)]_{i+k} = (\cdot) \bmod (X^{\phi(m)/\kappa} - r_{i+k})$ and $\psi_{i\mapsto i+k}(\tilde{\mathbf{A}}_i(r_{i+k}))$ is a fixed root of $f_i = (X^{\phi(m)/\kappa} - r_i)$ in the polynomial f_{i+k} $= (X^{\phi(m)/\kappa} - r_{i+k})$. Let $\hat{\mathbf{g}}_{i,i+k} = \sum_{j_1=0}^{\kappa_1-1}\psi_{j_1\mapsto j_1+1}\left((\tilde{\mathbf{A}}_i)_{j_1}(\tilde{\mathbf{r}}_{a,i+k})_{j_1} + (\tilde{\mathbf{B}}_i)_{j_1}\right.$ $\left.(\tilde{\mathbf{a}}_{i+k})_{j_1}\right)$, and $\hat{\mathbf{h}}_{i,i+k} = \sum_{j_1=0}^{\kappa_1-1}\psi_{j_1\mapsto j_1+1}\left((\tilde{\mathbf{C}}_i)_{j_1}(\tilde{\mathbf{r}}_{b,i+k})_{j_1} + (\tilde{\mathbf{D}}_i)_{j_1}(\tilde{\mathbf{b}}_{i+k})_{j_1}\right)$ for all $k = 1 - \kappa,\ldots,\kappa - 1$. Vectors $\hat{\mathbf{g}}_{i,i+k}$ and $\hat{\mathbf{h}}_{i,i+k}$ can be represented using the following isomorphism $\hat{\mathbf{g}}_{i,i+k} \cong \mathrm{CRT}_{r_0}^{r_{\kappa_1}-1}\left(\{(\tilde{\mathbf{g}}_{i,i+k})_{j_1}\}_{j_1\in[0,\kappa_1-1]}\right)$ $= \sum_{j_1=0}^{\kappa_1-1}\psi_{j_1\mapsto j_1+1}(\tilde{\mathbf{g}}_{i,i+k})_{j_1}$, where for all $j_1 \in [0,\kappa_1 - 1]$ holds $(\tilde{\mathbf{g}}_{i,i+k})_{j_1} = (\tilde{\mathbf{A}}_i)_{j_1}(\tilde{\mathbf{r}}_{a,i+k})_{j_1} + (\tilde{\mathbf{B}}_i)_{j_1}(\tilde{\mathbf{a}}_{i+k})_{j_1}$ and $\hat{\mathbf{h}}_{i,i+k} \cong \mathrm{CRT}_{r_0}^{r_{\kappa_1}-1}\left(\{(\tilde{\mathbf{h}}_{i,i+k})_{j_1}\}_{j_1\in[0,\kappa_1-1]}\right)$ $= \sum_{j_1=0}^{\kappa_1-1}\psi_{j_1\mapsto j_1+1}(\tilde{\mathbf{h}}_{i,i+k})_{j_1}$ with $(\tilde{\mathbf{h}}_{i,i+k})_{j_1} = (\tilde{\mathbf{C}}_i)_{j_1}(\tilde{\mathbf{r}}_{b,i+k})_{j_1} + (\tilde{\mathbf{D}}_i)_{j_1}(\tilde{\mathbf{b}}_{i+k})_{j_1}$. Then, diagonal commitments $\tilde{\mathbb{A}}_k$ are given as follows:

$$\tilde{\mathbb{A}}_k = \sum_{i=\max(1,1-k)}^{\min(\kappa,\kappa-k)}\sum_{j_1=0}^{\kappa_1-1}\left((\tilde{\mathbf{A}}_i)_{j_1}(\tilde{\mathbf{r}}_{a,i+k})_{j_1} + (\tilde{\mathbf{B}}_i)_{j_1}(\tilde{\mathbf{a}}_{i+k})_{j_1}\right)$$

$$\cong \mathrm{CRT}_{r_{\max(1,1-k)}}^{r_{\min(\kappa,\kappa-k)}}\left(\hat{\mathbf{g}}_{\max(1,1-k)},\ldots,\hat{\mathbf{g}}_{\min(\kappa,\kappa-k)}\right) = \sum_{i=\max(1,1-k)}^{\min(\kappa,\kappa-k)}\psi_{i\mapsto i+k}(\hat{\mathbf{g}}_{i,i+k})$$

and similarly for $\tilde{\mathbb{B}}_k$. For the zero-coefficient we obtain the following equation:

$$
\begin{aligned}
z_k &= \sum_{i=\max(1,1-k)}^{\min(\kappa,\kappa-k)} \mathrm{CRT}_{i,i+k}\Big(\sum_{j_1=0}^{\kappa_1-1} (\tilde{\mathbf{a}}_i)_{j_1} \cdot (\tilde{\mathbf{b}}_{i+k})_{j_1}\Big) \\
&= \sum_{i=\max(1,1-k)}^{\min(\kappa,\kappa-k)} \mathrm{CRT}\Big[\big(\psi_{i\mapsto i+k}(\tilde{\mathbf{a}}_i)\cdot\tilde{\mathbf{b}}_{i+k}\big)\Big]_{i+k} \\
&= \sum_{i=\max(1,1-k)}^{\min(\kappa,\kappa-k)} \mathrm{Coef}(\psi_{i\mapsto i+k}(\tilde{\mathbf{a}}_i))\cdot\mathrm{Coef}(\tilde{\mathbf{b}}_{i+k})
\end{aligned}
$$

Challenge: The verifier sends a monomial challenge $x \leftarrow \mathcal{CH}$ to the prover.

Rejection Sampling: The prover aborts with probability $1 - \mathsf{p}_{oip}$, where

$$
\mathsf{p}_{oip} := \frac{\mathfrak{D}_{\sigma_{oip}}^{m\kappa_1}(\tilde{\mathbf{r}}'_a)}{\mathfrak{D}_{\{x^j\cdot\mathbf{r}'_{a,j}\}_{j\in[1,\kappa]},\sigma_{oip}}^{m\kappa_1}(\tilde{\mathbf{r}}'_a)}.
$$

Verification: If $\mu \neq 1$: The prover and the verifier compute a reduced commitment which has the following form: $\tilde{\mathbf{A}}', \tilde{\mathbf{B}}', \tilde{\mathbf{C}}', \tilde{\mathbf{D}}', \tilde{\mathbb{A}}, \tilde{\mathbb{B}}, z', \kappa_{\mu-1}, \ldots, \kappa_1$, s.t. the following verification equation holds for a given isomorphism $\psi_{j\mapsto j_1} : \mathcal{R}_{q,j} \to (\mathcal{R}_{q,j})_{j_1}$, $f_j(r_j) \mapsto f_j(\psi_{j\mapsto j_1}(r_{j_1}))$:

$$
\begin{aligned}
\tilde{\mathbf{A}}' &= \sum_{j=0}^{\kappa-1}\sum_{j_1=0}^{\kappa_1-1} (\tilde{\mathbf{A}}_j)_{j_1} x^{-i} \cong \mathrm{CRT}_{r_0}^{r_{\kappa-1}}\Big(\tilde{\mathbf{A}}_0,\tilde{\mathbf{A}}_1,\ldots,\tilde{\mathbf{A}}_{\kappa-1}\Big)\circ\Big(1,x^{-1},\ldots,x^{1-\kappa}\Big)^{tr} \\
&= \sum_{j=0}^{\kappa-1} \psi_{j\mapsto j+1}\Big(\sum_{j_1=0}^{\kappa_1-1}\psi_{j_1\mapsto j_1+1}((\tilde{\mathbf{A}}_j)_{j_1})\Big)x^{-j} = \sum_{j=0}^{\kappa-1}\mathrm{Coef}(\psi(\tilde{\mathbf{A}}_j))x^{-j}
\end{aligned}
$$

The same equations hold for $\tilde{\mathbf{B}}', \tilde{\mathbf{C}}', \tilde{\mathbf{D}}'$ which we skip here due to the page limitation. The coefficients $\tilde{\mathbf{A}}_j$ of the above equation satisfy the following isomorphism and we note that the same equation holds for $\tilde{\mathbf{B}}_j, \tilde{\mathbf{C}}_j, \tilde{\mathbf{D}}_j$ for all $j \in [0, \kappa - 1]$:

$$
\tilde{\mathbf{A}}_j \cong \mathrm{CRT}_{r_0}^{r_{\kappa_1-1}}\big((\tilde{\mathbf{A}}_j)_0,\ldots,(\tilde{\mathbf{A}}_j)_{\kappa_1-1}\big) = \sum_{j_1=0}^{\kappa_1-1}\psi_{j_1\mapsto j_1+1}((\tilde{\mathbf{A}}_j)_{j_1})
$$

The corresponding randomnesses of the commitment is $\tilde{\mathbf{r}}_{a,j}$ and is split into chunks over the same rings $\mathcal{R}_{q,j}$, for all $j \in [0, \kappa - 1]$, such that the following isomorphism holds:

$$
\tilde{\mathbf{r}}_{a,j} \cong \mathrm{CRT}_{r_0}^{r_{\kappa_1-1}}\big((\tilde{\mathbf{r}}_{a,j})_0,\ldots,(\tilde{\mathbf{r}}_{a,j})_{\kappa_1-1}\big) = \sum_{j_1=0}^{\kappa_1-1}\psi_{j_1\mapsto j_1+1}((\tilde{\mathbf{r}}_{a,j})_{j_1}).
$$

Also here we note that the same isomorphism holds for the randomness $\tilde{\mathbf{r}}_{b,j}$. From this isomorphism follows the next representation of the compressed randomnesses

$\tilde{\mathbf{r}}'_a$ and $\tilde{\mathbf{r}}'_b$. Due to the similarity in their representation we provide only the full computation of $\tilde{\mathbf{r}}'_a$:

$$
\tilde{\mathbf{r}}'_a = \sum_{j=0}^{\kappa-1} \sum_{j_1=0}^{\kappa_1-1} (\tilde{\mathbf{r}}_{\tilde{a},j})_{j_1} x^j = \mathrm{CRT}_{r0}^{r_{\kappa-1}} \left(\tilde{\mathbf{r}}_{\tilde{a},0}, \tilde{\mathbf{r}}_{\tilde{a},1}, \dots, \tilde{\mathbf{r}}_{\tilde{a},\kappa-1} \right) \circ \left(1, x^1, \dots, x^{\kappa-1} \right)^{tr}
$$

$$
= \sum_{j=0}^{\kappa-1} \psi_{j \mapsto j+1} \left(\sum_{j_1=0}^{\kappa_1-1} \psi_{j_1 \mapsto j_1+1} \left(\tilde{\mathbf{r}}_{a,j})_{j_1} \right) \right) x^j = \sum_{j=0}^{\kappa-1} \mathrm{Coef}(\psi(\tilde{\mathbf{r}}_{a,j})) x^j
$$

Next, we define a commitment which is a sum of the diagonal commitments of matrices $\tilde{\mathfrak{C}}_{a,\kappa}$ and $\tilde{\mathfrak{C}}_{b,\kappa}$ defined above. We show only the equation of $\tilde{\mathbb{A}}'$ and note that the equation of $\tilde{\mathbb{B}}'$ is computed similarly using the diagonal commitments $\tilde{\mathbb{B}}_k$ for all $k \in [1-\kappa, \kappa-1]$.

$$
\tilde{\mathbb{A}}' = \sum_{k=1-\kappa}^{\kappa-1} \tilde{\mathbb{A}}_k x^k = \sum_{k=1-\kappa}^{\kappa-1} \sum_{i=\max(1,1-k)}^{\min(\kappa,\kappa-k)} \sum_{j_1=0}^{\kappa_1-1} \left((\tilde{\mathbf{A}}_i)_{j_1} (\tilde{\mathbf{r}}_{a,i+k})_{j_1} + (\tilde{\mathbf{B}}_i)_{j_1} (\tilde{\mathbf{a}}_{i+k})_{j_1} \right)
$$

$$
\cong \mathrm{CRT}_{r1-k}^{r_{k-1}} \left(\mathrm{CRT}_{r\max(1,1-k)}^{r\min(\kappa,\kappa-k)} \left(\hat{\mathbf{g}}_{\max(1,1-k)}, \dots, \hat{\mathbf{g}}_{\min(\kappa,\kappa-k)} \right) \right)
$$

$$
= \sum_{k=1-\kappa}^{\kappa-1} \psi_{k \mapsto k+1} \left(\sum_{i=\max(1,1-k)}^{\min(\kappa,\kappa-k)} \psi_{i \mapsto i+k}(\hat{\mathbf{g}}_{i,i+k}) \right) = \sum_{k=1-k}^{k-1} \mathrm{Coef}(\psi(\hat{\mathbf{g}}_{i+k})) \quad (28)
$$

where each z_k is given as follows: $z_k = \sum_{i=\max(1,1-k)}^{\min(\kappa,\kappa-k)} \mathrm{Coef}(\psi(\tilde{\mathbf{a}}_i)) \cdot \mathrm{Coef}(\psi(\tilde{\mathbf{b}}_{i+k}))$
The prover computes a new witness

$$
\tilde{\mathbf{a}}' = \sum_{j=0}^{\kappa-1} \sum_{j_1=0}^{\kappa_1-1} (\tilde{\mathbf{a}}_j)_{j_1} x^j = \mathrm{CRT}_{r0}^{r_{\kappa-1}} (\tilde{\mathbf{a}}_0, \tilde{\mathbf{a}}_1, \dots, \tilde{\mathbf{a}}_{\kappa-1}) \circ (1, x, \dots, x^{\kappa-1})^{tr}
$$

$$
= \sum_{j=0}^{\kappa-1} \psi_{j \mapsto j+1} \left(\sum_{j_1=0}^{\kappa_1-1} \psi_{j_1 \mapsto j_1+1} (\tilde{\mathbf{a}}_j)_{j_1} \right) x^j = \sum_{j=0}^{\kappa-1} \mathrm{Coef}(\psi(\tilde{\mathbf{a}}_j)) x^j
$$

and $\tilde{\mathbf{b}}'$ computed similarly. The following condition is satisfied: $ZC(\tilde{\mathbf{a}}' \cdot \tilde{\mathbf{b}}') = \sum_{j=0}^{\kappa-1} \tilde{\mathbf{a}}_j, \tilde{\mathbf{b}}_j$. This equation is equivalent to the following equality:

$$
ZC[(\sum_{j=0}^{\kappa-1} \mathrm{Coef}(\tilde{\mathbf{a}}') x^i) \cdot (\sum_{j=0}^{\kappa-1} \mathrm{Coef}(\tilde{\mathbf{b}}') x^i)] = \sum_{j=0}^{\kappa-1} \langle \mathrm{Coef}(\tilde{\mathbf{a}}_j), \mathrm{Coef}(\tilde{\mathbf{b}}_j) \rangle
$$

In the next step we encode vector $\mathrm{Coef}(\tilde{\mathbf{a}}') \in \mathbb{Z}_q^{\phi(m)/\kappa}$ into a polynomial of degree $\phi(m)/\kappa - 1$ by embedding each vector coordinate into the coefficients of a polynomial in $\mathcal{R}_q^{(1)} = \mathbb{Z}_q[X]/(X^{\phi(m)/\kappa} + 1)$. Then repeat the protocol by splitting $\mathcal{R}_q^{(1)}$ into $\kappa^{(1)} = \kappa_{\mu-1}$ chunks using CRT technique as above.

Theorem 5. *Assuming that our commitment scheme is computationally hiding and β_{oip}-binding with $\beta_{oip} < \min\{q, 2^{2\sqrt{n \log q \log \delta}}\}$, where δ denotes a root*

Hermite factor, then our inner product protocol with the rejection sampling probability p_{oip} *is a complete,* $(2\kappa - 1)$*-special sound and special honest verifier zero-knowledge argument of knowledge.*

Proof. We prove the following three security properties discussed in Definition 3.

Completeness: Similar to the security proof in Sect. 4 we need to show that the verification Eq. (28), and the corresponding equation for $\tilde{\mathbb{B}}'$ (skipped due to similarity reasons) are correct. We show this only for the first verification equation of $\tilde{\mathbb{A}}'$. We take $\tilde{\mathbb{A}}_k$ defined in the recursive step of the protocol and insert it into the equation:

$$\tilde{\mathbb{A}}' = \sum_{k=1-\kappa}^{\kappa-1} \tilde{\mathbb{A}}_k x^k = \sum_{k=1-\kappa}^{\kappa-1} \sum_{i=\max(1,1-k)}^{\min(\kappa,\kappa-k)} \sum_{j_1=0}^{\kappa_1-1} \left((\tilde{\mathbf{A}}_i)_{j_1} (\tilde{\mathbf{r}}_{a,i+k})_{j_1} + (\tilde{\mathbf{B}}_i)_{j_1} (\tilde{\mathbf{a}}_{i+k})_{j_1} \right)$$

$$\cong \mathrm{CRT}_{r_{1-k}}^{r_{k-1}} \left(\mathrm{CRT}_{r_{\max(1,1-k)}}^{r_{\min(\kappa,\kappa-k)}} \left(\hat{\mathbf{g}}_{\max(1,1-k)}, \cdots, \hat{\mathbf{g}}_{\min(\kappa,\kappa-k)} \right) \right)$$

$$= \sum_{k=1-\kappa}^{\kappa-1} \psi_{k \mapsto k+1} \left(\sum_{i=\max(1,1-k)}^{\min(\kappa,\kappa-k)} \psi_{i \mapsto i+k}(\hat{\mathbf{g}}_{i,i+k}) \right) = \sum_{k=1-k}^{k-1} \mathrm{Coef}(\hat{\psi}(\mathbf{g}_{i+k}))$$

We compare it with the following equation of $\tilde{\mathbb{A}}'$ which is a commitment on $\tilde{\mathbf{a}}$ with randomness $\tilde{\mathbf{r}}_a$ using public parameters $\tilde{\mathbf{A}}', \tilde{\mathbf{B}}'$:

$$\tilde{\mathbb{A}}' = \mathrm{Com}_{\tilde{\mathbf{A}}', \tilde{\mathbf{B}}'}(\tilde{\mathbf{a}}, \tilde{\mathbf{r}}_a) = \sum_{j=0}^{\kappa-1} \sum_{j_1=0}^{\kappa_1-1} \left((\tilde{\mathbf{A}}_j)_{j_1} \cdot (\tilde{\mathbf{r}}_{a,j})_{j_1} + (\tilde{\mathbf{B}}_j)_{j_1} (\tilde{\mathbf{a}}_j)_{j_1} \right)$$

$$\cong \mathrm{CRT}_{r_0}^{r_{\kappa-1}} \left(\mathrm{CRT}_{r_0}^{r'_{\kappa_1-1}} \left((\tilde{\mathbf{g}}_j)_0, \ldots, (\tilde{\mathbf{g}}_j)_{\kappa_1-1} \right) \right) = \sum_{j=0}^{\kappa-1} \psi_{j \mapsto j+1} \left(\sum_{j_1=0}^{\kappa_1-1} \psi_{j_1 \mapsto j_1+1}((\tilde{\mathbf{g}}_j)_{j_1}) \right)$$

By carefully expanding the above sums we can see that the verification equation $\tilde{\mathbb{A}}' = \sum_{j=0}^{\kappa-1} \sum_{j_1=0}^{\kappa_1-1} (\tilde{\mathbf{A}}_j)_{j_1} x^{-j}$ is correct. We also have to show the shortness of the new randomness $\tilde{\mathbf{r}}'_a$ and $\tilde{\mathbf{r}}'_b$. The Euclidean norm of this randomness is $\|\tilde{\mathbf{r}}'_a\| = \| \sum_{j=0}^{\kappa-1} \sum_{j_1=0}^{\kappa_1-1} (\tilde{\mathbf{r}}_{\tilde{a},j})_{j_1} x^j \| \leq \sqrt{n} \kappa \kappa_1 \beta_{oip}$.

$(2\kappa - 1)$**-Special Soundness:** We prove soundness using inductive process. When $\mu = 1$ the prover reveals a witness which passes the verification phase. The inductive process guarantees that in the recursive step, if a M-SIS relation holds for $\tilde{\mathbf{A}}_j, \tilde{\mathbf{B}}_j$ for $j \in [0, \kappa-1]$, then there is a non-trivial solution to the M-SIS relation for $\tilde{\mathbf{A}}', \tilde{\mathbf{B}}'$. The same argument is used for the public parameters $\tilde{\mathbf{C}}_j, \tilde{\mathbf{D}}_j$ for $j \in [1, \mu']$. From the inductive step follows that we can obtain the witness $\tilde{\mathbf{a}}', \tilde{\mathbf{b}}'$ which satisfy the equation $\tilde{\mathbb{A}}' = \sum_{j=0}^{\kappa-1} \psi_{j \mapsto j+1} \left(\sum_{j_1=0}^{\kappa_1-1} \psi_{j_1 \mapsto j_1+1}((\tilde{\mathbf{g}}_j)_{j_1}) \right) = \sum_{k=1-k}^{k-1} \mathrm{Coef}(\hat{\psi}(\mathbf{g}_{i+k}))$ as we showed above in the completeness proof The inner product of the reduced vectors $\tilde{\mathbf{a}}', \tilde{\mathbf{b}}'$ is given as $\tilde{\mathbf{a}}' \cdot \tilde{\mathbf{b}}' = \sum_{k=1-s}^{s-1} z_k x^{-k}$. We present the witness extraction only for $\tilde{\mathbf{a}}'$ and skip the extraction of $\tilde{\mathbf{b}}'$ due to the reasons of similarity of computations. Taking $2\kappa - 1$ challenges $x_1, \ldots, x_{2\kappa-1}$, we compute for all $\zeta \in [1, 2\kappa - 1]$:

$$\sum_{k=1-\kappa}^{\kappa-1} \tilde{\mathbb{A}}_k x_\zeta^k = \sum_{j=0}^{\kappa-1} \mathrm{Coef}(\tilde{\mathbf{A}}_j) x_\zeta^{-j} \sum_{j=0}^{\kappa-1} \mathrm{Coef}(\tilde{\mathbf{r}}_{\tilde{a},j}) x_\zeta^j + \sum_{j=0}^{\kappa-1} \mathrm{Coef}(\tilde{\mathbf{B}}_j) x_\zeta^{-j} \sum_{j=0}^{\kappa-1} \mathrm{Coef}(\tilde{\mathbf{a}}_j) x_\zeta^j$$

Knowing $\mathbf{a}'$, we can compute $\sum_{k=1-\kappa}^{\kappa-1} \tilde{\mathbb{A}}_k x^k - \tilde{\mathbf{B}}_x \cdot \tilde{\mathbf{a}}_x$, where $\tilde{\mathbf{B}}_x = \sum_{i=0}^{\kappa-1} \tilde{\mathbf{B}}_j x^{-j}$ and $\tilde{\mathbf{a}}_x = \sum_{i=0}^{\kappa-1} \tilde{\mathbf{a}}_j x^j$. For all challenges $x_1, \ldots, x_{2\kappa-1}$ it yields:

$$\sum_{k=1-\kappa}^{\kappa-1} \tilde{\mathbb{A}}_k x_1^k - \tilde{\mathbf{B}}_{x_1} \cdot \tilde{\mathbf{a}}'_{x_1} = \left(\sum_{i=0}^{\kappa-1} \tilde{\mathbf{A}}_j x_1^{-j} \right) \cdot \sum_{j=0}^{\kappa-1} \tilde{\mathbf{r}}_{a,j} x_1^j,$$

$$\vdots \qquad \vdots$$

$$\sum_{k=1-\kappa}^{\kappa-1} \tilde{\mathbb{A}}_k x_{2\kappa-1}^k - \tilde{\mathbf{B}}_{x_{2\kappa-1}} \cdot \tilde{\mathbf{a}}'_{x_{2\kappa-1}} = \left(\sum_{j=0}^{\kappa-1} \tilde{\mathbf{A}}_j x_{2\kappa-1}^{-j} \right) \cdot \sum_{j=0}^{\kappa-1} \tilde{\mathbf{r}}_{a,j} x_{2\kappa-1}^j$$

We define the left side of each j-th of the $2\kappa - 1$ equations above as $\tilde{\mathcal{A}}_j :=$ $\sum_{k=1-\kappa}^{\kappa-1} \tilde{\mathbb{A}}_k x_1^k - \tilde{\mathbf{B}}_{x_j} \cdot \tilde{\mathbf{a}}_{x_j}$ and rewrite the right side of the equations above as $\sum_{k=1-\kappa}^{\kappa-1} \tilde{\mathbf{R}}_k x^k$, where $\tilde{\mathbf{R}}_k = \sum_{j-i=k} \tilde{\mathbf{A}}_i \tilde{\mathbf{r}}_{a,j}$. We obtain the following system of equations $\tilde{\mathcal{A}} = (\tilde{\mathcal{A}}_1, \ldots, \tilde{\mathcal{A}}_{2\kappa-1})$:

$$\tilde{\mathcal{A}}_1 = \sum_{k=1-\kappa}^{\kappa-1} \tilde{\mathbf{R}}_k x_1^k = \tilde{\mathbf{R}}_{1-\kappa} x_1^{1-\kappa} + \ldots + \tilde{\mathbf{R}}_0 + \ldots + \tilde{\mathbf{R}}_{\kappa-1} x_1^{\kappa-1}$$

$$\vdots \qquad \vdots \qquad \vdots$$

$$\tilde{\mathcal{A}}_{2\kappa-1} = \sum_{k=1-\kappa}^{\kappa-1} \tilde{\mathbf{R}}_k x_{2\kappa-1}^k = \tilde{\mathbf{R}}_{1-\kappa} x_{2\kappa-1}^{1-\kappa} + \ldots + \tilde{\mathbf{R}}_0 + \ldots + \tilde{\mathbf{R}}_{\kappa-1} x_{2\kappa-1}^{\kappa-1}$$

Next, we define a generalised Vandermonde matrix as follows:

$$V_{2\kappa-1} = \begin{bmatrix} x_1^{1-\kappa} & x_1^{2-\kappa} & \cdots & x_1^{\kappa-2} & x_1^{\kappa-1} \\ \vdots & \vdots & \ddots & \vdots & \vdots \\ x_{2\kappa-1}^{1-\kappa} & x_{2\kappa-1}^{2-\kappa} & \cdots & x_{2\kappa-1}^{\kappa-2} & x_{2\kappa-1}^{\kappa-1} \end{bmatrix} \tag{29}$$

We can represent the equation system $\tilde{\mathcal{A}}$ using the above Vandermonde matrix $V_{2\kappa-1}$ and setting $\tilde{\mathbf{R}} = (\tilde{\mathbf{R}}_{1-\kappa}, \ldots, \tilde{\mathbf{R}}_0, \ldots, \tilde{\mathbf{R}}_{\kappa-1})$, $\tilde{\mathcal{A}} = (\tilde{\mathcal{A}}_1, \ldots, \tilde{\mathcal{A}}_{2\kappa-1})$ as follows: $\tilde{\mathcal{A}} = V_{2\kappa-1} \cdot \tilde{\mathbf{R}}$ The inverse of the Vandermonde matrix $V_{2\kappa-1}$ is small, therefore we can multiply $\tilde{\mathcal{A}}$ by $V_{2\kappa-1}^{-1}$ and obtain $\tilde{\mathbf{R}}$.

Special Honest Verifier Zero-Knowledge (SHVZK). To prove the zero-knowledge property of our protocol, we need to show how to simulate the protocol transcript. The public transcript in the real protocol is given by $\tilde{\mathbf{A}}', \tilde{\mathbf{B}}', \tilde{\mathbf{C}}', \tilde{\mathbf{D}}', \tilde{\mathbb{A}}$,

$\tilde{\mathbb{B}}, \tilde{\mathbb{A}}_k, \tilde{\mathbb{B}}_k, z_k$. In the simulated protocol the simulator chooses uniformly at random $\tilde{\mathbf{A}}', \tilde{\mathbf{C}}' \in (\mathcal{R}_{q,0}^{1 \times m}, \ldots, \mathcal{R}_{q,\kappa-1}^{1 \times m}), \tilde{\mathbf{B}}', \tilde{\mathbf{D}}' \in (\mathcal{R}_{q,0}, \ldots, \mathcal{R}_{q,\kappa-1}), \tilde{\mathbb{A}}, \tilde{\mathbb{B}} \in \mathcal{R}_{q,\kappa-1}^2,$
$\tilde{\mathbb{A}}_k, \tilde{\mathbb{B}}_k \in \mathcal{R}_{q,\kappa-1}, z_{k_\nu}, s_{\mu-1}, \ldots, s_1, x.$

Using the challenge x, the simulator computes $\tilde{\mathbf{A}}' = \sum_{j=0}^{\kappa-1} \sum_{j_1=0}^{\kappa_1-1} (\tilde{\mathbf{A}}_j)_{j_1} x^{-i},$ and $\tilde{\mathbf{B}}' = \sum_{j=0}^{\kappa-1} \sum_{j_1=0}^{\kappa_1-1} (\tilde{\mathbf{B}}_j)_{j_1} x^{-i}$ and similar for $\tilde{\mathbf{C}}', \tilde{\mathbf{D}}'$. Taking $\mathbb{A}_k, \mathbb{B}_k$ the simulator computes $\tilde{\mathbb{A}}' = \sum_{k=1-\kappa}^{\kappa-1} \tilde{\mathbb{A}}_k x^k, \tilde{\mathbb{B}}' = \sum_{k=1-\kappa}^{\kappa-1} \tilde{\mathbb{B}}_k x^{-k}, z_k$. which is indistinguishable from the real protocol output.   □

4.6   Efficiency Analysis and Parameters Setting

Similar to the first protocol the length of the non-zero vector in SIS is bounded by $\beta_{oip} \le \min\{q, 2^{2\sqrt{n \log q \log \delta}}\}$, with Hermite factor $\delta = 1.0045$ and $\lambda = 128$ being the security parameter. The standard deviation in the rejection sampling procedure is $\sigma_{oip} = \mathcal{B}_{oip}\sqrt{m\kappa_1}$. The security level is balanced for the LWE problem using LWE estimator [1]. The number of repetitions of the protocol is $128/8 = 16$ as in the first protocol. The main achievement of this protocol is the lower computational and communication cost. The prover computes $2\sum_{j=2}^{\mu}(2\kappa_j - 1) + 2\kappa_1$ diagonal commitments $\tilde{\mathbb{A}}_{k_\nu}, \tilde{\mathbb{B}}_{k_\nu}$ for $k \in [1 - \kappa, \kappa - 1]$ of length $n/(\kappa\kappa_1) \log q$, where $n = \kappa\kappa_1 \cdot \ldots \cdot \kappa_{\mu-1}$ for each commitment. We achieve a shorter commitment length due to the proved isomorphism we introduced in Sects. 4.2–4.4. The total proof length is $(2\sum_{j=2}^{\mu}(2\kappa_j - 1) + 2\kappa_1) \log(q) + \mathcal{B}_{ip}\kappa_1\sqrt{m\kappa_1}.$

In the following Table 2, we compare non-optimized and optimized inner product based on several parameters. We demonstrate that the proof size in the case of optimized inner product can be significantly improved in contrast to the non-optimized inner product argument.

Table 2. Non-optimized Inner Product (IP) vs. Optimized Inner Product (OIP) parameters

Parameter	Set 1		Set 2		Set 3		Set 4	
	IP	OIP	IP	OIP	IP	OIP	IP	OIP
Commitment modulus q	2^{24}		2^{28}		2^{32}		2^{36}	
Ring dimension n	2^7		2^8		2^9		2^{10}	
m	768		896		1024		1024	
s_ν/κ	2	2	2	4	2	6	2	8
σ_{ip}/σ_{oip}	$\approx 2^{12}$	$\approx 2^9$	$\approx 2^{13}$	$\approx 2^{10}$	$\approx 2^{14}$	$\approx 2^{10}$	$\approx 2^{17}$	$\approx 2^{12}$
$\mathcal{B}/\mathcal{B}_{oip}$	20		25		30		145	
Proof size	1.76 kB	387B	3.21 kB	488B	5.66 kB	595B	37.40 kB	1.97 kB

References

1. Albrecht, M.R., Player, R., Scott, S.: On the concrete hardness of learning with errors. J. Math. Cryptol. **9**(3), 169–203 (2015)
2. Arute, F., et al.: Quantum supremacy using a programmable superconducting processor. Nature **574**(7779), 505–510 (2019)

3. Attema, T., Cramer, R., Kohl, L.: A compressed σ-protocol theory for lattices. In: Malkin, T., Peikert, C. (eds.) CRYPTO 2021. LNCS, vol. 12826, pp. 549–579. Springer, Cham (2021). https://doi.org/10.1007/978-3-030-84245-1_19
4. Baum, C., Damgård, I., Larsen, K.G., Nielsen, M.: How to prove knowledge of small secrets. In: Robshaw, M., Katz, J. (eds.) CRYPTO 2016. LNCS, vol. 9816, pp. 478–498. Springer, Heidelberg (2016). https://doi.org/10.1007/978-3-662-53015-3_17
5. Baum, C., Damgård, I., Lyubashevsky, V., Oechsner, S., Peikert, C.: More efficient commitments from structured lattice assumptions. In: Catalano, D., De Prisco, R. (eds.) SCN 2018. LNCS, vol. 11035, pp. 368–385. Springer, Cham (2018). https://doi.org/10.1007/978-3-319-98113-0_20
6. Baum, C., Nof, A.: Concretely-efficient zero-knowledge arguments for arithmetic circuits and their application to lattice-based cryptography. In: Kiayias, A., Kohlweiss, M., Wallden, P., Zikas, V. (eds.) PKC 2020. LNCS, vol. 12110, pp. 495–526. Springer, Cham (2020). https://doi.org/10.1007/978-3-030-45374-9_17
7. Bayer, S., Groth, J.: Zero-knowledge argument for polynomial evaluation with application to blacklists. In: Johansson, T., Nguyen, P.Q. (eds.) EUROCRYPT 2013. LNCS, vol. 7881, pp. 646–663. Springer, Heidelberg (2013). https://doi.org/10.1007/978-3-642-38348-9_38
8. Ben-Sasson, E., Bentov, I., Horesh, Y., Riabzev, M.: Scalable, transparent, and post-quantum secure computational integrity. IACR Cryptology ePrint Archive 2018/46 (2018)
9. Benhamouda, F., Camenisch, J., Krenn, S., Lyubashevsky, V., Neven, G.: Better zero-knowledge proofs for lattice encryption and their application to group signatures. In: Sarkar, P., Iwata, T. (eds.) ASIACRYPT 2014. LNCS, vol. 8873, pp. 551–572. Springer, Heidelberg (2014). https://doi.org/10.1007/978-3-662-45611-8_29
10. Bootle, J., Cerulli, A., Chaidos, P., Groth, J., Petit, C.: Efficient zero-knowledge arguments for arithmetic circuits in the discrete log setting. In: Fischlin, M., Coron, J.-S. (eds.) EUROCRYPT 2016. LNCS, vol. 9666, pp. 327–357. Springer, Heidelberg (2016). https://doi.org/10.1007/978-3-662-49896-5_12
11. Bootle, J., Lyubashevsky, V., Nguyen, N.K., Seiler, G.: A non-PCP approach to succinct quantum-safe zero-knowledge. In: Micciancio, D., Ristenpart, T. (eds.) CRYPTO 2020. LNCS, vol. 12171, pp. 441–469. Springer, Cham (2020). https://doi.org/10.1007/978-3-030-56880-1_16
12. Bos, J., et al.: Frodo: take off the ring! Practical, quantum-secure key exchange from LWE. In: ACM SIGSAC CCS 2016, pp. 1006–1018 (2016)
13. Bünz, B., Bootle, J., Boneh, D., Poelstra, A., Wuille, P., Maxwell, G.: Bulletproofs: short proofs for confidential transactions and more. In: IEEE S&P, pp. 315–334. IEEE (2018)
14. Ducas, L., Durmus, A., Lepoint, T., Lyubashevsky, V.: Lattice signatures and bimodal gaussians. In: Canetti, R., Garay, J.A. (eds.) CRYPTO 2013. LNCS, vol. 8042, pp. 40–56. Springer, Heidelberg (2013). https://doi.org/10.1007/978-3-642-40041-4_3
15. Ducas, L., Lyubashevsky, V., Prest, T.: Efficient identity-based encryption over NTRU lattices. In: Sarkar, P., Iwata, T. (eds.) ASIACRYPT 2014. LNCS, vol. 8874, pp. 22–41. Springer, Heidelberg (2014). https://doi.org/10.1007/978-3-662-45608-8_2
16. Esgin, M.F., Steinfeld, R., Sakzad, A., Liu, J.K., Liu, D.: Short lattice-based one-out-of-many proofs and applications to ring signatures. In: Deng, R.H., Gauthier-Umaña, V., Ochoa, M., Yung, M. (eds.) ACNS 2019. LNCS, vol. 11464, pp. 67–88. Springer, Cham (2019). https://doi.org/10.1007/978-3-030-21568-2_4

17. Goldreich, O., Goldwasser, S.: On the limits of non-approximability of lattice problems. In: Proceedings ACM STOC 1998, pp. 1–9. ACM (1998)
18. Goldwasser, S., Micali, S., Rackoff, C.: The knowledge complexity of interactive proof-systems (extended abstract). In: ACM STOC 1985, pp. 291–304. ACM (1985)
19. Groth, J.: Linear algebra with sub-linear zero-knowledge arguments. In: Halevi, S. (ed.) CRYPTO 2009. LNCS, vol. 5677, pp. 192–208. Springer, Heidelberg (2009). https://doi.org/10.1007/978-3-642-03356-8_12
20. Groth, J.: Efficient zero-knowledge arguments from two-tiered homomorphic commitments. In: Lee, D.H., Wang, X. (eds.) ASIACRYPT 2011. LNCS, vol. 7073, pp. 431–448. Springer, Heidelberg (2011). https://doi.org/10.1007/978-3-642-25385-0_23
21. Groth, J.: On the size of pairing-based non-interactive arguments. In: Fischlin, M., Coron, J.-S. (eds.) EUROCRYPT 2016. LNCS, vol. 9666, pp. 305–326. Springer, Heidelberg (2016). https://doi.org/10.1007/978-3-662-49896-5_11
22. Ishai, Y., Kushilevitz, E., Ostrovsky, R., Sahai, A.: Zero-knowledge from secure multiparty computation. In: Johnson, D.S., Feige, U. (eds.) ACM STOC 2007, pp. 21–30. ACM (2007)
23. Kilian, J.: A note on efficient zero-knowledge proofs and arguments (extended abstract). In: Proceedings ACM STOC 1992, pp. 723–732. ACM (1992)
24. Libert, B., Ling, S., Mouhartem, F., Nguyen, K., Wang, H.: Zero-knowledge arguments for matrix-vector relations and lattice-based group encryption. In: Cheon, J.H., Takagi, T. (eds.) ASIACRYPT 2016. LNCS, vol. 10032, pp. 101–131. Springer, Heidelberg (2016). https://doi.org/10.1007/978-3-662-53890-6_4
25. Libert, B., Ling, S., Nguyen, K., Wang, H.: Zero-knowledge arguments for lattice-based PRFs and applications to E-cash. In: Takagi, T., Peyrin, T. (eds.) ASIACRYPT 2017. LNCS, vol. 10626, pp. 304–335. Springer, Cham (2017). https://doi.org/10.1007/978-3-319-70700-6_11
26. Lyubashevsky, V.: Fiat-Shamir with aborts: applications to lattice and factoring-based signatures. In: Matsui, M. (ed.) ASIACRYPT 2009. LNCS, vol. 5912, pp. 598–616. Springer, Heidelberg (2009). https://doi.org/10.1007/978-3-642-10366-7_35
27. Lyubashevsky, V.: Lattice signatures without trapdoors. In: Pointcheval, D., Johansson, T. (eds.) EUROCRYPT 2012. LNCS, vol. 7237, pp. 738–755. Springer, Heidelberg (2012). https://doi.org/10.1007/978-3-642-29011-4_43
28. Lyubashevsky, V., Seiler, G.: Short, invertible elements in partially splitting cyclotomic rings and applications to lattice-based zero-knowledge proofs. In: Nielsen, J.B., Rijmen, V. (eds.) EUROCRYPT 2018. LNCS, vol. 10820, pp. 204–224. Springer, Cham (2018). https://doi.org/10.1007/978-3-319-78381-9_8
29. Micciancio, D., Vadhan, S.P.: Statistical zero-knowledge proofs with efficient provers: lattice problems and more. In: Boneh, D. (ed.) CRYPTO 2003. LNCS, vol. 2729, pp. 282–298. Springer, Heidelberg (2003). https://doi.org/10.1007/978-3-540-45146-4_17
30. Regev, O.: On lattices, learning with errors, random linear codes, and cryptography. J. ACM (JACM) 56(6), 34 (2009)
31. Smart, N.P., Vercauteren, F.: Fully homomorphic SIMD operations. Des. Codes Crypt. 71(1), 57–81 (2012). https://doi.org/10.1007/s10623-012-9720-4
32. Stern, J.: A new identification scheme based on syndrome decoding. In: Stinson, D.R. (ed.) CRYPTO 1993. LNCS, vol. 773, pp. 13–21. Springer, Heidelberg (1994). https://doi.org/10.1007/3-540-48329-2_2

Streaming SPHINCS+ for Embedded Devices Using the Example of TPMs

Ruben Niederhagen[1,2]($\boxtimes$), Johannes Roth[3]($\boxtimes$), and Julian Wälde[4]($\boxtimes$)

[1] Academia Sinica, Taipei, Taiwan
ruben@polycephaly.org
[2] University of Southern Denmark, Odense, Denmark
[3] MTG AG, Darmstadt, Germany
johannes.roth@mtg.de
[4] Fraunhofer SIT, Darmstadt, Germany
julianwaelde@gmail.com

Abstract. We present an implementation of the hash-based post-quantum signature scheme SPHINCS$^+$ that enables heavily memory-restricted devices to sign messages by streaming-out a signature during its computation and to verify messages by streaming-in a signature. We demonstrate our implementation in the context of Trusted Platform Modules (TPMs) by proposing a SPHINCS$^+$ integration and a streaming extension for the TPM specification. We evaluate the overhead of our signature-streaming approach for a stand-alone SPHINCS$^+$ implementation and for its integration in a proof-of-concept TPM with the proposed streaming extension running on an ARM Cortex-M4 platform. Our streaming interface greatly reduces the memory requirements without introducing a performance penalty. This is achieved not only by removing the need to store an entire signature but also by reducing the stack requirements of the key generation, sign, and verify operations. Therefore, our streaming interface enables small embedded devices that do not have sufficient memory to store an entire SPHINCS$^+$ signature or that previously were only able to use a parameter set that results in smaller signatures to sign and verify messages using all SPHINCS$^+$ variants.

Keywords: SPHINCS+ · PQC · Signature streaming · ARM Cortex-M4 · TPM

1 Introduction

Experts predict that within the next decade quantum computers may be available that will be capable of breaking current asymmetric cryptography based on the integer factorization and discrete logarithm problems by applying Shor's algorithm. This creates a significant pressure to propose, analyze, implement, and migrate to new cryptographic schemes that are able to withstand attacks

© The Author(s), under exclusive license to Springer Nature Switzerland AG 2022
L. Batina and J. Daemen (Eds.): AFRICACRYPT 2022, LNCS 13503, pp. 269–291, 2022.
https://doi.org/10.1007/978-3-031-17433-9_12

aided by quantum computing. Such schemes are jointly referred to as Post-Quantum Cryptography (PQC). The research effort on PQC has culminated in a standardization process by the National Institute of Standards and Technology (NIST) in the US that started in December 2016 and is expected to be finished in 2024.

Currently, at the time of writing this paper in November 2021, the NIST standardization process is in the third round with seven finalists that might get standardized as result of this round and eight alternate candidates that might either replace finalists if vulnerabilities or implementation issues were to be found or that may be considered for future standardization in a possible fourth round. One of these alternate candidates is the hash-based PQC signature scheme SPHINCS$^+$ [HBD+2020].

Among the alternate candidates, SPHINCS$^+$ has a somewhat special role: NIST has stated in the 2nd round report [MAA+2020] that "NIST sees SPHINCS$^+$ as an extremely conservative choice for standardization" and that if "NIST's confidence in better performing signature algorithms is shaken by new analysis, SPHINCS$^+$ could provide an immediately available algorithm for standardization at the end of the third round." This statement has been emphasized also in a posting to the NIST mailing list by NIST on January 21, 2021[1]. Two major obstacles for the widespread adoption of SPHINCS$^+$ and also the reason why SPHINCS$^+$ was not selected by NIST as finalist in round 3 are its relatively large signature sizes and the relatively high computational signing cost. Therefore, SPHINCS$^+$ is a conservative and reliable choice as PQC signature scheme and provides very strong security guarantees—if its high cost in computing power and memory can be afforded. These costs are not prohibitive on larger computing systems like servers, PC, notebooks, tablets, and smart phones—but they might be a burden for small embedded devices with limited computing power and small memory.

An example for such constrained devices are Trusted Platform Modules (TPMs), which are Hardware Security Modules (HSMs) that are tightly coupled with a computing system and that provide an anchor of trust for sensitive applications. TPMs have a small protected and persistent memory for the secure and tamper-protected storage of secret encryption and signature keys as well as public verification keys. Furthermore, TPMs can act as cryptographic engines that can encrypt and decrypt data as well as sign and verify messages using the securely stored key material. The idea is that secret keys never leave the TPM and that public keys can be stored securely and protected from manipulation to reliably authenticate communication partners. TPMs typically have a very limited amount of RAM and fairly limited computational capabilities.

Hash-based signature schemes come in two flavors: They can be *stateful*, meaning that a security-critical signature state needs to be maintained by the signer and updated after each signature computation, and they can be *state-free*, meaning that such a state does not need to be maintained. SPHINCS$^+$ is

---

[1] https://groups.google.com/a/list.nist.gov/g/pqc-forum/c/2LEoSpskELs/m/VB1jng0aCAAJ.

a state-free hash-based signature scheme while XMSS [BDH2011] (published as an IETF-RFC [HBG+2018]) is a closely related example for a stateful scheme.

For TPMs, stateful signature schemes like XMSS might appear to be the better choice among hash-based signature schemes: On the one hand, signatures of state-free schemes like SPHINCS+ are so large that they might not fit into the TPM memory and on the other hand, the tamper-proof and unclonable storage of TPMs mitigates many of the commonly stated concerns when dealing with stateful schemes. However, the persistent storage is typically implemented as flash memory that has a significant wear-down over time. If too many write operations are performed at the same memory address, errors might occur that would render stateful signature schemes insecure. Storing the sensitive state persistently and securely in a TPM hence is not a simple task and might pose a security risk. Therefore, using a state-less signature scheme like SPHINCS+ might be more secure—if the larger signatures can be handled.

Depending on variant and parameter set, the size of SPHINCS+ signatures ranges between 8 kB and 50 kB although private and public keys are very small with 64 B to 128 B and 32 B to 64 B respectively. Some embedded devices (including TPMs) do not have sufficient memory to store an entire signature while signing or verifying a message. As a solution to this problem, splitting a signature into several smaller parts and streaming these parts out of or into an embedded device has been proposed and evaluated for SPHINCS-256 signing and verification in [HRS2016] and for SPHINCS+ verification in [GHK+2021]. In this paper, we are refining this approach and we are evaluating it exemplarily on TPMs.

Contributions. Our contributions in this paper are:

- the integration of a signature streaming interface for signing and verification into the reference implementation of SPHINCS+,
- a performance and stack evaluation of this interface on ARM Cortex-M4,
- the design and prototypical implementation of a SPHINCS+ and streaming extension for the TPM specification, and
- the evaluation of this TPM-streaming protocol with our streaming modification of SPHINCS+ on the Cortex-M4 platform.

The source code of our implementation is publicly available under BSD license at: https://github.com/QuantumRISC/mbedSPHINCSplusArtifact.

Related Work. There is some work on computing hash-based signatures on embedded devices. Wang et al. propose hardware accelerators for XMSS on a RISC-V platform in [WJW+2019] and Amiet et al. introduce hardware accelerators for SPHINCS-256 in [ACZ2018] (SPHINCS-256 is a predecessor of SPHINCS+). Kölbl describes an implementation of SPHINCS on a relatively large ARMv8-A platform in [K2018] and Campos et al. compare LMS and XMSS on an ARM Cortex-M4 in [CKRS2020]. The pqm4 project [KRSS] provides performance measurements of several PQC schemes including SPHINCS+ on a Cortex-M4 platform. All of these implementations assume that the embedded platform has sufficient memory to store an entire hash-based signature.

As mentioned above, the idea to stream signatures has been applied to SPHINCS⁺ (or its predecessors) before. In [HRS2016], an implementation is presented that computes a 41 kB signature of SPHINCS-256 [BHH+2015] on a Cortex-M3 processor with 16 kB of RAM. The authors show that key generation, signature generation, and signature verification are possible on the device by splitting the SPHINCS-256 signature into several relatively large parts, which are streamed separately. In [GHK+2021] Gonzalez et al. investigate signature and public key streaming for verification for several PQC schemes including SPHINCS⁺ in only 8 kB of RAM using relatively large blocks for streaming. We extend and refine their work to also cover signing (and key generation) and we provide a more detailed analysis for more SPHINCS⁺ parameter sets and for the use of signature streaming for TPMs.

Streaming of PQC schemes has also been discussed in other publications. For example, Gonzalez et al. also apply their streaming approach for signature verification to the PQC signature schemes Rainbow, GeMSS, Dilithium, and Falcon [GHK+2021]. Roth et al. in [RKK2020] are streaming the large public key of the code-based scheme Classic McEliece into and out of a Cortex-M4 processor.

Paul et al. study the use of a TPM as random number generator and for hashing in the migration of Transport Layer Security (TLS) towards PQC schemes, using among others SPHINCS⁺ in TLS, but they do not alter or extend existing TPM hardware or specifications and they do not perform SPHINCS⁺ operations on or stream SPHINCS⁺ signatures to a TPM [PSS2021]. The FutureTPM project[2] is a European effort to evaluate post-quantum cryptography for the use in TPMs. In their project report, they discuss the use of several PQC signature schemes including SPHINCS⁺ in a TPM prototype [CMP+2021]. However, they do not consider the streaming of signatures and their TPM prototype runs as software TPM on a powerful, non-embedded CPU.

Structure of this Paper. We provide an overview of SPHINCS⁺ and TPMs in Sect. 2. We then describe the implementation of our streaming interface and its integration into a TPM prototype in Sect. 3 and evaluate our implementation and conclude our paper in Sect. 4.

2   Preliminaries

This section provides a brief introduction to the signature scheme SPHINCS⁺ and a quick overview on TPM.

2.1   SPHINCS⁺

The state-free hash-based post-quantum signature scheme SPHINCS⁺ has been described in [BHK+2019] and has been submitted to the NIST PQC standardization process as defined in the submission document [HBD+2020]. It is composed

---

[2] https://futuretpm.eu/.

of a hypertree of total height h with d layers of Merkle signature trees. These trees have WOTS+ one-time signatures at their leaves such that the inner trees sign Merkle trees at the next hypertree layer and the leaves of the bottom layer sign FORS few-time signatures, which in turn are used to sign message digests.

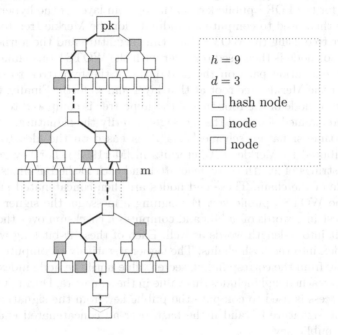

$h = 9$

$d = 3$

☐ hash node

☐ node

☐ node

Fig. 1. Illustration of a small SPHINCS+ structure (figure from [BHK+2019]).

Figure 1 shows an example of the hypertree structure of SPHINCS+ with reduced (hyper-)tree sizes for illustration. The output length n (in bytes) of the underlying hash function defines the security level of a SPHINCS+ signature.

Key generation of SPHINCS+ is relatively expensive, since the entire first-layer tree of the hypertree including all WOTS+ public keys on its leaf nodes needs to be computed in order to obtain the root node of the first-layer tree as public key.

The process of signing a message using SPHINCS+ is very similar to signing with an XMSS multi-tree [BDH2011, HBG+2018] with a notable distinction that XMSS does not use a few-time signature scheme at the bottom layer of the hypertree. To sign a message using SPHINCS+, a FORS private key at the leaves of the trees at the bottom layer is selected and the message is signed with this few-time signature key. The resulting public key is then signed with the corresponding WOTS+ one-time signature, an authentication path through the Merkle tree is computed as part of the signature, and the root node of the Merkle tree is obtained. This tree root is then signed using the corresponding WOTS+ one-time signature of the corresponding tree at the next higher layer.

The WOTS$^+$ public key is computed and again authenticated by computing an authentication path with the corresponding Merkle tree root. This process is repeated over the layers of the inner trees until finally the root tree of the hypertree is reached and the authentication path of the root tree has been computed.

Verification works equivalently: First, the FORS signature is used to compute a candidate for the FORS public key on the bottom layer of the hypertree. This candidate is then used to compute a candidate for the Merkle tree root of that bottom-layer tree using the WOTS$^+$ one-time signature and the authentication path. This root node is then used together with the WOTS$^+$ one-time signature and the authentication path on the next layer of the hypertree to compute a candidate for the Merkle-tree root at that layer and so forth. Finally, the candidate of the root node of the root tree of the hypertree is compared to the public key of the proclaimed signer of the message to verify the signature.

The one-time signature scheme WOTS$^+$ is based on the idea to use hash chains (attributed by Merkle to Winternitz in [Mer1990]). For key generation, random bit-strings of length n are generated and each hashed w times to obtain the end node of the chain. These end nodes are then concatenated and hashed to obtain the WOTS$^+$ public key. For signing a message, the signer splits the message digest into words of w bits and computes a checksum over these words, which is split into w-length words as well. Each of these w-bit long words then serves as index into the hash chains: The signer iteratively recomputes the hash chain starting from the corresponding secret value until the node indexed by the w-bit word is reached and includes this value in the signature. During verification the same process is used to compute the public key from the signature and the message. The signature is valid if the hash over all concatenated end nodes is equal to the public key.

FORS is short for Forest Of Random Subsets. It is a few-time signature scheme based on Merkle hash trees. FORS uses k trees of height a with $t = 2^a$ leaf nodes to sign a message digest of ka bits. The root nodes of the k trees are hashed together to obtain the FORS public key. To generate a FORS signature, the signer computes a message digest of ka bits for the message, splits this digest into k a-bit strings, and interprets each of the a-bit strings as index into the corresponding tree. The secret indexed by each a-bit string is copied into the signature together with a verification path in the corresponding Merkle tree. The verifier then recomputes the root nodes of the k trees by hashing the leaf node from the signature and using the verification path and obtains a public key candidate by hashing the root nodes together. This public key candidate is in turn authenticated by the SPHINCS$^+$ hypertree. The parameters k and t are chosen according to the desired number of signatures that can be computed with this few-time signature scheme such that the secrets revealed in each signature do not provide enough information to forge signatures.

Hash-based signature schemes like SPHINCS$^+$ require a huge number of hash-function calls: WOTS$^+$ is using many hash calls for computing the hash chains and the computations for FORS and Merkle trees are based on pairwise hashing of child nodes. Kannwischer et al. report in [KRSS2019] that 87% to 98% of the time in SPHINCS+ operations is spent on hashing.

SPHINCS+ uses the parameters n (the security parameter in bytes), h (the height of the hypertree), d (the number of layers in the hypertree), t (the number of leaves of a FORS tree), k (the number of trees in FORS), and w (the Winternitz parameter for WOTS+). The SPHINCS+ specification offers a total of 36 parameter sets for three security levels, three different hash functions, "simple" and "robust" variants, and "small" as well as "fast" parameter sets. For the remainder of this paper we only consider variants that are using SHA-256 as a hash functions. However, we also implemented our solution for SHAKE256 and our results also apply to the other choices of hash functions for SPHINCS+. Section 4 references a selection of these parameter sets in Tables 2, 3 and 4 using the same notation as the SPHINCS+ specification.

Table 1. SPHINCS+ parameter sets as proposed for NIST Round 3 [HBD+2020].

Parameter set	n	h	d	$\log(t)$	k	w	Bit-security	Security level	Signature [bytes]
SPHINCS+-128f	16	66	22	6	33	16	128	1	17 088
SPHINCS+-128s	16	63	7	12	14	16	133	1	7 856
SPHINCS+-192f	24	66	22	8	33	16	194	3	35 664
SPHINCS+-192s	24	63	7	14	17	16	193	3	16 224
SPHINCS+-256f	32	68	17	9	35	16	255	5	49 856
SPHINCS+-256s	32	64	8	14	22	16	255	5	29 792

The "s" (small) and "f" (fast) variants provide a trade-off between signature sizes and computational cost. The "s" parameter sets have a smaller number d of layers in the hypertree and hence taller subtrees of height h/d. Therefore, the "s" parameter sets provide smaller signatures (since fewer WOTS+ signatures, one per layer, are required) at the cost of key generation and signing time (since the subtress are taller and exponentially more leaf nodes need to be generated). However, verification time is reduced since accordingly fewer WOTS+ verifications are required. The "f" parameter sets significantly speed up key generation and signing while increasing signature sizes and verification time. This trade-off is achieved by choosing different layouts of the hypertree with different parameters for FORS and WOTS+ signatures (see Table 1).

The security argument for the "simple" parameter sets involves an invocation of the Random Oracle Model (ROM) while the "robust" variants have a security proof that assumes pre-image resistance and the Pseudo Random Function (PRF) property for the hash-function constructions. The "robust" variants require more hash-function invocations, because additional inputs for tweakable hash functions need to be computed. This difference is equivalent to the difference between XMSS [HBG+2018] ("robust") and LMS [MCF2019] ("simple") [HBD+2020, Sect. 8.1.6].

2.2   Trusted Platform Modules

Trusted Platform Modules (TPMs) are passive co-processors that perform cryptographic operations and store key material in a secure way. A TPM typically contains a small processor that handles the communication protocol, a random number generator, hardware accelerators for cryptography, and a secure non-volatile memory region. The vendors of these devices apply proprietary hardening measures to the hardware structures within the TPM to defeat side-channel and fault-injection attacks. TPMs do not work stand-alone but they always are connected to a host system. Either they are an integral part of the host system or they are connected to the host system via a low level bus system. For example, a TPM can be attached to the host system using the Serial Peripheral Interface (SPI) bus. The TPM 2.0 specification was developed by the Trusted Computing Group (TCG) in 2013 [Tru2019a] and has since been adopted as ISO/IEC 11889 standard in 2015.

Communication with the host system is realized using a command/response protocol in which the host system issues commands for a variety of tasks and receives responses upon completion of the requested task. The "Commands" part of the specification [Tru2019b] lists all standard TPM commands and their semantics. These commands are used to implement a variety of protocols such as secure boot, remote attestation, and secure firmware updates, where they are the central component for key storage and for performing operations in a way that cannot be influenced by the attached host system. An integrated random number generator allows to create cryptographic keys that are never exported from the TPM. This provides the capability to pin an identity to a specific host system respective TPM.

The TPM 2.0 standard mandates the use of the Rivest-Shamir-Adleman (RSA) public key cryptosystem and optionally that of Elliptic-Curve Cryptography (ECC) for the purposes of digital signatures. These options are however not secure against attackers equipped with sufficiently capable quantum computers. Therefore, an integration of post-quantum cryptography into the TPM standard is urgently desired.

3   Design and Implementation

In this section, we describe the implementation of our streaming interface as well as its integration into our PQC-TPM prototype.

3.1   Streaming Interface

A SPHINCS$^+$ signature consists of multiple parts as illustrated in Fig. 2. First, there is the randomness R followed by a FORS signature. The FORS signature in itself consists of k private key values, each combined with an authentication path in the corresponding Merkle tree. A hypertree signature follows which consists of d Merkle signatures, which each again consists of a WOTS$^+$ signature and

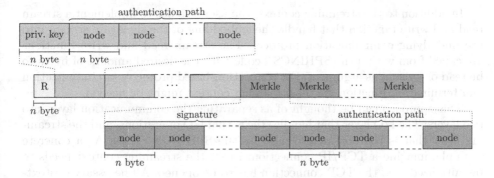

Fig. 2. SPHINCS+ signature format.

an authentication path. A WOTS+ signature is the concatenation of multiple hash-chain nodes that are computed by the WOTS+ chaining function.

Each of the described parts, in turn, consists of one or more n-byte blocks. More precisely, the randomness R, the FORS private key values, every node in the authentication paths, as well as every hash-chain node are all separate byte arrays of size n—because they are each the result of an invocation of the instantiated hash functions that output n bytes. This makes it natural to split signatures into chunks of n bytes as well.

Our implementation of the streaming interface is based on the SPHINCS+ reference implementation[3], which directly accesses a large memory buffer that stores the signature to either write or read signature data. It maintains a pointer to keep track of the current position in the buffer. After a (potentially large) chunk of data has been processed, the pointer is incremented by the corresponding amount of bytes and the next part of the signature is processed.

We implement a streaming interface that can be thought of as an abstraction from a buffer that is *sequentially* written to during signing a message or read from during verifying a signature respectively. Instead of directly accessing the memory at an address inside a buffer, the implementation requests to sequentially read or write one or more blocks of size n from or to the signature stream. Since the signature is exactly in the order in which the bytes are processed (for the sign and verify operation alike), this abstraction works. Also, once a chunk of one or more blocks of n bytes has been written, it is not needed for further computations, i.e., it does not need to remain in memory. The same holds for reading: Once the requested chunk has been processed, it is not needed any longer and the chunk does not need to be kept in memory anymore. Only the part of the signature that is currently processed needs to reside in memory.

The Streaming API. We slightly modify the SPHINCS+ API so that instead of a signature buffer and its length it uses a streaming-context data structure. The streaming context is supposed to store all context-related data that is necessary to handle reading from the stream and writing to the stream.

---

[3] https://github.com/sphincs/sphincsplus/.

In addition to the streaming context, the user also has to implement a stream read and write function that handle the embedding of the signature stream into the underlying communication protocol. The stream read and write functions are called from within the SPHINCS$^+$ code with the desired amount of bytes to be read or written as argument. For connection-based protocols, an initialization and termination function for the streaming context might be needed.

This approach can be thought of as separating the communication layer into two layers: The I/O layer that handles the actual I/O operations, and the streaming layer that is the abstraction used by the SPHINCS$^+$ code. As a concrete example, imagine a TCP/IP connection. First, the streaming context needs to be initialized, i.e., the TCP connection has to be opened. All necessary context-related data, i.e., typically a file descriptor for socket-APIs, is stored in the session context. The stream read and write functions can be implemented as wrappers of the corresponding TCP/IP layer functions. In doing so, embedding the signature data into the TCP/IP protocol is handled by the TCP/IP layer. Then, the session context can be terminated, i.e., the TCP/IP connection can be closed. This example demonstrates the general applicability of the approach. The details of the underlying protocol are hidden behind a simple abstraction. Buffer sizes can be adapted in the I/O layer to maximize performance at a reasonable memory overhead. How much is buffered at the I/O layer or the streaming layer (in the streaming context), is up to the implementation of these layers.

We want to emphasize that in principle our streaming API can be used in every case in which the non-streaming reference API can be used. Neither the public key format nor the signature format are changed (nor the private key format). In general, it is not possible to distinguish between a communication that makes use of the streaming API and the reference implementation, apart from possible timing differences. Since the streaming API is designed as an abstraction from the signature buffer, it can naturally also be used on a signature buffer that resides in memory. In this case, the stream write function merely performs the appropriate memcpy calls and keeps track of the currently written bytes and the stream read function just returns a pointer to the correct location inside the signature buffer.

The streaming API introduces a slight computational overhead due to additional function calls, but apart from this and a slightly increased complexity due to implementing and using the streaming related functions, there is no loss in generality. Moreover, due to the generality, it is easy to integrate our streaming interface into different protocols. We only briefly outlined this for TCP/IP but demonstrate the principle in more detail with our TPM integration in Sect. 3.2 which is evaluated in Sect. 4.2.

Our API changes are straightforward to integrate into typical C APIs by either extending them with new function calls (backwards compatible) or by adding a streaming context to existing API calls (not backwards compatible). If an API already includes a customizable context data structure as parameter, no changes at all are required. These changes are generic and support streaming implementations for other cryptographic schemes as well. From a user perspective, only appropriate streaming functions for reading and writing the protocol-specific stream need to be additionally implemented. However, a maintainer of a crypto library can provide suitable streaming functions for supported protocols.

Eliminating the Signature Buffer. The streaming API hides the details of what is buffered at which point. In theory, the data could be read from or written to I/O directly without any buffering (effectively replacing memory operations with data I/O) or the entire signature could be buffered (effectively maintaining the data handling of the reference implementation). In practice, a buffer of a certain size optimal for the underlying I/O interface can be maintained and flushed as data is being written or read.

We first demonstrate that the signature buffer can be reduced to only operating on one n byte chunk of signature data at a time. That means that at no point in time some signature data that has previously been accessed is needed to continue the signature operation, and at no point in time, more than one n byte chunk needs to be accessed.

The following is described from a signer's perspective for simplicity. Although the computations are slightly different for the verifier, the same general abstraction applies. The components of a SPHINCS+ signature are:

- R: This value is generated by combining the message with a secret PRF key and optional randomness using a hash function. After it has been used to compute the message digest, which is going to be signed by FORS, the value can be written to the stream and removed from memory.
- FORS: A FORS signature consists of private keys that are released as part of the signature and an authentication path in a corresponding Merkle tree:
  - Private Keys: A FORS private key is computed by applying the PRF to the SPHINCS+ secret key seed and the appropriate FORS address. It can be immediately streamed out.
  - Authentication Path: The authentication-path node at a given height is the root of a subtree and can be computed with the tree-hash algorithm directly, given that the index of the left-most leaf in this subtree is specified. In this way it is possible to compute the nodes of the authentication path in order and the buffer for the authentication path can be omitted. To avoid costly recomputations of leaf nodes, the root-node computation is intertwined with the computation of the authentication-path nodes.
  - Public Key: FORS public keys are only an implicit part of the signature, but handling them in an efficient streaming implementation warrants some attention to avoid recomputations of nodes and memory overhead. The FORS root nodes are combined to form the public key by computing a tweakable hash over the nodes. This value is then signed by the bottom layer of the SPHINCS+ hypertree. Instead of buffering all root nodes in order to compute the tweakable hash function, we maintain a state of the tweakable hash function and update this state with each newly computed root node, after streaming the corresponding authentication path.
- SPHINCS+ Hypertree: The signature components of the SPHINCS+ hypertree consist of WOTS+ signatures and nodes in the authentication paths:

- WOTS$^+$ Signature: The details of the WOTS$^+$ signature generation are described in Sect. 2.1. Here, we only roughly outline how buffering is avoided. A WOTS$^+$ signature consists of a number of hash-chain nodes that are derived from the private key values and authenticates the tree on the layer below. The computation is typically intertwined with the computation of the WOTS$^+$ public key that is also needed for generating the corresponding leaf in the hypertree. In order to compute the public key, all hash-chain nodes are computed in order. Writing out the signature thus basically only means writing out the correct node while the public key is computed. Finally, for computing the corresponding leaf in the hypertree, the public key values are combined with a tweakable hash-function call. Instead of buffering the end node of each hash chain and then applying the tweakable hash function, we update the tweakable hash function after each hash-chain end node has been computed.
- Authentication Path: This is analogous to FORS authentication paths.

Since all elements of the signature can be computed in order, the signature buffer can be reduced to just processing the current chunk of n bytes.

In comparison to this approach, in [HRS2016], the authors split a SPHINCS-256 signature into larger chunks. For example, WOTS$^+$ signatures are processed as a single chunk. This does not hinder the computation in 16 kB of RAM though, as the memory is only temporarily required, and the WOTS$^+$ public key is quickly reduced to a single leaf node. Another notable difference is that in [HRS2016], the signature format is slightly changed. This is due to a design decision in HORST, the few-time signature scheme that is used for SPHINCS-256 instead of FORS: The top of the tree is cut off at some layer—here layer six—such that only authentication paths up to this layer are computed. This prevents duplications in the top layers, however, it also complicates streaming, since the nodes on the sixth layer are appended at the end of the signature, instead of being part of the respective authentication paths. The solution in [HRS2016] is that HORST nodes are tagged with their actual position in the hypertree, rather than producing the nodes in the correct order of the signature. These signature elements are put into the correct order on the receiving end by reordering the nodes accordingly. We want to emphasize that this is not necessary for SPHINCS$^+$ and that the signature format does not need to be changed in our implementation.

Details of the implementation. While it is not necessary to rigorously avoid buffering small quantities of n byte chunks, implementing the streaming interface goes hand in hand with reducing the size of the internal buffers that hold parts of the signature. The advantage of working with the granularity of only n bytes—or small multiples of n bytes—is only noticeable when there are no large internal buffers for the signature data. As an example, the reference implementation computes a tweakable hash over a WOTS$^+$ public key by first buffering it entirely using a buffer of up to $67 \times n = 2144$ bytes for $n = 32$.

In most places, it is straight-forward to reduce or eliminate the buffers by utilizing the stream read and write functions and by intertwining certain computations as outlined in the previous paragraph. An exception from this is the treehash function. The reference implementation always generates the tree nodes in a fixed order. This means that in general, the authentication-path nodes are not computed in the order in which they appear in the signature. Thus, to enable streaming of the authentication paths as well, we modified the treehash function to produce the authentication-path nodes in the correct order. This allows us to eliminate the authentication-path buffer as well.

Furthermore, SPHINCS+ applies the tweakable hash function to some large buffers, namely to the WOTS+ public key and the FORS root nodes. In order to eliminate the buffers for those, we implement an incremental API for the hash calls. Instead of applying one single thash call for the tweakable hash function, we implement the functions thash_init, thash_update, and thash_finalize. As this incremental API stretches the computation over multiple separate calls, a state has to be kept. The SHA-256-simple state consists of the SHA-256 state, as well as a buffer to account for the possibility that the current input does not fill an entire block. For SHA-256-robust, an additional state is kept for the Mask Generation Function (MGF) that SPHINCS+ uses for generating masks. With this, there is no need to keep a buffer for the WOTS+ public key or the FORS root nodes merely for the sake of computing the hash value.

Figure 3 shows as an example an excerpt from the WOTS+ leaf-generation reference code. As can be seen in Line 8, the currently computed WOTS+ hash-chain node is copied sequentially to the signature if it is part of the signature. The memcpy call can simply be replaced by a call of the write stream function. Likewise, the pk_buffer that holds the WOTS+ public key is only needed for the thash function call in Line 14. This can be replaced by using the thash_init, thash_update, and thash_finalize functions. Public key nodes are computed sequentially and consumed with a thash_update call.

```
1 for (i=0, buffer=pk_buffer; i<SPX_WOTS_LEN; i++,
     buffer+=SPX_N) {
2   ...
3   // iterate down the WOTS chain
4   for (k=0;; k++) {
5     // check if this is the value that needs to
6     // be saved as a part of the WOTS signature
7     if (k == wots_k) {
8       memcpy( info->wots_sig + i * SPX_N, buffer, SPX_N );
9     }
10    ...
11  }
12 }
13 // do the final thash to generate the public keys
14 thash(dest, pk_buffer, SPX_WOTS_LEN, pub_seed, pk_addr);
```

Fig. 3. Excerpt from the SPHINCS+ reference code (wots_gen_leafx1 function).

By applying the outlined changes systematically throughout the code, the signature buffer is completely eliminated. While we presented this from the signer's perspective, the same can be done for the verifier. The main difference is that the signer has to traverse each tree with the `treehash` function. For the verifier, all required nodes are provided in the signature. For each tree, in addition to the provided authentication path, one leaf has to be computed from either the released FORS private key value, the FORS root nodes, or the WOTS$^+$ signature. The WOTS$^+$ and FORS signatures are implicitly verified if the computed root of the hypertree matches the SPHINCS$^+$ public key.

The described streaming implementation does not reduce the storage size, i.e., the size that a signature will require when stored on a medium, such as flash memory. Further, this does not reduce network bandwidth requirements. However, it greatly reduces the memory requirements for the sign and verify operation, since no buffer is required to hold the signature. Furthermore, the key-generation operation also benefits from the changes. While there is no signature buffer that can be eliminated, large intermediate buffers are eliminated, for example to hash the WOTS$^+$ public keys.

3.2   TPM Prototype and Streaming Extension

We forked the official TPM 2.0 reference implementation by Microsoft[4] as basis for our prototype TPM with SPHINCS$^+$ signatures and a TPM streaming protocol. The TPM reference implementation can be compiled with different crypto libraries for the required cryptographic primitives, either with OpenSSL or with wolfSSL. We chose to use the wolfSSL library, since it is better suited for the use on resource-restricted embedded systems. However, within SPHINCS$^+$ we are using the implementations of the hash functions from the SPHINCS$^+$ reference implementation for better comparison with prior art in Sect. 4.

We needed to apply two major changes to the TPM reference implementation for the integration of SPHINCS$^+$ as signature scheme. The first was to add data structures so that SPHINCS$^+$ can be used for generating keys, as well as for signature generation and verification. The key generation is covered by adding a data structure that stores a SPHINCS$^+$ key pair. We used the data structures that are used for RSA keys as templates for SPHINCS$^+$.

The second major change was the definition of additional commands for signing and verifying using SPHINCS$^+$. The TPM commands `RSA_Encrypt` and `RSA_Decrypt` can be used to perform data signing and signature verification with RSA keys. This is not the only way to use a signature primitive with TPMs, it is however the most direct way to instruct the TPM to sign a message or verify a signature using only one command per operation. We added two commands `PQC_Private` and `PQC_Public` for signing and verification respectively, again using the RSA code as template. We implemented a unit-test on the host for covering key generation, signing, and verification on the TPM using the three commands `TPM_CreateLoaded`, `PQC_Private`, and `PQC_Public`. The

---

[4] https://github.com/microsoft/ms-tpm-20-ref/.

command TPM_CreateLoaded has a parameter for the selection of the crypto-graphic scheme that we defined for SPHINCS+. This parameter is used to set the SPHINCS+ parameters during key-pair generation and is stored along-side the key pair on the TPM for use during signing and verification.

In order to send commands to the TPM and to receive its responses, we implemented a variant of the TPM Interface Specification (TIS) protocol [Tru2013]. TIS defines a 24 bit address space that is mapped to control registers and data buffers inside the TPM. Read and write operations on specific addresses are used to transfer commands and data to the TPM, to receive responses from it, and to initiate the execution of commands.

The specification describes a simple SPI-based protocol for implementing read and write operations for TPMs that are not directly connected to a memory bus. Messages in this SPI protocol start with a byte that uses the first bit to indicate whether a read or write operation is performed and the remaining 7 bit to define the length of the data in bytes. This initial byte is followed by a 24 bit address indicating the source (for a read operation) or destination (for a write operation). After this, data is transferred.

The host system initiates all communication with the TPM and polls a 32 bit status register using the SPI-based protocol to detect if the TPM is ready to receive commands or if a response is ready. We only implemented a minimal subset of the address space that is defined in the TIS specification. The two most important addresses are the 32 bit status register STS at address 000018h and the 32 bit FIFO command-and-response register DATA_FIFO at address 000024h. Specific bits of the STS are used by the TPM to communicate its readiness to receive commands or transmit responses as well as for the host system to initiate the execution of a previously written TPM command.

We propose an extension to this communication protocol for the streaming of data between the host and the TPM. We extend the TIS interface by two addresses, the 32 bit IOSTREAM FIFO register at address 000030h for the streaming of data and the 32 bit STREAMSIZE register at address 000040h to communicate the size of the data to be streamed. The STS register is polled by the host platform regularly. Several of its bits are marked as reserved by the TIS specification. We decided to use two of those reserved bits to signal that the TPM is ready to send (STS bit 23) or receive (STS bit 24) data. If one of these bits is set when the host system reads the STS register, it reads out the STREAMSIZE register, which holds the number of bytes that the TPM is able to send or receive. The data is then read from or written to the IOSTREAM register, which acts as a FIFO. This helps to reduce additional polling during streaming, since the host system is already polling the STS register during the execution of any TPM command to detect if a response is ready.

An alternative would be to formalize the sequence of streaming messages in a state machine and to issue special commands asking for further data or to transmit data via the DATA_FIFO register. This approach however would introduce a significant overhead in transmitted data and all data would have to pass through the serialization and deserializing layers of the TPM firmware. Furthermore, the implementation of a cryptographic scheme using such a state-machine-based communication layer would require significant changes to the program flow into a state-machine as well instead of being able to handle I/O transparently during the cryptographic computations as described in Sect. 3.1 for SPHINCS$^+$.

We used the SPI controller (in the SPI "slave" role) of the STM32F4 SoC to implement the TIS protocol. Our implementation is driven by an interrupt service routine that is triggered every time a byte is received on the SPI bus. The interrupt operates a small state machine that handles writing to and reading from the available addresses, including the streaming of signature data. This approach results in an interruption of the code for every byte that is transferred. These frequent interrupts could be avoided using a dedicated hardware implementation of the TIS protocol on an actual TPM.

3.3   Considerations on Fault Attacks

We would like to emphasize that there are no efficient (non-generic) countermeasures against the random-fault attack described by Genêt et al. in [GKPM2018]. This attack targets signature generation: Collecting several signatures with well-timed faults enables the attacker to sign arbitrary messages. Most faulted signatures verify correctly. Thus, the attack cannot be detected by the standard method of verifying the signature after signing and before releasing it. While the streaming of the signature can be used as a side-channel to facilitate triggering faults at the right moment, SPHINCS$^+$ is already inherently vulnerable to this attack, also in the non-streaming case.

Therefore, fault-attack countermeasures must be put in place when computing SPHINCS$^+$ signatures (with or without signature streaming) in scenarios that are susceptible to fault attacks. TPMs typically do provide some (often proprietary) physical protection against fault injection.

4   Evaluation

The parameter sets of SPHINCS$^+$ can be instantiated with different choices for the hash functions. These variants determine the implementation of the tweakable hash function. This directly influences the considered metrics, i.e., cycle count and stack usage. We consider the two SHA-256 variants SHA-256-simple and SHA-256-robust. However, we also applied our modifications to the SHAKE256 variants with equivalent results.

We built the binaries with GCC 9.2.1 and the "-O2" flag which offer a good trade-off between the different metrics. We are evaluating our implementation on a STM32F4 Discovery board with an ARM Cortex-M4 CPU. The board offers several clock frequencies. We are using the default frequency of 168 MHz if not explicitly stated differently. For our measurements with the TPM integration we used a Raspberry Pi 4 Model B in the role of the host system, because it provides an SPI controller for communication with our TPM prototype.

4.1   Streaming Interface

The mupq project provides implementations and optimizations for several PQC schemes for several embedded platforms. Its subproject pqm4[5] is dedicated to the Cortex-M4 platform using the STM32F4 Discovery board. For SPHINCS+, it uses the implementation from the PQClean project[6], which is based on the SPHINCS+ reference implementation.

In order to verify that our streaming interface does not introduce a significant performance penalty, we compare the cycle counts and the stack sizes of the selected SPHINCS+ parameter sets with the reference implementation and the mupq/PQClean implementation of SPHINCS+ on the Cortex-M4 platform. The mupq project provides performance measurements that are frequently updated. We compare the performance of our streaming interface to the measurements in the file "benchmarks.csv" from git commit 12d5e56.

Table 2. Cycle counts (in mega cycles) for key generation, signing, and verification for the reference implementation and the streaming API at 168 MHz as well as for the pqm4/pqclean implementation the streaming API at 24 MHz rounded to three significant figures.

Parameter set	stream vs. reference impl. (168 MHz)						stream vs. pqm4/pqclean (24 MHz)					
	Keygen		Sign		Verify		Keygen		Sign		Verify	
	ref.	strm.	ref.	strm.	ref.	strm.	pqm4	strm.	pqm4	strm.	pqm4	strm.
sphincs-sha256-128f-robust	54.6	55.0	1 270	1 280	81.7	82.7	30.5	36.0	750	835	43.9	54.2
sphincs-sha256-128s-robust	3 610	3 520	27 100	26 400	28.9	27.8	1 950	2 300	14 700	17 300	14.8	18.2
sphincs-sha256-192f-robust	81.5	81.8	2 150	2 160	121	123	45.2	53.8	1 250	1 420	67.1	80.6
sphincs-sha256-192s-robust	5 220	5 240	48 100	48 400	44.3	44.3	2 890	3 440	26 800	31 700	23.9	29.1
sphincs-sha256-256f-robust	300	300	6 110	6 120	177	177	165	195	3 450	3 980	95.8	115
sphincs-sha256-256s-robust	4 810	4 800	58 900	58 900	91.5	90	2 630	3 130	32 400	38 200	49.6	58.5
sphincs-sha256-128f-simple	26.7	27.3	625	640	36.9	39.8	16.1	17.7	400	416	22.6	25.8
sphincs-sha256-128s-simple	1 770	1 750	13 400	13 300	12.9	13.6	1 030	1 140	7 850	8 630	7.71	8.84
sphincs-sha256-192f-simple	39.5	40.2	1 060	1 080	58.1	58.4	23.7	26.2	669	701	33.6	37.9
sphincs-sha256-192s-simple	2 520	2 570	24 000	24 400	20.4	21.2	1 520	1 670	14 400	15 800	12.0	13.8
sphincs-sha256-256f-simple	106	106	2 210	2 230	61.4	60.6	62.6	69.4	1 340	1 450	35.5	39.4
sphincs-sha256-256s-simple	1 700	1 700	21 900	22 000	30.9	28.9	998	1 110	12 900	14 300	17.6	18.7

Performance. The pqm4 project is running the STM32F4 Discovery board at only 24 MHz in order to avoid flash-memory access effects. Therefore, we performed the measurements of our streaming interface at the frequencies 168 MHz for comparison to the reference implementation and at 24 MHz for comparison to mupq. Detailed cycle counts are listed in Table 2.

For the reference implementation the difference in the cycle count to our streaming implementation varies between one or two percent for key generation and signing. Besides the integration of the streaming interface, our code also

---

[5] https://github.com/mupq/pqm4/.
[6] https://github.com/PQClean/PQClean/.

replaces the compile-time selection of the parameter set in the reference code with a runtime-selection, introducing some `if-then` clauses, which might be the cause of some of the cycle-count differences. Overall our modifications to the control flow of the reference implementation when integrating the streaming interface do not have a major impact on the performance.

The difference to pqm4/PQClean is more pronounced: In this case, the performance for key generation and signing is 10% to 20% faster than our version for the SHA-256 variants. This is due to the fact that the pqm4 project is using optimized SHA-256 code for the Cortex-M4 CPU. We did not incorporate these optimizations in order to remain closer to the reference implementation. On an actual PQC-TPM, we would recommend to use hardware acceleration for all hash computations to achieve significant performance improvements.

The runtime varies more significantly for the verification operation—since the verification time itself varies for different inputs (as opposed to key generation and signing which have a runtime that is quite independent from inputs). However, the performance differences for verification are qualitatively similar to those of key generation and signing.

Stack Size. For stack measurements we are using an implementation of the streaming interface that is simply writing into a large buffer just as the reference implementation. This signature buffer is not part of the stack-size measurements for all, the reference, the pqm4/PQClean, and our streaming implementation.

Table 3 shows the stack sizes of the reference implementation (columns "ref.") and the pqm4/PQClean implementation (columns "pqm4") compared to our streaming variant (columns "strm."). We also provide the signature sizes to emphasize that both the reference and the pqm4/PQClean implementations require a large data buffer for storing the signature in addition to the stack requirements.

Table 3. Stack sizes for the sphincs-sha256-parameter sets for the SPHINCS$^+$ reference implementation ("ref"), pqm4/PQClean ("pqm4"), and our streaming interface implementation ("strm.") as well as the corresponding signature sizes in bytes. The buffer size for our streaming version can be freely chosen to satisfy the available memory resources.

Parameter Set	Sig.	Key Generation			Signing			Verification		
		ref.	pqm4	strm.	ref.	pqm4	strm.	ref.	pqm4	strm.
sphincs-sha256-128f-robust	17 088	3 688+sig.	2 256+sig.	1 960+buf.	3 176+sig.	2 320+sig.	2 000+buf.	3 344+sig.	2 808+sig.	1 728+buf.
sphincs-sha256-128s-robust	7 856	3 984+sig.	2 472+sig.	2 056+buf.	3 264+sig.	2 544+sig.	2 088+buf.	2 592+sig.	2 112+sig.	1 656+buf.
sphincs-sha256-192f-robust	35 664	6 536+sig.	3 680+sig.	2 192+buf.	5 336+sig.	3 832+sig.	2 264+buf.	4 848+sig.	4 040+sig.	1 856+buf.
sphincs-sha256-192s-robust	16 224	6 928+sig.	4 104+sig.	2 336+buf.	5 472+sig.	3 992+sig.	2 360+buf.	4 728+sig.	3 376+sig.	1 888+buf.
sphincs-sha256-256f-robust	49 856	10 456+sig.	5 792+sig.	2 456+buf.	8 272+sig.	5 760+sig.	2 512+buf.	7 424+sig.	5 656+sig.	2 088+buf.
sphincs-sha256-256s-robust	29 792	10 816+sig.	6 064+sig.	2 584+buf.	8 400+sig.	5 904+sig.	2 616+buf.	7 424+sig.	5 360+sig.	1 960+buf.
sphincs-sha256-128f-simple	17 088	2 904+sig.	2 104+sig.	1 632+buf.	2 392+sig.	2 168+sig.	1 688+buf.	2 592+sig.	2 656+sig.	1 384+buf.
sphincs-sha256-128s-simple	7 856	3 096+sig.	2 432+sig.	1 736+buf.	2 480+sig.	2 392+sig.	1 768+buf.	1 904+sig.	1 960+sig.	1 296+buf.
sphincs-sha256-192f-simple	35 664	5 072+sig.	3 520+sig.	1 840+buf.	3 872+sig.	3 560+sig.	1 896+buf.	3 816+sig.	3 880+sig.	1 480+buf.
sphincs-sha256-192s-simple	16 224	5 464+sig.	3 944+sig.	1 992+buf.	4 008+sig.	3 832+sig.	2 016+buf.	3 160+sig.	3 216+sig.	1 456+buf.
sphincs-sha256-256f-simple	49 856	8 160+sig.	5 512+sig.	2 080+buf.	5 872+sig.	5 592+sig.	2 104+buf.	5 424+sig.	5 488+sig.	1 876+buf.
sphincs-sha256-256s-simple	2 9792	8 416+sig.	5 896+sig.	2 216+buf.	6 000+sig.	5 736+sig.	2 232+buf.	5 024+sig.	5 080+sig.	1 868+buf.

Due to the modifications to the data handling on the stack and in buffers, we are reducing the stack size significantly even if the buffer for storing the complete signature required by the reference and the pqm4/PQClean implementations is not taken into account. The buffer for our streaming variant can be entirely avoided if all data is transferred or consumed right away or it can be any size up to the size of an entire signature. For the TPM example, we are using a 1 kB buffer (see Sect. 4.2).

The stack requirements of pqm4/PQClean are significantly lower than those of the reference implementation. However, our streaming implementation requires even less stack than pqm4/PQClean. Our implementation requires only 1 296 B to 2 616 B of stack, which is overall between 23% to 71% of the stack size of the reference implementation; the difference is most significant for the higher security levels. Compared to pqm4/PQClean, in some cases we achieve a reduction in stack usage to 34%.

Nevertheless, the main memory savings of our streaming implementation are achieved by not storing the entire signature in device memory during signing and verification. Our overall memory savings are hence revealed when also the size of the signature ("Sig." in Table 3) is considered. Overall, our implementation requires up to 30× less data memory than the reference implementation for SPHINCS+ parameter sets with large signatures.

Time-Memory Trade-Off. Since our streaming interface does not introduce a significant performance penalty but reduces the stack and memory demand significantly, we provide savings in regard to memory without cost in time.

Comparison to Prior Streaming Approaches. Our implementation cannot directly be compared to the work by Hülsing et al. in [HRS2016], since they are investigating signature streaming for the predecessor SPHINCS-256 of SPHINCS+. SPHINCS-256 uses different performance parameters and a different few-time signature scheme than SPHINCS+. Their primary goal is to fit into the 16 kB RAM of their Cortex-M3 CPU. They require much fewer cycles for key generation but many more cycles for signing with their SPHINCS-256 parameter set compared to us using the SPHINCS+ parameter sets. Their stack usage is between 6 kB and 9 kB depending on compiler parameters.

Gonzalez et al. are providing performance and stack measurements for two SPHINCS+ parameter sets for verifying a streamed signature in [GHK+2021] on a Cortex-M3 platform with 8 kB of memory. Their cycle counts are not comparable to our implementation since we are using a different CPU for our measurements but their stack size is similar to our version. However, they are splitting the signature in relatively large parts of up to 5 kB along the layers of the SPHINCS+ hypertree, while our implementation is more flexible in regard to the streaming interface and buffer sizes and independent of the SPHINCS+ hypertree structure.

4.2 TPM Integration

Table 4 shows performance measurements of the SPHINCS$^+$ variants integrated into our prototype TPM implementation. We compute the I/O overhead (column "Embedded – I/O") as the relative difference between the cycle counts from the measurements of the stand-alone streaming implementation (column "Embedded – strm.") and the cycle count of the corresponding operation in the TPM integration (column "Embedded – TPM") as "(TPM - strm.)/(TPM * 100)". We also report the overall wall clock time of the corresponding TPM operation (including TPM-protocol overhead etc.) as seen from the host in seconds (column "Host – total").

Table 4. Performance data for key generation, signing, and verification on the embedded device and on the host. For the embedded device, we list the cycle counts of the reference implementation including the streaming interface as "strm." in mega cycles, the integration of SPHINCS$^+$ into the TPM prototype as "TPM" in mega cycles, and the communication overhead, i.e., the difference between the two in percent, as "I/O Δ". For the host, we list the overall wall-clock time from issuing a TPM command until its completion (including I/O) as "total" in seconds.

Parameter Set	Key Generation				Signing				Verification			
	Embedded			Host	Embedded			Host	Embedded			Host
	strm.	TPM	I/O	total	strm.	TPM	I/O	total	strm.	TPM	I/O	total
	[mcyc]	[mcyc]	Δ	[s]	[mcyc]	[mcyc]	Δ	[s]	[mcyc]	[mcyc]	Δ	[s]
sphincs-sha256-128f-robust	55.0	60.5	9.1%	0.531	1 280	1 960	34.9%	11.8	82.7	470	82.4%	2.90
sphincs-sha256-128s-robust	3 520	3 870	9.1%	23.3	26 400	29 500	10.3%	176	27.8	206	86.5%	1.33
sphincs-sha256-192f-robust	81.8	91.3	10.4%	0.727	2 160	3 580	39.8%	21.4	123	928	86.8%	5.63
sphincs-sha256-192s-robust	5 240	5 840	10.4%	35.0	48 400	54 600	11.4%	326	44.3	406	89.1%	2.52
sphincs-sha256-256f-robust	300	330	9.0%	2.17	6 120	8 340	26.7%	49.8	177	1 320	86.6%	7.98
sphincs-sha256-256s-robust	4 800	5 280	9.0%	31.6	58 900	65 800	10.5%	392	90	767	88.3%	4.67
sphincs-sha256-128f-simple	27.3	29.7	8.2%	0.340	640	1 250	48.9%	7.54	39.8	420	90.5%	2.61
sphincs-sha256-128s-simple	1 750	1 900	8.2%	11.5	13 300	14 800	10.2%	88.2	13.6	189	92.8%	1.23
sphincs-sha256-192f-simple	40.2	44.4	9.6%	0.447	1 080	2 360	54.3%	14.1	58.4	850	93.1%	5.17
sphincs-sha256-192s-simple	2 570	2 840	9.6%	17.1	24 440	27 700	11.6%	165	21.2	386	94.5%	2.40
sphincs-sha256-256f-simple	106	120	10.9%	0.914	2 230	4 110	45.8%	24.6	60.6	1 180	94.9%	7.14
sphincs-sha256-256s-simple	1 700	1 910	10.9%	11.6	22 000	25 800	14.7%	154	28.9	689	95.8%	4.21

The modified reference implementation of the TPM firmware performs serialization and deserialization, formatting of commands, and parsing the responses of the TPM. On the host system we measured "wall-clock" time with a resolution of milliseconds for the complete execution of three commands, including transmission of the command, reception of the response, and streaming I/O.

I/O Overhead. Since the prototype TPM is connected to the host via SPI, the throughput of the communication is rather low. In addition, since the development board that is running the TPM code does not have dedicated hardware for SPI communication, all SPI interrupts and data transfers need to be handled by the CPU. The speed of the SPI communication can be controlled by the SPI host. Therefore, we gradually increased the SPI bus speed on the Raspberry Pi to find the maximum speed without transmission errors and conducted the experiments at the resulting speed of 4 MHz. To further improve the communication throughput we implemented the streaming API as buffered I/O that stores messages in a 1 kB buffer to be transfered in bulk when the buffer is full. The same mechanism is also used during verification and the signature is transmitted 1 kB at a time using an appropriate implementation of the streaming API. This reduces the overall number of SPI transfers. If sufficient memory is available, a larger buffer size can be chosen to further reduce the communication overhead.

For key generation, there is an about 10% overhead caused by the general host-TPM communication and the SPI interrupt handling due to frequent polling from the host on the SPI bus, despite the fact that there is no data I/O during the computation of the keys. For signing, the I/O overhead is large for the "f" parameter sets due to their large signature sizes.

For verification, the communication overhead is even more pronounced with well over 80% of the time. Therefore, the performance advantage of the "s" over the "f" parameter sets for verification is rather dominated by the communication time of the around two times smaller signatures than by the up to three times faster verification time.

Wall-clock time. The key-generation time for the fast "f" parameter sets overall is relatively low with under 3 s. The key-generation time for the slower size-optimized "s" parameter sets is one order of magnitude slower. Signing time is quite high. Verification time is relatively low for all SHA-256 parameter sets but in particular for the "s" parameter sets.

As mentioned in Sect. 2.1, most of the time in all SPHINCS+ operations is spent in the hash-functions. Therefore, providing optimized implementations or hardware acceleration for hashing in a PQC-TPM will significantly speed up the wall-clock time for SPHINCS+ operations. In our experiments, verification is dominated by the communication time and also for signing using the "f" parameters the communication time is significant. However, communication time can be reduced as well with dedicated hardware for SPI or when the TPM is tightly coupled with the host system.

The "f" parameter sets are intended to provide faster key generation and signing time at the cost of larger signatures and slower verification. This effect is clearly visible in our TPM-prototype measurements. Therefore, we recommend the "s" parameter sets for applications where a TPM verifies SPHINCS+ signatures and the "f" parameter sets when a TPM is the owner of a SPHINCS+ private key (i.e., performs key generation and signing). If a TPM is required to perform all the operations key generation, signing, and verification, then the "f" parameter sets may overall be the better choice.

5   Conclusion

In conclusion, it is possible to stream SPHINCS+ signatures during signing and verification while requiring only a fraction of the memory that would be required to store such a signature on the device that computes the signature. The peak memory usage across all measured operations and parameter sets in the ARM Cortex-M4 implementation is only 2,55 kB despite the fact that the signatures alone are larger. In this work, we have improved upon previous results aiming to stream hash-based signatures and demonstrated our approach by integrating our implementation into the TPM reference implementation. Our proposed modification to the TPM interface, or a similar construction for streaming, will allow to better navigate the increased resource demands of using post-quantum cryptography with these devices.

While computing SPHINCS$^+$ signatures on an embedded devices requires a significant (for some applications potentially prohibitive) amount of time, verifying SPHINCS$^+$ signatures on such devices is indeed very much feasible using signature streaming even if the memory of the device is too small to store an entire SPHINCS$^+$ signature. As a result, TPM use cases that require private key operations might not be feasible, depending on runtime requirements. However, our work enables the implementation of typical TPM use cases such as secure boot and secure firmware updates with SPHINCS$^+$ signatures, where the TPM is used to securely store a public authentication key and verify a signature.

Acknowledgements. We would like to thank Aymeric Genêt and anonymous reviewers for their valuable feedback on earlier versions of this paper. This work has been partially funded by the German Federal Ministry of Education and Research (BMBF) under the project "QuantumRISC" (IDs 16KIS1033K and 16KIS1037) and by the Taiwanese Ministry of Science and Technology (MOST) under the project 109-2221-E-001-009-MY3.

References

[ACZ2018]   Amiet, D., Curiger, A., Zbinden, P.: FPGA-based accelerator for SPHINCS-256. **2018**(1), 18–39 (2018)

[BDH2011]   Buchmann, J., Dahmen, E., Hülsing, A.: XMSS - a practical forward secure signature scheme based on minimal security assumptions. In: Yang, B.-Y. (ed.) PQCrypto 2011. LNCS, vol. 7071, pp. 117–129. Springer, Heidelberg (2011). https://doi.org/10.1007/978-3-642-25405-5_8

[BHH+2015]   Bernstein, D.J., et al.: SPHINCS: practical stateless hash-based signatures. In: Oswald, E., Fischlin, M. (eds.) EUROCRYPT 2015. LNCS, vol. 9056, pp. 368–397. Springer, Heidelberg (2015). https://doi.org/10.1007/978-3-662-46800-5_15

[BHK+2019]   Bernstein, D.J., Hülsing, A., Kölbl, S., Niederhagen, R., Rijneveld, J., Schwabe, P.: The SPHINCS+ signature framework, pp. 2129–2146 (2019)

[CKRS2020]   Campos, F., Kohlstadt, T., Reith, S., Stöttinger, M.: LMS vs XMSS: comparison of stateful hash-based signature schemes on ARM cortex-M4. In: Nitaj, A., Youssef, A. (eds.) AFRICACRYPT 2020. LNCS, vol. 12174, pp. 258–277. Springer, Cham (2020). https://doi.org/10.1007/978-3-030-51938-4_13

[CMP+2021]   Chen, L., et al.: Final demonstrators implementation report (2021). https://futuretpm.eu/images/Deliverables/FutureTPM-D65-Final-Demonstrators-Implementation-Report-PU-M36.pdf

[GHK+2021] Gonzalez, R., et al.: Verifying post-quantum signatures in 8 kB of RAM. In: Cheon, J.H., Tillich, J.-P. (eds.) PQCrypto 2021 2021. LNCS, vol. 12841, pp. 215–233. Springer, Cham (2021). https://doi.org/10.1007/978-3-030-81293-5_12

[GKPM2018] Genêt, A., Kannwischer, M.J., Pelletier, H., McLauchlan, A.: Practical fault injection attacks on SPHINCS. Cryptology ePrint Archive, Report 2018/674 (2018)

[HBD+2020] Hülsing, A., et al.: SPHINCS+. techreport. National Institute of Standards and Technology (2020)

[HBG+2018] Hülsing, A., Butin, D., Gazdag, S.-L., Rijneveld, J., Mohaisen, A.: XMSS: eXtended Merkle Signature Scheme. RFC **8391**, 1–74 (2018)

[HRS2016] Hülsing, A., Rijneveld, J., Schwabe, P.: ARMed SPHINCS - computing a 41 KB signature in 16 KB of RAM, pp. 446–470 (2016)

[K2018] Kölbl, S.: Putting wings on SPHINCS. In: Lange, T., Steinwandt, R. (eds.) PQCrypto 2018. LNCS, vol. 10786, pp. 205–226. Springer, Cham (2018). https://doi.org/10.1007/978-3-319-79063-3_10

[KRSS] Kannwischer, M.J., Rijneveld, J., Schwabe, P., Stoffelen, K.: PQM4: post-quantum crypto library for the ARM Cortex-M4. https://github.com/mupq/pqm4/

[KRSS2019] Kannwischer, M.J., Rijneveld, J., Schwabe, P., Stoffelen, K.: pqm4: testing and benchmarking NIST PQC on ARM Cortex-M4. Cryptology ePrint Archive, Report 2019/844 (2019)

[MAA+2020] Moody, D., et al.: Status report on the second round of the NIST postquantum cryptography standardization process (2020)

[MCF2019] McGrew, D., Curcio, M., Fluhrer, S.: Hash-based signatures. IETF Crypto Forum Research Group (2019). https://datatracker.ietf.org/doc/html/draft-mcgrew-hash-sigs-15/

[Mer1990] Merkle, R.C.: A certified digital signature. In: Brassard, G. (ed.) CRYPTO 1989. LNCS, vol. 435, pp. 218–238. Springer, New York (1990). https://doi.org/10.1007/0-387-34805-0_21

[PSS2021] Paul, S., Schick, F., Seedorf, J.: TPM-based post-quantum cryptography: a case study on quantum-resistant and mutually authenticated TLS for IoT environments. In: Reinhardt, D., Müller, T. (eds.) ARES 2021, pp. 3:1–3:10. ACM (2021)

[RKK2020] Roth, J., Karatsiolis, E., Krämer, J.: Classic McEliece implementation with low memory footprint. In: Liardet, P.-Y., Mentens, N. (eds.) CARDIS 2020. LNCS, vol. 12609, pp. 34–49. Springer, Cham (2021). https://doi.org/10.1007/978-3-030-68487-7_3

[Tru2013] Trusted Computing Group. TCG PC client specific TPM interface specification (TIS). Specification Version 1.3, 1 (2013). https://trustedcomputinggroup.org/resource/pc-client-platform-tpm-profile-ptp-specification/

[Tru2019a] Trusted Computing Group. Trusted Platform Module Library, Part 1: Architecture. Specification version: 1.59 Family 2.0, 1 (2019a). https://trustedcomputinggroup.org/resource/tpm-library/

[Tru2019b] Trusted Computing Group. Trusted Platform Module Library, Part 3: Commands. Specification version: 1.59 Family 2.0, 1 (2019b)

[WJW+2019] Wang, W., et al.: XMSS and embedded systems. In: Paterson, K.G., Stebila, D. (eds.) SAC 2019. LNCS, vol. 11959, pp. 523–550. Springer, Cham (2020). https://doi.org/10.1007/978-3-030-38471-5_21

Post-quantum (Crypt)analysis

Solving the Learning Parity with Noise Problem Using Quantum Algorithms

Bénédikt Tran[(✉)] and Serge Vaudenay

LASEC, Ecole Polytechnique Fédérale de Lausanne, 1015 Lausanne, Switzerland
{benedikt.tran,serge.vaudenay}@epfl.ch

Abstract. The Learning Parity with Noise (LPN) problem is a famous cryptographic problem consisting in recovering a secret from noised samples. This problem is usually solved via reduction techniques, that is, one reduces the original instance to a smaller one before substituting back the recovered unknowns and starting the process again. There has been an extensive amount of work where time-memory trade-offs, optimal chains of reductions or different solving techniques were considered but hardly any of them involved quantum algorithms. In this work, we are interested in studying the improvements brought by quantum computers when attacking the LPN search problem in the sparse noise regime. Our primary contribution is a novel efficient quantum algorithm based on Grover's algorithm which searches for permutations achieving specific error patterns. This algorithm non-asymptotically outperforms the known techniques in a low-noise regime while using a low amount of memory.

Keywords: Post-quantum cryptography · LPN · Gaussian elimination · Walsh-Hadamard transform

1 Introduction

The *Learning Parity with Noise* (LPN) problem is a fundamental problem in modern cryptography. It is closely related to code-based and lattice-based cryptography and is relatively easy to state. If considered as a code-based problem, the LPN search problem is equivalent to the Computational Syndrome Decoding problem which consists in decoding a noisy codeword and recovering the original message. The usual framework for solving LPN is to use reduction chains. More precisely, the initial LPN instance with a secret of size k is reduced through a chain of reductions to an LPN instance with a secret of size $k' < k$ during the *reduction phase*. After that, the smaller instance is solved in the *solving phase* by some algorithm $\mathcal{A}$ to recover a part of the original secret. The unknown bits in the original secret are then substituted back and the process is repeated until the whole secret is recovered.

B. Tran—Supported by the Swiss National Science Foundation (SNSF) through the project grant № 192364 on Post-Quantum Cryptography.

Previous Work. In the current state of the art, reductions and solving algorithms are mainly *classical* algorithms, although some works present *quantum* variants. In [15], Esser, Kübler and May described a novel attack on LPN which for the first time relied on quantum algorithms. They revisited the reduction techniques of Blum, Kalai and Wasserman [9] and proposed an hybrid quantum algorithm achieving better classical and quantum complexity. Their results were recently improved by Jiao in [20]. These algorithms essentially try to find an error-free batch of LPN queries in order to recover the secret via Gaussian elimination, similarly to Information Set Decoding (ISD) techniques in code-based cryptography. Currently, correcting w errors in a code of length n and dimension k is done in classical time $\tilde{O}(2^{\alpha n})$, where α depends on the code rate $R = \frac{k}{n}$ and error rate $\omega = \frac{w}{n}$. For unique decoding instances targetting the Gilbert-Varshamov distance, [21] reported that the *classical* ISD techniques satisfy $\alpha = 0.1207$ for the naive Prange's algorithm [27] and $\alpha = 0.0966$ for the best known technique due to May and Ozerov [25]. However, when considering *quantum* ISD, Bernstein's algorithm [5] (Quantum Prange) satisfies $\alpha = 0.06035$ while the best known quantum technique based on quantum random walks due to Kachigar and Tillich [21] satisfies $\alpha = 0.05869$ [21, §1]. Morally speaking, advanced classical ISD techniques usually improve significantly the running time of the naive approach, but that is not necessarily the case with their quantum counterpart. In the field of reduction techniques, Bogos and Vaudenay [11] described a framework for finding the best time-complexity-wise reduction chains while Wiggers and Samardjiska [29] investigated LPN under memory constraints. While most of the solving techniques rely on Gaussian elimination, exhaustive search or Walsh-Hadamard transform (WHT), other algorithms can be used instead such as the SFT algorithm introduced by Akavia in [1] and later studied by Galbraith, Laity and Shani [16] and Dachman-Soled, Gong, Kippen and Shahverdi [14].

Our Contributions. In this paper, our main contribution is a novel quantum algorithm (Algorithm 5) that solves an LPN instance by searching for a permutation of the LPN queries for which the corresponding error vector follows a specific pattern. This follows the same idea as the Lee-Brickell [22] algorithm which is a generalization of Prange's algorithm, yet does not rely on advanced decoding in order to minimize the memory cost. Our algorithm is based on Gaussian elimination and Grover's algorithm and improves the time complexity of LPN solving algorithms for large dimensions in a low-noise regime. It consumes a very low amount of quantum memory (Table 1) and requires a small amount of LPN queries that do not need to be accessed in superposition. This is an alternative to using the quantum version of the MMT [24] or BJMM [3] algorithms, which both require an exponential amount of memory, or the Well-Pooled Gauss [15] algorithm which requires a large number of LPN queries. In the continuation of [11], we present novel quantum algorithms based on the exhaustive search and the Walsh-Hadamard transform (Algorithms 6 and 7) and compare them with existing works. On the other hand, by considering the SFT algorithm as an alternative to the WHT solver, we observe that the classical time complexity improvements brought by the former over the latter are of a factor 4 to 8, while the memory complexity remains roughly unchanged. We also extended and refined the algorithm from [11] to include the memory complexity and more solvers than what was originally proposed by the authors. These optimizations may also serve as non-trivial bounds on the range of parameters for other optimization programs and are presented in the Appendix B. For the sake of completeness, we report in Table 2 the best complexity of the chains that we found and compare them with those reported in [15] and [29]. For instance, for $k = 512$ and $\tilde{\tau} = 0.05$, the quantum algorithm from [15] claims a quantum complexity of $\tilde{O}(2^{18.27})$ but should rather be estimated as $O(2^{49.39})$ due to the matrix inversion and matrix multiplications appearing in Grover's predicate, showing the importance of polynomial factors. Although the authors of [15] reported their results by taking into account polynomial factors, these were later corrected by [29] as there was a bug in the original script (which was acknowledged by the authors). In comparison, our algorithm runs in quantum time $O(2^{46.72})$ for this set of parameters. In this paper, we try to keep track of all the polynomial factors to have a good estimate of the non-asymptotic complexity.

Structure of the Paper. This paper is structured as follows. Section 2 introduces the notations and presents basic notions on Fourier analysis and quantum computing. Section 2.4 defines the Learning Parity with Noise problem. In Sect. 3, we present the decoding techniques used to solve an LPN instance. Section 4 reports the complexity of the reduction chains that we found and compares them with existing results. We eventually conclude our paper in the last section. The different reduction techniques are presented in Appendix A and the optimization results related to reduction chains are presented in Appendix B.

2   Preliminaries

We write $P \stackrel{\triangle}{=} Q$ to mean that the symbol P is *defined as* the symbol Q. By convention, $\log(\cdot)$ denotes the *binary logarithm*. The set of *positive integers* is denoted by $\mathbb{N}$, the set of *nonnegative integers* by $\mathbb{Z}_+$ (i.e. $0 \in \mathbb{Z}_+$) and the *integral range* $\{a, \ldots, b\}$ for $a \leq b \in \mathbb{Z}$ by $[\![a, b]\!]$. To ease notations, we simply write $[\![n]\!]$ instead of $[\![1, n]\!]$. The *ring* $\mathbb{Z}/n\mathbb{Z}$ of integers modulo n is denoted by $\mathbf{Z}_n$.

The *algebra of $m \times n$ matrices* defined over a commutative ring A is identified with $A^{m \times n}$. Unless stated otherwise, vectors are written as *row* vectors. Given a vector $z \in A^n$ and an indexation set $I \subseteq [\![n]\!]$ of size k, we denote by $z_I \in A^k$ the *subvector of z indexed by I*. We define a similar notation for matrices by denoting the *submatrix of $M \in A^{n \times m}$ indexed by I* by $M_I \in A^{k \times m}$. The *transpose* of a matrix M is denoted by M^T and the *transpose of the inverse* of an invertible matrix M is denoted by $M^{-T} = (M^{-1})^T = (M^T)^{-1}$. The *Hamming weight* of a vector $x \in A^n$, denoted by $wt(x)$, is the number of nonzero coefficients of x.

A random variable X following a distribution $\mathcal{D}$ is denoted by $X \sim \mathcal{D}$ and a variable x taking a value according to the distribution $\mathcal{D}$ is denoted by $x \leftarrow \mathcal{D}$. For the *uniform distribution $\mathcal{U}$* over a finite set S, we simply write $x \stackrel{\$}{\leftarrow} S$ instead of $x \leftarrow \mathcal{U}$. The *expectation* of a random variable X is denoted by $\mathbb{E}[X]$.

2.1   Fourier Analysis over Finite Abelian Groups

Given a finite Abelian group $G \cong \mathbf{Z}_{N_1} \oplus \ldots \oplus \mathbf{Z}_{N_\ell}$ of order N, we denote by $L^2(G)$ the space of all complex-valued functions on G endowed with the inner product defined by $\langle f, g \rangle \triangleq \mathbb{E}[f(x)\overline{g(x)}] \triangleq \frac{1}{N} \sum_{x \in G} f(x)\overline{g(x)}$. This inner product induces a norm on $L^2(G)$ via $\|f\|_2 \triangleq \sqrt{\langle f, f \rangle}$ and $\|f\|_\infty \triangleq \max_{x \in G} |f(x)|$. By the Pontryagin duality, any isomorphism $\alpha \mapsto \chi_\alpha$ of $G \cong \hat{G}$ ensures that a character $\chi_\alpha \in \hat{G}$ is expressible as $\chi_{(\alpha_1,\ldots,\alpha_\ell)}(x_1,\ldots,x_\ell) = \prod_{i=1}^{\ell} \omega_{N_i}^{\alpha_i x_i}$ where $\omega_{N_i} \triangleq \exp(2\pi i/N_i)$.

Definition 1. *The Fourier transform $\hat{f} \in L^2(\hat{G})$ of $f \in L^2(G)$ is defined by*

$$\hat{f}(\alpha) \triangleq \langle f, \chi_\alpha \rangle = \frac{1}{N} \sum_{x_1,\ldots,x_\ell \in G} f(x_1,\ldots,x_\ell) \prod_{j=1}^{\ell} \omega_{N_i}^{-\alpha_j x_j}.$$

For any subset $S \subseteq G$, the restriction $f_S \colon S \longrightarrow \mathbb{C}$ of f to S is the function defined by $f_S(x) \triangleq \sum_{\alpha \in S} \hat{f}(\alpha)\chi_\alpha(x)$, where $\chi_\alpha \in \hat{G}$ is the character corresponding to $\alpha \in G$ under a chosen isomorphism $\alpha \mapsto \chi_\alpha$ from G to $\hat{G}$.

Definition 2. *The Walsh-Hadamard transform $\mathcal{W}_f \in L^2(\mathbf{Z}_2^n)$ of $f \in L^2(\mathbf{Z}_2^n)$ is the function defined by $\mathcal{W}_f(y) \triangleq \sum_{x \in \mathbf{Z}_2^n} (-1)^{\langle x,y \rangle} f(x)$ where $\langle \cdot, \cdot \rangle$ is the usual dot product in $\mathbf{Z}_2^n$.*

For the rest of the document, we implicitly identify $[\![0, 2^n - 1]\!]$ with $\mathbf{Z}_2^n$ via integer-to-binary conversion, that is $k \in [\![0, 2^n - 1]\!]$ is identified with its binary representation $x_k \in \mathbf{Z}_2^n$. For $f \in L^2(\mathbf{Z}_2^n)$ and $i \in [\![0, 2^n - 1]\!]$, we will abusively write $f(i)$ instead of $f(x_i)$. The *fast Walsh-Hadamard transformation* described by Algorithm 1 computes the spectrum $\{\mathcal{W}_f(k)\}_k$ in time $O(t_0 + n2^n\sigma)$ and memory $O(2^n\sigma)$, where t_0 is the complexity of constructing the table $\{f(k)\}_k$ and σ is an estimation of the size of $\mathcal{W}_f$.

Algorithm 1: FWHT

Input: A function $f \in L^2(\mathbf{Z}_2^n)$.
Output: A list $Y = \{y_0, \ldots, y_{2^n-1}\}$ such that $y_i = \mathcal{W}_f(i)$.
1 $X \leftarrow \{f(i)\}_i$ ▷ $X = \{x_0, \ldots, x_{2^n-1}\}$.
2 $Y \leftarrow \{\bot, \ldots, \bot\}$
3 **for** $i = 0, \ldots, n-1$ **do**
4 | **for** $j = 0, \ldots, 2^n - 1$ **do**
5 | | **if** $(j \gg i) \bmod 2 = 1$ **then**
6 | | | $y_j \leftarrow x_{j-2^i} - x_j$
7 | | **else**
8 | | | $y_j \leftarrow x_j + x_{j+2^i}$
9 | $X \leftarrow Y$
10 **return** Y

2.2 Significant Fourier Coefficients

Characters χ_α over $G = \mathbf{Z}_2^n$ satisfy $\chi_\alpha(x) = (-1)^{\langle \alpha, x \rangle}$ so that $\hat{f} \in L^2(\mathbf{Z}_2^n)$ satisfies $\hat{f}(\alpha) = \frac{1}{2^n} \sum_{x \in \mathbf{Z}_2^n} (-1)^{\langle \alpha, x \rangle} f(x) = \frac{1}{2^n} \mathcal{W}_f(\alpha)$. In particular, the Fourier and the Walsh-Hadamard transforms might have been defined with a $\frac{1}{\sqrt{N}}$ factor in order to agree in the binary case, but this is in general not the case in the literature. Nevertheless, this opens a connection between the study of the Walsh-Hadamard spectrum (i.e. the values of $\mathcal{W}_f$) and the Fourier coefficients of f. For instance, if one is interested in computing $\arg\max_y |\mathcal{W}_f(y)|$, then the whole spectrum of either transform is *a priori* needed.

Definition 3 (Significant Fourier Coefficient). *Let G be a finite abelian group and let $f \in L^2(G)$. Given $\tau \geq 0$, we say that $\alpha \in G$ is a τ-significant Fourier coefficient of f if $|\hat{f}(\alpha)|^2 \geq \tau$.*

The SFT problem consists in enumerating the τ-significant Fourier coefficients of $f \in L^2(G)$. It is achieved by generic algorithms in time $N \cdot$ poly$(\log N, 1/\tau)$ and improves over a naive application of FFT whose complexity is $\Theta(N \log N)$. Algorithm 2 describes the algorithm proposed by Galbraith, Laity and Shani in [16] to solve the SFT problem for $G \overset{\Delta}{=} \mathbf{Z}_{2^n}$ (which can be extended to arbitrary groups via domain stretching) with a memory complexity of order $O(2^n)$. By [13], the time complexity for finding the τ-significant Fourier coefficients of $f \in L^2(\mathbf{Z}_{2^n})$ with probability at least $1 - \delta$ is $O\left(\frac{n\|f\|_2^2\|f\|_\infty^4}{\tau^3} \ln \frac{n\|f\|_2^2}{\delta\tau}\right)$.

Algorithm 2: SFT algorithm over $G = \mathbf{Z}_{2^n}$.

Input: A function $f \in L^2(G)$, a threshold $\tau > 0$ and a parameter $\lambda > 0$.
Output: A subset $L \subset G$ containing the τ-significant Fourier coefficients of f.

1   $V_0 \leftarrow \{G\}$
2   **for** $i = 1, \ldots, n$ **do**
3      $V_i \leftarrow \emptyset$
4   **for** $L \in V_{i-1}$ **do**
5   Encode each $x \in L$ as $x = x_n \cdots x_1$ where x_n is the most significant bit.
6         $A \leftarrow \{x = x_n \cdots x_1 \in L : x_{n-i} = 0\}$
7         $B \leftarrow \{x = x_n \cdots x_1 \in L : x_{n-i} = 1\}$
8   **if** $\|f_A\|_2^2 \geq \lambda\tau$ **then**
9           $\lfloor$ $V_i \leftarrow V_i \cup \{A\}$
10   **if** $\|f_B\|_2^2 \geq \lambda\tau$ **then**
11          $\lfloor$ $V_i \leftarrow V_i \cup \{B\}$

12   $L \leftarrow \{x \in G : \{x\} \in V_n\}$
13   **return** L

As stated in [13, §3.5], a naive iteration of Algorithm 2 requires 2^n samples of $f(x)$ to compute $\|f_A\|_2^2$, giving a query complexity of order $\Omega(n2^n)$. As such, the straightforward approach does not give any improvements over the FFT algorithm, and therefore the authors of [16] suggested to *approximate* the norm instead of directly computing it. By [13, Lemma 3], approximating $\|f_A\|_2^2$ up to an error bounded by $\eta\|f\|_\infty^2$ with probability at least

$1 - \varepsilon$ requires $m = \Omega\left(\frac{2}{\eta^2} \ln \frac{2}{\varepsilon}\right)$ samples from $f(x)$ and by [13, Lemma 6], there are $L = O\left(\frac{\|f\|_2^2}{\lambda\tau - \eta\|f\|_\infty^2}\right)$ subsets that will be approximated. Choosing $\lambda = 2/3$, $\eta = \frac{\tau}{3\|f\|_\infty^2}$ and $\varepsilon = \frac{\delta(\lambda\tau - \eta\|f\|_\infty^2)}{2n\|f\|_2^2}$ minimizes the overall complexity [13, Appendix A]. A more refined bound can be found using the Central Limit Theorem and a complete description of the SFT algorithm with approximations is given in [13, §4].

2.3   Quantum Computing

Proposition 1 ([19, **Prop. 3**], [26, §6]). *Let $n \geq 1$ and let $f : \mathbf{Z}_2^n \longrightarrow \{0,1\}$ be a boolean function implemented by a classical circuit consisting of $O(K)$ gates. Let $M = \left|f^{-1}(\{1\})\right|$ and $N = 2^n$. Then, Grover's algorithm runs in quantum time $O(K\sqrt{N/M})$ and quantum memory $O(\log N)$ and succeeds in finding a pre-image of 1 with probability at least $1/4$.*

Notation 1. We denote C independent *lazy* runs of Grover's algorithm for predicate φ over a unsorted database Y by $\mathsf{Grover}^{\otimes C}(Y, \varphi) \xrightarrow{\$} (y_1, \ldots, y_C)$. More precisely, it is equivalent to run Grover's algorithm sufficiently many times to ensure the existence of at least one $y_i \in Y$ satisfying the predicate.

2.4   Learning Parity with Noise

Definition 4 (Bias of a distribution in the sense of Bleichenbacher [8]). *The bias $\delta_{\mathcal{X}}$ of a distribution $\mathcal{X}$ defined over $\mathbf{Z}_q$ is defined to be $\delta_{\mathcal{X}} \triangleq \mathbb{E}\left[\mathbf{e}_q(\mathcal{X})\right]$, where $\mathbf{e}_q(x) \triangleq \exp(2\pi i x/q)$. More generally, the bias of $y = (y_1, \ldots, y_n) \in \mathbf{Z}_q^n$ is defined by $\delta_y = \frac{1}{n}\sum_{i=1}^{n} \mathbf{e}_q(y_i)$.*

For the uniform distribution $\mathcal{X}$ over $\mathbf{Z}_q$, we have $\delta_{\mathcal{X}} = 0$, while for the Bernoulli distribution $\mathcal{X} = \mathsf{Ber}_\tau$ of parameter τ, we have $\delta_{\mathcal{X}} = 1 - 2\tau$.

Definition 5 (LPN oracle [11, §2.1]). *Let $k \in \mathbb{N}$ and $0 < \tau < \frac{1}{2}$. Given a random $s \in \mathbf{Z}_2^k$ (not necessarily uniform), an LPN oracle $\mathcal{O}_{\mathsf{LPN}(k,\tau,s)}$ is an oracle which outputs independent random samples according to the distribution $\mathcal{Q}(k, \tau, s)$ whose values $\psi = (a, c) \in \mathbf{Z}_2^{k+1}$ are sampled as follows:*

$$\left\{\psi = (a, c) \mid a \xleftarrow{\$} \mathbf{Z}_2^k, c = \langle a, s \rangle \oplus \varepsilon, \varepsilon \leftarrow \mathsf{Ber}_\tau\right\}.$$

The parameter k is called the dimension and τ is called the noise rate. The biases of the noise and the secret s are denoted by δ_τ and δ_s respectively. We write $(\mathbf{A}, c) \leftarrow \mathsf{LPN}_{k,\tau,s}^{\otimes n}$ to denote the random matrix $\mathbf{A} = \begin{bmatrix} -a_1- \\ \vdots \\ -a_n- \end{bmatrix} \in \mathbf{Z}_2^{n \times k}$ with the oracle bits vector $c = (c_1, \ldots, c_n) = s\mathbf{A}^T \oplus \varepsilon \in \mathbf{Z}_2^n$ arising from the LPN queries $\mathcal{Q} = \{(a_i, c_i)\}_i$ and the (unknown) noise vector $\varepsilon = (\varepsilon_1, \ldots, \varepsilon_n) \in \mathbf{Z}_2^n$.

Definition 6 (LPN search problem [11, §2.1]**).** *A k-dimensional Learning Parity with Noise (LPN) instance with secret vector $s \in \mathbf{Z}_2^k$ and constant noise rate $0 < \tau < \frac{1}{2}$ is denoted by* LPN(k, τ, s). *Given parameters q, t, m and ϑ, an algorithm $\mathcal{A}$, limited in time t and memory m and performing at most q queries to an* LPN *oracle $\mathcal{O}_{\mathsf{LPN}(k,\tau,s)}$, is said to (q, t, m, ϑ)–solve the search problem associated with the* LPN(k, τ, s) *instance if*

$$\Pr\left[\mathcal{A}^{\mathcal{O}_{\mathsf{LPN}(k,\tau,s)}} \rightarrow s \mid s \xleftarrow{\$} \mathbf{Z}_2^k\right] \geq \vartheta.$$

3   Solving Techniques

As mentioned in [11], an idea for solving LPN is to reduce the original problem to an easier one by applying multiple reductions before solving the final instance using decoding techniques, such as *Gaussian elimination, Walsh-Hadamard transform* (WHT), *majority vote* (as used in BKW algorithms), *Significant Fourier Coefficients* [13], or *exhaustive search*. Since WHT solvers perform usually better than majority vote ones, we will not consider the latter. It remains to decide which of the remaining solvers is the most efficient given a chain of reductions.

The overall solving process consists in choosing some threshold ϑ to bound the failure probability of the solver to recover a first block of the secret. By iterating the process on the remaining unknowns and reducing the failure probability at each step (ϑ^i for the i-th iteration), the whole secret is recovered in i iterations and the total failure probability is bounded by $\psi(\vartheta, i) = \vartheta + \ldots + \vartheta^i$ which satisfies $\lim_{i \to \infty} \psi(\frac{1}{3}, i) = \frac{1}{2}$. For the rest of the section, $\mathcal{Q} = \{(a_1, c_1), \ldots, (a_n, c_n)\}$ denotes a set of n LPN queries and $\varepsilon = (\varepsilon_1, \ldots, \varepsilon_n) \in \mathbf{Z}_2^n$ is the corresponding noise vector. We also recall that $\mathbf{A} \in \mathbf{Z}_2^{n \times k}$ is the matrix whose rows consist of the a_i's and that $c = (c_1, \ldots, c_n) \in \mathbf{Z}_2^n$ are the corresponding oracle bits. Unless stated otherwise, the oracle queries do not need to be accessed in superposition.

3.1   Gaussian Elimination and Information Set Decoding

Given an independent set of k queries, the LPN secret $s \in \mathbf{Z}_2^k$ can be efficiently recovered. More precisely, one samples $(\mathbf{A}, c) \leftarrow \mathsf{LPN}_{k,\tau,s}^{\otimes k}$ until $\mathbf{A}$ is invertible and defines the secret candidate to be $\hat{s} \triangleq c\mathbf{A}^{-T} = (\hat{s}_1, \ldots, \hat{s}_k)$. If the queries were all error-free (i.e. $\varepsilon = \mathbf{0}$) then we would have $s = \hat{s}$. This construction mimics Prange's algorithm [27] for solving the Computational Syndrome Decoding problem.

Esser, Kübler and May presented classical and quantum ISD-based techniques in [15] based on the well-known MMT algorithm [24] to solve the LPN search problem. While MMT seems to perform quite-well, it may be outperformed by normal techniques, as reported in [29, Table 1]. Instead, we suggest an approach inspired by the Lee-Brickell [22] algorithm, extending the Gaussian elimination solver. To that end, we use a well-known technique called sparse-secret that consists in transforming an $\mathsf{LPN}(k, \tau, s)$ instance into an $\mathsf{LPN}(k, \tau, s')$ instance where s' is a LPN secret following the same distribution as the error, i.e. a Bernoulli distribution of parameter τ. This reduction is described on Algorithm 3 and the complexity analysis can be found in Appendix A.1. For now, we denote the time complexity of this reduction by $\tau_{sparse} = \mathsf{poly}(n, k)$.

Algorithm 3: sparse-secret

Input: A list of n queries $\mathcal{Q} = \{(a_i, c_i)\}_i$ of an $\mathsf{LPN}(k, \tau, s)$ instance with noise $\varepsilon \in \mathbf{Z}_2^n$.
Output: A list of $n - k$ queries $\mathcal{Q}' = \{(a_i', c_i')\}_i$ of a reduced $\mathsf{LPN}(k, \tau, s')$ instance and an indexation set $J = \{j_1, \dots, j_k\} \subseteq [\![n]\!]$ such that $s' = \varepsilon_J$.

1 **repeat**
2   Select an indexation set $J = \{j_1, \dots, j_k\} \subseteq [\![n]\!]$ of size k.
3     $M \leftarrow \begin{bmatrix} a_{j_1}^T & \cdots & a_{j_k}^T \end{bmatrix} \in \mathbf{Z}_2^{k \times k}$
4 **until** $\mathrm{rank}(M) = k$
5 $n' \leftarrow n - k$
6 $[\![n]\!] \setminus J \to \{i_1, \dots, i_{n'}\}$
7 **for** $\ell = 1, \dots, n'$ **do**
8     $a_\ell' \leftarrow a_{i_\ell} M^{-T}$
9     $c_\ell' \leftarrow \langle a_\ell', c_J \rangle \oplus c_{i_\ell}$ ▷ $c_J \overset{\triangle}{=} (c_{j_1}, \dots, c_{j_k})$
10 $\mathcal{Q}' \leftarrow \{(a_1', c_1'), \dots, (a_{n'}', c_{n'}')\}$ ▷ the new list of queries
11 **return** $(\mathcal{Q}', J)$

Given a secret candidate $\hat{s}$, we need to determine whether it is the correct one or not. For that, it suffices to sample m fresh queries $(\hat{\mathbf{A}}, \hat{c}) \leftarrow \mathsf{LPN}_{k, \tau, s}^{\otimes m}$ and decide whether the distribution of $\hat{\varepsilon} \overset{\triangle}{=} \hat{s}\hat{\mathbf{A}}^T \oplus \hat{c}$ is closer to $\mathsf{Ber}_\tau^{\otimes m}$ or $\mathsf{Ber}_{1/2}^{\otimes m}$. Such task is achieved by Algorithm 4 which tests whether $wt(\hat{\varepsilon})$ is closer to $m\tau$ or $\frac{m}{2}$.

Algorithm 4: TEST-SECRET [15, Alg. 3]

Input: An $\mathsf{LPN}(k, \tau, s)$ instance, a candidate $\hat{s} \in \mathbf{Z}_2^k$ and $\alpha, \beta \in (0, 1]$.
Output: An accept (1) or reject (0) flag.

1 $m \leftarrow \left(\dfrac{\sqrt{\frac{3}{2} \ln(\alpha^{-1})} + \sqrt{\ln(\beta^{-1})}}{\frac{1}{2} - \tau} \right)^2$

2 $(\hat{\mathbf{A}}, \hat{c}) \leftarrow \mathsf{LPN}_{k, \tau, s}^{\otimes m}$

3 $\gamma \leftarrow \tau m + \sqrt{3 \left(\frac{1}{2} - \tau \right) \ln(\alpha^{-1}) m}$

4 $\hat{\varepsilon} \leftarrow \hat{s}\hat{\mathbf{A}}^T \oplus \hat{c}$

5 **return** $\mathbb{1}_{wt(\hat{\varepsilon}) \leq \gamma}$

By [15, Lem. 3], generalized by [29, Prop. 2], for all $0 < \alpha, \beta \leq \frac{1}{\sqrt{2\pi e}}$, Algorithm 4 accepts the correct LPN secret with probability at least $1 - \alpha$ and rejects incorrect candidates $\hat{s}$ with probability at least $1 - \beta$ if at least m samples are available, where

$$m = \left(\frac{\sqrt{2\tau(1 - \tau) \ln\left(\frac{1}{\alpha\sqrt{2\pi}} \right)} + \sqrt{\frac{1}{2} \ln\left(\frac{1}{2} \frac{1}{\beta\sqrt{2\pi}} \right)}}{\frac{1}{2} - \tau} \right)^2.$$

This crucial observation turns Algorithm 4 into a "checking" procedure for an arbitrary secret which may not necessarily arise from an information set. Instead of searching for an information set, we may even search for an indexation set for which the weight of the corresponding noise vector lies within a given interval. This approach is similar to the Lee-Brickell ISD algorithm [22] and gives rise to the following novel algorithm.

Algorithm 5: LPN-ISD

Input: A list of n queries $\mathcal{Q} = \{(a_i, c_i)\}_i$ of an LPN(k, τ, s) instance and $w_1, w_2 \in [0, k]$.
Output: An LPN secret candidate $s \in \mathbf{Z}_2^k$ or $\perp$ if none can be found.

1   $P \leftarrow \sum\limits_{i=w_1}^{w_2} \binom{k}{i} \tau^i (1-\tau)^{k-i}$ $\triangleright$ $P = \Pr[wt(\varepsilon) \in [w_1, w_2] : \varepsilon \sim \mathsf{Ber}_\tau]$

2   **repeat** $1/P$ **times**

3   Apply sparse-secret (Algorithm 3) to get an LPN(k, τ, ε_*) instance.

4   **forall the** $\varepsilon \in \mathbf{Z}_2^k : w_1 \le wt(\varepsilon) \le w_2$ **do**

5   Call Algorithm 4 with the remaining $m = n - k$ queries to check ε.

6   **if** ε *is the correct secret of* LPN(k, τ, ε_*) **then**

7   Reconstruct s from ε by reverting Algorithm 3.

8   **return** s

9   **return** $\perp$

Let $P = P(k, \tau, w_1, w_2) = \sum\limits_{i=w_1}^{w_2} \binom{k}{i} \tau^i (1-\tau)^{k-i}$. Since Algorithm 4 runs in time $O(k(n-k))$, the classical time complexity of Algorithm 5 is

$$\tau_c = \frac{1}{P}\left(\tau_{sparse} + k(n-k) \sum_{i=w_1}^{w_2} \binom{k}{i}\right). \tag{1}$$

Since there are $m = n-k$ queries after sparse-secret, one chooses $m \ge \frac{8k\ln(2)}{(1-2\tau)^2}$, which is the minimum number of samples required for Algorithm 4 to fail with negligible probability [29, §4]. While the classical variant performs poorly as the dimensions grows, this may not necessarily be the case with its quantum variant. Indeed, most of the complexity arises from the term $1/P$ which is ideally replaced by $1/\sqrt{P}$ if Grover's algorithm can be applied. The ideal Grover predicate must output 1 if the indexation set J chosen by the sparse-secret reduction yields an LPN(k, τ, ε_*) instance for which $wt(\varepsilon_*) \in [w_1, w_2]$. Since the probability of such event to occur is P, it suffices to ensure that Algorithm 4 succeeds and use the results from [15]. Therefore, Algorithm 5 runs in quantum time

$$\tau_q = \frac{1}{\sqrt{P}}\left(\tau_{sparse} + k(n-k) \sum_{i=w_1}^{w_2} \binom{k}{i}\right). \tag{2}$$

The classical memory complexity of Algorithm 5 is $O(kn)$ which is simply the memory complexity of sparse-secret. The quantum memory complexity is dominated by the complexity of storing a superposition of all indexation sets chosen by sparse-secret, namely $\log\binom{n}{k} = O(kn)$.

Remark 1. We think that it is unlikely that we are able to straightforwardly use Grover's algorithm in the inner loop of Algorithm 5 (the search for ε_*). Indeed, the outer loop requires a predicate to be evaluated roughly $1/\sqrt{P}$ times until finding a suitable indexation set. This predicate depends on whether the inner loop finds ε_*, which in turns depends on the queries that are passed to Algorithm 4. The final quantum complexity would then be affected by replacing the term $\sum_{i=w_1}^{w_2} \binom{k}{i}$ by $\sqrt{\sum_{i=w_1}^{w_2} \binom{k}{i}}$. For $w_1 = w_2 = 0$, this does not matter and for $w_1 = 0$ and $w_2 = O(1)$, the speed-up may be marginal compared to the oracle instantiation cost. One possibility that was suggested by the reviewers is to consider a search-with-two oracle approach but we leave it as future work.

The results that we found using this quantum algorithm are promising as it seems to improve the known algorithms for large dimensions and small noise as shown on Table 2 of Sect. 4. The results reported on Tables 1 and 2 were generated by selecting $w_1, w_2 \leq k$ such that τ_c and τ_q are minimal. For $\tau = \frac{1}{\sqrt{k}}$, choosing $w_1 = w_2 = 0$ gives $\tau_c = \mathsf{poly}(n, k) \exp(k\tau)$ and $\tau_q = \mathsf{poly}(n, k) \exp(k\tau/2)$, matching the complexity of the Pooled Gauss algorithm in [15]. On the other hand, for $\tau = O(1)$, choosing $w_1 = 0$ and $w_2 \in \{1, 2\}$ usually gives $P \approx \exp(-k\tau)$ and slightly improves the final complexity.

For a fair comparison of our algorithm, we present the classical and quantum versions of the Pooled Gauss [15, §4.2] and Well-Pooled Gauss [15, §5.1] algorithms. Both are based on Gaussian elimination and have low requirements in query and memory complexity. In the following paragraphs, we will explicitly express the complexities of these algorithms by keeping the poly-logarithmic factors. As we will see later, those factors are actually of importance when comparing the non-asymptotic complexities. The $\tilde{O}$-complexities are taken from [15, Table 1].

Pooled Gauss. The Pooled Gauss algorithm [15, §4.2] works similarly to Algorithm 5, but uses a different number of queries and searches for information sets. More precisely, given an LPN instance $(A, c) \leftarrow \mathsf{LPN}_{k,\tau,s}^{\otimes n}$ for $n = k^2 \log^2 k$, the goal is to find an information set $I \subseteq [\![n]\!]$ of size k such that A_I is invertible and check that $c_I A_I^{-T}$ is the secret using $m = m(\alpha, \beta)$ samples (line 1 of Algorithm 4), where $\alpha = \frac{1}{2^k}$ and $\beta = \left(\frac{1-\tau}{2}\right)^k$. By [15, Thm. 3], an information set is found on average after $N_G(k, \tau) = \frac{\log^2 k}{(1-\tau)^k}$ iterations. The complexity of computing A_I^{-T} and running Algorithm 4 is $\tau_G(k, m) = O(k^3 + mk)$, hence Pooled Gauss runs in classical time

$$\tau_{PG} = O(\tau_G(k, m) \cdot N_G(k, \tau)) = \tilde{O}(2^{kf(\tau)}), \tag{3}$$

where $f(t) = \log\left(\frac{1}{1-t}\right)$. By applying Grover's algorithm on top of Pooled Gauss gives Quantum Pooled Gauss. In [15], to ensure a good probability of success for Grover's algorithm, α and β are chosen so that $\alpha = \beta = \binom{n}{k}^{-2}$. Since the number of Grover's iterations is $\sqrt{N_G(k,\tau)}$, the overall quantum complexity is

$$\tau_{QPG} = O\Big(\tau_G(k,m) \cdot \sqrt{N_G(k,\tau)}\Big) = \tilde{O}\Big(2^{\frac{kf(\tau)}{2}}\Big). \tag{4}$$

Well-Pooled Gauss. The idea of the Well-Pooled Gauss [15, §5.1] algorithm is to use the Pooled Gauss algorithm as a decoding routine and split the problem into finding the first $k'_c = \frac{k}{1+f(\tau)}$ secret bits. Let n and m be the parameters of a Pooled Gauss in dimension k'_c. The first k'_c secret bits are recovered by sampling a pool of $n+m$ LPN samples $(a,c) \leftarrow \mathsf{LPN}_{k,\tau,s}$ for which the last $k-k'_c$ coordinates are 0. By [15, Thm. 5], this takes time $\tau_{pool}(k,\tau) = 2^{k-k'_c}(n+m+\log^2 k)$. Then, a Pooled Gauss is executed using that pool and the remaining bits are recovered similarly. In particular, the complexity of Well-Pooled Gauss is

$$\tau_{WPG} = O(\tau_{pool}(k,\tau) + \tau_G(k'_c,m)N_G(k'_c,\tau)) = \tilde{O}\Big(2^{\frac{kf(\tau)}{1+f(\tau)}}\Big). \tag{5}$$

Replacing k'_c by $k'_q = \frac{2k}{2+f(\tau)}$ and Pooled Gauss by Quantum Pooled Gauss gives rise to Quantum Well-Pooled Gauss which runs in quantum time

$$\tau_{QWPG} = O\Big(\tau_{pool}(k,\tau) + \tau_G(k'_q,m)\sqrt{N_G(k'_q,\tau)}\Big) = \tilde{O}\Big(2^{\frac{kf(\tau)}{2+f(\tau)}}\Big). \tag{6}$$

The number of LPN queries required in Pooled Gauss and Well-Pooled Gauss is much more larger than in our algorithm. In comparison, for $k = 512$ and $\tau = \frac{1}{\sqrt{k}}$, our algorithm requires $O(2^{11.93})$ queries while Quantum Pooled Gauss requires at least $\Omega(2^{24.25})$ queries. Note that Esser and May chose α and β so that the overall complexity matches the $\tilde{O}$-expressions given above and thus, changing the number of queries may also change the final expression.

3.2   Exhaustive Search

Let $f\colon \mathbf{Z}_2^k \longrightarrow \mathbf{Z}_2^n$ be the function defined by $f(x) = x\mathbf{A}^T \oplus c$. Since $f(s) = \varepsilon$, the identity $s = \arg\min_y wt(f(y))$ is likely to hold in a sparse noise regime. Given a weight $0 \leq r \leq k$, the exhaustive search solver EXH introduced in [12, §3.8.1] computes the table of $wt(f|_S)$ where $S = \mathbb{B}_k(r) \subseteq \mathbf{Z}_2^k$ contains all vectors of Hamming weight at most r. By using the techniques of [7], the complexity of computing $wt(f|_S)$ is improved from $O(|S|kn)$ to[1] $O(|S|n)$. This relies on the fact that computing $x\mathbf{A}^T$ for $wt(x) = i$ means XOR'ing i columns of $\mathbf{A}$, so that computing $x'\mathbf{A}^T$ for $wt(x') = i+1$ is achieved by adding one extra column to the previous results. By [12, Thm. 3.10], the probability of success of the algorithm depends on whether there exists a unique $s \in S$ such that $s = \arg\min_y wt(f(y))$. Note that the classical space complexity of the EXH solver is $O(|S|kn)$.

We suggest a quantum algorithm for this solver, described by Algorithm 6. If we were given a predicate φ such that $\varphi(x) = \mathbb{1}_{x=s}$, then Grover's algorithm

---

[1] Here, it is important to keep the $O(n)$ factor as it will influence the quantum algorithm presented later.

would recover the secret in quantum time $\Theta(2^{k/2})$ with probability at least $\frac{1}{2}$. The issue is that we do not have such predicate. Nevertheless, this problem can be solved by observing that $wt(f|_S)$ takes values in $[0, n]$. Let $\phi\colon \mathbf{Z}_2^k \longrightarrow \{0,1\}$ be the predicate defined as $\phi(x, \omega) = \mathbb{1}_{wt(f(x))<\omega}$ for some fixed ω. The idea of Algorithm 6 is to run a quantum binary search on $[0, n]$. To ensure that each binary search step is correct with high probability, we run Grover's algorithm multiple times before squeezing the search interval.

Algorithm 6: Q-EXH

Input: An LPN(k, s, τ) instance, the ball $S = \mathbb{B}_k(r) \subseteq \mathbf{Z}_2^k$ of radius r and $C \in \mathbb{N}$.
Output: An LPN secret candidate s of weight at most r.

1   $s \xleftarrow{\$} S$
2   $w_1 \leftarrow 1$
3   $w_2 \leftarrow wt(f(s))$
4   **while** $w_2 > w_1$ **do**
5      $\omega \leftarrow (w_1 + w_2)/2$
6   Grover$^{\otimes C}(S, \phi(\cdot, \omega)) \xrightarrow{\$} (y_1, \ldots, y_C)$
7   **if** $\exists i : \phi(y_i, \omega) = 1$ **then**
8          $s \leftarrow y_i$
9          $w_2 \leftarrow wt(f(s))$
10   **else**
11          $w_1 \leftarrow \omega$

12   **return** s

3.3 Walsh-Hadamard Transform

Let $f\colon \mathbf{Z}_2^k \longrightarrow \mathbb{R}$ be defined by $f(x) = \sum_{i=1}^{n} \mathbb{1}_{a_i=x}(-1)^{c_i}$. Then,

$$\mathcal{W}_f(y) = \sum_{i=1}^{n}(-1)^{\langle a_i, y\rangle + c_i} = n - 2 \cdot wt(y\mathbf{A}^T \oplus c).$$

The correct LPN secret s satisfies $\mathcal{W}_f(s) = \sum_{i=1}^{n}(-1)^{\varepsilon_i}$ and $s = \arg\max |\mathcal{W}_f|$ is likely to hold in a sparse noise regime. Note that the fast Walsh-Hadamard transform (Algorithm 1) can be simply modified to yield the maximizing value. The number of queries needed to ensure $s = \arg\max |\mathcal{W}_f|$ holds with high probability is discussed in [11, Appendix A] and [12]. The time complexity of the WHT solver is $O(kn + k2^k\ell)$, where $\ell \approx \frac{\log n+1}{2}$ is the expected bit size of $\mathcal{W}_f(x)$. Here, the term $O(kn)$ arises from the construction of the table $\{(x, f(x))\}$. Depending on n, this term plays an important role in the overall complexity as observed by [11, footnote 3] and thus cannot be ignored. Algorithm 7 describes a quantum algorithm for the WHT solver similar to Algorithm 6 and uses the Grover's predicate ϕ defined by $\phi(x, \omega) = \mathbb{1}_{|\mathcal{W}_f(x)|>\omega}$.

To our knowledge, there is no efficient way to implement the fast Walsh-Hadamard transform as a quantum algorithm itself and recover its spectrum as classical data. While it is possible to get a superposition of the Walsh-Hadamard spectrum [2], it is meaningless as this cannot be used to recover $\arg\max |\mathcal{W}_f|$.

Algorithm 7: Q-WHT

Input: An LPN(k, s, τ) instance, the ball $S = \mathbb{B}_k(r) \subseteq \mathbf{Z}_2^k$ of radius r and $C \in \mathbb{N}$.
Output: An LPN secret candidate s of weight at most r.

1 $s \xleftarrow{\$} S$
2 $w_1 \leftarrow |\mathcal{W}_f(s)|$
3 $w_2 \leftarrow n$
4 **while** $w_2 > w_1$ **do**
5 $\quad \omega \leftarrow (w_1 + w_2)/2$
6 $\quad \mathrm{Grover}^{\otimes C}(S, \phi(\cdot, \omega)) \xrightarrow{\$} (y_1, \ldots, y_C)$
7 $\quad$ **if** $\exists i : \phi(y_i, \omega) = 1$ **then**
8 $\qquad s \leftarrow y_i$
9 $\qquad w_1 \leftarrow |\mathcal{W}_f(s)|$
10 $\quad$ **else**
11 $\qquad w_2 \leftarrow \omega$

12 **return** s

3.4 Quantum Complexity Analysis for EXH and WHT Solvers

Let $f_1(x) = x\mathbf{A}^T \oplus c$ and $f_2(x) = \sum_{i=1}^{n} \mathbb{1}_{a_i = x}(-1)^{c_i}$. Since $\mathcal{W}_{f_2}(x) = n - 2\,wt(f_1(x))$ and the support of f_2 is a subset of $\{a_1, \ldots, a_n\}$, the quantum complexity of Algorithms 6 or 7 solely depends on the complexity of computing $wt(f_1(x))$. As mentioned in Sect. 3.2, this requires classical time $K = O(n)$. Since Algorithm 6 implements a binary search over $[\![0, n]\!]$, there are at most $\log(n)$ sub-intervals to be tested. Then, the overall quantum complexity is of order $O(CK\sqrt{|S|}\log n)$ compared to the classical complexity of $O(|S|n)$ where $S = \mathbb{B}_k(r) \subseteq \mathbf{Z}_2^k$ is the ball of radius $0 \leq r \leq k$. By Proposition 1, taking $C \approx 4 = O(1)$ is a suitable choice. With the minimal number of LPN queries according to [12, §3.8.1], we deduce the following result.

Proposition 2. *Choosing* $S = \left\{x \in \mathbf{Z}_2^k : wt(x) \leq k\tau_s + \sqrt{\frac{k}{2}\ln\left(\frac{2}{\vartheta}\right)}\right\}$ *and with at least* $n \geq \frac{4}{\delta_\tau^2}\ln\left(\frac{2^k}{\vartheta}\right)$ *queries, Algorithms 6 and 7 solve the* LPN(k, τ, s) *search problem in quantum time* $O(n\log n\sqrt{|S|})$ *and memory* $O(\log |S|)$ *with probability at least* $1 - \vartheta$.

In the low-noise regime $\tau = \frac{1}{\sqrt{k}}$, we have $|S| \leq 2^{kH(2/\sqrt{k})} \approx k^{\sqrt{k}/2}$ by Stirling's formula, where $H(p) = -p\log p - (1-p)\log(1-p)$ is the binary entropy function. We experimentally observed that the complexity of the quantum algorithm highly depends on the $O(n)$ term needed to compute Hamming weights. In almost all experiments, this term blows up the quantum complexity and we did not achieve significant improvements as we expected. There has been a recent work to *estimate* the Hamming weight of $\mathcal{W}_f(x)$ for an arbitrary boolean function in almost constant quantum time [30]. As such, future research would focus on reducing the cost of this computation to lower the complexity of our quantum algorithms.

3.5   Significant Fourier Transform

We mentioned the equivalence between the Walsh-Hadamard and the Fourier transforms up to a normalization factor for $G = \mathbf{Z}_2^n$. In particular, our "arg max" condition can be reformulated as a *Significant Fourier Coefficients* search problem. The complexity of the SFT solver has been studied in [13, §5]. The author concluded that applying the Walsh-Hadamard transform with the optimal number of queries on a *non-reduced* LPN instance is no better than the WHT solver. However, our results show that, for the same reduction chain, SFT is usually better than WHT by a factor 4. This is solely due to the fact that for these parameters, the time complexity of the SFT algorithm is lower than the time complexity of the Walsh-Hadamard transform. On the other hand, the number of LPN queries required by the SFT solver is unchanged since the condition of $|\hat{f}(s)| = ||\hat{f}||_\infty$ must be satisfied, where $f(x) = \sum_{i=1}^{n} \mathbb{1}_{a_i=x}(-1)^{c_i}$ and $\hat{f}$ is its Fourier transform. On average, $||\hat{f}||_\infty = \frac{n(1-2\tau)}{2^k}$ where n is the number of available LPN queries and $||f||_\infty^2 = 1$ and $||f||_2^2 \leq \frac{n}{2^k}$. The complexity of the SFT solver is then given by the following proposition.

Proposition 3 ([13, §5.3]). *Let* $\{(a_1, c_1), \ldots, (a_n, c_n)\}$ *be the set of queries of an* LPN(k, τ, s) *instance and let* $f(x) = \sum_{i=1}^{n} \mathbb{1}_{a_i=x}(-1)^{c_i}$. *Let* $\vartheta_1, \vartheta_2 \in (0,1)$, *where* ϑ_1 *denotes the probability that* $||\hat{f}||_\infty$ *is not realized by the secret* s *and* ϑ_2 *denotes the probability that the SFT algorithm fails to find the* $||\hat{f}||_\infty$*-significant coefficients. If* $n \geq \frac{8\ln(2^k/\vartheta_1)}{(1-2\tau)^2}$, *then the SFT algorithm recovers the secret* s *with probability at least* $(1 - \vartheta_1)(1 - \vartheta_2)$ *in time*

$$O\left(kn + \frac{2^{5k} k}{n^5 (1 - 2\tau)^6} \ln\left(\frac{2^k k}{\vartheta_2 n (1 - 2\tau)^2} \right) \right).$$

Remark 2. If the logarithmic term is negligible for sufficient large k, the SFT solver complexity for $n \approx 2^{5k/6}$ is given by $O(kn)$. Using the Central Limit Theorem, one may lower the complexity to $O(kn)$ with $n \approx 2^{4k/5}$.

The SFT solver usually improves the complexity of the WHT solver (see Table 1) since both solvers are based on the same idea, namely finding the vector which maximizes $|\mathcal{W}_f|$ which, with high probability, is the LPN secret. In essence, the SFT algorithm searches (Algorithm 2) for the binary representation of the τ-significant Fourier coefficients and each iteration depends on the previous one. As such, it is very hard to apply Grover's algorithm to search for such representation. In a very low noise regime, it would be interesting to combine the SFT algorithm together with *quantum* information set decoding techniques to first recover a large set of τ-significant candidates before searching for the correct one. Future research may also focus on improving the SFT algorithm for the specific case of LPN as it was done for BKW by Dachman-Soled et al. in [14].

4 Results

In this section, we present the results (Tables 1 and 2) that were obtained by extending the implementation from [11]. The implementation has been revisited and optimized so that the space of parameters it searches is smaller. Precise details are reported in the Appendix B. Thanks to those optimizations, we were able to run the optimizer for larger LPN instances.

Since the EXH and WHT solvers, along with their quantum variants, need the same amount of LPN queries, we wondered which of these were the best depending on the noise rate τ and the dimension k. The WHT solver usually performs the best for medium-sized secrets, while EXH is better in small dimensions. Interestingly, the SFT solver slightly outperforms the WHT solver in larger dimensions but requires a bit more of memory. Unfortunately, neither the Q-EXH nor the Q-WHT solvers that were introduced in that paper outperform their classical version, mainly due to the computation of $wt(x\mathbf{A}^T \oplus c)$.

The C-ISD and Q-ISD solvers correspond to the classical and quantum versions of Algorithm 5 respectively. Except for these algorithms which recover the whole secret, the other algorithms presented in Table 1 correspond to a partial key-recovery attack on LPN with failure probability $\vartheta = \frac{1}{3}$. As observed by [11], the complexity of a full key-recovery attack is dominated by the complexity of recovering the first block of the secret.

Most of the reductions presented in Appendix A have no quantum counterpart. The only reduction which may enjoy a quantum variant with an interesting complexity is the drop-reduce reduction (Appendix A.3). This reduction drops queries that are not zero on a set of predefined bits. In particular, reduction chains starting with one or more drop-reduce reductions require less classical memory since the non-interesting LPN queries can be dropped immediately. On the other hand, the quantum version of that reduction would need to access the LPN queries in superposition. In that model, the reduction chains using the Q-EXH or Q-WHT solvers and a quantum drop-reduce reduction perform slightly better than their classical counterparts but only in small dimensions. From a cryptographic point of view, having quantum reductions does not seem to bring substantial improvements and thus we assumed that all reductions are classical, that LPN queries are not accessed in superposition and that only solving algorithms may be quantum.

Table 1. Logarithmic complexity $time_{space}$ for mounting a partial key-recovery attack on $\mathsf{LPN}(k, s, \tau)$. The smallest *classical* time complexity is underlined and the smallest time complexity is **in bold**, where the minimum is computed over the presented algorithms. For the Q-EXH and Q-WHT quantum solvers, the classical space complexity of the whole reduction chain is the same as the classical variant, hence omitted, and the quantum space complexity of the solver is put as a superscript (assumed to be 0 if omitted). The classical and quantum space complexities of the Q-ISD solver are the same as the classical space complexity of C-ISD, hence omitted. Unavailable results are represented by grey boxes.

k	τ	EXH	WHT	SFT	C-ISD	Q-EXH	Q-WHT	Q-ISD
8	0.05	**$6.98_{6.47}$**	$7.01_{6.47}$	$7.00_{6.47}$	$12.07_{8.97}$	6.98	7.00	11.77
	0.1	<u>$7.39_{6.46}$</u>	$7.39_{6.42}$	$7.41_{6.42}$	$12.86_{9.27}$	**7.38**	7.38	12.25
	0.125	<u>$6.71_{5.74}$</u>	$6.71_{5.74}$	$7.41_{5.74}$	$13.28_{9.44}$	**6.69**	6.69	12.51
	0.2	**$7.43_{6.48}$**	$7.43_{6.43}$	$7.63_{6.43}$	$14.67_{10.04}$	7.44	7.44	13.65
	0.25	$8.21_{6.45}$	**<u>$8.20_{6.34}$</u>**	$8.54_{6.34}$	$15.58_{10.53}$	8.27	8.27	14.34
	$\frac{1}{\sqrt{k}}$	**$9.69_{8.87}$**	$9.86_{8.05}$	$11.49_{8.69}$	$18.21_{12.04}$	10.18	10.35	16.53
16	0.05	$9.82_{9.00}$	$9.82_{9.00}$	**<u>$9.81_{9.00}$</u>**	$15.44_{10.97}$	9.85	9.87	14.84
	0.1	$10.42_{9.38}$	$10.41_{9.34}$	**<u>$10.40_{9.34}$</u>**	$16.77_{11.27}$	10.48	10.48	15.63
	0.125	$10.81_{9.83}$	$10.78_{9.76}$	**<u>$10.74_{9.76}$</u>**	$17.35_{11.44}$	10.99	10.99	16.12
	0.2	**$11.70_{10.47}$**	$11.70_{10.45}$	$11.70_{10.45}$	$19.34_{12.04}$	11.75	11.75	17.45
	0.25	$12.44_{11.20}$	**<u>$12.41_{11.14}$</u>**	$12.41_{11.14}$	$20.94_{12.53}$	12.60	12.60	18.50
32	0.05	$13.77_{12.89}$	$13.77_{12.89}$	**<u>$13.74_{12.89}$</u>**	$19.29_{12.97}$	13.92	13.99	18.11
	0.1	$15.04_{13.98}$	**<u>$15.01_{13.93}$</u>**	$15.08_{14.52}$	$21.39_{13.27}$	15.27	15.27	19.60
	0.125	**<u>$15.65_{14.73}$</u>**	$15.65_{14.73}$	$15.65_{14.73}$	$22.55_{13.44}$	15.66	15.66	20.32
	0.2	$17.02_{15.82}$	$17.00_{15.78}$	**<u>$16.99_{15.78}$</u>**	$26.54_{14.04}$	17.19	17.19	22.68
	0.25	**<u>$18.31_{17.03}$</u>**	$18.42_{17.13}$	$18.35_{17.13}$	$29.63_{14.53}$	18.31	$20.13^{2.88}$	24.54
	$\frac{1}{\sqrt{k}}$	**<u>$16.60_{15.57}$</u>**	$16.73_{15.57}$	$17.41_{15.22}$	$25.22_{13.83}$	16.71	16.81	21.91
48	0.05	$14.72_{14.38}$	$14.72_{14.38}$	**<u>$14.71_{14.38}$</u>**	$21.81_{14.14}$	14.79	14.82	20.28
	0.1	$18.76_{18.38}$	**<u>$18.57_{17.91}$</u>**	$18.81_{17.79}$	$25.05_{14.44}$	18.78	18.60	22.40
	0.125	$19.29_{18.56}$	$19.29_{18.54}$	**<u>$19.08_{18.04}$</u>**	$26.85_{14.61}$	19.43	19.43	23.49
	0.2	**<u>$21.25_{20.45}$</u>**	$21.25_{20.45}$	$23.55_{20.42}$	$32.87_{15.21}$	21.26	21.26	26.84
	0.25	$22.39_{21.54}$	**<u>$22.34_{21.50}$</u>**	$23.62_{20.31}$	$37.47_{15.70}$	22.55	$23.68^{3.58}$	29.55
	$\frac{1}{\sqrt{k}}$	$20.04_{19.27}$	$19.84_{19.00}$	**<u>$19.40_{18.59}$</u>**	$28.31_{14.75}$	20.49	$21.72^{3.10}$	24.32
64	0.05	**<u>$15.99_{15.54}$</u>**	$15.99_{15.54}$	$15.98_{15.54}$	$23.93_{14.97}$	16.04	16.06	22.01
	0.1	$21.78_{21.30}$	$21.78_{21.29}$	**<u>$21.77_{21.29}$</u>**	$28.34_{15.27}$	21.91	21.91	24.75
	0.125	$22.94_{22.06}$	$22.94_{22.06}$	**<u>$22.92_{21.71}$</u>**	$30.77_{15.44}$	22.95	22.95	26.12
	0.2	$25.75_{25.74}$	$24.42_{23.29}$	**<u>$24.35_{23.41}$</u>**	$38.89_{16.04}$	$25.85^{2.58}$	$28.02^{3.66}$	30.63
	0.25	**<u>$26.80_{25.68}$</u>**	$26.86_{25.69}$	$29.54_{25.37}$	$44.91_{16.53}$	26.80	$28.36^{2.73}$	33.87
100	0.05	**<u>$20.53_{20.07}$</u>**	$20.53_{20.07}$	$20.53_{20.07}$	$27.96_{16.26}$	20.57	20.59	25.13
	0.1	$27.75_{27.39}$	$27.59_{26.93}$	**<u>$27.24_{26.32}$</u>**	$35.12_{16.56}$	27.80	$31.86^{3.72}$	29.26
	0.125	$29.80_{29.33}$	$28.91_{28.02}$	**<u>$27.94_{26.92}$</u>**	$39.02_{16.73}$	29.95	$31.99^{3.90}$	31.35
	0.2	$32.58_{31.76}$	**<u>$32.06_{31.22}$</u>**	$32.87_{31.04}$	$51.75_{17.32}$	32.61	$33.32^{4.26}$	38.01
	0.25	$35.15_{36.14}$	**<u>$32.94_{32.20}$</u>**	$34.02_{30.83}$	$61.12_{17.82}$	$35.05^{3.50}$	$37.10^{4.33}$	42.92
128	0.05	**<u>$23.64_{23.18}$</u>**	$23.64_{23.18}$	$23.64_{23.18}$	$30.77_{16.97}$	23.68	23.69	27.17
	0.1	$31.84_{31.37}$	$31.56_{31.06}$	**<u>$30.73_{29.91}$</u>**	$40.09_{17.27}$	31.95	$37.22^{3.99}$	32.33
	0.125	$34.44_{33.60}$	$33.40_{32.80}$	**<u>$33.21_{32.25}$</u>**	$45.12_{17.44}$	34.53	$39.80^{4.18}$	34.93
	0.2	$38.73_{38.80}$	**<u>$36.98_{36.15}$</u>**	$37.28_{35.94}$	$61.50_{18.04}$	$38.54^{2.88}$	$43.87^{4.17}$	43.42
	0.25	$40.30_{39.24}$	**<u>$39.15_{38.07}$</u>**	$40.78_{38.18}$	$73.47_{18.53}$	40.38	$41.07^{4.71}$	49.64
	$\frac{1}{\sqrt{k}}$	$30.41_{30.02}$	$30.41_{30.01}$	**<u>$29.87_{29.32}$</u>**	$37.83_{17.20}$	30.52	30.52	31.14

(continued)

Table 1. (*continued*)

k	τ	EXH	WHT	SFT	C-ISD	Q-EXH	Q-WHT	Q-ISD
192	0.05	**$30.47_{30.10}$**	$30.47_{30.10}$	$30.47_{30.10}$	$36.72_{18.14}$	30.50	30.51	31.19
	0.1	$41.04_{40.54}$	$39.28_{38.69}$	**$38.27_{37.74}$**	$50.99_{18.44}$	41.14	$48.02^{4.34}$	38.64
	0.125	$44.49_{43.95}$	$41.79_{41.17}$	**$40.87_{40.39}$**	$58.62_{18.61}$	44.56	$51.96^{4.53}$	42.54
	0.2	$49.99_{50.49}$	$46.84_{45.93}$	**$46.55_{45.97}$**	$83.24_{19.21}$	$49.93^{3.99}$	$52.31^{4.93}$	55.14
	0.25	$52.54_{53.31}$	**$48.38_{47.66}$**	$49.92_{48.53}$	$101.20_{19.70}$	$52.49^{3.58}$	$61.46^{5.04}$	64.37
	$\frac{1}{\sqrt{k}}$	$35.92_{35.53}$	$35.95_{35.52}$	**$35.22_{34.78}$**	$42.87_{18.27}$	35.98	$43.01^{4.13}$	**34.49**
256	0.05	$36.75_{36.31}$	$36.75_{36.31}$	**$36.53_{36.22}$**	$42.30_{18.97}$	36.79	36.80	**34.74**
	0.1	$49.91_{49.45}$	$46.75_{46.14}$	**$45.31_{45.36}$**	$61.55_{19.27}$	50.00	$58.74^{4.62}$	**44.53**
	0.125	$53.66_{53.13}$	$49.90_{49.33}$	**$48.61_{48.81}$**	$71.77_{19.44}$	53.81	$63.07^{4.86}$	49.73
	0.2	$60.14_{60.01}$	$56.52_{55.93}$	**$55.56_{56.30}$**	$104.68_{20.04}$	$60.67^{2.43}$	$73.35^{5.21}$	66.48
	0.25	$63.62_{65.04}$	**$59.47_{58.36}$**	$59.92_{60.19}$	$128.61_{20.53}$	$63.49^{4.47}$	$67.31^{5.43}$	78.70
	$\frac{1}{\sqrt{k}}$	$41.07_{40.75}$	$40.55_{40.06}$	**$39.73_{39.49}$**	$46.94_{19.04}$	41.13	$49.19^{4.24}$	**37.11**
512	0.05		$57.77_{57.37}$	**$56.51_{57.56}$**	$63.25_{20.97}$		$73.86^{4.79}$	**46.72**
	0.1	$81.89_{83.66}$	$73.68_{73.26}$	**$71.43_{75.08}$**	$102.45_{21.27}$	$82.49^{3.19}$	$97.77^{5.40}$	**66.47**
	0.125	$87.59_{87.14}$	$78.85_{78.32}$	**$76.45_{81.04}$**	$123.07_{21.44}$	87.73	$104.93^{5.58}$	76.86
	0.2	$98.28_{98.00}$	$89.52_{89.08}$	**$87.23_{92.03}$**	$189.07_{22.04}$	$98.27^{5.19}$	$120.57^{6.00}$	110.16
	0.25	$102.93_{103.54}$	$94.98_{94.22}$	**$92.70_{97.05}$**	$236.81_{22.53}$	$102.89^{4.78}$	$117.04^{6.18}$	134.28
768	0.05		$76.63_{76.19}$	**$74.64_{79.05}$**	$83.38_{22.14}$		$101.59^{5.21}$	**57.65**
	0.1	$109.25_{109.30}$	$98.97_{98.55}$	**$96.30_{105.00}$**	$142.53_{22.44}$	$109.48^{2.90}$	$134.36^{5.80}$	**87.37**
	0.125	$117.29_{117.09}$	$106.00_{105.58}$	**$102.85_{113.00}$**	$173.55_{22.61}$	$117.28^{3.99}$	$145.31^{6.04}$	102.97
	0.2	$131.63_{131.83}$	$121.20_{120.69}$	**$117.26_{129.00}$**	$272.64_{23.21}$	$131.61^{4.65}$	$160.01^{6.46}$	152.82
	0.25	$139.20_{138.64}$	$128.40_{127.95}$	**$124.83_{136.00}$**	$344.23_{23.70}$	139.26	$176.38^{6.66}$	188.86

In [15, Table 1], the asymptotic complexities of Pooled Gauss and Well-Pooled Gauss are expressed *without* their poly-logarithmic factors, that is, as the right hand-side of (3), (4), (5) and (6). However, those factors are of importance when comparing the non-asymptotic complexities since they may be the dominant term. For instance, for $k = 512$ and $\tau = 0.05$, the QPG and QWPG quantum complexities are $2^{50.19}$ and $2^{49.39}$ (using the O-expression) instead of $2^{18.94}$ and $2^{18.27}$ (using the $\tilde{O}$-expression) respectively, which is a non-negligible gap. While the authors have taken into account polynomial factors when reporting the non-asymptotic values [15, §6], they acknowledged that there was a bug in their script, leading to different results [29].

Table 2. Comparisons with [29] in dimension $k \in \{128, 256, 384, 512\}$ of the best solver introduced in that paper with existing ones. The columns WIG, HYB (hybrid) and MMT are copied from [29] and contain the logarithmic classical time complexities under memory constraints of 40, 60 and 80 bits (40-bit constraint for MMT). The HYB and MMT columns are per [15] and were regenerated by [29] since Esser's original publication contains different results as they were generated by a boggy implementation acknowledged by the authors. The QPG and QWPG columns report the logarithmic quantum time complexity of the Quantum Pooled Gauss and Quantum Well-Pooled Gauss algorithms from [15] using the O-expression of Sect. 3.1.

k	τ	Solver	Complexity	QPG	QWPG	WIG			HYB			MMT
						40	60	80	40	60	80	40
	0.05	EXH	$23.64_{23.18}$	30.79	30.49		26			37		34
	0.1	SFT	$30.73_{29.91}$	36.05	35.10		31			41		38
	0.125	SFT	$33.21_{32.25}$	38.80	37.40		33			41		41
128	0.25	WHT	$39.15_{38.07}$	54.07	48.86		38			47		57
	0.4	Q-ISD	$72.26_{21.13}$	77.22	63.44	51	48	48	62	57	57	75
	$\frac{1}{\sqrt{k}}$	SFT	$29.87_{29.32}$	34.79	34.03							
	0.05	Q-ISD	$34.74_{18.97}$	38.08	37.62		38			54		40
	0.1	Q-ISD	$44.53_{19.27}$	48.30	46.66	50	46	46	76	61	61	53
	0.125	SFT	$48.61_{48.81}$	53.64	51.14	56	49	49	86	61	61	61
256	0.25	WHT	$59.47_{58.36}$	83.05	73.27	102	58	58	113	69	69	95
	0.4	Q-ISD	$121.93_{23.13}$	126.74	100.28	136	84	71	129	93	81	132
	$\frac{1}{\sqrt{k}}$	Q-ISD	$37.11_{19.04}$	40.58	39.89							
	0.05	Q-ISD	$40.95_{20.14}$	44.35	43.71	58	49	49	70	68	68	48
	0.1	Q-ISD	$55.71_{20.44}$	59.53	57.21	81	60	60	106	106	74	70
	0.125	Q-ISD	$63.51_{20.61}$	67.46	63.88	92	71	64	121	110	81	81
384	0.25	Q-ISD	$106.71_{21.7}$	111.04	96.69	140	92	77	175	135	104	134
	0.4	Q-ISD	$170.54_{24.3}$	175.26	136.11	189	176	116	197	160	139	189
	$\frac{1}{\sqrt{k}}$	Q-ISD	$41.24_{20.15}$	44.65	44.99							
	0.05	Q-ISD	$46.72_{20.97}$	50.19	49.39	68	58	58	87	87	84	57
	0.1	Q-ISD	$66.47_{21.27}$	70.35	67.33	99	92	73	136	136	101	87
	0.125	SFT	$76.45_{81.04}$	80.86	76.20	114	105	78	157	157	101	102
512	0.25	SFT	$92.70_{97.05}$	138.62	119.70	179	186	115	230	202	171	172
	0.4	Q-ISD	$218.72_{25.13}$	223.39	171.54	245	241	209	264	228	207	245
	$\frac{1}{\sqrt{k}}$	Q-ISD	$44.52_{20.94}$	47.92	47.28							

5   Conclusion

In this paper, we complemented the results from Bogos and Vaudenay [11] solving the LPN search problem using classical algorithms and suggested novel quantum algorithms achieving better complexities for cryptographically interesting parameters. While two of our quantum algorithms failed to yield satisfying improvements, this is mostly due to the high-complexity of computing Hamming weights every time the Grover's predicate is evaluated. Recent work has shown that the Hamming distance between two boolean functions can be approximated in almost constant time, opening another line of research. On the other hand, our simple ISD-like quantum algorithm provides promising results for low-noise instances even in large dimensions and may be subject to further improvements. Further research would need to focus on the precise quantum complexity and the implementability of such algorithm on quantum computers.

A   Reductions

Algorithms to solve LPN are tuned so that their time complexity is the most efficient one. In the literature, authors usually bruteforce the parameters space in order to find the best parameters. Most of the LPN solving techniques may be described within the same framework: the original $\mathsf{LPN}(k, \tau, s)$ is *reduced* to a smaller $\mathsf{LPN}(k', \tau', s')$ instance for which the secret s' is recovered by a *solving* algorithm. Then, the queries are updated accordingly and the process is repeated until the original secret is completely recovered. In this section, we restrict our attention to some well-studied reductions π and describe the *update* rule

$$(k, n, \delta_\tau, \delta_s) \xrightarrow{\ \pi\ } (k', n', \delta'_\tau, \delta'_s),$$

where $k' = \pi(k)$ is the updated secret size, $n' = \pi(n)$ is the updated number of queries, $\delta'_\tau = \pi(\delta_\tau)$ is the updated noise bias and $\delta'_s = \pi(\delta_s)$ is the updated secret bias. The updated noise rate τ' can be recovered via $\tau' = \frac{1 - \delta'_\tau}{2} = \pi(\tau)$. If available, the *classical* and *quantum* time (resp. memory) complexities of a reduction π are denoted by τ_π (resp. μ_π) and $\tau_{q,\pi}$ (resp. $\mu_{q,\pi}$) respectively. Unless stated otherwise, the reductions that we present can be found in the existing literature such as [10] or [11] and in [29] for their memory complexities. In this section, we will recall the reductions presented in [11]. These reductions were used to construct the chains (see Appendix B for the formal description) giving the results on Table 1.

A.1   Reduction: Sparse-Secret

The `sparse-secret` reduction described by Algorithm 3 transforms an LPN instance with $\delta_s = 0$ (corresponding to an uniformly distributed secret) to an LPN instance where the secret and the noise bits follow a Ber_τ distribution. To that end, the idea is to consider a portion of the noise vector as the new secret at the cost of dropping some of the queries. The time complexity of the reduction depends on the choice of the underlying matrix multiplication algorithm. There exist two versions of the reduction, one is given by Guo, Johansson and Löndahl in [18] and the other by Bernstein in [4]. We assume that inverting a $k \times k$ binary matrix takes $k^{\omega + o(1)}$ field operations, where $\omega \geq 2$ is the matrix multiplication exponent[2]. This term can be ignored if this reduction is typically applied once.

---

[2] The $o(1)$ term in the exponent was actually missing in [11], but may be negligible in practice since we are usually interested in the logarithmic complexity.

π : sparse-secret

$$k' = k, \quad n' = n - k, \quad \delta'_\tau = \delta_\tau, \quad \delta'_s = \delta_\tau$$
$$\tau_\pi = O\left(\min_{\chi \in \mathbb{N}}\left(kn'\left\lceil\frac{k}{\chi}\right\rceil + k\chi 2^\chi, \frac{n'k^2}{\log k - \log\log k}\right) + k^{\omega+o(1)}\right), \quad \mu_\pi = O(kn)$$

If we were to replace the classical algorithm with a quantum one, we essentially need to perform boolean matrix multiplications. While there exist quantum algorithms that do improve the classical time complexity, they usually depend on the sparsity of the input matrices or the output matrix. As such, a quantum algorithm equivalent to Algorithm 3 would need to be thought differently. On the other hand, this reduction is usually used at most once and it has a polynomial complexity, hence there is no advantage in making it quantum.

A.2   Reduction: Part-Reduce (LF1) and Xor-Reduce (LF2)

Notation 2. Given $\mathcal{Q} \subseteq \mathbf{Z}_2^{k+1}$ and $I \subseteq [\![k]\!]$, we denote by $\sim_I$ the equivalence relation defined over $\mathcal{Q} \times \mathcal{Q}$ by $\psi \sim_I \psi'$ if and only if $\psi_I = \psi'_I$. The corresponding canonical projection is denoted by $[\cdot]_I\colon \mathcal{Q} \twoheadrightarrow \mathcal{Q}/\sim_I$.

The part-reduce(b) reduction, also called LF1(b) reduction, is the original reduction in the BKW algorithm [9] which consists in partitioning the set of queries according to some equivalence relation $\sim_I$. More precisely, an indexation set $I \subseteq [\![k]\!]$ of size b is picked uniformly at random and the queries $\psi \in \mathcal{Q}$ are sorted according to $[\psi]_I$. Then, for each equivalence class, one fixes a representative and XOR's it with the rest of the class before dropping it. The effective size of the secret is then reduced by b bits, at the cost of discarding 2^b queries. By *effective size*, we mean that we ignore the bits at position $i \in I$ since they would always be XOR'ed with zero bits. The noise bias $\delta' = \delta_{\tau'}$ is amplified as $\delta' = \delta_\tau^2$ while the secret bias δ_s remains the same.

π : part-reduce(b)

$$k' = k - b, \ n' = n - 2^b, \ \delta'_\tau = \delta_\tau^2, \ \delta'_s = \delta_s, \ \tau_\pi = \mu_\pi = O(kn)$$

Another reduction similar to part-reduce(b) is the xor-reduce(b) reduction, also called LF2(b) reduction and introduced by Levieil and Fouque in [23]. Instead of XOR'ing a single representative with the rest of the class, xor-reduce(b) applies a pairwise XOR on the whole equivalence class. The effective size of the secret is then reduced by b bits, while the expected number of queries $n' = \frac{n(n-1)}{2^{b+1}}$ increases if $n > 1 + 2^{b+1}$, remains unchanged if $n \approx 1 + 2^{b+1}$ and decreases otherwise. According to practical experiments, xor-reduce(b) performs better than part-reduce(b), even though it relies on heuristic assumptions.

π : xor-reduce(b)

$$k' = k - b, \ n' = \frac{n(n-1)}{2^{b+1}}, \ \delta'_\tau = \delta_\tau^2, \ \delta'_s = \delta_s, \ \tau_\pi = O(k \cdot \max(n, n')), \ \mu_\pi = O(\max(kn, k'n'))$$

A partition[3] for $\sim_I$ can be constructed by picking any query $\psi \in Q$ and searching for all queries in the same equivalence class. The process is repeated until all queries are exhausted. On average, there are 2^b equivalence classes, each of which containing $\frac{n}{2^b}$ queries, so that the partitioning would be achieved in quantum time complexity $\tau_{q,\pi} \approx \sum_{m=0}^{2^b-1} \frac{n - \frac{mn}{2^b}}{2^{b/2}} = \frac{n(2^b+1)}{2^{1+b/2}} > n$. Therefore, using Grover's algorithm does *not* improve the complexity of the reduction. A similar argument stands for the `part-reduce` reduction.

A.3   Reduction: Drop-Reduce

In the `drop-reduce`(b) reduction, queries that are nonzero on a set of b bits are dropped, where the b positions are chosen uniformly at random. The resulting LPN instance consists of a secret s' of effective size $k' = k - b$ with an expected number of remaining queries $n' = \frac{n}{2^b}$. The noise and secret biases remain unchanged.

π : `drop-reduce`(b)

$$k' = k - b, \; n' = \frac{n}{2^b}, \; \delta'_\tau = \delta_\tau, \; \delta'_s = \delta_s, \; \tau_\pi = n \sum_{i=1}^{b} \frac{1}{2^{i-1}} = \frac{n(2^b - 1)}{2^{b-1}} = O(n), \; \mu_\pi = O(kn)$$

Quantum Algorithm. The `drop-reduce`(b) reduction is essentially a filter. Grover's algorithm [17] searches for *one* marked item in an unsorted database of N items in quantum time $\Theta(\sqrt{N})$. If there are $1 \le M \le N$ marked items, then the running time decreases [26] to $\Theta(\sqrt{N/M})$ so that finding *all* marked items takes quantum time $\Theta(\sqrt{NM})$. Since we expect to keep $n/2^b$ queries, the expected quantum time of `drop-reduce`(b) is $\tau_{q,\pi} = O(n2^{-b/2})$.

Remark 3. While the quantum version of `drop-reduce`(b) may *a priori* improve the classical time complexity, one critical observation is that this result entirely based on the assumption that a sufficient amount of quantum memory is accessible, that the LPN queries can be accessed in superposition and that the oracle construction cost is negligible.

A.4   Reduction: Code-Reduce

The `code-reduce`(k, k', params) reduction approximates the queries $\psi_i = (a_i, c_i)$ with codewords in a $[k, k']_2$-code C with $k' < k$ characterized by params and generated by a known matrix $M \in \mathbf{Z}_2^{k \times k'}$. Let $\mathfrak{D}_C$ be a decoder which decodes a codeword in C in time τ_{dec}. Let $\nu_i \triangleq \nu'_i M^T \in \mathbf{Z}_2^k$ be the nearest codeword in C to a_i. Then, $c_i = \langle a_i, s_i \rangle \oplus \varepsilon_i = \langle \nu'_i M^T, s \rangle \oplus \langle a_i - \nu_i, s \rangle \oplus \varepsilon_i = \langle \nu'_i, sM \rangle \oplus \langle a_i - \nu_i, s \rangle \oplus \varepsilon_i$. By setting, $\varepsilon'_i \triangleq \langle a_i - \nu_i, s \rangle \oplus \varepsilon_i$, the queries for the $\text{LPN}(k', \tau, s')$ instance with secret $s' \triangleq sM$ are exactly those of the form $\psi'_i = (\nu'_i, c_i)$, hence $n' = n$. On

---

[3] In [11], the cost of this partitioning step, namely $O(n)$, was not considered.

the other hand, the new noise bias δ'_τ is expressed as $\delta'_\tau = \delta_\tau \cdot \mathsf{bc}$, where bc denotes the bias of $\langle a_i - \nu_i, s \rangle$, that is $\mathsf{bc} = \mathbb{E}[(-1)^{\langle a_i - \nu_i, s \rangle}]$. The secret bias δ'_s is expressed as a function of δ_s and $\mathcal{C}$.

$\pi : \mathsf{code-reduce}(k, k', \mathsf{params})$
$k', \quad n' = n, \quad \delta'_\tau = \delta_\tau \cdot \mathsf{bc}, \quad \delta'_s = \delta'_s(\delta_s, \mathcal{C}), \quad \tau_\pi = O(kn \cdot \tau_{dec}), \quad \mu_\pi = O(kn)$

In practice, the idea is to choose $\mathcal{C}$ with bc as large as possible and $\tau_{dec} = O(1)$. For general LPN instances, the authors of [11] provided three classes of codes, namely repetition codes, perfect codes and quasi-perfect codes defined by some set of parameters, and computed their corresponding bc.

A.5   Reduction: Guess-Reduce

The $\mathsf{guess-reduce}(b, w)$ reduction [6,18] is a reduction that forces the secret to satisfy some distribution. More precisely, one selects $0 \le w' \le w$ and $b \ge w$ positions of the secret, say $s_1, \ldots, s_b$. Then, out of those b unknowns, w' are set to 1, say the first w', and the others are set to 0. In this example, this is equivalent to assume that the secret is of the form $s = \mathbf{1}^{w'} || \mathbf{0}^{b-w'} || (s_{b+1}, \ldots, s_k)$. More generally, the reduction succeeds if the secret contains a pattern of b bits with at most w errors, which occurs with probability[4]

$$\sum_{i=0}^{w} \binom{b}{i} \left(\frac{1-\delta_s}{2}\right)^i \left(\frac{1+\delta_s}{2}\right)^{b-i} = \sum_{i=0}^{w} \binom{b}{i} \tau_s^i (1-\tau_s)^{b-i}.$$

Furthermore, the solving algorithm must be iterated $\sum_{i=0}^{w} \binom{b}{i}$ times since each pattern of b bits with at most w errors must be tested. The complexity of the reduction step itself is $O(1)$ as there is "nothing" to do except choosing and replacing variables (the complexity is at most $O(b \log b)$ since this is the complexity of randomly sampling b positions, but this can be amortized to $O(1)$). It can furthermore be integrated after (resp. before) a $\mathsf{sparse-secret}$ (resp. $\mathsf{code-reduce}$) reduction and the two reductions are merged as $\mathsf{sparse+guess}$ (resp. $\mathsf{guess+code}$).

$\pi : \mathsf{guess-reduce}(b, w)$
$k' = k - b, \quad n' = n, \quad \delta'_\tau = \delta_\tau, \quad \delta'_s = \delta_s, \quad \tau_\pi = \mathcal{O}(1), \quad \mu_\pi = \mathcal{O}(kn)$

Arbitrary guessing-based reductions do not enjoy well quantum speed-ups since they essentially require to repeat the same algorithm but for different choices of the bits and weights. One idea is to create a superposition of $N = \sum_{i=0}^{w} \binom{b}{i}$ states, each of which encoding a fixed pattern and run Grover's algorithm over this set until we find a "good" one, which corresponds to recovering the secret. Such set could be found in time of order $\sqrt{N} \le 2^{b/2}$. The issue

---

[4] In [11], the binomial coefficients were wrongly written as $\binom{w}{i}$ instead of $\binom{b}{i}$.

is that the predicate deciding whether a set is good or not entirely depends on whether the solver succeeded or not, hence the cost of evaluating Grover's algorithm is likely to explode. As such, we do not consider a quantum version of this reduction. Additionally, the `guess-reduce` reduction may appear at the middle of a reduction chain, making the rest of the chain somehow part of the Grover's predicate. According to [11, §6], classical `guess-reduce` do not seem to bring substantial improvements. Future research may however investigate whether there is a way to introduce a quantum `guess-reduce` in such a way that the underlying Grover's predicate is efficiently evaluated.

Other reductions such as `LF4`(b) and (u)`trunc-reduce`(b) were presented in [11] and [12], but as a matter of fact, were considered inefficient compared to the existing ones. The `LF4`(b) reduction is similar to `LF1`(b) and `LF2`(b) but is based on Wagner's algorithm [28]. It has worse complexity because it is essentially equivalent to two `LF2`(b). On the other hand, the `trunc-reduce`(b) and `utrunc-reduce`(b) reductions introduce secret bits in the error vector by truncating bits. According to [11, §6, table 3], those reductions do not seem to bring notable improvements, and thus were not considered in this study.

B   Graph of Reductions

In [11], Bogos and Vaudenay considered each reduction as an edge of a graph and tried to find a path for which the end vertex is an LPN instance whose secret is recovered by one of the presented solvers. Stated otherwise, one chooses a set of reductions Π and starts from an initial $\mathsf{LPN}(k, \tau, s)$ instance, identified to some vertex $(k, \log n)$ where n is the number of available queries. By applying consecutive reduction steps $\pi \in \Pi$, an $\mathsf{LPN}(k', \tau', s')$ instance whose secret s' is recovered by the solving algorithm is eventually reached. In this section, we suggest an optimized way to construct such graph and extend the formalism introduced by [11] to an arbitrary set of reductions.

Notation 3. For $\mathcal{L} \subseteq \mathbb{R}$, we define a *flooring* $\lfloor \cdot \rfloor_{\mathcal{L}}$ *function*, a *ceiling* $\lceil \cdot \rceil_{\mathcal{L}}$ *function* and a *rounding* $\lfloor \cdot \rceil_{\mathcal{L}}$ *function* by $\lfloor x \rfloor_{\mathcal{L}} \triangleq \max_{z \in \mathcal{L}} \{z \le x\}$, $\lceil x \rceil_{\mathcal{L}} \triangleq \min_{z \in \mathcal{L}} \{z \ge x\}$ and $\lfloor x \rceil_{\mathcal{L}} \triangleq \arg\min_{z \in \mathcal{L}} |x - z|$ respectively.

Definition 7 (reduction graph). *Let* Π *be a set of reductions and let* $\mathcal{L} \subseteq \mathbb{R}$ *and* $k \in \mathbb{N}$. *A* k-*dimensional* $(\Pi, \mathcal{L})$-*reduction graph is a directed and labelled graph* $\mathcal{G} = (\mathcal{V}, \mathcal{E})$ *defined over* $\mathcal{V} \triangleq [\![1, k]\!] \times \mathcal{L}$ *such that any edge* $(\varepsilon : v \xrightarrow{\lambda} v') \in \mathcal{E}$ *from* $v = (k, \eta) \in \mathcal{V}$ *to* $v' = (k', \eta') \in \mathcal{V}$ *labelled by* $\lambda = (\alpha_\lambda, \beta_\lambda, \pi_\lambda) \in \mathbb{R} \times \mathbb{R} \times \Pi$ *satisfies* $k' = \pi_\lambda(k)$ *and* $\eta' = \lfloor \log \pi_\lambda(2^\eta) \rceil_{\mathcal{L}}$. *Here,* α_λ *and* β_λ *are real values that describe the evolution of the noise bias* $\delta_\tau \xmapsto{\pi_\lambda} \delta'_\tau$ *according to* $\delta'_\tau = \alpha_\lambda \delta_\tau + \beta_\lambda$.

Remark 4. We assume that π_λ encodes all the statically known parameters of a reduction. For instance, the reduction `code-reduce`(k, k', params) for fixed k, k' and params can only be applied to instances of size k, whereas `drop-reduce`(b) does not depend on the initial LPN instance.

Notation 4. Given a label λ, integers $k' \leq k$ and $\eta \in \mathbb{R}$, let $\eta' = \eta_{out}^\lambda(k, \eta, k')$ be the binary logarithm of the *exact* number of queries obtained after applying the reduction $(v = (k, \eta) \xrightarrow{\lambda} (k', \eta') = v')$ and let $\tau_{log}^\lambda(v, v')$ be the corresponding logarithmic time complexity.

Definition 8 (reduction chain). *Let Π be a set of reductions and let $\mathcal{C}$ be a finite sequence of length m of the form*

$$v_0 = (k_0, \log n_0) \xrightarrow{\lambda_1} \dots \xrightarrow{\lambda_m} (k_m, \log n_m) = v_m, \quad \lambda_i = (\alpha_{\lambda_i}, \beta_{\lambda_i}, \pi_{\lambda_i}).$$

Then, $\mathcal{C}$ is said to be a Π-reduction chain if $(k_{i-1}, \log n_{i-1}) \xrightarrow{\lambda_i} (k_i, \log n_i)$ follows the update rule defined by the reduction $\pi_{\lambda_i} \in \Pi$ for all $1 \leq i \leq m$. If this is the case, we abusively write $v_i = \lambda_i(v_{i-1})$. The time complexity $\tau_\mathcal{C}$ and the time max-complexity $\tau_{\mathcal{C},\infty}$ of $\mathcal{C}$ are respectively defined by $\tau_\mathcal{C} \overset{\triangle}{=} \sum_\lambda \tau_\lambda$ and $\tau_{\mathcal{C},\infty} \overset{\triangle}{=} \max_\lambda \tau_\lambda$, where $\tau_\lambda \overset{\triangle}{=} \tau_{\pi_\lambda}$ is the time complexity of a reduction step $\lambda \in \mathcal{C}$.

Definition 9 (simple reduction chain). *A Π-reduction chain $\mathcal{C}$ is said to be simple if it is accepted by the automaton described on Fig. 1, where the dotted lines are transitions described by an arbitrary solving algorithm $\mathcal{A}$. The transition map $\mathbf{T}: [\![1, 4]\!] \times \Pi \longrightarrow [\![0, 4]\!]$ denoted by $(\sigma, \pi) \mapsto \mathbf{T}_\pi^\sigma$ associates (σ, π) to σ' if π is a valid transition from σ to σ' and to 0 otherwise.*

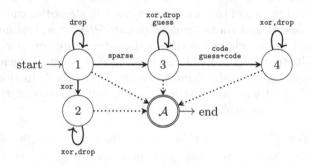

Fig. 1. Automaton accepting simple chains.

Given an algorithm $\mathcal{A}$ recovering a k'-dimensional LPN secret in time τ_ϑ with probability at least $1 - \vartheta$, a reduction chain $\mathcal{C}$ from $\mathsf{LPN}(k, s, \tau)$ to $\mathsf{LPN}(k', s', \tau')$ is said to be ϑ-valid for $\mathcal{A}$. Given an upper bound $\tau_\infty \in \mathbb{R}$ on the *logarithmic* time complexity, the goal is to find a chain $\mathcal{C}$ for which $\tau_{\mathcal{C},\vartheta} \overset{\triangle}{=} \tau_\mathcal{C} + \tau_\vartheta = \mathcal{O}(2^{\tau_\infty})$. This can be achieved by searching for relatively small chains $\mathcal{C}$ for which the *time max-complexity* $\tau_{\mathcal{C},\vartheta,\infty} \overset{\triangle}{=} \max(\tau_{\mathcal{C},\infty}, \tau_\vartheta)$ is upper-bounded by 2^{τ_∞} as the max-complexity metric is a relatively good approximation of the normal complexity.

B.1 Finding Optimal ϑ-valid Chains

To find optimal ϑ-valid chains, [11] constructed a directed graph $\mathcal{G}^* = (\mathcal{V}^*, \mathcal{E}^*)$ where the set of vertices $\mathcal{V}^* = \mathcal{V} \times [\![1,4]\!]$ furthermore encodes the automaton state. The action of a reduction step λ on $\mathcal{V}$ is extended to $\mathcal{V}^*$ via

$$(k, \eta, \sigma) \overset{\lambda}{\longmapsto} (k', \eta', \sigma') \triangleq \left(\pi_\lambda(k), \lfloor \log \pi_\lambda(2^\eta) \rceil_{\mathcal{L}}, \mathbf{T}_{\pi_\lambda}^\sigma \right)$$

and $\delta'_\tau = \alpha_\lambda \delta + \beta_\lambda$. In particular, $\mathcal{E}^* \subseteq \left\{ \varepsilon \colon v \overset{\lambda}{\longrightarrow} v' \mid v, v' \in \mathcal{V}^*,\ v' = \lambda(v) \right\}$. The construction of $\mathcal{G}^*$ is described by [11, §4.1, Alg. 2]. In practice, $\mathcal{G}^*$ is lazily constructed by iteratively looking for the optimal edges for which δ_τ is the largest at each reduction step. Algorithm 8 describes the high-level idea of how to construct the graph by iterating over possible vertices and adding them to the graph depending on the strategy described by the transition matrix. For practical reasons, $\mathcal{L}$ is a partition of the real segment $[0, \tau_\infty]$ with a step of size ϱ (which plays the role of a "precision") that will be used to approximate the number of required queries.

B.2 Optimizing the build() Algorithm

In their original paper, the authors considered LPN instances up to a dimension of $k = 756$ and $\tau \in \{0.05, 0.1, 0.2, 0.25\}$ and with a precision $\varrho = 10^{-1}$. For small dimensions, their algorithm is sufficiently fast, but for larger instances, there is a way to reduce the running time of the optimization algorithm by half in practice. Indeed, since the conditions at line 11 of Algorithm 8 depend on the loop index i, it suffices to find a smaller interval $[\![i_{min}^\lambda, i_{max}^\lambda]\!] \subseteq [\![j+1, k]\!]$ for which the conditions hold.

Lemma 1. *Let $\tau_\infty, \varrho > 0$ and let $\mathcal{L} = \left\{ \eta_\ell = \varrho(\ell - 1) : 1 \le \ell \le N = \lfloor \frac{\tau_\infty}{\varrho} \rfloor + 1 \right\}$. Let $\mathcal{G}^*$ be a $(\mathbf{\Pi}, \mathcal{L})$-reduction graph. For all $1 \le j < i \le k$ and for all $1 \le \ell_1 \le N$, we define $\eta_j^\lambda = \eta_{out}^\lambda(i, \eta_{\ell_1}, j)$ and $\ell_2 = \lfloor \eta_j^\lambda / \varrho \rfloor + 1$. Let $v_1 = (i, \eta_{\ell_1}) \in \mathcal{V}$ be a vertex and let $v_2 = (j, \eta_{\ell_2})$ be a point, not necessarily in $\mathcal{V}$ as ℓ_2 may be outside the range $[\![1, N]\!]$. Then, the following assertions are verified for $i_{min}^\lambda = j + 1$:*

1. *The conditions $\{\eta_j^\lambda \ge 0\}$, $\{1 \le \ell_2 \le N\}$ and $\left\{ \tau_{log}^\lambda(v_1, v_2) \le \tau_\infty \right\}$ are satisfied for $\lambda = \mathtt{drop\text{-}reduce}$ if $i_{max}^\lambda = \min(k, \eta_{\ell_1} + j, I)$, where $I = \infty$ if $\tau_\infty \ge \eta_{\ell_1} + 1$ and $I = j - \log(1 - 2^{\tau_\infty - \eta_{\ell_1} - 1})$ otherwise.*
2. *The conditions $\{\eta_j^\lambda \ge 0\}$ and $\{1 \le \ell_2 \le N\}$ are satisfied for $\lambda = \mathtt{xor\text{-}reduce}$ if $i_{max}^\lambda = \min\left(k, 2^{\tau_\infty - \eta_{\ell_1}}, I\right)$, where $I = \eta_{\ell_1} + \log(2^{\eta_{\ell_1}} - 1) + j - 1$ if $\eta_{\ell_1} \ge 1$ and 0 otherwise.*
3. *The conditions $\{\eta_j^\lambda \ge 0\}$, $\{1 \le \ell_2 \le N\}$ and $\left\{ \tau_{log}^\lambda(v_1, v_2) \le \tau_\infty \right\}$ are satisfied for $\lambda = \mathtt{code\text{-}reduce}$ if $i_{max}^\lambda = \min\left(k, 2^{\tau_\infty - \eta_{\ell_1} - \log \tau_{dec}}\right)$, where τ_{dec} is the time complexity of the corresponding decoder.*

Algorithm 8: build()

---

1   $N \leftarrow \lfloor \frac{\tau_\infty}{\varrho} \rfloor + 1$

2   $\mathcal{L} \leftarrow \left\{ \eta_i \triangleq \varrho(i-1) \mid i = 1, \ldots, N \right\}$

3   **for** $j = k$ *down to* 1 **do**

4   **for** $\ell_1 = 1$ *to* N **do**

5   **foreach** *possible reduction label* $\lambda = (\alpha_\lambda, \beta_\lambda, \pi_\lambda)$ **do**

6   **for** $i = j+1, \ldots, k$ **do**

7                  $\eta_j^\lambda \leftarrow \eta_{out}^\lambda(i, \eta_{\ell_1}, j)$

8                  $\ell_2 \leftarrow \lfloor \eta_j^\lambda / \varrho \rfloor + 1$

9                  $v_1 \leftarrow (i, \eta_{\ell_1})$

10                 $v_2 \leftarrow (j, \eta_{\ell_2})$

11   **if** $\eta_j^\lambda \geq 0$ *and* $\ell_2 \in [\![1, N]\!]$ *and* $\tau_{log}^\lambda(v_1, v_2) \leq \tau_\infty$ **then**

12   Add the edge (v_1, v_2) to the current graph if possible.

Proof. Let $\eta = \eta_{\ell_1}$ and $\eta' = \eta_{\ell_2}$, $n = 2^\eta$ and $n' = 2^{\eta'}$ and $b = i - j$. We claim that if $i_{min}^\lambda \leq i \leq i_{max}^\lambda$, then $1 \leq \ell_2 \leq N$ and $\eta' \geq 0$, and optionally $\tau_{log}^\lambda(v_1, v_2) \leq \tau_\infty$.

1. Since $\eta' = \eta - b$, it follows that $i \leq \min(k, \eta + j)$ ensures $\eta' \geq 0$. On the other hand, $\tau_{log}^\lambda \triangleq \log \frac{n(2^b - 1)}{2^{b-1}} = \eta + 1 + \log(1 - 2^{-b}) \leq \tau_\infty$ holds if $\tau_\infty \geq \eta + 1$ or if $i \leq I \triangleq j - \log(1 - 2^{\tau_\infty - \eta - 1})$ and $\tau_\infty < \eta + 1$. Setting $I = \infty$ if $\tau_\infty \geq \eta + 1$ then justifies $i_{max}^\lambda = \min(k, \eta + j, I)$ as a suitable upper bound.

2. Since $\eta' = \eta + \log(n - 1) - b - 1$, either $\eta' \geq 0$ if $\eta \geq 1$ or $i \leq \eta + \log(n - 1) + j - 1$ otherwise. If $\eta \in [0, 1)$, then $\eta + \log(n - 1) \leq b + 1$, meaning that $\eta' < 0$ which is not possible as we have an integral number of queries. In that case, the loop is empty. On the other hand, $\tau_{log}^\lambda = \log i + \max(\eta, \eta')$ is smaller than τ_∞ when $\eta' \leq \eta$ if $i \leq \min(k, 2^{\tau_\infty - \eta})$. For the case $\eta' > \eta$, we would need to optimize i so that $\log i + \eta' \leq \tau_\infty$, but since η' depends on i itself, we did not dwell into these details.

3. Since the number of queries is maintained, only the condition on the time complexity needs to be checked. Since $\tau_{log}^\lambda = \log i + \eta + \log \tau_{dec}$, it suffices that $i \leq 2^{\tau_\infty - \eta - \log \tau_{dec}}$ to ensure $\tau_{log}^\lambda \leq \tau_\infty$ and this concludes the proof. $\quad\square$

References

1. Akavia, A.: Learning noisy characters, MPC, and cryptographic hardcore predicates. Ph.D. thesis, Massachusetts Institute of Technology, Cambridge, MA, USA (2008)
2. Asaka, R., Sakai, K., Yahagi, R.: Quantum circuit for the fast Fourier transform. Quantum Inf. Process. 19(8), 1–20 (2020). https://doi.org/10.1007/s11128-020-02776-5
3. Becker, A., Joux, A., May, A., Meurer, A.: Decoding random binary linear codes in $2^n/20$: how $1 + 1 = 0$ improves information set decoding. In: Pointcheval, D., Johansson, T. (eds.) EUROCRYPT 2012. LNCS, vol. 7237, pp. 520–536. Springer, Heidelberg (2012). https://doi.org/10.1007/978-3-642-29011-4_31

4. Bernstein, D.J.: Optimizing linear maps modulo 2 (2009). http://binary.cr.yp.to/linearmod2-20090830.pdf
5. Bernstein, D.J.: Grover vs. McEliece. In: Sendrier, N. (ed.) PQCrypto 2010. LNCS, vol. 6061, pp. 73–80. Springer, Heidelberg (2010). https://doi.org/10.1007/978-3-642-12929-2_6
6. Bernstein, D.J., Lange, T.: Never trust a bunny. In: Hoepman, J.-H., Verbauwhede, I. (eds.) RFIDSec 2012. LNCS, vol. 7739, pp. 137–148. Springer, Heidelberg (2013). https://doi.org/10.1007/978-3-642-36140-1_10
7. Bernstein, D.J., Lange, T., Peters, C.: Smaller decoding exponents: ball-collision decoding. In: Rogaway, P. (ed.) CRYPTO 2011. LNCS, vol. 6841, pp. 743–760. Springer, Heidelberg (2011). https://doi.org/10.1007/978-3-642-22792-9_42
8. Bleichenbacher, D.: On the generation of one-time keys in DL signature schemes (2000). https://blog.cr.yp.to/20191024-bleichenbacher.pdf
9. Blum, A., Kalai, A., Wasserman, H.: Noise-tolerant learning, the parity problem, and the statistical query model. CoRR cs.LG/0010022 (2000)
10. Bogos, S., Tramèr, F., Vaudenay, S.: On solving LPN using BKW and variants. IACR Cryptology ePrint Archive **2015**, 49 (2015)
11. Bogos, S., Vaudenay, S.: Optimization of LPN solving algorithms. Cryptology ePrint Archive, Report 2016/288 (2016). https://ia.cr/2016/288
12. Bogos, S.M.: LPN in Cryptography: an algorithmic study. Ph.D. thesis, Lausanne (2017). http://infoscience.epfl.ch/record/228977
13. Choi, G.: Applying the SFT algorithm for cryptography (2017). https://lasec.epfl.ch/intranet/projects/year16_17/Fall-16_17_Gwangbae_Choi_Applying_The_SFT/report.pdf. Access on demand
14. Dachman-Soled, D., Gong, H., Kippen, H., Shahverdi, A.: BKW meets Fourier new algorithms for LPN with sparse parities. In: Nissim, K., Waters, B. (eds.) TCC 2021. LNCS, vol. 13043, pp. 658–688. Springer, Cham (2021). https://doi.org/10.1007/978-3-030-90453-1_23
15. Esser, A., Kübler, R., May, A.: LPN decoded. Cryptology ePrint Archive, Report 2017/078 (2017)
16. Galbraith, S.D., Laity, J., Shani, B.: Finding significant Fourier coefficients: clarifications, simplifications, applications and limitations. Chic. J. Theor. Comput. Sci. **2018** (2018)
17. Grover, L.K.: A fast quantum mechanical algorithm for database search. In: Proceedings of the Twenty-Eighth Annual ACM Symposium on Theory of Computing, STOC 1996, pp. 212–219. Association for Computing Machinery, New York (1996). https://doi.org/10.1145/237814.237866
18. Guo, Q., Johansson, T., Löndahl, C.: Solving LPN using covering codes. In: Sarkar, P., Iwata, T. (eds.) ASIACRYPT 2014. LNCS, vol. 8873, pp. 1–20. Springer, Heidelberg (2014). https://doi.org/10.1007/978-3-662-45611-8_1
19. Hallgren, S., Vollmer, U.: Quantum computing. In: Bernstein, D.J., Buchmann, J., Dahmen, E. (eds.) Post-Quantum Cryptography. Springer, Heidelberg (2009). https://doi.org/10.1007/978-3-540-88702-7_2
20. Jiao, L.: Specifications and improvements of LPN solving algorithms. IET Inf. Secur. **14**(1), 111–125 (2020). https://doi.org/10.1049/iet-ifs.2018.5448
21. Kachigar, G., Tillich, J.-P.: Quantum information set decoding algorithms. In: Lange, T., Takagi, T. (eds.) PQCrypto 2017. LNCS, vol. 10346, pp. 69–89. Springer, Cham (2017). https://doi.org/10.1007/978-3-319-59879-6_5
22. Lee, P.J., Brickell, E.F.: An observation on the security of McEliece's public-key cryptosystem. In: Barstow, D., et al. (eds.) EUROCRYPT 1988. LNCS, vol. 330,

pp. 275–280. Springer, Heidelberg (1988). https://doi.org/10.1007/3-540-45961-8_25

23. Levieil, É., Fouque, P.-A.: An improved LPN algorithm. In: De Prisco, R., Yung, M. (eds.) SCN 2006. LNCS, vol. 4116, pp. 348–359. Springer, Heidelberg (2006). https://doi.org/10.1007/11832072_24

24. May, A., Meurer, A., Thomae, E.: Decoding random linear codes in $\tilde{O}(2^{0.054n})$. In: Lee, D.H., Wang, X. (eds.) ASIACRYPT 2011. LNCS, vol. 7073, pp. 107–124. Springer, Heidelberg (2011). https://doi.org/10.1007/978-3-642-25385-0_6

25. May, A., Ozerov, I.: On computing nearest neighbors with applications to decoding of binary linear codes. In: Oswald, E., Fischlin, M. (eds.) EUROCRYPT 2015. LNCS, vol. 9056, pp. 203–228. Springer, Heidelberg (2015). https://doi.org/10.1007/978-3-662-46800-5_9

26. Nielsen, M.A., Chuang, I.L.: Quantum Computation and Quantum Information: 10th Anniversary Edition, Anniversary Cambridge University Press, Cambridge (2010). https://doi.org/10.1017/CBO9780511976667

27. Prange, E.: The use of information sets in decoding cyclic codes. IRE Trans. Inf. Theory 8(5), 5–9 (1962). https://doi.org/10.1109/TIT.1962.1057777

28. Wagner, D.: A generalized birthday problem. In: Yung, M. (ed.) CRYPTO 2002. LNCS, vol. 2442, pp. 288–304. Springer, Heidelberg (2002). https://doi.org/10.1007/3-540-45708-9_19

29. Wiggers, T., Samardjiska, S.: Practically solving LPN. In: IEEE International Symposium on Information Theory, ISIT 2021, pp. 2399–2404. IEEE (2021). https://doi.org/10.1109/ISIT45174.2021.9518109

30. Xie, Z., Qiu, D., Cai, G.: Quantum algorithms on Walsh transform and Hamming distance for Boolean functions. Quantum Inf. Process. 17(6), 1–17 (2018). https://doi.org/10.1007/s11128-018-1885-y

An Estimator for the Hardness of the MQ Problem

Emanuele Bellini[1], Rusydi H. Makarim[1(✉)], Carlo Sanna[2], and Javier Verbel[1]

[1] Cryptography Research Center, Technology Innovation Institute, Abu Dhabi, UAE
{emanuele.bellini,rusydi.makarim,javier.verbel}@tii.ae
[2] Department of Mathematical Sciences, Politecnico di Torino, Torino, Italy

Abstract. The Multivariate Quadratic (MQ) problem consists in finding the solutions of a given system of m quadratic equations in n unknowns over a finite field, and it is an NP-complete problem of fundamental importance in computer science. In particular, the security of some cryptosystems against the so-called algebraic attacks is usually given by the hardness of this problem. Many algorithms to solve the MQ problem have been proposed and studied. Estimating precisely the complexity of all these algorithms is crucial to set secure parameters for a cryptosystem. This work collects and presents the most important classical algorithms and the estimates of their computational complexities. Moreover, it describes a software that we wrote and that makes possible to estimate the hardness of a given instance of the MQ problem.

Keywords: MQ problem · Estimator · Polynomial solving · Multivariate cryptography

1 Introduction

The problem of solving a multivariate quadratic system over a finite field is known as the Multivariate Quadratic (MQ) problem. This problem is known to be NP-complete, and it seems to be hard on average for an extensive range of parameters.

Despite of its clear hardness, there exists a considerable amount of algorithms to solve the MQ problem [16,17,31,32,36,37,49,51,53,63]. Their complexities depend on several values: the ratio of the number of variables and the number of polynomials, the size of the field, the characteristic of the field, and the number of solutions to the underlying problem. So it is difficult to determine what is the complexity of the best algorithm to solve a particular instance of the MQ problem. Moreover, some of the algorithms have optimized some parameters to provide the best asymptotic complexity. Since this does not mean that such optimizations provide the best complexity for a particular set of parameters, once a specific instance is provided, the parameters optimizing the complexity should be computed.

The MQ problem has been extensively used in cryptography. In cryptanalysis, it appears in the so-called *algebraic attacks*. These attacks break the security of

L. Batina and J. Daemen (Eds.): AFRICACRYPT 2022, LNCS 13503, pp. 323–347, 2022.
https://doi.org/10.1007/978-3-031-17433-9_14

a cryptosystem by solving one system of polynomial equations over a finite field (e.g., see [61]). In post-quantum cryptography, the MQ problem constitutes the building block of the Multivariate public key cryptosystems (MPKCs). These are promising post-quantum secure alternatives to the current public-key schemes, which would no longer be hard in the presence of a quantum computer [11].

In general, the MPKCs used for signature schemes are divided into two categories, named trapdoor and one-way multivariate signature schemes. The trapdoor ones are built upon a trapdoor multivariate polynomial map. They have very short signatures and fast signature verification that can be implemented in low-cost devices [20, 28]. Some examples of this kind of schemes are UOV [49], Rainbow [29] GeMSS [20], MAYO [15]. The one-way signature schemes are based on an identification scheme that uses the knowledge of a solution of a random multivariate polynomial map to authenticate a legitimate party (e.g., [59]). Then, the multivariate identification scheme is converted into a signature scheme using a standard protocol [40]. The main advantage of this kind of multivariate signature scheme is that their security is based (directly) on the hardness of the MQ problem, and they enjoy a small compressed public key. Some of the these schemes are SOFIA [21], MQDSS [22], MUDFISH [13], and the signature proposed by Furue, Duong and Takagi in [42].

In the design of MPKCs, once the specific parameters of the scheme are selected, the size of the finite field q, the number of variables n, and the number of polynomials m of the corresponding MQ problem are fixed. Thus, a good estimate of the hardness of solving such an instance with given parameters q, n, and m of the MQ problem will allow the designers to set parameters to get efficient schemes while keeping high levels of security. Also, MPKCs are potentially strong candidates for the upcoming NIST call for proposals to standardize a new signature scheme that is not based on structural lattices [54].

Our first contribution is to gather the algorithms available in the literature for solving the MQ problem and expressing their estimates of time and space complexities as a function of their parameters if any. For the Crossbred algorithm, we establish a more tightly bound that takes into account the field equations when $q > 2$. Our second contribution is to provide a software named the MQ estimator [9], that given an instance of the MQ problem estimates the complexities of each algorithm to solve it. We use our software to estimate the best algorithm, in terms of time complexity, for different regimes of parameters, see Figs. 1a, 1c, 1b and 1d. Also, we estimate the security of the multivariate schemes Rainbow, MAYO, MUDFISH, and MQDSS against the direct attack. We found that all the parameter sets of MAYO, MUDFISH, MQDSS and the category I parameters of Rainbow are under the claimed security, see Table 2, 3 and 4.

Our paper is somehow analog to the work that Albrecht, Player, and Scott did for the problem Learning with Errors [1], and the work by Bellini and Esser for the Syndrome Decoding problem [10, 35]. Regarding the problem of solving polynomial systems over an arbitrary field, we refer the reader to the book edited by Dickenstein and Emiris [27] and to the survey of Ayad [4]. For collections of algorithms for the case of finite fields, we point out the Ph.D. theses of Bard [6],

Mou [55], and Ullah [64]. Also, there are surveys on very specific techniques like, for instance, signature-based algorithms for computing Gröbner bases [34].

The structure of the paper is as follows. Section 2 shows some preliminary facts about computational complexity and the MQ problem. In Sect. 3 we list the main algorithms for solving the MQ problem, and we examine their time and space complexities. Also, we establish a generalization over $\mathbb{F}_{q\geqslant 2}$ to compute the complexity of the Crossbred algorithm. Finally, in Sect. 5 the usage of the MQ estimator is explained, and some of the estimates obtained are shown.

2 Preliminaries

2.1 General Notation

We employ Landau's notation $f(n) = \mathcal{O}(g(n))$, with its usual meaning that $|f(n)| \leqslant C|g(n)|$ for some constant $C > 0$. Also, we write $f(n) = \tilde{\mathcal{O}}(g(n))$ whenever $f(n) = \mathcal{O}(n^k g(n))$ for some constant $k \geqslant 0$. For every real number x, let $\lfloor x \rfloor$ be the greatest integer not exceeding x. We let log denote the logarithm in base 2, while $e = 2.718\ldots$ denotes the Euler number. The Greek letter ω denotes the exponent in the complexity of matrix multiplication. That is, we assume that there is an algorithm that multiplies two $n \times n$ matrices over a field with $\mathcal{O}(n^\omega)$ field operations. We have $2 \leqslant \omega \leqslant 3$, with $\omega = 2.80736$ given by Strassen's algorithm [62] (currently, the best upper bound is $\omega < 2.37286$, given by the algorithm of Alman and Williams [2], but such improvements of Strassen's algorithm are never used in practice, due to the large hidden constants of their asymptotic complexities). We write $\mathbb{F}_q$ for a finite field of q elements. Lastly, we use n_{sol} to denote the number of solutions of a given MQ instance.

2.2 Computational Complexity

Throughout this paper, the time and space complexities of each algorithm are given, assuming a computational model in which the operations of $\mathbb{F}_q$ (addition, multiplication, and division) are performed in constant time $\mathcal{O}(1)$ and in which every element of $\mathbb{F}_q$ is stored in constant space $\mathcal{O}(1)$ ($\mathbb{F}_q$-complexity). A more detailed analysis could assume a computational model in which the operations at bit-level are performed in constant time $\mathcal{O}(1)$ and in which every bit is stored in constant space $\mathcal{O}(1)$ (bit-complexity). However, the bit-complexities of addition, multiplication, and division in $\mathbb{F}_q$ are different (with the addition the least expensive and division the most) and depend on the algorithms implementing them, possible hardware optimizations, and eventually, q having a special form, like q being equal to a power of 2 or a Mersenne prime (see [44] for a survey). Therefore, there is no straightforward way to convert between $\mathbb{F}_q$-time complexity and bit-time complexity. Roughly, the bit-time complexity can be estimated by $(\log q)^\theta$ times the $\mathbb{F}_q$-time complexity, with $\theta \in [1, 2]$. On the other hand, the bit-space complexity is simply equal to $\log q$ times the $\mathbb{F}_q$-space complexity. Of course, for $q = 2$ the $\mathbb{F}_q$-complexity and the bit-complexity are equivalent.

2.3   The MQ Problem

The input of the MQ problem consists of m quadratic polynomials $p_1, \ldots, p_m$ in n variables $x_1, \ldots, x_n$ and coefficients in a finite field $\mathbb{F}_q$. The output concerns the solutions (in $\mathbb{F}_q$) of the system of equations

$$p_i(x_1, \ldots, x_n) = 0, \quad i = 1, \ldots, m. \tag{1}$$

There are three versions of the MQ problem:

- **Decision:** It asks to determine if (1) has a solution.
- **Search:** It asks to find a solution of (1), if there is any.

The decision version of MQ is known to be NP-complete. Moreover, the decision and search version of MQ are strictly related. On the one hand, obviously, solving the search version also solves the decision. On the other hand, by iteratively testing each variable, one can solve the search version by calling a subroutine for the decision version at most $(q-1)n$ times. In this paper, we focus only on the search version of the problem.

2.4   General Strategies for Underdetermined Systems

A system of equations is said to be *underdetermined* if it has more unknowns than equations, that is, in our notation, $n > m$. There are algorithms that transform an underdetermined system into one with the same number of equations and variables so that a solution to the former system can efficiently be computed from a solution to the last system. This section describes some of these algorithms.

Fixing Variables. This approach consists in fixing the values of $n - m$ unknowns. The resulting systems $\mathcal{Q}$ has m unknowns and m equations and, assuming that we started from a random MQ problem, it has a solution with probability $e^{-1} = 0.367 \ldots$ [43]. Thus, the complexity of this strategy is dominated by the complexity of solving $\mathcal{Q}$.

Thomae–Wolf and Improvements. Let P be an MQ problem with m equations in $n = \alpha m$ unknowns over $\mathbb{F}_q$, where $\alpha > 1$ is a rational number. Based on the ideas of Kipnis, Patarin, and Goubin [49], Thomae and Wolf [63] designed a mechanism to reduce P to another MQ problem $\mathcal{P}'$ of $m - \lfloor \alpha \rfloor + a$ equations and unknowns, where $a = 0$ if $m/\lfloor \alpha \rfloor$ is an integer, and $a = 1$ otherwise. The time complexity of the reduction is $\mathcal{O}\left(m(\lfloor \alpha \rfloor m)^3\right)$ when q is even. For q odd, the complexity of the reduction is dominated by the complexity of quadratic system with $\lfloor \alpha \rfloor - 1$ equations over $\mathbb{F}_q$. Still, for the rage of parameters interesting in practice, e.g., see Table 2, and 3 the complexity of the reduction is insignificant compared with the complexity of solving the problem $\mathcal{P}'$.

This technique was further improved by Furue, Nakamura, and Takagi [41], who combined Thomae and Wolf's approach with fixing k variables. Their method reduces a system of m quadratic equations in n unknowns over $\mathbb{F}_{2^r}$ to a systems of $m - \alpha_k$ quadratic equations in $m - k - \alpha_k$ unknowns, where $\alpha_k := \lfloor (n-k)/(m-k) \rfloor - 1$ for $r > 1$ and $\alpha_k := \lfloor (n-k)/(m-k-1) \rfloor - 1$ for $r = 1$.

3   Algorithms for Solving MQ

This section lists the most important classical algorithms for solving the MQ problem and describes their computational complexities. There are also quantum algorithms to solve the MQ problem, which speed up some of the classical algorithms via quantum walks, but they are out of the scope of this paper. We refer the reader to [12,38,60] for more information on quantum algorithms solving the MQ problem.

The complexity of some of the algorithms described in this section depends on the number of solutions n_{sol} of the underlying instance. We remark that for the non-underdetermined case, hard instances of the MQ problem are expected to have a small n_{sol} (e.g., 1, 2, or 3). In the other case, n_{sol} is expected to be around q^{m-n}.

3.1   Exhaustive Search

Fast Exhaustive Search (FES). Bouillaguet et al. [17] proposed a more efficient way to perform exhaustive search over $\mathbb{F}_2^n$ by enumerating the solution space with Gray codes. The evaluation of an element in $\mathbb{F}_2^n$ is used to compute the evaluation of the next potential solution. The time complexity of finding one solution to the MQ problem with this algorithm is given by $4 \log(n) \left(\frac{2^n}{n_{sol}+1} \right)$. The space complexity is given by the memory required to store the polynomial system, so $\mathcal{O}(n^2 m)$. This approach can be extended to any field $\mathbb{F}_q$ using q-ary Gray codes [33]. In this case, the time complexity is given by $\mathcal{O} \left(\log_q(n) \frac{q^n}{n_{sol}+1} \right)$.

3.2   Algorithms Designed for Underdetermined Systems

In this section, we describe some of the algorithms specially designed for underdetermined systems.

Kipnis–Patarin–Goubin (KPG). Kipnis, Patarin, and Goubin [49] proposed a polynomial-time algorithm to solve the MQ problem over a field of even characteristic when $n > m(m + 1)$. We write KPG to refer to this algorithm. The main idea in the KPG algorithm is to find a non-singular matrix $\mathbf{S} \in \mathbb{F}_q^{n \times n}$ such that the change of variables $(y_1, \ldots, y_n)^\top = \mathbf{S}(x_1, \ldots, x_n)^\top$ results in a system of the form

$$\sum_{i=1}^{m} a_{i,1} y_i^2 + \sum_{i=1}^{m} y_i L_{i,1}(y_{m+1}, \ldots, y_n) + Q_1(y_{m+1}, \ldots, y_n) = 0 \qquad (2)$$

$$\vdots$$

$$\sum_{i=1}^{m} a_{i,m} y_i^2 + \sum_{i=1}^{m} y_i L_{i,m}(y_{m+1}, \ldots, y_n) + Q_m(y_{m+1}, \ldots, y_n) = 0,$$

where the $L_{i,j}(\cdot)$ are linear maps and the $Q_i(\cdot)$ are quadratic maps. Then, they solve (2) by solving, sequentially, two systems of linear equations in the y_i's. The overall time complexity of this algorithm is given by

$$\mathcal{O}\left(\sum_{i=1}^{m-1}(im)^\omega + m^\omega + m^{2\omega} + 3n^\omega\right) = \mathcal{O}(mn^\omega).$$

The space complexity is dominated either by the space needed to solve a square linear system of size $(m-1)m$ plus the space required to store the original polynomials. It is given by $\mathcal{O}(mn^2)$.

Courtois et al. applied the ideas of KPG over fields of odd characteristic. They provided an algorithm with time complexity $2^{40}(40 + 40/\log q)^{m/40}$ for $n \geqslant (40 + 40/\log q)^{m/40}(m+1)$, see [25, Sec. 4.2] for the details.

Miura–Hashimoto–Takagi (MHT). The algorithm of Miura, Hashimoto, and Takagi [53] works for $n \geqslant m(m+3)/2$ over any finite field. Its complexity is exponential in m over fields of odd characteristic. Precisely, its time complexity is

$$\begin{cases} \mathcal{O}(n^\omega m) & \text{if } q \text{ is even;} \\ \mathcal{O}(2^m n^\omega m) & \text{if } q \text{ is odd.} \end{cases}$$

The space complexity of MHT is dominated by the memory required to store the initial set of polynomials.

Huang–Bao (HB). In [46], Huang and Bao propose an algorithm that generalizes the MHT algorithm, and it works the broader range of parameters $n \geqslant m(m+1)/2$. The space complexity is the same of MHT, while the time complexity is given by

$$\begin{cases} \mathcal{O}\left(q(\log q)^2 \cdot n^\omega m\right) & \text{if } q \text{ is even;} \\ \mathcal{O}\left(q(\log q)^2 \cdot 2^m n^\omega m\right) & \text{if } q \text{ is odd.} \end{cases}$$

Courtois–Goubin–Meier–Tacier (CGMT-A). Courtois et al. [25] introduced an algorithm, so-called Algorithm A, to solve the MQ problem in the underdetermined case. Here we use CGMT-A to refer to this algorithm.

Let k be an integer, and let $f_1, \ldots, f_m$ be the input polynomials of the underlying MQ problem. For each $j = 1, \ldots, m$, we can write

$$f_j(x_1, \ldots, x_n) = g_j(x_1, \ldots, x_k) + h_j(x_{k+1}, \ldots, x_n) + \sum_{i=1}^{k} L_{i,j}(x_{k+1}, \ldots, x_n)x_i,$$

where the $L_{i,j}$'s are linear polynomials. In the CGMT-A algorithm one has to set $L_{i,j}(x_{k+1}, \ldots, x_n) = c_{i,j}$, where each $c_{i,j} \in \mathbb{F}_q$ is randomly chosen. It is also defined $g_j'(x_1, \ldots, x_k) := g_j(x_1, \ldots, x_k) + \sum_{i=1}^{k} c_{i,j}x_i$ for $j = 1, \ldots, 2k$. Then, one has to compute and store (sorted) the q^k vectors of the set $\mathcal{G} =$

$\{-(g'_1(a), \ldots, g'_{2k}(a)) : a \in \mathbb{F}_q^k\}$ along with its corresponding preimage a. After, we have to search for a vector $b \in \mathbb{F}_q^{n-k}$ such that

$$\{L_{i,j}(b) = c_{i,j}\}_{i,j=0}^{k,2k} \quad \text{and} \quad (h_1(b), \ldots, h_{2k}(b)) \in \mathcal{G}. \tag{3}$$

Notice that any b be fulfilling Eq. (3) yields to a vector $c := (a, b) \in \mathbb{F}_q^b$ such that $f_j(c) = 0$ for $j = 1, \ldots, 2k$, and $f_j(c) = 0$ for $j = 2k + 1, \ldots, m$ with probability $q^{-(m-2k)}$.

Courtois et al. noticed that in order to find one b satisfying Eq. (3) one has to compute on average q^k evaluations of the form $(h_1(b), \ldots, h_{2k}(b))$ for vectors b satisfying $\{L_{i,j}(b) = c_{ij}\}_{i,j=0}^{k,2k}$.

If $k := \min\lfloor m/2, \sqrt{n/2 - \sqrt{n/2}}\rfloor$ satisfies that $m - 2k < 2k^2 \leqslant n - 2k$, then CGMT-A succeed on finding a solution, and its average time complexity is given by

$$\mathcal{O}\left(2k \binom{n-k}{2} q^{m-k}\right).$$

The space complexity of this algorithm is dominated by the memory needed to store the q^k evaluations of the g'_i polynomials, i.e., $\mathcal{O}(2kq^k)$.

3.3   Gröbner Basis

This section shows the complexity to solve the MQ problem via the so-called *Gröbner basis algorithms*. Throughout this section, we assume that the underlying sequence of polynomials is either *regular* or *semi-regular*, see Definition 3.2.

A solution to the MQ problem $f_1 = \cdots = f_m = 0$ can be efficiently extracted from a Gröbner basis G_{lex}, in the lexicographic order, of the ideal $I = \langle f_1, \ldots, f_m \rangle$ [26]. In practice, it is been verified that the most efficient way to compute G_{lex} is by first computing a Gröbner basis G_{grvlex} of I in the graded reverse lexicographic order. Then, one uses G_{grvlex} as an input of the FGLM [39] algorithm to compute G_{lex} [36].

The complexity of the Gröbner basis algorithms in the graded reverse lexicographic order is estimated via the *degree of regularity* of the ideal generated by the polynomial of the underlying MQ problem.

Definition 3.1. *The degree of regularity of a homogeneous ideal $I \subseteq \mathbb{F}_q[\boldsymbol{x}]$ is the minimum integer d, if any, such that $\dim(I_d) = \dim(R_d)$, where $I_d = R_d \cap I$, R_d is the set of elements in R of degree d.*

Definition 3.2 (Regular and semi-regular sequences). *A homogeneous sequence $\mathcal{F} \in \mathbb{F}_q[\boldsymbol{x}]^m$ is called semi-regular if*

$$\sum_{d \geqslant 0} \dim\left(R_d/I_d\right) z^d = \left[\frac{(1-z^q)^n}{(1-z)^n}\left(\frac{1-z^2}{1-z^{2q}}\right)^m\right]_+,$$

where $[H(z)]_+$ means that the series $H(z)$ is cut from the first non-positive coefficient. An affine sequence $\mathcal{G} = (g_1, \ldots, g_m)$ is semi-regular if the sequence $(\tilde{g}_1, \ldots, \tilde{g}_m)$ does, where $\tilde{g}_i$ is the homogeneous part of g_i of highest degree.

The Role of the Field Equations. In the ring $\mathbb{F}_q[x_1, \ldots, x_n]$, the set of elements $\{x_1^q - x_1, \ldots, x_n^q - x_n\}$ is called the *field equations*. By Lagrange's Theorem, every element in $\mathbb{F}_q$ is a root of the univariate polynomial $x^q - x$. Thus, the set of solutions of a given MQ problem (as defined in Sect. 2.3) does not change if we add the field equations to the original set of polynomials.

In terms of computing a Gröbner basis, adding the field equations to a set of polynomials in $\mathbb{F}_q[x_1, \ldots, x_n]$ is equivalent to considering the polynomials in the quotient ring

$$R = \mathbb{F}_q[x_1, \ldots, x_n]/\langle x_1^q - x_1, \ldots, x_n^q - x_n \rangle.$$

Given a positive integer d, let R_d and $\mathbb{F}_q[x_1, \ldots, x_n]_d$ denote the $\mathbb{F}_q$-vector spaces of homogeneous polynomials of degree d in R and $\mathbb{F}_q[x_1, \ldots, x_n]$, respectively. Hence, $\dim(R_d)$ represent the number of monomials in $\mathbb{F}_q[x_1, \ldots, x_n]$ of degree d such that no variable is raised to a power greater than $q - 1$. This value is essential in to determine the complexity of computing a Gröbner basis of an ideal $I \subset R$. The following proposition shows a way to compute $\dim(R_d)$.

Proposition 3.1. *Let d be a positive integer. Then, $\dim(R_d) = [z^d]H(z)$, where $H(z)$ is the series defined by*

$$H(z) := \left(\frac{1 - z^q}{1 - z} \right)^n.$$

That is, $\dim(R_d)$ is the coefficient of z^d in the series $H(z)$. Similarly,

$$\dim\left(\mathbb{F}_q[x_1, \ldots, x_n]_d \right) = [z^d] \left(\frac{1}{(1 - z)^n} \right),$$

or equivalently, $\dim\left(\mathbb{F}_q[x_1, \ldots, x_n]_d \right) = \binom{n+d-1}{d}$.

Let $I \subset \mathbb{F}_q[x_1, \ldots, x_n]$ be an ideal. For small values of q, the computation of a Gröbner basis of I can be significantly easier if I is seen into the ring R. This is because, for a given integer $d > 0$, R_d could be significantly smaller than $\mathbb{F}_q[x_1, \ldots, x_n]_d$. For instance see Example 3.1.

Example 3.1. Let $q = 2$ and $n = 10$. Then,

$$\left(\frac{1 - z^q}{1 - z} \right)^n = 1 + 10z + 45z^2 + 120z^3 + 210z^4 + 252z^5 + \cdots,$$

and

$$\frac{1}{(1 - z)^n} = 1 + 10z + 55z^2 + 220z^3 + 715z^4 + 2002z^5 + \cdots.$$

Thus, $\dim\left(F[x_1, \ldots, x_n]_5 \right) = 2002$, while $\dim(R_5) = 252$.

F4/F5. This section regards the complexity of solving the MQ problem via the F4 and F5 algorithms. All the estimations are computed over the hypothesis that the underlying sequences of polynomials are regular or semi-regular. The monomial order in the underlying polynomial ring is the graded reverse lexicographic (grevlex) monomial order.

The F4 and F5 are algorithms to compute a Gröbner basis of an ideal of polynomial equations over an arbitrary field. They were introduced by Faugère [36,37] and they are based on the original ideas of Lazard [50]. These two algorithms could be seen as generalizations of the XL [24] and the Mutant-XL algorithms [19].

It might be the case that one of the algorithms outperforms the other for a particular set of parameters, but it is slower for a different set of parameters. For instance, F5 is expected to be faster than F4 for underdetermined systems, but this is not the case for overdetermined systems [37]. Even though such an improvement is estimated to be no more than a factor of two for large values of n [30]. Asymptotically, the time and memory complexities of both algorithms are the same. Thus, in this paper and in our estimator, we use the F5's complexities to refer also to the complexities of F4.

The Square Case. Bardet, Faugère, and Salvy [7] estimated the complexity of computing a Gröbner basis of a homogeneous ideal of polynomials in the grevlex order. To estimate such complexity for a non-homogenous ideal I, we use the fact that a Gröbner basis of I can be obtained by specializing to $h = 1$ in every polynomial in $\mathcal{G}^{(h)}$, where $\mathcal{G}^{(h)}$ is Gröbner basis of $I^{(h)}$, and $I^{(h)}$ denotes the homogenization of I.

By Theorem 2 in [7] with $\ell = 1$, computing a Gröbner basis in the grevlex order of a non-homogeneous ideal I can be done, without using the field equations, in

$$\mathcal{O}\left((n+1)2^{4.29(n+1)} + n \cdot n_{sol}^3\right) = \tilde{\mathcal{O}}\left(2^{4.29n}\right)$$

in arithmetic operations in $\mathbb{F}_q$.

The Overdetermined Case. In the overdetermined case the time complexity is given by

$$\mathcal{O}\left(\binom{n+d_{reg}}{d_{reg}}^\omega + n \cdot n_{sol}^3\right),$$

while the space complexity:

$$\mathcal{O}\left(\binom{n+d_{reg}-1}{d_{reg}}^2\right),$$

where $d_{reg} = \deg(P(z)) + 1$, and $P(z)$ is the series given in Definition 3.2.

3.4   Hybrid Algorithms

A hybrid algorithm for solving the MQ problem combines a partial exhaustive search with another procedure. In this section, we consider the complexity estimations of hybrid algorithms.

BooleanSolve/FXL. The BooleanSolve algorithm and its generalization, the FXL algorithm, were proposed by Bardet et al. [8] and Courtois et al. [24], respectively. The idea of both algorithms is to guess a number k of variables repeatedly and then check the consistency of the resulting MQ problem.

In BooleanSolve, such a check is done by checking the consistency a linear system of the form $\mathbf{z}\mathbf{M}_d = (0, 0, .., 1)$, where $\mathbf{M}_d$ is the Macaulay matrix [8] of the resulting system up to degree d, and d is a large enough integer. Once a set of k variables being part of a solution is found, an exhaustive search algorithm is apply on the resulting system with $n - k$ variables.

In this section, we consider the FXL as a naïve generalization of BooleanSolve. That is, after guessing k variables, the consistency of the resulting system of $n - k$ variables is checked by using the Macaulay matrix at large enough degree. Notice that this is different from what Hybrid-F5 does, where the resulting system is solved after each guess of k variables.

There are methods to check the consistency of the system of the form $\mathbf{z}\mathbf{M}_d = (0, 0, .., 1)$. One uses Gaussian elimination (known as the *deterministic* variant), and the other one uses the probabilistic Wiedemann's algorithm (known as *Las Vegas* variant). For the deterministic variant, the time complexity of this algorithm is dominated by the guessing and consistency checking parts. Thus, it is given by

$$q^k \cdot \tilde{\mathcal{O}}\left(\binom{n - k + d_{wit}}{d_{wit}}^\omega\right),$$

while the space complexity is

$$\mathcal{O}\left(\binom{n - k + d_{wit} - 1}{d_{wit}}^2\right),$$

where $d_{wit} = \deg(P_k(z)) + 1$, and if we consider the field equations

$$P_k(z) = \left[\frac{(1 - z^q)^{n-k}}{(1 - z)^{n-k+1}}\left(\frac{1 - z^2}{1 - z^{2q}}\right)^m\right]_+. \tag{4}$$

While Las Vegas variant of this method has time complexity

$$q^k \cdot \mathcal{O}\left(3\binom{n - k + 2}{2}\binom{n - k + d_{wit}}{d_{wit}}^2\right),$$

and the space complexity is computed as the number of bits needed to store the whole Macaulay matrix[1]. So that one requires

---

[1] Every row of the Macaulay matrix can be compute on the fly, but it will introduce an overhead in the time complexity.

$$m \cdot w + T \cdot w \cdot \frac{\log_2 N}{\log_2 q} + N \frac{\log_2 m}{\log_2 q}$$

bits of memory, where $w := \binom{n-k+2}{2}$, $T := \binom{n-k+d_{wit}-2}{d_{wit}}$, and $N := \binom{n-k+d_{wit}}{d_{wit}}$ [56, Section 4.5.3].

Hybrid-(F4/F5). Another way to apply a hybrid algorithm is just by guessing a set of k variables, and then solve the resulting system by applying whether the F4 or F5 the algorithm. In this paper, we refer to this method as the Hybrid-F5 algorithm. The complexity of this method is given by

$$q^k \cdot \mathcal{O}\left(\left(\frac{n-k+d_{reg}}{d_{reg}} \right)^{\omega} + nn_{sol}^3 \right)$$

Memory complexity:

$$\mathcal{O}\left(\left(\frac{n-k+d_{reg}-1}{d_{reg}} \right)^2 \right),$$

where $d_{reg} = \deg(P_k(z)) + 1$, and $P_k(z)$ is the polynomial shown in Eq. (4).

Crossbred. The Crossbred algorithm was introduced by Joux and Vitse [48]. Its complexity was initially analyzed by Chen et al. in [22], and later Duarte provided a more detailed complexity analysis by encoding the information in several bivariate series to determine the complexity [33].

For $q = 2$, Duarte used the field equations to derive formulas of the aforementioned bivariate series, but he not consider them in the case of $q > 2$. Inspired by the ideas of Duarte, we extend the complexity of the Crossbred algorithm by taking into account the field equations even when $q > 2$.

Let us fix three positive integers D, d, and k. The Crossbred algorithm consists in two steps, the *preprocessing* and the *linearization* steps. In the former step, it performs a sequence of row operations on a submatrix of the degree D Macaulay matrix of the given set of polynomials, in such a way that every specialization of the last $n-k$ variables yields equations of degree d in the first k variables. In the linearization step, the Crossbred algorithm tests the consistency of the resulting degree d system by linearization. To derive the complexity of this algorithm we assume that after each specialization of the last $n-k$ variables the remain system is semi-regular. The complexity of this approach is given by

$$\tilde{\mathcal{O}}\left(n_{cols}^2 \right) + q^{n-k} \cdot \tilde{\mathcal{O}}\left(\tilde{n}_{cols}^{\omega} \right) = \mathcal{O}\left(n_{cols}^2 \log_2 n_{cols} \log_2 \log_2 n_{cols} \right) + q^{n-k} \cdot \mathcal{O}\left(m \cdot \tilde{n}_{cols}^{\omega} \right),$$

where for the given the parameters (D, d, k)

$$n_{cols} = \sum_{d_k=d+1}^{D} \sum_{d'=0}^{D-d_k} [x^{d_k} z^{d'}] H_k(x) H_{n-k}(z), \text{ and } \tilde{n}_{cols} = [z^d]\left(\frac{H_k(z)}{1-z} \right),$$

where $H_k(z) := \frac{(1-z^q)^k}{(1-z)^k}$.

Given a non-negative integer k, not all pairs (D, d), with $D > d$, are expected to configure the algorithm so that the Crossbred can solve an MQ problem $\mathcal{S}$ with an underlying semi-regular sequence of polynomials. We say that (D, d, k) are *admissible parameters* for $\mathcal{S}$ if the Crossbred algorithm with parameters (D, d, k) is expected to solve $\mathcal{S}$.

In [33], Duarte shows the case $q = 2$ of the following fact: if the coefficient of the monomial $x^D y^d$ in the bivariate series

$$\frac{(1+x)^{n-k}}{(1-x)(1-y)} \left(\frac{(1+xy)^k}{(1+x^2y^2)^m} - \frac{(1+x)^k}{(1+x^2)^m} \right) - \frac{(1+y)^k}{(1-x)(1-y)(1+y^2)^m} \quad (5)$$

is non-negative, then (D, d, k) are admissible parameters for $\mathcal{S}$.

Here we remark that for the case $q \geqslant 2$, it can be generalized as

$$S_k(x, y) := \frac{\tilde{H}_{k,m}(xy) \cdot H_{n-k}(x) - \tilde{H}_{n,m}(x) - \tilde{H}_{k,m}(y)}{(1-x)(1-y)}, \quad (6)$$

where $\tilde{H}_{k,m}(y)$ is the Hilbert series of a semi-regular sequence with m equations in k variables, i.e.,

$$\tilde{H}_{k,m}(y) := \left[\frac{(1-y^q)^k}{(1-y)^k} \left(\frac{1-y^2}{1-y^{2q}} \right)^m \right]_+ .$$

Notice that the Eq. (6) reduces to the Eq. (5) when $q = 2$.

The space complexity is dominated by the memory needed to store the matrices in the preprocessing and the linearization steps. Thus, the space complexity is given by

$$\mathcal{O}\left(n_{cols}^2 + \tilde{n}_{cols}^2 \right).$$

3.5   Probabilistic Algorithms

In this section, we describe the complexity of the so-called *probabilistic algorithms* for solving the MQ problem. A common and interesting feature of these algorithms is that they asymptotically outperform the exhaustive search algorithms in the worst case, and their complexity does not depend on any assumption about the input polynomials.

Lokshtanov et al.'s. Lokshtanov et al. [51] were the first to introduce a probabilistic algorithm that, in the worst case, solves a square $(m = n)$ polynomial system over $\mathbb{F}_q$ in time $\tilde{\mathcal{O}}(q^{\delta n})$, for some $\delta < 1$ depending only on q and the degree of the system, without relying on any unproven assumption. Overall, Lokshtanov et al.'s is an algorithm to check the consistency, i.e., determining whether or not the system has a solution to a given MQ problem. Computing a solution can be done by using this algorithm several times. Letting $q = p^d$, for a prime number p and a positive integer d, the time complexity of Lokshtanov et al.'s algorithm is:

- $\tilde{O}\left(2^{0.8765n}\right)$ for $q = 2$.
- $\tilde{O}\left(q^{0.9n}\right)$ for $q > 2$ being a power of 2.
- $\tilde{O}\left(q^{0.9975n}\right)$, when $p > 2$, $\log p < 8e$.
- For $\log p \geqslant 8e$, the complexity is given by

$$\tilde{O}\left(q^n \cdot \left(\frac{\log q}{2ed}\right)^{-dn}\right).$$

To derive a more precise time complexity estimation, let us assume that $C(n, m, q)$ is the time complexity of checking the Loskshtanov et al.'s algorithm to check the consistency of a given MQ problem. Then, the complexity of finding one solution to the MQ problem is upper bounded by

$$(q-1)\sum_{i=0}^{n-1} C(n-i, m, q).$$

Lokshtanov et al. [51] proved that

$$C(n, m, q) = O\left(100n \log_2(q)\left(q^{n-n'} + q^{n'} \cdot M(n-n', 2(q-1)(n'+2), q) \cdot n^{6q}\right)\right),$$

where $n' = \lfloor \delta n \rfloor$, and $M(n, d, q)$ is the number of monomials of degree at most d on n variables in $\mathbb{F}_q[x_1, \ldots, x_n]/\langle x_1^q - x_1, \ldots, x_n^q - x_n\rangle$, i.e., $M(n, d, q)$ is the coefficient of z^d in the series

$$\frac{(1 - z^q)^n}{(1 - z)^{n+1}}.$$

See [65, Lemma 1] for further details. The space complexity of this algorithm is given by

$$O\left(M(n - n', k(q-1)(n'+2), q) + \log_2 nq^{n-n'}\right).$$

Björklund et al.'s. Based on the ideas from Lokshtanov et al., Björklund et al. [16] devised an algorithm to compute the parity of the number of solutions of a given MQ problem over $\mathbb{F}_2$. They showed how their algorithm could be used to solve the MQ problem with time complexity $\tilde{O}\left(2^{0.803225n}\right)$.

Let $\mathcal{F}$ be a sequence of polynomials over $\mathbb{F}_2$, and for a given integer n_1, let $x = (y, z)$ be a partition of the variables in x, where y and z correspond to the first $n - n_1$ and the last n_1 variables in x, respectively. The main idea behind the Björklund et al.'s algorithm is to approximate the values of the polynomial $P(y)$ given by

$$P(y) = \sum_{\hat{z} \in \{0,1\}^{n_1}} F(y, \hat{z}), \quad \text{where } F(y, z) = \prod_{f \in \mathcal{F}}(1 + f(y, z)). \quad (7)$$

This approximation is made by computing $48n + 1$ times the values of $\tilde{P}(\tilde{y})$ for every $\hat{y} \in \{0, 1\}^{n-n_1}$, where $\tilde{P}$ is the polynomial given by

$$\tilde{P}(y) = \sum_{\hat{z} \in \{0,1\}^{n_1}} \tilde{F}(y, \hat{z}), \quad \text{where } \tilde{F}(y, z) = \prod_{g \in \mathcal{G}}(1 + g(y, z)), \quad (8)$$

and $\mathcal{G}$ is a sequence of polynomials formed by random $\mathbb{F}_2$-linear combinations of the polynomials in $\mathcal{F}$. Notice, for a fixed $\hat{y} \in \{0,1\}^{n-n_1}$ the value $\tilde{P}(\hat{y})$ is the parity of the function $\tilde{F}(\hat{y}, z)$, i.e., the parity of the addition of all $\tilde{F}(\hat{y}, \hat{z})$ with $\hat{z} \in \{0,1\}^{n_1}$. Also, the parity of $\tilde{F}$ is the parity of the sum of all values $\tilde{P}(\hat{y})$, and at the same time is an approximation to the parity of F. Since this last parity is clearly the parity of the number of solutions of the MQ problem, we can say the Bjöklund et al. parity counting algorithm reduces to many smaller instances of the same problem, namely, the parity of $\tilde{F}(\hat{y}, z)$ for every $\hat{y} \in \{0,1\}^{n-n_1}$ for each of the $48n + 1$ polynomial s $\tilde{F}$.

Let $T(n, m)$ be the time complexity of Björklund et al.'s parity-counting algorithm. Thus, it can be transformed to solve the MQ problem in polynomial time. More precisely, the expected number of operations is given by

$$\mathcal{O}\left(8k\log(n)\sum_{i=1}^{n-1} T(n-i, m+k+2)\right),$$

where $k = \lfloor \log(n_{sol} + 1) \rfloor^2$.

It is proven that

$$T(n,m) \leqslant s \cdot \tau(\ell)\left(T(\ell, \ell+2) + \mathcal{O}\left(\cdot(n + (\ell+2)m\binom{n}{\downarrow 2} + 2^{n-\ell}(n-\ell)\right)\right),$$

where $\ell = \lfloor \lambda n \rfloor$, $0 < \lambda < 1$, $s = 48n + 1$, $\tau(\ell) := \binom{n-\ell}{\downarrow \ell+4}$, and $\binom{n}{\downarrow k} := \sum_{j=0}^{k}\binom{n}{j}$. For the space complexity, denoted by $S(n, m)$, the following formula is proven

$$S(n,m) \leqslant S(\ell, \ell+2) + \mathcal{O}\left(2^{n-\ell}\log s + m\binom{n}{\downarrow 2}\right).$$

Dinur's First Algorithm. Inspired by the ideas from Björklund et al., Dinur [32] proposed an algorithm to compute the parity of the number of solutions of a given MQ problem over $\mathbb{F}_2$. Unlike Björklund et al.'s, Dinur's parity-counting algorithm does not compute one by one the 2^{n-n_1} values of an specialization of the polynomial $\tilde{P}$ given in (8). Instead, it computes all the values $\tilde{P}(\hat{y})$ at once via an algorithm to solve so-called *multiple parity counting* problem, such an algorithm is named the *multiparity algorithm*. Like in the Björklund et al.'s the Dinur's parity-counting algorithm computes $48n + 1$ time all the values of $\tilde{P}(\hat{y})$ to approximate the values of the polynomial $P(y)$ given in (7). Then, it adds the 2^{n-n_1} approximated values $\tilde{P}(\hat{y})$ to get the parity of the number of solutions.

The complexity of then Dinur's parity-counting algorithm is given by $T(n_1, n - n_1, m)$, where $0 \leqslant n_1 < n$, and $T(\cdot, \cdot, \cdot)$ is defined by

$$T(n_1, w, m) := \mathcal{O}\left(t \cdot \left(T(n_2, 2\ell - n_2, \ell) + n\binom{n - n_1}{\downarrow w}2^{n_1 - n_2} + n\binom{n - n_2}{\downarrow 2\ell - n_2}\right) + \ell m\binom{n}{\downarrow 2}\right),$$

---

[2] The factor $8k\log n$ comes from the expected complexity of the Valiant-Vazirani isolation's algorithm with probability $1 - 1/n$, see [16, Sec. 2.5] for more details.

with $t = 48n + 1$, $n_1 = \lfloor \kappa_0 n \rfloor$, $n_2 = \lfloor n_1 - \lambda n \rfloor$, $\ell = \min\{n_2 + 2, m\}$, $0 < \kappa_0 \leqslant \frac{1}{3}$, and $0 < \lambda < 1$. In the particular case, $n_2 \leqslant 0$, in this case $T(n, w) := n \cdot \binom{n-n_1}{\downarrow w} 2^{n_1}$.

Similarly to the Björklund et al.'s algorithm, the complexity of solving the MQ problem using Dinur's parity-counting is given by

$$
\mathcal{O}\left(8k \log(n) \sum_{i=1}^{n-1} T(n_{1i}, n - i - n_{1i}, m + k + 2) \right),
$$

where $k = \lfloor \log(n_{sol} + 1) \rfloor$, and $n_{1i} = \lfloor \kappa_0(n-i) \rfloor$. The $\tilde{\mathcal{O}}(\cdot)$ complexity estimated by Dinur is $\tilde{\mathcal{O}}\left(2^{0.6943n}\right)$. The space complexity of the algorithm is dominated by $\mathcal{O}\left((48n + 1)2^{n-n_1}\right)$.

Dinur's Second Algorithm. Dinur [31] proposed a more efficient algorithm to solve the MQ problem over $\mathbb{F}_2$.

Let $\mathcal{F}$ be the sequence of polynomials of a given MQ problem. The main difference with his previous algorithm is that the new algorithm does not approximate the parity of $n_{sol}(\mathcal{F})$ by computing the parity of $48n + 1$ specializations of the polynomial $\tilde{F}$ from Eq. 8. Instead, it computes all the solution of few specializations (up to 4 or 5) of the probabilistic sequence $\mathcal{G}$ from Eq. 8. All of such solutions are tested on the original sequence $\mathcal{F}$ until a solution is found.

Let n_1 be an integer satisfying that $m \leqslant 2(n_1 + 1) + 2$. Then, the time complexity $T(n, n_1)$ of the Dinur's second algorithm is tightly upper bounded by

$$
T(n, n_1) \leqslant 16 \log n \cdot 2^{n_1} \cdot \binom{n - n_1}{\downarrow n_1 + 2} + n_1 \cdot n \cdot 2^{n-n_1} + 2^{n-2n_1+1} \binom{n}{\downarrow 2}.
$$

Moreover, the fact $n_1 \approx n/5.4$ yields to $T(n, n_1) \leqslant n^2 \cdot 2^{n-n_1}$. The space complexity is given by

$$
8 \cdot (n_1 + 1) \cdot \binom{n - n_1}{\downarrow n_1 + 3}.
$$

4   Algorithms Not Considered in Our Estimator

Here we collect the algorithms designed to solve the MQ that are not considered explicitly in the software of our estimator.

Hashimoto's Algorithm. Hashimoto [45] proposed two algorithms, namely Has-1 and Has-2, to solve the MQ problem in the underdetermined case. However, Miura, Hashimoto, and Takagi [53] showed that Has-1 does not work, and they provided a better analysis for Has-2, see Sect. 3.2.

Linearization Algorithms. The linearization algorithms reduce the MQ problem to solve a, usually large, linear system of equations. The most general of this kind of algorithms is the **X**tended **L**inearization (XL) algorithm introduced by Courtois et al. in [24]. Moreover, XL is essentially the same algorithm independently devised by Lazard [50], and it can be viewed as a redundant variant of a Gröbner basis algorithms F4 and F5 [3]. Also, in the estimator, we do include the more general variant of XL called FXL, see Sect. 3.4.

Courtois et al.'s Algorithms. In our estimator, we do not consider the so-called algorithm B nor algorithm C by Courtois et al. [25]. Algorithm B is a particular case of the Crossbred algorithm where D and d are set to be 2 and 1, respectively. While algorithm C is the same strategy described by Thomae and Wolf in [63] over fields of characteristic 2.

5   The Estimator

Here we describe the software, named the MQ estimator, to estimate the hardness of the MQ problem. Also, we show how its estimates compare with the best-known practical results and previous estimations for some multivariate-based signature schemes.

5.1   Description/Usage

This section documents the overall structure of our MQ estimator. Full documentation is publicly available in [9].

Main Class:

MQEstimator: This class is to compute the complexity estimates for a given instances q, n, and m of the MQ problem. By default, for each algorithm X that works on a problem defined by q, n, and m, it builds one method to estimate the complexity of X.

The main parameters of this class are:

q: the size of the field
n: the number of variables
m: the number of polynomials

other optional parameters are:

w: the matrix multiplication complexity exponent (Default value: 2).
theta: the real number $\theta \in [0, 2]$ such that $(\log q)^{\theta}$ is the ratio between field
   operations complexity and bit complexity, see Sect. 2.2 (Default value: 0).
h: An integer specifying the external hybridization parameter. It assumes that
   the computation is split into q^h subsystem of $n-h$ variables and m equations.
   Hence, the time complexity of solving q^h of the aforementioned subsystems.
   In contrast, the space complexity is the amount of memory needed to solve
   only one subsystem (Default value: 0).

`excluded_algorithms`: list of algorithms not to be consider (Default value: `[]`).

`tilde_o_complexity`: the Boolean value determining if the complexity is estimated by just plugged in number is the $\tilde{O}$ complexity formula, if any (Default value: `False`).

`nsolutions`: the number of solutions of the underlying problem (Default value: 1).

5.2 Numerical Results

Table 1 compares the complexity estimates of some of the algorithms used to break instances of the FMQ challenge [66]. The column *algorithm used* shows the algorithm used to break the corresponding challenge, while the column *equivalent algorithm* gives the algorithm in our MQ estimator tool used to estimate the complexity of the algorithm used. The column *best algorithm* shows, according to our estimator, the best theoretical algorithm to solve a given instance. The time and memory estimates under the column *practical* (resp. *theoretical*) are practical (resp. theoretical) estimates of the number of clock cycles (resp. bit time complexity) and memory (resp. bit space complexity) used to solve the corresponding MQ problem. The value h denotes the external hybridization parameter (see Sect. 5.1).

All theoretical estimates are computed with our MQ estimator tool, where we used $\omega = 2.81$, and $\theta = 2$. For the *best algorithm* we set $h = 0$, while for the *equivalent algorithm* we set h to be the same used to break the challenge.

For all the algorithms but M4GB, our estimator provides tight estimates compared to the practical ones computed from the information provided by the challenge's breakers. The small gap between the time estimates of *algorithm used* and the *equivalent algorithm* is due to the different metrics used in each case. We use the number of clock cycles for the practical estimates and the number of bit operations for the theoretical ones. It is well known that several bit operations can be done in a single clock cycle. Still, the exact number depends on the device used and the implementation of the specific task[3].

The best time complexity for the Type I and IV parameters is way better than the one used to break the challenge. Still, the space complexities of the former are significantly larger than the latter, which makes it difficult to solve in practice. For Type II, III, and VI parameters, both the space complexity of the best algorithm and the algorithm used are relatively similar. Still, the time complexity is way better in the former than in the latter. This fact suggests that the estimated best algorithm would outperform (in practice) the one used in the MQ challenge. Finally, for Type V, we have that the FXL algorithm is better in terms of time and memory than the Hybrid-F5 algorithm.

---

[3] For instance, for the Type IV parameters where $n = 66$, the authors used several Spartan-6 FPGAs to break the challenge. There the authors implemented the FES algorithm to solve a system with 48 variables and equations. Such particular implementation allowed them to test 2^{10} potential solutions per clock cycle, which means they are computing at least 2^{10} bit operations per clock cycle.

Table 1. Comparison between the estimates of some of the algorithms used to break FMQ challenges [66] and the estimates using the MQ estimator.

Parameters			Complexity estimates					
Type	q	n	m	Practical algorithm used (parameters used)		Theoretical equivalent algorithm		Theoretical best algorithm (optimal parameters)	
				Time	Memory	Time	Memory	Time	Memory
I	2	74	148	Crossbred [57] $(k=22, D=4, d=1, h=10)$		Crossbred		Crossbred $(k=35, D=7, d=1)$	
				64.3	34.6	71.9	27.0	62.3	54.7
IV	2	99	66	FES [18] $(h=0)$		FES		Dinur2 $(n_1=12)$	
				55.9	n/a	68.6	18.1	63.2	49.8
IV	2	103	69	Crossbred[a] $(k=15, D=4, d=1, h=17)$		Crossbred		Dinur2 $(n_1=12)$	
				67	n/a	78.1	17.7	65.8	51.1
II	2^8	37	74	F4-style [47] $(h=0)$		F5		Crossbred $(k=36, D=7, d=2)$	
				60.1	38.5	76.8	52.8	57.7	48.0
V	2^8	28	19	M4GB [52] $(h=1)$		Hybrid-F5		FXL $(k=2, variant = las vegas)$	
				54.3	$\leqslant$37.9	78.7	47.6	75.5	32.6
III	31	38	76	XL [23] $(h=0)$		FXL		Crossbred $(k=36, D=7, d=2)$	
				59.0	35.5	66.7	39.2	56.7	47.8
VI	31	30	20	M4GB [52] $(h=2)$		Hybrid-F5		Crossbred $(k=10, D=9, d=1)$	
				55.3	$\leqslant$37.9	75.1	44.2	63.1	44.3

[a] No publication describing this implementation in detail.

Figures 1a, 1c, and 1b illustrate the bit complexity estimates of the MQ problem for different parameters q, n and m. Each line represents a different value of q, while a bullet over a given line indicates the algorithm providing such a complexity estimate. To generate the plots we set w = 2.81 in our estimator, and we left by default the rest of the inputs. In each figure, we emphasize on a different regime of the ratio m/n. Figure 1a $m/n = 1$ (the square case), Fig. 1c $m/n > 1$ (the overdetermined case), and Fig. 1b $m/n < 1$ (the underdetermined case).

In the square case we observe that, for $q = 2$ the Dinur's second algorithm provide the best estimates given $n \geqslant 30$, while the exhaustive search strategy is the best for $n < 30$. A similar observation was noted in practice [5]. For $q = 2^8$ and $q = 31$, the algorithm FXL provides the best time estimates for all the instances but when $n \leqslant 22$ and $q = 2^8$. In the case $m = 2n$, the Crossbred

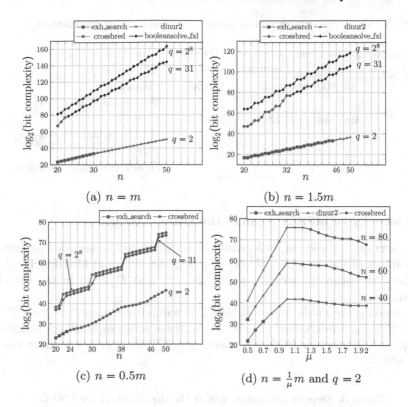

Fig. 1. Numerical estimates of the bit-complexity of the MQ problem.

algorithm outperform the others as long as $n \geqslant 24$ and the exhaustive search algorithm is the best for $n \leqslant 24$ and $q = 2$. The case $n = 1.5m$ exhibits a similar behavior than the square case. Here instead, for $q = 2$, the Dinur's second algorithm starts being better than exhaustive search just until $n \geqslant 46$.

Remark 5.1. In Fig. 1c, the exponent of the time complexity grows a the same rate for several consecutive values of n, but at a specific value, this rate suddenly increases. This is because the values of D providing the best time complexity for Crossbred increases by one after n reaches a particular value, and this causes a considerable increase in the size of the matrix in the preprocessing step. Hence the cost of the processing step increases considerably.

Figure 1d shows bit complexity as a function of the ratio m/n for $q = 2$. Here, each line represents a different value of n, and a bullet represents the algorithm's name providing the corresponding complexity. Note that, for every q, the Crossbred algorithm gets better than the others once μ is bigger than a threshold. For $n = 40, 60$ this threshold is 1.2, while for $n = 80$ the threshold moves up to 1.3.

Table 2. Security estimates against the direct attack for Rainbow.

Category	q	n	m	Claimed security	Estimated security	Algorithm (*parameters*)
I	16	100	64	164	**158.3**	Crossbred ($k = 38, D = 26, d = 4$)
III	256	148	80	**234**	235.7	FXL ($k = 5, \text{variant} = lasvegas$)
V	256	196	100	**285**	287.7	FXL ($k = 7, \text{variant} = lasvegas$)

5.3 Security of MPKCs Against the Direct Attack

In this section, we use our MQ estimator to estimate the security against the direct attack of Rainbow [28], MAYO [15], MQDSS [22], and MUDFISH [13]. We configure out estimator with $\omega = 2.81$, $\theta = 2$, and $D \leqslant 40$ in the Crossbred algorithm.

Commonly, the public key of an MPKC in a quadratic map $P : \mathbb{F}_q^n \to \mathbb{F}_q^m$ over a finite field $\mathbb{F}_q$. Undermined the security of these schemes is always possible by solving an MQ problem $P(x) = y$, where $y \in \mathbb{F}_q^m$. This attack is known as the *direct attack*.

Table 3. Security estimates against the direct attack for MAYO.

Category	q	n	m	Claimed security	Estimated security	Algorithm (*parameters*)
I	7	962	76	145	**137.4**	Crossbred ($k = 24, D = 20, d = 1$)
I	7	1140	78	145	**137.4**	Crossbred ($k = 24, D = 20, d = 1$)
III	7	2220	117	210	**204.5**	Crossbred ($k = 45, D = 30, d = 3$)
III	7	2240	117	209	**203.1**	Crossbred ($k = 45, D = 30, d = 3$)
V	7	2960	152	273	**268.7**	Crossbred ($k = 56, D = 39, d = 3$)
V	7	3874	157	273	**269.7**	Crossbred ($k = 61, D = 39, d = 4$)

Instead of directly trying to find a preimage of P, an attacker could try to recover the secret key by using the knowledge of P and the underlying structure of the cryptosystem. These attacks are called *structural attacks*. For some cryptosystems, e.g., Rainbow there is a structural attack that is more efficient than the direct one [14]. Still, for some cryptosystems, the direct attack is better than any other known structural attack, e.g., MAYO.

In [58], NIST defines five security categories, namely, category I, II, III, IV, and V. It establishes that cryptographic schemes with classical security categories I, III, and V must provide 143, 207 and 272 bits of security, respectively.

Tables 2 and 3 show the security estimates of Rainbow and MAYO, respectively. We observed that all MAYO parameters fail to achieve the target security category. Instead, all the Rainbow parameters achieve the claimed security category against the direct attack, but the category III and V parameters have fewer bits of security than claimed. Finally, in Table 4 we see that all the parameters of MUDFISH and MQDSS are far below the claimed security. Still, category I and III parameters achieve the claimed category.

Notice that our better complexity estimates are mainly due to new complexity estimates for the Crossbred algorithm, see Sect. 3.4. These estimates take into account the role of the field equations over a field with few elements, i.e., for small values of q. We believe that such more general formulas were not used in previous complexity estimates. Thus, we provide more accurate security estimates for the schemes considered in this section.

Table 4. Security estimates against the direct attack for MUDFISH and MQDSS

Category	q	n	m	Claimed security	Estimated security	Algorithm (*parameters*)
I	4	88	88	156	**146.0**	Crossbred $(k = 26, D = 19, d = 1)$
III	4	128	128	230	**208.0**	Crossbred $(k = 36, D = 27, d = 1)$
V	4	160	160	290	**258.5**	Crossbred $(k = 50, D = 33, d = 2)$

References

1. Albrecht, M.R., Player, R., Scott, S.: On the concrete hardness of learning with errors. Cryptology ePrint Archive, Report 2015/046 (2015). https://eprint.iacr.org/2015/046

2. Alman, J., Williams, V.V.: A refined laser method and faster matrix multiplication. In: Proceedings of the Annual ACM-SIAM Symposium on Discrete Algorithms, pp. 522–539 (2021)

3. Ars, G., Faugère, J.-C., Imai, H., Kawazoe, M., Sugita, M.: Comparison between XL and Gröbner basis algorithms. In: Lee, P.J. (ed.) ASIACRYPT 2004. LNCS, vol. 3329, pp. 338–353. Springer, Heidelberg (2004). https://doi.org/10.1007/978-3-540-30539-2_24

4. Ayad, A.: A survey on the complexity of solving algebraic systems. Int. Math. Forum 5(5–8), 333–353 (2010)

5. Barbero, S., Bellini, E., Sanna, C., Verbel, J.: Practical complexities of probabilistic algorithms for solving Boolean polynomial systems. Discret. Appl. Math. **309**, 13–31 (2022)
6. Bard, G.V.: Algorithms for Solving Linear and Polynomial Systems of Equations over Finite Fields with Applications to Cryptanalysis. Theses, University of Maryland (2007)
7. Bardet, M., Faugère, J.C., Salvy, B.: On the complexity of the F5 Gröbner basis algorithm. J. Symb. Comput. **70**, 49–70 (2015). https://doi.org/10.1016/j.jsc.2014.09.025
8. Bardet, M., Faugère, J.C., Salvy, B., Spaenlehauer, P.J.: On the complexity of solving quadratic Boolean systems. J. Complex. **29**(1), 53–75 (2013). https://doi.org/10.1016/j.jco.2012.07.001
9. Bellini, E., Makarim, R., Verbel, J.: An estimator for the complexity of the MQ problem (2021). https://github.com/Crypto-TII/multivariate_quadratic_estimator
10. Bellini, E., Esser, A.: Syndrome decoding estimator (2021). https://github.com/Crypto-TII/syndrome_decoding_estimator
11. Bernstein, D.J., Buchmann, J., Dahmen, E.: Post-Quantum Cryptography. Springer, Heidelberg (2009). https://doi.org/10.1007/978-3-540-88702-7
12. Bernstein, D.J., Yang, B.-Y.: Asymptotically faster quantum algorithms to solve multivariate quadratic equations. In: Lange, T., Steinwandt, R. (eds.) PQCrypto 2018. LNCS, vol. 10786, pp. 487–506. Springer, Cham (2018). https://doi.org/10.1007/978-3-319-79063-3_23
13. Beullens, W.: Sigma protocols for MQ, PKP and SIS, and fishy signature schemes. In: Canteaut, A., Ishai, Y. (eds.) EUROCRYPT 2020. LNCS, vol. 12107, pp. 183–211. Springer, Cham (2020). https://doi.org/10.1007/978-3-030-45727-3_7
14. Beullens, W.: Improved cryptanalysis of UOV and rainbow. In: Canteaut, A., Standaert, F.-X. (eds.) EUROCRYPT 2021. LNCS, vol. 12696, pp. 348–373. Springer, Cham (2021). https://doi.org/10.1007/978-3-030-77870-5_13
15. Beullens, W.: MAYO: practical post-quantum signatures from oil-and-vinegar maps. In: AlTawy, R., Hülsing, A. (eds.) SAC 2021. LNCS, vol. 13203, pp. 355–376. Springer, Cham (2022). https://doi.org/10.1007/978-3-030-99277-4_17
16. Björklund, A., Kaski, P., Williams, R.: Solving systems of polynomial equations over GF(2) by a parity-counting self-reduction. In: Baier, C., Chatzigiannakis, I., Flocchini, P., Leonardi, S. (eds.) International Colloquium on Automata, Languages and Programming - ICALP 2019. Schloss Dagstuhl-Leibniz-Zentrum fuer Informatik (2019). https://doi.org/10.4230/LIPIcs.ICALP.2019.26
17. Bouillaguet, C., et al.: Fast exhaustive search for polynomial systems in $\mathbb{F}_2$. In: Mangard, S., Standaert, F.-X. (eds.) CHES 2010. LNCS, vol. 6225, pp. 203–218. Springer, Heidelberg (2010). https://doi.org/10.1007/978-3-642-15031-9_14
18. Bouillaguet, C., Cheng, C.-M., Chou, T., Niederhagen, R., Yang, B.-Y.: Fast exhaustive search for quadratic systems in $\mathbb{F}_2$ on FPGAs. In: Lange, T., Lauter, K., Lisoněk, P. (eds.) SAC 2013. LNCS, vol. 8282, pp. 205–222. Springer, Heidelberg (2014). https://doi.org/10.1007/978-3-662-43414-7_11
19. Buchmann, J.A., Ding, J., Mohamed, M.S.E., Mohamed, W.S.A.E.: MutantXL: solving multivariate polynomial equations for cryptanalysis. In: Handschuh, H., Lucks, S., Preneel, B., Rogaway, P. (eds.) Symmetric Cryptography. Schloss Dagstuhl - Leibniz-Zentrum fuer Informatik, Germany (2009). https://drops.dagstuhl.de/opus/volltexte/2009/1945
20. Casanova, A., Faugère, J.C., Macario-Rat, G., Patarin, J., Perret, L., Ryckeghem, J.: GeMSS: a great multivariate short signature. NIST CSRC (2017). https://www-polsys.lip6.fr/Links/NIST/GeMSS.html

21. Chen, M.-S., Hülsing, A., Rijneveld, J., Samardjiska, S., Schwabe, P.: SOFIA: $\mathcal{MQ}$-based signatures in the QROM. In: Abdalla, M., Dahab, R. (eds.) PKC 2018. LNCS, vol. 10770, pp. 3–33. Springer, Cham (2018). https://doi.org/10.1007/978-3-319-76581-5_1

22. Chen, M.S., Hülsing, A., Rijneveld, J., Samardjiska, S., Schwabe, P.: MQDSS specifications (2020). https://mqdss.org/specification.html

23. Cheng, C.-M., Chou, T., Niederhagen, R., Yang, B.-Y.: Solving quadratic equations with XL on parallel architectures. In: Prouff, E., Schaumont, P. (eds.) CHES 2012. LNCS, vol. 7428, pp. 356–373. Springer, Heidelberg (2012). https://doi.org/10.1007/978-3-642-33027-8_21

24. Courtois, N., Klimov, A., Patarin, J., Shamir, A.: Efficient algorithms for solving overdefined systems of multivariate polynomial equations. In: Preneel, B. (ed.) EUROCRYPT 2000. LNCS, vol. 1807, pp. 392–407. Springer, Heidelberg (2000). https://doi.org/10.1007/3-540-45539-6_27

25. Courtois, N., Goubin, L., Meier, W., Tacier, J.-D.: Solving underdefined systems of multivariate quadratic equations. In: Naccache, D., Paillier, P. (eds.) PKC 2002. LNCS, vol. 2274, pp. 211–227. Springer, Heidelberg (2002). https://doi.org/10.1007/3-540-45664-3_15

26. Cox, D.A., Little, J., O'Shea, D.: Ideals, Varieties, and Algorithms: An Introduction to Computational Algebraic Geometry and Commutative Algebra, 3/e. Undergraduate Texts in Mathematics, Springer, New York (2007)

27. Dickenstein, A., Emiris, I.Z.: Solving Polynomial Equations. Foundations, Algorithms, and Applications, Algorithms and Computation in Mathematics, vol. 14. Springer, Heidelberg (2005)

28. Ding, J., Chen, M., Petzoldt, A., Schmidt, D., Yang, B.: Rainbow. NIST CSRC (2017). https://csrc.nist.gov/CSRC/media/Projects/Post-Quantum-Cryptography/documents/round-1/submissions

29. Ding, J., Schmidt, D.: Rainbow, a new multivariable polynomial signature scheme. In: Ioannidis, J., Keromytis, A., Yung, M. (eds.) ACNS 2005. LNCS, vol. 3531, pp. 164–175. Springer, Heidelberg (2005). https://doi.org/10.1007/11496137_12

30. Ding, J., Zhang, Z., Deaton, J.: How much can F5 really do. Cryptology ePrint Archive, Report 2021/051 (2021). https://eprint.iacr.org/2021/051

31. Dinur, I.: Cryptanalytic applications of the polynomial method for solving multivariate equation systems over GF(2). In: Canteaut, A., Standaert, F.-X. (eds.) EUROCRYPT 2021. LNCS, vol. 12696, pp. 374–403. Springer, Cham (2021). https://doi.org/10.1007/978-3-030-77870-5_14

32. Dinur, I.: Improved algorithms for solving polynomial systems over GF(2) by multiple parity-counting. In: ACM-SIAM Symposium on Discrete Algorithms (SODA), pp. 2550–2564 (2021). https://doi.org/10.1137/1.9781611976465.151

33. Duarte, J.D.: On the complexity of the crossbred algorithm. Cryptology ePrint Archive, Report 2020/1058 (2020). https://eprint.iacr.org/2020/1058

34. Eder, C., Faugère, J.C.: A survey on signature-based algorithms for computing Gröbner bases. J. Symb. Comput. 80, 719–784 (2017)

35. Esser, A., Bellini, E.: Syndrome decoding estimator. Cryptology ePrint Archive, Report 2021/1243 (2021). https://ia.cr/2021/1243

36. Faugère, J.C.: A new efficient algorithm for computing Gröbner bases (F4). J. Pure Appl. Algebra 139(1), 61–88 (1999)

37. Faugère, J.C.: A new efficient algorithm for computing Gröbner bases without reduction to zero (F5). In: Proceedings of the 2002 International Symposium on Symbolic and Algebraic Computation, ISSAC 2002, pp. 75–83. Association for Computing Machinery, New York (2002)

38. Faugère, J., Horan, K., Kahrobaei, D., Kaplan, M., Kashefi, E., Perret, L.: Fast quantum algorithm for solving multivariate quadratic equations. CoRR abs/1712.07211 (2017)
39. Faugère, J.C., Gianni, P., Lazard, D., Mora, T.: Efficient computation of zero-dimensional Gröbner bases by change of ordering. J. Symb. Comput. 16(4), 329–344 (1993)
40. Fiat, A., Shamir, A.: How to prove yourself: practical solutions to identification and signature problems. In: Odlyzko, A.M. (ed.) CRYPTO 1986. LNCS, vol. 263, pp. 186–194. Springer, Heidelberg (1987). https://doi.org/10.1007/3-540-47721-7_12
41. Furue, H., Nakamura, S., Takagi, T.: Improving Thomae-Wolf algorithm for solving underdetermined multivariate quadratic polynomial problem. In: Cheon, J.H., Tillich, J.-P. (eds.) PQCrypto 2021 2021. LNCS, vol. 12841, pp. 65–78. Springer, Cham (2021). https://doi.org/10.1007/978-3-030-81293-5_4
42. Furue, H., Duong, D., Takagi, T.: An efficient MQ-based signature with tight security proof. Int. J. Netw. Comput. 10(2), 308–324 (2020). https://www.ijnc.org/index.php/ijnc/article/view/238
43. Fusco, G., Bach, E.: Phase transition of multivariate polynomial systems. In: Cai, J.-Y., Cooper, S.B., Zhu, H. (eds.) TAMC 2007. LNCS, vol. 4484, pp. 632–645. Springer, Heidelberg (2007). https://doi.org/10.1007/978-3-540-72504-6_58
44. Gashkov, S.B., Sergeev, I.S.: Complexity of computations in finite fields. Fundam. Prikl. Mat. 17(4), 95–131 (2011/12)
45. Hashimoto, Y.: Algorithms to solve massively under-defined systems of multivariate quadratic equations. IEICE Trans. Fundam. Electron. Commun. Comput. Sci. E94.A(6), 1257–1262 (2011). https://doi.org/10.1587/transfun.E94.A.1257
46. Huang, H., Bao, W.: Algorithm for solving massively underdefined systems of multivariate quadratic equations over finite fields (2015)
47. Ito, T., Shinohara, N., Uchiyama, S.: An efficient F_4-style based algorithm to solve MQ problems. In: Attrapadung, N., Yagi, T. (eds.) IWSEC 2019. LNCS, vol. 11689, pp. 37–52. Springer, Cham (2019). https://doi.org/10.1007/978-3-030-26834-3_3
48. Joux, A., Vitse, V.: A crossbred algorithm for solving Boolean polynomial systems. In: Kaczorowski, J., Pieprzyk, J., Pomykała, J. (eds.) NuTMiC 2017. LNCS, vol. 10737, pp. 3–21. Springer, Cham (2018). https://doi.org/10.1007/978-3-319-76620-1_1
49. Kipnis, A., Patarin, J., Goubin, L.: Unbalanced oil and vinegar signature schemes. In: Stern, J. (ed.) EUROCRYPT 1999. LNCS, vol. 1592, pp. 206–222. Springer, Heidelberg (1999). https://doi.org/10.1007/3-540-48910-X_15
50. Lazard, D.: Gröbner bases, Gaussian elimination and resolution of systems of algebraic equations. In: van Hulzen, J.A. (ed.) EUROCAL 1983. LNCS, vol. 162, pp. 146–156. Springer, Heidelberg (1983). https://doi.org/10.1007/3-540-12868-9_99
51. Lokshtanov, D., Paturi, R., Tamaki, S., Williams, R., Yu, H.: Beating brute force for systems of polynomial equations over finite fields. In: Symposium on Discrete Algorithms, SODA 2017, pp. 2190–2202. Society for Industrial and Applied Mathematics, USA (2017)
52. Makarim, R.H., Stevens, M.: M4GB: an efficient Gröbner-basis algorithm. In: Burr, M.A., Yap, C.K., Din, M.S.E. (eds.) Proceedings of the 2017 ACM on International Symposium on Symbolic and Algebraic Computation, ISSAC 2017, Kaiserslautern, Germany, pp. 293–300. ACM (2017). https://doi.org/10.1145/3087604.3087638
53. Miura, H., Hashimoto, Y., Takagi, T.: Extended algorithm for solving underdefined multivariate quadratic equations. In: Gaborit, P. (ed.) PQCrypto 2013. LNCS, vol. 7932, pp. 118–135. Springer, Heidelberg (2013). https://doi.org/10.1007/978-3-642-38616-9_8

54. Moody, D.: The homestretch: the beginning of the end of the NIST PQC 3rd round. In: International Conference on Post-Quantum Cryptography (2021). https://pqcrypto2021.kr/download/program/2.2_PQCrypto2021.pdf
55. Mou, C.: Solving Polynomial Systems over Finite Fields: Algorithms, Implementation and Applications. Theses, Université Pierre et Marie Curie (2013)
56. Niederhagen, R.: Parallel cryptanalysis. Ph.D. thesis, Eindhoven University of Technology (2012). https://polycephaly.org/thesis/index.shtml
57. Ning, K.C.: An adaption of the crossbred algorithm for solving multivariate quadratic systems over $\mathbb{F}_2$ on GPUs (2017). https://pure.tue.nl/ws/portalfiles/portal/91105984/NING.K_parallel_cb_v103.pdf
58. NIST: Submission requirements and evaluation criteria for the post-quantum cryptography standardization process (2017). https://csrc.nist.gov/CSRC/media/Projects/Post-Quantum-Cryptography/documents/call-for-proposals-final-dec-2016.pdf
59. Sakumoto, K., Shirai, T., Hiwatari, H.: Public-key identification schemes based on multivariate quadratic polynomials. In: Rogaway, P. (ed.) CRYPTO 2011. LNCS, vol. 6841, pp. 706–723. Springer, Heidelberg (2011). https://doi.org/10.1007/978-3-642-22792-9_40
60. Schwabe, P., Westerbaan, B.: Solving binary $\mathcal{MQ}$ with Grover's algorithm. In: Carlet, C., Hasan, M.A., Saraswat, V. (eds.) SPACE 2016. LNCS, vol. 10076, pp. 303–322. Springer, Cham (2016). https://doi.org/10.1007/978-3-319-49445-6_17
61. Seres, I.A., Horváth, M., Burcsi, P.: The Legendre pseudorandom function as a multivariate quadratic cryptosystem: security and applications. Cryptology ePrint Archive, Report 2021/182 (2021). https://ia.cr/2021/182
62. Strassen, V.: Gaussian elimination is not optimal. Numer. Math. **13**(4), 354–356 (1969)
63. Thomae, E., Wolf, C.: Solving underdetermined systems of multivariate quadratic equations revisited. In: Fischlin, M., Buchmann, J., Manulis, M. (eds.) PKC 2012. LNCS, vol. 7293, pp. 156–171. Springer, Heidelberg (2012). https://doi.org/10.1007/978-3-642-30057-8_10
64. Ullah, E.: New techniques for polynomial system solving. Theses, Universität Passau (2012)
65. Yang, B.-Y., Chen, J.-M.: Theoretical analysis of XL over small fields. In: Wang, H., Pieprzyk, J., Varadharajan, V. (eds.) ACISP 2004. LNCS, vol. 3108, pp. 277–288. Springer, Heidelberg (2004). https://doi.org/10.1007/978-3-540-27800-9_24
66. Yasuda, T., Dahan, X., Huang, Y.J., Takagi, T., Sakurai, K.: MQ challenge: hardness evaluation of solving multivariate quadratic problems. In: NIST Workshop on Cybersecurity in a Post-Quantum World, Washington, D.C (2015). https://www.mqchallenge.org

Recovering Rainbow's Secret Key with a First-Order Fault Attack

Thomas Aulbach[1(✉)], Tobias Kovats[2], Juliane Krämer[1],
and Soundes Marzougui[3]

[1] Universität Regensburg, Regensburg, Germany
{thomas.aulbach,juliane.kraemer}@ur.de
[2] SBA Research, Vienna, Austria
tkovats@sba-research.org
[3] Technische Universität Berlin, Berlin, Germany
soundes.marzougui@tu-berlin.de

Abstract. Rainbow, a multivariate digital signature scheme and third round finalist in NIST's PQC standardization process, is a layered version of the unbalanced oil and vinegar (UOV) scheme. We introduce two fault attacks, each focusing on one of the secret linear transformations T and S used to hide the structure of the central map in Rainbow. The first fault attack reveals a part of T and we prove that this is enough to achieve a full key recovery with negligible computational effort for all parameter sets of Rainbow. The second one unveils S, which can be extended to a full key recovery by the Kipnis-Shamir attack. Our work exposes the secret transformations used in multivariate signature schemes as an important attack vector for physical attacks, which need further protection. Our attacks target the optimized Cortex-M4 implementation and require only first-order instruction skips and a moderate amount of faulted signatures.

Keywords: Rainbow · Fault injection attacks · Multivariate schemes · Post-quantum cryptography · Cortex M4 implementation

1 Introduction

Quantum computers pose a threat to public-key schemes based on the integer factorization or the discrete logarithm problem, like the widely deployed RSA and ECC. Since Shor published his famous algorithms [28] to solve these problems in polynomial time, their security depends on the technical feasibility of large scale quantum computers. Although there still is a certain amount of scepticism about the possibility of quantum computers being capable of factorizing integers and solving the discrete logarithm for cryptographically relevant instances in the upcoming decades [17,19,26], the National Institute of Standards and Technology (NIST) states that:

> "[...] regardless of whether we can estimate the exact time of the arrival of the quantum computing era, we must begin now to prepare our information security systems to be able to resist quantum computing" [1].

L. Batina and J. Daemen (Eds.): AFRICACRYPT 2022, LNCS 13503, pp. 348–368, 2022.
https://doi.org/10.1007/978-3-031-17433-9_15

Therefore, a standardization process for post-quantum, i.e., quantum-resistant cryptographic algorithms was initiated. Currently five families of post-quantum cryptography are being studied, each relying on different mathematical assumptions. Concerning signatures, the remaining candidates in the currently ongoing third round of the standardization process mainly consist of lattice-based, hash-based, and multivariate schemes.

The evaluation criteria of NIST are not only the security and performance of the candidates, but also other properties such as resistance to side channel attacks and misuse resistance. Hence, NIST asked for efficient implementations that are protected against physical attacks, such as side channel and fault attacks. In these attacks, an attacker does not exploit mathematical weaknesses of a cryptographic scheme. Instead, in a side channel attack an attacker measures physical information during the computation of a cryptographic algorithm that she then analyzes to reveal secret data. In a fault attack, an attacker intentionally introduces faults into the computation such that it results in faulty outputs that she can analyze to learn secret data. In a first-order fault attack, an attacker induces a single fault during a computation, while in higher-order fault attacks, at least two faults are induced in the same computation. Since this is technically more complex, first-order faults are generally believed to be more realistic and, hence, more practically relevant.

In this work, we study first-order fault attacks on Rainbow, a multivariate signature scheme that was selected as finalist in the NIST standardization [14,15]. We are aware of the significant improvements in mathematical cryptanalysis on the multivariate signature schemes GeMSS and Rainbow that have been published recently [3,4,30]. Especially the improved cryptanalytic approach presented by Beullens massively reduces the complexity of key recovery attacks against Rainbow, in particular against the parameter set for security level I [4]. However, NIST announced that there will be a fourth round where further post-quantum signature schemes can be submitted[1]. This became necessary since on the one hand, for security and practicality reasons diversity of (post-quantum) signatures is needed, while on the other hand the remaining signature candidates in the current third round are mostly based on structured lattices. Thus, for the fourth round NIST is especially interested in schemes that are not based on structured lattices and we expect that, despite the recent cryptanalytic results, other multivariate schemes will be submitted. For instance, the well-studied scheme UOV is likely to gain more attention soon, since it is explicitly not affected by Beullens latest approach. Hence, we believe that our results are relevant for the future development of multivariate signature schemes even if Rainbow turns out to be insecure or even broken. Our results reveal attack vectors for and weaknesses of a specific multivariate signature scheme, which have to be prevented in future developments or optimizations of other multivariate signature schemes, too.

---

[1] Announced by Dustin Moody at the third PQC Standardization Conference in June 2021 https://www.nist.gov/video/third-pqc-standardization-conference-session-i-welcomecandidate-updates.

Related Work. The number of publications on the physical security of multivariate cryptography has increased in recent years, but is still manageable. Some effort was put into side channel analysis (SCA) of signature schemes. To name a few of them, Steinwandt et al. theoretically conducted differential power analysis (DPA) to reveal the secret seed and subsequently the affine bijections S and T used in FLASH and SFLASH already in 2001 [29]. Some years later, Okeya et al. were the first to experimentally verify a DPA attack against SFLASH [23]. More recently, in 2017, Yi and Li presented a DPA on enTTS [32], a signature scheme that contains some common features with Rainbow, such as the layer structure of the central map and the enclosing affine transformations. Finally, there are side channel attacks by Park et al. [24] and by Pokorny et al. [25] on Rainbow, both targeting the affine transformations via correlation power analysis (CPA).

The literature on fault attacks on multivariate signatures is less extensive. In 2011, Hashimoto et al. described some general ideas that might be applicable to multivariate schemes [18]. However, their ideas remain rather high-level and refer to several schemes at once. The authors in [32] mentioned a fault model that is supposed to facilitate the DPA on the central map F of the enTTS scheme, but they also did not provide a detailed description of their approach. They merely stated to "cause a fault, to change the unknown items during the signature generation". Krämer and Loiero transferred two ideas of [18] to UOV and Rainbow [21]. First, they analyzed how a faulted coefficient in the central map propagates through the signature and can be utilized to regain information about the secret transformation S. Second, they discussed the effect of fixing the vinegar variables across multiple signatures and show how information about the secret transformation T can be revealed by this. Shim and Koo developed the latter approach further to a full key recovery attack [27]. But the algebraic post-processing method they used still has a significant complexity of 2^{40}, rendering the attack impractical. The most practical attack yet, called *Quantumhammer* [22] by Mus, Islam, and Sunar, was performed on LUOV. The authors randomly induce bit flips in the linear transformation T and learn one bit of the secret key through each faulty signature. They also append an algebraic attack to the online fault injection phase, but they manage to limit the effort in the range of hours. In summary, there is no fault attack on Rainbow that presents a full key recovery in reasonable time.

Contribution. We introduce the first two efficiently executable fault attacks on Rainbow that lead to full key recovery. Both fault attacks only require first-order instruction skips and a moderate number of faulted signatures to be executed. We target the optimized Cortex-M4 implementation from [12].

1. We revisit the already existing theoretical approach of fixing the vinegar variables via a fault injection attack. This attack leads to partial leakage of one of the secret transformations used in Rainbow. The authors of [27] suggested to exploit this leakage by speeding up the key recovery attack using the notion of good keys [31]. Although they can reduce the number of variables and equations, the remaining system of quadratic equations is still

of significant complexity of around 2^{40} [27, Table. VII] for the Rainbow level I parameter set. We introduce a cryptanalytical method for circumventing this costly procedure and show how it is possible to recover the remaining bits of the secret key by just solving linear equations. Contrary to the previously suggested key recovery attack, this method can be applied to any possible parameter set of Rainbow and leads to full key recovery.

2. We present a new fault attack that targets the application of the linear transformation S. By collecting a small number of faulted signatures, we obtain enough input and output values of S to completely recover it. By knowledge of S, the complexity of Rainbow can be reduced to a small UOV instance with reduced parameter sizes [3]. To complete the key recovery, we apply the Kipnis-Shamir attack[2] for unbalanced oil and vinegar values [20], with remaining complexity $\mathcal{O}(q^{v_1-o_1})$. Considering Rainbows security level I parameter set, it holds $q^{v_1-o_1} = 2^{16}$. Compared to the first fault attack, this attack works with half the number of faulted signatures.

We see the algebraic post-processing that is used to further exploit the information gained by the fault attacks as a contribution of its own. It can be used as a plug-and-play method for all kinds of physical attacks. For instance, Sect. 3.1 proves that if an attacker obtains the block T_1 of the secret Rainbow parameters through any kind of leakage, she can achieve full key recovery without any further physical or computational effort.

Furthermore, we verify our attacks on an emulated ARM M4 architecture. On the one hand, this implies that we execute the compiled binary of the source code as a real signing device would and, therefore, can target the specific instruction of the assembly code that needs to be skipped. On the other hand, it verifies the feasibility of our attacks and proves the claims we made above for a given Rainbow key pair.

Finally, we suggest efficient countermeasures to prevent the mentioned attacks and make implementations of multivariate schemes more resilient against fault attacks.

1.1 Organization

In Sect. 2, we develop the background that is necessary for the presented attacks. This includes the Rainbow signature scheme, relevant simplifications applied by the authors of the corresponding NIST submission, and background information on fault attacks. In Sect. 3, we present the two fault attacks, together with a detailed description of the algebraic post-processing. We uncover the low-level instructions that need to be skipped in the practical fault attack in Sect. 4 and present our simulation. In Sect. 5, we suggest countermeasures to the previously described fault attacks and Sect. 6 concludes the work.

---

[2] In a very recent paper Esser et al. claim that there is another way to complete the key recovery, instead of using the Kipnis-Shamir attack [16]. If their findings hold true, this works with significantly lower complexity $\mathcal{O}(n^3)$, which is efficient even for higher parameter sets.

2   Background

In this section, we recall useful background information for understanding the rest of the paper. This includes an overview on the Rainbow signature scheme and fault injection attacks.

Notation. Let $\mathbb{F}_q$ be a finite field with q elements. By $x = (x_1, \ldots, x_n) \in \mathbb{F}_q^n$ we denote a vector and by $T \in M_n(\mathbb{F}_q)$ we denote a matrix with entries in $\mathbb{F}_q$. The multivariate quadratic maps $\mathcal{P} : \mathbb{F}_q^n \to \mathbb{F}_q^m$ are given by m quadratic polynomials $p^{(i)}$ in n variables. To concatenate two strings x and y, $x\|y$ is written. $\mathcal{H}(x)$ represents the application of a hash function $\mathcal{H}$ on a value x.

2.1   The Rainbow Signature Scheme

The Rainbow signature scheme [15] can be seen as a generalization of the unbalanced oil and vinegar (UOV) scheme [20]. It consists of several layers, where the oil and vinegar variables of the i-th layer are used as vinegar variables of the subsequent layer. Inserting them into the central polynomials of this layer, leads to easily solvable linear equations, since there are no quadratic oil terms in each layer just as it is the case for UOV. Initially, the authors suggested to use $u = 5$ layers, but it turned out to work best for $u = 2$ which is used by all currently suggested parameter sets. The case $u = 1$ constitutes the original UOV, the scheme whose security and efficiency Rainbow is supposed to improve.

More formally, let $\mathbb{F}_q$ be a finite field with q elements and $v_1 < \ldots < v_{u+1} = n$ be integers. Set $V_i = \{1, \ldots, v_i\}$ and $O_i = \{v_i + 1, \ldots, v_{i+1}\}$ for $i \in \{1, \ldots, u\}$. Therefore, it holds $|V_i| = v_i$ and $|O_i| = o_i$ for $i \in \{1, \ldots, u\}$. The central map F of Rainbow consists of $m = n - v_1$ multivariate quadratic polynomials $f^{(v_1+1)}, \ldots, f^{(n)}$ of the form

$$f^{(k)}(x) = \sum_{i,j \in V_l} \alpha_{ij}^{(k)} x_i x_j + \sum_{i \in V_l, j \in O_l} \beta_{ij}^{(k)} x_i x_j + \sum_{i \in V_l \cup O_l} \gamma_i^{(k)} x_i + \delta^{(k)}, \quad (1)$$

where $l \in \{1, \ldots, u\}$ is the only integer such that $k \in O_l$. In each layer l there remain no quadratic terms in the polynomials $f^{(k)}$ after inserting the values of the vinegar variables x_i for $i \in V_l$. This leads to an easily invertible central map $F : \mathbb{F}^n \to \mathbb{F}^m$ consisting of the m coordinate functions f. This special structure of $\mathcal{F}$ facilitates the signature generation and must be hidden in the public key. To this end, two invertible linear maps $S : \mathbb{F}^m \to \mathbb{F}^m$ and $T : \mathbb{F}^n \to \mathbb{F}^n$ are concatenated to the central map in order to generate the *public key*

$$\mathcal{P} = S \circ \mathcal{F} \circ T : \mathbb{F}^n \to \mathbb{F}^m. \quad (2)$$

Since the composed maps look like a random system of multivariate quadratic equations, it is hard to find a preimage under $\mathcal{P}$. By holding the *private key* maps $S, \mathcal{F}$, and T, this task becomes feasible. The signing and verifying procedure for the Rainbow signature scheme can be briefly summarized as follows. For the signing procedure we also present the pseudo code in Algorithm 1.

Signature Generation: To generate a signature for a message (or hash value) $w \in \mathbb{F}_m$, one performs the following three steps.

1. Compute $x = S^{-1}(w) \in \mathbb{F}^m$.
2. Compute a pre-image y of x under the central map $\mathcal{F}$.
3. Compute the signature $z \in \mathbb{F}^n$ by $z = T^{-1}(y)$.

Signature Verification: To check, if $z \in \mathbb{F}^n$ is a valid signature for a message $w \in \mathbb{F}^m$, one simply computes $w_0 = \mathcal{P}(z)$. If $w_0 = w$ holds, the signature is accepted, otherwise rejected.

Since both fault attacks presented in this work target the signing procedure, we shortly present it in Algorithm 1 to give the reader a first intuition of the code lines that render the signature scheme vulnerable.

The algorithm is located in Sect. 3.1 to keep it close to the presented fault attacks. We use a similar description as [14, Section 3.5], but align the notation tighter to the actual implementation and simplify the representation of the secret maps, as they are all chosen to be homogeneous in [14, Section 4], anyway. The first fault attack in Sect. 3.1 targets the sampling of random vinegar variables in Line 2. The second fault attack in Sect. 3.2 bypasses the application of S in Line 8. Since both lines are located in a loop, one has to consider under which conditions the fault might be annihilated by a repeated execution of the respective lines. We exit the while loop if the matrices given by $\hat{F}_1$ and $\hat{F}_2$ are invertible. If we assume the entries to be uniformly distributed in $\mathbb{F}_q$, the probability that a matrix $M_n(\mathbb{F}_q)$ is invertible is given by

$$\prod_{i=0}^{n}(\frac{q^n - q^i}{q^{n^2}}) = \prod_{i=1}^{n}(1 - \frac{1}{q^i}). \tag{3}$$

For the given parameters this evaluates to approximately 93%. We will carefully analyze what impact the injected fault might have on the conditions of the while loop in Sect. 4.2.

Remark 1. Very recently, Beullens presented an improved cryptanalytic approach that massively reduces the complexity of key recovery attacks [4], in particular against the Rainbow parameter set for security level I. His paper builds on an earlier analysis of him [3], where he introduced a new description of the Rainbow scheme, avoiding the presence of the central map and rather considering secret subspaces that satisfy certain equations under the public map $\mathcal{P}$ and its polar form $\mathcal{P}'$. He defines

$$O'_1 \subset \mathbb{F}_q^n := \{x \in \mathbb{F}_q^n : x_i = 0 \text{ for } i \in \{1, \ldots, v_1\}\},$$
$$O'_2 \subset \mathbb{F}_q^n := \{x \in \mathbb{F}_q^n : x_i = 0 \text{ for } i \in \{1, \ldots, v_1 + o_1\}\},$$
$$W' \subset \mathbb{F}_q^m := \{x \in \mathbb{F}_q^m : x_i = 0 \text{ for } i \in \{1, \ldots, o_1\}\}.$$

The interesting point about these (public) subspaces is that all polynomials of the central map vanish on O'_2 and the polynomials of the first layer vanish even on O'_1, i.e., it holds $\mathcal{F}(O'_2) = 0$ and $\mathcal{F}(O'_1) \subset W'$, respectively. The secret linear maps S and T now transform the given subspaces to the secret subspaces $O_1 = T^{-1}O'_1, O_2 = T^{-1}O'_2$, and $W = SW'$. The new technique in [4] finds a vector in the secret subspace O_2 with way less computational effort than needed in previous works. The attack is completed in similar style as in [3], where he uses the vector in O_2 to recover W efficiently by using the polar form of the public key and finally, applying the Kipnis-Shamir attack to compute O_1. The important take-away for our analysis in Sect. 3.2 is that recovering the secret transformation S is equivalent to detecting the secret subspace W using this notation. For more details we refer to [3, Section 5].

2.2   Conventions in the Specification

In the Rainbow specification [14], several simplifications are made. They are introduced to speed up the key generation process and reduce the key sizes, while it is argued that they do not weaken the security of Rainbow. First, the secret transformations S and T are chosen to be of the form

$$S = \begin{pmatrix} I & S_1 \\ 0 & I \end{pmatrix} \quad \text{and} \quad T = \begin{pmatrix} I & T_1 & T_2 \\ 0 & I & T_3 \\ 0 & 0 & I \end{pmatrix}. \tag{4}$$

This is justified by the fact that, for every public map $\mathcal{P}$, there exists an equivalent secret key $(S, \mathcal{F}, T)$ with S and T as in Eq. (4). Consequently, the inverse maps have the same structure and are given by

$$S^{-1} = \begin{pmatrix} I & S_1 \\ 0 & I \end{pmatrix} \quad \text{and} \quad T^{-1} = \begin{pmatrix} I & T_1 & T_4 \\ 0 & I & T_3 \\ 0 & 0 & I \end{pmatrix}, \tag{5}$$

where $T_4 = T_1 T_3 - T_2$. Furthermore, the Rainbow submitters restrict themselves to a homogeneous central map $\mathcal{F}$. As a result, the public map $\mathcal{P} = S \circ \mathcal{F} \circ T$ is homogeneous as well. Thus, the coefficients of every quadratic polynomial $f^{(i)}$ and $p^{(j)}$ for $i, j \in \{1, \ldots, m\}$ can be collected in $n \times n$ matrices, by defining $F_i \in M_{n \times n}(\mathbb{F}_q)$ and $P_j \in M_{n \times n}(\mathbb{F}_n)$ as the matrices that satisfy $f^{(i)}(x) = x^\top F_i x$ and $p^{(j)}(x) = x^\top P_j x$, respectively. Following this notation, Eq. (2) can be turned into an equation of matrices of the form

$$F_i = \sum_{j=1}^{m} \tilde{s}_{ij}(\tilde{T}^\top P_j \tilde{T}). \tag{6}$$

Here, $\tilde{s}_{ij}$ denote the entries of S^{-1} and $\tilde{T} = T^{-1}$. This method of switching back and forth from public to secret matrices will play a major role in the analysis of our fault attacks. Interchanging the roles of F_i and P_j in Eq. (6) represents the basic procedure of computing the public key from the private key. In the above form, the equation occurs less frequently in the literature, but is used, e.g., by

Thomae in [31]. Due to the structure of the central polynomials in Eq. (1), several parts of the matrices F_i are forced to be zero and this is obvious to any attacker. In more detail, the zero blocks of the matrices are given as

$$F_i = \begin{pmatrix} F_i^{(1)} & F_i^{(2)} & 0 \\ 0 & 0 & 0 \\ 0 & 0 & 0 \end{pmatrix} \text{ for } i \in \{1, \ldots, o_1\} \tag{7}$$

and

$$F_i = \begin{pmatrix} F_i^{(1)} & F_i^{(2)} & F_i^{(3)} \\ 0 & F_i^{(5)} & F_i^{(6)} \\ 0 & 0 & 0 \end{pmatrix} \text{ for } i \in \{o_1 + 1, \ldots, o_2\}.$$

If an attacker somehow obtains secret information, she can use Eq. (6) together with the structure of the occurring matrices given by Eq. (5) and Eq. (7), to further exploit this leakage. In Sect. 3.1 we will show, e.g., how an attacker that has T_1 at hand, is able to recover S_1 and subsequently T_3 and T_4, just by solving linear equations. Although this assumes a strong leakage in the first place, to the best of our knowledge this is the first work that demonstrates such a result.

2.3   Fault Attacks

Fault attacks against cryptographic schemes were first described 25 years ago [8]. Since then, a great variety of fault attacks has been developed. All fault attacks have in common that an attacker actively and intentionally disturbs the computation of a cryptographic algorithm so as to gain secret information from the faulty output. Both the kind of physical fault and the effect of a fault can be manifold. For instance, a fault can be injected via clock glitching, e.g., [9], or laser fault injection, e.g., [11], and it can be either transient or permanent. Most published fault attacks result in a zeroed or randomized value or an instruction skip, see, e.g., [6]. Instruction skips as also used in this work correspond to skipping, i.e., ignoring, selected lines of the program code. Since fault attacks were first described, most cryptographic schemes have been analyzed with respect to them and in recent years, fault attacks have been published for all five families of post-quantum cryptography, e.g., [6,9–11,21]. These works range from purely theoretical publications [6] to more practical attacks [22].

3   Full Key Recovery Attacks

In this section we present two different fault attack scenarios. Both rely on a first-order skipping fault model, i.e., the attacker is assumed to be capable of introducing a single instruction skip during the signing procedure. Compared to fault attacks that require randomizing or zeroing values in memory, the instruction skips belongs to the more practical ones and it has been shown that even higher-order skipping faults against real-world cryptographic implementations are possible [7]. The first attack already exists in the literature. It aims at fixing the vinegar variables across consecutive signature generations and leads to valid signatures. We significantly reduce the complexity of the post-processing that is necessary to achieve a full key recovery. Additionally, we introduce a completely new attack that benefits from the same efficient techniques and works with even less faulted signatures. They constitute the first fault attacks on the Rainbow scheme that lead to a complete revealing of the secret key which are executable on a desktop machine. In both cases, the messages that are chosen to generate the faulty signatures not need to fulfill special requirements, that are hard to control. The messages must be different from each other and should lead to linearly independent vectors at some point of the respective procedures, but the attacker can just discard a faulty signature if it does not meet this requirement and start over with a new message. We will emphasize this condition in the description of the two fault attacks.

In Sect. 3.1, we reinvestigate the case of fixed vinegar variables, which was presented in detail in [21]. The authors of [27] are the first to expand this to a complete key recovery attack. However, their approach is reliant on a costly post-processing step that involves solving a system of quadratic equations of moderate size. They investigate three different level I parameter sets of Rainbow, and even in the best case their complexities remain as high as 2^{38}. This is still considerably large to constitute another hurdle in the practicability of the fault attack. We introduce a method on how to bypass this step, leading to an easily executable full key recovery attack.

Furthermore, we present in Sect. 3.2 a new fault attack that gets along with significantly less faulted signatures. The faulted output reveals the secret transformation S and the attack can be completed to a full key recovery by a subsequent Kipnis-Shamir attack. Due to the knowledge of S, the parameters of the system to solve allow for an efficiently executable instance of the Kipnis-Shamir attack. After explaining the attacks, we also translate the procedure to the abstract secret subspace notation used by Beullens which we stated in Remark 1.

3.1   Attack 1: Full Key Recovery from Fixed Vinegar Variables

This fault attack aims to skip the random generation of vinegar variables during the signing process. Depending on the implementation, this results in either the vinegar variables from the previous signature being reused, or being equal to zero in case they are zeroed at the end of the signing process. Both cases have already been mentioned in [27] and are very similar. The main difference is that for the reuse model an additional, unfaulted reference signature is needed. In the following we focus on the optimized bitsliced implementation developed in [12]. Here, the vinegar variables are not zeroed at the end of the signing process and therefore skipping the generation of the new vinegar variables results in the same variables being used for successive signature computations.

Algorithm 1. Rainbow Sign

Input message d, private key $(S, \mathcal{F}, T)$, length l of the salt.
Output signature $\sigma = (z, salt) \in \mathbb{F}_q^n \times \{0, 1\}^l$ s.t. $\mathcal{P}(z) = \mathcal{H}(\mathcal{H}(d)\|salt)$.

1: **repeat**
2:   $(z_1, \ldots, z_{v_1}) \leftarrow_R \mathbb{F}_q^{v_1}$
3:   $(\hat{f}^{(v_1+1)}, \ldots, \hat{f}^{(n)}) \leftarrow (f^{(v_1+1)}(z_1, \ldots, z_{v_1}), \ldots, f^{(n)}(z_1, \ldots, z_{v_1}))$
4: **until** IsInvertible($\hat{F}_1$) == True
5: **repeat**
6:   $salt \leftarrow_R \{0, 1\}^l$
7:   $y \leftarrow \mathcal{H}(\mathcal{H}(d)\|salt)$
8:   $y \leftarrow S^{-1}(y)$
9:   $z_{v_1+1}, \ldots, z_{v_2} \leftarrow \hat{F}_1^{-1}(y_{v_1+1}, \ldots, y_{v_2})$
10:   $(\hat{f}^{(v_2+1)}, \ldots, \hat{f}^{(n)}) \leftarrow (f^{(v_2+1)}(z_{v_1+1}, \ldots, z_{v_2}), \ldots, f^{(n)}(z_{v_1+1}, \ldots, z_{v_2}))$
11: **until** IsInvertible($\hat{F}_2$) == True
12: $z_{v_2+1}, \ldots, z_n \leftarrow \hat{F}_2^{-1}(y_{v_2+1}, \ldots, y_n)$
13: $z \leftarrow T^{-1}(z)$
14: $\sigma = (z, salt)$
15: **return** σ

First, we show how the secret matrices $T_1 \in M_{o_1 \times o_2}(\mathbb{F}_q)$ and $T_2 \in M_{o_2 \times o_2}(\mathbb{F}_q)$ in Sect. 2.2 can be determined from the faulty signatures. Let z' be the error-free generated signature of an arbitrary message d'. According to the Rainbow specification, z' is defined by $z' = T^{-1} \circ \mathcal{F}^{-1} \circ S^{-1}(y)$, where $y = \mathcal{H}(\mathcal{H}(d')\|salt) \in \mathbb{F}_q^m$. From an attacker's point of view, all intermediate values are unknown. What is known is that the first v_1 entries of $\mathcal{F}^{-1} \circ S^{-1}(y)$ consist of the generated vinegar values, whereas the remaining $m = o_1 + o_2$ entries are the corresponding solutions of the first and second layer of the central map under the chosen vinegar variables. Thus, we can write

$$z' = T^{-1} \begin{pmatrix} v \\ o'_1 \\ o'_2 \end{pmatrix},$$

with $v \in \mathbb{F}_q^{v_1}$, $o'_1 \in \mathbb{F}_q^{o_1}$, and $o'_2 \in \mathbb{F}_q^{o_2}$. By using the instruction skip indicated in Sect. 2.1 and elaborated in detail in Sect. 4.1, the attacker successively generates m signatures, all of which fall back to the same vinegar variables v as the reference signature z'. For $i \in \{1 \ldots m\}$, we denote these signatures by

$$z^{(i)} = T^{-1} \begin{pmatrix} v \\ o_1^{(i)} \\ o_2^{(i)} \end{pmatrix}.$$

The remaining entries $o_1^{(i)}$ and $o_2^{(i)}$ of the input of T^{-1} are under no control of the attacker and do not need to be considered in more detail. By subtracting the reference signature and multiplying with T, we receive

$$T(z^{(i)} - z') = \begin{pmatrix} v \\ o_1^{(i)} \\ o_2^{(i)} \end{pmatrix} - \begin{pmatrix} v \\ o_1' \\ o_2' \end{pmatrix} = \begin{pmatrix} 0 \\ \tilde{o}_1^{(i)} \\ \tilde{o}_2^{(i)} \end{pmatrix}, \tag{8}$$

for $i \in \{1 \ldots m\}$. Let $Z \in M_{n \times m}$ be the matrix whose i-th column is defined by the vector $z^{(i)} - z'$. Then Equation (8) implies that the first v_1 rows of T map Z to $0_{v_1 \times m}$. If this linear system of equations can be solved uniquely, it reveals the first v_1 rows of T, more precisely the submatrices $T_1 \in M_{o_1 \times o_2}(\mathbb{F}_q)$ and $T_2 \in M_{o_2 \times o_2}(\mathbb{F}_q)$. Therefore, we need the columns of Z and thus the last m entries of $Tz^{(i)}$ to be linearly independent, since the first entries are identical to the entries of the reference signature. Following Eq. 3 this happens with high probability and in case we draw a faulted signature that is linearly dependent of the previous, we can just disregard it and draw a new one. We note that Eq. (8) does not provide any further information about the remaining rows of T.

Remark 2. The authors of [27] only utilize parts of the gained information for their algebraic key recovery attack. More precisely, they use certain entries of the submatrices to reduce the complexity of a key recovery attack introduced in [31] using the good key approach. However, this still requires solving a system of quadratic equations. In the following we show how this can be completely omitted by utilizing the whole submatrix T_1.

Recover the Secret Transformation S. We take a closer look at Eq. (6). By also dividing the public matrices P_j and the secret transformation T into 3×3 block matrices we receive

$$\tilde{F}_i = \sum_{j=1}^{m} \tilde{s}_{ij} \left[\begin{pmatrix} I & 0 & 0 \\ T_1^\top & I & 0 \\ T_4^\top & T_3^\top & I \end{pmatrix} \begin{pmatrix} P_j^{(1)} & P_j^{(2)} & P_j^{(3)} \\ 0 & P_j^{(5)} & P_j^{(6)} \\ 0 & 0 & P_j^{(9)} \end{pmatrix} \begin{pmatrix} I & T_1 & T_4 \\ 0 & I & T_3 \\ 0 & 0 & I \end{pmatrix} \right]. \tag{9}$$

The resulting matrices are not necessarily equal to the matrices F_i of the central map but the polynomials they represent are identical. Consequently, by denoting

$$\tilde{F}_i = \begin{pmatrix} \tilde{F}_i^{(1)} & \tilde{F}_i^{(2)} & \tilde{F}_i^{(3)} \\ \tilde{F}_i^{(5)} & \tilde{F}_i^{(5)} & \tilde{F}_i^{(6)} \\ \tilde{F}_i^{(7)} & \tilde{F}_i^{(8)} & \tilde{F}_i^{(9)} \end{pmatrix}, \tag{10}$$

it follows from Eq. (7) that $\tilde{F}_i^{(5)}$ needs to be skew symmetric and $\tilde{F}_i^{(7)\top} + \tilde{F}_i^{(3)} = 0_{v_1 \times o_2}$ and $\tilde{F}_i^{(8)\top} + \tilde{F}_i^{(6)} = 0_{o_1 \times o_2}$ holds for the central maps of the first layer, i.e., for $i \in \{1, \ldots, o_1\}$.

Now, we solely focus on the middle block $\tilde{F}_i^{(5)} \in M_{o_1 \times o_1}(\mathbb{F}_q)$ and observe that T_1 is the only part of the secret transformation T contributing to that block. Thus, neglecting the other submatrices turns Eq. (9) into

$$\tilde{F}_i^{(5)} = \sum_{j=1}^{m} \tilde{s}_{ij} \left(T_1^\top P_j^{(1)} T_1 + T_1^\top P_j^{(2)} + P_j^{(4)} T_1 + P_j^{(5)} \right). \tag{11}$$

Note that the term inside the brackets is completely known to the attacker, since she has already recovered T_1. The remaining unknowns are now the entries of S^{-1}, in particular the $o_1 \cdot o_2$ entries of S_1. Since Eq. (11) holds for all $i \in \{1, \ldots, o_1\}$, the resulting linear system of equations is overdetermined and solving it provides exactly the entries of S_1.

Recover the Remaining Part of the Secret Transformation T. Having access to the complete transformation S, the attacker is able to exploit (9) even more. She now targets the $v_1 \times o_2$ block $F_i^{(3)}$ on the top right and the $o_2 \times o_1$ block $F_i^{(7)}$ on the bottom left. Similarly to (11), she derives

$$F_i^{(7)\top} + F_i^{(3)} = 0_{v_1 \times o_2} = \sum_{j=1}^{m} \tilde{s}_{ij}\left(P_j^{(1)\top}T_4 + P_j^{(1)}T_4 + P_j^{(2)}T_3 + P_j^{(3)}\right). \quad (12)$$

Now the attacker wants to solve for the unknowns in T_3 and T_4. By now, she has knowledge of all the entries $\tilde{s}_{ij}$, which turns (12) into a linear system of equations. Once more the number of equations exceeds the number of variables and its solution reveals the submatrices T_3 and T_4 and therefore the remaining part of the secret transformation T^{-1}. This finishes the key recovery attack. The algebraic post-processing of the fault attack can be summarized as follows.

Attack 1: Full Key Recovery from Fixed Vinegar Variables. After successful execution of the fault attack, the attacker takes the reference signature z' and m faulted signatures $z^{(1)}, \ldots, z^{(m)}$, obtained in the way described above and proceeds as follows.

1. Build the matrix $Z \in M_{n \times m}(\mathbb{F}_q)$ with columns $z^{(i)} - z'$ for $i \in \{1, \ldots, m\}$.
2. Compute the echelon form of the matrix $T' \in M_{v_1 \times n}(\mathbb{F}_q)$ that fulfills $T'Z = 0$. It holds $T' = \begin{pmatrix} I & T_1 & T_2 \end{pmatrix}$.
3. Insert T_1 into Eq. (11). Solve the resulting system of linear equations to recover S.
4. Insert S into Eq. (12). Solve the resulting system of linear equations to recover T_3 and T_4.
5. Use Eq. (6) to obtain $\mathcal{F}$. The attacker recovered the full secret key $(S, \mathcal{F}, T)$.

Remark 3. This attack can also be translated to the more abstract language established in Remark 1. The difference of two signatures $z^{(i)} - z'$ that are generated with identical vinegar variables, can be seen as a vector in the secret subspace O_1. This becomes obvious when considering Eq. (8), which shows that T maps this vector to a vector whose first v_1 entries are zero, i.e., an element in O_1'. Thus, the m linearly independent vectors of the matrix Z that are gained by our fault attack, together span the secret subspace O_1 from which the remaining secret subspaces can be deduced.

3.2 Attack 2: Secret Key Recovery by Skipping the Linear Transformation S

This fault attack aims to skip the application of the matrix S^{-1} during the generation of the signature. If the instruction skip is successful, the signing process evaluates to $\tilde{z} = T^{-1} \circ \mathcal{F}^{-1}(y)$. By inserting this faulted signature into the public map $\mathcal{P}$, an attacker receives $\mathcal{P}(\tilde{z}) = S \circ \mathcal{F} \circ T(\tilde{z}) = S(y) =: w \in \mathbb{F}_q^m$.

Since $y = \mathcal{H}(\mathcal{H}(d) \| salt)$ is known to the attacker, this fault attack presents a method for deriving input-output pairs for the secret linear transformation S. Now, let $W \in M_{m \times o_2}(\mathbb{F}_q)$ be the matrix whose columns consist of vectors $w^{(i)} \in \mathbb{F}_q^m, i \in \{1 \dots o_2\}$, which are obtained in the manner described above, and $Y \in M_{m \times o_2}(\mathbb{F}_q)$ be the matrix whose columns consist of the corresponding starting vectors $y^{(i)}, i \in \{1 \dots o_2\}$. By dividing the matrices and vectors into blocks according to Eq. (4), we receive

$$SY = \begin{pmatrix} I & S_1 \\ 0 & I \end{pmatrix} \begin{pmatrix} Y_1 \\ Y_2 \end{pmatrix} = \begin{pmatrix} Y_1 + S_1 Y_2 \\ Y_2 \end{pmatrix} = \begin{pmatrix} W_1 \\ W_2 \end{pmatrix}. \tag{13}$$

Thus, the secret submatrix S_1 can be obtained via $S_1 = (W_1 - Y_1) * Y_2^{-1}$. Consequently, for the attack to be successful o_2 faulty signatures are needed and the starting vectors $y^{(i)}$ need to be chosen s.t. $Y_2 \in M_{o_2 \times o_2}(\mathbb{F}_q)$ is invertible.

Recover T by Using S. Having access to the secret transformation S, an attacker can use the very same strategy to recover T_4 and T_3 as described in Sect. 3.1. By the time this step was applied during the post-processing of the first fault attack, the attacker had already learned T_1, which is not the case anymore. However, in order to exploit Eq. (12) it is enough to know S, i.e., the attacker does not need any of the entries of T_1 to recover T_3 and T_4.

This procedure - although presented somewhat differently - was already proposed by Park et al. in [24, Section 4.2]. In their work, they used Correlation Power Analysis to obtain S and thus, faced the same challenge for the subsequent algebraic evaluation, i.e., the recovery of T under the knowledge of S. In order to obtain T_1, they suggest to use a similar approach, namely by focusing on the $o_1 \times o_2$ block $F_i^{(6)}$ and the $o_2 \times o_1$ block $F_i^{(8)}$ of (10). However, it is not possible to continue the attack like this, as we sketch in the following. Therefore, observe

$$F_i^{(8)\top} + F_i^{(6)} = 0_{o_1 \times o_2} = \sum_{j=1}^{m} \tilde{s}_{ij} \Big(T_1^\top (P_j^{(1)\top} + P_j^{(1)}) T_4 + T_1^\top (P_j^{(2)}) T_3 + \dots$$

$$\dots P_j^{(2)\top} T_4 + (P_j^{(5)\top} + P_j^{(5)}) T_3 + T_1^\top P_j^{(3)} + P_j^{(6)} \Big). \tag{14}$$

While it is true that only linear equations remain, after inserting the known values for T_3, T_4, and S, one can deduce from

$$T_1^\top \sum_{j=1}^m \tilde{s}_{ij}\left((P_j^{(1)\top} + P_j^{(1)})T_4 + (P_j^{(2)})T_3 + P_j^{(3)}\right) \stackrel{(12)}{=} T_1^\top 0,$$

that Eq. (14) does not provide further information about the block T_1, since it is satisfied independent of its choice. The authors of [31] and [24] confirmed our findings in this regard.

Thus, one way to proceed and obtain T_1, is to fall back to the well-known Kipnis-Shamir attack on UOV [20]. Note that the knowledge of S is equivalent to the recovery of the secret subspace W, referring to the notation in Remark 1. Following [3, Section 5.3], this reduces the problem of finding O_1 to a small UOV instance with reduced parameter $n' = n - o_2$ and $m' = m - o_2$ and complexity $\mathcal{O}(q^{n'-2m'}) = \mathcal{O}(q^{n+o_2-2m}) = \mathcal{O}(q^{v_1-o_1})$. In case of Rainbow parameter set I, this leads to a very efficient method to finish the key recovery attack, since it holds $n' \approx 2m'$. For higher parameter sets this approach still remains infeasible, as we have $n' \gg 2m'$, rendering the Kipnis-Shamir attack inefficient.

Very recently, Esser et al. published a work on partial key exposure attacks [16], in which they cover Rainbow, among other schemes. They also treat the task of exposing T_1 after the remaining part of the secret matrices are known. Their approach builds up on a work by Billet and Gilbert [5] and has complexity $\mathcal{O}(n^3)$, which would be very efficient, even for larger parameter sets of Rainbow.

Attack 2: Secret Key Recovery by Skipping the Linear Transformation S. After successful execution of the fault attack, the attacker takes the generated faulted signatures $z^{(1)}, \ldots, z^{(o_2)}$ and the used starting values $y^{(1)}, \ldots, y^{(o_2)}$ being of the form described above and performs the following steps:

1. Compute $w^{(i)} = \mathcal{P}(z^{(i)})$ for $i \in \{1, \ldots, o_2\}$.
2. Build the matrices $W \in M_{m \times o_2}(\mathbb{F}_q)$ and $Y \in M_{m \times o_2}(\mathbb{F}_q)$ as described for Eq. (13).
3. Recover S by computing $S_1 = (W_1 - Y_1) * Y_2^{-1}$.
4. Insert S into Eq. (12). Solve the resulting system of linear equations to recover T_3 and T_4.
5. Obtain T by applying the Kipnis-Shamir attack to the reduced UOV instance.
6. Use Eq. (6) to obtain $\mathcal{F}$. The attacker recovered the full secret key $(S, \mathcal{F}, T)$.

4   Code Analysis and Simulation

To implement the attacks described in Sect. 3, an in-depth analysis of the instruction code needs to be performed. The following section discusses how to uncover the low-level instructions that need to be skipped to achieve the desired behaviour of the fault attacks as specified in Sect. 3 based on the source code of the ARM Cortex M4 optimized round 3 submission by the authors of [12]³. Furthermore, we present an elaborated simulation of our results.

4.1   Attack 1: Fixing the Vinegar Variables

Listing 1.1 shows the relevant code snippet for our first attack. The implementation proposed by [12] does not set the vinegar variables to zero after signature generation. Therefore skipping the function call to *prng_gen* in line 55 will leave them with the same values due to the temporary variable being reallocated to the same address at each function call. This, of course, assumes that the respective memory region is not overwritten between two function calls, which holds if the device acts solely as a signing oracle.

By analyzing the disassembly of the compiled binary, we find the relevant instruction given in Listing 1.2. By skipping the branch performed in line 0xdfb2, the desired behaviour is achieved and the vinegars remain constant for subsequent signatures.

4.2   Attack 2: Skipping the Linear Transformation S

To prohibit the application of the linear transformation S^{-1} we aim at skipping the function call to *gf256v_add* in line 178 of the source code shown in Listing 1.1. However, for this function being *inlined* - meaning the compiler inserts the function body instead of a branch - a single instruction skip does not suffice. Therefore the beforehand executed call to *gf16mat_prod_16_32* in line 173 is skipped, leaving the variable *temp_o* at its initial all-zero value and rendering the subsequent call to *gf256v_add* without effect. To achieve this effect, we target line 0xe070 of the assembly code shown in Listing 1.2 with a first order fault.

Exiting the While Loop. In this paragraph, we discuss the probability of exiting the respective while loop on the first iteration, assuming that the fault injection was successful. Regarding the attack in Sect. 4.1, if the skip of the vinegar variables in Line 2 of Algorithm 1 is introduced successfully, the same vinegar variables are used again for consecutive signatures. Thus, the chosen vinegar variables already led to an invertible matrix $\hat{F}_1$ in the previous signature. Since $\hat{F}_1$ only depends on the vinegar variables $(y_1, \ldots, y_{v_1})$ and the polynomials of the first layer, the condition in Line 8 is always fulfilled. Regarding the attack in Sect. 4.2, the condition in Line 11 also depends on the solution of the first layer in Line 9. Thus the probability of $\hat{F}_2$ to be invertible can be approximated by the probability of that a randomly generated matrix with entries in $\mathbb{F}_q$ is invertible which is given by Eq. (3).

---

³ The source code can be found at https://github.com/rainbowm4/rainbowm4.git.

```
26  int rainbow_sign (...)
27  {
...         ...
51      while (!l1_succ) // until solution found
52      {
...         ...
...         // skipped by Attack 1
55          prng_gen(&prng_sign, vinegar, _V1_BYTE);
...         ...
80      }
...     ...
...     // temp_o is initialized with zeros
155     uint8_t temp_o[_MAX_O_BYTE + 32] = {0};
...         ...
157     while (!succ) // until solution found
158     {
...     // skipped by Attack 2
173     gf16mat_prod_16_32(temp_o, sk->s1, _z + _O1_BYTE);
...         ...
...     // applying S
178     gf256v_add(y, temp_o, _O1_BYTE);
...         ...
228     }
...     ...
292 }
```

Listing 1.1. Relevant snippets of the rainbow_sign function in *rainbowm4/crypto_sign/rainbowI-classic/m4/rainbow.c*

```
...
0xdfb0 add        signature ,sp,#0xe4
0xdfb2 bl         prng_gen
0xdfb6 add        _digest ,sp,#0x6c
...
0xe06e add        signature ,sp,#0x144
0xe070 bl         gf16mat_prod_16_32
0xe074 ldr        sk ,[sp,#y [4]]
...
```

Listing 1.2. Relevant snippets of the assembly code corresponding to line 55 and line 173 of the rainbow_sign function in Listing 1.1.

4.3   Simulation

To verify our assumptions and provide a first proof of concept, we implement a generic ARM M4 architecture simulation environment based on Unicorn [13], which itself is based on QEMU [2][4]. The validity of our results exceed the ones one would obtain by simple code modification - i.e., removing code lines one

---

[4] The codebase of our framework can be found at https://anonymous.4open.science/r/double_rainbow_submission-E3CC.

wishes to skip - as the compiled binary of the unmodified source code is executed within our simulation just as a real device would execute it. The 32-bit Reduced Instruction Set Computer (RISC) architecture as defined by ARM is emulated in its entirety.

The framework allows per-instruction execution of the compiled binary, cycle-accurate skipping faults and memory analysis at any given point during execution. This facilitates the validation of both attacks' feasibility through injection of the intended faults and subsequent analysis of the memory space mapped to the vinegar variables and y for the first and second attack, respectively. After verification of the skipping faults' effects on memory, signature collection is performed. Both attacks lead to successful recovery of the secret key, proving the feasibility of our attacks. In the following we give a brief overview of the core features of the simulation framework.

Key Generation. For the generation of the public and secret key being computationally expensive and very time consuming within the simulation, we implement it on the host machine and subsequently map the keys to the simulated device memory.

Signing. The signing algorithm runs entirely within the simulation. Upon executing the binary starting from the respective function's memory address, the secret key is mapped to the simulated device's memory. The address of the memory region holding the message to be signed, a buffer for the result and the key's address are written to the corresponding registers according to the calling convention. To implement the attacks, the simulation first stops at the address where we want to inject the fault. Then the instruction pointer is incremented as required by the length of the instruction to be skipped. Execution is subsequently resumed at the following instruction.

Verification. For completeness, verification inside the simulation is also implemented. Of course, the adversary may implement verification on any device. It is merely used to verify successful fault injection and extract temporary variables that facilitate executing Attack 2.

4.4   Applicability to Other Implementations

The attack we introduced in Section 3.1 is not directly applicable to the reference implementation of Rainbow that was submitted to the NIST Standardization Process [14]. This is due to the fact that the vinegar variables are zeroed at the end of the signing process there, so they can't be reused in a subsequent signing process by a first-order fault attack. See Sect. 5.1 for more details. The second attack, however, can be applied to the reference implementation, since the same steps as mentioned in Listing 1.1 are executed there.

5   Countermeasures

Countermeasures attempt to either verify the integrity of the executed algorithm before returning its result or ensuring that a system cannot leak secrets even when compromised. If the latter is the case, the returned value should either be a random number or an error constant. A traditional way to tackle this problem for the case of fault injections is to repeat the computation and compare the results. However, this approach is very expensive in terms of computation time and relies on the assumption that an attacker will fail to successfully inject faults in two subsequent runs of the algorithm. In this section we suggest countermeasures that can be adopted in order to avoid the attacks described in Sect. 3.

5.1   Countermeasures for Attack 1

For the first attack relying on keeping the vinegar variables constant, some countermeasures aiming for either zeroing or randomization can be employed.

Firstly, resetting the memory region mapped to the vinegars at the end of the function call to zero - as it is done in the original NIST submission in [15] - is the most straight-forward solution. Then, if the respective fault is injected, the system of equations is rendered non-solvable, leading to re-iteration of the loop until either a threshold number of iterations is reached and the function is exited or the fault injection fails and vinegar variables are sampled correctly. However, depending on the implementation, this can enable a different attack of higher complexity relying on partial zeroing of the vinegars, as described in [27].

Secondly, if the vinegars were to be saved in between subsequent function calls, they could be checked for equivalence before returning the signature. While this might seem a viable solution, care must be taken to ensure safe storage not to leak their values. Moreover, since simple checks are assumed to be easily skippable, the checking procedure has to be elegantly integrated in the signing procedure.

Thirdly, inlining the function call to *prng_gen* could prohibit the attack for some parameter sets. Depending on the implementation and the corresponding number of vinegars, the loop copying the random values to the vinegars can be exited earlier by injecting a fault, leaving them partially constant. While this prohibits our attack which requires all vinegars to stay constant, similar attacks with less stringent constraints might still be applicable. To further mitigate these, loop unrolling could provide remedy. However, this combined mitigation technique would introduce non-negligible overhead in code size which might render it inapplicable to constrained devices.

5.2   Countermeasures for Attack 2

For the second attack that aims to skip the application of the secret transformation S, an evident mitigation technique is to verify the signature before returning it. However, this leads to an overhead of around 25% [12], rendering this strategy very costly.

More practical, one could initialize the *temp_o* variable so that the skipping fault would result to an all-zero y after execution of *gf256v_add*. To achieve this, *temp_o* first $o_1/2$ bytes - i.e., the bytes that are affected by the subsequent addition - are initialized with y's first $o_1/2$ bytes (i.e., 16 for the parameter set of 32 oil variables in the bitsliced representation). The subsequent $\mathbb{F}_{256}$ addition - i.e., implemented as multiple consecutive binary XORs - then leads to an all-zero y, prohibiting leakage of the secret key through the collected signatures.

Furthermore, inlining the call to *gf16mat_prod_16_32* would prohibit a first-order skipping fault attack. However, due to this function being implemented in assembly language for optimization purposes, there is a discrepancy for the required build steps. Therefore this mitigation technique might not be trivial to implement.

6   Conclusion

This paper demonstrated how important it is to protect the secret transformations S and T in multivariate schemes against fault attacks. They are the only obstacles an attacker faces when trying to discover the structure of the central map $\mathcal{F}$. Due to their linearity, it is possible to recover them either partially (see Sect. 3.1) or in total (see Sect. 3.2), by collecting enough input and output vectors and analyzing their transformation. As the generated signature constitutes the output of T^{-1} and the hash value that is to be signed represents the input to S^{-1}, an attacker only needs to obtain an intermediate result, e.g., the input vector of T^{-1} or the output vector of S^{-1}, in order to gain secret information. If she is able to thoughtfully induce a fault that compromises one of these intermediate vectors, either by skipping a code line or forcing the algorithm to compute with the same values over and over again, the security of the scheme is no longer guaranteed.

For instance, it was already shown in [27] that UOV and LUOV are vulnerable to the attack that fixes the vinegar variables. Whereas the authors of [22] doubt that it is possible to fix a large portion of the vinegar variables by physical fault injection, we showed that this is indeed possible by a single instruction skip.

Specifically for Rainbow, we proved that it is not even necessary to recover the whole secret transformation T, by the means of a fault attack. The introduced algebraic attack restores the complete secret key of Rainbow on input of the submatrix T_1 by just solving linear equations. This is of course not limited to the evaluation of fault attacks, but also holds if T_1 is leaked through any other kind of side-channel analysis. In the light of the recent breakthrough in cryptanalysis [4], we acknowledge that the Rainbow parameter set for security level I is deprecated. However, the fault attacks we suggest, directly reveal either the secret subspaces O_1 (see Sect. 3.1) or W (see Sect. 3.2) and thus, work for any given parameter set, in particular for higher security levels and adapted parameters that are designed to meet new requirements.

Acknowledgement. This research work has been funded by the German Ministry of Education, Research and Technology in the context of the project Aquorypt (grant number 16KIS1022) and the project Full Lifecycle Post-Quantum PKI - FLOQI (grant number 16KIS1074). Furthermore, we want to thank Enrico Thomae and Namhun Koo for the helpful correspondence concerning the algebraic evaluation in Sect. 3.2.

References

1. Post-Quantum Cryptography. NIST Official Website (2021). https://csrc.nist.gov/projects/post-quantum-cryptography
2. Bellard, F.: QEMU, a fast and portable dynamic translator. In: Proceedings of the Annual Conference on USENIX Annual Technical Conference, ATEC 2005, p. 41, USA. USENIX Association (2005)
3. Beullens, W.: Improved cryptanalysis of UOV and rainbow. In: Canteaut, A., Standaert, F.-X. (eds.) EUROCRYPT 2021. LNCS, vol. 12696, pp. 348–373. Springer, Cham (2021). https://doi.org/10.1007/978-3-030-77870-5_13
4. Beullens, W.: Breaking rainbow takes a weekend on a laptop. Cryptology ePrint Archive, Report 2022/214 (2022). https://ia.cr/2022/214
5. Billet, O., Gilbert, H.: Cryptanalysis of rainbow. In: De Prisco, R., Yung, M. (eds.) SCN 2006. LNCS, vol. 4116, pp. 336–347. Springer, Heidelberg (2006). https://doi.org/10.1007/11832072_23
6. Bindel, N., Buchmann, J., Krämer, J.: Lattice-based signature schemes and their sensitivity to fault attacks. In: 2016 Workshop on Fault Diagnosis and Tolerance in Cryptography, FDTC 2016, Santa Barbara, CA, USA, 16 August 2016, pp. 63–77. IEEE Computer Society (2016)
7. Blömer, J., Da Silva, R.G., Günther, P., Krämer, J., Seifert, J.P.: A practical second-order fault attack against a real-world pairing implementation. In: 2014 Workshop on Fault Diagnosis and Tolerance in Cryptography, pp. 123–136. IEEE (2014)
8. Boneh, D., DeMillo, R.A., Lipton, R.J.: On the importance of checking cryptographic protocols for faults. In: Fumy, W. (ed.) EUROCRYPT 1997. LNCS, vol. 1233, pp. 37–51. Springer, Heidelberg (1997). https://doi.org/10.1007/3-540-69053-0_4
9. Campos, F., Krämer, J., Müller, M.: Safe-error attacks on SIKE and CSIDH. In: Batina, L., Picek, S., Mondal, M. (eds.) SPACE 2021. LNCS, vol. 13162, pp. 104–125. Springer, Cham (2022). https://doi.org/10.1007/978-3-030-95085-9_6
10. Castelnovi, L., Martinelli, A., Prest, T.: Grafting trees: a fault attack against the SPHINCS framework. In: Lange, T., Steinwandt, R. (eds.) PQCrypto 2018. LNCS, vol. 10786, pp. 165–184. Springer, Cham (2018). https://doi.org/10.1007/978-3-319-79063-3_8
11. Cayrel, P.-L., Colombier, B., Drăgoi, V.-F., Menu, A., Bossuet, L.: Message-recovery laser fault injection attack on the *Classic McEliece* cryptosystem. In: Canteaut, A., Standaert, F.-X. (eds.) EUROCRYPT 2021. LNCS, vol. 12697, pp. 438–467. Springer, Cham (2021). https://doi.org/10.1007/978-3-030-77886-6_15
12. Chou, T., Kannwischer, M.J., Yang, B.Y.: Rainbow on cortex-M4. Cryptology ePrint Archive, Report 2021/532 (2021). https://ia.cr/2021/532
13. Quynh, N.A., Vu, D.H.: Unicorn: next generation CPU emulator framework (2015)
14. Ding, J., et al.: Rainbow. Technical report, National Institute of Standards and Technology (2020). https://csrc.nist.gov/projects/post-quantum-cryptography/round-3-submissions

15. Ding, J., Schmidt, D.: Rainbow, a new multivariable polynomial signature scheme. In: Ioannidis, J., Keromytis, A., Yung, M. (eds.) ACNS 2005. LNCS, vol. 3531, pp. 164–175. Springer, Heidelberg (2005). https://doi.org/10.1007/11496137_12

16. Esser, A., May, A., Verbel, J., Wen, W.: Partial key exposure attacks on BIKE. Rainbow and NTRU, Cryptology ePrint Archive (2022)

17. Grimes, R.A.: Cryptography Apocalypse: Preparing for the Day When Quantum Computing Breaks Today's Crypto. Wiley, Hoboken (2019)

18. Hashimoto, Y., Takagi, T., Sakurai, K.: General fault attacks on multivariate public key cryptosystems. In: Yang, B.-Y. (ed.) PQCrypto 2011. LNCS, vol. 7071, pp. 1–18. Springer, Heidelberg (2011). https://doi.org/10.1007/978-3-642-25405-5_1

19. Kalai, G.: The argument against quantum computers, the quantum laws of nature, and Google's supremacy claims. arXiv preprint arXiv:2008.05188 (2020)

20. Kipnis, A., Patarin, J., Goubin, L.: Unbalanced oil and vinegar signature schemes. In: Stern, J. (ed.) EUROCRYPT 1999. LNCS, vol. 1592, pp. 206–222. Springer, Heidelberg (1999). https://doi.org/10.1007/3-540-48910-X_15

21. Krämer, J., Loiero, M.: Fault attacks on UOV and rainbow. In: Polian, I., Stöttinger, M. (eds.) COSADE 2019. LNCS, vol. 11421, pp. 193–214. Springer, Cham (2019). https://doi.org/10.1007/978-3-030-16350-1_11

22. Mus, K., Islam, S., Sunar, B.: QuantumHammer: a practical hybrid attack on the LUOV signature scheme. In: Proceedings of the 2020 ACM SIGSAC Conference on Computer and Communications Security, pp. 1071–1084 (2020)

23. Okeya, K., Takagi, T., Vuillaume, C.: On the importance of protecting Δ in SFLASH against side channel attacks. IEICE Trans. Fundam. Electron. Commun. Comput. Sci. 88(1), 123–131 (2005)

24. Park, A., Shim, K.A., Koo, N., Han, D.G.: Side-channel attacks on post-quantum signature schemes based on multivariate quadratic equations:-rainbow and UOV. IACR Trans. Cryptographic Hardware Embed. Syst. 500–523 (2018)

25. Pokorný, D., Socha, P., Novotný, M.: Side-channel attack on rainbow post-quantum signature. In: 2021 Design, Automation & Test in Europe Conference & Exhibition (DATE), pp. 565–568. IEEE (2021)

26. Roetteler, M., Naehrig, M., Svore, K.M., Lauter, K.: Quantum resource estimates for computing elliptic curve discrete logarithms. In: Takagi, T., Peyrin, T. (eds.) ASIACRYPT 2017. LNCS, vol. 10625, pp. 241–270. Springer, Cham (2017). https://doi.org/10.1007/978-3-319-70697-9_9

27. Shim, K.-A., Koo, N.: Algebraic fault analysis of UOV and rainbow with the leakage of random vinegar values. IEEE Trans. Inf. Forensics Secur. 15, 2429–2439 (2020)

28. Shor, P.W.: Polynomial-time algorithms for prime factorization and discrete logarithms on a quantum computer. SIAM Rev. 41(2), 303–332 (1999)

29. Steinwandt, R., Geiselmann, W., Beth, T.: A theoretical DPA-based cryptanalysis of the NESSIE candidates FLASH and SFLASH. In: Davida, G.I., Frankel, Y. (eds.) ISC 2001. LNCS, vol. 2200, pp. 280–293. Springer, Heidelberg (2001). https://doi.org/10.1007/3-540-45439-X_19

30. Tao, C., Petzoldt, A., Ding, J.: Improved key recovery of the hfev-signature scheme. Cryptology ePrint Archive (2020)

31. Thomae, E.: A generalization of the rainbow band separation attack and its applications to multivariate schemes. Cryptology ePrint Archive (2012)

32. Yi, H., Li, W.: On the importance of checking multivariate public key cryptography for side-channel attacks: the case of enTTS scheme. Comput. J. 60(8), 1197–1209 (2017)

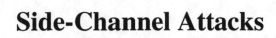

Side-Channel Attacks

Side-Channel Attacks

TransNet: Shift Invariant Transformer Network for Side Channel Analysis

Suvadeep Hajra[1](✉), Sayandeep Saha[2], Manaar Alam[3],
and Debdeep Mukhopadhyay[1]

[1] Indian Institute of Technology Kharagpur, Kharagpur, India
suvadeep.hajra@gmail.com
[2] Nanyang Technological University, Singapore, Singapore
[3] New York University Abu Dhabi, Abu Dhabi, United Arab Emirates

Abstract. Deep learning (DL) has revolutionized Side Channel Analysis (SCA) in recent years. One of the major advantages of DL in the context of SCA is that it can automatically handle masking and desynchronization countermeasures, even while they are applied simultaneously for a cryptographic implementation. However, the success of the attack strongly depends on the DL model used for the attack. Traditionally, Convolutional Neural Networks (CNNs) have been utilized in this regard. This work proposes to use Transformer Network (TN) for attacking implementations secured with masking and desynchronization. Our choice is motivated by the fact that TN is good at capturing the dependencies among distant points of interest in a power trace. Furthermore, we show that TN can be made *shift-invariant* which is an important property required to handle desynchronized traces. Experimental validation on several public datasets establishes that our proposed TN-based model, called *TransNet*, outperforms the present state-of-the-art on several occasions. Specifically, TransNet outperforms the other methods by a wide margin when the traces are highly desynchronized. Additionally, TransNet shows good attack performance against implementations with desynchronized traces even when it is trained on synchronized traces.

Keywords: Side channel analysis · Masking countermeasure · Transformer network

1 Introduction

Ever since its introduction in [16], SCA poses a significant threat to cryptographic implementations. To protect the cryptographic implementations from those attacks, several countermeasures have been proposed. Masking countermeasures [6] and desynchronization of traces [7] are two commonly used countermeasures against those attacks. In masking countermeasure, each intermediate sensitive variable of the cryptographic implementation is divided into multiple shares so that any proper subset of the shares remains independent of the sensitive variable. A successful attack against the masking scheme combines the leakages of all the shares to infer information about the sensitive variable. On the other hand, desynchronization of the power traces causes the PoIs of the traces to be misaligned, reducing the signal-to-noise ratio (SNR) of the individual sample points. The reduced SNR causes an increase in the number of power traces required for a successful attack. Recently, DL [19,21] has been found to be very effective against both the countermeasures. DL methods can eliminate the necessity of critical preprocessing steps in SCA while attacking desynchronized traces [5]. DL methods can also break masking countermeasures without requiring careful selection of combining function [29].

Various DL models like Feed-Forward Neural Networks (FFNs), Recurrent Neural Networks (RNNs), Convolutional Neural Networks (CNNs) have been explored [3,18,19] for SCA. Among those, CNNs have been widely adopted for performing profiling SCA[1] [3,5,14,37,40]. Because of the shift-invariance property of CNNs, they can perform very well on misaligned attack traces, and thus, can eliminate critical preprocessing steps like realignment of power traces in a standard SCA [5]. Moreover, the CNN-based models have achieved state-of-the-art results in many publicly available datasets [34,37]. However, the existing CNN-based models are limited in several aspects. Firstly, we have experimentally demonstrated that their performance gets worse as the amount of desynchronization gets larger. Secondly, to perform well on desynchronized attack traces, they are required to be trained using profiling desynchronization almost the same as attack desynchronization [33,40]. Finally, separate models are needed to be designed to attack implementations protected by different amounts of desynchronization.

Recently, in a seminal work, Vaswani et al. [32] have introduced Transformer Network (TN), which has defeated all its CNN and RNN-based counterparts by a wide margin in almost every natural language processing task. In this work, we propose to use TN for SCA. TN can easily capture the dependency between distant PoIs, and, thus, is a natural choice against implementations protected using countermeasures like masking for which the PoIs are spread across a long range in the time axis. Moreover, by introducing a weaker notion (applicable to SCA) of shift-invariance, we have shown that TN can be shift-invariant in the context of SCA. Thus, TN can be effective against misaligned traces as well. We have proposed a TN-based DL model, namely TransNet, for performing SCA based on the above observations. We have also experimentally evaluated TransNet against implementations protected by masking and trace desynchronization countermeasures. Our experimental results suggest that TransNet performs better than existing state-of-the-art CNN-based models on several scenarios. Specifically, TransNet performs better than the CNN-based state-of-the-art models when the attack traces are highly desynchronized. Additionally, TransNet

---

[1] In profiling SCA, the adversary possesses a device similar to the attack device and uses that device to train a model for the target device. The trained model is used to attack the target device. A profiling SCA assumes the strongest adversary and provides the worst-case security analysis of a cryptographic device. In this work, we have considered profiling SCA only.

can perform very well on highly desynchronized traces even when trained on synchronized traces – a feature that none of the existing CNN-based models exhibits (kindly refer to Sect. 6.6 for a detailed discussion).

In summary, the contributions of the paper are as follows:

– Firstly, we propose to use TN for SCA. TN can naturally capture long-distance dependency [32], thus, it is a better choice against masking countermeasure. Additionally, we have defined a weaker notion of shift-invariance that is well applicable to SCA. Under this new notion, we have mathematically shown that the TN can be made to be shift-invariant. Thus, it can be effective against misaligned traces as well.
– Our proposed TN-based model, namely TransNet, significantly differs from off-the-shelf TN models in several design choices which are crucial for its success in SCA.
– Experimentally, we have compared TransNet with the CNN-based state-of-the-art models on four datasets. Among the four datasets, two datasets contain trace desynchronization, whereas the other two do not contain any trace desynchronization. The performance of TransNet is better than or comparable to the CNN-based state-of-the-art models on the four datasets. Particularly, TransNet outperforms the other methods by a wide margin when the amount of desynchronization is very high. In those scenarios, TransNet can bring down the guessing entropy to zero using very small number of attack traces, whereas the CNN-based methods struggle to bring it down below 20.
– We have also shown that TransNet can perform very well on highly desynchronized attack traces even when the model is trained on only synchronized (aligned) traces. In our experiments, TransNet can reduce the guessing entropy below 1 using only 400 traces on *ASCAD_desync100* dataset [3] even when it is trained on aligned traces (i.e., on ASCAD dataset). On the other hand, the CNN-based state-of-the-art models struggle to reduce the guessing entropy below 20 using as much as 5000 traces in the same setting.

Several recent works [13,36] have explored different loss functions for DL-based SCA. Some other recent works have explored different training techniques [1,25]. However, those techniques are orthogonal to our work as we aim to explore different machine learning models. Also, several recent works [10,17,22,26] have introduced novel machine learning models to attack very long traces. In contrast, our proposed model is more appropriate for performing attacks on shorter traces or selected time windows of a small number of sample points.

The organization of the paper is as follows. In Sect. 2, we introduce the notations and briefly describe how the power attacks are performed using deep learning. Section 3 describes the general architecture of TN. In Sect. 4, we introduce our proposed TN-based model, namely TransNet, for SCA. Section 5 explains how a TN-based model can accumulate information from distant PoIs. The section also proves the shift-invariance property of the TransNet like models. In Sect. 6, we experimentally evaluate the TransNet model on several datasets. Section 7 discusses the advantages and disadvantages of the proposed model. Finally, in Sect. 8, we conclude.

2   Preliminaries

In this section, we first introduce the notations used in the paper. Then, we briefly describe how a profiling SCA is performed using DL.

2.1   Notations

Throughout the paper, we have used the following notational convention. A random variable is represented by a letter in the capital (e.g., X), whereas an instantiation of the random variable is represented by the corresponding letter in small (e.g., x) and the domain of the random variable by the corresponding calligraphic letter (e.g., $\mathcal{X}$). Similarly, a capital letter in bold (e.g., $\mathbf{X}$) is used to represent a random vector, and the corresponding small letter in bold (e.g., $\mathbf{x}$) is used to represent an instantiation of the random vector. A matrix is represented by a capital letter in roman type style (e.g., M). The i-th elements of a vector $\mathbf{x}$ is represented by $\mathbf{x}[i]$ and the element of i-th row and j-th column of a matrix is represented by $M[i, j]$. $\mathbb{P}[\cdot]$ represents the probability mass/density function and $\mathbb{E}[\cdot]$ represents expectation.

2.2   Profiling SCA Using Deep Learning

Like other profiling attacks, profiling attacks using deep learning are performed in two phases: profiling and attack. However, unlike other profiling attacks like template attacks, the adversary does not build any template distribution for each value of the intermediate secret in this case. Instead, he trains a deep learning model to directly predict the values of the intermediate secret from the power traces. More precisely, in the profiling phase, the adversary sets the keys of the clone device of his own choice and collects a large number of traces for different plaintexts. For each trace, he computes the value of the intermediate secret variable $Z = F(X, K)$ where X is the random plaintext, K is the key, and $F(\cdot, \cdot)$ is a cryptographic primitive. Then, the adversary trains a DL model $f : \mathbb{R}^n \mapsto \mathbb{R}^{|\mathcal{Z}|}$ using the power traces as input and the corresponding Z variables as the label or output. Thus, the output of the deep neural model for a power trace $\mathbf{l}$ can be written as $\mathbf{p} = f(\mathbf{l}; \theta^*)$ where θ^* is the parameter learned during training, and $\mathbf{p} \in \mathbb{R}^{|\mathcal{Z}|}$ such that $\mathbf{p}[i]$, for $i = 0, \cdots, |\mathcal{Z}| - 1$, represents the predicted probability for the intermediate variable $Z = i$. During the attack phase, the score of each possible key $k \in \mathcal{K}$ is computed as

$$\hat{\delta}_k = \sum_{i=0}^{T_a - 1} \log \mathbf{p}^i [F(p^i, k)] \tag{1}$$

where $\{\mathbf{l}^i, p^i\}_{i=0}^{T_a - 1}$ is the set of attack trace-plaintext pairs, and $\mathbf{p}^i = f(\mathbf{l}^i; \theta^*)$ is the predicted probability vector for the i-th trace. Like template attack, $\hat{k} = \text{argmax}_k \hat{\delta}_k$ is chosen as the guessed key.

Several deep neural network architectures including Feed Forward Network (FFN) [19–21], Convolutional Neural Network (CNN) [3,5,19,28,40], Recurrent

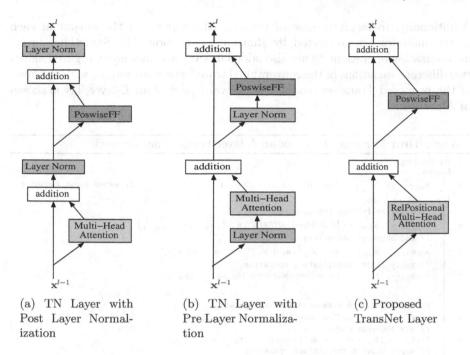

(a) TN Layer with Post Layer Normalization

(b) TN Layer with Pre Layer Normalization

(c) Proposed TransNet Layer

Fig. 1. A Single Transformer Layer. (a) and (b) show the conventional TN layers. In (c), we show a layer of the proposed TransNet. In the proposed TransNet layer, no layer normalization has been used. Additionally, the proposed TransNet layer uses relative positional encoding [8] within the self attention layer (please refer to Sect. 3.4 for details).

Neural Network (RNN) [17–19] have been explored for profiling SCA. In this work, we propose to use TN for the same. In the next section, we describe the architecture of a TN.

3 Transformer Network

A Transformer Network (TN) is a deep learning model which was originally developed for a sequence processing task. The TN takes a sequence $(x_0, \cdots, x_{n-1})$ as input and generates a sequence of output vectors $(\mathbf{y}_0, \cdots, \mathbf{y}_{n-1})$. The sequence of the output vectors can then be processed differently depending on the target task. For example, for a sequence classification task (as in SCA), the mean vector of the output vectors can be used to predict the class labels.

Structurally, TN is a stacked collection of transformer layers following an initial embedding layer. Thus, in an L-layer TN, the output of the initial embedding layer is used as the input of the first transformer layer, and the output of the i-th transformer layer is used as the input of $(i+1)$-th layer, $1 \le i < L$. Finally, the output of the L-th layer is taken as the network output.

A transformer layer consists of two main modules - a multi-head self-attention layer and a position-wise feed-forward layer. Specifically, a transformer layer is a multi-head self-attention layer followed by a position-wise feed-forward layer.

Additionally, to facilitate ease of training, the input and the output of each of the modules are connected by shortcut connection [11]. Sometimes layer-normalization operations [2] are also added in a transformer layer. Figure 1 shows two different variations of the conventional transformer layer along with the layer of the proposed TransNet model. The forward pass of an L-layer TN is shown in Algorithm 1.

Algorithm 1: Forward pass of an L layer transformer network

1 At the beginning
2 begin
3 $\quad$ $\mathbf{x}_0^0, \mathbf{x}_1^0 \cdots , \mathbf{x}_{n-1}^0 \leftarrow$ Embed$(x_0, x_1, \cdots , x_{n-1})$ $\hfill$ // embed input sequence
4 for $l \leftarrow 1$ to L do
$\quad$ // apply self-attention operation
5 $\quad$ $\mathbf{s}_0, \mathbf{s}_1, \cdots , \mathbf{s}_{n-1} \leftarrow$ MultiHeadSelfAttn^l $(\mathbf{x}_0^{l-1}, \mathbf{x}_1^{l-1}, \cdots , \mathbf{x}_{n-1}^{l-1})$
$\quad$ // add shortcut connection
6 $\quad$ $\mathbf{s}_0, \mathbf{s}_1, \cdots , \mathbf{s}_{n-1} \leftarrow \mathbf{s}_0 + \mathbf{x}_0^{l-1}, \mathbf{s}_1 + \mathbf{x}_1^{l-1}, \cdots , \mathbf{s}_{n-1} + \mathbf{x}_{n-1}^{l-1}$
$\quad$ // apply layer normalization operation
7 $\quad$ $\mathbf{s}_0, \mathbf{s}_1, \cdots , \mathbf{s}_{n-1} \leftarrow$ LayerNormalization $(\mathbf{s}_0, \mathbf{s}_1, \cdots , \mathbf{s}_{n-1})$

$\quad$ // apply position-wise feed-forward operation
8 $\quad$ $\mathbf{t}_0, \mathbf{t}_1, \cdots , \mathbf{t}_{n-1} \leftarrow$ PoswiseFF^l $(\mathbf{s}_0, \mathbf{s}_1, \cdots , \mathbf{s}_{n-1})$
$\quad$ // add shortcut connection
9 $\quad$ $\mathbf{t}_0, \mathbf{t}_1, \cdots , \mathbf{t}_{n-1} \leftarrow \mathbf{t}_0 + \mathbf{s}_0, \mathbf{t}_1 + \mathbf{s}_1, \cdots , \mathbf{t}_{n-1} + \mathbf{s}_{n-1}$
$\quad$ // apply layer normalization operation
10 $\quad$ $\mathbf{x}_0^l, \mathbf{x}_1^l, \cdots , \mathbf{x}_{n-1}^l \leftarrow$ LayerNormalization $(\mathbf{t}_0, \mathbf{t}_1, \cdots , \mathbf{t}_{n-1})$
11 return $(\mathbf{x}_0^L, \mathbf{x}_1^L, \cdots , \mathbf{x}_{n-1}^L)$

Each building block of the above overall architecture is described below.

3.1 Embedding Layer

A transformer layer takes a sequence of vectors as input. However, the input to a TN is generally a sequence of discrete symbols (in case of text processing) or a sequence of real numbers (in case of images or power traces). The embedding layer converts the sequence of discrete symbols or real numbers $(x_0, x_1, \cdots , x_{n-1})$ into the sequence of vectors $(\mathbf{x}_1, \mathbf{x}_2, \cdots , \mathbf{x}_{n-1})$. Generally, $\mathbf{x}_i = f(x_i; \mathrm{E}), 0 \leq i < n$, holds for some embedding function $f(\cdot)$ and parameter E. The parameter E is learned during training along with the other parameters of the network.

3.2 Multi-head Self-attention Layer

The multi-head self-attention layer is the key layer for the ability to capture long-distance dependencies. Before describing multi-head self-attention, we first describe the (single head) self-attention.

Self-attention: Self-attention layer takes a sequence of input vectors $(\mathbf{x}_0, \mathbf{x}_1, \cdots, \mathbf{x}_{n-1})$ as input and generates another sequence of vectors $(\mathbf{y}_0, \mathbf{y}_1, \cdots, \mathbf{y}_{n-1})$. For each ordered pair $(\mathbf{x}_i, \mathbf{x}_j)$ of input vectors, the self-attention operation computes the attention probability p_{ij} from vector $\mathbf{x}_i$ to vector $\mathbf{x}_j$ based on their similarity (sometimes also based on their positions). Finally, the i-th output vector $\mathbf{y}_i$ is computed using the weighted sum of the input vectors where the weights are given by the attention probabilities i.e. $\mathbf{y}_i = \sum_j p_{ij} \mathbf{x}_j$. Thus, if $\mathbf{x}_i$ and $\mathbf{x}_j$ are two vectors corresponding to the leakages of two PoIs, the state $\mathbf{y}_i$ can accumulate their information in a single step even when the distance between i and j is large. Thus, this step can be useful to combine leakages of multiple PoIs of the input traces (kindly refer to Sect. 5.1 for a detailed discussion).

To describe the self-attention operation more precisely, let $(\mathbf{x}_0, \mathbf{x}_1, \cdots, \mathbf{x}_{n-1})$ and $(\mathbf{y}_0, \mathbf{y}_1, \cdots, \mathbf{y}_{n-1})$ be the sequence of input and output vectors of a self-attention layer where $\mathbf{x}_i, \mathbf{y}_i \in \mathbb{R}^d$ for all i. Then, for each $i = 0, \cdots, n-1$, the i-th output vector $\mathbf{y}_i$ is computed as follows:

1. First the attention scores a_{ij} from i-th element to j-th element, $0 \leq j < n$, is calculated using a scaled dot product similarity measure, i.e.

$$a_{ij} = \frac{\langle W_Q \mathbf{x}_i, W_K \mathbf{x}_j \rangle}{\sqrt{d_k}} = \frac{\langle \mathbf{q}_i, \mathbf{k}_j \rangle}{\sqrt{d_k}} \tag{2}$$

where $W_Q, W_K \in \mathbb{R}^{d_k \times d}$ are trainable weight matrices and $\langle \cdot, \cdot \rangle$ denotes dot product of two vectors. $\mathbf{q}_i, \mathbf{k}_i \in \mathbb{R}^{d_k}$ are respectively known as *query* and *key* representation of the i-th element. Note that the term "key" used here has no relation with the term "(secret) key" used in cryptography.

2. The attention probabilities p_{ij} are computed by taking softmax of the attention scores a_{ij} over the j variable, i.e.,

$$p_{ij} = softmax(a_{ij}; a_{i,0}, \cdots, a_{i,n-1}) = \frac{e^{a_{ij}}}{\sum_{k=0}^{n-1} e^{a_{ik}}} \tag{3}$$

3. The intermediate output $\bar{\mathbf{y}}_i$ is computed by taking the weighted sum of the input vectors $\mathbf{x}_0, \mathbf{x}_1, \cdots, \mathbf{x}_{n-1}$. More precisely,

$$\bar{\mathbf{y}}_i = \sum_{j=0}^{n-1} p_{ij} W_V \mathbf{x}_j = \sum_{j=0}^{n-1} p_{ij} \mathbf{v}_j \tag{4}$$

where $W_V \in \mathbb{R}^{d_v \times d}$ is also a trainable weight matrix and $\mathbf{v}_j = W_V \mathbf{x}_j$ is called the *value* representation of the j-th input vector $\mathbf{x}_j$.

4. The final output $\mathbf{y}_i$ is computed by projecting the $\bar{\mathbf{y}}_i \in \mathbb{R}^{d_v}$ into $\mathbb{R}^d$ by a trainable weight matrix $W_O \in \mathbb{R}^{d \times d_v}$, i.e.

$$\mathbf{y}_i = W_O \bar{\mathbf{y}}_i \tag{5}$$

Thus, the self-attention operation can be written as matrix multiplication in the following way:

$$\bar{Y} = Self\text{-}Attention(W_Q, W_K, W_V) = softmax\,(A)\,XW_V^T = PXW_V^T \qquad (6)$$
$$Y = \bar{Y}W_O^T$$

where $\bar{y}_i$, y_i and x_i denote the ith rows of matrices $\bar{Y}$, Y and X, respectively. W_V^T represents the transpose of the matrix W_V. A and P are two $n \times n$ matrices such that $A[i,j]$ and $P[i,j]$ equals to a_{ij} and p_{ij} respectively.

Multi-head Self-attention: In self-attention, the matrix $\bar{Y}$ created by a set of parameters (W_Q, W_K, W_V) is called a single attention head. In a H-head self-attention operation, H attention heads are used to produce the output. More precisely, the output of a multi-head self attention is computed as

$$\bar{Y}^{(i)} = Self\text{-}Attention(W_Q^{(i)}, W_K^{(i)}, W_V^{(i)}), \text{ for } i = 0, \cdots, H-1$$
$$\bar{Y} = [\bar{Y}^{(0)}, \cdots, \bar{Y}^{(H-1)}]$$
$$Y = \bar{Y}W_O^T \qquad (7)$$

where the function Self $-$ Attention$(\cdot, \cdot, \cdot)$ is defined in Eq. 6, $[A_1, A_2, \cdots, A_n]$ denotes the row-wise concatenation of the matrices A_is and the output projection matrix $W_O \in \mathbb{R}^{d \times Hd_v}$ projects the Hd_v-dimensional vector into $\mathbb{R}^d$. A single head self-attention layer captures the dependency among the elements of the input sequence in one way. An H-head self-attention layer can capture the dependency among those in H-different ways.

3.3   Position-Wise Feed-Forward Layer

Position-wise feed-forward layer is a two layer feed-forward network applied to each element of the input sequence separately and identically. Let FFN$(\mathbf{x})$ be a two layer feed-forward network with ReLU activation [9] and hidden dimension d_i. Then, the output sequence $(y_0, y_1, \cdots, y_{n-1})$ of the position-wise feed-forward layer is computed as $y_i = \text{FFN}(\mathbf{x}_i)$, for $i = 0, 1, \cdots, n-1$ where $(\mathbf{x}_0, \mathbf{x}_1, \cdots, \mathbf{x}_{n-1})$ is the input sequence. The position-wise feed-forward layer helps to increase the non-linearity of the function represented by the TN. The integer hyper-parameter d_i is commonly referred to as inner dimension. In Table 1, we summarize the notations used to describe the transformer network.

In the standard architecture, as described above, there are several design choices for TN which are relevant in the context of SCA. We found that the *positional encoding* and *layer normalization* need to be chosen properly to use TN for SCA. Thus, we describe those, one by one.

3.4   Positional Encoding

Both the self-attention layer and position-wise feed-forward layer are oblivious to the ordering of the elements of the input sequence. Thus, to capture the input

Table 1. Notations used to denote the hyper-parameters of a transformer network

Notation	Description	Notation	Description
d	model dimension	d_k	key dimension
d_v	value dimension	d_i	inner dimension
n	input or trace length	H	# of heads in
L	# of transformer layers		self-attention layer

order, positional encoding is used in TN. Two kinds of positional encodings are commonly used in TN: 1) absolute positional encoding and 2) relative positional encoding. To achieve shift-invariance, we have used relative positional encoding. Thus, here we provide the details of the relative positional encoding.

Relative Positional Encoding: The relative positional encoding is introduced in [30]. In relative positional encoding, the attention score from i-th input element to j-th input element is made dependent on their relative position or distance $i - j$. [8] have further improved the scheme of [30]. In their proposed relative positional encoding, the attention score of Eq. 2 is modified to be computed as

$$a_{ij} = \frac{\langle W_Q x_i, W_K x_j \rangle + \langle W_Q x_i, r_{i-j} \rangle + \langle W_Q x_i, s \rangle + \langle r_{i-j}, t \rangle}{\sqrt{d_k}} \tag{8}$$

where the vectors $(r_{-n+1}, \cdots, r_0, \cdots, r_{n-1})$ are the relative positional encoding and are also learned during training. Finally, as before, the attention probabilities are computed as

$$p_{ij} = \text{softmax}(a_{ij}; a_{i,0}, \cdots, a_{i,n-1}) = \frac{e^{a_{ij}}}{\sum_{k=0}^{n-1} e^{a_{ik}}} \tag{9}$$

In our TN model for SCA, we have used the relative positional encoding given by Eq. (8). In Sect. 5.2, we have shown that the TN with this relative positional encoding possesses shift-invariance property.

3.5   Layer Normalization

Layer normalization is commonly used in transformer layers. It is used in two ways: "post-layer normalization" (Fig. 1a) and "pre-layer normalization" (Fig. 1b). In the context of a SCA, we have found that using any layer normalization in the network makes the network difficult to train. We speculate that the layer normalization removes the informative data-dependent variations from traces, effectively making the input independent of the target labels. Thus, in our TN model, we have not used any layer normalization layer (Fig. 1c).

In the previous section, we have described the general architecture of TN. In the next section, we describe our proposed TN-based model – TransNet.

Algorithm 2: Forward pass of an L-layer TransNet Architecture

---

1 **begin**

      // embed input sequence using a 1D convolutional layer

2      $\mathbf{x}_0^0, \mathbf{x}_1^0 \cdots, \mathbf{x}_{n-1}^0 \leftarrow \text{Conv1D}(x_0, x_1, \cdots, x_{n-1})$

      // optionally perform average-pooling to reduce sequence length

3      $\mathbf{x}_0^0, \mathbf{x}_1^0 \cdots, \mathbf{x}_{m-1}^0 \leftarrow \text{AvgPool}(\mathbf{x}_0^0, \mathbf{x}_1^0 \cdots, \mathbf{x}_{n-1}^0)$

4 **for** $l \leftarrow 1$ *to* L **do**

      // apply self-attention operation

5      $\mathbf{s}_0, \mathbf{s}_1, \cdots, \mathbf{s}_{m-1} \leftarrow \text{RelPositionalMultiHeadSelfAttn}^l(\mathbf{x}_0^{l-1}, \mathbf{x}_1^{l-1}, \cdots, \mathbf{x}_{m-1}^{l-1})$

      // add shortcut connection

6      $\mathbf{s}_0, \mathbf{s}_1, \cdots, \mathbf{s}_{m-1} \leftarrow \mathbf{s}_0 + \mathbf{x}_0^{l-1}, \mathbf{s}_1 + \mathbf{x}_1^{l-1}, \cdots, \mathbf{s}_{m-1} + \mathbf{x}_{m-1}^{l-1}$

      // apply position-wise feed-forward operation

7      $\mathbf{t}_0, \mathbf{t}_1, \cdots, \mathbf{t}_{m-1} \leftarrow \text{PoswiseFF}^l(\mathbf{s}_0, \mathbf{s}_1, \cdots, \mathbf{s}_{m-1})$

      // add shortcut connection

8      $\mathbf{x}_0^l, \mathbf{x}_1^l, \cdots, \mathbf{x}_{m-1}^l \leftarrow \mathbf{t}_0 + \mathbf{s}_0, \mathbf{t}_1 + \mathbf{s}_1, \cdots, \mathbf{t}_{m-1} + \mathbf{s}_{m-1}$

      // apply global average-pooling

9 $\bar{\mathbf{y}} \leftarrow \text{GlobalAvgPooling}(\mathbf{x}_0^l, \mathbf{x}_1^l, \cdots, \mathbf{x}_{m-1}^l)$

      // get class-probabilities by applying a classification layer

10 $p_0, p_1, \cdots, p_{C-1} \leftarrow \text{ClassificationLayer}(\bar{\mathbf{y}})$

11 **return** $(p_0, p_1, \cdots, p_{C-1})$

---

4 TransNet: A Transformer Network for SCA

TransNet is a multi-layer TN followed by a global pooling layer. The schematic diagram of TransNet is shown in Fig. 2, and the forward pass is described in Algorithm 2. It uses a one-dimensional convolutional layer as an embedding layer. The convolutional layer is followed by an average-pooling layer[2] which is followed by several transformer layers. The transformer layers are followed by a global pooling layer, a classification layer, and a softmax layer. Note that, unlike standard transformer layers, the TransNet layers do not use any layer normalization (Fig. 1c). Moreover, in the self-attention layers, relative positional encoding as given by Eq. (8) and (9) has been used instead of more common absolute positional encoding. In Sect. 5.2, we have shown that the relative positional encoding scheme makes the TN shift-invariant. We trained the TransNet model using cross-entropy loss, and Adam optimizer [15]. We have used cosine decay with a linear warm-up [38] as the learning rate scheduling algorithm.

Shift-invariance and the ability to capture the dependency among distant PoIs are two important properties to make a deep learning model effective against trace misalignments and masking countermeasures, respectively. In the next section, we explain how TransNet (in general TN) can capture the depen-

---

[2] Setting the pool size and stride of the average pooling layer to 1, the model will behave as if there is no average pooling layer. However, setting those values to a larger value will make the model computationally efficient at the cost of attack efficacy and shift-invariance.

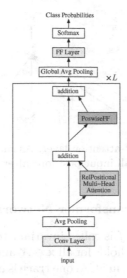

Fig. 2. Complete architecture of TransNet.

dency among distant sample points. We also mathematically show that a TN with relative positional encoding (TransNet in particular) is shift-invariant.

5   Long Distance Dependency and Shift-Invariance

5.1   Learning Long Distance Dependency Using TN

The PoIs remain spread over a long distance in power traces for many implementations. For example, in many software implementations of masking countermeasure, different shares leak at different sample points in the power traces. Moreover, the distance between the PoIs corresponding to different shares might be significantly large. Thus, a successful attack against those implementations requires capturing the dependency among those distant PoIs. The problem of learning dependency between distant sample points is known as the problem of learning long-distance dependency. This problem has been widely studied in the deep learning literature [12,32]. To be able to capture the dependence between two elements of the input sequence, the signal from the two input elements should be propagated to each other by the forward and backward passes through the layers of the deep neural network. Moreover, a shorter path between the two elements makes it easier to learn their dependency, whereas a longer path makes it difficult [32]. As can be seen in Fig. 3, the self-attention layer can connect any elements of the input sequence using a constant number of steps. Thus, TN is very good at capturing long-distance dependency. In fact, in [32], Vaswani et al. have argued that TN is better than both CNN and RNN in capturing long-distance dependency. This property of TN makes it a natural choice for a SCA against many cryptographic implementations.

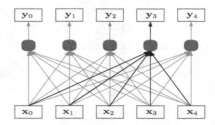

Fig. 3. Signal flow through a self-attention layer. As shown in the figure, each output position becomes dependent on all input positions after a single self-attention layer.

5.2   Shift-Invariance of Transformer Network

In computer vision, a function f is called invariant to a set of transformations T from $\mathcal{X}$ to $\mathcal{X}$ if $f(\mathbf{x}) = f(T(\mathbf{x}))$ holds for all $\mathbf{x} \in \mathcal{X}$ and $T \in \mathcal{T}$. In SCA, the inputs are generally very noisy. In fact, in SCA, one trace is often not sufficient to predict the correct key; instead, information from multiple traces is required to extract for the same. Thus, in this context, we are interested in the information contained in $f(\mathbf{X})$ about the sensitive variable Z where $\mathbf{X}$ represents the random variable corresponding to the power traces. Thus, for SCA, the invariance property can be defined in terms of $\mathbb{P}[f(\mathbf{X})|Z]$. However, for the sake of simplicity, we define the shift-invariance property only in terms of the conditional expectation $\mathbb{E}[f(\mathbf{X})|Z]$. Thus, in the context of SCA, we define the following weaker notion of invariance.

Definition 1. *A function f is said to be invariant to a set of transformation T with associated probability distribution function $\mathcal{D}_T$ if*

$$\mathbb{E}[f(\mathbf{X})|Z] = \mathbb{E}[f(T(\mathbf{X}))|Z] \tag{10}$$

holds where $T \sim \mathcal{D}_T$ and $\mathbf{X}$, Z are random variables respectively, representing the input and intermediate sensitive variable. $\mathbb{E}[\cdot|Z]$ represents the conditional expectation where the expectation is taken over all relevant random variables other than Z.

This section shows that a single layer TN model followed by a global pooling layer is shift-invariant. Towards that goal, we define the network architecture, leakage model, and the set of shift-transformations considered for the proof.

The Transformer Model: As stated in the previous paragraph, we consider a single layer TN followed by a global pooling layer. The result can be extended for multilayer TN, albeit with some minor errors arising because of the finite length of the input. Note that for the input of finite length, such errors also arise for CNN models [35]. In the rest of the section, we denote the single layer TN followed by the global pooling layer as TN_{1L}. The output of TN_{1L} can be given by the following operations:

$$\mathbf{Y}_0, \cdots, \mathbf{Y}_{n-1} = RelPositionalSelfAttention(\mathbf{X}_0, \cdots, \mathbf{X}_{n-1})$$
$$\mathbf{U}_0, \cdots, \mathbf{U}_{n-1} = \mathbf{Y}_0 + \mathbf{X}_0, \cdots, \mathbf{Y}_{n-1} + \mathbf{X}_{n-1} \qquad (11)$$
$$\mathbf{U}_0', \cdots, \mathbf{U}_{n-1}' = \mathrm{FFN}(\mathbf{U}_0), \cdots, \mathrm{FFN}(\mathbf{U}_{n-1})$$
$$\mathbf{U}_0'', \cdots, \mathbf{U}_{n-1}'' = \mathbf{U}_0' + \mathbf{U}_0, \cdots, \mathbf{U}_{n-1}' + \mathbf{U}_{n-1}$$

Finally the output of $\mathrm{TN}_{1\mathrm{L}}$ is defined as

$$\mathrm{TN}_{1\mathrm{L}}(\mathbf{X}_0, \cdots, \mathbf{X}_{n-1}) = \frac{1}{n} \sum_{i=0}^{n-1} \mathbf{U}_i'' \qquad (12)$$

where $(\mathbf{X}_0, \cdots, \mathbf{X}_{n-1})$ is the sequence of random vectors corresponding to the input of the network, $\mathrm{TN}_{1\mathrm{L}}(\mathbf{X}_0, \cdots, \mathbf{X}_{n-1})$ is the random vector corresponding to the final output (i.e. the output of global average pooling) of the network which is fed to a classification layer for the classification task. $RelPositionalSelfAttention(\cdots)$ and $\mathrm{FFN}(\cdot)$ respectively represent the self-attention and position-wise feed-forward operations. The description of the single layer TN is given in Fig. 1c. Note that $RelPositionalSelfAttention(\cdots)$ is the self-attention operation implemented using relative positional encoding. In other words, the attention scores and attention probabilities in the self-attention layer are computed by Eqs. (8) and (9).

The Leakage Model: We consider the leakage model of the software implementation of a first-order masking scheme. However, the results can be easily extended for any higher-order masking scheme. Thus, we take the following assumptions:

Assumption 1 (Second Order Leakage Assumption). *In the sequence of input vectors $(\mathbf{X}_{-n+1+m_2}, \cdots, \mathbf{X}_0, \cdots, \mathbf{X}_{n-1}, \cdots, \mathbf{X}_{n-1+m_1})$, the input vectors $\mathbf{X}_{m_1}$ and $\mathbf{X}_{m_2}$ $(0 \le m_1 < m_2 < n, m_2 - m_1 = l > 0)$ are the leakages corresponding to the mask M and masked sensitive variable $Z_M = Z \oplus M$ where Z is the sensitive variable. Thus, we can write $\mathbf{X}_{m_1} = f_1(M) + \mathbf{N}_1$ and $\mathbf{X}_{m_1+l} = f_2(Z_M) + \mathbf{N}_2$ where $f_1, f_2 : \mathbb{R} \mapsto \mathbb{R}^d$ are two deterministic functions of M, Z_M respectively and $\mathbf{N}_1, \mathbf{N}_2 \in \mathbb{R}^d$ are the noise component of $\mathbf{X}_{m_1}$ and $\mathbf{X}_{m_1+l}$ respectively. Note that, $\mathbf{N}_1$ and $\mathbf{N}_2$ are independent of both M and Z_M. The objective of the network is to learn a mapping from $\{\mathbf{X}_{m_1}, \mathbf{X}_{m_1+l}\}$ to Z.*

Assumption 2 (IID Assumption). *All the vectors $\{\mathbf{X}_i\}_{-n+m_2 < i < n+m_1}$ are identically distributed. Moreover, all the variables of the set $\{\mathbf{X}_i\}_{i \ne m_1, m_1+l}$ are mutually independent. Additionally, $\mathbf{X}_{m_1}$ and $\mathbf{X}_{m_1+l}$ are independent to the rest of the random variables i.e. $\{\mathbf{X}_i\}_{i \ne m_1, m_1+l}$.*

Note that the assumptions considered in the above leakage model, are very well-known assumptions for a first-order masking scheme. In fact, previous studies [18,31] have taken such assumptions to generate synthetic power traces.

The Shift Transformations: We define the set of shift transformations to be all shift transformations for which the PoIs (i.e. the leakage points corresponding to the two shares: M and $Z_M = Z \oplus M$) do not go out of the trace window, the range of time instances of traces considered for the attack. More precisely, we define the set of transformations $\mathcal{T}^{\text{shift}}$ as

$$\mathcal{T}^{\text{shift}} = \{T^s : s \in \mathbb{Z} \text{ and } -m_1 \leq s < n - m_2\}$$

where, $T^s(\mathbf{X}_{-n+1+m_2}, \cdots, \mathbf{X}_0, \cdots, \mathbf{X}_{n-1}, \cdots, \mathbf{X}_{n-1+m_1}) = \mathbf{X}_{0-s}, \cdots, \mathbf{X}_{n-1-s}$

In other words, the set of shift transformations $\mathcal{T}^{\text{shift}}$ consists of transformations T^s, where $-m_1 \leq s < n - m_2$, which shifts the input trace by s positions. The bound $-m_1 \leq s < n - m_2$ on the value of s ensures that the PoIs m_1 and m_2 do not go out of the window because of the shift operations. Note that the input to the transformations is a trace of size larger than n, which is required as, during the shift operations, some sample points go out of the window, and some sample points enter into the window.

Next, we state Lemma 1 which will lead us to our last assumption.

Lemma 1. *For any $0 < \epsilon < 1$, the parameters W_Q, W_K, $\{\mathbf{r}_{-n+1}, \cdots, \mathbf{r}_0, \cdots, \mathbf{r}_{n-1}\}$ and $\mathbf{t}$ of the transformer layer of TN_{1L} can be set such that $p_{i,i+l} > 1 - \epsilon$ for all $i = 0, \cdots, n-1-l$, and $p_{ij} = 1/n$ for all $i = n-l, \cdots, n-1$ and $j = 0, \cdots, n-1$ hold where $W_Q, W_K, p_{ij}, \{\mathbf{r}_{-n+1}, \cdots, \mathbf{r}_0, \cdots, \mathbf{r}_{n-1}\}$ and $\mathbf{t}$ are as defined in Eq. (8) and (9) and l is the distance between the two PoIs.*

Thus, according to Lemma 1, the attention probabilities can be such that the attention from the i-th sample point, for $0 \leq i < n - l$, can be mostly concentrated to the $(i + l)$-th sample point. Moreover, the attention probability $p_{i,i+l}$ can be made arbitrarily close to 1. Thus, to keep our main result (Proposition 1) simple, we take the following assumption on the trained TN_{1L} model:

Assumption 3. *$P_{i,i+l} = 1$ for $0 \leq i < n - l$ where $P_{i,j}$ is the random variable representing the attention probability from i-th sample point to j-th sample point (and is defined by Eq. (9)) in the transformer layer of TN_{1L}. For $n - l \leq i < n$, $P_{i,j} = 1/n$ for all $j = 0, \cdots, n-1$.*

Note that Assumption 3 can be approximately realized in practice when we use a relative positional encoding.

With Assumption 1, 2 and 3, we summarize the main result in Proposition 1.

Proposition 1. *There exists a set of parameters for which TN_{1L} satisfies the following equation:*

$$\mathbb{E}\left[TN_{1L}(T(\mathbf{X}_{-n+1+m_2}, \cdots, \mathbf{X}_{n-1+m_1}))|Z\right] = \mathbb{E}\left[TN_{1L}(\mathbf{X}_0, \cdots, \mathbf{X}_{n-1})|Z\right] \quad (13)$$

where T is a shift transformation drawn from any arbitrary distribution $\mathcal{D}_{\mathcal{T}^{\text{shift}}}$ over the set $\mathcal{T}^{\text{shift}}$ and the conditional expectations are taken over all the relevant variables other than Z.

Thus, according to Proposition 1, TN_{1L} is shift invariant. In Sect. 6.6, we have experimentally verified the shift-invariance of TransNet.

In the next section, we provide the experimental results of TransNet.

6 Experimental Results

In this section, we experimentally evaluate the efficacy of TransNet. In Sect. 6.1 to 6.3, we summarize the dataset details, hyperparameter settings and the state-of-the-art-methods to which TransNet has been compared with. Section 6.4 and 6.5 compare TransNet with other state-of-the-art methods on four different datasets. Finally, in Sect. 6.6, we verify the shift invariance of TransNet.

6.1 Datasets Details

For comparing TransNet with other methods, we have used the following datasets.

ASCAD: ASCAD datasets have been introduced by [3]. The original dataset is a collection of 60, 000 traces of a first-order masked implementation of AES in a software platform. Each trace contains 100, 000 sample points. From the original dataset, they have further created three datasets named *ASCAD_desync0*, *ASCAD_desync50*, and *ASCAD_desync100*. The *ASCAD_desync0* has been created without any desynchronization of the traces. However, *ASCAD_desync50* and *ASCAD_desync100* have been created by randomly shifting the traces where the length of random displacements have been generated from a uniform distribution in the range [0, 50) in case of *ASCAD_desync50* and [0, 100) in case of *ASCAD_desync100*. Note that the random displacements have been added to both the profiling and attack traces. Each of the three derived datasets contains 50, 000 traces for profiling and 10, 000 traces for the attack. For computational efficiency, the length of each trace is reduced by keeping only 700 sample points that correspond to the interval [45400, 46100) of the original traces.

We created two more datasets namely *ASCAD_desync200* and *ASCAD_desync400* using the API provided by [3]. As the name suggests, we have misaligned the traces by a random displacement in the range [0, 200) for *ASCAD_desync200* dataset and [0, 400) for *ASCAD_desync400* dataset. Each trace of the two derived datasets is 1500 sample point long and corresponds to the interval [45000, 46500) of the original traces. We provide a summary of the derived datasets in Table 2.

Table 2. Summary of the ASCAD datasets.

	desync0	desync50	desync100	desync200	desync400
Profiling dataset size	50000	50000	50000	50000	50000
Attack dataset size	10000	10000	10000	10000	10000
Indices of profiling traces	[0, 50000)	[0, 50000)	[0, 50000)	[0, 50000)	[0, 50000)
Indices of attack traces	[50000, 60000)	[50000, 60000)	[50000, 60000)	[50000, 60000)	[50000, 60000)
Trace length	700	700	700	1500	1500
Target points	[45400, 46100)	[45400, 46100)	[45400, 46100)	[45000, 46500)	[45000, 46500)
Profiling dataset desync	0	50	100	200	400
Attack dataset desync	0	50	100	200	400

DPA contest v4.2: *DPA contest v4.2* dataset [4] contains traces of a software implementation of AES. The implementation is protected by Rotating SBOX Masking (RSM). Following [37], we have assumed the mask to be known. Thus, the implementation behaves like an unprotected implementation.

Table 3. Details of the DPA contest v4.2, AES RD and AES HD datasets.

	DPA contest v4.2	AES RD	AES HD
Profiling dataset size	4500	25000	50000
Attack dataset size	500	25000	25000
Trace length	4000	3500	1250

AES RD: AES RD [7] contains the traces of a software implementation of AES protected by random delay countermeasure. The sensitive variable is taken to be the first round sbox operation. We have used the same train-test split which has been used in [37].

AES HD: AES HD [27] contains the traces of an unprotected AES implemented on FPGA. The trace window corresponds to the register update of the last round. Like *AES RD* dataset, for this dataset also, we have used the train-test split used in [37]. The statistics of the *DPA contest v4.2, AES RD* and *AES HD* are summarized in Table 3.

6.2   Other State-of-the-Art Methods

We have compared TransNet with the following methods:

CNNBest: The *CNNBest* model has been introduced in [3]. To evaluate *CNNBest* model on *ASCAD_desync0, ASCAD_desync50* and *ASCAD_desync100* datasets, we have used the trained model provided by the authors in their official GitHub repository[3]. For the evaluation on *ASCAD_desync200* and *ASCAD_desync400* datasets, we have trained the model on the two datasets using their code.

EffCNN: In [37], Zaid et al. have proposed a methodology for constructing CNN-based models that are robust to trace misalignments. For comparison with TransNet, we built the models following their methodology for different datasets.

SimplifiedEffCNN: In [34], the authors have suggested removing the first convolutional and batch normalization layer of the *EffCNN* models. These simplified *EffCNN* models are easier to train and provide an improvement in results over *EffCNN*. Thus, we also compare *SimplifiedEffCNN* models with TransNet.

DilatedCNN: In [23], Paguada et al. have used dilated convolutional layer to capture long distance dependency. Thus, we compare TransNet with their approach. We created two models similar to *EffCNN* models and replaced the first convolutional layer of the models with dilated convolution. We trained and tuned the *DilatedCNN* models for additional four sets of hyper-parameters: $[l_k = 16, dr = 4]$, $[l_k = 16, dr = 6]$, $[l_k = 32, dr = 3]$ and $[l_k = 64, dr = 2]$ where l_k and dr are the kernel width and dilation rate of the first convolutional layer.

---

[3] https://github.com/ANSSI-FR/ASCAD.git

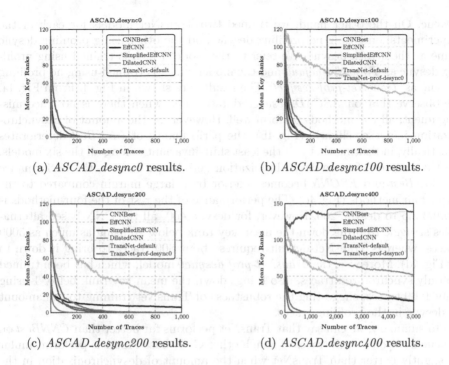

Fig. 4. Comparison with the CNN-based models on the *ASCAD* datasets. *TransNet-default* and *TransNet-prof-desync0* respectively denote the TransNet model trained with and without using profiling desynchronization. All the CNN-based models have been trained using profiling desync same as attack desync.

6.3 Hyper-parameter Setting of TransNet

Like in [3,17,37], we have used the identity leakage model. For all the experiments, we have set the number of transformer layers to 2, model dimension d to 128, the dimension of the key vectors and value vectors (i.e. d_k and d_v) to 64 and the number of heads H to 2. We set the kernel width of the convolutional layer to 11. For *ASCAD, DPA contest 4.2, AES RD* and *AES HD* datasets, the pool-size hyper-parameter has been set to 1, 4, 4 and 2 respectively. The pool-size hyper-parameter has been set to make the trace length less than 1000. The other hyper-parameter values have been set based on some initial experiments on the ASCAD dataset, which also worked well for the other datasets. We have also experimentally seen that TransNet performs equally well for a wide range of values of those hyper-parameters.

6.4 Results on ASCAD Datasets

This section compares TransNet with the other state-of-the-art methods on ASCAD datasets based on trace counts required to perform the attacks. All the CNN-based models have been trained using profiling desync, same as attack desync. On the other hand, we trained two TransNet models for each of the experiments: one using no profiling desync and the other using profiling desync same as the attack desync. We refer to the model which is trained using profiling desync as *TransNet-default* and the model which is trained using no profiling desync as *TransNet-prof-desync0*. The results are shown in Fig. 4. From Fig. 4a, we observe that on *ASCAD_desync0* dataset, i.e., when there is no trace misalignment, all the methods perform well. However, as the amount of desynchronization increases slightly (Fig. 4b), the performance of *CNNBest* deteriorates drastically, indicating that it is the least shift-invariant among all the six models. As the amount of trace desynchronization gets larger further, the performance of *CNNBest* and *EffCNN* becomes inferior by a large margin compared to the other four methods (Fig. 4c). The performance of the rest of the four methods is similar up to desync 200. However, for desync 400, all the CNN-based alternatives struggle to bring down the mean key rank below 20 using as much as 5000 traces, whereas TransNet-default requires about 800 traces to bring it down to 0 (Fig. 4d). Moreover, the *TransNet-prof-desync0* model, which has been trained on only synchronized traces, also brings down the mean key rank below 1 using only 1000 traces, suggesting the robustness of TransNet training to the amount of desync in the profiling traces.

In summary, we can say that TransNet performs far better than *CNNBest* on desynchronized attack traces. Though other CNN-based models perform similar or slightly better than TransNet when the amount of desynchronization in the attack traces is comparatively small, their performances get poor as the amount of desynchronization crosses a threshold[4]. Moreover, TransNet can perform very well on highly desynchronized attack traces even when the model is trained on only synchronized traces.

In the next section, we provide experimental results on the other datasets.

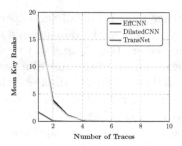

Fig. 5. Results on *DPA contest v4.2* dataset.

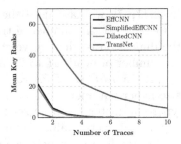

Fig. 6. Results on *AES RD* dataset.

---

[4] Note that the length of the power traces of the software implementations is typically in the order of 1e5. For example, the traces of the ASCAD dataset are 100000 points long. Thus, a desync value such as 400 is possible in those traces.

6.5 Experimental Results on the Other Datasets

In this section, we compare TransNet with the CNN-based models on *DPA contest v4.2*, *AES RD* and *AES HD* datasets (please refer to Sect. 6.1 for the details of the datasets). For the experiments on *DPA contest v4.2* and *AES RD* datasets, we set the *pool_size* hyper-parameter of TransNet to 4 and for *AES HD* dataset, we set it to 2. We have tuned the hyper-parameter *train_step* though we found that setting it to 30000 works very well across all three datasets. All other hyper-parameters are kept the same as in the experiments on the ASCAD dataset. For the experiments on *AES HD* dataset, we have trained TransNet as an ensemble of bit-models as proposed in [39]. In the ensemble of bit-models, each bit of the label is predicted independently. Thus, the rest of the model and the training process remain the same apart from the classification layer.

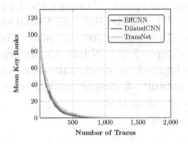
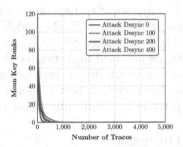

Fig. 7. Results on *AES HD* dataset.   **Fig. 8.** Shift-invariance of *TransNet*.

The results on *DPA contest v4.2*, *AES RD* and *AES HD* datasets are respectively shown in Figs. 5, 6 and 7. The figures show that TransNet performs better than the CNN-based counterparts on *DPA contest v4.2* and *AES RD* whereas slightly worse on *AES HD*. In particular, on the *DPA contest v4.2* and *AES RD*, the TransNet models bring down the mean key rank below 1 using at most two attack traces, whereas the CNN-based models require at least four for the same. Such a difference in the number of required traces may be critical for the success of the attack when the cipher is used in some leakage resilient mode [24]. For example, many existing leakage resilient modes assume 2-simulatability where at most two observations are available for a single key. A successful attack using 2 traces implies that the schemes are not secure.

In the next section, we verify the shift-invariance property of TransNet.

6.6 Verifying the Shift Invariance of TransNet

In Sect. 5.2, we have mathematically shown that TransNet is shift-invariant. To examine whether this property persists in practice, we performed experiments on the ASCAD datasets described in Sect. 6.1. To evaluate the achieved shift-invariance of the TransNet models, we trained the models on synchronized traces and evaluated on desynchronized traces. Note that the length of traces of the first three datasets namely *ASCAD_desync0*, *ASCAD_desync50* and *ASCAD_desync100* is 700 and the last two derived datasets namely *ASCAD_desync200* and *ASCAD_desync400* is 1500. Thus, we trained two TransNet models. The first one was trained for trace length 700 and we evaluated it on *ASCAD_desync0*, *ASCAD_desync50* and *ASCAD_desync100* datasets. The second model was trained for trace length 1500 and we evaluated that model on the *ASCAD_desync200* and *ASCAD_desync400* datasets. Both the models were trained using only aligned traces. The results are plotted in Fig. 8.

The figure shows that the results get only slightly worse as desynchronization in the attack traces increases. Thus, it can be considered as strong evidence for achieving almost shift-invariance by the TransNet models. On the other hand, interleaving of pooling layers with the convolution layers or using of the flattening layer reduces the shift-invariance of the CNN models [35]. As a result, the existing state-of-the-art CNN models fail to perform well on desynchronized attack traces while trained on synchronized profiling traces. To verify the fact, we also trained the EffCNN models on *ASCAD_desync0* dataset and tested on *ASCAD_desync100*, *ASCAD_desync200* and *ASCAD_desync400* datasets. The results are provided in Appendix D. The results imply EffCNN fails to perform well as the attack desync gets larger when it is trained on synchronized traces. Thus, TransNet is a better choice when the amount of desynchronization in attack traces is significantly larger than that of profiling traces.

7   Discussion

Though TransNet has outperformed the CNN-based state-of-the-art models on several datasets, the quadratic time and memory complexity with respect to the trace length limit its applicability to shorter attack windows (in the order of 1000). However, the trace length can be larger in many practical scenarios. One way to extend TransNet to traces of such length is by using linear or log-linear TN. We take the exploration of those variations for SCA as future work. Instead, in the current work, we choose to demonstrate the efficacy of TN for limited length traces. Our experimental results suggest that TransNet is a better alternative to the other models in many such scenarios in terms of attack efficacy.

Our experimental results suggest that the existing CNN-based state-of-the-art models fail to perform well on highly desynchronized traces. One way to improve the performance of the CNN models in such scenarios is by replacing the flattening layer with the global pooling layer in the models. We have compared one such model in Appendix C with TransNet on highly desynchronized *ASCAD_desync400* dataset. The results suggest that the performance of CNN models is still worse than TransNet. However, we agree that it might be possible to tune the CNN models further to improve their performance.

8   Conclusion

In this work, we have introduced TN in the context of profiling SCA. TN is good at capturing the dependency among the distant PoIs, which makes it a natural choice against many masked implementations. Moreover, we have shown that TN can also be made shift-invariant using some design choices. The shift-invariance of TN makes it highly effective against misaligned traces as well. Based on the above advantages of TN, we have proposed TransNet, a TN-based deep learning model for performing SCA. We have also experimentally evaluated the proposed model on four datasets. It is better than or comparable to other state-of-the-art methods on the four datasets. The advantage of TransNet over existing state-of-the-art methods is particularly observable when the traces are highly desynchronized. In those situations, TransNet can bring down the guessing entropy to zero using a very small number of attack traces, whereas the other methods fail to bring it down below 20. Additionally, TransNet can perform very well on highly desynchronized attack traces even when trained on synchronized profiling traces showing its low dependence on profiling desync for better training. The results suggest that TransNet provides a viable alternative to existing CNN-based models for SCA.

A   Proof of Lemma 1

The attention probabilities in the self-attention layer of TN_{1L} is calculated following Eqs. (8) and (9). If we set W_Q, W_K, $\{r_i\}_{i \neq l}$ all to zero of appropriate dimensions, $r_l = c\sqrt{d_k}\mathbf{1}$ and $\mathbf{t} = \mathbf{1}$ where $\mathbf{1}$ is a vector whose only first element is 1 and rest are zero, and c is a real constant in Eq. (8) and Eq. (9), we have p_{ij} equals to $\frac{e^c}{e^c+n-1}$ if $j = i+l$ and $\frac{1}{e^c+n-1}$ otherwise for $0 \leq i < n - l$. Setting $c > \ln\left(\frac{1-\epsilon}{\epsilon}\right) + \ln(n-1)$, we get $p_{i,i+l} > 1 - \epsilon$ for all $0 \leq i < n-l$ and $0 < \epsilon < 1$. Similarly, it is straight forward to show that $p_{ij} = 1/n$ for any $n - l \leq i < n$ and $0 \leq j < n$ for the same value of the parameters.

B   Proof of Proposition 1

From the Eqs (11), we have $\mathbf{U}_i = \mathbf{Y}_i + \mathbf{X}_i$, $\mathbf{U}_i'' = FFN(\mathbf{U}_i) + \mathbf{U}_i$, for $i = 0, \cdots, n - 1$ where $\mathbf{Y}_0, \mathbf{Y}_1, \cdots, \mathbf{Y}_{n-1} = RelPositionalSelfAttention(\mathbf{X}_0, \mathbf{X}_1, \cdots, \mathbf{X}_{n-1})$. And the output of TN_{1L} is given by $TN_{1L}(\mathbf{X}_0, \cdots, \mathbf{X}_{n-1}) = \frac{1}{n}\sum_{i=0}^{n-1}\mathbf{U}_i''$. From Eq. (4) and (5), we get $\mathbf{Y}_j = W_O\left(\sum_{k=0}^{n-1}P_{jk}W_V\mathbf{X}_k\right)$. Thus, we can write $\mathbf{Y}_{m_1}$ (where m_1 is defined in Assumption 1) as

$$\mathbf{Y}_{m_1} = W_O\left(\sum_{k=0}^{n-1}P_{m_1k}W_V\mathbf{X}_k\right) = W_O W_V \mathbf{X}_{m_1+l}, \text{ and thus} \tag{a2}$$

$$\mathbf{U}_{m_1} = W_O W_V \mathbf{X}_{m_1+l} + \mathbf{X}_{m_1} \tag{a3}$$

Equation (a2) follows since $i = m_1$ satisfies $P_{i,i+l} = 1$ in Assumption 3. Similarly we can write $\mathbf{Y}_i$ for $0 \leq i < n - l, i \neq m_1$ as

$$\mathbf{Y}_i = W_O\left(\sum_{k=0}^{n-1}P_{ik}W_V\mathbf{X}_k\right) = W_O W_V \mathbf{X}_{i+l}, \text{ and thus} \tag{a4}$$

$$\mathbf{U}_i = W_O W_V \mathbf{X}_{i+l} + \mathbf{X}_i \tag{a5}$$

For $n - l \leq i < n$, we can write

$$\mathbf{Y}_i = \frac{1}{n} \mathbf{W}_O \mathbf{W}_V \sum_{k=0}^{n-1} \mathbf{X}_k \quad \text{and,} \quad \mathbf{U}_i = \frac{1}{n} \mathbf{W}_O \mathbf{W}_V \sum_{k=0}^{n-1} \mathbf{X}_k + \mathbf{X}_i$$

since, by Assumption 3, $P_{ij} = 1/n$ for $j = 0, \cdots, n-1$ and $n - l \leq i < n$. Now we compute $\mathbf{U}_i''$ for $i = 0, \cdots, n-1$.

$$\mathbf{U}_i'' = FFN(\mathbf{U}_i) + \mathbf{U}_i \tag{a6}$$

Note that among all the $\{\mathbf{U}_i''\}_{0 \leq i < n}$, only $\mathbf{U}_{m_1}''$ and $\{\mathbf{U}_i''\}_{n-l \leq i < n}$ involve both the terms $\mathbf{X}_{m_1}$ and $\mathbf{X}_{m_1+l}$, thus can be dependent on the sensitive variable Z (from Assumption 1). Rest of the $\mathbf{U}_i''$s are independent of Z (from Assumption 2). The output of $\text{TN}_{1\text{L}}$ can be written as

$$\text{TN}_{1\text{L}}(\mathbf{X}_0, \cdots, \mathbf{X}_{n-1}) = \frac{1}{n} \sum_{i=0}^{n} \mathbf{U}_i'' = \frac{1}{n} \mathbf{U}_{m_1}'' + \frac{1}{n} \sum_{0 \leq i < n-l, i \neq m_1} \mathbf{U}_i'' + \frac{1}{n} \sum_{n-l \leq i < n} \mathbf{U}_i'' \tag{a7}$$

The expectation of the output conditioned on Z can be given by

$$\mathbb{E}[\text{TN}_{1\text{L}}(\mathbf{X}_0, \cdots, \mathbf{X}_{n-1})|Z] = \frac{1}{n} \mathbb{E}[\mathbf{U}_{m_1}''|Z] + \frac{1}{n} \sum_{n-l \leq i < n} \mathbb{E}[\mathbf{U}_i''|Z] + \frac{1}{n} \sum_{0 \leq i < n-l, i \neq m_1} \mathbb{E}[\mathbf{U}_i''] \tag{a8}$$

The second step follows because the random variables $\{\mathbf{U}_i\}_{0 \leq i < n-l, i \neq m_1}$ are independent of Z. To complete the proof, we compute

$$\mathbb{E}\left[\text{TN}_{1\text{L}}(T^s(\mathbf{X}_{-n+1+m_2}, \cdots, \mathbf{X}_{n-1+m_1}))|Z\right] \tag{a9}$$
$$= \mathbb{E}\left[\text{TN}_{1\text{L}}(\mathbf{X}_{-s}, \cdots, \mathbf{X}_{n-1-s})|Z\right]$$
$$= \frac{1}{n} \mathbb{E}[\mathbf{U}_{m_1}''|Z] + \frac{1}{n} \sum_{n-l-s \leq i < n-s} \mathbb{E}[\mathbf{U}_i''|Z] + \frac{1}{n} \sum_{-s \leq i < n-l-s, i \neq m_1} \mathbb{E}\left[\mathbf{U}_i''\right]$$

From Assumption 2, we get

$$\frac{1}{n} \sum_{n-l \leq i < n} \mathbb{E}\left[\mathbf{U}_i''|Z\right] = \frac{1}{n} \sum_{n-l-s \leq i < n-s} \mathbb{E}\left[\mathbf{U}_i''|Z\right],$$

$$\text{and } \frac{1}{n} \sum_{0 \leq i < n-l, i \neq m_1} \mathbb{E}\left[\mathbf{U}_i''\right] = \frac{1}{n} \sum_{-s \leq i < n-l-s, i \neq m_1} \mathbb{E}[\mathbf{U}_i'']$$

Thus, comparing the right hand side of Eq. (a8) and Eq. (a9) we have

$$\mathbb{E}[\text{TN}_{1\text{L}}(\mathbf{X}_0, \cdots, \mathbf{X}_{n-1})|Z] = \mathbb{E}\left[\text{TN}_{1\text{L}}(T^s(\mathbf{X}_{-n+1+m_2}, \cdots, \mathbf{X}_{n-1+m_1}))|Z\right]$$

which completes the proof.

C   Comparison with CNN Using Global Pooling Model

The state-of-the-art CNN models use a flattening layer after all the convolutional model to convert the two-dimensional feature representation into a one-dimensional feature representation. However, the use of a flattening layer reduces the shift-invariance of the CNN models resulting in their poor performance on highly desynchronized traces (ref. Fig. 4d). This section compares TransNet to a CNN model that uses global pooling instead of the flattening layer. For this purpose, we have used the same model as EffCNN (desync400) except for the flattening layer replaced by the global pooling layer. We refer to the resulting model as *EffCNN+GlobalPooling*. The results of *EffCNN+GlobalPooling* on highly desynchronized *ASCAD_desync0* dataset is compared with that of TransNet in Fig. 9. The results suggest that TransNet performs significantly better than *EffCNN+GlobalPooling*.

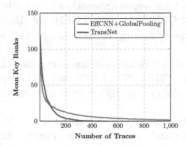
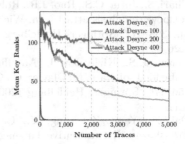

Fig. 9. Comparison of TransNet with *EffCNN+GlobalPooling* on the *ASCAD_desync400* datasets.

Fig. 10. Results of *EffCNN*. The models have been trained with profiling desync 0.

D   Sensitivity of EffCNN to Profiling Desynchronization

As the experiments of TransNet in Sect. 6.6, we verify the robustness of EffCNN training to the amount of profiling desync. To verify that, we trained the EffCNN models using only synchronized traces and tested them on desynchronized traces. The results are shown in Fig. 10. From the figure, it can be seen that as the amount of desynchronization in the attack traces increases, the performance of the models gets worse rapidly, suggesting the superiority of TransNet over EffCNN when the profiling desync is significantly less than the attack desync.

References

1. Abdellatif, K.M.: Mixup data augmentation for deep learning side-channel attacks. IACR Cryptology ePrint Archive, p. 328 (2021)
2. Ba, L.J., Kiros, J.R., Hinton, G.E.: Layer normalization. CoRR abs/1607.06450 (2016)
3. Benadjila, R., Prouff, E., Strullu, R., Cagli, E., Dumas, C.: Deep learning for side-channel analysis and introduction to ASCAD database. J. Cryptogr. Eng. **10**(2), 163–188 (2019). https://doi.org/10.1007/s13389-019-00220-8
4. Bhasin, S., Bruneau, N., Danger, J.-L., Guilley, S., Najm, Z.: Analysis and improvements of the DPA contest v4 implementation. In: Chakraborty, R.S., Matyas, V., Schaumont, P. (eds.) SPACE 2014. LNCS, vol. 8804, pp. 201–218. Springer, Cham (2014). https://doi.org/10.1007/978-3-319-12060-7_14
5. Cagli, E., Dumas, C., Prouff, E.: Convolutional neural networks with data augmentation against jitter-based countermeasures. In: Fischer, W., Homma, N. (eds.) CHES 2017. LNCS, vol. 10529, pp. 45–68. Springer, Cham (2017). https://doi.org/10.1007/978-3-319-66787-4_3
6. Chari, S., Jutla, C.S., Rao, J.R., Rohatgi, P.: Towards sound approaches to counteract power-analysis attacks. In: Wiener, M. (ed.) CRYPTO 1999. LNCS, vol. 1666, pp. 398–412. Springer, Heidelberg (1999). https://doi.org/10.1007/3-540-48405-1_26
7. Coron, J.-S., Kizhvatov, I.: An efficient method for random delay generation in embedded software. In: Clavier, C., Gaj, K. (eds.) CHES 2009. LNCS, vol. 5747, pp. 156–170. Springer, Heidelberg (2009). https://doi.org/10.1007/978-3-642-04138-9_12
8. Dai, Z., Yang, Z., Yang, Y., Carbonell, J.G., Le, Q.V., Salakhutdinov, R.: Transformer-XL: attentive language models beyond a fixed-length context. In: ACL, Italy, vol. 1, pp. 2978–2988. ACL (2019)
9. Glorot, X., Bordes, A., Bengio, Y.: Deep sparse rectifier neural networks. In: AISTATS, USA. JMLR Proceedings, vol. 15, pp. 315–323. JMLR.org (2011)
10. Gohr, A., Jacob, S., Schindler, W.: Subsampling and knowledge distillation on adversarial examples: new techniques for deep learning based side channel evaluations. In: Dunkelman, O., Jacobson, Jr., M.J., O'Flynn, C. (eds.) SAC 2020. LNCS, vol. 12804, pp. 567–592. Springer, Cham (2021). https://doi.org/10.1007/978-3-030-81652-0_22
11. He, K., Zhang, X., Ren, S., Sun, J.: Deep residual learning for image recognition. In: CVPR, USA, pp. 770–778. IEEE Computer Society (2016)
12. Hochreiter, S., Bengio, Y., Frasconi, P., Schmidhuber, J.: Gradient flow in recurrent nets: the difficulty of learning long-term dependencies (2001)
13. Kerkhof, M., Wu, L., Perin, G., Picek, S.: Focus is key to success: a focal loss function for deep learning-based side-channel analysis. In: Balasch, J., O'Flynn, C. (eds.) COSADE 2022. LNCS, vol. 13211, pp. 29–48. Springer, Cham (2022). https://doi.org/10.1007/978-3-030-99766-3_2
14. Kim, J., Picek, S., Heuser, A., Bhasin, S., Hanjalic, A.: Make some noise. unleashing the power of convolutional neural networks for profiled side-channel analysis. TCHES **2019**(3), 148–179 (2019)
15. Kingma, D.P., Ba, J.: Adam: a method for stochastic optimization. In: ICLR, USA (2015)
16. Kocher, P., Jaffe, J., Jun, B.: Differential power analysis. In: Wiener, M. (ed.) CRYPTO 1999. LNCS, vol. 1666, pp. 388–397. Springer, Heidelberg (1999). https://doi.org/10.1007/3-540-48405-1_25

17. Lu, X., Zhang, C., Cao, P., Gu, D., Lu, H.: Pay attention to raw traces: a deep learning architecture for end-to-end profiling attacks. TCHES **2021**(3), 235–274 (2021)
18. Maghrebi, H.: Deep learning based side channel attacks in practice. IACR Cryptology ePrint Archive 2019/578 (2019)
19. Maghrebi, H., Portigliatti, T., Prouff, E.: Breaking cryptographic implementations using deep learning techniques. In: Carlet, C., Hasan, M.A., Saraswat, V. (eds.) SPACE 2016. LNCS, vol. 10076, pp. 3–26. Springer, Cham (2016). https://doi.org/10.1007/978-3-319-49445-6_1
20. Martinasek, Z., Hajny, J., Malina, L.: Optimization of power analysis using neural network. In: Francillon, A., Rohatgi, P. (eds.) CARDIS 2013. LNCS, vol. 8419, pp. 94–107. Springer, Cham (2014). https://doi.org/10.1007/978-3-319-08302-5_7
21. Martinasek, Z., Zeman, V.: Innovative method of the power analysis. Radioengineering **22**(2), 586–594 (2013)
22. Masure, L., et al.: Deep learning side-channel analysis on large-scale traces. In: Chen, L., Li, N., Liang, K., Schneider, S. (eds.) ESORICS 2020. LNCS, vol. 12308, pp. 440–460. Springer, Cham (2020). https://doi.org/10.1007/978-3-030-58951-6_22
23. Paguada, S., Armendariz, I.: The forgotten hyperparameter: introducing dilated convolution for boosting CNN-based side-channel attacks. In: Zhou, J., et al. (eds.) ACNS 2020. LNCS, vol. 12418, pp. 217–236. Springer, Cham (2020). https://doi.org/10.1007/978-3-030-61638-0_13
24. Pereira, O., Standaert, F., Vivek, S.: Leakage-resilient authentication and encryption from symmetric cryptographic primitives. In: Ray, I., Li, N., Kruegel, C. (eds.) ACM SIGSAC, USA, pp. 96–108. ACM (2015)
25. Perin, G., Chmielewski, L., Picek, S.: Strength in numbers: improving generalization with ensembles in machine learning-based profiled side-channel analysis. TCHES **2020**(4), 337–364 (2020)
26. Perin, G., Wu, L., Picek, S.: Exploring feature selection scenarios for deep learning-based side-channel analysis. IACR Cryptology ePrint Archive, p. 1414 (2021)
27. Picek, S., Heuser, A., Jovic, A., Bhasin, S., Regazzoni, F.: The curse of class imbalance and conflicting metrics with machine learning for side-channel evaluations. TCHES **2019**(1), 209–237 (2019)
28. Picek, S., Samiotis, I.P., Kim, J., Heuser, A., Bhasin, S., Legay, A.: On the performance of convolutional neural networks for side-channel analysis. In: Chattopadhyay, A., Rebeiro, C., Yarom, Y. (eds.) SPACE 2018. LNCS, vol. 11348, pp. 157–176. Springer, Cham (2018). https://doi.org/10.1007/978-3-030-05072-6_10
29. Prouff, E., Rivain, M., Bevan, R.: Statistical analysis of second order differential power analysis. IACR Cryptology ePrint Archive, p. 646 (2010)
30. Shaw, P., Uszkoreit, J., Vaswani, A.: Self-attention with relative position representations. In: NAACL-HLT, USA, vol. 2, pp. 464–468. ACL (2018)
31. Thapar, D., Alam, M., Mukhopadhyay, D.: TranSCA: cross-family profiled side-channel attacks using transfer learning on deep neural networks. IACR Cryptology ePrint Archive 2020/1258 (2020)
32. Vaswani, A., et al.: Attention is all you need. In: NIPS, USA, pp. 5998–6008 (2017)
33. Won, Y., Hou, X., Jap, D., Breier, J., Bhasin, S.: Back to the basics: seamless integration of side-channel pre-processing in deep neural networks. IACR Cryptology ePrint Archive, 2020/1134 (2020)
34. Wouters, L., Arribas, V., Gierlichs, B., Preneel, B.: Revisiting a methodology for efficient CNN architectures in profiling attacks. TCHES **2020**(3), 147–168 (2020)

35. Yarotsky, D.: Universal approximations of invariant maps by neural networks. CoRR abs/1804.10306 (2018)
36. Zaid, G., Bossuet, L., Dassance, F., Habrard, A., Venelli, A.: Ranking loss: maximizing the success rate in deep learning side-channel analysis. TCHES **2021**(1), 25–55 (2021)
37. Zaid, G., Bossuet, L., Habrard, A., Venelli, A.: Methodology for efficient CNN architectures in profiling attacks. TCHES **2020**(1), 1–36 (2020)
38. Zhang, A., Lipton, Z.C., Li, M., Smola, A.J.: Dive into Deep Learning (2020). http://d2l.ai
39. Zhang, L., Xing, X., Fan, J., Wang, Z., Wang, S.: Multi-label deep learning based side channel attack. In: AsianHOST, China, pp. 1–6. IEEE (2019)
40. Zhou, Y., Standaert, F.: Deep learning mitigates but does not annihilate the need of aligned traces and a generalized ResNet model for side-channel attacks. J. Cryptogr. Eng. **10**(1), 85–95 (2020)

To Overfit, or Not to Overfit: Improving the Performance of Deep Learning-Based SCA

Azade Rezaeezade[1](✉), Guilherme Perin[1,2], and Stjepan Picek[1,2]

[1] Delft University of Technology, Delft, The Netherlands
`a.rezaeezade-1@tudelft.nl`
[2] Radboud University, Nijmegen, The Netherlands

Abstract. Profiling side-channel analysis allows evaluators to estimate the worst-case security of a target. When security evaluations relax the assumptions about the adversary's knowledge, profiling models may easily be sub-optimal due to the inability to extract the most informative points of interest from the side-channel measurements. When used for profiling attacks, deep neural networks can learn strong models without feature selection with the drawback of expensive hyperparameter tuning. Unfortunately, due to very large search spaces, one usually finds very different model behaviors, and a widespread situation is to face overfitting with typically poor generalization capacity.

Usually, overfitting or poor generalization would be mitigated by adding more measurements to the profiling phase to reduce estimation errors. This paper provides a detailed analysis of different deep learning model behaviors and shows that adding more profiling traces as a single solution does not necessarily help improve generalization. We recognize the main problem to be the sub-optimal selection of hyperparameters, which is then difficult to resolve by simply adding more measurements. Instead, we propose to use small hyperparameter tweaks or regularization as techniques to resolve the problem.

Keywords: Side-channel analysis · Deep learning · Overfitting · Generalization

1 Introduction

Side-channel analysis (SCA) encompasses non-invasive attacks exploring unintentional information leakage from cryptographic devices. Consequently, it is of interest of manufacturers to evaluate the robustness of their products against threats posed by multiple side-channel attacks. Such attacks are classified as profiling [9] and non-profiling attacks [15]. The latter appeared first in late 1990s s and rapidly after publication, protection mechanisms (countermeasures) started to be proposed [8,19] and implemented to mitigate differential power attacks and their variations [5,12]. On the other hand, profiling attacks allow a more

© The Author(s), under exclusive license to Springer Nature Switzerland AG 2022
L. Batina and J. Daemen (Eds.): AFRICACRYPT 2022, LNCS 13503, pp. 397–421, 2022.
https://doi.org/10.1007/978-3-031-17433-9_17

formal security evaluation of a device by implementing a profiling model from side-channel measurements obtained from a device identical to the device under evaluation. The model is later tested on a separate target as a secret recovery or attack phase. Since an evaluator can learn a statistical model from the existing leakages, several countermeasures against non-profiling attacks may become ineffective against profiling attacks, such as Boolean masking [17,18]. This depends on how much knowledge an adversary has about the target implementation (e.g., secret random shares and source code). This addition of knowledge in profiling attacks allows the estimation of worst-case security scenarios. If profiling attacks cannot reduce the secret's entropy under these circumstances and by considering a sufficient number of measurements, the target can be considered as secure.

Theoretically, the Gaussian template attack [9] is assumed to be the strongest profiling method in SCA. This is true if 1) an adversary can extract the most informative (leaking) points of interest (features) from side-channel measurements, 2) the true leakage distribution (which is unknown) follows a normal distribution, and 3) the adversary has an unlimited number of measurements to build the model. In recent years, deep learning appeared as a powerful alternative to implementing profiling models [17]. In practice, a deep neural network may skip feature selection and still provide strong models that defeat Boolean masking countermeasure. Additionally, the ability of Convolutional Neural Networks to bypass trace desynchronization effects [7] also became very attractive to the SCA community. The main drawback in deep learning (across all domains and not only SCA) is the expensive hyperparameter tuning process. Different solutions have been investigated to do this process in profiling attacks including grid search [30], random search [21], Bayesian optimization [28], genetic algorithms [17], and reinforcement learning [26]. Such solutions converge to different model behaviors, and usually, the best model is selected from a limited number of search attempts.

As the search spaces are usually very large, even for a few hyperparameters, the search mechanism can easily find multiple sub-optimal models for the problem. In other words, a large number of deep learning models will show overfitting or underfitting effects, leading to poor generalization ability. Finding an optimal model during the search is theoretically possible by assuming an unbounded adversary in terms of training resources, which is never the case in practice [24]. For profiling attacks in general, it is common to assume that a model is suboptimal or wrong if the assumptions about the leakage model contain errors or the number of side-channel measurements is not sufficient [11]. This is because we aim to find the actual statistical distribution of the leakage in the profiling phase. Since this distribution is unknown, we must approximate it using density estimation techniques. The estimation process is aligned with assumption and estimation errors. The former is the consequence of incorrect assumptions about the leakage model, and the latter is the consequence of insufficient side-channel measurements [6]. Reducing any of those errors will result in the improvement of the model performance.

Intuitively, a deep learning model showing sub-optimal generalization would start to converge to a stronger model by increasing the number of profiling traces and re-training. The expectation is that fewer estimation errors (i.e., more profiling traces) would suppress eventual assumption errors made by the model (due to hyperparameters combination and leakage model).

This paper examines this common profiling attack assumption that more profiling traces always improve model generalization. Motivated by the deep double descent phenomenon [20], we experimentally show that poor generalization (typically justified as overfitting and underfitting) is much more a matter of specific hyperparameters choice and not the lack of profiling traces. We generate models ranging from few thousand to millions of trainable parameters, and we verify that in several cases, independent of leakage model and deep learning model size, adding more profiling traces does not change (or even reduce) the model's generalization ability. We investigate simple techniques based on limited hyperparameter changes and regularization to override this unexpected effect. Additionally, understanding what causes unexpected model behaviors in deep learning (such as overfitting) allows evaluators to draw more consistent conclusions about the target's security, reducing the chances of overestimating the security of a device due to assumptions errors of the model. Our main contributions are:

1. We experimentally verify that the assumption that "adding more profiling traces increases the generalization of a model" is not always true for deep learning-based SCA. We investigate in detail the overfitting effect in profiling attacks. We validate that in many cases, the overfitting effect can be reduced by adding more profiling traces during training if the chosen hyperparameters combination does not result in large assumption errors.
2. We run experiments for software and hardware AES datasets and demonstrate that this behavior is not dataset dependent.
3. Considering the first contribution, we show that when increasing the profiling set size does not improve generalization, using regularization techniques and applying small changes in hyperparameters can improve the performance by reducing the assumption errors.

This work does not aim to find any specific model that will break a target with fewer measurements than state-of-the-art. Rather, it provides insights into a commonly observed problem in deep learning-based SCA: overfitting. Instead of simply concluding that a model does not work due to overfitting, as done in most related works, we try to find the underlying reasons for such behavior and how to mitigate it.

2   Background

2.1   Profiling SCA

Profiling attacks are conducted in two main phases: profiling and attack. The main goal of the profiling phase is to implement a classifier by learning or computing a set of parameters. The first method for profiling attacks is the *template attack*, where an adversary assumes that the leakage follows a multi-variate Gaussian distribution [9,10]. The profiling stage consists then of computing the Gaussian components (mean and covariance) as approximate statistics by assuming that the target device provides leakages that follow a Gaussian distribution. This allows an adversary to obtain a probability density function representing the distribution of side-channel leakages.

In machine learning (including deep learning) SCA, the statistics of the unknown leakage distribution are automatically learned from the profiling set. This time, the classifier parameters are learned from side-channel leakages rather than computed, meaning that the adversary does not necessarily need to assume the statistical distribution that describes the leakages well.

Although the Gaussian template attack theoretically represents the strongest profiling model due to the nature of side-channel leakages that tend to follow a Gaussian distribution, deep learning methods offer infinite opportunities to learn a classifier and, therefore, in practice, can reach more efficient results. If points of interest can be selected to build Gaussian templates, a security evaluator can evaluate the worst-case security scenarios by estimating the required number of side-channel measurements to recover the secret. On the other hand, deep learning methods require no feature selection as the points of interest are implicitly selected during the deep learning training phase.

The quality of a profiling classifier is given by its generalization ability to an attack set. For that, information-theoretic metrics like guessing entropy or success rate are computed from the output probabilities obtained from the classifier. Differing from the template attack where the adversary or the evaluator does not need to conduct hyperparameter tuning, deep learning methods suffer from the difficulty of defining those hyperparameters. Therefore, one needs to be careful when interpreting the outcome metrics from a profiling model and, consequently, the conclusions about the security of the implementation. The information-theoretic metrics help the evaluator to understand how to find the best possible deep learning model, and for that, it is important to understand when the metrics indicate overfitting, underfitting, and generalization.

2.2   Overfitting and Underfitting

In supervised learning, when we train a model, we fit it on a set of labeled data, and then we expect it to be able to decide about a set of unseen data from the same distribution. According to that, overfitting describes a model that fits the training data well but performs poorly on test data. It can be caused for various reasons, traditionally summarized as using a too complex model or using an inappropriate training set. In the same way, we can define underfitting as the model that does not learn the underlying function in training data, and its performance in test data is poor accordingly.

One suggested way to limit the effect of overfitting or improve the generalization power of a model is to expand the training set by collecting more data or running data augmentation [29]. However, there are limitations as traditional machine learning (and small neural network) models' performance saturates at some point, and we cannot see significant changes from that point ahead as we increase the training set size. In the case of deep neural networks, performance variation regarding increasing training set size depends on the proportion between the network's capacity[1] and the number of traces in the training set. Although the exact behavior of the neural models is still ongoing research, it has been shown that when the size of the training set and model's capacity is comparable, increasing the training set size can hurt the model's performance [20].

Deep learning models commonly have many trainable parameters [2], and such models can easily fit training data with empirical risk (average of the loss on the training set) close to zero. This simplifies the optimization problem so that we can use very complex models for simple problems and still reach extremely good generalization [31].

2.3 Deep Double Descent Phenomenon

The deep double descent phenomenon was first discovered by Belkin et al. [3]. The challenge started with the common claim in modern machine learning that "larger models are always better" [13,16,27], while standard statistical machine learning theory predicts that larger models are candidates for overfitting. Belkin et al. unified the classical bias-variance trade-off and the modern practice of larger models' advantage. They showed how increasing models' capacity beyond the size of the smallest model that can fit the training data with zero empirical risk could lead to performance improvement.

Bias-variance trade-off is the concept traditionally used to describe underfitting as a result of high bias and overfitting as a result of high variance. The conventional bias-variance trade-off is shown on the left of Fig. 1. Choosing the function class $\mathcal{F}$, like neural networks, and minimizing their training risk using an objective function, the training and test risk varies based on the capacity of $\mathcal{F}$. In this trade-off, there is a "sweet spot" where a model with a specific capacity has the best performance for the given problem. Before the "sweet spot", performance increases with increasing the capacity of the models. After the "sweet spot", the performance of the models in the training set keeps increasing, but performance in the test set decreases.

More recently, deep double descent replaced the conventional bias-variance trade-off with the neural model performance below the "interpolation point", where the interpolation point is the capacity of the smallest model from function class $\mathcal{F}$ that can fit a training set with n traces and zero training loss. Belkin et al. showed that although models with a capacity near the interpolation point have a high test risk (average of the loss in the test set), if we keep increasing the model's capacity, the risk will decrease again, and we can even reach models with better performance than the models in the "sweet spot". One can see these double descent behavior in the right of Fig. 1. All the models beyond the interpolation point fit the training data perfectly and have zero training risk.

---

[1] We consider the capacity to be the size of the network in trainable parameters.

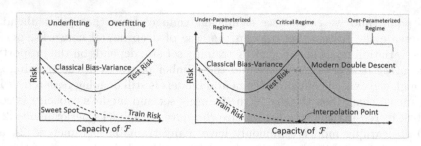

Fig. 1. Curves for training risk (dashed line) and test risk (solid line). Left: The classical U-shaped risk curve. Right: The Double Descent risk curve.

Considering this deep double descent phenomenon, a model f from function class $\mathcal{F}$ works in one of the following regimes, depending on the proportion between the capacity of the model and the number of measurements in the training set (n):

- Under-parameterized regime: where the capacity of f is sufficiently smaller than n. The models working in this regime show an increase in performance by increasing the training set size, i.e., increasing the number of measurements in the training set until the saturation point (where increasing the training set size does not improve the model's performance anymore).
- Over-parameterized regime: where the capacity of f is sufficiently larger than n. The models working in this regime show an increase in performance by increasing training set size unless the increase can change the regime that the model is in.
- Critically-parameterized regime: where the capacity of f and the size of the training set n are comparable. Models working in this regime may show an increase or decrease in performance by increasing the training set size. In the critical regime, the chosen model barely fits the training data, so it is fragile[2]. In the right of Fig. 1, by increasing the model's capacity, the test risk initially increases in the critical regime, and just as the model reaches the interpolation point and can fit with zero training risk, it undergoes the second descent. In many research works, this effect cannot be observed as it is avoided through early stopping or other regularization techniques[3].

In the right of Fig. 1, the critical regime is denoted in orange color. As one can see, the test risk reaches its peak at the interpolation point. Meanwhile, the training risk reaches zero for the first time. After that point, the training risk remains zero, and the test risk starts to decrease again. Increasing the training set size pushes the double descent curve downward by decreasing test risk. However, since a larger training set requires larger models to fit, increasing the training

---

[2] Small changes in the model's hyperparameter can invalidate it.
[3] Regularization are techniques used to mitigate overfitting by reducing the complexity of the models.

set also shifts the interpolation point (and the peak of test risk) to the right [20]. When we increase the training set size, these two effects combine, and we may observe that training a model with a fixed capacity with less training data shows better performance than training it with a larger training set. Consequently, increasing the training set size can hurt the performance of the model.

2.4 Overfitting and Generalization in Side-channel Analysis

To decide about the generalization power of neural network models in the side-channel domain, we cannot rely on accuracy and loss for the training and validation set. As discussed in [23], such machine learning metrics are not suitable in SCA as they limit the final prediction to individual decisions for each trace. Therefore, we need a metric that can accumulate the small biases of the model prediction toward the correct key. To overcome this shortcoming, besides the accuracy and loss of the model, we inspect the evolution of guessing entropy for an attack set. Following a standard differential power analysis setting, we accumulate information about each key candidate as $S_k = \sum_{i=1}^{Q} \log p(x_i, y)$, where Q is the number of attack traces and $p(x, y)$ indicates the probability of a trace x_i to be represented by an intermediate (in our case, a label) y. For example, the intermediate y can be the output of an S-box operation in the AES cipher. Namely, $y = Sbox(d \oplus k)$, where d is a plaintext byte and k is the key byte candidate. The best key candidate is the key that maximizes S_k. If we sort the key candidates according to their S_k values, guessing entropy (GE) is the average rank of the actual key among all the candidate keys after multiple attacks to an attack set. The attack is successful if it places the actual key first, i.e., $GE = 1$.

Detecting Overfitting and Underfitting in SCA. The inability of a deep neural network to generalize in profiling SCA is usually attributed to model overfitting or underfitting. In practice, overfitting is characterized by a model that memorizes all training data but cannot generalize to different (unseen) attack traces. The main outcome is a model that mostly fits noise instead of existing leakages. This scenario becomes even more critical in realistic profiling attacks where the attack traces are collected from a separate device. Underfitting happens when the model is trained for an insufficient number of iterations (i.e., epochs), and training metrics indicate a model that cannot even memorize training data.

   A profiling model is considered sub-optimal if there are assumption or estimation errors [11]. In the case of deep learning, assumption errors also include hyperparameter combinations that lead to insufficient generalization. However, there are cases when the trained model still eventually recovers the correct key at the price of the increased number of attack traces. Thus, it is common to observe the following scenarios:

- Model overfits but still recovers the correct key information: in this case, training accuracy reaches 100% (resp. training loss approaches zero) at the end of the training process. The overfitting is identified by checking the validation accuracy, which is typically close to random guessing, and the validation loss, which tends to grow as training continues. However, when processing a sufficient number of attack traces during the GE calculation, it is still possible to rank the correct key as first (or among the first ones). Of course, as the model overfits and the GE is usually verified for side-channel measurements obtained from the same device (ignoring portability [4]), one cannot assume the model provides sufficient generalization.

- Model *tends* to overfit but still recovers the correct key byte: the only difference from the previous situation is that the model shows a continuous improvement in training accuracy (resp., decreasing in loss), but the training stops before it reaches 100%. As this stopping decision happens before the complete overfitting, the tendency is a slightly better (but still far from optimal) generalization.
- Model overfits or tends to overfit and does not recover the correct key byte: this is a case when the evaluator selects a combination of hyperparameters that creates a model that cannot fit existing leakages and predominantly fits noise from side-channel measurements.

The final profiling models achieved through any of these scenarios are defined as sub-optimal models. Even the scenarios that recover the secret information are far from ideal for security evaluations. The problem is to assume that a sub-optimal model represents the existing leakage distribution of the target. The direct consequence is a false sense of security, usually overestimating the security of the implementation. *Additionally, it remains unclear if the increase in the number of profiling traces, which reduces estimation errors, always ensures the reduction of negative effects due to the model's sub-optimality.*

Finding the Best Possible Models. A typical procedure in deep learning-based profiling attacks is to run hyperparameter search methods to find the best possible models using available resources (processing power, time, and memory). To speed up the hyperparameter search process, an alternative is to reduce the number of profiling traces during the search and select the best possible model. Once the best model is found, one can increase the number of profiling traces again and re-train the model to improve its generalization. In essence, for some models, adding more profiling traces requires small changes in hyperparameters to accommodate the larger profiling set and the expected improvement in generalization. As it is more likely that we are dealing with sub-optimal models (we do not follow the worst-case security settings), generalization will be limited and will also happen in models showing overfitting.

3 Experimental Setup

3.1 Datasets

We use two publicly available datasets that are large enough to run our experiments. This will allow us to inspect the influence of the increasing number of traces on the neural network model behavior.

ASCAD Random Keys[4]. This dataset was released in 2019 [1] and contains side-channel measurements from an AES-128 software implementation running on an 8-bit AVR microcontroller. Details about the cryptographic design are provided in [25]. The AES implementation is protected with a first-order Boolean masking countermeasure. This dataset contains 200,000 traces with random keys and random plaintexts, which is then considered as a profiling set. Additional 100,000 traces with a fixed key are considered for attack and validation sets. Each side-channel measurement contains 250,000 features, and we consider the trimmed version of the dataset containing 1,400 features. This target interval represents the processing of the third byte (the first masked one) of the S-box in the first encryption round. Therefore, in our experiments, this dataset is labeled according to this intermediate byte, i.e., $Y^{(i)} = Sbox[P_3^{(i)} \oplus k_3^{(i)}]$ (Identity (ID) leakage model) and the Hamming weight of this intermediate byte (Hamming weight (HW) leakage model).

AES_HD[5]. This dataset was introduced in [23] and contains power side-channel measurements from an unprotected AES_128 implementation running on an FPGA platform. This dataset contains 500,000 side-channel traces (in [23], the authors considered a smaller version of the dataset) with a fixed key. In our case, we split this dataset in a profiling set containing 400,000 traces and the remaining 100,000 are used for attack and validation phases. Each measurement in this dataset contains 1,250 features. We label this dataset according to the Hamming distance (HD) between output ciphertext byte and the corresponding byte before S-box in the last encryption round, $Y^{(i)} = Sbox^{-1}[C_j^{(i)} \oplus k_j^{(i)}] \oplus C_{j'}^{(i)}$, where $C_j^{(i)}$ and $C_{j'}^{(i)}$ are related according to the ShiftRows operation. In our experiments, $j = 10$ and $j' = 6$.

3.2   Analysis Methodology

In profiling SCA, an analysis that makes correct assumptions about the leakage model and leakage distributions can increase models' performance by increasing the number of profiling traces. In Sect. 2.3, we discussed that recent deep learning results show the existence of a critical regime, where increasing the number of training data leads to an unexpected decrease in model generalization. Not surprisingly, this also happens in the side-channel domain.

This paper explores the effects mentioned above in the case of deep learning-based SCA. Our analysis methodology aims to verify the possibilities of reducing the overfitting effects in profiling models and understanding if a deep learning model trained with more data should always deliver better generalization. Our approach consists of the following steps:

---

[4] https://github.com/ANSSI-FR/ASCAD/tree/master/ATMEGA_AES_v1/ATM_AES_v1_variable_key.

[5] https://github.com/AISyLab/AES_HD_Ext.

1. A search space $\mathcal{S}$ is created for hyperparameter options for MultiLayer Perceptron (MLP) and Convolutional Neural Networks (CNN)[6].
2. 500 different hyperparameters combinations are generated for MLP and CNN neural network topology and leakage model (Hamming weight, Identity, and Hamming distance) combinations and two datasets (ASCAD Random Keys and AES_HD). Thus, the total number of generated models equals 3,000.

Table 1. *MLP* and *CNN* models hyperparameters.

Hyperparameters	Range
Dense layers	
Number of neurons	[100, 900], step = 100
Number of layers	[1, 8], step = 1
Convolution layers	
Number of layers	[1, 4], step = 1
Number of kernels	[4, 20], step = 1
First layer's filter size	[2, 4, 8, 12, 16]
$i^{(}th)$ layer filter size	$((i-1)filter\_size)^2$
Pooling	"Average", "Max"
Pooling size	[2, 10], step = 2
Pooling stride	[2, 10], step = 2
Learning hyperparameters	
Optimizer	"Adam", "RMSprop"
Weight initialization	"random_uniform", "glorot_uniform", and "he_uniform"
Activation function	"relu", "selu", and "elu"
Batch size	$[100, 900]$, $step = 100$
Learning rate	$[0.005, 0.001, 0.0005, 0.0001, 0.00005, 0.00001]$

To generate the models, we considered the hyperparameters and ranges depicted in Table 1. For both MLP and CNN dense layers, we used the ranges shown in *Dense layers* part of Table 1. The number of epochs for all settings is fixed and equals 200. The hyperparameters' ranges are being selected based on the ranges reported in the previous researches [1, 22, 30].
3. In the first phase, each randomly generated neural network is trained with a portion of the available profiling set. We start with 50,000 profiling traces, and the performance of each profiling model is estimated with the average over ten different validation sets, where each has 10,000 traces. For guessing

---

[6] Due to the limitation on the number of pages of the paper, we avoid describing MLP and CNN architectures here. We refer interested readers to many available papers in the literature describing these neural network models like [25, 30].

entropy and the required number of attack traces, we repeat the attack 100 times in each validation set for 5,000 randomly selected traces and report the average over those ten sets.

4. If $GE = 1$, the neural network model is selected as a *good* model. Otherwise, the model is discarded. To avoid subjective interpretation of the term *good model*, we clarify that this is not an optimal profiling model but a trained neural network that can recover the target key with the considered number of traces (i.e., 5,000).

5. For all good models, we analyze the training metrics to verify what regime the model is working in and if the profiling model overfits (or tends to overfit). The schematics of the overfitting or tending to overfit behaviors of the deep models are illustrated in Fig. 2.

6. All good models are re-trained with an increased number of profiling traces. We re-train the good models with 100,000, 150,000, and 200,000 traces for the ASCAD Random Keys dataset. For the AES_HD dataset, we repeat the training process with 100,000 up to 400,000 traces with steps of 50,000 traces. Note that the models are always re-initialized with the same trainable parameters from step 2. This will keep all the other hyperparameters and settings the same and provide us with the possibility to observe the effect of profiling size increments.

7. After re-training the good models with more profiling traces, we verify if the required number of attack traces to reach $GE = 1$ is reduced when compared to the baseline case (model trained with 50,000). We assume that this reduction in the required number of traces reflects a generalization improvement. This can be justified from two viewpoints. First, from a deep learning perspective, the improvement in the validation accuracy results in assigning the largest probability to the correct key more frequently than in cases when the model shows less accuracy in the validation set. From a side-channel perspective, we are interested in models that can rank the correct key first with fewer attack traces, and this can be a measure to compare the generalization power of different models.

8. For models where adding more profiling traces improves their generalization (this situation is illustrated in the top part of Fig. 3), one of the following situations might happen:

   (a) The baseline model was working in an under-parameterized regime, and the hyperparameter combination error (assumption error) was small compared to the neural network model's estimation error. As a result, increasing the number of profiling traces leads to decreasing estimation error and better generalization.

   (b) The baseline model was working in an over-parameterized regime, and the assumption error was small compared to the estimation error. As a result, an increasing number of profiling traces leads to decreasing estimation error and better generalization.

   (c) The baseline model was working in a critical regime. Increasing traces in the training set did not invalidate the neural network model, and the hyperparameter combination error did not increase with an increasing number of profiling traces. Instead, estimation error decreased by adding more traces to the training set, leading to decreasing estimation error and better generalization.

9. For models where adding more profiling traces does not improve the generalization (this situation is illustrated in bottom part of Fig. 3), one of the following situations might happen:

(a) Regardless of the regime the baseline model is working in, the specific hyperparameters combination leads to assumption errors after increasing the profiling set size. The model needs to be adjusted to reduce the assumption error effects.

(b) The baseline model is working in the critical regime, and adding more traces to the profiling set skewed the model and decreased its performance.

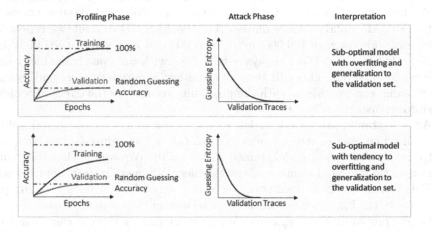

Fig. 2. Common model behaviors.

Figure 2 illustrates a typical scenario identified in [23] for sub-optimal deep learning models when machine learning metrics do not reflect the performance of a model concerning guessing entropy. The fact that we illustrate accuracy as a reference machine learning metric does not imply that we are ignoring training and validation loss to decide if a model shows the potential behaviors from Fig. 2. As proposed in [18], minimizing the cross-entropy loss should be the equivalent of solving side-channel analysis optimization. However, this principle usually does not apply to sub-optimal models with too many assumption errors, as is the case of models showing overfitting. It is important to note that for most of the models considered good models, the situation in the top part of Fig. 3 happens more often. This means that for those models, overfitting is also caused by the lack of profiling traces, leading to insufficient profiling. On the other hand, if a model shows the behavior from the bottom part of Fig. 3, we can modify some hyperparameters that are unrelated to the model size (e.g., learning rate, batch size, training epochs, dropout, and activation functions), which can cause the model to reduce its assumption errors.

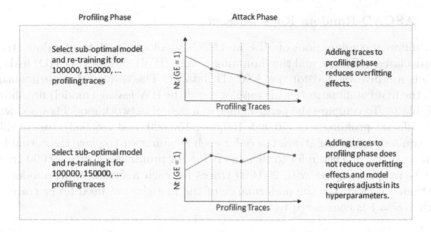

Fig. 3. Interpreting the model behaviors.

4   Experimental Results

Considering the neural network capacity and the size of the profiling set, we should specify the regime that the neural network model is working on. Unfortunately, we cannot clearly specify the borders between these regimes. This is because the interpolation point definition and "sufficiently larger" and "sufficiently smaller" terms in the definition of over-parameterized and under-parameterized regimes cannot give a clear separation. Additionally, there is no widely accepted definition for the capacity of the models in deep learning, which can justify the different performance of neural network models with a similar number of trainable parameters but different topology and output layer size. To tackle these ambiguities, we selected "good" neural network models with different numbers of trainable parameters ranging from a few thousand to a few million. Then, we consider the training and validation accuracy and loss evolution to roughly specify the interpolation point for different neural network and leakage model combinations. Finally, we can roughly specify the working regime for every selected neural network model. Still, considering that the specified interpolation points are valid for the specific profiling size, by increasing the profiling size, the working regime of the model may change [20]. In the tables, every row represents a randomly selected neural network model, denoted with numbers. Observe that there are some models that have the same number of trainable parameters (denoted as "Params"). This simply means that different architectures have the same capacity. For various settings (datasets, leakage models), we give various numbers of models based on the number of models that converge and have different capacities (to provide good coverage from small to large model sizes).

4.1   ASCAD Random Keys Dataset

Four different combinations of MLP and CNN topologies with the random structure declared in Sect. 3, and the Hamming weight (HW) and Identity (ID) leakage models are investigated for the ASCAD dataset. The results of experimenting with the first combination (MLP topology and the HW leakage model) are shown in Table 2a. To compare the performance of a neural network model trained with four different profiling sets (50,000, 100,000, 150,000, and 200,000), we consider the required number of attack traces for each profiling set to place the actual key in the first place. Then refer to them as NT_1[7] for profiling set with 50,000 traces to NT_4 for profiling set with 200,000 traces for each neural network model. As mentioned in Sect. 2.4, the performance of the models that need fewer traces to reach $GE = 1$ is considered to be better.

Table 2. Results for multilayer perceptron.

#	$Params$	NT_1	NT_2	NT_3	NT_4	#	$Params$	NT_1	NT_2	NT_3	NT_4
1	14,109	4,856	4,721	1,932	2,352	1	68,176	4,840	810	225	123
2	14,549	2,419	5,000	520	631	2	186,156	4,999	1,185	337	168
3	28,209	3,141	1,577	1,225	1,035	3	196,256	4,865	1,373	514	241
4	31,149	3,615	5,000	622	5,000	4	226,556	4,769	1,814	469	248
5	42,309	4,045	2,215	1,029	972	5	331,656	4,896	4,450	1,742	808
6	44,169	4,336	893	654	561	6	371,856	4,991	4,775	3,609	1,615
7	58049	4,034	2,259	1,662	1,324	7	371,856	4786	3208	1370	757
8	70,509	4,435	1,712	899	745	8	412,056	4,937	1,837	543	325
9	78,159	3,385	1,601	1,306	1,044	9	412,056	4,650	1,877	464	282
10	85,809	4,742	2,575	1,906	1,286	10	497,356	4,912	3,114	1,300	1,263
11	141,009	3,859	1,671	1,020	801	11	497,356	4,864	3,161	1,104	433
12	161,209	4,070	1,792	1,063	939	12	587,656	4,717	3,093	1,625	770
13	181,409	3,357	1,895	1,917	1,830	13	663,056	4,821	3,406	1,343	713
14	282,009	3,088	1,420	1,078	912	14	663,056	4,937	3,048	954	498
15	322,209	4,391	2,032	1,148	907	15	823,456	4,989	2,549	1,121	576
16	402,609	2,559	1,601	891	1,139	16	828,756	4,858	2,675	1,129	615
17	523,209	4,419	2,515	1,322	1,241	17	828,756	4,900	3,543	1,620	732
18	693,909	3,698	1,426	1,140	1,046	18	1039,156	4,719	1,047	458	281
19	724,409	4,276	2,238	1,511	1,368	19	1079,256	4,798	4,005	2,132	1,105
20	884,809	3,217	2,508	1,848	1,606	20	1,129,456	3,544	1,244	561	426
21	964,809	1,279	870	1,016	1,355	21	1,129,456	2,571	1,026	1,108	402
22	1,206,009	3,117	1,551	1,158	970	22	1,129,456	4,829	3,413	2,601	1,333
23	1,526,409	3,535	1,780	1,298	1,305	23	1,329,756	4,986	4,672	3,673	2,720
24	1,707,009	3,205	2,619	5,000	1,111	24	1,329,756	4,836	3,759	2,440	1,357
25	1,957,509	4,751	4,504	2,143	1,911	25	1,580,256	5,000	3,351	2,581	1,355
26	2,208,009	4,842	2,620	3,038	2,278	26	158,0256	4,651	2,928	905	4,818
27	2,458,509	3,450	1,744	1,072	893	27	1,785,856	2,271	5,000	5,000	5,000
(a) MLP trained for the HW leakage model.						(b) MLP trained for the ID leakage model.					

---

[7] NT: Average of the minimum number of attack traces that the model needs to place the actual key first.

Observe how all the neural network models ranked the correct key in the first place when trained with 50,000 traces. In many cases, by increasing the profiling size for each MLP model, the required number of traces to reach $GE = 1$ follows the classical machine learning belief that more data is better (for example, #6). Still, in some cases, the performance of the neural network model (the required number of attack traces) decreased when increasing the profiling set size. A part of this behavior has been predicted by deep double descent, and the proportion between the model's size and profiling set size, especially when increasing profiling size, changes the regime the neural network works in (e.g., #13 in Table 2a). This model works near over-parameterized regime boundaries with 50,000 profiling traces since its performance in the profiling set is $\approx 97\%$. Then, by increasing the profiling set size to 200,000, its performance decreases to $\approx 60\%$. Considering the proportion between the model's size and the profiling set size, this model is working in the critical regime for 100,000, 150,000, and 200,000 profiling traces. Still, the irregular increases and decreases in the required number of attack traces considering the model's complexity are not fully justified by the double descent phenomenon. For example one can consider #4 in Table 2a. The accuracy of the baseline model is $\approx 45\%$, and for the rest of the profiling set sizes, its profiling accuracy is less than 30%. Considering the proportion between this model size and the profiling set sizes, and the profiling accuracy, the model works in an under-parameterized regime, and an increasing number of profiling traces does not change the working regime. However, when we train the model with 100,000 and 200,000 profiling traces, it cannot reduce the key entropy at all as the model does not fit the leakage anymore.

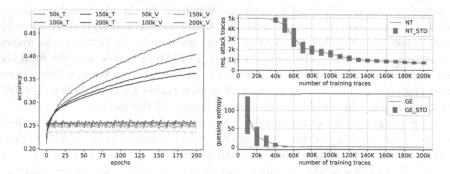

Fig. 4. Increasing the profiling set size and accuracy in the training (T) and validation (V) set and the required number of attack traces to reach $GE = 1$, #8 in Table 2a.

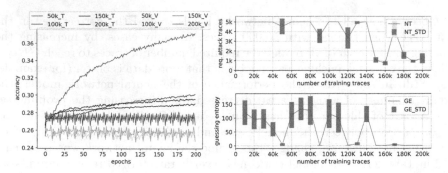

Fig. 5. Increasing the profiling set size and accuracy in the training (T) and validation (V) set and the required number of attack traces to reach $GE = 1$, #2 in Table 2a.

One can observe the changes in the performance for two MLP architectures in Figs. 4 and 5. The lighter colors in the left plot show accuracy for profiling (blue color) and validation (orange color) sets for MLPs trained with smaller profiling sets, and sequentially darker colors show these metrics after increasing the profiling set sizes to 100,000, 150,000, and 200,000 traces. Considering the profiling and validation accuracy and the proportion between the model's size and the profiling set size for #8 in Fig. 4, we can see that the baseline model works in the critical regime, and increasing the profiling set size pushes this model toward the under-parameterized regime. To eliminate the influence of a biased attack set on the required number of attack traces, we evaluated 10 different validation sets and provided mean and standard deviation values. In the right and top of Fig. 4, one can see the mean and variance of the required number of attack traces for MLP #8 to decrease GE to 1. In the right and bottom of Fig. 4, one can see the average of GE that the model managed to reach with 5,000 traces[8]. In Fig. 4, increasing profiling size results in better performance concerning the accuracy, the required number of attack traces, and the final GE that the model managed to reach with 5,000 attack traces. We can even detect small changes in the required number of attack traces from 150,000 to 200,000 profiling traces, which can be a sign of saturation of the model.

MLP #2 is another example that works in the under-parameterized regime. In Fig. 5, the accuracy of the MLP model shows normal (more profiling traces increase accuracy) behavior when increasing profiling set size. The training accuracy of the baseline model is $\approx 38\%$ and decreases to 28% for the profiling set with 200,000 traces. This model's test accuracy varies from 24% for the baseline model to $\approx 28\%$ when we train it with 200,000 traces. These accuracy percentages and the proportion between the model's size and the profiling set sizes indicate that this model works in the under-parameterized regime for all profiling set sizes. Still, this model cannot reduce the key entropy when trained with 200,000 traces.

Considering MLP #2 in Table 2a, while this MLP model converges to $GE = 1$ with on average 2,419 attack traces for a profiling set of 50,000 traces, it can-

---

[8] We took incremental steps of 10,000 in case of MLP #8 and MLP #2 to make the behavior tracking easier in Figs. 4 and 5.

not converge at all, i.e., cannot rank the correct key better than random guessing after increasing profiling size from 50,000 to 100,000 traces. The behavior is even more surprising when the model again converged to $GE = 1$ with on average 520 attack traces when it is trained with 150,000 profiling traces. This is an example of a scenario when the hyperparameter combination contains an assumption error and increasing the profiling size invalidates the model, i.e., changes the weights of the neural network model in a way that it cannot capture the underlying leakage model distribution and find the correct key. However, there are cases like #1 (works in the under-parameterized regime) and #26 (works in the over-parameterized regime), where increasing the profiling set size does not change the performance according to the required number of attack traces or sometimes makes it a bit worse compared to a smaller profiling set. In these cases, the assumption has an error, but it has been suppressed by increasing the profiling set size. MLP #23, #25, and #27 in Table 2a work in over-parameterized regime. Their profiling accuracy is more than 95% for all the profiling set sizes. Besides, the sizes of these models are at least six times larger than the largest profiling set size for ASCAD. In the case of MLP #24 and MLP#26, while the models have large sizes, the baseline model cannot reach more than 90% accuracy and, after increasing profiling size to 200,000 traces, the accuracy decreases under 70%. Thus, these models work in the critical regime for all the profiling sizes because the hyperparameter combination does not allow the models to fit the leakage perfectly.

Similar behavior is observed for multilayer perceptrons trained for the ID leakage model. In Table 2b, one can see the required number of attack traces for MLP models trained with 50,000, 100,000, 150,000, and 200,000 traces. There are many cases that follow the more data better generalization principle, but we can see cases that do not show a decrease in the required number of attack traces when we increase the profiling set size. Considering the size of the input layer, which is 1,400 (number of features for the ASCAD dataset), and the size of the output layer, which is 256 (number of classes for the ID leakage model), the smallest model that we managed to find that converges to $GE = 1$ has 68,176 trainable parameters and the baseline model has $\approx 10\%$ accuracy. Then the profiling accuracy decreases to $\approx 3\%$, which is still larger than the validation accuracy ($\approx 1\%$ but still larger than random guessing in the case of the Identity leakage model). MLP #23, #24, and #26 work in an over-parameterized regime for the same reasons as models in Table 2a.

We investigated CNNs and the Hamming weight and Identity leakage models to check if this behavior is still observable. The trained models and the required number of attack traces in this experiment can be analyzed in three regimes. For example, CNNs #1 to #7 in Table 3a work in under-parameterized regime. This can be concluded by considering the profiling accuracy of these models, which is less than 35%, and the proportion between the model sizes and the profiling set sizes. These models' accuracy and loss evolution for the profiling and validation sets do not show significant overfitting, meaning that these models do not have the capacity to memorize the noise in the profiling set. This can be considered as an indication that the number of trainable parameters does not represent the capacity of the models in a way that we can compare models from two different families (cf. results for the MLP and the ID leakage model). To confirm this, we draw attention to the fact that the smallest successful models, in the case of CNNs, have less than 10,000 trainable parameters.

Neural network models like #3 in Table 2a, and #1 and #7 in Table 3a are working in under-parameterized regime and follow the "more data better generalization" principle, but MLP models like #1, #2, and #4 in Table 2a and CNN models like #2 and #5 in Table 3a show a decrease in their generalization power after increasing the profiling set size. Their hyperparameter combination imposes an assumption error on the final model, and the neural network model cannot capture the actual leakage model's distribution. To resolve this, we need to change the hyperparameters so that the final model's parameters can capture the actual leakage model's distribution. The results in Sect. 4.4 show that in a considerable number of cases, a small change in hyperparameters, like changing the activation function or the number of epochs, can result in a neural network model that can capture the underlying leakage model distribution better.

The observations for the over-parameterized regime for MLP also hold for CNN (#23 and #24 in Table 3a). In the case of CNN models in Table 3b, many baseline models reach 100% accuracy, but then this accuracy decreases significantly by increasing the profiling set sizes. Consequently, none of these models work in the over-parameterized regime for all profiling sets. The models are being pushed into the critical regime by increasing the profiling set size.

Table 3. Results for convolutional neural networks.

#	$Params$	NT_1	NT_2	NT_3	NT_4	#	$Params$	NT_1	NT_2	NT_3	NT_4
1	2,959	629	320	286	248	1	6124	1,676	843	938	329
2	5,689	2,670	2,718	801	5,000	2	6,350	1,007	5,000	5,000	157
3	6,579	2,885	1,616	883	934	3	8,390	4,310	5,000	5,000	106
4	9,781	1,319	654	481	521	4	10,646	2,473	598	5,000	5,000
5	15,327	4,821	5,000	5,000	5,000	5	13,274	379	156	60	52
6	15,439	1,862	671	460	502	6	27,140	1,211	111	47	29
7	19,209	3,958	1,303	897	766	7	32,978	5,000	3,320	319	57
8	24,433	813	474	4,141	477	8	54,254	5,000	735	126	55
9	31,113	3,196	1,300	5,000	5,000	9	66,584	5,000	1,469	558	293
10	44,905	3,149	1,855	1,283	982	10	71,272	4,003	199	5,000	5,000
11	57,943	3,660	1,450	1,411	803	11	86,304	5,000	2,139	351	157
12	63,865	2,712	1,270	1,253	756	12	91,080	5,000	4,964	5,000	933
13	75,813	1,587	1,663	1,497	745	13	114,564	4,998	2,636	706	292
14	94,661	2,625	2,586	2,068	2,604	14	134,146	3,058	622	1,546	439
15	100,113	3,673	2,930	2,337	1,501	15	154,696	4,045	1,194	115	58
16	124,585	4,905	3,393	1,458	1,596	16	192,120	5,000	581	270	5,000
17	189,233	4,730	5,000	2,783	2,588	17	202,792	3,239	1,095	422	308
18	243,129	3,983	4,814	2,929	2,487	18	290,536	2,943	5,000	5,000	3,073
19	391,521	2,233	1,721	1,470	1,295	19	356,572	4,767	943	577	195
20	434,121	3,605	2,296	2,677	1,964	20	466,312	5,000	168	5,000	5,000
21	541,243	4,833	3,467	1,162	441	21	598,838	1,946	693	466	249
22	570,753	2,441	1,830	1,165	894	22	662,432	5,000	1,017	516	287
23	984,649	3,525	2,068	1,672	1,661	23	707,656	5,000	3,988	1,914	4,482
24	1,211,881	4,175	3,419	1,554	1,600	24	718,128	5,000	837	196	82
25	1,409,249	3,540	1,867	1,165	905	25	828,774	5,000	3,379	2,764	967

(a) $CNNs$ trained for the HW leakage model. | (b) $CNNs$ trained for the ID leakage model.

4.2   AES_HD Dataset

In the case of the AES_HD dataset, we trained 500 random MLP and 500 random CNN models with the Hamming distance (HD) leakage model and again selected some of the models that converged to GE equal to 1. The AES_HD dataset has twice the number of traces in the profiling set compared to the ASCAD dataset, and this allows us to investigate the model's generalization power after increasing the number of profiling samples for a longer interval. As observed in Table 4, we trained MLP models with profiling sets including 50,000, 100,000, 150,000, 200,000, 250,000, 300,000, 350,000, and 400,000 traces. The required number of attack traces to reach GE equal to 1 for each neural network model shows that the model's generalization did not increase for many cases when we increased the number of profiling traces. The experiment has been repeated for the CNN models, and the same behavior was observed, so we omit those results.

In most cases in Table 4, the models converge to GE equal to 1 for a similar number of attack traces. This means that the increase in the number of profiling traces can change the parameters of the models, and since the output probabilities of the models will change as a result of this, we can see the changes in the required number of attack traces for different profiling set sizes. However, these changes are not improvements in the attack performance as they do not indicate a successful attack performance. On the other hand, the choice of attack traces can have the same effect (i.e., changes in the required number of attack traces). However, there are models like #5 that, for some increases (from 150,000 to 200,000 and from 250,000 to 400,000), cannot even converge. While the training curve of these models shows normal behavior, they cannot rank the correct key better than the random guessing (thus, accuracy cannot serve as an indication of the SCA performance).

In Table 4, MLP #1, #2, #3, and #4, are in the under-parameterized regime. Looking at the required number of attack traces for different profiling set sizes, we cannot see an absolute decrease in this metric. Since the number of trainable parameters in these models in comparison to even 50,000 profiling traces is small, they have learned the leakage model's distribution with a smaller number of profiling traces and gone to the saturation part of the learning curve where adding more traces to the profiling set does not improve the performance. Models like #19, #20, and #21 in Table 4 are working in an over-parametrized regime because they reach $\approx 100\%$ accuracy for all profiling set sizes. In many cases, these neural network models need more than 5,000 attack traces to place the correct key to the first rank. However, by observing the GE evolution, we see that these models could reduce the key entropy, and by adding more attack traces, they can rank the correct key in the first place. This observation shows that models working in an over-parameterized regime cannot perform as well as models working in the under-parameterized regime for the AES_HD dataset. Consequently, there is overfitting that damages the model's generalization from a side-channel perspective. For the models working in a critical regime, the deep double descent effect and assumption error combine. Thus, we can observe (middle of Table 4) that for many cases, the models cannot rank the correct key in the first place with less than 5,000 attack traces.

4.3   Influence of Regularization Techniques

To check the influence of the increasing number of profiling traces in the presence of regularization on the required number of attack traces, we added dropout regularization to neural network models. More precisely, we added a dropout layer with a rate of 0.5 after every dense layer in MLP and CNN models that were selected in Sects. 4.1 and 4.2. The required number of attack traces in this experiment shows that using this technique can improve the performance of the neural models on average, especially for models with medium to large capacity, but still cannot negate the assumption error. In Table 5, one can see the influence of the increasing number of profiling traces on the MLP performance and the HD leakage model for the AES_HD dataset. The same behavior was captured for both CNN and MLP models for the ASCAD and AES_HD datasets.

Table 4. MLP trained for the HD leakage model.

#	$Params$	NT_1	NT_2	NT_3	NT_4	NT_5	NT_6	NT_7	NT_8	NT_9
1	12829	3294	2610	2549	2239	2041	2317	2220	2358	2011
2	26049	2795	2144	2128	2424	1904	2200	2526	2024	1938
3	26049	3268	2753	2060	2204	2470	2679	2816	2732	2608
4	27309	4700	3353	5000	3454	4384	3543	4014	3885	3965
5	60249	3681	3551	2366	5000	3224	5000	5000	2253	5000
6	136109	3445	3798	3321	3778	3391	3757	4478	3122	3118
7	196709	4918	3980	5000	4030	4293	4223	3495	2800	4222
9	292209	4527	5000	5000	5000	5000	5000	5000	5000	5000
10	378009	4867	5000	5000	4285	5000	4213	5000	4367	4288
11	378009	3706	5000	5000	5000	5000	5000	5000	5000	5000
12	412809	3735	3127	3459	2910	2854	2606	3066	2829	3297
13	468309	3880	4542	5000	5000	5000	3418	4001	3664	4732
14	824809	3456	4864	5000	5000	5000	5000	5000	5000	5000
15	824809	3533	3617	3978	5000	4235	4394	3674	4933	5000
16	880509	4339	5000	5000	5000	5000	5000	5000	5000	5000
17	985209	3771	4076	4502	4156	4601	3204	2614	3053	3219
18	1131009	2838	4824	5000	5000	5000	5000	5000	5000	5000
19	1381509	3401	5000	5000	5000	5000	5000	5000	4380	5000
20	1466409	2746	5000	5000	5000	5000	5000	4604	5000	5000
21	2383509	4134	3779	4496	5000	5000	5000	4137	5000	5000

Using dropout regularization influences the working regime of the models significantly. For both MLP and CNN models, almost all the re-trained models worked in the under-parameterized regime, even for the large models, like #9 in Table 5. This model is the counterpart of model #17 in Table 4, and its performance increased considerably. However, dropout regularization does not always improve the model's performance. For example, model #10 in Table 5 cannot converge at all with dropout. Its counterpart is #20 in Table 4 that was able to rank the actual key under 10 for many profiling sizes.

Table 5. *MLP* trained for the *HD* leakage model and the dropout regularization.

#	Params	NT_1	NT_2	NT_3	NT_4	NT_5	NT_6	NT_7	NT_8	NT_9
1	12829	5000	5000	4604	3496	3880	3578	3653	4133	3659
2	40599	4633	3283	3491	2758	3046	2854	2573	3430	2978
3	73209	3161	2574	2873	2600	2426	2548	2812	2411	2615
4	126009	3108	2677	2494	2254	2307	2765	2550	2608	2207
5	252009	5000	5000	5000	5000	5000	5000	5000	5000	5000
6	468309	2212	1740	1970	1942	1978	1784	2269	2291	2065
7	504009	3414	3258	2278	2733	2686	2496	2627	2753	2711
8	648909	1533	1462	1393	1402	1285	1455	1487	1405	1369
9	985209	957	920	902	1249	955	1084	1170	1232	1462
10	1466409	5000	5000	5000	5000	5000	5000	5000	5000	5000

4.4 Reducing Assumption Error by Changing Hyperparameters

Looking into Table 6, one can see the effect of changing a simple hyperparameter on the performance of a neural network model for a specific profiling size. For the sake of brevity, we provide only a few examples (one example from each combination of neural network topology and leakage models for the ASCAD dataset). Model #1 in Table 6, is the counterpart of model #4 in Table 2a. We trained this model for different numbers of epochs (shown in the "EPC" column). While the model that has been trained with 100,000 traces for 200 epochs cannot converge at all, if we train it for 100 epochs, it will be able to find the correct key with 647 attack traces. If we train it for 400 epochs, it will recover the key with 1,196 traces. Model #2 is the counterpart of model #13 in Table 2b. We changed this model's learning rate (shown in the "LR" column). As one can see in Table 6, this change improved its performance. Finally, models #3 and #4 are the counterpart of models #9 in Table 3a and model#2 in Table 3b. Changing the activation function (shown in the "Act. Func." column) in the case of these two models increased the performance considerably. In many other cases, changing hyperparameters led to the improvement of the models that could not converge to $GE = 1$ for a specific profiling set size.

Table 6. Results with small changes in hyperparameters.

#	Params	NT_1	NT_2	NT_3	NT_4	EPC	LR	Act. func
1	31149	3615	5000	622	5000	200	0.005	Adam
1	31149	3688	1196	5000	2434	400	0.005	Adam
1	31149	3856	647	5000	5000	100	0.005	Adam
2	663056	4821	3406	1343	713	200	0.0005	Adam
2	663056	4427	2053	886	496	200	0.0001	Adam
3	31113	3196	1300	5000	5000	200	0.005	Adam
3	31113	2415	5000	5000	621	200	0.0001	Adam
3	31113	3237	887	603	838	200	0.005	RMSprop
4	6350	1007	5000	5000	157	200	0.001	RMSprop
4	6350	675	133	2096	116	400	0.001	RMSprop
4	6350	1114	111	47	31	200	0.001	Adam

4.5   General Observations

- Increasing the profiling set size is not a guaranteed solution to increase the generalization power of a neural network model in deep learning-based SCA. The effects of the working regime on the performance of a model in the side-channel domain and the assumption error imposed by the hyperparameters combination cause the overall irregular behavior of the models regarding the increasing profiling set size.
- The under-parameterized models perform better than the critical and over-parameterized models in the SCA domain. While the theory indicates that over-parameterized models can reach better performance compared to under-parameterized models in a number of settings [2], this was not the case for SCA so far, especially for a noisy dataset like AES_HD.
- Compared to the neural network models working in the under-parameterized regime, the models working in the over-parameterized regime have a large capacity, and their number of trainable parameters is much larger than the number of traces in the profiling set. On average, such models need more traces to rank the correct key in the first place compared to the neural network models working in the under-parameterized regime. Still, it is possible to converge to $GE = 1$ with a small number of attack traces using large models and regularization.
- In many deep learning classification applications, we are interested in the final decision of the model, i.e., the class that the model assigns to measurement and not the probability that the model calculates to assign that measurement to a specific class. Contrary, in SCA, we are interested in the probabilities that a model assigns to each class for each measurement. Thus, small deviations in the estimated distribution function based on the profiling set will lead to significant changes in the model's performance from an SCA perspective. Since over-parameterized models have a large capacity and many parameters

shape the underlying leakage model distribution, they have more potential to contain assumption errors.

- A model working in a critical regime is very fragile, and in some cases, even a small change can decrease its performance noticeably. Thus, a cautionary solution could be to avoid using such models.
- Overfitting is a complex phenomenon, and we cannot trace its causes to only one source. Still, our results indicate that hyperparameter combinations play a more significant role than the profiling set size.

5   Conclusions and Future Work

This work investigates overfitting in deep learning-based SCA. We challenge the common assumption that more profiling traces is better, and we show that, while this may be the case, it cannot be taken for granted. Indeed, our experiments showed a number of settings where adding more profiling traces makes the attack less powerful or even unsuccessful. A simple yet powerful option to fight against overfitting is to use regularization or tweak the neural network architecture. Unfortunately, using such techniques does not also provide a guarantee to avoid overfitting. Thus, it is necessary to carefully design the model and assess its performance with different settings to understand in what regime the model works and then use the most appropriate one (which seems to be the under-parameterized regime). Finally, our research provides the setup to be more precise when discussing the failure of deep learning models in SCA. Instead of "simply" saying there is overfitting, one should strive to give insights what are the causes of that behavior. In future work, it would be interesting to provide a systematic approach on how to tweak hyperparameter changes to improve the attack performance. Besides, we again saw the beneficial effects of regularization (see, e.g., [14]), so it is somewhat surprising that there are no systematic evaluations on the relevance of regularization techniques in SCA.

Acknowledgment. This work received funding in the framework of the NWA Cybersecurity Call with project name PROACT with project number NWA.1215.18.014, which is (partly) financed by the Netherlands Organisation for Scientific Research (NWO). Additionally, this work was supported in part by the Netherlands Organization for Scientific Research NWO project DISTANT (CS.019).

References

1. Agence nationale de la sécurité des systèmes d'information (ANSSI): ASCAD. Github repository (2018). https://github.com/ANSSI-FR/ASCAD
2. Bartlett, P.L., Montanari, A., Rakhlin, A.: Deep learning: a statistical viewpoint. CoRR abs/2103.09177 (2021). https://arxiv.org/abs/2103.09177
3. Belkin, M., Hsu, D., Ma, S., Mandal, S.: Reconciling modern machine-learning practice and the classical bias-variance trade-off. Proc. Natl. Acad. Sci. **116**(32), 15849–15854 (2019)

4. Bhasin, S., Chattopadhyay, A., Heuser, A., Jap, D., Picek, S., Shrivastwa, R.R.: Mind the portability: a warriors guide through realistic profiled side-channel analysis. In: 27th Annual Network and Distributed System Security Symposium, NDSS 2020, San Diego, California, USA, 23–26 February 2020. The Internet Society (2020)

5. Brier, E., Clavier, C., Olivier, F.: Correlation power analysis with a leakage model. In: Joye, M., Quisquater, J.-J. (eds.) CHES 2004. LNCS, vol. 3156, pp. 16–29. Springer, Heidelberg (2004). https://doi.org/10.1007/978-3-540-28632-5_2

6. Bronchain, O., Hendrickx, J.M., Massart, C., Olshevsky, A., Standaert, F.-X.: Leakage certification revisited: bounding model errors in side-channel security evaluations. In: Boldyreva, A., Micciancio, D. (eds.) CRYPTO 2019. LNCS, vol. 11692, pp. 713–737. Springer, Cham (2019). https://doi.org/10.1007/978-3-030-26948-7_25

7. Cagli, E., Dumas, C., Prouff, E.: Convolutional neural networks with data augmentation against jitter-based countermeasures. In: Fischer, W., Homma, N. (eds.) CHES 2017. LNCS, vol. 10529, pp. 45–68. Springer, Cham (2017). https://doi.org/10.1007/978-3-319-66787-4_3

8. Chari, S., Jutla, C.S., Rao, J.R., Rohatgi, P.: Towards sound approaches to counteract power-analysis attacks. In: Wiener, M. (ed.) CRYPTO 1999. LNCS, vol. 1666, pp. 398–412. Springer, Heidelberg (1999). https://doi.org/10.1007/3-540-48405-1_26

9. Chari, S., Rao, J.R., Rohatgi, P.: Template attacks. In: Kaliski, B.S., Koç, K., Paar, C. (eds.) CHES 2002. LNCS, vol. 2523, pp. 13–28. Springer, Heidelberg (2003). https://doi.org/10.1007/3-540-36400-5_3

10. Choudary, O., Kuhn, M.G.: Efficient template attacks. In: Francillon, A., Rohatgi, P. (eds.) CARDIS 2013. LNCS, vol. 8419, pp. 253–270. Springer, Cham (2014). https://doi.org/10.1007/978-3-319-08302-5_17

11. Durvaux, F., Standaert, F.-X., Veyrat-Charvillon, N.: How to certify the leakage of a chip? In: Nguyen, P.Q., Oswald, E. (eds.) EUROCRYPT 2014. LNCS, vol. 8441, pp. 459–476. Springer, Heidelberg (2014). https://doi.org/10.1007/978-3-642-55220-5_26

12. Gierlichs, B., Batina, L., Tuyls, P., Preneel, B.: Mutual information analysis. In: Oswald, E., Rohatgi, P. (eds.) CHES 2008. LNCS, vol. 5154, pp. 426–442. Springer, Heidelberg (2008). https://doi.org/10.1007/978-3-540-85053-3_27

13. Huang, Y., et al.: Gpipe: efficient training of giant neural networks using pipeline parallelism. CoRR abs/1811.06965 (2018). https://arxiv.org/abs/1811.06965

14. Kim, J., Picek, S., Heuser, A., Bhasin, S., Hanjalic, A.: Make some noise. unleashing the power of convolutional neural networks for profiled side-channel analysis. IACR Trans. Cryptographic Hardware Embed. Syst. 148–179 (2019)

15. Kocher, P., Jaffe, J., Jun, B.: Differential power analysis. In: Wiener, M. (ed.) CRYPTO 1999. LNCS, vol. 1666, pp. 388–397. Springer, Heidelberg (1999). https://doi.org/10.1007/3-540-48405-1_25

16. Krizhevsky, A., Sutskever, I., Hinton, G.E.: Imagenet classification with deep convolutional neural networks. In: Bartlett, P.L., Pereira, F.C.N., Burges, C.J.C., Bottou, L., Weinberger, K.Q. (eds.) Advances in Neural Information Processing Systems 25: 26th Annual Conference on Neural Information Processing Systems 2012. Proceedings of a meeting held 3–6 December 2012, Lake Tahoe, Nevada, United States, pp. 1106–1114 (2012)

17. Maghrebi, H., Portigliatti, T., Prouff, E.: Breaking cryptographic implementations using deep learning techniques. In: Carlet, C., Hasan, M.A., Saraswat, V. (eds.)

SPACE 2016. LNCS, vol. 10076, pp. 3–26. Springer, Cham (2016). https://doi.org/10.1007/978-3-319-49445-6_1

18. Masure, L., Dumas, C., Prouff, E.: A comprehensive study of deep learning for side-channel analysis. IACR Trans. Cryptographic Hardware Embed. Syst. **2020**(1), 348–375 (2020). https://doi.org/10.13154/tches.v2020.i1.348-375

19. Messerges, T.S., Dabbish, E.A., Sloan, R.H.: Power analysis attacks of modular exponentiation in smartcards. In: Koç, Ç.K., Paar, C. (eds.) CHES 1999. LNCS, vol. 1717, pp. 144–157. Springer, Heidelberg (1999). https://doi.org/10.1007/3-540-48059-5_14

20. Nakkiran, P., Kaplun, G., Bansal, Y., Yang, T., Barak, B., Sutskever, I.: Deep double descent: where bigger models and more data hurt. In: 8th International Conference on Learning Representations, ICLR 2020, Addis Ababa, Ethiopia, 26–30 April 2020. OpenReview.net (2020). https://openreview.net/forum?id=B1g5sA4twr

21. Perin, G., Chmielewski, L., Picek, S.: Strength in numbers: improving generalization with ensembles in machine learning-based profiled side-channel analysis. IACR Trans. Cryptographic Hardware Embed. Syst. **2020**(4), 337–364 (2020). https://doi.org/10.13154/tches.v2020.i4.337-364

22. Perin, G., Picek, S.: On the influence of optimizers in deep learning-based side-channel analysis. In: Dunkelman, O., Jacobson, Jr., M.J., O'Flynn, C. (eds.) SAC 2020. LNCS, vol. 12804, pp. 615–636. Springer, Cham (2021). https://doi.org/10.1007/978-3-030-81652-0_24

23. Picek, S., Heuser, A., Jovic, A., Bhasin, S., Regazzoni, F.: The curse of class imbalance and conflicting metrics with machine learning for side-channel evaluations. IACR Trans. Cryptographic Hardware Embed. Syst. **2019**(1), 209–237 (2019). https://doi.org/10.13154/tches.v2019.i1.209-237

24. Picek, S., Heuser, A., Perin, G., Guilley, S.: Profiling side-channel analysis in the efficient attacker framework. Cryptology ePrint Archive, Report 2019/168 (2019). https://ia.cr/2019/168

25. Prouff, E., Strullu, R., Benadjila, R., Cagli, E., Dumas, C.: Study of deep learning techniques for side-channel analysis and introduction to ASCAD database. IACR Cryptol. ePrint Arch. p. 53 (2018). https://eprint.iacr.org/2018/053

26. Rijsdijk, J., Wu, L., Perin, G., Picek, S.: Reinforcement learning for hyperparameter tuning in deep learning-based side-channel analysis. IACR Trans. Cryptographic Hardware Embed. Syst. **2021**(3), 677–707 (2021). https://doi.org/10.46586/tches.v2021.i3.677-707

27. Szegedy, C., et al.: Going deeper with convolutions. In: IEEE Conference on Computer Vision and Pattern Recognition, CVPR 2015, Boston, MA, USA, 7–12 June 2015, pp. 1–9. IEEE Computer Society (2015). https://doi.org/10.1109/CVPR.2015.7298594

28. Wu, L., Perin, G., Picek, S.: I choose you: automated hyperparameter tuning for deep learning-based side-channel analysis. IACR Cryptol. ePrint Arch. p. 1293 (2020). https://eprint.iacr.org/2020/1293

29. Ying, X.: An overview of overfitting and its solutions. In: Journal of Physics: Conference Series, vol. 1168, p. 022022 (2019). https://doi.org/10.1088/1742-6596/1168/2/022022

30. Zaid, G., Bossuet, L., Habrard, A., Venelli, A.: Methodology for efficient CNN architectures in profiling attacks. IACR Trans. Cryptographic Hardware Embed. Syst. **2020**(1), 1–36 (2020). https://doi.org/10.13154/tches.v2020.i1.1-36

31. Zhang, C., Bengio, S., Hardt, M., Recht, B., Vinyals, O.: Understanding deep learning (still) requires rethinking generalization. Commun. ACM **64**(3), 107–115 (2021). https://doi.org/10.1145/3446776

Protocols and Foundations

A Secure Authentication Protocol for Cholesteric Spherical Reflectors Using Homomorphic Encryption

Mónica P. Arenas[1]($\boxtimes$) iD, Muhammed Ali Bingol[2]($\boxtimes$) iD, Hüseyin Demirci[1] iD, Georgios Fotiadis[1] iD, and Gabriele Lenzini[1]($\boxtimes$) iD

[1] SnT, University of Luxembourg, Esch-sur-Alzette, Luxembourg
{monica.arenas,huseyin.demirci,georgios.fotiadis,
gabriele.lenzini}@uni.lu
[2] Cyber Technology Institute, De Montfort University, Leicester, UK
muhammed.bingol@dmu.ac.uk

Abstract. Sometimes fingerprint-like features are found in a material. The exciting discovery poses new challenges on how to use the features to build an object authentication protocol that could tell customers and retailers equipped with a mobile device whether a good is authentic or fake. We are exactly in this situation with Cholesteric Spherical Reflectors (CSRs), tiny spheres of liquid crystals with which we can tag or coat objects. They are being proposed as a potential game-changer material in anti-counterfeiting due to their unique optical properties. In addition to the problem of processing images and extracting the minutiæ embedded in a CSR, one major challenge is designing cryptographically secure authentication protocols. The authentication procedure has to handle unstable input data; it has to measure the distance between some reference data stored at enrollment and noisy input provided at authentication. We propose a cryptographic authentication protocol that solves the problem, and that is secure against semi-honest and malicious adversaries. We prove that our design ensures data privacy even if enrolled data are leaked and even if servers and provers are actively curious. We implement and benchmark the protocol in Python using the Microsoft SEAL library through its Python wrapper PySEAL.

Keywords: Anti-counterfeiting · Cholesteric Spherical Reflectors · Image processing · Authentication · Biometric hashing · Homomorphic encryption

1 Introduction

To verify that an object is authentic, one has to seek in the object for certain features that are hard to reproduce in a counterfeited copy. To verify that an object is exactly that object and not another of the same family, those features must be unique. The identifying features can be derived from the object itself as it happens for our fingerprints [25]; or, they can be borrowed because of a tag,

L. Batina and J. Daemen (Eds.): AFRICACRYPT 2022, LNCS 13503, pp. 425–447, 2022.
https://doi.org/10.1007/978-3-031-17433-9_18

a coating, or a watermarking applied onto the object. The features have to be extracted, recognized, and authenticated in both cases.

A common process is to extract the features from an image of the object or of its tag, coat, or watermark, and verify them (authentication phase) by measuring how similar they are from a reference version of the features previously extracted from the same object and securely stored (enrollment phase). A "match" means authentication, a "mismatch" a non-authentication[1]. The process sounds simple, but the devil is in the details. The nature of the identifying features is extremely variable and strongly object-dependent. The analysis of features from an image requires dedicated minutiæ extraction procedures [5,21]. The authentication, i.e., matching a freshly input and the securely stored version, must be robust to noise. Furthermore, if the database that holds the original set of reference features is stored remotely, e.g., if the authentication works as a service, the process needs a security protocol that foresees the different drawbacks caused by security vulnerabilities and authorization attacks [18].

Needless to say, there is no general authentication protocol that works across different objects. Here, we address the problem of a particular material with fingerprint-like features that can be used to create tags and, to a certain extent, to coat objects. The material is composed of *Cholesteric Liquid Crystals (CLCs)*, the liquid we know from our digital device's screens, made in a spherical shape. Called CSRs in [12,14], spherical CLCs reflect light creating patterns (see Fig. 1) that have been argued to be unique and physically unclonable [12,24]. Although the nature of CSR is different from biometric data, they converge in their noisy and unique behavior. A reliable and secure process needs to be implemented to reconstruct binary strings from noise inputs. Once reliable information extraction is granted, it must be protected. Homomorphic encryption can ensure the process of the data in the encrypted domain, which has proven effective in ensuring the privacy of sensitive data [28]. CSRs tags have been demonstrated as a promising material in applications such as anti-counterfeiting, track-and-tracing, authentication systems, and fiducial markers [32].

Contributions. We showed how to extract minutiæ from CSR images in previous works [2,3]. However, a procedure was still missing to obtain robust information from the extracted features and to develop a cryptographically secure and effective authentication protocol. In this paper, we design a cryptographic authentication protocol for CSRs, which securely authenticates objects with a coat or tag containing CSRs.

Specifically, the contribution of this paper can be viewed from both theoretical and practical angles. More concretely, we have developed the following procedures: *i) features embedding* and *robust feature identification* of the minutiæ to increase information stability in the presence of noise; *ii)* cryptographic protocol for remote authentication that relies on *biometric hashing* and on *homomorphic encryption*; which we proved to be robust to attacks from semi-honest and malicious adversaries; and *iii)* formulation of the Hamming distance in the encrypted

---

[1] Match and mismatch will be defined over the features metric space.

domain, based on which authentication is achieved by comparing two homomorphically encrypted bitstrings. Our proposed protocol is accompanied by a proof-of-concept implementation in Python, using the PySEAL library for homomorphic encryption[2] which implements the Brakerski/Fan-Vercauteren (BFV) (somewhat) homomorphic encryption scheme [9,11]. Based on our implementation, we provide extensive performance benchmarking results, focusing especially on the core homomorphic operations that are required for computing the Hamming distance on encrypted data. The source code of our implementation is available at https://gitlab.uni.lu/irisc-open-data/2021-nofakes.

To the best of our knowledge, there is no previous work that combines CSR's optical responses in a cryptographic authentication protocol, which is unsurprising since the use of CSRs in security is quite recent and largely unexplored. But, our research has a wider application than just in relation to CSRs. The minutiæ extraction process and the protocol that we design are applicable to several anti-counterfeiting technologies. As we will see in Sect. 2—where we briefly recall how a CSR response looks like—our information extraction strategy assumes that the identifying information contained in an image (i.e., the minutiæ) are *colored blobs* (i.e., connected pixels forming a circular shape) "randomly"[3] distributed in a bi-dimensional space. Our information extraction and authentication protocol are built assuming vectors of blobs, internally represented as a list of tuples whose elements model the blobs as circles (i.e., centers and radii) and colors. Thus, what we have developed, modeled, and implemented here works for any watermarking, steganography, or optical unclonable functions that embody colored blobs as minutiæ.

Outline. Section 2 recalls the necessary background for CSRs and discusses the related work. In Sect. 3, we introduce our design, showing a robust-to-noise scheme to extract binary information from CSR images (Sect. 3.1), and an innovative cryptographic protocol design for object authentication. It uses tools such as biometric hashing to create stable bitstrings of information and homomorphic encryption to securely compare them in the authentication phase (Sect. 3.2). Section 4 discusses the security of the design under malicious and semi-honest adversary models enabling security against outsider attackers and insider provers, respectively. In Sect. 5, we demonstrate our implementation details and results of the proposed authentication protocol. Finally, Sect. 6 concludes the work and discusses open questions and future research.

2   Background and Related Work

Cholesteric Liquid Crystals and Reflectors. CLCs have been intensively studied in chemistry and matter physics for their optical properties and versatility [12,13,31]. Here, we recall the very basics necessary to understand our contribution. What is important to know is that "CSR" is a name to indicate

---

[2] https://github.com/Lab41/PySEAL.
[3] "Random" is intended informally, meaning "in a way that we cannot anticipate".

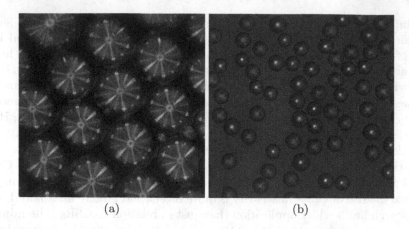

$$(a) \qquad\qquad\qquad (b)$$

Fig. 1. CSRs images acquired with (a) a DinoLite microscope and (b) a professional microscope.

CLCs in a spherical shape. The spheres —droplets, if full of liquid, or shells, if cave with the liquid only on the external surface— are tiny: they measure between 10 μm and 300 μm in diameter. CSRs can be produced in a large number, and they are delivered in a medium, e.g., a piece of plastic or a dried varnish, which we call a *CSR tag*. The absolute and the relative position of the CSRs in the tag is unpredictable because it is not possible to control that variable at the production phase. When illuminated, CSRs reflect the light, creating a peculiar colorful pattern. We can capture that image with a microscope, e.g., one of those we can plug into a computer with a USB cable. Such images (see Fig. 1-*a*) are what we assume to have as input. From the images, we can extract blobs, for instance, by following the procedure described in [2,3], using image processing.

Cryptographic Techniques in Object Authentication. Regarding object authentication and anti-counterfeiting, two topics closely related to one another and addressed by academic and industrial research alike, the literature is vast. What is relevant to position our contribution is the works that use cryptographic techniques such as those we also employ, namely biometric hashing and homomorphic encryption.

Before applying any cryptographic technique, we need to ensure the extraction of reliable information. For this purpose, we applied some techniques reported in the literature [35]. Tuyls *et al.* [35] proposed a helper data that guarantees the extraction of a unique and robust string from fingerprint biometrics data during the enrollment and authentication phases. As this helper data was stored in a database (public), the authors hashed it to keep the reference data sheltered from somebody that has access to the database. Once reliable information extraction is granted, it must be protected. Fully Homomorphic Encryption (FHE) can ensure to process the data in the encrypted domain. Again, research in biometrics is rich in inspiring results. Lattice-based FHE have been proved effective in ensuring privacy in biometric iris authentication [34], and private face recognition [8]. Homomorphic probabilistic encryption, a version compatible with the ISO/IEC 24745 standard on biometric data protection, has been used in a general framework for multi-biometric template protection [16].

Pradel and Mitchell [28] have recently proposed a privacy-preserving biometrics authentication protocol based on FHE, where a user's biometric sample is matched against an encrypted biometric template held by a remote system. This remote authentication protocol protects the privacy of users' sensitive data. They also conducted a proof-of-concept implementation using the TFHE[4] library and analyzed it in terms of efficiency. The underlying basic operations needed to execute the biometric matching are well described. Still, the performance results from the implementation show how complex it is to make FHE practical in this context. Pradel and Mitchell's implementation, if improved and optimized, could be used for real-world applications.

3   The Proposed Protocol

We propose an object authentication protocol that consists of two main parts where in each part, a set of various functionalities is deployed. The first part copes with data instability due to macro problems in image acquisition and processing. This is described in Sect. 3.1. The second part, which implements the authentication protocol and its enrollment and verification phases, is robust to noise at the level of bitstring values introduced when we extract and encode minutiæ from the inputs. It relies on biometric hashing and ensures the security of the protocol by storing encrypted data using homomorphic encryption. Authentication is achieved by comparing two homomorphically encrypted bitstrings obtained in the enrollment and authentication phases, in terms of their Hamming distance which is computed in the encrypted domain. When the Hamming distance is below a predefined threshold, the authentication is successful, otherwise it fails. Our protocol is introduced in Sect. 3.2, while the enrollment and authentication phases are described in Sects. 3.3 and 3.4, respectively.

3.1   Extraction of Robust Features

One necessary step must be done before we can describe any cryptographic protocol, which is to digitalize the information that is embedded into a CSR. The contact point with the reality of CSR is a picture of a CSR's optical response, an object that we indicate as [CSR]. Such pictures are noisy. Retaken pictures from the same CSR, i.e., $\{[\text{CSR}]'_1, \ldots, [\text{CSR}]'_m\}$, are slightly different one from the other due to uncontrollable factors, such as ambient light, read-out process, and variances in the sensor of the digital camera.

The reader can refer to the original work [3] for details. Still, here we recall that any [CSR] contains identifying minutiæ (technically, blobs) that can be identified and extracted by processing the image. These minutiæ are modeled and

---

[4] https://tfhe.github.io/tfhe/.

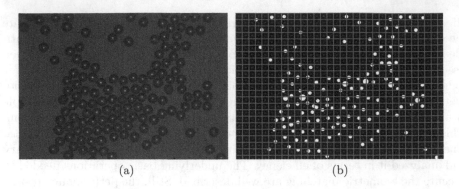

Fig. 2. (a) an example of [CSR] and (b) its extracted minutiæ embedded on a grid.

represented as a *list of colored circles*. We abstract the *feature extraction* process as a function Extract, whose domain is the set of all CSR images. An output Extract($[CSR]_i$) is a list $\boldsymbol{\omega}_i = (\omega_i(1), \ldots, \omega_i(n))$. Each element ω in that list is a pair $(\omega.c, \omega.rgb)$, where the first item is a circle and the second its color. A circle c is described in terms of coordinates of its center, $c.x$ and $c.y$, and radius, $c.r$.

The features extraction algorithm operates on noisy inputs and returns noisy outputs: depending on i, Extract($[CSR]_i$) varies not only in the numerical values but also in the length of the outputted list, that is, in the number of blobs detected. We have to correct and unify that high-level noise. Abstracting from any detail, we represent this process with two functions:

FeaturesEmbedding– using an $N \times M$ mesh grid (see Fig. 2-b), it returns a list of *exactly* $n = N \times M$ elements $\boldsymbol{\omega} = (\omega(1), \ldots, \omega(n))$. Each element is either a blob, the blob found in that position in the grid, or the undefined element $\bot$, if no blob is found there.

RobustPositions– taking a list of extracted embedded features, $(\boldsymbol{\omega}_1, \ldots, \boldsymbol{\omega}_m)$, from m sample images $\{[CSR]_i'\}$ for $i \in \{1, \ldots, m\}$, each $\boldsymbol{\omega}_i$ returns a set $K \subseteq \{1, \ldots, n\}$ of *reliable positions* i.e., indexes where, in all the m extracted features $\{(\omega_i(1), \ldots, \omega_i(n))\}$, there is either all blobs or all $\bot$. It returns also a list $\boldsymbol{\omega} = \{\omega(j)\}_{j \in K}$ of *reliable features* which are obtained by "averaging"[5] the values across the samples for all the reliable positions.

We use the two functions to pre-process CSR images in both authentication and enrollment. We call ReliableFeatures the front-end function, so defined:

$$
\begin{aligned}
&\text{ReliableFeatures}(\{[CSR]_1, \ldots, [CSR]_m\}) := \\
&\quad \text{RobustPositions(} \\
&\qquad \text{FeaturesEmbedding(} \\
&\qquad\quad (\text{Extract}([CSR]_1), \ldots, \text{Extract}([CSR]_m))))
\end{aligned}
\tag{1}
$$

---

[5] It is a means on the values of blobs, and it returns $\bot$ when one of the elements is $\bot$.

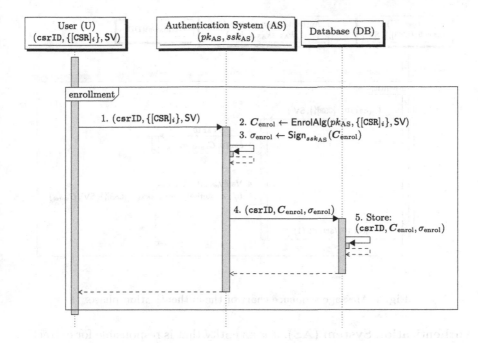

Fig. 3. Message sequence chart of the enrollment phase.

The output of the function ReliableFeatures is a vector $\boldsymbol{\omega} = (\omega(1), \ldots, \omega(k))$, of reliable features.

3.2 Protocol Description

We present an authentication protocol that uses CSR images and a biometric hashing (in short, *biohashing*) mechanism. Biohashing schemes are simple yet powerful biometric template protection methods [4,20,27,33].

Our protocol is divided into two main phases: *enrollment*, where the reference data from each CSR image are collected, and *authentication*, where it is verified whether a specific CSR image matches the one that has been enrolled.

We distinguish three entities that participate in the protocol: namely the *User*, the *Authentication System*, and an outsourced *Database*, with the following roles and responsibilities:

User (U): holds the CSR and provides the CSR images, [CSR]$_i$[6]. CSR comes with a numerical identifier, csrID, which U is able to read, and with a SV (i.e., a PIN/password, QR code, RFID data, or item image), a token that we intend to use for second-factor authentication.

---

[6] Here, the number of pictures that a User takes in the enrollment and authentication can be defined by the process. We used five images in our implementation, see Sect. 5.

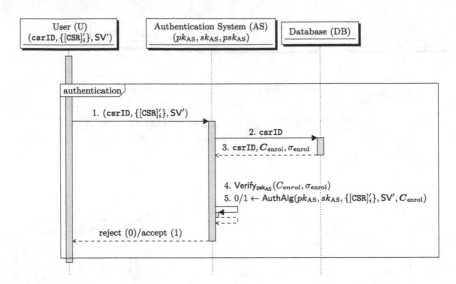

Fig. 4. Message sequence chart of the authentication phase.

Authentication System (AS): it is an entity that is responsible for extracting reliable features and carrying out the enrollment and authentication procedures. It can be a trusted hardware, for instance, in the device operated by the User. In the enrollment phase, it receives from the User CSR images and other data that it needs to calculate a binary vector V_{enrol}. The vector is encrypted homomorphically and stored in an outsourced database for later uses (see Fig. 3). In the *authentication phase*, it gets from the User an authentication request, with fresh CSR images, the object identifier, and the second-factor value, which AS processes to produce a new binary vector V_{auth}. The encryption of this value is compared against the one stored, which is retrieved thanks to the object identifier (see Fig. 4). The comparison is accomplished by computing the Hamming distance of the plaintext vectors V_{enrol} and V_{auth} in the encrypted domain, using the homomorphic operations. A successful authentication implies that the Hamming distance is below an acceptable threshold, while a failure indicates that the Hamming distance exceeds that threshold. The enrollment and authentication phases are discussed in more detail in Sects. 3.3 and 3.4, respectively. We further assume that the AS is equipped with a public/private key pair $(pk_{\mathrm{AS}}, sk_{\mathrm{AS}})$, to be used in the homomorphic cryptosystem, and with a public/private signing key pair $(psk_{\mathrm{AS}}, ssk_{\mathrm{AS}})$, to be used in a digital signature scheme.

Outsourced database (DB): it is the database of encrypted features maintained by an outsourced entity. For instance, it can be "in the Cloud". It is responsible for securely storing the data received from the AS in the enrollment phase. In contrast, in the authentication phase, it is responsible for retrieving the necessary information requested from the AS and transmitting this information to the AS.

3.3   Enrollment Phase

The first step in the CSR authentication protocol is the enrollment phase, in which the User sends data necessary for the enrollment for the first time to the AS. Without loss of generality, we assume that the User performs the enrollment. In reality, it can be another role, for instance, the producer of the object that carries the CSR or the producer the CSR. Then the AS executes a series of actions which are described in Algorithm 1. In this phase CSR images (i.e., a set of images $\{[\text{CSR}]_i\}$) are taken for the first time and converted by the AS into a CSR template $\omega = (\omega(1), \ldots, \omega(k))$, according to the procedure ReliableFeatures, described in Sect. 3.1. Then AS executes the biohashing scheme of Ngo et al. [27] based on random projection. It consists of two steps:

Random Projection (RP)– In this step, an identically distributed pseudo RP matrix, $R \in \mathbb{R}^{n \times k}$, is generated from a Gaussian distribution with zero mean and unit variance to transform the reliable features vector built from the CSR images provided by the User. The elements of RP can be generated from a Pseudorandom Number Generator (PRNG), with a seed derived from the User's SV value, and Gram-Schmidt (GS) procedure [29] is applied to obtain an orthonormal projection matrix. After that, the RP matrix is multiplied with the CSR template ω to project this vector onto an n-dimensional intermediate vector $I = R\omega$ where $I \in \mathbb{R}^{n \times 1}$.

Quantization– This step involves the binarization of the elements of the intermediate vector I with respect to a quantization threshold β. The User's SV is mapped to an n-bit string $h = H(\text{SV})$, where $h = (h(1), \cdots, h(n)) \in \{0,1\}^n$ and H is a cryptographic hash function. Then the enrollment biohash vector $V_{\text{enrol}} = (V_{\text{enrol}}(1), \cdots, V_{\text{enrol}}(n))$ of the User is constructed, via the relation:

$$V_{\text{enrol}}(i) = \begin{cases} 1 \oplus h(i), & I(i) \geq \beta \\ h(i), & \text{otherwise} \end{cases},$$

where $V_{\text{enrol}}(i) \in \{0,1\}$. Without loss of generality, β can be selected as the mean value of the intermediate vector I or the sign operator (i.e., 0), depending on the design of the system.

After the quantization, the User's biohash vector V_{enrol} is encrypted bit-by-bit with the public key pk_{AS} of the AS, using a secure homomorphic encryption scheme. The result is a vector $C_{\text{enrol}} = (C_{\text{enrol}}(1), \cdots, C_{\text{enrol}}(n))$ which is composed of n ciphertexts. Finally, the AS signs the ciphertext C_{enrol} with its secret signing key ssk_{AS}, using a standard secure digital signature algorithm (such as ECDSA [19]), and stores the triple $(\text{csrID}, C_{\text{enrol}}, \sigma_{\text{enrol}})$ in an outsourced DB. We note here that once the AS transmits the data to the DB and the enrollment is completed, it clears all the residual data from its memory. In other words, the AS does not store any processed information related to the User, such as CSR images, the SV or V_{enrol} which are considered sensitive information. On the contrary, we assume that the private parts of the encryption and signing key pairs are securely stored, for example, in a Hardware Security Module (HSM).

Algorithm 1: Enrollment algorithm (EnrolAlg)

Input: pk_{AS}, $\{[\text{CSR}]_i\}$, SV.
Output: C_{enrol}.
System Parameters: The RP matrix $R \in \mathbb{R}^{n \times k}$, a threshold β.
1 Feature extraction: $\omega \leftarrow \text{ReliableFeatures}(\{[\text{CSR}]_i\})$
2 Compute the intermediate vector: $I \leftarrow R\omega$, where $I \in \mathbb{R}^{n \times 1}$
3 Compute: $h \leftarrow H(\text{SV})$ where $h = (h(1), \ldots, h(n))$ and $h(i) \in \{0, 1\}$
4 $C_{\text{enrol}} \leftarrow \{\}$
5 **for** $i \in \{1, \ldots, n\}$ **do**
6   **if** $I(i) \geq \beta$ **then**
7 | $V_{\text{enrol}}(i) \leftarrow 1 \oplus h(i)$
8   **else**
9 | $V_{\text{enrol}}(i) \leftarrow h(i)$
10   Compute: $C_{\text{enrol}}(i) \leftarrow \text{HEnc}_{pk_{AS}}(V_{\text{enrol}}(i))$
11   Append $C_{\text{enrol}}(i)$ to C_{enrol}
12 **return** C_{enrol}

It is worth saying that, the User's SV also provides privacy-friendly revocation ability of the CSR's biohash in case it is needed (due to customization or membership termination) without revealing CSR data. In addition, the same CSR template of an item/subject can be utilized in various recognition systems without violating the privacy, as two biohash vectors V_{enrol} of the CSR with different User SV will be unlinkable.

3.4 Authentication Phase

The authentication phase is initiated by the User who sends the freshly taken set of images $\{[\text{CSR}]_i'\}$ from the object holding the CSR, the potentially different secret value SV' and object identifier csrID to the AS. The AS requests from the DB to search for an entry with CSR identifier csrID. If such an entry exists, the DB transmits to the AS the C_{enrol} and σ_{enrol} that correspond to the identifier csrID. Before proceeding to the authentication, the AS verifies the signature with the public signing key psk_{AS}. If the signature is not verified, the AS returns a failure message to the User. Once the signature is verified, the AS executes the authentication Algorithm 2, on input its public and private keys pk_{AS}, sk_{AS}, the images $\{[\text{CSR}]_i'\}$, the secret value SV', and the ciphertext C_{enrol}.

The first step in the authentication algorithm is to extract a reliable CSR template $\omega' \leftarrow \text{ReliableFeatures}(\{[\text{CSR}]_i'\})$ following the procedure described in Sect. 3.1. Using ω' and SV' the authentication algorithm creates a ciphertext vector C_{auth} that corresponds to the CSR' and SV', in the same way as in the enrollment phase. More concretely, $C_{\text{auth}} = (C_{\text{auth}}(1), \cdots, C_{\text{auth}}(n))$ is the result of the bit-by-bit homomorphic encryption of the biohash vector $V_{\text{auth}} = (V_{\text{auth}}(1), \cdots, V_{\text{auth}}(n))$, which is obtained through the quantization process, where $V_{\text{auth}}(i) \in \{0, 1\}$ for each $i = 1, \ldots, n$.

Algorithm 2: Authentication algorithm (AuthAlg)

Input: pk_{AS}, sk_{AS}, $\{[\text{CSR}]_i'\}$, SV', C_{enrol}.
Output: 0 (reject) or 1 (accept).
System Parameters: The RP matrix $\boldsymbol{R} \in \mathbb{R}^{n \times k}$, thresholds β and ε.

1 Feature extraction: $\boldsymbol{\omega}' \leftarrow \text{ReliableFeatures}(\{[\text{CSR}]_i'\})$
2 Compute the intermediate vector: $\boldsymbol{I}' \leftarrow \boldsymbol{R}\boldsymbol{\omega}'$, where $\boldsymbol{I}' \in \mathbb{R}^{n \times 1}$
3 Compute: $\boldsymbol{h}' \leftarrow H(\text{SV}')$ where $\boldsymbol{h}' = (h'(1), \ldots, h'(n))$ and $h'(i) \in \{0, 1\}$
4 $C_{\text{auth}} \leftarrow \{\}$
5 **for** $i \in \{1, \ldots, n\}$ **do**
6 $\quad$ **if** $\boldsymbol{I}'(i) \geq \beta$ **then**
7 $\quad\quad$ $V_{\text{auth}}(i) \leftarrow 1 \oplus h'(i)$
8 $\quad$ **else**
9 $\quad\quad$ $V_{\text{auth}}(i) \leftarrow h'(i)$
10 $\quad$ Compute: $C_{\text{auth}}(i) \leftarrow \text{HEnc}_{pk_{AS}}(V_{\text{auth}}(i))$
11 $\quad$ Append $C_{\text{auth}}(i)$ to C_{auth}
12 Compute the encrypted Hamming distance $\text{HD}_E(\boldsymbol{V}_{\text{enrol}}, \boldsymbol{V}_{\text{auth}})$ using Eq. (2)
13 Compute: $\text{HD}(\boldsymbol{V}_{\text{enrol}}, \boldsymbol{V}_{\text{auth}}) \leftarrow \text{HDec}_{sk_{AS}}(\text{HD}_E(\boldsymbol{V}_{\text{enrol}}, \boldsymbol{V}_{\text{auth}}))$
14 **if** $\text{HD}(\boldsymbol{V}_{\text{enrol}}, \boldsymbol{V}_{\text{auth}}) \leq \varepsilon$ **then**
15 $\quad$ **return** 1
16 **else**
17 $\quad$ **return** 0

For user authentication, the AS computes the Hamming distance of the two plaintext vectors $\boldsymbol{V}_{\text{enrol}}$ and $\boldsymbol{V}_{\text{auth}}$, using only the corresponding ciphertexts C_{enrol} and C_{auth}, i.e., in the encrypted domain. This is denoted as:

$$\text{HD}_E(\boldsymbol{V}_{\text{enrol}}, \boldsymbol{V}_{\text{auth}}) = \text{HEnc}_{pk_{AS}}(\text{HD}(\boldsymbol{V}_{\text{enrol}}, \boldsymbol{V}_{\text{auth}}))$$

$$= \text{HEnc}_{pk_{AS}}\left(\sum_{i=1}^{n}(V_{\text{enrol}}(i) \oplus V_{\text{auth}}(i))\right).$$

In the above relation, $\text{HD}(\boldsymbol{V}_{\text{enrol}}, \boldsymbol{V}_{\text{auth}})$ is the Hamming distance of the two bitstrings $\boldsymbol{V}_{\text{enrol}}, \boldsymbol{V}_{\text{auth}}$, while $\text{HD}_E(\boldsymbol{V}_{\text{enrol}}, \boldsymbol{V}_{\text{auth}})$ is the Hamming distance of the two bitstrings in the encrypted domain and $\text{HEnc}_{pk_{AS}}$ is the homomorphic encryption with the public key pk_{AS}. In general, the Hamming distance computation in the encrypted domain is not straightforward, and dedicated formulas need to be considered, which largely depend on the underlying homomorphic cryptosystem used. Further, doing this computation efficiently is challenging since such formulas typically require various homomorphic operations, including homomorphic multiplications, which are usually very expensive.

Once the encrypted Hamming distance is computed, the AS decrypts it to obtain the Hamming distance $\text{HD}(\boldsymbol{V}_{\text{enrol}}, \boldsymbol{V}_{\text{auth}})$, using its secret key sk_{AS} and checks whether the resulting Hamming distance falls within an accepted margin that is predefined by the threshold ε. If this is the case, then the authentication of the User is successful; otherwise, it fails.

Computation of the Encrypted Hamming Distance. Our protocol follows the approach described in [36] for computing the encrypted Hamming distance. Given two ciphertext vectors $\boldsymbol{C}_{\text{enrol}} = (C_{\text{enrol}}(1), \ldots, C_{\text{enrol}}(n))$ and $\boldsymbol{C}_{\text{auth}} = (C_{\text{auth}}(1), \ldots, C_{\text{auth}}(n))$, corresponding to the plaintext vectors $\boldsymbol{V}_{\text{enrol}} = (V_{\text{enrol}}(1), \ldots, V_{\text{enrol}}(n))$ and $\boldsymbol{V}_{\text{auth}} = (V_{\text{auth}}(1), \ldots, V_{\text{auth}}(n))$, the encrypted Hamming distance can be computed via the formula:

$$\text{HD}_E(\boldsymbol{V}_{\text{enrol}}, \boldsymbol{V}_{\text{auth}}) =$$

$$\boxplus_{i=1}^{n} [C_{\text{enrol}}(i) \boxplus C_{\text{auth}}(i) \boxminus (C_{\text{enrol}}(i) \boxtimes C_{\text{auth}}(i)) \boxminus (C_{\text{enrol}}(i) \boxtimes C_{\text{auth}}(i))], \quad (2)$$

where $\boxplus$, $\boxminus$, and $\boxtimes$ denote homomorphic addition, subtraction, and multiplication respectively. The homomorphic subtraction can be alternatively described as negating the ciphertext to be subtracted and then adding the result homomorphically to the first ciphertext. Besides negation, we define the homomorphic addition and multiplication in the usual way:

$$C_{\text{enrol}}(i) \boxplus C_{\text{auth}}(i) = \text{HEnc}_{pk_{AS}}(V_{\text{enrol}}(i) + V_{\text{auth}}(i))$$
$$C_{\text{enrol}}(i) \boxtimes C_{\text{auth}}(i) = \text{HEnc}_{pk_{AS}}(V_{\text{enrol}}(i) \cdot V_{\text{auth}}(i))$$

These suggest that Eq. (2) can be equivalently written as:

$$\text{HD}_E(\boldsymbol{V}_{\text{enrol}}, \boldsymbol{V}_{\text{auth}}) = \boxplus_{i=1}^{n} \text{HEnc}_{pk_{AS}}(V_{\text{enrol}}(i) + V_{\text{auth}}(i) - 2V_{\text{enrol}}(i) \cdot V_{\text{auth}}(i))$$

$$= \boxplus_{i=1}^{n} \text{HEnc}_{pk_{AS}}(V_{\text{enrol}}(i) \oplus V_{\text{auth}}(i))$$

$$= \text{HEnc}_{pk_{AS}}\left(\sum_{i=1}^{n}(V_{\text{enrol}}(i) \oplus V_{\text{auth}}(i))\right),$$

which corresponds to the encryption of the Hamming distance $\text{HD}(\boldsymbol{V}_{\text{enrol}}, \boldsymbol{V}_{\text{auth}})$. The second equality follows since $V_{\text{enrol}}(i), V_{\text{auth}}(i) \in \{0, 1\}$, for each $i = 1, \ldots, n$. We also note here that $+$ and $\cdot$ denote usual addition and multiplication, while $\oplus$ denotes the XOR addition.

Based on the above notation, Eq. (2) implies that for each pair of ciphertexts $(C_{\text{enrol}}(i), C_{\text{auth}}(i))$, the computation of

$$C_{\text{enrol}}(i) \boxplus C_{\text{auth}}(i) \boxminus (C_{\text{enrol}}(i) \boxtimes C_{\text{auth}}(i)) \boxminus (C_{\text{enrol}}(i) \boxtimes C_{\text{auth}}(i))$$

requires one homomorphic multiplication (HM), one homomorphic negation (HN), and three homomorphic additions (HA). For each $i = 1, \ldots, n$, the resulting value is a ciphertext. There are n such ciphertexts that need to be computed and then added together homomorphically to obtain the encrypted Hamming distance. Consequently, the total cost for computing $\text{HD}_E(\boldsymbol{V}_{\text{enrol}}, \boldsymbol{V}_{\text{auth}})$ in terms of homomorphic operations is: $n(3 \text{ HA} + 1 \text{ HN} + 1 \text{ HM}) + (n-1)$ HA, where the homomorphic multiplications constitute the main bottleneck in the computation of the encrypted Hamming distance.

4 Security Analysis

The proposed protocol is assumed to have three sources that are subject to attack: 1. the AS, 2. the communication channel between AS and DB, and 3. the DB. We start with the definitions of the adversary types.

Definition 1 (Semi-honest Adversary). *A semi-honest adversary (a.k.a. an honest-but-curious adversary) [6, 7, 15, 30] is an attacker that can do any passive attack (including recording all the intermediate transactions, making analysis, and retrieving any knowledge about the other parties' private data, etc.) without changing the prescribed definition of the protocol.*

Definition 2 (Malicious Adversary). *A malicious adversary is the strongest type of adversary [6, 7, 15, 30] that can arbitrarily deviate from the definition of the protocol and utilizes any effective strategy to retrieve some additional knowledge about other parties' private data and/or manipulate the outcome of the computation.*

We consider both adversary types in our security analysis as follows. We first assume the "semi-honest" security model on the User and AS sides, where the parties honestly follow the protocol and learn nothing beyond their own outputs. The security of AS is extremely important as the system takes the raw CSR image, the User's secret value SV and stores the private keys used in the homomorphic encryption and digital signature schemes. Under this security model, the communication channel between the User and AS is considered secure from any malicious attack. We assume that AS and DB are different entities, and collusion is not allowed between the AS and the DB. On the other hand, we assume the "malicious" security model on the DB side, which is the strongest adversary type. Therefore, depending on the application, DB can be outsourced to a third party (such as the cloud) for flexibility and cost-efficiency reasons. We also assume that the underlying cryptographic primitives (hash function, homomorphic encryption scheme, and digital signature algorithm) of the proposed authentication protocol in Sect. 3 are securely employed and implemented. Note that the algorithmic choices in Sect. 5 are for proof-of-concept and experimental purposes; without loss of generality, our protocol can be instantiated with different state-of-the-art secure algorithms.

In what follows, we analyze our scheme against attackers targeting to corrupt the DB to obtain or modify any sensitive data as DB is considered an outsourced and untrusted entity. The adversary can aim at obtaining the CSR template vector (ω) and the corresponding user secret value (SV) of a prover to attack the system for an unauthorized authentication. We also analyze our scheme against a legitimate but dishonest user trying to impersonate another user.

In addition, the adversary can also aim to clone or create an image of the CSR modality that can be used both to attack the system and to compromise the user's privacy. However, at this point, we follow the general assumption that CSRs reflect light-creating patterns that have been considered to be unique and physically unclonable [12,24]. Therefore, in this section, we only focus on analyzing the security of the proposed authentication protocol given in Sect. 3 under the adversary types defined above.

Theorem 1 (Security against database corruption). *The proposed authentication protocol is secure in case of corruption of the database.*

Proof. Let $\mathcal{A}$ be the malicious attacker that corrupted the DB. As $\mathcal{A}$ has access to the database, she has all the encrypted $C_{\text{enrol}}(i) = \mathsf{HEnc}_{pk_{\text{AS}}}(V_{\text{enrol}}(i))$, for $i = 1, \ldots, n$ where n is the size of the bitstring. The proposed authentication protocol provides computational indistinguishability against $\mathcal{A}$ due to the semantic (IND-CPA) security property of the underlying homomorphic encryption system as $C_{\text{auth}}(i) = \mathsf{HEnc}_{pk_{\text{AS}}}(V_{\text{auth}}(i))$ is encrypted each time with freshly generated random values (which is also different from the one used in the enrollment stage). Furthermore, even if the $\boldsymbol{\omega}$ vectors are matched in two different sessions (similarly to the enrollment session), the adversary cannot distinguish between V_{auth} and V_{enrol} values due to the semantic security property. The attacker cannot obtain any information about a user's biohash vector $\boldsymbol{V}_{\text{enrol}}$, since it is stored in the DB in encrypted form $\boldsymbol{C}_{\text{enrol}}$, under a homomorphic encryption cryptosystem. Therefore, the attacker can retrieve neither the CSR template ($\boldsymbol{\omega}$) nor the user SV by corrupting the database. In addition, $\boldsymbol{C}_{\text{enrol}}$ is stored with the signature of the data, so $\mathcal{A}$ cannot modify the enrollment data as the private keys are stored in AS using a secure environment (such as HSM [17]). We also masked the template data with the User secret value SV that provides revocation ability of the CSR template in case it is needed (due to customization or membership termination) without revealing the CSR data. In addition, the same CSR of a subject can be utilized in different recognition systems without constituting a privacy threat, as two templates of the CSR with different user secret values will be unlinkable to different databases. □

Theorem 2 (Security against malicious outsider attacker). *The proposed authentication protocol is secure against an outsider malicious adversary.*

Proof. The biohash values are not revealed at the authentication phase as they are processed in a semantically secure encrypted domain. Namely, the authentication procedure (see Algorithm 2) is determined by executing

$$\text{HD}(\boldsymbol{V}_{\text{enrol}}, \boldsymbol{V}_{\text{auth}}) \leftarrow \mathsf{HDec}_{sk_{\text{AS}}}(\mathsf{HD}_E(\boldsymbol{V}_{\text{enrol}}, \boldsymbol{V}_{\text{auth}})).$$

Considering that we (homomorphically) decrypt a single value after the computation of Eq. (2), the only outcome is the Hamming distance of the authentication and the enrollment biohash vectors, namely $\boldsymbol{V}_{\text{auth}}$ and $\boldsymbol{V}_{\text{enrol}}$. We then conclude that the security of the system against an outsider malicious adversary can be reduced to the security of the underlying homomorphic encryption cryptosystem. □

For example, in our implementation, we have considered the lattice-based homomorphic encryption scheme of Fan and Vercauteren [11], whose security relies on the Ring Learning With Errors (RLWE) assumptions. Hence, in order for a malicious adversary to gain partial information about the biohash vectors, she needs to be able to identify vulnerabilities either in the implementation of the homomorphic encryption scheme (e.g., side-channel attacks), or in the underlying RLWE hard mathematical problems.

Theorem 3 (Security against semi-honest prover). *A dishonest insider semi-honest prover (a user) can impersonate a legitimate prover $\mathcal{P}_i$ with only a negligible probability.*

Proof. Let $\mathcal{P}_c$ be a semi-honest insider user that aims to impersonate a different legitimate user $\mathcal{P}_i$. In the enrollment phase, the prover needs to provide a signature of the encryption of enrollment vector i.e., C_{enrol}. So, based on the assumption of secure key generation/distribution $\mathcal{P}_c$ cannot impersonate $\mathcal{P}_i$ during the enrollment phase. Considering the authentication phase, $\mathcal{P}_c$ needs to masquerade both a legal CSR reading and the user SV. As CSRs have been argued to behave as physical unclonable functions [12,24], it is very unlikely to make a physical counterfeit of CSRs. Assuming that a verifier always requires a CSR reading and entering SV, $\mathcal{P}_c$ can only impersonate a legitimate prover with a negligible probability. □

5   Implementation

In this section, we present the details of our proof-of-concept implementation and the experimental results regarding the execution of the CSR authentication protocol that is presented in Sect. 3.2. Specifically, we have implemented both the enrollment and authentication phases, described in Algorithms 1 and 2, where the implementation is conducted in *Python 3.6.9*. The homomorphic encryption scheme that we have chosen is the one presented by Fan and Vercauteren (FV) [11], and for the implementation of this scheme, as well as the required homomorphic operations, we use the PySEAL library[7]. The selected library for the hash functions is the hashlib[8], where for our purpose, we used SHA-256 and SHA-224, which are currently considered acceptable for hash function applications in [26], to obtain the digest of the User's secret value in the enrollment and authentication phases. Further, as a digital signature scheme, we have chosen ECDSA using the NIST Curve P-256; we used the Python ecdsa 0.17.0 library[9]. In contrast, the feature extraction process described in Sect. 3.1 and specifically the function ReliableFeatures that is required in both the enrollment and authentication algorithms for extracting the reliable features was implemented from scratch.

---

[7] https://github.com/Lab41/PySEAL.
[8] https://docs.python.org/3/library/hashlib.html.
[9] https://pypi.org/project/ecdsa/.

5.1 Dataset

We analyzed a set of 17 CSR IDs from which we generated a set of CSR images. The CSR images were acquired by using two different optical microscopes. 7 CSR images were taken by using a USB Dino-Lite digital microscope with perpendicular illumination to the sample, and flexible LED control, as shown in Fig. 1-a. These images may be closer to the images acquired by an end-user without the expertise and/or professional microscopes. In Fig. 1-a, one can observe some green spots due to the photonic cross-communication, which consists of the coupling effect of the optical signal between neighbor spheres [13]. This effect can be advantageous due to the fact of having more information, but it can also be a disadvantage as it may introduce more noise to the system. The other 10 CSR images were taken with a professional polarized microscope equipped with a digital camera and illumination perpendicular to the sample. Those images present a well-defined and colored CSRs, see Figs. 1-b and 2-a. The images acquired with different microscopes clearly show different responses, meaning that a reliable process needs to be implemented for the minutiæ detection from CSR images when acquired with distinct readout devices.

Table 1. Operations applied to CSR image to simulate input noise.

Sequence	Operation	Range
1	Rotation	$1 - 5°$ (anticlockwise)
2	Blurring	$(2 \times 2) - (4 \times 4)$
3	Gaussian noise	0.2–0.4

We inject two types of noise: similarity noise and Gaussian noise [10]. The first one simulates noise coming from external conditions such as sudden illumination changes, lack of focus, rotation, etc. The Gaussian noise simulates the photonic and electronic noise inherent to each device, and it occurs during the image acquisition under low-light conditions, which makes it difficult for the visible light sensors to capture details of the object efficiently [10]. Thus, we generated a set of CSR images by applying the operations listed in Table 1 to the reference images, whose ranges are based on the idea of keeping the noise within realistic external conditions. The procedure of generating noisy responses ensures the extraction of reliable blobs.

Table 2. Dataset for the enrollment and authentication phases.

Protocol phase	CSR responses	Number of attempts	Acquired images per attempt
Enrollment	17	1	7
Authentication		10	5

For the enrollment phase, from each CSR image, we generated seven noise images to extract the truly reliable blobs. For the authentication phase, we simulated ten attempts to authenticate CSR images taken at different time intervals and, at each time, five images were acquired (also intending to extract the reliable blobs), as described in Table 2.

5.2 Homomorphic Encryption Implementation

Fan and Vercauteren proposed the FV scheme in 2012 [11] and essentially, it is based on the homomorphic encryption scheme of Brakerski [9]. The FV scheme is instantiated over the RLWE setting instead of the LWE setting, which is the case in the Brakerski scheme, and it is generally a more efficient version of Brakerski's scheme. However, because of the similarities between the two schemes, we often refer to the FV scheme as Brakerski/Fan–Vercauteren (BFV). We present a high-level description of the BFV scheme here and refer to [11,23] for a more detailed analysis.

Since the BFV scheme works in the RLWE setting, its core operations are performed over a polynomial ring $R_m = \mathbb{Z}_m[x]/(x^d + 1)$, containing polynomials modulo $x^d + 1$, with integer coefficients in $\{\lceil -m/2 \rceil, \ldots, \lfloor (m-1)/2 \rfloor\}$. For efficiency reasons, the degree d of the *polynomial modulus* is usually chosen as a power of 2. Based on this notation, the plaintext space in the BFV scheme is described by the polynomial ring R_t, for some positive integer *plaintext modulus* t and the ciphertext space is described as R_q^2, for some positive integer *coefficient modulus* q. In practice, the coefficient modulus is chosen to be larger than the plaintext modulus so that each plaintext can be mapped to multiple valid ciphertexts. Hence, a plaintext message is represented as a polynomial in R_t, and its encryption is transformed into a pair of polynomials in R_q. Integer plaintext messages can be encrypted using the BFV scheme after applying an encoding to convert them to polynomials in R_t. For key generation, the secret key sk is sampled from R_2, i.e., it is a polynomial of degree at most $d-1$, with coefficients in $\{-1, 0, 1\}$, while the public key pk is composed of two polynomials in R_q.

BFV Parameter Sets in PySEAL. The most crucial part of implementing the BFV scheme is selecting a suitable parameter set that maintains a reasonable balance between performance and security. The BFV parameter set consists of the polynomial, plaintext, and coefficient moduli, and these parameters are usually chosen following the homomorphic encryption standard of Albrecht *et al.* [1]. PySEAL offers different flavors of such parameter sets targeting 128-bit security, while it also allows implementers to initialize the scheme with their own parameters in order to achieve higher security levels.

Table 3. Chosen parameter set for BFV scheme in PySEAL.

Sec. level. (bits)	Parameter set		
	Poly modulus (d)	Plaintext modulus (t)	Coefficient modulus (q)
128	$x^{2048} + 1$	256	72057594036879361

The parameter set chosen in our implementation is given in Table 3. This is one of the instantiations that is used in the PySEAL library for 128-bit security. The coefficient modulus q in PySEAL is defined as a product of distinct primes of size up to 60-bits, where each prime is congruent to 1 modulo $2d$. In our instance, q is composed of only one prime, as shown in Table 3. The performance of the homomorphic encryption scheme is largely affected by the polynomial modulus, as well as by the number of prime factors in the coefficient modulus. Hence, one needs to keep the degree d and the number of prime factors in q small.

Performance of BFV Homomorphic Operations in PySEAL. Besides homomorphic encryption and decryption, PySEAL supports all the required homomorphic operations for computing the encrypted Hamming distance using Eq. (2), i.e., homomorphic addition, negation, and multiplication. In Table 4, we list the average time required for performing the homomorphic operations that are needed in the authentication, Algorithm 2 (the homomorphic encryption in the enrollment takes similar times). The reason for focusing on the authentication phase in our experiments is that it contains the main bulk of homomorphic operations, including the computation of the Hamming distance in the encrypted domain. The timings in Table 4 refer to two different sizes of the biohash vector V_{auth}, namely 224- and 256-bits, where for this purpose, we used SHA-224 and SHA-256 for hashing the User's secret value.

Table 4. Average execution times (in seconds) of homomorphic operations, with respect to the BFV homomorphic encryption scheme and the parameter set of Table 3, that are performed in the authentication phase (Algorithm 2), using the PySEAL library.

Size of biohash	Homomorphic operations					
	Encryption	Addition	Negation	Multiplication	HD_E	Decryption
224-bits	1.423	0.0044	0.0010	0.456	0.462	0.0002
256-bits	1.635	0.0052	0.0012	0.523	0.529	0.0002

The encryption column refers to the average time required to encrypt the bio-hash vector V_{auth} bit-by-bit. In other words, it refers to the average time needed to perform n homomorphic encryption operations for $n \in \{224, 256\}$. The rest of the columns concern the homomorphic operations required for computing the encrypted Hamming distance based on Eq. (2). Specifically, our implementation requires approximately 4.4 ms to perform $4n - 1$ homomorphic additions for $n = 224$ and approximately 5.2 ms for $n = 256$. Performing n homomorphic negations takes roughly 1 ms in both cases. On the other hand, our implementation requires 0.456 s to perform n homomorphic multiplications for $n = 224$ and 0.523 s for $n = 256$.

The average time for calculating the encrypted Hamming distance is 0.462 s for $n = 224$ and 0.529 s for $n = 256$, suggesting that the homomorphic multiplications consume approximately 98.78% of the computation time for the encrypted

Hamming distance in both cases. The last column concerns the average time taken to decrypt $HD_E(V_{\text{enrol}}, V_{\text{auth}})$. This is approximately 0.2 milliseconds in both cases, which is expected since the encrypted Hamming distance represents a single ciphertext corresponding to the encryption of the actual Hamming distance $HD(V_{\text{enrol}}, V_{\text{auth}})$ and hence to the encryption of an integer in $\{0, \ldots, n\}$. Finally, the experimental results presented in Table 4 indicate that switching to biohash vectors of size 224-bits offers around 12.82% speed-up compared to the 256-bit case, both in terms of bit-by-bit encryption as well as in the computation of the encrypted Hamming distance.

5.3   Performance of Enrollment and Authentication Phases

In Table 5, we summarize our experimental results regarding the performance of the enrollment (Algorithm 1) and authentication (Algorithm 2), considering biohash vectors of size $n \in \{224, 256\}$ to be encrypted.

Table 5. Average execution times (in seconds) of enrollment and authentication phases, with respect to the homomorphic operations performance of Table 4. In these timings, we exclude the performance of the feature extraction.

Size of biohash	Enrollment (Algorithm 1)		Authentication (Algorithm 2)		
	Encryption: C_{enrol}	Enrollment	Encryption: C_{auth}	HD_E	Authentication
224-bits	1.407	1.409	1.423	0.462	1.892
256-bits	1.648	1.651	1.635	0.529	2.172

It is clear from Table 5 that almost all of the execution time of the enrollment is dedicated to the encryption of V_{enrol}, for both $n \in \{224, 256\}$. This is expected since all operations in Algorithm 1, except for the homomorphic encryption, are simple operations that can be efficiently performed, i.e., matrix multiplication, hash computation, and XOR. Specifically, the execution of the enrollment algorithm for 224-bits requires around 1.407 s, offering approximately a 14.66% performance advantage over the 256 case, which requires 1.648 s.

The authentication phase has the extra computational burden of computing the Hamming distance of the two bitstrings $V_{\text{enrol}}, V_{\text{auth}}$ using the encrypted vectors $C_{\text{enrol}}, C_{\text{auth}}$. For both $n \in \{224, 256\}$, the bit-by-bit encryption of V_{auth} consumes approximately 75.25% of the total execution time, while the computation of the encrypted Hamming distance requires approximately 24.39% of the execution time of Algorithm 2. As expected, the computation time for homomorphic encryption and the Hamming distance together corresponds to around 99.63% of the total execution time of the authentication algorithm. We also noted that the 224 case offers a performance gain of around 13.77% over the 256-bit case.

6   Conclusions and Future Work

We started to work with a challenge: proving that it is possible to securely authenticate objects enhanced with CSRs, a material that demonstrates fingerprint-like features and shows optical responses acclaimed to be unpredictable (at the production phase), physically non-reproducible, and identifying. Images of such responses —as often happen in biometrics— contain noise. Extracting information and minutiæ is a process with data instability, increasing the stake for those who intend to develop a cryptographically secure authentication protocol taking advantage of the materials' optical features.

We designed, proved it secure, and implemented a solution for authenticating CSRs tags. After illustrating a methodology to derive stable and reliable bitstrings from the minutiæ of CSRs images using techniques borrowed by the biometric traditions, the main contribution of the paper is the design of an authentication protocol. It uses biohashing and homomorphic encryption, and despite being thought to work only with CSRs, we argue that the proposed protocol can be applied to a wider range of use-cases. In fact, since CSRs minutiæ are abstractly represented as "randomly" distributed colored spots in a bi-dimensional plane, our solution works for any technology for authentication that relies on the same data structure, for example, dense cloud of ink dots used in watermarking, or certain allegedly Physical Unclonable Functions emerging from the optical analysis of fabric like silk [22].

We demonstrated that an encrypted bitstring can be stored securely in an outsourced database. When instantiated with a practical homomorphic encryption scheme, an authentication system can be designed to perform secure computations in the encrypted domain. One such operation is the computation of the Hamming distance of two bitstrings, using as input only their corresponding ciphertexts. This operation is the most significant in the authentication phase, as it determines whether the authentication is successfully performed and in a privacy-preserving manner, i.e., without revealing any sensitive information about the User's private data.

We presented a proof-of-concept implementation of the proposed CSR authentication protocol, which we instantiated with the BFV homomorphic encryption scheme. The implementation was conducted in Python, using the PySEAL library for performing the required homomorphic operations with the BFV scheme. Based on our implementation, we derived useful conclusions regarding the computational time that is consumed by heavy homomorphic operations such as bit-by-bit homomorphic encryption and homomorphic multiplication, which has a major performance impact in the computation of the Hamming distance of two bitstrings in the encrypted domain.

Future Work. We envision several extensions for this work, mainly targeting implementations with improved performance offering at the same time high-security guarantees. The first direction aims at achieving an optimized implementation. We believe that better timings can be obtained when switching to other programming languages and more up-to-date libraries, such as Microsoft's

SEAL library[10] which implements the BFV scheme in C++. In addition, we do not claim that our formula for computing the encrypted Hamming distance is the optimal one. It is likely that more efficient methods tailored to the BFV scheme are already available or can be designed. For example, in [36], the authors presented an optimized way for computing the encrypted Hamming distance with BFV homomorphic operations by applying different encodings ("packed" representations) for the polynomials representing ciphertexts and plaintexts. The second direction looks at the security of our implementation. We plan to emphasize more on instantiating the BFV scheme with optimal parameter sets, achieving at least 128-bits security. Still, from a security perspective, we also plan to look at implementations offering side-channel protection, focusing specifically on timing attacks.

Acknowledgements. We thank the reviewers for their valuable comments and suggestions. We would also like to acknowledge Prof. Dr. J. Lagerwall for providing the CSRs images. In addition, Mónica Arenas and Georgios Fotiadis would like to thank Dr. Kim Laine, from Microsoft Research, for his responsiveness and valuable comments regarding the BFV homomorphic encryption scheme and its implementation. The authors acknowledge the financial support from the Luxembourg National Research Fund (FNR) on the projects Security in the Shell "SSh" (C17/MS/11688643), No more Fakes "NoFakes" (PoC20/15299666/NOFAKES-PoC) and the CORE project Secure, Quantum-Safe, Practical Voting Technologies "EquiVox" (C19/IS/13643617/EquiVox/Ryan).

References

1. Albrecht, M.R., et al.: Homomorphic Encryption Standard. IACR, p. 939 (2019). Cryptol. ePrint Arch. https://eprint.iacr.org/2019/939
2. Arenas, M., Demirci, H., Lenzini, G.: Cholesteric spherical reflectors as physical unclonable identifiers in anti-counterfeiting. In: The 16th International Conference on Availability, Reliability and Security, pp. 1–11. ACM (2021). https://doi.org/10.1145/3465481.3465766
3. Arenas, M., Demirci, H., Lenzini, G.: An analysis of cholesteric spherical reflector identifiers for object authenticity verification. Mach. Learn. Knowl. Extr. 4(1), 222–239 (2022). https://doi.org/10.3390/make4010010
4. Bai, Z., Hatzinakos, D.: LBP-based biometric hashing scheme for human authentication. In: 11th International Conference on Control Automation Robotics Vision (ICARCV), pp. 1842–1847 (2010). https://doi.org/10.1109/ICARCV.2010.5707216
5. Bicego M., Lagorio, A., Grosso, E., Tistarelli, M.: On the use of SIFT features for face authentication. In: Conference On Computer Vision And Pattern Recognition Workshop. CVPRW 2006, pp. 35–35 (2006)
6. Bicer, O., Bingol, M.A., Kiraz, M., Levi, A.: Highly efficient and re-executable private function evaluation with linear complexity. IEEE Trans. Dependable Secure Comput. 19(02), 835–847 (2022). https://doi.org/10.1109/TDSC.2020.3009496

---

[10] https://github.com/Microsoft/SEAL.

7. Bingol, M.A.: Efficient and secure schemes for private function evaluation. Ph.D. thesis, Sabanci University, Istanbul (2019). https://research.sabanciuniv.edu/id/eprint/36861/

8. Boddeti, V.N.: Secure face matching using fully homomorphic encryption. In: 2018 IEEE 9th International Conference on Biometrics Theory, Applications and Systems (BTAS), pp. 1–10. IEEE (2018)

9. Brakerski, Z.: Fully homomorphic encryption without modulus switching from classical GapSVP. In: Safavi-Naini, R., Canetti, R. (eds.) Advances in Cryptology - CRYPTO 2012–32nd Annual Cryptology Conference, Santa Barbara, CA, USA, 19–23 August 2012. Proceedings. Lecture Notes in Computer Science, vol. 7417, pp. 868–886. Springer (2012). https://doi.org/10.1007/978-3-642-32009-5_50

10. Deledalle, C.A., Denis, L., Tupin, F.: How to compare noisy patches? Patch similarity beyond gaussian noise. Int. J. Comput. Vision, **99**(1), 86–102 (2012). https://doi.org/10.1007/s11263-012-0519-6, https://hal-imt.archives-ouvertes.fr/hal-00672357, http://link.springer.com/10.1007/s11263-012-0519-6

11. Fan, J., Vercauteren, F.: Somewhat Practical Fully Homomorphic Encryption (2012). https://ia.cr/2012/144. Cryptology ePrint Archive, Report 2012/144

12. Geng, Y., Noh, J., Drevensek-Olenik, I., Rupp, R., Lenzini, G., Lagerwall, J.P.: High-fidelity spherical cholesteric liquid crystal Bragg reflectors generating unclonable patterns for secure authentication. Sci. Rep. **6**, 1–9 (2016). https://doi.org/10.1038/srep26840

13. Geng, Y., Noh, J., Drevensek-Olenik, I., Rupp, R., Lagerwall, J.: Elucidating the fine details of cholesteric liquid crystal shell reflection patterns. Liq. Cryst. **44**(12–13), 1948–1959 (2017)

14. Geng, Y., Kizhakidathazhath, R., Lagerwall, J.P.F.: Encoding hidden information onto surfaces using polymerized cholesteric spherical reflectors. Adv. Funct. Mater. **31** (2021). https://doi.org/10.1002/adfm.202100399

15. Goldreich, O.: Foundations of Cryptography, vol. 1. Cambridge University Press, New York, NY, USA (2006)

16. Gomez-Barrero, M., Maiorana, E., Galbally, J., Campisi, P., Fierrez, J.: Multi-biometric template protection based on homomorphic encryption. Pattern Recogn. **67**, 149–163 (2017)

17. Ivarsson, J., Nilsson, A.: A Review of Hardware Security Modules (2010). https://www.opendnssec.org/wp-content/uploads/2011/01/A-Review-of-Hardware-Security-Modules-Fall-2010.pdf. Accessed Mar 2022

18. Joshi, M., Mazumdar, B., Dey, S.: Security Vulnerabilities Against Fingerprint Biometric System (2018). arXiv1805.07116, http://arxiv.org/abs/1805.07116

19. Johnson, D., Menezes, A., Vanstone, S.: The elliptic curve digital signature algorithm (ECDSA). Int. J. Inf. Secur. **1**(1), 36–63 (2001). https://doi.org/10.1007/s102070100002

20. Karabat, C., Kiraz, M.S., Erdogan, H., Savas, E.: THRIVE: threshold homomorphic encryption based secure and privacy preserving biometric verification system. EURASIP J. Adv. Sig. Process. **2015**(1), 1–18 (2015). https://doi.org/10.1186/s13634-015-0255-5

21. Khan, M.A.: Fingerprint image enhancement and minutiae extraction (2011)

22. Kim, M.S., Lee, G.J., Leem, J.W., Choi, S., Kim, Y.L., Song, Y.M.: Revisiting silk a lens-free optical physical unclonable function. Nature Commun. **13**(1), 1–12 (2022). https://doi.org/10.1038/s41467-021-27278-5, https://www.nature.com/articles/s41467-021-27278-5

23. Laine, K.: Simple encrypted arithmetic library 2.3. 1. Microsoft Research (2017). https://www.microsoft.com/en-us/research/uploads/prod/2017/11/sealmanual-2-3-1.pdf
24. Lenzini, G., et al.: Security in the shell an optical physical unclonable function made of shells of cholesteric liquid crystals. In: 2017 IEEE Workshop on Information Forensics and Security, WIFS 2017 2018-Janua, pp. 1–6 (2017). https://doi.org/10.1109/WIFS.2017.8267644
25. Ratha, N., Bolle, R., Pandit, V., Vaish, V.: Robust fingerprint authentication using local structural similarity. In: Proceedings Fifth IEEE Workshop On Applications Of Computer Vision, pp. 29–34 (2000)
26. National Institute of Standards and Technology SP 800–131A Rev. 2: Transitioning the Use of Cryptographic Algorithms and Key Lengths (2018). https://csrc.nist.gov/publications/detail/sp/800-131a/rev-2/final
27. Ngo, D., Teoh, A., Goh, A.: Biometric hash high-confidence face recognition. IEEE Trans. Circuits Syst. Video Technol. **16**(6), 771–775 (2006). https://doi.org/10.1109/TCSVT.2006.873780
28. Pradel, G., Mitchell, C.: Privacy-Preserving Biometric Matching Using Homomorphic Encryption. arXiv preprint arXiv:2111.12372 (2021)
29. Pursell, L., Trimble, S.Y.: Gram-schmidt orthogonalization by Gauss elimination. Am. Math. Mon. **98**(6), 544–549 (1991). https://doi.org/10.1080/00029890.1991.11995755
30. Schneider, T.: Engineering Secure Two-Party Computation Protocols - Advances in Design, Optimization, and Applications of Efficient Secure Function Evaluation. Ph.D. thesis, Ruhr-University Bochum, Germany, Information Sciences (2011). http://thomaschneider.de/papers/S11Thesis.pdf
31. Schwartz, M., Lenzini, G., Geng, Y., Rønne, P.B., Ryan, P.Y., Lagerwall, J.P.: Cholesteric liquid crystal shells as enabling material for information-rich design and architecture. Adv. Mater. **30**(30), 1–19 (2018). https://doi.org/10.1002/adma.201707382
32. Schwartz, M., et al.: Linking physical objects to their digital twins via fiducial markers designed for invisibility to humans. Multifunctional Mater. **2**(4), 1–19 (2021). https://doi.org/10.1088/2399-7532/ac0060
33. Topcu, B., Karabat, C., Azadmanesh, M., Erdogan, H.: Practical security and privacy attacks against biometric hashing using sparse recovery. EURASIP J. Adv. Sig. Process. **2016**(1), 1–20 (2016). https://doi.org/10.1186/s13634-016-0396-1
34. Torres, W.A.A., Bhattacharjee, N., Srinivasan, B.: Effectiveness of fully homomorphic encryption to preserve the privacy of biometric data. In: Proceedings of the 16th International Conference on Information Integration and Web-based Applications & Services, pp. 152–158 (2014)
35. Tuyls, P., Akkermans, A.H., Kevenaar, T.A., Schrijen, G.J., Bazen, A.M., Veldhuis, R.N.: Practical biometric authentication with template protection. Lect. Notes Comput. Sci. **3546**, 436–446 (2005). https://doi.org/10.1007/11527923_45
36. Yu, H., Yin, L., Zhang, H., Zhan, D., Qu, J., Zhang, G.: Road distance computation using homomorphic encryption in road networks. CMC-Comput. Mater. Continua **69**(3), 3445–3458 (2021)

Card-Minimal Protocols for Three-Input Functions with Standard Playing Cards

Rikuo Haga[1]([envelope]) [iD], Yuichi Hayashi[1,4] [iD], Daiki Miyahara[2,4] [iD],
and Takaaki Mizuki[3,4] [iD]

[1] Nara Institute of Science and Technology, 8916-5 Takayama,
Ikoma, Nara 630-0192, Japan
haga.rikuo.hm5@is.naist.jp
[2] The University of Electro-Communications, 1-5-1 Chofugaoka,
Chofu, Tokyo 182-8585, Japan
[3] Tohoku University, Aramak-Aza-Aoba, Aoba, Sendai 980-8576, Japan
[4] National Institute of Advanced Industrial Science and Technology (AIST),
2-3-26 Aomi, Koto-ku, Tokyo 135-0064, Japan

Abstract. A protocol realizing a secure computation using a deck of
physical cards is called a card-based cryptographic protocol. Since Niemi
and Renvall first proposed a few protocols using a commercially available deck of playing cards in 1999, several protocols for the two-input
AND and XOR functions have been proposed. By combining these existing protocols, one can construct a protocol for any Boolean function
using a standard deck of playing cards. However, the minimal numbers
of cards needed for Boolean functions having more than two inputs have
not been revealed so much. Recently, Koyama et al. developed a card-
minimal three-input AND protocol. In this study, by extending Koyama's
AND protocol, we construct a card-minimal protocol for the three-input
majority function. Furthermore, carrying the idea behind these protocols
further, we provide a generic card-minimal three-input protocol, which
covers many important three-input Boolean functions.

Keywords: Card-based cryptography · Secure computation ·
Standard deck of playing cards

1 Introduction

Card-based cryptographic protocols realize a secure computation using a deck of
physical cards (refer to [5,25,37] for surveys). Many researches on card-based
cryptography typically use a two-colored deck of cards whose fronts are red $\heartsuit$
or black $\clubsuit$ and whose backs are indistinguishable $\boxed{?}$. The Boolean values are
encoded as follows:

$$\boxed{\clubsuit}\,\boxed{\heartsuit} = 0, \qquad \boxed{\heartsuit}\,\boxed{\clubsuit} = 1. \tag{1}$$

When two face-down cards $\boxed{?}\,\boxed{?}$ represent a bit $x \in \{0,1\}$ according to Eq. (1),
we call them a *commitment* to x and denote it as follows:

© The Author(s), under exclusive license to Springer Nature Switzerland AG 2022
L. Batina and J. Daemen (Eds.): AFRICACRYPT 2022, LNCS 13503, pp. 448–468, 2022.
https://doi.org/10.1007/978-3-031-17433-9_19

Given commitments as input, a *committed-format* protocol produces a commitment to the output value of some predetermined function. For example, the (two-input) AND protocol designed in [26] produces a commitment to $a \wedge b$ via a series of actions, given two commitments to $a, b \in \{0, 1\}$ and two helping cards as input:

$$\underbrace{\boxed{?}\boxed{?}}_{a}\underbrace{\boxed{?}\boxed{?}}_{b}\boxed{\clubsuit}\boxed{\heartsuit} \rightarrow \cdots \rightarrow \boxed{\clubsuit}\boxed{\heartsuit}\underbrace{\boxed{?}\boxed{?}\boxed{?}\boxed{?}}_{a \wedge b} \text{ or } \boxed{\heartsuit}\boxed{\clubsuit}\underbrace{\boxed{?}\boxed{?}\boxed{?}\boxed{?}}_{a \wedge b}.$$

1.1 Card-Based Protocols with a Standard Deck of Cards

The protocols using a two-colored deck of cards cannot be implemented with a single *standard deck* of commercially available playing cards. The reason is that such playing cards contain numbers (such as $A, 2, 3, 4, \ldots, J, Q, K$) in addition to suits ($\clubsuit, \heartsuit, \spadesuit, \diamondsuit$), i.e., all the cards are distinct. Therefore, we need to prepare either multiple decks of playing cards or a tailor-made deck of cards to implement the protocols.

Fortunately, Niemi and Renvall [30] solved this problem by constructing a few protocols using a single standard deck of commercially available playing cards. They regarded a deck of playing cards as a total order on natural numbers from 1 to 52 because there are 52 combinations of numbers and suits in playing cards (excluding the joker); we denote these cards by $\boxed{1}\boxed{2}\boxed{3} \cdots \boxed{52}$. In their protocols, a bit $x \in \{0, 1\}$ is encoded using $\boxed{i}$ and $\boxed{j}$ satisfying $1 \leq i < j \leq 52$, as follows:

$$\boxed{i}\boxed{j} = 0, \quad \boxed{j}\boxed{i} = 1. \tag{2}$$

That is, if the number on the left card is smaller, it represents 0, and if the number on the left card is larger, it represents 1. Thus, similar to the two-colored-deck case (as defined in Eq. (1)), using two cards $\boxed{i}$ and $\boxed{j}$ (of different numbers), we can create a *commitment* to $x \in \{0, 1\}$, denoted by

$$\underbrace{\boxed{?}\boxed{?}}_{[x]^{\{i,j\}}},$$

where the set $\{i, j\}$ is called the *base* of the commitment. (We sometimes omit the description of the base.) For example,

$$\underbrace{\boxed{?}\boxed{?}}_{[x]^{\{1,4\}}}$$

is a commitment to x of base $\{1, 4\}$; if $x = 0$, the order of the sequence is $\boxed{1}\boxed{4}$, and if $x = 1$, it is $\boxed{4}\boxed{1}$.

1.2 Existing Protocols

Including the Niemi–Renvall protocols mentioned above, there are several existing protocols (working on a standard deck) in the literature, as shown in Table 1. In this subsection, we briefly review these protocols one by one.

Table 1. Existing protocols for Boolean functions using standard playing cards

Protocol	# of cards	# of shuffles	Finite?	Authors
2-AND	5	7.5 (exp.)		Niemi & Renvall [30]
	8	4	✓	Mizuki [22]
	4	6 (exp.)		Koch et al. [6]
2-XOR	4	7 (exp.)		Niemi & Renvall [30]
	4	1	✓	Mizuki [22]
3-AND	6	8.5 (exp.)		Koyama et al. [12]

Throughout the paper, '2-AND,' '2-XOR,' and '3-AND' mean the two-input AND, two-input XOR, and three-input AND functions, respectively; we also use similar notations for other functions. In addition, when simply writing 'AND protocol' or 'XOR protocol,' it means a two-input protocol, i.e., a 2-AND protocol or 2-XOR protocol.

Two-Input AND and XOR. As mentioned in Sect. 1.1, Niemi and Renvall [30] proposed the first protocols working on a standard deck. Specifically, they constructed a protocol for the two-input AND function (namely, 2-AND) using five cards:

$$\underbrace{\boxed{?}\boxed{?}}_{[a]^{\{1,2\}}} \underbrace{\boxed{?}\boxed{?}}_{[b]^{\{3,4\}}} \boxed{5} \quad \rightarrow \quad \cdots \quad \rightarrow \quad \underbrace{\boxed{?}\boxed{?}}_{[a \wedge b]^{\{1,4\}}} .$$

Therefore, aside from the two input commitments to $a, b \in \{0, 1\}$, this AND protocol uses one helping card, namely $\boxed{5}$. The protocol (with the slight modification by Koch et al. [6]) uses 7.5 shuffles in expectation; thus, it is a *Las Vegas* protocol (and it is not a finite-runtime protocol). See the first protocol listed in Table 1. We call this the *Niemi–Renvall AND protocol*, whose detailed explanation will be shown in Sect. 2.4.

Niemi and Renvall [30] also constructed a 2-XOR protocol with four cards:

$$\underbrace{\boxed{?}\boxed{?}}_{[a]^{\{1,2\}}} \underbrace{\boxed{?}\boxed{?}}_{[b]^{\{3,4\}}} \quad \rightarrow \quad \cdots \quad \rightarrow \quad \underbrace{\boxed{?}\boxed{?}}_{[a \oplus b]^{\{1,2\}}} .$$

Because the two input commitments need four cards as long as we follow the encoding rule in Eq. (2), this XOR protocol, which does not use any helping card, is *card-minimal*[1]. As shown in Table 1, the protocol uses seven shuffles in expectation.

---

[1] This paper (and the literature) assume the encoding (2), i.e., a two-card-per-bit encoding, when discussing the card-minimality of protocols; thus, an n-input (Boolean function) protocol always needs $2n$ cards for input commitments, and such a protocol using only $2n$ cards is card-minimal.

In 2016, Mizuki [22] proposed AND and XOR protocols with eight and four cards, respectively:

$$\boxed{?}\boxed{?}\;\boxed{?}\boxed{?}\;\boxed{5}\boxed{6}\boxed{7}\boxed{8}\;\rightarrow\;\cdots\;\rightarrow\quad\boxed{?}\boxed{?}\;\text{ or }\;\boxed{?}\boxed{?}$$
$$\underbrace{}_{[a]\{1,2\}}\;\underbrace{}_{[b]\{3,4\}}\qquad\qquad\qquad\underbrace{}_{[a\wedge b]\{5,6\}}\qquad\underbrace{}_{[a\wedge b]\{7,8\}}$$

and

$$\boxed{?}\boxed{?}\;\boxed{?}\boxed{?}\;\rightarrow\;\cdots\;\rightarrow\quad\boxed{?}\boxed{?}\;.$$
$$\underbrace{}_{[a]\{1,2\}}\;\underbrace{}_{[b]\{3,4\}}\qquad\qquad\underbrace{}_{[a\oplus b]\{3,4\}}$$

The AND and XOR protocols use four and one shuffles, respectively, and both the protocols are finite-runtime; see Table 1. While the XOR protocol is card-minimal, the AND protocol needs four helping cards.

As seen thus far, there had been card-minimal XOR protocols, whereas no card-minimal AND protocol had been found until 2019: Koch et al. [6] constructed a card-minimal AND protocol in 2019:

$$\boxed{?}\boxed{?}\;\boxed{?}\boxed{?}\;\rightarrow\;\cdots\;\rightarrow\quad\boxed{?}\boxed{?}\;.$$
$$\underbrace{}_{[a]\{1,2\}}\;\underbrace{}_{[b]\{3,4\}}\qquad\qquad\underbrace{}_{a\wedge b}$$

As seen in Table 1, this is a Las Vegas protocol, which uses six shuffles in expectation.

Three-Input AND. If we execute the above-mentioned card-minimal 2-AND protocol designed by Koch et al. [6] twice, we can securely compute 3-AND without any helping card, although it needs 12 shuffles in expectation.

In 2021, Koyama et al. [12] improved upon this by nicely making use of the Niemi–Renvall AND protocol. That is, they proposed a card-minimal 3-AND protocol with 8.5 shuffles (in expectation):

$$\boxed{?}\boxed{?}\;\boxed{?}\boxed{?}\;\boxed{?}\boxed{?}\;\rightarrow\;\cdots\;\rightarrow\quad\boxed{?}\boxed{?}\;.$$
$$\underbrace{}_{[a]\{1,2\}}\;\underbrace{}_{[b]\{3,4\}}\;\underbrace{}_{[c]\{5,6\}}\qquad\qquad\underbrace{}_{[a\wedge b\wedge c]\{1,4\}}$$

Hereinafter, we call this protocol *Koyama's AND protocol*.

Thus, there have already been card-minimal protocols for 3-AND. In addition, one can easily construct a card-minimal 3-XOR protocol by executing one of the existing 2-XOR protocols twice. However, aside from 2-AND and 2-XOR, there are many other three-input Boolean functions, and it is open to determine whether all the three-input Boolean functions can be securely computed without any helping card.

For example, the three-input majority function $\mathsf{maj}: \{0,1\}^3 \rightarrow \{0,1\}$ defined as

$$\mathsf{maj}(a,b,c) = \begin{cases} 0 & \text{if } a+b+c \leq 1, \\ 1 & \text{if } a+b+c \geq 2 \end{cases}$$

can be securely computed by combining the existing protocols (including the "copy" protocols, which will be mentioned in Sect. 1.4), because it suffices to apply AND, OR, and copy protocols by following a circuit such as

$$\mathsf{maj}(a, b, c) = (a \wedge b) \vee (b \wedge c) \vee (c \wedge a).$$

Note that a 2-OR protocol is obtained immediately by a 2-AND protocol with De Morgan's laws, or we will directly display a 2-OR protocol in Sect. 3.1. When following the circuit for 3-majority above, we need to duplicate some input commitments, and hence, we need some helping cards, implying that such a construction is not card-minimal. Thus, designing card-minimal protocols for three-input Boolean functions (including 3-majority) is considered to be non-trivial.

1.3 Contribution

In this study, we focus on designing card-minimal protocols for three-input Boolean functions by extending the idea behind Koyama's AND protocol [12] further. Specifically, the contribution of this paper is twofold:

- For the three-input majority function, we construct a protocol using six cards, i.e., we design a card-minimal 3-majority protocol:

$$[a]\{1,2\} \ [b]\{3,4\} \ [c]\{5,6\} \qquad\qquad [\mathsf{maj}(a,b,c)]\{1,4\}$$

  As will be explained, our protocol is based on Koyama's AND protocol [12], and uses the same number of shuffles, namely 8.5 shuffles (in expectation). Note that the 3-majority is one of the most important three-input Boolean functions in terms of practical use.
- We generalize the idea behind Koyama's AND protocol so that we obtain a generic card-minimal three-input protocol, which accommodates many three-input Boolean functions (namely, 140 functions), including important functions such as 3-OR, 3-XOR, 3-NAND, 3-NOR, 3-XNOR, and the 3-minority.

1.4 Related Work

Aside from the existing AND and XOR protocols introduced in Sect. 1.2, there are "copy" protocols working on a standard deck [13,22,30]. A copy protocol duplicates a commitment without revealing any information about the value of the commitment. Using such a copy protocol as well as 2-AND, 2-XOR, and NOT protocols[2], we can construct a protocol for any Boolean function. However, determining whether there exist card-minimal protocols for multi-input functions remains an open problem (except the n-AND and n-XOR functions).

---

[2] A NOT protocol can be simply constructed: swapping two cards comprising a commitment produces a commitment to the negation.

There are also attractive applications using a standard deck of cards: zero-knowledge proof protocols for Sudoku [34] and millionaire protocols [18]. Moreover, under another computation model which accepts "private operations" such as revealing a card behind player's back, card-minimal AND, XOR, and copy protocols were constructed [16].

As mentioned at the beginning of this section, many card-based protocols work on a two-color deck of cards; under several kinds of settings of decks (including the standard-deck and two-color-deck settings), the research area on card-based cryptography has grown rapidly recently from both theoretical and practical aspects. Examples are: constructing zero-knowledge proof protocols [15,32,33,35], investigating computation models [3,9,23,39] and shuffles [8,21,36], designing private-operation-model protocols [1,17,28,29,31], seeking practical and/or efficient protocols [2,7,14,20,40], and making use of other physical objects [4,11,19,27,38].

1.5 Outline

In Sect. 2, we introduce operations used in card-based cryptography and describe the existing protocol [30] and technique [12]. In Sect. 3, we show how to construct a three-input majority protocol by extending the ideas behind the Niemi–Renvall AND protocol and Koyama's AND protocol. In Sect. 4, we construct a generic protocol which covers many three-input Boolean functions by generalizing the ideas further. Section 5 summarizes our study.

2 Preliminaries

In this section, we introduce the description of operations formalized in the computational model of card-based cryptography [24]. We also introduce the two practical shuffles called the "random cut" and "random bisection cut." Finally, we describe the Niemi–Renvall AND protocol [30] and the useful technique [12] called the "swap operation by commitment value."

2.1 Operations

We here introduce three operations, namely *rearrangement*, *turn*, and *shuffle*. We assume that we have a sequence of n face-down cards for some natural number $n\,(\geq 2)$.

Rearrangement. This applies some permutation $\pi \in S_n$ to the sequence, where S_n denotes the symmetric group of degree n. This is written as (perm, π), and the sequence changes as follows:

$$\underset{1}{\boxed{?}}\,\underset{2}{\boxed{?}}\cdots\underset{n}{\boxed{?}}\quad\xrightarrow{(\mathsf{perm},\pi)}\quad\overset{\pi^{-1}(1)}{\boxed{?}}\ \overset{\pi^{-1}(2)}{\boxed{?}}\ \cdots\ \overset{\pi^{-1}(n)}{\boxed{?}}\ .$$

Turn. This reveals the t-th card from the left in the sequence to check its number. This is written as $(\mathsf{turn}, \{t\})$, and the sequence changes as follows (for example):

$$\boxed{?}\boxed{?}\cdots\boxed{?}\cdots\boxed{?} \xrightarrow{(\mathsf{turn},\{t\})} \boxed{?}\boxed{?}\cdots\boxed{7}\cdots\boxed{?}.$$

Shuffle. This applies a permutation π drawn from a permutation set $\Pi \subseteq S_n$ according to a probability distribution $\mathcal{F}$ on Π. This is written as $(\mathsf{shuf}, \Pi, \mathcal{F})$, and the sequence changes as follows:

$$\boxed{?}\boxed{?}\cdots\boxed{?} \xrightarrow{(\mathsf{shuf},\Pi,\mathcal{F})} \overset{\pi^{-1}(1)}{\boxed{?}}\ \overset{\pi^{-1}(2)}{\boxed{?}}\ \cdots\ \overset{\pi^{-1}(n)}{\boxed{?}} \quad \text{for } \pi \leftarrow \mathcal{F}.$$

Note that no one learns which permutation in Π was applied. If $\mathcal{F}$ is uniform, then we simply write it as (shuf, Π).

2.2   Random Cut

A *random cut*, denoted by $\langle \cdot \rangle$, is an operation that shuffles a sequence by cyclically shifting it. Applying a random cut to a sequence of n cards results in one of n possibilities, each occurring with a probability of $1/n$:

$$\left\langle \boxed{?}\boxed{?}\cdots\boxed{?}\boxed{?} \right\rangle \to \begin{cases} \boxed{?}\boxed{?}\cdots\boxed{?}\boxed{?} & (1/n), \\ \boxed{?}\boxed{?}\cdots\boxed{?}\boxed{?} & (1/n), \\ \quad\vdots \\ \boxed{?}\boxed{?}\cdots\boxed{?}\boxed{?} & (1/n), \\ \boxed{?}\boxed{?}\cdots\boxed{?}\boxed{?} & (1/n). \end{cases}$$

Thus, this operation can be written as $(\mathsf{shuf}, \langle (1\ 2 \cdots n) \rangle)$, where $\langle (i_1\ i_2 \cdots i_\ell) \rangle$ denotes the cyclic group generated by a (cyclic) permutation $(i_1\ i_2 \cdots i_\ell)$.

2.3   Random Bisection Cut (RBC)

A random bisection cut (RBC) [26], denoted by $[\,\cdot\,|\,\cdot\,]$, is a shuffling operation, which bisects a sequence of cards and then randomly swaps the two halves. Thus, when an RBC is applied to a sequence of $2n$ cards, the sequence becomes either the original one, or the one in which the first n cards are swapped with the last n cards, as follows:

$$\left[\boxed{?}\cdots\boxed{?} \,\middle|\, \boxed{?}\cdots\boxed{?} \right] \to \begin{cases} \boxed{?}\cdots\boxed{?} \,\big|\, \boxed{?}\cdots\boxed{?} & (1/2), \\ \boxed{?}\cdots\boxed{?} \,\big|\, \boxed{?}\cdots\boxed{?} & (1/2). \end{cases}$$

This operation can be written as $(\mathsf{shuf}, \{\mathsf{id}, (1\ n{+}1)(2\ n{+}2)\cdots(n\ 2n)\})$, where id denotes the identity permutation.

2.4 The Niemi–Renvall AND Protocol

The Niemi–Renvall AND protocol [30] takes as input two commitments to $a, b \in \{0,1\}$ as well as an additional card and outputs a commitment to $a \wedge b$. This protocol proceeds as follows.

1. Place the two input commitments and the additional card $\boxed{5}$ as follows, and turn over the face-up card:

$$\boxed{5}\ \underbrace{\boxed{?}\boxed{?}}\ \underbrace{\boxed{?}\boxed{?}}\ \rightarrow\ \boxed{?}\ \underbrace{\boxed{?}\boxed{?}}\ \underbrace{\boxed{?}\boxed{?}}\ .$$
$$\quad\quad [a]\{1,2\}\ [b]\{3,4\}\quad\quad\quad [a]\{1,2\}\ [b]\{3,4\}$$

2. Swap the third and fourth cards:

$$\overset{1\ 2\ 3\ 4\ 5}{\boxed{?}\boxed{?}\boxed{?}\boxed{?}\boxed{?}}\ \rightarrow\ \overset{1\ 2\ 4\ 3\ 5}{\boxed{?}\boxed{?}\boxed{?}\boxed{?}\boxed{?}}\ .$$

   The initial and swapped sequences for each input are described in the third and fourth columns of Table 2. Observe that the order of $\boxed{1}$, $\boxed{4}$, and $\boxed{5}$ in the swapped sequence is $\boxed{5} \rightarrow \boxed{4} \rightarrow \boxed{1}$ if and only if $a \wedge b = 1$. Therefore, we try to remove the two cards $\boxed{2}$ and $\boxed{3}$ in the next steps.

3. Apply a random cut to the sequence:

$$\langle\boxed{?}\boxed{?}\boxed{?}\boxed{?}\boxed{?}\rangle\ \rightarrow\ \boxed{?}\boxed{?}\boxed{?}\boxed{?}\boxed{?}$$

4. Turn over the first card. Remove the revealed card if it is either $\boxed{2}$ or $\boxed{3}$; otherwise, turn the card face down. Return to Step 3 unless both $\boxed{2}$ and $\boxed{3}$ are already removed.

5. Now, the sequence is one of the three possibilities as described in the fifth column of Table 2. Apply a random cut to the sequence again and then turn over the first card. We can obtain a commitment to $a \wedge b$ (as output), as follows:[3]

$$\langle\boxed{?}\boxed{?}\boxed{?}\rangle\ \rightarrow\ \boxed{?}\boxed{?}\boxed{?}\ \xrightarrow{(\text{turn},\{1\})}\ \begin{cases} \boxed{1}\ \underbrace{\boxed{?}\boxed{?}}_{[a \wedge b]\{4,5\}}\quad (1/3), \\[2mm] \boxed{4}\ \underbrace{\boxed{?}\boxed{?}}_{[a \wedge b]\{1,5\}}\quad (1/3), \\[2mm] \boxed{5}\ \underbrace{\boxed{?}\boxed{?}}_{[a \wedge b]\{1,4\}}\quad (1/3). \end{cases}$$

If the first card is $\boxed{4}$, then we obtain a commitment to the negation of $a \wedge b$; we can obtain a commitment to $a \wedge b$ by swapping the two cards comprising the commitment.

The correctness of this protocol is clear from Table 2. In addition, no information about the input and output is leaked when a card is turned over because we always apply a random cut before turning over a card.

---

[3] This step was proposed by Koch et al. [6], reducing the number of shuffles.

Table 2. The sequence of five cards for each input during the Niemi–Renvall protocol

Input (a,b)	$a \wedge b$	Initial	After swap	$\boxed{2}$ and $\boxed{3}$ removed
$(0,0)$	0	$\boxed{5}\boxed{1}\boxed{2}\boxed{3}\boxed{4}$	$\boxed{5}\boxed{1}\boxed{3}\boxed{2}\boxed{4}$	$\boxed{1}\boxed{4}\boxed{5}$ or $\boxed{4}\boxed{5}\boxed{1}$ or $\boxed{5}\boxed{1}\boxed{4}$
$(0,1)$	0	$\boxed{5}\boxed{1}\boxed{2}\boxed{4}\boxed{3}$	$\boxed{5}\boxed{1}\boxed{4}\boxed{2}\boxed{3}$	$\boxed{1}\boxed{4}\boxed{5}$ or $\boxed{4}\boxed{5}\boxed{1}$ or $\boxed{5}\boxed{1}\boxed{4}$
$(1,0)$	0	$\boxed{5}\boxed{2}\boxed{1}\boxed{3}\boxed{4}$	$\boxed{5}\boxed{2}\boxed{3}\boxed{1}\boxed{4}$	$\boxed{1}\boxed{4}\boxed{5}$ or $\boxed{4}\boxed{5}\boxed{1}$ or $\boxed{5}\boxed{1}\boxed{4}$
$(1,1)$	1	$\boxed{5}\boxed{2}\boxed{1}\boxed{4}\boxed{3}$	$\boxed{5}\boxed{2}\boxed{4}\boxed{1}\boxed{3}$	$\boxed{1}\boxed{5}\boxed{4}$ or $\boxed{4}\boxed{1}\boxed{5}$ or $\boxed{5}\boxed{4}\boxed{1}$

2.5 Swapping by Commitment Value

Koyama et al. [12] proposed a sub-protocol called the *swapping by commitment value* based on the idea of behind the two-input XOR protocol [22] proposed by Mizuki. This led to the construction of the 3-AND protocol [12]. Given two target cards $\boxed{?}\boxed{?}$ and a commitment to $c \in \{0,1\}$ of base $\{i,j\}$, the swapping by commitment value is to swap the two cards $\boxed{?}\boxed{?}$ if and only if $c = 1$, without leaking any information about the value of c as follows:

$$
\overset{1 \ 2}{\boxed{?}\boxed{?}} \quad \underbrace{\boxed{?}\boxed{?}}_{[c]^{\{i,j\}}} \quad \rightarrow \quad
\begin{cases}
\overset{1 \ 2}{\boxed{?}\boxed{?}} & \text{if } c = 0, \\
\overset{2 \ 1}{\boxed{?}\boxed{?}} & \text{if } c = 1.
\end{cases}
$$

The procedure is shown below.

1. Place the two target cards and the commitment to c as follows:

$$
\boxed{?}\boxed{?} \quad \underbrace{\boxed{?}\boxed{?}}_{[c]^{\{i,j\}}} \ .
$$

2. Swap the second and third cards, i.e., apply $(\mathsf{perm}, (2\,3))$.
3. Apply $(\mathsf{shuf}, \{\mathsf{id}, (1\,3)(2\,4)\})$, i.e., apply an RBC as follows:

$$
\left[\boxed{?}\boxed{?} \middle| \boxed{?}\boxed{?} \right] \quad \rightarrow \quad \boxed{?}\boxed{?}\boxed{?}\boxed{?}.
$$

4. Apply $(\mathsf{perm}, (2\,3))$ again. Then, the sequence becomes one of the following two possibilities depending on the value of c:

$$
c = 0 \rightarrow
\begin{cases}
\overset{1 \ 2}{\boxed{?}\boxed{?}} \ \boxed{i}\boxed{j} & (1/2), \\
\overset{2 \ 1}{\boxed{?}\boxed{?}} \ \boxed{j}\boxed{i} & (1/2).
\end{cases}
$$

$$
c = 1 \rightarrow
\begin{cases}
\overset{1 \ 2}{\boxed{?}\boxed{?}} \ \boxed{j}\boxed{i} & (1/2), \\
\overset{2 \ 1}{\boxed{?}\boxed{?}} \ \boxed{i}\boxed{j} & (1/2).
\end{cases}
$$

Observe that the order of the first and second cards are desirable if the order of $\boxed{i}$ and $\boxed{j}$ is $\boxed{i}\boxed{j}$.

5. Turn over the third and fourth cards to reveal the order of $\boxed{i}$ and $\boxed{j}$.
   (a) If $\boxed{i}\boxed{j}$ appears, then output the first and second cards.
   (b) If $\boxed{j}\boxed{i}$ appears, then swap the first and second cards and output them.

Thus, the above sub-protocol achieves the desired functionality without leaking any information about c.

3 Three-Input Majority Protocol

In this section, we construct a card-minimal protocol for the three-input majority function $\mathsf{maj}(a, b, c)$ working on a standard deck. The idea behind our proposed protocol is based on the Niemi–Renvall AND protocol [30] and Koyama's AND protocol [12].

To construct a 3-majority protocol, we utilize the following equation:

$$\mathsf{maj}(a, b, c) = \begin{cases} a \wedge b & \text{if } c = 0, \\ a \vee b & \text{if } c = 1. \end{cases} \tag{3}$$

To compute $\mathsf{maj}(a, b, c)$, observe that, if $c = 0$, it suffices to compute $a \wedge b$ using the Niemi–Renvall AND protocol introduced in Sect. 2.4; otherwise, we want to compute $a \vee b$. Therefore, we first construct an OR protocol by modifying the Niemi–Renvall protocol and then construct a 3-majority protocol.

3.1 Two-Input or Protocol

We construct a two-input OR protocol by changing the rearrangement positions in the Niemi–Renvall AND protocol. The protocol takes as input two commitments to a, b as well as an additional card and outputs a commitment to $a \vee b$, as follows.

1. Place the two input commitments and the additional card $\boxed{5}$ and turn it over as follows:

$$\boxed{5}\ \underbrace{\boxed{?}\boxed{?}}_{[a]^{\{1,2\}}}\ \underbrace{\boxed{?}\boxed{?}}_{[b]^{\{3,4\}}}\ \ \rightarrow\ \ \underbrace{\boxed{?}}_{}\underbrace{\boxed{?}\boxed{?}}_{a}\underbrace{\boxed{?}\boxed{?}}_{b}.$$

2. Rearrange the sequence as follows, i.e., apply $(\mathsf{perm}, (2\ 3\ 5\ 4))$:

$$\overset{1\ \ 2\ \ 3\ \ 4\ \ 5}{\boxed{?}\boxed{?}\boxed{?}\boxed{?}\boxed{?}}\ \ \rightarrow\ \ \overset{1\ \ 4\ \ 2\ \ 5\ \ 3}{\boxed{?}\boxed{?}\boxed{?}\boxed{?}\boxed{?}}.$$

The input and rearranged sequences for each input are described in the third and fourth columns of Table 3. Observe that the order of $\boxed{1}, \boxed{4}$, and $\boxed{5}$ in the rearranged sequence is $\boxed{5} \rightarrow \boxed{4} \rightarrow \boxed{1}$ if and only if $a \vee b = 1$.

3. Apply Steps 3, 4, and 5 of the Niemi–Renvall AND protocol shown in Sect. 2.4 to obtain a commitment to $a \vee b$.

Table 3. The sequence of five cards for each input during the 2-OR protocol

Input (a,b)	$a \vee b$	Initial	Rearranged (Step 2)	Removing [2] and [3]
$(0,0)$	0	[5][1][2][3][4]	[5][3][1][4][2]	[1][4][5] or [4][5][1] or [5][1][4]
$(0,1)$	1	[5][1][2][4][3]	[5][4][1][3][2]	[1][5][4] or [4][1][5] or [5][4][1]
$(1,0)$	1	[5][2][1][3][4]	[5][3][2][4][1]	[1][5][4] or [4][1][5] or [5][4][1]
$(1,1)$	1	[5][2][1][4][3]	[5][4][2][3][1]	[1][5][4] or [4][1][5] or [5][4][1]

3.2 Idea

Remember that in Step 2 of the Niemi–Renvall AND protocol and our OR protocol, we rearrange the sequence of cards, i.e., the AND protocol uses $(\mathsf{perm}, (3\ 4))$ and the OR protocol uses $(\mathsf{perm}, (2\ 3\ 5\ 4))$.

Observe that if we apply $(\mathsf{perm}, (3\ 4))$, namely

$$\overset{1\ 2\ 3\ 4\ 5}{[?][?][?][?][?]} \quad \rightarrow \quad \overset{1\ 2\ 4\ 3\ 5}{[?][?][?][?][?]},$$

and apply $(\mathsf{perm}, (2\ 3)(4\ 5))$, namely

$$\overset{1\ 2\ 3\ 4\ 5}{[?][?][?][?][?]} \quad \rightarrow \quad \overset{1\ 3\ 2\ 5\ 4}{[?][?][?][?][?]},$$

the resulting sequence becomes the same as the one after executing Step 2 of our OR protocol. In other words, $((2\ 3)(4\ 5))(3\ 4) = (2\ 3\ 5\ 4)$.

Therefore, after applying $(\mathsf{perm}, (3\ 4))$, if we do nothing, it results in the AND protocol. If we apply $(\mathsf{perm}, (2\ 3)(4\ 5))$ after applying $(\mathsf{perm}, (3\ 4))$, it results in the OR protocol. Therefore, it suffices to perform the swap operation by commitment value [12] introduced in Sect. 2.5 to apply $(\mathsf{perm}, (2\ 3)(4\ 5))$ if and only if $c = 1$ (see Eq. (3) again).

3.3 Description of Protocol

We are ready to describe the procedure for our 3-majority protocol. The protocol takes three commitments to a, b, c as input and outputs a commitment to $\mathsf{maj}(a, b, c)$.

1. Place three input commitments as follows:

$$\underset{[a]^{\{1,2\}}}{[?][?]} \quad \underset{[b]^{\{3,4\}}}{[?][?]} \quad \underset{[c]^{\{5,6\}}}{[?][?]} \ .$$

2. Swap the second and the third cards:

$$\overset{1\ 2\ 3\ 4\ 5\ 6}{[?][?][?][?][?][?]} \quad \rightarrow \quad \overset{1\ 3\ 2\ 4\ 5\ 6}{[?][?][?][?][?][?]}\ .$$

Table 4. The sequence of six cards for each input in our 3-majority protocol, where the sequences in the fourth column are in a case when the order of the revealed fifth and sixth cards are [5][6] in Step 3d.

Input(a,b,c)	maj(a,b,c)	Initial	After Swap (Step 3d)	Removing [2][3][6]
$(0,0,0)$	0	[1][2][3][4][5][6]	[1][3][2][4][5][6]	[1][4][5]
$(0,0,1)$	0	[1][2][3][4][6][5]	[3][1][4][2][5][6]	[1][4][5]
$(0,1,0)$	0	[1][2][4][3][5][6]	[1][4][2][3][5][6]	[1][4][5]
$(0,1,1)$	1	[1][2][4][3][6][5]	[4][1][3][2][5][6]	[4][1][5]
$(1,0,0)$	0	[2][1][3][4][5][6]	[2][3][1][4][5][6]	[1][4][5]
$(1,0,1)$	1	[2][1][3][4][6][5]	[3][2][4][1][5][6]	[4][1][5]
$(1,1,0)$	1	[2][1][4][3][5][6]	[2][4][1][3][5][6]	[4][1][5]
$(1,1,1)$	1	[2][1][4][3][6][5]	[4][2][3][1][5][6]	[4][1][5]

3. Apply the swap operation by the commitment to c [12] to apply $(\mathsf{perm}, (1\ 2)(3\ 4))$ if and only if $c = 1$ as follows:

   (a) Rearrange the sequence as follows:

   $$\underset{1\ 2\ 3\ 4\ 5\ 6}{[?][?][?][?][?][?]} \rightarrow \underset{1\ 3\ 5\ 2\ 4\ 6}{[?][?][?][?][?][?]}.$$

   (b) Apply $(\mathsf{shuf}, \{\mathsf{id}, (1\,4)(2\,5)(3\,6)\})$, i.e., apply an RBC as follows:

   $$\left[[?][?][?]\,\big|\,[?][?][?]\right] \rightarrow [?][?][?][?][?][?].$$

   (c) Rearrange the sequence as follows:

   $$\underset{1\ 2\ 3\ 4\ 5\ 6}{[?][?][?][?][?][?]} \rightarrow \underset{1\ 4\ 2\ 5\ 3\ 6}{[?][?][?][?][?][?]}.$$

   (d) Turn over the fifth and sixth cards. If their order is [5][6], do nothing; if it is [6][5], swap the first and second cards as well as the third and fourth cards. The sequence for each input is described in Table 4 where the order of the revealed two cards [5][6] does not matter.

4. Execute Steps 3, 4, and 5 of the Niemi–Renvall AND protocol to obtain a commitment to maj(a, b, c), where we use the first through fourth cards as input, and the [5] turned over in Step 3d as an additional card (i.e., place the [5] in the first from the left).

3.4 Correctness and Security

The correctness of this protocol is clear from Table 4 because when the input (a, b, c) satisfies maj$(a, b, c) = 0$, the resulting sequence after Step 3 is [1][4][5]

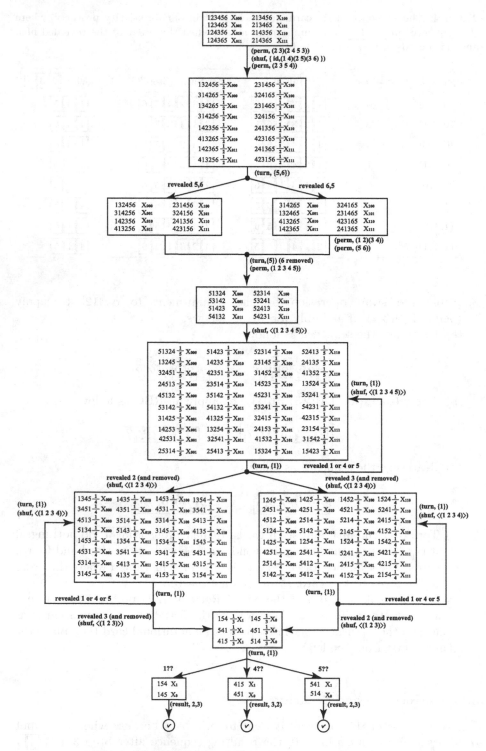

Fig. 1. The KWH-tree of three-input majority protocol

(where $\boxed{2}$, $\boxed{3}$, and $\boxed{6}$ are removed); otherwise, the sequence is $\boxed{4}\boxed{1}\boxed{5}$. As for the security, we execute the swap operation by commitment value [12] in Step 3 and then the part of the Niemi–Renvall AND protocol (and Steps 1 and 2 just place and swap the sequence, respectively), no information about the input and output is leaked.

More formally, we use the *KWH-tree* [10] to prove the security (and correctness) of this protocol; we depict the KWH-tree of our three-input majority protocol in Fig. 1. In the diagram, states of a sequence of cards are expressed as nodes, and operations on the sequence of cards are expressed as edges. Because the sum of the probability distributions of the nodes is equal to the probability distribution of the input, the protocol is guaranteed to be secure.

4   Generic Protocol for Three-Input Functions

In this section, we generalize our 3-majority protocol described in Sect. 3 so as to obtain a generic card-minimal protocol for three-input Boolean functions.

After we describe the idea behind the generalization in Sect. 4.1, we generalize the Niemi–Renvall AND protocol and the swap operation by commitment value [12] in Sects 4.2 and 4.3, respectively.

Before going into the subsections, we define a notation; hereinafter, $\pi_{ijk\ell}$ denotes a permutation in S_4 such that

$$\pi_{ijk\ell} = \begin{pmatrix} 1\ 2\ 3\ 4 \\ i\ j\ k\ \ell \end{pmatrix}$$

for four distinct integers $i, j, k, \ell \in \{1, 2, 3, 4\}$. For example, $\pi_{1234} = \mathrm{id}$ and $\pi_{1324} = (2\ 3)$.

4.1   Idea

Our idea is that, as $\mathsf{maj}(a, b, c)$ is represented with the two elementary functions of a and b depending on the value of c (as in Eq. (3)), every three-input Boolean function $f : \{0,1\}^3 \rightarrow \{0,1\}$ can be also written as follows:

$$f(a, b, c) = \begin{cases} g(a, b) & \text{if } c = 1, \\ h(a, b) & \text{if } c = 0, \end{cases} \tag{4}$$

where there exist two functions $g, h : \{0,1\}^2 \rightarrow \{0,1\}$.

Remember that in our 3-majority protocol proposed in Sect. 3, we first apply the permutation π_{1324} (to compute 2-AND) and then, if $c = 1$, apply the permutation π_{2143} by the swap operation (to compute 2-OR); π_{1324} leads to 2-AND, and $\pi_{2143}\pi_{1324}$ leads to 2-OR. If we replace these two permutations with other ones, then we will obtain (possibly) another three-input protocol.

Bearing this in mind, we first investigate what two-input function (as a candidate for g or h in Eq. (4)) will be computed for every permutation $\pi_{ijk\ell} \in S_4$ (in Sect. 4.2). Then, we enumerate all possible swap operations (in Sect. 4.3).

Table 5. Output NR^π of the generalized Niemi–Renvall protocol with π

Permutation π	$\mathsf{NR}^\pi(a, b)$
$\pi_{1234}, \pi_{1243}, \pi_{2134}, \pi_{2143}$	0
π_{1324}	$a \wedge b$
π_{1423}	$a \wedge \bar{b}$
π_{1342}, π_{1432}	a
π_{2314}	$\bar{a} \wedge b$
π_{3124}, π_{3214}	b
N/A	$a \oplus b$
π_{3142}	$a \vee b$
π_{2413}	$\overline{a \vee b}$
N/A	$\overline{a \oplus b}$
π_{4123}, π_{4213}	$\bar{b}$
π_{4132}	$a \vee \bar{b}$
π_{2341}, π_{2431}	$\bar{a}$
π_{3241}	$\bar{a} \vee b$
π_{4231}	$\overline{a \wedge b}$
$\pi_{3412}, \pi_{3421}, \pi_{4312}, \pi_{4321}$	1

4.2   Generalizing the Niemi–Renvall and Protocol

In this subsection, we generalize the Niemi–Renvall AND protocol by considering all permutations for Step 2 of the protocol.

Assume that we apply a permutation $\pi \in S_4$ (instead of the original permutation) in Step 2 of the Niemi–Renvall AND protocol. Then, at the end of the protocol, we should obtain a commitment to a certain two-input function; we denote this function by $\mathsf{NR}^\pi : \{0, 1\}^2 \to \{0, 1\}$.

We examined all 4! possibilities for π and write $\mathsf{NR}^\pi(a, b)$ in Table 5. This table tells us that aside from 2-XOR and 2-XNOR, all two-input functions can be obtained.

4.3   Generalizing Swap Operation by Commitment Value

In this subsection, consider all possible swapping operations.

Assume that we have four cards along with a commitment to $c \in \{0, 1\}$ of base $\{5, 6\}$:

$$\boxed{?}\boxed{?}\boxed{?}\boxed{?} \ \underbrace{\boxed{?}\boxed{?}}_{[c]^{\{5,6\}}} \ .$$

We want to apply a permutation in S_4 to the first four cards if and only if $c = 1$. What are the possible permutations? We can consider two kind of swap operations.

($i\,j$)-*swap.* Remember that the swap operation introduced in Sect. 2.5 swaps two cards (or does not) depending on the value of c. As a natural extension, let us consider a swap operation such that the i-th and j-th cards (among the leftmost four cards) for $1 \leq i < j \leq 4$ are swapped or not; we call this the ($i\,j$)-*swap*, which can be achieved as follows.

1. Apply the permutation corresponding to ($i\,j$) according to Table 6.
2. Apply (shuf, {id, $(3\,5)(4\,6)$}) , i.e., apply an RBC as follows:

$$\boxed{?\,?}\,\Big[\boxed{?\,?}\,\Big|\,\boxed{?\,?}\,\Big] \;\rightarrow\; \boxed{?}\,\boxed{?}\,\boxed{?}\,\boxed{?}\,\boxed{?}\,\boxed{?}$$

3. Apply the inverse of the permutation applied in Step 1.
4. Turn over the fifth and sixth cards (namely, apply (turn, {5, 6})). If the order of the revealed cards are $\boxed{6}\,\boxed{5}$, swap the i-th and j-th cards (namely, (perm, ($i\,j$))); otherwise, do nothing.

($i\,j$)($k\,\ell$)-*swap.* Remember that our 3-majority protocol uses (perm, $(2\,3)(4\,5)$) in the swap operation, and note that the permutations $(2\,3)$ and $(4\,5)$ are disjoint. Therefore, we can consider a swap operation such that the i-th and j-th cards as well as the k-th and ℓ-th cards are swapped or not for $1 \leq i < j \leq 4$ and $\{k, \ell\} = \{1, 2, 3, 4\} - \{i, j\}$; we call this the ($i\,j$)($k\,\ell$)-*swap*, which can be achieved as follows.

1. Apply the permutation corresponding to ($i\,j$)($k\,\ell$) according to Table 7.
2. Apply (shuf, {id, $(1\,4)(2\,5)(3\,6)$}), i.e., apply an RBC as follows:

$$\Big[\boxed{?}\,\boxed{?}\,\boxed{?}\,\Big|\,\boxed{?}\,\boxed{?}\,\boxed{?}\,\Big] \;\rightarrow\; \boxed{?}\,\boxed{?}\,\boxed{?}\,\boxed{?}\,\boxed{?}\,\boxed{?}$$

3. Apply the inverse of the permutation applied in Step 1.
4. Turn over the fifth and sixth cards (namely, apply (turn, {5, 6})). If the order of the revealed cards are $\boxed{6}\,\boxed{5}$, swap the i-th and j-th cards as well as k-th and ℓ-th cards (namely, (perm, ($i\,j$)($k\,\ell$))); otherwise, do nothing.

4.4   Description of Protocol

We are now ready to describe our generic protocol for three-input Boolean function.

Our protocol owns two permutations $\pi, \sigma \in S_4$ as parameter, where either $\sigma = (i\,j)$ for $1 \leq i < j \leq 4$, or $\sigma = (i\,j)(k\,\ell)$ for $1 \leq i < j \leq 4$ and $\{k, \ell\} = \{1, 2, 3, 4\} - \{i, j\}$; it proceeds as follows.

1. Place three input commitments as:

$$\underbrace{\boxed{?\,?}}_{[a]\,\{1,2\}} \;\; \underbrace{\boxed{?\,?}}_{[b]\,\{3,4\}} \;\; \underbrace{\boxed{?\,?}}_{[c]\,\{5,6\}} \;.$$

2. Apply (perm, π).
3. Apply σ-swap.
4. Apply Steps 3, 4, and 5 of the Niemi–Renvall AND protocol.

Table 6. Actions for Steps 1 and 3 of the $(i\ j)$-swap

$(i\ j)$	Action for Step 1	Action for Step 3 (Inverse of Step 1)
$(1\ 2)$	(perm, $(1\ 3)(2\ 5\ 4)$)	(perm, $(1\ 3)(2\ 4\ 5)$)
$(1\ 3)$	(perm, $(1\ 3\ 5\ 4\ 2)$)	(perm, $(1\ 2\ 4\ 5\ 3)$)
$(1\ 4)$	(perm, $(1\ 3\ 2)(4\ 5)$)	(perm, $(1\ 2\ 3)(4\ 5)$)
$(2\ 3)$	(perm, $(2\ 3\ 5\ 4)$)	(perm, $(2\ 4\ 5\ 3)$)
$(2\ 4)$	(perm, $(2\ 3)(4\ 5)$)	(perm, $(2\ 3)(4\ 5)$)
$(3\ 4)$	(perm, $(4\ 5)$)	(perm, $(4\ 5)$)

Table 7. Actions for Steps 1 and 3 of the $(i\ j)(k\ \ell)$-swap

$(i\ j)(k\ \ell)$	Action for Step 1	Action for Step 3 (Inverse of Step 1)
$(1\ 2)(3\ 4)$	(perm, $(2\ 4\ 5\ 3)$)	(perm, $(2\ 3\ 5\ 4)$)
$(1\ 3)(2\ 4)$	(perm, $(3\ 4\ 5)$)	(perm, $(3\ 5\ 4)$)
$(1\ 4)(2\ 3)$	(perm, $(3\ 5)$)	(perm, $(3\ 5)$)

4.5   Covered Functions

In this subsection, we comprehensively reveal what three-input functions our generic protocol computes.

Executing our generic protocol with parameter $\pi, \sigma \in S_4$ is equivalent to executing a protocol for the three-input Boolean function f such that

$$f(a,b,c) = \begin{cases} \mathsf{NR}^{\sigma\pi}(a,b) & \text{if } c = 1, \\ \mathsf{NR}^{\pi}(a,b) & \text{if } c = 0. \end{cases}$$

For example, if we take π, σ as in the first and second columns of Table 8, we have NR^{π} and $\mathsf{NR}^{\sigma\pi}$ as in the fourth and fifth columns, and hence, the corresponding three-input Boolean functions are shown in the sixth column. This table tells us that major three-input Boolean functions are covered by our generic protocol.

From the user's perspective, given a three-input function f, we want to find two permutations $\pi, \sigma \in S_4$ which lead to f. Table 9 helps us: We first find g, h such that

$$f(a,b,c) = \begin{cases} g(a,b) & \text{if } c = 1, \\ h(a,b) & \text{if } c = 0; \end{cases}$$

then, using Table 9, find the corresponding parameter π, σ.

Although not all three-input Boolean functions have a corresponding parameter π, σ, our generic protocol covers 140 three-input Boolean functions among the 256 ones.

Table 8. Covered main functions

π	σ	$\sigma\pi$	NR^{π}	$NR^{\sigma\pi}$	$f(a,b,c)$
π_{1234}	$(2\ 3)$	π_{1324}	AND	0	3-AND [12]
π_{3412}	$(2\ 3)$	π_{3142}	1	OR	3-OR
π_{3412}	$(1\ 4)(2\ 3)$	π_{2143}	NAND	OR	3-XOR
π_{4321}	$(2\ 3)$	π_{4231}	NAND	1	3-NAND
π_{2413}	$(2\ 3)$	π_{2143}	0	NOR	3-NOR
π_{2413}	$(1\ 3)(2\ 4)$	π_{1324}	AND	NOR	3-XNOR
π_{1324}	$(1\ 2)(3\ 4)$	π_{3142}	OR	AND	3-majority
π_{2413}	$(1\ 2)(3\ 4)$	π_{4231}	NOR	NAND	3-minority

Table 9. Parameter π, σ leading to g, h

h \ g	0	$a\wedge b$	$a\wedge\bar b$	a	$\bar a\wedge b$	b	$a\oplus b$	$a\vee b$	$\overline{a\vee b}$	$\overline{a\oplus b}$	$\bar b$	$a\vee\bar b$	$\bar a$	$\bar a\vee b$	$\overline{a\wedge b}$	1
0	π_{1234} (34)	π_{1234} (23)	π_{1243} (23)	π_{1234} (24)	π_{2134} (23)	π_{1234} (13)	N/A	π_{2143} (14)	π_{2143} (23)	N/A	π_{2143} (13)	π_{2134} (14)	π_{1243} (24)	π_{1243} (14)	π_{1234} (14)	π_{2143} (14)(23)
$a\wedge b$	π_{1324} (23)	N/A	π_{1324} (24)	π_{1324} (34)	π_{1324} (13)	π_{1324} (12)	N/A	π_{1324} (12)(34)	π_{1324} (13)(24)	N/A	N/A	N/A	N/A	N/A	π_{1324} (14)(23)	π_{1324} (14)
$a\wedge\bar b$	π_{1423} (23)	π_{1423} (24)	N/A	π_{1423} (34)	π_{1423} (13)(24)	N/A	N/A	π_{1423} (13)	N/A	π_{1423} (12)	π_{1423} (12)(34)	N/A	π_{1423} (14)(23)	N/A	N/A	π_{1423} (14)
a	π_{1342} (24)	π_{1342} (34)	π_{1432} (34)	π_{1432} (23)	N/A	π_{1342} (12)(34)	N/A	π_{1342} (12)	N/A	N/A	π_{1342} (13)(24)	π_{1432} (12)	π_{1432} (14)(23)	N/A	N/A	π_{1432} (13)
$\bar a\wedge b$	π_{2314} (23)	π_{2314} (13)	π_{2314} (13)(24)	N/A	N/A	π_{2314} (12)	N/A	N/A	π_{2314} (24)	N/A	N/A	π_{2314} (14)(23)	π_{2314} (34)	π_{2314} (12)(34)	N/A	π_{2314} (14)
b	π_{3124} (13)	π_{3124} (12)	N/A	π_{3124} (12)(34)	π_{3214} (12)	π_{3124} (23)	N/A	π_{3124} (34)	N/A	N/A	π_{3214} (14)(23)	N/A	π_{3214} (12)(34)	π_{3214} (34)	N/A	π_{3124} (24)
$a\oplus b$	N/A	N/A	N/A	N/A	N/A	N/A	N/A	N/A	N/A	N/A	N/A	N/A	N/A	N/A	N/A	N/A
$a\vee b$	π_{3142} (14)	π_{3142} (12)(34)	N/A	π_{3142} (12)	N/A	π_{3142} (34)	N/A	N/A	π_{3142} (14)(23)	N/A	N/A	π_{3142} (13)	N/A	π_{3142} (24)	π_{3142} (13)(24)	π_{3142} (23)
$\overline{a\vee b}$	π_{2413} (23)	π_{2413} (13)(24)	π_{2413} (13)	N/A	π_{2413} (14)	N/A	N/A	π_{2413} (14)(23)	N/A	N/A	π_{2413} (12)	N/A	π_{2413} (34)	N/A	π_{2413} (12)(34)	π_{2413} (14)
$\overline{a\oplus b}$	N/A	N/A	N/A	N/A	N/A	N/A	N/A	N/A	N/A	N/A	N/A	N/A	N/A	N/A	N/A	N/A
$\bar b$	π_{4123} (13)	N/A	π_{4123} (12)	π_{4213} (13)(24)	N/A	π_{4123} (14)	N/A	N/A	π_{4213} (12)	N/A	π_{4123} (23)	π_{4123} (34)	π_{4123} (13)(24)	N/A	π_{4213} (34)	π_{4123} (24)
$a\vee\bar b$	π_{4132} (14)	N/A	π_{4132} (12)(34)	π_{4132} (12)	π_{4132} (14)(23)	N/A	N/A	π_{4132} (13)	N/A	N/A	π_{4132} (34)	N/A	N/A	π_{4132} (13)(24)	π_{4132} (24)	π_{4132} (23)
$\bar a$	π_{2341} (24)	N/A	N/A	π_{2341} (14)	π_{2341} (34)	π_{2341} (12)(34)	N/A	N/A	π_{2431} (34)	N/A	π_{2341} (13)(24)	N/A	π_{2341} (23)	π_{2341} (12)	π_{2431} (12)	π_{2431} (13)
$\bar a\vee b$	π_{3241} (14)	N/A	π_{3241} (14)(23)	N/A	π_{3241} (14)	π_{3241} (12)(34)	N/A	π_{3241} (34)	π_{3241} (24)	N/A	N/A	π_{3241} (13)(24)	π_{3241} (12)	N/A	π_{3241} (13)	π_{3241} (23)
$\overline{a\wedge b}$	π_{4231} (14)	π_{4231} (14)(23)	N/A	N/A	π_{4231} (14)	N/A	N/A	π_{4231} (13)(24)	π_{4231} (12)(34)	N/A	π_{4231} (34)	π_{4231} (24)	π_{4231} (12)	π_{4231} (13)	N/A	π_{4231} (23)
1	π_{3412} (14)(23)	π_{4321} (14)	π_{3421} (14)	π_{3412} (13)	π_{4312} (14)	π_{3421} (24)	N/A	π_{3412} (23)	π_{3412} (14)	N/A	π_{4312} (24)	π_{4312} (23)	π_{4321} (13)	π_{3421} (23)	π_{4321} (23)	π_{3412} (34)

5 Conclusion

In this study, we showed how to construct a card-minimal 3-majority protocol by extending the Niemi–Renvall AND protocol [30] and Koyama's AND protocol [12]. Furthermore, we constructed a generic card-minimal protocol that covers many three-input Boolean functions as shown in Table 9.

Although the proposed protocol accommodates many major functions as seen in Table 8, not all the three-input Boolean functions can be computed by it. It is open to determine whether there exists a six-card protocol for every three-input Boolean function. While 3-XOR and 3-XNOR can be computed without any helping card by using the existing protocols, we conjecture that some functions, say

$$f(a, b, c) = \begin{cases} a \wedge b & \text{if } c = 1, \\ a \oplus b & \text{if } c = 0, \end{cases}$$

would need helping cards.

Acknowledgements. We thank the anonymous referees, whose comments have helped us improve the presentation of the paper. We also thank Hiroto Koyama for his cooperation in preparing a Japanese draft version of Sect. 3 at an earlier stage of this work. This work was supported in part by JSPS KAKENHI Grant Numbers JP21K11881 and JP19H01104.

References

1. Abe, Y., et al.: Efficient card-based majority voting protocols. New Gener. Comput. **40**, 173–198 (2022). https://doi.org/10.1007/s00354-022-00161-7
2. Abe, Y., Hayashi, Y., Mizuki, T., Sone, H.: Five-card AND computations in committed format using only uniform cyclic shuffles. New Gener. Comput. **39**(1), 97–114 (2021). https://doi.org/10.1007/s00354-020-00110-2
3. Dvořák, P., Koucký, M.: Barrington plays cards: the complexity of card-based protocols. In: Bläser, M., Monmege, B. (eds.) Theoretical Aspects of Computer Science. LIPIcs, vol. 187, pp. 26:1–26:17. Schloss Dagstuhl, Dagstuhl (2021). https://doi.org/10.4230/LIPIcs.STACS.2021.26
4. Isuzugawa, R., Miyahara, D., Mizuki, T.: Zero-knowledge proof protocol for cryptarithmetic using dihedral cards. In: Kostitsyna, I., Orponen, P. (eds.) UCNC 2021. LNCS, vol. 12984, pp. 51–67. Springer, Cham (2021). https://doi.org/10.1007/978-3-030-87993-8_4
5. Koch, A.: Cryptographic protocols from physical assumptions. Ph.D. thesis, Karlsruhe Institute of Technology (2019). https://doi.org/10.5445/IR/1000097756
6. Koch, A., Schrempp, M., Kirsten, M.: Card-based cryptography meets formal verification. In: Galbraith, S.D., Moriai, S. (eds.) ASIACRYPT 2019. LNCS, vol. 11921, pp. 488–517. Springer, Cham (2019). https://doi.org/10.1007/978-3-030-34578-5_18
7. Koch, A., Schrempp, M., Kirsten, M.: Card-based cryptography meets formal verification. New Gener. Comput. **39**(1), 115–158 (2021). https://doi.org/10.1007/s00354-020-00120-0
8. Koch, A., Walzer, S.: Foundations for actively secure card-based cryptography. In: Farach-Colton, M., Prencipe, G., Uehara, R. (eds.) Fun with Algorithms. LIPIcs, vol. 157, pp. 17:1–17:23. Schloss Dagstuhl, Dagstuhl (2020). https://doi.org/10.4230/LIPIcs.FUN.2021.17

9. Koch, A., Walzer, S.: Private function evaluation with cards. New Gener. Comput. 1–33 (2022, in press). https://doi.org/10.1007/s00354-021-00149-9
10. Koch, A., Walzer, S., Härtel, K.: Card-based cryptographic protocols using a minimal number of cards. In: Iwata, T., Cheon, J.H. (eds.) ASIACRYPT 2015. LNCS, vol. 9452, pp. 783–807. Springer, Heidelberg (2015). https://doi.org/10.1007/978-3-662-48797-6_32
11. Komano, Y., Mizuki, T.: Coin-based secure computations. Int. J. Inf. Secur. 1–14 (2022, in press). https://doi.org/10.1007/s10207-022-00585-8
12. Koyama, H., Miyahara, D., Mizuki, T., Sone, H.: A secure three-input AND protocol with a standard deck of minimal cards. In: Santhanam, R., Musatov, D. (eds.) CSR 2021. LNCS, vol. 12730, pp. 242–256. Springer, Cham (2021). https://doi.org/10.1007/978-3-030-79416-3_14
13. Koyama, H., Toyoda, K., Miyahara, D., Mizuki, T.: New card-based copy protocols using only random cuts. In: ASIA Public-Key Cryptography Workshop, pp. 13–22. ACM, New York (2021). https://doi.org/10.1145/3457338.3458297
14. Kuzuma, T., Toyoda, K., Miyahara, D., Mizuki, T.: Card-based single-shuffle protocols for secure multiple-input AND and XOR computations. In: ASIA Public-Key Cryptography, pp. 1–8. ACM, New York (2022, to appear). https://doi.org/10.1145/3494105.3526236
15. Lafourcade, P., Miyahara, D., Mizuki, T., Robert, L., Sasaki, T., Sone, H.: How to construct physical zero-knowledge proofs for puzzles with a "single loop" condition. Theor. Comput. Sci. **888**, 41–55 (2021). https://doi.org/10.1016/j.tcs.2021.07.019
16. Manabe, Y., Ono, H.: Card-based cryptographic protocols with a standard deck of cards using private operations. In: Cerone, A., Ölveczky, P.C. (eds.) ICTAC 2021. LNCS, vol. 12819, pp. 256–274. Springer, Cham (2021). https://doi.org/10.1007/978-3-030-85315-0_15
17. Manabe, Y., Ono, H.: Card-based cryptographic protocols with malicious players using private operations. New Gener. Comput. **40**, 67–93 (2022). https://doi.org/10.1007/s00354-021-00148-w
18. Miyahara, D., Hayashi, Y., Mizuki, T., Sone, H.: Practical card-based implementations of Yao's millionaire protocol. Theor. Comput. Sci. **803**, 207–221 (2020). https://doi.org/10.1016/j.tcs.2019.11.005
19. Miyahara, D., Komano, Y., Mizuki, T., Sone, H.: Cooking cryptographers: secure multiparty computation based on balls and bags. In: Computer Security Foundations Symposium, pp. 1–16. IEEE, New York (2021). https://doi.org/10.1109/CSF51468.2021.00034
20. Miyahara, D., Ueda, I., Hayashi, Y., Mizuki, T., Sone, H.: Evaluating card-based protocols in terms of execution time. Int. J. Inf. Secur. **20**(5), 729–740 (2020). https://doi.org/10.1007/s10207-020-00525-4
21. Miyamoto, K., Shinagawa, K.: Graph automorphism shuffles from pile-scramble shuffles. New Gener. Comput. **40**, 199–223 (2022). https://doi.org/10.1007/s00354-022-00164-4
22. Mizuki, T.: Efficient and secure multiparty computations using a standard deck of playing cards. In: Foresti, S., Persiano, G. (eds.) CANS 2016. LNCS, vol. 10052, pp. 484–499. Springer, Cham (2016). https://doi.org/10.1007/978-3-319-48965-0_29
23. Mizuki, T., Komano, Y.: Information leakage due to operative errors in card-based protocols. Inf. Comput. 1–15 (2022, in press). https://doi.org/10.1016/j.ic.2022.104910
24. Mizuki, T., Shizuya, H.: A formalization of card-based cryptographic protocols via abstract machine. Int. J. Inf. Secur. **13**(1), 15–23 (2013). https://doi.org/10.1007/s10207-013-0219-4

25. Mizuki, T., Shizuya, H.: Computational model of card-based cryptographic protocols and its applications. IEICE Trans. Fundam. **E100.A**(1), 3–11 (2017). https://doi.org/10.1587/transfun.E100.A.3

26. Mizuki, T., Sone, H.: Six-card secure AND and four-card secure XOR. In: Deng, X., Hopcroft, J.E., Xue, J. (eds.) FAW 2009. LNCS, vol. 5598, pp. 358–369. Springer, Heidelberg (2009). https://doi.org/10.1007/978-3-642-02270-8_36

27. Murata, S., Miyahara, D., Mizuki, T., Sone, H.: Efficient generation of a card-based uniformly distributed random derangement. In: Uehara, R., Hong, S.-H., Nandy, S.C. (eds.) WALCOM 2021. LNCS, vol. 12635, pp. 78–89. Springer, Cham (2021). https://doi.org/10.1007/978-3-030-68211-8_7

28. Nakai, T., Misawa, Y., Tokushige, Y., Iwamoto, M., Ohta, K.: Secure computation for threshold functions with physical cards: power of private permutations. New Gener. Comput. 1–19 (2022, in press). https://doi.org/10.1007/s00354-022-00153-7

29. Nakai, T., Misawa, Y., Tokushige, Y., Iwamoto, M., Ohta, K.: How to solve millionaires' problem with two kinds of cards. New Gener. Comput. **39**(1), 73–96 (2021). https://doi.org/10.1007/s00354-020-00118-8

30. Niemi, V., Renvall, A.: Solitaire zero-knowledge. Fundam. Inf. **38**(1,2), 181–188 (1999). https://doi.org/10.3233/FI-1999-381214

31. Ono, H., Manabe, Y.: Card-based cryptographic logical computations using private operations. New Gener. Comput. **39**(1), 19–40 (2020). https://doi.org/10.1007/s00354-020-00113-z

32. Robert, L., Miyahara, D., Lafourcade, P., Mizuki, T.: Card-based ZKP for connectivity: applications to Nurikabe, Hitori, and Heyawake. New Gener. Comput. **40**, 149–171 (2022). https://doi.org/10.1007/s00354-022-00155-5

33. Robert, L., Miyahara, D., Lafourcade, P., Libralesso, L., Mizuki, T.: Physical zero-knowledge proof and NP-completeness proof of Suguru puzzle. Inf. Comput. 1–14 (2021, in press). https://doi.org/10.1016/j.ic.2021.104858

34. Ruangwises, S.: Two standard decks of playing cards are sufficient for a ZKP for Sudoku. New Gener. Comput. 1–17 (2022, in press). https://doi.org/10.1007/s00354-021-00146-y

35. Ruangwises, S., Itoh, T.: Physical zero-knowledge proof for ripple effect. Theor. Comput. Sci. **895**, 115–123 (2021). https://doi.org/10.1016/j.tcs.2021.09.034

36. Saito, T., Miyahara, D., Abe, Y., Mizuki, T., Shizuya, H.: How to implement a non-uniform or non-closed shuffle. In: Martín-Vide, C., Vega-Rodríguez, M.A., Yang, M.-S. (eds.) TPNC 2020. LNCS, vol. 12494, pp. 107–118. Springer, Cham (2020). https://doi.org/10.1007/978-3-030-63000-3_9

37. Shinagawa, K.: On the construction of easy to perform card-based protocols. Ph.D. thesis, Tokyo Institute of Technology (2020)

38. Shinagawa, K.: Card-based cryptography with dihedral symmetry. New Gener. Comput. **39**(1), 41–71 (2021). https://doi.org/10.1007/s00354-020-00117-9

39. Takashima, K., Miyahara, D., Mizuki, T., Sone, H.: Actively revealing card attack on card-based protocols. Nat. Comput. 1–13 (2021, in press). https://doi.org/10.1007/s11047-020-09838-8

40. Toyoda, K., Miyahara, D., Mizuki, T.: Another use of the five-card trick: card-minimal secure three-input majority function evaluation. In: Adhikari, A., Küsters, R., Preneel, B. (eds.) INDOCRYPT 2021. LNCS, vol. 13143, pp. 536–555. Springer, Cham (2021). https://doi.org/10.1007/978-3-030-92518-5_24

A Random Oracle for All of Us

Marc Fischlin, Felix Rohrbach[✉], and Tobias Schmalz

Cryptoplexity, Technische Universität Darmstadt, Darmstadt, Germany
{marc.fischlin,felix.rohrbach,tobias.schmalz}@cryptoplexity.de
https://www.cryptoplexity.de

Abstract. We introduce the notion of a universal random oracle. Analogously to a classical random oracle it idealizes hash functions as random functions. However, as opposed to a classical random oracle which is created freshly and independently for each adversary, the universal random oracle should provide security of a cryptographic protocol against *all* adversaries simultaneously. This should even hold if the adversary now depends on the random function. This reflects better the idea that the strong hash functions like SHA-2 and SHA-3 are fixed before the adversary decides upon the attack strategy.

Besides formalizing the notion of the universal random oracle model we show that the model is asymptotically equivalent to Unruh's auxiliary-input random oracle model (Crypto 2007). In Unruh's model the adversary receives some inefficiently computed information about the random oracle as extra input. Noteworthy, while security in the universal random oracle model implies security in the auxiliary-input random oracle model tightly, the converse implication introduces an inevitable security loss. This implies that the universal random oracle model provides stronger guarantees in terms of concrete security. Validating the model we finally show, via a direct proof with concrete security, that a universal random oracle is one-way.

1 Introduction

The random oracle methodology [2,11] has turned out to be a useful tool to design cryptographic protocols with practical efficiency, while allowing security proofs if one assumes that the hash function behaves ideally. That is, in the security proof one assumes that the involved hash function acts optimally like a random function. The underlying assumption is that, if one later uses a strong hash function like SHA-2 or SHA-3 in practice, then any attack against the protocol must be due to unexpected weakness in the hash function. While the soundness of this approach has been disputed, e.g., [1,7,14,17], we have not yet experienced practical schemes showing such weaknesses (i.e., without incorporating an obvious structural shortcoming in this regard).

1.1 The Universal Random Oracle Model

Security in the random oracle model considers executions where the random oracle is chosen when the attack starts, independently of the adversary and its

© The Author(s), under exclusive license to Springer Nature Switzerland AG 2022
L. Batina and J. Daemen (Eds.): AFRICACRYPT 2022, LNCS 13503, pp. 469–489, 2022.
https://doi.org/10.1007/978-3-031-17433-9_20

strategy. If one goes back to the original idea of later plugging in SHA-2 or SHA-3, however, the order compared to practical settings is in fact reversed: These hash functions have been designed first and are already available, such that the adversary may actually take advantage of this a-priori knowledge in the attack. In contrast, common security games first fix the adversary and then initialize the random oracle.

At first it seems as if the idea of making the adversary depend on the random oracle would refute the idea of eliminating the presence of any structural weakness of the hash function. But recall that we still consider the random oracle to be a random function, only that the adversary may now depend on this random function. In a sense, the adversary still cannot exploit functional properties of the hash functions, but it may take into account that the actual hash function in the protocol is fixed before the protocol is attacked, or even designed. We call this a *universal* random oracle, because the same random oracle should work against all adversaries.

On a technical level the difference between the two approaches, the classical random oracle model and the universal one, becomes apparent through the usage of the Borel-Cantelli lemma, as done for example in the famous work by Impagliazzo and Rudich [16]. The Borel-Cantelli lemma allows to reverse the order of quantifiers in the sense that if for any adversary the probability of an attack for a random oracle is negligible, then there exists an oracle which works against all adversaries. In fact, a random oracle will work almost surely against all adversaries.

Hence, while one could use in principle the Borel-Cantelli lemma to switch from the random oracle model to the universal one, the lemma comes with two disadvantages. First, the final step in the argument, namely that a random function works against all adversaries, only works against the countable class of uniform adversaries (unless one makes further restrictions on the security reduction itself [3,4]), and thus excludes non-uniform adversaries. The second disadvantage is that the asymptotic statement of the Borel-Cantelli lemma infringes with the notion of concrete security. But the latter is important for schemes aiming at practicality. Hence, using the Borell-Cantelli lemma in principle indeed allows to go from classical random oracles to universal ones, but comes at a price.

1.2 Defining Universal Random Oracles

Defining the universal random oracle model (UROM) is more challenging than one would envision. A straightforward approach would be to demand that for a random oracle $\mathcal{O}$ no adversary A can win the corresponding security experiment Game (with more than negligible probability ε in the security parameter λ):

$$\mathbb{P}_{\mathcal{O}}\left[\forall A\ \exists \varepsilon \in \text{negl}\ \forall \lambda : \mathbb{P}_{\text{Game}}\left[\text{Game}^{A^{\mathcal{O}},\mathcal{O}}(\lambda)\right] \leq \varepsilon(\lambda)\right] = 1.$$

However, as we argue this definition appears to be too liberal: We provide an experiment which was secure in this version of the UROM, although the experiment is both intuitively insecure and also provably breakable in the ordinary random oracle model. This would violate our intuition that the UROM provides stronger security guarantees than the ordinary ROM.

The above mismatch also motivates our actual definition of the UROM. As in the random oracle model we aim for security for a given security parameter, such that the quantification over λ appears outside of the probability over the random oracle:

$$\forall s \in \text{poly} \ \exists \varepsilon \in \text{negl} \ \forall \lambda :$$
$$\mathbb{P}_{\mathcal{O}} \left[\forall A \in \text{SIZE} \left(s(\lambda) \right) : \mathbb{P}_{\text{Game}} \left[\text{Game}^{A, \mathcal{O}}(\lambda) \right] \leq \varepsilon(\lambda) \right] \geq 1 - \varepsilon(\lambda).$$

To let the adversary A depend on the random oracle we quantify over all adversaries in the probability for $\mathcal{O}$, and only use a size bound $s(\lambda)$ on the outside. We give more details about this choice within. Another justification for the correctness of our approach is by relating this model to existing definitions, especially to the auxiliary-input random oracle model.

1.3 Relationship to Auxiliary-Input Random Oracles

Unruh [19] defined the auxiliary-input random oracle model (AI-ROM) as an extension of the classical random oracle model. In this model the adversary A receives as input some information about the previously sampled random oracle $\mathcal{O}$, provided by some unbounded algorithm $z^{\mathcal{O}}$ with oracle access to the random oracle. This can, for example, be a collision found in exponential time such that random oracles are not collision-resistant in this model.

Unruh's main technical result, called lazy sampling with auxiliary input [19, Theorem 2], is to relate the statistical distance of outputs for adversaries receiving auxiliary input $z^{\mathcal{O}}$ for random oracle $\mathcal{O}$, to the one when instead having access to a fresh random oracle (but which is consistent on some fixed values with the original oracle). He shows that the statistical distance between the two settings is of order $\mathcal{O}\left(\sqrt{ST/P}\right)$ where S is the bit size of auxiliary information, T is the number or random oracle queries of the adversary, and P is the number of coordinates to be fixed. The bound was subsequently improved to $\mathcal{O}\left(ST/P\right)$ by Coretti et al. [9], matching a lower bound of Dodis et al. [10].

Here we show that the two models, AI-ROM and UROM, are equivalent. That is, if a game is secure in one model, then it is also secure in the other model. Remarkably, there is a security degradation when going from AI-ROM to UROM: If a game is ϵ-secure in the AI-ROM, then it is "only" $\sqrt{\epsilon}$-secure in the UROM. We also show that this quadratic loss is inevitable in general. The other direction holds tightly, i.e., ϵ-security in the UROM implies ϵ-security in the AI-ROM. In this sense, the UROM gives stronger security guarantees for concrete bounds.

Another interesting aspect of UROM is that the separation of the game's randomness from the randomness of choosing the random oracle allows for more freedom in setting the security bounds. The above equivalence of UROM and AI-ROM holds for negligible bounds for both the game's and the random oracle's randomness, but the UROM model also allows for notions where the game should have a negligible success probability for any adversary, with all but exponentially-small probability in the selection of the random oracle.

1.4   Relationship to Global Random Oracles

Canetti et al. [8], and later Camenisch et al. [5], considered the notion of global random oracles in the Universal Composability (UC) framework [6]. The starting point of the global random oracle model is the observation that, even if multiple components of a cryptographic protocols are proven UC secure in the (standard) random oracle model, their composition is not necessarily secure if the random oracle is replaced by the same hash function in all components. The global random oracle model now says that a single, global random oracle functionality is available to all parties. A security proof in the model allows for one random oracle to be used in all components, and therefore also to be replaced with the same hash function everywhere.

The global random oracle model and the UROM are close in spirit in light of the idea that the same hash function may be used at several places, but are technically somewhat orthogonal. The global random oracle model is investigating cross-effects of hash function deployments between different protocol executions (but a fresh random oracle instance is chosen when considering an attack on the composed setting). In contrast, the UROM is concerned with dependencies of the adversary with respect to the universally available random oracle within an abstract security game. This abstract security game may be compound of several protocols but is not cast in a simulation-based setting like the UC framework.

1.5   Proving Security in the UROM

We finally give an example of how to show security in the UROM, by showing that one-wayness exists in the UROM. Of course, we can immediately transfer any security result from the AI-ROM via the equivalence, however, this example lets us use the above mentioned flexibility in choosing our security bounds to show that one-wayness exists for all but exponentially few (universal) random oracles.

The proof of one-wayness follows the compression technique of Gennaro and Trevisan [12]. Similar approaches have also been given for the AI-ROM [9,10]; our goal here is to exercise security arguments in the UROM model. The line of reasoning is as follows. If there was a successful adversary against the one-wayness of the UROM, then we can compress the random oracle with the help of the adversary. The important point here is that the adversary may depend on the random oracle for this compression, making the approach employable in the UROM. If the adversary is too successful then we can actually compress beyond information-theoretic lower bounds. Of course, we state the latter fact in terms of concrete security in the UROM.

2   Preliminaries

In this section we present the basic notions of negligible functions, security games, and the (classical) random oracle model, and one-wayness. The notions of the UROM and AI-ROM are given in the subsequent sections.

2.1   Negligible Functions

We use the standard of notion of negligible function and state some very basic but useful properties afterwards:

Definition 1 (Negligible Functions). *A function* $\varepsilon : \mathbb{N} \to \mathbb{R}$ *is called* negligible *if for any polynomial* $p : \mathbb{N} \to \mathbb{R}^+$ *there exists* $\Lambda \in \mathbb{N}$ *such that*

$$\forall \lambda \geq \Lambda : \varepsilon(\lambda) \leq \frac{1}{p(\lambda)}.$$

We denote the set of all negligible functions by negl *and the set of all functions which are not negligible by* non-negl.

Note that we allow negligible functions ε to be negative at some inputs. When quantifying over all negligible functions we can restrict ourselves to non-negative functions by considering the pointwise maximum $\max\{0, \varepsilon(\lambda)\}$. If and only if ε is negligible so is this maximum. Analogously, we can always presume $\varepsilon(\lambda) \leq 1$ when quantifying over all negligible functions. This follows by considering the pointwise minimum $\min\{1, \varepsilon(\lambda)\}$.

When considering definitions we sometimes bound success probabilities for a sequence of events E_λ (e.g., an adversary winning a security game for parameter λ), by negligible functions:

$$\exists \varepsilon \in \text{negl} \; \forall \lambda \in \mathbb{N} : \mathbb{P}[E_\lambda] \leq \varepsilon(\lambda).$$

Note that we can quantify over all λ since we can change the negligible function ε at finitely many points. When negating this statement, e.g., when describing that there exists a successful adversary, we get

$$\forall \varepsilon \in \text{negl} \; \exists \lambda \in \mathbb{N} : \mathbb{P}[E_\lambda] > \varepsilon(\lambda). \tag{1}$$

This means that for any (negligible) bound we find a security parameter where the probability of the event, e.g., the adversary winning, exceeds this bound. When showing our relationship of the UROM to the AI-ROM we use that the above holds if and only if

$$\forall \varepsilon \in \text{negl} \; \exists \lambda \in \mathbb{N} : \mathbb{P}[E_\lambda] > \varepsilon^2(\lambda). \tag{2}$$

To see this note that we may only consider non-negative functions ε bounded from above by 1. But then the function $\delta(\lambda) := \sqrt{\varepsilon(\lambda)}$ is well defined and it holds that $\delta(\lambda) \geq \varepsilon(\lambda)$ for all security parameters. Furthermore, δ is negligible if and only if ε is.

Hence, when quantifying over all negligible functions we can always switch between ε and δ and get the desired bound. More precisely, assume that statement (1) holds. Take some arbitrary negligible function ε. Our goal is to show that there exists some λ such that $\mathbb{P}\left[E_\lambda\right] > \varepsilon^2(\lambda)$. But this follows straightforwardly from the first statement since $\varepsilon(\lambda) \geq \varepsilon^2(\lambda)$. For the converse note that, if statement (2) holds, then for any given negligible function ε we can consider the function $\delta(\lambda) = \sqrt{\varepsilon(\lambda)}$ in the second statement. By assumption there exists some λ where the probability exceeds $\delta^2(\lambda) = \varepsilon(\lambda)$. This shows that the first statement holds in this case as well for any negligible function.

2.2   Security Games

We consider abstract security games involving the adversary A and an oracle $\mathcal{O}$. We denote by $\mathsf{Game}^{A,\mathcal{O}}(\lambda)$ the binary outcome of executing the security game. We often emphasize the dependency of algorithms and functions by using subscripts, e.g., we write $A_\mathcal{O}$ to denote the fact that the adversary may depend on oracle $\mathcal{O}$, or $\varepsilon_{A,\mathcal{O}}(\lambda)$ to indicate that the function ε depends on both the adversary and the oracle. We use the terms security game and experiment interchangeably.

Further, by $A^\mathcal{O}$, we denote that the adversary A has oracle-access to $\mathcal{O}$. We view A as a (family of) circuit(s) that have a special oracle gate, which allows A to query the oracle. We capture adversaries with an upper bound $s(\lambda)$ of the size for non-uniform adversaries resp. run time for uniform adversaries via a set SIZE $(s(\lambda))$. The set of efficient adversaries is given by SIZE (poly).

We write $\mathbb{P}_{\mathsf{Game}}\left[\mathsf{Game}^{A_\mathcal{O}^\mathcal{O},\mathcal{O}}(\lambda)\right]$ for the probability that adversary A with access to random oracle $\mathcal{O}$ wins in the security game Game. Here, the probability is over all random choices in the game, including the randomness of the adversary. The random oracle, however, is fixed at this point and the adversary may depend on $\mathcal{O}$. The oracle is usually chosen "outside" of the game.

2.3   The Random Oracle Model

A random oracle $\mathcal{O}$ is an oracle that gives access to a truly random function. We assume that for every security parameter λ, oracle $\mathcal{O}$ maps inputs from $\{0,1\}^*$ or from $\{0,1\}^{\leq d(\lambda)}$ to outputs from $\{0,1\}^\lambda$, where $\{0,1\}^{\leq d(\lambda)}$ denotes the set of strings of bit length at most $d(\lambda)$. For so-called length-preserving random oracles the domain for every security parameter λ is simply $\{0,1\}^\lambda$, i.e., inputs are of length $d(\lambda) = \lambda$ exactly. In the classical random oracle model we pick the oracle $\mathcal{O}$ as part of the game. In this case we usually write $\mathbb{P}_{\mathsf{Game},\mathcal{O}}\left[\mathsf{Game}^{A^\mathcal{O},\mathcal{O}}(\lambda)\right]$ for the probability of A winning the corresponding game. Note that here now A usually does not depend on $\mathcal{O}$ beyond the oracle access.

With the above notation we can phrase the (classical) random oracle model as follows.

Definition 2 (ROM). *An experiment Game is secure in the ROM iff*

$$\forall A \in \text{SIZE}\,(\text{poly}) \ \exists \varepsilon \in \text{negl} \ \forall \lambda \in \mathbb{N} : \mathbb{P}_{\mathcal{O}, \textsf{Game}} \left[\textsf{Game}^{A^{\mathcal{O}}, \mathcal{O}}(\lambda) \right] \leq \varepsilon(\lambda).$$

2.4 One-Wayness in the Random Oracle Model

To define that a random oracle $\mathcal{O}$ immediately gives a one-way function we simply state the security game $\textsf{Game}_{\text{OW}}^{A^{\mathcal{O}}, \mathcal{O}}(\lambda)$ as follows. Run $A^{\mathcal{O}}(1^{\lambda}, \mathcal{O}(x))$ for $x \leftarrow_{\$} \{0,1\}^{\lambda}$ to obtain a value x^*. Let the game output 1 if and only if $\mathcal{O}(x) = \mathcal{O}(x^*)$. If we assume length-preserving random oracles, as in Sect. 5, we necessarily have $x^* \in \{0,1\}^{\lambda}$ then:

$$\underline{\textsf{Game}_{\text{OW}}^{A, \mathcal{O}}(\lambda)}$$

1: $x \leftarrow_{\$} \{0,1\}^{\lambda}$
2: $x^* \leftarrow_{\$} A^{\mathcal{O}}(1^{\lambda}, \mathcal{O}(x))$
3: **return** 1 **if** $\mathcal{O}(x^*) = \mathcal{O}(x)$ **else** 0

Note that if we later switch to the UROM, then the one-wayness security game does not change, only the oracle setting.

3 The Universal Random Oracle Model UROM

A straightforward formalization of the universal ROM may now be to demand that, with probability 1, a random oracle $\mathcal{O}$ is good for all adversaries A. That is, for each adversary the success probability is negligible for the given random oracle:

$$\mathbb{P}_{\mathcal{O}} \left[\begin{matrix} \forall A_{\mathcal{O}} \in \text{SIZE}\,(\text{poly}(\lambda)) \\ \exists \varepsilon_{A, \mathcal{O}} \in \text{negl} \ \forall \lambda \in \mathbb{N} \end{matrix} : \mathbb{P}_{\textsf{Game}} \left[\textsf{Game}^{A_{\mathcal{O}}, \mathcal{O}}(\lambda) \right] \leq \varepsilon_{A, \mathcal{O}}(\lambda) \right] = 1.$$

The issue with this approach is that it identifies a case which is both intuitively insecure and also provably insecure in the (plain) random oracle, to be secure in this version of the UROM, as we discuss in Appendix A.

We next present the, in our view, right definition of the UROM. The essence from the above failed definitional attempt is that we have to pull out the quantification of the security parameter from the outer probability, and therefore all preceding quantifiers. But moving out the quantification over all adversaries would infringe with our idea to make the adversary depend on the random oracle. To re-install this idea we set a bound on the adversarial success probability and run time resp. size, and define "good" random oracles for all adversaries within such bounds:

Definition 3 (UROM). *A security game Game is secure in the UROM if*

$$\forall s \in \text{poly} \ \exists \varepsilon_s \in \text{negl} \ \forall \lambda \in \mathbb{N} :$$

$$\mathbb{P}_{\mathcal{O}} \left[\forall A_{\mathcal{O}} \in \text{SIZE}\,(s(\lambda)) : \mathbb{P}_{\textsf{Game}} \left[\textsf{Game}^{A_{\mathcal{O}}, \mathcal{O}}(\lambda) \right] \leq \varepsilon_s(\lambda) \right] \geq 1 - \varepsilon_s(\lambda). \quad (3)$$

Note that with the "outer" negligible error function ε_s we account for "bad" random oracles, for which the security game may be easy to win, e.g., breaking one-wayness for the all-zero oracle $\mathcal{O}$. Since we may consider finite domains and ranges for $\mathcal{O}$ for the fixed-size adversaries (for given security parameter λ), such bad random oracles may have a non-zero probability. The negligible function expresses that such oracles are very sparse. As the weakness of the random oracle may depend on the adversarial size, e.g., many hardcoded preimages in the one-wayness experiment may affect the security, we make the negligible function also depend on the size s. The "inner" probability then captures that no adversary (of the given size) can win the security game with high probability, but here the probability is only over all the random choices of the game and adversary.

Both the inner and outer negligible error terms are based on the same function. We could have chosen different negligible functions ε_s (for the inner game probability) and δ_s for the outer oracle probability, and quantify over the existence of such negligible functions ($\exists \varepsilon_s, \delta_s \in$ negl). But the pointwise maximum, $\gamma_s(\lambda) := \max\{\varepsilon_s(\lambda), \delta_s(\lambda)\}$, would also be negligible and satisfy the bounds:

- For $\gamma_s(\lambda) = \delta_s(\lambda) \geq \varepsilon_s(\lambda)$ we have

$$1 - \delta_s(\lambda) \leq \mathbb{P}_\mathcal{O}\left[\forall A_\mathcal{O} \in \mathrm{SIZE}\,(s(\lambda)) : \mathbb{P}_{\mathsf{Game}}\left[\mathsf{Game}^{A_\mathcal{O},\mathcal{O}}(\lambda)\right] \leq \varepsilon_s(\lambda)\right]$$

$$\leq \mathbb{P}_\mathcal{O}\left[\forall A_\mathcal{O} \in \mathrm{SIZE}\,(s(\lambda)) : \mathbb{P}_{\mathsf{Game}}\left[\mathsf{Game}^{A_\mathcal{O},\mathcal{O}}(\lambda)\right] \leq \delta_s(\lambda)\right].$$

- For $\gamma_s(\lambda) = \varepsilon_s(\lambda) \geq \delta_s(\lambda)$ we have

$$\mathbb{P}_\mathcal{O}\left[\forall A_\mathcal{O} \in \mathrm{SIZE}\,(s(\lambda)) : \mathbb{P}_{\mathsf{Game}}\left[\mathsf{Game}^{A_\mathcal{O},\mathcal{O}}(\lambda)\right] \leq \varepsilon_s(\lambda)\right] \geq 1 - \delta_s(\lambda)$$

$$\geq 1 - \varepsilon_s(\lambda).$$

It thus suffices to consider a single negligible function.

4   UROM vs. AI-ROM

In this section we show that UROM and AI-ROM are equivalent, although not tightly related. We first present the AI-ROM and then show both directions of the equivalence.

4.1   AI-ROM

The auxiliary-input random oracle model AI-ROM [19] allows a preprocessing through an unbounded oracle algorithm $z^{(\cdot)}$ which on input the security parameter outputs a polynomial-size string. This string is then given as auxiliary information about the random oracle to the adversary A. Experiments in which the adversary needs to find a collision in the (unkeyed) random oracle are for example insecure in the AI-ROM: The function $z^\mathcal{O}(1^\lambda)$ exhaustively searches for a collision $x \neq x'$ of complexity λ and outputs this pair; adversary A simply outputs the collision. This is in contrast to security in the regular ROM in which no efficient A is able to find such a collision with non-negligible probability.

Definition 4 (AI-ROM). *An experiment* Game *is secure in the AI-ROM iff*

$$\forall A, z^{(\cdot)} \; \exists \varepsilon \in \text{negl} \; \forall \lambda : \mathbb{P}_{\mathcal{O}, \text{Game}} \left[\text{Game}^{A^{\mathcal{O}}(z^{\mathcal{O}}), \mathcal{O}}(\lambda) \right] \leq \varepsilon(\lambda).$$

We will now show the equivalence of the two notions. Section 4.2 will show that AI-ROM implies UROM, and Sect. 4.3 will show the reverse implication.

4.2 AI-ROM Implies UROM

Theorem 1 (AI-ROM ⇒ UROM). *If* Game *is secure in the AI-ROM then it is also secure in the UROM.*

Proof. Assume an experiment Game is insecure in the UROM, i.e., negating the security requirement we have

$$\exists s \in \text{poly} \; \forall \varepsilon \in \text{negl} \; \exists \lambda \in \mathbb{N} :$$
$$\mathbb{P}_{\mathcal{O}} \left[\forall A_{\mathcal{O}} \in \text{SIZE}\,(s(\lambda)) : \mathbb{P}_{\text{Game}} \left[\text{Game}^{A_{\mathcal{O}}, \mathcal{O}}(\lambda) \right] \leq \varepsilon(\lambda) \right] < 1 - \varepsilon(\lambda).$$

We will show that the experiment is also insecure in the AI-ROM, by constructing an adversary pair (A_{AI}, z) against the auxiliary-input setting. First, to get a better intuition we switch to the complementary event of the outer probability for our successful attack again the UROM:

$$\exists s \in \text{poly} \; \forall \varepsilon \in \text{negl} \; \exists \lambda \in \mathbb{N} :$$
$$\mathbb{P}_{\mathcal{O}} \left[\exists A_{\mathcal{O}} \in \text{SIZE}\,(s(\lambda)) : \mathbb{P}_{\text{Game}} \left[\text{Game}^{A_{\mathcal{O}}, \mathcal{O}}(\lambda) \right] > \varepsilon(\lambda) \right] \geq \varepsilon(\lambda).$$

This formula now states the fraction of "bad" random oracles $\mathcal{O}$ for which there exists a successful adversary, exceeding the bound $\varepsilon(\lambda)$ for some parameter λ, cannot be upper bounded by any negligible function $\varepsilon(\lambda)$. We can capture this set $\Omega = \Omega_{s,\varepsilon,\lambda}$ of bad random oracles as

$$\Omega := \left\{ \mathcal{O} \; \middle| \; \exists A_{\mathcal{O}} \in \text{SIZE}\,(s(\lambda)) : \mathbb{P}_{\text{Game}} \left[\text{Game}^{A_{\mathcal{O}}, \mathcal{O}}(\lambda) \right] > \varepsilon(\lambda) \right\}$$

Note that all parameters s, ε, λ are fixed via the quantifiers when defining this set. This is especially true for the security parameter λ, so the condition is *not* a statement over all security parameters. To emphasize this we can also write the definition of Ω implicitly as

$$\exists s \in \text{poly} \; \forall \varepsilon \in \text{negl} \; \exists \lambda \in \mathbb{N} \; \forall \mathcal{O} \in \Omega \; \exists A_{\mathcal{O}} \in \text{SIZE}\,(s(\lambda)) :$$
$$\mathbb{P}_{\text{Game}} \left[\text{Game}^{A_{\mathcal{O}}, \mathcal{O}}(\lambda) \right] > \varepsilon(\lambda).$$

Note that for the fixed values s, ε, λ we have $\mathbb{P}_{\mathcal{O}} \left[\mathcal{O} \in \Omega \right] \geq \varepsilon(\lambda)$ and therefore

$$\mathbb{P}_{\mathcal{O}, \text{Game}} \left[\text{Game}^{A_{\mathcal{O}}, \mathcal{O}}(\lambda) \right] \geq \mathbb{P}_{\text{Game}} \left[\text{Game}^{A_{\mathcal{O}}, \mathcal{O}}(\lambda) \mid \mathcal{O} \in \Omega \right] \cdot \mathbb{P}_{\mathcal{O}} \left[\mathcal{O} \in \Omega \right] > \varepsilon^2(\lambda).$$

Next we define an inefficient function $z_s^{(\cdot)}$ that, given any oracle $\mathcal{O}$ and security parameter λ, outputs (a circuit description of) the adversary $A_\mathcal{O}$ of size at most $s(\lambda)$ with the highest success probability against the game. This adversary will win the game with probability more than $\varepsilon(\lambda)$ for any oracle in Ω according to the definition. Further, we define A_{AI}, which is the universal circuit that will interpret the circuit returned by z_s. Note that the universal circuit A_{AI} has polynomial size, since the size of $A_\mathcal{O}$ is bounded by the (fixed) polynomial $s(\lambda)$ and the execution of a circuit can be done efficiently. Therefore we can conclude that there exists a pair (A_{AI}, z_s), where A_{AI} is polynomially bounded. This pair is successful in the given game for any bad oracle from the set Ω:

$$\exists (A_{\mathsf{AI}}, z_s^{(\cdot)}) \; \forall \varepsilon \in \mathrm{negl} \; \exists \lambda \in \mathbb{N} \; \forall \mathcal{O} \in \Omega : \mathbb{P}_{\mathsf{Game}} \left[\mathsf{Game}^{A_{\mathsf{AI}}^\mathcal{O}(z_s^\mathcal{O}), \mathcal{O}}(\lambda) \right] > \varepsilon(\lambda).$$

It remains to show that a similar bound also holds when we go back to picking $\mathcal{O}$ at random from *all* random oracles instead of the set Ω. To this end we use our assumption that the probability of an oracle being in Ω is at least $\varepsilon(\lambda)$:

$$\exists (A_{\mathsf{AI}}, z_s^{(\cdot)}) \; \forall \varepsilon \in \mathrm{negl} \; \exists \lambda \in \mathbb{N} : \mathbb{P}_{\mathcal{O}, \mathsf{Game}} \left[\mathsf{Game}^{A_{\mathsf{AI}}^\mathcal{O}(z_s^\mathcal{O}), \mathcal{O}}(\lambda) \right] > \varepsilon^2(\lambda).$$

According to the discussion about negligible functions we can rewrite this as

$$\exists (A_{\mathsf{AI}}, z_s^{(\cdot)}) \; \forall \varepsilon \in \mathrm{negl} \; \exists \lambda \in \mathbb{N} : \mathbb{P}_{\mathcal{O}, \mathsf{Game}} \left[\mathsf{Game}^{A_{\mathsf{AI}}^\mathcal{O}(z_s^\mathcal{O}), \mathcal{O}}(\lambda) \right] > \varepsilon(\lambda).$$

But this means that the protocol cannot be secure in the AI-ROM. $\qquad\square$

In terms of exact security, the derived adversary A_{AI} has roughly the same running time as A. But its success probability drops from $\varepsilon(\lambda)$ (for A) to $\varepsilon^2(\lambda)$. In general this is inevitable, though. For any $k = \omega(\lambda)$ consider the game $\mathsf{Game}^{A, \mathcal{O}}(\lambda)$ which returns 1 if the leading k bits of $\mathcal{O}(0^\lambda)$ are all 0 and if, in addition, k random coin flips also land all on 0. Then the probability that any pair (A_{AI}, z) wins in the AI-ROM setting is at most 2^{-2k}. But in the UROM setting we can set $\varepsilon(\lambda)$ to be 2^{-k}, because for all "good" oracles $\mathcal{O}$ with the leading k bits of $\mathcal{O}(0^\lambda)$ being different from 0 no adversary can win the game.

4.3   UROM Implies AI-ROM

Theorem 2 (UROM $\Rightarrow$ AI-ROM, tightly). *If Game is secure in the UROM then it is also secure in the AI-ROM.*

For the proof we use the so-called splitting lemma [18] which allows to relate the probability of events over a product space $X \times Y$ to the ones when the X-part is fixed:

Lemma 1 (Splitting Lemma [18]). *Let $\mathcal{D} = \mathcal{D}_X \times \mathcal{D}_Y$ be some product distributions over $X \times Y$. Let $Z \subseteq X \times Y$ be such that $\mathbb{P}_\mathcal{D}[(x, y) \in Z] > \varepsilon$. For any $\alpha < \varepsilon$ call $x \in X$ to be α-good if*

$$\mathbb{P}_{y \leftarrow\!\!\$\, \mathcal{D}_Y}[(x, y) \in Z] > \varepsilon - \alpha.$$

Then we have $\mathbb{P}_{x \leftarrow\!\!\$\, \mathcal{D}_X}[x \text{ is } \alpha\text{-good}] \geq \alpha$.

Proof (of Theorem 2). Assume that we have a successful attacker in the AI-ROM:

$$\exists (A_{AI}, z^{(\cdot)}) \; \forall \varepsilon \in \text{negl} \; \exists \lambda \in \mathbb{N} : \mathbb{P}_{\mathcal{O}, \text{Game}} \left[\text{Game}^{A_{AI}^{\mathcal{O}}(z^{\mathcal{O}}), \mathcal{O}}(\lambda) \right] > \varepsilon(\lambda).$$

We show that we can build a successful adversary A in the UROM model. We first apply the splitting lemma (Lemma 1) for fixed $A_{AI}, z, \varepsilon, \lambda$. We will only consider such choices which exceed the bound $\varepsilon(\lambda)$. We define the distribution $\mathcal{D}_X$ as the choice of a random oracle $\mathcal{O}$, and $\mathcal{D}_Y$ as the randomness in the game (for both the game and the adversary), as well as Z as the events in which (A_{AI}, z) wins the game for the random oracle. This happens with probability at least $\varepsilon(\lambda)$ by assumption. If we now choose α to be $\frac{1}{2}\varepsilon$ then we get that $\mathbb{P}_{\mathcal{O}} [\mathcal{O} \text{ is } \alpha\text{-good}] \geq \frac{1}{2}\varepsilon$. Therefore,

$$\exists (A_{AI}, z) \; \forall \varepsilon \in \text{negl} \; \exists \lambda \in \mathbb{N} : \; \mathbb{P}_{\mathcal{O}} \left[\mathbb{P}_{\text{Game}} \left[\text{Game}^{A_{AI}^{\mathcal{O}}(z), \mathcal{O}}(\lambda) \right] > \tfrac{1}{2}\varepsilon \right] \geq \tfrac{1}{2}\varepsilon$$

As $\frac{1}{2}\varepsilon$ is negligible iff ε is, and since we quantify over all negligible functions, we get

$$\exists (A_{AI}, z) \; \forall \varepsilon \in \text{negl} \; \exists \lambda \in \mathbb{N} : \; \mathbb{P}_{\mathcal{O}} \left[\mathbb{P}_{\text{Game}} \left[\text{Game}^{A_{AI}^{\mathcal{O}}(z^{\mathcal{O}}), \mathcal{O}}(\lambda) \right] > \varepsilon(\lambda) \right] \geq \varepsilon(\lambda).$$

Since A_{AI} is polynomially bounded, and $z^{(\cdot)}$ only returns a polynomial-size string, we can view A_{AI} as a circuit of polynomial size $s(\lambda)$. But then we can interpret the AI-ROM adversary pair as consisting of an oracle-dependent component, namely the polynomial-size string $z^{\mathcal{O}}$, and a general part A_{AI}. If we hardcode the string $z^{\mathcal{O}}$ we can write this as a single oracle-dependent adversary $A_{\mathcal{O}}$ of polynomial size $s(\lambda)$. Moving this oracle-dependent algorithm inside the outer probability we obtain:

$$\exists s(\lambda) \in \text{poly} \; \forall \varepsilon \in \text{negl} \; \exists \lambda \in \mathbb{N} :$$
$$\mathbb{P}_{\mathcal{O}} \left[\exists A_{\mathcal{O}} \in \text{SIZE}(s(\lambda)) : \mathbb{P}_{\text{Game}} \left[\text{Game}^{A_{\mathcal{O}}^{\mathcal{O}}, \mathcal{O}}(\lambda) \right] > \varepsilon(\lambda) \right] \geq \varepsilon(\lambda).$$

This shows that the have a successful adversary against the UROM. □

Remarkably, the reduction here is tight. If we have an adversary A_{AI} and z against the AI-ROM, then we get a successful adversary A against UROM with the same running time (as AI-ROM) and, except for a factor $\frac{1}{2}$, the same success probability. This shows that the AI-ROM and UROM model are qualitatively equivalent. Yet, quantitatively, a security bound in the AI-ROM may be significantly looser than in the UROM (see the discussion after Theorem). This means that a direct proof in the UROM may yield tighter bounds.

4.4   Advantages of UROM

While AI-ROM and UROM are equivalent as shown in the last two sections, we argue that UROM has some advantages over AI-ROM, as it provides more flexibility in choosing security bounds. By having separate bounds for the selection of the random oracle and the success probability of an adversary in the security game, we can for example demand that a game might only be won with negligible probability, for all but an exponential fraction of random oracles. Or, conversely, we could show that a game is secure for every second random oracle, if we can be reasonably sure that we can use one of the good oracles, while in the AI-ROM, a proof might not be possible at all.

For the former, we will give an example in the next section, showing that UROM is a one-way function for nearly all oracles.

5   Universal Random Oracles are One-Way Functions

In this chapter, we will show that random oracles exist in the UROM (more specifically, that the oracle itself is a one-way function). This result serves as an example how to prove security in the UROM, and how to show that a game is secure for all but an exponential fraction of random oracles. Our proof will use the compression technique introduced by Gennaro and Trevisan [12], although our notation is closer to the argument by Haitner et al. [15].

We note that similar results exist for the AI-ROM [9,10], which shows that in the AI-ROM, a one-way function exists which no adversary can invert with probability higher than $\frac{AT}{2^\lambda} + \frac{T}{2^\lambda}$, where A denotes the size of the non-uniform advice the adversary gets about the oracle, and T denotes the number of queries to the oracle. Obviously, their result could be translated to a security bound in the UROM due to the equivalence of the two notions, but the goal here is to present a proof that directly works in the UROM.

The idea of the proof is that, if we have a successful adversary against the random oracle $\mathcal{O}$, then we can use this (specific) adversary to compress the oracle $\mathcal{O}$ into a smaller description, contradicting lower bounds for the description size of random oracles. The reason that this works in the UROM is that the compression can of course depend on the random oracle, such that the adversary, too, can depend on $\mathcal{O}$.

For simplicity reasons, we will assume for this chapter that the random oracle $\mathcal{O}$ is always length-preserving (i.e., $d(\lambda) = \lambda$). Note that the existence of length-preserving one-way functions is equivalent to the existence of general one-way functions [13], so this assumption does not influence the result.

We state the result in terms of exact security, using the general UROM approach where we have different probabilities for the inner and outer probability (for the game hardness resp. for the random oracle):

Theorem 3. *Let S be the maximum size of an adversary. Then, a random oracle model is a one-way function UROM with security bounds $\frac{1}{P}$ and $2^{-\lambda}$ for the inner and outer probability, under the condition that $P \cdot S \leq 2^{\lambda/4}$ and $\lambda > 55$:*

$$\mathbb{P}_{\mathcal{O}}\left[\exists A_{\mathcal{O}} \in \mathrm{SIZE}\,(S) : \mathbb{P}_{x \leftarrow \{0,1\}^\lambda}\left[A_{\mathcal{O}}^{\mathcal{O}}(1^\lambda, \mathcal{O}(x)) \in \mathcal{O}^{-1}(\mathcal{O}(x))\right] > \frac{1}{P}\right] < 2^{-\lambda}$$

The asymptotic version follows as an easy corollary:

Corollary 1. *UROM is a one-way function in the* UROM *model: For every poly-nomial* $s(\lambda)$ *bounding the size of an adversary, there exists a negligible function* $\epsilon_s(\lambda)$ *such that for all security parameters* λ,

$$\mathbb{P}_{\mathcal{O}}\left[\exists A_{\mathcal{O}} \in \text{SIZE}\,(s(\lambda)) : \mathbb{P}_{x \leftarrow \{0,1\}^\lambda}\left[A_{\mathcal{O}}^{\mathcal{O}}(1^\lambda, \mathcal{O}(x)) \in \mathcal{O}^{-1}(\mathcal{O}(x))\right] > \varepsilon_s(\lambda)\right] < 2^{-\lambda}$$

Our compression argument will work as follows: Assuming that the random oracle $\mathcal{O}$ in the UROM is not a one-way function, we will show that we can describe the oracle $\mathcal{O}$ with less bits than should be required for a truly random function. For this we assume that A is deterministic; if it is not, then we can make it deterministic by hard-coding the best randomness. We also assume that A needs to output a preimage of size λ and thus only makes queries of this size; any other queries do not help to find a preimage of λ bits and could be easily answered randomly by A itself. Both of these assumptions only increase the size of A at most by a small, constant factor which does not affect our proof.

We give an encoder algorithm which encodes the entire UROM-oracle $\mathcal{O}$ using the successful adversary A, as well as a decoder algorithm which reconstructs $\mathcal{O}$ without access to the oracle itself, using the shorter output of the encoder only. The code for both algorithms is given in Fig. 1. The encoder starts by defining the set I of all images y on which $A_{\mathcal{O}}$ is able to find some preimage x. Note that, as $A_{\mathcal{O}}$ is deterministic, for given $\mathcal{O}$, we can indeed specify if $A_{\mathcal{O}}$ is successful on some input y or not. Further, the encoder creates two initially empty sets: Y, which will contain all the y's for which we reply on $A_{\mathcal{O}}$ to recover one of y's preimages (and which we therefore do not have to save explicitly); and Z, which will contain all full pairs (x, y) with $\mathcal{O}(x) = y$. Therefore, Y denotes the set for which values we actually compress (by not saving the corresponding x-values).

As long as the set I of invertible images still contains values, the encoder takes the lexicographically smallest value y out of I and adds it to Y. We simply write $\min I$ for this element (line 4). Now, the encoder emulates a run of $A_{\mathcal{O}}$ with y as input and checks for all queries. There are two types of queries we need to take care of: The first one are hitting queries, i.e., queries to $\mathcal{O}$ which return y (line 8). In this case, however, A has already given us the preimage, therefore, we abort the simulation at this point. The second type of queries we have to handle are queries that return values y which are still in I (line 10). To make sure we have no circular dependencies between these values, we remove these values from the set I. After the execution of $A_{\mathcal{O}}$ finishes and found a preimage x, we add all further preimages $x' \neq x$ of y that $A_{\mathcal{O}}$ did not return to Z and continue (line 14). Finally, after the set I has become empty, we add all preimages of $y \notin Y$ (as pairs with the image) to Z (line 16). The encoder eventually returns the sets Y, Z, plus a description of $A_{\mathcal{O}}$.

The decoder, on input Y, Z and $A_{\mathcal{O}}$, starts by initializing $\mathcal{O}$ with all the preimage-image-pairs in Z (line 1). Now, similar to the encoder, the decoder goes through all values in Y in lexicographical order and emulates a run of $A_{\mathcal{O}}$ using the partial definition of $\mathcal{O}$. Note that at this point, we already have a partial description of $\mathcal{O}$ that consists of all value-image-pairs we got via Z as well as all preimages we reconstructed in previous steps. Therefore, for each

$\text{Encoder}^{\mathcal{O}}(1^\lambda, A_{\mathcal{O}})$

```
 1:  I ← {y ∈ {0,1}^λ | A_O^O(y) successful}
 2:  Y, Z ← ∅
 3:  while I ≠ ∅ :
 4:      y ← min I
 5:      Y ← Y ∪ {y}, I ← I \ {y}
 6:      Emulate A_O^O(y) :
 7:          On O-query x :
 8:              if O(x) = y :
 9:                  abort emulation with result x
10:              if O(x) ∈ I :
11:                  I ← I \ {O(x)}
12:              return O(x)
13:      x ← A_O^O(y)// or x result of abort
14:      Z ← Z ∪ {(x', y) | O(x') = y, x' ≠ x}
15:  endwhile
16:  Z ← Z ∪ {(x', y') | y' ∉ Y, O(x') = y'}
17:  return (Y, Z, A_O)
```

$\text{Decoder}(1^\lambda, Y, Z, A_{\mathcal{O}})$

```
 1:  O ← Initialize with Z
 2:  while Y ≠ ∅ :
 3:      y ← min Y
 4:      Emulate A_O^O(y):
 5:          On O-query x:
 6:              if O(x) ≠ ⊥ :
 7:                  return O(x)
 8:              else
 9:                  abort emulation with x
10:      x ← A_O^O(y)// or x in abort
11:      O(x) ← y
12:  endwhile
13:  return O
```

Fig. 1. Encoder and Decoder for UROM-oracle $\mathcal{O}$.

query x, the adversary $A_{\mathcal{O}}$ makes to the oracle, we first check if $\mathcal{O}(x) \neq \bot$, i.e., if $\mathcal{O}$ is already defined on that value (line 6). If this is the case, we just return the value saved in $\mathcal{O}$. However, if this is not the case, we know that the call to $\mathcal{O}$ is a hitting query. The reason is that the encoder would have recognized this case and made sure that the value would have been saved in Z (by potentially removing it from I, see line 11) – except for the case where that query is a hitting query. Therefore, in this case, we can already abort the simulation with result x (line 9). If none of the queries is a hitting query and we therefore do not abort, then we eventually obtain x from the adversary (line 10), since the encoder has only put y into Y because the adversary is successful for y. Finally the decoder sets $\mathcal{O}(x)$ to y.

Note that the lexicographic order here is rather arbitrary – the important part is that the encoder always knows exactly which partial information the decoder will have when it will try to decode a specific y, so any fixed order on the images is fine.

The decoder will always return the original oracle $\mathcal{O}$ when given the information the encoder returns. However, we still need to argue that the information returned by encoder is actually smaller than a straightforward description of $\mathcal{O}$.

Lemma 2. *Let $A_{\mathcal{O}}$ be a deterministic adversary against the one-wayness of $\mathcal{O}$ of size $S \leq s(\lambda)$. Further, let $A_{\mathcal{O}}$ be successful on a fraction of $\frac{1}{P}$ of all input challenges $x \in \{0,1\}^\lambda$. With probability $1 - 2^{-\lambda-1}$ the encoder algorithm describes $\mathcal{O}$ using at most*

$$2 \log \binom{2^\lambda}{a} + (2^\lambda - a)\lambda + S$$

bits, where a is defined as $a = \frac{2^\lambda}{n^2 \cdot PS}$.

Proof. First note that with probability $1 - 2^{-\lambda}$, oracle $\mathcal{O}$ will have no y such that y has more than λ^2 preimages. To show this we start with the probability that a specific y has more than λ^2 preimages. For this, we model each of the 2^n inputs x as a random variable X_i such that $X_i = 1$ iff this x maps to y. Then the number of preimages is the sum of all X_i, denoted by X. Now, we can use the Chernoff bound for a binomial distribution $B(n, p)$ to bound the probability of y having too many preimages:

$$\mathbb{P}[X \geq (1 + \delta)np] \leq \left[\frac{e^\delta}{(1 + \delta)^{(1+\delta)}} \right]^{np}.$$

Using $n = 2^\lambda$, $p = 2^{-\lambda}$ and $\delta = \lambda^2$, we get

$$\mathbb{P}_{\mathcal{O}}\left[|\mathcal{O}^{-1}(y)| > \lambda^2\right] \leq \frac{e^{\lambda^2}}{(1 + \lambda^2)^{1+\lambda^2}} \leq 2^{-\lambda^2}$$

for $\lambda \geq 3$. Therefore, the probability that each value $y \in \{0, 1\}^\lambda$ has at most λ^2 preimages is

$$\mathbb{P}_{\mathcal{O}}\left[\forall y, |\mathcal{O}^{-1}(y)| \leq \lambda^2\right] \geq 1 - 2^\lambda(2^{-\lambda^2}) \geq 1 - 2^{-\lambda-1}.$$

Now that we can assume that the number of preimages of all y is bounded by λ^2, we know that I, the set of all y on which A is successful, has at least size $\frac{2^\lambda}{\lambda^2 \cdot P}$, where $\frac{1}{P}$ is the success probability of $A_{\mathcal{O}}$. Furthermore, $A_{\mathcal{O}}$ makes at most S queries on any input. Hence, for each y the encoder adds to Y, it removes at most S values from I. Therefore, Y has at least size $\frac{2^\lambda}{\lambda^2 \cdot PS}$.

We will now encode Y by giving the positions of the values in Y in $\{0, 1\}^\lambda$. For this we need $\log \binom{2^\lambda}{|Y|}$ bits, since we have at most $\binom{2^\lambda}{|Y|}$ such sets of size $|Y|$. Similarly, we can encode the corresponding preimages x in $\{0, 1\}^\lambda$ which the encoder found for each $y \in Y$ with the same amount of bits. Denote this set as X. Note that these positions of the x's in X enables a shorter presentation of the set Z of pairs (x', y') with $y' \notin Y$, which the encoder also outputs. Instead of storing the pairs we only need to go through the values $x' \in \{0, 1\}^\lambda$ in lexicographic order, skipping over the values in X, and only store the corresponding values y' in this order. This allows us to recover the pairs in Z with the help of the positions in X, but now we only to store $(2^\lambda - |Y|)\lambda$ extra bits to represent Z, plus the $\log \binom{2^\lambda}{|Y|}$ bits to encode X. Finally, we need S bits for the description of $A_{\mathcal{O}}$.

Now, the above size corresponds to the size if the adversary has a success probability of exactly $\frac{1}{P}$ and makes exactly S queries for each input. However, for any sensible parameters, this should yield an upper bound on the size of the description for any adversary that makes less queries and is successful on a larger fraction of images (if this is not the case, we can of course always adjust our en- and decoder to initialize I with exactly a P-fraction of all ys and always remove exactly S items from I for every y we add to Y).   □

Proof (for Theorem 3). To prove Theorem 3, we have to show that for parameters S, P and λ,

$$\mathbb{P}_{\mathcal{O}}\left[\exists A_{\mathcal{O}} \in \mathrm{SIZE}\,(S) : \mathbb{P}_{x \leftarrow \{0,1\}^\lambda}\left[A_{\mathcal{O}}^{\mathcal{O}}(1^\lambda, \mathcal{O}(x)) \in \mathcal{O}^{-1}(\mathcal{O}(x))\right] > \frac{1}{P}\right] < 2^{-\lambda}.$$

Lemma 2 tells us two things: First, that at most a $2^{-\lambda-1}$ fraction of the oracles $\mathcal{O}$ has more than λ^2 preimages for some y. Further, we know that for those oracles with at most λ^2 preimages for each value, if $A_{\mathcal{O}}$ is successful, we can encode the oracle using at most

$$2\log\binom{2^\lambda}{a} + (2^\lambda - a)\lambda + S$$

bits with $a = \frac{2^\lambda}{\lambda^2 \cdot P \cdot S}$. Now, however, this means that the number of oracles that can be encoded in this way is at most

$$\binom{2^\lambda}{a}^2 \cdot 2^{(2^\lambda - a)\lambda} \cdot 2^S.$$

Therefore, using $P, S \leq 2^{\lambda/4}$ and $\lambda^2 PS \geq 2$ one can encode only a fraction of

$$\frac{\binom{2^\lambda}{a}^2 2^{(2^\lambda - a)\lambda} 2^S}{2^{\lambda 2^\lambda}} < \frac{(\frac{e2^\lambda}{a})^{2a}\, 2^S}{2^{a\lambda}} = \frac{e^{2a} 2^{\lambda a} 2^S}{a^{2a}} = \frac{e^{2a} 2^S (\lambda^2 PS)^{2a}}{(2^\lambda)^a}$$

$$= 2^S \left(\frac{e^2 \lambda^4 P^2 S^2}{2^\lambda}\right)^{\frac{2^\lambda}{\lambda^2 PS}} < 2^S \left(\frac{e^2 \lambda^4 P^2 S^2}{2^\lambda}\right)^{2^{\frac{\lambda}{2}}}$$

$$< 2^{\frac{\lambda}{4}}\left(\frac{e^2\lambda^4 2^{\frac{\lambda}{2}}}{2^\lambda}\right)^{2^{\lambda/2}} < \left(\frac{8\lambda^4 2^{2^{-\lambda/4}} 2^{\frac{\lambda}{2}}}{2^\lambda}\right)^{2^{\frac{\lambda}{2}}} < \left(\frac{8\lambda^4 2^{\frac{\lambda}{2}+1}}{2^\lambda}\right)^{2^{\frac{\lambda}{2}}}$$

$$< 2^{-\lambda-1} \text{ for } \lambda \geq 55.$$

of all $2^{\lambda 2^\lambda}$ oracles.

In summary, $A_{\mathcal{O}}$ can invert either those oracles $\mathcal{O}$ that have some y with more than λ^2 preimages (which happens with probability at most $2^{-\lambda-1}$), or those that can be encoded as above (which is a fraction of $2^{-\lambda-1}$). Note that both bounds are independent of the choice of S and P. Therefore, the probability that a random oracle $\mathcal{O}$ is invertible with more than probability $\frac{1}{P}$ is bounded by $2^{-\lambda}$:

$$\mathbb{P}_{\mathcal{O}}\left[\exists A_{\mathcal{O}} \in \mathrm{SIZE}\,(s(\lambda)) : \mathbb{P}_{x \leftarrow \{0,1\}^\lambda}\left[A_{\mathcal{O}}^{\mathcal{O}}(1^\lambda, \mathcal{O}(x)) \in \mathcal{O}^{-1}(\mathcal{O}(x))\right] > \frac{1}{P}\right]$$

$$< 2^{-\lambda-1} + 2^{-\lambda-1} = 2^{-\lambda}.$$

This proves the theorem.   □

6   Conclusion

In our paper we have presented an alternative approach to define security for idealized hash functions. Whereas the classical random oracle model assumes that the idealized hash function is specific for each adversary, the UROM model allows arbitrary dependencies of the adversary on the random oracle. This appears to be a natural and necessary generalization of the ROM when instantiating the random oracle with known hash functions like SHA-2 or SHA-3. Our UROM has been defined in light of this idea.

Once we had carved out our model, we could evaluate it. We thus related our definition to Unruh's auxiliary-input random oracle model. There, the dependency of the adversary on the random oracle is defined by an unbounded pre-processing stage, giving a polynomial-sized advice to the adversary. We then proved our security notion equivalent to AI-ROM which further solidifies the validity of our UROM definition and, vice versa, also means that the AI-ROM provides strong security guarantees. Remarkably, the security bounds are not tightly related.

One of the differences between the UROM and the AI-ROM, and potentially one of the advantages of the UROM, is that our model allows for more flexibility concerning the sources of insecurities. Specifically, in our model one can separately fine-tune the probabilities for the random oracle and the random choices of the adversary. For instance, one could go so far and simply ask for a non-zero probability for a good random oracle, still stipulating a negligible success probability for the adversary. One could then argue, or hope, that SHA-2 or SHA-3 is indeed one of these good random oracles to provide strong security against all adversaries.

An interesting aspect may be to transfer the UROM or the AI-ROM to the UC setting and the global random oracle model. As mentioned before, the global random oracle model and the idea of having an adversarial dependency on the random oracle (as in UROM and AI-ROM) are incomparable. In principle, however, it should be possible to consider a universal random oracle in the global UC setting as well. Given the subtleties in the simpler game-based setting for defining the UROM, we expect this to be far from trivial, though.

Acknowledgments. We thank the anonymous reviewers for valuable comments. Funded by the Deutsche Forschungsgemeinschaft (DFG, German Research Foundation) − SFB 1119 − 236615297 and by the German Federal Ministry of Education and Research and the Hessian Ministry of Higher Education, Research, Science and the Arts within their joint support of the National Research Center for Applied Cybersecurity ATHENE.

A   Defining Universal Random Oracles

In this section we present an alternative definition for UROM and argue why it is inappropriate, motivating also our definition of UROM (Definition 3 on page 7).

The Naive Approach. We start with the straightforward adoption of the idea to make the adversary depend on the random oracle by splitting the success probabilities for the experiment Game and the random oracle $\mathcal{O}$, stating that the random oracle should work for all adversaries:

A security game Game is secure in the *naive UROM* if

$$\mathbb{P}_{\mathcal{O}}\left[\begin{array}{l} \forall A_{\mathcal{O}} \in \mathrm{SIZE}\,(\mathrm{poly}(\lambda)) \\ \exists \varepsilon_{A,\mathcal{O}} \in \mathrm{negl}\,\forall\lambda \end{array} : \mathbb{P}_{\mathsf{Game}}\left[\mathsf{Game}^{A_{\mathcal{O}}^{\mathcal{O}},\mathcal{O}}(\lambda)\right] \le \varepsilon_{A,\mathcal{O}}(\lambda)\right] = 1.$$

We next argue that that there is a game which is trivially insecure when considered in the plain random oracle model, but provably secure according to naive UROM. This is counterintuitive because we expect universal random oracles to provide stronger security guarantees compared to the classical ROM. Let $\mathcal{O}$ be length-preserving and the domain size of the random oracle be $d(\lambda) = \lambda$. The game is defined as:

$$\mathsf{Game}^{A_{\mathcal{O}}^{\mathcal{O}},\mathcal{O}}(=)1 \quad :\Longleftrightarrow \quad \mathcal{O}(0^{\lambda}) \equiv 0 \bmod \lambda^2,$$

where we interpret the λ-bits output of (0^{λ}) as an integer between 0 and $2^{\lambda} - 1$. We ignore here for simplicity that this integer reduced mod λ^2 is only statistically close to a random number between 0 and $\lambda^2 - 1$, and from now on calculate with a probability of $\frac{1}{\lambda^2}$ that the experiment Game returns 1 and the adversary wins.

First note that this experiment Game is insecure in the standard random oracle mode (Definition 2 on page 7), because the trivial adversary who does nothing wins with non-negligible probability has a success probability of at least $\frac{1}{\lambda^2}$, where the probability is over the choice of $\mathcal{O}$ only. We next show that it is secure in the naive UROM, though. To this end we first negate the security statement of the naive UROM and consider the complementary probability. That is, we have to show:

$$\mathbb{P}_{\mathcal{O}}\left[\begin{array}{l} \exists A_{\mathcal{O}} \in \mathrm{SIZE}\,(\mathrm{poly}(\lambda)) \\ \forall \varepsilon_{A,\mathcal{O}} \in \mathrm{negl}\,\exists\lambda \end{array} : \mathbb{P}_{\mathsf{Game}}\left[\mathsf{Game}^{A_{\mathcal{O}}^{\mathcal{O}},\mathcal{O}}(\lambda)\right] > \varepsilon_{A,\mathcal{O}}(\lambda)\right] = 0.$$

We first note that the experiment is independent of the adversary, such that we can simplify the statement to:

$$\mathbb{P}_{\mathcal{O}}\left[\forall \varepsilon_{\mathcal{O}} \in \mathrm{negl}\,\exists\lambda : \mathbb{P}_{\mathsf{Game}}\left[\mathsf{Game}^{\mathcal{O}}(\lambda)\right] > \varepsilon_{\mathcal{O}}(\lambda)\right] = 0.$$

Next observe that the experiment is deterministic, once $\mathcal{O}$ is chosen randomly "on the outside". This means that we can restrict ourselves to negligible functions $\varepsilon_{\mathcal{O}}$ which only take on values 0 and 1, and also drop the probability over Game and instead use the output of the game directly:

$$\mathbb{P}_{\mathcal{O}}\left[\forall \varepsilon_{\mathcal{O}} \in \mathrm{negl}, \varepsilon_{\mathcal{O}} : \mathbb{N} \to \{0,1\}\,\exists\lambda : \mathsf{Game}^{\mathcal{O}}(\lambda) > \varepsilon_{\mathcal{O}}(\lambda)\right] = 0.$$

It suffices now to show that, with probability 0 over the choice of $\mathcal{O}$, experiment Game outputs 1 for infinitely many security parameters λ. If the game only outputs 1 finitely often for a fixed oracle $\mathcal{O}$, say, up to a bound $\Lambda \in \mathbb{N}$, then we can consider the binary-valued negligible function $\varepsilon_{\mathcal{O}}^{\Lambda}(\lambda) = 1$ if $\lambda \leq \Lambda$, and 0 elsewhere. For this function the game's output would not exceed the bound $\varepsilon_{\mathcal{O}}^{\Lambda}(\lambda)$ for any λ. In other words, it suffices to show that the (deterministic) experiment Game outputs 1 for infinitely many security parameters:

$$\mathbb{P}_{\mathcal{O}}\left[\text{for infinitely many } \lambda \in \mathbb{N} : \mathsf{Game}^{\mathcal{O}}(\lambda) = 1\right] = 0.$$

We next apply the Borel-Cantelli lemma to show that this is indeed the case. Let E_λ describe the event that the game is won for security parameter λ. Then $\mathbb{P}_{\mathcal{O}}[E_\lambda] = \frac{1}{\lambda^2}$ over the choice of the random oracle $\mathcal{O}$. Therefore, since the hyperharmonic series converges,

$$\sum_{\lambda=1}^{\infty} \mathbb{P}[E_\lambda] < \infty.$$

The Borel-Cantelli lemma now tells us that the probability that infinitely many E_λ happen is 0. Therefore, the game is indeed secure in the naive UROM.

Towards the Sophisticated UROM. Let us recap what goes wrong with the naive approach above. Borel-Cantelli tells us that for a random oracle $\mathcal{O}$ the probabilities of Game outputting 1 become small such that the adversary will only be successful on finitely many security parameters (with probability 1). This yields a fundamental, yet from a cryptographic perspective somewhat counterintuitive property of adversaries: *An adversary might be only successful on finitely many security parameters (except with probability 0), even though the adversary has a polynomial success probability for each individual security parameter!*

The difference to the ordinary random oracle model is that, there, we rather state security in reverse order, i.e., for a given security parameter λ the probability of an adversary breaking the game for random oracle $\mathcal{O}$ is negligible. We would like to resurrect this behavior while preserving the idea of having a universal random oracle. The approach is basically to move out the quantification over all security parameters ($\forall \lambda$) out of the probability for oracle $\mathcal{O}$. This, however, means that the preceding quantification over the adversary and the negligible function ($\forall A \exists \varepsilon \forall \lambda$) needs to be moved outside of $\mathbb{P}_{\mathcal{O}}[\cdot]$ as well. But this infringes with our idea of the universal random oracle model where the adversary may depend on $\mathcal{O}$. To re-install this property we only move out a bound $s(\lambda)$ on the adversary's size, and still quantify over all adversaries of this maximal size $s(\lambda)$. This yields our definition of the universal random oracle model (Definition 3):

$$\forall s \in \mathrm{poly} \, \exists \varepsilon_s \in \mathrm{negl} \, \forall \lambda \in \mathbb{N} :$$

$$\mathbb{P}_{\mathcal{O}}\left[\forall A_{\mathcal{O}} \in \mathrm{SIZE}\,(s(\lambda)) : \mathbb{P}_{\mathsf{Game}}\left[\mathsf{Game}^{A_{\mathcal{O}}^{\mathcal{O}}, \mathcal{O}}(\lambda)\right] \leq \varepsilon_s(\lambda)\right] \geq 1 - \varepsilon_s(\lambda). \quad (4)$$

The outer negligible function $\varepsilon_s(\lambda)$ now becomes necessary since for fixed λ we only consider oracle $\mathcal{O}$ of restricted input and output size, determined by the size bound of the adversary and the fixed game.

Besides the equivalence to the auxiliary-input random oracle model and the immediate implication that security in this version of the UROM implies security for ordinary random oracles, we can also discuss directly why our counter example for the naive approach is also labeled as insecure. Recall that $\mathsf{Game}^{\mathcal{O}}(\lambda)$ outputs 1 if $\mathcal{O}(0^{\lambda}) \equiv 0 \bmod \lambda^2$. Then for any given parameter λ we have $\mathbb{P}_{\mathcal{O}}\left[\mathsf{Game}^{\mathcal{O}}(\lambda) = 0\right] \leq 1 - \frac{1}{\lambda^2}$. It follows that there is no negligible bound $\varepsilon_s(\lambda)$ such that this probability at least $1 - \varepsilon_s(\lambda)$.

References

1. Bellare, M., Boldyreva, A., Palacio, A.: An uninstantiable random-oracle-model scheme for a hybrid-encryption problem. In: Cachin, C., Camenisch, J.L. (eds.) EUROCRYPT 2004. LNCS, vol. 3027, pp. 171–188. Springer, Heidelberg (2004). https://doi.org/10.1007/978-3-540-24676-3_11
2. Bellare, M., Rogaway, P.: Random oracles are practical: a paradigm for designing efficient protocols. In: Denning, D.E., Pyle, R., Ganesan, R., Sandhu, R.S., Ashby, V. (eds.) ACM CCS 1993, pp. 62–73. ACM Press (1993). https://doi.org/10.1145/168588.168596
3. Buldas, A., Laur, S., Niitsoo, M.: Oracle separation in the non-uniform model. In: Pieprzyk, J., Zhang, F. (eds.) ProvSec 2009. LNCS, vol. 5848, pp. 230–244. Springer, Heidelberg (2009). https://doi.org/10.1007/978-3-642-04642-1_19
4. Buldas, A., Niitsoo, M.: Black-box separations and their adaptability to the non-uniform model. In: Boyd, C., Simpson, L. (eds.) ACISP 2013. LNCS, vol. 7959, pp. 152–167. Springer, Heidelberg (2013). https://doi.org/10.1007/978-3-642-39059-3_11
5. Camenisch, J., Drijvers, M., Gagliardoni, T., Lehmann, A., Neven, G.: The wonderful world of global random oracles. In: Nielsen, J.B., Rijmen, V. (eds.) EUROCRYPT 2018. LNCS, vol. 10820, pp. 280–312. Springer, Cham (2018). https://doi.org/10.1007/978-3-319-78381-9_11
6. Canetti, R.: Universally composable security: a new paradigm for cryptographic protocols. In: 42nd FOCS, pp. 136–145. IEEE Computer Society Press (2001). https://doi.org/10.1109/SFCS.2001.959888
7. Canetti, R., Goldreich, O., Halevi, S.: The random oracle methodology, revisited. J. ACM **51**(4), 557–594 (2004). https://doi.org/10.1145/1008731.1008734
8. Canetti, R., Jain, A., Scafuro, A.: Practical UC security with a global random oracle. In: Ahn, G.J., Yung, M., Li, N. (eds.) ACM CCS 2014, pp. 597–608. ACM Press (2014). https://doi.org/10.1145/2660267.2660374
9. Coretti, S., Dodis, Y., Guo, S., Steinberger, J.: Random oracles and non-uniformity. In: Nielsen, J.B., Rijmen, V. (eds.) EUROCRYPT 2018. LNCS, vol. 10820, pp. 227–258. Springer, Cham (2018). https://doi.org/10.1007/978-3-319-78381-9_9
10. Dodis, Y., Guo, S., Katz, J.: Fixing cracks in the concrete: random oracles with auxiliary input, revisited. In: Coron, J.-S., Nielsen, J.B. (eds.) EUROCRYPT 2017. LNCS, vol. 10211, pp. 473–495. Springer, Cham (2017). https://doi.org/10.1007/978-3-319-56614-6_16
11. Fiat, A., Shamir, A.: How to prove yourself: practical solutions to identification and signature problems. In: Odlyzko, A.M. (ed.) CRYPTO 1986. LNCS, vol. 263, pp. 186–194. Springer, Heidelberg (1987). https://doi.org/10.1007/3-540-47721-7_12

12. Gennaro, R., Trevisan, L.: Lower bounds on the efficiency of generic cryptographic constructions. In: 41st FOCS, pp. 305–313. IEEE Computer Society Press (2000). https://doi.org/10.1109/SFCS.2000.892119

13. Goldreich, O.: Foundations of Cryptography: Basic Tools, vol. 1. Cambridge University Press, Cambridge (2001)

14. Goldwasser, S., Kalai, Y.T.: On the (in)security of the Fiat-Shamir paradigm. In: 44th FOCS, pp. 102–115. IEEE Computer Society Press (2003). https://doi.org/10.1109/SFCS.2003.1238185

15. Haitner, I., Hoch, J.J., Reingold, O., Segev, G.: Finding collisions in interactive protocols - tight lower bounds on the round and communication complexities of statistically hiding commitments. SIAM J. Comput. 44(1), 193–242 (2015). https://doi.org/10.1137/130938438

16. Impagliazzo, R., Rudich, S.: Limits on the provable consequences of one-way permutations. In: 21st ACM STOC, pp. 44–61. ACM Press (1989). https://doi.org/10.1145/73007.73012

17. Nielsen, J.B.: Separating random oracle proofs from complexity theoretic proofs: the non-committing encryption case. In: Yung, M. (ed.) CRYPTO 2002. LNCS, vol. 2442, pp. 111–126. Springer, Heidelberg (2002). https://doi.org/10.1007/3-540-45708-9_8

18. Pointcheval, D., Stern, J.: Security arguments for digital signatures and blind signatures. J. Cryptol. 13(3), 361–396 (2000). https://doi.org/10.1007/s001450010003

19. Unruh, D.: Random oracles and auxiliary input. In: Menezes, A. (ed.) CRYPTO 2007. LNCS, vol. 4622, pp. 205–223. Springer, Heidelberg (2007). https://doi.org/10.1007/978-3-540-74143-5_12

Public Key (Crypt)analysis

DiSSECT: Distinguisher of Standard and Simulated Elliptic Curves via Traits

Vladimir Sedlacek[1,2]($\boxtimes$), Vojtech Suchanek[1], Antonin Dufka[1], Marek Sys[1], and Vashek Matyas[1]

[1] Masaryk University, Brno, Czech Republic
{vlada.sedlacek,vojtechsu,dufkan,syso,matyas}@mail.muni.cz
[2] Université de Picardie Jules Verne, Amiens, France

Abstract. It can be tricky to trust elliptic curves standardized in a non-transparent way. To rectify this, we propose a systematic methodology for analyzing curves and statistically comparing them to the expected values of a large number of generic curves with the aim of identifying any deviations in the standard curves.

For this purpose, we put together the largest publicly available database of standard curves. To identify unexpected properties of standard generation methods and curves, we simulate over 250 000 curves by mimicking the generation process of four standards. We compute 22 different properties of curves and analyze them with automated methods to pinpoint deviations in standard curves, pointing to possible weaknesses.

Keywords: Elliptic curves · Standards · Simulations · Testing tool

1 Introduction

Many prominent cryptographers [Sch13, Loc+14, Ber+15, CLN15, Sco99] criticize the selection of curves in all major elliptic curve standards [ANS05, Cer10, Age11, SSL14]. The lack of explanation of parameters used in cryptographic standards provides a potential space for weaknesses or inserted vulnerabilities.

This is a serious matter, considering that the popular NIST curves have been designed by the NSA, which has been involved in a number of incidents: the Dual EC DRBG standard manipulation [Hal13, BLN16, Che+], Clipper chip backdoor [Tor94], or the deliberate weakening of the A5 cipher [BD00]. Bernstein et al. [Ber+15] justify such skepticism, showing that the degrees of freedom in the generation of elliptic curves offer a means to insert a backdoor. Relying on the supposed implausibility [KM16] of weak curves escaping detection for such a long time may prove catastrophic. As the usage of NIST curves increases with time [Val+18], the impact of any vulnerability would be extensive at this moment.

Even though newer, more rigidly generated curves like Curve25519 [Ber06], Ed448-Goldilocks [Ham15b] or NUMS curves [Bla+14] are on the rise, Lochter et al. [Loc+14] argue that *"perfect rigidity, i.e., defining a process that is accepted as completely transparent and traceable by everyone, seems to be impossible"*.

© The Author(s), under exclusive license to Springer Nature Switzerland AG 2022
L. Batina and J. Daemen (Eds.): AFRICACRYPT 2022, LNCS 13503, pp. 493–517, 2022.
https://doi.org/10.1007/978-3-031-17433-9_21

Thus, a thorough wide-scale analysis of the standard curves is important to establish trust in elliptic curve cryptosystems.

There is no clear way of looking for unknown vulnerabilities, especially within elliptic curve cryptosystems with such a rich and complex theory behind them. Our main idea is that if a hidden weakness is present in a curve, it can manifest itself via a statistical deviation when we compare the curve to a large number of generic curves. We consider two cases: either the deviation stems from the generation method of the curve, or from the choice of its parameters. Consequently, we compare the curve to two types of curves – random curves in the former case and curves generated according to the same standard in the latter case.

Core Contributions. Our work provides the following contributions:

- We assemble the first public database of all standard[1] curves (to the best of our knowledge), with comprehensive parameter details.
- We develop an open-source, extensible framework DiSSECT for generating curves according to known standards, and for statistical analysis of the standards. This includes a large number of test functions and visualization tools.
- We find properties of the standard GOST curves [PLK06,SF16] that are inconsistent with the claimed [ANS18] generation method and present unreported properties of the BLS12-381 [BLS02] curve.

In addition, we offer a new methodology for testing properties and potential weaknesses of standard curve parameters and their generation methods. By a systematic analysis of standard curves, we rule out multiple types of problems, raising the level of trust in most of the curves.

This paper is organized as follows: In Sect. 2, we briefly survey the major elliptic curve standards. Section 3 introduces our database and explains our methodology for simulating and distinguishing curves. Section 4 gives an overview of our proposed trait functions and presents the findings of the outlier detection. We report on the technicalities of our tool in Sect. 5 and draw conclusions in Sect. 6. Appendix A contains descriptions of individual traits.

2   Background

Throughout the paper, we will use the following notation: $p \geq 5$ is a prime number, $\mathbb{F}_p$ is a finite field of size p, $E(a,b)\colon y^2 = x^3 + ax + b$ is an elliptic curve over $\mathbb{F}_p$, $n = \#E(\mathbb{F}_p)$ is the order of the group of points over $\mathbb{F}_p$, l the largest prime factor of n, $h = n/l$ is the cofactor, and $t = p + 1 - n$ is the trace of Frobenius of E. Parts of this section are adopted from [Sed22].

Even though pairing-friendly curves and curves over binary and extension fields have found some applications, we focus mainly[2] on the prevalent category

---

[1] In this work, we use the adjective "standard" for widely used curves (from actual standards and even that are/were a de facto standard).

[2] However, binary, extension and pairing-friendly curves are included in our database as well and have been included partly in our analysis.

of prime field curves that are recommended for classical elliptic curve cryptosystems. We include Montgomery and (twisted) Edwards curves as well, though for unification purposes, we convert them to the short Weierstrass form, which is universal.

Known Curve Vulnerabilities. When using elliptic curve cryptography (ECC) in the real world, both sides of the scheme must agree on a choice of a particular curve. We need curves where the elliptic curve discrete logarithm problem (ECDLP) is difficult enough. The SafeCurves website [BL] presents a good overview of known curve vulnerabilities (and discusses implementation-specific vulnerabilities as well). In short, to avoid the known mathematical attacks, curve should satisfy the following criteria:

- p should be large enough, e.g., over 256 bits if we aim for 128-bit security;
- l should be large enough, as this determines the complexity of the Pohlig-Hellman attack [PH78] (again, roughly 256 bits for 128-bit security); ideally, the same should hold for the quadratic twist of the curve (to avoid attacks on implementations[3]);
- the curve should not be anomalous (i.e., $n \neq p$), otherwise the Semaev-Satoh-Araki-Smart additive transfer attack applies [Sma99, Sem98, SA+98];
- the embedding degree of E (i.e., the order of p in $\mathbb{F}_l^\times$) should be large enough (e.g., at least 20), otherwise the MOV attack based on multiplicative transfer using the Weil and Tate pairings applies [Sem96, FR94, MOV93] – in particular, this rules out the cases $t = 0$ and $t = 1$;
- the absolute value of the CM field discriminant (i.e., the absolute discriminant of the field $\mathbb{Q}(\sqrt{t^2 - 4p})$ should not be too low ([BL] suggests at least 2^{100}), otherwise Pollard's ρ attack can be speeded up due to the presence of efficiently computable endomorphisms of the curve [GLV01]. This does not pose a serious threat for the moment though, as the limits of the speedup are reasonably well understood.

2.1   Overview of Standard Curve Generation

The main approach for finding a curve that satisfies the mentioned conditions is repeatedly selecting curve parameters until the conditions hold. The bottleneck here is point-counting: we can use the polynomial SEA algorithm [Sch95], but in practice, it is not fast enough to allow on-the-fly ECC parameter generation.

Several standardization organizations have therefore proposed elliptic curve parameters for public use. To choose a curve, one has to first pick the appropriate base field. Several standards also choose primes of special form for more efficient arithmetic, e.g., generalized Mersenne primes [Sol11] or Montgomery-friendly primes [CLN15]. When the field and the curve form are fixed, it remains to pick two[4] coefficients, though one of them is often fixed.

---

[3] This is often ignored in the standards though, except for the NUMS standard and individual curves such as Curve25519.

[4] At least for short Weierstrass, Montgomery and twisted Edwards curves.

In this subsection, we survey the origin of all the standard curves. For easier orientation, we divide the generation methods of standard curves into three rough categories. Curves of unknown or ambiguous origin are hard to trust, while verifiably pseudorandom ones make use of one-way functions in hopes of addressing this. Other rigid methods go even further in attempts to increase their transparency.

Unknown or Ambiguous Origin. The following is a list of curves we analyze and whose method of generations is either completely unexplained or ambiguous.

- The 256-bit curve FRP256v1 has been recommended in 2011 by the French National Cybersecurity Agency (ANSSI) in the Official Journal of the French Republic [Jou11]. The document does not specify any method of generation.
- The Chinese SM2 standard [SSL14] was published in 2010 [DY15] by the Office of State Commercial Cryptography Administration (OSCCA). The standard recommends one 256-bit curve but does not specify the generation method.
- In addition to the Russian GOST R 34.10 standard from 2001, six standardized curves were provided in [PLK06] and [SF16]. Again, no method of generation was specified in the original standard, although there were some attempts for explanation afterward [ANS18]. We discuss this in further sections.
- The Wireless Application Protocol Wireless Transport Layer Security Specification [Wir00] recommends 8 curves, 3 of which are over prime fields and are not copied from previous standards. Their method of generation is not described.
- Apart from verifiably pseudorandom curves, the Standards for Efficient Cryptography Group (SECG) [Cer] recommends so-called Koblitz curves[5], which possess an efficiently computable endomorphism. However, the standard only vaguely states *"The recommended parameters associated with a Koblitz curve were chosen by repeatedly selecting parameters admitting an efficiently computable endomorphism until a prime order curve was found"*.

Verifiably Pseudorandom Curves. Aiming to re-establish the trust in ECC, several standards have picked the coefficients a, b in the Weierstrass form $y^2 = x^3 + ax + b$ in a so-called *verifiably pseudorandom* way, as Fig. 1 demonstrates.

The details differ and we study them more closely in Sect. 3.2. The common idea is that the seed is made public, which limits the curve designer's freedom to manipulate the curve. However, this might not be sufficient, as Bernstein et al. [Ber+15] show that one could still iterate over many seeds (and potentially also over other "natural" choices) until they find a suitable curve. If a large enough proportion of curves (say, one in a million) is vulnerable to an attack known to the designer, but not publicly, this offers an opportunity to insert a backdoor. In particular, we should be suspicious of curves whose seed's origin is unknown.

---

[5] Analyzing these curves is of great importance due to the usage of secp256k1 in Bitcoin [Nak08].

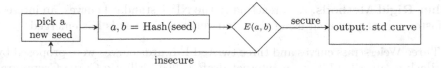

Fig. 1. A simplified template for generating verifiably pseudorandom curves over a fixed field $\mathbb{F}_p$.

In our analysis, we will focus on two major standards containing verifiably pseudorandom generation procedures:

- The Brainpool curves, proposed in 2005 by Manfred Lochter and Johannes Merkle under the titles "ECC Brainpool Standard Curves and Curve Generation" [Brainpool] to focus on issues that have not been previously addressed such as verifiable choice of seed or usage of prime of nonspecial form.
- NIST in collaboration with NSA presented the first standardization of curves was in FIPS 186-2 in 2000 [Nat00]. However, the used generation method already appeared in ANSI X9.62 in 1998 [Com+98]. Other standards recommend these curves (e.g., SECG [Cer] or WTLS [Wir00]).

Another notable paper considering the verifiably pseudorandom approach is "The Million dollar curve" which proposed a new source of public entropy for the seeds, combining lotteries from several different countries [Bai+15] (Fig. 2).

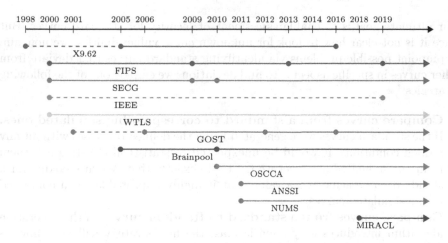

Fig. 2. Timeline of standardization of publicly available prime-field curves. Dashed line indicates that the source does not specify curve parameters. Individual curves (e.g., Curve25519) are omitted.

Other Rigid Methods. As a reaction to the NIST standard curves, an interest in faster curves generated using rigid and verifiable methods has emerged:

- Three Weierstrass curves and three twisted Edwards curves were proposed by Black et al. [Bla+14] as an Internet draft called "Elliptic Curve Cryptography (ECC) Nothing Up My Sleeve (NUMS) Curves and Curve Generation" [Bla+14].
- MIRACL library [MIR18] combines approaches of NUMS and Brainpool by extracting seeds from well-known constants and iteratively incrementing one of the parameters of a curve in the Weierstrass form.
- Bernstein's Curve25519 and its sibling Ed25519 were created in 2006 [Ber06] and since then have been widely accepted by the cryptography community. The curve is in the Montgomery form and allows extremely fast x-coordinate point operations while meeting the SafeCurves security requirements. In 2013, Bernstein et al. [Ber+13] proposed the curve Curve1174 with an encoding for points as strings indistinguishable from uniform random strings (the Elligator map).
- To address higher security levels and maintain good performance, several authors developed curves of sizes in the 400–521 bit range such as the Edwards curve Curve41417 by Bernstein, Chuengsatiansup, and Lange [BCL14], Ed448-Goldilocks by Hamburg [Ham15a], E-3363 by Scott [Sco15] or M, E curves by Aranha1 et al. [Ara+13].

3   Methodology

Our ultimate goal is to enable assessment of security for standard curves. But since it is not clear how to look for unknown curve vulnerabilities, we now aim to pinpoint possible problems via identifying standard curves that deviate from other curves in specific aspects. To find deviations we employ one of the following strategies:

1. **Compare curves from a standard to corresponding simulated ones.** If the standard curves were generated using the defined processes without any hidden conditions, it would be unexpected to statistically distinguish them from our simulated ones, yet we try to do exactly that. We are looking for a standard curve achieving a value that is highly improbable when compared to the simulated curves.

2. **Compare curves from a standard to Random curves.** If the generation algorithm introduces a systematic bias, the first strategy will not allow us to find it – the problem might occur in both the standard and simulated curves. Thus this strategy tries to detect any sort of unexpected behaviour by comparing curves from a given standard to $Random^6$ curves.

---

[6] In the remainder of this work, the word Random with capital R refers to the curves we generated by our own method to be as generic as possible.

To target specific curve properties, we describe and implement traits, which are functions that take a curve as an input (sometimes with additional parameters) and output numerical results. We run these traits on standard curves as well as simulated ones whenever it is computationally feasible and store the results in our database.

3.1 Standard Curve Database

DiSSECT is, as far as we know, the first public database of all standard elliptic curves, divided into 18 curve categories by their source. The database includes:

1. verifiably pseudorandom curves (X9.62, NIST, SEC, Brainpool);
2. pairing-friendly curves: Barreto-Lynn-Scott curves [BLS02], Barreto-Naehrig curves [Per+11], Miyaji-Nakabayashi-Takano curves [MNT01]);
3. amicable curves: Tweedledee/Tweedledum [BGH19], Pallas/Vesta [Hop20];
4. rigidly generated NUMS curves and curves from the MIRACL library [MIR18];
5. Bernstein's high performance curves [Ber06] and M, E curves [Ara+13];
6. curves from the standards ANSSI [Jou11], OSCCA [SSL14], GOST [PLK06, SF16], OAKLEY [Orm98], WTLS [Wir00], ISO/IEC [ISO17] and others;

Although our analysis focuses mainly on prime-field curves, the database contains 31 curves over binary fields and one over an extension field. Currently, there are 188 standard curves in total. Note that we also include curves that were but are no longer supported by the standards, and curves that are not recommended for public use, but have been included in the documents for various reasons (e.g., curves for implementation checks). The database provides filtering by bit-length, field type, cofactor size, and curve form.

Additionally, our database contains five categories of simulated curves: X9.62$_{sim}$, Brainpool$_{sim}$, NUMS$_{sim}$, Curve25519$_{sim}$ and Random[7].

For each curve, we also precomputed usual properties such as the CM discriminant, the j-invariant, the trace of Frobenius t, and the embedding degree. This precomputation significantly speeds up computation of some traits (Table 1).

Table 1. Numbers of elliptic curves in our database grouped by their source.

Source	#	Source	#	Source	#	Source	#
X9.62	40	BARP	6	OSCCA	1	X9.62$_{sim}$	120k
Brainpool	14	BLS	6	BN	16	NUMS$_{sim}$	1.2k
NUMS	24	GOST	9	AMIC	4	Curve25519$_{sim}$	784
SECG	33	ISO	4	DJB	10	Brainpool$_{sim}$	12k
NIST	15	MNT	10	ANSSI	1	Random	250k
MIRACL	8	OAKLEY	2	WTLS	8	Other	11

---

[7] The set of Random curves and their trait results is currently still evolving.

3.2 Simulations

We have picked four major standards X9.62 [Com+98], Brainpool [Brainpool], NUMS [Bla+14] and Curve25519 [Ber06] for simulations, since their generation method was explained in enough detail and can be easily extended for large scale generation. At a few points, the standards were a little ambiguous, so we filled the gaps to reflect the choices made for the actual standard curves whenever possible. We have simulated over 120 000 X9.62 curves, 12 000 Brainpool curves, 1 200 NUMS curves and 750 Curve25519 curves[8].

The aim of this part is not to undertake a thorough analysis of the published algorithms, rather explain our approach to the large-scale generation using the given methods. For the details of the original algorithms, see the individual standards. Although NUMS, Brainpool and Curve25519 provide a method for generating group generators, we are currently not focusing on their analysis.

X9.62 - The Standard. We focus on the generation method of the 1998 version [Com+98]. Its input is a 160-bit seed and a large prime p and the output is an elliptic curve in short Weierstrass form over the field $\mathbb{F}_p$, satisfying the following security conditions:

- "Near-primality": The curve order shall have a prime factor l of size at least $\min\{2^{160}, 4\sqrt{p}\}$. Furthermore, the cofactor shall be s-smooth, where s is a small integer (the standard proposes $s = 255$ as a guide).
- The embedding degree of the curve shall be greater than 20. The standard also specifies that to check this condition, we may simply verify that $p^e \neq 1$ (mod l) for all $e \leq 20$.
- The trace t shall not be equal to 1.

Given a seed and a prime p, the standard computes a $\log(p)$-bit integer r using[9] the function (1). The next step is choosing $a, b \in \mathbb{F}_p$ such that $b^2 r = a^3$. This process is repeated until the curve satisfies the security conditions mentioned above.

$$H(\text{seed}) = \underbrace{\texttt{SHA-1}(\text{seed})}_{\text{discard}} || \underbrace{\texttt{SHA-1}(\text{seed} + 1) || \ldots || \texttt{SHA-1}(\text{seed} + i)}_{\log(p) - \text{bit integer as output}}. \qquad (1)$$

X9.62 – Our approach. For each of the five bit-lengths 128, 160, 192, 224 and 256 bits we have fixed the same prime as the standard (hence all curves of the same bit-length are defined over the same field). Since there is no guidance in the standard how to pick the seed for each iteration, we have taken the published seed for each bit-length and iteratively incremented its value by 1. To pick a and b, we have fixed $a = -3$ (as was done for most X9.62 curves for performance reasons [CC86]) and computed b accordingly, discarding the curve if $b^2 = -27/r$ does not have a solution for $b \in \mathbb{F}_p$. We also restricted the accepted cofactors to 1, 2, or 4 as this significantly accelerated the point counting. This choice also

---

[8] This took up to a week per standard on 40-core cluster of Intel Xeon Gold 5218.

[9] More precisely, H also changes the most significant bit of the output to 0.

conforms to with the fact that the standard curves all have cofactor 1 and the SECG standard (which overlaps with the X9.62 specifications) recommends the cofactor to be bounded by 4. The point counting – the main bottleneck of the computations – was done by an early-abort version of the SEA algorithm [Sch95]. For each of the five bit-lengths we have tried 5 million seeds, resulting in over 120 000 elliptic curves. Figure 3 captures a simplified overview of the algorithm.

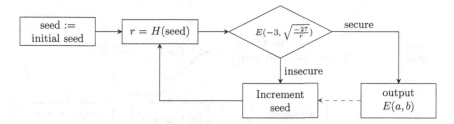

Fig. 3. X9.62 algorithm adjusted (indicated by the dashed line) for large-scale generation.

Brainpool – The Standard. The Brainpool standard proposes algorithms for generating both the prime p and the curve over $\mathbb{F}_p$. Since in our simulations we have used the same finite fields as are in the recommended curve parameters we will skip the algorithm for prime generation.

Given a seed and a prime, the curve generation process outputs an elliptic curve in Weierstrass form that satisfies the following security conditions:

- The cofactor shall be 1, i.e. the group order n shall be prime.
- The embedding degree shall be greater than $(n-1)/100$.
- The trace t shall not be equal to 1. Technical requirements then state that $t > 1$.
- The class number of the endomorphism algebra of the curve should be larger than 10^7.

The algorithm itself follows similar idea as X9.62, but in more convoluted way, as can be seen in Fig. 4. This time, the H function (1) is used to compute both a and b in pseudorandom way. Roughly speaking, a given seed is repeatedly incremented by 1 and mapped by H until an appropriate a is found and the resulting seed is used for finding b in a similar way. If the curve does not satisfy the condition, the seed is incremented and used again as the initial seed. See the standard for details of generation, GenA and GenB represent generation of a and b in Fig. 4.

Brainpool – Our Approach. We have used the same approach as in X9.62 and used the published seed as initial seed for the whole generation, incrementing seed after each curve was found. Since generation of both a and b can in theory take an arbitrary number of attempts, the seed is incremented after each failed

attempt. We have again used 5 million seeds for each of the four bit-lengths
(160, 192, 224, 256) Brainpool recommends. The number of generated curves in
total is over 12 000. The drop in the proportion of generated curves compared
to X9.62 standard is caused by stricter conditions.

There is currently no known efficient method that computes the class number;
instead we checked that a related quantity – the CM discriminant – is greater
than 2^{100}, following the SafeCurves recommendations [BL].

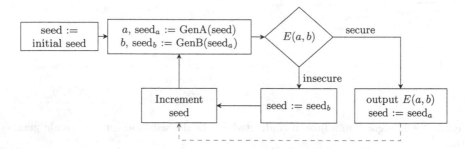

Fig. 4. Brainpool algorithm adjusted (indicated by the dashed line) for large-scale
generation.

NUMS – The Standard. The NUMS generation method, in accordance with
its name, does not fall into the verifiably pseudorandom category. As Brainpool, NUMS proposes algorithms for generating both the prime field and the
curve. The lowest recommended bit-length for prime fields by NUMS is 256.
The method of prime generation works by starting with $c = 1$ and incrementing
this value by 4 until $p = 2^s - c$ is a prime congruent to 3 mod 4.

Although NUMS proposes algorithms for generating both Weierstrass and
Edwards curves, we have focused only on the Weierstrass curves. The curve is
found by searching for $E(-3, b)$ satisfying the following security conditions by
incrementing b, starting from $b = 1$:

- The curve order as well as the order of its twist shall be primes.
- The trace t shall not equal 0 or 1. This condition is further extended by
  requiring $t > 1$, supposedly for practical reasons.
- The embedding degree shall be greater than $(n - 1)/100$ following the Brainpool standard.
- The CM discriminant shall be greater than 2^{100}, following the SafeCurves
  recommendations.

NUMS – Our Approach. We have used the same process, but this time
iterating over 10 million values for b, for each of the four bit-lengths 160, 192,
224 and 256. Though the lowest recommended bit-length for prime fields by
NUMS is 256, we have generated 160, 192 and 224-bit primes using the proposed
method to study curves of lower bit-lengths. This process produced over 1 200
curves, implying that the twist condition is strongly restrictive.

Curve25519 – The Standard. Curve25519 was created in a similar rigid manner as NUMS curves by minimizing one coefficient of the curve equation. The prime $2^{255} - 19$ for the prime field was chosen to be close to a power of 2 and with bit-length slightly below multiple of 32 for efficiency of the field arithmetic. Curve25519 is a Montgomery curve of the form $y^2 = x^3 + Ax^2 + x$ with the smallest $A > 2$ such that $A - 2$ is divisible by 4 and:

- The cofactor of the curve and its twist shall be 8 and 4 respectively.
- The trace t shall not equal 0 or 1.
- The embedding degree shall be greater than $(n - 1)/100$.
- The CM discriminant shall be greater than 2^{100}.

Curve25519 – Our Approach. Similarly to the NUMS approach we have iterated over A for bit-lengths 159, 191 and 255 where we have picked primes $2^{159} - 91$ and $2^{191} - 19$ for lower bitlengths. Iterating over 10 million values for A resulted in roughly 804 curves in total.

Random – Our Approach. Since all of the simulated standards contain certain unique properties (small b for NUMS, small A for Curve25519, bit overlaps in Brainpool, $rb^2 = -27$ for X9.62) and curves of the same bit-length share a base field, we have also generated curves for bit-lengths 128, 160, 192, 224, 256 using the method depicted in Fig. 5 that aims to avoid such biases. We call such curves Random, as this term clearly describes our intention. However, for practical reasons, we made the process deterministic using a hash function. For each curve, we generated a prime for the base field by hashing (SHA-512) a seed and taking the smallest prime bigger than this hash when interpreted as an integer. Curve coefficients were chosen using the hash function as well, see fig. 5. We kept such a curve if it was not anomalous, had cofactor 1, 2, 4 or 8 and satisfied the SafeCurves criteria on embedding degree and CM discriminant. We tried 5 million seeds, resulting in over 250 000 Random curves.

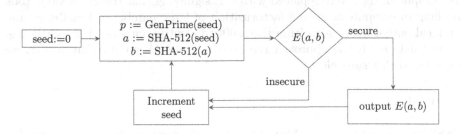

Fig. 5. Random simulation.

3.3 Outlier Detection

Our framework offers options for graphical comparisons for described distinguishing strategies. However, manual inspection does not scale well, so we utilize automated approaches to identify suspicious curves. Since we do not have (and cannot have) a labeling that could be used for the typical supervised approaches, we had to resort to unsupervised methods, namely outlier detection.

We built several datasets of simulated curves according to the selected distinguishing strategies. Each dataset of simulated curves consists only of curves of the same bit-length that were generated by the same method. Table 2 shows numbers of curves contained within each dataset. The rows correspond to the used generation method and the columns to the bit-length of the selected curves.

Table 2. Numbers of curves in our datasets of simulated curves.

	256 bits	224 bits	192 bits	160 bits	128 bits
X9.62$_{sim}$	18 502	22 211	18 836	27 780	36 126
Brainpool$_{sim}$	1 677	2 361	2 640	3 184	0
NUMS$_{sim}$	83	109	191	325	0
Curve25519$_{sim}$	140	0	366	278	0
Random	18 636	21 226	24 805	29 639	37 311

Additionally, in cases where trait results are (mostly) independent of the curve bit-length, we analyzed curves of all bit-lengths together. This approach allowed us to study even curves that did not match any of the generated bit-lengths.

We augmented each dataset with standard curves according to distinguishing strategies, i.e., Random curves with each category of standard curves, and the other three simulated categories only with standard curves of the same type. From these augmented datasets, we derived feature vectors consisting of all computed trait results, as well as some of their subsets. The features were scaled using a min-max scaler to fit within the $[0; 1]$ range. In case some results were not computed, they were replaced with -1, signifying that the given value took too long to compute (e.g., the factorization of large numbers). Finally, we ran the local outlier factor algorithm [Bre+00] to identify outliers within each augmented dataset. If the approach reported a standard curve as an outlier, we inspected such results closer.

4   Traits

DiSSECT currently contains 22 trait functions[10] – traits for brevity – designed to test a wide range of elliptic curve properties, including mathematical characteristics of curves, all SafeCurves ECDLP requirements, and properties connected to curve standards or implementations. In particular, the traits are not limited to properties connected to known attacks or vulnerabilities, and aim to find new interesting deviations.

---

[10] See https://dissect.crocs.fi.muni.cz/ or Appendix A for a full list.

We have divided the traits into five categories:

Potential Attacks. These traits test the classical properties of elliptic curves relevant to known attacks (the order and cofactor of the curve; the quadratic twist; the embedding degree). However, we also cover lesser-known and threatening attacks, for example, the factorization of values of the form $kn \pm 1$ as a generalization of [Che06]. To test scalar multiplication, essential to all ECC protocols, we inspect multiplicative orders of small values modulo the group order n. Another trait follows the idea from [Che02], with a possible connection of the discrete logarithm on ECC to factorization.

Complex Multiplication. Although at this moment there is no serious attack utilizing any knowledge about the CM discriminant or class number, these values are the defining features of an elliptic curve. They determine the structure of the endomorphism ring, the torsion points, isogeny classes, etc. Multiple traits deal with the factorization of t, the size and the factorization of the Frobenius discriminant $D = t^2 - 4p$, as well as how D changes as we move the defining base field to its extensions. We also compute bounds on the class number using the Dirichlet class number formula [Dav80].

Torsion. We have designed several traits to directly analyze the torsion points of a given elliptic curve. One of the traits computes the degree of the extension $\mathbb{F}_{p^k}/\mathbb{F}_p$ over which the torsion subgroup is (partially) defined. Lower degrees might lead to computable pairings. Another trait approaches torsion from the direction of division polynomials and computes their factorization. We also consider the lift $E(\mathbb{F}_p) \to E(\mathbb{Q})$ and computes the size of the torsion subgroup over $\mathbb{Q}$ which might be relevant for lifting of ECDLP.

Isogenies. Both torsion and complex multiplication can be described using isogenies. Kernel polynomial of every isogeny is a factor of the division polynomial, and the special cases of isogenies, endomorphisms, form an order in an imaginary quadratic field of $\mathbb{Q}(\sqrt{D})$. One of isogeny traits computes the degree of the extension where some/all isogenies of a given degree are defined. Isogeny traits also analyze isogenies of ordinary curves and the corresponding isogeny volcanoes – their depth and the shape of so-called crater, and also the number of neighbors for a given vertex in the isogeny graph.

Standards and Implementation. During our analysis of standard methods for generating curves, we have noticed unusual steps in the algorithms, so we designed traits to capture the resulting properties. The nature of the Brainpool standard (see Fig. 4) causes overlaps in the binary representations of the curve coefficients in roughly half of the generated curves. The NUMS standard, as well as the Koblitz curves, use small curve coefficients by design. The X9.62 standard uses the relation $b^2r = a^3$ to determine the curve coefficients from r. The SECG standard recommends the curves `secp224k1` and `secp256k1` together with the group generators; the x-coordinate of half of both of these generators is the same small number.

Most attacks on the ECDLP are aiming at specific implementation vulner-abilities. To address this, we propose traits that target possible irregularities in practical implementations. One trait follows the idea of [Wei+20], where the authors analyze the side-channel leakage caused by improper representation of large integers in memory. Based on [Bai+09], we designed a trait that analyzes the number of points with a low Hamming weight on a given curve.

4.1 Notable Findings

GOST Curves. The trait that analyzes the size of the coefficients in the Weierstrass form was motivated by the NUMS standard. However, our outlier detection also recognized two 256-bit GOST curves (`CryptoPro-A-ParamSet`, `CryptoPro-C -ParamSet`) in this trait, and a closer inspection in Fig. 6 revealed that both curves have small b coefficients (166 and 32858). This contradicts Alekseev, Nikolaev, and Smyshlyaev [ANS18], who claim that all of the seven standardized GOST R curves were generated in the following way[11]:

1. Select p that allows fast arithmetic.
2. Compute r by hashing a random seed with the Streebog hash function.
3. For the generation of twisted Edwards curve $eu^2 + v^2 = 1 + du^2v^2$, put $e = 1, d = r$. For the generation of Weierstrass curve $y^2 = x^3 + ax + b$, put $a = -3$ and b equal to any value such that $rb^2 = a^3$.
4. Check the following security conditions:
   - $n \in (2^{254}, 2^{256}) \cup (2^{508}, 2^{512})$.
   - The embedding degree is at least 32 (resp. 132) if $n \in (2^{254}, 2^{256})$ (resp. if $n \in (2^{508}, 2^{512})$).
   - The curve is not anomalous.
   - The j-invariant is not 0 or 1728.

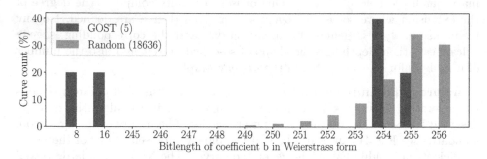

Fig. 6. Two GOST curves (`CryptoPro-A-ParamSet`, `CryptoPro-C-ParamSet`) exhibit particularly low bit-length of b parameter, even though Alekseev, Nikolaev, and Smyshlyaev [ANS18] claim that they were generated pseudorandomly.

---

[11] The authors support their claims by providing seeds for two of the seven curves. We find it problematic that the seeds were not previously made public.

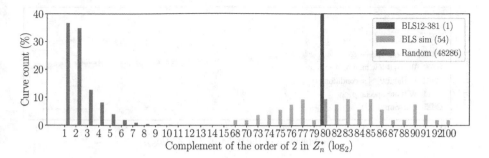

Fig. 7. BLS12-381 and BLS simulated curves exhibit unexpectedly large complement of the order of 2 in $\mathbb{Z}_n^*$ when compared to Random curves.

Thus the small size of b (which should be pseudorandom if r is) implies that it is very unlikely that they were generated with this claimed method. More precisely, since $b^2 = -27/r$ in $\mathbb{F}_p$ and p has 256 bits, then the probability for $b = 166$, resp. $b = 32858$ is 2^{-248}, resp. 2^{-240}, considering the bitlengths of the parameters. We hypothesise that the `CryptoPro-A-ParamSet` curve was generated by incrementing b from 1 until the GOST security conditions were satisfied. We have verified that $b = 166$ is the smallest such value with the added condition that the cofactor is 1 (otherwise, the smallest value is $b = 36$). The `CryptoPro-C-ParamSet` does not have this property, as its b coefficient 32858 is only the 80th smallest such value. However, there is an additional problem with the generator point $(0, \sqrt{32858})$. It was shown [Gou03], prior to the standardization of this curve, that there exist side-channel attacks utilizing such special points with $x = 0$. If we consider the existence of such point as another condition imposed on the curves, then 32858 is the 46th smallest value. We employed DiSSECT to distinguish this particular curve for from the rest of the 45 curves using the implemented traits in order to explain their choice, but without results.

Furthermore, the trait inspecting CM discriminant revealed that the third curve `CryptoPro-B-ParamSet` from [PLK06] has a CM discriminant of -619. Such a small value is extremely improbable, unless the curve was generated by the CM method [Brö06]. (The CM discriminant -915 of `gost256` is small as well, but this curve was used just as an example and there are no claims about its generation).

The BLS12-381 Curve. The trait that measures $\phi(n)$ divided by the multiplicative order of 2 modulo n (low multiplicative orders translate to high values and vice versa) identified the BLS12-381 curve [Bow17] as an outlier in the set of Random curves. While some traits were expected to show statistical differences between pairing-friendly curves and Random curves, the cause was not clear for this particular trait. To further investigate this, we have adopted the generation method of the BLS12-381 curve to DiSSECT. Figure 7 shows the results of the trait on Random curves, the BLS12-381 curve and the BLS simulated curves.

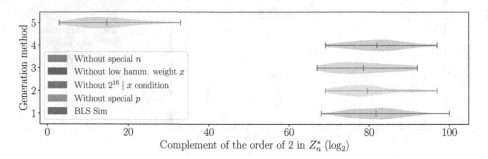

Fig. 8. Simulation of BLS curves while ignoring different properties have shown that the special construction of n caused the unexpected behavior.

Figure 7 shows that the unexpected detection of BLS12-381 as an outlier was not a coincidence. Rather it was caused by the generation method, and consequently the properties, of the BLS12-381 curve. To briefly summarize, the generation method works by finding an integer x satisfying:

- x has low hamming weight,
- x is divisible by 2^{16},
- $n = x^4 - x^2 + 1$ is a prime,
- $p = \frac{1}{3}n(x - 1)^2 + x$ is a prime.

When such x is found, the CM method is used to construct a BLS curve[12] over $\mathbb{F}_p$ with cardinality $\frac{1}{3}n(x - 1)^2$. We have identified exactly what conditions in the BLS generation method were behind the outlier detection of BLS12-381 curve by removing each condition and computing the trait for these modified curves. On one hand, Fig. 8 shows that the conditions on x and special form of p have little or no impact on the results of the trait. On the other hand, we can see that the conditions that were the main cause of the unexpected results of BLS12-381 is the special form of the order $n = x^4 - x^2 + 1$. Indeed, in this case $\phi = x^2(x-1)(x+1)$ which means that small multiplicative orders are more likely than for general n. Although this does not seem to cause any vulnerabilities in the BLS12-381 curve, it reveals an undocumented property of the generation method.

The Bitcoin curve. A trait that inspects the x-coordinate of inverted generator scalar multiples, i.e., x-coordinates of points $k^{-1}G$, where $k \in \{1, \ldots, 8\}$, was inspired by Brengel et al. [BR18], who reported an unexpectedly low value for $k = 2$ on the Bitcoin curve `secp256k1`. Furthermore, Maxwell [Max15] pointed out that `secp224k1` yields exactly the same result. Pornin [Por19] guesses that this was caused by reusing the code for Koblitz curves with the same seeds, together with poor documentation.

---

[12] Iterating through 100 million values of x we have generated 54 BLS curves.

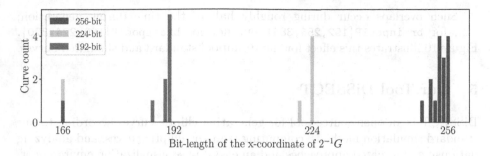

Fig. 9. Curves `secp256k1` and `secp224k1` exhibit significantly shorter x-coordinate of the point $2^{-1}G$ than expected. The other standard curves of given bit-lengths are also plotted.

We analyzed the results of this trait in our visualization framework (Fig. 9) and discovered that `secp256k1` and `secp224k1` are the only standard curves for which the x-coordinate of $k^{-1}G$ is significantly shorter than the full bit-length.

Brainpool Overlaps. The trait designed to detect bit-overlaps in the Weierstrass coefficients, revealed a structure in the Brainpool curves, already observed by Bernstein et al. [Ber+15].

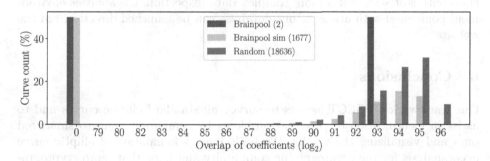

Fig. 10. Bit-overlap of 256-bit standard Brainpool, simulated Brainpool, and Random curves.

More precisely the trait compares coefficients a and b when stripped of 160 bits (SHA-1 output size) from the left and right respectively. Inspecting `brainpoolP256r1`, we can see the identical segments in a, b:

$a = $ 0x7d5a0975fc2c3057eef67530417affe7fb8055c1**26dc5c6ce94a4b44f330b5d9**

$b = $ 0x**26dc5c6ce94a4b44f330b5d9**bbd77cbf958416295cf7e1ce6bccdc18ff8c07b6

Such overlaps occur during roughly half of the time during generation; e.g., for `brainpoolP{192,256,384}` but not for `brainpoolP{160,224,320}`. Figure 10 illustrates this effect for the Brainpool standard and simulated curves.

5   Our Tool DiSSECT

DiSSECT is an open-source tool for generating elliptic curves according to our standard simulation methods, computing traits on elliptic curves, and analyzing data using automated approaches and an easy-to-use visualization environment. The tool does not aim to perform rigorous statistical tests given the limited sample size of standard curves. Its code contains implementations of all 22 traits described in Appendix A, and it can be easily extended. Adding a new trait requires only a short description of its function and writing a few lines of Sage code that computes the new trait result for a given curve.

The tool provides an approach for automated outlier detection to systematically identify deviations. A Jupyter notebook environment can be used to perform a more detailed analysis of computed trait results. Both of these approaches allow configuring the subset of analyzed curves, traits, and their parameters, and can access locally stored data as well as our publicly accessible database.

Our website[13] https://dissect.crocs.fi.muni.cz/ contains detailed information about curves in our database and corresponding trait results, and trait descriptions with statistics. For a more complex data inspection, the analysis environment configured with access to our database can be launched directly from the website.

6   Conclusions

Our framework DiSSECT aspires to survey all standard elliptic curves and to assist in identification of potential problems by comparing them to simulated ones and visualizing the results. We built it as a foundation of elliptic curve cryptanalysis for the cryptographic community and hope that more cryptographers and mathematicians will join the project. DiSSECT's code is available at our repository[14].

Our tool revealed two surprising types of deviations. We realized that the generation process of three GOST curves described by Alekseev, Nikolaev, and Smyshlyaev [ANS18] is inconsistent with the sizes of the b coefficient in two cases and with the size of the CM discriminant in the third one. Properly documenting such properties is crucial for re-establishing trust in the standard curves and the whole ECC ecosystem. We cannot expect its users, developers, or policy-makers to notice even fairly obvious deviations (e.g., small Weierstrass coefficients), as they often do not access the parameters directly.

---

[13] https://dissect.crocs.fi.muni.cz/.
[14] https://github.com/crocs-muni/DiSSECT.

We found an interesting, previously undescribed property of the BLS12-381 curve (related to smoothness) that is caused by its generation. Recent attacks [KB16] on special properties of pairing-friendly curves have proven that awareness of all properties caused by the pairing-friendly generation methods is crucial. In particular, our approach of isolation of individual properties in BLS generation has shown to have a lot of potential for future research of security of pairing-friendly curves. One further interesting improvement of DiSSECT would be an implementation of clustering algorithms that would help uncover biases systematically introduced by these properties. Another approach might be combining DiSSECT with statistical tools such as [Obr+15].

Selected parts of DiSSECT could also be used to quickly assess new individual curves. This might be useful for implementations following the idea of Miele and Lenstra [ML15], trading standard curves for ephemeral on-the-fly generated ones. Besides cryptographic applications, DiSSECT might also be useful to number theorists by providing them with empiric distributions of various traits. It is unrealistic to go through the whole space of trait results for different parameter choices and curve sets manually. Thus we employed an automated outlier detection method, which found all discrepancies we discovered manually. Still, there may be other outliers, and we believe it is an interesting open problem to statistically evaluate the results in a way that takes into account the inner structure of the data for a given trait.

Acknowledgements. This project has been made possible in part by a grant from the Cisco University Research Program Fund, an advised fund of Silicon Valley Community Foundation. V. Sedlacek, V. Matyas, M. Sys and A. Dufka were supported by Czech Science Foundation project GA20-03426S. V. Sedlacek and V. Suchanek were also supported by the Ph.D. Talent Scholarship - funded by the Brno City Municipality. Computational resources were supplied by the project "e-Infrastruktura CZ" (e-INFRA LM2018140) provided within the program Projects of Large Research, Development and Innovations Infrastructures.

A   List of traits

The following is a list of all traits used for curve analysis. Each trait takes as an input an ordinary elliptic curve $E/\mathbb{F}_p : y^2 = x^3 + ax + b$ of order n.

Trait name	Input	Output
cofactor	int r	Tuple (n_1, n_2) such that the group $E(\mathbb{F}_{p^r})$ is isomorphic to $\mathbb{Z}_{n_1} \times \mathbb{Z}_{n_2}$ and $n_1 \mid n_2$ ($n_1 = 1$ for cyclic groups)
discriminant		The factorization of $D = t^2 - 4p = v^2 d_K$, where d_K is the discriminant of the endomorphism algebra of E
twist order	int r	The factorization of the cardinality of the quadratic twist of $E(\mathbb{F}_{p^r})$
kn fact.	int k	The factorizations of $kn + 1$, $kn - 1$
torsion extension	prime l	$k_1, k_2, k_2/k_1$, where k_1, k_2 are the smallest integers satisfying $E[l] \cap E(\mathbb{F}_{p^{k_1}}) \neq \emptyset$ and $E[l] \subseteq E(\mathbb{F}_{p^{k_2}})$
conductor	int r	The factorization of D_r/D_1, where $D_r = t_r^2 - 4p^r$ and t_r is the trace of Frobenius of $E/\mathbb{F}_{p^r}$
embedding		The ratio $\phi(r)/e$, where $r \mid n$ is the order of the prime order subgroup and e is the multiplicative order of q (mod r)
class number		Upper bound [Dav80] and lower bound [Col85] on the class number of the endomorphism algebra of E
small prime order	prime l	The ratio $\phi(n)/m$ where m is the multiplicative order of l (mod n)
division pol.	prime l	The factorization of the l-th division polynomial
volcano	prime l	The depth and the degree of the l-volcano
isogeny extension	prime l	$i_1, i_2, i_2/i_1$ where i_1, i_2 are the smallest integers such that there exists a $\mathbb{F}_{p^{i_1}}$-rational l-isogeny and $l + 1$ $\mathbb{F}_{p^{i_2}}$-rational l-isogenies from E
trace fact.	int r	A factorization of the trace of Frobenius of $E/\mathbb{F}_{p^r}$
isogeny neighbors	prime l	A number of roots of $\Phi_l(j(E), x)$ where Φ_l is the l-th modular polynomial
q torsion		Torsion order of $E'(\mathbb{Q})$ where E' is given by the same equation $y^2 = x^3 + ax + b$
hamming x	int k	A number of points on E with the Hamming weight of the x-coordinate equal to k
square 4p-1		The factorization of square-free parts of $4p - 1$ and $4n - 1$ where n is the order of the generator point of E
pow distance		The distances of n to the nearest power of 2 and multiples of 32 and 64
multiples x	int k	The x-coordinate of $\frac{1}{k}G$
x962 inv.		The value $r = \frac{a^3}{b^2}$
brainpool overlap		$a_{160} - b_{-160}$ where a_{160} are the $s - 160$ rightmost bits of a and b_{-160} are the $s - 160$ leftmost bits of b
weierstrass		The parameters a, b

References

[Age11] Agence Nationale de la Securite des Systemes d'Information. Avis relatif aux paramètres de courbes elliptiques définis par l'Eetat français (2011). https://www.legifrance.gouv.fr/download/pdf?id=QfYWtPSAJVtAB_c6Je5tAv00OY2r1-ad3LaVVmnStGvQ=

[ANS18] Alekseev, E.K., Nikolaev, V.D., Smyshlyaev, S.V.: On the security properties of Russian standardized elliptic curves. Math. Questions Cryptogr. **9**(3), 5–32 (2018)

[ANS05] ANSI. Public key cryptography for the financial services industry: the elliptic curve digital signature algorithm (ECDSA). ANSI X9.62 (2005)

[Ara+13] Aranha, D.F., Barreto, P.S.L.M., Pereira, G.C.C.F., Ricardini, J.E.: A note on high-security general-purpose elliptic curves. Cryptology ePrint Archive, Report 2013/647 (2013). https://eprint.iacr.org/2013/647

[Bai+15] Baigneres, T., Delerablée, C., Finiasz, M., Goubin, L., Lepoint, T., Rivain, M.: Trap me if you can-million dollar curve. IACR Cryptol. ePrint Arch. **2015**, 1249 (2015)

[Bai+09] Bailey, D.V., et al.: Breaking ECC2K-130. IACR Cryptol. ePrint Arch. **2009**, 541 (2009)

[BLS02] Barreto, P.S.L.M., Lynn, B., Scott, M.: Constructing elliptic curves with prescribed embedding degrees. In: Cimato, S., Persiano, G., Galdi, C. (eds.) SCN 2002. LNCS, vol. 2576, pp. 257–267. Springer, Heidelberg (2003). https://doi.org/10.1007/3-540-36413-7_19

[Ber06] Bernstein, D.J.: Curve25519: new Diffie-Hellman speed records. In: Yung, M., Dodis, Y., Kiayias, A., Malkin, T. (eds.) PKC 2006. LNCS, vol. 3958, pp. 207–228. Springer, Heidelberg (2006). https://doi.org/10.1007/11745853_14

[BL] Bernstein, D.J., Lange, T.: SafeCurves: choosing safe curves for elliptic-curve cryptography. https://safecurves.cr.yp.to/. Accessed 17 Aug 2021

[Ber+15] Bernstein, D.J., et al.: How to manipulate curve standards: a white paper for the black Hat http://bada55.cr.yp.to. In: Chen, L., Matsuo, S. (eds.) SSR 2015. LNCS, vol. 9497, pp. 109–139. Springer, Cham (2015). https://doi.org/10.1007/978-3-319-27152-1_6

[BCL14] Bernstein, D.J., Chuengsatiansup, C., Lange, T.: Curve41417: karatsuba revisited. In: Batina, L., Robshaw, M. (eds.) CHES 2014. LNCS, vol. 8731, pp. 316–334. Springer, Heidelberg (2014). https://doi.org/10.1007/978-3-662-44709-3_18

[Ber+13] Bernstein, D.J., Hamburg, M., Krasnova, A., Lange, T.: Elligator: elliptic-curve points indistinguishable from uniform random strings. In: Proceedings of the 2013 ACM SIGSAC Conference on Computer & Communications Security, pp. 967–980 (2013)

[BLN16] Bernstein, D.J., Lange, T., Niederhagen, R.: Dual EC: a standardized back door. In: Ryan, P.Y.A., Naccache, D., Quisquater, J.-J. (eds.) The New Codebreakers. LNCS, vol. 9100, pp. 256–281. Springer, Heidelberg (2016). https://doi.org/10.1007/978-3-662-49301-4_17

[BD00] Biham, E., Dunkelman, O.: Cryptanalysis of the A5/1 GSM stream cipher. In: Roy, B., Okamoto, E. (eds.) INDOCRYPT 2000. LNCS, vol. 1977, pp. 43–51. Springer, Heidelberg (2000). https://doi.org/10.1007/3-540-44495-5_5

[Bla+14] Black, B., Bos, J., Costello, C., Longa, P., Naehrig, M.: Elliptic curve cryptography (ECC) nothing up my sleeve (NUMS) curves and curve generation. Internet-Drafts are working documents of the Internet Engineering Task Force (2014). https://datatracker.ietf.org/doc/html/draft-black-numscurves-02

[Bow17] Bowe, S.: BLS12-381: New zk-snark elliptic curve construction (2017). https://electriccoin.co/blog/new-snark-curve/. Accessed 16 Sept 2021

[BGH19] Bowe, S., Grigg, J., Hopwood, D.: Recursive proof composition without a trusted setup. Cryptology ePrint Archive, Report 2019/1021 (2019). https://ia.cr/2019/1021

[BR18] Brengel, M., Rossow, C.: Identifying key leakage of bitcoin users. In: Bailey, M., Holz, T., Stamatogiannakis, M., Ioannidis, S. (eds.) RAID 2018. LNCS, vol. 11050, pp. 623–643. Springer, Cham (2018). https://doi.org/10.1007/978-3-030-00470-5_29

[Bre+00] Breunig, M.M., Kriegel, H.-P., Ng, R.T., Sander, J.: LOF: identifying density-based local outliers. In: Proceedings of the 2000 ACM SIGMOD International Conference on Management of Data, pp. 93–104 (2000)

[Brö06] Bröker, R.: Constructing elliptic curves of prescribed order. Ph.D. thesis. Thomas Stieltjes Institute for Mathematics (2006)

[Cer10] Certicom Research. Sec 2: Recommended elliptic curve domain parameters, version 2.0 (2010). https://secg.org/

[Cer] Certicom Research. Standards for Efficient Cryptography Group. https://secg.org/. Accessed 13 Aug 2021

[Che+] Checkoway, S., et al.: A systematic analysis of the Juniper Dual EC incident. In: Proceedings of the 2016 ACM SIGSAC Conference on Computer and Communications Security, Vienna, Austria, 24–28 October 2016, pp. 468–479 (2016)

[Che02] Cheng, Q.: A new special-purpose factorization algorithm. Citeseer (2002)

[Che06] Cheon, J.H.: Security analysis of the strong Diffie-Hellman problem. In: Vaudenay, S. (ed.) EUROCRYPT 2006. LNCS, vol. 4004, pp. 1–11. Springer, Heidelberg (2006). https://doi.org/10.1007/11761679_1

[CC86] Chudnovsky, D.V., Chudnovsky, G.V.: Sequences of numbers generated by addition in formal groups and new primality and factorization tests. Adv. Appl. Math. 7(4), 385–434 (1986)

[Col85] Collectif. Nombres de classes des corps quadratiques imaginaires. In: Séminaire Bourbaki: 1983/84, exposés 615–632. Astérisque 121–122. Société mathématique de France (1985). https://www.numdam.org/item/SB_1983-1984__26__309_0/

[Com+98] Accredited Standards Committee et al.: American national standard x9. 62-1998. Public Key Cryptography for the Financial Services Industry, The Elliptic Curve Digital Signature Algorithm (ECDSA) (1998)

[CLN15] Costello, C., Longa, P., Naehrig, M.: A brief discussion on selecting new elliptic curves. In: Microsoft Research. Microsoft 8 (2015)

[Dav80] Davenport, H.: Multiplicative number theory, pp. 43–53 (1980)

[DY15] Di, L., Yan, L.: Introduction to the commercial cryptography scheme in China (2015). https://icmconference.org/wp-content/uploads/C23Introduction-on-the-Commercial-Cryptography-Scheme-in-China-20151105.pdf. Accessed 23 Aug 2021

[Brainpool] Elliptic curve cryptography (ECC) brainpool standard curves and curve generation. Technical report IETF RFC 5639 (2010)

[FR94]   Frey, G., Rück, H.-G.: A remark concerning m-divisibility and the discrete logarithm in the divisor class group of curves. Math. Comput. **62**(206), 865–874 (1994)

[GLV01]   Gallant, R.P., Lambert, R.J., Vanstone, S.A.: Faster point multiplication on elliptic curves with efficient endomorphisms. In: Kilian, J. (ed.) CRYPTO 2001. LNCS, vol. 2139, pp. 190–200. Springer, Heidelberg (2001). ISBN 978-3-540-44647-7. https://doi.org/10.1007/3-540-44647-8_11

[Gou03]   Goubin, L.: A refined power-analysis attack on elliptic curve cryptosystems. In: Desmedt, Y.G. (ed.) PKC 2003. LNCS, vol. 2567, pp. 199–211. Springer, Heidelberg (2003). https://doi.org/10.1007/3-540-36288-6_15

[Hal13]   Hales, T.C.: The NSA back door to NIST. Not. AMS **61**(2), 190–192 (2013)

[Ham15a] Hamburg, M.: A note on high-security general-purpose elliptic curves. Cryptology ePrint Archive, Report 2015/625 (2015). https://eprint.iacr.org/2015/625.pdf

[Ham15b] Hamburg, M.: Ed448-goldilocks, a new elliptic curve. IACR Cryptology ePrint Archive, Report 2015/625 (2015)

[Hop20]   Hopwood, D.: The pasta curves (2020). https://electriccoin.co/blog/the-pasta-curves-for-halo-2-and-beyond/. Accessed 27 Aug 2021

[ISO17]   ISO/IEC 15946. Information technology—Security techniques—Cryptographic techniques based on elliptic curves—Part 5: Elliptic curve generation (2017)

[Jou11]   Journal officiel de la republique francaise. Avis relatif aux paramètres de courbes elliptiques définis par l'etat français (2011). https://www.legifrance.gouv.fr/download/pdf?id=QfYWtPSAJVtAB_c6Je5tAv00OY2r1ad3LaVVmnStGvGvQ=

[KB16]   Kim, T., Barbulescu, R.: Extended tower number field sieve: a new complexity for the medium prime case. In: Robshaw, M., Katz, J. (eds.) CRYPTO 2016. LNCS, vol. 9814, pp. 543–571. Springer, Heidelberg (2016). https://doi.org/10.1007/978-3-662-53018-4_20

[KM16]   Koblitz, N., Menezes, A.: A riddle wrapped in an enigma. IEEE Secur. Priv. **14**(6), 34–42 (2016)

[Loc+14] Lochter, M., Merkle, J., Schmidt, J.-M., Schutze, T.: Requirements for standard elliptic curves. IACR Cryptology ePrint Archive, Report 2014/832 (2014)

[Max15]   Maxwell, G.: The most repeated R value on the blockchain (2015). https://bitcointalk.org/index.php?topic=1118704.0. Accessed 09 Sept 2021

[MOV93]   Menezes, A.J., Okamoto, T., Vanstone, S.A.: Reducing elliptic curve logarithms to logarithms in a finite field. IEEE Trans. Inf. Theory **39**(5), 1639–1646 (1993)

[ML15]   Miele, A., Lenstra, A.K.: Efficient ephemeral elliptic curve cryptographic keys. In: Lopez, J., Mitchell, C.J. (eds.) ISC 2015. LNCS, vol. 9290, pp. 524–547. Springer, Cham (2015). https://doi.org/10.1007/978-3-319-23318-5_29

[MIR18]   MIRACL UK Ltd.: Multiprecision integer and rational arithmetic cryptographic library (2018). https://github.com/miracl/MIRACL

[MNT01]   Miyaji, A., Nakabayashi, M., Takano, S.: New explicit conditions of elliptic curve traces for FR-reduction. IEICE Trans. Fundam. Electron. Commun. Comput. Sci. **84**, 1234–1243 (2001)

[Nak08]   Nakamoto, S.: Bitcoin: a peer-to-peer electronic cash system. Decentralized Business Review, p. 21260 (2008)

[Nat00] National Institute of Standards and Technology. Fips publication 186-2 (2000). https://csrc.nist.gov/publications/detail/fips/186/2/archive/2000-01-27

[Obr+15] Obrátil, L., Klinec, D., Švenda, P., Ukrop, M.: Randomness testing toolkit (2015). https://rtt.ics.muni.cz

[Orm98] Orman, H.: The OAKLEY key determination protocol. RFC 2412 (1998). https://rfc-editor.org/rfc/rfc2412.txt

[Per+11] Pereira, G.C., Simplício, M.A., Jr., Naehrig, M., Barreto, P.S.: A family of implementation-friendly BN elliptic curves. J. Syst. Softw. **84**(8), 1319–1326 (2011)

[PH78] Pohlig, S., Hellman, M.: An improved algorithm for computing logarithms over $GF(p)$ and its cryptographic significance. IEEE Trans. Inf. Theory 106–110 (1978)

[PLK06] Popov, V., Leontiev, S., Kurepkin, I.: Additional cryptographic algorithms for use with GOST 28147-89, GOST R 34.10-94, GOST R 34.10-2001, and GOST R 34.11-94 Algorithms (2006). https://rfc-editor.org/rfc/rfc4357.txt

[Por19] Pornin, T.: https://crypto.stackexchange.com/questions/60420/what-does-the-special-form-of-the-base-point-of-secp256k1-allow. Accessed 16 Sept 2021

[SA+98] Satoh, T., Araki, K., et al.: Fermat quotients and the polynomial time discrete log algorithm for anomalous elliptic curves. Rikkyo Daigaku sugaku zasshi **47**(1), 81–92 (1998)

[Sch13] Schneier, B.: The NSA Is Breaking Most Encryption on the Internet (2013). https://www.schneier.com/blog/archives/2013/09/the_nsa_is_brea.html. Accessed 13 Aug 2021

[Sch95] Schoof, R.: Counting points on elliptic curves over finite fields. Jo. Théorie Nombres Bordeaux 219–254 (1995)

[Sco99] Scott, M.: Re: NIST annouces set of Elliptic Curves (1999). https://web.archive.org/web/20160313065951/groups.google.com/forum/message/raw?msg=sci.crypt/mFMukSsORmI/FpbHDQ6hM_MJ. Accessed 13 Aug 2021

[Sco15] Scott, M.: A new curve (2015). https://moderncrypto.org/mail-archive/curves/2015/000449.html. Accessed 01 Sept 2021

[Sed22] Sedláček, V.: On cryptographic weaknesses related to elliptic curves. Ph.D. thesis. Masaryk University (2022)

[Sem96] Semaev, I.: On computing logarithms on elliptic curves. Discret. Math. Appl. **6**(1), 69–76 (1996)

[Sem98] Semaev, I.: Evaluation of discrete logarithms in a group of p-torsion points of an elliptic curve in characteristic p. Math. Comput. **67**(221), 353–356 (1998)

[SSL14] Shen, S., Shen, S., Lee, X.: SM2 digital signature algorithm. Internet-Draft. Work in Progress (2014). https://datatracker.ietf.org/doc/html/draft-shen-sm2-ecdsa-02

[Sma99] Smart, N.P.: The discrete logarithm problem on elliptic curves of trace one. J. Cryptol. **12**(3), 193–196 (1999)

[SF16] Smyshlyaeva, E.S., Fotieva, V.: Information technology. Cryptographic data security. Parameters of elliptic curves for cryptographic algorithms and protocols. Federal Agency on Technical Regulating and Metrology (2016)

[Sol11] Solinas, J.A.: Generalized mersenne prime. In: van Tilborg, H.C.A., Jajo-
         dia, S. (eds.) Encyclopedia of Cryptography and Security, pp. 509–510.
         Springer, Boston (2011). https://doi.org/10.1007/978-1-4419-5906-5_32
[Tor94] Torkelson, C.E.: The clipper chip: how key escrow threatens to undermine
         the fourth amendment. Seton Hall L. Rev. **25**, 1142 (1994)
[Val+18] Valenta, L., Sullivan, N., Sanso, A., Heninger, N.: In search of curveswap:
         Measuring elliptic curve implementations in the wild. Cryptology ePrint
         Archive, Report 2018/298 (2018). https://ia.cr/2018/298
[Wei+20] Weiser, S., Schrammel, D., Bodner, L., Spreitzer, R.: Big numbers - big
         troubles: systematically analyzing nonce leakage in (EC)DSA implemen-
         tations. In: USENIX Security Symposium (2020)
[Wir00] Wireless Application Protocol Forum. Wireless application protocol
         wireless transport layer security specification (2000). https://web.archive.
         org/web/20170829023257/www.wapforum.org/tech/documents/WAP-
         199-WTLS-20000218-a.pdf

Co-factor Clearing and Subgroup Membership Testing on Pairing-Friendly Curves

Youssef El Housni[1,2](✉) [ID], Aurore Guillevic[3,4](✉) [ID], and Thomas Piellard[1]

[1] ConsenSys R&D, Paris, France
{youssef.elhousni,thomas.piellard}@consensys.net
[2] Inria, Saclay, France
[3] Université de Lorraine, CNRS, Inria, LORIA, Nancy, France
aurore.guillevic@inria.fr
[4] Aarhus University, Aarhus, Denmark

Abstract. An important cryptographic operation on elliptic curves is hashing to a point on the curve. When the curve is not of prime order, the point is multiplied by the cofactor so that the result has a prime order. This is important to avoid small subgroup attacks for example. A second important operation, in the composite-order case, is testing whether a point belongs to the subgroup of prime order. A pairing is a bilinear map $e\colon \mathbb{G}_1 \times \mathbb{G}_2 \to \mathbb{G}_T$ where $\mathbb{G}_1$ and $\mathbb{G}_2$ are distinct subgroups of prime order r of an elliptic curve, and $\mathbb{G}_T$ is a multiplicative subgroup of the same prime order r of a finite field extension. Pairing-friendly curves are rarely of prime order. We investigate cofactor clearing and subgroup membership testing on these composite-order curves. First, we generalize a result on faster cofactor clearing for BLS curves to other pairing-friendly families of a polynomial form from the taxonomy of Freeman, Scott and Teske. Second, we investigate subgroup membership testing for $\mathbb{G}_1$ and $\mathbb{G}_2$. We fix a proof argument for the $\mathbb{G}_2$ case that appeared in a preprint by Scott in late 2021 and has recently been implemented in different cryptographic libraries. We then generalize the result to both $\mathbb{G}_1$ and $\mathbb{G}_2$ and apply it to different pairing-friendly families of curves. This gives a simple and shared framework to prove membership tests for both cryptographic subgroups.

1 Introduction

A pairing is a bilinear map from two groups $\mathbb{G}_1, \mathbb{G}_2$ into a target group $\mathbb{G}_T$ and is available on dedicated pairing-friendly elliptic curves. $\mathbb{G}_1$ corresponds to a subgroup of prime order r of the elliptic curve over a prime field $\mathbb{F}_q$, $\mathbb{G}_2$ is a distinct subgroup of points of order r, usually over some extension $\mathbb{F}_{q^k}$, and $\mathbb{G}_T$ is the target group in a finite field $\mathbb{F}_{q^k}$, where k is the embedding degree.

preprint version available on ePrint at https://eprint.iacr.org/2022/352 and HAL at https://hal.inria.fr/hal-03608264, SageMath verification script at https://gitlab.inria.fr/zk-curves/cofactor.

L. Batina and J. Daemen (Eds.): AFRICACRYPT 2022, LNCS 13503, pp. 518–536, 2022.
https://doi.org/10.1007/978-3-031-17433-9_22

The choices of pairing-friendly curves of prime order over $\mathbb{F}_q$ are limited to the MNT curves (Miyaji, Nakabayashi, Takano) of embedding degree 3, 4, or 6, Freeman curves of embedding degree 10, and Barreto–Naehrig curves of embedding degree 12. Because of the new NFS variant of Kim and Barbulescu, Gaudry, and Kleinjung (TNFS), the discrete logarithm problem in extension fields $\mathrm{GF}(q^k)$ is not as hard as expected, and key sizes and pairing-friendly curve recommendations are now updated. In this new list of pairing-friendly curves, BN curves are no longer the best choice in any circumstances. The widely deployed curve is now the BLS12-381 curve: a Barreto–Lynn–Scott curve of embedding degree 12, with a subgroup of 255-bit prime order, defined over a 381-bit prime field. The parameters of this curve have a polynomial form, and in particular, the cofactor has a square term: $c_1(x) = (x - 1)^2/3$ were x is the seed $-(2^{63} + 2^{62} + 2^{60} + 2^{57} + 2^{48} + 2^{16})$.

One important cryptographic operation is to hash from a (random) string to a point on the elliptic curve. This operation has two steps: first mapping a string to a point $P(x, y)$ on the curve, then multiplying the point by the cofactor so that it falls into the cryptographic subgroup. For the first step, there is the efficient Elligator function for curves with j-invariant not 0 nor 1728 and having a point of order 4. For other curves including BLS curves of j-invariant 0, Wahby and Boneh propose an efficient map in [14]. Because the BLS12-381 curve is not of prime order, the point is multiplied by the cofactor c_1 to ensure the hash function to map into the cryptographic subgroup of 255-bit prime order. Wahby and Boneh wrote in [14] that it is sufficient to multiply by $(x - 1)$, instead of the cofactor $(x - 1)^2/3$. They observed that for any prime factor ℓ of $(x - 1)$, the BLS12-381 curve has no point of order ℓ^2. Finally in [8] the authors show that for all BLS curves, the curve cofactor contains the square form $(x - 1)^2/3$ and it is enough to multiply by $(x - 1)$ to clear this factor, instead of $(x - 1)^2/3$, thanks to a theorem of Schoof [11].

Other pairing-friendly curves are investigated to replace the BN curves, and at CANS'2020, Clarisse, Duquesne and Sanders revisited Brezing-Weng curves and showed that curves of embedding degree 13 and 19 are competitive for fast operations on the curve (in the first group $\mathbb{G}_1$). Again, a fast multiplication by the curve cofactor is important to provide a fast hashing to the curve.

Another important operation is to test whether a given point belongs to the right subgroup of order r, i.e. $\mathbb{G}_1$ or $\mathbb{G}_2$. This is a crucial operation to avoid small subgroups attacks. In late 2021, Scott in the preprint [12] investigated subgroup membership testing in $\mathbb{G}_1, \mathbb{G}_2$ and $\mathbb{G}_T$ for BLS12 curves and discussed the generalization of the results to other BLS curves. Given a point on a curve $E(\mathbb{F}_q)$ or on a degree-d twisted curve E' defined over an extension of degree k/d, the question is whether the point is of prime order r. This test can be done much faster if an efficient endomorphism is available, which is usually the case for pairing-friendly curves. Budrato and Pintore showed that computing a general formula of the eigenvalue modulo the cofactor is not always well-defined at all primes [6].

Contributions. In this paper, we first apply El Housni and Guillevic technique [8] for cofactor clearing to other pairing-friendly constructions listed in the taxonomy paper of Freeman, Scott and Teske [9]. We show that it applies to many polynomial families: all curves of the constructions numbered 6.2 to 6.7, except for the cases $k \equiv 2, 3 \bmod 6$ of Construction 6.6 that generalizes the BLS curves. We provide a SageMath verification script at

https://gitlab.inria.fr/zk-curves/cofactor

Next, we fix a proof argument in the paper [12] for $\mathbb{G}_2$ membership test and generalize the result. This gives a simple and shared framework to prove both $\mathbb{G}_1$ and $\mathbb{G}_2$ membership tests.

Organization of the Paper. Section 2 provides preliminaries on pairing-friendly curves and associated subgroups and endomorphisms. In Sect. 3, we investigate the cofactor clearing technique for different polynomial constructions in [9]. In Sect. 4, we revisit some previously known results on subgroup membership and propose a simple criterion for these tests. We conclude in Sect. 5.

2   Preliminaries

Let E be an elliptic curve $y^2 = x^3 + ax + b$ defined over a field $\mathbb{F}_q$, where q is a prime or a prime power. Let π_q be the Frobenius endomorphism:

$$\pi_q : E(\overline{\mathbb{F}_q}) \to E(\overline{\mathbb{F}_q})$$
$$(x, y) \mapsto (x^q, y^q) \quad (\text{and } \mathcal{O} \mapsto \mathcal{O}) .$$

Its minimal polynomial is $X^2 - tX + q$ where t is called the *trace*. Let r be a prime divisor of the curve order $\#E(\mathbb{F}_q) = q + 1 - t = c_1 r$. The r-torsion subgroup of E is denoted $E[r] := \{P \in E(\overline{\mathbb{F}_q}), [r]P = \mathcal{O}\}$ and has two subgroups of order r (eigenspaces of π_q in $E[r]$) that are useful for pairing applications. We define the two groups $\mathbb{G}_1 = E[r] \cap \ker(\pi_q - [1])$, and $\mathbb{G}_2 = E[r] \cap \ker(\pi_q - [q])$. The group $\mathbb{G}_2$ is defined over $\mathbb{F}_{q^k}$, where the embedding degree k is the smallest integer $k \in \mathbb{N}^*$ such that $r \mid q^k - 1$. A pairing e is a bilinear map $\mathbb{G}_1 \times \mathbb{G}_2 \to \mathbb{G}_T$ where $\mathbb{G}_T$ is the *target* group of r-th roots of unity in $\mathbb{F}_{q^k}$.

It is also important to recall some results with respect to the complex multiplication (CM) discriminant $-D$. When $D = 3$ (resp. $D = 4$), the curve has CM by $\mathbb{Q}(\sqrt{-3})$ (resp. $\mathbb{Q}(\sqrt{-1})$) so that twists of degrees 3 and 6 exist (resp. 4). When E has d-th order twists for some $d \mid k$, then $\mathbb{G}_2$ is isomorphic to $E'[r](\mathbb{F}_{q^{k/d}})$ for some twist E'. Otherwise, in the general case, E admits a single twist (up to isomorphism) and it is of degree 2. We denote c_2 the $\mathbb{G}_2$ cofactor, *i.e.* $\#E'(\mathbb{F}_{q^{k/d}}) = c_2 r$.

When $D = 3$, the curve has a j-invariant 0 and is of the form $y^2 = x^3 + b$ ($a = 0$). In this case, an efficient endomorphism ϕ exist on $\mathbb{G}_1$. Given β a cube root of unity in $\mathbb{F}_q$,

$$\phi : E(\mathbb{F}_q)[r] \to E(\mathbb{F}_q)[r]$$
$$(x, y) \mapsto (\beta x, y) \quad (\text{and } \mathcal{O} \mapsto \mathcal{O}) .$$

ϕ has a minimal polynomial $X^2 + X + 1$ and an eigenvalue λ satisfying $\lambda^2 + \lambda + 1 \equiv 0 \mod r$. When $D = 1$, the curve has j-invariant 1728 and is of the form $y^2 = x^3 + ax$ ($b = 0$). In this case an efficient endomorphism σ exist on $\mathbb{G}_1$. Given $i \in \mathbb{F}_q$ such that $i^2 = -1$,

$$\sigma : E(\mathbb{F}_q)[r] \to E(\mathbb{F}_q)[r]$$
$$(x, y) \mapsto (-x, iy) \quad (\text{and } \mathcal{O} \mapsto \mathcal{O}) .$$

On $\mathbb{G}_2$, an efficient endomorphism is ψ the "untwist-Frobenius-twist" introduced in [10]. ψ has a minimal polynomial $X^2 - tX + q$ and is defined by

$$\psi : E'[r](\mathbb{F}_{q^{k/d}}) \to E'[r](\mathbb{F}_{q^{k/d}})$$
$$(x, y) \mapsto \xi^{-1} \circ \pi_q \circ \xi(x, y) \quad (\text{and } \mathcal{O} \mapsto \mathcal{O}) .$$

where ξ is the twisting isomorphism from E' to E. When $D = 3$, there are actually two sextic twists, one with $q + 1 - (-3f + t)/2$ points on it, the other with $q + 1 - (3f + t)/2$, where $f = \sqrt{(4q - t^2)/3}$. Only one of these is the "right" twist, i.e. has an order divisible by r. Let ν be a quadratic and cubic non-residue in $\mathbb{F}_{q^{k/d}}$ and $X^6 - \nu$ an irreducible polynomial, the "right" twist is either $y^2 = x^3 + b/\nu$ (D-type twist) or $y^2 = x^3 + b\nu$ (M-type twist). For the D-type, $\xi : E' \to E : (x, y) \mapsto (\nu^{1/3}x, \nu^{1/2}y)$ and ψ becomes

$$\psi : (x, y) \mapsto (\nu^{(q-1)/3}x^q, \nu^{(q-1)/2}y^q) \quad (\text{and } \mathcal{O} \mapsto \mathcal{O}) .$$

For the M-type, $\xi : E' \to E : (x, y) \mapsto (\nu^{2/3}x/\nu, \nu^{1/2}y/\nu)$ and ψ becomes

$$\psi : (x, y) \mapsto (\nu^{(-q+1)/3}x^q, \nu^{(-q+1)/2}y^q) \quad (\text{and } \mathcal{O} \mapsto \mathcal{O}) .$$

For other d-twisting ξ formulae, see [13].

Most of pairing-friendly curves fall into polynomial families, i.e. the curves parameters are expressed as polynomials $q(x), r(x)$ and $t(x)$. These polynomials are then evaluated in a "seed" u to derive a given curve (cf. Sect. 3).

3   Polynomial Families of Pairing-Friendly Curves, and Faster Co-factor Clearing

3.1   Faster Co-factor Clearing

We recall the result on cofactor clearing from [8]. Let $\text{End}_{\mathbb{F}_q}(E)$ denote the ring of $\mathbb{F}_q$-endomorphisms of E, let $\mathcal{O}$ denotes a complex quadratic order of the ring of integers of a complex quadratic number field, and $\mathcal{O}(\Delta)$ denotes the complex quadratic order of discriminant Δ.

Theorem 1 ([11, **Proposition 3.7**]). *Let E be an elliptic curve over $\mathbb{F}_q$ and $n \in \mathbb{Z}_{\geq 1}$ with $q \nmid n$. Let π_q denote the Frobenius endomorphism of E of trace t. Then,*

$$E[n] \subset E(\mathbb{F}_q) \iff \begin{cases} n^2 \mid \#E(\mathbb{F}_q), \\ n \mid q - 1 \text{ and} \\ \pi_q \in \mathbb{Z} \text{ or } \mathcal{O}\left(\frac{t^2 - 4q}{n^2}\right) \subset \text{End}_{\mathbb{F}_q}(E). \end{cases}$$

We will apply this theorem to the polynomial families of the taxonomy paper of Freeman, Scott and Teske [9]. The families are designed for specific discriminants $D = 1$ for constructions 6.2, 6.3 and 6.4, $D = 3$ for construction 6.6 and some of the KSS families, $D = 2$ for construction 6.7. First we identify a common cofactor within the family which has a square factor, then we compute its gcd with $q(x) - 1$ and $y(x)$. We summarize our results in the following tables and provide a SageMath verification script at https://gitlab.inria.fr/zk-curves/cofactor.

3.2　Construction 6.6

The family of pairing-friendly BLS curves appeared in [2]. A BLS curve can have an embedding degree k multiple of 3 but not 18. Common examples are $k = 9, 12, 15, 24, 27, 48$. A generalization was given in [9] and named Construction 6.6. Let k be a positive integer with $k \leq 1000$ and $18 \nmid k$. Construction 6.6 is given in Table 1. Then (t, r, q) parameterizes a complete family of pairing-friendly curves with embedding degree k and discriminant 3. Next, in Table 2, we compute the cofactor polynomial $c_1(x)$ for Construction 6.6 family. We recall that $y(x)$ satisfies the Complex Multiplication equation $4q(x) = t(x)^2 + Dy(x)^2$.

Table 1. Construction 6.6 from [9, Sect. 6], formulas for $k = 9, 15$ mod 18 from ePrint.

k	$r(x)$	$t(x)$	$y(x)$	$q(x)$	x mod 3
1 mod 6	$\Phi_{6k}(x)$	$-x^{k+1}+x+1$	$(-x^{k+1}+2x^k-x-1)/3$	$(x+1)^2(x^{2k}-x^k+1)/3-x^{2k+1}$	2
2 mod 6	$\Phi_{3k}(x)$	$x^{k/2+1}-x+1$	$(x^{k/2+1}+2x^{k/2}+x-1)/3$	$(x-1)^2(x^k-x^{k/2}+1)/3+x^{k+1}$	1
3 mod 18	$\Phi_{2k}(x)$	$x^{k/3+1}+1$	$(-x^{k/3+1}+2x^{k/3}+2x-1)/3$	$(x^2-x+1)^2(x^{2k/3}-x^{k/3}+1)/3+x^{k/3+1}$	2
9,15 mod 18	$\Phi_{2k}(x)$	$-x^{k/3+1}+x+1$	$(-x^{k/3+1}+2x^{k/3}-x-1)/3$	$(x+1)^2(x^{2k/3}-x^{k/3}+1)/3-x^{2k/3+1}$	2
4 mod 6	$\Phi_{3k}(x)$	x^3+1	$(x^3-1)(2x^{k/2}-1)/3$	$(x^3-1)^2(x^k-x^{k/2}+1)/3+x^3$	1
5 mod 6	$\Phi_{6k}(x)$	$x^{k+1}+1$	$(-x^{k+1}+2x^k+2x-1)/3$	$(x^2-x+1)(x^{2k}-x^k+1)/3+x^{k+1}$	2
0 mod 6	$\Phi_k(x)$	$x+1$	$(x-1)(2x^{k/6}-1)/3)$	$(x-1)^2(x^{k/3}-x^{k/6}+1)/3+x$	1

To prove the results of Table 2, we will need some basic polynomial results that we prove in Lemmas 1, 2, 3, and 4.

Lemma 1. *Over the field of rationals* $\mathbb{Q}$, $\Phi_d(x)$ *denotes the d-th cyclotomic polynomial, and for all the distinct divisors d of n including 1 and n,*

$$x^n - 1 = \prod_{d|n} \Phi_d(x) .\tag{1}$$

Lemma 2. *For any odd $k \geq 1$ not multiple of 3 ($k \equiv 1, 5$ mod 6), we have*

$$x^2 - x + 1 \mid x^{2k} - x^k + 1 .\tag{2}$$

Proof (of Lemma 2). By Lemma 1, $x^{6k} - 1$ is a multiple of $\Phi_1 = x - 1$, $\Phi_2 = x + 1$, $\Phi_3 = x^2 + x + 1$ and $\Phi_6 = x^2 - x + 1$. Since

$$x^{6k} - 1 = (x^{3k} - 1)(x^{3k} + 1) = (x^k - 1)(x^{2k} + x^k + 1)(x^k + 1)(x^{2k} - x^k + 1)$$

and $\Phi_1\Phi_3 \mid x^{3k} - 1$ but $\Phi_6 \nmid x^{3k} - 1$ because k is odd, nor $x^k + 1$ because k is not multiple of 3, then $\Phi_6 = x^2 - x + 1$ should divide the other term $x^{2k} - x^k + 1$.

Lemma 3. *For any odd $k \geq 1$ such that $(k \equiv 1 \bmod 6)$, we have*

$$x^2 - x + 1 \mid x^{k+1} - x + 1 \quad and \quad x^2 - x + 1 \mid x^{k+1} - 2x^k + x + 1 . \tag{3}$$

Proof (of Lemma 3). Let $\omega, \overline{\omega} \in \mathbb{C}$ be the two primitive 6-th roots of unity that are the two roots of $x^2 - x + 1$. Since $k \equiv 1 \bmod 6$ and $\omega^6 = \overline{\omega}^6 = 1$, then $\omega^k = \omega$, $\overline{\omega}^k = \overline{\omega}$, $\omega^{k+1} = \omega^2$ and $\overline{\omega}^{k+1} = \overline{\omega}^2$. Then $\omega^{k+1} - \omega + 1 = \omega^2 - \omega + 1 = 0$ and $\overline{\omega}^{k+1} - \overline{\omega} + 1 = \overline{\omega}^2 - \overline{\omega} + 1 = 0$. Hence $\omega, \overline{\omega}$ are roots of $x^{k+1} - x + 1$ and $x^2 - x + 1$ divides $x^{k+1} - x + 1$. Similarly, $\omega^{k+1} - 2\omega^k + \omega + 1 = \omega^2 - 2\omega + \omega + 1 = 0$ and the same holds for $\overline{\omega}$. We conclude that $x^2 - x + 1$ divides $x^{k+1} - 2x^k + x + 1$.

Lemma 4. *For any odd $k \geq 1$ such that $(k \equiv 5 \bmod 6)$, we have*

$$x^2 - x + 1 \mid x^{k+1} - 2x^k - 2x + 1 . \tag{4}$$

Proof (of Lemma 4). Let $\omega, \overline{\omega} \in \mathbb{C}$ be the two primitive 6-th roots of unity that are the two roots of $x^2 - x + 1$. Similarly as in the proof of Lemma 3, since $k \equiv 5 \bmod 6$ and $\omega^3 = -1$, $\omega^6 = 1$, then $\omega^{k+1} = 1$, $\omega^k = \omega^5 = -\omega^2$. Then $\omega^{k+1} - 2\omega^k - 2\omega + 1 = 1 - 2(-\omega^2) - 2\omega + 1 = 2\omega^2 - 2\omega + 2 = 0$. The same holds for $\overline{\omega}$, and we conclude that $x^2 - x + 1$ divides $x^{k+1} - 2x^k - 2x + 1$.

Table 2. Cofactors of construction 6.6 families

k	$q(x) + 1 - t(x)$	$c_0(x)$	$\gcd(c_0(x), q(x) - 1)$	$\gcd(c_0(x), y(x))$
1 mod 6	$(x^{2k} - x^k + 1)(x^2 - x + 1)/3$	$(x^2 - x + 1)^2/3$	$x^2 - x + 1$	$(x^2 - x + 1)/3$
2 mod 6	$(x^k - x^{k/2} + 1)(x^2 + x + 1)/3$	$(x^2 + x + 1)/3$	1	1
3 mod 18	$(x^{2k/3} - x^{k/3} + 1)(x^2 - x + 1)^2/3$	$(x^2 - x + 1)^2/3$	1	1
9 mod 18	$(x^{2k/3} - x^{k/3} + 1)(x^2 - x + 1)/3$	$(x^2 - x + 1)/3$	1	1
15 mod 18	$(x^{2k/3} - x^{k/3} + 1)(x^2 - x + 1)/3$	$(x^2 - x + 1)^2/3$	1	1
4 mod 6	$(x^k - x^{k/2} + 1)(x^3 - 1)^2/3$	$(x^3 - 1)^2/3$	$x^3 - 1$	$(x^3 - 1)/3$
5 mod 6	$(x^{2k} - x^k + 1)(x^2 - x + 1)/3$	$(x^2 - x + 1)^2/3$	$x^2 - x + 1$	$(x^2 - x + 1)/3$
0 mod 6	$(x^{k/3} - x^{k/6} + 1)(x - 1)^2/3$	$(x - 1)^2/3$	$x - 1$	$(x - 1)/3$

Proof (of Table 2). For $k = 1 \bmod 6$, one computes

$$q(x) + 1 - t(x) = (x + 1)^2(x^{2k} - x^k + 1)/3 - x^{2k+1} + 1 - (-x^{k+1} + x + 1)$$
$$= (x + 1)^2(x^{2k} - x^k + 1)/3 - x(x^{2k} - x^k + 1)$$
$$= (x^{2k} - x^k + 1)(x^2 - x + 1)/3 .$$

By Lemma 2, $(x^2 - x + 1)$ divides $x^{2k} - x^k + 1$ since $k \equiv 1 \bmod 6$. Note that for $x \equiv 2 \bmod 3$, $x^2 - x + 1 \equiv 0 \bmod 3$. Hence the cofactor is a multiple of $c_0(x) = (x^2 - x + 1)^2/3$. Next, one computes

$$q(x) - 1 = \underbrace{(x+1)^2}_{=(x^2-x+1)+3x}(x^{2k} - x^k + 1)/3 - x^{2k+1} - 1$$

$$=(x^2 - x + 1)(x^{2k} - x^k + 1)/3 + x(x^{2k} - x^k + 1) - x^{2k+1} - 1$$

$$=(x^2 - x + 1)(x^{2k} - x^k + 1)/3 - (x^{k+1} - x + 1)$$

and by Lemma 3, $x^2 - x + 1$ divides $x^{k+1} - x + 1$. We computed the derivative of $q(x) - 1$ and checked that none of $\omega, \overline{\omega}$ is a zero of the derivative. Finally, $x^2 - x + 1$ divides $q(x) - 1$ with multiplicity one. To conclude, Lemma 3 ensures that $(x^2 - x + 1)$ divides $y(x)$, and we checked that the derivative of $y(x)$ does not vanish at a primitive sixth root of unity, hence $x^2 - x + 1$ divides $y(x)$ with multiplicity one.

For $k = 2 \bmod 6$, one computes

$$q(x) + 1 - t(x) = (x - 1)^2(x^k - x^{k/2} + 1)/3 + x^{k+1} + 1 - (x^{k/2+1} - x + 1)$$

$$=(x^2 - 2x + 1)(x^k - x^{k/2} + 1)/3 + x(x^k - (x^{k/2} + 1)$$

$$=(x^k - x^{k/2} + 1)(x^2 + x + 1)/3$$

Note that k is even. Lemma 2 will apply for $k' = k/2$ to be odd, that is $k \equiv 2 \bmod 12$. Nevertheless the cofactor $c_0(x)$ will not be a square. We checked that none of the primitive cubic and sextic roots of unity are roots of $q(x) - 1$ nor $y(x)$, hence the gcd of $c_0(x)$ and $q(x) - 1$, resp. $y(x)$, is 1.

For $k = 3 \bmod 18$, it is straightforward to get $q(x) + 1 - t(x) = (x^2 - x + 1)^2(x^{2k/3} - x^{k/3} + 1)/3$, the cofactor $c_0(x) = (x^2 - x + 1)^2/3$ is a square as for $k = 1 \bmod 6$. For $k = 9, 15 \bmod 18$, we compute

$$q(x) + 1 - t(x) = (x + 1)^2(x^{2k/3} - x^{k/3} + 1)/3 - x^{2k/3+1} + 1 - (-x^{k/3+1} + x + 1)$$

$$=(x^2 + 2x + 1)(x^{2k/3} - x^{k/3} + 1)/3 - x(x^{2k/3} - x^{k/3} + 1)$$

$$=(x^2 - x + 1)(x^{2k/3} - x^{k/3} + 1)/3$$

For $k = 9 \bmod 18$, $k/3$ is a multiple of 3 and $x^2 - x + 1$ does not divide $(x^{2k/3} - x^{k/3} + 1)$, while for $k = 15 \bmod 18$, $k/3$ is co-prime to 6, and $(x^{2k/3} - x^{k/3} + 1)$ is a multiple of $(x^2 - x + 1)$ by Lemma 2. For $k \equiv 3, 9, 15 \bmod 18$, we checked that neither $q(x) - 1$ nor $y(x)$ have a common factor with $c_0(x)$, and no faster co-factor clearing is available.

For $k \equiv 4, 0 \bmod 6$, the calculus is similar to the case $k \equiv 1 \bmod 6$, and for $k \equiv 5 \bmod 6$, we use Lemma 4 to conclude about $y(x)$.

For the cases $k \equiv 2 \bmod 6$ and $k \equiv 9 \bmod 18$, $c_1(x)$ has no square factor and thus the cofactor clearing is already optimised. For $k \equiv 3, 15 \bmod 18$, the cofactor is a square but Theorem 1 does not apply. For all remaining cases, $c_1(x) = n(x)^2/3$ for some polynomial factor $n(x)/3$ that satisfies Theorem 1. Hence, it is sufficient to multiply by $n(x)$ to clear the cofactor on Construction 6.6 curves. We summarize our results in Theorem 2.

Theorem 2. *For $k \equiv 1, 5 \bmod 6$, the curve cofactor has a factor $c_0(x) = (x^2 - x + 1)^2/3$, whose structure is $\mathbb{Z}/(x^2 - x + 1)/3\mathbb{Z} \times \mathbb{Z}/(x^2 - x + 1)\mathbb{Z}$, and it is enough to multiply by $n(x) = (x^2 - x + 1)$ to clear the co-factor $c_0(x)$.*

For $k \equiv 4 \bmod 6$, the curve cofactor has a factor $c_0(x) = (x^3 - 1)^2/3$, whose structure is $\mathbb{Z}/(x^3 - 1)/3\mathbb{Z} \times \mathbb{Z}/(x^3 - 1)\mathbb{Z}$, and it is enough to multiply by $n(x) = (x^3 - 1)$ to clear the co-factor $c_0(x)$.

For $k \equiv 0 \bmod 6$, the curve cofactor has a factor $c_0(x) = (x - 1)^2/3$, whose structure is $\mathbb{Z}/(x - 1)/3\mathbb{Z} \times \mathbb{Z}/(x - 1)\mathbb{Z}$, and it is enough to multiply by $n(x) = (x - 1)$ to clear the co-factor $c_0(x)$.

Proof (of Theorem 2). From Table 2, $k = 1, 5 \bmod 6$ has $n(x) = (x^2 - x + 1)/3$, $k = 4 \bmod 6$ has $n(x) = (x^3 - 1)/3$, $k = 0 \bmod 6$ has $n(x) = (x - 1)/3$ where $n(x)$ satisfies the conditions of Theorem 1. The n-torsion is $\mathbb{F}_q$-rational, that is $E[n] \subset E(\mathbb{F}_q)$ and has structure $\mathbb{Z}/n\mathbb{Z} \times \mathbb{Z}/n\mathbb{Z}$ over $\mathbb{F}_q$. Taking into account the co-factor 3, the structure of the subgroup of order $c_0(x) = 3n^2(x)$ is $\mathbb{Z}/3n\mathbb{Z} \times \mathbb{Z}/n\mathbb{Z}$ and multiplying by $3n(x)$ clears the cofactor.

Example. In [7], Clarisse, Duquesne and Sanders introduced two new pairing-friendly curves with optimal $\mathbb{G}_1$, the curves BW13-P310 with seed $u = -\text{0x8b0}$ and BW19-P286 with seed $v = -\text{0x91}$. They fall in Construction 6.6 with $k = 1 \bmod 6$. Our faster co-factor clearing method applies.

For BW13-P310, the prime subgroup order is $r = \Phi_{6 \cdot 13}(u) = (u^{26} - u^{13} + 1)/(u^2 - u + 1)$. The cofactor is $(u^2 - u + 1)^2/3$, where $(u^2 - u + 1)$ divides $q(u) - 1$ and $(u^2 - u + 1)/3$ divides $y(u)$. It is enough to multiply by $(u^2 - u + 1)$ to clear the cofactor.

For BW19-P286, the prime subgroup order is $r = \Phi_{6 \cdot 19}(v) = (v^{38} - v^{19} + 1)/(v^2 - v + 1)$. The cofactor is $(v^2 - v + 1)^2/3$, where $(v^2 - v + 1)$ divides $q(v) - 1$ and $(v^2 - v + 1)/3$ divides $y(v)$. It is enough to multiply by $(v^2 - v + 1)$ to clear the cofactor.

3.3 Constructions 6.2, 6.3, 6.4, and 6.5 with $D = 1$

The constructions with numbers 6.2 to 6.5 have discriminant $D = 1$, we report the polynomial forms of the parameters in Table 3. The cofactor $c_1(x)$ in $q(x) + 1 - t(x) = r(x)c_1(x)$ has always a factor $c_0(x)$ that we report in Table 4, with special cases for $k = 2$ and $k = 4$. For $q(x)$ to be an integer, $x \equiv 1 \bmod 2$ is required, except for 6.5 where x is required to be even.

Table 3. Constructions 6.2, 6.3, 6.4, and 6.5 from [9, Sect. 6]

	k	$r(x)$	$t(x)$	$y(x)$	$q(x)$
6.2	$1 \bmod 2$	$\Phi_{4k}(x)$	$-x^2 + 1$	$x^k(x^2 + 1)$	$(x^{2k+4} + 2x^{2k+2} + x^{2k} + x^4 - 2x^2 + 1)/4$
6.3	$2 \bmod 4$	$\Phi_{2k}(x)$	$x^2 + 1$	$x^{k/2}(x^2 - 1)$	$(x^{k+4} - 2x^{k+2} + x^k + x^4 + 2x^2 + 1)/4$
6.4	$4 \bmod 8$	$\Phi_k(x)$	$x + 1$	$x^{k/4}(x - 1)$	$(x^{k/2+2} - 2x^{k/2+1} + x^{k/2} + x^2 + 2x + 1)/4$
6.5	$k = 10$	$\Phi_{20}(x)$	$-x^6 + x^4 - x^2 + 2$	$x^3(x^2 - 1)$	$(x^{12} - x^{10} + x^8 - 5x^6 + 5x^4 - 4x^2 + 4)/4$

Table 4. Cofactors of constructions 6.2, 6.3, 6.4, and 6.5. Note that $x \equiv 1 \bmod 2$ except for 6.5 where $x \equiv 0 \bmod 2$.

	k	$c_0(x)$	$\gcd(c_0(x), q(x) - 1)$	$\gcd(c_0(x), y(x))$
6.2	1 mod 2	$(x^2 + 1)^3/4$	$x^2 + 1$	$x^2 + 1$
6.3	$k = 2$	$(x^2 - 1)^2/2$	$x^2 - 1$	$x^2 - 1$
6.3	2 mod 4, $k > 2$	$(x^2 - 1)^2(x^2 + 1)/4$	$x^2 - 1$	$x^2 - 1$
6.4	$k = 4$	$(x - 1)^2/2$	$x - 1$	$x - 1$
6.4	4 mod 8, $k > 4$	$(x - 1)^2(x^2 + 1)/4$	$x - 1$	$x - 1$
6.5	$k = 10$	$x^4/4$	x^2	x^3

Lemma 5. *For any odd $k \geq 1$ we have*

$$x^2 + 1 \mid x^{2k} + 1 . \tag{5}$$

Explicitly,

$$x^{2k} + 1 = (x^2 + 1)(1 - x^2 + x^4 - \ldots + \ldots - x^{2k-4} + x^{2k-2}) . \tag{6}$$

Proof. By Lemma 1, $x^{4k} - 1$ is a multiple of $\Phi_1 = x - 1$, $\Phi_2 = x + 1$ and $\Phi_4 = x^2 + 1$. Since $x^{4k} - 1 = (x^{2k} - 1)(x^{2k} + 1)$ and $\Phi_1\Phi_2 \mid x^{2k} - 1$ but $\Phi_4 \nmid x^{2k} - 1$ because k is odd, then $\Phi_4 = x^2 + 1$ should divide the other term $x^{2k} + 1$.

Proof (of Table 4). All families of constructions 6.2 to 6.5 have j-invariant 1728, an a point of order 2 (their order is even).

In Construction 6.2 one has k odd. One gets $q(x) + 1 - t(x) = (x^2 + 1)^2(x^{2k} + 1)/4$, and by Lemma 5, $x^2 + 1$ is a factor of $x^{2k} + 1$, hence $c_0(x) = (x^2 + 1)^3/4$ which is even, divides $q(x) + 1 - t(x)$. The factorization of $q(x) - 1$ is

$$
\begin{aligned}
q(x) - 1 &= (x^{2k}(x^2 + 1)^2 + (x^2 - 1)^2)/4 - 1 \\
&= ((x^4 + 2x^2 + 1)x^{2k} + (x^4 - 2x^2 + 1) - 4)/4 \\
&= ((x^4 - 1)x^{2k} + (2x^2 + 2)x^{2k} + (x^4 - 1) - 2x^2 - 2)/4 \\
&= ((x^4 - 1)(x^{2k} + 1) + 2(x^2 + 1)(x^{2k} - 1))/4 \\
&= (x^4 - 1)(x^{2k} + 1 + 2a(x))/4 \text{ where}
\end{aligned}
$$

$$a(x) = (x^{2k} - 1)/(x^2 - 1) = 1 + x^2 + x^4 + \ldots + x^{2k-2} = \sum_{i=0}^{k-1} x^{2i}$$

and by Lemma 1, $x^{2k} - 1$ is a multiple of $x^2 - 1 = \Phi_1\Phi_2$, and $(x^4 - 1)/2$ divides $q(x) - 1$. More precisely, because x is odd, $4 \mid q(x) - 1$, and

$$q(x) - 1 = 2\underbrace{(x^2 + 1)}_{\text{even}} \underbrace{(x^2 - 1)/4}_{\in \mathbb{Z}} \underbrace{(x^{2k} + 1 + 2a(x))/2}_{\in \mathbb{Z}} .$$

As a consequence, $x^2 + 1$ divides $q(x) - 1$. Finally, $y(x) = x^k(x^2 + 1)$ is a multiple of $x^2 + 1$.

We isolate the case $k = 2$ in Construction 6.3, with parameters $r(x) = \Phi_4(x) = x^2+1$ (even), $t(x) = x^2+1$, $y(x) = x(x^2-1)$, $q(x) = (x^6-x^4+3x^2+1)/4$, $q(x) + 1 - t(x) = (x^2 + 1)(x^2 - 1)^2/4$. We set $r(x) = (x^2 + 1)/2$ and $c_1(x) = (x^2 - 1)^2/2$, $q(x) - 1 = (x^2 - 1)(x^4 + 3)/4$ where $(x^4 + 3)/4$ is an integer. For larger $k = 2 \bmod 4$, one has

$$q(x) + 1 - t(x) = (x^{k+4} - 2x^{k+2} + x^k + x^4 + 2x^2 + 1)/4 + 1 - (x^2 + 1)$$
$$= (x^k(x^2 - 1)^2 + (x^2 + 1)^2 - 4x^2)/4$$
$$= (x^k + 1)(x^2 - 1)^2/4$$

and since k is even, by Lemma 5, $x^2 + 1$ divides $x^k + 1$, hence $c_0(x) = (x^2 + 1)(x^2 - 1)^2/4$ divides the curve order. We compute $q(x) - 1$ and factor it:

$$q(x) - 1 = (x^k(x^2 - 1)^2 + (x^2 + 1)^2)/4 - 1$$
$$= (x^k(x^2 - 1)^2 + (x^2 - 1)^2 + 4x^2 - 4)/4$$
$$= (x^2 - 1)(x^k \underbrace{(x^2 - 1)}_{\text{mult. of } 4} + \underbrace{x^2 - 1}_{\text{mult. of } 4} + 4)/4$$

which proves that $x^2 - 1$ divides $q(x) - 1$. Because $y(x) = x^{k/2}(x^2 - 1)$, it is obvious that $x^2 - 1$ divides $y(x)$.

With Construction 6.4, $k = 4 \bmod 8$. First $k = 4$ is a special case where the curve order is $q(x) + 1 - t(x) = (x - 1)^2(x^2 + 1)/4$, the cofactor is $c_0(x) = (x - 1)^2/2$, $r(x) = (x^2 + 1)/2$, $q(x) - 1 = (x^2 - 1)(x^2 - 2x + 3)/4$ factors as $q(x) - 1 = (x - 1)(x + 1)/2(x^2 - 2x + 3)/2$, and $y(x) = x(x - 1)$.

For larger k, we compute, with $q(x) = (x^{k/2}(x - 1)^2 + (x + 1)^2)/4$,

$$q(x) + 1 - t(x) = (x^{k/2}(x - 1)^2 + (x + 1)^2)/4 + 1 - (x + 1)$$
$$= (x^{k/2}(x - 1)^2 + x^2 + 2x + 1 - 4x)/4$$
$$= (x^{k/2}(x - 1)^2 + (x - 1)^2)/4$$
$$= (x - 1)^2(x^{k/2} + 1)/4$$

and because $k \equiv 4 \bmod 8$, $k/2$ is even and by Lemma 5, $x^2 + 1$ divides $x^{k/2} + 1$, hence $c_0(x) = (x - 1)^2(x^2 + 1)/4$ divides the curve order. Now we compute $q(x) - 1$ and obtain the factorisation

$$q(x) - 1 = (x^{k/2}(x - 1)^2 + (x + 1)^2)/4 - 1$$
$$= (x^{k/2}(x - 1)^2 + x^2 - 2x + 1 + 4x - 4)/4$$
$$= (x^{k/2}(x - 1)^2 + (x - 1)^2 + 4(x - 1))/4$$
$$= (x - 1)(x^{k/2}(x - 1) + (x - 1) + 4)/4$$
$$= (x - 1)(\underbrace{(x^{k/2} + 1)(x - 1)}_{\text{mult. of } 4} + 4)/4$$

hence $x - 1$ divides $q(x) - 1$. Finally $y(x) = x^{k/4}(x - 1)$ and $(x - 1)$ divides $y(x)$.

For construction 6.5, x is even this time, the curve order is $q(x) + 1 - t(x) = x^4/4(x^8 - x^6 + x^4 - x^2 + 1)$, $y(x) = x^3(x^2 - 1)$, $q(x) - 1 = x^2(x^{10} - x^8 + x^6 - 5x^4 + 5x^2 - 4)/4$ were the factor $(x^{10} - x^8 + x^6 - 5x^4 + 5x^2 - 4)/4$ is an integer whenever x is even.

From Table 4 and Theorem 1, we obtain Theorem 3.

Theorem 3. *For construction 6.2, the curve cofactor has a factor $c_0(x) = (x^2 + 1)^3/4$, whose structure is $\mathbb{Z}/(x^2 + 1)/2\mathbb{Z} \times \mathbb{Z}/(x^2 + 1)^2/2\mathbb{Z}$, and it is enough to multiply by $n(x) = (x^2 + 1)^2/2$ to clear the co-factor $c_0(x)$.*

For construction 6.3, the curve cofactor has a factor $c_0(x) = (x^2 - 1)^2(x^2 + 1)/4$, whose structure is $\mathbb{Z}/(x^2 - 1)/2\mathbb{Z} \times \mathbb{Z}/((x^2 - 1)(x^2 + 1)/2\mathbb{Z}$, and it is enough to multiply by $n(x) = (x^2 - 1)(x^2 + 1)/2$ to clear the co-factor $c_0(x)$.

For construction 6.4, the curve cofactor has a factor $c_0(x) = (x - 1)^2(x^2 + 1)/4$, whose structure is $\mathbb{Z}/(x - 1)/2\mathbb{Z} \times \mathbb{Z}/(x - 1)(x^2 + 1)/2\mathbb{Z}$, and it is enough to multiply by $n(x) = (x - 1)(x^2 + 1)/2$ to clear the co-factor $c_0(x)$.

For construction 6.5, the curve order has cofactor $c_0(x) = x^4/4$, whose structure is $\mathbb{Z}/x^2/2\mathbb{Z} \times \mathbb{Z}/x^2/2\mathbb{Z}$, and it is enough to multiply by $n(x) = x^2/2$ to clear the cofactor.

3.4 Construction 6.7 with $D = 2$

Construction 6.7 in [9] has discriminant $D = 2$. We report the polynomial forms of the parameters in Table 5. The cofactor $c_1(x)$ in $q(x) + 1 - t(x) = r(x)c_1(x)$ has always a factor $c_0(x)$ that we report in Table 6. For $q(x)$ to be an integer, $x \equiv 1 \bmod 2$ is required, and $x \equiv 1 \bmod 4$ for $k \equiv 0 \bmod 24$.

Table 5. Construction 6.7 from [9, Sect. 6].

6.7, $k = 0 \bmod 3$, $\ell = \mathrm{lcm}(8, k)$
$r(x) = \Phi_\ell(x)$
$t(x) = x^{\ell/k} + 1$
$y(x) = (1 - x^{\ell/k})(x^{5\ell/24} + x^{\ell/8} - x^{\ell/24})/2$
$q(x) = (2(x^{\ell/k} + 1)^2 + (1 - x^{\ell/k})^2(x^{5\ell/24} + x^{\ell/8} - x^{\ell/24})^2)/8$

Table 6. Cofactor of construction 6.7. Note that $x \equiv 1 \bmod 2$, except for $k \equiv 0 \bmod 24$, where $x \equiv 1 \bmod 4$.

	k	$c_0(x)$	$\gcd(c_0(x), q(x) - 1)$	$\gcd(c_0(x), y(x))$
6.7	0 mod 3	$(x^{\ell/k} - 1)^2/8$	$(x^{\ell/k} - 1)/2$	$(x^{\ell/k} - 1)/2$

Proof (of Table 6). We compute

$$q(x) + 1 - t(x) = (2(x^{\ell/k} + 1)^2 + (1 - x^{\ell/k})^2(x^{5\ell/24} + x^{\ell/8} - x^{\ell/24})^2)/8 + 1 - (x^{\ell/k} + 1)$$
$$= (2(x^{\ell/k} + 1)^2 - 8x^{\ell/k} + (1 - x^{\ell/k})^2(x^{\ell/24}(x^{4\ell/24} + x^{2\ell/24} - 1))^2)/8$$
$$= (2(x^{\ell/k} - 1)^2 + (x^{\ell/k} - 1)^2 x^{\ell/12}(x^{\ell/6} + x^{\ell/12} - 1)^2)/8$$
$$= (x^{\ell/k} - 1)^2(x^{\ell/12}(x^{\ell/6} + x^{\ell/12} - 1)^2 + 2)/8$$

and for $q(x) - 1$ we obtain

$$q(x) - 1 = (2(x^{\ell/k} + 1)^2 - 8 + (x^{\ell/k} - 1)^2(x^{\ell/12}(x^{\ell/6} + x^{\ell/12} - 1)^2))/8$$
$$q(x) - 1 = (2(x^{\ell/k} - 1)^2 + 8x^{\ell/k} - 8 + (x^{\ell/k} - 1)^2(x^{\ell/12}(x^{\ell/6} + x^{\ell/12} - 1)^2))/8$$
$$q(x) - 1 = (x^{\ell/k} - 1)(8 + (x^{\ell/k} - 1)(2 + x^{\ell/12}(x^{\ell/6} + x^{\ell/12} - 1)^2)/8$$

It is straightforward to see that $(x^{\ell/k} - 1)/2$ divides $y(x)$.

From Table 6 and Theorem 1, we obtain Theorem 4.

Theorem 4. *For construction 6.7, let $\ell = \mathrm{lcm}(k, 8)$. The curve cofactor has a factor $c_0(x) = (x^{\ell/k} - 1)^2/8$, whose structure is $\mathbb{Z}/(x^{\ell/k} - 1)/4\mathbb{Z} \times \mathbb{Z}/(x^{\ell/k} - 1)/2\mathbb{Z}$, and it is enough to multiply by $n(x) = (x^{\ell/k} - 1)/2$ to clear the co-factor $c_0(x)$.*

3.5   Other Constructions

We also investigated the KSS curves named Constructions 6.11, 6.12, 6.13, 6.14, 6.15 in [9], and the KSS-54 curve of 2018, but none of the cofactors is a square, and the gcd of the cofactor and $q(x) - 1$, resp. $y(x)$, is equal to 1. Hence our faster co-factor clearing does not apply.

4   Subgroup Membership Testing

For completeness, we first state the previously known membership tests for $\mathbb{G}_1$ [5,12] and $\mathbb{G}_T$ [1,8,12] for BLS curves. Next, we show that the proof argument for the $\mathbb{G}_2$ test in [12] is incomplete and provide a fix and a generalization.

For the sequel, we recall that the curves of interest have a j-invariant 0 and are equipped with efficient endomorphisms ϕ on $\mathbb{G}_1$ and ψ on $\mathbb{G}_2$ (see Sect. 2).

4.1 $\mathbb{G}_1$ and $\mathbb{G}_T$ Membership

Given a point $P \in E(\mathbb{F}_q)$, Scott [12, Sect. 6] proves by contradiction that for BLS12 curves it is sufficient to verify that $\phi(P) = -u^2 P$ where $-u^2$ is the eigenvalue λ of ϕ. A similar test was already proposed in a preprint by Bowe [5, Sect. 3.2] for the BLS12-381: $((u^2 - 1)/3)(2\phi'(P) - P - \phi'^2(P)) - \phi'^2(P) = \mathcal{O}$ (where ϕ' here is ϕ^2). This boils down to exactly $\phi(P) = -u^2 P$ using $\phi^2(P) + \phi(P) + P = \mathcal{O}$ and $\lambda^2 + \lambda + 1 \equiv 0 \mod r$ ($u^4 \equiv u^2 - 1 \mod r$). However, the proof uses a tautological reasoning, as reproached by Scott [12, footnote p. 6], because it replaces λP by $\phi(P)$ where P is a point yet to be proven of order r.

For $w \in \mathbb{G}_T$ membership test, Scott [12] hinted that it is sufficient on BLS12 curves to verify that $w^{q^4 - q^2 + 1} = 1$ (cyclotomic subgroup test) and that $w^q = w^u$. This was based on a personal communication with the authors of [8] who proved the proposition for any pairing- friendly curve. They also implemented this test for some BLS12 and BLS24 curves in [4] prior to Scott's pre-print. The same test also appears in [1] without a proof.

4.2 $\mathbb{G}_2$ Membership

Following [12, Sect. 4], let $E(\mathbb{F}_q)$ be an elliptic curve of j-invariant 0 and embedding degree $k = 12$. Let E' be the sextic twist of E defined over $\mathbb{F}_{q^{k/d}} = \mathbb{F}_{q^2}$, and ψ the "untwist-Frobenius-twist" endomorphism with the minimal polynomial

$$\chi(X) = X^2 - tX + q \tag{7}$$

Let $Q \in E'(\mathbb{F}_{q^2})$. We have $\gcd(q + 1 - t, \#E'(\mathbb{F}_{q^2})) = r$. To check if Q is in $E'(\mathbb{F}_{q^2})[r]$, it is therefore sufficient to verify that

$$[q + 1 - t]Q = \mathcal{O}$$

Since $[q] = -\psi^2 + [t] \circ \psi$ from Eq. (7), the test to perform becomes

$$\psi \circ ([t]Q - \psi(Q)) + Q - [t]Q = 0 . \tag{8}$$

It is an efficient test since ψ is fast to evaluate and $[t]Q$ can be computed once and cheaper than $[r]Q$. For BLS12 curves $t = u + 1$ and the test to perform becomes in [12, Sect. 4] the quadratic equation

$$\psi(uQ) + \psi(Q) - \psi^2(Q) = uQ$$

So far, the only used fact is $\chi(\psi) = 0$, which is true everywhere. So the reasoning is correct and we have

$$\psi(uQ) + \psi(Q) - \psi^2(Q) = uQ \implies Q \in E'(\mathbb{F}_{q^2})[r]$$

However the preprint [12, Sect. 4] goes further and writes that the quadratic equation has only two solutions, $\psi(Q) = Q$ and $\psi(Q) = uQ$. Since ψ does not act trivially on $E'(\mathbb{F}_{q^2})$ the conclusion is

$$\psi(Q) = uQ \implies Q \in E'(\mathbb{F}_{q^2})[r] \tag{9}$$

The Issue. The previous property is, by luck, true as we will show later (Sect. 4.3). However, the overall reasoning is flawed, because it circles back to the fact that ψ acts as the multiplication by u on $\mathbb{G}_2$, while we are trying to prove that Q is in $\mathbb{G}_2$. This is the same kind of tautological reasoning reproached in the footnote of Scott's preprint [12]. This reasoning implicitly supposes ψ acts as the multiplication by u only on $E'(\mathbb{F}_{q^2})[r]$, and therefore that this action characterizes $E'(\mathbb{F}_{q^2})[r]$. However, $E'(\mathbb{F}_{q^2})[r]$ might not be the only subgroup of $E'(\mathbb{F}_{q^2})$ on which ψ has the eigenvalue u. Indeed, if a prime number ℓ divides the cofactor c_2 and $\chi(u) = 0 \bmod \ell$, it is possible that, on $E'(\mathbb{F}_{q^2})[\ell]$, ψ acts as the multiplication by u, for instance if $E'(\mathbb{F}_{q^2})[\ell]$ contains the eigenspace associated to u. So the implication (9) is true, provided that no such prime exists.

The Solution. The implication (9) becomes true if we know that there is no other subgroup of $E'(\mathbb{F}_{q^2})$ on which ψ acts as the multiplication by u. To make sure of this, it is enough to check that $\chi(u) \neq 0 \bmod \ell_i$ for all primes ℓ_i dividing c_2. If that is the case, we know that ψ acts as the multiplication by u only on $E'(\mathbb{F}_{q^2})[r]$. Using the Chinese Remainder Theorem it gives the following criterion:

Proposition 1. *If ψ acts as the multiplication by u on $E'(\mathbb{F}_{q^2})[r]$ and $\gcd(\chi(u), c_2) = 1$ then*

$$\psi(Q) = [u]Q \implies Q \in E'(\mathbb{F}_{q^2})[r] \ .$$

Note that checking the gcd of the polynomials $\chi(\lambda(X))$ and $c_2(X)$ is not sufficient and one needs to check the gcd of the integers, that are evaluations of the polynomials at u. In fact, $\gcd(\chi(\lambda(X)), c_2(X)) = 1$ in $\mathbb{Q}[X]$ only means that there is a relation $A\chi(\lambda) + Bc_2 = 1$ where $A, B \in \mathbb{Q}[X]$. The seeds u are chosen so that $\chi(\lambda(u)), c_2(u)$ are integers, but it might not be the case for $A(u)$ and $B(u)$. If d is the common denominator of the coefficients of A and B, we can only say that for a given seed u, $\gcd(\chi(u), c_2(u)) \mid d$. Therefore, we have to take care of the "exceptional seeds" u such that $\gcd(\chi(u), c_2(u))$ is a proper divisor of d.

4.3   A Generalisation of $\mathbb{G}_1$ and $\mathbb{G}_2$ Membership Tests

Proposition 1 can be generalized to both $\mathbb{G}_1$ and $\mathbb{G}_2$ groups for any polynomial-based family of elliptic curves (e.g. BLS, BN, KSS). Let $\tilde{E}(\mathbb{F}_{\tilde{q}})$ be a family of elliptic curves (i.e. it can be $E(\mathbb{F}_q)$ or $E'(\mathbb{F}_{q^{k/d}})$ for instance). Let $\mathbb{G}$ be a cryptographic group of $\tilde{E}$ of order r equipped with an efficient endomorphism $\tilde{\phi}$. It has a minimal polynomial $\tilde{\chi}$ and an eigenvalue $\tilde{\lambda}$. Let c be the cofactor of $\mathbb{G}$. Proposition 1 becomes then

Proposition 2. *If $\tilde{\phi}$ acts as the multiplication by $\tilde{\lambda}$ on $\tilde{E}(\mathbb{F}_{\tilde{q}})[r]$ and $\gcd(\tilde{\chi}(\tilde{\lambda}), c) = 1$ then*

$$\tilde{\phi}(Q) = [\tilde{\lambda}]Q \implies Q \in \tilde{E}(\mathbb{F}_{\tilde{q}})[r] \ .$$

Examples

Example 1. (BN[3]). Let $E(\mathbb{F}_{q(x)})$ define the BN pairing-friendly family. It is parameterized by

$$q(x) = 36x^4 + 36x^3 + 24x^2 + 6x + 1$$
$$r(x) = 36x^4 + 36x^3 + 18x^2 + 6x + 1$$
$$t(x) = 6x^2 + 1$$

and $E(\mathbb{F}_{q(x)})$ has a prime order so $c_1 = 1$. The cofactor on the sextic twist $E'(\mathbb{F}_{q^2})$ is $c = c_2$

$$c_2(x) = q(x) - 1 + t(x)$$
$$= 36x^4 + 36x^3 + 30x^2 + 6x + 1 .$$

On $\mathbb{G} = \mathbb{G}_2 = E'(\mathbb{F}_{q^2})[r]$, $\tilde{\phi} = \psi$ (the "untwist-Frobenius-twist") has a minimal polynomial $\tilde{\chi} = \chi$ and an eigenvalue $\tilde{\lambda} = \lambda$

$$\chi = X^2 - tX + q$$
$$\lambda = 6X^2 .$$

We have $\gcd(c_2, \chi(\lambda)) = \gcd(c_2(X), \chi(6X^2)) = 1$, and running the extended Euclidean algorithm we find a relation $Ac_2 + B\chi(\lambda) = 1$ where $A, B \in \mathbb{Q}[X]$. The common denominator of the coefficients of A and B is $d = 2$. We now look at the congruence relations the seed u should satisfy so that $\chi(\lambda(u))$ and $c_2(u)$ are both divisible by 2: those will be the exceptional seeds, under which the implication (9) could be false. Since c_2 is always odd there is no exceptional seeds and we obtain:

Proposition 3. *For the BN family, if $Q \in E'(\mathbb{F}_{q^2})$,*

$$\psi(Q) = [u]Q \implies Q \in E'(\mathbb{F}_{q^2})[r] .$$

Example 2 (BLS12 [2]). The BLS12 parameters are:

$$q(x) = (x - 1)^2/3 \cdot r(x) + x$$
$$r(x) = x^4 - x^2 + 1$$
$$t(x) = x + 1 .$$

On $\mathbb{G} = \mathbb{G}_1 = E(\mathbb{F}_p)[r]$, the endomorphism $\tilde{\phi} = \phi$ has minimal polynomial $\tilde{\chi} = \chi$ and eigenvalue $\tilde{\lambda} = \lambda$ as follows:

$$\chi = X^2 + X + 1$$
$$\lambda = -X^2 .$$

We have $c = c_1 = (X - 1)^2/3$. Running the extended Euclidean algorithm on c_1 and $\chi(\lambda)$, we find a relation $Ac_1 + B\chi(\lambda) = 1$ in $\mathbb{Q}[X]$. In fact, here A and B are in $\mathbb{Z}[X]$, so there are no exceptional cases: for any acceptable seed u, $\gcd(c_1(u), \chi(\lambda(u))) = 1$, so we retrieve the result from Scott's paper [12]:

Proposition 4. *For the BLS12 family, if $Q \in E(\mathbb{F}_p)$,*

$$\phi(Q) = [-u^2]Q \implies Q \in E(\mathbb{F}_p)[r] \ .$$

On $\mathbb{G} = \mathbb{G}_2 = E'(\mathbb{F}_{q^2})[r]$, $\tilde{\phi} = \psi$ (the "untwist-Frobenius-twist") has a minimal polynomial $\tilde{\chi} = \chi$ and an eigenvalue $\tilde{\lambda}$, where

$$\chi = X^2 - tX + q$$
$$\lambda = X \ .$$

The $\mathbb{G}_2$ cofactor is $c = c_2$

$$c_2(x) = (x^8 - 4x^7 + 5x^6 - 4x^4 + 6x^3 - 4x^2 - 4x + 13)/9 \ .$$

We have $\gcd(c_2, \chi(\lambda)) = 1$ and running the extended Euclidean algorithm we find a relation $Ac_2 + B\chi(\lambda) = 1$ where $A, B \in \mathbb{Q}[X]$. The common denominator of the coefficients of A and B is $3 \cdot 181$. We look at what congruence properties the seed u should have so that $\chi(\lambda(u))$ and $c_2(u)$ are both divisible by 181 or 3 to rule out the exceptional cases (as before, with those seeds, the implication (9) could be false). We find that there is no seed u such that $3 \mid c_2(u)$. Furthermore, the seeds u such that $181 \mid \chi(\lambda(u))$ and $181 \mid c_2(u)$ are such that $u \equiv 7 \bmod 181$ and in that case, $181 \mid r(u)$. Therefore there are no exceptional cases as long as r is prime, and we obtain:

Proposition 5. *For the BLS12 family, if $r = r(u)$ is prime and $Q \in E'(\mathbb{F}_{q^2})$,*

$$\psi(Q) = [u]Q \implies Q \in E'(\mathbb{F}_{q^2})[r] \ .$$

Example 3 (BLS24[2]). The BLS24 family is parameterized by

$$q(x) = (x-1)^2/3 \cdot r(x) + x$$
$$r(x) = x^8 - x^4 + 1$$
$$t(x) = x + 1 \ .$$

On $\mathbb{G} = \mathbb{G}_1 = E(\mathbb{F}_p)[r]$, the endomorphism $\tilde{\phi} = \phi$ has minimal polynomial $\tilde{\chi} = \chi$ and eigenvalue $\tilde{\lambda} = \lambda$, where

$$\chi = X^2 + X + 1$$
$$\lambda = -X^4 \ .$$

We have $c = c_1 = (X-1)^2/3$. Running the extended Euclidean algorithm on c_1 and $\chi(\lambda)$, we find a relation $Ac_1 + B\chi(\lambda) = 1$ in $\mathbb{Q}[X]$. As for BLS12, A and B are in $\mathbb{Z}[X]$, so there are no exceptional cases, and we have

Proposition 6. *For the BLS24 family, if $Q \in E(\mathbb{F}_p)$,*

$$\phi(Q) = [-u^4]Q \implies Q \in E(\mathbb{F}_p)[r] \ .$$

On $\mathbb{G} = \mathbb{G}_2 = E'(\mathbb{F}_{q^4})[r]$, $\tilde{\phi} = \psi$, the "untwist-Frobenius-twist" has a minimal polynomial $\tilde{\chi} = \chi$ and an eigenvalue $\tilde{\lambda} = \lambda$, where

$$\chi = X^2 - tX + q$$
$$\lambda = X .$$

The cofactor on the sextic twist $E'(\mathbb{F}_{q^4})$ is $c = c_2$

$$c_2(x) = (x^{32} - 8x^{31} + 28x^{30} - 56x^{29} + 67x^{28} - 32x^{27} - 56x^{26} + 160x^{25} - 203x^{24} + 132x^{23}$$
$$+ 12x^{22} - 132x^{21} + 170x^{20} - 124x^{19} + 44x^{18} - 4x^{17} + 2x^{16} + 20x^{15} - 46x^{14} + 20x^{13}$$
$$+ 5x^{12} + 24x^{11} - 42x^{10} + 48x^9 - 101x^8 + 100x^7 + 70x^6 - 128x^5 + 70x^4 - 56x^3$$
$$- 44x^2 + 40x + 100)/81 .$$

We have $\gcd(c_2, \chi(\lambda)) = 1$. Running the extended Euclidean algorithm on c_2 and $\chi(\lambda)$, we find a relation $Ac_2 + B\chi(\lambda) = 1$ where the common denominator of the coefficients of A and B is $3^5 \times 1038721$. As before, we find that there is no seed u such that $3 \mid c_2(u)$. Moreover, the seeds u such that $1038721 \mid c_2(u)$ and $1038721 \mid \chi(\lambda)$ are such that $u = 162316 \bmod 1038721$. In this case $1038721 \mid r(u)$ and hence there are no exceptional cases. We obtain:

Proposition 7. *For the BLS24 family, if $r = r(u)$ is prime and $Q \in E'(\mathbb{F}_{q^4})$, then*

$$\psi(Q) = [u]Q \implies Q \in E'(\mathbb{F}_{q^4})[r] .$$

Example 4 (BLS48 [2]). The BLS48 family is parametrised by

$$q(x) = (x-1)^2/3 \cdot r(x) + x$$
$$r(x) = x^{16} - x^8 + 1$$
$$t(x) = x + 1 .$$

On $\mathbb{G} = \mathbb{G}_1 = E(\mathbb{F}_p)[r]$, the endomorphism $\tilde{\phi} = \phi$ has minimal polynomial $\tilde{\chi} = \chi$ and eigenvalue $\tilde{\lambda} = \lambda$, where

$$\chi = X^2 + X + 1$$
$$\lambda = -X^8 .$$

We have $c = c_1 = (X-1)^2/3$. Running the extended Euclidean algorithm on c_1 and $\chi(\lambda)$, we find a relation $Ac_1 + B\chi(\lambda) = 1$ in $\mathbb{Q}[X]$. As for BLS12 and BLS24, A and B are in $\mathbb{Z}[X]$, so there are no exceptional cases, and we have

Proposition 8. *For the BLS48 family, if $Q \in E(\mathbb{F}_p)$,*

$$\phi(Q) = [-u^8]Q \implies Q \in E(\mathbb{F}_p)[r] .$$

On $\mathbb{G} = \mathbb{G}_2 = E'(\mathbb{F}_{q^8})[r]$, $\tilde{\phi} = \psi$, the "untwist-Frobenius-twist" has a minimal polynomial $\tilde{\chi} = \chi$ and an eigenvalue $\tilde{\lambda} = \lambda$, where

$$\chi = X^2 - tX + q$$
$$\lambda = X .$$

The cofactor on the sextic twist $E'(\mathbb{F}_{q^8})$ is $c = c_2 = (p^8(x) + 1 - (3y_8(x) + t_8(x))/2)/r(x)$

$$c_2(x) = (x^{128} - 16x^{127} + 120x^{126} - 560x^{125} + \cdots + 6481)/6561 .$$

We have $\gcd(c_2, \chi(\lambda)) = 1$. Running the extended Euclidean algorithm on c_2 and $\chi(\lambda)$, we find a relation $Ac_2 + B\chi(\lambda) = 1$ where the common denominator of the coefficients of A and B is $1153 \times 4726299241057$. We now look at the congruence relations the seed u should satisfy so that $\chi(\lambda(u))$ and $c_2(u)$ are both divisible either by 1153 or 4726299241057: Those will be the exceptional seeds, under which the implication (9) could be false. We note U_{p_i} the set of values of $u \bmod p_i$ such that $\chi(\lambda)(x) = 0 \bmod p_i$ and similarly V_{p_i} the set of values of $u \bmod p_i$ such that $c_2(u) = 0 \bmod p_i$.

$$p_i = 1153 : \qquad U_{1153} \cap V_{1153} = \{1135\}$$
$$p_i = 4726299241057 : U_{4726299241057} \cap V_{4726299241057} = \{2085225345771\}$$

For the exceptional seeds $u \equiv 1135 \bmod 1153$ and $u \equiv 2085225345771 \bmod 4726299241057$, we need to check that $\gcd(\chi(\lambda)(u), c_2(u)) = 1$ over the integer instances (i.e. for the concrete values of x). However, in both cases r is not a prime. So we have

Proposition 9. *For the BLS48 family, if $r = r(u)$ is prime and $Q \in E'(\mathbb{F}_{q^8})$,*

$$\psi(Q) = [u]Q \implies Q \in E'(\mathbb{F}_{q^8})[r] .$$

5   Conclusion

Cofactor clearing and subgroup membership tests are two important operations in many pairing-based protocols. In this work, we generalized and proved a technique for cofactor clearing to many pairing-friendly constructions. We gave a simple criterion to prove both $\mathbb{G}_1$ and $\mathbb{G}_2$ membership tests after fixing an incomplete proof of a $\mathbb{G}_2$ test that was recently widely deployed in cryptographic libraries. These operations are now provably fast for different pairing-friendly curves which consequently speeds up many cryptographic protocols. This also gives more flexibility to find curves with nice properties at the expense of composite cofactors.

References

1. Aranha, D.F., Pagnin, E., Rodríguez-Henríquez, F.: LOVE a pairing. In: Longa, P., Ràfols, C. (eds.) LATINCRYPT 2021. LNCS, vol. 12912, pp. 320–340. Springer, Cham (2021). https://doi.org/10.1007/978-3-030-88238-9_16
2. Barreto, P.S.L.M., Lynn, B., Scott, M.: Constructing elliptic curves with prescribed embedding degrees. In: Cimato, S., Persiano, G., Galdi, C. (eds.) SCN 2002. LNCS, vol. 2576, pp. 257–267. Springer, Heidelberg (2003). https://doi.org/10.1007/3-540-36413-7_19

3. Barreto, P.S.L.M., Naehrig, M.: Pairing-friendly elliptic curves of prime order. In: Preneel, B., Tavares, S. (eds.) SAC 2005. LNCS, vol. 3897, pp. 319–331. Springer, Heidelberg (2006). https://doi.org/10.1007/11693383_22

4. Botrel, G., Piellard, T., Housni, Y.E., Tabaie, A., Kubjas, I.: Consensys/gnark-crypto (2022). https://doi.org/10.5281/zenodo.6092968

5. Bowe, S.: Faster subgroup checks for BLS12-381. Cryptology ePrint Archive, Report 2019/814 (2019). https://eprint.iacr.org/2019/814

6. Budroni, A., Pintore, F.: Efficient hash maps to $\mathbb{G}_2$ on bls curves. Appl. Algebra Eng. Commun. Comput. **33**, 261–281 (2022). https://doi.org/10.1007/s00200-020-00453-9, ePrint https://eprint.iacr.org/2017/419

7. Clarisse, R., Duquesne, S., Sanders, O.: Curves with fast computations in the first pairing group. In: Krenn, S., Shulman, H., Vaudenay, S. (eds.) CANS 2020. LNCS, vol. 12579, pp. 280–298. Springer, Cham (2020). https://doi.org/10.1007/978-3-030-65411-5_14

8. El Housni, Y., Guillevic, A.: Families of SNARK-friendly 2-chains of elliptic curves. In: Dunkelman, O., Dziembowski, S. (eds.) EUROCRYPT 2022. LNCS, vol. 13276, pp. 367–396. Springer, Cham (2022). https://doi.org/10.1007/978-3-031-07085-3_13

9. Freeman, D., Scott, M., Teske, E.: A taxonomy of pairing-friendly elliptic curves. J. Cryptol. **23**(2), 224–280 (2010). https://doi.org/10.1007/s00145-009-9048-z

10. Galbraith, S.D., Scott, M.: Exponentiation in pairing-friendly groups using homomorphisms. In: Galbraith, S.D., Paterson, K.G. (eds.) Pairing 2008. LNCS, vol. 5209, pp. 211–224. Springer, Heidelberg (2008). https://doi.org/10.1007/978-3-540-85538-5_15

11. Schoof, R.: Nonsingular plane cubic curves over finite fields. J. Comb. Theor Series A **46**(2), 183–211 (1987). https://doi.org/10.1016/0097-3165(87)90003-3

12. Scott, M.: A note on group membership tests for $\mathbb{G}_1$, $\mathbb{G}_2$ and $\mathbb{G}_T$ on BLS pairing-friendly curves. ePrint https://eprint.iacr.org/2021/1130d 2021/1130

13. Scott, M.: A note on twists for pairing friendly curves (2009). http://indigo.ie/mscott/twists.pdf

14. Wahby, R.S., Boneh, D.: Fast and simple constant-time hashing to the BLS12-381 elliptic curve. IACR TCHES, **2019**(4), 154–179 (2019). https://doi.org/10.13154/tches.v2019.i4.154-179

A Generalized Attack on the Multi-prime Power RSA

Abderrahmane Nitaj[1(✉)], Willy Susilo[2], and Joseph Tonien[2]

[1] Normandie Univ, UNICAEN, CNRS, LMNO, 14000 Caen, France
abderrahmane.nitaj@unicaen.fr
[2] Institute of Cybersecurity and Cryptology, School of Computing and Information
Technology, University of Wollongong, Wollongong, Australia
{willy.susilo,joseph.tonien}@uow.edu.au

Abstract. The Multi-Prime Power RSA is an efficient variant of the
RSA cryptosystem with a modulus of the form $N = p^r q^s$ and $r > s \geq 2$.
It can be used with a public exponent e and a private exponent d satisfying $e \equiv \frac{1}{d} \pmod{p^{r-1} q^{s-1} (p-1)(q-1)}$. In 2017, Lu, Peng and Sarkar
showed that one can factor the modulus $N = p^r q^s$ if $d < N^{1 - \frac{3r+s}{(r+s)^2}}$. In
this paper, we propose a generalization of this attack to the situation
where the public exponent e is of the form $e \equiv \frac{z_0}{x_0} \pmod{p^{r-1} q^{s-1} (p-1)(q-1)}$. We show that for $x_0 = N^\delta$ and $|z_0| = N^\gamma$, one can factor
the modulus $N = p^r q^s$ if $\delta + \gamma < 1 + \frac{2(r-s)}{r(r+s)^2} \sqrt{s(r+s)} - \frac{2(2r-s)}{r(r+s)}$. As a
consequence, our method can break the Multi-Prime Power RSA variant
even if the private exponent d is of arbitrarily large size.

Keywords: RSA · Factorization · Lattice reduction · Coppersmith's
method

1 Introduction

Since its design in 1978, the RSA cryptosystem [18] has attracted much attention
and has been widely used in various public key cryptography applications [2].
In the original RSA, the modulus is an integer of the form $N = pq$ where
p and q are large primes of the same bit-size. For efficiency reasons, several
variants of RSA have been proposed with different moduli. The RSA variants
with a modulus of the form $N = p^r q$ with $r \geq 2$ are called prime power RSA,
while variants with a modulus of the form $N = p^r q^s$ for fixed $r > s \geq 2$ are
called multi prime-power RSA. The simplest modulus $N = p^2 q$ was first used
in 1991 by Fujioka et al. [6]. In 1998, Takagi proposed an RSA variant using
the modulus $N = p^r q$, and in 2000, Lim et al. [11] extended such moduli to
$N = p^r q^s$. The moduli $N = p^r q^s$ have been used to design more systems such as
the Okamoto-Uchiyama cryptosystem [17]. In general, the public exponent is an
integer satisfying $\gcd(e, pq(p-1)(q-1)) = 1$, and the private key is an integer d
such that $ed \equiv 1 \pmod{pq(p-1)(q-1)}$ or $ed \equiv 1 \pmod{p^{r-1} q^{s-1} (p-1)(q-1)}$.

© The Author(s), under exclusive license to Springer Nature Switzerland AG 2022
L. Batina and J. Daemen (Eds.): AFRICACRYPT 2022, LNCS 13503, pp. 537–549, 2022.
https://doi.org/10.1007/978-3-031-17433-9_23

For this case, the correspondent key equation is of the form $ed - kp^{r-1}q^{s-1}(p-1)(q-1) = 1$, and can be solved when d is sufficiently small. In 1998, Takagi [20] showed that one can factor $N = p^r q$ if $d < N^{\frac{1}{2(r+1)}}$, and in 2004, May [15] improved the bound to $d < N^{\max\left(\frac{r}{(r+1)^2}, \frac{(r-1)^2}{(r+1)^2}\right)}$. In 2014, Sarkar [19] improved the bound for $r \le 5$, and in 2015, Lu et al. [12] improved it to $d < N^{\frac{r(r-1)}{(r+1)^2}}$. In 2017, Lu et al. [13] studied the case where $N = p^r q^s$ with $r > s \ge 2$ and showed that one can factor N if $d < N^{1 - \frac{3r+s}{(r+s)^2}}$. Their method is based on Coppersmith's method [3], and is valid for a public key e satisfying $e \equiv \frac{1}{d}$ $(\bmod\ p^{r-1}q^{s-1}(p-1)(q-1))$ with $d < N^{1 - \frac{3r+s}{(r+s)^2}}$.

In this paper, we present a new attack on the Multi-Prime Power RSA moduli $N = p^r q^s$, when the public key e is in the form $e \equiv \frac{z_0}{x_0}$ $(\bmod\ p^{r-1}q^{s-1}(p-1)(q-1))$. Using Coppersmith's method, we show that one can factor N in polynomial time if $x_0 = N^\delta$, $|z_0| = N^\gamma$ and

$$\delta + \gamma < 1 + \frac{2(r-s)}{r(r+s)^2}\sqrt{s(r+s)} - \frac{2(2r-s)}{r(r+s)}.$$

This bound is independent of the size of the private exponent d satisfying $ed \equiv 1$ $(\bmod\ p^{r-1}q^{s-1}(p-1)(q-1))$. As a consequence, our method works even if d is much larger than the upper bound $d < N^{1 - \frac{3r+s}{(r+s)^2}}$ of Lu et al. [13], and can be considered as its generalization. We note that for the RSA cryptosystem with a modulus of the form $N = pq$, Blömer and May [1] studied the public exponents e satisfying $ex - z \equiv 0$ $(\bmod\ (p-1)(q-1))$ for suitably small x and z. Alternatively, such exponents can be rewritten as $e \equiv \frac{z}{x}$ $(\bmod\ (p-1)(q-1))$. For this reason, our attack can also be considered as an extension of the Blömer-May attack.

The rest of this paper is organized as follows. In the next section, we give some preliminaries on Coppersmith's method and lattice basis reduction. In Sect. 3, we present the new attack on the Multi-Prime Power RSA variant. In Sect. 4, we present a detailed experimental example for the attack. In Sect. 5, we give an estimation of the number of exponents that are vulnerable to the new attack. We conclude the paper in Sect. 6.

2   Preliminaries

In 1996, Coppersmith [3] presented a method to find the small solutions of a modular polynomial equation with integer coefficients of the form $f(x) \equiv 0$ $(\bmod\ N)$, even when N is of unknown factorization. He also presented a method to find the small roots of a bivariate polynomial with integer coefficients of the form $g(x, y)$. Coppersmith's method is intensively used in cryptanalysis, especially of RSA and its variants [2,8]. Howgrave-Graham [9] and others have proposed various generalizations of Coppersmith's method. The following result due to Howgrave-Graham is often used in Coppersmith's method.

Theorem 1. *Let* $f(x_1, \ldots, x_n) = \sum_{i_1 \cdots i_n} a_{i_1 \cdots i_n} x_1^{i_1} \cdots x_n^{i_n} \in \mathbb{Z}[x_1, \ldots, x_n]$ *be a polynomial with at most* ω *monomials and an Euclidean norm* $\|f(x_1, \ldots, x_n)\| = \sqrt{\sum_{i_1 \cdots i_n} a_{i_1 \cdots i_n}^2}$. *Suppose that*

$$f\left(x_1^{(0)}, \ldots, x_n^{(0)}\right) \equiv 0 \pmod{M},$$

$$\left|x_1^{(0)}\right| < X_1, \ldots, \left|x_n^{(0)}\right| < X_n,$$

$$\|f(x_1 X_1, \ldots, x_n X_n)\| < \frac{M}{\sqrt{\omega}}.$$

Then $f\left(x_1^{(0)}, \ldots, x_n^{(0)}\right) = 0$ *holds over the integers.*

Coppersmith's method uses lattice basis reduction methods such as the LLL algorithm [10]. A lattice $\mathcal{L}$ of dimension ω is a discrete group of the form

$$\mathcal{L} = \left\{ \sum_{i=1}^{\omega} \lambda_i b_i \mid \lambda_i \in \mathbb{Z} \right\},$$

where $b_1, \cdots, b_\omega \in \mathbb{R}^n$ are ω linearly independent vectors with $\omega \leq n$. If B is the matrix formed by the rows of the vectors $b_1, \cdots, b_\omega$, the positive value $\det(\mathcal{L}) = \sqrt{|\det(BB^t)|}$ is the determinant of $\mathcal{L}$. A classical and hard problem in the theory of lattices is lattice reduction. The goal of lattice reduction is to find ω linearly independent vectors $b_1, \cdots, b_\omega \in \mathbb{R}^n$ with good properties. In 1982, Lenstra, Lenstra and Lovász [10] proposed a useful polynomial time algorithm, known as the LLL algorithm, which has various properties and applications [16]. Here, we mention one of the properties of the LLL algorithm due to May [14] that will be used in the paper.

Theorem 2. *Let* $\mathcal{L}$ *be a lattice of dimension* ω *spanned by a matrix* B. *The LLL algorithm outputs a reduced basis* $\{v_1, \cdots, v_\omega\}$ *of* $\mathcal{L}$ *in polynomial time satisfying*

$$\|v_1\| \leq \|v_2\| \leq \cdots \leq \|v_i\| \leq 2^{\frac{\omega(\omega-1)}{4(\omega+1-i)}} \det(\mathcal{L})^{\frac{1}{\omega+1-i}},$$

for $1 \leq i \leq \omega$.

To find a solution $\left(x_1^{(0)}, \ldots, x_n^{(0)}\right)$ of the modular equation $f(x_1, \ldots, x_n) \equiv 0 \pmod{M}$ by Coppersmith's method with prescribed bounds $|x_i| < X_i$, one starts by deriving ω polynomials $g_i(x_1, \ldots, x_n)$, $1 \leq i \leq \omega$, having the common solution $\left(x_1^{(0)}, \ldots, x_n^{(0)}\right)$ modulo M. Then, using the coefficients of the polynomials $g_i(X_1 x_1, \ldots, X_n x_n)$, one constructs a matrix B which serves as a basis for a lattice $\mathcal{L}$. By applying the LLL algorithm to B, one gets a reduced basis from which one collects the rows to form ω polynomials $h_i(x_1, \ldots, x_n)$ that share the solution $\left(x_1^{(0)}, \ldots, x_n^{(0)}\right)$ over the integers. Under some conditions on the bounds $X_1, \cdots, X_n$, one can solve a system of polynomial equations to find the target solution $\left(x_1^{(0)}, \ldots, x_n^{(0)}\right)$. This is possible by applying Gröbner basis techniques or resultant calculations if the following widely used assumption is achieved.

Assumption 1. *Let* $h_i(x_1, \ldots, x_n)$, $1 \leq i \leq \omega$, *be the polynomials produced by Coppersmith's algorithm. Then at least* n *of such polynomials are algebraically independent.*

In this paper, the former assumption is supported by experimental results and is always satisfied for suitable parameters.

3   The New Attack

In this section, we present our attack to factor $N = p^r q^s$ with the help of the structure of the public exponent e.

Theorem 3. *Let* $N = p^r q^s$ *be an RSA prime power modulus with* $r > s \geq 2$ *where* p *and* q *are of the same bit-size. Let* e *be a public exponent of the form* $e \equiv \frac{z_0}{x_0} \pmod{p^{r-1}q^{s-1}(p-1)(q-1)}$ *with* $x_0 < N^\delta$ *and* $|z_0| < N^\gamma$. *Then, under Assumption 1, one can factor* N *in polynomial time if* $N \nmid (ex_0 - z_0)$, *and*

$$\delta + \gamma < 1 + \frac{2(r-s)}{r(r+s)^2}\sqrt{s(r+s)} - \frac{2(2r-s)}{r(r+s)}.$$

Proof. Let $N = p^r q^s$ with $r > s \geq 2$. Assume that the public exponent e has the form $e \equiv \frac{z_0}{x_0} \pmod{p^{r-1}q^{s-1}(p-1)(q-1)}$. This can be rewritten as $ex_0 - p^{r-1}q^{s-1}(p-1)(q-1)y_0 = z_0$ for some integer y_0. Hence (x_0, y_0, z_0) is a solution of the modular equation $ex - p^{r-1}q^{s-1}(p-1)(q-1)y = z$. In turn, this can be transformed to $ex - z \equiv 0 \pmod{p^{r-1}q^{s-1}}$. Since $\gcd(e, N) = 1$, then multiplying by $e^{-1} \pmod N$ gives $x + az \equiv 0 \pmod{p^{r-1}q^{s-1}}$ where $a \equiv -e^{-1} \pmod N$. Consider the polynomial $f(x, z) = x + az$. Then $(x, y) = (x_0, y_0)$ is a solution of the modular equation $f(x, z) \equiv 0 \pmod{p^{r-1}q^{s-1}}$.

For integers m, t_1, and t_2 to be fixed later, consider the following polynomials

$$G_{k,i}(x, z) = z^i f(x, z)^k N^{\max\left(0, \left\lceil \frac{(r-1)(t_1-k)}{r}\right\rceil, \left\lceil \frac{(s-1)(t_2-k)}{s}\right\rceil\right)},$$

with $k = 0, \ldots, m$, and $i = 0, \ldots, m - k$. Since $r > s \geq 2$, then $\frac{r-1}{r} > \frac{s-1}{s}$. Moreover, if $t_1 \geq t_2$, then $\frac{(r-1)(t_1-k)}{r} > \frac{(s-1)(t_2-k)}{s}$ and

$$\max\left(0, \left\lceil \frac{(r-1)(t_1-k)}{r}\right\rceil, \left\lceil \frac{(s-1)(t_2-k)}{s}\right\rceil\right) = \max\left(0, \left\lceil \frac{(r-1)(t_1-k)}{r}\right\rceil\right).$$

Consequently, to use $\left\lceil \frac{(r-1)(t_1-k)}{r}\right\rceil$ and $\left\lceil \frac{(s-1)(t_2-k)}{s}\right\rceil$ as possible exponents of N in $G_{k,i}(x, z)$, we need $t_1 < t_2$.
Now, if $t_2 < k$, then

$$\max\left(0, \left\lceil \frac{(r-1)(t_1-k)}{r}\right\rceil, \left\lceil \frac{(s-1)(t_2-k)}{s}\right\rceil\right) = 0,$$

and
$$G_{k,i}(x_0, z_0) \equiv 0 \pmod{p^{(r-1)k} q^{(s-1)k}}$$
$$\equiv 0 \pmod{p^{(r-1)t_1} q^{(s-1)t_2}}.$$

If $t_1 \leq k \leq t_2$, then
$$\max\left(0, \left\lceil \frac{(r-1)(t_1-k)}{r} \right\rceil, \left\lceil \frac{(s-1)(t_2-k)}{s} \right\rceil\right) = \left\lceil \frac{(s-1)(t_2-k)}{s} \right\rceil$$
$$\geq \frac{(s-1)(t_2-k)}{s},$$

and
$$G_{k,i}(x_0, z_0) \equiv 0 \pmod{p^{(r-1)k} q^{(s-1)k} N^{\frac{(s-1)(t_2-k)}{s}}}$$
$$\equiv 0 \pmod{p^{(r-1)t_1} q^{(s-1)k+(s-1)(t_2-k)}}$$
$$\equiv 0 \pmod{p^{(r-1)t_1} q^{(s-1)t_2}}.$$

If $k < t_1$ and $\left\lceil \frac{(r-1)(t_1-k)}{r} \right\rceil \leq \left\lceil \frac{(s-1)(t_2-k)}{s} \right\rceil$, we get
$$\max\left(0, \left\lceil \frac{(r-1)(t_1-k)}{r} \right\rceil, \left\lceil \frac{(s-1)(t_2-k)}{s} \right\rceil\right) = \left\lceil \frac{(s-1)(t_2-k)}{s} \right\rceil,$$

and
$$G_{k,i}(x_0, z_0) \equiv 0 \pmod{p^{(r-1)k} q^{(s-1)k} N^{\left\lceil \frac{(s-1)(t_2-k)}{s} \right\rceil}}$$
$$\equiv 0 \pmod{p^{(r-1)k} q^{(s-1)k} p^{r\left\lceil \frac{(r-1)(t_1-k)}{r} \right\rceil} q^{s\left\lceil \frac{(s-1)(t_2-k)}{s} \right\rceil}}$$
$$\equiv 0 \pmod{p^{(r-1)k+(r-1)(t_1-k)} q^{(s-1)k+(s-1)(t_2-k)}}$$
$$\equiv 0 \pmod{p^{(r-1)t_1} q^{(s-1)t_2}}.$$

Finally, if $k < t_1$ and $\left\lceil \frac{(r-1)(t_1-k)}{r} \right\rceil > \left\lceil \frac{(s-1)(t_2-k)}{s} \right\rceil$, we get
$$\max\left(0, \left\lceil \frac{(r-1)(t_1-k)}{r} \right\rceil, \left\lceil \frac{(s-1)(t_2-k)}{s} \right\rceil\right) = \left\lceil \frac{(r-1)(t_1-k)}{r} \right\rceil,$$

and
$$G_{k,i}(x_0, z_0) \equiv 0 \pmod{p^{(r-1)k} q^{(s-1)k} N^{\left\lceil \frac{(r-1)(t_1-k)}{r} \right\rceil}}$$
$$\equiv 0 \pmod{p^{(r-1)k} q^{(s-1)k} p^{r\left\lceil \frac{(r-1)(t_1-k)}{r} \right\rceil} q^{s\left\lceil \frac{(s-1)(t_2-k)}{s} \right\rceil}}$$
$$\equiv 0 \pmod{p^{(r-1)k+(r-1)(t_1-k)} q^{(s-1)k+(s-1)(t_2-k)}}$$
$$\equiv 0 \pmod{p^{(r-1)t_1} q^{(s-1)t_2}}.$$

This shows that in all cases, we have $G_{k,i}(x_0, z_0) \equiv 0 \pmod{p^{(r-1)t_1} q^{(s-1)t_2}}$.

Let $X = N^\delta$ and $Z = N^\gamma$ be the upper bounds of x_0 and $|z_0|$. We consider the lattice $\mathcal{L}$ generated by the matrix where the rows are spanned by the coefficients of the polynomials $G_{k,i}(xX, zZ)$. In order to make the matrix triangular, we consider the following ordering. A polynomial $G_{k,i}(xX, zZ)$ is prior to a polynomial $G_{k',i'}(xX, zZ)$ if $k < k'$, or if $k = k'$, and $i < i'$. Similarly, a monomial $z^i x^k$ is prior to a monomial $z^{i'} x^{k'}$ if $k < k'$, or if $k = k'$, and $i < i'$. For $m = 4$, $r = 3$, $s = 2$, $t_1 = 3$, and $t_2 = 4$, the matrix of $\mathcal{L}$ is presented in Table 1.

Table 1. The matrix for $m = 4$, $r = 3$, $s = 2$, $t_1 = 3$, and $t_2 = 4$.

$G_{k,i}(x,z)$	1	z	z^2	z^3	z^4	x	xz	xz^2	xz^3	x^2	x^2z	x^2z^2	x^3	x^3z	x^4
$G_{0,0}(x,z)$	N^2	0	0	0	0	0	0	0	0	0	0	0	0	0	0
$G_{0,1}(x,z)$	0	N^2Z	0	0	0	0	0	0	0	0	0	0	0	0	0
$G_{0,2}(x,z)$	0	0	N^2Z^2	0	0	0	0	0	0	0	0	0	0	0	0
$G_{0,3}(x,z)$	0	0	0	N^2Z^3	0	0	0	0	0	0	0	0	0	0	0
$G_{0,4}(x,z)$	0	0	0	0	N^2Z^4	0	0	0	0	0	0	0	0	0	0
$G_{1,0}(x,z)$	0	ZaN^2	0	0	0	N^2X	0	0	0	0	0	0	0	0	0
$G_{1,1}(x,z)$	0	0	Z^2aN^2	0	0	0	N^2XZ	0	0	0	0	0	0	0	0
$G_{1,2}(x,z)$	0	0	0	Z^3aN^2	0	0	0	N^2XZ^2	0	0	0	0	0	0	0
$G_{1,3}(x,z)$	0	0	0	0	Z^4aN^2	0	0	0	N^2XZ^3	0	0	0	0	0	0
$G_{2,0}(x,z)$	0	0	Z^2a^2N	0	0	0	$2XZaN$	0	0	NX^2	0	0	0	0	0
$G_{2,1}(x,z)$	0	0	0	Z^3a^2N	0	0	0	$2Z^2XaN$	0	0	NX^2Z	0	0	0	0
$G_{2,2}(x,z)$	0	0	0	0	Z^4a^2N	0	0	0	$2Z^3XaN$	0	0	NX^2Z^2	0	0	0
$G_{3,0}(x,z)$	0	0	0	Z^3a^3N	0	0	0	$3XZ^2a^2N$	0	0	$3ZX^2aN$	0	NX^3	0	0
$G_{3,1}(x,z)$	0	0	0	0	Z^4a^3N	0	0	0	$3Z^3Xa^2N$	0	0	$3Z^2X^2aN$	0	NX^3Z	0
$G_{4,0}(x,z)$	0	0	0	0	Z^4a^4	0	0	0	$4XZ^3a^3$	0	0	$6Z^2X^2a^2$	0	$4ZX^3a$	X^4

Observe that the matrix of the lattice is triangular and that its determinant is the product of the diagonal terms, that is

$$\det(L) = X^{e_X} Z^{e_Z} N^{e_N}, \tag{1}$$

with

$$e_X = \sum_{k=0}^{m} \sum_{i=0}^{m-k} k = \frac{1}{6}(m+1)(m+2),$$

$$e_Z = \sum_{k=0}^{m} \sum_{i=0}^{m-k} i = \frac{1}{6}(m+1)(m+2).$$

The dimension of the lattice is

$$\omega = \sum_{k=0}^{m} \sum_{i=0}^{m-k} 1 = \frac{1}{2}(m+1)(m+2).$$

Notice that e_X, e_Y, and ω depend only on m. To compute e_N, one needs to fix the exponent $\max\left(0, \left\lceil \frac{(r-1)(t_1-k)}{r} \right\rceil, \left\lceil \frac{(s-1)(t_2-k)}{s} \right\rceil\right)$ of N in the polynomial $G_{k,i}(x, z)$. Let

$$k_0 = \left\lceil \frac{s(r-1)t_1 - r(s-1)t_2}{r-s} \right\rceil,$$

be the smallest integer such that $\left\lceil \frac{(s-1)(t_2-k)}{s} \right\rceil \geq \left\lceil \frac{(r-1)(t_2-k)}{r} \right\rceil$. To be useful, we need $k_0 \geq 0$, which is possible if the condition $t_1 \geq \frac{r(s-1)}{s(r-1)} t_2$ is satisfied. On the other hand, we have

$$\frac{s(r-1)t_1 - r(s-1)t_2}{r-s} \leq \frac{s(r-1)t_1 - r(s-1)t_1}{r-s} = t_1,$$

and $k_0 \leq \lceil t_1 \rceil$. Remember that $t_1 < t_2$. Then,

$$\max\left(0, \left\lceil \frac{(r-1)(t_1-k)}{r} \right\rceil, \left\lceil \frac{(s-1)(t_2-k)}{s} \right\rceil\right)$$

$$= \begin{cases} 0 & \text{if } t_2 \leq k, \\ \left\lceil \dfrac{(s-1)(t_2-k)}{s} \right\rceil & \text{if } k_0 \leq k < t_2, \\ \left\lceil \dfrac{(r-1)(t_1-k)}{r} \right\rceil & \text{if } k < k_0. \end{cases}$$

Using k_0, the exponent e_N can be computed as

$$e_N = \sum_{k=0}^{k_0-1} \sum_{i=0}^{m-k} \left\lceil \frac{(r-1)t_1}{r} \right\rceil + \sum_{k=k_0}^{t_2} \sum_{i=0}^{m-k} \left\lceil \frac{(s-1)t_2}{s} \right\rceil.$$

In average, we take $\left\lceil \frac{(r-1)t_1}{r} \right\rceil = \frac{(r-1)t_1}{r} + \frac{1}{2}$, $\left\lceil \frac{(s-1)t_2}{s} \right\rceil = \frac{(s-1)t_2}{s} + \frac{1}{2}$, and $k_0 = \frac{s(r-1)t_1 - r(s-1)t_2}{r-s} + \frac{1}{2}$. We set $t_1 = \tau_1 m$, and $t_2 = \tau_2 m$. Then, the dominant parts in e_X and e_Z are

$$e_X = e_Z = \frac{1}{6}m^3 + o\left(m^3\right). \tag{2}$$

Similarly, the dominant part in e_N is

$$\begin{aligned} e_N = \frac{r-1}{6r(r-s)^2}\Big(&- s^2(r-1)^2\tau_1^3 + 3rs(s-1)(r-1)\tau_1^2\tau_2 \\ &- 3r^2(s-1)^2\tau_1\tau_2^2 + r(s-1)(rs-2r+s)\tau_2^3 \\ &+ 3s(r-1)(r-s)\tau_1^2 - 6r(s-1)(r-s)\tau_1\tau_2 \\ &+ 3r(s-1)(r-s)\tau_2^2 \Big)m^3 + o(m^3). \end{aligned} \tag{3}$$

The next step consists in applying the LLL algorithm to the lattice $\mathcal{L}$ spanned by the rows of the polynomials $G_{k,i}(xX, zZ)$ for $k = 0, \ldots, m$ and $i = 0, \ldots, m-k$. This gives a new basis whose rows are polynomials of the form $h_j(xX, zZ)$ with $j = 1, \ldots, \omega$ such that $h_j(xX, zZ) \equiv 0 \pmod{p^{(r-1)t_1}q^{(s-1)t_2}}$. By Theorem 2 with $i = 2$, we have

$$\|h_1(xX, zZ)\| \leq \|h_2(xX, zZ)\| \leq 2^{\frac{\omega}{4}} \det(L)^{\frac{1}{\omega-1}}.$$

To combine this with Theorem 1, we set $\|h_2(xX, zZ)\| < \frac{p^{(r-1)t_1}q^{(s-1)t_2}}{\sqrt{\omega}}$. This is possible if

$$2^{\frac{\omega}{4}} \det(L)^{\frac{1}{\omega-1}} < \frac{p^{(r-1)t_1}q^{(s-1)t_2}}{\sqrt{\omega}}.$$

Since p and q are of the same bit size, then $p \approx q \approx N^{\frac{1}{r+s}}$. Plugging this approximation in the former inequality, we get

$$2^{\frac{\omega}{4}} \det(L)^{\frac{1}{\omega-1}} < \frac{N^{\frac{(r-1)t_1+(s-1)t_2}{r+s}}}{\sqrt{\omega}},$$

which leads to

$$\det(\mathcal{L}) < 2^{-\frac{\omega(\omega-1)}{4}} \omega^{-\frac{\omega-1}{2}} N^{\frac{(r-1)t_1+(s-1)t_2}{r+s}(\omega-1)}. \tag{4}$$

Using (1), this becomes

$$X^{e_X} Z^{e_Z} N^{e_N - \frac{(r-1)t_1+(s-1)t_2}{r+s}(\omega-1)} < 2^{-\frac{\omega(\omega-1)}{4}} \omega^{-\frac{\omega-1}{2}}.$$

Still with $t_1 = \tau_1 m$ and $t_2 = \tau_2 m$, the dominant part in $\frac{(r-1)t_1+(s-1)t_2}{r+s}(\omega-1)$ is

$$\frac{(r-1)t_1+(s-1)t_2}{r+s}(\omega-1) = \frac{(r-1)\tau_1+(s-1)\tau_2}{2(r+s)}m^3 + o\left(m^3\right). \tag{5}$$

Using $X = N^\delta$, $Z = N^\gamma$, the inequality (4) can be rewritten as

$$N^{e_X\delta+e_Z\gamma+e_N - \frac{(r-1)t_1+(s-1)t_2}{r+s}(\omega-1)} < 2^{-\frac{\omega(\omega-1)}{4}} \omega^{-\frac{\omega-1}{2}}.$$

Using the approximations in (2), (3), (5), this leads to the inequality

$$\begin{aligned}
&\frac{1}{6}(\delta+\gamma) - \frac{(r-1)^3 s^2}{6r(r-s)^2}\tau_1^3 + \frac{s(r-1)^2(s-1)}{2(r-s)^2}\tau_1^2\tau_2 - \frac{r(s-1)^2(r-1)}{2(r-s)^2}\tau_1\tau_2^2 \\
&+ \frac{(s-1)(r-1)(rs-2r+s)}{6(r-s)^2}\tau_2^3 \\
&+ \frac{s(r-1)^2}{2r(r-s)}\tau_1^2 - \frac{(s-1)(r-1)}{r-s}\tau_1\tau_2 + \frac{(s-1)(r-1)}{2(r-s)}\tau_1^2 \\
&- \frac{(r-1)}{2(r+s)}\tau_1 - \frac{(s-1)}{2(r+s)}\tau_2 \\
&< -\varepsilon_1,
\end{aligned}$$

for a small positive constant

$$\varepsilon_1 = -\frac{\log\left(2^{-\frac{\omega(\omega-1)}{4}} \omega^{-\frac{\omega-1}{2}}\right)}{m^3 \log(N)}.$$

Neglecting ε_1, this gives the upper bound $\delta + \gamma < g(\tau_1, \tau_2)$ where

$$
g(\tau_1, \tau_1) = \frac{(r-1)^3 s^2}{r(r-s)^2}\tau_1^3 - \frac{3s(r-1)^2(s-1)}{(r-s)^2}\tau_1^2\tau_2 + \frac{3r(s-1)^2(r-1)}{(r-s)^2}\tau_1\tau_2^2
$$
$$
- \frac{(s-1)(r-1)(rs-2r+s)}{(r-s)^2}\tau_2^3
$$
$$
- \frac{3s(r-1)^2}{r(r-s)}\tau_1^2 + \frac{6(s-1)(r-1)}{r-s}\tau_1\tau_2 - \frac{3(s-1)(r-1)}{(r-s)}\tau_1^2
$$
$$
+ \frac{3(r-1)}{(r+s)}\tau_1 + \frac{3(s-1)}{(r+s)}\tau_2.
$$

The function $g(\tau_1, \tau_2)$ is optimized if $\frac{\partial g}{\partial \tau_1}(\tau_1, \tau_2) = 0$ and $\frac{\partial g}{\partial \tau_2}(\tau_1, \tau_2) = 0$. Solving the former equations, we get

$$
\tau_1 = 1 - \frac{(r-s)\sqrt{s(r+s)}}{s(r-1)(r+s)}, \qquad \tau_2 = 1.
$$

We note that $\tau_2 > \tau_1 \geq \frac{r(s-1)}{s(r-1)}\tau_2$ and that the two conditions $t_2 > t_1 \geq \frac{r(s-1)}{s(r-1)}t_2$ are fulfilled. Plugging the former values in $g(\tau_1, \tau_2)$, we get

$$
\delta + \gamma < 1 + \frac{2(r-s)}{r(r+s)^2}\sqrt{s(r+s)} - \frac{2(2r-s)}{r(r+s)}.
$$

When the former inequality is satisfied, by using two polynomials $h_1(xX, zZ)$, and $h_2(xX, zZ)$ from the reduced lattice basis, we obtain two polynomials $H_1(x, z)$, $H_2(x, z)$, with the common root (x_0, z_0). Assuming that the two polynomials are independent according to Assumption 1, this common root can be extracted by resultant calculations or by Gröbner basis technique. Using x_0 and z_0, we get $p^{r-1}q^{s-1}(p-1)(q-1)y_0 = ex_0 - z_0$. Since $N \nmid (ex_0 - z_0)$ and $p^{r-1}q^{s-1} \mid (ex_0 - z_0)$, then $\frac{N}{\gcd(N, ex_0 - z_0)}$ will be p, q, or pq. In all cases, this leads to the factorization of N, and terminates the proof. $\qquad\square$

4 Comparison with Former Methods

4.1 Comparison with Factorization Methods

In 2016, Coron et al. [4] presented a method to factor the modulus $N = p^r q^s$ when r is greater than $\log^3 \max(p, q)$. Later, the former method was improved by Coron and Zeitoun [5] to the much smaller bound $r = \Omega(\log q)$. For security and efficiency reasons, the modulus $N = p^r q^s$ should be used with small r and s. As a consequence, for a modulus with significantly small exponent r, the former methods can not be applied.

4.2   Comparison with the Method of Lu et al.

Lu et al. presented in [13] a lattice based method to factor $N = p^r q^s$ when the public key e has the form $e \equiv \frac{1}{d} \pmod{p^{r-1} q^{s-1}(p-1)(q-1)}$ with $d = N^{\delta'}$ and $\delta' < 1 - \frac{3r+s}{(r+s)^2}$. Our method, as described in Sect. 3 is more general since it works for all exponents of the form $e \equiv \frac{z_0}{x_0} \pmod{p^{r-1} q^{s-1}(p-1)(q-1)}$ with $x_0 = N^\delta$, $|z_0| = N^\gamma$ and $\delta + \gamma < 1 + \frac{2(r-s)}{r(r+s)^2}\sqrt{s(r+s)} - \frac{2(2r-s)}{r(r+s)}$. A straightforward calculation shows that the bound $\delta' < 1 - \frac{3r+s}{(r+s)^2}$ is slightly better than ours. However, this happens only in the case $z_0 = 1$. For all other cases, the method of Lu et al. can not be applied, while our method is more suitable. Also, our attack can be applied even if the private exponent d is much larger than the bound $N^{1 - \frac{3r+s}{(r+s)^2}}$. Let us present a small example to prove this.

Example 1. Take the following values

$$r = 3,$$
$$s = 2,$$
$$N = 12083614103031209541588242946758305191998961190930302362618027,$$
$$e = 49407605704839141925737382436732234125326071824959097150124 05.$$

Our attack is suitable to factor N when $x_0 < X = N^\delta$, $|z_0| < Z = N^\gamma$ with

$$\delta + \gamma < 1 + \frac{2(r-s)}{r(r+s)^2}\sqrt{s(r+s)} - \frac{2(2r-s)}{r(r+s)} \approx 0.55.$$

The polynomial is then $f(x, z) = x + az$ where

$$a \equiv -e^{-1} \pmod{N}$$
$$\equiv 66409066437509636958361554506838631885179192657293741617550 22.$$

We apply the method of Sect. 3 to find the small solutions (x_0, z_0) of the modular equation $f(x, z) \equiv 0 \pmod{p^{r-1} q^{s-1}(p-1)(q-1)}$ with the bounds $x_0 < X = \lfloor N^{0.25} \rfloor$, $|z_0| < Z = \lfloor N^{0.30} \rfloor$ so that $0.25 + 0.30 = 0.55$. We also take $m = 6$, $t_1 = \left\lfloor \left(1 - \frac{(r-s)\sqrt{s(r+s)}}{s(r-1)(r+s)}\right) m \right\rfloor = 5$, $t_2 = m = 6$, form the lattice $\mathcal{L}$, and apply the LLL algorithm to $\mathcal{L}$. This outputs a new basis with $\omega = 28$ polynomials. Applying Gröbner basis method with the two first polynomials, we get

$$x_0 = 1575173230751, \quad z_0 = 1265874132723179.$$

Using (x_0, y_0), we get

$$p^{r-1} q^{s-1} = \gcd(N, ex_0 - z_0) = 50676727611924621395836620531580 29097,$$

and

$$pq = \frac{N}{p^{r-1} q^{s-1}} = 2384450352746897329696691.$$

Combining with $N = p^r q^s$, we get finally

$$p = 2125300178867, \quad q = 1121935798273.$$

This enables us to compute the private key d related to e as

$$d \equiv e^{-1} \pmod{p^{r-1} q^{s-1} (p-1)(q-1)}$$
$$\equiv 94717910775308563463367243899785422020977217973881916677681437.$$

We note that $d = N^{\delta'}$ with $\delta' \approx 0.998$ which is much larger than the bound $1 - \frac{3r+s}{(r+s)^2} = 0.56$ for which the method of Lu et al. [13] can be applied. This shows that the method of Lu et al. can not be applied for the former example.

5   Estimating the Number of Weak Keys

In this section, we discuss an estimation of the number of exponents that are vulnerable to our attack.

Let $N = p^r q^s$ be a modulus and $\phi(N) = p^{r-1} q^{s-1} (p-1)(q-1)$. Let x_0 be a positive integer with $x_0 = N^\delta$ and $\gcd(x_0, \phi(N)) = 1$. Let $|z_0|$ be an integer with $z_0 = N^\gamma$ and $N \nmid (ex_0 - z_0)$. Consider the exponent $e \equiv \frac{z_0}{x_0} \pmod{\phi(N)}$. Then, by Theorem 3, e is weak to the new attack if $\delta + \gamma < \beta_0$ where

$$\beta_0 = 1 + \frac{2(r-s)}{r(r+s)^2} \sqrt{s(r+s)} - \frac{2(2r-s)}{r(r+s)}.$$

In Table 2, we list the values of β_0 for $2 \le s < r \le 6$.

Table 2. Values of β_0 for small r and s

(r,s)	$(3,2)$	$(5,2)$	$(4,3)$	$(5,3)$	$(5,4)$	$(6,5)$
β_0	0.5510	0.6345	0.6896	0.7112	0.7630	0.8083

Moreover, the following result gives a comparison between N^{β_0} and $\phi(N)$.

Lemma 1. Let $N = p^r q^s$ be a Multi-Prime Power RSA modulus with $r > s \ge 2$. Let $\phi(N) = p^{r-1} q^{s-1} (p-1)(q-1)$ and $\beta_0 = 1 + \frac{2(r-s)}{r(r+s)^2} \sqrt{s(r+s)} - \frac{2(2r-s)}{r(r+s)}$. Then

$$N^{\beta_0} < \phi(N).$$

Proof. For $p \ge 5$ and $q \ge 5$, we have $p - 1 > \frac{\sqrt{2}}{2} p$ and $q - 1 > \frac{\sqrt{2}}{2} q$. Then

$$\phi(N) = p^{r-1} q^{s-1} (p-1)(q-1) > \frac{1}{2} p^{r-1} q^{s-1} pq = \frac{1}{2} N.$$

To compare N^{β_0} and $\phi(N)$, we set $x = \frac{r}{s} > 1$, and observe that

$$\beta_0 = 1 - \frac{2}{sx(x+1)}\left(2x - 1 - \frac{x-1}{x+1}\sqrt{x+1}\right).$$

A straightforward calculation shows that for $x > 1$, $2x - 1 - \frac{x-1}{x+1}\sqrt{x+1} > 0$. Hence $\beta_0 < 1$, and

$$N^{\beta_0} < \frac{1}{2}N < \phi(N),$$

for sufficiently large N. This terminates the proof. □

Next, we argue that the number of weak exponents to our attack is at least N^{β_0}. Consider $x_0 = 1$, $-N^{\beta_0} < z_0 < 0$, and $e = z_0 + \phi(N)$. Using Lemma 1, we get $0 < \phi(N) - N^{\beta_0} < z_0 + \phi(N) < \phi(N)$, that is $0 < e < \phi(N)$. By Theorem 3, one can find z_0, and since $e - z_0 = \phi(N) < N$, then $N \nmid (e - z_0)$. Hence $\frac{N}{\gcd(N, e-z_0)} = \frac{N}{\gcd(N, \phi(N))} = pq$. This leads to the factorization of N. Consequently, each integer z_0 in the range $-N^{\beta_0} < z_0 < 0$ gives rise to a weak exponent $e = z_0 + \phi(N)$. If we restrict such exponents to the condition $\gcd(e, \phi(N)) = 1$, this is possible when $\gcd(z_0, \phi(N)) = 1$. The number of such z_0 with $-N^{\beta_0} < z_0 < 0$ is approximately $\frac{N^{\beta_0}}{\phi(N)}\phi(\phi(N))$. Using the well known inequality $\phi(n) > \frac{Cn}{\log(\log(n))}$ with a positive constant C (see Theorem 328 of [7]), the number of weak exponents $e = z_0 + \phi(N)$ with $\gcd(e, \phi(N)) = 1$ is approximately

$$\frac{N^{\beta_0}}{\phi(N)}\phi(\phi(N)) > \frac{CN^{\beta_0}\phi(N)}{\phi(N)\log(\log(\phi(N)))} > \frac{CN^{\beta_0}}{\log(\log(N) - \log(2))} = N^{\beta_0 - \varepsilon},$$

where ε is a small positive constant. Obviously, this is a lower bound for the number of weak exponents since every pair of integers (x_0, z_0) with $\gcd(x_0, \phi(N)) = 1$, and $x_0|z_0| < N^{\beta_0}$ gives rise to an exponent e of the form $e \equiv \frac{z_0}{x_0} \pmod{\phi(N)}$, which, with an overwhelming probability satisfies $N \nmid (ex_0 - z_0)$, and consequently is weak to the new attack.

6   Conclusion

In this paper, we have studied the cryptanalysis of the Multi-Prime Power RSA with a modulus $N = p^r q^s$, $r > s \geq 2$. We have considered the situation where the public exponent e is in the form $e \equiv \frac{z_0}{x_0} \pmod{p^{r-1}q^{s-1}(p-1)(q-1)}$. We have showed that one can factor the modulus if x_0 and z_0 are suitably small. Our method works even if the private exponent is arbitrarily large. This generalizes the former small private cryptanalytical attacks on the Multi-Prime Power RSA.

References

1. Blömer, J., May, A.: A generalized wiener attack on RSA. In: Bao, F., Deng, R., Zhou, J. (eds.) PKC 2004. LNCS, vol. 2947, pp. 1–13. Springer, Heidelberg (2004). https://doi.org/10.1007/978-3-540-24632-9_1

2. Boneh, D.: Twenty years of attacks on the RSA cryptosystem. Notices Am. Math. Soc. **46**(2), 203–213 (1999)
3. Coppersmith, D.: Small solutions to polynomial equations, and low exponent RSA vulnerabilities. J. Cryptol. **10**(4), 233–260 (1997)
4. Coron, J.-S., Faugère, J.-C., Renault, G., Zeitoun, R.: Factoring $N = p^r q^s$ for large r and s. In: Sako, K. (ed.) CT-RSA 2016. LNCS, vol. 9610, pp. 448–464. Springer, Cham (2016). https://doi.org/10.1007/978-3-319-29485-8_26
5. Coron, J.S., Zeitoun, R.: Improved factorization of $N = p^r q^s$. Cryptology ePrint Archive, Report 2016/551 (2016). https://ia.cr/2016/551
6. Fujioka, A., Okamoto, T., Miyaguchi, S.: ESIGN: an efficient digital signature implementation for smart cards. In: Davies, D.W. (ed.) EUROCRYPT 1991. LNCS, vol. 547, pp. 446–457. Springer, Heidelberg (1991). https://doi.org/10.1007/3-540-46416-6_38
7. Hardy, G.H., Wright, E.M.: An Introduction to the Theory of Numbers. Oxford University Press, London (1975)
8. Hinek, M.: Cryptanalysis of RSA and Its Variants. Cryptography and Network Security Series, Chapman & Hall/CRC, Boca Raton (2009)
9. Howgrave-Graham, N.: Finding small roots of univariate modular equations revisited. In: Darnell, M. (ed.) Cryptography and Coding 1997. LNCS, vol. 1355, pp. 131–142. Springer, Heidelberg (1997). https://doi.org/10.1007/BFb0024458
10. Lenstra, A.K., Lenstra, H.W., Lovász, L.: Factoring polynomials with rational coefficients. Math. Ann. **261**, 513–534 (1982)
11. Lim, S., Kim, S., Yie, I., Lee, H.: A generalized Takagi-cryptosystem with a modulus of the form $p^r q^s$. In: Roy, B., Okamoto, E. (eds.) INDOCRYPT 2000. LNCS, vol. 1977, pp. 283–294. Springer, Heidelberg (2000). https://doi.org/10.1007/3-540-44495-5_25
12. Lu, Y., Zhang, R., Peng, L., Lin, D.: Solving linear equations modulo unknown divisors: revisited. In: Iwata, T., Cheon, J.H. (eds.) ASIACRYPT 2015. LNCS, vol. 9452, pp. 189–213. Springer, Heidelberg (2015). https://doi.org/10.1007/978-3-662-48797-6_9
13. Lu, Y., Peng, L., Sarkar, S.: Cryptanalysis of an RSA variant with moduli $N = p^r q^l$. J. Math. Cryptol. **11**(2), 117–130 (2017)
14. May, A.: New RSA vulnerabilities using lattice reduction methods. Ph.D. thesis, University of Paderborn (2003). https://www.cits.rub.de/imperia/md/content/may/paper/bp.ps
15. May, A.: Secret exponent attacks on RSA-type schemes with moduli $N = p^r q$. In: Bao, F., Deng, R., Zhou, J. (eds.) PKC 2004. LNCS, vol. 2947, pp. 218–230. Springer, Heidelberg (2004). https://doi.org/10.1007/978-3-540-24632-9_16
16. Nguyen, P.Q., Vallée, B.: The LLL Algorithm: Survey and Applications. Information Security and Cryptography, Springer, Heidelberg (2010)
17. Okamoto, T., Uchiyama, S.: A new public-key cryptosystem as secure as factoring. In: Nyberg, K. (ed.) EUROCRYPT 1998. LNCS, vol. 1403, pp. 308–318. Springer, Heidelberg (1998). https://doi.org/10.1007/BFb0054135
18. Rivest, R., Shamir, A., Adleman, L.: A method for obtaining digital signatures and public-key cryptosystems. Commun. ACM **21**(2), 120–126 (1978)
19. Sarkar, S.: Small secret exponent attack on RSA variant with modulus $N = p^r q$. Des. Codes Cryptogr. **73**(2), 383–392 (2014)
20. Takagi, T.: Fast RSA-type cryptosystem modulo $p^k q$. In: Krawczyk, H. (ed.) CRYPTO 1998. LNCS, vol. 1462, pp. 318–326. Springer, Heidelberg (1998). https://doi.org/10.1007/BFb0055738

Finding Low-Weight Polynomial Multiples Using the Rho Method

Laila El Aimani[✉]

University of Cadi Ayyad - ENSA Safi,
Route Sidi Bouzid, BP 63, 46000 Safi, Morocco
laila.elaimani@gmail.com, l.elaimani@uca.ac.ma

Abstract. The Low-weight polynomial multiple problem consists of finding multiples of binary polynomials, of degree less than a given bound, and with the least possible weight, where the weight of a multiple is the number of its nonzero coefficients. Recently, [11] introduced a new memory-efficient approach that computes the solution to the problem as a collision of a random function. In this paper, we elaborate further on this approach and generalize it to any weight; this can be particularly useful if finding the least-weight multiple is intractable. Then, we introduce a novel nested collision finding method − inspired by the NestedRho algorithm from Crypto'16 − that recursively produces collisions. Similarly to [11], our memory-efficient algorithms allow for a time/memory trade-off thanks to the Parallel Collision Search (PCS) method. Both our memory-efficient and trade-off algorithms improve significantly on the state-of-the-art for a wide range of cryptanalytic instances.

Keywords: Low-weight polynomial multiple · (Nested) Rho algorithm · Collision-finding algorithm · Time/memory trade-off

1 Introduction

Finding low-weight multiples of binary polynomials − the weight of a binary polynomial is the number of its nonzero coefficients − is of great importance in cryptology. The most popular application is attacks against LFSR-based stream ciphers. In fact, the small weight of the multiples ensures a low bias and therefore a low cost of the distinguishing or key-recovery attacks against stream ciphers [18,20].

Low-weight irreducible polynomials are also useful in representing finite fields when exponentiation is a core operation [23]. Since these do not always exist, [4] proposed to look for a low-weight multiple of the given irreducible polynomial and do most field operations modulo the found multiple.

Finally, the low-weight polynomial multiple problem is used to establish the security of the public-key cryptosystem TCHo [13]. Actually, this problem is believed to be computationally hard since there exists no known polynomial-time algorithm that solves it. Finally, it is worth noting that this problem is no harder than some celebrated NP-complete problems such as syndrome decoding [16,17] or the subset-sum problem [11]; the other direction has not been investigated.

L. Batina and J. Daemen (Eds.): AFRICACRYPT 2022, LNCS 13503, pp. 550–575, 2022.
https://doi.org/10.1007/978-3-031-17433-9_24

1.1   Variants of the Low-Weight Polynomial Multiple Problem

The low-weight polynomial multiple problem comes in many flavors in the literature. The most popular one is

Problem 1 (The Least-Weight Polynomial Multiple (LWPM) problem)

  Input: *A binary polynomial $P \in \mathbb{F}_2[X]$ of degree d, and a bound n*
  Output: *A multiple of P (in $\mathbb{F}_2[X]$) with degree less than n, and with the least possible weight*

To estimate the least weight $\omega_{\min}$ of a LWPM instance (P, d, n), one uses the following heuristic; the minimal weight $\omega_{\min}$ is the smallest ω_e such that the following inequality holds.

$$\binom{n}{\omega_e - 1} \geq 2^d \qquad (1)$$

In fact, the number of weight-$\omega_{\min}$ binary polynomials of degree at most n and with nonzero constant term is $\binom{n}{\omega_{\min}-1}$. For large n, we expect the multiples to be uniformly distributed. In other terms, for a random degree-d polynomial, we expect the number of its multiples with nonzero constant term, weight $\omega_{\min}$, and degree at most n to be $\mathcal{N}_M = 2^{-d}\binom{n}{\omega_{\min}-1}$. This explains the wide use of the above heuristic in the literature to estimate the least-weight of a LWPM instance.

When it is computationally intractable to find the least-weight multiple of a polynomial, we settle for finding a multiple with small enough weight. We consider thus the following variant of the problem:

Problem 2 (The Small-Weight Polynomial Multiple (SWPM) problem)

  Input: *A binary polynomial $P \in \mathbb{F}_2[X]$ of degree d, a bound n, and a weight ω*
  Output: *A multiple of P (in $\mathbb{F}_2[X]$) with degree less than n, and with weight smaller than ω (provided it exists).*

1.2   Previous Work

Let (P, d, n, w) be a SWPM instance. The techniques used in the literature to solve this instance can be classified into direct techniques that solve the SWPM problem, and indirect techniques that reduce solving SWPM to solving some popular problems in cryptography. We recall below both strategies. We describe the time or space complexity using the Big-O notation, which denotes the worst case complexity of the algorithms.

Direct Techniques. The standard time/memory trade-off approach [15] writes the weight as $\omega = t + m + 1$, $m \leq t$, and builds a list M with all possible weight-m combinations of $X^i \bmod P$ for $0 < i \leq n$. Then for each weight-t combination of the residues $X^i \bmod P$, look for an entry in the list M that sums up to 1. Clearly if M is implemented as an efficient hash-table, then the method runs in $O(n^t)$

and uses $O(n^m)$ of memory. The usual time/memory trade-off uses $t = \lceil \frac{\omega-1}{2} \rceil$ and $m = \lfloor \frac{\omega-1}{2} \rfloor$ to balance the time and memory costs. Chose et al. [8] cut the memory utilization down to $O(n^{\lfloor \frac{\omega-1}{4} \rfloor})$ while still running in $O(n^{\lceil \frac{\omega-1}{2} \rceil})$. When the bound n on the degree increases, for example $n \geq 2^{d/(1+\log_2(\omega-1))}$, then *Wagner's generalized birthday paradox* [24] solves SWPM in time and memory linear in n.

If the polynomial P is primitive, then the multiplicative group of $\mathbb{F}_2[X]/P$ is generated by X, and has order $2^d - 1$. In this case, [9] propose to work with the discrete logarithm of the involved polynomials — the polynomials are powers of X in the multiplicative group of $\mathbb{F}_2[X]/P$ — instead of their direct representations. This technique requires $2^d - 1$ to be sufficiently smooth in order to ignore the initial cost due to precomputing the discrete logarithms; it solves then the problem in time $O(n^{\lceil \frac{\omega-2}{2} \rceil})$ and memory $O(n^{\lfloor \frac{\omega-2}{2} \rfloor})$.

As for the memory-efficient algorithms for SWPM, we note the work [7] that solves SWPM in $O(n^{\omega-1})$ while requiring linear memory. The discrete-log-based variant [19] — that works with the discrete-log of the polynomials viewed as group elements in the multiplicative group of $\mathbb{F}_2[X]/P$ — runs in approximately $O(\frac{2^d}{n})$ and requires P to be a product of powers of irreducible polynomials with coprime orders.

Techniques via Reductions. The SWPM problem can be solved via a reduction to the syndrome decoding problem, i.e., by finding a low-weight codeword in a linear code. Syndrome decoding is an established problem in cryptography for which there exists the popular information-set decoding algorithms [3,6,16,17,21] that solve it. Applying these algorithms to a (P, d, n, ω) SWPM instance solves it in approximately $O(\text{Poly}(n) \cdot (\frac{n}{d})^\omega)$ with $O(d^\omega)$ of memory.

Recently, [11] proposed to solve the low-weight problem via a reduction to the celebrated knapsack problem. Technically, the technique uses cycle-finding algorithms [5] to compute a solution to LWPM as a collision of some random function, leading therefore to a memory-efficient algorithm for LWPM. The time/memory trade-off is achieved using the Parallel Collision Search (PCS) technique [22]. Both the memory-efficient and the trade-off algorithms are described for LWPM; they can be easily adaptable to SWPM, however, the cost (both time and memory) will need a major revision.

1.3   Contributions

We elaborate on the Rho-method introduced in [11] to further improve the presented algorithms for solving SWPM. Technically, we make the following contributions.

1. First, we provide the foundational theory of our results. Namely, we study the distribution of $\text{weight}(X_1 \oplus \ldots \oplus X_k)$, for nonzero integer k, and n-bit vectors $X_1, \ldots, X_k$. We distinguish two cases: (i) when the X_i enjoy a Bernoulli distribution, i.e., the coordinates of the X_i are independent and follow the

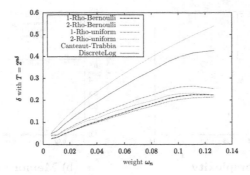

Fig. 1. Estimates for the runtime of the known memory-efficient techniques (DicreteLog [19] and Canteaut-Trabbia [7]) and our algorithms. The considered instance is the Bluetooth polynomial with: $d = 128$, $n \in [300, 2745]$, $\omega_n = \omega/n$, and $\omega \in [\omega_{min}, \omega_{min} + 10]$ where ω_{min} is the least-weight possible expected at degree n (found using Inequality 1).

Bernoulli law with the same parameter, and (ii) when the X_i are uniformly drawn at random from some set of n-bit vectors with a given weight ψ. We believe this study is of independent interest.

2. Second, we adapt the memory-efficient algorithms of [11] to compute any weight-ω solution to SWPM (and not necessarily the least-weight solution).

3. Third, we introduce our two-layer finding collision approach, inspired by the NestedRho algorithm [10], to solve SWPM. Specifically, we first find in layer-1 partial solutions that satisfy (solve) SWPM on half the bits, then in layer-2 our algorithm looks among those partial solutions for candidates that satisfy SWPM on the remaining bits.

We show that our (nested) Rho-based algorithms improve significantly on the state-of-the-art; we depict in Fig. 1 the state-of-the-art algorithms along with our four contributed algorithms, namely 1-Rho-Bernoulli, 1-Rho-uniform, 2-Rho-Bernoulli, and 2-Rho-uniform: the x-axis represents the relative weight $\omega_n = \omega/n$, and the y-axis represents the relative exponent $\log(T)/n$ of the time cost T.

Furthermore, we demonstrate the practicality of our approach with an implementation of the algorithms that confirm our theoretical estimates.

4. Finally, we tune our memory-efficient algorithms to allow for a time/memory trade-off thanks to the Parallel Collision Search (PCS) method [22]. Again, the resulting trade-off algorithms improve substantially on the state-of-the-art especially in memory consumption; see Fig. 2: the x-axis represents the relative weight $\omega_n = \omega/n$, whereas the y-axis represents the relative exponent $\log(T)/n$ (resp. $\log(M)/n$) of the time (resp. memory) cost T (resp. M).

The paper is structured as follows. Section 2 establishes the necessary background and notations that will be used throughout the text. Section 3 presents the foundational theory we build upon our results. Sections 4 and 5 describe respectively our simple and nested Rho-based approaches to solve SWPM. Finally, in Sect. 6, we compare our algorithms with the state-of-the-art, and

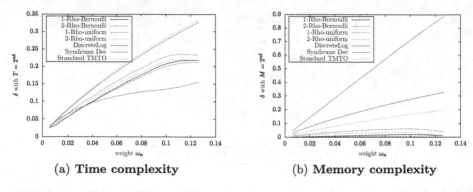

(a) **Time complexity**   (b) **Memory complexity**

Fig. 2. Estimates for the time and memory costs of the state-of-the-art (DiscreteLog [9], Standard TMTO [8], and Syndrome Decoding [16,17]) and our trade-off algorithms. The considered instance is the Bluetooth polynomial with: $d = 128$, $n \in [300, 2745]$, $\omega_n = \omega/n$, and $\omega \in [\omega_{\min}, \omega_{\min} + 10]$ where $\omega_{\min}$ is the least-weight possible expected at degree n (found using Inequality 1).

show how to improve their time cost by allowing a time/memory trade-off or by adopting a deeper nesting of the Rho technique.

2   Preliminaries

Let E and F be finite sets, and $f : E \to F$ be a random function.

It is well-known that a collision in f can be computed in roughly $\sqrt{|F|}$ function evaluations. This is commonly referred to as the birthday paradox [14]. The expected number of f-collisions, i.e., the number of distinct pairs $\{x, y\}$ with $f(x) = f(y)$, is roughly $\frac{|E|^2}{2|F|}$ according to [11, Fact 1].

If $F \subseteq E$, then common collision-search algorithms, e.g. [5], use a chain of invocations of f from a random starting point until a collision occurs. Consider, for random starting point x_0, the chain $f(x_0)$, $f^2(x_0) := f(f(x_0))$, $f^3(x_0), \dots$. Let further $f^t(x_0)$ be the first repeated value in the chain and $f^{t+s}(x_0)$ its second occurrence. We denote by $\mathsf{Rho}(f, x_0)$ the output of some cycle-finding algorithm on f from starting point x_0:

$$\mathsf{Rho}(f, x_0) := (f^{t-1}(x_0), f^{t+s-1}(x_0))$$

The name Rho stems from the shape of the chain resulting from the iterative collision search. Van Oorschot and Wiener [22] extend this technique of collision search to find collisions between two random functions $f_1, f_2 \colon E \to F$ (with $F \subseteq E$). They define a new function f that alternates between applications of f_1 and f_2 according to the input:

$$f \colon E \longrightarrow F$$

$$x \longmapsto \begin{cases} f_0(x) & \text{if } b_f(x) = 0 \\ f_1(x) & \text{if } b_f(x) = 1 \end{cases}$$

where $b_f \colon E \to \{0,1\}$ is a random bit function. Then a collision $f(x) = f(y)$ for f leads to a collision between f_1 and f_2 with probability roughly $\frac{1}{2}$ if collisions are random, and the number of "inter"collisions (collisions between f_1 and f_2) is roughly equal to the number of "intra" collisions (collisions inside f_1 in addition to collisions inside f_2). To obtain random collisions, [2,12] consider a family of permutations $(P_k)_{k \in \mathbb{N}}$ in E addressed by k to define the so-called *flavors* of a random function:

Definition 1 (Flavor of a function [12, Definition 2.1]). *Let f be a function with $f \colon E \longrightarrow E$. Let $(P_k)_{k \in \mathbb{N}} \colon E \longrightarrow E$ be a family of bijective functions addressed by k. Then the kth flavor of f is defined as*

$$f^{[k]}(x) := P_k(f(x))$$

Notice that for all k, a collision (x,y) of $f^{[k]}$ satisfies

$$f^{[k]}(x) = f^{[k]}(y) \Leftrightarrow P_k(f(x)) = P_k(f(y)) \Leftrightarrow f(x) = f(y)$$

With this definition, we can apply the collision-finding algorithm Rho to $f^{[k]}$ in order to search collisions for f. This ensures that different invocations of $\mathsf{Rho}(f^{[k]}, .)$ produce uniformly distributed collisions of f.

Notations. Let $z = (z_1, \ldots, z_n) \in \{0,1\}^n$ be a binary vector. $\mathsf{weight}(z) := |\{i \in [1,n] \colon z_i = 1\}|$ denotes the hamming weight of z. The relative weight of z is referred to as $\mathsf{weight}(z)/n$. $z_{i \ldots j}$ denotes the sub-vector extracted from vector z between indices i and j. Also, we conveniently denote by $+$ the termwise addition over $\mathbb{Z}_2$ (the group of integers modulo 2) between bit-vectors.

$\mathbb{F}_2$ is the field of two elements where the additive identity and the multiplicative identity are denoted 0 and 1 respectively. $\mathbb{F}_2[X]$ denotes the ring of polynomials over $\mathbb{F}_2$. For a polynomial $P \in \mathbb{F}_2[X]$, $\deg(P)$ and $\mathsf{weight}(P)$ refer respectively to the degree and weight of P, where the weight of polynomial over $\mathbb{F}_2$ corresponds to the number of its nonzero coefficients. We conveniently identify polynomials in $\mathbb{F}_2[X]$ with their coefficient vectors. $\mathbb{F}_2[X]/P$ denotes the ring of polynomials modulo P. In the text, if a is a length-n vector and x is an n-bit vector, then $\langle a, x \rangle$ denotes $\sum_{i=1}^{n} x_i a_i$. For instance, if $a := (a_1, \ldots, a_n)$, where the a_i are the residues $X^i \bmod P$ for $i \in [1,n]$, then $\langle a, x \rangle$ denotes the d-bit vector $\sum_{i=1}^{n} x_i a_i$.

We analyze our algorithms using the Θ notation, which gives the average case complexity. Sometimes we use the $\tilde{\Theta}$ notation which ignores the polynomial factors in the input. In this line of sought, we obtain, using Stirling's formula, the following approximation for the binomial coefficient $\binom{n}{k} = \frac{n!}{k! \cdot (n-k)!}$:

$$\binom{n}{k} = \Theta\left(n^{-1/2} 2^{nH(\frac{k}{n})}\right) \quad \text{or} \quad \binom{n}{k} = \tilde{\Theta}\left(2^{nH(\frac{k}{n})}\right)$$

where H is the binary entropy function defined as $H(x) := -x \log_2(x) - (1 - x) \log_2(1 - x)$; $\log_2$ is the logarithm in base 2.

For a finite set E, $e \in_R E$ corresponds to drawing uniformly at random element e from set E.

Let X be a random variable, $p \in [0,1]$, n and integer, and x a real number. P_X denotes the probability mass function (PMF) of X, defined as $P_X \colon x \mapsto \Pr[X = x]$. F_X denotes its cumulative distribution function (CDF): $F_X \colon x \mapsto \Pr[X \leq x]$. In the text, we use the notation $X \sim$ Law if X follows the probability law Law. For example $X \sim$ Bernoulli(p) means that X follows the Bernoulli law with parameter p, i.e., X takes the value 1 with probability p and the value 0 with probability $1 - p$. Also, if $X_1, \ldots, X_n$ are independent random variables that follow the Bernoulli law with parameter p, then we write $(X_1, \ldots, X_n) \sim$ Bernoulli(p, n). Finally, it is not hard to see that if $X \sim$ Bernoulli(p, n), then the random variable weight(X) corresponding to the number of successes of X follows the binomial distribution: weight(X) $\sim$ Binomial(p, n), i.e., $P_{\mathsf{weight}(X)}[k] = \binom{n}{k} p^k (1 - p)^{n-k}$, $k \in [0, k]$.

3   Foundational Work: Distribution of weight($X_1 + \ldots + X_k$)

We consider the distribution of the random variable $W_k := \mathsf{weight}(X_1 + \ldots + X_k)$ for nonzero integer k and elements $X_1, \ldots, X_k$ from the set

$$\mathcal{T} = \{ z \in \{0, 1\}^n : \mathsf{weight}(z) = \psi \}$$

where ψ is a given weight in $[1, n]$. We will treat the case where the elements $X_1, \ldots, X_k$ follow a Bernoulli law $X_i \sim$ Bernoulli(ψ_n, n) with $\psi_n = \psi/n$, and the case where they are simply drawn uniformly at random from $\mathcal{T}$. We stress that in both cases the $X_1, \ldots, X_k$ are independent and identically distributed.

Note that this study has been initiated in [11] for $k = 2$. We elaborate on it further in this section, and generalize it to any nonzero integer k.

3.1   Expectation of weight($X_1 + \ldots + X_k$)

Let E_k denote the expectation of $W_k := \mathsf{weight}(X_1 + \ldots + X_k)$. Note that for $k = 1$, we have $E_1 = E(\mathsf{weight}(X_1)) = E(\psi) = \psi$. We assume then in the rest of this subsection that $k > 1$.

Define, for $i = 1, \ldots, n$, the following indicator random variable:

$$I_{k,i} = \begin{cases} 1 \text{ if } (X_1 + \ldots + X_k)_i = 1 \\ 0 \qquad \text{otherwise} \end{cases}$$

Note that $I_{k,i}$, $i = 1 \ldots n$, are not necessarily independent although the $X_1, X_2, \ldots, X_k$ are. We can still apply the linearity property of the expectation to get

$E_k = E(W_k) = \sum_{i=1}^{n} E(I_{k,i})$. Furthermore, we have:

$$
\begin{aligned}
E(I_{k,i}) &= \Pr[(X_1 + \ldots + X_k)_i = 1] \\
&= \Pr[(X_1 + \ldots + X_{k-1})_i = 1 \wedge (X_k)_i = 0] + \Pr[(X_1 + \ldots + X_{k-1})_i = 0 \wedge (X_k)_i = 1] \\
&= \Pr[(X_1 + \ldots + X_{k-1})_i = 1]\Pr[(X_k)_i = 0] + \Pr[(X_1 + \ldots + X_{k-1})_i = 0]\Pr[(X_k)_i = 1] \\
&= (1 - \Pr[(X_k)_i = 1])E(I_{k-1,i}) + \Pr[(X_k)_i = 1](1 - E(I_{k-1,i})) \\
&= (1 - 2\Pr[(X_k)_i = 1])E(I_{k-1,i}) + \Pr[(X_k)_i = 1]
\end{aligned}
$$

In fact $\Pr[(X_1+\ldots+X_{k-1})_i = 1] = E(I_{k-1,i})$, and $\Pr[(X_1+\ldots+X_{k-1})_i = 0] = 1 - E(I_{k-1,i})$. On another note, we know that $\Pr[(X_j)_i = 1] = \psi_n$, $1 \leq j \leq k$ and $1 \leq i \leq n$ since:

1. If $X_j \sim \text{Bernoulli}(\psi_n, n)$, then by definition $\Pr[(X_j)_i = 1] = \psi_n$ for all $1 \leq i \leq n$.
2. If $X_j \in_R T$, then $\Pr[(X_j)_i = 1] = \frac{\binom{n-1}{\psi-1}}{\binom{n}{\psi}} = \frac{\psi}{n} = \psi_n$.

   Therefore

$$E_k = \sum_{i=1}^{n} E(I_{k,i}) = \sum_{i=1}^{n} [(1 - 2\psi_n)E(I_{k-1,i}) + \psi_n]$$
$$= (1 - 2\psi_n)E(W_{k-1}) + n\psi_n = (1 - 2\psi_n)E_{k-1} + \psi$$

Solving the above recurrence gives

$$E_k = (1 - 2\psi_n)E_{k-1} + \psi$$
$$= (1 - 2\psi_n)^j E_{k-j} + \psi \left(1 + (1 - 2\psi_n) + \ldots + (1 - 2\psi_n)^{j-1}\right)$$
$$= (1 - 2\psi_n)^{k-1}E_1 + \frac{n}{2}\left(1 - (1 - 2\psi_n)^{k-1}\right)$$
$$= \frac{n}{2}\left(1 - (1 - 2\psi_n)^{k-1} + \frac{2\psi}{n}(1 - 2\psi_n)^{k-1}\right)$$
$$= \frac{n}{2}\left(1 - (1 - 2\psi_n)^k\right)$$

Note that the above expression for E_k generalizes that found in [11] for $k = 2$:

$$E_2 = \frac{n}{2}\left(1 - (1 - 2\psi_n)^2\right) = 2n\psi_n(1 - \psi_n)$$

3.2   PMF of weight$(X_1 + \ldots + X_k)$

We distinguish two cases: (1) when $X_j \sim \text{Bernoulli}(\psi_n, n)$, for $j = 1, \ldots, k$, and (2) when the X_j are random elements from T, i.e., random n-bit vectors with weight ψ.

Case $X_1, \ldots, X_k \sim \text{Bernoulli}(\psi_n, n)$. Consider the random variables $S_k = X_1 + \ldots + X_k$, and $S_{k,i} = (X_1 + \ldots + X_k)_i$ for $i \in [1, n]$. We have:

$$P_{S_{k,i}}(1) = \Pr[S_{k,i} = 1] = \Pr[S_{k-1,i} = 1 \wedge (X_k)_i = 0] + \Pr[S_{k-1,i} = 0 \wedge (X_k)_i = 1]$$
$$= \Pr[S_{k-1,i} = 1](1 - \psi_n) + \psi_n(1 - \Pr[S_{k-1,i} = 1])$$
$$= (1 - 2P_{S_{k-1,i}}(1)) + \psi_n$$

Solving the above recurrence with $P_{S_{1,i}}(1) = \psi_n$ gives $P_{S_{k,i}}(1) = \frac{1}{2}(1 - (1 - 2\psi_n)^k)$.

Moreover, it is obvious that the $S_{k,i}$, are independent due to the Bernoulli assumption. Thus $S_k \sim \text{Bernoulli}\left(\frac{1}{2}(1 - (1 - 2\psi_n)^k), n\right)$. It follows that:

$$W_k \sim \text{Binomial}\left(\frac{1}{2}(1 - (1 - 2\psi_n)^k), n\right) \tag{2}$$

Case $X_1, , \ldots, X_k \in_R \mathcal{T}$. We will proceed again in an incremental manner, that is, we will compute the PMF of $W_k = \mathsf{weight}(X_1 + \ldots + X_k)$ as a function of the PMF of $W_{k-1} = \mathsf{weight}(X_1 + \ldots + X_{k-1})$. But first, we need the following lemma.

Lemma 1. *Let X and Y denote random n-bit vectors with respective weights p and q $(q \geq p)$. Then $\Pr[\mathsf{weight}(X + Y) = k]$ is given by:*

$$
\begin{cases}
\binom{p}{\frac{k-(q-p)}{2}} \binom{n-q}{\frac{k-(q-p)}{2}} / \binom{n-(q-p)}{p} & \text{if } \begin{cases} q-p \leq k \leq \min(p+q, 2n-(q-p)) \\ \text{and } k \equiv q-p \bmod 2 \end{cases} \\
0 & \text{otherwise}
\end{cases}
$$

Note that this lemma generalizes the result in [11] where $p = q$.

Proof. First note that the probability is zero for $k < q-p$. In fact, k corresponds to the number of positions where X and Y disagree. We know that there are p ones in X and $p + (q-p)$ ones in Y. Therefore, X and Y disagree on at least $q - p$ positions.

Next, we note that if k and $q - p$ don't have the same parity, then the probability is zero. In fact, let $\bar{X}$ and $\bar{Y}$ be the substrings of X and Y respectively from which we subtract a length-$(q-p)$ string where X and Y disagree. $\bar{X}$ and $\bar{Y}$ both have length $n - (q-p)$, and they both have weight p. We can then apply [11, Fact 2] and conclude that $\bar{X}$ and $\bar{Y}$ disagree on an even number, say $2t$, of positions. That is, X and Y disagree on $(q - p) + 2t$ positions.

Finally, if we use the result from [11, Subsect. 4.1] for $\bar{X}$ and $\bar{Y}$, we get for $\Pr[\mathsf{weight}(X + Y) = k]$ or equivalently $\Pr[\mathsf{weight}(\bar{X} + \bar{Y}) = k - (q - p)]$:

$$
\begin{cases}
\binom{p}{\frac{k-(q-p)}{2}} \binom{n-(q-p)-p}{\frac{k-(q-p)}{2}} / \binom{n-(q-p)}{p} & \text{if } \begin{cases} 0 \leq k - (q - p) \leq \min(2p, 2n - 2(q-p)) \\ \text{and } k \equiv (q - p) \bmod 2 \end{cases} \\
0 & \text{otherwise}
\end{cases}
$$

I.e.,

$$
\begin{cases}
\binom{p}{\frac{k-(q-p)}{2}} \binom{n-q}{\frac{k-(q-p)}{2}} / \binom{n-(q-p)}{p} & \text{if } \begin{cases} q-p \leq k \leq \min(p+q, 2n-(q-p)) \\ \text{and } k \equiv (q-p) \bmod 2 \end{cases} \\
0 & \text{otherwise}
\end{cases}
$$

$\square$

Let now t be an element in $[1, n]$:

$$
P_{W_k}(t) = \Pr[W_k = t] = \sum_{i=0}^{n} \Pr[W_{k-1} = i \wedge W_k = t]
$$

$$
= \sum_{i=0}^{n} P_{W_{k-1}}(i) \Pr[W_k = t \mid W_{k-1} = i, \mathsf{weight}(X_k) = \psi] \tag{3}
$$

$$
= \sum_{i=0}^{n} P_{W_{k-1}}(i) P_{i,\psi}(t)
$$

where

$$P_{i,\psi}(t) = \begin{cases} \binom{\min(i,\psi)}{\frac{t-|i-\psi|}{2}}\binom{n-\max(i,\psi)}{\frac{t-|i-\psi|}{2}}/\binom{n-|i-\psi|}{\min(i,\psi)} & \text{if} \begin{cases} |i-\psi| \le k \le \min(i+\psi, 2n-|i-\psi|)) \\ \text{and } k \equiv |i-\psi| \bmod 2 \end{cases} \\ 0 & \text{otherwise} \end{cases}$$

3.3   CDF of weight$(X_1 + \ldots + X_k)$

Case $X_1, \ldots, X_k \sim$ Bernoulli(ψ_n, n). In this case, we know that
$W_k \sim$ Binomial$(w_{k,n}, n)$, with $w_{k,n} = \frac{1}{2}\left(1 - (1 - 2\psi_n)^k\right)$. Then, according to [1]

$$F_{W_k}(n\omega_n) = \Pr[W_k \le n\omega_n] = \tilde{\Theta}(2^{-nD(\omega_n \| w_{k,n})}) \tag{4}$$

where $D(a\|b)$ refers to the *relative entropy (or Kullback-Leibler divergence)* between the Bernoulli(a) and Bernoulli(b) distributions:

$$D(a\|b) = a\log_2\frac{a}{b} + (1-a)\log_2\frac{1-a}{1-b}.$$

Case $X_1, \ldots, X_k \in_R \mathcal{T}$. Unfortunately, we don't have a closed formula to approximate accurately the CDF of $W_k = $ weight$(X_1 + \ldots + X_k)$. So we simply use the definition:

$$F_{W_k}(\omega) = \sum_{t=0}^{\omega} P_{W_k}(t) \tag{5}$$

where $P_{W_k}(t)$ is defined in Eq. 3.

4   Solving SWPM Using the Rho Technique

In [11], the author presents two memory-efficient algorithms to solve LWPM using the Rho method. Whilst both algorithms can straightforwardly be adapted to SWPM, their complexity analyses need to be revised. This is the purpose of the present section.

More specifically, we will first overview the key idea of both algorithms, then proceed to the analysis of their complexities. We finish by experimentally validating our theoretical analysis on a specific instance of SWPM.

4.1   Overview of the Algorithms in [11]

The key idea in [11] consists in viewing LWPM as an instance of the Group Subset Sum Problem (GSS), then solving it using a cycle-finding algorithm.

Problem 3 (The Group Subset Sum Problem (GSS) [11])

> **Given:** $a_1, \ldots, a_n, t \in (\mathbb{G}, +)$ *and* $\omega, 0 < \omega \le \frac{n}{2}$
> **Find:** $z = (z_1, \ldots, z_n) \in \{0,1\}^n: \sum_{i=1}^n z_i a_i = t$ *and* weight$(z) = \omega$.

In fact, let P be a degree-d polynomial in $\mathbb{F}_2[X]$. Consider further the additive group of the ring $\mathbb{F}_2[X]/P$ (whose order is 2^d, and identity is the zero polynomial), and the GSS instance $a_1, \ldots, a_n, t = a_0 \in (\mathbb{F}_2[X]/P, +)$, with $a_i \equiv X^i \bmod P$, $0 \leq i \leq n$. A weight-$(\omega - 1)$ solution $(z_1, \ldots, z_n)$ to this GSS instance, satisfies $\sum_{i=1}^{n} z_i a_i = a_0$. Which is equivalent to $1 + \sum_{i=1}^{n} z_i X^i \equiv 0 \bmod P$. This provides a weight-ω solution, with nonzero constant term, to the LWPM instance (P, d, n).

The next step is to solve GSS for the specific group $\mathbb{G} = (\mathbb{F}_2[X]/P, +)$. This is achieved by computing the solution z from a collision (x, y) of some function $f \colon \mathcal{T} \longrightarrow \mathcal{T}$. The challenge is to design $\mathcal{T}$ and consequently f to allow as many *representations* as possible of z.

The result in [11] considers the following building blocks

1. The set $\mathcal{T} = \{v \in \{0,1\}^n \colon \mathsf{weight}(v) = \psi = n \cdot \psi_n\}$, where ψ is a weight to be determined as a function of n and ω.
2. The following functions, where $a_i = X^i \bmod P$, $i \in [0, n]$

$$f_0, f_1 \colon \mathcal{T} \longrightarrow \mathbb{F}_2[X]/P$$

$$f_0(x) = \sum_{i=1}^{n} x_i a_i \quad \text{and} \quad f_1(x) = a_0 + \sum_{i=1}^{n} x_i a_i$$

3. And finally

$$f \colon \mathcal{T} \longrightarrow \mathbb{F}_2[X]/P$$

$$x \longmapsto \begin{cases} f_0(x) & \text{if } b_f(x) = 0 \\ f_1(x) & \text{if } b_f(x) = 1 \end{cases}$$

where $b_f \colon \{0,1\}^n \to \{0,1\}$ is a random bit function.

The function f alternates between applications of f_0 and f_1 depending on the input. Let $z = x + y$ (in $(\mathbb{F}_2[X]/P, +)$) be a weight-$(\omega - 1)$ solution to GSS, computed from a collision (x, y) of function f. It is clear that z produces a multiple of P with expected weight less than ω: a collision of type $f_i(x) = f_i(y)$, $i = 0, 1$ gives a multiple with expected weight $\omega - 1$, and a collision of type $f_i(x) = f_{1-i}(y)$, $i = 0, 1$ gives a multiple with expected weight ω.

The last ingredient the paper introduces is *an injective map* $\tau \colon \mathbb{F}_2[X]/P \to \mathcal{T}$ (provided that $2^d \leq |\mathcal{T}|$). Thus, (x, y) is a collision of f if and only if it is a collision of $\tau \circ f$. In this way, the range and domain of $\tau \circ f$ are the same, and any cycle-finding algorithm can be applied to $\tau \circ f$ to search collisions in f. Actually, $\tau \circ f$ is identified with f throughout this section, provided that $2^d \leq |\mathcal{T}|$.

A high level description of the algorithms in [11] is straightforward.

Algorithm for LWPM

Input A polynomial P with degree d, and a bound n
Output A multiple M of P with $\deg(M) \leq n$ and with the least possible weight
Compute the expected minimal weight $\omega_{\min}$ by solving Inequality 1
repeat
    choose a random starting point $s \in_R \mathcal{T}$
    $(x, y) \longleftarrow \mathrm{Rho}(f, s)$
    $M \longleftarrow \begin{cases} \sum_{i=1}^{n}(x_i \oplus y_i)X^i & \text{if } f_i(x) = f_i(y), \ i = 0, 1 \\ 1 + \sum_{i=1}^{n}(x_i \oplus y_i)X^i & \text{if } f_i(x) = f_{1-i}(y), \ i = 0, 1 \end{cases}$
until $\mathsf{weight}(M) = \omega_{\min}$
return M

The cost of the algorithm above depends on the PMF of the random variable $X = \mathsf{weight}(x + y)$ for $x, y \in_R \mathcal{T}$. Actually, the algorithm keeps looking for collisions (x, y) until finding one that satisfies the weight condition $\mathsf{weight}(M) = \omega$. This will bifurcate the algorithm above into two algorithms: (1) the first algorithm assumes and puts in place a Bernoulli distribution on the elements of $\mathcal{T}$, (2) and the second algorithm does not assume anything on the elements of $\mathcal{T}$. The cost of the first algorithm is better, in terms of expected calls to function f, than that of the second algorithm. However, the implementation of the Bernoulli distribution incurs a computation overhead in the first algorithm.

4.2 First Algorithm for SWPM

The first algorithm for LWPM in [11] assumes a Bernoulli distribution on the elements of $\mathcal{T}$. According to the study in Sect. 3, we have $\omega - 1 = E_{W_2} = 2n\psi_n(1 - \psi_n)$ which implies that the weight of elements in T equals: $\psi = \frac{n}{2}(1 \pm \sqrt{1 - 2\omega_n})$, with $\omega_n := \frac{\omega - 1}{n}$.

However, note that we need the function f to output elements in $\mathcal{T}$, that is, we need $2^d \leq |\mathcal{T}|$. Therefore

$$\psi_n = \frac{1}{2}(1 \pm \sqrt{1 - 2 \cdot \mu/n})$$

where μ is the smallest integer, greater or equal than $(\omega - 1)$, that satisfies $2^d \leq \binom{n}{\psi}$.

The Bernoulli distribution is established by a random map σ that inputs n-bit strings and outputs n-bit vectors that satisfy the Bernoulli distribution:

$$\begin{aligned} \sigma \colon \mathcal{T} &\longrightarrow \{0, 1\}^n \\ x &\longmapsto \sigma(x) \colon \sigma(x) \sim \mathrm{Bernoulli}(\psi_n, n) \end{aligned} \tag{6}$$

The function subject to collision search becomes $f \circ \sigma \colon \mathcal{T} \longrightarrow \mathcal{T}$.
We can now describe Algorithm 1-Rho-b for solving the SWPM problem.

Algorithm 1-Rho-b for SWPM

Input A polynomial P with degree d, a bound n, and a weight ω
Output A multiple M of P such that $\deg(M) \leq n$ and $\text{weight}(M) \leq \omega$ (if it exists)

$\omega_n \longleftarrow (\omega - 1)/n$; $\mu \longleftarrow \omega - 1$
repeat

$\qquad \mu_n \longleftarrow \mu/n; \mu \longleftarrow \mu + 1$
$\qquad \psi_n \longleftarrow \frac{1}{2}(1 \pm \sqrt{1 - 2 \cdot \mu_n})$; $\psi \longleftarrow n \cdot \psi_n$
until $\binom{n}{\psi} \geq 2^d$ $\qquad\qquad\qquad\qquad\qquad$ ▷ to ensure that f has range $f(\mathcal{T}) \subseteq \mathcal{T}$
repeat

$\qquad$ choose a random flavor k
$\qquad$ choose a random starting point $s \in_R \mathcal{T}$
$\qquad (x, y) \longleftarrow \text{Rho}((f \circ \sigma)^{[k]}, s)$
$\qquad (p, q) \longleftarrow (\sigma(x), \sigma(y))$
$\qquad M \longleftarrow \begin{cases} \sum_{i=1}^{n}(p_i \oplus q_i)X^i & \text{if } f_i(p) = f_i(q), \ i = 0, 1 \\ 1 + \sum_{i=1}^{n}(p_i \oplus q_i)X^i & \text{if } f_i(p) = f_{1-i}(q), \ i = 0, 1 \end{cases}$
until $M \equiv 0 \bmod P$ and $\text{weight}(M) \leq \omega$
return M

Theorem 1. *Algorithm* 1-Rho-b *runs in time* $\tilde{\Theta}(2^{C_t})$ *with*

$$C_t = \frac{d}{2} + n(-H(w_n) + H_1(\omega_n)))$$

where $H_1(\omega_n, \psi_n) = -\omega_n \log_2(2\psi_n(1 - \psi_n)) - (1 - \omega_n)\log_2(1 - 2\psi_n(1 - \psi_n))$, *and* H *is the binary entropy function* $H(x) := -x \log_2(x) - (1 - x)\log_2(1 - x)$.

Proof. The running time of the algorithm is the product of the cost of a collision of $(f \circ \sigma)^{[k]}$ and the cost of finding a "useful collision", i.e., a collision that finds a multiple M with weight less than ω:

$$T = \left(\frac{\# \text{ useful\_collisions}}{\# \text{ total\_collisions}} \right)^{-1} \cdot C_{\text{collision}}$$

The cost of finding a collision of $(f \circ \sigma)^{[k]}$ is $\tilde{\Theta}(2^{d/2})$. In fact, $(f \circ \sigma)^{[k]}$ has domain $\mathcal{T}$ and outputs elements in $\mathcal{T}$, however the size of its range is 2^d, which corresponds to the size of $\mathbb{F}_2[X]/P$.

The number of total collisions of $(f \circ \sigma)^{[k]}$ is in $\Theta\left(\frac{|\mathcal{T}|^2}{2^{d+1}}\right)$ according to [11, Fact 1].

Let $(x, y) \in_R \mathcal{T}^2$ with $(p, q) = (\sigma(x), \sigma(y))$. (x, y) is a useful collision for $(f \circ \sigma)^{[k]}$ if the following hold:

Event E_1: "$p, q \in \mathcal{T}$" (so that the function $f \circ \sigma$ and thus $(f \circ \sigma)^{[k]}$ is well-defined)
Event E_2: "$\text{weight}(p + q) \leq n \cdot \omega_n$"
Event E_3: "$\sum_{i=1}^{n}(p_i \oplus q_i)X^i$ or $1 + \sum_{i=1}^{n}(p_i \oplus q_i)X^i$ is a multiple of P".

Therefore the number of useful collisions is given by $|\mathcal{T}|^2 \cdot \Pr[E1 \wedge E2 \wedge E_3]$.

Also, we have

$$\Pr[\sigma(x) \in \mathcal{T}, x \in_R \mathcal{T}] = \binom{n}{\psi} \psi_n^\psi (1 - \psi_n)^{n-\psi} = \binom{n}{n\psi_n} 2^{-nH(\psi_n)}$$

$$\approx \frac{1}{\sqrt{2\pi n \psi_n (1 - \psi_n)}} = \tilde{\Theta}(1)$$

Thus $\Pr[E_1] = \Pr[\mathsf{weight}(p) = \mathsf{weight}(q) = \psi] = \tilde{\Theta}(1)$.

Furthermore, the probability that a random weight-ω polynomial with nonzero constant term and degree at most n equals a weight-ω multiple of P with nonzero constant term and degree at most n is $\binom{n}{\omega-1}^{-1} \mathcal{N}_M$, where $\mathcal{N}_M$ is the number of such multiples which equals $\binom{n}{\omega-1} 2^{-d}$. Therefore, $\Pr[E_3 \mid E_2, E_1] = 2^{-d+1}$. For $\Pr[E_2|E_1]$, we need to consider the CDF of the random variable $\mathsf{weight}(p+q)$. It is worth noting here that ω is not the smallest integer such that inequality $\binom{n}{\omega-1} \geq 2^d$ holds, and thus $\psi_n \neq \omega_n$.

Since $\mathsf{weight}(p + q) \sim (\mathsf{Binomial}(2\psi_n(1 - \psi_n), n))$, then

$$\Pr[\mathsf{weight}(p + q) \leq \omega] = \tilde{\Theta}(2^{-nD(\omega_n \| 2\psi_n(1 - \psi_n))})$$

Worked out, the algorithm runs in $\tilde{\Theta}(2^{C_t})$ with:

$$C_t = \frac{d}{2} - \log_2(\Pr[\mathsf{weight}(p + q) \leq \omega])$$

$$\approx \frac{d}{2} + n(-H(\omega_n) + H_1(\omega_n, \psi_n))$$

with H the binary entropy function and $H_1(\omega_n, \psi_n) = -\omega_n \log_2(2\psi_n(1 - \psi_n)) - (1 - \omega_n) \log_2(1 - 2\psi_n(1 - \psi_n))$. $\qquad\square$

We compare in Fig. 3 the runtime estimates for Algorithm 1-Rho-b and the experimental results run on Polynomial $P = X^{17} + X^{15} + X^{14} + X^{13} + X^{11} + X^{10} + X^9 + X^8 + X^6 + X^5 + X^4 + X^2 + 1$.

4.3   Second Algorithm for SWPM

The second algorithm in [11] for LWPM does not assume anything on the input of the random function subject to collision search. According to the previous study, the PMF of the random variable $\mathsf{weight}(x + y)$ for $x, y \in_R \mathcal{T}$ satisfies:

$$\Pr[\mathsf{weight}(x + y) = 2k] = \begin{cases} \binom{\psi}{k}\binom{n-\psi}{k}/\binom{n}{\psi} & \text{if } 0 \leq k \leq \min(\psi, n/2) \\ 0 & \text{otherwise} \end{cases}$$

Note that this probability law is reminiscent of the hyper-geometric distribution. We also have

$$\psi_n = \frac{1}{2}(1 \pm \sqrt{1 - 2 \cdot \mu/n})$$

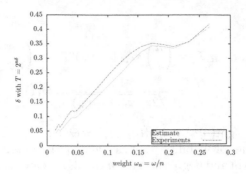

Fig. 3. Averaged function calls T for Algorithm 1-Rho-b run on: Polynomial $P = X^{17} + X^{15} + X^{14} + X^{13} + X^{11} + X^{10} + X^9 + X^8 + X^6 + X^5 + X^4 + X^2 + 1$, $n \in [30, 300]$, and $\omega \in [\omega_{\min}, \omega_{\min} + 3]$, where $\omega_{\min}$ is the least weight expected at degree n. Sample size per ω_n (number of instances averaged over) is 10. The discrepancies between the experiments and the estimates are due to adopting the $\tilde{\Theta}$ notation which ignores the polynomial factors in n, e.g., the factor $2\pi n \phi_n (1 - \phi_n)$ present in $\Pr[E_1]$.

where μ is the smallest integer, greater or equal than $(\omega - 1)$, that satisfies $2^d \leq \binom{n}{\psi}$.

The second algorithm for SWPM is then straightforward. It differs from Algorithm 1-Rho-b in the function subject to collision search; it is in this case simply f (instead of $f \circ \sigma$).

Algorithm　1-Rho-u for SWPM

Input A polynomial P with degree d, a bound n, and a weight ω
Output A multiple M of P such that $\deg(M) \leq n$ and $\mathsf{weight}(M) \leq \omega$ (if it exists)
$\omega_n \longleftarrow (\omega - 1)/n$; $\mu \longleftarrow \omega - 1$
repeat
$\quad \mu_n \longleftarrow \mu/n$; $\mu \longleftarrow \mu + 1$
$\quad \psi_n \longleftarrow \frac{1}{2}(1 \pm \sqrt{1 - 2 \cdot \mu_n})$; $\psi \longleftarrow n \cdot \psi_n$
until $\binom{n}{\psi} \geq 2^d$　　　　　　　　　　　　$\triangleright$ to ensure that f has range $f(\mathcal{T}) \subseteq \mathcal{T}$
repeat
$\quad$ choose a random flavor k
$\quad$ choose a random starting point $s \in_R \mathcal{T}$
$\quad (p, q) \longleftarrow \mathrm{Rho}(f^{[k]}, s)$
$\quad M \longleftarrow \begin{cases} \sum_{i=1}^{n}(p_i \oplus q_i)X^i & \text{if } f_i(p) = f_i(q), \ i = 0, 1 \\ 1 + \sum_{i=1}^{n}(p_i \oplus q_i)X^i & \text{if } f_i(p) = f_{1-i}(q), \ i = 0, 1 \end{cases}$
until $M \equiv 0 \bmod P$ and $\mathsf{weight}(M) \leq \omega$
return M

Let F_{W_2} be the CDF of the random variable $W_2 := \mathsf{weight}(p + q)$ $(p, q \in_R \mathcal{T})$, defined in Eq. 5 for $k = 2$.

Note that $\mathsf{P}_{W_2}(2k) = \mathsf{P}_G(\psi - k)$, where G is the hyper-geometric distribution with parameters $\{n, \psi, \psi\}$. Therefore, we can relate $\mathsf{F}_{W_2}(\omega - 1)$ to $\mathsf{F}_G(\psi - \frac{\omega - 1}{2})$

via the relation $\mathsf{F}_{W_2}(\omega - 1) = 1 - \mathsf{F}_G(\psi - \frac{\omega-1}{2})$. Unfortunately, this is not of much interest since we don't have accurate approximations of F_G. Thus, we don't have a closed formula for F_{W_2}, and we settle for the expression derived from its definition to state the theorem below.

Theorem 2. *Algorithm* 1-*Rho-u runs in time* $\tilde{\Theta}(2^{C_t})$ *with* $C_t = \frac{d}{2} - \log_2(\mathsf{F}_{W_2}(\omega-1))$, *where* F_{W_2} *is the CDF of the random variable* $W_2 := \mathsf{weight}(p + q)$ $(p, q \in_R \mathcal{T})$, *defined in Eq. 5 for* $k = 2$.

Proof. Again, the running time of the algorithm is the product of the cost of a collision of $f^{[k]}$, namely $2^{d/2}$, and the cost of finding a collision that satisfies the weight condition $\mathsf{weight}(p + q) \leq \omega$, namely $\mathsf{F}_{W_2}(\omega - 1)^{-1}$. □

We consider the same test polynomial in Subsect. 4.2 for the same range of values; the results are depicted in Fig. 4.

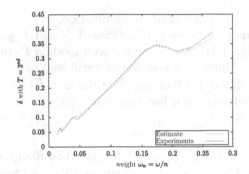

Fig. 4. Averaged function calls T for Algorithm 1-Rho-u run on: Polynomial $P = X^{17} + X^{15} + X^{14} + X^{13} + X^{11} + X^{10} + X^9 + X^8 + X^6 + X^5 + X^4 + X^2 + 1$, $n \in [30, 300]$, and $\omega \in [\omega_{\min}, \omega_{\min} + 3]$, where $\omega_{\min}$ is the least weight expected at degree n. Sample size per ω_n is 10. The discrepancies between the experiments and the estimates are due to adopting the $\tilde{\Theta}$ notation which ignores the polynomial factors n.

5   Solving SWPM Using the Nested Rho Method

In the previous section, we computed the solution to SWPM as a collision of the function f: for $a_i = X^i \bmod P$, $i \in [1, n]$ and (x, y) a collision of f, the solution is computed as $\langle a, x + y \rangle$ or $1 + \langle a, x + y \rangle$.

In this section, we compute the solution using a "nested" collision search. That is, we first look for a collision that matches the solution on half of the bits, i.e., compute a polynomial that once reduced modulo P has half of its bits identically zero. Then, among these collisions use another collision search to identify the complete solution.

5.1 Overview of the Idea

Consider the set $\mathcal{T} = \{v \in \{0,1\}^n : \mathsf{weight}(v) = \psi = n \cdot \psi_n\}$, where ψ is a weight to be determined later as a function of n and ω.

Let R be a random $\frac{d}{2}$-bit vector. We define the following functions:

$$f : \mathcal{T} \longrightarrow \mathbb{Z}_2^{d/2}$$

$$x \longmapsto \begin{cases} f_0(x) = \langle a, x \rangle_{1 \ldots \frac{d}{2}} & \text{if } b_f(x) = 0 \\ f_{1,R}(x) = (R + \langle a, x \rangle)_{1 \ldots \frac{d}{2}} & \text{if } b_f(x) = 1 \end{cases}$$

where $b_f : \{0,1\}^n \to \{0,1\}$ is a random bit function.

$$g : \mathcal{T} \longrightarrow \mathbb{Z}_2^{d/2}$$

$$x \longmapsto \begin{cases} g_0(x) = \langle a, x \rangle_{1 \ldots \frac{d}{2}} & \text{if } b_g(x) = 0 \\ g_{1,R}(x) = (1 + R + \langle a, x \rangle)_{1 \ldots \frac{d}{2}} & \text{if } b_g(x) = 1 \end{cases}$$

where $b_g : \{0,1\}^n \to \{0,1\}$ is a random bit function.

That is, f alternates between applications of f_0 and $f_{1,R}$, and a collision of f will lead to a polynomial that, when reduced modulo P, matches either 0 or R on the first $\frac{d}{2}$ bits. Similarly, a collision of g will lead to a polynomial reduced modulo P that matches either 0 or $1 + R$ on the first $\frac{d}{2}$ bits.

And finally, we introduce our last function:

$$h : \mathcal{T} \longrightarrow \mathbb{Z}_2^{d/2}$$

$$s \longmapsto \begin{cases} h_0(s) = \langle a, x + y \rangle_{\frac{d}{2}+1 \ldots d}, & \text{where } (x,y) := \mathsf{Rho}(f, s), & \text{if } b_h(s) = 0 \\ h_1(s) = 1 + \langle a, z + t \rangle_{\frac{d}{2}+1 \ldots d}, & \text{where } (z,t) := \mathsf{Rho}(g, s), & \text{if } b_h(s) = 1 \end{cases}$$

where $b_h : \{0,1\}^n \to \{0,1\}$ is a random bit function.

Similarly to Sect. 4, if $\binom{n}{\psi} \geq 2^{d/2}$, we can easily assume that f, g, and h output elements in $\mathcal{T}$. This allows an iterative application of the functions, which is needed in the cycle-finding algorithms.

Now, let us explain the workings of function h. Let (s_0, s_1) be a collision returned by $\mathsf{Rho}(h, \cdot)$. Then $h(s_0) = h(s_1)$. Suppose $h_0(s_0) = h_1(s_1)$. Then

$$\langle a, x + y \rangle_{\frac{d}{2}+1 \ldots d} = 1 + \langle a, z + t \rangle_{\frac{d}{2}+1 \ldots d}$$

Thus, the upper $\frac{d}{2}$ bits of $1 + \langle a, x + y + z + t \rangle$ are zero:

$$1 + \langle a, x + y + z + t \rangle_{\frac{d}{2}+1 \ldots d} = 0_{\frac{d}{2}+1 \ldots d}$$

Moreover, (x,y) and (z,t) are collisions of f and g respectively. Suppose that $f_0(x) = f_{1,R}(y)$ and $g_0(z) = g_{1,R}(t)$:

$$\langle a, x + y \rangle_{1 \ldots \frac{d}{2}} = R \quad \text{and} \quad \langle a, z + t \rangle_{1 \ldots \frac{d}{2}} = 1 + R$$

Which implies $\langle a, x + y + z + t\rangle_{1...\frac{d}{2}} = 1$ or $1 + \langle a, x + y + z + t\rangle_{1...\frac{d}{2}} = 0_{1...\frac{d}{2}}$. Putting all together, we get $1 + \langle a, x + y + z + t\rangle_{1...d} = 0_{1...d}$.

In other words $1 + \langle a, x + y + z + t\rangle$ is a multiple of P with nonzero constant term, and weight less than $1 + \mathsf{weight}(x + y + z + t)$. Figure 5 illustrates the principle of the nested Rho algorithm versus the simple Rho algorithm.

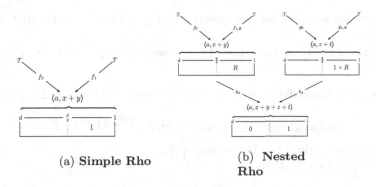

(a) **Simple Rho**

(b) **Nested Rho**

Fig. 5. Structure of the simple and nested Rho algorithms

In general, a collision of h outputs two pairs (x, y) and (z, t) with $\langle a, x + y + z + t\rangle \in \{R, 1 + R, 0, 1\}$. The cases that lead to a multiple of P are when $\langle a, x + y + z + t\rangle \in \{0, 1\}$ (the multiple will have either zero or nonzero constant term). We can argue that these cases occur with probability greater than $\frac{1}{2}$. In fact, Let p denote the probability that $\mathsf{Rho}(f, \cdot)$ returns an "inter" collision (collision between f_0 and $f_{1,R}$), and q denote the probability that $\mathsf{Rho}(h, \cdot)$ returns an "inter" collision. It is obvious that the probability that $\mathsf{Rho}(g, \cdot)$ returns an "inter" collision is also p since both f and g are similar. Now, the case $\langle a, x + y + z + t\rangle \in \{0, 1\}$ occurs when either (1) (x, y, z, t) is an intra-collision of h, and (x, y) and (z, t) are both intra-collisions or both inter-collisions (of either f or g) (2) (x, y, z, t) is an inter-collision of h, and (x, y) and (z, t) are both intra-collisions or both inter-collisions. In other terms $\langle a, x + y + z + t\rangle \in \{0, 1\}$ occurs with probability $q(p^2 + (1 - p)^2) + (1 - q)(p^2 + (1 - p)^2) = p^2 + (1 - p)^2$, which is greater than $\frac{1}{2}$ for all values of p. In the experiments, we set R to a random bit, and we were able to exploit all types of collisions; the details will appear in the long version of the paper.

5.2 The Algorithm

In view of the foregoing analysis, it remains to compute the weight ψ, and determine the probability law of $W_4 = \mathsf{weight}(x + y + z + t)$ for $x, y, z, t \in_R \mathcal{T}$.

For the weight, we have $\omega = 1 + \mathsf{weight}(x + y + z + t)$. On another note, and according to the study in Sect. 3, the expectation of $W_4 = \mathsf{weight}(x + y + z + t)$ is $E_4 = \frac{n}{2}(1 - (1 - 2\psi/n)^4)$. We conclude that

$$\omega_n = \frac{1}{2}(1 - (1 - 2\psi_n)^4) \text{ with } \omega_n = \frac{\omega - 1}{n} \text{ and } \psi_n = \frac{\psi}{n}$$

Solving this equation for ψ_n gives $\psi_n = \frac{1}{2}(1 \pm \sqrt[4]{1 - 2 \cdot \omega_n})$.

However, note that we need the functions f, g, and h to output elements in $\mathcal{T}$, that is, we need $2^{d/2} \leq |\mathcal{T}|$. Therefore

$$\psi_n = \frac{1}{2}(1 \pm \sqrt[4]{1 - 2 \cdot \mu/n})$$

where μ is the smallest integer, greater or equal than $(\omega - 1)$, that satisfies $2^{d/2} \leq \binom{n}{\psi}$.

Concerning the probability law of $W_4 = \mathsf{weight}(x + y + z + t)$, we distinguish two cases:

1. If $x, y, z, t \sim \mathsf{Bernoulli}(\psi_n, n)$, then $W_4 \sim \mathsf{Binomial}\left(\frac{1}{2}(1 - (1 - 2\psi_n)^4), n\right)$. and

$$\mathsf{F}_{W_4}(n\omega_n) = \Pr[W_4 \leq n\omega_n] = \tilde{\Theta}(2^{-nD(\omega_n \| \frac{1}{2}(1-(1-2\psi_n)^4))})$$

   with $D(a\|b) = a \log_2 \frac{a}{b} + (1 - a) \log_2 \frac{1-a}{1-b}$.
2. when $x, y, z, t \in_R \mathcal{T}$, then

$$\mathsf{F}_{W_4}(\omega) = \sum_{t=0}^{\omega} \mathsf{P}_{W_4}(t)$$

where P_{W_4} is computed according to the recurrence $\mathsf{P}_{W_k}(t) = \sum_{i=0}^{n} \mathsf{P}_{W_{k-1}}(i)$ $\mathsf{P}_{i,\psi}(t)$ with

$$\mathsf{P}_{i,\psi}(t) = \begin{cases} \binom{\min(i,\psi)}{\frac{t-|i-\psi|}{2}}\binom{n-\max(i,\psi)}{\frac{t-|i-\psi|}{2}} / \binom{n-|i-\psi|}{\min(i,\psi)} & \text{if} \begin{cases} |i-\psi| \leq k \leq \min(i+\psi, 2n-|i-\psi|) \\ \text{and } k \equiv |i-\psi| \bmod 2 \end{cases} \\ 0 & \text{otherwise} \end{cases}$$

The algorithm is then straightforward.

Algorithm 2-Rho-(b/u) **for SWPM**

Input A polynomial P with degree d, a bound n, and a weight ω
Output A multiple M of P with $\deg(M) \leq n$ and $\mathsf{weight}(M) \leq \omega$ (if it exists)
$\omega_n \longleftarrow (\omega - 1)/n$; $\mu \longleftarrow \omega - 1$
repeat
    $\mu_n \longleftarrow \mu/n$; $\mu \longleftarrow \mu + 1$
    $\psi_n \longleftarrow \frac{1}{2}(1 \pm \sqrt[4]{1 - 2 \cdot \mu_n})$; $\psi \longleftarrow n \cdot \psi_n$
until $\binom{n}{\psi} \geq 2^{d/2}$ ▷ to ensure that f, g, and h have range included in $\mathcal{T}$
repeat
    choose a random flavor k
    choose a random $R \in \{0,1\}^{d/2}$
    choose a random starting point $s \in_R \mathcal{T}$
    $(s_1, s_2) \longleftarrow \mathsf{Rho}(h^{[k]}, s)$
    $(x, y) \longleftarrow \mathsf{Rho}(f^{[k]}, s_1)$; $(z, t) \longleftarrow \mathsf{Rho}(g^{[k]}, s_2)$
    $M_0 \longleftarrow \sum_{i=1}^{n}(x_i \oplus y_i + z_i \oplus t_i)X^i$; $M_1 \longleftarrow \sum_{i=1}^{n}(x_i \oplus y_i + z_i \oplus t_i)X^i + 1$
until $M_i \equiv 0 \bmod P$ and $\mathsf{weight}(M_i) \leq \omega$, for $i = 0$ or $i = 1$
return M_i

Remark 1. In case we run Algorithm 2-Rho-*b*, i.e., we assume that the elements of $\mathcal{T}$ enjoy a Bernoulli distribution, we need to use the map σ defined in Eq. 6. The functions subject to collision search become $f \circ \sigma$, $g \circ \sigma$, $h \circ \sigma$ instead of f, g, and h respectively.

Theorem 3. *Algorithm* 2-Rho-(b/u) *runs in* $\tilde{\Theta}(2^{C_t})$, *with:*

$$C_t = \frac{d}{2} - \log_2(\mathsf{F}_{W_4}(\omega))$$

where F_{W_4} *is the CDF of* $\mathsf{weight}(x + y + z + t)$, $x, y, z, t \in_R \mathcal{T}$, *defined above in this Subsect. 5.2.*

Proof. First, note that the cost of finding a collision of f or g is $\tilde{\Theta}(2^{d/4})$. In fact, these random functions have range $\mathbb{Z}_2^{d/2} \subset \mathcal{T}$. Then according to the birthday paradox, a collision can be found in $\tilde{\Theta}(\sqrt{2^{d/2}})$ evaluations of the function in question. By the same argument, a collision of h requires $\tilde{\Theta}(2^{d/4})$ evaluations of h. However, an evaluation of h consists of finding collisions in both f and g which costs $\tilde{\Theta}(2^{d/4})$. We conclude that a collision of h costs $\tilde{\Theta}(2^{d/2})$.

The cost of Algorithm 2-Rho-(b/u) is dominated by the time needed to find a collision of h ($\mathsf{Rho}(h^{[k]}, s)$) that satisfies the weight condition $W_4 = \mathsf{weight}(x + y + z + t) \leq \omega$. Therefore, Algorithm 2-Rho-(b/u) runs in $\tilde{\Theta}(2^{d/2}\mathsf{F}_{W_4}(\omega)^{-1})$, i.e., in $\tilde{\Theta}(2^{C_t})$, with: $C_t = \frac{d}{2} - \log_2(\mathsf{F}_{W_4}(\omega))$. □

We consider the same test polynomial in Subsect. 4.2 for the same range of values; the results are depicted in Fig. 6.

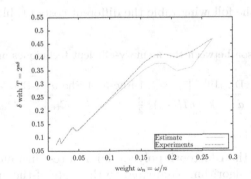

Fig. 6. Averaged function calls T for Algorithm 2-Rho-u run on: Polynomial $P = X^{17} + X^{15} + X^{14} + X^{13} + X^{11} + X^{10} + X^9 + X^8 + X^6 + X^5 + X^4 + X^2 + 1$, $n \in [30, 300]$, and $\omega \in [\omega_{\min}, \omega_{\min} + 3]$, where $\omega_{\min}$ is the least weight expected at degree n. Sample size per ω_n (number of instances averaged over) is 10. The discrepancies between the experiments and the estimates are due to adopting the $\tilde{\Theta}$ notation which ignores the polynomial factors in n.

6   Performance and Extensions

6.1   Comparison with the State-of-the-Art

We proposed so far four algorithms for SWPM that compute the solution as a collision of some function f:

1. **Algorithm** 1-Rho-b uses a simple Rho technique that puts in place a Bernoulli distribution on the input of f. It runs in $\tilde{\Theta}(2^{(d/2-C_{1b})})$, with $C_{1b} = \log_2(\mathsf{F}_{W_2}(\omega))$, and F_{W_2} is the CDF defined in Eq. 4 for $k = 2$.
2. **Algorithm** 1-Rho-u uses a simple Rho technique that assumes only a uniform distribution on the input of f. It runs in $\tilde{\Theta}(2^{(d/2-C_{1u})})$, with $C_{1u} = \log_2(\mathsf{F}_{W_2}(\omega))$, and F_{W_2} is the CDF defined in Eq. 5 for $k = 2$.
3. **Algorithm** 2-Rho-b uses a nested Rho technique that puts in place a Bernoulli distribution on the input of f. It runs in $\tilde{\Theta}(2^{(d/2-C_{2b})})$, with $C_{2b} = \log_2(\mathsf{F}_{W_4}(\omega))$, and F_{W_4} is the CDF defined in Eq. 4 for $k = 4$.
4. **Algorithm** 2-Rho-u uses a nested Rho technique that assumes only a uniform distribution on the input of f. It runs in $\tilde{\Theta}(2^{(d/2-C_{2u})})$, with $C_{2u} = \log_2(\mathsf{F}_{W_4}(\omega))$, and F_{W_4} is the CDF defined in Eq. 5 for $k = 4$.

Remark 2. It is worth noting that the weight ψ of the elements of T in Algorithms 1-Rho-b and 1-Rho-u is computed as $\psi_n = \frac{1}{2}(1 \pm \sqrt{1 - 2 \cdot \mu/n})$, where μ is the smallest integer, greater or equal than $(\omega - 1)$, that satisfies $2^d \leq \binom{n}{\psi}$. Whereas ψ in Algorithms 2-Rho-b and 2-Rho-u is computed as $\psi_n = \frac{1}{2}(1 \pm \sqrt[4]{1 - 2 \cdot \mu/n})$, where μ is the smallest integer, greater or equal than $(\omega - 1)$, that satisfies $2^{d/2} \leq \binom{n}{\psi}$.

We summarize in the following table the different costs (Table 1):

Table 1. Comparison between the memory-efficient techniques and our algorithms

Method	DL [19]	[7]	1-Rho-b	1-Rho-u	1-Rho-b	2-Rho-u
$\log_2(\tilde{\Theta}(T))$	d	$nH(\omega_n)$	$\frac{d}{2} - C_{1b}$	$\frac{d}{2} - C_{1u}$	$\frac{d}{2} - C_{2b}$	$\frac{d}{2} - C_{2u}$

Let us consider the Bluetooth polynomial as a test instance to visualize the performance of our algorithms compared to the state-of-the-art.

The Bluetooth polynomial P_{BT} ($d = 128$, $\mathsf{weight}(P_{BT}) = 49$) is the product of the four following polynomials:

$$P_1(x) = x^{25} + x^{20} + x^{12} + x^8 + 1; \quad P_2(x) = x^{31} + x^{24} + x^{16} + x^{12} + 1;$$
$$P_3(x) = x^{33} + x^{28} + x^{24} + x^4 + 1; \quad P_4(x) = x^{39} + x^{36} + x^{28} + x^4 + 1;$$

We depict in Fig. 7 the performance of the known memory-efficient methods and our algorithms on this instance.

It is not hard to see that the larger ω_n, the more difficult the problem gets. I.e., it is hard to find small-degree multiples when the weight expected at the multiple degree is large. For instance, if $n = \mathrm{ord}(P)$ (order of P) then $X^n + 1$ is a multiple of P with weight 2. However, the challenge is to find small-degree multiples with small weights. In fact, n refers in case of a correlation attack to the keystream length, which is in case of Bluetooth small and equal to 2745.

For instance, we obtain for $(n = 668, \omega = \omega_{\min} = 22)$ and $(n = 668, \omega = 26)$ the results depicted respectively in Tables 2 and 3.

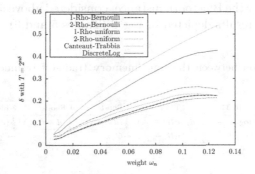

Fig. 7. Estimates for the runtime of the known memory-efficient techniques (DicreteLog [19] and Canteaut-Trabbia [7]) and our algorithms. The considered instance is the Bluetooth polynomial with: $d = 128$, $n \in [300, 2745]$, $\omega_n = \omega/n$, and $\omega \in [\omega_{\min}, \omega_{\min} + 10]$ where $\omega_{\min}$ is the least-weight possible expected at degree n (found using Inequality 1).

Table 2. Time costs, in terms of function calls (calls to the function subject to collision search), of the known memory-efficient techniques and our algorithms on the Bluetooth instance ($d = 128, n = 668, \omega = \omega_{\min} = 22$)

Method	DL [19]	Canteaut-Trabbia [7]	1-Rho-b	1-Rho-u	2-Rho-b	2-Rho-u
$\log_2(\tilde{\Theta}(T))$	128	134	72	99	68	89

Table 3. Time costs, in terms of function calls (calls to the function subject to collision search), of the known memory-efficient techniques and our algorithms on the Bluetooth instance ($d = 128, n = 668, \omega = 26$)

Method	DL [19]	Canteaut-Trabbia [7]	1-Rho-b	1-Rho-u	2-Rho-b	2-Rho-u
$\log_2(\tilde{\Theta}(T))$	128	153	69	89	66	79

6.2 Time/Memory Trade-Off Algorithms

Fortunately, our Rho-based algorithms for SWPM allow for a time/memory trade-off using the van Oorschot-Wiener Parallel Collision Search (PCS) technique [22]. The PCS technique allows to efficiently find multiple collisions, of a random function, at a low amortized cost per collision. More precisely, if C is the time needed to find a collision with polynomial memory, then PCS finds $\tilde{\Theta}(2^m)$ collisions in time $\tilde{\Theta}(2^{\frac{m}{2}}C)$ using $\tilde{\Theta}(2^m)$ memory.

As an illustration, we know that Algorithm 1-Rho-b requires to find $\tilde{\Theta}(2^{-C_{1b}})$ collisions where each one costs on average $\tilde{\Theta}(2^{d/2})$. Therefore, applying PCS to Algorithm 1-Rho-b reduces the time complexity down to $\tilde{\Theta}(2^{\frac{d-C_{1b}}{2}})$ at the expense of $\tilde{\Theta}(2^{-C_{1b}})$ of memory.

Similarly, we get for the algorithms 1-Rho-u, 2-Rho-b, and 2-Rho-u the complexities described in Table 4.

Again, we get for the Bluetooth instance, considered above for the same range of parameters, the results depicted in Fig. 8 (Tables 5 and 6).

Table 4. Comparison between the time/memory trade-off techniques and our algorithms

	DL [9]	SD [16,17]	TMTO [8]	1-Rho-b	1-Rho-u	2-Rho-b	2-Rho-u
$\log_2(T)$	$nH(\frac{\omega-2}{2n})$	$\omega(\log_2 n - \log_2 d)$	$nH(\frac{\omega-1}{2n})$	$\frac{1}{2}(d - C_{1b})$	$\frac{1}{2}(d - C_{1u})$	$\frac{1}{2}(d - C_{2b})$	$\frac{1}{2}(d - C_{2u})$
$\log_2(M)$	$nH(\frac{\omega-2}{2n})$	$\omega\log_2 d$	$nH(\frac{\omega-1}{4n})$	$-C_{1b}$	$-C_{1u}$	$-C_{2b}$	$-C_{2u}$

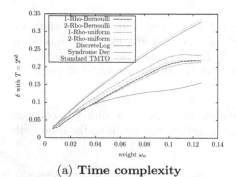

(a) **Time complexity**

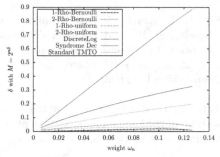

(b) **Memory complexity**

Fig. 8. Estimates for the time and memory costs of the state-of-the-art (DiscreteLog [9], Standard TMTO [8], and Syndrome Decoding [16,17]) and our trade-off algorithms. The considered instance is the Bluetooth polynomial with: $d = 128$, $n \in [300, 2745]$, $\omega_n = \omega/n$, and $\omega \in [\omega_{\min}, \omega_{\min} + 10]$ where $\omega_{\min}$ is the least-weight possible expected at degree n (found using Inequality 1).

Table 5. Time/memory costs, in terms of function calls (calls to the function subject to collision search), of the trade-off techniques on the Bluetooth instance ($d = 128, n = 668, \omega = \omega_{\min} = 22$)

	DL [9]	SD [16,17]	TMTO [8]	1-Rho-b	1-Rho-u	2-Rho-b	2-Rho-u
$\log_2(T)$	75	52	78	68	81	66	76
$\log_2(M)$	75	154	44	8	35	4	25

Table 6. Time/memory costs, in terms of function calls (calls to the function subject to collision search), of the trade-off techniques on the Bluetooth instance ($d = 128, n = 668, \omega = 26$)

	DL [9]	SD [16,17]	TMTO [8]	1-Rho-b	1-Rho-u	2-Rho-b	2-Rho-u
$\log_2(T)$	87	62	90	66	76	65	72
$\log_2(M)$	87	182	51	5	25	2	15

6.3   Deeper Nesting of Rho

So far, we have demonstrated the efficiency of the nested Rho-based approach over the simple Rho-based approach for solving SWPM. It seems then natural to try a deeper nesting of Rho.

For example, for a 3-Rho-based approach, the algorithm will operate in three layers: (i) layer-1 where one looks for potential solutions that satisfy SWPM on quarter of the bits (i) layer-2 where one chooses among those partial solutions candidates that satisfy SWPM on half of the bits, and finally (iii) layer-3 where one chooses among the partial solutions of layer-2 candidates that satisfy SWPM on the remaining bits.

The relative weight ψ_n will be computed as $\psi_n = \frac{1}{2}(1 \pm \sqrt[8]{1 - 2 \cdot \mu/n})$, where μ is the smallest integer, greater or equal than $(\omega - 1)$, that satisfies $2^{d/4} \leq \binom{n}{n\psi_n}$. Furthermore, we will consider the CDF of the random variable W_8 defined in Eqs. 4 and 5 for $k = 8$.

We get for the above Bluetooth instances the following costs (computed using the $\tilde{\Theta}$ notation): for example, an algorithm that runs in 2^{74} and uses 2^{20} memory means that it makes on average roughly 2^{74} calls to the random function, and it uses on average a storage of size roughly 2^{20} (the algorithm stores special elements from $\mathcal{T}$, that are called "distinguished points").

- **Bluetooth instance** ($d = 128, n = 668, \omega = 22$). Algorithm 3-Rho-$b$ runs in 2^{66}, and its trade-off variant runs in 2^{65} and uses 2^2 memory. Algorithm 3-Rho-u runs in 2^{85}, and its trade-off variant runs in 2^{74} and uses 2^{20} memory.
- **Bluetooth instance** ($d = 128, n = 668, \omega = 26$). Algorithm 3-Rho-$b$ runs in 2^{65}, and its trade-off variant runs in 2^{64} and uses $2^{0.6}$ memory. Algorithm 3-Rho-u runs in 2^{75}, and its trade-off variant runs in 2^{69} and uses 2^{11} memory.

It is clear that the 3-Rho based method improves on the 2-Rho and simple Rho ones.

In general, for an r-Rho-based algorithm, we should set the relative weight ψ_n to $\psi_n = \frac{1}{2}(1 \pm \sqrt[2^r]{1 - 2 \cdot \mu/n})$, where μ is the smallest integer, greater or equal than $(\omega - 1)$, that satisfies $2^{d/2^{-r+1}} \leq \binom{n}{\psi}$. Then consider the CDF of random variable W_k defined in Eqs. 4 and 5 for $k = 2^r$.

References

1. Arratia, R., Gordon, L.: Tutorial on large deviations for the binomial distribution. Bull. Math. Biol. **51**, 125–131 (1989). https://doi.org/10.1007/BF02458840
2. Becker, A., Coron, J.-S., Joux, A.: Improved generic algorithms for hard knapsacks. In: Paterson, K.G. (ed.) EUROCRYPT 2011. LNCS, vol. 6632, pp. 364–385. Springer, Heidelberg (2011). https://doi.org/10.1007/978-3-642-20465-4_21
3. Becker, A., Joux, A., May, A., Meurer, A.: Decoding random binary linear codes in $2^{n/20}$: how $1 + 1 = 0$ improves information set decoding. In: Pointcheval, D., Johansson, T. (eds.) EUROCRYPT 2012. LNCS, vol. 7237, pp. 520–536. Springer, Heidelberg (2012). https://doi.org/10.1007/978-3-642-29011-4_31
4. Brent, R.P., Zimmermann, P.: Algorithms for finding almost irreducible and almost primitive trinomials. Lectures in Honour of the Sixtieth Birthday of Hugh Cowie Williams, p. 2003 (2003)
5. Brent, R.P.: An improved Monte Carlo factorization algorithm. BIT Numer. Math. **20**, 176–184 (1980)
6. Canteaut, A., Chabaud, F.: A new algorithm for finding minimum-weight words in a linear code: application to McEliece's cryptosystem and to narrow-sense BCH codes of length 511. IEEE Trans. Inf. Theory **44**, 367–378 (1998)
7. Canteaut, A., Trabbia, M.: Improved fast correlation attacks using parity-check equations of weight 4 and 5. In: Preneel, B. (ed.) EUROCRYPT 2000. LNCS, vol. 1807, pp. 573–588. Springer, Heidelberg (2000). https://doi.org/10.1007/3-540-45539-6_40
8. Chose, P., Joux, A., Mitton, M.: Fast correlation attacks: an algorithmic point of view. In: Knudsen, L.R. (ed.) EUROCRYPT 2002. LNCS, vol. 2332, pp. 209–221. Springer, Heidelberg (2002). https://doi.org/10.1007/3-540-46035-7_14
9. Didier, J., Laigle-Chapuy, Y.: Finding low-weight polynomial multiples using discrete logarithm. In: IEEE International Symposium on Information Theory, ISIT 2007, Nice, France, p. to appear (2007)
10. Dinur, I., Dunkelman, O., Keller, N., Shamir, A.: Memory-efficient algorithms for finding needles in haystacks. In: Robshaw, M., Katz, J. (eds.) CRYPTO 2016, Part II. LNCS, vol. 9815, pp. 185–206. Springer, Heidelberg (2016). https://doi.org/10.1007/978-3-662-53008-5_7
11. El Aimani, L.: A new approach for finding low-weight polynomial multiples. In: Yu, Yu., Yung, M. (eds.) Inscrypt 2021. LNCS, vol. 13007, pp. 151–170. Springer, Cham (2021). https://doi.org/10.1007/978-3-030-88323-2_8
12. Esser, A., May, A.: Low weight discrete logarithm and subset sum in $2^{0.65n}$ with polynomial memory. In: Canteaut, A., Ishai, Y. (eds.) EUROCRYPT 2020. LNCS, vol. 12107, pp. 94–122. Springer, Cham (2020). https://doi.org/10.1007/978-3-030-45727-3_4
13. Finiasz, M., Vaudenay, S.: When stream cipher analysis meets public-key cryptography. In: Biham, E., Youssef, A.M. (eds.) SAC 2006. LNCS, vol. 4356, pp. 266–284. Springer, Heidelberg (2007). https://doi.org/10.1007/978-3-540-74462-7_19
14. Galbraith, S.D.: Mathematics of Public Key Cryptography. Cambridge University Press, Cambridge (2012)
15. Golic, J.D.: Computation of Low-Weight Parity-Check Polynomials. Electron. Lett. **32**, 1981–1982 (1996)
16. Löndahl, C., Johansson, T.: Improved algorithms for finding low-weight polynomial multiples in $F_2[x]$ and some cryptographic applications. Des. Codes Cryptogr. **73**, 625–640 (2014)

17. May, A., Ozerov, I.: On computing nearest neighbors with applications to decoding of binary linear codes. In: Oswald, E., Fischlin, M. (eds.) EUROCRYPT 2015. LNCS, vol. 9056, pp. 203–228. Springer, Heidelberg (2015). https://doi.org/10.1007/978-3-662-46800-5_9

18. Meier, W., Staffelbach, O.: Fast correlation attacks on certain stream ciphers. J. Cryptol. **1**, 159–176 (1989)

19. Peterlongo, P., Sala, M., Tinnirello, C.: A discrete logarithm-based approach to compute low-weight multiples of binary polynomials. Finite Fields Their Appl. **38**, 57–71 (2016)

20. Siegenthaler, T.: Decrypting a class of stream ciphers using ciphertext only. IEEE Trans. Comput. **C–34**(1), 81–84 (1985)

21. Stern, J.: A method for finding codewords of small weight. In: Cohen, G., Wolfmann, J. (eds.) Coding Theory 1988. LNCS, vol. 388, pp. 106–113. Springer, Heidelberg (1989). https://doi.org/10.1007/BFb0019850

22. van Oorschot, P.C., Wiener, M.J.: Parallel collision search with cryptanalytic applications. J. Cryptol. **12**(1), 1–28 (1999). https://doi.org/10.1007/PL00003816

23. von zur Gathen, J., Nöcker, M.: Polynomial and normal bases for finite fields. J. Cryptol. **18**(4), 337–355 (2005). https://doi.org/10.1007/s00145-004-0221-0

24. Wagner, D.: A generalized birthday problem. In: Yung, M. (ed.) CRYPTO 2002. LNCS, vol. 2442, pp. 288–304. Springer, Heidelberg (2002). https://doi.org/10.1007/3-540-45708-9_19

EHNP Strikes Back: Analyzing SM2 Implementations

Jinzheng Cao[1], Qingfeng Cheng[1]([✉]), and Jian Weng[2]

[1] Strategic Support Force Information Engineering University,
Zhengzhou 450001, China
qingfengc2008@sina.com
[2] Jinan University, Guangzhou 510630, China

Abstract. The SM2 digital signature algorithm is part of the Chinese standard public key cryptography suite designed on elliptic curves and has been included in various Chinese commercial applications. Due to the structure of the algorithm and quality of coding, some implementations are vulnerable to potential side-channel attacks and leak information about the double-and-add chains. Popular SM2 libraries such as GmSSL, TASSL and old versions of OpenSSL still use sliding-window (recommended by standard) or wNAF to conduct scalar multiplication of points, which is vulnerable to side-channel attacks like FLUSH+RELOAD: key recovery is then an instance of the Extended Hidden Number Problem (EHNP). The EHNP can be reduced to the Shortest Vector Problem (SVP) and solved with lattice algorithms. In this paper, we propose an extended key-recovery attack with leaked double-and-add chains from signature schemes such as SM2 and ECDSA. The side-channel leakage is possible in libraries which use wNAF or sliding-window multiplication. Our approach translates side information of different implementations to an EHNP instance, then propose novel strategies to reduce the EHNP to SVP in a lattice of smaller dimension than previous method, and introduce our algorithms to solve the problem. To evaluate the probability, we provide new estimations for the norm of the target vector, and formulate a tradeoff function. Finally, we show the new record of attacking SM2 with provided information. We are able to recover the secret key with only three signatures, while previous attacks required more than six signatures. We also attack the SM2 traces with improved probability and efficiency. Our new algorithm does not rely on any specific digital signature scheme, thus can be used to attack other signature algorithms.

Keywords: SM2 · Side-channel attack · Lattice · Extended hidden number problem

1 Introduction

SM2 is one of the Chinese national standard cryptographic algorithms published in 2010, which aims to provide protection for the domestic network infrastructure. In 2018, the SM2 scheme was included in ISO/IEC10118-3:2018, and

L. Batina and J. Daemen (Eds.): AFRICACRYPT 2022, LNCS 13503, pp. 576–600, 2022.
https://doi.org/10.1007/978-3-031-17433-9_25

became an international standard. In 2020, SM2 was merged in Linux kernel 5.10 release. SM2 is a public key cryptography suite based on elliptic curve, including a digital signature algorithm, an encryption algorithm, and a key exchange protocol. SM2 is part of the effort by the Chinese government to provide reliable protection for various information services (video monitoring, online banking, IC card, VPN applications and more). Similar to the elliptic curves digital signature algorithm (ECDSA), the theoretical security of SM2 digital signature is based on the computational intractability of the discrete logarithm problem on elliptic curves (ECDLP). However, real-world security problems may stem from implementation issues such as hardware structure and code quality. At present, some public SM2 implementations are based on old open source libraries to perform elliptic curve operations, and lack regular maintenance. As a result, potential vulnerabilities are introduced into the SM2 code unnoticed. Side-channel attacks on elliptic curve signatures usually focus on the scalar multiplication of points on the curve (sliding-window and wNAF). The goal of these algorithms is to accelerate the scalar multiplication of points with pre-computed data. In the process, however, different inputs result in different time cost and cache accessing operations. Consequently, side-channel approaches such as FLUSH+RELOAD are able to extract the sequence of add and double in the multiplication. At present, the community is not yet fully aware of the threat of EHNP attack in the face of new side-channel analysis techniques. We can still find, even in some popular projects, codes that have been proven to be at risk. This situation is worrying, especially when SM2 has been demanded by the Chinese state authorities in various public network services.

1.1 Background

Implementations of SM2. The original standard documentation recommends computing scalar multiplication of points by sliding-window multiplication, which may leak "double-and-add" chains by side-channel attacks. SM2 was included in TPM 2.0 and ISO/IEC 10118-3:2018, and deployed in extensive applications. At present, there are several open-source libraries that implement SM2. In 2018, SM2 was included in OpenSSL 1.1.1 beta. However, [29] argues that the code uses default wNAF algorithm to execute scalar multiplication, which is vulnerable to attacks such as FLUSH+RELOAD. Other libraries include GmSSL, Crypto++ and TASSL. These libraries use scalar multiplication algorithms based on codes from OpenSSL library, which also use the wNAF method. Chen et al. [5] first extracted side-channel information of SM2 nonces from smartcard and constructed lattice problem instances. Zhang et al. [31] attacked SM2 with wNAF and captured the traces. Presently, OpenSSL has used Montgomery ladder algorithm to replace wNAF. However, recent research [28] shows that even the "safe" algorithms (such as the "double-add-always" algorithm) will leak available traces through power analysis, and OpenSSL is still vulnerable if information about memory is known by the attacker.

Table 1. Open source implementations of SM2

Name	Language	Version	Scalar multiplier
OpenSSL	C	3.0	wNAF(old versions), Montgomery ladder
libgcrypt	C	1.9.4	Montgomery ladder
Crypto++	C++	8.6	wNAF
GmSSL	C	3.0	wNAF
TASSL	C	1.1.1	wNAF(default)
BouncyCasle	C#	1.9.0	Combination, wNAF
gmssl	Python	3.3.1	Double-and-add
snowland	Python	0.3.2	Double-and-add

Side-Channel Analysis. Initiated by Kocher et al. [17], the side-channel attack has become a useful approach to analyzing implementations of ECC algorithms. Side-channel attacks have been mounted against numerous cryptographic schemes [7,21] and poses a serious threat to the security of Internet protocols and mobile devices. In ECC algorithms, side-channel attacks mainly target the sliding-window and wNAF representation of nonces. At present, constant-time and constant-memory implementations can avoid some side-channel attacks, but attacks wNAF implementation are still relevant, especially in some libraries that are not updated in time. Moreover, recent research shows that even some "constant-time" executions are vulnerable to power analysis and still leak the information [28]. Genkin et al. were able to extract traces from Android and iOS devices via physical side-channel analysis [14]. A recent survey [16] shows that wNAF is still implemented in SunEC, Intel PP Crypto, Crypto++ libraries. The official document of SM2 suggests a sliding window method to execute scalar multiplication, while more open source projects still choose wNAF to do the task. Unfortunately, both methods will suffer from leakage by cache time attack such as FLUSH+RELOAD and PRIME+PROBE [8]. Table 1 lists some potentially vulnerable signature schemes.

Previous EHNP Attacks. Van de Pol et al. [24] derived an effective way of extracting information from 13 traces, but still used the HNP to recover the key. This method omitted much of the side information. Fan et al. [12] proposed an attack of ECDSA using EHNP. Their attack relies on the positions of non-zero coefficients in the wNAF or other presentations. Based on the information, an instance of the Extended Hidden Number Problem (EHNP) can be constructed. The authors solved the EHNP instances by lattice reduction algorithm and successfully recovered the key with four traces. De Micheli et al. [9] introduced preselecting of data to make sure traces of smaller weight are taken as input to construct a lattice basis. Zhang et al. [31] used the method to attack SM2 digital signature but did not achieve high success rate. Previous attacks can recover the secret key from a few traces, but the probability of recovering the secret key is relatively low. To formulate a reliable attack.

1.2   Our Results

Our main contribution is an improved method to solve the Extended Hidden Number problem (EHNP) and use the method to attack the SM2 digital signature with the "double-and-add" chain of the nonce. The chain is available through side-channel attack when the nonce is decomposed by sliding-window algorithm or wNAF algorithm. In fact, the sliding window is the algorithm recommended by the standard documentation, while the wNAF is implemented in popular libraries such as GmSSL and older versions of OpenSSL. Recovering the nonce is then translated to EHNP and further reduced to the Shortest Vector Problem (SVP) in lattice.

New Solution to EHNP. The first step of our solution is a new reduction from EHNP to SVP. In other words, we reduce EHNP equations to an SVP instance in a sublattice of smaller dimension compared with previous solutions. This is in contrast with the known construction of [12] and [9], which use a significantly larger lattice basis. Further, we adopt sieving to find the target vector when it is not sufficiently short.

Data-Probability Tradeoff. To describe the EHNP instance, we provide a data-probability tradeoff model to estimate the complexity of solving the problem. In fact, the number and length of traces along with merged digits will affect the length of the target vector compared with the Gaussian heuristic, thus changing the hardness of solving the instance. With the tradeoff model, we find suitable parameters to attack the SM2 signature and discuss how to protect the scheme.

Analyzing SM2 Implementations. We develop a new attack on SM2 libraries based on the new solution to EHNP. With a few signatures that leak side-channel information about sliding-window or wNAF multiplication, we are able to recover the private key. The attack is based on our new reduction from EHNP to SVP. We find that previous attacks are not able to make full use of the linear conditions of side-channel information: the attacker has to find the target vector in a larger search space. By adding new equations as constraint condition, we define a new SVP instance where the target vector is in a lattice of reduced dimension. In addition, previous research assumes that the target vector is the shortest if it is shorter than the Gaussian heuristic, while we prove that there exist unexpectedly short vectors.

By experimental results, it is superior to known attacks both in number of signatures required and in efficiency. Based on simulation and experimental results, we show that our attack is able to recover the key with only three double-and-add traces of wNAF or sliding-window multiplication. Compared with previous works, the new attack is superior in success probability and efficiency.

2   Preliminaries

2.1   SM2 Digital Signature

The SM2 signing algorithm is a digital signature algorithm based on elliptic curve. Let E be an elliptic curve on finite field $\mathbb{F}_q$, where q is prime. G is a known point on E of a large prime order n. H is a hash function (SM3 hash by standard). The secret key is an integer $0 < d_A < n$. The public key is the point $Q_A = d_A G$. Denote Z_A the personalization string. The main steps to sign a message m are as follows:

1) Compute the hash $h = H(Z_A \| m)$.
2) Select a secret nonce k uniformly from $[1, \dots, n-1]$.
3) Compute $(x, y) = kG$.
4) Compute $r = h + x \bmod n$.
5) Compute $s = (1 + d_A)^{-1}(k - rd_A) \bmod n$.
6) If any of $r = 0, s = 0$, or $s = k$ hold, retry.
7) Return the SM2 digital signature (r, s).

The pair (r, s) is an SM2 signature of message m. Given k and public information (s, r, m), the secret key can be recovered by computing

$$d_A = (s + r)^{-1}(k - s) \bmod n. \tag{1}$$

2.2   Scalar Multiplication and Side-Channel Attack

The scalar multiplication of an elliptic curve point is the most time-consuming operation in SM2 digital signature. To enable faster multiplication, the SM2 standard recommends sliding-window algorithm, which uses pre-computed points and decomposition of the scalar.

Sliding-Window Algorithm. The algorithm represents the nonce k by a sequence of non-zero digits $\{h_0, h_1, \dots, h_{l_k-1}\}$, where $l_k > 0, h_j \in [1, 2^w - 1]$, w is the window size. We can rewrite the nonce as

$$k = \sum_{j=0}^{l_k-1} 2^{c_j} h_j, \tag{2}$$

where $c_{j+1} > c_j \geq 0$.

Some libraries such as `Crypto++` and older versions of `OpenSSL` implement another representation for the nonce, the wNAF method.

wNAF Algorithm. In wNAF, the nonce k is also represented by a sequence of non-zero digits $\{h_0, h_1, \dots, h_{l_k-1}\}$ similar to sliding-window algorithm, where $\{h_j\}$ are the non-zero digits in $\{m_0, m_1, \dots\}$. But the h_j is in the range $[-2^w + 1, 2^w - 1]$.

Both sliding-window and wNAF compute the scalar multiplication kP with a sequence of "add" and "double" operations. By side-channel analysis of the time consumption and the behavior of caches, an attacker can retrieve the sequence of form "ADDDADDDDDDDAD ... DDDADD", where "A" represents an add operation in the **if-then** block, and "D" a double operation. We refer to the Hamming weight or number of non-zero digits of the trace as length. Naturally, from the order of 'A's and 'D's, we can recover the $\{c_j\}$ in the representation 2. From side-channel information, we can only decide if a digit is zero or not, yet the exact values of the non-zero digits are not revealed. In the following sections, we try to find the unknown values and recover the secret d_A with the side information.

2.3   EHNP

The Extended Hidden Number Problem (EHNP) was initially introduced to study the DSA signatures. We will construct an EHNP instance from the positions of non-zero digits.

Definition 1 (Extended Hidden Number Problem). *Let N be a prime, given u congruences*

$$\beta_i x + \sum_{j=1}^{l_i} a_{i,j} k_{i,j} \equiv c_i \bmod N, 1 \le i \le u,$$

where $k_{i,j}$ and x are unknown. $0 \le k_{i,j} \le 2^{\epsilon_{i,j}}$. $\beta_i, a_{i,j}, c_i, l_i$ are known. The EHNP is to find the hidden number x that satisfies the conditions above.

The EHNP can be reduced to an approximate SVP instance with suitable parameters.

2.4   Lattice

We provide basic concepts, necessary assumptions, and hard problems about lattice. Readers can refer to [23] to learn more about lattice.

Definition 2 (Lattice). *Let $\mathbf{b}_1, \mathbf{b}_2, \ldots, \mathbf{b}_d \in \mathbb{R}^d$ be linearly independent vectors. We define the lattice basis as $B = [\mathbf{b}_1, \mathbf{b}_2, \ldots, \mathbf{b}_d]$. The lattice generated by B is $\mathcal{L}(B) = \{\sum_{i=1}^{d} x_i \mathbf{b}_i : x_i \in \mathbb{Z}\}$.*

We refer to $\mathcal{L}$ as the full lattice compared with the sublattice generated by the submatrix of full basis B. For a given basis B, π_i are the projections orthogonal to the span of $\mathbf{b}_1, \mathbf{b}_2, \ldots, \mathbf{b}_{i-1}$ and the Gram-Schmidt orthogonalization of B is $B^* = [\mathbf{b}_1^*, \mathbf{b}_2^*, \ldots, \mathbf{b}_d^*]$, where $\mathbf{b}_i^* = \pi_i(\mathbf{b}_i)$. The determinant of $\mathcal{L}$ denotes the volume of the fundamental area, $\det \mathcal{L} = \det B = \|\mathbf{b}_1^*\| \|\mathbf{b}_2^*\| \ldots \|\mathbf{b}_d^*\|$.

The Shortest Vector Problem (SVP) and the Closest Vector Problem (CVP) is one of the fundamental problems of lattice-based cryptography. The problem demands to find a non-zero lattice vector of minimal length.

Definition 3 (Shortest Vector Problem). *Given a basis B of a lattice $\mathcal{L}$, find a non-zero lattice vector $v \in \mathcal{L}$ of minimal length $\lambda_1(\mathcal{L}) = \min_{0 \neq \mathbf{w} \in L} \|\mathbf{w}\|$.*

In practice, approximate versions of SVP are usually used, which asks to find a vector longer than the shortest vector by a polynomial factor. To evaluate the quality of the lattice, we adopt the Gaussian heuristic [22] to explain our analysis. Let $K \subset \mathbb{R}^d$ be a measurable body, then $|K \cap \mathcal{L}| \approx \mathrm{vol}(K)/\det(\mathcal{L})$. When applying the heuristic to a d-dimension ball of volume $\det(\mathcal{L})$ we get

$$\lambda_1(\mathcal{L}) \approx \frac{\Gamma\left(\frac{d}{2}+1\right)^{\frac{1}{d}} \det(\mathcal{L})^{\frac{1}{d}}}{\sqrt{\pi}} \approx \sqrt{\frac{d}{2\pi e}} \det(\mathcal{L})^{1/d}.$$

We denote the heuristic length by $gh(\mathcal{L})$ or $\mathrm{GH}(\mathcal{L})$ in short. In a random lattice $\mathcal{L}$, we assume the shortest vector will have norm $\mathrm{GH}(\mathcal{L})$.

2.5 Lattice Reduction and Sieve

Currently, lattice reduction, sieve and enumeration are used to find a short vector in a given lattice. The first widely applied reduction algorithm is LLL [19]. The LLL algorithm has a polynomial time complexity, but the quality of output basis is limited. LLL has been widely used in attacks such as Coppersmith's attack on RSA. BKZ algorithm is commonly used to get a basis better than LLL. A BKZ-reduced lattice basis B for block size $\beta \geq 2$ satisfies $\mathbf{b}_i^* = \lambda_1(\pi_i(\mathcal{L}_{[i:\min(i+\beta,d)]}))$, $i = 1, \ldots, d-1$. When taking a d-dimensional lattice as input, the algorithm outputs a short vector of length $\approx \left(\beta^{1/2\beta}\right)^d \det(\mathcal{L})^{1/d}$ in time $\beta^{\beta/(2e)}$ [15]. Although some algorithms, such as slide reduction [13], allow better theoretical results, BKZ and its variants are preferred in practical circumstances. The BKZ algorithm and the BKZ 2.0 variant [6] can achieve a good balance between the quality of reduced basis and running-time.

The Sieve algorithm takes a list of lattice vectors as input, then searches for short integer combinations of the vectors. Typically, when the input list is sufficiently large, then SVP can be solved by recursively performing the process. At present, heuristic sieve algorithms such as 3-Sieve are important SVP solvers. Sieve has a time complexity ranging from $(4/3)^{n+o(n)}$ to $(3/2)^{n/2+o(n)}$ with its different variants [4,18]. In 2018, Ducas proposed Subsieve [10], combining sieve and Babai's lift to decrease the complexity. The algorithm can find the shortest vector by sieve in a context of rank $\Theta(d/\log d)$. In 2019, Albrecht et al. gave an implementation of the algorithm, along with a general kernel for sieve [1]. Currently, the fastest public sieve implementation is the GPU version of G6K library [11].

3 Generic EHNP Attack on SM2 Implementations

In this section, we summarize our main contribution, a generic EHNP analysis on SM2 implementations. The method is based on our new solution to EHNP. Prior works usually construct an EHNP instance from wNAF traces, while we show that the model can be applied to traces from both sliding-window and wNAF

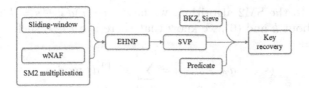

Fig. 1. Outline of attack

multiplications. The EHNP attack model does not depend on specific schemes of signature or implementations, and thus can equally apply to SM2, ECDSA or other ECC cryptosystems. The outline of our attack is shown in Fig. 1.

3.1 EHNP from Sliding-Window

After retrieving side-channel information from sliding-window multiplication, we have the equation:

$$k = \sum_{j=0}^{l_k-1} 2^{\lambda_j} h_j,$$

with the coefficients h_j unknown, and $0 \leq h_j \leq 2^w - 1$. From (1), we have

$$(s+r)d_A = k - s \bmod n. \tag{3}$$

According to the sliding-window algorithm, h_j is odd. So the h_j is rewritten as $h_j = 2d_j + 1$, and

$$k = \overline{k} + \sum_{j=0}^{l_k-1} 2^{\lambda_j+1} d_j, \tag{4}$$

where $\overline{k} = \sum_{j=0}^{l_k-1} 2^{\lambda_j}$. Therefore, we have

$$(s+r)d_A + s - \overline{k} = \sum_{j=0}^{l_k-1} 2^{\lambda_j+1} d_j \bmod n, \tag{5}$$

where $\{d_j\}$ is unknown, $|d_j| < 2^{w-1}$. Such equations form an EHNP instance.

3.2 EHNP from wNAF

Similar to sliding-window, with side information of wNAF point multiplication, we rewrite k as $k = \sum_{i=1}^{l} k_i 2^{\lambda_i}$, where $k_i \in \{\pm 1, \pm 3, \ldots, \pm(2^w - 1)\}$. Obviously the i-th non-zero digit k_i is odd, so we rewrite it as $k_i = 1 + 2 \cdot k_i'$, where $k_i' \in [-2^{w-1}, 2^{w-1} - 1]$. Let $d_i = k_i' + 2^{w-1} \in [0, 2^w - 1]$, so k can be rewritten as

$$k = \sum_{i=1}^{l} k_i 2^{\lambda_i} = \overline{k} + \sum_{i=1}^{l} d_i 2^{\lambda_i+1}, \tag{6}$$

where $\overline{k} = \sum_{i=1}^{l} 2^{\lambda_i} - \sum_{i=1}^{l} 2^{\lambda_i+w}$.

According to the SM2 algorithm, we have $(s + r)d_A + s = k \bmod n$. With information about k and (6), we know that there is a $t \in \mathbb{Z}$ such that

$$(s + r)d_A + s - \overline{k} = \sum_{j=0}^{l_k-1} 2^{\lambda_j+1} d_j \bmod n, \tag{7}$$

where $0 < d_A < q$ and $0 \le d_j \le 2^w - 1$ are unknown.

3.3   Modifying EHNP

After formulating the EHNP instance, we make some modifications to the instance to improve the efficiency of solving the problem. The techniques we use are first initiated by [12] and [9] to attack ECDSA. We will show that they are also useful when attacking SM2. With u signatures (r_i, s_i) of different messages using one secret key d_A, we can build following equations:

$$\begin{cases} (s_1 + r_1)d_A + s_1 - \overline{k_1} - \displaystyle\sum_{j=0}^{l_1-1} 2^{\lambda_{1,j}+1} d_{1,j} + t_1 n = 0, \\ \qquad\qquad \cdots \\ (s_u + r_u)d_A + s_u - \overline{k_u} - \displaystyle\sum_{j=0}^{l_u-1} 2^{\lambda_{u,j}+1} d_{u,j} + t_u n = 0, \end{cases} \tag{8}$$

where l_i denotes the number of non-zero digits of ephemeral key k_i, $\lambda_{i,j}$ is the position of the j-th non-zero digit $k_{i,j}$. The definition of $\overline{k_i}$ and $d_{i,j}$ are discussed as above. The value of $\alpha, d_{i,j}$ and h_i are unknown. To reduce the dimension of EHNP, eliminating and merging are commonly used.

Merging. The technique of merging minimizes the number of unknown bits in a trace, reducing the number of non-zero digits l of each ephemeral key [9]. In the merging process, we replace $2^{\lambda_i+1} d_i + 2^{\lambda_{i+1}+1} d_{i+1}$ with $2^{\lambda_i+1} d'_i$, where the expected value of d'_i is $d_i + d_{i+1} 2^{\lambda_{i+1}-\lambda_i}$. The main operation is to merge consecutive non-zero digits into a new non-zero digit. The distance of two adjacent non-zero digits is $\lambda_{i+1} - \lambda_i \ge w + 1 (1 \le i \le l - 1)$. From literature, we have the following conclusion ([12], Theorem 1):

Theorem 1. *For $h \ge 1$, suppose $h + 1$ consecutive digits $d_i, \ldots, d_{i+h}(d_j \in [0, 2^{w'} - 1])$ are merged as a new digit d'_i. Then we have $0 \le d'_i \le 2^{\mu_i} - 1$, where $\mu_i = \lambda_{i+h} - \lambda_i + w'$ is the window size of d'_i.*

This result gives the upper bound of the unknown d'. In addition, $\lambda_{i+h} - \lambda_i + w = w + \sum_{j=1}^{h}(\lambda_{i+j} - \lambda_{i+j-1}) \ge h(w + 1) + w$. The equality holds if and only if $\lambda_{i+j} - \lambda_{i+j-1} = w + 1, 1 \le j \le h$. In this case, we can minimize the number of unknown bits. We adopt the merging technique from [12], in which the consecutive non-zero digits whose distance is $w + 1$ are merged. This strategy ensures that we can reduce about half the number of non-zero digits while keeping the number of unknown bits as small as possible.

Eliminating d_A. One straightforward improvement is to eliminate d_A from the equations [12], thus reducing the dimension by 1. We denote the i-th equation in (8) as E_i. To eliminate d_A, we compute $(s_1 + r_1)E_i - (s_i + r_i)E_1$ for $1 < i \le u$. As a result, we have the following equations:

$$\sum_{j=1}^{l_1} \underbrace{(2^{\lambda_{1,j}+1}(s_i + r_i))}_{\tau_{j,i}} d_{1,j} + \sum_{j=1}^{l_i} \underbrace{(-2^{\lambda_{i,j}+1}(s_1 + r_1))}_{\sigma_{i,j}} d_{i,j} - \underbrace{[(s_1 + r_1)(\overline{k}_i - s_i) - (s_i + r_i)(\overline{k}_1 - s_1)]}_{\gamma_i} + t_i n = 0,$$

where $0 \le d_{1,j}, d_{i,j} \le 2^{\mu_{i,j}} - 1$ and t_i are unknown. The equations form a new EHNP instance.

$$M = \begin{bmatrix}
n & & & & & & & & & & & \\
 & \ddots & & & & & & & & & & \\
 & & n & & & & & & & & & \\
\tau_{1,2} & \cdots & \tau_{1,u} & \delta/2^{\mu_{1,1}} & & & & & & & & \\
\vdots & & \vdots & & \ddots & & & & & & & \\
\tau_{l_1,2} & & \tau_{l_1,u} & & & \delta/2^{\mu_{1,l_1}} & & & & & & \\
\sigma_{2,1} & & & & & & \delta/2^{\mu_{2,1}} & & & & & \\
\vdots & & & & & & & \ddots & & & & \\
\sigma_{2,l_2} & & & & & & & & \delta/2^{\mu_{2,l_2}} & & & \\
 & \ddots & & & & & & & & \ddots & & \\
\sigma_{u,1} & & & & & & & & & & \delta/2^{\mu_{u,1}} & \\
\vdots & & & & & & & & & & & \ddots \\
\sigma_{u,l_u} & & & & & & & & & & & \delta/2^{\mu_{u,l_u}} \\
\gamma_2 & \cdots & \gamma_u & \delta/2 & \cdots & \delta/2 & \delta/2 & \cdots & \delta/2 & \cdots & \delta/2 & \cdots & \delta/2 & \delta/2
\end{bmatrix} \quad (9)$$

3.4 EHNP to SVP in Sublattice

We propose a new method to solve the EHNP initiated from SM2 side-channel information. By adding a dimension, the EHNP can be converted to an SVP instance in lattice. Fan et al. [12] constructs a basis matrix M as in (9). Let $T = \sum_{i=1}^{u} l_i$, then M is a $(T + u) \times (T + u)$ matrix as in (9). The row vectors in M form a basis of a lattice $\mathcal{L}(M)$ of dimension $d = T + u$. To solve the EHNP instance, the attacker should find the vector

$$\mathbf{z} = [t_2, \ldots, t_u, d_{1,1}, \ldots, d_{1,l_1}, \ldots, d_{u,1}, \ldots, d_{u,l_u}, -1] \cdot M$$

$$= [0, \ldots, 0, \frac{d_{1,1}}{2^{\mu_{1,1}}}\delta - \frac{\delta}{2}, \ldots, \frac{d_{1,l_1}}{2^{\mu_{1,l_1}}}\delta - \frac{\delta}{2}, \ldots, \frac{d_{u,1}}{2^{\mu_{u,1}}}\delta$$

$$- \frac{\delta}{2}, \ldots, \frac{d_{u,l_u}}{2^{\mu_{u,l_u}}}\delta - \frac{\delta}{2}, -\frac{\delta}{2}] \in \mathcal{L}(M).$$

This subsection introduces a new reduction from EHNP to SVP in a sublattice of $\mathcal{L}(M)$. One of the problems with the classic method is that it introduces an additional factor δ, which will affect the ratio $\|z\|/vol(\mathcal{L})^{1/(T+u)}$. According to [12] and [9], δ has to be large to make z short enough to be recovered with a BKZ call. Our approach reduces the dimension of the basis by $(u-1)$, and eliminate the effect of δ on the basis. Recall that to recover the correct d_A, the first $u-1$ components of z must be 0. The target vector z can be rewritten as $z = [t, d] \cdot M = [0_{u-1}, b]$, where $t \in \mathbb{Z}^{u-1}, d \in \mathbb{Z}^{T+1}, b \in \mathbb{Z}^{T+1}$. From the equation, we have

$$0_{u-1} = t \cdot nI_{u-1} + d \cdot A,$$
$$b = d \cdot \delta B. \tag{10}$$

In this way, we describe the target vector with an additional condition. Using the condition, we can define a smaller basis where the target can be found. In the following part, we define the sublattice of the EHNP-lattice.

Definition 4. *For a $(T + u) \times (T + u)$-EHNP basis* $M = \begin{bmatrix} nI_{u-1} & 0 \\ A & \delta B \end{bmatrix}$, *the sublattice of M is defined as* $\mathcal{L}' = \mathcal{L}_{\text{sub}}(M) = \{d' \cdot \delta B \in \mathcal{L}(\delta B) : d' \cdot A = 0_{u-1} \pmod{q}\}$.

To solve the EHNP instance, we will expect to find the target vector $b = d \cdot B$ as in (10). The following theorem describes the rank of the sublattice $\mathcal{L}'$.

Theorem 2. *At least $u - 1$ vectors in the basis of $\mathcal{L}$ are independent to the target vector* $z = [0_{u-1}, b]$.

Proof. To solve the equation $d \cdot A = 0_{u-1} \pmod{n}$ is equivalent to solving

$$t \cdot nI_{u-1} + d \cdot A = 0_{u-1},$$

where t and d are integer vectors. So vector $[t, d]$ is in the left kernel of block $\begin{bmatrix} nI_{u-1} \\ A \end{bmatrix} \in \mathbb{Z}^{(T+u) \times (u-1)}$. The kernel of the block has rank $T + 1$. Therefore, there exist $u - 1$ independent vectors b' such that $d' \cdot A \neq 0_{u-1} \pmod{n}$.

In fact, we can describe the shape of the $u - 1$ independent vectors explicitly. Recall that n is a prime number, so $\gcd(n, \tau_{i,j}) = \gcd(n, \sigma_{i',j'}) = 1$. Thus, after some linear combination, there is a vector with a 1 element in the first $u - 1$ positions.

$$c_i = [\underbrace{0, \ldots, 1, 0, \ldots,}_{u-1} \underbrace{c'_i}_{T+1}].$$

When we check the formation of the target vector $b = d \cdot \delta B$, obviously every component of b has a factor δ. In the following theorem, we argue that different δ values lead to isomorphic sublattices

Theorem 3. *For two basis $M_{\delta_1}, M_{\delta_2}$ generated by the same EHNP instance and two δ values δ_1, δ_2, they contain sublattices $\mathcal{L}_{\text{sub}}(M_{\delta_1})$ and $\mathcal{L}_{\text{sub}}(M_{\delta_2})$ which are isomorphic.*

Proof. We first give the basis of $\mathcal{L}_{\mathsf{sub}}(M_{\delta_1})$ and $\mathcal{L}_{\mathsf{sub}}(M_{\delta_2})$. From the definition of M, M_{δ_1} and M_{δ_2} share the same left block $\begin{bmatrix} nI_{u-1} \\ A \end{bmatrix}$. As an n-ary matrix, the block has the Hermite Normal Form $\begin{bmatrix} I_{u-1} \\ 0 \end{bmatrix}$. Therefore, there is an unimodular matrix R such that $R\begin{bmatrix} nI_{u-1} \\ A \end{bmatrix} = \begin{bmatrix} I_{u-1} \\ 0 \end{bmatrix}$. Similarly, $RM = \begin{bmatrix} I_{u-1} & C' \\ 0 & \delta B' \end{bmatrix}$. B' is not affected by choice of δ, and $\delta b_1, \ldots, \delta b_{T+1}$ are the basis vectors of sublattice $\mathcal{L}_{\mathsf{sub}}(M_\delta)$, where $b_1, \ldots, b_{T+1}$ are the rows of B'. Define a homomorphic map

$$\phi : \mathcal{L}_{\mathsf{sub}}(M_{\delta_1}) \to \mathcal{L}_{\mathsf{sub}}(M_{\delta_2})$$

$$[\delta_1 a_1, \delta_1 a_2, \ldots, \delta_1 a_{T+1}] \to [\delta_2 a_1, \delta_2 a_2, \ldots, \delta_2 a_{T+1}].$$

For every basis $\delta_1 b_i \in \mathcal{L}_{\mathsf{sub}}(M_{\delta_1})$, $\phi(\delta_1 b_i) = \delta_2 b_i$ is a corresponding basis vector in $\mathcal{L}_{\mathsf{sub}}(M_{\delta_1})$. Therefore, ϕ is an isomorphic map.

In other words, the δ no longer affects the recovery of $\mathbf{b}$ in the sublattice. For simplicity, we can set $\delta = 1$ in the following sections and omit it. Therefore, the recovery of secret is converted to finding $\mathbf{b}$ in the sublattice $\mathcal{L}_{\mathsf{sub}}(M)$. The attack we have described assumes that the traces we obtain are perfectly correct. In that case, our algorithm ensures a good probability to recover the secret key. However, more likely than not, the traces may contain some wrong digits. According to [24], the probability to obtain a perfectly correct trace is 56%. Therefore, it is important to conduct efficient attacks with a few traces. When possible errors are considered, the target vector z is significantly longer compared to the error-free case.

3.5   SVP with Predicate

In Subsect. 3.4, we construct the sublattice basis B, and propose that the target vector $\mathbf{b}$ is a short vector in the sublattice. As we will discuss in following sections, the target vector is not necessarily the shortest vector in the lattice. In similar situations, Albrecht et al. used predicate to solve the Bounded Distance Decoding problem [3]. In this work, we introduce the predicate to find the target vector in EHNP sublattice.

Definition 5 (α-Shortest Vector Problem with predicate). *Given a basis B of a lattice $\mathcal{L}$, a parameter $0 < \alpha$ and predicate $g(\cdot)$, find the non-zero lattice vector $\mathbf{v} \in \mathcal{L}$ satisfying $GH(\mathcal{L}) > \alpha \cdot \|\mathbf{v}\|$ and $g(\mathbf{v}) = 1$.*

The uniqueness of target vector $\mathbf{b}$ is not only ensured by its norm, but also the non-linear conditions the elements satisfy. For SM2, that condition is the elliptic curve discrete logarithm problem (ECDLP). What we are going to solve is actually a lattice problem with predicate. In this form, the empirical technique of examining the entire reduced basis to find the target is systematized. We use a predicate $g(\cdot)$ to describe the non-linear condition $\mathbf{b}$ should satisfy and therefore

---

Algorithm 1: SVP predicate $g(\cdot)$

Input: Vector $\mathbf{v} = [v_1, v_2, \ldots, v_d]$

Output: $g(\mathbf{b})$

Compute $\mathbf{u} = \mathbf{v} \cdot B^{-1} = [t_2, \ldots, t_u, d_{1,1}, \ldots, d_{1,l_1}, \ldots, d_{u,1}, \ldots, d_{u,l_u}, m]$;

if $m \neq -1$ **then**
 | **return** *FALSE*;
end

Solve equation $(s_i + r_i)d_A + s_i - \overline{k_i} - \sum_{j=0}^{l_i-1} 2^{\lambda_{i,j}+1} d_{i,j} + t_i n = 0$, get d_A;

if $Q_A == d_A \cdot G$ **then**
 | **return** *TRUE*;
end

else
 | **return** *FALSE*;
end

---

ensure the uniqueness of the target vector. After lattice reduction or SVP solver is called, we search for vectors satisfying $g(\mathbf{b}) = 1$ in the output. This technique is meant to make use of the non-linear information that is omitted and improve the success probability. For an EHNP instance generated from SM2 traces, the $\{\mu_{i,j}\}$ and basis matrix B are known. Therefore, we can define a predicate to find vector $\mathbf{b}$ as in Algorithm 1.

3.6 Attack Algorithm for SM2

We summarize our method of attacking SM2 and provides our algorithms for recovering the SM2 private key. We propose two algorithms for attacking SM2, one based on lattice reduction, and one based on sieve. The algorithms take in as input a database of traces and the predicate, as well as other parameters. We begin with the basic procedures of our attack.

Baseline. We first introduce the basic strategies of our algorithms. One of the fundamental techniques is building an SVP instance in sublattice from traces as described in Sect. 3.4. By constructing a compact sublattice, the dimension of the basis is $T + 1$, while previous attacks need a basis of dimension $T + u$. To improve the probability of recovering the secret with a few traces, we preselect the traces to construct a better basis. After the SVP solver is called, we use predicate to find the target vector $\mathbf{b}$ instead of only trying to get the shortest vector.

Primary Attack. Our first algorithm aims to recover the private key as fast as possible. This method is useful when the target is expected to be significantly shorter than other lattice vectors. Previous researchers [9,12] tend to simply use BKZ to solve the SVP instance. To improve the efficiency, we adopt the progressive reduction, which increases the block size in the process of reduction. The algorithm is shown in Algorithm 2.

Algorithm 2: Primary attack

Input: Set of traces S, dimension d, block size β_{max}, predicate $g(\cdot)$
Output: Vector **b**
Select u traces from S to maximize function f;
Construct matrix M as described in (9);
Compute the Hermite Normal Form of the left block of M, get the
  transformation matrix R;
Compute RM, remove irrelevant vectors, get the sublattice basis B from M;
Set β to be the number of quasi-reduced rows in B;
while $\beta < \beta_{max}$ **do**
  BKZ tour on B with block size β;
  Increase β;
  if *row vector* **v** *in B satisfies* $g(\mathbf{v}) = 1$ **then**
  | **return v**
  end
end

Hybrid Attack. Our second, and stronger, algorithm is a combination of lattice reduction and sieve, before using predicate to check the output vectors. The goal of the algorithm is to improve the probability of success. By sieving in the basis, we can recover target vectors not enough to be found by simply running BKZ. The basic structure of our algorithm to solve the EHNP-SVP is progressive BKZ combined with sieve. The BKZ procedure is similar to Algorithm 2. The algorithm then uses sieve as the SVP solver after progressive reduction. In addition, we consider the list of output vectors (database), and run the predicate on each of the vectors. This technique considers the set of relatively short vectors or "database" that a sieve call outputs [2]. Heuristically, after a sieve call terminates, it will output a list L that contains all vectors shorter than $\sqrt{4/3}\mathrm{GH}(\mathcal{L})$. The sieve attack is expected to improve the probability of successful attacks. The algorithm is shown as in Algorithm 3.

To implement efficient sieve attacks, we adopt the "dimension-for-free" technique, which runs a sieve in a projected block of dimension $d' = d - \Theta(d/\log d)$. It is one of the fastest sieve variants proposed by Ducas [10]. According to [1], the target vector **b** can be found if its projection $\|\pi_{d-d'}(\mathbf{b})\|$ satisfies $\|\pi_{d-d'}(\mathbf{b})\| \leq \sqrt{4/3} \cdot \mathrm{GH}(\pi_{d-d'}(\mathcal{L}_{\mathbf{sub}}))$. [10] predicts that $d' = d - \frac{d\log(4/3)}{\log(d/(2\pi e))}$. However, our attack may result a target vector longer than $\mathrm{GH}(\mathcal{L}_{\mathbf{sub}})$. In practice, we should adjust the parameters.

4   Analysis of SM2-EHNP

In this section, we analyze our EHNP attack based on the parameters of SM2 digital signature, and discuss the success condition of key recovery. We provide a model to analyze the relationship between amount of unknown data and probability of successful attack. Additionally, we prove in this section that the target

Algorithm 3: Hybrid attack

Input: Set of traces S, dimension d, block size β_{max}, predicate $g(\cdot)$
Output: Vector **b**
Select u traces from S to maximize function f;
Extract sublattice basis B from traces;
Set β to be the number of quasi-reduced rows in B;
while $\beta < \beta_{max}$ **do**
$\quad$ BKZ tour on B with block size β;
$\quad$ Increase β;
$\quad$ **if** *row vector* **v** *in B satisfies* $g(\mathbf{v}) = 1$ **then**
$\quad\quad$ | **return v**
$\quad$ **end**
end
Run sieve algorithm on projected sublattice of B, return the shortest vector **b**;
Lift the vectors in L', get list of vectors L;
for $\mathbf{v} \in L$ **do**
$\quad$ **if** $g(\mathbf{v}) = 1$ **then**
$\quad\quad$ | **return v**
$\quad$ **end**
end

---

vector is not necessarily the shortest vector in the sublattice. To find the target vector that is not short enough, we use predicate to check the basis.

4.1   Expected Norm of Target Vector

We start our analysis from a new estimation of $\|\mathbf{b}\|$. According to Sect. 3, the target vector has norm $\|\mathbf{b}\| \leq \sqrt{T+1}/2$. Assuming that the value of non-zero digits in the trace is distributed uniformly, we estimate the norm of **b** in the average case.

$$
\mathbb{E}(\|\mathbf{b}\|^2) = \mathbb{E}\left[\sum_{1 \leq i \leq u,\ 1 \leq j \leq l_u} \left(\frac{d_{i,j}}{2^{\mu_{i,j}}} - \frac{1}{2} \right)^2 + \left(\frac{1}{2} \right)^2 \right]
$$

$$
= T \cdot \mathbb{E}\left[\left(\frac{d_{i,j}}{2^{\mu_{i,j}}} - \frac{1}{2} \right)^2 \right] + \frac{1}{4}.
$$

Assuming $d_{i,j}$ is distributed uniformly in $[0, 2^{\mu_{i,j}} - 1]$, we have

$$
\mathbb{E}\left[\left(\frac{d_{i,j}}{2^{\mu_{i,j}}} - \frac{1}{2} \right)^2 \right] = \frac{1}{2^{2\mu_{i,j}}} \mathbb{E}\left[\left(d_{i,j} - 2^{\mu_{i,j}-1} \right)^2 \right]
$$

$$
= \frac{1}{2^{2\mu_{i,j}}} \left[\frac{1}{2^{\mu_{i,j}}} \sum_{k=0}^{2^{\mu_{i,j}}-1} \left(k - 2^{\mu_{i,j}-1} \right)^2 \right]
$$

$$
= \frac{1}{12} + \frac{1}{6 \cdot 2^{2\mu_{i,j}}},
$$

and

$$\mathbb{E}(\|\mathbf{b}\|^2) = \mathbb{E}\left[\sum_{1 \le i \le u,\ 1 \le j \le l_u} \left(\frac{d_{i,j}}{2^{\mu_{i,j}}} - \frac{1}{2}\right)^2 + \left(\frac{1}{2}\right)^2\right]$$

$$= \frac{T}{12} + \frac{1}{4} + \sum_{1 \le i \le u,\ 1 \le j \le l_u} \frac{1}{6 \cdot 2^{2\mu_{i,j}}}$$

$$\approx \frac{T}{12} + \frac{1}{4}.$$

Therefore, the target vector $\mathbf{b}$ has expected norm $O(\sqrt{T/12})$, relatively shorter than the upper bound $O(\sqrt{T}/2)$. As a result, the success condition of the attack can be relaxed.

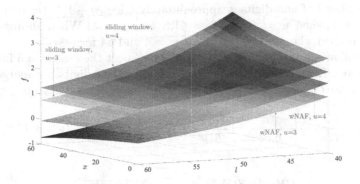

Fig. 2. Simulator function

4.2 Data-Probability Tradeoff

To recover the secret key with lattice reduction algorithms, we expect that the target vector $\mathbf{b}$ is significantly shorter than the Gaussian heuristic of the basis. In this subsection, we try to evaluate the shortness of the target vector, ensure a high success rate for the attack, and further, give a trade-off formula to assess the probability of successful attacks. We first compute the determinant of sublattice $\mathcal{L}_{\mathbf{sub}}(M)$.

Theorem 3 introduces unimodular R such that $RM = \begin{bmatrix} I_{u-1} & C' \\ \mathbf{0} & B' \end{bmatrix}$. Therefore, we have

$$|M| = |RM| = |I_{u-1}||B'|,$$

and $\det(\mathcal{L}') = |B'| = |M| = n^{u-1}2^{-U-1}$, where $U = \sum_{i=1}^{u}\sum_{j=1}^{l_u}\mu_{i,j}$.

The determinant of $\mathcal{L}_{\mathbf{sub}}(M)$ is affected by $\{\mu_{i,j}\}$. In the attack, we apply the merging technique to shorten the traces, or reduce the number of non-zero coefficients. As a side effect, this operation increases U.

Theorem 4. *After m merging operations, the sum of merged $\mu_{i,j}$ values increases by m.*

Proof. The merging technique only merges two digits when their distance is $w + 1$. Suppose $k_0, k_1, \ldots, k_m$ are consecutive non-zero digits to be merged of position $\lambda_0, \lambda_1, \ldots, \lambda_m$, where $\lambda_{i+1} - \lambda_i = 4, i = 0, 1, \ldots, m$. Suppose the original $\mu_0, \mu_1, \ldots, \mu_m$ are all w (the window size). After m merging operations, the m digits are merged into new digit with $\mu'_0 = 3 + \lambda_m - \lambda_0 = 3 + 4m = \sum_{i=-0}^m \mu_i + m$.

Suppose x digits in total are merged in the traces, then the Gaussian heuristic of $\mathcal{L}'$ is

$$\mathrm{GH}(\mathcal{L}') \approx \sqrt{\frac{T' + 1}{2\pi e}} n^{\frac{u-1}{T'+1}} 2^{-\frac{U'+1}{T'+1}}, \tag{11}$$

where $T' = T - x, T = lu$. For the wNAF version of scalar multiplication, the average number l of non-digits is approximately $(\lfloor \log_2 n + 1 \rfloor)/(w + 2) - 1$. We have $l \approx 50.4$ when $w = 3$ and $l \approx 41.8$ for $w = 4$. When sliding-window algorithm is used, the average l is 51 for $w = 4$ and 64 for $w = 3$.

In the following part of this subsection, we inspect the case $w = 3$ for wNAF multiplication. Before merging, $T = lu, U = 3lu$. After digits are merged, T, U are updated to $T' = lu - x, U' = 3lu + x$. After merging, we have $\mu'_{i,j} > 4$. So

$$\mathbb{E}(\|\mathbf{b}\|^2) \leq \frac{T'}{12} + \frac{1}{4} + \frac{T'}{6 \cdot 2^{10}} = \frac{171T'}{2048} + \frac{1}{4} < \frac{1}{10}(T' + 1) \quad (\text{when } T' > 10),$$

and

$$\mathrm{GH}(\mathcal{L}')/\mathbb{E}(\|\mathbf{b}\|) < \sqrt{\frac{5}{\pi e}} n^{\frac{u-1}{T'+1}} 2^{-\frac{U'+1}{T'+1}}.$$

To mount an efficient attack, we expect the ratio to be as large as possible. To evaluate the chance of success, we define a simulator function

$$\begin{aligned} f = \log_2(n^{\frac{u-1}{T'+1}} 2^{-\frac{U'+1}{T'+1}}) &= \frac{u-1}{T - x + 1} \log_2 n - \frac{U + x + 1}{T - x + 1} \log_2 2 \\ &= \frac{u-1}{lu - x + 1} 256 - \frac{3lu + x + 1}{lu - x + 1}, \end{aligned} \tag{12}$$

where we approximately assume $\log_2 n = 256$. When f is larger, the target vector is easier to be found by an SVP solver such as lattice reduction. Therefore, we use f to estimate the tradeoff of data provided and the probability of success. Figure 2 illustrates the value of f.

From Fig. 2, we can see the merging technique has relatively complicated influence on the EHNP instance, for it changes both the length of traces and μ values. On average, we assume $l = 50, U = 3T = 150u$. For $u = 3$ as an example, then $f_{u=3} = (2 \times 256)/(151 - x) - (451 + x)/(151 - x)$, which is a decreasing function. However, when $u = 3$, $\frac{\partial f}{\partial x} = 0 \Rightarrow T = 3l = 127$. Therefore, when the traces contain fewer non-zero digits, f increases with x.

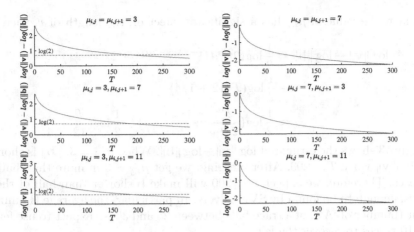

Fig. 3. $\log \|\mathbf{v}\| - \log \|\mathbf{b}\|$ in different conditions

4.3 Non-shortness of Target Vector

In this section, we explain the necessity of sieve and predicate techniques in our attack. In Subsect. 4.2, we try to make the target vector $\mathbf{b}$ as short as possible. However, $\mathbf{b}$ may not be the shortest vector in $\mathcal{L}_{\mathrm{sub}}(M)$ of basis B. For example, the rows of submatrix A are not linearly independent, which leads to a set of non-unique solutions to the equation $\mathbf{x} \cdot A = \mathbf{0}_{u-1} \pmod{n}$. Consider in B's row vectors corresponding to $\lambda_{i,j}$ and $\lambda_{i,j+1}$, or in other words, the $(u - 1 + \sum_{k=1}^{i-1} l_k + j)$-th row $v_{i,j}$ and $(u + \sum_{k=1}^{i-1} l_k + j)$-th row $v_{i,j+1}$ of M, $0 \le j \le l_i - 1$. To compare the two rows, one can take $\sigma_{i,j}$ and $\sigma_{i,j+1}$ as an example.

Here we assume the traces have been merged and T, U are properly updated. By definition of σ, we have $\sigma_{i,j+1} = -2^{\lambda_{i,j+1}+1} \cdot s_i r_1 = 2^{\lambda_{i,j+1}-\lambda_{i,j}} \cdot \sigma_{i,j}$, so we can get a short vector by $v_{i,j+1}$ minus $2^{\lambda_{i,j+1}-\lambda_{i,j}}$ times $\mathbf{v}_{i,j}$:

$$\mathbf{v} = \mathbf{v}_{i,j+1} - 2^{\lambda_{i,j+1}-\lambda_{i,j}} \cdot \mathbf{v}_{i,j}$$
$$= [0, \ldots, 0, - \cdot 2^{\lambda_{i,j+1}-\lambda_{i,j}-\mu_{i,j}}, \cdot 2^{-\mu_{i,j+1}}, 0, \ldots, 0]. \tag{13}$$

In 3/4 of the cases, the distance between two consecutive non-zero digits after merging is larger than $2w$. And the distribution of $\mu_{i,j}$ is shown in Table 2. Knowing $\mu_{i,j}$ and $\mu_{i,j+1}$ allows more accurate discussion on the length of $\mathbf{v}$ and

Table 2. Frequency of $\mu_{i,j}$ after merging

$\mu_{i,j}$	Frequency	$\mu_{i,j}$	Frequency
3	0.50	15	0.06
7	0.26	19	0.03
11	0.12	>19	0.03

b. In fact, the value of $\mu_{i,j}$ has a significant effect on the length of v, then we have

$$\log\|\mathbf{v}\| - \log\|\mathbf{b}\| \approx \frac{1}{2}\log(2^{2\lambda_{i,j+1}-2\lambda_{i,j}-2\mu_{i,j}} + 2^{-2\mu_{i,j+1}})$$

$$- \frac{1}{2}\log(T/12 + 1/4)$$

$$\approx \frac{1}{2}\log(\frac{2^{4w}}{2^{2\mu_{i,j}}} + \frac{1}{2^{2\mu_{i,j+1}}}) - \frac{1}{2}\log(\frac{T}{12} + \frac{1}{4}).$$

Figure 3 shows the estimated $\log\|\mathbf{v}\| - \log\|\mathbf{b}\|$. When $\mu_{i,j} = 3$, $\|\mathbf{b}\|$ is shorter than $0.5\|\mathbf{v}\|$ when $T < 200$. After merging, we get $\mu_{i,j} = 3$ in more than half of the cases. Therefore, we expect $T < 200$ will make $\mathbf{b}$ shorter than half of the $\mathbf{v}$ vectors, enough to be found by SVP solvers. In particular, the average Hamming weight (number of 'A's) of a trace falls between 25 and 30, so expect to use fewer than 10 traces to recover the key.

We have observed the vectors $\mathbf{v} = (0, \ldots, 0, -2^{\lambda_{i,j+1}-\lambda_{i,j}-\mu_{i,j}}, 2^{-\mu_{i,j+1}}, 0, \ldots, 0)$. By choosing proper parameters we can avoid too short $\mathbf{v}$ vectors. However, the structure of $\mathbf{v}$ will lead to another problem. Consider

$$\mathbf{v}_{i,j} = [0, \ldots, 0, -2^{\lambda_{i,j+1}-\lambda_{i,j}-\mu_{i,j}}, 2^{-\mu_{i,j+1}}, 0, \ldots, 0]$$

and

$$\mathbf{v}_{i,j+1} = [0, \ldots, -2^{\lambda_{i,j+2}-\lambda_{i,j+1}-\mu_{i,j+1}}, 2^{-\mu_{i,j+2}}, 0, \ldots],$$

$\|\mathbf{v}_{i,j}\| > 2^{\lambda_{i,j+1}-\lambda_{i,j}-\mu_{i,j}}$, $\langle \mathbf{v}_{i,j}, \mathbf{v}_{i,j+1}\rangle = 2^{\lambda_{i,j+2}-\lambda_{i,j+1}}/2^{\mu_{i,j+1}}$. The two vectors share one common component that is not zero.

Particularly, $\frac{\langle\mathbf{v}_{i,j},\mathbf{v}_{i,j+1}\rangle}{\|\mathbf{v}_{i,j}\|\|\mathbf{v}_{i,j+1}\|} \approx 2^{-2w} \ll 1$. The vector $\mathbf{v}_{i,j}$ only has two non-zero elements, and is nearly orthogonal to $\mathbf{v}_{i,j-1}$ and $\mathbf{v}_{i,j+1}$. Except for the two vectors, $\mathbf{v}_{i,j}$ and other vectors $\mathbf{v}_{i',j'}$ are orthogonal.

From the u sets of dependent rows in A, we can extract as many as $T - u$ vectors of the form $\mathbf{v} = (\ldots, 0, *, *, 0, \ldots)$ are likely to appear in a reduced basis. Usually, such short vectors are put in the first rows of the basis, nearly orthogonal to each other. We refer to the situation as quasi-reduced basis. Prior work chose small BKZ blocks to find $\mathbf{z}$. In most of the instances, however, the BKZ algorithm terminates early when reaching the nearly orthogonal vectors, leaving the target $\mathbf{b}$ still hidden. To overcome the barrier, we later sieve to find the desired short vector if necessary, instead of merely using lattice reduction.

4.4   Experiments and Performance

We test our attack on the curve recommended by SM2, and show our results for attacking with at least 3 traces. We used the personal computer on an Intel Core i7-10750H CPU running at 2.60 GHz in six threads. The implementation of BKZ and Sieve functions are based on FPLLL [25,26] and G6K [27]. We target the SM2 wNAF implementation of TASSL and GmSSL. The default window size for wNAF is 3. In fact, the libraries seem to have similar codes for the wNAF module, and we reach roughly the same result of attack. For the sliding-window multiplication, we simulate the side-channel leakage in python. For every parameter set, we do 200 experiments, and take the average value of success rate and running-time.

New Record of Attacking 3 Traces. Our algorithm is able to attack SM2 with 3 traces. When attacking the sliding-window multiplication, we reach a success probability > 0.5. When attacking wNAF, however, the attack is difficult. Previously, the best result is attacking with 6 traces [31]. Based on the discussion in Subsect. 4, we can evaluate the traces with simulator function f. In the attack, we adopt the preselecting technique to find the best traces to mount an attack. We try two possible rules in preselecting: (1) choosing traces with fewer merged digits, or (2) choosing traces with fewer non-zero digits (shorter traces) before merging. The result is shown in the Table 3.

Table 3. Key recovery with 3 traces

	Probability	Time
wNAF		
None	0.002	83 h
Rule (1)	0.23	43 h
Rule (2)	0.81	1 h 37 min
Sliding-window		
$w = 3$	0.96	20 s
$w = 4$	0.64	40 s

For the wNAF attack, it seems that the rule (2) of preselecting is superior to other options, especially when running-time is concerned. Our result is also better than the best known result of attacking ECDSA [20]. In fact, by choosing shorter traces, the basis has a smaller rank, thus making it possible to find the target vector after BKZ reduction and before sieve is called, while longer traces requires sieve to recover the target vector, consuming too much computation.

Key Recovery from a Few Signatures. From the result of recovering the secret key from 3 traces, we notice that wNAF is relatively harder to attack. To mount a reliable attack, more traces are required to construct an EHNP basis. When we use more than 3 wNAF traces to attack SM2, we also enjoy an advantage compared with previous attacks. As the results show, with more information, the probability of success rises. In particular, with 5 traces the probability is close to 1, far more than the probability that previous attacks can reach with 7 or 8 traces. Table 5 shows our new result. Table 4 shows the results of different parameter sets. The total time is the average time of a single attack multiplied by the number of trials necessary to recover the key. When attacking

Table 4. Experiment results (A. No preselecting; B. Preselecting)

u	Method	SVP solver	Probability	Time
3	A	BKZ+Sieve	0.002	5 min
	B	BKZ	0.70	58 min
		BKZ+Sieve	0.81	1 h 37 min
4	A	BKZ	0.45	6 min
		BKZ+Sieve	0.75	12 min
	B	BKZ	0.76	48 min
		BKZ+Sieve	0.89	55 min
5	A	BKZ	0.84	4 min
		BKZ+Sieve	0.92	9 min
	B	BKZ	0.91	29 min
		BKZ+Sieve	0.95	34 min

Table 5. New record of attacking wNAF SM2

	u	Probability	Time		u	Probability	Time
Our attack $w = 3$	3	0.81	1 h 37 min	Our attack $w = 4$	3	0.95	56 min
	4	0.89	55 min		4	0.98	44 min
	5	0.95	34 min		5	0.98	25 min
[31], $w = 3$	6	0.8	–	[30], $w = 3$	20	0.15	–
	7	0.65	–		40	>0.5	–
	8	0.5	–				

more than 3 traces, using randomly generated traces proves enough to recover the key d_A. Still, the preselecting technique can be adopted to increase success probability.

Table 6. Attacks on SM2 and ECDSA

u	Our attack (SM2)		Our attack (ECDSA)		De Micheli's attack (ECDSA)		Fan's attack (ECDSA)	
	Probability	Time	Probability	Time	Probability	Time	Probability	Time
3	0.81	1 h 37 min	0.85	1 h 50 min	0.002	39 h	0	–
4	0.89	55 min	0.91	45 min	0.04	25 h 28 min	0.08	88 min
5	0.95	34 min	0.99	29 min	0.20	1 h 4 min	0.38	102 min

Attacking ECDSA. The attack depends only on the algorithm of scalar multiplication and can be applied to ECDSA as well as SM2. To illustrate the efficiency of our attack, we compare our attack on SM2 with previous EHNP attacks on ECDSA. We also try our attack on ECDSA traces if wNAF is used.

The results are shown in Table 6. Our attack succeeds faster and with higher probability. This illustrates the capability of our new algorithm.

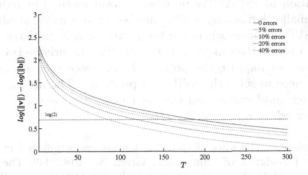

Fig. 4. $\log(\|\mathbf{v}\|) - \log(\|\mathbf{b}\|)$ with errors

Attacking Erroneous Traces. In practical cases, it is expected to obtain traces with errors in practice. We carry out a series of experiments and tested the probability of success when errors exist. Generally, the lattice method is not good at tackling noisy data. Based on simulation, we can estimate the norms of the vectors, and the relation of target vector **b** and undesired vector **v**. Our simulation is shown in Fig. 4. To verify our approach, Fig. 5 shows the result of attacks with different number of errors.

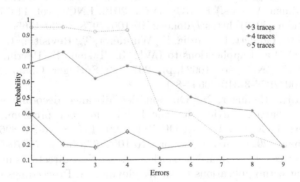

Fig. 5. Result of attacks

5   Conclusion

This paper introduces an improved EHNP method of attacking sliding-window and wNAF multiplications in SM2. Previous EHNP attacks of ECDSA and SM2 already gain remarkable advantage against the HNP method. In this work, we successfully recover the key with 3 traces, while previous EHNP attacks on SM2 need 6 traces or more to reach similar results. The attack also recovers the key with 3 traces when attacking with erroneous information. Our attack is based on a new solution to EHNP. We propose a novel method of reducing EHNP to SVP in a smaller lattice. By adding new equations as constraint condition, we construct SVP instances where the target vector is in sublattices of reduced dimension. As a result, the complexity of recovering the private key is decreased. In addition, we can improve the probability of success by combining lattice reduction and sieve to solve the SVP with predicate. The attack does not rely on special structure of curves and can be mounted on any curve and similar digital signature schemes such as ECDSA.

Acknowledgements. The work of Qingfeng Cheng was supported by the National Natural Science Foundation of China under Grant No. 61872449; The work of Jian Weng was supported by National Key Research and Development Plan of China under Grant No. 2020YFB1005600, Major Program of Guangdong Basic and Applied Research Project under Grant No. 2019B030302008, National Natural Science Foundation of China under Grant No. 61825203, Guangdong Provincial Science and Technology Project under Grant Nos. 2017B010111005 and 2021A0505030033, National Joint Engineering Research Center of Network Security Detection and Protection Technology, and Guangdong Key Laboratory of Data Security and Privacy Preserving.

References

1. Albrecht, M.R., Ducas, L., Herold, G., Kirshanova, E., Postlethwaite, E.W., Stevens, M.: The general sieve kernel and new records in lattice reduction. In: Ishai, Y., Rijmen, V. (eds.) EUROCRYPT 2019. LNCS, vol. 11477, pp. 717–746. Springer, Cham (2019). https://doi.org/10.1007/978-3-030-17656-3_25
2. Albrecht, M.R., Göpfert, F., Virdia, F., Wunderer, T.: Revisiting the expected cost of solving uSVP and applications to LWE. In: Takagi, T., Peyrin, T. (eds.) ASIACRYPT 2017. LNCS, vol. 10624, pp. 297–322. Springer, Cham (2017). https://doi.org/10.1007/978-3-319-70694-8_11
3. Albrecht, M.R., Heninger, N.: On bounded distance decoding with predicate: breaking the "lattice barrier" for the hidden number problem. In: Canteaut, A., Standaert, F.-X. (eds.) EUROCRYPT 2021. LNCS, vol. 12696, pp. 528–558. Springer, Cham (2021). https://doi.org/10.1007/978-3-030-77870-5_19
4. Becker, A., Ducas, L., Gama, N., Laarhoven, T.: New directions in nearest neighbor searching with applications to lattice sieving. In: Proceedings of the Twenty-Seventh Annual ACM-SIAM Symposium on Discrete Algorithms, SODA 2016, pp. 10–24. Society for Industrial and Applied Mathematics, USA (2016)
5. Chen, J., Liu, M., Li, H., Shi, H.: Mind your nonces moving: template-based partially-sharing nonces attack on sm2 digital signature algorithm. In: Proceedings of the 10th ACM Symposium on Information, Computer and Communications Security, ASIACCS 2015, pp. 609–614, April 2015. https://doi.org/10.1145/2714576.2714587
6. Chen, Y., Nguyen, P.Q.: BKZ 2.0: better lattice security estimates. In: Lee, D.H., Wang, X. (eds.) ASIACRYPT 2011. LNCS, vol. 7073, pp. 1–20. Springer, Heidelberg (2011). https://doi.org/10.1007/978-3-642-25385-0_1

7. Dachman-Soled, D., Ducas, L., Gong, H., Rossi, M.: LWE with side information: attacks and concrete security estimation. In: Micciancio, D., Ristenpart, T. (eds.) CRYPTO 2020. LNCS, vol. 12171, pp. 329–358. Springer, Cham (2020). https://doi.org/10.1007/978-3-030-56880-1_12

8. De Feo, L., Poettering, B., Sorniotti, A.: On the (in)security of ELGamal in OpenPGP. In: Proceedings of the 2021 ACM SIGSAC Conference on Computer and Communications Security, CCS 2021, New York, NY, USA, pp. 2066–2080. Association for Computing Machinery (2021). https://doi.org/10.1145/3460120.3485257

9. De Micheli, G., Piau, R., Pierrot, C.: A tale of three signatures: practical attack of ECDSA with wNAF. In: Nitaj, A., Youssef, A. (eds.) AFRICACRYPT 2020. LNCS, vol. 12174, pp. 361–381. Springer, Cham (2020). https://doi.org/10.1007/978-3-030-51938-4_18

10. Ducas, L.: Shortest vector from lattice sieving: a few dimensions for free. In: Nielsen, J.B., Rijmen, V. (eds.) EUROCRYPT 2018. LNCS, vol. 10820, pp. 125–145. Springer, Cham (2018). https://doi.org/10.1007/978-3-319-78381-9_5

11. Ducas, L., Stevens, M., van Woerden, W.: Advanced lattice sieving on GPUs, with tensor cores. In: Canteaut, A., Standaert, F.-X. (eds.) EUROCRYPT 2021. LNCS, vol. 12697, pp. 249–279. Springer, Cham (2021). https://doi.org/10.1007/978-3-030-77886-6_9

12. Fan, S., Wang, W., Cheng, Q.: Attacking OpenSSL implementation of ECDSA with a few signatures. In: Proceedings of the 2016 ACM SIGSAC Conference on Computer and Communications Security, pp. 1505–1515 (2016)

13. Gama, N., Nguyen, P.Q.: Finding short lattice vectors within Mordell's inequality. In: Proceedings of the Fortieth Annual ACM Symposium on Theory of Computing, STOC 2008, New York, NY, USA, pp. 207–216. Association for Computing Machinery (2008). https://doi.org/10.1145/1374376.1374408

14. Genkin, D., Pachmanov, L., Pipman, I., Tromer, E., Yarom, Y.: ECDSA key extraction from mobile devices via nonintrusive physical side channels. In: Proceedings of the 2016 ACM SIGSAC Conference on Computer and Communications Security, CCS 2016, New York, NY, USA, pp. 1626–1638. Association for Computing Machinery (2016). https://doi.org/10.1145/2976749.2978353

15. Hanrot, G., Pujol, X., Stehlé, D.: Analyzing blockwise lattice algorithms using dynamical systems. In: Rogaway, P. (ed.) CRYPTO 2011. LNCS, vol. 6841, pp. 447–464. Springer, Heidelberg (2011). https://doi.org/10.1007/978-3-642-22792-9_25

16. Jancar, J., Sedlacek, V., Svenda, P., Sys, M.: Minerva: the curse of ECDSA nonces systematic analysis of lattice attacks on noisy leakage of bit-length of ECDSA nonces. IACR Trans. Cryptogr. Hardw. Embedded Syst. **2020**(4), 281–308 (2020). https://doi.org/10.13154/tches.v2020.i4.281-308. https://tches.iacr.org/index.php/TCHES/article/view/8684

17. Kocher, P., Jaffe, J., Jun, B.: Differential power analysis. In: Wiener, M. (ed.) CRYPTO 1999. LNCS, vol. 1666, pp. 388–397. Springer, Heidelberg (1999). https://doi.org/10.1007/3-540-48405-1_25

18. Laarhoven, T.: Sieving for shortest vectors in lattices using angular locality-sensitive hashing. In: Gennaro, R., Robshaw, M. (eds.) CRYPTO 2015. LNCS, vol. 9215, pp. 3–22. Springer, Heidelberg (2015). https://doi.org/10.1007/978-3-662-47989-6_1

19. Lenstra, A.K., Lenstra, H.W., Lovasz, L.: Factoring polynomials with rational coefficients. Math. Ann. **261**, 515–534 (1982). https://doi.org/10.1007/BF01457454. http://infoscience.epfl.ch/record/164484

20. Li, S., Fan, S., Lu, X.: Attacking ECDSA leaking discrete bits with a more efficient lattice. In: Yu, Yu., Yung, M. (eds.) Inscrypt 2021. LNCS, vol. 13007, pp. 251–266. Springer, Cham (2021). https://doi.org/10.1007/978-3-030-88323-2_13

21. Micciancio, D., Regev, O.: Lattice-based cryptography. In: Bernstein, D.J., Buchmann, J., Dahmen, E. (eds.) Post-Quantum Cryptography, pp. 147–191. Springer, Heidelberg (2009). https://doi.org/10.1007/978-3-540-88702-7_5

22. Micciancio, D., Walter, M.: Practical, predictable lattice basis reduction. In: Fischlin, M., Coron, J.-S. (eds.) EUROCRYPT 2016. LNCS, vol. 9665, pp. 820–849. Springer, Heidelberg (2016). https://doi.org/10.1007/978-3-662-49890-3_31

23. Nguyen, P.Q., Vallée, B.: The LLL Algorithm: Survey and Applications. Information Security and Cryptography, Springer, Heidelberg (2010). https://doi.org/10.1007/978-3-642-02295-1. https://hal.archives-ouvertes.fr/hal-01141414

24. van de Pol, J., Smart, N.P., Yarom, Y.: Just a little bit more. In: Nyberg, K. (ed.) CT-RSA 2015. LNCS, vol. 9048, pp. 3–21. Springer, Cham (2015). https://doi.org/10.1007/978-3-319-16715-2_1

25. The FPLLL development team: FPLLL, a lattice reduction library, Version: 5.4.1 (2021). https://github.com/fplll/fplll/

26. The FPLLL development team: FPYLLL, a Python wraper for the FPLLL lattice reduction library, Version: 0.5.6 (2021). https://github.com/fplll/fpylll

27. The FPLLL Development Team: The general sieve kernel (G6K) (2021). https://github.com/fplll/fpylll

28. Thibault, J.P., O'Flynn, C., Dewar, A.: Ark of the ECC: an open-source ECDSA power analysis attack on a FPGA based curve P-256 implementation. Cryptology ePrint Archive, Report 2021/1520 (2021). https://ia.cr/2021/1520

29. Tuveri, N., ul Hassan, S., García, C.P., Brumley, B.B.: Side-channel analysis of SM2: a late-stage featurization case study. In: Proceedings of the 2018 Annual Computer Security Applications Conference, ACSAC 2018, New York, NY, USA, pp. 147–160. Association for Computing Machinery (2018). https://doi.org/10.1145/3274694.3274725

30. Wei, W., Chen, J., Li, D., Wang, B.: Partially known information attack on SM2 key exchange protocol. SCIENCE CHINA Inf. Sci. **62**(3), 1–14 (2019). https://doi.org/10.1007/s11432-018-9515-9

31. Zhang, K., et al.: Practical partial-nonce-exposure attack on ECC algorithm. In: 2017 13th International Conference on Computational Intelligence and Security (CIS), pp. 248–252 (2017). https://doi.org/10.1109/CIS.2017.00061

Author Index

Printed in the United States
by Baker & Taylor Publisher Services

Printed in the United States
by Baker & Taylor Publisher Services